D0534817

PRENTICE HALL

# AMERICA

## PATHWAYS TO THE PRESENT

### MODERN AMERICAN HISTORY

*Andrew Cayton*
*Elisabeth Israels Perry*
*Linda Reed*
*Allan M. Winkler*

Prentice Hall

Needham, Massachusetts
Upper Saddle River, New Jersey
Glenview, Illinois

# About the Authors

**Andrew Cayton, Ph.D.**

Andrew Cayton is Professor of History at Miami University in Oxford, Ohio. He received his B.A. from the University of Virginia and his M.A. and Ph.D from Brown University. Dr. Cayton is an early American historian, specializing in political and social history. He is author of *Frontier Republic: Ideology and Politics in the Ohio Country, 1780–1825* and co-author of *The Midwest and the Nation: Rethinking the History of an American Region.* His most recent book is *Frontier Indiana.*

**Linda Reed, Ph.D.**

Linda Reed directs the African American Studies Program at the University of Houston. She received her B.S. from Alabama A&M University, her M.A. from the University of Alabama, and her Ph.D. from Indiana University. Dr. Reed's specialization is twentieth-century African American history, particularly the modern-day civil rights era. She is the author of *Simple Decency and Common Sense: The Southern Conference Movement, 1938–1963.*

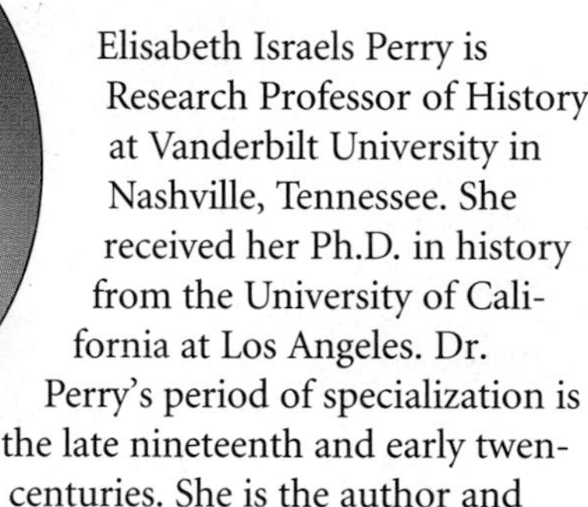

**Elisabeth Israels Perry, Ph.D.**

Elisabeth Israels Perry is Research Professor of History at Vanderbilt University in Nashville, Tennessee. She received her Ph.D. in history from the University of California at Los Angeles. Dr. Perry's period of specialization is the late nineteenth and early twentieth centuries. She is the author and coeditor of a number of books, among them *Belle Moskowitz: Feminine Politics and the Exercise of Power in the Age of Alfred E. Smith* and *Women in Action: Rebels and Reformers, 1920–1980.*

**Allan M. Winkler, Ph.D.**

Allan M. Winkler is Professor of History at Miami University in Oxford, Ohio. He received his B.A. from Harvard University, his M.A. from Columbia University, and his Ph.D. from Yale University. Dr. Winkler's specialization is twentieth-century political and social history. He is author of eight books, including *Home Front U.S.A.: America During World War II* and *Life Under a Cloud: American Anxiety About the Atom.*

**AmericanHeritage®** *American Heritage* magazine was founded in 1954, and it quickly rose to the position it occupies today: the country's preeminent magazine of history and culture. Dedicated to presenting the past in incisive, entertaining narratives underpinned by scrupulous scholarship, *American Heritage* today goes to more than 300,000 subscribers and counts the country's very best writers and historians among its contributors. Its innovative use of historical illustration and its wide variety of subject matter have gained the publication scores of honors across more than 40 years, among them the National Magazine Awards. American Heritage is also known for the classic illustrated histories it has published over the years.



Prentice Hall

ISBN 0-13-053628-8

3 4 5 6 7 8 9 10 05 04 03 02 01

# Program Reviewers

## CONTENT CONSULTANTS

**Senior Curriculum Consultant**
**Dr. Pedro Castillo,** *Professor of History, University of California at Santa Cruz, Santa Cruz, California*

**Constitution Consultant**
**William A. McClenaghan,** *Department of Political Science, Oregon State University Beaverton, Oregon, author,* Magruder's American Government

**Religion Consultant**
**Dr. Jon Butler**
*Department of History, Yale University, New Haven, Connecticut*

**Holocaust Consultant**
**Dr. Karen Friedman,** *Director, Braun Holocaust Institute, New York, New York*

**Reading Consultant**
**Dr. Bonnie Armbruster**
*Professor of Education, University of Illinois at Urbana-Champaign, Urbana, Illinois*

**Block Scheduling Consultant**
**Dr. Michael Rettig**
*Assistant Professor of Education, James Madison University, Harrisonburg, Virginia*

**Internet Consultant**
**Brent Muirhead,** *Teacher, Social Studies Department, South Forsyth High School, Cumming, Georgia*

## HISTORIAN REVIEWERS

**Elizabeth Blackmar**
*Department of History, Columbia University, New York, New York*

**William Childs**
*Department of History, Ohio State University, Columbus, Ohio*

**Donald L. Fixico**
*Department of History, Western Michigan University, Kalamazoo, Michigan*

**George Forgie**
*Department of History, University of Texas at Austin, Austin, Texas*

**Mario Garcia**
*Department of History University of California at Santa Barbara Santa Barbara, California*

**Gerald Gill**
*Department of History, Tufts University Medford, Massachusetts*

**Huping Ling**
*Division of Social Science, Truman State University, Kirksville, Missouri*

**Melton A. McLaurin**
*Department of History, The University of North Carolina at Wilmington, Wilmington, North Carolina*

**Roy Rosenzweig**
*Department of History, George Mason University Fairfax, Virginia*

**Susan Smulyan**
*Department of American Civilization, Brown University, Providence, Rhode Island*

## TEACHER ADVISORY PANEL

**Tracy Babbitt**
*Hillwood High School, Nashville, Tennessee*

**Alfred B. Cate, Jr.**
*Central High School, Memphis, Tennessee*

**Elsie E. Clark**
*Johnson High School, Savannah, Georgia*

**Vern Cobb**
*Okemos High School, Okemos, Michigan*

**Kelly Curtright**
*Putnam City Schools Administration, Oklahoma City, Oklahoma*

**Alice D'Addario**
*Walt Whitman High School, Huntington Station, New York*

**Michael DaDurka**
*David Starr Jordan High School, Long Beach, California*

**Richard Di Giacomo**
*Yerba Buena High School, San Jose, California*

**Rita Geiger**
*Norman Public Schools, Oklahoma City, Oklahoma*

**James Fogarty**
*Arroyo Grande High School, Arroyo Grande, California*

**Jake Gordon**
*Pine Forest High School, Fayetteville, North Carolina*

**Paula M. Hanzel**
*Kit Carson Middle School, Sacramento, California*

**Richard Hart**
*El Cajon High School, El Cajon, California*

**Rosemary Hess**
*John Adams High School, South Bend, Indiana*

**Phillip James**
*Lincoln-Sudbury High School, Sudbury, Massachusetts*

**Gary L. Kelly**
*Novi High School, Novi, Michigan*

**Ann Kennedy**
*Southeast High School, Oklahoma City, Oklahoma*

**Ronald Maggiano**
*West Springfield High School, Springfield, Virginia*

**Steve McClung**
*Santa Teresa High School, San Jose, California*

**Lawrence Moaton**
*Social Studies, Supervisor, Memphis, Tennessee*

**Brent Muirhead**
*South Forsyth High School, Cumming, Georgia*

**Jim Mullen**
*Del Mar High School, Campbell, California*

**John Nehl**
*Mountain View High School, Bend, Oregon*

**Ellen Oicles**
*Piedmont Hills High School, San Jose, California*

**Wayne D. Rice**
*Carlsbad High School, Carlsbad, California*

**Ed Robinson**
*Tulare Western High School, Tulare, California*

**Kerry Steed**
*Ponderosa High School, Shingle Springs, California*

**George A. Stewart**
*Hoffman Estates High School, Hoffman Estates, Illinois*

**Walter T. Thurnau**
*Southwestern Central High School, Jamestown, New York*

**Donald S. Winters**
*Davis High School, Davis, California*

**Ruth Writer**
*Buchanan High School, Buchanan, Michigan*

## STUDENT REVIEW BOARD

**Brenda Borchardt**
*Cudahy High School, Cudahy, Wisconsin*

**Jeff Burton**
*Northwest High School, Clarksville, Tennessee*

**Rebecca A. Day**
*Moore High School, Moore, Oklahoma*

**Ashanté Dobbs**
*Frederick Douglass High School, Atlanta, Georgia*

**Lena K. Franks**
*Frankford High School, Philadelphia, Pennsylvania*

**Katie Holcombe**
*South Forsyth High School, Cumming, Georgia*

**Phillip Payne**
*Moore High School, Moore, Oklahoma*

**Brooke J. Peterson**
*Lincoln-Sudbury High School, Sudbury, Massachusetts*

# Contents

unit ONE

## Building a Powerful Nation 16

BUFFALO BILL'S
WILD WEST

MARCH 1907
TEN CENTS
WOMAN'S HOME COMPANION
THE CROWELL PUBLISHING COMPANY

# The United States on the Brink of Change, 1890–1920 256

# Boom Times to Hard Times, 1919–1938 338

# Hot and Cold War, 1939–1960 426

# unit FIVE

# The Upheaval of the Sixties, 1960–1975 538

# Continuity and Change, 1968–Present 646

# Pathways to the Future 750

# Reference Section

# SPECIAL FEATURES

***Eyewitness accounts from* American Heritage *magazine of ordinary Americans and extraordinary events***



TURNING POINT

***Critical events in the nation's history and their lasting impact***

***Artifacts from the Smithsonian Institution's National Museum of American History***

***An in-depth look at the links between geography and history***

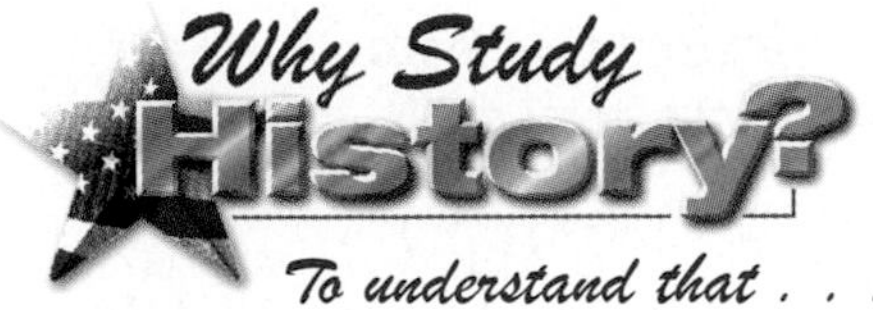


***Links between events of the chapter and present-day issues***



## exploring TECHNOLOGY

***Detailed drawings of key advances in technology***



## CONNECTIONS TO American Literature

***A collection of literature, songs, speeches, and memoirs***



## Time Lines

***More than 100 time lines that highlight the critical events in American history***

1700 1800 1900

# SKILLS FOR LIFE

***Step-by-step lessons to learn and practice important skills***



## ECONOMICS CONCEPTS

***Historical context and present-day application of important economics concepts***



## GOVERNMENT CONCEPTS

***Historical context and present-day application of important government concepts***

# PRIMARY SOURCES

***Primary source quotations from famous and ordinary Americans***

# PRIMARY SOURCES



## VOICES FROM ABROAD

### *Primary source quotations from around the world*



## KEY DOCUMENTS

### *Important speeches, amendments, and other documents*

# PRIMARY SOURCES

## COMPARING PRIMARY SOURCES

***Primary source quotations on controversial issues of the period***

## Political Cartoons

***Cartoons are visual historical documents, which appear in every chapter of the textbook.***

# BIOGRAPHIES

## AMERICAN BIOGRAPHY

***Profiles describing the lives and accomplishments of prominent Americans***

## Notable PRESIDENTS

***Biographies of some of the most highly respected Presidents***

# MAPS



# GRAPHS, CHARTS, AND TABLES

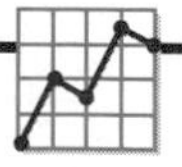

# GRAPHS, CHARTS, AND TABLES

# HOW TO USE THIS BOOK
## Chapters and Sections

CHAPTER 8 **Becoming a World Power**

**1890–1913**

**CHAPTER FOCUS**
Every chapter begins with a brief summary of the important content to be covered in the chapter.

**WHY STUDY HISTORY?**
This statement previews the issue that will be covered in the Why Study History? connections page at the end of the chapter.

**CHAPTER FOCUS**

*This chapter describes the years when the United States grew to be a world power. Growth in American industry pushed business and political leaders to look for new markets abroad. Some Americans, inspired by grand dreams of an empire, pursued new territory as well.*

*The **Why Study History?** page at the end of this chapter explores the connection between United States participation in world affairs in the early 1900s and its role in the global community today.*

▲ **VIEWING HISTORY**
Edward Moran captured the triumph of the Great White Fleet in his 1899 painting *Return of the Conquerors.* ***Foreign Relations*** ***Why did the United States expand its influence overseas?***

258

**SECTION TIME LINES**
At the start of every section is a time line listing some of the most important events discussed in the section.

**SECTION PREVIEW**
Included here are a list of **Objectives** covering each of the headings in the section, the boldfaced **Key Terms,** the **Main Idea** of the section, and a **Reading Strategy** to help you get the most out of reading the section.

**1867** *United States buys Alaska and annexes Midway Islands*

**1875** *United States signs trade agreement with Hawaii*

**1881** *Congress establishes Naval Advisory Board*

**1884** *American businessman granted long-term lease in Costa Rica*

**1890** *Alfred Mahan publishes The Influence of Sea Power Upon History*

1865 | 1875 | 1885 | 1895

# 1 The Pressure to Expand

**SECTION PREVIEW**

**Objectives**

1 Explain some of the reasons for the growth of imperialism around the world.
2 Summarize the American view regarding imperialism prior to 1890.
3 *Key Terms* Define: imperialism; nationalism; annex; banana republic.

**Main Idea**

In the late 1800s, as European nations took over vast areas in Africa and Asia, American leaders looked to expand American influence abroad.

**Reading Strategy**

*Reinforcing Main Ideas* As you read, create a list of the pressures that led the United States to adopt a policy of political and economic expansion overseas.

**SECTION REVIEW**
Six questions, including critical thinking and writing exercises, test your understanding of each of the section objectives. Every Section Review includes:

- Key Terms definitions
- Summarizing the Main Idea question
- Organizing Information activity
- Critical Thinking questions
- Writing Activity

By the late 1800s, the industrialists, inventors, and workers of the United States had built a powerful industrial economy. But the overproduction of food and goods led to financial panic and depression. Labor and farmers protested their plight, helping to convince business and political leaders that the United States must secure new markets abroad. Some people also began to believe that the United States had a duty to carry democratic values and Christianity to others around the globe.

## *Growth of Imperialism*

Meanwhile, as the maps on the next page show, Europe had reached new heights in its quest for territories to rule. The late 1800s marked the peak of European imperialism, with much of Africa and Asia under foreign domination. Under **imperialism,** stronger nations attempt to create empires by dominating weaker nations—economically, politically, culturally, or militarily.

**Why Imperialism Grew** Several factors accounted for the burst of imperialistic activity in the late 1800s.

(1) *Economic factors.* The growth of industry in Europe created an increased need for natural resources, such as rubber and petroleum. Manufacturing nations also required new markets in which to sell their manufactured goods.

(2) *Nationalist factors.* Competition among European nations for large empires was the result of **nationalism,** or devotion to one's nation. For example, when France acquired colonies in West Africa in the late 1800s, rival nations Great Britain and Germany seized lands nearby to stop French expansion.

(3) *Military factors.* Advances in military technology produced European armies and navies that were far superior to those in Africa ...'s growing navies

*Businesses, such as this fruit grower, eagerly sought new markets abroad.*

**SECTION 1 REVIEW**

**Comprehension**

1. *Key Terms* Define: (a) imperialism; (b) nationalism; (c) annex; (d) banana republic.
2. *Summarizing the Main Idea* Why did United States policymakers feel the need to secure new markets abroad in the late 1800s?
3. *Organizing Information* Create a web diagram that describes the major arguments for American expansionism. Label the center circle *Arguments for Expansionism.* Include supporting details in at least three surrounding circles.

**Critical Thinking**

4. *Analyzing Time Lines* Review the time line at the start of the section. Which event, in your opinion, best reflects American expansionist policies?
5. *Drawing Conclusions* What factors aided European imperialism in the late 1800s?

**Writing Activity**

6. *Writing an Expository Essay* Research and write a brief essay tracing the history of American expansionism before 1880. Be sure to include specific examples of expansionism in your essay.

# HOW TO USE THIS BOOK

## Technology and Learning

### *The Internet and the World Wide Web*

The **Internet** is a global computer network that began in the 1960s as a U.S. Department of Defense project linking university computer science departments. The Internet has since grown to include millions of business, governmental, educational, and individual computers around the world. The **World Wide Web,** or "the Web" for short, is a collection of linked electronic files. Using programs called browsers, Internet users can find out what files are available on the Web and then access those files.

### *How to Search the Internet*

There are two basic ways to find information on the Internet.

- **Use the URL.** If you know the address of the Web site you want to visit, you can go there directly by typing in the site's URL. (URL stands for Universal Resource Locator; each Web site has its own URL.)
- **Use a search engine.** You can search for information using a search engine, such as Yahoo! or Infoseek, by typing key words representing the topic you want to research. The search engine will then scan the Internet and list all of the Web sites with information on your topic.

Whichever method you use, you will encounter Web sites containing **hyperlinks.** These appear on your screen as colored or underlined text or as

## Chapter 8 Review

### Chapter Summary

The major concepts of Chapter 8 are presented below. See also ***Guide to the Essentials of American History*** or ***Interactive Student Tutorial CD-ROM,*** which contains interactive review activities, time lines, helpful hints, and test practice.

***Reviewing the Main Ideas***

By the 1890s, farms and factories in the United States were producing more than the nation could consume. Soon, many business and political leaders began to pursue new markets abroad. Inspired by dreams of an empire, some Americans pushed for new territory as well. American expansion caused some citizens to raise doubts about the morality of imperialism.

***Section 1: The Pressure to Expand***

In the late 1800s, as European nations took over vast areas in Africa and Asia, American leaders looked to expand American influence abroad.

***Section 2: The Spanish-American War***

A swift American victory in the Spanish-American War confirmed the nation's status as a world power, but it left some people arguing over how to govern newly acquired territories.

***Section 3: Expansion Under Roosevelt and Taft***

President Theodore Roosevelt conducted a vigorous foreign policy that suited the new status of the United States as a world power. Although President William Howard Taft continued Roosevelt's policies, he preferred a more subtle approach to influencing other nations.

***Section 4: Debating America's New Role***

After the Spanish-American War, the debate intensified over whether it was appropriate for the United States to build an empire.

Since the 1890s, the United States has played an active role in world affairs. On numerous occasions, Americans have provided military and economic aid to countries in need.

282

### Key Terms

For each of the terms below, write a sentence explaining how it relates to this chapter.

1. annex
2. Open Door Policy
3. Great White Fleet
4. Roosevelt Corollary
5. imperialism
6. sphere of influence
7. nationalism
8. dollar diplomacy
9. jingoism
10. banana republic

### Comprehension

1. Briefly explain the arguments of Alfred T. Mahan, Henry Cabot Lodge, and Albert J. Beveridge regarding expansionism.
2. Describe how the 1895 dispute between the United States and Great Britain reaffirmed the Monroe Doctrine.
3. Why did the American public favor war with Spain in 1898?
4. What was the Open Door Policy, and why was it important for the United States?
5. Describe Theodore Roosevelt's approach to foreign policy.
6. How did the Roosevelt Corollary affect United States policy in Latin America?
7. Explain President Taft's policy of dollar diplomacy.
8. Explain why anti-imperialists believed that imperialism betrayed basic American principles.

### Using Graphic Organizers

On a separate sheet of paper, copy the multi-flow map to show the causes and effects of American expansion during the late 1800s and early 1900s. Provide at least three causes and three effects.

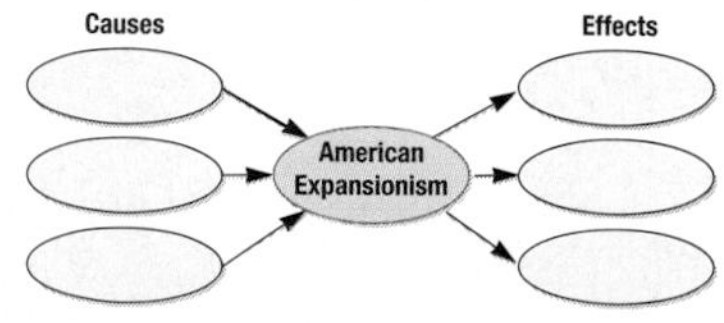


**CD-ROM SUPPORT**

*The* ***Interactive Student Tutorial CD-ROM*** *provides section-by-section review of chapter content through interactive review activities and practice tests.*

icons. Hyperlinks act as doorways to other documents. When you click your mouse on hyperlinked text or graphics, a new document appears on your screen. That document may come from the same computer as the Web site you just left, or from one thousands of miles away.

## Tips for Successful Searches

- **Keep your search focused.** Because the Internet contains so much interesting information, it is easy to "wander off" and lose track of your goal in searching. To avoid this, you should establish a specific research goal before your begin your Internet search.
- **Make bookmarks for your favorite Web sites.** A bookmark is a note to your computer to "remember" the location of the Web site. You can reach any bookmarked site from any other site with a simple click of your mouse.
- **Use specific key words.** If your key words are too general, your search might turn up thousands of Web sites. Many search engines have useful tips on searching with key words.
- **Evaluate the quality of Internet information.** Not all of the information available on the Internet is appropriate for your research. Ask a teacher, parent, or librarian for help in evaluating the reliability and appropriateness of Web sites and information.

**Analyzing Political Cartoons ▶**

1. The caption to this 1904 political cartoon was: "HIS 128th BIRTHDAY. 'Gee but this is an awful stretch!'" (a) Whose birthday is it? (b) How do you know? (c) What is the "awful stretch" referring to? (d) How do you know?
2. What is the cartoonist's view on United States imperialsim?

**Critical Thinking**

1. *Applying the Chapter Skill* Review the time zone map on page 270. Name two cities on the map that are in the same time zone as New York City.
2. *Identifying Central Issues* How did the popular philosophy of social Darwinism make it easier for some Americans to embrace imperialist policies in the late 1800s?
3. *Drawing Conclusions* During the late 1800s, the press fanned the flames of the Spanish-American War by publishing sensational stories about Spanish cruelties in Cuba. On what current issues has the press played a major role in influencing public opinion?
4. *Distinguishing Fact from Opinion* President McKinley's Secretary of State, John Hay, referred to the Spanish-American War as "a splendid little war." Can you think of any Americans, in addition to anti-imperialists, who might disagree with Hay?

**INTERNET ACTIVITY**

*For your portfolio:*
CREATE A TIME LINE

Access Prentice Hall's *America: Pathways to the Present* site at **www.Pathways.phschool.com** for the specific URL to complete the activity. Additional resources and related Web sites are also available.

Read the biography of William Howard Taft and create a time line of his career. Write a paragraph summarizing Taft's professional life. How would you characterize his career? What do you consider his most important achievement? What did Taft consider his most important achievement?

**ANALYZING DOCUMENTS ◀ INTERPRETING DATA**

Turn to the "American Voices" quotation on page 272.

1. Theodore Roosevelt is suggesting that his policies made it (a) impossible to build the canal. (b) possible to return Panama to Colombia. (c) easier to build the canal. (d) necessary to submit a State paper to Congress.
2. What is the most likely reason Roosevelt felt he had to justify his policies regarding the Panama Canal even after he left office? (a) Colombia was asking for the return of the Canal Zone. (b) Anti-imperialists were complaining about his high-handed methods. (c) Panama was asking for more money. (d) Congress was considering returning the land to Panama.
3. *Writing* Do you think Roosevelt's argument justifies his actions? Explain your reasoning.

**Connecting to Today**

*Essay Writing* The United States still intervenes in foreign countries when its interests are threatened. Write a letter to the editor of a newspaper in which you argue either for or against an interventionist foreign policy. Research recent examples of United States actions in foreign countries and use them to support your arguments.

283

**INTERNET ACTIVITY**

*Every Chapter Review has an Internet activity based on key content of the chapter. A* ***Companion Web Site*** *(shown below) featuring online links and assessment activities provides structured chapter-by-chapter support for all Chapter Review activities and important review material for key content.*

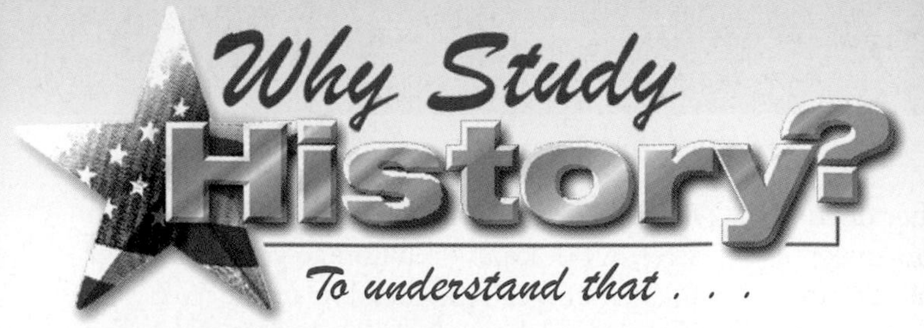


*"I know no way of judging the future but by the past," wrote Patrick Henry in 1775. The four statements in bold red type on these pages help explain the continuing relevance and drama of historical events. To explore the many links between the issues of yesterday and today, every chapter in this textbook contains a Why Study History? page immediately before the Chapter Review.*

## History Is Everyone's Story

American history is not only the story of famous heroes but also that of ordinary people. Remarkable leaders like Washington and Lincoln have guided the country well in times of crisis, while other men and women have been outstanding in business, science, and education. But America's greatness also rests on the hard work and dedicated effort of countless others. Since the country began, they have plowed the fields, built the cities, raised the families, fought the wars, and done all the everyday things that add up to a country's history. While we may never know all their names, we know these people's stories—because they are our story, too.

## The Present Is Linked to the Past

Throughout history, Americans have looked for new frontiers. Pioneers pushed westward into unknown territory, across rugged mountains and wide prairies. They built new towns and added new states to the nation. The frontier spirit has stayed with us, giving Americans a strong sense of energy, personal freedom, and individualism. More recently, Americans have looked toward farther frontiers, pioneering in space with the first moon landing and probes to distant planets.

## *History Is Unpredictable*

You might mistakenly think of history as a collection of cut-and-dried facts—names, dates, laws, statistics. But in fact, history is full of unexpected twists and turns, situations that could easily have turned out differently and so changed the course of many people's lives. The Pilgrims' first landfall in America, for instance, was due to a storm that blew their ship off course. President Harry Truman's election victory in 1948 was an upset that surprised almost everyone. Like many other events, it showed that history is never predictable and often has surprise endings.

## *Real People Change the Course of History*

History is not only about yesterday's events—it is about today's headlines and tomorrow's news. As you are reading this, someone in the United States is taking an action that could change history. That person may not be famous or powerful, but may be just an ordinary citizen, like one of the marchers at the March on Washington in 1963. Ordinary people from many different backgrounds—like you and your friends and neighbors—are the people who really write history. And that is one answer to the question, Why study history? Because you are a part of it.

# THEMES IN *AMERICA: PATHWAYS TO THE PRESENT*

*Much of what you learn about American history can be better understood if you view events as part of a larger pattern. The themes listed below apply to all periods of American history and can help you link events across time. You will see these themes throughout this textbook, at the start of each unit and in the captions that accompany photographs and other graphics.*

## *Government*

The United States was founded on such ideals as human equality, limited government, and democratic representation. For more than two centuries, Americans have worked to make their form of government live up to those ideals. Formerly excluded groups such as women and African Americans, for example, have demanded and won equal rights.

## *Geography*

Geography has shaped the growth of American power and prosperity, as Americans have benefited from their nation's large size and many natural resources. In addition, because the United States faces both the Atlantic and Pacific oceans, it has had profitable trade with both Europe and Asia.

## *Diversity*

People from many nations, representing an extraordinary range of ethnic, racial, national, and religious groups, have come to the United States and become Americans. This diversity is a source of tremendous strength for the United States, but also produces conflict.

## Economics

Abundant natural resources, combined with an economic system that encourages individual initiative, have made the American economy staggeringly successful. Throughout our nation's history, economic opportunity has attracted immigrants to the United States.

## Culture

American culture is as diverse as American people, drawing on the traditions of the nation's many immigrants. American culture also reflects the nation's democratic ideals, as Americans have pioneered in forms of entertainment, such as baseball and movies, that are aimed at mass audiences.

## Foreign Relations

In its early history the United States, focusing its energies on westward expansion, sought to remain free from European entanglements. By the twentieth century, however, this nation had become a major world power, with worldwide commitments and responsibilities.

## Science & Technology

Innovations in science and technology have played critical roles in American history. These innovations—the cotton gin, the airplane, nuclear power, the polio vaccine, and the computer, to name just a few—have contributed to this nation's security and prosperity.

# THE FIVE GEOGRAPHIC THEMES

*Like history, geography can be divided into themes. Geographers use five themes, described below, to organize their study of the world. You will find these themes in the captions that accompany the maps in this textbook. In addition, a Geography and History feature in each unit explores one of the themes in greater depth.*

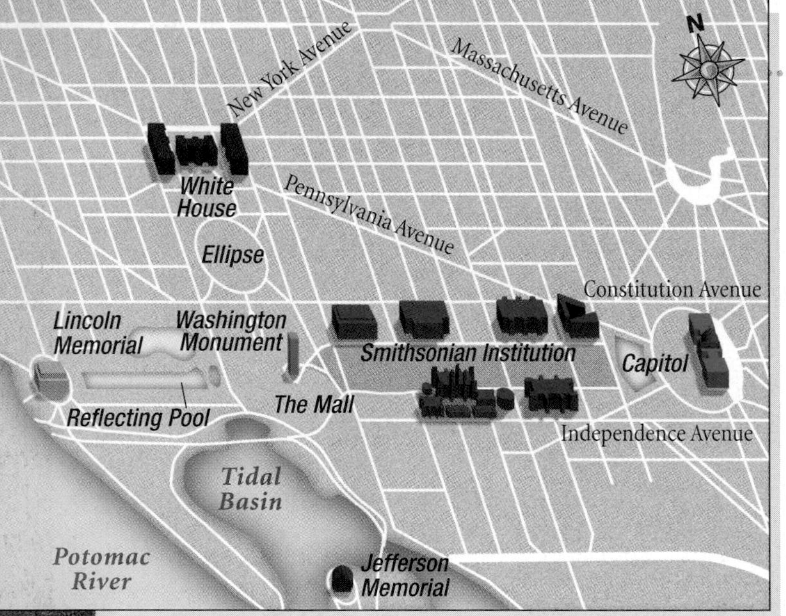


## Location

The most basic of the geographic themes, location tells where a place is. Location can be expressed in two ways. *Absolute location* describes a place's position on the globe as determined by latitude and longitude. *Relative location* describes a place's position in relation to other places. While each place can have only one absolute location, its relative location can be expressed in a number of ways. For example, the relative location of the Smithsonian Institution can be described as "west of the Capitol," "at the Mall," or "east of the Washington Monument."

## Place

Place describes the characteristics that make a location distinctive. There are two kinds of characteristics. *Physical characteristics* include landforms, vegetation, and climate. *Human characteristics* include the culture, economy, and government of the people who live in a place. Each place in the United States—indeed, on Earth—has a unique combination of physical and human characteristics.

## *Movement*

People, goods, and ideas regularly travel from one place to another. Examples from American history include the continuing immigration of new Americans, the westward migration of Americans through the 1800s, and the spread of American ideals of individual liberty through the world following the American Revolution. Today's advances in communication and transportation make movement easier and more common than ever.

## *Regions*

A region is any group of places with at least one common characteristic. Regions can be any size, and a single place can belong to several different regions. The city of San Diego, for example, is part of California (a political region), the Sunbelt (a demographic region), and the Pacific Rim (an economic region).

## *Human-Environment Interaction*

Human-environment interaction explores the ways in which people use and modify their environment. The Brooklyn Bridge, the coal mines of West Virginia, the wheat fields of the Plains states, Hoover Dam—all are examples of Americans modifying their environment in order to produce or extract needed resources or to make movement more efficient.

# THEMES IN AMERICAN HISTORY

*The text at right reviews key events in American history to 1750. The pages that follow examine the time period from 1750 to 1900, viewed through each of the seven American history themes used in this textbook. This thematic presentation reveals the trends that shaped the American nation and laid the foundations for life in the 20th century.*



## Early America

### Beginnings to 1750

A thin, broken trail of evidence indicates that the Western Hemisphere was first populated by Asians who arrived tens of thousands of years ago. Most scientists believe that they migrated across Beringia, a strip of land that once connected what is now Russia and Alaska. The migration ceased when water washed over Beringia, creating the Bering Strait. Over thousands of years, humans spread out across North and South America. These original people and their descendents are known as Native Americans.

### *Native American Culture*

Most North American groups were **nomadic.** That is, they seldom stayed in one place, but traveled to where food was available to hunt or gather at certain times of the year. They generally moved within a region that could supply all their needs.

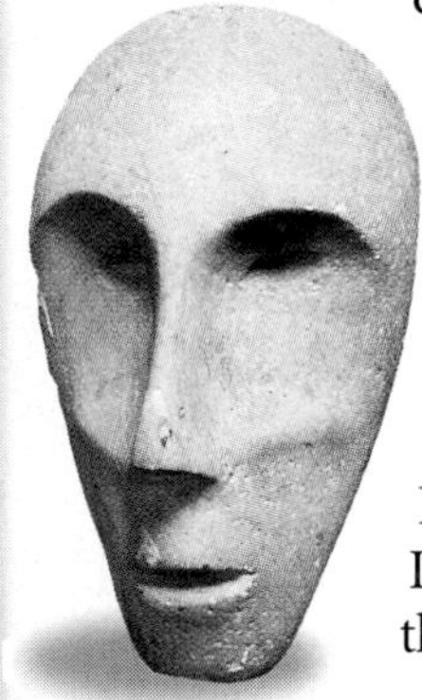

Native American groups had varying degrees of organization. Some set up trade networks across hundreds of miles. The Mississippian culture, which began around A.D. 800, included peoples from Wisconsin to Louisiana with a shared culture. The first large political alliance in North America was the Iroquois Confederacy, a league of Indian groups from the Atlantic to the Great Lakes, formed about 1500.

### *Exploration and Settlement*

By the 1400s, Portugal and Spain were competing to find a westward sea route to Asia. In 1492, Italian navigator Christopher Columbus found land and claimed it for his Spanish sponsors. He had come upon a whole hemisphere unknown to Europeans. The discovery set off a wave of exploration and settlement of the Western Hemisphere.

**Above** *Native American sculpture;* **facing page, top** *colonial spinning wheel;* **facing page, bottom** *Jamestown colony*

Europeans had a variety of reasons for coming to the Americas. During the 1500s Spain sent **conquistadors,** or conquerers, to search for gold. Spanish missionaries came to convert Native Americans to Christianity.

To obtain and export raw materials from North America, British investors funded the creation of colonies along the East Coast of North America. The first permanent British colony—at Jamestown, Virginia—was settled in 1607.

French settlement began in 1608 with the founding of Quebec, in Canada. The French developed relations with the Indians, who traded animal pelts for guns and other goods. Dutch traders settled New Amsterdam (now New York City) in 1625.

Some immigrants came to America fleeing religious persecution in England. A group known as the Pilgrims formed Plymouth Colony in Massachusetts in 1620. In 1630 the Puritans founded the Massachusetts Bay Colony.

British colonies grew rapidly, bringing settlers into conflict with the Indians. The bloody **King Philip's War** (1675–1676) destroyed Native American power in southern New England. One exception to the hostile English-Indian relations was Pennsylvania, founded by William Penn in 1681 as a refuge for the Quakers, a persecuted Christian sect. Penn paid Indians for their land and treated them with respect.

## *Colonial America*

Britain's American colonies quickly became a vital source of raw materials and farm products not native to England. Many of these goods came from **plantations,** large farms that grew crops for sale. Crops grown not for food but for sale are called **cash crops.** In colonial times, tobacco plantations became big business in Virginia and North Carolina. Rice plantations spread across hot, swampy areas of South Carolina and Georgia.

At first, farm labor was provided by indentured servants. These workers, usually European men, received passage to America and food and shelter in return for several years of labor. But by 1750 most plantations used African slave labor.

Most enslaved people were West Africans, purchased by slave traders for goods such as guns and rum. In African ports the captives were branded with hot irons and crammed aboard hot, filthy ships for a transatlantic voyage that millions did not survive. Arriving slaves were sold at auctions. Slavery was never as widespread in the North as in the South. Northern farms were smaller, and farm families provided much of the labor.

As American commerce thrived and people grew wealthier, many strayed from strict Puritan beliefs. This spurred a revival of religion in the 1730s and 1740s known as the **Great Awakening.** Fiery preachers urged a return to Puritan values. Others held large, revival meetings that stressed independent thought and inner faith rather than outward observances. New Christian denominations, the Methodists and Baptists, challenged the authority of older churches.

### Reviewing Themes

1. *Key Terms* Define: (a) nomadic; (b) conquistador; (c) King Philip's War; (d) plantation; (e) cash crop; (f) Great Awakening.
2. *Comprehension* List three reasons that Europeans came to America.
3. *Connecting to Today* How did the arrival of Africans affect American society today?

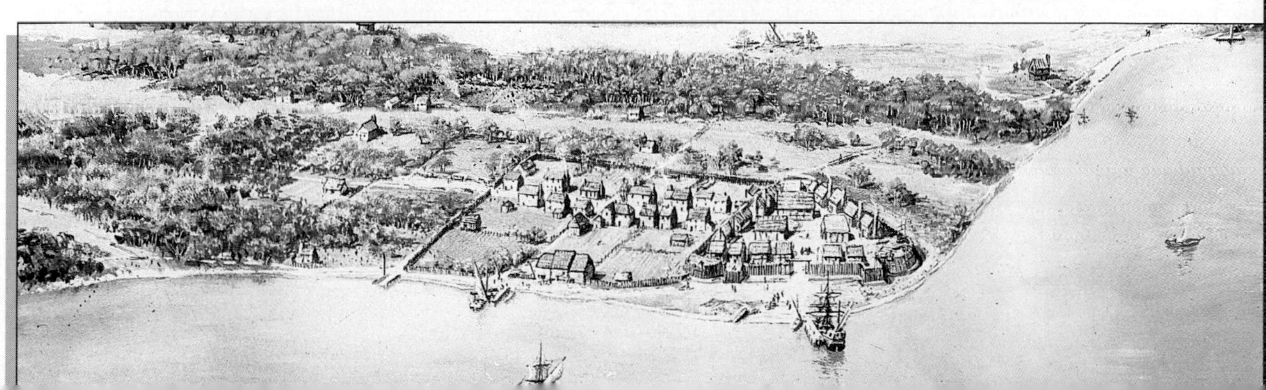

# GOVERNMENT 1750–1900

As the United States grew, its government came to represent a greater diversity of its citizens, a trend that continued into modern times. The adoption of a Constitution, the formation of political parties, and the extension of voting rights were some of the key steps in creating a strong, democratic government. Those steps are traced in the time line below.

## *Establishing a Government*

Most colonial Americans wanted to be left alone to run their farms and shops, to pursue the exciting freedoms and economic prospects of their new homeland. An ocean away, the British government saw America as a ripe source of tax revenues, raw materials, and markets for British exports. By the mid-1700s, tensions were building.

Heavy taxes, with military enforcement, led to protests in the 1760s, especially in the merchant city of Boston. Fiery leaders such as Virginia's Patrick Henry made "no taxation without representation" a rallying cry. In 1775 rebellion exploded into a bloody six-year conflict, the **American Revolution.**

In 1776, Virginian Thomas Jefferson wrote the historic document that asserted citizens' rights to certain basic freedoms: the **Declaration of Independence.** The newly independent states agreed to form a central government in a document called the **Articles of Confederation.** Ratified in 1781, the Articles gave most governing powers to the states, since Americans generally feared a strong central government.

In 1787, delegates to the **Constitutional Convention** in Philadelphia voted to replace the weak Articles with a Constitution created under the guidance of Virginian James Madison. It established a strong federal government, but a Bill of Rights was soon added to protect individual rights such as free speech.

The Constitution created a federal government with three branches: the executive (headed by the President), the legislative (Congress), and the judicial (federal courts). A system of **checks and balances** was designed to prevent any one branch from overpowering another.

A national political system emerged in the early 1800s as competing political parties formed. Voting rights, at first limited to property-owning men, gradually were expanded to include most white men. These voters helped elect President Andrew Jackson, a sworn opponent of federal power.

## *Division, Reunion, Expansion*

The rapid addition of new western territories raised the explosive issue of whether slavery would extend

into these lands. Congressional compromises in the 1840s added a balance of free and slave states, but the solutions were only temporary. In the slaveholding South, believers in states' rights feared the growing political power of northern abolitionists seeking to ban slavery.

In 1860 the election of Illinois Republican Abraham Lincoln as President prompted South Carolina to secede, or withdraw, from the Union. Other southern states followed. They formed a nation called the Confederate States of America.

From 1861 to 1865 Union and Confederate forces fought a blistering Civil War that killed more than a half-million soldiers. The warmaking resources of the industrial North—from guns to trains—devastated the South. In 1863 Lincoln issued the **Emancipation Proclamation,** freeing slaves in the rebelling states. Lincoln's assassination at the war's end put Vice President Andrew Johnson in charge of the rebuilding of the war-torn South, an effort called **Reconstruction.**

During Reconstruction, southern states returned to the Union. Constitutional amendments ended slavery and gave citizenship and voting rights to African Americans, although these rights were largely ignored as former Confederates gradually returned to power in the South.

The reunited nation continued to expand westward. The discovery of gold and silver in the West in the 1860s and 1870s and a railroad building boom caused a surge of migration to the West and the admission of Colorado and other new states.

At the end of the century, the United States began to look beyond its borders for new territory to acquire. The Spanish-American War, fought in 1898, was an easy win for the United States, which gained Spanish territories in the Pacific and the Caribbean. America was now a world power.

## Reviewing Themes

1. *Key Terms* Define: (a) Declaration of Independence; (b) Constitutional Convention; (c) checks and balances; (d) Emancipation Proclamation; (e) Reconstruction.
2. *Analyzing Time Lines* What steps did American leaders take to establish the United States government?
3. *Comprehension* Why did the Union become divided, and how was it reunited?
4. *Connecting to Today* What freedoms do you enjoy today because of the Bill of Rights?

**1828**
*Tariff of Abominations*

**1836**
- *Battle of the Alamo*
- *Republic of Texas established*

**1845**
- *Texas becomes a state*
- *Concept of Manifest Destiny originated*

**1846**
*War with Mexico begins*

**1850**

**1854**
*Kansas-Nebraska Act allows popular sovereignty in those territories*

**1860**
- *Lincoln elected*
- *South Carolina secedes*

**1861**
- *Confederacy elects Davis as president*
- *Civil War begins*

**1865**
- *Lee surrenders at Appomattox*
- *Civil War ends*
- *Lincoln assassinated*
- *Johnson becomes President*
- *Reconstruction begins*
- *Thirteenth Amendment ratified*

**1877**
- *Compromise of 1877 makes Hayes President*
- *Reconstruction ends*

**1883**
*Pendleton Act reforms civil service*

**1891**
*Populist party formed*

**1896**
- *McKinley elected President*
- *Plessy v. Ferguson legalizes "separate but equal" segregation*

**1900**

# GEOGRAPHY
## 1750–1900

As settlers fanned out across America, they went over or around one geographic barrier after another. They learned how to survive in unfamiliar environments. They discovered what Native Americans had known for thousands of years: The continent was blessed with an array of natural resources.

North America's climate regions, from subarctic to tropical, supported abundant vegetation and wildlife. Geographic features from natural harbors to mineral-rich hills gave each region unique advantages. By the mid-1700s, the colonies had begun to specialize in the production of certain raw materials and goods, according to resources available in each region. The time line below shows how Americans adapted to and changed their environment.

### *Regional Development*

Farming was never easy in the fertile but rocky soil of New England. The growing season was relatively short, and winter could be brutal. As other regions became food-producing areas, people turned to other uses of New England's resources. A whaling industry grew up in the 1700s. Deep harbors from Canada to the mid-Atlantic helped create thriving seaports. Navigable rivers allowed the transport of inland goods to seaports for export. They also provided the water power that launched the growth of industry in the North in the early 1800s.

Farming slowly shifted south and west. Tobacco grew well in the warm, sandy soil of eastern Virginia and the Carolinas. Swampy coastal plains and tidal basins with a semi-tropical climate proved ideal for cultivating rice. Cotton, which needs high precipitation and a long growing season, thrived in the deep South. West of the Appalachians, a region called the **Northwest Territory** (today's Midwest) became the center of grain farming and livestock production.

From the mid-1700s through the late-1800s, a steady stream of pioneers moved westward. In geographers' terms, the migration was caused by **push-pull factors.** The constant need for more farmland "pushed" people westward, while a desire for a new start in life "pulled" them in that direction.

Several routes to the West became worn with the grooved tracks of wagon trains. The Oregon Trail took pioneers to the Northwest; the Santa Fe Trail ran to the Southwest. A widening network of roads and canals, and later railroads, made it possible to ship goods to eastern markets. Starting in the 1860s, ranchers herded millions of cattle along the Chisholm Trail from Texas to railroad depots at Abilene and Dodge City, Kansas, for shipment to eastern markets.

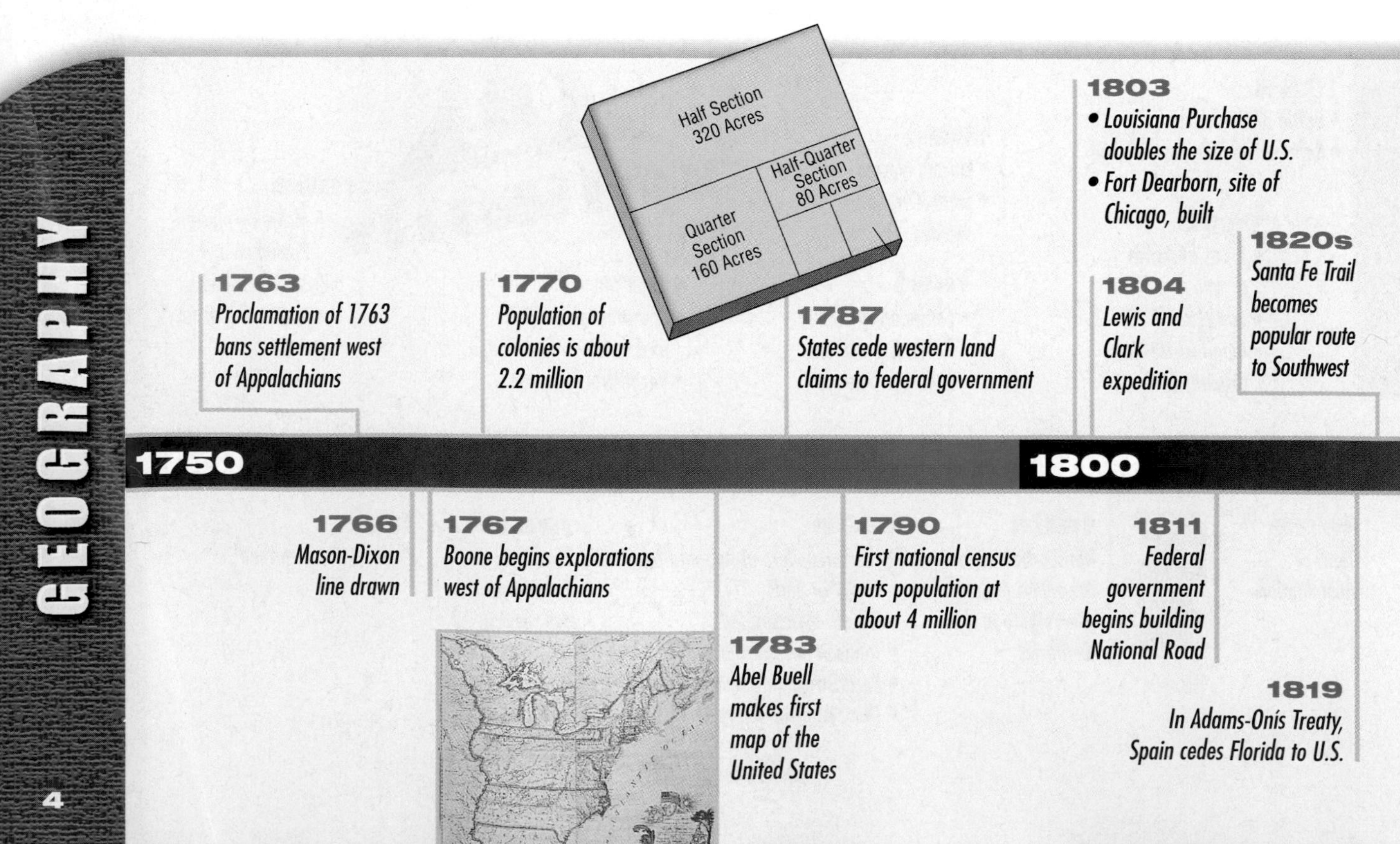


**1763** *Proclamation of 1763 bans settlement west of Appalachians*

**1766** *Mason-Dixon line drawn*

**1767** *Boone begins explorations west of Appalachians*

**1770** *Population of colonies is about 2.2 million*

**1783** *Abel Buell makes first map of the United States*

**1787** *States cede western land claims to federal government*

**1790** *First national census puts population at about 4 million*

**1803**
- *Louisiana Purchase doubles the size of U.S.*
- *Fort Dearborn, site of Chicago, built*

**1804** *Lewis and Clark expedition*

**1811** *Federal government begins building National Road*

**1819** *In Adams-Onís Treaty, Spain cedes Florida to U.S.*

**1820s** *Santa Fe Trail becomes popular route to Southwest* que Gran Bretaña estaba de acuerdo en salir de los fuertes en los territorios del noroeste y ambos países en mejorar las relaciones comerciales

**Jazz Age (Era del Jazz)** un término usado para describir la década de 1920 (p. 360)

**Jim Crow (Leyes Jim Crow)** sistema de leyes que aplicaba la segregación en los servicios públicos a principios de la década de 1890 (p. 243)

**jingoism (jingoísmo)** un sentimiento intenso de orgullo nacional y deseo de una política exterior agresiva (p. 265)

**joint-stock company (sociedad anónima)** una compañía fundada y dirigida por un grupo de inversores que comparten las ganancias y pérdidas de la compañía

**judicial branch (poder judicial)** la rama del gobierno que interpreta y aplica las leyes

**judicial review (revisión judicial)** el poder de los tribunales federales para decidir qué leyes son constitucionales (p. 69)

# K

***kamikaze* (kamikaze)** en la segunda guerra mundial, un avión suicida japonés (p. 447)

**Kansas-Nebraska Act (Decreto de Kansas-Nebraska)** una ley de 1854 que pedía que los ciudadanos de cada territorio decidieran sobre el tema de la esclavitud en ellos (p. 81)

**Kellogg-Briand Pact (Pacto Kellogg-Briand)** un acuerdo firmado en 1928 por el que las naciones firmantes se ponían de acuerdo en no recurrir a la guerra para resolver sus diferencias (p. 346)

**King Philip's War (guerra del rey Felipe)** la guerra que empezó en 1675 entre los colonos ingleses y los indígenas norteamericanos

**kinship (parentesco)** las relaciones familiares

**Korean War (guerra de Corea)** el conflicto sobre el futuro de la península de Corea, que transcurrió entre 1950 y 1953 y acabó en punto muerto (p. 500)

***Kristallnacht* (Noche de los cristales)** nombre que recibe la noche de violencia, el 9 de noviembre de 1938, en contra de los judíos en Alemania y Austria, en 1938 (p. 452)

# L

**labor union (sindicato)** una organización de trabajadores formada para proteger los intereses de sus miembros

**laissez-faire (liberalismo)** la política gubernamental de no interferencia en los negocios privados (p. 205)

**land speculator (especulador del suelo)** una persona que compra grandes terrenos con la esperanza de venderlos después y obtener provecho (p. 177)

**Latino (latino)** una persona con orígenes familiares en la Latinoamérica hispanohablante (p. 596)

**League of Nations (Liga de las Naciones)** una organización internacional, formada después de la primera guerra mundial, que pretendía promover la seguridad y la paz para todos sus miembros (p. 329)

**legislative branch (poder legislativo)** la rama del gobierno que hace las leyes

**legislature (legislatura)** una asamblea legislativa

**Lend-Lease Act (Ley de Préstamo-Alquiler)** una ley de 1941 que autorizaba al Presidente a prestar ayuda a cualquier nación cuya defensa fuera, en su opinión, vital para la seguridad de los Estados Unidos (p. 434)

**Lewis and Clark expedition (expedición de Lewis y Clark)** el viaje de Meriwether Lewis y William Clark a través del territorio de Luisiana durante 1804–1806 (p. 71)

**Liberty Bond (bonos de la libertad)** unos bonos de guerra especiales que se vendían para apoyar la causa de los Aliados durante la primera guerra mundial (p. 322)

**Liberty ship (barco de la libertad)** un barco mercante grande y robusto construido durante la segunda guerra mundial (p. 461)

**Limited Test Ban Treaty (Tratado para la Limitación de Pruebas Nucleares)** en el tratado, firmado en 1963, los Estados Unidos y la Unión Soviética acordaron no probar armas nucleares por encima de la superficie terrestre

**literacy (alfabetismo)** la capacidad de leer y escribir (p. 231)

**long drive (gran travesía)** la conducción de ganado desde las lejanas montañas a los bulliciosos centros ferroviarios que transportaban el ganado al mercado (p. 186)

**loose construction (vaga interpretación)** la creencia en que el gobierno puede hacer cualquier cosa que la Constitución no dice que no puede hacer

**Lost Generation (generación perdida)** un grupo de escritores de la década de 1920 que compartían la creencia de que estaban perdidos en un mundo codicioso y materialista que carecía de valores morales (p. 361)

**Louisiana Purchase (adquisición de Luisiana)** la compra por los Estados Unidos a Francia del territorio de Luisiana, en 1803 (p. 70)

**Lower South (Bajo Sur)** Los estados de Texas, Luisiana, Misisipí, Alabama, Florida, Georgia y Carolina del Sur

**lynching (linchamiento)** el secuestro y ejecución ilegal de una persona por una multitud (p. 243)

# M

**Magna Carta (carta grande)** una "carta grande" firmada en 1215 que cedo ciertas derechas a los nobles ingleses (p. 22)

**mail-order catalog (catálogo de pedidos por correo)** un catálogo que anuncia una gran variedad de objetos que se pueden comprar por correo (p. 248)

**mandate (mandato)** una serie de deseos que los votantes piden a un candidato (p. 542)

**Manhattan Project (Proyecto Manhattan)** en la segunda guerra mundial, el programa secreto norteamericano para fabricar una bomba atómica (p. 448)

**manifest destiny (destino manifiesto)** el razonamiento que defendía que los Estados Unidos estaba destinado a expandirse por Norteamérica (p. 77)

**manufacturing (manufactura)** la fabricación de bienes por medio de máquinas

***maquiladora* (*maquiladora*)** factoría mexicana instalada en las cercanías de la frontera entre los Estados Unidos y México, que produce y monta productos para compañías estadounidenses (p. 788)

**March on Washington (marcha sobre Washington)** la manifestación en favor de los derechos civiles, en 1963, en Washington, D.C. (p. 576)

***Marbury* v. *Madison* (*Marbury* contra *Madison*)** en 1803, un caso en el que el Tribunal Supremo estableció el principio de revisión judicial

**Market Revolution (revolución de mercado)** el cambio de la economía doméstica a la economía basada en el dinero y en la compra y venta de bienes

**Marshall Plan (Plan Marshall)** el programa de ayuda económica norteamericana a Europa Occidental, anunciado en 1947 (p. 492)

**martial law (ley marcial)** gobierno de emergencia de las autoridades militares (p. 98)

**Massacre at Wounded Knee (masacre de Wounded Knee)** el asesinato a tiros por tropas del ejército de un grupo de siux desarmados, en 1890 (p. 182)

**mass media (medios de comunicación)** métodos para la comunicación de información a gran número de personas por medio de letra impresa o transmisión (p. 358)

**mass production (producción en masa)** producción de bienes en gran cantidad (p. 155)

**Mayflower Compact (pacto del Mayflower)** el acuerdo por el que los colonos de la colonia Plymouth se comprometían a obedecer las leyes de su gobierno

**McCarran-Walter Act (Decreto McCarran-Walter)** una ley de inmigración de 1952 que discriminaba en contra de potenciales inmigrantes de Asia y Europa Meridional y Central (p. 498)

***McCulloch* v. *Maryland* (*McCulloch* contra *Maryland*)** en 1819, un caso en el que el Tribunal Supremo falló que el Congreso tiene la autoridad para llevar a cabo las acciones necesarias para cumplir sus deberes constitucionales

**median age (edad mediana)** la edad que divide a la población en dos mitades: una mitad por encima de esa edad y la otra por debajo

**Medicaid** un programa federal que provee ayuda médica para los norteamericanos pobres (p. 548)

**Medicare** un programa federal que provee ayuda médica para los ancianos norteamericanos (pp. 548, 775)

**mercantilism (mercantilismo)** una teoría económica que razonaba que un país debía tratar de acumular tantos lingotes de oro y plata como le fuera posible, exportando más bienes de los que importa (p. 23)

**mercenary (mercenario)** un soldado extranjero que lucha por dinero

**mestizo (mestizo)** una persona de herencia mixta hispana e indígena americana

**Mexican War (guerra Mexicana)** el conflicto entre los Estados Unidos y México, de 1846 a 1848, que acabó con la victoria de Estados Unidos (p. 78)

**Middle Ages (Edad Media)** era de la historia europea que comprende desde el año 500 d. de C. hasta el año 1300

**Middle America (Norteamérica moderada)** un término usado a veces para describir la tendencia principal entre los norteamericanos (p. 649)

**middle class (clase media)** una nueva clase de comerciantes, negociantes y artesanos que surgió en Europa al final de la Edad Media; en los tiempos modernos, la clase social entre los muy ricos y la clase trabajadora menos pudiente

**Middle Colonies (colonias centrales)** las colonias inglesas de Nueva York, Nueva Jersey, Pennsylvania y Delaware

**Middle Passage (paso medio)** la parte del comercio triangular en la que los africanos eran sacados a la fuerza de África para ser llevados como esclavos a las Américas (p. 24)

**migrant farm worker (trabajador agrícola migratorio)** un trabajador que va de granja en granja sembrando y cosechando cosechas distintas (p. 597)

**militarism (militarismo)** la política de aumento de las fuerzas armadas de una nación, como preparación previa a la guerra (p. 309)

**militia (milicia)** ciudadanos armados que sirven de soldados durante una emergencia (p. 763)

**Miranda rule (Ley de Miranda)** obligación que tiene la policía de informar de sus derechos legales a los acusados de cometer un crimen (p. 549)

**mission (misión)** la sede desde la cual personas de otro país pretenden la difusión de su religión

**Missouri Compromise (Compromiso de Misuri)** un acuerdo al que se llegó en 1820 que pedía la admisión de Misuri como estado esclavista y de Maine como estado libre, declarando ilegal la esclavitud en los futuros estados que se crearan al norte de los 36° 30' N de latitud (p. 74)

**mobile society (sociedad móvil)** una sociedad en la que las personas están constantemente yendo de lado a lado

**mobilization (mobilización)** la preparación de tropas para la guerra (p. 310)

**modem (módem)** un dispositivo que convierte datos

en señales que pueden transmitirse por teléfono (p. 801)

**modern republicanism (republicanismo moderno)** propuesta de gobierno del Presidente Eisenhower, descrito como "conservador en lo referente al dinero, liberal en lo referente a los seres humanos" (p. 527)

**monarch (monarca)** alguien que gobierna un reino, como un rey o una reina

**monetary policy (política monetaria)** el plan del gobierno federal para la fabricación y reserva del suministro de dinero de la nación (p. 191)

**monopoly (monopolio)** control completo de un producto o servicio (p. 160)

**Monroe Doctrine (Doctrina Monroe)** la declaración que hizo el Presidente Monroe en 1823 en la que decía que Estados Unidos se opondría a los esfuerzos de cualquier potencia extranjera que quisiera controlar a otra nación en el Hemisferio Occidental (pp. 73, 787)

**Montgomery bus boycott (boicó a los autobuses de Montgomery)** la protesta que en 1955–1956 hicieron los afroamericanos contra la segregación racial en el sistema de autobuses de Montgomery, Alabama (p. 531)

**Morrill Land-Grant Act (Acta Morrill de Concesión de Tierra)** una ley 1862 por la que el gobierno federal distribuyó millones de acres de tierras en el oeste entre los gobiernos de los estados para fundar colegios agrícolas estatales (p. 177)

**mountain man (hombre montañés)** uno de los comerciantes de pieles norteamericanos que exploraron las Montañas Rocosas y otras regiones más al oeste en los 1800

**muckraker (reportero investigador)** un periodista que investiga fechorías cometidas por políticos o corporaciones (p. 287)

**multiculturalism (multiculturalismo)** movimiento que pide más atención a las culturas no europeas en distintas áreas, como la educación (p. 742)

**municipal (municipal)** relativo a la ciudad, como el gobierno municipal (p. 286)

***Munn* v. *Illinois* (*Munn* contra *Illinois*)** una decisión del Tribunal Supremo en 1877 que permitía que los estados regularan ciertos negocios dentro de sus fronteras (p. 208)

**mutiny (motín)** revuelta contra la autoridad superior

**My Lai massacre (masacre de My Lai)** la matanza de varios cientos de vietnamitas por soldados norteamericanos en 1968 (p. 624)

# N

**napalm** una sustancia química muy inflamable usada en ataques con bombas incendiarias (p. 624)

**National American Woman Suffrage Association (Asociación Nacional Norteamericana para el Sufragio Femenino)** una organización formada en 1890 para impulsar el derecho de la mujer al voto (p. 302)

**National Association for the Advancement of Colored People (Asociación Nacional para el Progreso de las Personas de Color)** una organización formada en 1909 para el progreso de la causa de los afroamericanos (p. 244)

**national debt (deuda nacional)** la cantidad total de dinero que debe el gobierno nacional (pp. 416, 776)

**National Defense Education Act (Ley Nacional para la Defensa de la Educación)** una ley de 1958 para mejorar la enseñanza de ciencias y matemáticas en las escuelas (p. 528)

**National Rifle Association (NRA) (Asociación Nacional del Rifle)** organización destacada que está en contra del control de armas (p. 764)

**nationalism (nacionalismo)** devoción hacia la propia nación (p. 259)

**nationalization (nacionalización)** conversión en propiedad del gobierno (p. 413)

**National Organization for Women (NOW) (Organización Nacional de Mujeres)** una organización formada en 1966 para promover la participación total de las mujeres en la sociedad norteamericana (p. 591)

**Nation of Islam (Nación del Islam)** una organización, llamada también Musulmanes Negros, dedicada a la separación de las personas de raza negra y a la ayuda a sí mismos (p. 581)

**nativism (indigenismo)** un movimiento que promueve un mejor trato para los norteamericanos nacidos en el país que para los inmigrantes (p. 223)

**nativist (natalista)** que apoya la política de favorecer a los ciudadanos nacidos en el país y desfavorecer a los inmigrantes (p. 755)

**naturalize (naturalizar)** solicitud y concesión de la ciudadanía norteamericana

**natural rights (derechos naturales)** derechos que tiene la gente simplemente por ser humanos

**neutral (neutral)** que no toma partido en un conflicto o disputa

**New Deal (Nuevo Trato)** los programas de ayuda, recuperación y reforma del Presidente Franklin Roosevelt para combatir la Gran Depresión (pp. 403, 769)

**New England Colonies (colonias de Nueva Inglaterra)** las colonias inglesas que se convirtieron en los estados de Connecticut, Rhode Island, Massachusetts, Vermont, Nueva Hampshire y Maine

**New Federalism (Nuevo Federalismo)** el plan del Presidente Reagan para dar a los estados más control sobre el uso de la ayuda federal (p. 705)

**New Freedom (Nueva Libertad)** la plataforma de la campaña de Woodrow Wilson en 1912, en la que se pedía acción antimonopolio sin amenazar la libre competencia (p. 298)

**New Frontier (Nueva Frontera)** las propuestas del

Presidente Kennedy para mejorar la economía, ayudar a los pobres y acelerar el programa espacial (p. 542)

**New Left (Nueva Izquierda)** un movimiento político nuevo de finales de la década de 1960 que pedía cambios radicales para luchar contra la pobreza y el racismo (p. 627)

**New Nationalism (Nuevo Nacionalismo)** el programa de Theodore Roosevelt para aumentar la regulación federal de los negocios y lugares de trabajo, los impuestos sobre la renta y las herencias y reformas electorales (p. 297)

**New Right (nueva derecha)** una coalición de grupos conservadores que surgió hacia 1980 (p. 702)

**Niagara Movement (Movimiento Niágara)** una organización fundada en 1905 por W.E.B. Du Bois y otros líderes negros que pedía libertades civiles totales para los afroamericanos, el fin de la discriminación racial y el reconocimiento de la hermandad de los seres humanos (p. 235)

**Nisei (nisei)** un japonés-americano cuyos padres nacieron en Japón (p. 429)

**nomadic (nómada)** que cambia de lugar regularmente en busca de alimento

**nomad (nómada)** una persona que emigra constantemente, en lugar de vivir permanentemente en un lugar

**nonviolent protest (protesta no-violenta)** una forma de protesta en la que los protestantes no se resisten o devuelven los golpes al ser atacados (p. 565)

**North American Free Trade Agreement (NAFTA) (Zona de Libre Comercio del Atlántico Norte)** un acuerdo por el que se suprimen las restricciones al comercio entre Estados Unidos, Canadá y México (pp. 737, 784)

**North Atlantic Treaty Organization (NATO) (Organización del Tratado del Atlántico Norte) (OTAN)** la alianza entre Estados Unidos, Canadá y naciones de Europa Occidental, formada en 1949 (pp. 495, 796)

**Nuclear Regulatory Commission (Comisión para la Regulación Nuclear)** una organización gubernamental formada en 1974 para supervisar los usos civiles de materiales nucleares (p. 607)

**nullification (anulación)** negativa de un estado a reconocer una ley federal

# O

**obsolete (obsoleto)** anticuado

**Office of War Information (Oficina de Información para la Guerra)** una agencia federal creada en 1942 para conseguir apoyo público para el esfuerzo de guerra de la segunda guerra mundial (p. 466)

**Office of War Mobilization (Oficina de Mobilización para la Guerra)** una agencia federal creada en 1943 para coordinar asuntos relacionados con la producción de guerra durante la segunda guerra mundial (p. 460)

**Olive Branch Petition (Petición de la Rama de Olivo)** una petición que los colonos norteamericanos hicieron al rey Jorge III en 1775 para que él parara la lucha

**Open Door Policy (política de puertas abiertas)** la estrategia norteamericana con China hacia el 1900, que favorecía relaciones comerciales abiertas entre China y otras naciones (p. 269)

**oral history (historia oral)** tradiciones transmitidas por la palabra de generación en generación

**Oregon Trail (Pista Oregón)** una ruta que unía Independence, Misuri, y Oregón, usada por muchos pioneros durante la década de 1840

**Organization of Petroleum Exporting Countries (OPEC) (Organización de Países Exportadores de Petróleo) (OPEP)** un grupo de naciones que colaboraban para regular el precio y suministro de petróleo (p. 655)

# P

**pardon (perdón)** absolución oficial de un crimen (p. 127)

**Paris peace talks (conferencias de París para la paz)** las negociaciones entre los Estados Unidos y Vietnam del Norte, que comenzaron en 1968 (p. 635)

**pass (paso)** un lugar a poca altura en una cadena montañosa que permite el paso de viajeros al otro lado

**patent (patente)** una licencia para fabricar, usar o vender un invento (p. 152)

**patronage (patrocinio)** la práctica de contratar a partidarios políticos para puestos de trabajo en el gobierno

**Peace Corps (Cuerpo de Paz)** un programa federal establecido para mandar voluntarios para ayudar a las naciones en desarrollo en todo el mundo (p. 557)

**Pendleton Civil Service Act (Acta Pendleton de Servicio Civil)** una ley de 1883 que creó una Comisión para el Servicio Civil y declaró que a los empleados federales no se les podía exigir que contribuyeran a los fondos para las campañas electorales y no podían ser despedidos por razones políticas (p. 207)

**Pentagon Papers (Papeles del Pentágono)** un estudio del gobierno sobre la participación de los Estados Unidos en la guerra de Vietnam, hecho público en 1971 (p. 626)

**Pequot War (guerra Pequot)** la guerra entre los colonos ingleses y los indios pequot en 1637

**per capita income (renta per cápita)** promedio de los ingresos por persona (p. 511)

**persecute (perseguir)** oprimir a alguien a causa de sus creencias

**Persian Gulf War (guerra del Golfo Pérsico)** la guerra en la que fuerzas de las Naciones Unidas expulsaron de Kuwait al ejército invasor iraquí en 1991 (p. 718)

**philanthropist (filántropo)** persona que hace donaciones a causas que lo merecen (p. 233)

**Pickett's Charge (Carga de Pickett)** la desafortunada carga de la infantería confederada durante la batalla de Gettysburg (p. 109)

**piecework (trabajo a destajo)** un sistema en el que a los trabajadores no se les paga por horas sino por lo que producen (p. 164)

**Pilgrim (peregrino)** un miembro del grupo de separatistas ingleses que establecieron la colonia de Plymouth en 1620

**Pinckney Treaty (Tratado Pinckney)** un tratado entre los Estados Unidos y España en 1795 que estableció los límites de los Estados Unidos por el sur

**placer mining (minería de lavadero)** un método minero usado por buscadores particulares (p. 185)

**plantation (plantación)** una gran instalación agrícola en la que las cosechas se cultivan principalmente para la venta

***Plessy* v. *Ferguson* (*Plessy* contra *Ferguson*)** un caso de 1896 en el que el Tribunal Supremo falló que la segregación racial era legal siempre que las instalaciones separadas fueran iguales para ambas razas (p. 243)

**political asylum (asilo político)** protección que un país da a los refugiados de otro país (p. 753)

**political machine (maquinaria política)** una organización no oficial diseñada para mantener en el poder a un partido o grupo en particular, dirigida normalmente por un único y poderoso jefe (p. 220)

**political party (partido político)** un grupo de personas que tratan de ganar las elecciones y los cargos públicos para controlar la política y los programas del gobierno

**poll tax (impuesto por persona)** una tarifa especial que se debe pagar antes de que una persona pueda votar (p. 242)

**Pontiac's Rebellion (rebelión de Pontiac)** una rebelión de los indígenas norteamericanos contra los británicos en la región de los Grandes Lagos, en 1763

**Poor People's Campaign (Campaña de los Pobres)** una cruzada contra la injusticia económica organizada en 1968 por Martin Luther King, Jr. (p. 650)

**popular sovereignty (soberanía popular)** dejar que la gente de un territorio decida si se va a permitir la esclavitud en él

**population density (densidad de población)** el número de personas promedio que viven en un espacio dado

**Populist (populista)** un seguidor del partido populista, formado en 1891, que apoyaba la creación de una provisión mayor de dinero y otras reformas económicas (p. 193)

**precedent (precedente)** algo que se ha hecho o dicho que se convierte en un ejemplo, regla o tradición a seguir

**prejudice (prejuicio)** una opinión irracional, generalmente desfavorable, sobre otro grupo

**presidio (presidio)** fuerte construido en el Suroeste por los españoles

**price controls (control de precios)** un sistema de precios determinados por el gobierno (p. 323)

**prime minister (primer ministro)** el funcionario más alto de un gobierno parlamentario

**privateer (corsario)** un barco propiedad de un particular que es contratado por un gobierno para atacar a barcos enemigos

**Proclamation of 1763 (Proclamación de 1763)** una orden del rey británico que cerró la región al oeste de los Apalaches y prohibió el asentamiento de colonos

**productivity (productividad)** la cantidad que produce un trabajador en un periodo de tiempo (pp. 152, 803)

**profiteering (acaparamiento)** venta de bienes escasos a precios irracionalmente altos

**progressive (progresista)** reformista político y social de finales de los 1800 y principios de los 1900 (p. 768)

**Progressive Era (Era Progresista)** el periodo entre 1890 y 1920 durante el cual se realizaron una serie de reformas a nivel local, estatal y federal (p. 287)

**progressive income tax (impuesto progresivo sobre la renta)** un impuesto en el que el porcentaje de tasas que se deben aumenta con la renta percibida (p. 193)

**prohibition (prohibición)** prohibición legal de manufacturación y venta de bebidas alcohólicas (p. 224)

**proliferation (proliferación)** aumento rápido del número, esparcimiento (p. 662)

**proprietary colony (colonia propiedad)** concesión de una colonia con plenos derechos de gobierno que el rey o reina hace a un individuo o grupo

**public works program (programa de obras públicas)** un programa financiado por el gobierno para construir obras públicas (p. 405)

**Pueblo Revolt of 1680 (revuelta de los Pueblo de 1680)** una revuelta de los indios pueblo de Nuevo México contra España

**Pullman Strike (huelga Pullman)** la huelga de trabajadores del ferrocarril que se extendió por toda la nación (p. 172)

**Puritan (puritano)** una persona a favor de la purificación de la Iglesia Anglicana de Inglaterra

## Q

**Quaker (cuáquero)** un miembro de un grupo protestante que pone énfasis en la igualdad

**quarantine (cuarentena)** un periodo de aislamiento para prevenir la extensión de una enfermedad (p. 212)

**quorum (quórum)** el numero minimo de miembros necesarios para votar

**quota (cuota)** un número límite (p. 345)

# R

**racism (racismo)** la creencia que sostiene que las diferencias en carácter o inteligencia se deben a la raza de la persona (p. 278)
**ragtime (ragtime)** un estilo de música que consiste en melodías con acentos sincopados sobre un pulso constante (p. 239)
**ratify (ratificar)** aprobar o sancionar
**rationing (racionar)** distribuir cantidades fijas de bienes entre los consumidores (p. 323)
***realpolitik* (realpolitik)** en alemán, "política práctica," o política exterior basada en el interés en lugar de en principios morales (p. 659)
**recall (retirar)** un proceso por el que los votantes destituyen a un funcionario público de su puesto antes de la próxima elección (p. 292)
**recession (recesión)** un periodo de poca actividad económica (p. 677)
**recognition (reconocimiento)** aceptación oficial (p. 96)
**Reconstruction (reconstrucción)** el esfuerzo del gobierno federal entre 1865 y 1877 por reparar los daños causados al Sur y devolver los estados sureños a la Unión (p. 125)
**red scare (miedo a los rojos)** miedo al comunismo y a otras ideas extremas (p. 342)
**referendum (referéndum)** un proceso por el que los ciudadanos votan una ley aprobada por su legislatura (p. 292)
**Reformation (Reforma)** una revuelta contra la Iglesia Católica, que comenzó en 1517
**religious tolerance (tolerancia religiosa)** la idea que mantiene que personas de religiones distintas deberían vivir juntas en paz
**Renaissance (Renacimiento)** una era de la historia europea, desde el año 1300 al 1500
**reparations (compensación)** pago que un enemigo debe hacer por daños económicos sufridos durante una guerra (p. 330)
**republic (república)** gobierno del pueblo por medio de sus representantes electos (p. 42)
**republican virtues (virtudes republicanas)** las virudes que el pueblo norteamericano necesitaría para gobernarse a sí mismo, como sacrificar las necesidades individuales por el bien de la comunidad, autoconfianza, industria, frugalidad y armonía
**reservation (reserva)** una área que el gobierno federal reservó para los indígenas norteamericanos que habían perdido su tierra natal (p. 180)
**restrictive covenant (pacto restrictivo)** un acuerdo entre propietarios de viviendas para no vender propiedades inmobiliarias a ciertos grupos de personas, como a los afroamericanos o a los judíos (p. 219)
**revenue (ingresos)** renta (p. 416)
**revival (renacer)** una reunión en la que las personas "renacen," o son devueltas a una vida religiosa
**Revolutionary War (guerra de Independencia)** la guerra de los colonos norteamericanos por conseguir la independencia de Gran Bretaña, que duró de 1775 a 1783 (p. 30)
**rock and roll** un tipo de música que surge del rhythm and blues y que se hizo popular en la década de 1950 (p. 521)
***Roe* v. *Wade* (*Roe* contra *Wade*)** en 1973, la decisión del Tribunal Supremo que legalizó el aborto (p. 593)
**Roosevelt Corollary (Corolario de Roosevelt)** la ampliación que el Presidente Theodore Roosevelt hizo en 1904 de la Doctrina Monroe, en la que Roosevelt afirmaba el derecho de los Estados Unidos a intervenir en naciones latinoamericanas (pp. 273, 787)
**Rosie the Riveter (Rosie "la remachadora")** un término que simboliza a las muchas mujeres que trabajaron en la industria de defensa durante la segunda guerra mundial (p. 470)
**royal colony (colonia real)** una colonia con un gobernador nombrado por el rey
**rural (rural)** ambiente de campo, en vez de ambiente de ciudad
**rural free delivery (reparto rural gratuito)** la entrega gratuita de paquetes en las áreas rurales, que comenzó en 1896 (p. 248)
**Russian Revolution (revolución Rusa)** el colapso del gobierno del zar en Rusia en 1917, que finalmente llevó a la toma del poder por los bolcheviques (p. 316)

# S

**sachem (cacique)** un líder indígena norteamericano
**Salem witch trials (juicios por brujería de Salem)** el procesamiento y ejecución de veinte mujeres y hombres acusados de brujería en Massachusetts, en 1692
**SALT I (Strategic Arms Limitation Treaty) (tratado para la limitación de armas estratégicas)** un acuerdo firmado en 1972 por los Estados Unidos y la Unión Soviética sobre la limitación de armas nucleares (p. 662)
**salutary neglect (negligencia saludable)** la política británica a principios de los 1700 consistente en no interferir en la política y la economía de las colonias norteamericanas, siempre que dicha negligencia sirviera a los intereses económicos británicos
**Sandinista (sandinista)** un miembro del grupo de nicaragüenses que se hicieron con el gobierno en 1979 (p. 711)
**Santa Fe Trail (Pista de Santa Fe)** un camino que unía Independence, Misuri, con Santa Fe, Nuevo México, a mediados del siglo XIX

**satellite nation (nación satélite)** un país dominado política y económicamente por otro país, especialmente por la Unión Soviética durante la guerra fría (p. 487)
**saturation bombing (bombardeo de saturación)** arrojar grandes concentraciones de bombas sobre cierta área (p. 623)
**savanna (sabana)** una región cerca del ecuador con praderas tropicales y árboles dispersos
**scab (esquirol)** un trabajador contratado por un patrón para reemplazar a obreros en huelga (p. 170)
**scalawag (republicano del Sur)** un apodo insultante para un republicano blanco del Sur después de la guerra Civil (p. 136)
**scarce (escaso)** que hay poco
**Scopes trial (juicio Scopes)** un juicio en Tennessee en 1925 sobre la enseñanza de la teoría de la evolución en las escuelas públicas (p. 368)
***Scott* v. *Sandford* (*Scott* contra *Sandford*)** una decisión del Tribunal Supremo en 1857 que declaró que los esclavos no eran ciudadanos y reguló el Compromiso de Misuri era inconstitucional
**secede (secesión)** renunciar formalmente a ser miembro de un grupo u organización (p. 82)
**secessionist (secesionista)** una persona que quería que el Sur se separara
**Second Amendment (Segunda Enmienda)** enmienda a la Constitución de los Estados Unidos que concede a los estados el derecho a formar milicia armada (p. 763)
**Second Continental Congress (Segundo Congreso Continental)** una asamblea de representantes de las colonias que se reunió por primera vez en Filadelfia en mayo de 1775 (p. 30)
**Second Great Awakening (Segundo Gran Despertar)** un movimiento religioso de principios del S. XIX
**Second New Deal (Segundo Nuevo Trato)** un periodo de actividad legislativa emprendido por el Presidente Franklin Roosevelt en 1935 (p. 408)
**section (sección)** una región geográfica
**secularize (secularizar)** poner bajo el control del gobierno en vez del de la iglesia
**sedition (sedición)** palabras o acciones que fomentan la rebelión (p. 324)
**segregation (segregación)** separación por la fuerza (p. 214)
**Selective Service Act (Ley de Servicio Selectivo)** una ley de 1917 que autorizaba la leva de hombres jóvenes para el servicio militar (p. 317)
**self-determination (autodeterminación)** el poder de tomar decisiones sobre el propio futuro (p. 328)
**self-sufficient (autosuficiente)** capaz de hacer todo lo necesario para mantenerse a sí mismo
**Seneca Falls Convention (Convención de Seneca Falls)** la primera convención sobre los derechos de la mujer en la historia de los Estados Unidos, celebrada en 1848
**seniority (antigüedad)** estado derivado de la duración del servicio (p. 472)
**separation of powers (separación de poderes)** la separación de poderes en el gobierno federal entre el poder legislativo, executivo y judicial
**settlement house (centro de residencia)** un centro comunitario organizado para proveer varios servicios a los pobres de la ciudad (p. 225)
**sharecropping (aparcería)** un sistema de cultivo en el que un agricultor cultivaba una porción de tierra de otro propietario y recibía como pago parte de la cosecha en el momento de la recolección (p. 138)
**Shays' Rebellion (Rebelión de Shay)** una revuelta contra los impuestos en Massachusetts en 1786 y 1787
**shell (granada)** un artefacto que explota en el aire o cuando choca contra un objetivo sólido (p. 90)
**Sherman Antitrust Act (Acta Antimonopolios Sherman)** una ley aprobada en 1890 que prohibía cualquier combinación de compañías que limitaran el comercio (p. 161)
**shuttle diplomacy (diplomacia itinerante)** viajes repetidos de un mediador entre naciones en disputa con la intención de llegar a un acuerdo (p. 684)
**siege (asedio)** una táctica en la que se rodea al enemigo y se le hace pasar hambre para que se rinda (p. 110)
**silent majority (mayoría silenciosa)** un término usado por el Presidente Nixon para describir a los norteamericanos que no estaban de acuerdo con la contracultura (p. 656)
**sit-down strike (huelga de brazos caídos)** una protesta laboral en la que los trabajadores dejan de trabajar pero se niegan a abandonar el lugar de trabajo (p. 417)
**sit-in (sentada)** forma de protesta en la que los protestantes se sientan y se niegan a moverse; los defensores de los derechos civiles las usaron a veces para protestar pacíficamente (p. 570)
**social Darwinism (darwinismo social)** una teoría, derivada de la teoría sobre la selección natural de Darwin, según la cual la sociedad debe interferir lo menos posible en la búsqueda de la felicidad de sus individuos (p. 160)
**social gospel movement (movimiento del evangelio social)** un movimiento de reforma social que se desarrolló en instituciones religiosas y que buscaba la aplicación directa de la palabra de Jesús en la sociedad (p. 225)
**socialism (socialismo)** una filosofía económica y política que favorece el control público (o social) de la propiedad y los ingresos (p. 167)
**Social Security system (sistema de Seguridad Social)** un sistema público que proporciona pagos regulares a personas que no pueden mantenerse a sí mismas (p. 409)
**social welfare program (programa de bienestar social)**

un programa diseñado para asegurar un estándar de vida básico para todos los ciudadanos (p. 288)

**software (software)** programa para una computadora (p. 802)

**solid South (Sólido Sur)** un término que describe la dominación ejercida por el partido demócrata en el Sur desde la guerra Civil (p. 142)

**sooner (primer colono)** una persona que señalaba su propiedad en territorio indio antes de que éste se abriera legalmente a la colonización (p. 183)

**Southern Christian Leadership Conference (SCLC) (Conferencia de Liderazgo Cristiano del Sur)** una organización en favor de los derechos civiles formada en 1957 por el Dr. Martin Luther King, Jr., y otros líderes (p. 565)

**Southern Colonies (colonias del sur)** las colonias inglesas de Virginia, Maryland, las Carolinas y Georgia

**speakeasy (bar clandestino)** durante la Prohibición, un bar donde se servían ilegalmente bebidas alcohólicas (p. 366)

**special prosecutor (fiscal especial)** un investigador nombrado por el Departamento de Justicia para investigar irregularidades cometidas por funcionarios del gobierno (p. 668)

**specie (metálico)** moneda de oro o plata

**speculation (especulación)** inversiones de alto riesgo con la esperanza de obtener mucha ganancia (p. 377)

**sphere of influence (esfera de influencia)** área de control económico y político que ejerce una nación sobre otra u otras naciones (p. 269)

**spiritual (espiritual)** un himno popular

**spoils (botín)** recompensa (p. 329)

**spoils system (sistema de sinecuras)** sistema o práctica por el que el partido ganador en una elección concede cargos oficiales como recompensa; el nombre del sistema de padrinazgo bajo la presidencia de Jackson

***Sputnik*** el primer satélite artificial en orbitar la Tierra, lanzado por la Unión Soviética en 1957 (p. 506)

**stagflation (estanflación)** una combinación de alta inflación y alto desempleo, sin crecimiento económico (p. 677)

**stalemate (punto muerto)** una situación en la que ninguna de las partes en conflicto es capaz de conseguir ventaja (p. 310)

**Stamp Act (Ley del Impuesto de los Sellos)** una ley aprobada por el Parlamento británico en 1765 que exigía un impuesto sobre los periódicos, documentos legales y otros materiales impresos en las colonias (p. 28)

**staple crop (cultivo básico)** una cosecha que está en constante demanda, como el algodón, el trigo o el arroz

**states' rights (derechos de los estados)** la teoría que sostiene que la potencia dividida constitución entre los estados y el gobierno federal y que una interpretación terminante de esa división debe ser respetada

**steerage (tercera clase)** una área grande y espaciosa debajo de la cubierta del barco en la que viajaban muchos inmigrantes pobres (p. 211)

**stereotype (estereotipo)** una concepción fija en la que cree un grupo de personas (p. 200)

**Stono Rebellion (rebelión Stono)** una revuelta de esclavos en Carolina del Sur en 1739

**Strategic Arms Reduction Treaty (START) (tratado para la reducción de armas estratégicas)** el acuerdo firmado en 1991 que establecía una reducción cuantiosa del armamento nuclear de norteamericanos y soviéticos (p. 717)

**Strategic Defense Initiative (SDI) (Iniciativa de Defensa Estratégica)** propuesta del Presidente Reagan para crear un sistema de defensa contra un ataque nuclear (p. 705)

**strict construction (interpretación estricta)** la creencia en que el gobierno no debería hacer nada que la Constitución no diga explícitamente que puede hacer

**strike (huelga)** parar de trabajar para forzar al patrón a cumplir ciertas exigencias, como un salario más alto o mejores condiciones de trabajo

**Student Nonviolent Coordinating Committee (SNCC) (Comité No Violento de Coordinación Estudiantil)** una organización estudiantil a favor de los derechos civiles fundada en 1960 (p. 567)

**subsidy (subsidio)** un pago del gobierno para fomentar el desarrollo de ciertas industrias clave (p. 206)

**suburb (suburbio)** una comunidad residencial que rodea una ciudad (p. 218)

**suffrage (sufragio)** derecho a votar

**supply-side economics (economía de suministro indirecto)** la teoría que defiende que las reducciones de impuestos aumentarán la inversión y por lo tanto fomentarán el crecimiento económico (p. 703)

**Sussex pledge (la promesa de Sussex)** en 1916, una promesa del gobierno alemán de que sus submarinos avisarían a los barcos antes de atacar (p. 315)

**synagogue (sinagoga)** casa judía de oración

# T

**Taft-Hartley Act (Ley Taft-Hartley)** una ley de 1947 que permitía que el Presidente ordenara que volvieran al trabajo los trabajadores en huelga de ciertas industrias (p. 524)

**tariff (tarifa)** un impuesto sobre los bienes extranjeros importados en un país (pp. 68, 784)

**Tariff of 1828 (Tarifa de 1828)** un impuesto elevado sobre bienes manufacturados; llamada la "Tarifa de la Abominación" por los sureños

# iographical Dictionary

## A

**Adams, Abigail** First Lady, 1797–1801; as the wife of Patriot John Adams, she urged him to promote women's rights at the beginning of the American Revolution

**Adams, John Quincy** Sixth President of the United States, 1825–1829; proposed greater federal involvement in the economy through tariffs and improvements such as roads, bridges, and canals

**Adams, John** Second President of the United States, 1797–1801; worked to relieve increasing tensions with France; lost reelection bid to Jefferson in 1800 as the country moved away from Federalist policies

**Addams, Jane** Cofounder of Hull House, the first settlement house, in 1889; remained active in social causes through the early 1900s (p. 225)

**Agnew, Spiro** Vice President under President Richard Nixon until forced to resign in 1973 for crimes committed before taking office; known for his harsh campaign attacks (p. 668)

**Allen, Richard** African American religious leader; helped found the African Methodist Episcopal Church (AME) in 1816

**Anthony, Susan B.** Political activist and women's rights leader in the late 1800s (p. 301)

**Arthur, Chester A.** Twenty-first President of the United States, 1881–1885; signed 1883 Pendleton Act, which instituted the Civil Service (p. 207)

**Askia, Muhammad** Ruler of the African empire of Songhai, 1493–1528; promoted Islamic culture

**Austin, Stephen** Leader of first American group of Texas settlers in 1822

usan B. Anthony

## B

**Bakke, Allan** Student who won a suit against the University of California in 1978 on the grounds that the affirmative action program had kept him out (p. 694)

**Baldwin, James** African American author and spokesperson for the civil rights movement during the 1960s (p. 580)

**Banks, Dennis** Native American leader in 1960s and 1970s; helped organize American Indian Movement (AIM) and the 1973 Wounded Knee occupation (p. 602)

**echer, Catharine** Author whose 1841 book *A Treatise on Domestic Economy* argued that women should support reform from the home

**er, Lyman** Revivalist during the Second Great kening; feared the rise of selfishness in the United

**enachem** Israeli leader during the 1970s; began ddle East peace process by reaching the 1978 avid Accords with Egypt (p. 685)

**Bell, Alexander Graham** Inventor; developed the telephone in 1876; one of the founders of American Telephone & Telegraph (AT&T) (p. 154)

**Bellamy, Edward** Author of the novel *Looking Backward* (1888), which proposed nationalizing trusts to eliminate social problems (p. 285)

**Bethune, Mary McLeod** African American educator, New Deal worker; founded Bethune Cookman College in the 1920s, advised the National Youth Administration (p. 406)

**Beveridge, Albert J.** Indiana senator in the early 1900s; saw United States imperialism as a duty owed to "primitive" societies (p. 262)

**Booth, John Wilkes** Southern actor who assassinated President Abraham Lincoln in 1865 (p. 117)

**Brady, James** Press Secretary to President Reagan who was paralyzed by a gunshot during a 1981 assassination attempt; the 1994 law requiring a five-day waiting period before purchase of a gun was named for Mr. Brady (p. 763)

**Breckinridge, John C.** Presidential candidate of the southern wing of the Democratic party in 1860

**Brown, John** Abolitionist crusader who massacred proslavery settlers in Kansas before the Civil War; hoped to inspire slave revolt with 1859 attack on Virginia arsenal; executed for treason against the state of Virginia

**Bruce, Blanche** African American senator from Mississippi during Reconstruction (p. 135)

**Bryan, William Jennings** Advocate of silver standard and proponent of Democratic and Populist views from the 1890s through the 1910s; Democratic candidate for President in 1896, 1900, and 1908 (p. 194)

**Buchanan, James** Fifteenth President of the United States, 1857–1861; supported by the South; attempted to moderate fierce disagreement over expansion of slavery

**Bush, George H. W.** Forty-first President of the United States, 1989–1993; continued Reagan's conservative policies; brought together United Nations coalition to fight the Persian Gulf War (p. 714)

**Byrd, William** Wealthy plantation owner in colonial Virginia whose diary gives a vivid picture of colonial life

## C

**Calhoun, John C.** Statesman from South Carolina who held many offices in the federal government; supported slavery, cotton exports, states' rights; in 1850 foresaw future conflicts over slavery

**Carnegie, Andrew** Industrialist who made a fortune in steel in the late 1800s through vertical consolidation; as a philanthropist, he gave away some $350 million (p. 159)

**Carson, Rachel** Marine biologist, author of *Silent Spring* (1962), which exposed harmful effects of pesticides and inspired concern for the environment (p. 606)



**teach-in (sesión de instrucción)** una sesión especial de conferencia y debate sobre un tema polémico (p. 627)

**Teapot Dome scandal (escándalo del Teapot Dome)** un escándalo durante la administración Harding referente a la concesión de derechos de prospección petrolera en tierras del gobierno a cambio de dinero (p. 345)

**telecommunications (telecomunicaciones)** comunicación a larga distancia por medios electrónicos (p. 1058)

**televangelism (televangelismo)** el uso de la televisión por organizaciones religiosas, especialmente para recaudar fondos (p. 702)

**temperance movement (movimiento de la templanza)** una campaña organizada para eliminar el consumo de alcohol (p. 224)

**tenant farming (agricultor arrendatario)** sistema de labranza en el que un agricultor alquila tierras de cultivo a un hacendado (p. 138)

**tenement (casa de vecindad)** un edificio de apartamentos lleno de gente, con pobres condiciones sanitarias, de seguridad y de comodidad (p. 218)

**Tennessee Valley Authority (Autoridades del Valle del Tennessee)** un proyecto federal para proporcionar corriente eléctrica, control de inundación y oportunidades recreativas en el valle del río Tennessee (p. 406)

**Tet Offensive (Ofensiva Tet)** el ataque que en 1968 lanzaron fuerzas norvietnamitas y del Vietcong contra Vietnam del Sur (p. 621)

**Texas War for Independence (guerra de la Independencia de Texas)** la exitosa revuelta de los texanos contra el gobierno mexicano en 1835–1836 (p. 78)

**Thirteenth Amendment (Decimotercera Enmienda)** la enmienda constitucional, ratificada en 1865, que abolió la esclavitud (p. 116)

**38th parallel (paralelo 38)** la línea de latitud que dividía a Corea del Norte y Corea del Sur (p. 500)

**Three-Fifths Compromise (Compromiso de las Tres Quintas Partes)** el compromiso en la Convención Constitucional que establecía que las tres quintas partes de los esclavos de un estado contaran para propósitos de representación

**totalitarian (totalitario)** que describe una forma de gobierno que controla todos los aspectos de la vida de sus ciudadanos (p. 429)

**trade deficit (déficit comercial)** la cantidad de dinero que se pierde cuando una nación gasta más en importación de lo que gana con la exportación (p. 785)

**trade surplus (excedente comercial)** la cantidad de dinero que se gana cuando una nación gana más con la exportación de lo que gasta en importación (p. 785)

**Trail of Tears (Sendero de Lágrimas)** el desalojo forzoso de los cheroquís en 1838-1839 y su traslado a tierras al oeste del río Misisipí (p. 75)

**trans-Appalachia (transapalaches)** el área al oeste de los Montes Apalaches

**transcendentalism (trascendentalismo)** un movimiento filosófico a mediados del S. XIX que enfatizaba el descubrimiento espiritual y la clarividencia en lugar de la razón

**transcontinental railroad (ferrocarril transcontinental)** un ferrocarril que iba de costa a costa (p. 152)

**transistor (transistor)** un pequeñísimo circuito que amplifica, controla y genera señales eléctricas (p. 512)

**Treaty of Ghent (Tratado de Ghent)** el acuerdo firmado en 1814 que puso fin a la guerra de 1812

**Treaty of Greenville (Tratado de Greenville)** un tratado frimado en 1795 por los Estados Unidos y varios pueblos indígenas norteamericanos por el que los indios norteamericanos cedían el control de casi todo Ohio

**Treaty of Guadalupe Hidalgo (Tratado de Guadalupe Hidalgo)** un tratado firmado en 1848 por los Estados Unidos y México, que ponía final a la guerra Mexicana

**Treaty of Paris (1763) (Tratado de París de 1763)** el tratado que terminó la guerra Franco-india y por el cual Francia renunció en favor de Gran Bretaña a sus pretensiones sobre los territorios norteamericanos

**Treaty of Paris (1783) (Tratado de París de 1783)** el tratado que puso fin a la guerra de la Independencia y en el cual Gran Bretaña reconoció la independencia de Norteamérica (p. 31)

**Treaty of Tordesillas (Tratado de Tordesillas)** un tratado firmado por Portugal y España en 1494 en el que se repartían el mundo no cristiano

**triangular trade (comercio triangular)** el comercio entre las Américas, Europa y África (p. 24)

**Truman Doctrine (Doctrina Truman)** la declaración del Presidente Truman en 1947 que decía que los Estados Unidos apoyarían a las naciones amenazadas por el comunismo (pp. 490, 795)

**trust (sociedad de fideocomiso)** un grupo de compañías independientes que se sitúan bajo el control de una junta directiva (p. 161)

**trustee (depositario)** alguien en quien se deposita la confianza para que se encargue de un negocio

**Turner's Rebellion (Rebelión de Turner)** una fracasada revuelta de esclavos dirigida por Nat Turner en 1831

**Turner thesis (Tesis de Turner)** el razonamiento que hizo Frederick Jackson Turner en 1893, que decía que la frontera había dado forma al estilo de vida norteamericano (p. 198)

**turnpike (carretera de peaje)** una carretera en la que los usuarios deben pagar peaje

**Twenty-first Amendment (Vigesimoprimera Enmienda)** la enmienda constitucional, ratificada en 1933, que terminó con la Prohibición (p. 391)

# U

**U-boat** un submarino alemán (p. 314)
**Underground Railroad (Ferrocarril Subterráneo)** una red de rutas de escape que facilitaba protección y transporte a los esclavos que huían hacia el norte en busca de libertad
**undocumented immigrant (inmigrante indocumentado)** inmigrante que ha entrado ilegalmente en los Estados Unidos (p. 753)
**Union (Unión)** los Estados Unidos como entidad nacional; o, durante la guerra Civil, el Norte
**United Farm Workers (UFW) (Trabajadores Agrícolas Unidos)** un sindicato organizado por César Chávez para organizar a los braceros mexicanos en el oeste (p. 598)
**Upper South (Alto Sur)** los estados de Virginia, Carolina del Norte, Tennessee y Arkansas
**utopian community (comunidad utópica)** una pequeña sociedad dedicada a la perfección de las condiciones sociales y políticas
**U-2 incident (incidente U-2)** el derribo de un avión espía norteamericano sobre la Unión Soviética en 1960 (p. 506)

# V

**vaudeville (vodevil)** un espectáculo de variedades que presentaba números cómicos, musicales y de baile (p. 236)
**Versailles Treaty (Tratado de Versalles)** el tratado de 1919 que terminó la primera guerra mundial (p. 330)
**vertical consolidation (consolidación vertical)** hacerse con el control de los numerosos y distintos negocios que componen todas las fases del desarrollo de un producto (p. 161)
**veto (veto)** impedir que se convierta en ley (p. 41)
**vice (vicio)** comportamiento inmoral o corrupto (p. 224)
**victory garden (huerta de la victoria)** una huerta casera creada para incrementar la producción alimentaria durante la segunda guerra mundial (p. 466)
**Viet Cong (Vietcong)** fuerza formada por guerrillas comunistas en Vietnam del Sur que, con apoyo norvietnamita, luchó contra el gobierno de Vietnam del Sur en la guerra del Vietnam (p. 619)
**Vietnamization (vietnamización)** la política de reemplazar a las fuerzas militares norteamericanas por las de Vietnam del Sur (p. 635)
**Vietnam Veterans Memorial (Monumento Conmemorativo de los Veteranos de Vietnam)** el monumento en Washington, D.C., construido para honrar a los caídos en la guerra del Vietnam (p. 638)
**vigilante (vigilante)** un ciudadano que toma la ley en sus manos (p. 324)
**Virginia and Kentucky Resolutions (Resoluciones de Virginia y Kentucky)** resoluciones aprobadas en 1798 que atacaban la Ley de Extranjería y Sedición por ser anticonstitucionales
**Volunteers in Service to America (VISTA) (Voluntarios en Servicio a Norteamérica)** un programa federal organizado para mandar voluntarios a ayudar a las personas en las comunidades pobres (p. 547)
**Voting Rights Act of 1965 (Ley de Derechos Electorales de 1965)** una ley que se proponía reducir los impedimentos para el voto de los afroamericanos, en parte por medio del aumento de la autoridad federal para censar votantes (p. 579)

# W

**Wagner Act (Ley de Wagner)** una ley aprobada en 1935 que ayudaba a los sindicatos al legalizar la negociación colectiva y establecer la Mesa Nacional de Relaciones Laborales (p. 409)
**Wannsee Conference (Conferencia de Wansee)** la conferencia celebrada en 1942 en Alemania relativa al plan para asesinar a los judíos europeos (p. 453)
**war bond (bono de guerra)** un bono de ahorro del gobierno que se vende para recaudar dinero para la guerra (p. 463)
**War of 1812 (guerra de 1812)** la guerra entre los Estados Unidos y Gran Bretaña (p. 72)
**war of attrition (guerra de desgaste)** una guerra en la que uno de los lados causa continuas pérdidas al enemigo para disminuir su resistencia (p. 89)
**War Powers Act (Ley de los Poderes de Guerra)** una ley de 1973 que limita el poder del Presidente para desplegar tropas en el extranjero (p. 678)
**War Refugee Board (Oficina de Refugiados de Guerra)** una agencia federal creada en 1994 para tratar de ayudar a las personas amenazadas de muerte por los nazis (p. 454)
**Warren Commission (Comisión Warren)** la comisión presidida por el juez presidente Earl Warren que investigó el asesinato del Presidente Kennedy (p. 544)
**Warsaw Pact (Pacto de Varsovia)** una alianza militar entre la Unión Soviética y naciones de Europa del este formada en 1955 (pp. 495, 797)
**Watergate scandal (escándalo Watergate)** el escándalo que supuso el descubrimiento de actividades ilegales que finalmente produjeron la renuncia del Presidente Nixon en 1974 (p. 666)
**welfare capitalism (capitalismo del bienestar)** una estrategia laboral en la que las compañías satisfacen algunas de las necesidades de sus trabajadores sin intervención de los sindicatos (p. 376)
**Whiskey Rebellion (rebelión del Whisky)** los desórdenes de 1794 causados por la oposición a un impuesto sobre el whisky
**Whitewater affair (asunto Whitewater)** acusaciones contra el Presidente Clinton en las que se alegaba su participación en transacciones comerciales ilegales antes de convertirse en presidente (p. 727)
**wildcat strike (huelga no autorizada)** una huelga organizada por los trabajadores en vez de por los dirigentes sindicales (p. 462)
**Wilderness Road** un camino construido en 1770 que se convirtió en la ruta principal para atravesar los Montes Apalaches
**Woodstock festival (festival de Woodstock)** un festival de 1969 en el norte del estado de Nueva York (p. 632)
**work ethic (ética del trabajo)** sistema de valores que pone énfasis en la importancia del trabajo arduo para desarrollar la personalidad y conseguir el éxito (p. 772)
**World Trade Organization (WTO) (Organización Mundial del Trabajo)** una organización internacional formada en 1995 para fomentar la expansión del comercio mundial (p. 737)
**World Wide Web (Red Informática Mundial)** organización de redes globales de computadores por medio de la cual los usuarios pueden acceder a la información (p. 805)
**writ of habeas corpus (orden de hábeas corpus)** una protección legal que requiere que un tribunal determine si una persona ha sido encarc legalmente (p. 98)

# X

**XYZ Affair (Asunto XYZ)** en 1798, la controversi causada por las exigencias de los franceses en sobornos de los negociadores norteamericano.

# Y

**Yalta Conference (Conferencia de Yalta)** la reunión 1945 entre Churchill, Stalin y Roosevelt en la que líderes hablaron de planes para el mundo de la posguerra (p. 443)
**yellow journalism (periodismo amarillo)** un tipo de información periodística que da importancia a relatos sensacionalistas de crimen y escándalo (p. 238)

# Z

**Zimmermann note (nota de Zimmermann)** una nota de un diplomático alemán en la que en 1917 se proponía una alianza con México (p. 316)

**Carter, James Earl, Jr.** Thirty-ninth President of the United States, 1977–1981; advocated concern for human rights in foreign policy; assisted in mediating the Camp David Accords (p. 680)

**Castro, Fidel** Revolutionary leader who took control of Cuba in 1959; ally of Soviet Union through the 1980s (p. 505)

**Catt, Carrie Chapman** Women's suffrage leader in the early 1900s; helped secure passage of Nineteenth Amendment in 1920; headed National American Woman Suffrage Association (p. 303)

**Champlain, Samuel de** French explorer who founded the city of Quebec in 1608

**Chavez, Cesar** Latino leader from 1962 to his death in 1993; organized the United Farm Workers (UFW) to help migratory farm workers gain better pay and working conditions (p. 597)

**Churchill, Winston** Leader of Great Britain before and during World War II; powerful speechmaker who rallied Allied morale during the war (p. 431)

**Clark, William** Leader, with Meriwether Lewis, of expedition through the West beginning in 1804; brought back scientific samples, maps, and information on Native Americans

**Clay, Henry** Statesman from Kentucky; accused by Jackson of giving votes to John Q. Adams in return for post as Secretary of State; endorsed government promotion of economic growth; advocate of Compromise of 1850

**Cleveland, Grover** Twenty-second and twenty-fourth President of the United States, 1885–1889, 1893–1897; supported railroad regulation and a return to the gold standard (p. 193)

**Clinton, Bill** Forty-second President of the United States, 1993–2001; defeated George Bush after overcoming numerous political obstacles; advocated economic and health-care reform (p. 723)

**Columbus, Christopher** Explorer whose voyage for Spain to North America in 1492 opened the Atlantic World

**Coolidge, Calvin** Thirtieth President of the United States, 1923–1929; promoted big business and opposed social aid (p. 343)

**Coughlin, Father Charles E.** "Radio Priest" who supported and then attacked President Franklin Roosevelt's New Deal; prevented by the Catholic Church from broadcasting after he praised Hitler (p. 413)

**Coxey, Jacob S.** Populist who led Coxey's Army in a march on Washington, D.C., in 1894 to seek government jobs for the unemployed (p. 209)

**Custer, George Armstrong** General who directed army attacks against Native Americans in the 1870s; commanded army forces killed in 1876 at Little Bighorn in Montana (p. 181)

## D

**Davis, Jefferson** President of the Confederate States of America; ordered attack on Fort Sumter, the first battle of the Civil War

**Dewey, George** Officer in United States Navy, 1861–1917; led a surprise attack in the Philippines during the Spanish-American War that destroyed the entire Spanish fleet (p. 266)

**Diem, Ngo Dinh** Leader of South Vietnam, 1954–1963; supported by United States, but not by Vietnamese Buddhist majority; assassinated in 1963 (p. 618)

**Dix, Dorothea** Advocate of prison reform and of special institutions for the mentally ill in Massachusetts before the Civil War

W.E.B. Du Bois

**Dole, Robert** Senator from Kansas, 1969–1996; challenged Bill Clinton for the presidency in 1996 (p. 727)

**Douglas, Stephen** Illinois senator who introduced the Kansas-Nebraska Act, which allowed new territories to choose their own position on slavery; debated Abraham Lincoln on slavery issues in 1858

**Douglass, Frederick** African American abolitionist leader who spoke eloquently for abolition in the United States and Britain before the Civil War

**Du Bois, W.E.B.** African American scholar and leader in early 1900s; encouraged African Americans to attend colleges to develop leadership skills (p. 235)

## E

**Edison, Thomas A.** Inventor; developed the light bulb, the phonograph, and hundreds of other inventions in the late 1800s and early 1900s (p. 154)

**Ehrlichman, John** Adviser on domestic policy to President Richard Nixon; deeply involved in Watergate (p. 654)

**Einstein, Albert** Physicist who fled Nazi persecution and later encouraged President Roosevelt to develop the atomic bomb (p. 448)

**Eisenhower, Dwight D.** Thirty-fourth President of the United States, 1953–1961; leader of Allied forces in World War II; as President, he promoted business and continued social programs (p. 503)

**Ellington, Duke** African American musician, bandleader, and composer of the 1920s and 1930s (p. 360)

**Ellsberg, Daniel** Defense Department official; leaked Pentagon Papers to *The New York Times* in 1971, showing government lies to public about Vietnam (p. 665)

**Equiano, Olaudah** Antislavery activist who wrote an account of his enslavement

## F

**Father Divine** African American minister; his Harlem soup kitchens fed the hungry during the Great Depression (p. 386)

**Fillmore, Millard** Thirteenth President of the United States, 1850–1853; promoted the Compromise of 1850 to smooth over disagreements about slavery in new territories

**Finney, Charles Grandison** Revivalist during the Second Great Awakening; emphasized religious conversion and personal choice

**Fitzgerald, F. Scott** Novelist who depicted the United States and the world during the 1920s in novels such as *The Great Gatsby* (p. 362)

**Fitzhugh, George** Southern author who criticized northern industrialists for exploiting workers in his 1857 book *Cannibals All!*

**Ford, Gerald R.** Thirty-eighth President of the United States, 1974–1977; succeeded and pardoned Nixon; failed to establish strong leadership (p. 675)

**Ford, Henry** Pioneering auto manufacturer in the early 1900s; made affordable cars for the masses using assembly line and other production techniques (p. 349)

**Franklin, Benjamin** Colonial inventor, printer, writer, statesman; contributed to the Declaration of Independence and the Constitution

**Frémont, John C.** Explorer, military officer, and politician; led United States troops in 1846 Bear Flag Revolt when the United States took California from Mexico; ran for President as a Republican in 1856

**Friedan, Betty** Feminist author; criticized limited roles for women in her 1963 book *The Feminine Mystique* (p. 520)

## G

**Garfield, James A.** Twentieth President of the United States, 1881; his assassination by a disappointed office seeker led to the reform of the spoils system (p. 207)

**Garrison, William Lloyd** White leader of radical abolition movement based in Boston; founded *The Liberator* in 1831 to work for an immediate end to slavery

**Garvey, Marcus** African American leader from 1919 to 1926 who urged African Americans to return to their "motherland" of Africa; provided early inspiration for "black pride" movements (p. 370)

**Gates, Bill** Founder of Microsoft; revolutionized personal computing, investigated for questionable business practices (p. 744)

**George III** King of England during the American Revolution

**George, Henry** Author of *Progress and Poverty* (1879) linking land speculation and poverty; proposed a single tax based on land value (p. 285)

**Gingrich, Newt** Representative from Georgia, 1979–1998; called on Republican congressional candidates in 1994 elections to endorse "Contract with America" (p. 726)

**Gorbachev, Mikhail** Soviet leader whose bold reforms led to the breakup of the Soviet Union in the late 1980s (p. 711)

**Gore, Al** Senator from Tennessee; Vice President under President Bill Clinton, 1993–2001 (p. 725)

**Graham, Billy** Evangelist and presidential adviser; known for leading large-scale crusades, or religious rallies (p. 519)

**Grant, Ulysses S.** Eighteenth President of the United States, 1869–1877; commander of Union forces who accepted Lee's surrender in 1865 (p. 90)

*Newt Gingrich*

## H

**Haldeman, H. R.** Chief of Staff under President Richard Nixon; deeply involved in Watergate (p. 654)

**Hamilton, Alexander** Officer in the War for Independence: delegate to the Constitutional Convention; Federalist and first Secretary of the Treasury

**Handsome Lake** Leader of Seneca in late 1700s; encouraged blending of Native American and white American cultures

**Harding, Warren G.** Twenty-ninth President of the United States, 1921–1923; presided over a short administration marked by corruption (p. 344)

**Harrington, Michael** Author; wrote *The Other America* in 1962, which described areas of poverty in the otherwise prosperous United States (p. 542)

**Harrison, Benjamin** Twenty-third President of the United States, 1889–1893; signed 1890 Sherman Antitrust Act later used to regulate big business (p. 193)

**Harrison, William Henry** Ninth President of the United States, 1841; died after only a month in office

**Hayes, Rutherford B.** Nineteenth President of the United States, 1877–1881; promised to withdraw Union troops from the South in order to end dispute over his election; attacked spoils system (p. 142)

**Hearst, William Randolph** Newspaper publisher from 1887 until his death in 1951; used "yellow journalism" in the 1890s to stir up sentiment in favor of the Spanish-American War (p. 238)

**Hiss, Alger** Former State Department official investigated as a possible Communist spy by House Un-American Activities Committee after World War II; convicted of perjury in 1950 (p. 498)

**Hitler, Adolf** German leader of National Socialist (Nazi) party 1933–1945; rose to power by promoting racist and nationalist views (p. 430)

**Ho Chi Minh** Leader of the Communist party in Indochina after World War II; led Vietnamese against the French, then North Vietnamese against the United States in the Vietnam War (p. 617)

**Hollerith, Herman** 1890 census agent who devised a machine that used punch cards to tabulate data (p. 803)

**Hoover, Herbert** Thirty-first President of the United States, 1929–1933; worked to aid Europeans during World War I; responded ineffectively to 1929 stock market crash and Great Depression (p. 323)

**Houston, Sam** Leader of Texas troops in war for independence from Mexico in 1836; elected first president of independent Texas

**Humphrey, Hubert** Democratic presidential candidate in 1968; lost narrowly to Nixon in an election bid hurt by support for the Vietnam War and by third-party candidate George Wallace (p. 651)

**Hutchinson, Anne** Critic of Puritan leadership of Massachusetts Bay Colony; banished for her religious beliefs

## I

**Isabella** Ruler of Spanish Christian kingdoms with Ferdinand in late 1400s; sponsored Columbus's voyage to North America

## J

**Jackson, Andrew** Seventh President of the United States, 1829–1837; supported minimal government and the spoils system; vetoed rechartering of the national bank; pursued harsh policy toward Native Americans (p. 74)

**Jackson, Stonewall** Confederate general known for his swift strikes against Union forces; earned nickname Stonewall by holding his forces steady under extreme pressure at the First Battle of Manassas (p. 86)

**Jefferson, Thomas** Third President of the United States, 1801–1809; main author of the Declaration of Independence; a firm believer in the people and decentralized power; reduced the federal government (p. 69)

**Johnson, Andrew** Seventeenth President of the United States, 1865–1869; clashed with Radical Republicans on Reconstruction programs; was impeached, then acquitted, in 1868 (p. 127)

**Johnson, Lyndon B.** Thirty-sixth President of the United States, 1963–1969; expanded social assistance with his Great Society program; increased United States commitment during Vietnam War (p. 544)

**Jordan, Barbara** Member of Congress from Texas; first African American and woman to represent her state in Congress; gave keynote addresses at 1976 and 1992 Democratic National Conventions (p. 681)

**Joseph, Chief** Leader of Nez Percé; forced to give up his home by United States army, fled toward Canada; captured in 1877 (p. 182)

## K

**Kamiakin** Yakima chief who led Native Americans in 1855 war against Northwest settlers

**Kelley, Florence** Progressive reformer active from 1886 to 1920; worked in state and federal government for laws on child labor, workplace safety, and consumer protection (p. 288)

**Kennedy, John F.** Thirty-fifth President of the United States, 1961–1963; seen as youthful and inspiring; known for his firm handling of the Cuban Missile Crisis; assassinated in 1963 (p. 541)

**Kennedy, Robert F.** Attorney General under his brother, President John Kennedy, in the early 1960s; supported civil rights; assassinated while running for President in 1968 (p. 572)

**Keynes, John Maynard** British economist who believed that government spending could help a faltering economy; his theories helped shape New Deal legislation (p. 395)

**Khomeini, Ayatollah Ruholla** Islamic fundamentalist leader of Iran after the 1979 overthrow of the Shah; approved holding of American hostages (p. 687)

**Khrushchev, Nikita** Soviet leader from 1953 to 1964; opposed President Kennedy in the Cuban Missile Crisis (p. 553)

**King, Martin Luther, Jr.** African American civil rights leader from the mid-1950s until his assassination in 1968; used nonviolent means such as marches, boycotts, and legal challenges to win civil rights (p. 565)

**Kissinger, Henry** Secretary of State under Presidents Richard Nixon and Gerald Ford; used *realpolitik* to open relations with China, to end the Vietnam War, and to moderate Middle East conflict (p. 659)

## L

**Lafayette, Marquis de** French officer who assisted American forces in the War for Independence

**Lange, Dorothea** Photographed migrant farm workers during the Great Depression; inspired government aid programs and Steinbeck's *The Grapes of Wrath* (p. 384)

**Lee, Jason** First Methodist missionary to Oregon Country in 1834; built a mission school in Willamette Valley

**Lee, Robert E.** Brilliant general of Confederate forces during the Civil War (p. 93)

**Lenin, Vladimir I.** Revolutionary leader in Russia; established a Communist government in 1917 (p. 318)

**Levitt, William J.** Built new communities in the suburbs after World War II, using mass-production techniques (p. 514)

**Lewis, John L.** Head of United Mine Workers through World War II; used strikes during the war to win pay raises (p. 462)

**Lewis, Meriwether** Leader with William Clark of expedition through the West beginning in 1804; brought back scientific samples, maps, and information on Native Americans

**Lincoln, Abraham** Sixteenth President of the United States, 1861–1865; known for his effective leadership during the Civil War and his Emancipation Proclamation declaring the end of slavery in Confederate-held territory (p. 97)

**Lindbergh, Charles A.** Aviator who became an international hero when he made the first solo flight across the Atlantic Ocean in 1927 (p. 356)

**Little Turtle** Native American leader of the late 1700s; adopted policy of accommodation

**Lodge, Henry Cabot** Massachusetts senator of early 1900s; supported United States imperialism (p. 262)

**Long, Huey** Louisiana politician in 1930s; suggested redistributing large fortunes by means of grants to families; assassinated in 1935 (p. 413)

## M

**MacArthur, Douglas** United States general during the Great Depression, World War II, and Korean War; forced by Truman to resign in 1951 (p. 500)

**Madison, James** Fourth President of the United States, 1809–1817; called the Father of the Constitution for his leadership at the Constitutional Convention (p. 39)

**Mahan, Alfred T.** Author who argued in 1890 that the economic future of the United States rested on new overseas markets protected by a larger navy (p. 261)

**Malcolm X** African American leader during the 1950s and 1960s; eloquent spokesperson for African American self-sufficiency; assassinated in 1965 (p. 581)

*James Madison*

**Mann, Horace** School reformer and supporter of public education before the Civil War; devised an educational system in Massachusetts later copied by many states

**Mao Zedong** Leader of Communists who took over China in 1949; remained in power until his death in 1976 (p. 433)

**Marshall, George C.** Army Chief of Staff during World War II and Secretary of State under President Harry Truman; assisted economic recovery in Europe after World War II and established strong allies for the United States through his Marshall Plan (p. 440)

**Marshall, John** Chief Justice of the Supreme Court appointed by John Adams; set precedents that established vital powers of the federal courts (p. 69)

**Marshall, Thurgood** First African American Supreme Court justice; as a lawyer, won landmark school desegregation case *Brown* v. *Board of Education* in 1954 (p. 530)

**McCarthy, Eugene** Candidate in the 1968 Democratic presidential race who opposed the Vietnam War; convinced President Lyndon Johnson not to run again through his strong showing in the primaries (p. 634)

**McCarthy, Joseph R.** Republican senator from Wisconsin in the late 1940s and early 1950s; led a crusade to investigate officials he claimed were Communists; discredited in 1954 (p. 502)

**McClellan, George** Early Union army leader in the Civil War; careful organizer and planner who moved too slowly for northern politicians; ran against President Abraham Lincoln in the election of 1864 (p. 90)

William McKinley

**McKinley, William** Twenty-fifth President of the United States, 1897–1901; supported tariffs and a gold standard; expanded the United States by waging the Spanish-American War (p. 194)

**McNamara, Robert** Secretary of Defense under Presidents Kennedy and Lyndon Johnson; expanded American involvement in Vietnam War (p. 618)

**Meade, George G.** Union commander at Battle of Gettysburg in 1863; defended the high ground and forced Confederate army to attack, causing great casualties (p. 108)

**Means, Russell** Native American leader of 1960s and 1970s; helped organize American Indian Movement (AIM) and 1973 Wounded Knee occupation (p. 604)

**Metacom** Leader of Pokanokets in Massachusetts; also known by his English name, King Philip; led Native Americans in King Philip's War, 1675–1676

**Mitchell, John** Attorney General under President Richard Nixon; deeply involved in Watergate scandal (p. 654)

**Monroe, James** Fifth President of the United States, 1817–1825; acquired Florida from Spain; declared Monroe Doctrine to keep foreign powers out of the Americas

**Morse, Samuel F. B.** Artist and inventor; developed telegraph and Morse code in the 1830s

**Mott, Lucretia** Women's rights leader; helped organize first women's convention in Seneca Falls, New York, in 1848

**Mussolini, Benito** Italian fascist leader who took power in the 1920s; called *Il Duce* — "the leader"; known for his brutal policies (p. 429)

## N

**Nader, Ralph** Consumer advocate; published *Unsafe at Any Speed* in 1965 criticizing auto safety and inspiring new safety laws (p. 609)

**Nimitz, Chester** Leader of American naval forces in World War II Battle of Midway, during which several Japanese aircraft carriers were destroyed (p. 445)

**Nixon, Richard M.** Thirty-seventh President, 1969–1974; known for his foreign policy toward the Soviet Union and China and for illegal acts he committed in the Watergate affair that forced his resignation (p. 653)

## O

**O'Connor, Sandra Day** First woman Supreme Court justice; appointed by Reagan in 1981 (p. 710)

**Oppenheimer, J. Robert** Physicist who led American effort in World War II to develop first atomic bomb (p. 448)

## P

**Pahlevi, Muhammed Reza Shah** Leader of Iran, from 1941 until his overthrow in 1979; supported by the United States; brought modernization to his country along with repression and corruption (p. 687)

**Paine, Thomas** Author of political pamphlets during 1770s and 1780s; wrote *Common Sense* in 1776

**Paul, Alice** Women's suffrage leader of early 1900s; her Congressional Union used aggressive tactics to push the Nineteenth Amendment (p. 303)

**Penn, William** English Quaker who founded the colony of Pennsylvania in 1681 (p. 1)

**Perkins, Frances** Secretary of Labor 1933–1945 under President Franklin Delano Roosevelt; first woman Cabinet member (p. 406)

**Perot, H. Ross** Billionaire businessman who challenged Bill Clinton and George Bush for the presidency in 1992; strong opponent of NAFTA (p. 724)

**Pierce, Franklin** Fourteenth President of the United States, 1853–1857; signed the Kansas-Nebraska Act, which renewed conflicts over slavery in the territories

**Pinckney, Eliza Lucas** South Carolina plantation manager in the 1740s; promoted indigo as a staple crop

**Polk, James K.** Eleventh President of the United States, 1845–1849; led expansion of United States to southwest through war against Mexico

**Polo, Marco** Venetian traveler to China in the late 1200s; his book about the journey helped make Europeans aware of trade opportunities in eastern Asia

**Popé** Medicine man who led Pueblos and Apaches against Spanish rule in the Pueblo Revolt of 1680

**Prosser, Gabriel** Planned a slave revolt in Virginia in 1800; captured and executed after revolt failed

**Pulitzer, Joseph** Early 1900s newspaper publisher; used "yellow journalism" to stir up public sentiment in favor of the Spanish-American War (p. 238)

## R

**Randolph, A. Philip** Civil rights activist from the 1930s to the 1950s; planned the Washington march that pressured President Franklin Delano Roosevelt into opening World War II defense jobs to African Americans (p. 477)

**Reagan, Ronald** Fortieth President of the United States, 1981–1989; popular conservative leader who promoted supply-side economics and created huge budget deficits (p. 699)

**Riis, Jacob** Reformer who wrote *How the Other Half Lives,* describing the lives of poor immigrants in New York City in the late 1800s (p. 220)

**Robinson, Jackie** Athlete who in 1947 became the first African American to play baseball in the major leagues (p. 530)

**Rockefeller, Nelson** Vice President appointed by President Gerald Ford in 1974; the nation's only nonelected Vice President to serve with a nonelected President (p. 676)

**Roosevelt, Eleanor** First Lady 1933–1945; tireless worker for social causes, including women's rights and civil rights for African Americans and other groups (p. 396)

**Roosevelt, Franklin D.** Thirty-second President of the United States, 1933–1945; fought the Great Depression through his New Deal social programs; battled Congress over Supreme Court control; proved a strong leader during World War II (p. 396)

**Roosevelt, Theodore** Twenty-sixth President of the United States, 1901–1909; fought trusts, aided progressive reforms, built Panama Canal, and increased United States influence overseas (p. 265)

**Rosenberg, Julius and Ethel** Husband and wife convicted and executed in 1953 for passing atomic secrets to the Soviet Union; their guilt is still debated (p. 499)

**Rowson, Susanna Haswell** Author of *Charlotte Temple* (1794), a popular moralizing novel that encouraged women to look beyond appearances when choosing a husband

## S

**Sacajawea** Shoshone woman who served as guide and translator for Lewis and Clark on their exploratory journey through the West in the early 1800s

**Sacco, Nicola** Immigrant and anarchist executed, in a highly controversial case, for a 1920 murder at a Massachusetts factory (pp. 7, 342)

**Sadat, Anwar el-** Egyptian leader in the 1970s; began the Middle East peace process by reaching the 1978 Camp David Accords with Israel (p. 685)

**Salinger, J. D.** Author of 1951 novel *The Catcher in the Rye,* which criticized 1950s pressure to conform (p. 520)

**Santa Anna, Antonio López de** Mexican dictator who led government and troops in war against Texas; won the battle of the Alamo

**Schlafly, Phyllis** Conservative activist; led campaign during the 1970s and 1980s to block the Equal Rights Amendment (p. 593)

**Seward, William Henry** Republican antislavery leader during the 1860s; acquired Alaska in 1867 as Secretary of State (p. 260)

**Sherman, William Tecumseh** Union general in the Civil War; known for his destructive march from Atlanta to Savannah in 1864 (p. 113)

**Sirica, John J.** Washington judge who presided over the Watergate investigation in the 1970s; gave tough sentences to convicted participants and ordered President Richard Nixon to release secret tapes (p. 666)

**Sitting Bull** Chief Leader of Sioux in clashes with United States Army in Black Hills in 1870s (p. 181)

**Slater, Samuel** English textile worker who brought the Industrial Revolution to the United States by duplicating British textile machinery from memory

**Smith, John** Leader of the Jamestown, Virginia, colony in the early 1600s

**Smith, Joseph** Founder of Church of Jesus Christ of Latter-day Saints, or Mormons, in New York in 1830; killed by a mob in Illinois in 1844

**Spock, Benjamin** Pediatrician and author of *The Common Sense Book of Baby and Child Care* (1946), which encouraged mothers to stay home with their children rather than work (p. 520)

**Stalin, Joseph** Leader of the Soviet Union from 1924–1953; worked with Roosevelt and Churchill during World War II but afterwards became an aggressive participant in the cold war (p. 440)

**Stanton, Elizabeth Cady** Women's rights leader in the 1800s; helped organize first women's convention; wrote the Declaration of Sentiments on women's rights in 1848

**Starr, Ellen Gates** Cofounder of Chicago's Hull House, the first settlement house, in 1889 (p. 225)

**Steinem, Gloria** Journalist, women's rights leader since 1960s; founded *Ms.* magazine in 1972 to cover women's issues (p. 592)

**Stevenson, Adlai** Senator from Illinois and Democratic candidate for President in 1952 and 1956 against Eisenhower (p. 526)

**Stowe, Harriet Beecher** Author of the novel *Uncle Tom's Cabin* (1852), which contributed significantly to antisouthern feelings among Northerners before the Civil War (p. 7)

**Sumner, Charles** Abolitionist and senator from Massachusetts; beaten badly in the Senate by a southern congressman after making an antislavery speech

Harriet Beecher Stowe

## T

**Taft, William Howard** Twenty-seventh President of the United States, 1909–1913; continued progressive reforms of President Theodore Roosevelt; promoted "dollar diplomacy" to expand foreign investments (p. 275)

**Taney, Roger** Chief Justice of the Supreme Court who wrote an opinion in the 1857 Dred Scott case that declared the Missouri Compromise unconstitutional

**Taylor, Zachary** Twelfth President of the United States, 1849–1850; tried to avoid slavery issues

**Tecumseh** Native American leader in the late 1700s and early 1800s; led a pan-Indian movement that tried to unite several groups despite their differences

**Tenskwatawa** Native American leader of the early 1800s known as the Prophet; he called for a return to traditional ways and rejection of white values

**Thomas, Clarence** Conservative African American Supreme Court justice appointed in 1991; during his confirmation hearings he was charged with sexual harassment (p. 718)

**Thoreau, Henry David** Transcendentalist author known for his work *Walden* (1854) and other writings

**Travis, William** Leader in Texas's bid for independence from Mexico in 1836; died at the Alamo after appealing to the United States for help

**Truman, Harry S.** Thirty-third President of the United States, 1945–1953; authorized use of atomic bomb; signed Marshall Plan to rebuild Europe (p. 486)

Harry S. Truman

**Truth, Sojourner** Abolitionist and women's rights advocate before the Civil War; as a former slave, she spoke effectively to white audiences on abolition issues

**Tubman, Harriet** "Conductor" on the Underground Railroad, which helped slaves escape to freedom before the Civil War

**Turner, Frederick Jackson** Historian who wrote an essay in 1893 emphasizing the western frontier as a powerful force in the formation of the American character (p. 197)

**Turner, Nat** African American preacher who led a slave revolt in 1831; captured and hanged after the revolt failed

**Tweed, William Marcy** Boss of the Tammany Hall political machine in New York City; convicted of forgery and larceny in 1873 and died in jail in 1878 (p. 221)

**Tyler, John** Tenth President of the United States, 1841–1845; accomplished little due to quarrels between Whigs and Jacksonian Democrats (p. 854)

## V

**Van Buren, Martin** Eighth President of the United States, 1837–1841; Jacksonian Democrat; was voted out of office after the Panic of 1837 brought widespread unemployment and poverty (p. 853)

**Vance, Cyrus** Secretary of State under President Jimmy Carter; invited Israelis and Egyptians to Camp David in 1978 to begin Middle East peace process (p. 685)

**Vanzetti, Bartolomeo** Immigrant and anarchist executed, in a highly controversial case, for a 1920 murder at a Massachusetts factory (p. 342)

**Vesey, Denmark** African American who planned 1822 South Carolina slave revolt; captured and hanged after revolt failed

**von Steuben, Friedrich** Prussian officer who trained Washington's troops in the winter at Valley Forge

## W

**Walker, David** African American author of *Appeal to the Colored Citizens of the World* (1829), which called for an immediate end to slavery

**Walker, Madam C. J.** African American leader and businesswoman in the early 1900s; she spoke out against lynching (p. 245)

**Wallace, George C.** Third-party candidate for President in 1968; focused his campaign on issues of blue-collar anger in the North and racial tension (p. 652)

**Warren, Earl** Chief Justice of Supreme Court 1953–1968; investigated President Kennedy's assassination; led in many decisions that protected civil rights, rights of the accused, and right to privacy (p. 548)

**Washington, Booker T.** African American leader from the late 1800s until his death in 1915; founded Tuskegee Institute in Alabama; encouraged African Americans to learn trades (p. 234)

**Washington, George** First President of the United States, 1789–1797; led American forces in the War for Independence; set several federal precedents, including the two-term maximum for presidential office (p. 42)

**Webster, Noah** Author of the best-known American dictionary in the early 1800s; promoted a standard national language and public support for education

**Whitman, Narcissa Prentiss** Missionary; one of the first white women to cross the Rocky Mountains to Oregon in 1836

**Whitney, Eli** Inventor; developed the cotton gin in 1793, which rapidly increased cotton production in the South and led to a greater demand for slave labor

**Wilhelm, Kaiser** Emperor of Germany during World War I; symbol to the United States of German militarism and severe efficiency (p. 311)

**Wilson, Woodrow** Twenty-eighth President of the United States, 1913–1921; tried to keep the United States out of World War I; proposed League of Nations (p. 298)

## Y

**Yeltsin, Boris** Leader of Russia in late 1980s and 1990s; took over from Mikhail Gorbachev as reforms continued and Communist party control ended (p. 732)

**York, Alvin** American soldier who was awarded the Congressional Medal of Honor for bravery during World War I (p. 319)

**Young, Brigham** Mormon leader who supervised migration to Utah beginning in the 1840s; first governor when Utah became a United States territory

# Index

**Note:** Entries with a page number followed by a *c* indicate a chart or graph on that page; *m* indicates a map; and *p* indicates a picture.

## A



INDEX

# B

INDEX

## F

## I



## J

# K



# L

## M

## N

INDEX

# S

## X



## Y



## Z



INDEX

# Acknowledgments

**Team Credits** The people who made up the *America: Pathways to the Present* team include: Tom Barber, Joyce Barisano, Wendy Bohannan, Bruce Bond, Melinda Boroson, Todd Christy, Patrick Connolly, Anthony DeAngelis, Anne Falzone, Elizabeth Good, Mary Ann Gundersen, Ed Hagenstein, Mary Hanisco, Michal Howden, Linda Johnson, Lynne Kalkanajian, John Kelley, Russ Lappa, Marilyn Leitao, Dotti Marshall, Grace Massey, Kathy Maxcey, Efrat Metser, Gabriela Pérez Fiato, Debra Reardon, Nancy Rogier, Luess Sampson-Lizotte, Suzanne Schineller, Angela Sciaraffa, Olena Serbyn Sullivan, Amit Shah, Carol Signorino, John Springer, Mark Staloff, Susan Swan, Kira Thaler-Marbit, Jean C. Thomas, Stuart Wallace.

**Cover Design**

Bruce Bond

**Front Cover Photograph**

Astronaut David R. Scott saluting the U.S. flag during the Apollo 15 mission, July/August 1971. NASA

**Picture Research**

Pembroke Herbert and Sandi Rygiel/Picture Research Consultants, Inc.

**Geography and History Contributing Writers:** Carol Barrett, Department of Geography, University of Wisconsin at River Falls, River Falls, WI; Tom Baerwald, Program Director of Geography and Regional Science, National Science Foundation, Washington, D.C.; Peter Hugill, Department of Geography, Texas A&M University, College Station, TX

**Maps**

**Horizon Design/Sanderson Associates:**

20, 24, 26, 29, 71, 72, 74, 77, 82, 90, 92, 108, 114, 121, 130, 134, 142, 153, 157, 181, 186, 189, 194, 219, 260, 266, 270, 274, 277, 279, 295, 304, 310, 319, 329, 355, 389, 396, 407, 431, 433, 434, 439, 446, 476, 487, 494, 501, 504, 517, 552, 554, 558, 572, 583, 618, 620, 637, 655, 681, 715, 731, 733, 788

**Olena Serbyn Sullivan:** xxix, 71

**Illustration**

**Precision Graphics:**

40, 73, 116, 139, 159, 161, 162, 163, 164, 170, 187, 200, 206, 212, 213, 232, 234, 261, 272, 343, 344, 349, 377, 381, 382, 406, 442, 460, 462, 472, 489, 505, 512, 514, 515, 520, 543, 547, 548, 579, 590, 593, 599, 628, 655, 677, 705, 707, 741, 742, 756, 761, 776, 789

**Matthew Pippin**

79, 111, 156, 178, 321, 331, 348, 349, 438, 555, 692, 803, 804

**Photography**

**Abbreviation Key** LOC = Library of Congress; RH/LS = photo by Rob Huntley/Lightstream; NA = National Archives; PRC = Picture Research Consultants, Inc.; FRENT = Collection of David J. and Janice L. Frent; BB = Brown Brothers; CP = Culver Pictures; WW = Wide World Photos; GL = Gamma Liaison; WC = Woodfin Camp & Associates; C&G = Chermayeff & Geismar/MetaForm photo by Karen Yamauchi; BS = Black Star; MP = Magnum Photos; CB = Corbis Bettmann; TL = Time-Life.

**Unit Openers** Page **17 T,** "Election Day in Philadelphia" by John Lewis Krimmel, 1815. Courtesy, Winterthur Museum; **17 B**, Wood Painted American Eagle, FE 37. Shelburne Museum; **25 T**, New York & Cuba Mail Steamship Company Dock scene. C/B; **257 B**,"Vote Yes" suffrage poster. Smithsonian Institution; **339 T**, Mother and Child during the Depression. LOC; **339 B**,"Kick Out Depression" button. FRENT; **427 T**, "Buy War Bonds" painting by N.C. Wyeth. PRC; **427 B**, Army Medal of Honor. U.S. Department of Defense; **539 T**, Selma March. (detail) by James H. Karales; **539 B**, Woodstock poster. The Image Works Archive; **647 B**, Statue of Liberty. Elsa Peterson/Stock Boston; **647 T**, Newly sworn in immigrants in Brooklyn. Lynn Johnson/BS; **751**, Flag and Confetti. C&G

**American Artifacts:**

**Abbreviation Key:** SI= Smithsonian Institution; OPPS=Office of Printing and Photographic Services, Smithsonian Institution; NPS=Courtesy of the National Park Service

**The Growth of Sports** FOOTBALL PLAYER, BASEBALL MUSIC, Larry Gates, SI; SKATING, Jim Wallace, SI; SKIING, FOOTBALL PANTS, BASEBALL, all by Rick Vargas, SI; BICYCLE, Alfred Harrell, SI; CYCLIST, Collection of Sally Fox

**African Americans' Great Migration** DOLL, Eric Long, SI; PLOW, Jeff Tinsley, SI; RECORD BOOK, Diane Penland, SI; HOME SCHOOLING, LOC; SUITCASE, Eric Long, SI; SOLDIERS, Courtesy of the National Archives & Records Administration; JOBS, Jeff Tinsley

**The Jazz Age** DUKE, Courtesy of John Hasse; TRUMPET, Jeffrey Ploskonka, SI; DRESS, Jeff Tinsley, SI; HYMIE, Danny Thompson, SI; SAXOPHONE, Diane Penland, SI; CLARINET, Diane Penland, SI; BAND, Missouri Historical Society, Block Brothers photo

**On the Home Front** Jeff Tinsley, SI all with exception of PROPAGANDA POSTERS, Richard Strauss, SI

**The Vietnam Veterans Memorial** VIETNAM MEMORIAL, Sandra Rogers, SI; STUFFED ANIMALS, Richard Strauss, SI; BOOTS, HELMET, LETTER , LETTER TO GARY, Eric Long, SI, NPS; DOGTAGS, Rick Vargas, SI

**The Information Age** SATELLITE, OPPS; FIBER-OPTIC, Courtesy of Intel Corporation, Jeff Tinsley, SI; LASER HEAD, OPPS; BAR CODES, MAD'S UPC, symbol cover is ©E.C. Publications, Inc. 1978. Used with permission from MAD Magazine; HAND HELD COMPUTER, Courtesy of Apple Computer, Inc. EARLY COMPUTER, Eric Long, SI; WATERGATE BUGS, Margaret McCullough, SI, courtesy of the National Archives & Records Administration

**Chapter 1 18**, Chicago Historical Society; **19**, Courtesy of South Florida Science Museum. Photo by Randy Smith; **21**, Colonial National Historical Park; **22**, LOC; **23**, Museum of the City of New York; **25**, LOC; **30**, The Metropolitan Museum of Art, Gift of John S. Kennedy, 1897 (97.34); **35**, LOC; **36**, Independence National Historic Park; **38**, Collection of the Architect of the Capitol; **39**, LOC; **41**, Courtesy, American Antiquarian Society; **42**, LOC; **43 T**, The Brooklyn Museum 39.536.1 Gift of the Crescent-Hamilton Athletic Club; **43 B**, Museum of American Political Life. Photo by Sally Anderson-Bruce; **45**, Collection of the Architect of the Capitol; **67**; Locher/ *The Chicago Tribune;* **69**, © White House Historical Association/ Photo by National Geographic Society; **70 TL**, LOC: **70 TR**, LOC; **70 BL**, Courtesy of Bexar County & the Witte Museum, San Antonio; **70 BR**, Amon Carter Museum, Fort Worth, Texas; **76**, Peabody and Essex Museum; **81**, LOC; **83 L**, Kansas State Historical Society; **83 R**, WW.

**Chapter 2 86**, West Point Museum; **87**, Collection of David & Kevin Kyle; **89**, LOC; **91**, Collection of Michael J. McAfee. Courtesy William Gladstone. Photo © Seth Goltzer; **93**, Museum of the Confederacy; **95**, West Point Museum Collections. Courtesy William Gladstone. Photo © Seth Goltzer; **97**, McLellan Lincoln Collection, John Hay Library, Brown University; **98**, LOC; **99**, Chicago Historical Society; **100**, LOC; **101**, LOC; **102**, Courtesy, American Antiquarian Society; **107**, Museum of the Confederacy; **109**, Photogoraph courtesy Historical Art Prints, Southbury, CT 06488; **110**, The Beverly R. Robinson Collection, U.S. Naval Academy Museum; **112**, Brown University Library; **117**, Virginia Historical Society; **118**, Anne S. K. Brown Military Collection, Brown University Library, Providence, RI; **119L**, Artist: Douglas Volk, Minnesota Historical Society; **119R**, Jay Syverson/Stock Boston; **120T**, Museum of the Confederacy; **120B**, Confederate Memorial Hall, New Orleans. From ECHOES OF GLORY; ARMS & EQUIPMENT OF THE CONFEDERACY. Photo by Larry Sherer © 1991Time-Life Books; **123**, CP.

**Chapter 3 124**, LOC; **126**, Chicago Historical Society; **128 TL**, Collection of William Gladstone. Photograph by Seth Goltzer; **128 BL**, Collection of William Gladstone. Photograph by Seth Goltzer; **128 BR**, Collection of William Gladstone; **129**, Collection of William Gladstone; **132 TL**, FRENT; **132 TR**, M. Abramson/BS; **132 BL**, Radcliffe College Archives, Schlesinger Library; **132 BR**, C/B; **135**, LOC; **136**, Collection of Nancy Gewirz, Antique Textile Resource, Bethesda, Maryland; **137**, Courtesy of the Decorative and Industrial Arts Collection of the Chicago Historical Society; Acc. No. 1920.53; Photographer: John Alderson; **138**, The New-York Historical Society; **141**, Collection of State Historical Museum/Mississippi Department of Archives and History; **143**, LOC; **144**, LOC; **145 L**, LOC; **145 R**, Rick Friedman/ BS; **147**, LOC; **148**, LOC; **149**, NA.

**Chapter 4 150**, The Oakland Museum History Department; **151**, Division of Political History, Smithsonian Institution, Washington, DC. #89-6626; **152**, Division of Community Life, Smithsonian Institution, Washington, D.C. #86-2200; **153**, Lightfoot Collection; **155 T**, C/B; **155 BL**, LOC; **155 BR**, WW; **158**, Museum of American Textile History; **159**, LOC; **160**, LOC; **165**, Putman County Historical Society, Cold Spring, N.Y.; **166 L**, LOC; **166 R**, Urban Archives, Temple University; **167**, Collection of Ralph J. Brunke; **168 L**, LOC; **168 R**, PRC; **171**, C/B; **172**, BB; **173 L**, Hagley Museum and Library; **173 R**, Paul Chesley/Photographers/Aspen; **175**, LOC.

**Chapter 5 176**, National Cowboy Hall of Fame; **177**, The Oakland Museum History Department; **180**, © Justin Kerr, 1989; **182**, LOC; **184**, State Historical Society of Wisconsin; **185**, Western History Division, Denver Public Library, photo by L. C. McClure; **188**, The Oakland Museum History Department; **192**, East Carolina Manuscript Collection, J. Y. Joyner Library, East Carolina University; **193**, Kansas State Historical Society; **195**, LOC; **197**, Buffalo Bill Historical Center, Cody WY; **199 L**, Amon Carter Museum of Western Art; **199 R**, LOC; **201 L**, Denver Public Library; **201 R**, Bob Daemmrich Photography; **203**, LOC.

**Chapter 6 204**, CP; **205,** Puck March 10, 1897; **207**, LOC; **208**, Union Pacific Railroad Museum; **209**, New York Public Library. Astor, Lenox and Tilden Foundation; **210**, LOC; **211**, National Park Service Collection, Gift of Angelo Forgione; **212**, BB; **213**, LOC; **215 T**, C&G; **215 B**, C&G; **216**, California Department of Parks and Recreation, courtesy Fred Wasserman; **217**, PRC/RH/LS; **218**, LOC; **220 T**, Museum of the City of New York, Gift of Joseph Varner Reed; **220 B**, BB; **221**, The Granger Collection, New York; **223**, Division of Political History, Smithsonian Institution, Washington. D.C. #88-8676; **224**, C&G; **225**, LOC; **226**, California Museum of Photography WX5266; **227 L**, Courtesy George Eastman House; **227 R**, Bob Daemmrich Photography; **229**, Puck 1909.

**Chapter 7 230**, American Heritage; **232**, Nebraska State Historical Society; **233**, Sophia Smith Collection; **234**, BB; **235**, BB; **236**, Collection of Sally Fox; **237**, LOC; **238 L**, Chicago Historical Society; **238 TR**, Wood River Gallery, Mill Valley, California; **238 BR**, Wood River Gallery, Mill Valley, California; **239**, C/B; **242**, Frank Leslie's Illustrated Newspaper; **245**, National Portrait Gallery, Smithsonian Institution, Washington, DC. Art Resource, NY; **246**, Museum of American Political Life.Photo by Steve Laschever; **247**, Courtesy of The Maytag Company; **248**, PRC/RH/LS; **249**, Kansas State Historical Society; **251 L**, State Historical Society of North Dakota; **251 R**, Bob Daemmrich/Stock Boston; **253**, LOC; **254**, Kansas State Historical Society, **255**, Courtesy of Birmingham Public Library, Department of Archives & Manuscripts.

**Chapter 8 258**, Courtesy of the U.S. Naval Academy Museum; **259**, The Oakland Museum History Department; **262**, LOC; **264**, C/B; 521 TL, NA; **265 TR**, Larry Burrows, Life Magazine; **265 BL**, NA; **265 BR**, Bill Gentile/SIPA Press; **267**, California Museum of Photography #24039; **268**, Courtesy of the Liliuokalani Trust and the Bishop Museum (detail); **269**, CP; **271**, PRC; **273**, BB; **274**, LOC; **275**, White House Historical Association; **276**, C/B; **278**, Courtesy of Fred and Kathryn Giampietro; **281 L**, LOC; **281 R**, WW; **283**, Puck, June 29, 1904.

**Chapter 9** **284**, C/B; **286**, Labor-Management Documentation Center, Cornell University; **287**, CP; **288**, Courtesy George Eastman House; **289**, C/B; **292**, CP; **293**, LOC; **296**, National Portrait Gallery, Smithsonian Institution, Washington, DC. Art Resource, NY; **297**, Joseph Keppler from PUCK.Theodore Roosevelt Collection, Harvard College Library; **298**, Museum of American Political Life; **299 T**, C/B; **299 B**, FRENT; **300** FRENT; **301**, Meserve Collection; **303**, Sophia Smith College Archives; **305 L**, Chicago Historical Society; **305 R**, Corporation for National Service; **307**, Courtesy of the League of Women's Voters of the United States.

**Chapter 10** **308** C/B; **309**, Collection of Colonel Stuart S.Corning, Jr. Photo ©RH/LS; **311**, Bayerisches Haupstaatsarchiv; **312**, CP; **314**, The Granger Collection; **315 L**, LOC; **315 R**, Boston Athenaeum; **316**, National Portrait Gallery, Smithsonian Institution, Washington, DC/Art Resource, NY; **317**, Collection of Colonel Stuart S.Corning, Jr. RH/LS; **318**, NA; **320**, BB; **322**, LOC; **324**, C/B; **325**, Wayne State University, Archives of Labor and Urban Affairs; **332**, LOC; **333 L**, Archive Photos/Lambert; **333 R**, C/B; **335**, Stock Montage; **336 T**, Collection of Colonel Stuart S. Corning, Jr.; **336 B**, U.S. Air Force; **337 T**, U.S. Air Force; **337 B**, C/B.

**Chapter 11** **340**, John Sloan Sixth Avenue Elevated at Third Street, 1928 (detail). Collection of Whitney Museum of American Art, Purchase 36.154. Photograph 1998: Whitney Museum of American Art, NY; **342**, FRENT; **344**, LOC; **345**, FRENT; **346**, LIFE Magazine December 10,1925; **347**, PRC/RH/LS; **350**, Courtesy Ford Archives; **351**, Lake County (IL) Museum/Curt Teich Postcard Archives; **352**, Saturday Evening Post, June 30, 1928, Curtis Archives; **353**, C/B; **354**, LOC; **355**, Schomburg Center for Research in Black Culture, The New York Public Library, Astor, Lenox and Tilden Foundations; **356**, CP; **357 L**, C/B; **357 R**, C/B; **358**, SuperStock; **359**, Division of Electricity/Smithsonian Institution; **360 L**, Nipper's Choice Phonographs, Keene, New Hampshire. Photograph by Wright Studio; **360 R**, C/B; **361 T**, Purchased with funds from the Edmundson Art Foundation, Inc. Des Moines Art Center Permanent Collections, 1958.2; **361 B**, C/B; **362 L**, Cartier Bresson/ Magnum Photos; **362 TM**, Beinecke Library, Yale University; **362 BM**, C/B; **362 R**, C/B; **366**, The Michael Barson Collection/Past Perfect. RH/LS; **367**, Chicago Historical Society; **368**, BB; **369**, C&G; **370**, BB; **371 L**, LOC; **371 R**, PRC; **373**, The Granger Collection, New York.

**Chapter 12** **374**, LOC; **375**, Courtesy of Speigel; **376**, Wood River Gallery, Mill Valley, California; **377**, Boston Athenaeum; **378**, C/B; **379**, LOC; **380**, C/B; **383**, Detroit News; **384**, Museum of the City of New York. Photograph by Bernice Abbott, Federal Arts Project; **385 L**, LOC; **385 R**, LOC; **386**, C/B; **388**, LOC; **391**, CP; **392**, C/B; **395**, C/B; **397 TL**, C/B; **397 TR**, FRENT; **397 BR**, Lyndon Baines Johnson Presidential Library; **398**, FDR Library; **399 L**, C/B; **399 R**, People Weekly © 1998 Steve Kagan; **401**, Reprinted from the Albany Evening News, 6/7/31 with permission of the Times Union, Albany, NY.

**Chapter 13** **402**, LOC; **403**, C/B; **404**, C/B; **405 T**, U.S. Forest Service; **405 B**, LOC; **407**, Franklin D. Roosevelt Library; **409**, LOC; **411**, Margaret Bourke-White LIFE Magazine © Time Warner; **412**, ©1935, 1963 by the Condé Nast Publications, Inc.; **415**, National Portrait Gallery, Smithsonian Institution, Washington, DC. Art Resource, NY; **416**, The Oakland Museum History Department; **417**, C/B; **418**, LOC; **419**, James Prigoff; **421 L**, PTC; **421 R**, David Hurn/MP; **423**, Franklin D. Roosevelt Library; **424**, NA; **425**, National Baseball Hall of Fame and Museum.

**Chapter 14** **428**, C/B; **429**, Collection of Chester Stott, RH/LS; **430**, Bilderdienst Suddeutscher Verlag; **431**, NA; **432**, LOC; **436**, Collection of Chester H. Stott, RH/LS; **437**, NA; **441 T**, National Portrait Gallery, Smithsonian Institution, Washington, DC. Art Resource. N.Y.; **441 B**, U.S. Army; **443**, U.S. Army; **445**, Navy Art Collection/ Gift of Abbott Laboratories; **446**, C/B; **448**, LOC; **449**, C/B; **450**, NA; **451**, US Holocaust Memorial Museum; **452 L**, Rijksinstituut voor Oorlogsdocumentatie, courtesy of U.S. Holocaust Memorial Museum Archives; **452 R**, Courtesy of U.S. Holocaust Memorial Museum Archives; **454**, US Holocaust Memorial Museum Archives; **455 L**, Yivo Institute for Jewish Research; **455 R**, C/B; **457**, Reprinted with permission of The Detroit News, a Gannett Newspaper, © 1993.

**Chapter 15** **458**, © The Curtis Publishing Company; **459**, Private Collection, RH/LS; **460**, NA; **461 T**, The Bancroft Library, Kaiser Pictorial Collections; **461 B**, NA; **463**, NA; **464**, LOC; **465**, C/B; **466**, National Museum of American History,Smithsonian Institution, Washington, D.C.; **467**, WW; **470**, Collection of Col. Stuart S. Corning,Jr. RH/LS; **471**, NA; **473**, Ellen Kaiper Collection, Oakland; **474**, Courtesy of the Norman Rockwell Family Trust and Curtis Archives; **475**, Collection of Jeff Ikler, RH/LS; **476**, LOC; **477 T**, LOC; **477 B**, National Portait Gallery, Gift of the Harmon Foundation/ Art Resource, NY; **478**, LOC; **479**, NA; **481 L**, LOC; **481 R**, Bob Daemmrich/ Stock Boston; **483**, Des Moines Register.

**Chapter 16** **484**, Collection of Whitney Museum of American Art, New York. Photography by Geoffrey Clements, NY; **485**, U.S. Army; **486**, Harry S. Truman Presidential Library; **488 L**, C/B; **488 R**, Courtesy of the J. N. Ding Darling Foundation; **490**, © 1949 Time Inc. Reprinted with permission; **493 T**, Bob Daemmrich/ Image Works; **493 BL**, C/B; **493 BR**, WW; **494**, Fenno Jacobs/BS; **498 T**, The Michael Barson Collection/Past Perfect, RH/LS; **498 B**, The Michael Barson Collection/Past Perfect, RH/LS; **499 L**, BB; **499 R**, Elliot Erwitt/MP; **500**, NA; **502**, C/B; **503 T**, C/B; **503 B**, The Michael Barson Collection/Past Perfect, RH/LS; **505**, © 1959 Newsweek Inc. All rights reserved. Reprinted by permission; **507 L**, Boeing Airplane Company; **507 R**, WW; **509**, From Herblock: A Cartoonist's Life (Macmillan Publishing, 1993).

**Chapter 17** **510**, © The Curtis Publishing Company; **511**, PRC; **512**, The McDonald's Corporation; **513**, Dan Weiner, Courtesy Sandra Weiner; **514**, Van Bucher/Photo Researchers; **516**, Collection of Robert and Bonnie Pope, RH/LS; **518**, Bill Ray LIFE Magazine © Time Warner; **519**, Leo Chopin/BS; **520**, The Michael Barson Collection/Past Perfect, RH/LS; **522**, PRC, RH/LS; **523**, Harry S. Truman Presidential Library; **524**, C/B; **525**, C/B; **526 T**, FRENT; **526 B**; Division of Political History, Smithsonian Institution, Washington, D.C. #91-13778; **527**, Dwight D. Eisenhower Library; **528**, From The Herblock's Special for Today (Simon & Schuster, 1958); **529**, FRENT; **530**, The Michael Barson Collection/Past Perfect, RH/LS; **531**, Grey Vielet LIFE Magazine © Time Warner; **532**, WW; **533 L**, C/B; **533 R**, Lonnie Duke/Tony Stone Images; **535**, ©The New Yorker Collection, 1954, Robert J. Day from cartoonbank.com. All Rights Reserved; **536**, NA; **537**, U. S. Naval Historical Center; **539 T**, (detail) by James H. Karales; **539 B**, The Image Works Archive.

**Chapter 18** **540**, John F. Kennedy Library; **541**, FRENT; **542**, John F. Kennedy Presidential Library; **544**, John F. Kennedy Presidential Library; **546**, Lyndon Baines Johnson Presidential Library; **549**, Supreme Court Historical Society; **551**, Courtesy Boeing Defense & Space Group; **553**, C/B; **557 L**, Courtesy of the Peace Corps; **557 R**, Courtesy of the Peace Corps; **559 L**, Y. Okamoto/LBJ Library; **559 R**, WW; **561**, ©1962 Herblock in The Washington Post.

**Chapter 19** **562**, Bob Adelman/MP; **563**, Dan Budnick/WC; **564**, C/B; **565**, C/B; **566**, WW; **567 T**, FRENT; **567 B**, Danny Lyon/MP; **568**, Dial Juvenile Books, 1968, a Division of Penguin Books USA, Inc.; **570**, Don Uhrbrock LIFE Magazine © Time Warner; **571 L**, Rapho/Photo Researchers; **571 R**, Danny Lyons/MP; **572**, C/B; **573**, WW; **574**, Charles Moore/BS; **575**, Robert Phillips LIFE Magazine ©Time Warner; **576 L**, Fred Ward/BS; **576 R**, Steve Schapiro/BS; **577 TL**, WW; **577 TR**, Bob Daemmrich Photography; **577 BL**, Bob Daemmrich Photography; **577 BR**, Bob Daemmrich/The Image Works; **578**, C/B; **579**, Eve Arnold/MP; **580**, C/B; **581**, Eve Arnold/MP; **582**, C/B; **583**, Charles Moore/BS; **584**, AP/Wide World Photos; **585 L**, C/B; **585 R**, Bob Mahoney/The Image Works; **587**, David Horsey/The Seattle-Post Intelligencer.

**Chapter 20** **588**, Ken Regan/Camera 5; **589**, Al Freni LIFE Magazine © Time Warner; **591 T**, Werner Wolff/ Black Star; **591 B**, © Bettye Lane; **592 T**, Bob Daemmrich Photography; **592 B**, Courtesy Lang Communications; **593**, C/B; **597**, Michael Nichols/MP; **598**, Craig Aurness/WC; **600**, George Bacon Collection, Hawaii State Archives; **601**, Eddie Adams/TIME Magazine; **602**, Jim Noelker/The Image Works; **603**, Rick Smolan/Against All Odds; **604 L**, Dirck Halstead/TIME Magazine; **604 R**, Dirck Halstead/TIME Magazine; **605**, C/B; 862, FRENT; **606**, FRENT; **607 T**, Alfred Eisenstaedt/LIFE Magazine © Time Warner; **607 B**, FRENT; **608 L**, Collection of Michael McCloskey; **608 R**, Ken Regan/Camera 5; **610**, C/B; **611 L**, M. Abramson/BS; **611 R**, Mike Orazzi; **612**, PRC; **615**, Mike Peters.

**Chapter 21** **616,** Larry Burrows; **617,** Courtesy United Nations, RH/LS; **618**, Dennis Brack/BS; **619**, C/B; **622**, Philip Jones Griffiths/MP, Zenith Electronics Corporation; **623**, C/B; **624 L**, Catherine Leroy/AP, print courtesy Time Inc. Picture Collection; **624 R**, Larry Burrows LIFE Magazine © Time Warner; **625**, Harry Breedlove; **626**, FRENT; **627**, The Bancroft Library, University of California; **629**, ©Lisa Law/The Image Works; **631**, The Oakland Museum History Department; **632**, © Lisa Law/The Image Works; **633**, Michael Frederick/The Image Works; **634**, Brad Markel/GL; **637**, FRENT; **638**, Thai Khad Chuon/C/B; **639 L**, WW; **639 R**, Bob Daemmrich/Tony Stone Images; **643**, From Herblock on All Fronts (New American Library, 1980); **644**, C/B; **645 L**, LOC; **645 R**, WW.

**Chapter 22** **648**, Nixon Presidential Materials Project; **649**, Courtesy of the Lyndon B. Johnson Presidential Library; **650 L**, Joseph Louw LIFE Magazine © Time Warner; **650 R**, Bill Eppridge LIFE Magazine © Time Warner; **651**, C/B; 908, FRENT; **653**, Roddey E. Mims/C/B; **654**, Nixon Presidential Materials Project; **656**, John Filo; **657**, Ted Cowell/BS; **658**, NASA; **659**, Dennis Brack/BS; **660**, Steve Northup, Time Magazine © Time Inc.; **661 T**, John Dominis LIFE Magazine © Time Warner; **661 B**, Sovfoto/Eastfoto; **662 T**, Rene Burri/MP; **662 B**, John T. Barr/GL; **663**, C/B; **664**, FRENT; **665 T**, Richard Ellis/Sygma; **665 B**, Dennis Brack/BS; **666**, WW; **669**, Roland Freeman/MP; **671 L**, Mark Godfrey/Image Works; **671 R**, WW; **673**, Tony Auth. Reprinted by permission: Tribune Media Services.

**Chapter 23** **674**, Robert Llewellyn; **675**, Dennis Brack/BS; **676 T**, WW; **676 B**, Copyright © 1974 by The New York Times Company; **678**, Gerald Ford Presidential Library; **679**, Hardin/BS; **680**, FRENT; **681**, Dennis Brack/BS; **682**, Jimmy Carter Presidential Library; **683**, Dennis Brack/BS; **685**, Jimmy Carter Presidential Library; **686**, C/B; **687**, Alain Mingam/GL; **688 L**, Peter Marlow/MP; **688 R**, FRENT; **690**, Dennis Brack/BS; **694 L**, WW; **694 R**, C/B; **695 L**, WW; **695 R**, PRC; **697**, Mike Peters/Dayton Daily News.

**Chapter 24** **698**, Sygma; **699**, FRENT; **700**, Diana Walker/Time Magazine; **701 TL**, C/B; **701 TR**, WW; **701 B**, Ken Hawking/Sygma; **702**, Les Schofer/Sygma; **704**, Charles Steiner/Sygma; **705**, C/B; **708**, Dick Halstead/GL; **710**, Zimberhoff/Sygma; **711**, WW; **714**, Atlan/Sygma; **715**, WW; **716**, R. Bossu/Sygma; **717 L**, Abbas/MP; **717 R**, Langevin/Sygma; **719 L**, David Woo/Sygma; **719 R**, Larry Downing/Sygma; **721**, Bob Englehard/The Hartford Courant.

**Chapter 25** **722**, National Center for Supercomputing Applications at the University of Illinois; **723**, John C. Sykes Jr.; **724**, Ira Wyman/Sygma; **726**, John Harrington/BS; **727** inset, The Liaison Agency Network; **727**, © Garse/SIPA Press; **728**, AP Photo/Eric Gay; **732**, C/B; **733**, Les Stone/Sygma; **735**, AP Photo/Boris Grdanoski; **736**, WW; **740**, JB Pictures Ltd.; **743**, B. Kraft/Sygma; **744**, Rick Maiman/Sygma; **745 L**, Doug Menuez/Stock Boston; **745 R**, Bob Daemmrich/Stock Boston; **747**, Mike Smith/Las Vegas Sun; **748**, C/B.

**Chapter 26** **752 T**, C&G; **752B**, Rebecca Cooney/NYT Pictures; **753**, Davies & Starr; **754**, BB; **755**, LOC; **756**, David Butow; **757**, ©1993 Time Inc., Reprinted by permission; **758**, Elsa Peterson/Stock Boston.

**Chapter 27** **760 T**, The New York Historical Society; **760 B**, David J. Camo/Stock Boston; **761**, Boot Hill Museum, photo by Henry Groskinsky; **762**, North Carolina Museum of Art, Raleigh, Purchased with funds from the State of North Carolina; **763**, "The Cowboy" by Remington, 1902. Amon Cater Museum of Western Art; **764**, David Woo/GL; **765**, Dennis Brack/BS.

**Chapter 28** **767 B**, John Zoiner/Uniphoto; **768**, CP; **769 T**, Stock Montage; **769 B**, Museum of the City of New York; **770 T**, FRENT; **770 B**, LOC; **771**, Bob Daemmrich/Tony Stone Images; **772**, Barney Taxel/NYT Pictures.

**Chapter 29** **774 T**, PRC Archive; **774 B**, Gilles Mingasson/GL; **775**, David Hurn/MP; **777**, "Mother and Child" by Dorothea Lange (detail) LOC;

**778 T**, FRENT; **778 B**, Kingsport Press, Inc.; **779**, J. Pat Carter/GL; **780**, Leiderman/Rothco; **781**, John Harrington/BS.

**Chapter 30** 783 **T**, PRC Archive; **783 B**, Lisa Quinones/BS; **784**, Matthew McVay/Tony Stone Images; **785**, William Campbell/Sygma; **786 T**, NA; **786 B**, LOC; **787 T**, BB; **787 B**, Museum of American Political Life; **790**, Int'l Brotherhood of Teamsters.

**Chapter 31** 792 **T**, Courtesy of Fred and Kathryn Giampietro; **792 B**, © B. Thouanel/SIPA Press; **793 T**, Christopher Morris/BS; Klaus Reisinger/BS; **794 BOTH**, Collection of Col. Stuart S. Corning, Jr. RH/LS; **795 T**, WW; **795 B**, NA; **796**, Brad Markel/GL; ©1959 Newsweek, Inc. All rights reserved. Reprinted by permission; **798**, R. Bossu/Sygma.

**Chapter 32** **800**, David Chambers/Tony Stone Images; **801**, David Young Wolff/Tony Stone Images; **802**, National Center for Supercomputing Application at the University of Illinois; **804 L**, Courtesy Picture Tel; **804 M&R**, Div. of Political History, SI; **805 BL**, Courtesy Ford Archives; **805 BM**, NASA; **806**, C/B; **808**, Steve Dunwell/The Image Bank; **811**, Stock Connection©1995 Joe Sohn/Chromosohm.

**Reference Section** 812 **TL clockwise**, Jim Pickerell; Franklin D. Roosevelt Library; Van Bucher/Photo Researchers; Collection of the Architect of the Capitol; C/B; **814**, Independence National Historic Park; **816**, Nichipor Collection, Courtesy of Minuteman National Historical Park. Rob Huntley/ Lightstream; **818**, Miriam and Ira D. Walsh Division of Art, Prints and Photographs, New York Public Library. Astor, Lenox and Tilden Foundations; **819**, Free Library of Philadelphia; **820**, Courtesy, American Antiquarian Society; **823**, LOC; **826**, PRC; **827**, LOC; **829**, Margaret Bourke-White LIFE Magazine © Time Warner; **830**, US Holocaust Memorial Museum; **832**, C/B; **834**, WW; **836**, Rick Reinhart/Impact Visuals; **837**, Paul Conklin; **857**, Corbis Sygma **858**, Jim Pickerell; **900**, Meserve Collection; **901**, Dwight D. Eisenhower Library; **902**, John Harrington/BS; **903**, WW; **904**, LOC; **905**, Radcliffe College Archives, Schlesinger Library; © 1949 Time Inc. Reprinted with permission.

## Primary Source Bibliography


**Chapter 1** **Samuel Maverick;** Cronon, William. Changes in the Land: Indians, Colonists, and the Ecology of New England. Hill and Wang, 1983, p. 139; **Morris Birkbeck:** Birkbeck, Morris. "Notes on a Journey in America from the Coasts of Virginia to the Territory of Illinois," Philadelphia, 1817, p. 34; **Reverend Walter Colton:** Three Years in California. S.A. Rollo, 1850, pp. 242–253.

**Chapter 2** **Mary Boykin Chesnut:** Woodward, C. Vann, et al., eds. *Mary Chesnut's Civil War.* Yale University Press, 1981, pp. 326, 327, 330, 333, 339; **Abraham Lincoln:** Ward, Geoffrey C. *The Civil War: An Illustrated History.* Alfred A. Knopf, 1990, p. 110; **Louis Wigfall:** McPherson, James M. *Battle Cry of Freedom.* Oxford University Press, 1988, p. 430; **Abraham Lincoln:** McPherson, p. 510; **Emancipation Proclamation:** Boorstin, Daniel, ed. *An American Primer.* University of Chicago Press, 1968, p. 431; **Frederick Douglass:** *Douglass' Monthly*, August, 1863; **soldier at Gettysburg:** E. B. Long, *The Civil War Day by Day.* Da Capo Press, 1971, p. 377; **Abraham Lincoln:** *Selected Speeches and Writings.* First Vintage Books, Library of America, p. 449; **Abraham Lincoln:** Lincoln, p. 450.

**Chapter 3** **Abraham Lincoln:** *Selected Speeches and Writings.* First Vintage Books, Library of America, p. 450; **Charlotte Forten:** "Life on the Sea Islands," *Atlantic Monthly,* Vol. 13 (May and June) 1864, pp. 588–589, 591–594, 666–667; **Lydia Child:** Foner, Eric. *Reconstruction: America's Unfinished Revolution 1863–1877.* Harper and Row, 1988, p. 473; **Ira Steward:** Levine, Bruce et al., eds. *Who Built America? Working People and the Nation's Economy, Politics, Culture, and Society.* Pantheon Books, 1989, p. 539.

**Chapter 4** **Andrew Carnegie:** Carnegie, Andrew. *The Empire of Business.* Doubleday, 1902, pp. 138–140, quoted in Kirkland, Edward Chase. *Dream and Thought in the Business Community, 1860–1900.* Cornell, 1956, pp. 156–157; **Resident of Lynn, Massachusetts:** Bureau of Labor, *Fourth Annual Report,* 1873, p. 306; **Frederick Winslow Taylor:** Taylor, Frederick W. *The Principles of Scientific Management.* W.W. Norton and Company, 1911, p. 39; **Samuel Gompers:** *Labor and the Employer.* Ayer Company Publishers, 1971, p. 118; **August Spies:** Kogan, B. R. "The Chicago Haymarket Riot," 1959 (a reproduction of the circular in the Chicago Historical Society collection).

**Chapter 5** **newspaper reporter:** Fite, Gilbert. *The Farmer's Frontier, 1865–1900.* University of New Mexico Press, 1974, p. 205; **newspaper report:** "Commercial and Financial Chronicle," September 21, 1879, quoted in Fite, p. 82; **Washington Gladden:** *The Annals of America.* Vol. 11, *1884–1894: Agrarianism and Urbanization.* Encyclopedia Britannica, 1968, p. 356.; **Tom Watson:** Woodward, C. Vann. *Tom Watson, Agrarian Rebel.* Oxford University Press, 1963, p. 220; **Frederick Jackson Turner:** Billington, Ray, ed. *Frontier and Section: Selected Essays of Frederick Jackson Turner.* Prentice Hall, 1961, p. 61; **Edward L. Wheeler:** *Deadwood Dick, The Prince of the Road.* Garland, 1979, p. 16.

**Chapter 6** **anonymous:** Kutler, Stanley I. *Looking for America: The People's History,* Vol. 2. W. W. Norton & Company, 1979, p. 178; **Fiorello LaGuardia:** *The Making of an Insurgent.* J. B. Lippincott Co., 1948, pp. 64–65; **Sadie Frowne:** Adapted from "The Story of a Sweatshop Girl: Sadie Frowne," Katzman and Tuttle. *Plain Folk: The Life Stories of Undistinguished Americans.* Illinois, University of Illinois Press, 1982; **Emily Dinwiddie:** "Some Aspects of Italian Housing and Social Conditions in Philadelphia," *Charities and the Commons,* Vol. 12, 1904, p. 490; **Jacob Riis:** *How the Other Half Lives.* Penguin, 1997, p. 6; **Martin Lomasney:** *The Boston Globe,* December 2, 1923, quoted in Zink, Harold. *City Bosses in the United States. A Study of Twenty Municipal Bosses.* Duke University Press, 1930, p. 83.

**Chapter 7** **Pauli Murray:** *Proud Shoes.* Harper and Row, 1956, pp. 269–270; **Booker T. Washington:** *Address of Booker T. Washington, principal of the Tuskegee Normal and Industrial Institute, Tuskegee, Alabama, delivered at the opening of the Cotton States and International Exposition, at Atlanta, Ga., September 18, 1895.* Daniel A. P. Murray Pamphlet Collection, Library of Congress, 1894, pp. 7–9; **W.E.B. Du Bois:** Du Bois, W.E.B. *The Negro Problem: A Series of Articles by Representative American Negroes of Today.* J. Pott & Company, 1903, pp. 33–75; **notice to performers:** Royle, Edwin Milton. "The Vaudeville Theatre," *Scribner's Magazine,* Vol. XXVI, October 1899, pp. 485–495.

**Chapter 8** **James G. Blaine:** LaFeber, Walter. *The New Empire: An Interpretation of American Expansion, 1860–1898.* Cornell University Press, 1963, p. 165; **Theodore Roosevelt:** Hart, Albert Bushnell, and Herbert Ronald Ferleger, eds. *Theodore Roosevelt Cyclopedia.* Roosevelt Memorial Association, 1941, p. 407; **Theodore Roosevelt:** Commager, Henry Steele, ed. *Documents of American History,* vol. 2, Eighth Edition. Appleton-Century Crofts, 1968, p. 34; **Carl Schurz:** "The Policy of Imperialism," 1899 address by Carl Schruz to Anti-Imperialist Conference in Chicago, October 17, 1899; **Bishop Alexander Walters:** "Wisconsin Weekly Advocate," August 17, 1899, quoted in Gatewood, Willard B., Jr. *Black Americans and the White Man's Burden, 1898–1903.* University of Illinois Press, 1975, p. 200.

**Chapter 9** **Edward Bellamy:** *Looking Backward.* River City Press, 1888, p. 56; **Upton Sinclair:** *The Jungle.* Doubleday, 1906, pp. 96–97; **Jane Addams:** "Why Women Should Vote." *Ladies Home Journal,* Vol. XXVII, January 1910, pp. 21–22; **Susan B. Anthony:** Sherr, Lynn. *Failure Is Impossible: Susan B. Anthony in Her Own Words.* Times Books, 1995, pp. 110–112.

**Chapter 10** **Arthur Zimmerman:** Leckie, Robert. *The Wars of America.* Harper and Row, 1968, p. 628; **Woodrow Wilson:** Cooper, John Milton, Jr. *Pivotal Decades: The United States, 1900–1920.* W. W. Norton and Company, 1990, p. 265; **Corporal Elmer Sherwood:** Berger, Dorothy and Josef, eds. *Diary of America.* Simon and Schuster, 1957, p. 536; **Herbert Hoover:** "Gospel of the Clean Plate." *Ladies Home Journal,* August 1917, p. 25; **Woodrow Wilson:** Commager, Henry Steele, ed. *Documents of American History,* vol. II, Eighth Edition. Appleton-Century-Crofts, 1968, p. 138; **Alice Lord O'Brian:** *No Glory: Letters from France, 1917–1919.* Airport Publishers, 1936, pp. 8, 141, 152–153.

**Chapter 11** **Henry Ford:** *My Life and Work.* Doubleday, 1923; **Preston Slosson:** *The Great Crusade and After, 1914–1928.* Macmillan, 1930, p. 157; **Edna St. Vincent Millay:** "First Fig." *Edna St. Vincent Millay: Selected Poems.* HarperCollins, 1991, p. 19; **Langston Hughes:** From COLLECTED POEMS by Langston Hughes Copyright (c) 1994 by the Estate of Langston Hughes reprinted by permission of Alfred A. Knopf, Inc.; **Alice Longworth:** *Crowded Hours: Reminiscences of Alice Roosevelt Longworth.* Charles Scribner's Sons, 1933, p. 324.

**Chapter 12** **Lincoln Steffens:** Leuchtenberg, William. *The Perils of Prosperity, 1914–1932.* University of Chicago Press, 1958, p. 202; **Broadway show tune:** Words by E. Y. Harburg, music by Jay Gorney. Harms, Inc., 1932. Renewed, permission from Warner Brothers Music; **Gordon Parks:** *Voices in the Mirror: An Autobiography.* Doubleday, 1990; **Wilson Ledford:** "How I Lived During the Depression." Interview taped and transcribed by Reuben Hiatt, November 7, 1982. Quoted in Snell, William R. ed., *Hard Times Remembered: Bradley County and the Great Depression.* Bradley County Historical Society, 1983, pp. 117–121; **Gerald W. Johnson:** "The Average American and the Depression." *Current History,* February 1932; **Kitty McCulloch:** Terkel, Studs. *Hard Times: An Oral History of the Great Depression.* Pantheon Books, 1970; **William Saroyan:** *Inhale and Exhale.* Random House, 1936, p. 81; **Herbert Hoover:** Myers, William S., ed. *The State Papers and Other Public Writings of Herbert Hoover.* Doubleday, Doran and Company, Inc., Vol. II, 1934, pp. 408–413; **Franklin D. Roosevelt:** *The New York Times,* September 24, 1932; **Roosevelt's Inaugural Address:** March 4, 1933.

**Chapter 13** **Harry Hopkins:** Dawley, Alan. *Struggles for Justice: Social Responsibility and the Liberal State.* Harvard University Press, 1991, p. 367; **federal official:** Markowitz, Gerald, and David Rosner, eds. "Slaves of the Depression." *Workers' Letters About Life on the Job.* Cornell, 1987, p. 154; **Franklin Roosevelt:** White, Walter. *A Man Called White: The Autobiography of Walter White.* Viking Press, 1948, pp. 179–180; **Sam E. Roberts:** Duram, James C., and Eleanor A. Duram. "Congressman Clifford Hope's Correspondence With his Constituents: A Conservative View of the Court-Packing Fight of 1937." *Kansas Historical Quarterly,* 37/1 (Spring 1971), p. 71; **Hiram W. Johnson:** Barnes, William R., and A. W. Littlefield. *The Supreme Court Issue and the Constitution, Comments Pro and Con by Distinguished Men.* Barnes & Noble, 1937, p. 49; **Walter Reuther:** Madison, Charles A. *American Labor Leaders, Personalities and Forces in the Labor Movement.* Ungar, 1950, p. 382; **Mrs. Renee Lohrback:** Blackwelder, Julia Kirk. *Women of the Depression: Caste and Culture in San Antonio, 1929–1939.* Texas A&M Press, 1984.

**Chapter 14** **Winston Churchill:** Baldwin, Hanson W. *The Crucial Years: 1939–1941.* Harper and Row, 1976, p. 127; **Franklin D. Roosevelt:** Commager, Henry Steele, ed. *Documents of American History,* vol. II, Eighth Edition. Appleton-Century-Crofts, 1968, p. 452; **Franklin D. Roosevelt:** Commager, Henry Steele, ed. *Documents of American History,* vol. II, Eighth Edition. Appleton-Century-Crofts, 1968, p. 449; **American GI:** Martin, Ralph. *The GI War.* Boston: Little, Brown and Co., 1967, p. 338; **Hiroshima survivor:** Cook, Haruko Taya, and Theodore Cook. *Japan at War: An Oral History.* The New Press, 1992, p. 397; **Leon Bass:** *Holocaust and Human Behavior.* Facing History and Ourselves National Foundation, p. 414.

**Chapter 15** **Leonard Williamson:** Hoopes, Roy. *Americans Remember the Home Front: An Oral Narrative.* Hawthorn Books, 1977, p. 115; **Want ad:** *Sporting News,* February 25, 1943; **Sheril Cunning:** Terkel, Studs. *"The Good War": An Oral History of World War Two.* Ballantine Books, 1984, p. 234; **Beatrice Clifton:** Gluck, Sherna Berger. *Rosie the Riveter Revisited: Women, the War, and Social Change.* Twayne Publishers, 1987, pp. 211, 219; **Lloyd Brown:** Blum, John Morton. *V Was for Victory: Politics and American Culture During World War II.* Harcourt Brace Jovanovich, 1976, p. 191; **Henry Murakami:** Harris, Mark Jonathan, et al. *The Homefront: America During World War II.* G. P. Putnam's Sons, 1984, p. 113.

**Chapter 16** **Winston Churchill:** *The Annals of America.* Vol. 16, *1940–1949: The Second World War and After.* Encyclopedia Britannica, 1968, p. 367; **George Kennan:** *The Annals of America.* Vol. 16, *1940–1949: The Second World War and After.* Encyclopedia Britannica, 1968, p. 444; **Harry Truman:** Commager, Henry Steele, ed. *Documents of American History,* vol. II, Eighth Edition. Appleton-Century-Crofts, 1968, p. 525; **George C. Marshall:** Commager, Henry Steele, ed. *Documents of American History,* vol. II, Eighth Edition. Appleton-Century-Crofts, 1968, p. 532; **MacArthur:** Phillips, Cabell. *The Truman Presidency: The History of a Triumphant Succession.* The Macmillan Company, 1966, p. 348; **John Foster Dulles:** Shafritz, Jay M. *HarperCollins Dictionary of American Govern-*

The lure of the West became irresistible when gold was found in California in 1848. The **Comstock Lode,** a huge silver deposit in Nevada discovered in 1859, heightened mining fever. Miners eventually found gold or silver in 30 western states.

By 1890, America's western frontier had all but disappeared. The creation of the country's first national park, Yellowstone, in 1872, was an indication of how fast the West was becoming developed.

## *The Rise of Cities*

While people spread westward, they also began moving to the cities. East of the Mississippi, industrialization spurred much of the urban growth in the early to mid-1800s. Transportation influenced growth as well. The decision on where to dig a canal or run a railroad line could make or break a city. When canals linked the East to the Great Lakes (1825), and the Great Lakes to the Mississippi River (1848), the sleepy town of Chicago, at the junction of these waterways, became a giant.

In the West, the discovery of mineral resources created boomtowns, which shot up quickly with the creation of sudden wealth. Many fizzled out, but some remained. The first year of the gold rush brought 40,000 people to San Francisco. Discovery of the uses of petroleum in the mid-1860s turned sticky, worthless oil into black gold. Oil rigs appeared in back yards in Los Angeles, and some people became wealthy overnight. Oil wealth helped build cities in Texas and Oklahoma, as well.

In the late 1800s, the United States experienced tremendous urban growth caused in part by large waves of immigration. Large ethnic neighborhoods formed in major cities such as New York, Boston, Chicago, and San Francisco. By 1900, 40 percent of Americans lived in urban areas.

### Reviewing Themes

1. *Key Terms* Define: (a) Northwest Territory; (b) push-pull factors; (c) Comstock Lode.
2. *Analyzing Time Lines* List three entries from the time line that show people breaking geographic barriers. Explain your choices.
3. *Comprehension* Why did diverse regional economies develop in the United States?
4. *Connecting to Today* Identify push-pull factors that have caused people to move from cities to the suburbs in recent times.

**1825**
*Erie Canal opens*

**1845**
- *Texas becomes a state*
- *Concept of Manifest Destiny originated*

**1846**
*Northern border of Oregon established at 49th parallel*

**1848**
*Treaty of Guadalupe Hidalgo increases American territory by one third*

**1850**

**1853**
*Gadsden Purchase completes present-day borders of continental United States*

**1862**
*Homestead Act draws settlers to West*

**1867**
*U.S. buys Alaska from Russia for $7.2 million*

**1870**
*Standardized time zones developed*

**1871**
*Chicago Fire*

**1872**
*Yellowstone National Park created*

**1898**
- *Hawaii annexed*
- *U.S. gains Philippines, Puerto Rico, and Guam in Spanish-American War*

**1900**

**1900**
*Tidal wave devastates Galveston, Texas*

# CULTURE
## 1750–1900

In most things concerning society and culture, Americans in times past took their cues from Europe. Ships brought visitors with news of the latest music, fashions, and art fads. At the docks people nearly rioted to get new manuscripts from celebrated European authors. Thomas Jefferson returned from Paris in 1789 with trunks full of books.

Most Americans' values reflected a European heritage as well. They believed in obedience to a stern God. They valued education. They had a love of commerce and a belief that hard work reaps the reward of prosperity.

Americans also were revolutionaries and frontiersmen. That bred in them a desire to do things differently, to create their own styles, to think their own thoughts. As the time line below illustrates, over time a distinct, influential American culture took shape.

### *Religion and Reform*

The nation's founders so valued religious freedom that they guaranteed it in the Constitution. The first words of the First Amendment state that "Congress shall make no law" to establish a church, nor may it prohibit citizens' "free exercise" of their religious beliefs. Under these protections, a variety of religions flourished in the United States. European religions, including Protestant sects, Catholicism, and Judaism, took hold in the 1700s. Distinctly American religions such as the Mormon church arose as well.

Starting in the 1790s, America experienced a revival of religious interest called the **Second Great Awakening.** Like the First Great Awakening of the 1730s and 1740s, this movement was evangelical, emphasizing preaching rather than ceremonies. It focused on converting people to a belief in God and Christ so that they might gain salvation. Preachers held huge camp meetings that attracted people of all ages and economic groups. Revivalists taught that a person's faith mattered more than social status. This was a new, democratic approach to religion.

Religion strongly influenced a social reform movement in the early 1800s. Reformers tackled a variety of social ills. Educator Horace Mann helped create a model public school system in Massachusetts. Women played a key role in the **temperance movement,** which succeeded in cutting the nation's high alcohol consumption. Reformer Dorothea Dix convinced state legislatures to improve prison conditions. The **abolition movement** sought to end slavery. Abolitionists included African Americans such as Frederick Douglass, a former slave who became a lecturer

**1750**

**1776**
*Thomas Paine's* Common Sense

**1783**
- *First U.S. daily newspaper,* The Pennsylvania Evening Post, *is founded*
- *Noah Webster publishes first dictionary of American language*

**1789**
- *Jefferson completes design for Virginia Capitol, first U.S. building in Roman style*
- *Thanksgiving is national holiday for the first time*

**1790**
*Second Great Awakening begins*

**1791**
*Pierre Charles L'Enfant finishes design for Washington, D.C.*

**1798**
*Commonly known version of "Yankee Doodle" published*

**1800**

**c.1825**
*First U.S. art movement, Hudson River school of landscape painting, begins*

**1827**
*John James Audubon produces* Birds of America *prints*

**1831**
*William Lloyd Garrison begins anti-slavery publication* The Liberator

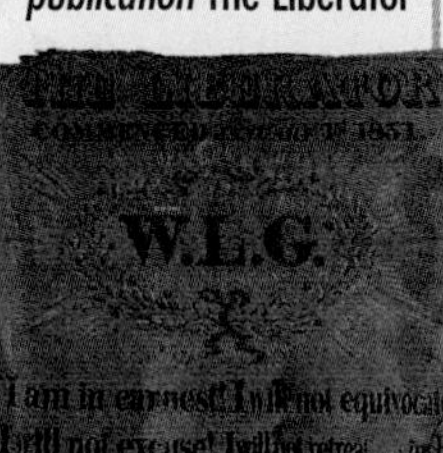


CULTURE

and writer, and white northerners such as William Lloyd Garrison, who published an influential antislavery newspaper.

Reform movements had several features in common. They reflected the optimistic American belief in self-improvement. Most stressed adherence to biblical, Protestant values.

## *The Arts and Recreation*

In painting, poetry, stories, and song, Americans of the 1800s celebrated traditional values and beliefs. They also created uniquely American artistic styles.

Revolutionary-era thinkers such as Thomas Paine and Thomas Jefferson inspired future generations with their writings on political philosophy. Reform-minded writers such as Henry David Thoreau, Louisa May Alcott, and Harriet Beecher Stowe reflected the moral values of their day. Stowe's powerful novel *Uncle Tom's Cabin* stirred public outrage against slavery. The essence of American life was captured in the folksy, dry humor of Mark Twain.

Much of the art and architecture of the 1800s expressed an appreciation of nature. The first truly American movement in painting was the Hudson River school, which captured the beauty and variety of American landscapes. Architect Frederick Law Olmsted created oases of natural beauty in American cities by designing parks such as Boston's "Emerald Necklace."

In factories or on farms, most Americans led a hard life. Long workdays consumed most of their daylight hours. But by the end of the 1800s, time-saving inventions had introduced working Americans to a new concept: leisure. People used their free time in new amusements, from bicycles to Ferris wheels. Organized sports became popular, and one new sport—baseball—was on its way to becoming a national obsession.

### Reviewing Themes

1. *Key Terms* Define: (a) Second Great Awakening; (b) temperance movement; (c) abolition movement.
2. *Analyzing Time Lines* On the time line, find three examples of uniquely American cultural contributions. Explain your choices.
3. *Comprehension* How were reform movements of the early 1800s linked to religion?
4. *Connecting to Today* How does American culture influence other countries today?

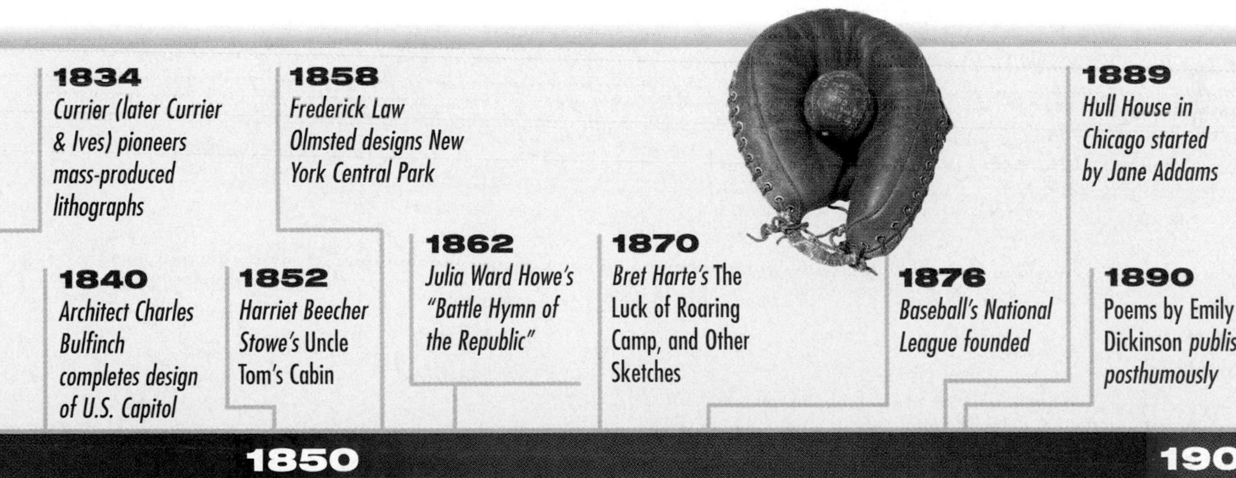


**1843** *Reformer Dorothea Dix reports on prison conditions*

**1854** *Thoreau's* Walden

**1855** *Walt Whitman's* Leaves of Grass

**1869** *Louisa May Alcott's* Little Women

**1881** *Booker T. Washington founds Tuskegee Institute*

**1884** *Mark Twain's* The Adventures of Huckleberry Finn

**1885** *Stanford University opened in Palo Alto, Calif.*

# ECONOMICS 1750–1900

With a continent of undeveloped resources at their doorstep, Americans came to believe that economic prosperity and the creation of wealth were their destiny. Hard work and innovation reaped huge rewards. They turned forests and fields into productive farms and created the world's leading industrial nation, as the time line below shows.

The expansion was not endless, of course. Nor did it come without periodic setbacks and downturns. Prosperity benefited some, not all. Much of the legislation that brought stability and fairness to American business would not come until modern times.

## *From Farms to Factories*

One of America's first economic activities was farming. In the South, a relatively small number of wealthy white men owned large plantations using slave labor. But most farmers, North or South, were simple families who worked smaller plots of land.

In the 1700s most Americans lived off the land, but other occupations were growing. Shipping and finance prospered in seaports such as Boston, New York, and Charleston. A profitable whaling and fishing industry grew up in New England. A brisk fur trade thrived in forested areas farther west, especially in the Great Lakes region.

In early America, items that people needed or wanted—clothing, tools, weapons—had to be made by hand, at home or by craftspeople. That changed with the **Industrial Revolution,** an explosion of manufacturing inventions and processes that originated in England in the 1700s. The Industrial Revolution spread to the United States in 1793, when Samuel Slater built the first successful American textile mill. Water power ran the machinery of the mills that spread along the rivers of the Northeast.

The Industrial Revolution in America triggered vast economic and social changes. The spread of factories hastened the growth of towns and cities. People left the farms and moved to the cities to work. Americans began buying manufactured items instead of making them. New stores opened; a banking industry developed. These rapid economic changes of the early 1800s are referred to as the **Market Revolution**.

One source of problems was that the country lacked a stable currency. Money varied in value from place to place and bank to bank. Yet as people bought more goods, they came to rely more and more on money. The instability of the nation's currency led to occasional panics and depressions.

As the economy grew, the federal government took on a greater role in the nation's economic

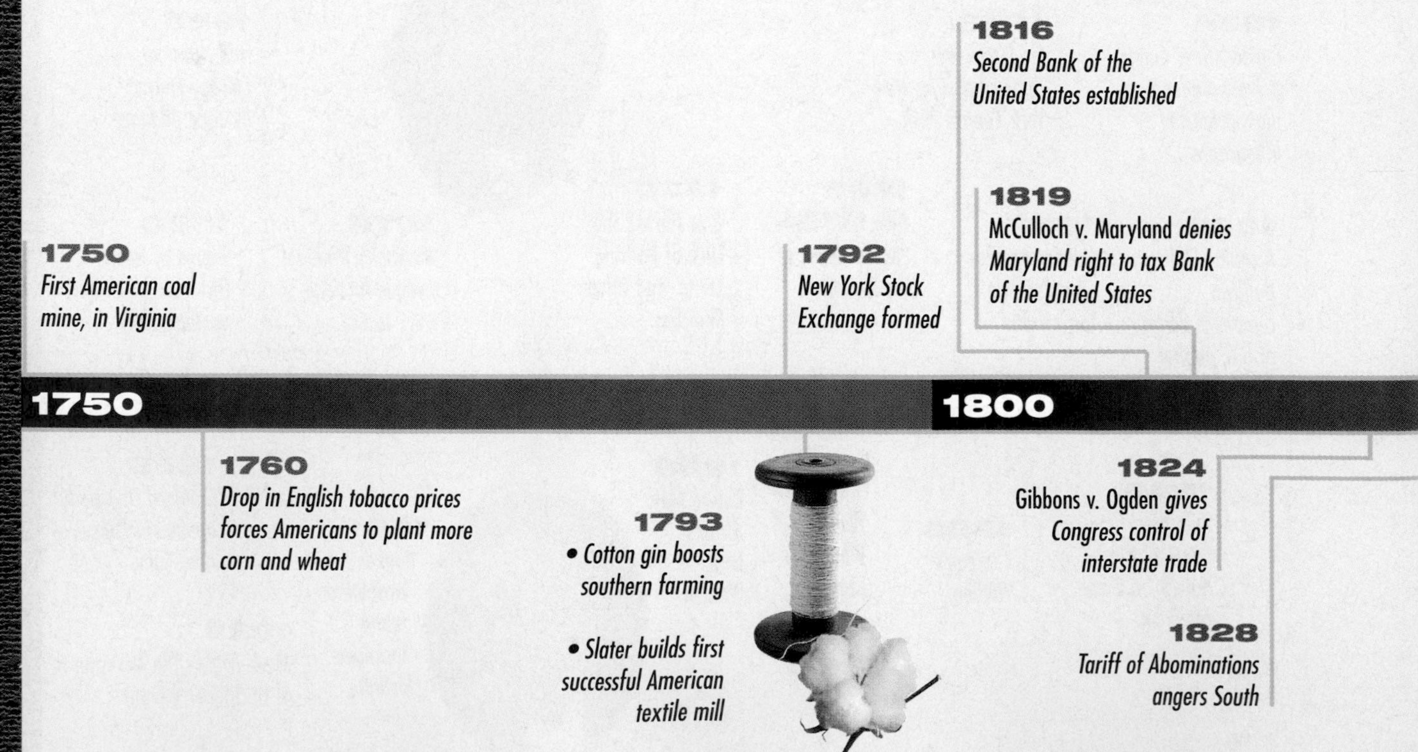

affairs. It created a national bank in 1816, for example, and built roads and canals.

During the early 1800s, the economies of the various geographic regions became more diverse: manufacturing in the North; plantation farming of cotton, tobacco, and rice in the South; livestock and corn and grain farming farther west.

## The Rise of Big Business

Regional economic divisions contributed to the tensions that led to the Civil War. Economic differences, such as the North's superiority in equipment and transportation, also helped determine the war's outcome. In the end the South's economic system, based on slave labor, lay in ruins. Industry began to take hold in the postwar South, but the growth was slow. The North would remain the wealthiest region until well into the 20th century.

In the late 1800s new technologies and northern wealth helped industries grow into giant corporations. These companies produced exciting new consumer goods. But unregulated corporate growth led to some abuses. Factory workers labored in dangerous conditions, earning little pay for long hours. **Monopolies**, companies that controlled an entire industry, often charged high prices and smothered competition. Corporations routinely bribed government officials to avoid the law or to keep reform legislation from getting passed. Monopoly control of the railroads forced farmers to pay unfair rates to ship their goods.

The growth of big business produced calls for government regulation. The number of labor unions grew, and their demands for workplace reforms began to be heard. Desperate farmers united in a movement of the people called **populism**, forming the Populist party in 1891. Many of the reforms these groups sought would not come until the 1900s.

### Reviewing Themes

1. *Key Terms* Define: (a) Industrial Revolution; (b) monopoly; (c) populism.
2. *Analyzing Time Lines* What benefits and challenges resulted from the nation's rapid economic growth in the early 1800s?
3. *Comprehension* Describe the rise of big business and some problems it caused.
4. *Connecting to Today* How does the federal government get involved in the economy of the United States today? Give examples.

**1834** *National Trades Union formed*

**1846** *Invention of sewing machine makes manufactured clothing affordable*

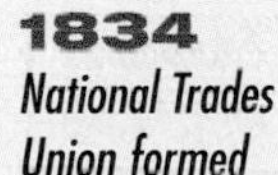

**1848** *California gold rush begins*

**1850**

**1862** *Pacific Railroad Act*

**1863** *National Bank Act sets up federally chartered banks and new regulation*

**1865** *Sharecropping/tenant farming becomes widespread with end of slavery*

**1869** *Transcontinental railroad completed*

**1873** *Bank failures trigger Panic of 1873*

**1877**
- *Munn v. Illinois allows regulation of railroads*
- *Great Strike of 1877*

**1886**
- *American Federation of Labor formed*
- *Haymarket Riot*

**1890** *Sherman Antitrust Act passed*

**1893** *Railroad failures trigger Panic of 1893*

**1894** *Pullman Strike of 1894*

**1896** *William Jennings Bryan's "Cross of Gold" speech*

**1900**

# DIVERSITY 1750-1900

The people of the early United States had many common traits. Most were white, English-speaking Protestant Christians. Yet the American population included large groups of people of other descent who would play a major role in the nation's history. Today's diverse society, representing many nationalities, ethnic groups, and religions, took centuries of struggle to build, as the time line below shows.

## *Growth Produces Conflict*

In the nation's first century, competition for land and wealth pitted groups of people against one another. Native Americans suffered the first and most permanent losses.

British officials and American settlers generally believed that the Indians had to make way for white civilization. This led to frequent conflict. In 1763, Pontiac, leader of the Ottawa Indians, led an unsuccessful three-year war known as Pontiac's Rebellion. During the next century, settlers pressed farther west. Native Americans were forced into signing treaties that crowded them into ever smaller tracts of land with dwindling food sources. Many of these treaties were eventually broken.

In the American South, growth and prosperity were achieved through the use of an unpaid labor force: enslaved Africans. By 1750, rice, tobacco, and indigo plantations had become dependent on slave labor. Slaves tended the fields and served white households. African Americans were born into a lifetime of servitude. Slavery broke up families and shattered cultural traditions.

Yet Africans strongly influenced American society. Most slaves came from West Africa, and they managed to keep and pass on folklore, religious beliefs, music, and other traditions of their homelands.

In the mid-1800s, another mixing of cultures took place that would greatly shape American culture today. From 1845 to 1853, the United States acquired California and the Southwest from Mexico. These areas combined the Spanish language, Catholic religion, and other traditions with those of Native Americans. Now this southwestern culture became a part of American life.

Cultural, religious, and ethnic diversity increased in the early 1800s. Fleeing political upheaval, a wave of German immigrants began in the late 1820s. Severe famine in Ireland in the mid-1840s brought mostly Catholic newcomers. Many settled in eastern cities, forming tight-knit neighborhoods to shield themselves from anti-Catholic prejudice.

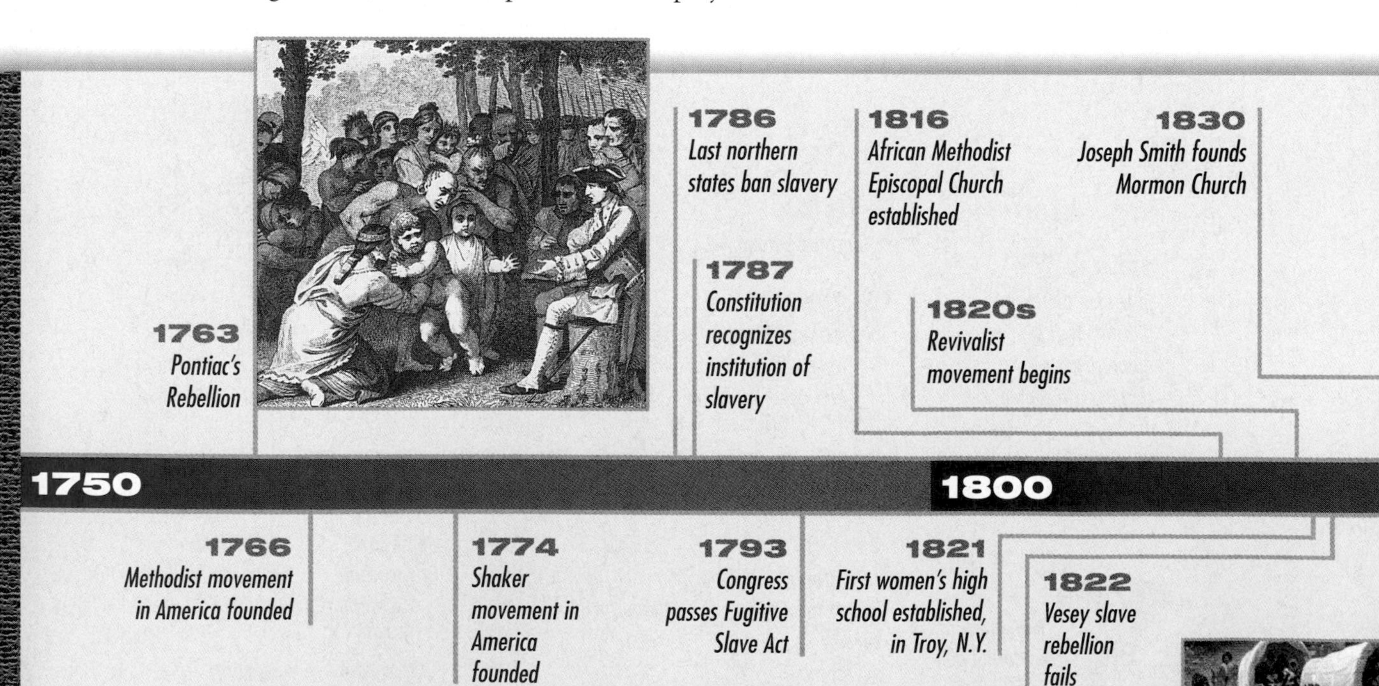

## *Progress and Challenges*

In the mid- to late-1800s, the nation began to move in the direction of a more diverse and fair society. Progress was slow, but measurable.

Slavery ended with the Emancipation Proclamation in 1863 and the Thirteenth Amendment in 1865. During Reconstruction, African Americans gained citizenship and voting rights. Throughout the South, dozens of black lawmakers won election to state and federal offices.

With the removal of federal troops from the South in 1877, however, former Confederates regained power. They passed voting restrictions and laws to **segregate,** or separate, blacks from white society. In 1896 the Supreme Court ruled in *Plessy* v. *Ferguson* that "separate but equal" public facilities, from restrooms to schools, were legal.

The second half of the 1800s brought many new groups of immigrants to America. In the West, Chinese workers were brought in to build the railroads. Large waves of immigrants from Eastern and Southern Europe, including Russian Jews, also began arriving for the first time.

These new peoples enriched American society with their ideas and customs. However, their presence caused a backlash among some Americans of white, Protestant heritage, who formed a movement known as **nativism.** In 1882 nativists helped pass the Chinese Exclusion Act.

By 1890, the last Native Americans had been forced onto reservations. Adding to this tragedy, the Dawes Act of 1887 attempted to bring Indians into white society by forcing them to give up their own cultural traditions.

A battle for women's rights gathered momentum in the mid-1800s. Women gathered in New York in 1848 for the Seneca Falls Convention. The historic meeting launched the movement for women's **suffrage,** or the right to vote. By the turn of the century, women could vote in several states, and pressure was growing for a constitutional amendment to guarantee women's suffrage.

### Reviewing Themes

1. ***Key Terms*** Define: (a) segregate; (b) nativism; (c) suffrage.
2. ***Analyzing Time Lines*** Identify three positive and three negative developments in the struggle for diversity and equal rights.
3. Compare the treatment of Native Americans to that of African Americans in the 1800s.
4. ***Connecting to Today*** Select an entry below and describe its impact on modern society.

**1838** *Trail of Tears*

**1841** *Scandinavian immigration increases*

**1845** *Irish famine spurs immigration*

**1848**
- *Seneca Falls Convention*
- *U.S. gains Spanish-speaking lands through Mexican War*

**1850**

**1857** *Dred Scott decision*

**1863** *Emancipation Proclamation*

**1865** *Thirteenth Amendment ratified*

**1868** *Reconstruction governments in South*

**1869** *Wyoming territory grants women right to vote*

**1870** *Fifteenth Amendment ratified*

**1880s**
- *Immigration from southern and eastern Europe increases*
- *Immigration from Mexico and Caribbean increases*

**1882** *Chinese Exclusion Act*

**1887** *Dawes Act aims to assimilate Native Americans*

**1890s** *Utah, Colorado, and Idaho grant women right to vote*

**1890** *Battle of Wounded Knee*

**1896** *Plessy v. Ferguson legalizes segregation*

**1900**

# FOREIGN RELATIONS 1750–1900

In a little over 200 years, a handful of rebel colonies became the world's undisputed superpower. As the time line below indicates, Britain, France, Spain, and Russia saw their desires for an American empire stopped short as the United States pushed relentlessly westward.

## *Expansion in North America*

By the mid-1700s, Britain had thriving colonies along the North American coast. France controlled much of the forested interior and modern-day Canada. From 1754 to 1763 the two rivals fought for control of eastern North America. France drew on its friendly trade relations with Native American groups to aid it in the conflict, known as the French and Indian War. American troops and the addition of Iroquois forces helped give Britain the victory in 1763.

Britain could not celebrate for long. Relations with the colonies worsened as Parliament heaped heavier taxes on Americans in the 1760s. King George III responded to American protests not with compromises but with force. War broke out in 1775, and in 1776 Americans declared their independence from British rule.

Despite Britain's advantage in troops, training, equipment, and naval power, it could not sustain a long, distant war in unfamiliar terrain. The Revolutionary War ended in 1781 with the British surrender at Yorktown, Virginia. Under the terms of the 1783 peace agreement, Britain recognized the United States' independence.

In the postwar years, America pursued a policy of neutrality toward other countries. During the 1790s the United States was still weak and could not afford to get drawn into wars going on in Europe. President George Washington tried to steer a neutral course in foreign relations. In his Farewell Address, he warned against permanent ties to any other country. His warning influenced future foreign policy.

Nevertheless, American leaders were eager to work out agreements to protect and expand the borders of the United States. In 1803, the administration of President Thomas Jefferson struck a deal with France to buy the Louisiana Territory, a huge tract of land from the Mississippi River westward to the Rocky Mountains. The $15 million **Louisiana Purchase** nearly doubled the size of the United States.

Despite America's policy of neutrality, conflicts with Britain over trade finally led to war. The three-year War of 1812 settled little, but over time, ties with Britain improved.

**1754** *French and Indian War begins*

**1763** *French and Indian War ends with Treaty of Paris*

**1765**
- *Britain passes Quartering Act, Stamp Act*
- *Colonists boycott British goods*

**1769**
- *Spanish found San Diego*
- *First mission in California*

**1773**
- *Britain passes Tea Act*
- *Boston Tea Party*

**1775** *Revolutionary War begins*

**1781** *British surrender at Yorktown*

**1794** *Jay's Treaty with Britain*

**1795** *Pinckney's Treaty with Spain*

**1797** *XYZ Affair*

**1800**

**1803** *Louisiana Purchase*

**1812** *War of 1812 begins*

**1817** *Rush-Bagot Treaty*

**1821** *Mexico wins independence, encourages Americans to settle Texas*

**1823** *Monroe Doctrine aims to end European expansion in Western Hemisphere*

Continuing concern about European aggression prompted President James Monroe in 1823 to issue the **Monroe Doctrine.** The policy declared U.S. neutrality in European wars and warned other nations not to interfere in the Western Hemisphere. The Monroe Doctrine became a cornerstone of American foreign policy.

While Monroe was warning against European aggression in the Americas, the United States was pursuing a policy of expansion across the continent that is known as **manifest destiny.** In 1845 the United States annexed Texas. This act led to the Mexican War, in which the United States gained California and the Southwest.

In 1846 Britain agreed to establish the northern border of Oregon at the 49th parallel. In the 1853 Gadsen Purchase the United States acquired Mexican land south of the Gila River. The United States then purchased Alaska from Russia in 1867.

Influence in Central America began unofficially, through the growth and control of banana plantations in Costa Rica that eventually became the United Fruit Company in 1899. The company gained financial and political control over several Latin American countries in which it did business.

In the late 1800s, European nations began a frenzied global competition to conquer and colonize, a policy called **imperialism.** The United States, now economically and militarily mature, joined the contest. In 1898 the United States annexed Hawaii after having deposed its Queen.

That same year, the battleship U.S.S. *Maine* mysteriously exploded and sank in waters off Spanish-controlled Cuba. The incident triggered the Spanish-American War, a 16-week conflict fought both in the Caribbean and in the Philippine Islands in the Pacific. The U.S. victory was swift and profitable. America gained Puerto Rico and the Pacific islands of Guam and the Philippines. The United States was now a world power.

## Reviewing Themes

1. *Key Terms* Define: (a) Louisiana Purchase; (b) Monroe Doctrine; (c) manifest destiny; (d) imperialism.
2. *Analyzing Time Lines* In the time line below, find two examples of manifest destiny.
3. *Comprehension* List three methods that the United States used to acquire land.
4. *Connecting to Today* Choose one of the key terms listed above and explain how it affects United States policies today.

**1893** *Americans overthrow Hawaii's Queen Liliuokalani*

**1836**
- *Battle of Alamo*
- *Texas wins independence from Mexico*

**1846** *Northern border of Oregon set at 49th parallel*

**1848** *United States wins Mexican War*

**1850**

**1853** *Gadsden Purchase from Mexico*

**1867** *United States buys Alaska from Russia*

**1880s** *American naval fleet enlarged and modernized*

**1898**
- *Hawaii annexed*
- *Sinking of U.S.S. Maine*
- *Spanish-American War*
- *Battle of San Juan Hill*

**1899**
- *United States announces Open Door Policy in China*
- *United Fruit Company established*

**1900** *American forces help put down China's Boxer Rebellion*

**1900**

# SCIENCE & TECHNOLOGY 1750–1900

When they weren't busy creating a nation, three of the nation's founders were part-time scientists. They sought practical applications for new scientific theories and discoveries coming from Europe.

George Washington used scientific methods to study crop rotation and cattle breeding. Thomas Jefferson contributed to the fields of zoology, botany, geology, architecture, mathematics, meteorology, and engineering. He invented an improved plow and a machine for encoding messages. Benjamin Franklin's innovations include an energy-efficient stove, the lightning rod, and bifocal glasses. As the time line below demonstrates, invention is America's heritage.

## *The Industrial Revolution*

In the 1700s, the British learned to harness the energy of rushing water to run new mechanical inventions. This discovery led to Britain's Industrial Revolution.

One of Britain's most closely guarded secrets was the textile mill. Defying British law, mill worker Samuel Slater memorized the workings of an entire mill, then came to Rhode Island and built his own in 1793. Slater brought the Industrial Revolution to America. Along the fast-flowing rivers of the Northeast, mills and other factories arose. Manufacturing forever changed the economies of northern states.

A major advance in manufacturing was the use of **interchangeable parts,** standard-sized parts that allowed products to be assembled quickly, instead of being made from scratch with individually crafted parts. Inventor Eli Whitney introduced the concept at his weapons factory in Connecticut. Whitney is also credited with inventing a machine in 1793 that changed the economy of the South. The **cotton gin** performed the time-consuming task of straining the seeds out of raw cotton. Cotton profits soared.

Two inventions helped turn the Great Plains into the nation's breadbasket. In 1831 Cyrus McCormick created the mechanical reaper to harvest grain. John Deere's steel plow in 1837 conquered the tough sod of the plains that had broken many a wooden plow.

New forms of transportation encouraged trade and migration. The Conestoga wagon hauled freight in the East. Its descendant, the prairie schooner, carried settlers westward. Moving people and goods became faster as canals crisscrossed the North. The famous Erie Canal was completed in 1825. Speedier vessels, such as the steamboat, moved inland goods to coastal seaports. Traffic bristled along the Mississippi and other major rivers.

In 1869, the Union Pacific and the Central Pacific railroad lines were joined at Promontory Point, Utah, creating the first **transcontinental railroad.** The

**1752** *Franklin uses kite to show that lightning is electricity*

**1799** *First U.S. smallpox vaccine*

**1798** *Whitney produces muskets with interchangeable parts*

**1807** *Robert Fulton's steamboat Clermont sets speed record*

**1825** *Erie Canal opens*

**1750** — **1800**

**1750** *Conestoga wagon introduced, in Pennsylvania*

**1765** *First American medical school, in Philadelphia*

**1790** *Slater builds first U.S. cotton mill, launching industrial revolution in America*

**1793** *Whitney invents the cotton gin*

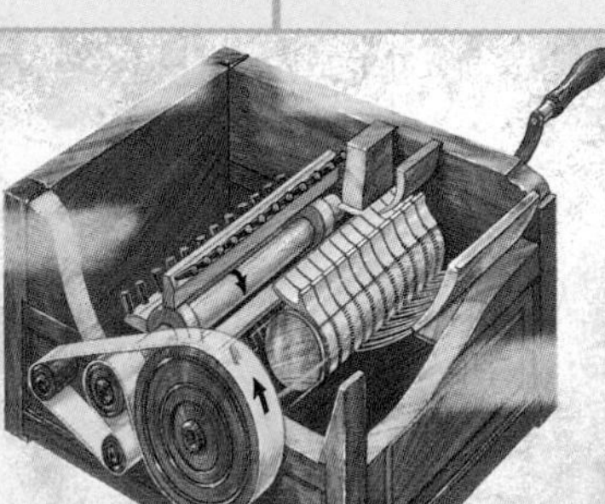

**1831** *McCormick invents the mechanical reaper*

**1832** *Morse invents the telegraph*

future of the West was now decided as trainloads of settlers arrived in Kansas City, Seattle, San Francisco, and other western stops. As railroad track stretched westward, lines for the new telegraph often followed. Invented by Samuel F. B. Morse in 1832, it launched a new era in communication.

## *Making Life Better*

Machines changed American life, not just on farms and in factories, but in the home as well. Many time-consuming tasks, from weaving to candlemaking to grinding grain, disappeared as manufactured items appeared in stores. Elias Howe's 1846 sewing machine freed women from the endless chore of stitching clothing by hand.

With the coming of machines, people looked for ways to power them in areas where water was not available. One innovation was the steam engine, which turned energy into motion. The engines were fueled at first by burning wood, then by coal, then kerosene, which was made from oil. Owners of oil-rich land in Texas and California became wealthy as uses for oil were developed in the late 1800s.

Another technological revolution began in the 1870s, when Alexander Graham Bell spoke the first scratchy words over a telephone wire. From the fertile mind of Thomas Alva Edison came two other revolutionary products, the phonograph and the electric light bulb. Edison eventually obtained patents on hundreds of inventions.

The age of electricity illuminated American cities. In 1882 Edison created the first power plant, electrifying 85 buildings in New York City. Electric power was put to work in cable cars, street lamps, stoves, sewing machines, and other appliances.

At the turn of the century, two new forms of entertainment had just arrived: motion pictures and radio. More exciting new products were just around the corner.

### Reviewing Themes

1. *Key Terms* Define: (a) interchangeable parts; (b) cotton gin; (c) transcontinental railroad.
2. *Analyzing Time Lines* Choose three entries from the time line and explain their impact on the economy of the United States.
3. *Comprehension* How did technology affect farm life and city life in America?
4. *Connecting to Today* Choose one invention listed here. Show how it affects your life today.

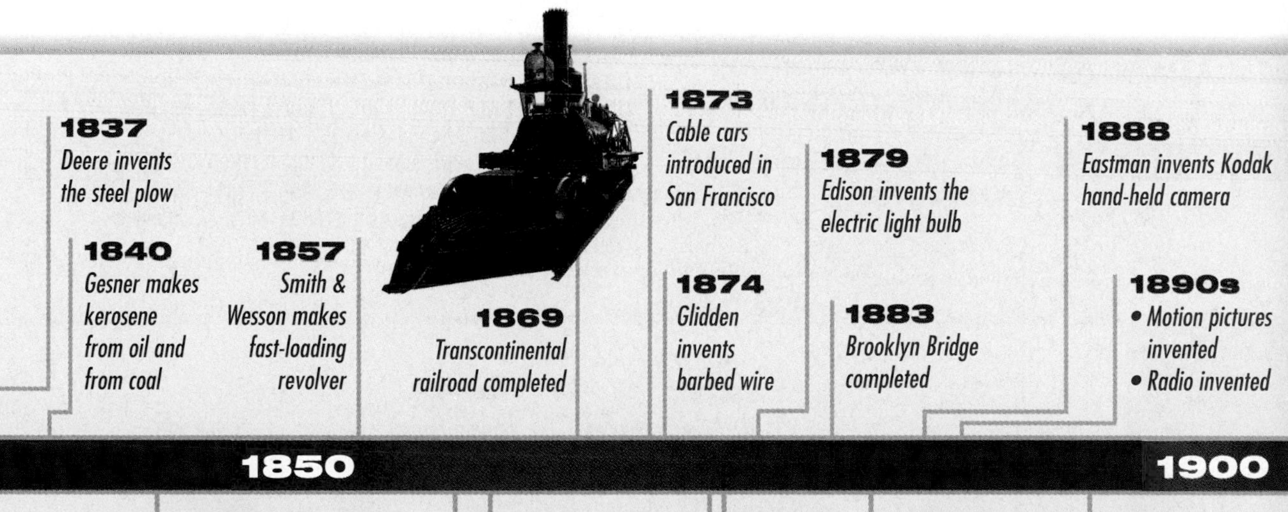

**1837** *Deere invents the steel plow*

**1840** *Gesner makes kerosene from oil and from coal*

**1857** *Smith & Wesson makes fast-loading revolver*

**1869** *Transcontinental railroad completed*

**1873** *Cable cars introduced in San Francisco*

**1874** *Glidden invents barbed wire*

**1879** *Edison invents the electric light bulb*

**1883** *Brooklyn Bridge completed*

**1888** *Eastman invents Kodak hand-held camera*

**1890s**
- *Motion pictures invented*
- *Radio invented*

**1850** — **1900**

**1846** *Howe invents the sewing machine*

**1862** *Battle of two ironclads, the Monitor and the Merrimack, ends of era of wooden ships*

**1864** *Bessemer steel process first used in U.S.*

**1876** *Bell invents telephone*

**1877** *Edison invents phonograph*

**1885** *First steel-frame skyscraper built, in Chicago*

**1897** *First underground subway opens in Boston*

# unit ONE

# Building a Powerful Nation

*The rich and varied histories of people from around the world shaped our nation. When the American colonists overthrew British rule in the American Revolution, they created a new nation that struggled to achieve a balance between liberty and order. In the last half of the nineteenth century, the United States underwent dramatic change, as it experienced civil war, territorial expansion, industrialization, and population growth.*



## UNIT THEMES

**Government** In 1787 the Constitutional Convention crafted a plan of government that struck a balance between liberty and order.

**Economics** The North's superior economic strength helped it defeat the South in the Civil War.

**Geography** The explosive growth of the post–Civil War era transformed the nation.

## PRESIDENTS

Washington (1789–1797), J. Adams (1797–1801), Jefferson (1801–1809), Madison (1809–1817), Monroe (1817–1825), J.Q. Adams (1825–1829), Jackson (1829–1837), Van Buren (1837–1841), Harrison (1841), Tyler (1841–1845), Polk (1845–1849), Taylor (1849–1850), Fillmore (1850–1853), Pierce (1853–1857), Buchanan (1857–1861), Lincoln (1861–1865), Johnson (1865–1869), Grant (1869–1877), Hayes (1877–1881), Garfield (1881), Arthur (1881–1885), Cleveland (1885–1889), Harrison (1889–1893), Cleveland (1893–1897), McKinley (1897–1901)

**EVENTS IN THE UNITED STATES**

**1492** *Columbus sails to the Americas*

**1524** *Verrazano explores the North American coast*

**1565** *Spain founds St. Augustine, Florida*

**1607** *England founds Jamestown*

**1450** — **1525** — **1600**

**EVENTS IN THE WORLD**

**1521** *Hernando Cortés conquers Mexico's Aztec empire*

**1533** *Francisco Pizarro destroys the Inca empire*

**1614** *Dutch East India Company founded*

**VIEWING HISTORY** John L. Krimmel painted *Election Day in Philadelphia* in 1815. *Culture* ***What do you think explains the emotional intensity of the crowd?***

E pluribus unum — *"from many, one"— was chosen as the nation's motto in 1776.*

**1776**
*Declaration of Independence signed*

**1803**
*Turning Point: Louisiana Purchase (p. 70)*

**1856**
*Turning Point: Bessemer Steel Process (p. 155)*

**1861**
*Civil War begins*

**1868**
*Turning Point: Fourteenth Amendment (p. 132)*

**1750** | **1825** | **1900**

**1689**
*England's Glorious Revolution produces a bill of rights*

**1781**
*Peruvians revolt against Spanish rule*

**1829**
*Slavery abolished in Mexico*

**1889**
*French Panama Canal Company goes bankrupt*

CHAPTER

1

# American History to the Civil War

## Beginnings–1861

## CHAPTER FOCUS

**F**irst populated by Native Americans, the Americas became home to a diverse and growing population as European nations set up colonies. In 1776 Britain's American colonies declared their independence. The new nation, the United States, expanded westward across the continent, but found no peaceful way to confront the issue of slavery.

*The **Why Study History?** page at the end of this chapter explores the issue of states' rights versus the power of the federal government—the same issue that played a role in the outbreak of the Civil War.*

▲ **VIEWING HISTORY** *This 1803 painting reflects Americans' pride in the nation's growing prosperity.* **Government** ***What does the eagle symbolize in this painting?***

**1492** *Columbus reaches the Americas*

**1524** *Verrazano explores the North American coast*

**1565** *Spain founds St. Augustine*

**1607** *England founds Jamestown*

**1660** *Navigation Act tightens English control over trade*

**1750** *African Americans make up about 20 percent of colonial population*

1450 | 1550 | 1650 | 1750

# 1 Exploration and the Colonial Era

## SECTION PREVIEW

### Objectives

1. Describe the first Americans and how they reached the Americas.
2. List the reasons why Spain, France, Holland, and England were interested in the Americas, and describe the growth of the English colonies.
3. Describe the experiences of African Americans in the colonies.
4. *Key Terms* Define: Columbian Exchange; colony; Magna Carta; House of Burgesses; mercantilism; Triangular Trade; Middle Passage; diversity.

### Main Idea

Columbus's journey to the Americas in 1492 began a wave of migration that would bring many Europeans and Africans to the Americas.

### Reading Strategy

*Formulating Questions* Reread the Main Idea above. Then rewrite it as a question. As you read, take notes about events that help answer the question.

For tens of thousands of years, the only humans living in the Americas were Native Americans. The 1400s, however, set the scene for the arrival of new cultures. Explorers from a number of European nations would race to claim land in the Americas. Africans also reached the American shores.

## *The First Americans Reach the Americas*

Before Europeans or Africans ever reached the Americas, hundreds of societies already populated the American land. The people who created these societies and the generations that descended from them are today generally called Native Americans, or Indians.

No one knows exactly when people first came to the Americas. It is known, however, that some early peoples left fingerprints in New Mexico mud that hardened 28,000 years ago, and that weapons have been chipped from Alaskan stone 12,000 years ago.

Archaeologists think the first Americans may have arrived as many as 40,000 years ago. At that time, known as the Ice Age, the lowering of the level of the world's oceans created a temporary land bridge between Asia and what is now Alaska. As groups arrived from Asia they dispersed, and their settlements eventually ranged from the Arctic Circle to South America's tip. By the late 1400s, when the first Europeans arrived, Native Americans had developed a variety of distinct languages and customs.

*A silent witness to the Spanish attempt to conquer Florida, this soldier's helmet was lost in the 1500s at Palm Beach and discovered in recent times.*

## *Spanish Exploration*

On August 3, 1492, three ships set sail from the seaport of Palos, in the Spanish kingdom of Castile. Before the crews lay the vast, uncrossed Atlantic Ocean. Before them also lay a great challenge—the challenge of finding a new trade route to "the lands of India."

## European Exploration of the Americas, 1492–1682

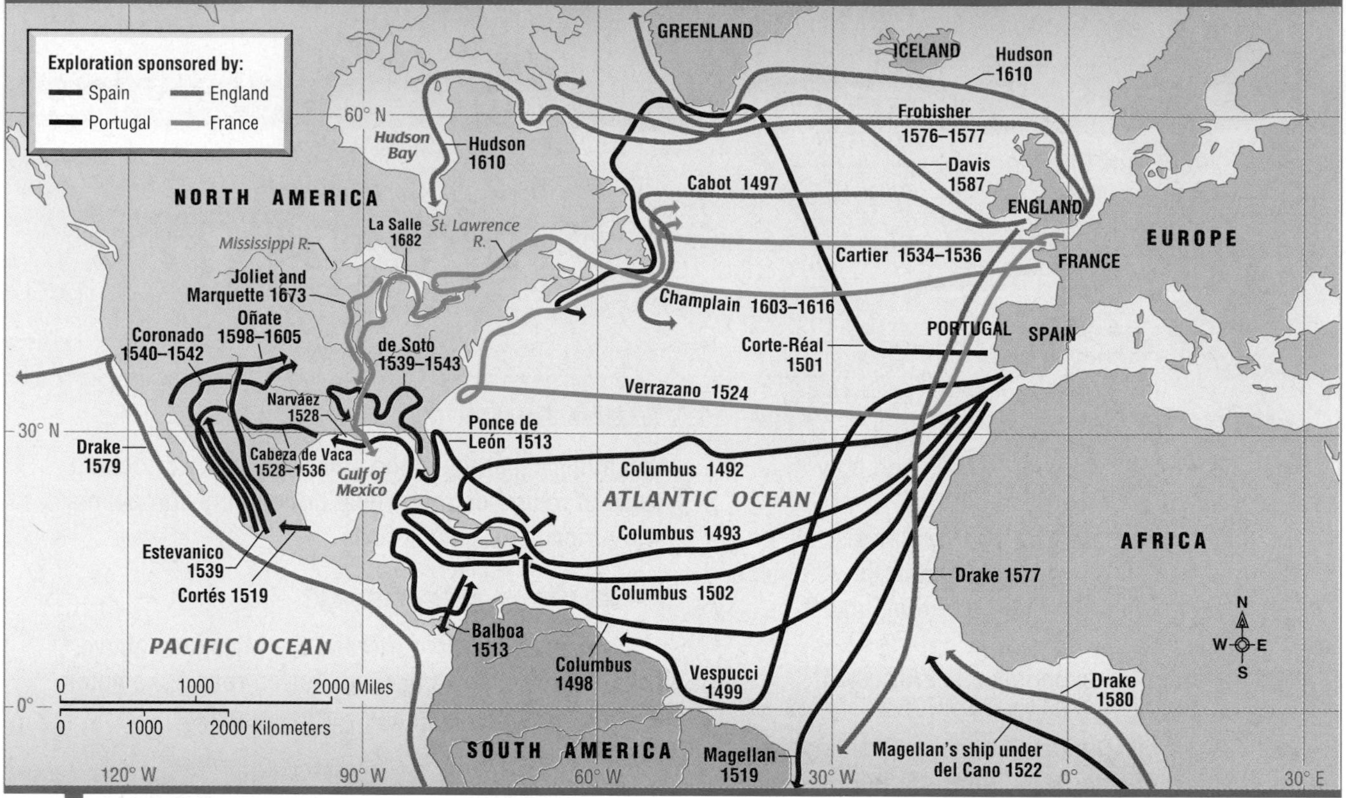

For more than a century after Columbus's voyages, explorers sailed on behalf of any power that would sponsor them. Cabot and Verrazano were Italian, and Hudson was English. Estevanico was originally an African slave who was later freed to explore the Southwest. ***Movement*** ***What nations sponsored Cabot, Verrazano, Hudson, and Estevanico?***

**Main Idea CONNECTIONS**

*Why did Spain explore the Western Hemisphere?*

For the rest of his life, Christopher Columbus believed that he and the three ships he commanded had discovered a sea route from Europe to Asia. But in reality, Columbus and his crews had landed on islands in the Caribbean Sea—not, as Columbus believed, on the "Indies" off the Asian coast. Columbus's discovery of a "New World" was confirmed by Amerigo Vespucci, a Florence merchant who reached the Caribbean in 1499. It was Vespucci whose name eventually was used to identify the unknown lands—"America."

Columbus's Atlantic crossing made possible a regular, permanent exchange among the people of the Americas, Africa, and Europe. Known as the **Columbian Exchange,** this interaction involved people, animals, goods, ideas, technology, and even disease. European ships returned from the Americas with new foods, including potatoes and cocoa. Europeans brought to the Americas crops such as wheat and sugar and domesticated animals such as the cow.

During the 1500s, Spanish explorers, searching for the wealth promised by Columbus's voyages, explored parts of the Western Hemisphere. They conquered and plundered civilizations of Central and South America, such as the Aztecs and Incas. They also pushed northward, exploring the southeastern and southwestern parts of what would become the United States. In 1513 explorer Juan Ponce de León claimed Florida for Spain. In 1565 Spain established St. Augustine, Florida, the oldest surviving European settlement in the present-day United States. Eventually Spain would also claim the land west of the Mississippi River.

Spanish settlements eventually dotted the South and West. Some of these settlements grew into **colonies,** areas settled by immigrants who continue to be ruled by their parent country.

## French and Dutch Exploration

The Spanish were not the only Europeans interested in North America. The French too were exploring northeastern North America, looking for trading opportunities. As early as 1524, Giovanni de Verrazano, an Italian explorer sailing for France, explored the coast of North America from what is now North Carolina to Newfoundland, now a part of Canada. On the basis of Jacques Cartier's explorations, the French king claimed present-day Canada and parts of the northern United States for France, calling the area New France. In 1608 the first successful French colony was founded on the site of the Canadian city of Quebec. It based its economy on fur, which the French obtained through trade with Native Americans and then sold to be made into clothing in Europe.

The Dutch also came looking for trade. Dutch settlers established New Amsterdam (now New York City) in 1626 to control the fur trade along the Hudson River. Later, Fort Orange (now Albany) became a center of trade with the Native Americans. Like the French, the Dutch were less interested in conquering Native Americans than in simply obtaining furs by trade.

## English Colonization

Despite these early efforts by the French and Dutch, the European power that came to dominate eastern North America was England. The first English attempt at settlement, at Roanoke in present-day North Carolina, failed twice. The first attempt, in 1585, ended when the starving settlers returned to England after only a year. Two years later, a second attempt at settlement was made, but it ended in a great mystery. A supply expedition arriving from England in 1590 found only empty buildings at the Roanoke settlement. What happened to the settlers there has never been discovered.

The next English to settle on the Atlantic coast resulted in the founding of Jamestown. For nearly 20 years after Roanoke, the only hold England had on North America was a claim to the eastern coast, which had been named

The English colony of Jamestown began in 1607 as a fortified settlement huddled on a peninsula deep within Chesapeake Bay. The James River flowed nearby. ***Geography*** *What advantages and disadvantages did this location have?*

The colonies supplied England with food and raw materials. This detail from a map of 1751 shows tobacco being loaded at a southern dock for shipment to England. ***Economics*** ***Why did England require the colonies to supply it with raw materials?***

**Main Idea CONNECTIONS**

*How did tobacco change England's colonies in Virginia and Maryland?*

Virginia in honor of unmarried Queen Elizabeth I, the "Virgin Queen." Then in 1607, a group of shareholders in the new Virginia Company, with permission from King James I, sent about 100 colonists to the region. The colonists built a settlement near the Chesapeake Bay and called their new village Jamestown, after their king. The residents of Jamestown, many of them unused to physical labor and wanting only to make a quick fortune, faced years of starvation and sickness.

When the Virginia Company proved unable to turn a steady profit, King James took control of Jamestown and appointed a royal governor. The governor's power, like that of the king of England, was not absolute. The power of the English king had been defined by the 1215 signing of the **Magna Carta,** which made the king obey the law and granted many powers to the aristocracy. Similarly, the royal governor's power also was limited. In Virginia, he shared authority with a lawmaking assembly of elected representatives called the **House of Burgesses,** which was formed in 1619. Later, this would be seen as the first example of self-government in the English colonies.

During the early years of their settlement, only one thing saved the Virginia colonists from failing altogether. It was tobacco, a plant native to the Western Hemisphere but unknown in Europe. In 1614 colonist John Rolfe shipped some tobacco to Europe. It became so popular there that by 1640, Virginia and its neighboring colony Maryland (established in 1632 by English Catholics) were sending home 3 million pounds of tobacco a year.

In order to cash in on the tobacco boom, settlers moved out from Jamestown. They carved out plantations (large farms) along waterways like the James, York, and Potomac rivers, so that they could grow and transport tobacco more easily.

## *Growth of the English Colonies*

In 1630, while the French and Dutch were building trade links with Native Americans, a wave of English migration began to reach the shores of New England. By 1643 some 16,000 colonists were living in the new Massachusetts Bay Colony. Unlike the French and the Dutch, the English began to transform the landscape. They replaced existing forests with fields, cultivated crops like wheat, barley, and corn, and raised domestic animals like cows and pigs. One settler commented:

**AMERICAN VOICES**

> **"In the year 1626 or thereabouts, there was not a Neat Beast [cow] Horse or sheep in the Country and a very few Goats or hogs, and now it is a wonder to see the great herds of Cattle belonging to every Town."**
>
> *—Samuel Maverick, 1660*

The English settlers, called Puritans because of their desire to purify the Protestant Church of England, also attempted to remake Native Americans in their own image. They convinced many to adopt Puritan religious beliefs and customs and forced some to farm. (Farming was usually done by women in Native American societies.)

**The Theory of Mercantilism** By 1650, many western European nations were working to improve their economies, spurred on by a new theory called **mercantilism.** This economic theory was meant to increase a nation's wealth and thus boost its power. Mercantilism held that a country should try to obtain and hold on to as much gold and silver as possible. This could be done by exporting more goods than were imported.

Soon English rulers realized that colonies could provide raw materials, such as tobacco and furs, for England to sell to other countries. Furthermore, the colonies could buy England's glass, china, books, and other manufactured items. This exchange would greatly improve England's balance of trade (the balance between imports and exports). English leaders decided, therefore, that it was necessary to have as many colonies as possible and to control colonial trade.

**Controlling Colonial Trade** To this end, in 1660, Charles II approved a stronger version of a previous law called the Navigation Act. Together with other laws, the Navigation Act required the colonies to sell certain goods, including sugar, tobacco, and cotton, only to England. Moreover, if colonists wanted to sell anything to people in other parts of the world, they had to take the product to England first and pay a tax on it. They also were forced to use English ships for all their trade.

In the early 1700s, however, British leaders did not strictly enforce such trade restrictions.† Nor did Britain interfere much with colonial affairs. Colonial economies were thriving, and the existing economy and politics of the colonists already served British interests. The

† In 1707 England joined with Scotland to form Great Britain.

## ECONOMICS CONCEPTS

***balance of trade:* the difference in value between a country's exports and imports**

▼ **The Historical Context** The theory of mercantilism argued that a nation would prosper by maintaining a *positive* balance of trade—that is, by consistently exporting more than it imported. The American colonies aided Britain's mercantilist policies by acting as a market for British exports.

▼ **The Concept Today** In recent years the United States has maintained a *negative* balance of trade, importing much more than it exports. Experts disagree on whether this "trade deficit" harms the American economy. Some have argued that the United States should limit imports in order to balance its trade.

Shortly after this painting was made, about 1650, the English took over New Amsterdam, renaming it New York. ***Culture*** *Compare this painting with the one of Jamestown around 1607 shown earlier in the section. What are the similarities and differences?*

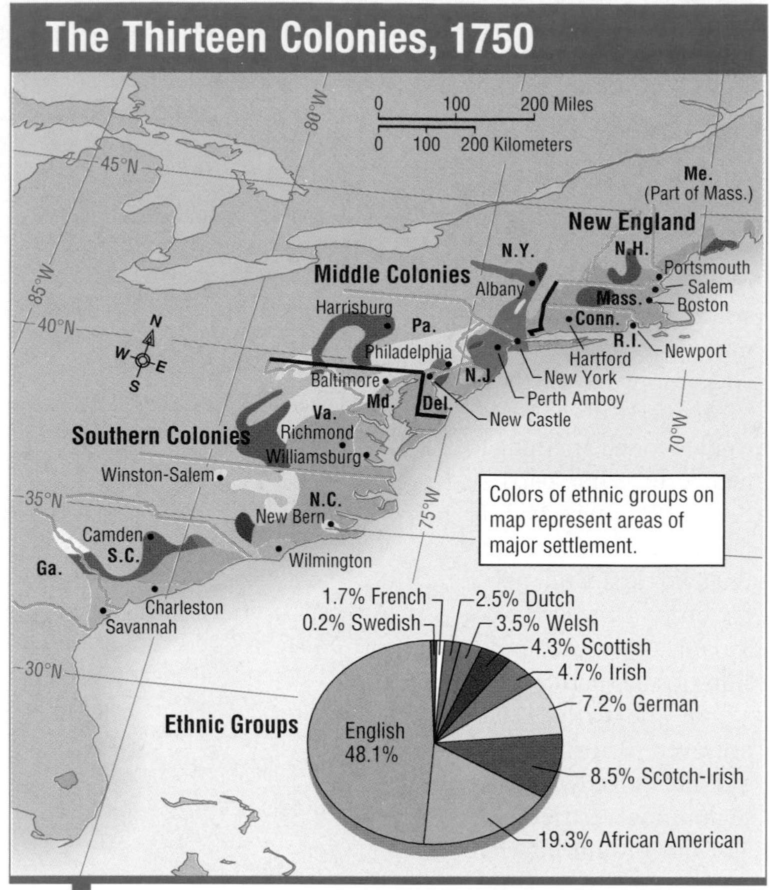


**MAP SKILLS** English settlements in North America in the 1700s generally clung to the Eastern seaboard and its rivers. In this narrow strip, however, lived a wide variety of ethnic groups. ***Regions*** ***After the English, which was the largest ethnic group? Where did they live?***

**African-American Population, 1690–1750**

| Year | New England Colonies | Middle Colonies | Southern Colonies |
|---|---|---|---|
| 1690 | 905 | 2,472 | 13,307 |
| 1700 | 1,680 | 3,361 | 22,476 |
| 1710 | 2,585 | 6,218 | 36,063 |
| 1720 | 3,956 | 10,825 | 54,058 |
| 1730 | 6,118 | 11,683 | 73,220 |
| 1740 | 8,541 | 16,452 | 125,031 |
| 1750 | 10,982 | 20,736 | 204,702 |

Source: *Historical Statistics of the United States, Colonial Times to 1970*

**Interpreting Tables** The growth in the number of African Americans, although relatively small in the 1600s, jumped considerably in the early 1700s. ***Geography*** ***In which group of colonies did the number of African Americans increase most sharply?***

British realized that the most salutary, or beneficial, policy would be to leave the colonies alone. Thus historians call British colonial policy during the early 1700s "salutary neglect."

**The Colonial Economies** By the 1700s the American colonies could be grouped into three regions, each with its own economy. Plantation farming dominated in the Southern Colonies (Virginia, Maryland, the Carolinas, and Georgia). The Middle Colonies (New York, Delaware, New Jersey, and Pennsylvania) had a mixed economy of farming and commerce. The New England Colonies (Massachusetts, New Hampshire, Connecticut, and Rhode Island) were a region of small, self-sufficient farms and of towns dependent on long-distance trade.

New England towns, unlike Philadelphia and New York, did not rely heavily on local crops for their commerce. Instead, they had developed a business of carrying crops and goods from one place to another. Merchants might haul china, books, and cloth from England to the West Indies in the Caribbean Sea. These goods would be exchanged for sugar, which merchants would take back to New England, where it was usually distilled into rum. The rum along with firearms would be transported to West Africa to be traded for slaves. The merchants would then carry the slaves for whom they had traded to the West Indies for more sugar. This trade between three points—the Americas, Europe, and Africa—was known as the **Triangular Trade.** The part of the journey that carried enslaved Africans between their homeland and the Americas was called the **Middle Passage.**

## *African Americans in the Colonies*

Although there were enslaved Africans working in the Americas as early as the sixteenth century, the widespread use of slave labor in the colonies began in the 1700s. By that time, southern plantations were prospering, and owners were looking for a source of cheap labor. They decided to use slavery to answer their economic needs.

By the middle of the 1700s, about one out of every five colonists, excluding Native Americans, was of African descent. However, the experiences of African Americans were not all the same because of the **diversity,** or variety, of the colonies that had been settled by then.

This authentic watercolor depicts a scene at a South Carolina plantation in the late 1700s. The musical instruments and the dance form were derived from the Yoruba people of West Africa. ***Culture*** ***How does this painting document the character of African American culture on South Carolina plantations?***

In South Carolina and Georgia, for example, many enslaved Africans endured brutal conditions laboring on cotton plantations or in rice fields. The major crop in Virginia and Maryland was tobacco. Cultivating tobacco did not take as much time as growing rice, so slaves in Virginia and Maryland were put to work at a variety of other tasks. In New England, where the economy was mixed, enslaved Africans worked as cooks, housekeepers, personal servants, artisans, and lumberjacks. In addition, a number of free African Americans lived in the colonies.

African Americans throughout the colonies did have two important things in common. Unlike other immigrants, they had been brought to the Americas against their will. In addition, whether enslaved or free, they faced a lifetime of discrimination because of their race.

## SECTION 1 REVIEW

### Comprehension

1. *Key Terms* Define: (a) Columbian Exchange; (b) colony; (c) Magna Carta; (d) House of Burgesses; (e) mercantilism; (f) Triangular Trade; (g) Middle Passage; (h) diversity.
2. *Summarizing the Main Idea* What regions of the Americas were claimed by Spain, France, Holland, and England?
3. *Organizing Information* Create a graphic organizer showing the reasons why the Spanish, French, Dutch, and English wanted to settle in North America.

### Critical Thinking

4. *Analyzing Time Lines* Review the time line at the start of the section. In your opinion, which of the events on the time line had the greatest impact at the time?
5. *Identifying Central Issues* How did the experiences of early Africans in America differ from those of European colonists?

### Writing Activity

6. *Writing an Expository Essay* Write an essay explaining how Britain's practice of mercantilism affected the American colonies.

# SKILLS FOR LIFE

**Geography**

**Graphs and Charts**

**Historical Evidence**

**Critical Thinking**

# Interpreting an Economic Activity Map

An economic activity map shows how the land in a particular region is used and helps demonstrate the ways that geography can influence historical events and developments. Economic activity maps also illustrate ways in which regions are similar or different.

Often a region's economic activity is related to its natural resources and climate. For example, mining can take place only in regions where enough minerals are present to make this activity profitable. By the mid-1700s, clear patterns of economic activity were emerging among the British colonies in North America. This map uses symbols and a color-coded key to communicate basic information about land use in the colonies.

Use the following steps to analyze the economic activity map.

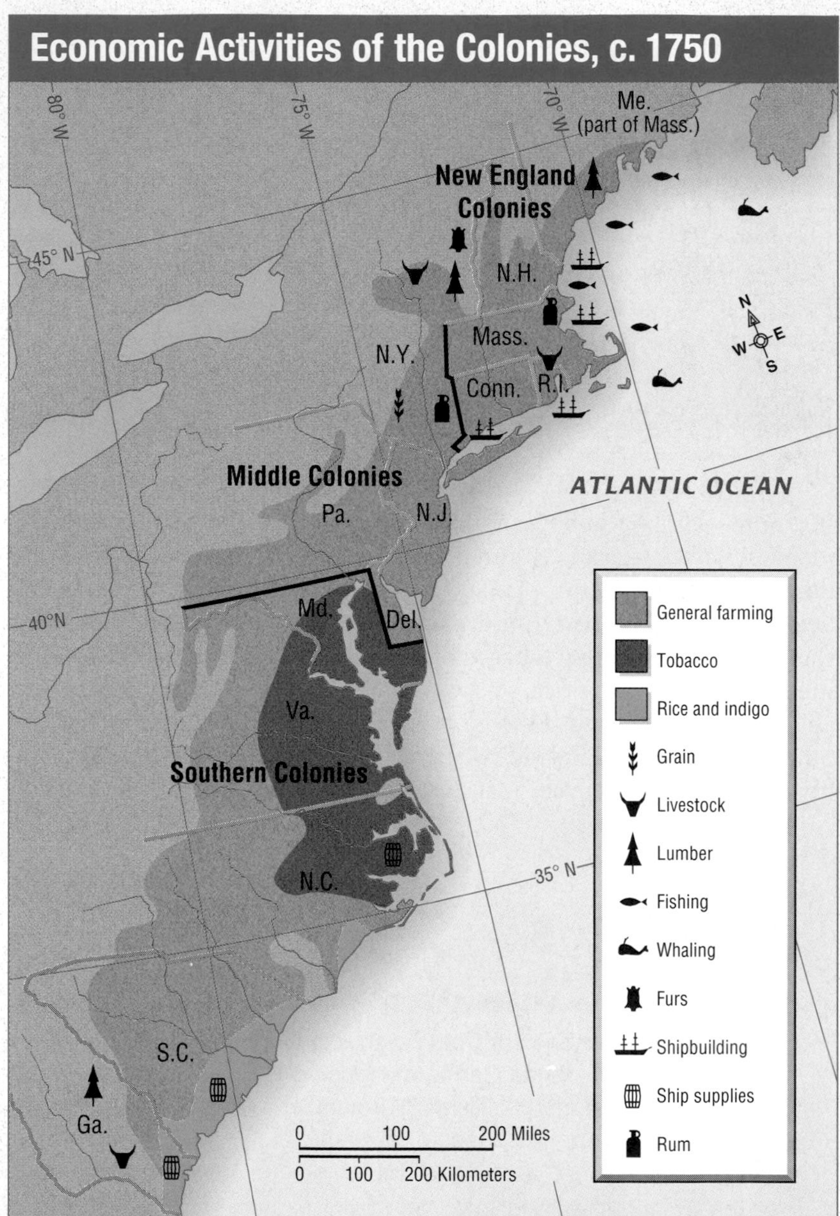


**1. *Identify the economic activities shown on the map.*** Use the map and key to answer the following questions. (a) What was the major economic activity in Delaware? (b) What were the major economic activities north of Massachusetts? (c) Which colony produced tobacco, rice, and indigo? (d) According to the map, what economic activity supported residents of Pennsylvania and New Jersey?

**2. *Look for relationships or patterns among the colonies and their economic activities.*** (a) As shown on the map, was farmland more extensive in the Southern or the New England colonies? (b) What other economic activities in the New England Colonies encouraged shipbuilding? (c) If you had been a livestock herder in Britain planning to move to the colonies, which of the American colonies do you think would have offered you the most opportunity for making a living?

**TEST FOR SUCCESS**

Review the symbols and color-coded key. Which region appears to have had a mixed economy? Explain your answer.

**1754** *French and Indian War begins*

**1763** *France gives up eastern North America*

**1775** *Battles of Lexington and Concord*

**1776** *Declaration of Independence signed*

**1783** *Britain recognizes American independence*

**1750** **1760** **1770** **1780**

# 2 The American Revolution

## SECTION PREVIEW

### Objectives

1. Describe the French and Indian War and other events that led to the American Revolution.
2. Summarize the events of the Revolutionary War.
3. Explain the effects of the American Revolution.
4. *Key Terms* Define: French and Indian War; First Continental Congress; Battles of Lexington and Concord; Revolutionary War; Second Continental Congress; Declaration of Independence; Battle of Yorktown; Treaty of Paris (1783).

### Main Idea

The American colonies, demanding the right to rule themselves, fought for and won their independence from Britain.

### Reading Strategy

*Formulating Questions* Skim the section, noting the headings and subheadings. Then rewrite the headings as questions and make predictions about the answers before you read the section. As you read, compare your predictions with the correct answers.

In the space of less than three decades, two wars would be fought to determine who would control the riches of North America. The first war would see the French pitted against the British. The second war was between Britain and its American colonists.

## The French and Indian War

In 1753 the governor of Virginia felt the need to protect his colony's claim to the Ohio River valley. He sent troops led by a young Virginian named George Washington to take a fort the French had built at the fork of the Ohio. The Virginia troops failed.

This unsuccessful military expedition became the first skirmish of a major war that lasted until 1763. Called the **French and Indian War** because the British and their colonists fought against the French and their Native American allies, it was the final struggle among the British, the French, and the Native Americans for control of eastern North America. Though Native Americans fought on both sides, many tended to ally themselves with the French, because they saw the French as less likely to disrupt their way of life.

Until late in 1758, the French and their Indian allies took the lead in the fighting. Then British troops began to move in overwhelming numbers against the French. The British drove the French out of Louisbourg, on the gulf of the St. Lawrence; out of their New York forts; and out of Quebec, the capital city of New France. With their capture of Quebec, the British won the war. In the Treaty of Paris, signed in 1763, the French turned over Canada to the British.

## Events Leading to the American Revolution

At the end of the French and Indian War, Americans believed they had every right to be regarded as full-fledged citizens of a great empire. However, the British had no intention of treating their colonists as equals.

FACT Finder

## British Policies in the Colonies, 1764–1774

| *Date* | *British Action* | *Colonial Response* |
|---|---|---|
| 1764 | **Sugar Act** Although it reduced the tax on imported foreign molasses, the law, unlike its predecessor the Molasses Act, was strictly enforced. | Colonists responded with written protests, occasional boycotts, and cries of "No taxation without representation!" |
| 1765 | **Stamp Act** The first direct taxation of colonists, the Stamp Act taxed legal and commercial documents and printed matter, such as newspapers. | Colonists protested violently. The Stamp Act Congress met and a boycott of British goods began. |
| | **Quartering Act** Following the French and Indian War, England maintained a standing army in the colonies. The Quartering Act required colonial assemblies to house and provision the British soldiers. | Most colonial legislatures refused to pay for supplies as required by the Quartering Act. |
| 1766 | **Declaratory Act** England repealed the Stamp Act in the face of colonial protest. To reassert its authority over the colonies it passed the Declaratory Act—a statement of England's right to rule the colonies in any way it saw fit. | Colonists were pleased with the repeal of the Stamp Act, but continued to protest other British-imposed laws, such as the Quartering Act. |
| 1767 | **Townshend Acts** Import taxes on lead, paper, tea, paint, and glass were collected at port. Revenue from the Townshend duties were used to support British troops, royal governors, and royal judges, taking the power of the purse away from colonial assemblies. The Townshend Acts also created a customs commission and suspended the New York assembly for failing to comply with the act. | "Letters from a Farmer in Pennsylvania," a widely read series of letters protesting the act, were published in nine colonial newspapers. Colonists resumed boycotting British goods, cutting trade in half. |
| 1773 | **Tea Act** The Tea Act was created to save the ailing East India Company. It allowed the company to sell its surplus tea in the American colonies. The act retained the import tax on tea—the only remaining tax of the nearly defunct Townshend Acts. | A group of Boston patriots destroyed a shipment of tea in a protest known as the Boston Tea Party. |
| 1774 | **Intolerable Acts** Also called the Coercive Acts, this series of punitive acts targeted Massachusetts. The Port Bill closed Boston Harbor until Boston paid for the tea destroyed by the Boston Tea Party. Other acts nearly eliminated self-government in Massachusetts. New provisions to the Quartering Act required colonists to house British soldiers in private homes as necessary. | Delegates from twelve colonies met as the First Continental Congress. They created the Continental Association to boycott British goods. They also sent a petition to the king, outlining what they considered the rights of the colonists and their assemblies. |

**Interpreting Tables** The years between 1764 and 1774 were beset with unrest in the American colonies. ***Government*** ***Why did England continue to pass controversial acts in the face of colonial protest?***

**New British Policies** Great Britain's attitude toward its colonies changed after the French and Indian War. In an effort to help pay off some of the huge debts Britain had acquired during the war, Parliament passed laws designed to collect more money from colonists.

The British also set aside their practice of salutary neglect and began to interfere in local matters, disrupting old traditions and accepted customs. In addition, the Proclamation of 1763 prohibited colonists from settling the lands west of the Appalachians. British leaders reasoned that if there were no settlers west of the original colonies, no British money would be required to protect the area.

**The Colonists' Response** These new policies angered many colonists. They pointed out that all these decisions were made with no American voice, since colonists did not have representatives in Parliament. New taxes especially disturbed the colonists. They argued that Britain could not tax them without their consent—in other words, there should be "no taxation without representation." Although Americans proclaimed their loyalty to Britain's King George, they were also demanding their rights as his subjects.

Colonists protested the changes in British policy by boycotting British goods. When Britain refused to back down, colonists decided to meet and plan a united response. This gathering became known as the **First Continental Congress.**

**A Plea for Peace** All the colonies but Georgia were represented by the 56 delegates who met for the First Continental Congress in Philadelphia in 1774. Together the delegates renewed the boycott of British goods and called on the people of all colonies to arm themselves and form militias. At the same time, the delegates made a direct appeal to the king, outlining their grievances and asking for understanding.

King George was in no mood to be understanding. "The New England colonies are in a state of rebellion," he wrote, concluding that "blows must decide" the outcome of the issue. However, the Americans he labeled "rebels" (they preferred to call themselves "Patriots") followed the advice of the First Continental Congress and began to gather guns and ammunition.

**Fighting at Lexington and Concord** On April 18, 1775, a force of about 700 British troops marched toward the Massachusetts town of Concord, about 20 miles from Boston. There they intended to seize a major stockpile of weapons. In Lexington, about 5 miles before Concord, they encountered about 130 colonists, who had gathered on the green to protest the British plan. The British ordered the colonists to give up their guns. Some colonists began to leave, but others stood their ground.

## ECONOMIC CONCEPTS

***inflation and deflation: Inflation is a steady rise in prices; deflation is a steady drop in prices***

- **The Historical Context:** Inflation, which has been described as "too much money chasing too few goods," plagued the American economy during the Revolutionary War. As Congress printed more and more Continental dollars, and the war limited the supply of goods available to consumers, the price of goods rose.
- **The Concept Today:** Government officials, knowing that inflation could hurt economic growth, keep a close watch over consumer prices. The federal government has several tools to fight inflation, such as reducing the supply of money and limiting government spending.

## War for Independence, 1775–1778

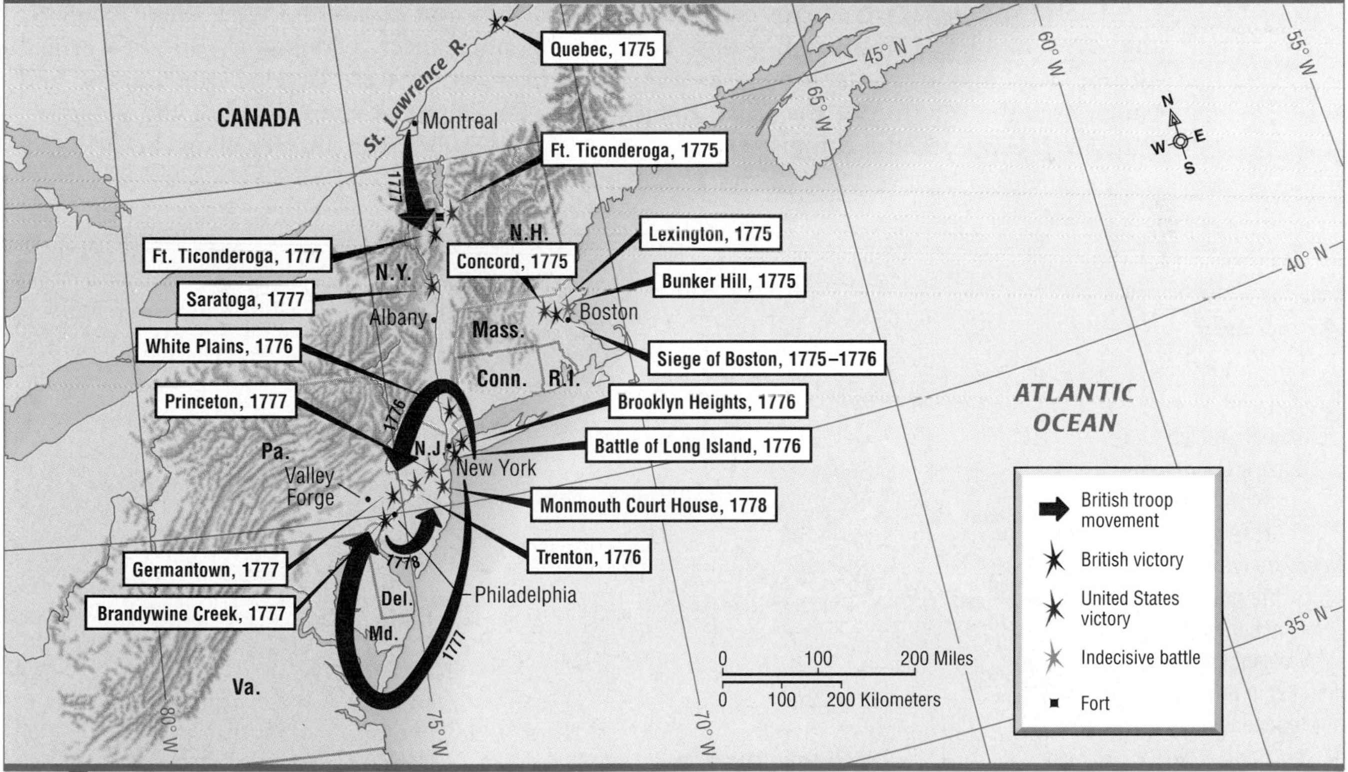

The major battles of the early part of the war took place in the North. ***Location*** *Where were most of these battles fought?*

Which side fired the first shot will never be known. But within minutes, eight dead Americans lay on Lexington Green and another nine were wounded. The British went on to Concord and burned the stockpile of supplies there.

As the troops returned, however, some 4,000 Patriots gathered along the road to shoot at them from behind stone walls and other cover. When the **Battles of Lexington and Concord** were over, more than one fourth of the British soldiers had been killed or wounded.

## *The Revolutionary War*

Word quickly spread through the colonies of the fighting at Lexington and Concord. The events of that day marked the start of the **Revolutionary War,** which would last until 1783.

**The Second Continental Congress** Less than a month after the clash between British troops and colonial militia, the **Second Continental Congress** met. At first the delegates, like the American people, were deeply divided. Some members, such as Samuel Adams and Patrick Henry, leaned toward independence. On the other hand, moderates, led by John Dickinson, favored seeking some compromise with Britain that would increase colonial self-rule.

Thus, two courses were followed. One was the creation of a Continental Army, with George Washington at its head. The other course was the drafting of the Olive Branch Petition. It expressed the colonists' continued loyalty to the king and begged him to halt the fighting until a solution could be found.

As the fighting continued, however, many delegates began to support a more radical point of view. Then, in November 1775, the Congress learned that King George had refused the Olive Branch Petition and had declared the colonies to be in open rebellion. A peaceful resolution now seemed impossible.

**Declaring Independence** In June 1776, after more than a year of fighting, the Congress decided it was time for the colonies to cut their ties with Britain. It appointed a committee to prepare a statement of the reasons for the separation—a **Declaration of Independence.** The committee chose Thomas Jefferson to draft the statement. The document he composed stated that all people had certain "inalienable rights," or rights that could not be taken away. The declaration also listed the wrongs that colonists believed had been committed by the British king. In the last section of the document, Jefferson stated that "these United Colonies are . . . and of Right ought to be Free and Independent States." The Declaration of Independence was adopted on July 4, which we now celebrate as Independence Day.

**Washington Leads the Way** King George III did not expect a long war. Britain's armed forces, which were larger, better trained, and better equipped than those of the colonists, could easily crush the rebellion, he believed.

Emanuel Gottlieb Leutze's *George Washington Crossing the Delaware* captures the patriotic feelings inspired by Washington's victories in the War for Independence. ***Geography*** ***What difficulties did fighting in winter pose?***

"Once these rebels have felt a smart blow, they will submit," he said. He was wrong.

Washington and other leaders realized that the Americans could win as long as they had the determination to outlast the British. George Washington never gave up, even in the face of repeated defeats. Although the British seized New York, Philadelphia, and almost every other important colonial city, Washington knew the secret to winning the war. The British might capture territory, he said, but they could never win as long as Americans were willing and able to continue fighting them.

**The Final Battle** After many years and many battles, the war came down to the **Battle of Yorktown** in 1781. British troops, under the leadership of General Lord Cornwallis, had moved to Yorktown, Virginia, on a peninsula between the York and James rivers. There they awaited reinforcements to arrive by sea. To the north, Washington at once saw the opportunity to deal the British a fatal blow. A French army had just joined the Continental Army in New York. (In 1777, following the Patriot victory in the Battle of Saratoga, France had agreed to join the Patriots in their fight against Britain.) Washington quickly moved the combined American-French force south, while the French fleet set up a blockade off the Virginia coast. When the British navy arrived in early September, the French ships drove it off.

A few days later Washington's troops arrived and in early October the American and French artillery began to pound Yorktown. Cornwallis had no escape. The American army blocked him by land, and the French fleet blocked him by sea. On October 18 Cornwallis surrendered his army of nearly 8,000 soldiers to Washington.

Nearly two years after Cornwallis's surrender at Yorktown, in September 1783, the **Treaty of Paris (1783)** was signed. It established the independence of the United States. It also officially defined the nation's borders.

## *The Effects of the Revolution*

In 1776 Thomas Jefferson's Declaration of Independence had stated that "all men are created equal," and the Congress had used this assertion to help justify a revolution. This was a radical concept in a world that had long accepted the idea of human inequality.

It took many years before the American Revolution's ideals of equality, rights, and freedom began to be fully realized. Over the next two centuries many groups in the United States, such as women and African Americans, would move closer to true equality. At the same time, the principles for which the Patriots fought would also inspire peoples around the world.

## SECTION 2 REVIEW

### Comprehension

1. *Key Terms* Define: (a) French and Indian War; (b) First Continental Congress; (c) Battles of Lexington and Concord; (d) Revolutionary War; (e) Second Continental Congress; (f) Declaration of Independence; (g) Battle of Yorktown; (h) Treaty of Paris (1783).
2. *Summarizing the Main Idea* How did Americans win independence in spite of Britain's military advantages?
3. *Organizing Information* Create a two-column chart that compares the actions and results of the Continental Congresses. Label the left column *The First Continental Congress.* Label the right column *The Second Continental Congress.* For each, describe both the actions of the Congress and the results of those actions.

### Critical Thinking

4. *Analyzing Time Lines* Review the time line at the start of the section. For each event, write a sentence explaining its relationship to the American Revolution.
5. *Determining Conclusions* How did the French and Indian War help set the stage for the American Revolution?

### Writing Activity

6. *Writing an Expository Essay* Write an essay in which you explain how the effects of the American Revolution continued long after the war had ended.

# THE DECLARATION OF *Independence*

***In Congress, July 4, 1776***

THE UNANIMOUS DECLARATION OF THE THIRTEEN UNITED STATES OF AMERICA,

When in the Course of human events, it becomes necessary for one people to dissolve the political bands which have connected them with another, and to assume among the Powers of the earth, the separate and equal station to which the Laws of Nature and of Nature's God entitle them, a decent respect to the opinions of mankind requires that they should declare the causes which impel them to the separation.

We hold these truths to be self-evident, that all men are created equal, that they are endowed by their Creator with certain unalienable Rights, that among these are Life, Liberty and the pursuit of Happiness. That to secure these rights, Governments are instituted among Men, deriving their just powers from the consent of the governed, That whenever any Form of Government becomes destructive of these ends, it is the Right of the People to alter or to abolish it, and to institute new Government, laying its foundation on such principles and organizing its powers in such form, as to them shall seem most likely to effect their Safety and Happiness. Prudence, indeed, will dictate that Governments long established should not be changed for light and transient causes; and accordingly all experience hath shown, that mankind are more disposed to suffer, while evils are sufferable, than to right themselves by abolishing the forms to which they are accustomed. But when a long train of abuses and usurpations, pursuing invariably the same Object evinces a design to reduce them under absolute Despotism, it is their right, it is their duty, to throw off such Government, and to provide new Guards for their future security.—Such has been the patient sufferance of these Colonies; and such is now the necessity which constrains them to alter their former Systems of Government. The history of the present King of Great Britain is a history of repeated injuries and usurpations, all having in direct object the establishment of an absolute Tyranny over these States. To prove this, let Facts be submitted to a candid world.

He has refused his Assent to Laws, the most wholesome and necessary for the public good.

He has forbidden his Governors to pass Laws of immediate and pressing importance, unless suspended in their operation till his Assent should be obtained; and when so suspended, he has utterly neglected to attend to them.

He has refused to pass other Laws for the accommodation of large districts of people, unless those people would relinquish the right of Representation in the Legislature, a right inestimable to them and formidable to tyrants only.

He has called together legislative bodies at places unusual, uncomfortable, and distant from the depository of their Public Records, for the sole purpose of fatiguing them into compliance with his measures.

He has dissolved Representative Houses repeatedly, for opposing with manly firmness his invasions on the rights of the people.

He has refused for a long time, after such dissolutions, to cause others to be elected; whereby the Legislative powers, incapable of Annihilation, have returned to the People at large for their exercise; the State remaining in the mean time exposed to all the dangers of invasions from without, and convulsions within.

He has endeavored to prevent the population of these States; for that purpose obstructing the Laws for Naturalization of Foreigners; refusing to pass others to encourage their migration hither, and raising the conditions of new Appropriations of Lands.

He has obstructed the Administration of Justice, by refusing his Assent to Laws for establishing Judiciary powers.

He has made Judges dependent on his Will alone for the tenure of their offices, and the amount and payment of their salaries.

He has erected a multitude of New Offices, and sent hither swarms of Officers to harass our people and eat out their substance.

He has kept among us in time of peace, Standing Armies, without the Consent of our legislature.

He has affected to render the Military independent of and superior to the Civil power.

He has combined with others to subject us to a jurisdiction foreign to our constitutions, and unacknowledged by our laws; giving his Assent to their Acts of pretended Legislation:

For Quartering large bodies of armed troops among us:

For protecting them, by a mock Trial, from Punishment for any Murders which they should commit on the Inhabitants of these States:

For cutting off our Trade with all parts of the world:

For imposing Taxes on us without our Consent:

For depriving us in many cases, of the benefits of Trial by Jury:

For transporting us beyond Seas to be tried for pretended offenses:

For abolishing the free System of English Laws in a neighbouring Province, establishing therein an Arbitrary government, and enlarging its Boundaries so as to render it at once an example and fit instrument for introducing the same absolute rule into these Colonies:

For taking away our Charters, abolishing our most valuable Laws, and altering fundamentally the Forms of our Governments;

For suspending our own Legislature, and declaring themselves invested with Power to legislate for us in all cases whatsoever.

He has abdicated Government here, by declaring us out of his Protection, and waging War against us.

He has plundered our seas, ravaged our Coasts, burned our towns, and destroyed the lives of our people.

He is at this time transporting large Armies of foreign mercenaries to compleat the works of death, desolation and tyranny, already begun with circumstances of Cruelty and perfidy scarcely paralleled in the most barbarous ages, and totally unworthy the Head of a civilized nation.

He has constrained our fellow Citizens taken Captive on the high Seas to bear Arms against their Country, to become the executioners of their friends and Brethren, or to fall themselves by their Hands.

He has excited domestic insurrections amongst us, and has endeavored to bring on the inhabitants of our frontiers the merciless Indian Savages, whose known rule of warfare, is an undistinguished destruction of all ages, sexes, and conditions.

In every stage of these Oppressions We have Petitioned for Redress in the most humble terms. Our repeated Petitions have been answered only by repeated injury. A Prince, whose character is thus marked by every act which may define a Tyrant, is unfit to be the ruler of a free People.

Nor have We been wanting in attentions to our British brethren. We have warned them from time to time of attempts by their legislature to extend an unwarrantable jurisdiction over us. We have reminded them of the circumstances of our emigration and settlement here. We have appealed to their native justice and magnanimity, and we have conjured them by the ties of our common kindred to disavow these usurpations, which, would inevitably interrupt our connections and correspondence. They too have been deaf to the voice of Justice and of consanguinity. We must, therefore, acquiesce in the necessity, which denounces our Separation, and hold them, as we hold the rest of mankind, Enemies in War, in Peace Friends.

We, therefore, the Representatives of the United States of America, in General Congress, Assembled, appealing to the Supreme Judge of the world for the rectitude of our intentions, do, in the Name, and by the Authority of the good People of these Colonies, solemnly publish and declare, That these United Colonies are, and of Right ought to be Free and Independent States; that they are Absolved from all Allegiance to the British Crown, and that all political connection between them and the State of Great Britain, is and ought to be totally dissolved, and that as Free and Independent States, they have full Power to levy War, conclude Peace, contract Alliances, establish Commerce, and to do all other Acts and Things which Independent States may of right do. And for the support of this Declaration, with a firm reliance on the protection of Divine Providence, we mutually pledge to each other our Lives, our Fortunes and our sacred Honor.

JOHN HANCOCK
President of the Continental Congress 1775–1777

NEW HAMPSHIRE
*Josiah Bartlett*
*William Whipple*
*Matthew Thornton*

MASSACHUSETTS BAY
*Samuel Adams*
*John Adams*
*Robert Treat Paine*
*Elbridge Gerry*

RHODE ISLAND
*Stephen Hopkins*
*William Ellery*

CONNECTICUT
*Roger Sherman*
*Samuel Huntington*
*William Williams*
*Oliver Wolcott*

NEW YORK
*William Floyd*
*Philip Livingston*
*Francis Lewis*
*Lewis Morris*

NEW JERSEY
*Richard Stockton*
*John Witherspoon*
*Francis Hopkinson*
*John Hart*
*Abraham Clark*

DELAWARE
*Caesar Rodney*
*George Read*
*Thomas McKean*

MARYLAND
*Samuel Chase*
*William Paca*
*Thomas Stone*
*Charles Carroll of Carrollton*

VIRGINIA
*George Wythe*
*Richard Henry Lee*
*Thomas Jefferson*
*Benjamin Harrison*
*Thomas Nelson, Jr.*
*Francis Lightfoot Lee*
*Carter Braxton*

PENNSYLVANIA
*Robert Morris*
*Benjamin Rush*
*Benjamin Franklin*
*John Morton*
*George Clymer*
*James Smith*
*George Taylor*
*James Wilson*
*George Ross*

NORTH CAROLINA
*William Hooper*
*Joseph Hewes*
*John Penn*

SOUTH CAROLINA
*Edward Rutledge*
*Thomas Heyward, Jr.*
*Thomas Lynch, Jr.*
*Arthur Middleton*

GEORGIA
*Button Gwinnett*
*Lyman Hall*
*George Walton*

# Reviewing the Declaration



### VOCABULARY

Choose ten words in the Declaration with which you are unfamiliar. Look them up in the dictionary. Then, on a piece of paper, copy the sentence in the Declaration in which each unfamiliar word is used, and after the sentence write the definition of the unfamiliar word.

### COMPREHENSION

1. Which truths in the second paragraph are "self-evident"?
2. Name the three unalienable rights listed in the Declaration.
3. From what source do governments derive their "just powers"?
4. What right do people have when their government becomes destructive?
5. In the series of paragraphs beginning, "He has refused his Assent," to whom does the word "He" refer?
6. Which phrase in the Declaration expresses the colonists' opposition to taxation without representation?
7. According to the Declaration, what powers does the United States have "as Free and Independent States"?
8. List the colonies that the signers of the Declaration represented.

### CRITICAL THINKING

1. ***Cause and Effect*** Why do you think the colonists were unhappy with the fact that their judges' salaries were paid by the king?
2. ***Drawing Conclusions*** As Section 2 of this chapter explains, the Declaration was divided into four parts. Write down the first phrase of each of those four parts.
3. ***Identifying Assumptions*** Do you think that the statement "all men are created equal" was intended to apply to all human beings? Explain your reasoning.
4. ***Recognizing Bias*** What reference do you see to Native Americans? What attitudes toward Native Americans does this express?
5. ***Drawing Conclusions*** What evidence is there that the colonists had already unsuccessfully voiced concerns to the King?

### ISSUES PAST AND PRESENT

1. Write a letter to the Continental Congress from the perspective of a woman or an African American who has just read the Declaration in 1776. In your letter, comment on the Declaration's statement that "all men are created equal" and also express your attitude toward American independence.
2. What evidence in the Declaration is there of religious faith? How do you think this religious faith influenced the ideals expressed in the Declaration?
3. Examine the unalienable rights of individuals as stated in the Declaration. Do you think these rights are upheld today? Give examples to support your answer.

### ANALYZING POLITICAL CARTOONS

1. This cartoon was published in 1779. (a) Read the caption and identify the horse. (b) Who is the master being thrown? (c) How do you know?
2. Examine the figure on the horse. (a) What is he holding? (b) What does it represent?
3. What is the cartoonist's overall message?

THE HORSE AMERICA, *throwing his Master.*

| 1781 | 1786 | 1787 | 1789 | 1791 | 1800 |
|---|---|---|---|---|---|
| *Articles of Confederation approved* | *Shays' Rebellion* | *Constitutional Convention* | *George Washington becomes first President* | *Bill of Rights is added to the Constitution* | *Washington, D.C. becomes nation's capital* |

1780 1785 1790 1795 1800

# 3 The Constitution

## SECTION PREVIEW

### Objectives

1 Describe the government in the early United States.
2 Describe the Constitutional Convention, including the role of James Madison.
3 Examine the new plan of government created by the Constitution.
4 *Key Terms* Define: Articles of Confederation; amend; Electoral College; veto; checks and balances; Federalist; Antifederalist; Bill of Rights; republic; inauguration; Cabinet; administration.

### Main Idea

When the Articles of Confederation could not provide a strong enough national government, the states drafted and approved the Constitution.

### Reading Strategy

*Organizing Information* As you read, list the problems of the Articles of Confederation and the ways in which the Constitution addressed them.

*After resigning from the army, Washington went on to lead the Constitutional Convention. A detail of the chair he used is shown above.*

On December 23, 1783, a month after watching the British army leave New York forever, George Washington performed perhaps the most important act of his life: he voluntarily gave up power. Having helped Americans achieve their freedom from a king, he did not want to become another ruler over them. In an act of formal resignation that astonished the world, he gave up his commission as commander of the American army.

Washington's resignation highlighted a new dilemma for the American people. Could they enjoy their freedom without the strong, unified, national government symbolized by Washington's leadership? Could they keep their new liberty and maintain order at the same time? In short, what kind of government should a free people have?

## *Government in the Early United States*

George Washington had become powerful in large part because a single military authority was needed to win the War for Independence. The Congress that approved the Declaration of Independence in 1776 was nothing more than a loose collection of representatives from thirteen separate states. Almost no one imagined creating a powerful national government. After all, Americans were rebelling against an imperial government that had tried repeatedly to strengthen its power over them.

Instead, many people saw Congress as only a necessary wartime inconvenience. Most Americans thought of themselves as citizens of individual states rather than as citizens of a nation. It is significant that in referring to the United States, most Americans in those times wrote "the united States are" rather than "the United States is," as people do today. They believed that the nation as a whole was less important than its thirteen parts.

**The Articles of Confederation** To govern the United States, the Continental Congress created a set of laws called the **Articles of Confederation.** Although written in 1776, the Articles were not approved until 1781. Under the Articles, the government consisted of a legislature, or group of representatives from the states who gathered to conduct business. The gathering of the legislature was called a Congress. This Continental Congress passed laws and tried to make sure they were enforced. Thus it combined the functions of a legislative branch (the part of government that makes laws) and an executive branch (the part that puts into action the laws passed by a legislature). The Articles did not create a judicial branch, which judges whether laws have been broken. That job was left to the states.

Under the Articles of Confederation, states could send as many representatives to Congress as they wished, but each state had only one vote in Congress. The powers of Congress were strictly limited. It took nine votes, not just a simple majority, to pass any measure dealing with money. Any attempt to **amend,** or change, the Articles required the approval of all thirteen states. Congress also did not have the power to tax—a serious weakness that forced the national government to beg funds from the states. Nor did Congress have any coercive power, the power to force the states to do what it wanted. These and other defects in the Articles made the United States government weak. But that was exactly what most Americans wanted their national government to be.

**Fact Finder: Weaknesses in the Articles of Confederation**

| Weaknesses in the Articles of Confederation |
|---|
| One vote for each state, regardless of size |
| Congress cannot collect taxes |
| Congress powerless to regulate foreign and interstate commerce |
| No separate executive branch to enforce acts of Congress |
| No national court system to interpret laws |
| Amendment only with consent of all the states |
| A 9/13 majority required to pass laws |
| Articles only a "firm league of friendship" |

**Interpreting Tables** The confederation entered into by the 13 states gave little real power to the national government. ***Government*** *How did the Articles limit the power of Congress?*

**State Constitutions** Far more important than the Articles during the country's early years were the individual state constitutions, which established the state governments. Most states adopted new constitutions during the Revolution. Many of those constitutions made popular control of government a central principle. One state, Pennsylvania, extended voting rights to all tax-paying white adult males. Pennsylvania thus was the first state to open the voting process to ordinary people, not just wealthy gentlemen.

**Criticism of the Articles** During the 1780s, economic problems raised concerns about the new state and national governments. In 1786, the United States still owed about $50 million—a huge sum at that time—to foreign countries and to its own citizens for the expenses of the Revolutionary War. Debt everywhere was such a problem that some state governments were distributing cheap paper money to help their citizens pay off their loans. This was creating economic chaos.

All the states were desperately looking for ways to raise money. States heavily taxed any goods bound for neighboring states, thus angering citizens of those states. Land sales also became an issue. In the Treaty of Paris of 1783, the United States had gained political control over the vast area between the Appalachian Mountains and the Mississippi River. The state governments, disregarding the rights of Native Americans in the territory, quarreled bitterly among themselves over which should be able to profit by the sale of this land.

**GOVERNMENT CONCEPTS**

***three branches of government:* *the legislative branch makes the laws; the executive branch enforces the laws; the judicial branch interprets the laws***

▼ **The Historical Context** The national government created by the Articles of Confederation did not include an executive or judicial branch. This omission, which reflected Americans' fear of a strong central government, made it difficult for the national government to operate effectively.

▼ **The Concept Today** The Constitution of the United States, which later replaced the Articles, did provide for three separate branches of government. All three branches remain strong and vital parts of the federal government.

In 1786, supporters of a stronger national government arranged a meeting of the representatives of the states at Annapolis, Maryland, to discuss the economic problems caused by the Articles of Confederation. Only twelve delegates from five states attended. All that the leaders could do was promise to meet again the following year in Philadelphia.

Before that second meeting, however, dramatic changes occurred—including the outbreak of an armed rebellion in Massachusetts. The uprising, known as Shays' Rebellion after its leader, Captain Daniel Shays, was a struggle over debts and taxes. In 1786 the Massachusetts legislature voted the heaviest direct tax in the state's history. The tax had to be paid in silver or gold coin, both of which were scarce. Massachusetts citizens rebelled. Congress could only look on helplessly, since it had no money to raise an army and no way to force the states to give it money. Although the government of Massachusetts dispersed the rebels, Shays' Rebellion did convince many prominent Americans that they had to act. In May 1787, delegates began to arrive in Philadelphia. Their challenge, in the words of Virginia delegate James Madison, was to "decide forever the fate of republican government."

## *The Constitutional Convention*

At the Constitutional Convention, as the Philadelphia meeting became known, the delegates wrote a new set of rules by which the nation was to be governed. Today Americans refer to those rules simply as the Constitution. The Constitutional Convention was by no means a gathering to make refinements in a

This painting shows George Washington heading the Constitutional Convention in Philadelphia in 1787. ***Government* What impressions did the artist try to convey about this historic gathering?**

successful government. Instead it was a rescue mission for a government that might well fail. According to Madison, the idea was to find a way to "at once support . . . the national authority, and leave in force the local authorities" only to the extent that the local authorities could be useful without interfering with the national government.

## *James Madison (1751–1836)*

AMERICAN BIOGRAPHY

During the sessions of the Constitutional Convention, James Madison could be seen busily taking the notes that later would become our best record of the proceedings. Later generations would call him "the father of the Constitution."

**Man of Knowledge** Madison was a quiet bachelor of only 36 when he arrived in Philadelphia to help rescue the struggling government. Yet few men came better prepared for the task. In his home at the foot of the Blue Ridge Mountains of Virginia, he had spent evenings poring over books of history, government, and law. By the time of the convention, Madison had invested a year thinking specifically about how best to craft a new government.

Madison had a superb foundation of knowledge to build upon. The son of a wealthy landowner, he grew up on a plantation in Orange County, Virginia. There he studied European political thought under a Scottish tutor. In 1769 he left home for New Jersey College (now Princeton University), finishing the four-year program in two years.

*James Madison (1751–1836)*

Education, talent, and hard work made Madison the "best-informed man of any point in debate," as a fellow delegate noted. Yet the Virginian remained "a gentleman of great modesty—with a remarkable sweet temper."

A small-boned man with a thin voice and sometimes frail health, Madison was shy and polite. He did not marry until he was 43, but found a good match in the lively and sociable Dolley Payne Todd, a 26-year-old widow. They were happily married for 42 years.

**Man of Politics** Despite his shyness and dislike for public speaking, Madison became an early leader in the independence movement. He took part in the Continental Congress of 1780, served in the Virginia legislature, and helped draft the Articles of Confederation.

After his work on the Constitution, Madison would serve in the new House of Representatives and hold other key jobs in the early government. Madison became President in 1809 and served until 1817. He remained active in politics well into his 80's.

**Man of Philosophy** Madison's studies of philosophy had led him to believe that people are naturally selfish creatures driven by powerful emotions and personal interests. That did not mean there was no hope for order in society, however. Madison drew from the writings of European philosophers who argued that through proper government, humans could take control of themselves.

Constitutions established political institutions that encouraged the best in people while restraining the worst. A dream of devising just such a constitution was exactly what brought James Madison to the Philadelphia Convention. ■

## *A New Plan of Government*

After a summer of meetings, on September 17, 1787, delegates approved the final draft of a new Constitution. It created what some began to call a federal government, in which power was shared among state and national authorities. The document also created three branches of government—the legislative, executive, and judicial branches.

**A Three-Branched Government** According to the Constitution the legislative branch was made up of two houses. One was the House of Representatives, whose representation was based on each state's population and whose members would be elected every two years. The second house was the Senate, which was made up of two representatives from each state. Their terms would last six years.

## The System of Checks and Balances

**Judicial Branch**

**Supreme Court Interprets the Law**

**Checks on Legislative Branch:**
- Can declare acts of Congress unconstitutional

**Checks on Executive Branch:**
- Can declare executive actions unconstitutional

**Legislative Branch**

BILL

**Congress Makes the Law**

**Checks on Judicial Branch:**
- Creates lower federal courts
- Can impeach and remove judges
- Can propose amendments to overrule judicial decisions
- Approves appointments of federal judges

**Checks on Executive Branch:**
- Can override presidential veto
- Confirms executive appointments
- Ratifies treaties
- Can declare war
- Appropriates money
- Can impeach and remove President

**Executive Branch**

**President Carries Out the Law**

**Checks on Judicial Branch:**
- Appoints federal judges
- Can grant pardons to federal offenders

**Checks on Legislative Branch:**
- Can propose laws
- Can veto laws
- Can call special sessions of Congress
- Makes appointments to federal posts
- Negotiates foreign treaties

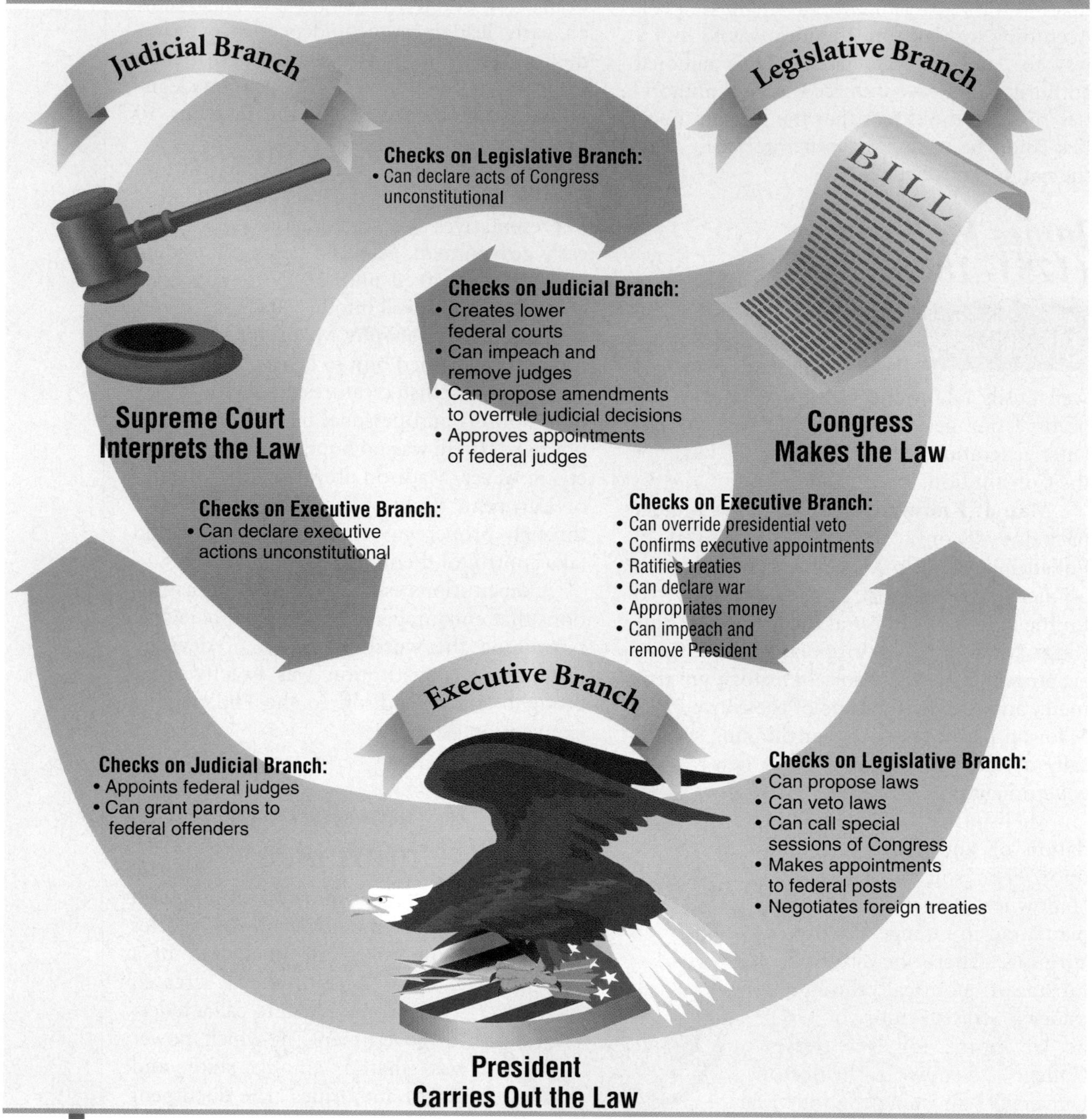

**Interpreting Charts** "You must first enable the government to control the governed," wrote Madison, "and in the next place, oblige it to control itself." This control is found in the Constitution's system of checks and balances. ***Government*** ***How does the legislative branch check the executive branch?***

The executive branch described by the Constitution had a strong executive officer at its head: the President of the United States. The writers of the Constitution placed a shield between the government and the people by making the election of the President complicated. Voters were to choose electors to do their electing for them. Each state would have as many electoral votes as it had members of Congress. Whoever received the majority of the votes in the **Electoral College,** or meeting of the electors, would become President. If the Electoral College failed to produce a majority for one candidate, the House of Representatives would choose the President.

According to the Constitution, the President, with the advice and consent of the Senate, would choose judges for the national court system. These judges would hold office for life, as long as they did not act dishonorably. The Constitution called for the formation of one Supreme Court and several lesser courts, but it left the details of the judicial structure up to Congress.

**Other Provisions** The Constitution called for a separation of powers among three branches. That is, powers of government at the national level would be divided among the legislative, executive, and judicial branches. In addition, each branch would be able to check, or stop, the others in certain ways. For instance, the President, as the head of the executive branch, could **veto,** or overturn, acts of Congress. This executive power was balanced, however, by Congress's power to overturn the veto with a two-thirds vote of both houses. This government structure is known today as the system of **checks and balances.**

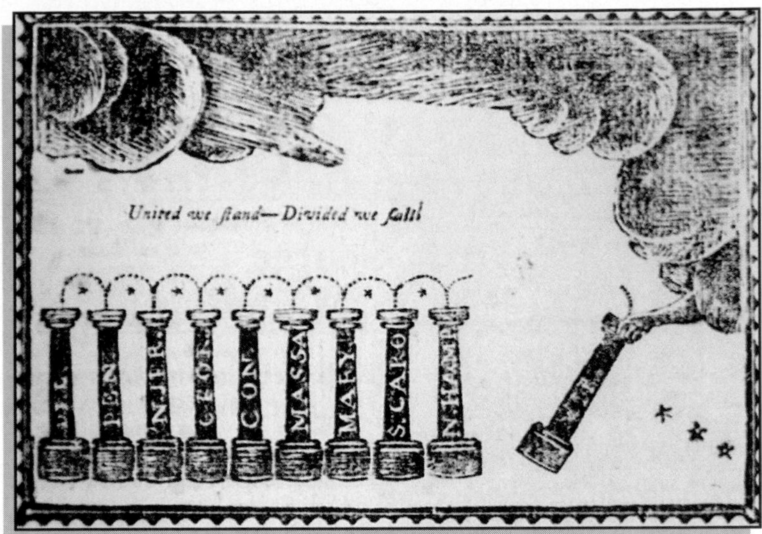

This cartoon shows the states as pillars, with nine upright and a tenth being raised. Nine states had to approve the new Constitution before it became law. ***Government*** ***What is the message of the words in the cartoon?***

**Ratifying the Constitution** To take effect, the proposed Constitution had to be ratified, or approved, by nine of the thirteen states. Ratification votes would be cast not by state legislatures but by special state conventions.

Supporters of the Constitution were called **Federalists** because they stood for a strong federal government. Those who opposed the Constitution were called **Antifederalists.** They feared that the new government would be the death of American liberty.

To many Americans, the new federal government seemed a potentially tyrannical force in their lives. They wanted protection from it. Thomas Jefferson, who generally approved of the Constitution, urged Madison to add protection for freedom of religion and of the press, as well as from armies and unjust courts, to the Constitution. So strong was the Antifederalist demand for a Bill of Rights that Madison and other Federalists gave in to it. Their agreement to amend the Constitution to protect certain basic freedoms proved to be the key to their victory. Without this promise, several states probably would not have ratified the Constitution.

**FACT Finder**

## The Bill of Rights

| | |
|---|---|
| **1st Amendment** | Guarantees freedom of religion, speech, press, assembly, and petition |
| **2nd Amendment** | Guarantees the right to bear arms |
| **3rd Amendment** | Restricts the manner in which the federal government may house troops in the homes of citizens |
| **4th Amendment** | Protects individuals against unreasonable searches and seizures |
| **5th Amendment** | Provides that a person must be accused by a grand jury before being tried for a serious federal crime; protects individuals against self-incrimination and against being tried twice for the same crime; prohibits unfair actions by the federal government; prohibits the government from taking private property for public use without paying a fair price for it |
| **6th Amendment** | Guarantees persons accused of a crime the right to a swift and fair trial |
| **7th Amendment** | Guarantees the right to a jury trial in civil cases tried in federal courts |
| **8th Amendment** | Protects against cruel and unusual punishment and excessive bail |
| **9th Amendment** | Establishes that the people have rights beyond those stated in the Constitution |
| **10th Amendment** | Establishes that all powers not guaranteed to the federal government and not withheld from the states are held by each of the states, or their citizens |

**Interpreting Tables** The Bill of Rights was intended to protect Americans from the strong national government the Constitution created. ***Government*** ***Which amendment protects people's right to express their views?***

## George Washington

*"To be prepared for war is one of the most effectual means of preserving peace."*
—First Annual Address, 1790

George Washington was not only the nation's first President, but the person for whom the office was created. A former Virginia planter and surveyor, he had fought in the French and Indian War and had led the Continental Army during the Revolutionary War. Washington's successful leadership in the fight for independence made the tall and imposing 57-year-old easily the nation's leading public figure.

Washington was famous too for his honesty, dignity, and self-control. In 1787 the Framers of the Constitution created the office of President with him in mind, confident that he could be trusted with the enormous powers of the presidency. Washington backed the Constitution during the debate over ratification, and as President he acted with dignity and restraint, thus easing many people's fears about the new government.

Washington could not, however, make the new government universally popular. Many Americans distrusted the new, stronger government and disliked Alexander Hamilton's economic plans. Washington's pro-British foreign policy angered those Americans who thought the United States should support France instead. Convinced that Washington was leading the nation away from the ideals of the Revolution, these opponents rallied behind Thomas Jefferson, who had resigned as secretary of state in 1793. Washington tried to keep the nation politically united under his leadership, but ultimately, divisions occurred. Offended and tired, in 1796 he refused to run for a third term.

When Washington died in 1799, Americans put aside the bitter conflicts of his presidency. They remembered instead his years of steadfast service to the nation, first as a general fighting a difficult war and later as a President seeking a workable balance between order and liberty.

### Connecting to Today

Do you believe that characteristics such as dignity and restraint are as important for American Presidents today as they were in Washington's era? Explain your answer.

On December 7, 1787, Delaware became the first state to ratify the Constitution. In May 1790 Rhode Island became the thirteenth state to say yes. In December 1791 the **Bill of Rights**—ten amendments intended to protect individuals' rights—was added to the document. Though other amendments have since been added, the Constitution has remained basically the same for more than two centuries.

**Electing a President** By the summer of 1788, enough states had ratified the Constitution to allow the organization of a government. Now the nation considered the question of who would lead the new **republic.** (A republic is a government in which supreme power rests with the voting citizens.) The obvious choice was George Washington, and the Electoral College voted unanimously for him as President. John Adams was chosen to serve as Vice President.

On April 30, 1789, thousands surrounded Federal Hall, an elegant building on New York City's Wall Street that served as the temporary home of the new government. From windows and rooftops, people strained to catch a glimpse of George Washington as he appeared on the front balcony of the building. Those within earshot listened as he repeated the oath of office of President of the United States and kissed a Bible. The crowd roared its approval.

A French ambassador observed this joyous **inauguration,** or official swearing-in ceremony. "Never," he wrote, "has [a] sovereign [a ruler] reigned more completely in the hearts of his subjects than did Washington in those of his fellow-citizens. . . . He has the soul, look, and figure of a hero united in him."

**Washington as President** President Washington selected prominent Americans to head the major departments of the executive branch. This group of federal leaders is called the **Cabinet.** Edmund Randolph of Virginia was named Attorney General, the nation's chief law officer and legal adviser. Henry Knox, who had been Secretary of War under the Articles of Confederation, continued in the job under Washington. Thomas Jefferson was named to head the Department of State, which handles relations with foreign countries. Alexander Hamilton accepted the job of Treasury Secretary.

During the first four years of Washington's **administration,** or term in office, the government had to resolve issues both large and

**Using Historical Evidence** This painting of a reception during the Washington administration is titled *The Republican Court.* ***Culture*** *How does the scene reflect Federalist plans for the new government?*

small. For example, the role of the Supreme Court had to be defined. Congress and the President had to learn how to deal with each other. After all, Washington and his officials were doing things no one else had done before. People were not even sure what to call the new President.

It also was necessary to create a permanent home for the new government. It was determined that a ten-square-mile tract of land on the Potomac River would become the capital. An African American mathematician and inventor, Benjamin Banneker, was charged with surveying the city, which would be called the District of Columbia. (The name *Washington* was not used until 1799, after the President had died.) Pierre Charles L'Enfant, a French artist and architect who had fought for the United States during the Revolutionary War, developed the city plan. In 1800, the government took up residence in its new and permanent home.

## SECTION 3 REVIEW

### Comprehension

1. ***Key Terms*** Define: (a) Articles of Confederation; (b) amend; (c) Electoral College; (d) veto; (e) checks and balances; (f) Federalist; (g) Antifederalist; (h) Bill of Rights; (i) republic; (j) inauguration; (k) Cabinet; (l) administration.
2. ***Summarizing the Main Idea*** What were some of the weaknesses of the Articles of Confederation?
3. ***Organizing Information*** Create a three-column chart that describes the structure of the three branches of the national government. Label the left column *Legislative Branch.* Label the middle column *Executive Branch.* Label the right column *Judicial Branch.* Write a description of each branch, according to the Constitution.

### Critical Thinking

4. ***Analyzing Time Lines*** Review the time line at the start of the section. For each entry, write a sentence or two explaining its relationship to the event after it.
5. ***Identifying Central Issues*** Explain how the promise of a Bill of Rights encouraged the states to ratify the Constitution.

### Writing Activity

6. ***Writing an Expository Essay*** Write an essay that explains the link between James Madison's views on human nature and the plan of government created by the Constitution.

# THE CONSTITUTION OF THE United States

## THE SIX BASIC PRINCIPLES

The classic textbook *Magruder's American Government* outlines the six basic principles of the Constitution. Below is a description of these principles:

### Popular Sovereignty

The Preamble to the Constitution begins with the bold phrase, "We the people. . . ." These words announce that in the United States, the people are sovereign. The government receives its power from the people and can govern only with their consent.

### Limited Government

Because the people are the ultimate source of all government power, the government has only as much authority as the people give it. Government's power is thus limited. Much of the Constitution, in fact, consists of specific limitations on government power.

### Separation of Powers

Government power is not only limited, but also divided. The Constitution assigns certain powers to each of the three branches: the legislative (Congress), executive (President), and judicial (federal courts). This separation of government's powers was intended to prevent the misuse of power.

### Checks and Balances

The system of checks and balances gives each of the three branches of government the ability to restrain the other two. Such a system makes government less efficient but also less likely to trample on the rights of citizens.

### Judicial Review

Who decides whether an act of government violates the Constitution? Historically, the courts have filled this function. The principle of judicial review means that federal courts have the power to review acts of the federal government and to cancel any acts that are unconstitutional, or violate a provision in the Constitution.

### Federalism

A federal system of government is one in which power is divided between a central government and smaller governments. This sharing of powers is intended to ensure that the central government is powerful enough to be effective yet not so powerful as to threaten states or individuals.

# PARTS OF THE CONSTITUTION



## *A Note on the Text of the Constitution*

The complete text of the Constitution, including amendments, appears on the pages that follow. Spelling, capitalization, and punctuation have been modernized, and headings have been added. Portions of the Constitution altered by later amendments or that no longer apply have been crossed out. Commentary appears in the outside column of each page.

## COMMENTARY

The Preamble describes the purpose of the government set up by the Constitution. Americans expect their government to defend justice and liberty and provide peace and safety from foreign enemies.

The Constitution gives Congress the power to make laws. Congress is divided into the Senate and the House of Representatives.

**Clause 1** ***Electors*** refers to voters. Members of the House of Representatives are elected every two years. Any citizen allowed to vote for members of the larger house of the state legislature can also vote for members of the House.

**Clause 2** A member of the House of Representatives must be at least 25 years old, an American citizen for 7 years, and a resident of the state he or she represents.

**Clause 3** The number of representatives each state elects is based on its population. An ***enumeration***, or census, must be taken every 10 years to determine population. Today, the number of representatives in the House is fixed at 435.

This clause contains the famous Three-Fifths Compromise worked out at the Constitutional Convention. ***Persons bound to service*** meant indentured servants. ***All other persons*** meant slaves. All free people in a state were counted. However, only three fifths of the slaves were included in the population count. This three-fifths clause became meaningless when slaves were freed by the Thirteenth Amendment.

**Clause 4** ***Executive authority*** means the governor of a state. If a member of the House leaves office before his or her term ends, the governor must call a special election to fill the seat.

**Clause 5** The House elects a Speaker. Today, the Speaker is usually chosen by the party that has a majority in the House. Also, only the House has the power to ***impeach***, or accuse, a federal official of wrongdoing.

## CONSTITUTION

# *PREAMBLE*

We the people of the United States, in order to form a more perfect union, establish justice, insure domestic tranquillity, provide for the common defense, promote the general welfare, and secure the blessings of liberty to ourselves and our posterity, do ordain and establish this Constitution for the United States of America.

# *Article I. Legislative Branch*

## Section 1. Legislative Powers; The Congress

All legislative powers herein granted shall be vested in a Congress of the United States, which shall consist of a Senate and House of Representatives.

## Section 2. House of Representatives

**1. Election of Members** The House of Representatives shall be composed of members chosen every second year by the people of the several states, and the electors in each state shall have the qualifications requisite for electors of the most numerous branch of the state legislature.

**2. Qualifications** No person shall be a representative who shall not have attained to the age of twenty-five years, and been seven years a citizen of the United States, and who shall not, when elected, be an inhabitant of that state in which he shall be chosen.

**3. Apportionment** Representatives ~~and direct taxes~~ shall be apportioned among the several states which may be included within this Union, according to their respective numbers, ~~which shall be determined by adding to the whole number of free persons, including those bound to service for a term of years and excluding Indians not taxed, three fifths of all other persons.~~ The actual enumeration shall be made within three years after the first meeting of the Congress of the United States, and within every subsequent term of ten years, in such manner as they shall by law direct. The number of representatives shall not exceed one for every thirty thousand, but each state shall have at least one representative; ~~and until such enumeration shall be made, the state of New Hampshire shall be entitled to choose three, Massachusetts eight, Rhode Island and Providence Plantations one, Connecticut five, New York six, New Jersey four, Pennsylvania eight, Delaware one, Maryland six, Virginia ten, North Carolina five, South Carolina five, and Georgia three.~~

**4. Filling Vacancies** When vacancies happen in the representation from any state, the executive authority thereof shall issue writs of election to fill such vacancies.

**5. Officers; Impeachment** The House of Representatives shall choose their Speaker and other officers; and shall have the sole power of impeachment.

## Section 3. Senate

**1. Composition; Term** The Senate of the United States shall be composed of two senators from each state ~~chosen by the legislature thereof,~~ for six years, and each senator shall have one vote.

**Clause 1** Each state has two senators. Senators serve for six-year terms. The Seventeenth Amendment changed the way senators were elected.

**2. Classification; Filling Vacancies** Immediately after they shall be assembled in consequence of the first election, they shall be divided as equally as may be into three classes. The seats of the senators of the first class shall be vacated at the expiration of the second year, of the second class at the expiration of the fourth year, and of the third class at the expiration of the sixth year, so that one third may be chosen every second year; ~~and if vacancies happen by resignation, or otherwise, during the recess of the legislature of any State, the executive thereof may make temporary appointments until the next meeting of the legislature, which shall then fill such vacancies.~~

**Clause 2** Every two years, one third of the senators run for reelection. Thus, the makeup of the Senate is never totally changed by any one election. The Seventeenth Amendment changed the way of filling ***vacancies,*** or empty seats. Today, the governor of a state must choose a senator to fill a vacancy that occurs between elections.

**3. Qualifications** No person shall be a senator who shall not have attained to the age of thirty years, and been nine years a citizen of the United States, and who shall not, when elected, be an inhabitant of that state for which he shall be chosen.

**Clause 3** A senator must be at least 30 years old, an American citizen for 9 years, and a resident of the state he or she represents.

**4. President of the Senate** The Vice President of the United States shall be president of the Senate, but shall have no vote, unless they be equally divided.

**Clause 4** The Vice President presides over Senate meetings, but he or she can vote only to break a tie.

**5. Other Officers** The Senate shall choose their other officers, and also a president *pro tempore,* in the absence of the Vice President, or when he shall exercise the office of the President of the United States.

**Clause 5** ***Pro tempore*** means temporary. The Senate chooses one of its members to serve as president *pro tempore* when the Vice President is absent.

**6. Impeachment Trials** The Senate shall have the sole power to try all impeachments. When sitting for that purpose, they shall be on oath or affirmation. When the President of the United States is tried, the Chief Justice shall preside; and no person shall be convicted without the concurrence of two thirds of the members present.

**Clause 6** The Senate acts as a jury if the House impeaches a federal official. The Chief Justice of the Supreme Court presides if the President is on trial. Two thirds of all senators present must vote for conviction, or finding the accused guilty. No President has ever been convicted. The House impeached President Andrew Johnson in 1868, but the Senate acquitted him of the charges. In 1974, President Richard Nixon resigned before he could be impeached.

**7. Penalty on Conviction** Judgment in cases of impeachment shall not extend further than to removal from office, and disqualification to hold and enjoy any office of honor, trust or profit under the United States: but the party convicted shall nevertheless be liable and subject to indictment, trial, judgment, and punishment, according to law.

**Clause 7** If an official is found guilty by the Senate, he or she can be removed from office and barred from holding federal office in the future. These are the only punishments the Senate can impose. However, the convicted official can still be tried in a criminal court.

## Section 4. Elections and Meetings

**1. Election of Congress** The times, places, and manner of holding elections for senators and representatives, shall be prescribed in each state by the legislature thereof; but the Congress may at any time by law make or alter such regulations, except as to the places of choosing senators.

**Clause 1** Each state legislature can decide when and how congressional elections take place, but Congress can overrule these decisions. In 1842, Congress required each state to set up congressional districts with one representative elected from each district. In 1872, Congress decided that congressional elections must be held in every state on the same date in even-numbered years.

**2. Sessions** The Congress shall assemble at least once in every year, ~~and such meeting shall be on the first Monday in December, unless they shall by law appoint a different day~~.

**Clause 2** Congress must meet at least once a year. The Twentieth Amendment moved the opening date of Congress to January 3.

## Section 5. Legislative Proceedings

**Clause 1** Each house decides whether a member has the qualifications for office set by the Constitution. A ***quorum*** is the smallest number of members who must be present for business to be conducted. Each house can set its own rules about absent members.

**1. Organization** Each house shall be the judge of the elections, returns, and qualifications of its own members, and a majority of each shall constitute a quorum to do business; but a smaller number may adjourn from day to day, and may be authorized to compel the attendance of absent members, in such manner, and under such penalties, as each house may provide.

**Clause 2** Each house can make rules for the conduct of members. It can only expel a member by a two-thirds vote.

**2. Rules** Each house may determine the rules of its proceedings, punish its members for disorderly behavior, and with the concurrence of two thirds, expel a member.

**Clause 3** Each house keeps a record of its meetings. *The Congressional Record* is published every day with excerpts from speeches made in each house. It also records the votes of each member.

**3. Record** Each house shall keep a journal of its proceedings, and from time to time publish the same, excepting such parts as may in their judgment require secrecy; and the yeas and nays of the members of either house on any question shall, at the desire of one fifth of those present, be entered on the journal.

**Clause 4** Neither house can ***adjourn***, or stop meeting, for more than three days unless the other house approves. Both houses of Congress must meet in the same city.

**4. Adjournment** Neither house, during the session of Congress, shall, without the consent of the other, adjourn for more than three days, nor to any other place than that in which the two houses shall be sitting.

## Section 6. Compensation, Immunities, and Disabilities of Members

**Clause 1** ***Compensation*** means salary. Congress decides the salary for its members. While Congress is in session, a member is free from arrest in civil cases and cannot be sued for anything he or she says on the floor of Congress. This allows for freedom of debate. However, a member can be arrested for a criminal offense.

**1. Salaries; Immunities** The senators and representatives shall receive a compensation for their services, to be ascertained by law, and paid out of the Treasury of the United States. They shall in all cases, except treason, felony, and breach of the peace, be privileged from arrest during their attendance at the session of their respective houses, and in going to and returning from the same; and for any speech or debate in either house, they shall not be questioned in any other place.

**Clause 2** ***Emolument*** also means salary. A member of Congress cannot hold another federal office during his or her term. A former member of Congress cannot hold an office created while he or she was in Congress. An official in another branch of government cannot serve at the same time in Congress. This strengthens the separation of powers.

**2. Restrictions on Other Employment** No senator or representative shall, during the time for which he was elected, be appointed to any civil office under the authority of the United States, which shall have been created, or the emoluments whereof shall have been increased during such time; and no person holding any office under the United States shall be a member of either house during his continuance in office.

## Section 7. Revenue Bills, President's Veto

**Clause 1** ***Revenue*** is money raised by the government through taxes. Tax bills must be introduced in the House. The Senate, however, can make changes in tax bills. This clause protects the principle that people can be taxed only with their consent.

**1. Revenue Bills** All bills for raising revenue shall originate in the House of Representatives; but the Senate may propose or concur with amendments as on other bills.

**Clause 2** A ***bill,*** or proposed law, that is passed by a majority of the House and Senate is sent to the President. If the President signs the bill, it becomes law.

A bill can also become law without the President's signature. The President can refuse to act on a bill. If Congress is in session at the time, the bill becomes law 10 days after the President receives it.

**2. How a Bill Becomes Law; the Veto** Every bill which shall have passed the House of Representatives and the Senate shall, before it become a law, be presented to the President of the United States; if he approve, he shall sign it, but if not, he shall return it, with his objections, to that house in which it shall have originated, who shall enter the objections at large on their journal, and proceed to reconsider it. If after such reconsideration two thirds of that house shall agree to pass the bill, it shall be sent, together with the objections, to the other house, by which it shall likewise be reconsidered, and if approved by two thirds of that house, it shall become a law. But in all such cases the votes of both houses shall be determined by yeas and nays, and the names of the persons voting for and against the bill shall be entered on the journal of each house respectively. If any bill shall not be returned by the President within ten days (Sundays excepted) after it shall have been presented to him, the same shall be a law, in like manner as if he had signed it, unless the Congress by their adjournment prevent its return, in which case it shall not be a law.

The President can ***veto***, or reject, a bill by sending it back to the house where it was introduced. Or if the President refuses to act on a bill and Congress adjourns within 10 days, then the bill dies. This way of killing a bill without taking action is called the ***pocket veto***.

Congress can override the President's veto if each house of Congress passes the bill again by a two-thirds vote. This clause is an important part of the system of checks and balances.

**3. Resolutions Passed by Congress** Every order, resolution, or vote to which the concurrence of the Senate and House of Representatives may be necessary (except on a question of adjournment) shall be presented to the President of the United States; and before the same shall take effect, shall be approved by him, or being disapproved by him, shall be repassed by two thirds of the Senate and House of Representatives, according to the rules and limitations prescribed in the case of a bill.

**Clause 3** Congress can pass resolutions or orders that have the same force as laws. Any such resolution or order must be signed by the President (except on questions of adjournment). Thus, this clause prevents Congress from bypassing the President simply by calling a bill by another name.

## Section 8. Powers of Congress

The Congress shall have power

1. To lay and collect taxes, duties, imposts, and excises, to pay the debts and provide for the common defense and general welfare of the United States; but all duties, imposts and excises shall be uniform throughout the United States;

**Clause 1** ***Duties*** are tariffs. ***Imposts*** are taxes in general. ***Excises*** are taxes on the production or sale of certain goods. Congress has the power to tax and spend tax money. Taxes must be the same in all parts of the country.

2. To borrow money on the credit of the United States;

**Clause 2** Congress can borrow money for the United States. The government often borrows money by selling bonds, or certificates that promise to pay the holder a certain sum of money on a certain date.

3. To regulate commerce with foreign nations, and among the several states, and with the Indian tribes;

**Clause 3** Only Congress has the power to regulate foreign and interstate trade, or trade between states. Disagreements over interstate trade were a major problem with the Articles of Confederation.

4. To establish an uniform rule of naturalization, and uniform laws on the subject of bankruptcies throughout the United States;

**Clause 4** ***Naturalization*** is the process whereby a foreigner becomes a citizen. ***Bankruptcy*** is the condition in which a person or business cannot pay its debts. Congress has the power to pass laws on these two issues. The laws must be the same in all parts of the country.

5. To coin money, regulate the value thereof, and of foreign coin, and fix the standard of weights and measures;

**Clause 5** Congress has the power to coin money and set its value. Congress has set up the National Bureau of Standards to regulate weights and measures.

6. To provide for the punishment of counterfeiting the securities and current coin of the United States;

**Clause 6** ***Counterfeiting*** is the making of imitation money. ***Securities*** are bonds. Congress can make laws to punish counterfeiters.

7. To establish post offices and post roads;

**Clause 7** Congress has the power to set up and control the delivery of mail.

8. To promote the progress of science and useful arts by securing for limited times to authors and inventors the exclusive right to their respective writings and discoveries;

**Clause 8** Congress may pass copyright and patent laws. A ***copyright*** protects an author. A patent makes an inventor the sole owner of his or her work for a limited time.

## COMMENTARY

**Clause 9** Congress has the power to set up ***inferior***, or lower, federal courts under the Supreme Court.

**Clause 10** Congress can punish ***piracy***, or the robbing of ships at sea.

**Clause 11** Only Congress can declare war. Declarations of war are granted at the request of the President. ***Letters of marque and reprisal*** were documents issued by a government allowing merchant ships to arm themselves and attack ships of an enemy nation. They are no longer issued.

**Clauses 12, 13, 14** These clauses place the army and navy under the control of Congress. Congress decides on the size of the armed forces and the amount of money to spend on the army and navy. It also has the power to write rules governing the armed forces.

**Clauses 15, 16** The ***militia*** is a body of citizen soldiers. Congress can call up the militia to put down rebellions or fight foreign invaders. Each state has its own militia, today called the National Guard. Normally, the militia is under the command of a state's governor. However, it can be placed under the command of the President.

**Clause 17** Congress controls the district around the national capital. In 1790, Congress made Washington, D.C., the nation's capital. In 1973, it gave residents of the District the right to elect local officials.

**Clause 18** Clauses 1–17 list the powers delegated to Congress. The writers of the Constitution added Clause 18 so that Congress could deal with the changing needs of the nation. It gives Congress the power to make laws as needed to carry out the first 17 clauses. Clause 18 is sometimes called the elastic clause because Congress has used it to stretch the meaning of its power.

**Clause 1** ***Such persons*** means slaves. This clause resulted from a compromise between the supporters and the opponents of the slave trade. In 1808, as soon as Congress was permitted to abolish the slave trade, it did so. The $10 import tax was never imposed.

**Clause 2** A ***writ of habeas corpus*** is a court order requiring government officials to bring a prisoner to court and explain why he or she is being held. A writ of habeas corpus protects people from unlawful imprisonment. The government cannot suspend this right except in times of rebellion or invasion.

**Clause 3** A ***bill of attainder*** is a law declaring that a person is guilty of a particular crime. An ***ex post facto law*** punishes

## CONSTITUTION

9. To constitute tribunals inferior to the Supreme Court;

10. To define and punish piracies and felonies committed on the high seas and offenses against the law of nations;

11. To declare war, grant letters of marque and reprisal, and make rules concerning captures on land and water;

12. To raise and support armies, but no appropriation of money to that use shall be for a longer term than two years;

13. To provide and maintain a navy;

14. To make rules for the government and regulation of the land and naval forces;

15. To provide for calling forth the militia to execute the laws of the Union, suppress insurrections, and repel invasions;

16. To provide for organizing, arming, and disciplining the militia, and for governing such part of them as may be employed in the service of the United States, reserving to the states, respectively, the appointment of the officers, and the authority of training the militia according to the discipline prescribed by Congress;

17. To exercise exclusive legislation in all cases whatsoever, over such district (not exceeding ten miles square) as may, by cession of particular states, and the acceptance of Congress, become the seat of the government of the United States, and to exercise like authority over all places purchased by the consent of the legislature of the state in which the same shall be, for the erection of forts, magazines, arsenals, dock-yards, and other needful buildings; —and

18. To make all laws which shall be necessary and proper for carrying into execution the foregoing powers, and all other powers vested by this Constitution in the government of the United States, or in any department or officer thereof.

### Section 9. Powers Denied to Congress

**1. The Slave Trade** ~~The migration or importation of such persons as any of the states now existing shall think proper to admit, shall not be prohibited by the Congress prior to the year one thousand eight hundred and eight, but a tax or duty may be imposed on such importation, not exceeding ten dollars for each person.~~

**2. Writ of *Habeas Corpus*** The privilege of the writ of *habeas corpus* shall not be suspended, unless when in cases of rebellion or invasion the public safety may require it.

**3. Bills of Attainder; *Ex Post Facto* Laws** No bill of attainder or *ex post facto* law shall be passed.

**4. Apportionment of Direct Taxes** No capitation, ~~or other direct,~~ tax shall be laid, unless in proportion to the census or enumeration herein before directed to be taken.

**5. Taxes on Exports** No tax or duty shall be laid on articles exported from any state.

**6. Special Preference for Trade** No preference shall be given by any regulation of commerce or revenue to the ports of one state over those of another; nor shall vessels bound to, or from, one state, be obliged to enter, clear, or pay duties in another.

**7. Spending** No money shall be drawn from the Treasury, but in consequence of appropriations made by law; and a regular statement and account of the receipts and expenditures of all public money shall be published from time to time.

**8. Titles of Nobility** No title of nobility shall be granted by the United States; and no person holding any office of profit or trust under them, shall, without the consent of the Congress, accept of any present, emolument, office, or title, of any kind whatever, from any king, prince or foreign state.

## Section 10. Powers Denied to the States

**1. Unconditional Prohibitions** No state shall enter into any treaty, alliance, or confederation; grant letters of marque and reprisal; coin money; emit bills of credit; make any thing but gold and silver coin a tender in payment of debts; pass any bill of attainder, *ex post facto* law, or law impairing the obligation of contracts, or grant any title of nobility.

**2. Powers Conditionally Denied** No state shall, without the consent of the Congress, lay any imposts or duties on imports or exports, except what may be absolutely necessary for executing its inspection laws; and the net produce of all duties and imposts, laid by any state on imports or exports, shall be for the use of the Treasury of the United States; and all such laws shall be subject to the revision and control of the Congress.

**3. Other Denied Powers** No state shall, without the consent of Congress, lay any duty of tonnage, keep troops, or ships of war in time of peace, enter into any agreement or compact with another state, or with a foreign power, or engage in war, unless actually invaded, or in such imminent danger as will not admit of delay.

# *Article II. Executive Branch*

## Section 1. President and Vice President

**1. Chief Executive; Term** The executive power shall be vested in a President of the United States of America. He shall hold his

an act which was not illegal when it was committed. Congress cannot pass a bill of attainder or *ex post facto* laws.

**Clause 4** A ***capitation tax*** is a tax placed directly on each person. ***Direct taxes*** are taxes on people or on land. They can be passed only if they are divided among the states according to population. The Sixteenth Amendment allowed Congress to tax income without regard to the population of the states.

**Clause 5** This clause forbids Congress to tax exports. In 1787, southerners insisted on this clause because their economy depended on exports.

**Clause 6** Congress cannot make laws that favor one state over another in trade and commerce. Also, states cannot place tariffs on interstate trade.

**Clause 7** The federal government cannot spend money unless Congress ***appropriates*** it, or passes a law allowing it. This clause gives Congress an important check on the President by controlling the money he or she can spend. The government must publish a statement showing how it spends public funds.

**Clause 8** The government cannot award titles of nobility, such as Duke or Duchess. American citizens cannot accept titles of nobility from foreign governments without the consent of Congress.

**Clause 1** The writers of the Constitution did not want the states to act like separate nations. So they prohibited states from making treaties or coining money. Some powers denied to the federal government are also denied to the states. For example, states cannot pass *ex post facto* laws.

**Clauses 2, 3** Powers listed here are forbidden to the states, but Congress can lift these prohibitions by passing laws that give these powers to the states.

Clause 2 forbids states from taxing imports and exports without the consent of Congress. States may charge inspection fees on goods entering the states. Any profit from these fees must be turned over to the United States Treasury.

Clause 3 forbids states from keeping an army or navy without the consent of Congress. States cannot make treaties or declare war unless an enemy invades or is about to invade.

**Clause 1** The President is responsible for ***executing***, or carrying out, laws passed by Congress.

**Clauses 2, 3** Some writers of the Constitution were afraid to allow the people to elect the President directly. Therefore, the Constitutional Convention set up the electoral college. Clause 2 directs each state to choose electors, or delegates to the electoral college, to vote for President. A state's electoral vote is equal to the combined number of senators and representatives. Each state may decide how to choose its electors. Members of Congress and federal officeholders may not serve as electors. This much of the original electoral college system is still in effect.

Clause 3 called upon each elector to vote for two candidates. The candidate who received a majority of the electoral votes would become President. The runner-up would become Vice President. If no candidate won a majority, the House would choose the President. The Senate would choose the Vice President.

The election of 1800 showed a problem with the original electoral college system. Thomas Jefferson was the Republican candidate for President, and Aaron Burr was the Republican candidate for Vice President. In the electoral college, the vote ended in a tie. The election was finally decided in the House, where Jefferson was chosen President. The Twelfth Amendment changed the electoral college system so that this could not happen again.

**Clause 4** Under a law passed in 1792, electors are chosen on the Tuesday following the first Monday of November every four years. Electors from each state meet to vote in December.

Today, voters in each state choose ***slates***, or groups, of electors who are pledged to a candidate for President. The candidate for President who wins the popular vote in each state wins that state's electoral vote.

**Clause 5** The President must be a citizen of the United States from birth, at least 35 years old, and a resident of the country for 14 years. The first seven Presidents of the United States were born under British rule, but they were allowed to hold office because they were citizens at the time the Constitution was adopted.

**Clause 6** The powers of the President pass to the Vice President if the President leaves office or cannot discharge his or her duties. The wording of this clause caused confusion the first time a President died in office. When President William Henry Harrison died, it was uncertain whether Vice President John Tyler should remain Vice President and act

office during the term of four years, and, together with the Vice President, chosen for the same term, be elected as follows:

**2. Electoral College** Each state shall appoint, in such manner as the legislature thereof may direct, a number of electors, equal to the whole number of senators and representatives to which the state may be entitled in the Congress: but no senator or representative, or person holding an office of trust or profit under the United States, shall be appointed an elector.

**3. Former Electoral Method** ~~The electors shall meet in their respective states, and vote by ballot for two persons, of whom one at least shall not be an inhabitant of the same state with themselves. And they shall make a list of all the persons voted for, and of the number of votes for each; which list they shall sign and certify, and transmit sealed to the seat of the government of the United States, directed to the president of the Senate. The president of the Senate shall, in the presence of the Senate and House of Representatives, open all the certificates, and the votes shall then be counted. The person having the greatest number of votes shall be the President, if such number be a majority of the whole number of Electors appointed; and if there be more than one who have such majority, and have an equal number of votes, then the House of Representatives shall immediately choose by ballot one of them for President; and if no person have a majority, then from the five highest on the list the said House shall in like manner choose the President. But in choosing the President, the votes shall be taken by states, the representation from each state having one vote; a quorum for this purpose shall consist of a member or members from two thirds of the states, and a majority of all the states shall be necessary to a choice. In every case, after the choice of the President, the person having the greatest number of votes of the electors shall be the Vice President. But if there should remain two or more who have equal votes, the Senate shall choose from them by ballot the Vice President.~~

**4. Time of Elections** The Congress may determine the time of choosing the electors, and the day on which they shall give their votes; which day shall be the same throughout the United States.

**5. Qualifications for President** No person except a natural-born citizen, ~~or a citizen of the United States at the time of the adoption of this Constitution,~~ shall be eligible to the office of President; neither shall any person be eligible to that office who shall not have attained to the age of thirty-five years, and been fourteen years a resident within the United States.

**6. Presidential Succession** ~~In case of the removal of the President from office, or of his death, resignation, or inability to discharge the powers and duties of the said office, the same shall devolve on the Vice President,~~ and the Congress may by law provide for the case of removal, death, resignation or inability, both of the President and Vice President, declaring what officer shall then act as President, and such officer shall act accordingly, until the disability be removed, or a President shall be elected.

as President or whether he should be sworn in as President. Tyler persuaded a federal judge to swear him in. So he set the precedent that the Vice President assumes the office of President when it becomes vacant. The Twenty-fifth Amendment replaced this clause.

**7. Salary** The President shall, at stated times, receive for his services, a compensation, which shall neither be increased nor diminished during the period for which he shall have been elected, and he shall not receive within that period any other emolument from the United States, or any of them.

**Clause 7** The President is paid a salary. It cannot be raised or lowered during his or her term of office. The President is not allowed to hold any other federal or state position while in office. Today, the President's salary is $200,000 a year.

**8. Oath of Office** Before he enter on the execution of his office, he shall take the following oath or affirmation:—"I do solemnly swear (or affirm) that I will faithfully execute the office of the President of the United States, and will to the best of my ability, preserve, protect, and defend the Constitution of the United States."

**Clause 8** Before taking office, the President must promise to protect and defend the Constitution. Usually, the Chief Justice of the United States administers the oath of office to the President.

## Section 2. Powers of the President

**1. Military Powers** The President shall be commander in chief of the army and navy of the United States, and of the militia of the several states, when called into the actual service of the United States; he may require the opinion, in writing, of the principal officer in each of the executive departments, upon any subject relating to the duties of their respective offices, and he shall have power to grant reprieves and pardons for offenses against the United States, except in cases of impeachment.

**Clause 1** The President is head of the armed forces and the state militias when they are called into national service. So the military is under ***civilian***, or nonmilitary, control.

The President can get advice from the heads of executive departments. In most cases, the President has the power to grant a reprieve or pardon. A ***reprieve*** suspends punishment ordered by law. A ***pardon*** prevents prosecution for a crime or overrides the judgment of a court.

**2. Treaties; Appointments** He shall have power, by and with the advice and consent of the Senate, to make treaties, provided two thirds of the senators present concur; and he shall nominate, and by and with the advice and consent of the Senate, shall appoint ambassadors, other public ministers and consuls, judges of the Supreme Court, and all other officers of the United States, whose appointments are not herein otherwise provided for, and which shall be established by law: but the Congress may by law vest the appointment of such inferior officers, as they think proper, in the President alone, in the courts of law, or in the heads of departments.

**Clause 2** The President has the power to make treaties with other nations. Under the system of checks and balances, all treaties must be approved by two thirds of the Senate. Today, the President also makes agreements with foreign governments. These executive agreements do not need Senate approval.

The President has the power to appoint ambassadors to foreign countries and to appoint other high officials. The Senate must ***confirm***, or approve, these appointments.

**3. Temporary Appointments** The President shall have power to fill up all vacancies that may happen during the recess of the Senate, by granting commissions which shall expire at the end of their next session.

**Clause 3** If the Senate is in ***recess,*** or not meeting, the President may fill vacant government posts by making temporary appointments.

## Section 3. Duties of the President

He shall from time to time give to the Congress information of the state of the Union, and recommend to their consideration such measures as he shall judge necessary and expedient; he may, on extraordinary occasions, convene both houses, or either of them, and in case of disagreement between them, with respect to the time of adjournment, he may adjourn them to such time as he shall think proper; he shall receive ambassadors and other public ministers; he shall take care that the laws be faithfully executed, and shall commission all the officers of the United States.

The President must give Congress a report on the condition of the nation every year. This report is now called the State of the Union Address. Since 1913, the President has given this speech in person each January.

The President can call a special session of Congress and can adjourn Congress if necessary. The President has the power to receive, or recognize, foreign ambassadors.

The President must carry out the laws. Today, many government agencies oversee the execution of laws.

***Civil officers*** include federal judges and members of the Cabinet. ***High crimes*** are major crimes. ***Misdemeanors*** are lesser crimes. The President, Vice President, and others can be forced out of office if impeached and found guilty of certain crimes. Andrew Johnson and Bill Clinton are the only Presidents to have been impeached.

## Section 4. Impeachment

The President, Vice President and all civil officers of the United States, shall be removed from office on impeachment for, and conviction of, treason, bribery, or other high crimes and misdemeanors.

***Judicial power*** means the right of the courts to decide legal cases. The Constitution creates the Supreme Court but lets Congress decide on the size of the Supreme Court. Congress has the power to set up inferior, or lower, courts. The Judiciary Act of 1789 set up a system of district and circuit courts, or courts of appeal. All federal judges serve for life.

# *Article III. Judicial Branch*

## Section 1. Courts, Terms of Office

The judicial power of the United States shall be vested in one Supreme Court, and in such inferior courts as the Congress may from time to time ordain and establish. The judges, both of the Supreme and inferior courts, shall hold their offices during good behavior, and shall, at stated times, receive for their services, a compensation, which shall not be diminished during their continuance in office.

**Clause 1** ***Jurisdiction*** refers to the right of a court to hear a case. Federal courts have jurisdiction over cases that involve the Constitution, federal laws, treaties, foreign ambassadors and diplomats, naval and maritime laws, disagreements between states or between citizens from different states, and disputes between a state or citizen and a foreign state or citizen.

In *Marbury v. Madison*, the Supreme Court established the right to judge whether a law is constitutional.

## Section 2. Jurisdiction

**1. Scope of Judicial Power** The judicial power shall extend to all cases, in law and equity, arising under this Constitution, the laws of the United States, and treaties made, or which shall be made, under their authority;—to all cases affecting ambassadors, other public ministers and consuls;—to all cases of admiralty and maritime jurisdiction;—to controversies to which the United States shall be a party;—to controversies between two or more states; ~~between a state and citizens of another state;~~ —between citizens of different states;—between citizens of the same state claiming lands under grants of different states, and between a state, or the citizens thereof, and foreign states, citizens, or subjects.

**Clause 2** ***Original jurisdiction*** means the power of a court to hear a case where it first arises. The Supreme Court has original jurisdiction over only a few cases, such as those involving foreign diplomats. More often, the Supreme Court acts as an appellate court. An ***appellate*** court does not decide guilt. It decides whether the lower court trial was properly conducted and reviews the lower court's decision.

**2. Supreme Court** In all cases affecting ambassadors, other public ministers and consuls, and those in which a state shall be a party, the Supreme Court shall have original jurisdiction. In all the other cases before mentioned, the Supreme Court shall have appellate jurisdiction, both as to law and fact, with such exceptions, and under such regulations as the Congress shall make.

**Clause 3** This clause guarantees the right to a jury trial for anyone accused of a federal crime. The only exceptions are impeachment cases. The trial must be held in the state where the crime was committed.

**3. Trial by Jury** The trial of all crimes, except in cases of impeachment, shall be by jury; and such trial shall be held in the state where the said crimes shall have been committed; but when not committed within any state, the trial shall be at such place or places as the Congress may by law have directed.

**Clause 1** Treason is clearly defined. An ***overt act*** is an actual action. A person cannot be convicted of treason for what he or she thinks. A person can be convicted of treason only if he or she confesses or two witnesses testify to it.

## Section 3. Treason

**1. Definition** Treason against the United States shall consist only in levying war against them, or in adhering to their enemies, giving them aid and comfort. No person shall be convicted of treason unless on the testimony of two witnesses to the same overt act, or on confession in open court.

**Clause 2** Congress has the power to set the punishment for traitors. Congress may not punish the children of convicted traitors by taking away their civil rights or property.

**2. Punishment** The Congress shall have power to declare the punishment of treason, but no attainder of treason shall work corruption of blood or forfeiture except during the life of the person attained.

# *Article IV. Relations Among the States*

## Section 1. Full Faith and Credit

Full faith and credit shall be given in each state to the public acts, records, and judicial proceedings of every other state. And the Congress may by general laws prescribe the manner in which such acts, records, and proceedings shall be proved, and the effect thereof.

Each state must recognize the official acts and records of any other state. For example, each state must recognize marriage certificates issued by another state. Congress can pass laws to ensure this.

## Section 2. Privileges and Immunities of Citizens

**1. Privileges** The citizens of each state shall be entitled to all privileges and immunities of citizens in the several states.

**Clause 1** All states must treat citizens of another state in the same way it treats its own citizens. However, the courts have allowed states to give residents certain privileges, such as lower tuition rates.

**2. Extradition** A person charged in any state with treason, felony, or other crime, who shall flee from justice, and be found in another state, shall on demand of the executive authority of the state from which he fled, be delivered up, to be removed to the state having jurisdiction of the crime.

**Clause 2** ***Extradition*** means the act of returning a suspected criminal or escaped prisoner to a state where he or she is wanted. State governors must return a suspect to another state. However, the Supreme Court has ruled that a governor cannot be forced to do so if he or she feels that justice will not be done.

**3. Fugitive Slaves** ~~No person held to service or labor in one state, under the laws thereof, escaping into another, shall in consequence of any law or regulation therein, be discharged from such service or labor, but shall be delivered up on claim of the party to whom such service or labor may be due.~~

**Clause 3** ***Persons held to service or labor*** refers to slaves or indentured servants. This clause required states to return runaway slaves to their owners. The Thirteenth Amendment replaces this clause.

## Section 3. New States and Territories

**1. New States** New states may be admitted by the Congress into this Union; but no new states shall be formed or erected within the jurisdiction of any other state; nor any state be formed by the junction of two or more states, or parts of states, without the consent of the legislatures of the states concerned as well as of the Congress.

**Clause 1** Congress has the power to admit new states to the Union. Existing states cannot be split up or joined together to form new states unless both Congress and the state legislatures approve. New states are equal to all other states.

**2. Federal Lands** The Congress shall have power to dispose of and make all needful rules and regulations respecting the territory or other property belonging to the United States; and nothing in this Constitution shall be so construed as to prejudice any claims of the United States, or of any particular state.

**Clause 2** Congress can make rules for managing and governing land owned by the United States. This includes territories not organized into states, and federal lands within a state.

## Section 4. Protection Afforded to States by the Nation

The United States shall guarantee to every state in this Union a republican form of government, and shall protect each of them against invasion; and on application of the legislature, or of the executive (when the legislature cannot be convened) against domestic violence.

In a ***republic,*** voters choose representatives to govern them. The federal government must protect the states from foreign invasion and from ***domestic,*** or internal, disorder if asked to do so by a state.

# Article V. Provisions for Amendment

The Constitution can be ***amended***, or changed, if necessary. An amendment can be proposed by (1) a two-thirds vote of both houses of Congress or (2) a national convention called by Congress at the request of two thirds of the state legislatures. (This second method has never been used.) An amendment must be ***ratified***, or approved, by (1) three fourths of the state legislatures or (2) special conventions in three fourths of the states. Congress decides which method will be used.

The Congress, whenever two thirds of both houses shall deem it necessary, shall propose amendments to this Constitution, or, on the application of the legislatures of two thirds of the several states, shall call a convention for proposing amendments, which, in either case, shall be valid to all intents and purposes, as part of this Constitution, when ratified by the legislatures of three fourths of the several states, or by conventions in three fourths thereof, as the one or the other mode of ratification may be proposed by the Congress; provided ~~that no amendment which may be made prior to the year one thousand eight hundred and eight shall in any manner affect the first and fourth clauses in the ninth section of the first Article; and~~ that no state, without its consent, shall be deprived of its equal suffrage in the Senate.



# Article VI. National Debts, Supremacy of National Law, Oath

## Section 1. Validity of Debts

The United States government promised to pay all debts and honor all agreements made under the Articles of Confederation.

All debts contracted and engagements entered into, before the adoption of this Constitution, shall be as valid against the United States under this Constitution, as under the Confederation.

## Section 2. Supremacy of National Law

Under the Constitution, federal laws and treaties that the Senate have ratified are the ***supreme,*** or highest, law of the land. A judge must overturn a state law if he or she believes that it conflicts with the Constitution or a federal law that he or she deems constitutional.

This Constitution, and the laws of the United States which shall be made in pursuance thereof, and all treaties made, or which shall be made, under the authority of the United States, shall be the supreme law of the land; and the judges in every state shall be bound thereby, anything in the constitution or laws of any state to the contrary notwithstanding.

## Section 3. Oaths of Office

State and federal officeholders take an ***oath,*** or solemn promise, to support the Constitution. However, this clause forbids the use of religious tests for officeholders. During the colonial period, every colony except Rhode Island required a religious test for officeholders.

The senators and representatives before mentioned, and the members of the several state legislatures, and all executive and judicial officers, both of the United States and of the several states, shall be bound by oath or affirmation, to support this Constitution; but no religious test shall ever be required as a qualification to any office or public trust under the United States.

# Article VII. Ratification of Constitution

During 1787 and 1788, states held special conventions. By October 1788, the required nine states had ratified the Constitution.

The ratification of the conventions of nine states shall be sufficient for the establishment of this Constitution between the states so ratifying the same.

Done in convention by the unanimous consent of the states present the seventeenth day of September, in the year of our Lord one thousand seven hundred and eighty-seven, and of the independence of the United States of America the twelfth. *In Witness* whereof, we have hereunto subscribed our names.

Attest:
*William Jackson, SECRETARY*
*George Washington, PRESIDENT and deputy from Virginia*

NEW HAMPSHIRE
*John Langdon*
*Nicholas Gilman*

MASSACHUSETTS
*Nathaniel Gorham*
*Rufus King*

CONNECTICUT
*William Samuel Johnson*
*Roger Sherman*

NEW YORK
*Alexander Hamilton*

NEW JERSEY
*William Livingston*
*David Brearley*
*William Paterson*
*Jonathan Dayton*

PENNSYLVANIA
*Benjamin Franklin*
*Thomas Mifflin*
*Robert Morris*
*George Clymer*
*Thomas Fitzsimons*
*Jared Ingersoll*
*James Wilson*
*Gouverneur Morris*

DELAWARE
*George Read*
*Gunning Bedford, Jr.*
*John Dickinson*
*Richard Bassett*
*Jacob Broom*

MARYLAND
*James McHenry*
*Dan of St. Thomas Jennifer*
*Daniel Carroll*

VIRGINIA
*John Blair*
*James Madison, Jr.*

NORTH CAROLINA
*William Blount*
*Richard Dobbs Spaight*
*Hugh Williamson*

SOUTH CAROLINA
*John Rutledge*
*Charles Cotesworth Pinckney*
*Charles Pinckney*
*Pierce Butler*

GEORGIA
*William Few*
*Abraham Baldwin*

# *AMENDMENTS*

## First Amendment

### *(1791) Freedom of Religion, Speech, Press, Assembly, and Petition*

Congress shall make no law respecting an establishment of religion, or prohibiting the free exercise thereof; or abridging the freedom of speech, or of the press; or the right of the people peaceably to assemble, and to petition the government for a redress of grievances.

**First Amendment** The First Amendment protects five basic rights: freedom of religion, speech, the press, assembly, and petition. Congress cannot set up an established, or official, church or religion for the nation. During the colonial period, most colonies had established churches. However, the authors of the First Amendment wanted to keep government and religion separate.

Congress may not ***abridge***, or limit, the freedom to speak and write freely. The government may not censor, or review, books and newspapers before they are printed. This amendment also protects the right to assemble, or hold public meetings. ***Petition*** means ask. ***Redress*** means to correct. ***Grievances*** are wrongs. The people have the right to ask the government for wrongs to be corrected.

## Second Amendment

### *(1791) Bearing Arms*

A well-regulated militia being necessary to the security of a free state, the right of the people to keep and bear arms shall not be infringed.

**Second Amendment** The meaning of this amendment is highly controversial. Some experts believe that it guarantees individuals the right to bear arms while others contend that it guarantees the individual states the right to maintain a militia.

## Third Amendment

### *(1791) Quartering of Troops*

No soldier shall, in time of peace, be quartered in any house, without the consent of the owner; nor in time of war, but in a manner to be prescribed by law.

**Third Amendment** During the colonial period, the British ***quartered,*** or housed, soldiers in private homes without the permission of the owners. This amendment limits the government's right to use private homes to house soldiers.

**Fourth Amendment** This amendment protects Americans from unreasonable searches and seizures. Search and seizure are permitted only if a judge has issued a ***warrant***, or written court order. A warrant is issued only if there is probable cause. This means an officer must show that it is probable, or likely, that the search will produce evidence of a crime. A search warrant must name the exact place to be searched and the things to be seized.

In some cases, courts have ruled that searches can take place without a warrant. For example, police may search a person who is under arrest.

**Fifth Amendment** This amendment protects the rights of the accused. ***Capital crimes*** are those that can be punished with death. ***Infamous crimes*** are those that can be punished with prison or loss of rights. The federal government must obtain an ***indictment***, or formal accusation, from a grand jury to prosecute anyone for such crimes. A ***grand jury*** is a panel of between 12 and 23 citizens who decide if the government has enough evidence to justify a trial. This procedure prevents the government from prosecuting people with little or no evidence of guilt. (Soldiers and the militia in wartime are not covered by this rule.)

***Double jeopardy*** is forbidden by this amendment. This means that a person cannot be tried twice for the same crime. However, if a court sets aside a conviction because of a legal error, the accused can be tried again. A person on trial cannot be forced to ***testify,*** or give evidence, against himself or herself. A person accused of a crime is entitled to ***due process of law***, or a fair hearing or trial.

Finally, the government cannot seize private property for public use without paying the owner a fair price for it.

**Sixth Amendment** In criminal cases, the jury must be ***impartial***, or not favor either side. The accused is guaranteed the right to a trial by jury. The trial must be speedy. If the government purposely postpones the trial so that it becomes hard for the person to get a fair hearing, the charge may be dismissed. The accused must be told the charges against him or her and be allowed to question prosecution witnesses. Witnesses who can help the accused can be ordered to appear in court.

The accused must be allowed a lawyer. Since 1942, the federal government has been required to provide a lawyer if the accused cannot afford one. In 1963, the Supreme Court decided that states must also provide lawyers for a defendant too poor to pay for one.



## Fourth Amendment
*(1791) Searches and Seizures*

The right of the people to be secure in their persons, houses, papers, and effects, against unreasonable searches and seizures, shall not be violated, and no warrants shall issue, but upon probable cause, supported by oath or affirmation, and particularly describing the place to be searched, and the persons or things to be seized.

## Fifth Amendment
*(1791) Criminal Proceedings; Due Process; Eminent Domain*

No person shall be held to answer for a capital, or otherwise infamous, crime, unless on a presentment or indictment of a grand jury, except in cases arising in the land or naval forces, or in the militia, when in actual service in time of war or public danger; nor shall any person be subject for the same offense to be twice put in jeopardy of life and limb; nor shall be compelled, in any criminal case, to be a witness against himself; nor be deprived of life, liberty, or property, without due process of law; nor shall private property be taken for public use, without just compensation.

## Sixth Amendment
*(1791) Criminal Proceedings*

In all criminal prosecutions, the accused shall enjoy the right to a speedy and public trial, by an impartial jury of the state and district wherein the crime shall have been committed, which district shall have been previously ascertained by law, and to be informed of the nature and cause of the accusation; to be confronted with the witnesses against him; to have compulsory process for obtaining witnesses in his favor, and to have the assistance of counsel for his defense.

## Seventh Amendment
*(1791) Civil Trials*

In suits at common law, where the value in controversy shall exceed twenty dollars, the right of trial by jury shall be preserved, and no fact tried by a jury shall be otherwise re-examined in any court of the United States, than according to the rules of the common law.

**Seventh Amendment** ***Common law*** refers to rules of law established by judges in past cases. This amendment guarantees the right to a jury trial in lawsuits where the sum of money at stake is more than $20. An appeals court cannot change a verdict because it disagrees with the decision of the jury. It can set aside a verdict only if legal errors made the trial unfair.

## Eighth Amendment
*(1791) Punishment for Crimes*

Excessive bail shall not be required, nor excessive fines imposed, nor cruel and unusual punishments inflicted.

**Eighth Amendment** ***Bail*** is money the accused leaves with the court as a pledge that he or she will appear for trial. If the accused does not appear for trial, the court keeps the money. ***Excessive*** means too high. This amendment forbids courts to set unreasonably high bail. The amount of bail usually depends on the seriousness of the charge and whether the accused is likely to appear for the trial. The amendment also forbids cruel and unusual punishments such as mental and physical abuse.

## Ninth Amendment
*(1791) Unenumerated Rights*

The enumeration in the Constitution, of certain rights, shall not be construed to deny or disparage others retained by the people.

**Ninth Amendment** The people have rights that are not listed in the Constitution. This amendment was added because some people feared that the Bill of Rights would be used to limit rights to those actually listed.

## Tenth Amendment
*(1791) Powers Reserved to the States*

The powers not delegated to the United States by the Constitution, nor prohibited by it to the states, are reserved to the states respectively, or to the people.

**Tenth Amendment** This amendment limits the power of the federal government. Powers not given to the federal government belong to the states. The powers reserved to the states are not listed in the Constitution.

## Eleventh Amendment
*(1798) Suits Against States*

The judicial power of the United States shall not be construed to extend to any suit in law or equity, commenced or prosecuted against one of the United States by citizens of another state, or by citizens or subjects of any foreign state.

**Eleventh Amendment** This amendment changed part of Article 3, Section 2, Clause 1. As a result, a private citizen from one state cannot sue the government of another state in federal court. However, a citizen can sue a state government in a state court.

## Twelfth Amendment
*(1804) Election of President and Vice President*

The electors shall meet in their respective states, and vote by ballot for President and Vice President, one of whom, at least, shall not be an inhabitant of the same state with themselves; they shall name in their ballots the person voted for as President, and in distinct ballots the person voted for as Vice President, and they shall make distinct lists of all persons voted for as President, and of all persons voted for as Vice President, and of the number of votes for each, which lists they shall sign and certify, and transmit sealed to the seat of the government of the United States, directed to the president of the Senate; the president of the Senate shall, in the presence of the Senate and the House of Representatives, open all the certificates and the votes shall then be counted;—the person having the greatest number of votes for

**Twelfth Amendment** This amendment changed the way the electoral college voted. Before the amendment was adopted, each elector simply voted for two people. The candidate with the most votes became President. The runner-up became Vice President. In 1800, however, a tie vote resulted between Thomas Jefferson and Aaron Burr.

In such a case, the Constitution required the House of Representatives to elect the President. Federalists had a majority in the House. They tried to keep Jefferson out of office by voting for Burr. It took 35 ballots in the House before Jefferson was elected President.

To keep this from happening again, the Twelfth Amendment was passed and ratified in time for the election of 1804.

This amendment provides that each elector choose one candidate for President and one candidate for Vice President. If no candidate for President receives a majority of electoral votes, the House of Representatives chooses the President. If no candidate for Vice President receives a majority, the Senate elects the Vice President. The Vice President must be a person who is eligible to be President.

This system is still in use today. However, it is possible for a candidate to win the popular vote and lose in the electoral college. This happened in 1876.

President shall be the President, if such number be a majority of the whole number of electors appointed; and if no person have such a majority, then from the persons having the highest numbers not exceeding three on the list of those voted for as President, the House of Representatives shall choose immediately, by ballot, the President. But in choosing the President, the votes shall be taken by states, the representation from each state having one vote; a quorum for this purpose shall consist of a member or members from two thirds of the states, and a majority of all the states shall be necessary to a choice. And if the House of Representatives shall not choose a President whenever the right of choice shall devolve upon them, ~~before the fourth day of March next following,~~ then the Vice President, shall act as President, as in the case of the death or other constitutional disability of the President.—The person having the greatest number of votes as Vice President, shall be the Vice President, if such number be a majority of the whole number of electors appointed, and if no person have a majority, then from the two highest numbers on the list, the Senate shall choose the Vice President; a quorum for the purpose shall consist of two thirds of the whole number of senators, and a majority of the whole number shall be necessary to a choice. But no person constitutionally ineligible to the office of President shall be eligible to that of Vice President of the United States.



**Thirteenth Amendment** The Emancipation Proclamation (1863) freed slaves only in areas controlled by the Confederacy. This amendment freed all slaves. It also forbids ***involuntary servitude***, or labor done against one's will. However, it does not prevent prison wardens from making prisoners work. Congress can pass laws to carry out this amendment.

## Thirteenth Amendment

*(1865) Slavery and Involuntary Servitude*

**Section 1. Outlawing Slavery** Neither slavery nor involuntary servitude, except as a punishment for crime whereof the party shall have been duly convicted, shall exist within the United States, or any place subject to their jurisdiction.

**Section 2. Enforcement** Congress shall have power to enforce this article by appropriate legislation.

**Fourteenth Amendment, Section 1** This section defines citizenship for the first time in the Constitution, and it extends citizenship to blacks. It also prohibits states from denying the rights and privileges of citizenship to any citizen. This section also forbids states to deny due process of law.

Section 1 guarantees all citizens "equal protection under the law." For a long time, however, the Fourteenth Amendment did not protect blacks from discrimination. After Reconstruction, separate facilities for blacks and whites sprang up. In 1954, the Supreme Court ruled that separate facilities for blacks and whites were by their nature unequal. This ruling, in the case of *Brown* v. *Board of Education*, made school segregation illegal.

## Fourteenth Amendment

*(1868) Rights of Citizens*

**Section 1. Citizenship** All persons born or naturalized in the United States, and subject to the jurisdiction thereof, are citizens of the United States and of the state wherein they reside. No state shall make or enforce any law which shall abridge the privileges or immunities of citizens of the United States; nor shall any state deprive any person of life, liberty, or property, without due process of law; nor deny to any person within its jurisdiction the equal protection of the laws.

**Fourteenth Amendment, Section 2** This section replaced the three-fifths clause. It provides that representation in the House of Representatives is decided on the basis of the number of people in the state. It also provides that states which deny the vote to male citizens over age 21 will be punished by losing part of their representation in the

**Section 2. Apportionment of Representatives** Representatives shall be apportioned among the several states according to their respective numbers, counting the whole number of persons in each state, excluding Indians not taxed. But when the right to vote at any election for the choice of electors for President and Vice President of the United States, representatives in Congress, the executive and judicial officers of a state, or the members of the legislature thereof, is denied to any of the male inhabitants of such state, being twenty-one years of age, and citizens of the United States, or in any way abridged, except for participation in rebellion, or other crime, the basis of representation therein shall be reduced in the proportion which the number of such male citizens shall bear to the whole number of male citizens twenty-one years of age in such state.

House. This provision has never been enforced.

Despite this clause, black citizens were often prevented from voting. In the 1960s, federal laws were passed to end voting discrimination.

**Section 3. Former Confederate Officials** No person shall be a senator or representative in Congress, or elector of President and Vice President, or hold any office, civil or military, under the United States, or under any state, who, having previously taken an oath, as a member of Congress, or as an officer of the United States, or as a member of any state legislature, or as an executive or judicial officer of any state, to support the Constitution of the United States, shall have engaged in insurrection or rebellion against the same, or given aid or comfort to the enemies thereof. But Congress may, by a vote of two thirds of each house, remove such disability.

**Fourteenth Amendment, Section 3** This section prohibited people who had been federal or state officials before the Civil War and who had joined the Confederate cause from serving again as government officials. In 1872, Congress restored the rights of former Confederate officials.

**Section 4. Public Debt** The validity of the public debt of the United States, authorized by law, including debts incurred for payment of pensions and bounties for services in suppressing insurrection or rebellion, shall not be questioned. But neither the United States nor any state shall assume or pay any debt or obligation incurred in aid of insurrection or rebellion against the United States, or any claim for the loss or emancipation of any slave; but all such debts, obligations and claims shall be held illegal and void.

**Fourteenth Amendment, Section 4** This section recognized that the United States must repay its debts from the Civil War. However, it forbade the repayment of debts of the Confederacy. This meant that people who had loaned money to the Confederacy would not be repaid. Also, states were not allowed to pay former slave owners for the loss of slaves.

**Section 5. Enforcement** The Congress shall have power to enforce, by appropriate legislation, the provisions of this article.

**Fourteenth Amendment, Section 5** Congress can pass laws to carry out this amendment.

## Fifteenth Amendment
*(1870) Right to Vote—Race, Color, Servitude*

**Section 1. Extending the Right to Vote** The right of citizens of the United States to vote shall not be denied or abridged by the United States or by any state on account of race, color, or previous condition of servitude.

**Fifteenth Amendment, Section 1** ***Previous condition of servitude*** refers to slavery. This amendment gave blacks, both former slaves and free blacks, the right to vote. In the late 1800s, southern states used grandfather clauses, literacy tests, and poll taxes to keep blacks from voting.

**Section 2. Enforcement** The Congress shall have power to enforce this article by appropriate legislation.

**Fifteenth Amendment, Section 2** Congress can pass laws to carry out this amendment. The Twenty-fourth Amendment barred the use of poll taxes in national elections. The Voting Rights Act of 1965 gave federal officials the power to register voters where there was voting discrimination.

## Sixteenth Amendment
*(1913) Income Tax*

The Congress shall have power to lay and collect taxes on incomes, from whatever source derived, without apportionment among the several states, and without regard to any census or enumeration.

**Sixteenth Amendment** Congress has the power to collect taxes on people's income. An income tax can be collected without regard to a state's population. This amendment changed Article 1, Section 9, Clause 4.

## Seventeenth Amendment
*(1913) Popular Election of Senators*

**Section 1. Method of Election** The Senate of the United States shall be composed of two senators from each state, elected by the people thereof, for six years; and each senator shall have one vote.

**Seventeenth Amendment, Section 1** This amendment modified Article 1, Section 3, Clause 1. Before it was adopted, state legislatures chose senators. This amendment provides that senators are directly elected by the people of each state.

**Seventeenth Amendment, Section 2** When a Senate seat becomes vacant, the governor of the state must order an election to fill the seat. The state legislature can give the governor power to fill the seat until an election is held.

**Seventeenth Amendment, Section 3** Senators who had already been elected by the state legislatures were not affected by this amendment.

**Eighteenth Amendment, Section 1** This amendment, known as Prohibition, banned the making, selling, or transporting of alcoholic beverages in the United States. Later, the Twenty-first Amendment ***repealed,*** or canceled, this amendment.

**Eighteenth Amendment, Section 2** Both the states and the federal government had the power to pass laws to enforce this amendment.

**Eighteenth Amendment, Section 3** This amendment had to be approved within seven years. The Eighteenth Amendment was the first amendment to include a time limit for ratification.

**Nineteenth Amendment, Section 1** Neither the federal government nor state governments can deny the right to vote on account of sex. Thus, women won ***suffrage,*** or the right to vote. Before 1920, some states had allowed women to vote in state elections.

**Nineteenth Amendment, Section 2** Congress can pass laws to carry out this amendment.

**Twentieth Amendment, Section 1** The date for the President and Vice President to take office is January 20. Members of Congress begin their terms of office on January 3. Before this amendment was adopted, these terms of office began on March 4.

**Twentieth Amendment, Section 2** Congress must meet at least once a year. The new session of Congress begins



The electors in each state shall have the qualifications requisite for electors of the most numerous branch of the state legislatures.

**Section 2. Vacancies** When vacancies happen in the representation of any state in the Senate, the executive authority of such state shall issue writs of election to fill such vacancies: provided, that the legislature of any state may empower the executive thereof to make temporary appointments until the people fill the vacancies by election as the legislature may direct.

**Section 3. Those Elected Under Previous Procedure** ~~This amendment shall not be so construed as to affect the election or term of any senator chosen before it becomes valid as part of the Constitution.~~

## Eighteenth Amendment
*(1919) Prohibition of Intoxicating Liquors*

**Section 1. Ban on Alcohol** ~~After one year from the ratification of this article, the manufacture, sale, or transportation of intoxicating liquors within, the importation thereof into, or the exportation thereof from the United States and all territory subject to the jurisdiction thereof for beverage purposes is hereby prohibited.~~

**Section 2. Enforcement** ~~The Congress and the several states shall have concurrent power to enforce this article by appropriate legislation.~~

**Section 3. Method of Ratification** ~~This article shall be inoperative unless it shall have been ratified as an amendment to the Constitution by the legislatures of the several states, as provided in the Constitution, within seven years from the date of the submission hereof to the states by Congress.~~

## Nineteenth Amendment
*(1920) Women's Suffrage*

**Section 1. The Right to Vote** The right of citizens of the United States to vote shall not be denied or abridged by the United States or by any state on account of sex.

**Section 2. Enforcement** Congress shall have power to enforce this article by appropriate legislation.

## Twentieth Amendment
*(1933) Commencement of Terms; Sessions of Congress; Death or Disqualification of President-Elect*

**Section 1. Beginning of Terms** The terms of the President and Vice President shall end at noon on the 20th day of January, and the terms of senators and representatives at noon on the 3d day of January, of the years in which such terms would have ended if this article had not been ratified; and the terms of their successors shall then begin.

**Section 2. Congressional Sessions** The Congress shall assemble at least once in every year, and such meeting shall begin at noon on the 3rd day of January, unless they shall by law appoint a different day.

**Section 3. Presidential Succession** If, at the time fixed for the beginning of the term of the President, the President-elect shall have died, the Vice President-elect shall become President. If a President shall not have been chosen before the time fixed for the beginning of his term, or if the President-elect shall have failed to qualify, then the Vice President-elect shall act as President until a President shall have qualified; and the Congress may by law provide for the case wherein neither a President-elect nor a Vice President-elect shall have qualified, declaring who shall then act as President, or the manner in which one who is to act shall be selected, and such person shall act accordingly until a President or Vice President shall have qualified.

**Section 4. Elections Decided by Congress** The Congress may by law provide for the case of the death of any of the persons from whom the House of Representatives may choose a President whenever the right of choice shall have devolved upon them, and for the case of the death of any of the persons from whom the Senate may choose a Vice President whenever the right of choice shall have devolved upon them.

**Section 5. Date of Implementation** ~~Sections 1 and 2 shall take effect on the 15th day of October following the ratification of this article.~~

**Section 6. Ratification Period** ~~This article shall be inoperative unless it shall have been ratified as an amendment to the Constitution by the legislatures of three fourths of the several states within seven years from the date of its submission.~~

## Twenty-first Amendment
*(1933) Repeal of Prohibition*

**Section 1. Repeal** The eighteenth article of amendment to the Constitution of the United States is hereby repealed.

**Section 2. State Laws** The transportation or importation into any state, territory, or possession of the United States for delivery or use therein of intoxicating liquors, in violation of the laws thereof, is hereby prohibited.

**Section 3. Ratification Period** ~~This article shall be inoperative unless it shall have been ratified as an amendment to the Constitution by conventions in the several states, as provided in the Constitution, within seven years from the date of the submission hereof to the states by the Congress.~~

## Twenty-second Amendment
*(1951) Presidential Tenure*

**Section 1. Two-Term Limit** No person shall be elected to the office of the President more than twice, and no person who has held the office of President, or acted as President, for more than two years of a term to which some other person was elect-



on January 3. Before this amendment, members of Congress who had been defeated in November continued to hold office until the following March. Such members were known as lame ducks.

**Twentieth Amendment, Section 3** If the President-elect dies before taking office, the Vice President-elect becomes President. If no President has been chosen by January 20 or if the elected candidate fails to qualify for office, the Vice President-elect acts as President, but only until a qualified President is chosen.

Finally, Congress has the power to choose a person to act as President if neither the President-elect nor Vice President-elect is qualified to take office.

**Twentieth Amendment, Section 4** Congress can pass laws in cases where a presidential candidate dies while an election is being decided in the House. Congress has similar power in cases where a candidate for Vice President dies while an election is being decided in the Senate.

**Twentieth Amendment, Section 5** Section 5 sets the date for the amendment to become effective.

**Twentieth Amendment, Section 6** Section 6 sets a time limit for ratification.

**Twenty-first Amendment, Section 1** The Eighteenth Amendment is repealed, making it legal to make and sell alcoholic beverages. Prohibition ended December 5, 1933.

**Twenty-first Amendment, Section 2** Each state was free to ban the making and selling of alcoholic drink within its borders. This section makes bringing liquor into a "dry" state a federal offense.

**Twenty-first Amendment, Section 3** Special state conventions were called to ratify this amendment. This is the only time an amendment was ratified by state conventions rather than state legislatures.

**Twenty-second Amendment, Section 1** Before Franklin Roosevelt became President, no President served more than two terms in office. Roosevelt broke with this custom and was elected to four terms. This amendment provides that no President may serve more than two terms. A President who has already served more than half of someone else's term can serve only one more full term. However, the amendment did not apply to Harry Truman, who had become President after Franklin Roosevelt's death in 1945.

**Twenty-second Amendment, Section 2** A seven-year time limit is set for ratification.

**Twenty-third Amendment, Section 1** This amendment gives residents of Washington, D.C., the right to vote in presidential elections. Until this amendment was adopted, people living in Washington, D.C., could not vote for President because the Constitution had made no provision for choosing electors from the nation's capital. Washington, D.C., has three electoral votes.

**Twenty-third Amendment, Section 2** Congress can pass laws to carry out this amendment.

**Twenty-fourth Amendment, Section 1** A ***poll tax*** is a tax on voters. This amendment bans poll taxes in national elections. Some states used poll taxes to keep African Americans from voting. In 1966, the Supreme Court struck down poll taxes in state elections, also.

**Twenty-fourth Amendment, Section 2** Congress can pass laws to carry out this amendment.

**Twenty-fifth Amendment, Section 1** If the President dies or resigns, the Vice President becomes President. This section clarifies Article 2, Section 1, Clause 6.

**Twenty-fifth Amendment, Section 2** When a Vice President takes over the office of President, he or she appoints a



ed President shall be elected to the office of the President more than once. ~~But this article shall not apply to any person holding the office of President when this article was proposed by the Congress, and shall not prevent any person who may be holding the office of President, or acting as President, during the term within which this article becomes operative from holding the office of President or acting as President during the remainder of such term.~~

**Section 2. Ratification Period** ~~This article shall be inoperative unless it shall have been ratified as an amendment to the Constitution by the legislatures of three fourths of the several states within seven years from the date of its submission to the states by the Congress.~~

## Twenty-third Amendment

*(1961) Presidential Electors for the District of Columbia*

**Section 1. Determining the Number of Electors** The district constituting the seat of government of the United States shall appoint in such manner as the Congress may direct:

A number of electors of President and Vice President equal to the whole number of senators and representatives in Congress to which the district would be entitled if it were a state, but in no event more than the least populous state; they shall be in addition to those appointed by the states, but they shall be considered, for the purposes of the election of President and Vice President, to be electors appointed by a state; and they shall meet in the district and perform such duties as provided by the twelfth article of amendment.

**Section 2. Enforcement** The Congress shall have power to enforce this article by appropriate legislation.

## Twenty-fourth Amendment

*(1964) Right to Vote in Federal Elections—Tax Payment*

**Section 1. Poll Tax Banned** The right of citizens of the United States to vote in any primary or other election for President or Vice President, for electors for President or Vice President, or for senator or representative in Congress, shall not be denied or abridged by the United States or any state by reason of failure to pay any poll tax or other tax.

**Section 2. Enforcement** The Congress shall have the power to enforce this article by appropriate legislation.

## Twenty-fifth Amendment

*(1967) Presidential Succession, Vice Presidential Vacancy, Presidential Inability*

**Section 1. President's Death or Resignation** In case of the removal of the President from office or of his death or resignation, the Vice President shall become President.

**Section 2. Vacancies in Vice Presidency** Whenever there is a vacancy in the office of the Vice President, the President shall nominate a Vice President who shall take office upon confirmation by a majority vote of both houses of Congress.

Vice President who must be approved by a majority vote of both houses of Congress. This section was first applied after Vice President Spiro Agnew resigned in 1973. President Richard Nixon appointed Gerald Ford as Vice President.

**Section 3. Disability of the President** Whenever the President transmits to the president *pro tempore* of the Senate and the Speaker of the House of Representatives his written declaration that he is unable to discharge the powers and duties of his office, and until he transmits to them a written declaration to the contrary, such powers and duties shall be discharged by the Vice President as acting President.

**Twenty-fifth Amendment, Section 3** If the President declares in writing that he or she is unable to perform the duties of office, the Vice President serves as acting President until the President recovers.

**Section 4. Vice President as Acting President** Whenever the Vice President and a majority of either the principal officers of the executive departments or of such other body as Congress may by law provide, transmit to the President *pro tempore* of the Senate and the Speaker of the House of Representatives their written declaration that the President is unable to discharge the powers and duties of his office, the Vice President shall immediately assume the powers and duties of the office as acting President.

Thereafter, when the President transmits to the president *pro tempore* of the Senate and the Speaker of the House of Representatives his written declaration that no inability exists, he shall resume the powers and duties of his office unless the Vice President and a majority of either the principal officers of the executive department or of such other body as Congress may by law provide, transmit within four days to the president *pro tempore* of the Senate and the Speaker of the House of Representatives their written declaration that the President is unable to discharge the powers and duties of his office. Thereupon Congress shall decide the issue, assembling within forty-eight hours for that purpose if not in session. If the Congress, within twenty-one days after receipt of the latter written declaration, or, if Congress is not in session, within twenty-one days after Congress is required to assemble, determines by two thirds vote of both Houses that the President is unable to discharge the powers and duties of his office, the Vice President shall continue to discharge the same as acting President; otherwise, the President shall resume the powers and duties of his office.

**Twenty-fifth Amendment, Section 4** Two Presidents, Woodrow Wilson and Dwight Eisenhower, have fallen gravely ill while in office. The Constitution contained no provision for this kind of emergency.

Section 3 provided that the President can inform Congress that he or she is too sick to perform the duties of office. However, if the President is unconscious or refuses to admit to a disabling illness, Section 4 provides that the Vice President and Cabinet may declare the President disabled. The Vice President becomes acting President until the President can return to the duties of office. In case of a disagreement between the President and the Vice President and Cabinet over the President's ability to perform the duties of office, Congress must decide the issue. A two-thirds vote of both houses is needed to find the President is disabled or unable to fulfill the duties of office.

## Twenty-sixth Amendment
### *(1971) Right to Vote—Age*

**Section 1. Lowering of Voting Age** The right of citizens of the United States, who are eighteen years of age or older, shall not be denied or abridged by the United States or by any state on account of age.

**Section 2. Enforcement** The Congress shall have the power to enforce this article by appropriate legislation.

**Twenty-sixth Amendment, Section 1** In 1970, Congress passed a law allowing 18-year-olds to vote. However, the Supreme Court decided that Congress could not set a minimum age for state elections. So this amendment was passed and ratified.

**Twenty-sixth Amendment, Section 2** Congress can pass laws to carry out this amendment.

## Twenty-seventh Amendment
### *(1992) Congressional Pay*

No law, varying the compensation for the services of the senators and representatives, shall take effect until an election of representatives shall have intervened.

**Twenty-seventh Amendment** If members of Congress vote themselves a pay increase, it cannot go into effect until after the next congressional election. This amendment was proposed in 1789. In 1992, Michigan became the thirty-eighth state to ratify it.

# Reviewing the Constitution

## SUMMARY OF THE CONSTITUTION

The Constitution is the set of fundamental laws of the United States. Drafted by the Constitutional Convention in 1787, the document was approved by all thirteen original states by 1790. Twenty-seven amendments have been added to the Constitution since then.

### ARTICLE I. Legislative Branch

The Congress constitutes the legislative, or law-making, branch of the federal government. The Congress consists of the Senate and the House of Representatives.

### ARTICLE II. Executive Branch

The President heads the executive branch, which enforces the laws of the federal government.

### ARTICLE III. Judicial Branch

A Supreme Court and other federal courts make up the judicial branch, which interprets the laws.

### ARTICLE IV. Relations Among the States

This article describes states' obligations toward each other and each other's residents, procedures for creating new states, and the obligations of the federal government toward the states.

### ARTICLE V. Provisions for Amendment

This article describes the procedure by which the Constitution may be amended.

### ARTICLE VI. National Debts, Supremacy of National Law, Oath

This article discusses the debts acquired prior to the Constitution, asserts the supremacy of national over state law, and requires oaths of state and federal officials.

### ARTICLE VII. Ratification of Constitution

This article states that the approval of nine of the thirteen states was necessary for ratification of the Constitution.

### AMENDMENTS

The 27 amendments to the Constitution include the Bill of Rights (amendments 1–10) plus other amendments on such topics as slavery, women's suffrage, and prohibition.

## COMPREHENSION: Articles I-III

1. Name the two bodies that constitute the legislative branch.
2. How are the seats in these two bodies divided among the states?
3. What powers does Congress have regarding taxes? Regarding trade?
4. What are the qualifications for President?
5. What are the President's military powers?
6. For what acts may the President be removed from office?
7. Which courts make up the national judicial branch?
8. How long do federal judges serve in office?
9. What kinds of cases do federal courts handle?

## COMPREHENSION: Articles IV-VII and Amendments

10. Do states have the power to discriminate against citizens of other states? Why or why not?
11. How does the Constitution ensure that fugitives cannot escape prosecution by fleeing from one state to another?
12. Which level of government is responsible for protecting the states against foreign invasion?
13. What must happen before Congress can propose an amendment to the Constitution?
14. How can the state legislatures propose an amendment to the Constitution?
15. What fraction of the states must approve an amendment before it becomes law?
16. Which is the supreme law of the land: state or federal law?
17. What oath must state and federal officials take?
18. Which amendments make up the Bill of Rights?
19. Which amendment prevents states from denying any citizen the "equal protection of the laws"?
20. Which amendment changed the minimum voting age? What is the minimum voting age?

## ANALYZING POLITICAL CARTOONS

1. This cartoon appeared during Bill Clinton's presidential administration. Clinton is the figure on the left. (a) What does the figure on the right represent? (b) How do you know?
2. Note the scene. (a) What activity are the two figures engaged in? (b) What happens if one figure lets go of the rope he is holding?
3. What comment does this cartoon make on the separation of powers and federal system of checks and balances?

## CRITICAL THINKING

1. ***Recognizing Cause and Effect*** Which Article and Section of the Constitution describe the infamous Three-Fifths Compromise? Why has that part of the Constitution been struck out?
2. ***Identifying Assumptions*** Why, do you think, are the qualifications for the Senate more strict than those for the House?
3. ***Drawing Conclusions*** Do the American voters directly elect the President? Explain your answer.
4. ***Expressing Problems Clearly*** Though the Constitution limits the terms of Congress and the President to a specific number of years, it does not set such a limit for federal judges. Why do you think this is so?
5. ***Demonstrating Reasoned Judgment*** Restate the First Amendment in your own words.
6. ***Making Comparisons*** Which constitutional amendment do you believe is the most important? Justify your choice.

### INTERNET ACTIVITY

***For your portfolio:***
**PREPARE A REPORT**

Access Prentice Hall's *America: Pathways to the Present site* at **www.Pathways.phschool.com** for the specific URL to complete the activity. Additional resources and related Web sites are also available.

Use the links to find the text of the United States Constitution and your state's constitution. Compare the Preamble of the national Constitution to your state's. How do they compare in spirit? In language? Write a brief report analyzing the similarities and differences between the two.

## ACTIVITIES

1. ***Organizing a Class Debate*** Hold a class debate on the following resolution: *Resolved, that the Constitution be amended to provide for a single, six-year term of office for the President, with no eligibility for reelection.* To organize the debate, divide the class into two equal teams. The debate should begin with a five-minute presentation by each team, after which team members are free to rebut the other team's arguments.
2. ***Reporting on Constitutional Issues*** Find a current newspaper story that concerns a constitutional issue, such as an important court case. Then prepare a five-minute oral report in which you (a) provide the background of the issue, (b) describe the outcome, and (c) analyze the importance of the issue.
3. ***Creating a Time Line*** Connect several sheets of construction paper end-to-end. Then create a time line showing all 27 amendments to the Constitution. For each amendment, include the year in which it was ratified and a brief description of the amendment.

| 1794 Whiskey Rebellion | 1803 Louisiana Purchase | 1812 War of 1812 begins | 1819 McCulloch v. Maryland | 1820 Missouri Compromise | 1823 Monroe Doctrine |
|---|---|---|---|---|---|

1790 · 1800 · 1810 · 1820 · 1830

# 4 The United States, 1789–1830

## SECTION PREVIEW

### Objectives

1. List the actions that helped define the powers of the federal government.
2. Describe important events in relations between the United States and the world.
3. Summarize the major domestic issues of the 1820s and early 1830s.
4. *Key Terms* Define: tariff; judicial review; Louisiana Purchase; Lewis and Clark expedition; War of 1812; Monroe Doctrine; depression; capital; Missouri Compromise; Indian Removal Act; Trail of Tears.

### Main Idea

In its first decades, the new United States sought to promote stable government and economic growth, encourage westward expansion, and avoid European conflicts.

### Reading Strategy

*Organizing Information* Create a concept map by drawing three large circles on a piece of paper and labeling each circle with a heading from the section. Add supporting information in smaller circles and draw lines connecting them to the large circles.

By 1790, all of the states had ratified the Constitution. Yet there still was disagreement about the powers of the national government. During the decades following the Revolutionary War, the powers of the national government, as well as the powers of the states, would become more defined.

## *Defining the Government's Powers*

An early order of business of the new United States government was to raise money. To do this, Congress used its constitutional right to "collect taxes, duties, imposts and excises" to pass two measures. First, in 1789 Congress had created a **tariff**— a tax on imported goods. Then in 1791 it made whiskey the target of a new excise. An excise is a tax on something manufactured within a country. The money raised by these two new taxes went to pay the expenses of the government and to repay creditors.

**The Powers of the President** In western Pennsylvania and other frontier areas, many people objected to paying an excise tax on whiskey. Whiskey was of critical importance to their economy. It was not just a traditional beverage, but also was one of the only products farmers could make from corn that could be transported to market without spoiling. Whiskey was even used as a kind of currency. In 1794, opposition to the whiskey tax became so strong that western Pennsylvania appeared to be in a state of rebellion against the authority of the federal government.

President Washington was determined to crush the resistance of the Whiskey Rebellion. He and others saw the rebellion as an opportunity to demonstrate the power of the federal government. Washington used his constitutional authority to gather an army of over 12,000 men, who marched into the Pittsburgh area. The rebellion soon dissolved. Washington's tough stand had demonstrated to American citizens and the rest of the world that the American government had the means and the will to force its citizens to obey its laws.

**The Powers of the Supreme Court** The Constitution did not clearly define the organization and role of the judicial branch of government. In 1803 the Supreme Court's Chief Justice, John Marshall, helped define the powers of the courts in the case *Marbury* v. *Madison.* The Supreme Court's decision in that case established the power of **judicial review,** by which federal courts had the authority to review laws and declare them unconstitutional if necessary.

**The Powers of Congress** The Supreme Court also helped define the powers of the national government when the State of Maryland tried to tax the Bank of the United States. The bank refused, claiming that the tax was unconstitutional, and in 1819 the dispute reached the Supreme Court. In the case of *McCulloch* v. *Maryland,* Chief Justice Marshall went to the heart of the issue by declaring the fine illegal and the bank itself constitutional. The powers of the federal government were greater than those spelled out in the Constitution, Marshall said. He based his argument on Article I, Section 8, which states that Congress has the right "to make all laws necessary and proper" for carrying out the powers granted it under the Constitution. Thus Congress had the power to create such a bank if it wished.

Furthermore, Marshall stressed that because the federal government had created the bank, no state had the power to tax it. "The power to tax is the power to destroy," he pointed out. No state could destroy by taxes what the federal government under the Constitution had created.

## *Turning Point: The Louisiana Purchase*

During this time, the United States also worked to define its position in the world. The young nation's primary goals were to encourage American expansion westward and to avoid becoming entangled in European conflicts.

A seemingly unstoppable wave of Americans continued to spread westward from the original thirteen states. President Thomas Jefferson decided to use the power of the national government to aid in the nation's expansion. He knew that to develop the West,

## *Notable* PRESIDENTS

### Thomas Jefferson

*"We hold these truths to be self-evident; that all men are created equal"*

—Declaration of Independence

Thomas Jefferson had impressive qualifications for the presidency. The Virginia-born planter and lawyer had not only drafted the Declaration of Independence, but had served as ambassador to France, Secretary of State, and Vice President. Jefferson promised a more democratic government, one that would leave most decisions in the hands of the people.

During his first term, from 1801 to 1805, Jefferson had considerable success. He trimmed the federal government's size and cost and acted as President in a simple, democratic manner. When given the chance to buy the Louisiana Territory from France, Jefferson approved the purchase. The Louisiana Purchase of 1803 considerably increased the country's size.

Jefferson failed, however, in his effort to reduce the power of the federal courts. Jefferson feared the power of federal judges, who were appointed for life and thus were beyond the reach of voters. The federal courts, led by Chief Justice John Marshall, gained power during Jefferson's administration.

Jefferson's second term, from 1805 to 1809, was far less successful than his first. His Embargo of 1807, which halted trade with European nations until they promised to stop harassing American ships on the high seas, was a disaster. Americans ignored the embargo and it was repealed before a disappointed Jefferson left office.

Jefferson died on July 4, 1826, the fiftieth anniversary of the Declaration of Independence. In his time, Jefferson's commitment to equality among white men, as well as his opposition to slavery, were brave and radical ideas. Today, Jefferson remains a puzzle for historians, for the author of some of the most eloquent words ever written about human freedom was himself the owner of slaves.

**Connecting to Today**

Find an issue in the news today in which one or both sides might use the famous phrase from the Declaration, "all men are created equal," to support its case. Then describe how the idea of equality affects that issue.

the Mississippi River, a vital trade route, had to be kept open.

**Napoleon and the French** When the French ruler Napoleon took over much of the Spanish land in the West, he gained control of the mouth of the Mississippi at New Orleans. The French used this control to extract large sums of money from American traders who had no choice but to travel the Mississippi.

Fearing this French control and Napoleon's ambitions, Jefferson in 1803 sent James Monroe to Paris to buy the city of New Orleans. Congress instructed Monroe along with the American minister in Paris, Robert Livingston, that they could pay up to $10 million for the land. What happened next was one of the most fateful events in American history.

Napoleon did in fact have ambitions to create a new French Empire in the Americas. When his attempt to quell a rebellion on the French island of Haiti failed, however, he quickly changed his mind. Napoleon refused to sell New Orleans to the United States but offered instead to sell *all* of the French claims known as Louisiana. Not daring to ask him to wait for weeks or months for an answer, Monroe and Livingston offered Napoleon $15 million for the **Louisiana Purchase.**† They desperately hoped that Congress and the President would support their decision.

When Jefferson heard of the agreement with the French, he was troubled. The Constitution did not mention the purchase of foreign lands. He was also wary of spending large amounts of public money. Jefferson overcame his doubts, however, and urged Congress to approve the sale. With the stroke of a pen, the Louisiana Purchase dramatically increased both the national debt and the size of the United States.

† The actual cost of Louisiana was $11.25 million. The remainder was for covering debts of France to United States citizens.

## TURNING POINT: *The Louisiana Purchase*

**The Louisiana Purchase was a historic step in the United States' westward expansion. While the nation's territorial expansion has ended, the westward movement of people continues to this day.**

**1803** *The United States buys the Louisiana Territory from France.*

**1846** *In a treaty with Britain, the United States gains claim to the Pacific Northwest.*

**1912** *Arizona and New Mexico, the newest of the "lower 48" states, join the Union.*

**1800** **1850** **1900** **1950** **2000**

**1845** *The United States annexes Texas.*

**1848** *Following the Mexican War, Mexico cedes southwestern territories to the United States.*

**1980** *For the first time, the mean population center of the United States lies west of the Mississippi River.*

As the time line on the previous page shows, the Louisiana Purchase was to have an enormous impact on the history of the United States.

**The Lewis and Clark Expedition** Congress agreed to finance Jefferson's call for an expedition to explore the area included in the Louisiana Purchase. Jefferson chose his private secretary, Meriwether Lewis, to lead the expedition. Lewis in turn chose William Clark as his companion officer.

The **Lewis and Clark expedition** began in the spring of 1804. Their goals were to search for river routes to the western ocean, make contact with the Native Americans living in the territory, and gather information about the region's natural resources. To help in this task, the expedition hired a French-Canadian fur trapper and his wife Sacajawea, a Shoshone Indian, as interpreters.

The expedition reached the Pacific Ocean late in 1805 and returned east by September 1806. The journey, that had lasted two years, four months, succeeded in filling in many of the details of the vast lands to the west. Additional information about the West was gathered by Zebulon Pike, who traveled as far west as the Rockies and then south into Spanish-held territory between 1806 and 1807.

## *Major Foreign Issues*

During Jefferson's first term, a brief peace settled on European nations. When the European

### Exploration of the American West, 1804–1807

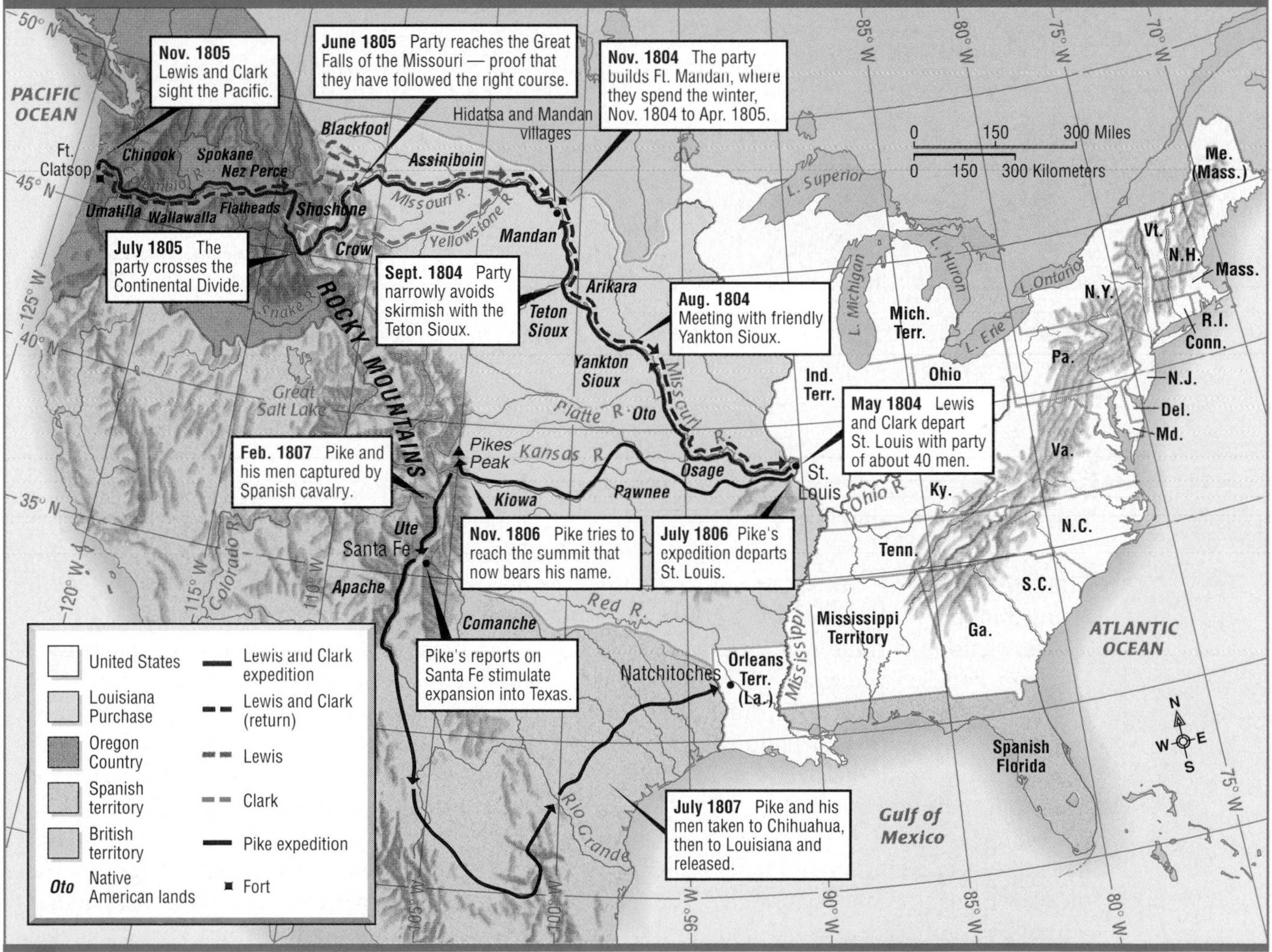

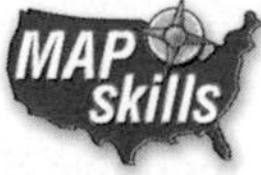


In their two-year expedition, Louis and Clark explored thousands of miles and collected information on the lands, peoples, and plant and animal species they encountered. Their crossing of the Continental Divide proved once and for all that a water route to the Pacific did not exist. ***Movement*** ***Study the map above. What difficulties did the exploring parties face?***

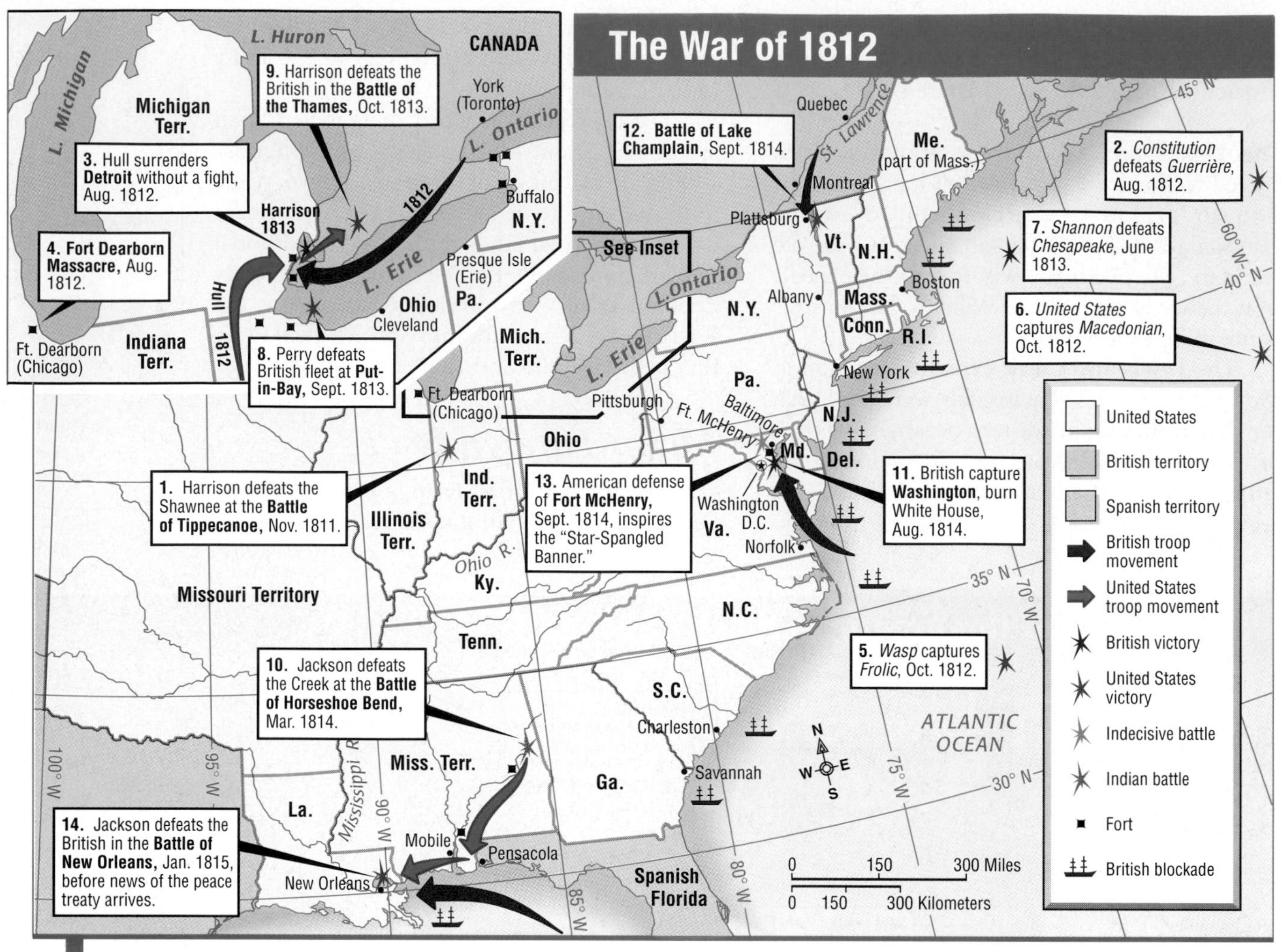


**MAP skills** Although the United States considered the War of 1812 a victory over England, in the end neither side gained nor lost any territory. ***Movement*** ***Why was the British naval blockade such a threat?***

wars resumed, so too did troubles between Europe and the United States.

**The Embargo of 1807** One such conflict resulted in the Embargo of 1807. (An embargo is a restriction on trade with other countries.) Jefferson imposed the embargo in response to British and French attacks on American trading ships. The two European nations had been at war for years, and each sought to choke off American trade with its rival.

Many Americans hated the embargo, which had little effect on Britain or France but crippled the New England economy, which depended on trade. The embargo also failed to resolve the nation's differences with Great Britain—differences that in 1812 would lead to war.

**The War of 1812** Great Britain had regularly interfered with American shipping. It had also encouraged Native Americans to resist American settlement of the West. In June 1812 Congress, urged on by President Madison, declared war on Great Britain. Thus began the **War of 1812.**

In many ways, the declaration of war was a foolhardy action. The United States had only a small army and navy and no foreign assistance. The nation would have to deal not only with the powerful British, but with Native Americans to the north and south who sought to block western expansion.

Despite these disadvantages, American military planners expected to strike a swift, damaging blow to the enemy by pushing into Canada and conquering that vast British territory. To their surprise, American invasion forces, poorly equipped and led, were beaten by the British in the summer of 1812. The United States did manage some land victories, against both the

United States Exports, 1800–1820

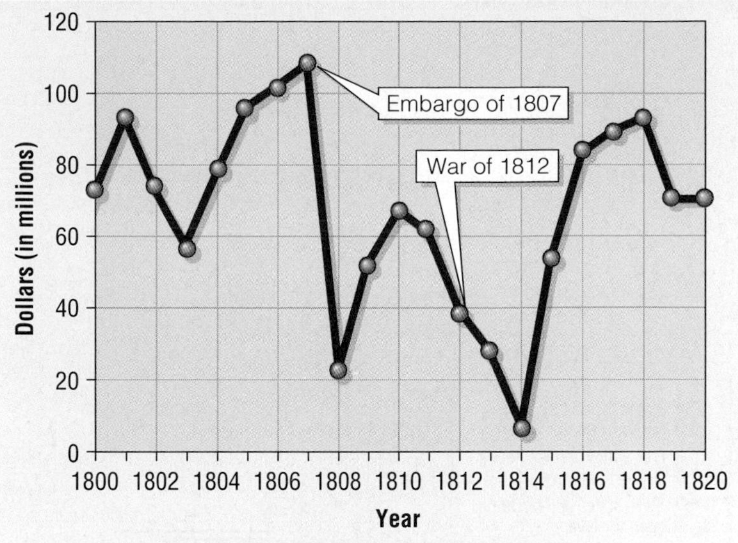


Source: *Historical Statistics of the United States, Colonial Times to 1970*

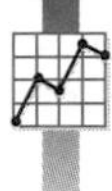

**Interpreting Graphs** The Embargo of 1807 sharply cut United States export trade. The British blockade during the War of 1812 nearly brought U.S. trade income to a halt. ***Economics* *What was the status of U.S. export income before the embargo? By how much had it decreased by 1814?***

British and the Native Americans. But these modest successes were not about to convince a power like Great Britain to give up.

Meanwhile, the British used their superior sea power to blockade the American coast, thereby cutting off its trade. (British ships outnumbered American vessels by about twenty to one.) British ships also sailed up the Chesapeake Bay and landed about 4,000 troops, who marched on Washington. On August 24, 1814, the enemy entered the capital and started fires that consumed the city. Even the Capitol and the White House were gutted by flames, and President Madison and his wife were forced to flee.

Still, both the British and the Americans recognized that this was a war no one wanted. On December 24, 1814, representatives of the two nations signed the Treaty of Ghent, ending the War of 1812. All the old boundaries between the United States and British territory in North America were restored.

Because of the slow communication of the times, fighting continued after the peace treaty had been signed. On January 8 a British force tried to take New Orleans. General Andrew Jackson and his force of soldiers and volunteers from all over the Mississippi Valley, including two battalions of free African Americans, defended the city. In a battle that lasted just over an hour, the British suffered 2,036 casualties; the Americans, 21. The Battle of New Orleans was a remarkable American victory, the greatest of the war. It made Jackson a national hero and finally gave the American people something to celebrate.

## *Major Domestic Issues*

With peace restored, the United States continued to work to secure its borders. In 1818 President James Monroe established the final boundary between the United States and Canada, and in 1821 the nation obtained Florida from Spain. In 1823 President Monroe issued the **Monroe Doctrine,** which warned other nations against any colonization efforts in the Americas.

**Postwar Boom, Then Panic** The American economy entered a period of growth and prosperity following the War of 1812. Encouraged by abundant credit made available by the nation's banks, Americans began moving westward at an increasing rate. These new settlers bought hundreds of thousands of acres of land, from Indiana to Louisiana, from the government. Meanwhile, American ships were busy carrying agricultural products and other goods to Europe. Everything seemed to be going well.

Then, in 1819, the first great **depression,** or severe economic downturn, struck the nation. It began when London banks demanded that banks in the United States pay money owed to them. The American banks in turn demanded the return of money they had loaned to the American public. People who had borrowed too much in the days of easy loans after 1815 were financially ruined, and the nation's supply of **capital** (wealth that can be used to produce goods and make money) dried up.

Although they had experienced hard times before, Americans had thought their economic problems were over for good. Shocked by the Panic of 1819, many began to think about ways of reforming the government to improve the performance of the economy.

**The Missouri Compromise** Still another dark cloud appeared on the horizon in 1819. In that year Congress took up the question of the admission of the state of Missouri to the United States. Should slavery be permitted in Missouri?

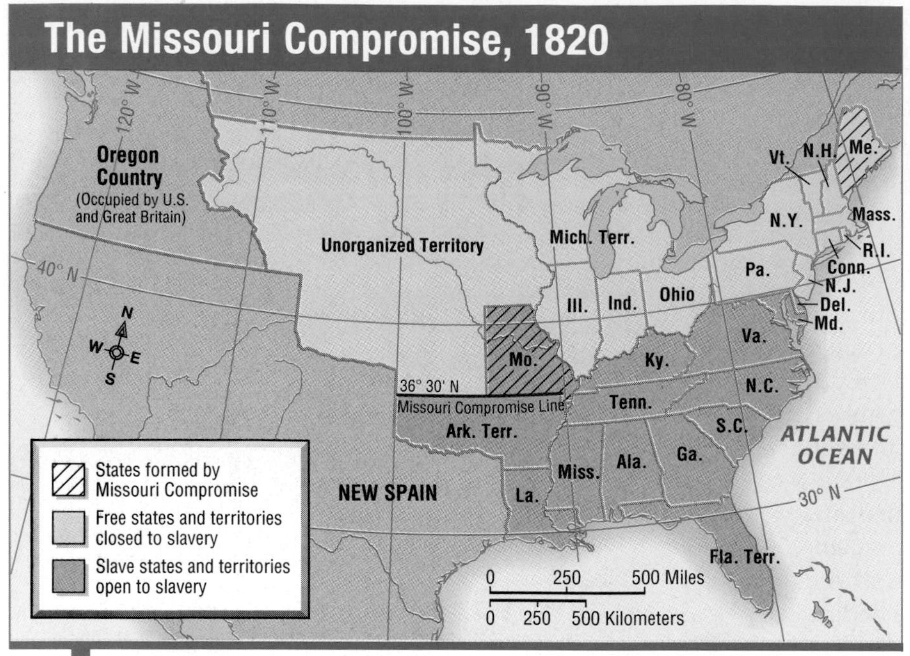


**MAP skills** Under the terms of the Missouri Compromise, Maine was admitted as a free state, Missouri was admitted as a slave state, and slavery was prohibited north of 36° 30′ N latitude. ***Region*** ***Which would cover more land under the compromise, new free states or new slave states?***

Southern members of Congress worried that if Congress forbade slavery in Missouri, it could do so elsewhere. Several northern members of Congress objected to admitting Missouri as a slave state. They were concerned not only about the liberty of African Americans, but also about the increase of power of the southern states in the national government.

After months of bitter debate, Congress reached what is now called the **Missouri Compromise.** It was signed into law in 1820. The Missouri Compromise had two main points: (1) Slavery would be permitted in Missouri; at the same time, Maine—once part of northern Massachusetts—would be admitted to the Union as a free, or nonslave, state. This arrangement kept the balance in the Senate between slave states and free states. (2) Furthermore, Congress agreed that as the United States expanded westward, states north of 36° 30′ N latitude would be free states, as the map above shows.

To Thomas Jefferson, still a keen observer of the national scene, the Missouri controversy "filled [him] with terror." Could compromises enable the United States to avoid confronting the issue of slavery indefinitely? As Jefferson had written earlier about the existence of slavery in a democratic republic: "I tremble for my country when I reflect that God is just: that His justice cannot sleep forever."

**The Nullification Crisis** State power versus the national government also was an issue when Congress passed a new tariff in 1828. The tariff put a high tax on imports in order to encourage manufacturing within the United States. Most manufacturers, however, were in the North, and southerners did not like paying higher prices for goods to help northerners make a profit. They termed the 1828 tariff the "Tariff of Abominations."

In 1832 South Carolina responded to the tariff by declaring the tariff "null, void, and no law, nor binding upon this State, its officers or citizens." In doing so, it raised a question known as nullification. Did a state have the right to nullify, or declare illegal, a law passed by Congress?

Although the national government threatened force, the conflict was eventually settled by compromise. Congress agreed to gradually reduce the tariff, and South Carolina canceled its Nullification Act. Yet the question of whether the states had the authority to reject acts of the federal government would return in the 1850s over the issue of slavery.

**Indian Relocation** In the 1820s, wealthy plantation owners were buying up much of the best cotton-farming land in the South. There were soaring profits to be made in cotton farming, and large and small planters alike wanted to expand westward into Native American lands. The Cherokee, Creek, Choctaw, Chickasaw, and Seminole peoples lived on about 100 million acres of fertile land in western parts of the Carolinas and in Georgia, Florida, Alabama, Mississippi, and Tennessee. These Native Americans were known as the "Five Civilized Tribes." The Cherokees, the Creek, and the Chickasaw practiced farming and led a settled lifestyle.

Just after Andrew Jackson took office as President, Georgia, Alabama, and Mississippi began to take control of the Indian lands within their states, breaking federal treaties. The President supported these actions. In 1830 he encouraged Congress's passage of the **Indian Removal Act,** which authorized him to give Native Americans land in parts of the Louisiana Purchase in exchange for lands taken from them in the East.

Under the Indian Removal Act and later acts, Jackson forcibly relocated about 100,000 members of the Five Tribes. For their 100 million acres of largely cultivated land, the Native Americans received about 32 million acres of prairie land in what is now Oklahoma.

The situation of the Cherokees was unique. More than any other Native American people, they had adopted white culture. Many Cherokees had taken up the farming methods, home styles, clothing styles, and religion of their white neighbors. Their government was modeled upon that of the United States. In 1821, a Cherokee named Sequoyah devised a writing system using symbols to represent syllables. In a very short time, nearly all the Cherokee people became literate.

In 1829, however, gold was found on Cherokee land in western Georgia. White miners and farmers flooded Indian lands. Violent confrontation between settlers and Indians seemed almost inevitable. The state seized about 9 million acres of Indian land that lay within its borders, violating treaties with the Cherokees.

The Cherokees sued. But Chief Justice John Marshall ruled that they had no legal standing in American courts, because the Cherokees were neither United States citizens nor a foreign country. The Cherokees also sought help in the United States Senate. When that failed, they issued a public statement, trying (unsuccessfully) to win the support of the American people.

In 1832, the Cherokees pursued their case again through a missionary from Vermont, Samuel Austin Worcester. This time, in *Worcester* v. *Georgia,* Chief Justice John Marshall ruled that Georgia had no authority over Cherokee territory. Georgia, however, simply ignored the ruling. President Jackson sided firmly with Georgia in defiance of the United States Supreme Court.

In 1838 the United States Army rounded up more than 15,000 Cherokees into camps, while settlers burned their homes and farms. Then, in a nightmare journey that the Cherokees called the **Trail of Tears,** men, women, and children, most on foot, began a 116-day forced march westward in groups of about 1,000.

The poorly organized and undersupplied effort took place in the fall and winter of 1838 and 1839. One out of every four Cherokees died of cold or disease, as troops refused to let them pause to rest. Afterward, the $6 million spent by the federal government to relocate the Cherokees was subtracted from the $9 million payment to the Cherokees for their lands.

## SECTION 4 REVIEW

### Comprehension

1. *Key Terms* Define: (a) tariff; (b) judicial review; (c) Louisiana Purchase; (d) Lewis and Clark expedition; (e) War of 1812; (f) Monroe Doctrine; (g) depression; (h) capital; (i) Missouri Compromise; (j) Indian Removal Act; (k) Trail of Tears.
2. *Summarizing the Main Idea* What gave Congress the authority to create excises and tariffs?
3. *Organizing Information* Create a cause-and-effect chart about one of the two major foreign policy events of the period, the Louisiana Purchase or the War of 1812.

### Critical Thinking

4. *Analyzing Time Lines* Review the time line at the start of the section. Why was the Missouri Compromise important to the nation's expansion?
5. *Identifying Central Issues* How did the establishment of the power of judicial review help define the power of the Supreme Court?

### Writing Activity

6. *Writing a Persuasive Essay* Write a newspaper editorial expressing an opinion about the nullification controversy. Your editorial should address the specific tariff issue, as well as the general question of a state's right to nullify a federal law.

| 1830 | 1836 | 1846 | 1848 | 1854 | 1860 | 1860 |
|---|---|---|---|---|---|---|
| Indian Removal Act | Republic of Texas is founded | Mexican War begins | Gold discovered in California | Kansas-Nebraska Act | Lincoln wins presidency | South Carolina secedes |

1830 1840 1850 1860

# 5 The United States, 1830–1860

## SECTION PREVIEW

### Objectives

1. Describe the nation's expansion westward in the early 1800s.
2. Summarize the effects of the Mexican War and the California Gold Rush.
3. Explain how growing sectional differences led to conflict between the North and South.
4. *Key Terms* Define: Indian Removal Act; manifest destiny; Texas War for Independence; annex; Mexican War; California Gold Rush; Kansas-Nebraska Act; secede.

### Main Idea

Between 1830 and 1860 the westward expansion of the United States continued, leading to a war with Mexico and new controversies over slavery.

### Reading Strategy

*Arranging Events in Order* As you read this section, create a time line of events. Write a statement for each event summarizing its impact on the United States.

*This cradle from around 1800 symbolizes the young nation's population growth.*

The American migration westward picked up steam in the early decades of the 1800s. Over mountains and rivers, across plains and deserts, a huge wave of Americans pressed westward in search of rich land and a rich life. As one European visitor explained:

> "We have now fairly turned our backs on the old world, and find ourselves in the very stream of emigration. Old America seems to be breaking up, and moving westward. . . . [W]e travel on this grand track . . . some with a view to a particular spot; close to a brother perhaps, or a friend, who has gone before, and reported well of the country. . . . Often the back of the poor pilgrim bears all his effects, and his wife follows, naked-footed, bending under the hopes of the family."
>
> —*Morris Birkbeck, Notes on a Journey in America, 1818*

The surge of people on the move was partly the result of a rapidly growing population. About 2.7 million people lived in the original thirteen states in 1780. By 1830, the population had grown to 12 million people in 24 states.

## *Westward Expansion*

Following the purchase of Louisiana from France in 1803, a few enterprising American trappers and traders began to explore the vast expanse of territory beyond the Mississippi River. The tales they brought back of a wild and beautiful land encouraged thousands of Americans to begin pushing westward into Texas, New Mexico, California, and Oregon.

Although many people found new opportunities in the West, they were invading land on which Native Americans and Mexicans had lived for centuries. The tensions that resulted

## Native American Land Transfer Before 1850

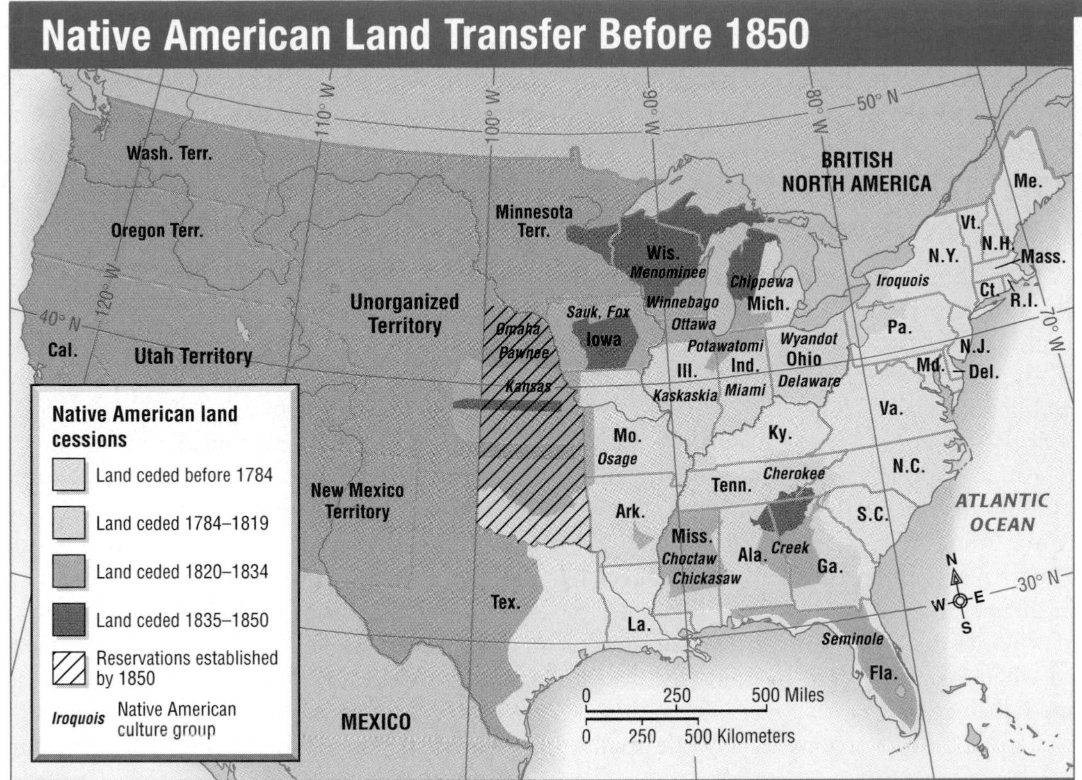

A map can only hint at the hardship and turmoil of being forced to move. For instance, the Seminole people fought United States troops well into the 1840s to avoid being removed from their homeland. Some remain in their homeland even today. ***Place*** ***Where is the Seminole homeland?***

from these encounters led to conflict with Native Americans. They also led to a war with Mexico.

**Native Americans Lose Their Lands** Throughout the early history of the United States, treaty upon treaty was made and broken with Native Americans. Then in 1830 Congress passed the **Indian Removal Act,** which allowed the President to move eastern Indian peoples to lands west of the Mississippi River. Over the next ten years, most eastern Native Americans were driven west.

One of the groups forced west during this time was the Cherokee. A prosperous group, the Cherokee had their own alphabet, newspaper, and written constitution. They were generally at peace with their white neighbors. But Georgia seized Cherokee land (an act later judged unconstitutional by the Supreme Court), and in 1837 and 1838, the United States Army gathered about 15,000 Cherokee and forced them to migrate west.

On this nightmare journey, which the Cherokee called the Trail of Tears, about one out of every four Cherokees died of exposure or disease. In an added outrage, the federal government charged the Cherokee $6 million for this forced removal.

Although the United States had proclaimed all land west of the 95th meridian to be "Indian Country," Native Americans would soon find that this offered them no protection. Thousands of white settlers continued to pour into Oregon, California, and other western regions. Meanwhile, the Bureau of Indian Affairs, created to deal with Native American issues, tried to "extinguish" Native American land claims through treaties and yearly payments. By the 1850s the government increasingly championed the idea of forcing Indians onto reservations.

**Manifest Destiny** Throughout the 1830s and 1840s, some Americans dreamed of a continental empire stretching from the Atlantic to the Pacific. They believed that the United States had a divine mission to spread liberty across the continent. A New York journalist named John L. O'Sullivan neatly captured this sense of mission when he coined the phrase **manifest destiny.** O'Sullivan claimed it was the nation's "manifest destiny" to overspread and to possess the whole of the continent.

One result of the belief in manifest destiny was the demand for control of the Oregon Country. In 1846 Great Britain and the United States reached a peaceful agreement that divided the Oregon Country along the 49th parallel. Another result of manifest destiny was the demand for land held by Mexico. That demand eventually led to war.

## *War with Mexico, Gold in California*

Conflict with Mexico began when, in 1835, the thousands of Americans who had settled in Texas united in the cause of independence from Mexico. In March 1836 they formally founded the Republic of Texas.

Mexico's dictator, General Antonio López de Santa Anna, responded by leading an army of several thousand men north to subdue the rebellion. Santa Anna won early victories at the Alamo, a fortress built on the ruins of a Spanish mission in San Antonio, and at Goliad. But the tide of the **Texas War for Independence** changed when 900 Texans led by Sam Houston regrouped at the San Jacinto River. There they surprised Santa Anna's troops in a battle that lasted just a matter of minutes. Victorious Texans forced Santa Anna to sign a treaty recognizing the Republic of Texas. Nine years later, in 1845, Texas was **annexed,** or added, to the United States, becoming the twenty-eighth state.

President Polk, however, wanted much more from Mexico than Texas. Polk had dreams of acquiring the entire territory stretching from Texas to the Pacific. In a final attempt to gain these lands without war, he sent an ambassador to Mexico City in 1845 with an offer to buy California and New Mexico for $30 million. But the Mexican government refused even to receive the ambassador, let alone consider his offer.

Determined to have his way, Polk sent some 2,000 American troops into southern Texas to support the American claim that the Rio Grande was the official American-Mexican border. When Mexican troops fired on American forces in early May 1846, Polk had the excuse he needed to seize Mexican lands. Expressing outrage at the loss of "American blood on American soil," the President pushed for an immediate declaration of war. Despite some opposition, Congress gave it to him on May 13, 1846.

The **Mexican War** ended in 1848 with a United States victory over its weaker neighbor. In the Treaty of Guadalupe Hidalgo in 1848, Mexico recognized the Rio Grande as the border of Texas. Mexico also gave up New Mexico and California—more than two fifths of Mexico's territory—to the United States.

Five years after the war ended, the Mexican government sold 30,000 square miles of what is now southern New Mexico and Arizona to the United States for $10 million. Together, the Mexican War and that purchase of land, known as the Gadsden Purchase, established the southern and western boundaries of the continental United States.

No event was more important in attracting settlers to the West than the discovery of gold at Sutter's Mill in California in January 1848. One Californian described how the news of the **California Gold Rush** affected his community:

**AMERICAN VOICES** "The blacksmith dropped his hammer, the carpenter his plane, the mason his trowel, the farmer his sickle, the baker his loaf, and the tapster his bottle. All were off for the mines, some on horses, some on carts, and some on crutches, and one went in a litter."

—*Walter Colton, mayor of Monterey, California*

## COMPARING PRIMARY SOURCES

### EXPANDING INTO MEXICAN TERRITORY

Strained relations between North and South intensified after the United States annexed vast Mexican territories in 1848.

#### Pro-Annexation

"The pretense that the annexation has been unrightful and unrighteous is wholly untrue and unjust to ourselves. If Texas became peopled with an American population, it was on the express invitation of Mexico herself. . . . What, then, can be more preposterous than all this clamor by Mexico against annexation as a violation of any rights of hers, any duties of ours?"

—*John L. O'Sullivan, editorial in* United States Magazine and Democratic Review, *1845*

#### Anti-Annexation

"They [who favor the Mexican War] have succeeded in robbing Mexico of her territory. And they are rejoicing over their success under the hypocritical pretense of a regard for peace. Had they not succeeded in robbing Mexico of the most important and most valuable part of her territory, many of those now loudest in their cries of favor for peace would be loudest and wildest for war. . . . We are not the people to rejoice. We ought rather blush and hang our heads for shame."

—*Frederick Douglass, editorial in* North Star, *March 17, 1848*

***ANALYZING VIEWPOINTS*** **Which writer do you think uses facts most effectively? Explain.**

Newspapers in the eastern United States were soon full of the news, and people touched by gold fever rushed west by the thousands. California had 14,000 residents in 1848. Within a year, 100,000 people were living in the state.

The Gold Rush had a tremendous impact on life in California. For Native Americans, the influx of thousands of white immigrants was a disaster. Newly arriving miners not only forced Native Americans to labor in the gold mines, but also spread illness. In 1848 there were roughly 150,000 Native Americans in California. By 1860 only 35,000 remained.

## Growing Sectional Differences

In the 1850s many Americans were convinced that the nation's two main sections, the North and the South, were moving in different directions. By 1860 those differences would prompt southern states to begin leaving the Union.

**exploring TECHNOLOGY** *A Textile Mill*

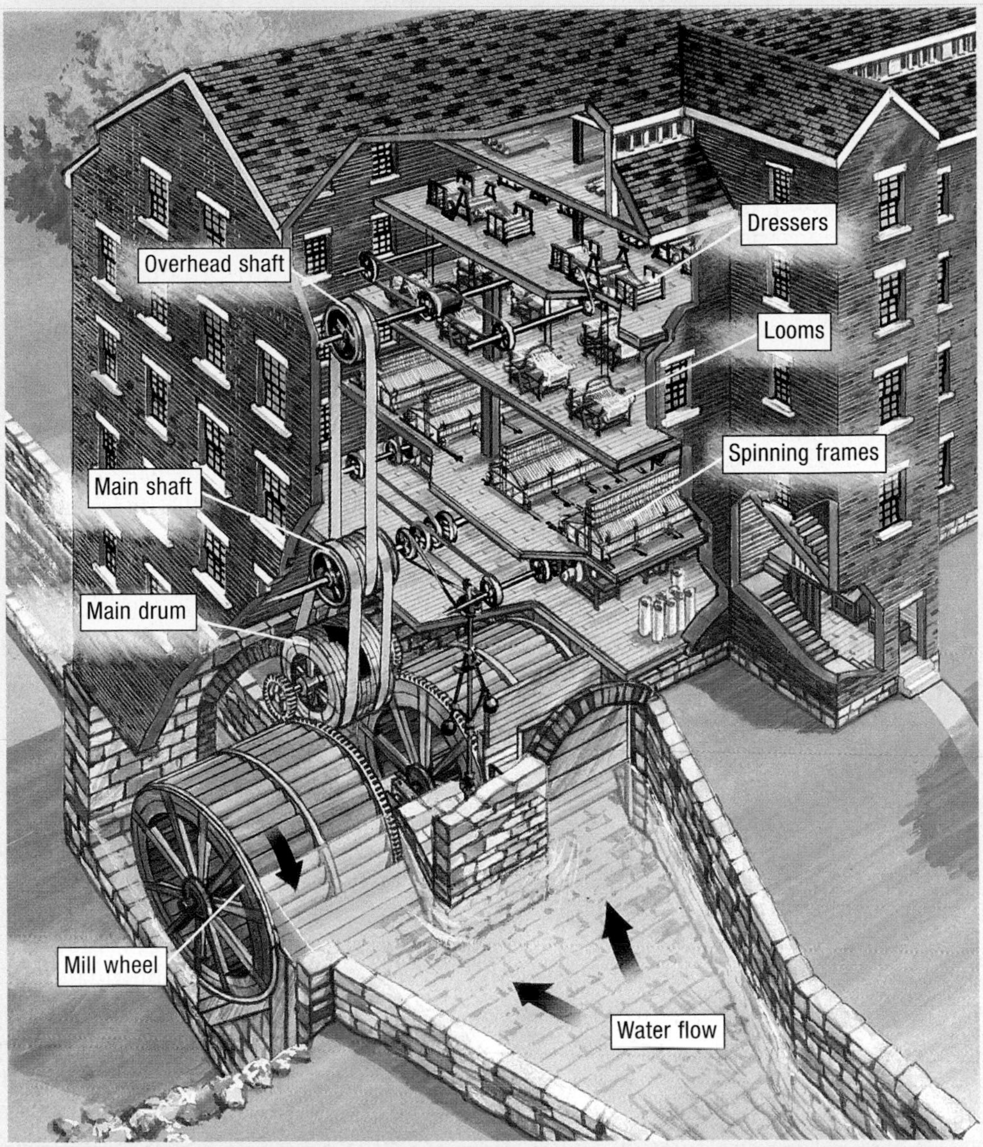

**New England mill builders adopted a system of belts to harness river power. On the first floor, cotton was combed; on the second floor it was spun into thread; on the third, thread was woven into cloth; and on the fourth, the cloth was dressed, or finished.** ***Geography* *Why was the Northeast a suitable place to build a factory?***

**Contrasting Economies** The North was becoming more and more urban and more industrial than the South. Its population, two and a half times as large as the population of the southern states, was becoming even larger and more diverse, as Irish and German immigrants crowded into swelling northern cities. Of the ten largest cities in the United States in 1860, nine were located in the North.

Like immigration, new technology had a heavier impact on the North than on the South. The biggest technological change was the appearance of the railroads. Developed in Great Britain in the 1820s, railroads were the quickest, most efficient form of transportation the world had yet known. Most of the new railroad track, some 70 percent, was in the North. The South had tracks, but southern farmers still tended to rely on water transportation to take their crops to market.

Like the railroad, another invention—the telegraph—also magnified differences between

## Fact Finder: Advantages and Disadvantages of the North and South

| | Northern States | Southern States |
|---|---|---|
| **Population** | 21.5 million | 9 million |
| **Railroad Mileage** | 21.7 thousand miles | 9 thousand miles |
| **Manufacturing** | | |
| Number of Factories | 110.1 thousand | 20.6 thousand |
| Number of Workers | 1.17 million | 111 thousand |
| Value of Products | $1.62 billion | $155 million |
| **Finance** | | |
| Bank Deposits | $207 million | $47 million |
| Specie | $56 million | $27 million |
| **Agriculture** | | |
| Corn (bushels) | 446 million | 280 million |
| Wheat (bushels) | 132 million | 31 million |
| Oats (bushels) | 150 million | 20 million |
| Cotton (bales) | 4 thousand | 5 million |
| Tobacco (pounds) | 229 million | 199 million |
| Rice (pounds) | 50 thousand | 187 million |
| **Livestock** | | |
| Horses | 4.2 million | 1.7 million |
| Donkeys and Mules | 300 thousand | 800 thousand |
| Milk Cows | 5.7 million | 2.7 million |
| Beef Cattle | 6.6 million | 7 million |
| Sheep | 16 million | 5 million |
| Swine | 16.3 million | 15.5 million |

Highlight indicates advantage

Source: *The American Heritage Picture History of the Civil War,* edited by Richard M. Ketchum

**Interpreting Tables** As war between the North and South threatened to erupt, a Northerner warned his southern friend, "You are bound to fail." ***Economics*** *Which advantages would allow the North to raise a larger, better equipped army than the South?*

North and South. This early form of electronic communication allowed people to send messages over wire by means of coded pulses of electricity. Because telegraph wires were strung along the ever-growing network of railroad tracks, the communications revolution in the North advanced more quickly than in the South.

Railroads and improved communications nourished the booming industries of the North. In 1860 the North had 110,000 factories, compared to 20,000 in the South, and produced $1.62 billion worth of goods, compared to the South's $155 million. In fact, in terms of numbers, the South outdid the North in only two notable ways. It had more cotton, and it had more enslaved people.

**Slavery and Westward Expansion** The Missouri Compromise of 1820 had established 36° 30' N latitude as the permanent boundary between free and slave states. But after the United States acquired a large part of Mexico in the Mexican War, Northerners were unwilling to accept this boundary. They feared that the new territory would be divided into several slave states. This would give the South a majority vote in the United States Senate and perhaps in the Electoral College as well.

Southerners were equally firm in insisting that the federal government had no business telling its free citizens they could not take their property to the territories if they wished. And property, after all, was what they considered enslaved people to be.

In 1850, with Americans streaming into California after gold, the federal government realized that some decision about slavery had to be made. President Fillmore and Congress struggled to put together a deal between the two rival parts of the nation. The package of laws they proposed was called the Compromise of 1850. It included these provisions:

(1) Congress would admit California as a free state.

(2) The people of the territories of New Mexico and Utah would decide for themselves whether to permit slavery.

(3) Congress would abolish the sale of enslaved people, but not slavery itself, in Washington, D.C.

(4) Congress would pass the Fugitive Slave Act, which ordered all American citizens to assist in the return of slaves who had escaped from their owners.

After months of debate, the Compromise of 1850 finally was passed. However, it brought only a temporary calm to the nation.

The question of slavery was renewed in 1854, when Congress considered statehood for the Kansas and Nebraska territories. Those against slavery stated that the Missouri Compromise prohibited either territory from becoming a slave state. But in 1854 Congress passed the **Kansas-Nebraska Act,** which said that the people in a territory should decide whether slavery would be allowed there. Antislavery organizations in the Northeast decided to take action by ensuring that antislavery forces were in the majority in the Kansas territory. At the same time, many proslavery settlers in Missouri crossed into Kansas to vote illegally in territorial elections.

By 1855 Kansas had two rival capitals. There was an antislavery capital at Topeka and a proslavery capital at Lecompton. The following year, tensions escalated into open violence, with murderous raids and counterraids throughout Kansas. The violence won the territory the grim nickname of "Bleeding Kansas."

**The Election of 1860** Differences over slavery split the Democratic party in 1860. With the Democrats divided, Abraham Lincoln, the candidate of the newly formed Republican party, won the presidency in that year's election. Lincoln's victory was a sectional one, however. His opposition to the spread of slavery meant that he did not win a single southern state.

Many Southerners, outraged that a President

### GOVERNMENT CONCEPTS

***federalism: a system of government in which power is divided between a central government and smaller governments***

▼ **The Historical Concept** A central issue in the debates of the 1850s was the proper division of authority between the federal government and the states. Northerners and Southerners disagreed over whether the federal government could limit slavery in the territories and whether states could secede from the Union.

▼ **The Concept Today** Through most of the 1900s, the federal government gained power at the expense of the states. In recent years, however, the states have become increasingly active and powerful in areas such as social welfare policy.

During the debate that led to the Compromise of 1850, all the great speakers of Congress had their say. Among them was Henry Clay, shown here in February 1850 as he warned that a failure to compromise would lead to "furious" and "bloody" war. ***Government What led Clay to propose a compromise?***

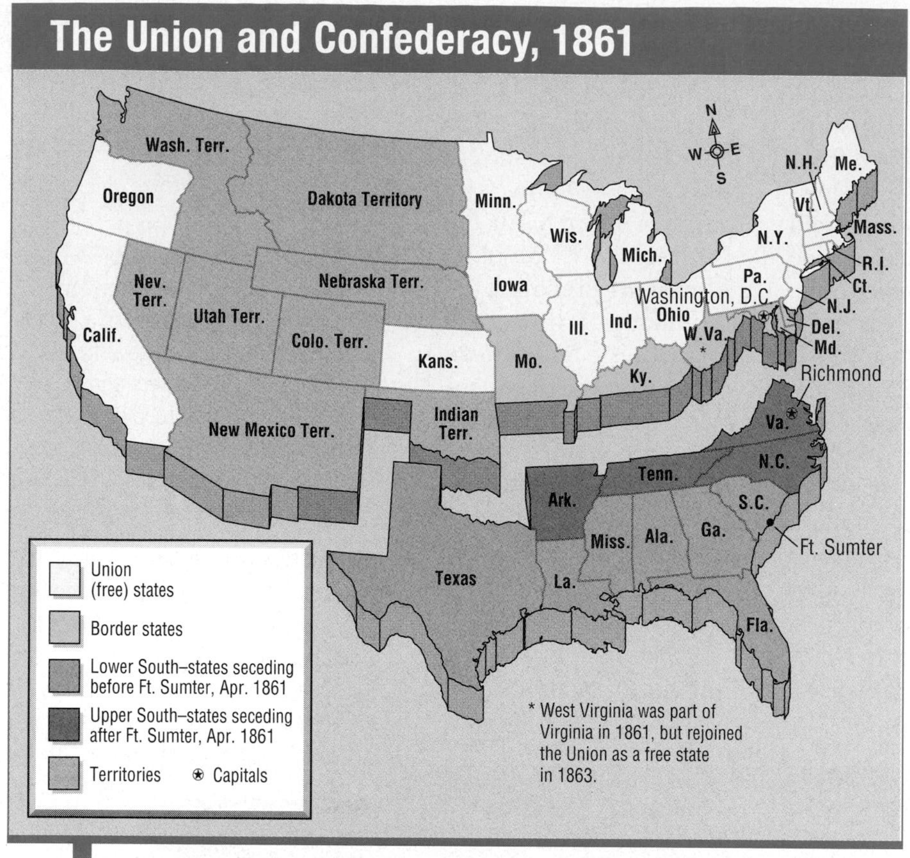

South Carolina was the first state to secede from the Union. It was soon joined by other states, however, making the Confederate republic one of the largest republics in the world. ***Place*** ***Name the states that seceded after the surrender of Fort Sumter.***

could be elected without southern votes, began to call for the South to **secede,** or withdraw from the Union. On December 20, 1860, South Carolina officially left the Union. Over the next few weeks, so did six other southern states. In early 1861, delegates from the seven seceding states created a new nation, the Confederate States of America. As their president they elected Jefferson Davis of Mississippi.

On March 4, 1861, Lincoln became President of a divided nation. On April 12, 1861, Confederate General P.G.T. Beauregard opened fire on Fort Sumter, a federal fort in the harbor of Charleston, South Carolina. Lincoln responded by calling for volunteers for federal troops. Southerners saw his action as an act of war against them. The Upper South states of Virginia, North Carolina, Tennessee, and Arkansas, now joined the Lower South in the Confederacy. Eighty-four years after it had declared its independence, the United States had come apart.

## SECTION 5 REVIEW

### Comprehension

1. *Key Terms* (a) Indian Removal Act; (b) manifest destiny; (c) Texas War for Independence; (d) annex; (e) Mexican War; (f) California Gold Rush; (g) Kansas-Nebraska Act; (h) secede.
2. *Summarizing the Main Idea* What caused the Mexican War?
3. *Organizing Information* Create a cause-and-effect chart of the events that led to the secession of the southern states.

### Critical Thinking

4. *Analyzing Time Lines* Review the time line at the start of the section. In your opinion, which event contributed most to the division of North and South?
5. *Drawing Conclusions* Why did the Kansas-Nebraska Act fail to solve the growing sectional division over slavery?

### Writing Activity

6. *Writing a Persuasive Essay* Write a newspaper editorial in response to the Indian Removal Act or the Trail of Tears. In your editorial, give your opinion on the government's action and explain what you think the government's policy should have been toward Native Americans.

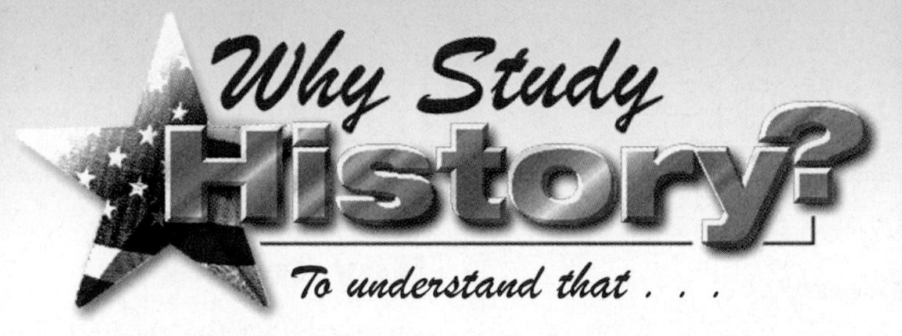


# The Debate over States' Rights Continues

A controversy over public land use focuses on states' rights, the issue that divided the United States in the mid-1800s.

*The debate over federal power led to violence in Kansas in 1856.*

Stunning snow-covered peaks and alpine flowers reward hikers in Colorado's Rocky Mountain National Park. Ancient Indian ruins and petrified sand dunes amaze visitors to Arizona's Canyon de Chelly. Mountains and seashore compete for tourists' attention in Maine's Acadia National Park. Each year, millions of people from all over the world experience the wilderness areas preserved in our national parks and monuments.

Who would imagine that these beautiful areas could be the subject of a bitter political struggle? Yet the federal government is caught in a tug-of-war with western states for control over public lands.

## The Impact Today

Throughout American history, there have been two different views on the relationship between the states and the federal government. One view, generally called states' rights, favors state power over national power. State governments are closer to the people than the federal government. This view holds, therefore, that state governments better reflect the people's wishes.

The other view favors national power over the states. Because the federal government represents all Americans, this view holds, it can deal better and more fairly with issues that affect the entire nation than states can.

Across the nation, states exercise their rights in areas such as education, public safety, and highway construction. In the West, many states are also trying to determine the use of public lands. The federal government owns more than 50 percent of land in the West, which it administers as national parks, forests, and monuments. The western states have no control over this land, even though it lies within their borders.

*President Clinton signs the bill creating the Grand Staircase-Escalante National Monument.*

A "sagebrush rebellion" has been brewing in the West for a number of years. Many westerners seek control over the public lands within their states and over laws regulating land use. The issue exploded in 1996, when President Clinton set aside 1.7 million acres of Utah's desert plateaus and canyonlands to create the Grand Staircase Escalante National Monument. Some Americans called the action a federal "land grab" that deprived Utah of its rights. Others applauded the move because it preserved a beautiful wilderness area.

## The Impact on You

What control, if any, should states have over the use of federal lands within their borders? Discuss the issue with a small group of classmates and see if your group can agree on a common position.

# Chapter 1 Review

## Chapter Summary

The major concepts of Chapter 1 are presented below. See also ***Guide to the Essentials of American History*** or ***Interactive Student Tutorial CD-ROM,*** which contains interactive review activities, time lines, helpful hints, and test practice.

***Reviewing the Main Ideas***

For thousands of years only Native Americans populated the Americas. After Europeans arrived, it was only a matter of several hundred years before they had pushed the Native Americans west, broken away from Great Britain, and created a new, strong, national government.

***Section 1: Exploration and the Colonial Era***

Columbus's journey to the Americas in 1492 began a wave of migration that would bring Europeans and Africans to the Americas.

***Section 2: The American Revolution***

The American colonies, demanding the right to rule themselves, fought and won their independence from Great Britain.

***Section 3: The Constitution***

When the Articles of Confederation could not provide a strong national government for the nation, the states drafted and approved the Constitution.

***Section 4: The United States, 1789–1830***

In its first decades, the new United States sought to promote stable government and economic growth, encourage westward expansion, and avoid European conflicts.

***Section 5: The United States, 1830–1860***

Between 1830 and 1860 the westward expansion of the United States continued, leading to a war with Mexico and new controversies over slavery.

Current controversy over the use of public land in western states focuses on states' rights, the issue that divided the United States in the mid-1800s and led to the Civil War.

## Key Terms

Use each of the terms below in a sentence that shows how it relates to either Native American, European, or West African culture.

1. First Continental Congress
2. mercantilism
3. veto
4. California Gold Rush
5. Middle Passage
6. Bill of Rights
7. Kansas-Nebraska Act
8. Declaration of Independence
9. secede
10. Louisiana Purchase
11. Revolutionary War
12. Monroe Doctrine

## Comprehension

1. What did Christopher Columbus, Juan Ponce de León, and Giovanni de Verrazano all have in common?
2. What role did tobacco play in the success of the Virginia colony?
3. Describe the Triangular Trade.
4. During the French and Indian War, why did most Native Americans fight on the side of the French?
5. What was the purpose of the Declaration of Independence?
6. How did President Washington react to the Whiskey Rebellion?
7. What was the outcome of the War of 1812?
8. What were the components of the Compromise of 1850?
9. How did Kansas get the nickname of "Bleeding Kansas"?

## Using Graphic Organizers

On a separate sheet of paper, copy the web organizer to organize the major developments in this nation's westward expansion. Provide at least two supporting details for each main idea.

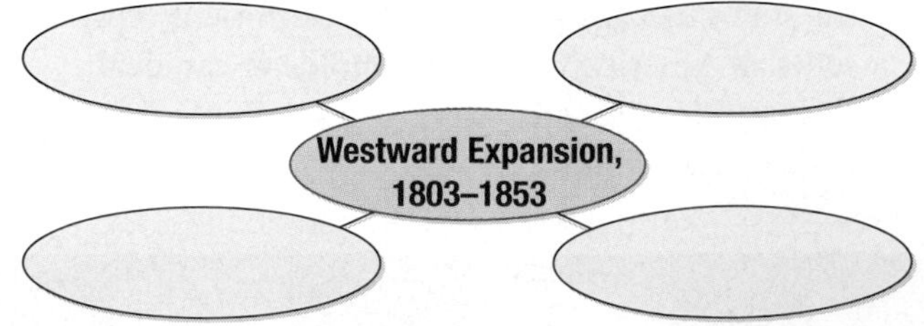

## Analyzing Political Cartoons ▶

1. This cartoon by Benjamin Franklin appeared in several versions during the American Revolution. (a) What do the segments of the snake represent? (b) How do you know?
2. What is the message of the cartoon?
3. What makes this an effective cartoon?

## Critical Thinking

1. ***Applying the Chapter Skill*** Use the map on page 26 to write three sentences. The first sentence should be a generalization of early economic activity in the New England Colonies, the second sentence should be a generalization of early economic activity in the Middle Colonies, and the third sentence should be a generalization of early economic activity in the Southern Colonies.
2. ***Predicting Consequences*** Thomas Jefferson said that the Missouri Compromise "filled [him] with terror." Why might Jefferson have viewed the compromise with such foreboding?
3. ***Identifying Alternatives*** Do you think that it would have been possible for the United States and Mexico to have resolved their differences in the 1840s without war? Why or why not?
4. ***Predicting Consequences*** What economic difficulties would the South have faced if Lincoln had allowed it to leave the Union peacefully?

### INTERNET ACTIVITY

***For your portfolio:***
**WRITE AN ESSAY**

Access Prentice Hall's *America: Pathways to the Present* site at **www.Pathways.phschool.com** for the specific URL to complete the activity. Additional resources and related Web sites are also available.

Read Thomas Jefferson's words on rights and the need for a bill of rights. Write an essay describing what rights you believe are inalienable and whether you think a bill of rights or other constitutional protections are necessary to guarantee them. Use examples from today's world in your argument.

## ANALYZING DOCUMENTS ◀▶ INTERPRETING DATA

Turn to the "American Voices" quotation on page 22.

1. Which statement best represents the meaning of the quotation? (a) Early settlers brought their domesticated animals with them on the ships. (b) In the years following 1626, many American colonies found a level of success. (c) Early towns concentrated on farming rather than on industry.
2. Which of the following describes the basis of the economy of colonial America? (a) factories (b) inventions (c) farming
3. ***Writing*** Do you think Samuel Maverick used an accurate measurement when describing the economy of the colonies? Explain your answer.

## Connecting to Today

***Essay Writing*** Lincoln was elected only by voters from the North. How might voters in other regions of the United States respond today if a President were elected on the basis of winning, for example, only the South and the West? What challenges might a President encounter if he or she had only regional appeal?

CHAPTER

# 2 The Civil War

## 1861–1865

## CHAPTER FOCUS

This chapter describes the years of the Civil War, the period between 1861 and 1865 when the nation divided and North fought South. The Confederate states of the South struggled to gain self-government and to retain a way of life supported by the institution of slavery. The Northern or Union states battled to maintain the unity of the nation.

*The Why Study History? page at the end of this chapter explores the ways in which Americans today remember the Civil War.*

▲

**VIEWING HISTORY**

Union soldiers practice a drill in this 1861 painting by James Walker. ***Culture*** ***What regional differences between the North and the South contributed to the Civil War?***

| July 21, 1861 *First Battle of Bull Run* | March 9, 1862 *Battle between the Merrimack and the Monitor* | April 6-7, 1862 *Battle of Shiloh* | September 17, 1862 *Battle of Antietam* |
|---|---|---|---|

1861 — 1862 — 1863

# 1 From Bull Run to Antietam

## SECTION PREVIEW

### Objectives

1 Describe the First Battle of Bull Run and the war preparations of the two sides.
2 Explain the importance of Union victories in the western part of the Confederacy during 1862.
3 Describe the outcome of the battles in the East during 1862.
4 *Key Terms* Define: Civil War; First Battle of Bull Run; casualty; war of attrition; shell; canister; Battle of Shiloh; Battle of Antietam.

### Main Idea

Bloody fighting during the first two years of the Civil War made it clear to both the North and the South that the struggle would be long and difficult.

### Reading Strategy

*Formulating Questions* Reread the Main Idea above. Then rewrite it as a question. As you read, take notes about events that help answer the question.

In May 1861, after the Upper South (Virginia, North Carolina, Tennessee, and Arkansas) seceded from the Union, the Confederate states shifted their capital from Montgomery, Alabama, to Richmond, Virginia. By July, some 35,000 northern volunteers were training in Washington, D.C., just 100 miles away. "Forward to Richmond!" urged a headline in the *New York Tribune*. Many Northerners believed that capturing the Confederate capital would bring a quick end to the **Civil War.** No one predicted that this war between the Northern (Union) and Southern (Confederate) states would last from 1861 to 1865.

## The First Battle of Bull Run

General Irvin McDowell, commander of the Union troops, was not yet ready to fight. Most of his troops, however, had volunteered for just 90 days and their term of service was nearly finished. "This is not an army," he told the President. "It will take a long time to make an army." Despite this warning, Lincoln ordered his general into action.

On July 16, McDowell marched his poorly prepared army into Virginia. His objective was the town of Manassas, an important railroad junction southwest of Washington. Opposing him was a smaller Confederate force under General P.G.T. Beauregard, the officer who had captured Fort Sumter. The Confederates were camped along Bull Run, a stream that passed about four miles north of Manassas.

*More than 90 percent of all battle wounds in the Civil War were caused by bullets such as the newer, more accurate type shown here.*

The Union army took nearly four days to march 25 miles to Manassas. The soldiers' lack of training contributed to their slow pace. McDowell later explained, "They stopped every moment to pick blackberries or get water. . . . They would not keep in the ranks, order as much as you pleased."

Beauregard had no trouble keeping track of McDowell's progress. Accompanying the troops was a huge crowd of reporters, politicians, and other civilians from Washington, planning to picnic and watch the battle.

McDowell's delays allowed Beauregard to strengthen his army. Some 11,000 additional Confederate troops were packed into freight cars and sped to the scene. (This was the first

## COMPARING PRIMARY SOURCES

### THE AIMS OF THE CIVIL WAR

Throughout the years of quarreling between North and South, Southerners protested repeatedly that Northerners were trampling on their rights, including the right to own slaves as property.

| The Aims of the South | The Aims of the North |
|---|---|
| "We have vainly endeavored to secure tranquillity and obtain respect for the rights to which we were entitled. . . . If . . . the integrity of our territory and jurisdiction [legal authority] be assailed [attacked], it will but remain for us with firm resolve to appeal to arms." —*President Jefferson Davis, Inaugural Address, February 18, 1861* | "This war is not waged upon our part in any spirit of oppression, nor for any purpose of conquest or subjugation, nor purpose of overthrowing or interfering with the rights or established institutions of those [seceding] States, but to defend and maintain the supremacy of the Constitution and to preserve the Union." —*House of Representatives, Crittenden Resolution, July 25, 1861* |

***ANALYZING VIEWPOINTS*** **How did the war aims of each side reflect their quarrel, as described above?**

time in the history of warfare that troops were moved by train.) When McDowell finally attacked on July 21, he faced a force nearly the size of his own. Beyond the Confederate lines lay the road to Richmond.

After hours of hard fighting, the Union soldiers appeared to be winning. Their slow advance pushed the Southerners back. However, some Virginia soldiers commanded by General Thomas Jackson refused to give up. Seeing this, another Confederate officer rallied his retreating troops, shouting: "Look! There is Jackson standing like a stone wall! Rally behind the Virginians!" The Union advance was stopped, and "Stonewall" Jackson had earned his nickname.

Tired and discouraged, in late afternoon the Union forces began to fall back. Then a trainload of fresh Confederate troops arrived and launched a counterattack. The orderly Union retreat fell apart. Hundreds of soldiers dropped their weapons and started to run north. They stampeded into the sightseers who had followed them to the battlefield.

As the army disintegrated, soldiers and civilians were caught in a tangle of carriages, wagons, and horses on the narrow road. Terrified that the Confederate troops would catch them, they ran headlong for the safety of Washington. The Confederates, however, were also disorganized and exhausted, and they did not pursue the Union army.

The first major battle of the Civil War thus ended. It became known as the **First Battle of Bull Run,** because the following year another bloody battle occurred at almost exactly the same site.†

Compared to what would come, this battle was not a huge action. About 35,000 were involved on each side. The Union suffered about 2,900 **casualties,** the military term for those killed, wounded, captured, or missing in action. Confederate casualties were fewer than 2,000. Later battles would prove much more costly.

## *Preparing for War*

Bull Run caused some Americans on both sides to suspect that winning the war might not be easy. "The fat is in the fire now," wrote Lincoln's private secretary. "The preparations for the war will be continued with increased vigor by the Government." Congress quickly authorized the President to raise a million three-year volunteers. In Richmond, a clerk in the Confederate War Department began to worry, "We are resting on our oars, while the enemy is drilling and equipping 500,000 or 600,000 men."

**Strengths and Weaknesses** In several respects, the North was much better prepared for war than was the South. For example, the North had more than double the South's miles of railroad track. This made the movement of troops, food, and supplies quicker and easier in the North. More than twice as many factories were in the North as in the South. The North was thus better able to produce the guns, ammunition, shoes, and other items it needed for its army. The North's economy was well balanced between farming and industry, and the North had far more money in its banks than the South. Finally, the North already had a functioning government and, although they were small, an existing army and navy.

† Many Civil War battles have two names, one given by the South and the other given by the North. The South tended to connect a battle with the nearest town, the North with some physical feature close by the battlefield.

Most importantly, two thirds of the nation's population lived in Union states. This made more men available to the Union army, but allowed for a sufficient labor force to remain behind for farm and factory work.

The Confederates had some advantages, too. Because seven of the nation's eight military colleges were in the South, a majority of the nation's trained officers were Southerners. When the war began, most of these officers sided with the Confederacy. In addition, the southern army did not need to initiate any military action to win the war. All they needed to do was maintain a defensive position and keep from being beaten. In contrast, to restore unity to the nation the North would have to attack and conquer the South. Southerners had the added advantage of fighting to preserve their way of life and, they believed, their right to self-government.

**Union Military Strategies** After the fall of Fort Sumter, President Lincoln ordered a naval blockade of the seceded states. By shutting down the South's ports along the Atlantic Coast and the Gulf of Mexico, Lincoln hoped to keep the South from shipping its cotton to Europe. He also wanted to prevent Southerners from importing the manufactured goods they needed.

Lincoln's blockade was part of a strategy developed by General Winfield Scott, the hero of the Mexican War and commander of all U.S. troops in 1861. The general realized it would take a long time to raise and train an army that was big enough and strong enough to invade the South successfully. Instead, he proposed to choke off the Confederacy with the blockade and to use troops and gunboats to gain control of the Mississippi River. Scott believed this would pressure the South to seek peace and would restore the nation without a bloody war.

Northern newspapers sneered at Scott's strategy. They scornfully named it the Anaconda Plan, after a type of snake that coils around its victims and crushes them to death. Despite the Union defeat at Bull Run, political pressure for action and a quick victory remained strong in 1861. This public clamor for results led to several more attempts to capture Richmond.

**Confederate War Strategies** The South's basic war plan was to prepare and wait. Many Southerners hoped that Lincoln would let them go in peace. "All we ask is to be let alone," announced Confederate president Jefferson Davis, shortly after secession. He planned for a defensive war.

Southern strategy called for a **war of attrition.** In this type of war, one side inflicts continuous losses on the enemy in order to wear down its strength. Southerners counted on their forces being able to turn back Union attacks until Northerners lost the will to fight. However, this strategy did not take into account the North's tremendous advantage in the resources needed to fight a long war. In the end, it was the North that waged a war of attrition against the South.

Southern strategy in another area also backfired. The South produced some 75 percent of the world's cotton. Historically, much of this cotton supplied the textile mills of Great Britain and France. However, Confederate leaders convinced most southern planters to stop exporting cotton. The South believed that the sudden loss of southern cotton would cause problems for the textile industries in Great Britain and France. They hoped that European industrial leaders would then pressure their governments to help the South gain its independence in exchange for restoring the flow of cotton.

Gunboats gave Union forces a great advantage in river warfare. One Union naval commander was reported to have preached a Sunday sermon to his sailors in which he said, "Let not your heart be troubled. Ye believe in God; believe also in gunboats." ***Geography*** ***Why did the Union want to control the Mississippi River?***

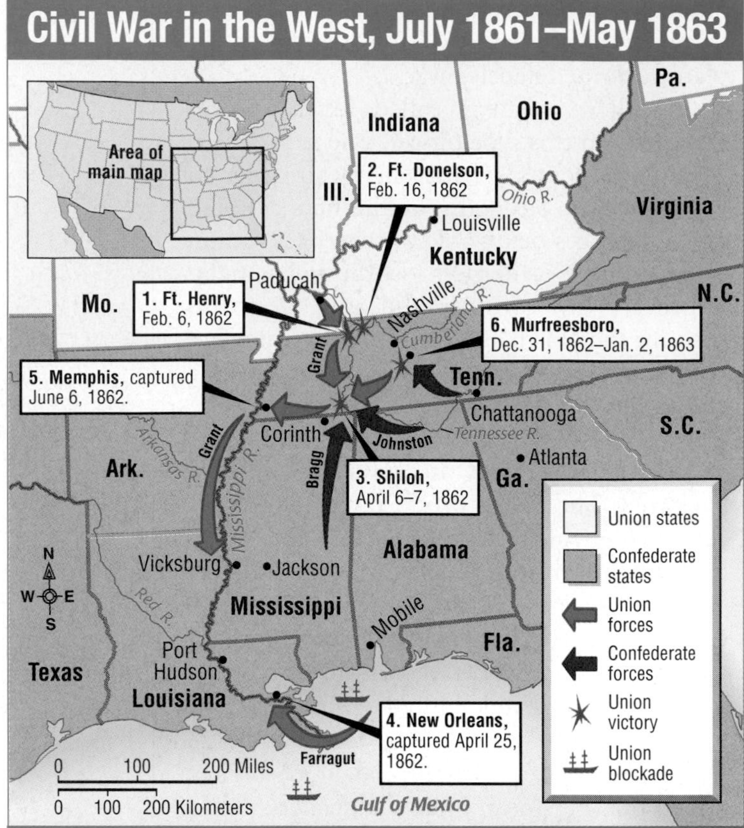


**MAP skills** Union generals in the West focused their attention on the Mississippi River. "That Mississippi ruins us, if lost," worried southern observer Mary Boykin Chesnut in 1862. ***Place*** ***What two key cities on the Mississippi had the Union captured by the summer of 1862?***

Instead the Europeans turned to India and Egypt for their cotton. By the time Southerners recognized the failure of this strategy, the Union blockade had become so effective that little cotton could get out. With no income from cotton exports, the South lost the money it needed to buy guns and maintain its armies.

**Tactics and Technology** For generations, European commanders had fought battles by concentrating their forces, assaulting a position, and driving the enemy away. Cannons and muskets in early times were neither accurate nor capable of repeating fire very rapidly. Generals relied on masses of charging troops to overwhelm the enemy.

**Main Idea CONNECTIONS**

*Why did Civil War generals use outdated tactics?*

Most generals in the Civil War had been trained in these methods. Many on both sides had seen such tactics work well in the Mexican War. However, the technology that soldiers faced in the 1860s was much improved over what these officers had faced on the battlefields of the 1840s.

By the Civil War, gun makers knew that bullet-shaped ammunition drifted less as it flew through the air than a round ball, the older type of ammunition. They had also learned that rifling, a spiral groove cut on the inside of a gun barrel, would make a fired bullet pick up spin, causing it to travel farther and straighter.

Older muskets, which had no rifling, were accurate only to about 100 yards. Bullets fired from rifles, as the new guns were called, hit targets at 500 yards. In addition, they could be reloaded and fired much faster.

Improvements in artillery were just as deadly. Instead of relying only on iron cannon balls, gunners could also fire **shells,** devices that exploded in the air or when they hit something. Artillery often fired **canister,** a special type of shell filled with bullets. This turned cannons into giant shotguns.

Thousands of soldiers went to their deaths by following orders to cross open fields against such weapons. Commanders on both sides, however, were slow to recognize that traditional methods exposed their troops to slaughter.

## *War in the West*

After the disaster at Bull Run, President Lincoln named General George McClellan to build and command a new army. While McClellan was involved with this task, Union forces in the west invaded the Confederacy.

The states of Arkansas, Louisiana, Mississippi, and Tennessee held the key to control of the Mississippi River. Although some battles did take place farther west, the fighting in these four states is generally referred to as the "war in the West."

The most successful Union forces in the West were led by General Ulysses S. Grant. A graduate of the United States Military Academy at West Point, Grant had left the military after serving in the Mexican War. Over the next several years he tried and failed at a number of civilian jobs. After the fall of Fort Sumter, Grant organized a group of Illinois volunteers and became a colonel. His success at organizing and training troops caused Lincoln to promote him to general. He was assigned to command the Union forces based in Paducah, Kentucky, where the Ohio and Tennessee rivers meet.

**Forts Henry and Donelson** In February 1862, Grant advanced south along the Tennessee River with more than 15,000 troops and several gunboats. Powered by steam and built to navigate shallow bodies of water, these gunboats were basically small floating forts fitted with cannons.

Grant's objectives were Fort Henry and Fort Donelson, located just over the border in the Confederate state of Tennessee. The forts protected the Tennessee and Cumberland rivers, important water routes into the western Confederacy.

On February 6 the Union gunboats pounded Fort Henry into surrender before Grant's troops arrived. The general then marched his army east and attacked Fort Donelson on the Cumberland River. Following three days of shelling by the gunboats, Fort Donelson also gave up.

The battles caused a sensation in both North and South. Northerners rejoiced that at last the Union had an important victory. Southerners worried that loss of the forts exposed much of the region to attack. Indeed Nashville soon fell to another Union army. Meanwhile, Grant and some 42,000 soldiers pushed farther south along the Tennessee River to threaten Mississippi and Alabama.

**The Battle of Shiloh** In late March, Grant's army neared Corinth, Mississippi, an important railroad center near the Tennessee-Mississippi border. Confederate general Albert Sidney Johnston gathered troops from throughout the region to halt the Union advance. As Grant's forces approached, Johnston had assembled an army of about 40,000 to oppose them.

Grant, however, stopped at Pittsburg Landing, Tennessee, a small river town about 20 miles north of Corinth. Here he waited for more Union troops that General Don Carlos Buell was bringing from Nashville. Johnston decided to launch an attack against Grant's army before it got any larger.

On April 6, 1862, Johnston's Confederates surprised some of Grant's troops, who were camped at Shiloh Church outside Pittsburg Landing. Fighting quickly spread along a battle line six miles long. By the end of the first day of the **Battle of Shiloh,** the Southerners had driven the Union forces back, nearly into the Tennessee River. That night, some of Grant's officers advised a retreat before the Confederates could renew their attack the next day. "Retreat?" Grant scoffed. "No. I propose to attack at daylight and whip them."

Fortunately for Grant, Buell's troops arrived during the night. The next day, Union forces counterattacked and defeated Johnston's army. However, the cost to both sides was high. The Union suffered more than 13,000 casualties, the Confederates nearly 11,000. Johnston was among the Confederate dead.

Shiloh was the bloodiest single battle that had taken place on the North American continent to that time. It shattered on both sides any remaining illusions about the glory of war and destroyed northern hopes that the Confederacy would be soon defeated.

*U.S. Grant demanded "unconditional and immediate surrender" of Fort Donelson, earning himself the nickname "Unconditional Surrender Grant."*

**Action on the Mississippi** While Grant advanced into the Confederacy from the north, Union forces were also moving up the Mississippi River from the Gulf of Mexico. In late April 1862, a naval squadron commanded by David Farragut fought its way past two forts in the Louisiana swamps to force the surrender of New Orleans. Pushing upriver, Farragut soon captured Baton Rouge, Louisiana, and Natchez, Mississippi. In her diary, Southerner Mary Chesnut voiced her concerns about the Confederate losses:

**"Battle after battle—disaster after disaster. How can I sleep? The power they are bringing to bear against our country is tremendous. . . . Are we not cut in two? . . . The reality is hideous."**

—*Mary Chesnut*

On June 6, the Union navy seized Memphis, Tennessee. Only two major posts on the Mississippi River now remained in

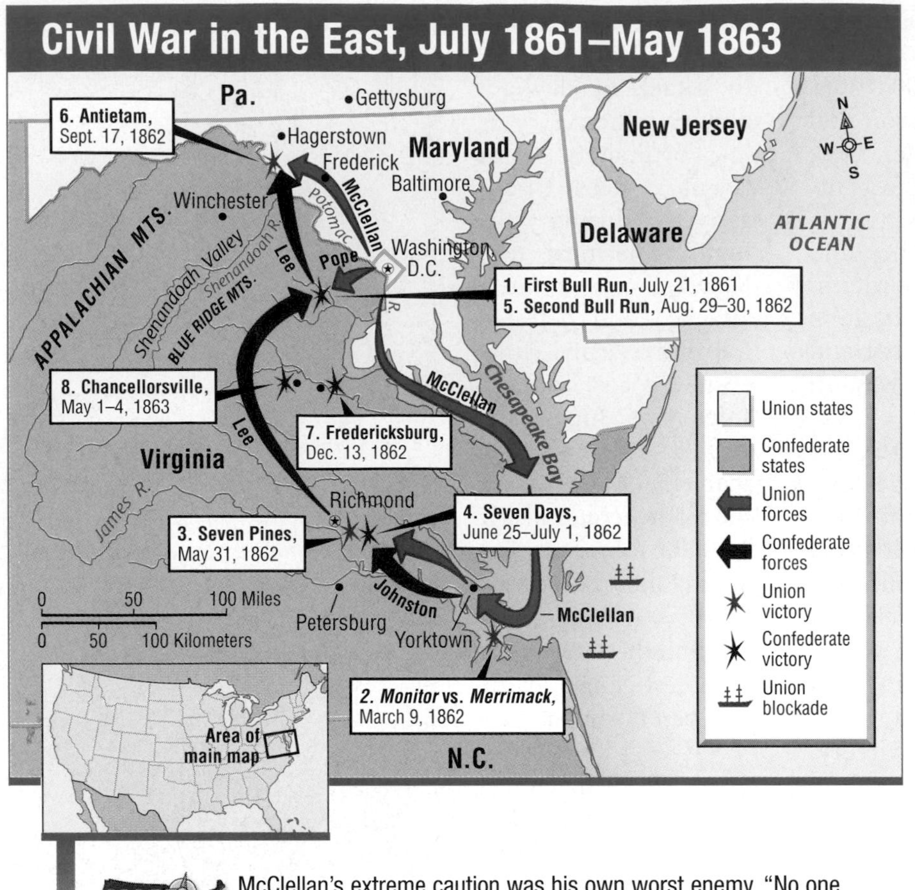


**MAP skills** McClellan's extreme caution was his own worst enemy. "No one but McClellan would have hesitated to attack," said Confederate general Joseph Johnston during McClellan's slow advance toward Richmond before the Seven Days' Battles. ***Movement*** ***What action did Lee take following the Seven Days' Battles?***

Confederate hands. These were Vicksburg, Mississippi, and Port Hudson, Louisiana. If northern forces could find some way to capture them, the entire Mississippi River valley would finally be under Union control. The Confederacy would be split into two parts.

## *War in the East*

While the Union army marched through the western Confederate states, Union warships maintained the blockade of Virginia's coast. The Confederates, however, had developed a secret weapon with which to fight the blockade. In early March 1862, a Confederate ship that resembled a floating barn roof steamed out of the James River. When the Union warships guarding the mouth of the river opened fire on the strange-looking vessel, their cannon shots bounced off it like rubber balls. In hours, the Confederate vessel destroyed or heavily damaged three of the most powerful ships in the Union navy.

**The *Monitor* and the *Merrimack*** Southerners had created the strange-looking vessel by bolting iron plates to an old wooden steamship called the *Merrimack.* (Although the ship was renamed the *Virginia,* it is still called the *Merrimack* in most historical accounts.) The Union's wooden navy was no match for this powerful ironclad warship. Northern leaders feared the new weapon might soon break apart the entire blockade.

Fortunately for the Union, early reports of the Confederates' work on the *Merrimack* had reached the North. Reacting to the threat of a powerful weapon, President Lincoln had ordered construction of a similar Union warship. It was made entirely of iron and was rushed to completion in about 100 days. Named the *Monitor,* it looked like a tin can on a raft.

On March 9, the *Monitor* arrived off the Virginia coast to confront the Confederate ironclad. Neither ship was able to do serious damage to the other. After several hours of fighting, the *Merrimack* finally withdrew.

The two ships never met again. The Confederates blew up the *Merrimack* at its base in Norfolk, Virginia, in May 1862. The following December the *Monitor* sank in a storm. Their one encounter, however, changed the history of warfare. In a single day, the wooden navies of the world became obsolete.

**The Peninsular Campaign** The Confederates destroyed the *Merrimack* because they feared it would fall into Union hands. They knew that Union general George McClellan had landed troops nearby, launching the North's second attempt to capture Richmond.

At 36 years old, McClellan was young for a commanding general. However, he was an outstanding organizer and an excellent strategist. In addition, he was well liked by his troops. McClellan's great weakness was that he was very cautious and never seemed quite ready to fight. This irritated Lincoln and other northern leaders, who were impatient to avenge the Union's defeat at Bull Run.

In March 1862, McClellan finally ordered the Army of the Potomac out of Washington. Because he thought that marching to Manassas again would be a mistake, he transported some 100,000 soldiers by boat to a peninsula southeast of Richmond. As the Union troops moved up the peninsula, they encountered some 15,000 Southerners at Yorktown, Virginia, about 60 miles from the Confederate capital.

Although the enemy force was much smaller than his own, McClellan asked for more troops. Lincoln dispatched a stern message to his general:

**AMERICAN VOICES** **"It is indispensable to you that you strike a blow. . . . The country will not fail to note—and is now noting—that the present hesitation to move upon an entrenched enemy is but the story of Manassas repeated. . . . I have never written you . . . in greater kindness of feeling than now. . . . *But you must act.*"**

—*President Lincoln*

McClellan, however, waited outside Yorktown for about a month. When he was finally ready to advance, the defenders abandoned their positions and retreated toward Richmond.

On May 31, as they neared the capital, the Southerners suddenly turned and attacked McClellan's army. Although the North claimed victory at the Battle of Seven Pines, both sides suffered heavy casualties. Among the wounded was the Confederate commander, General Joseph Johnston. Command of his army fell to Robert E. Lee.

## Robert E. Lee

**AMERICAN BIOGRAPHY** A warm and charming southern gentleman, Robert E. Lee came from an old, distinguished Virginia family. Among his relatives were two signers of the Declaration of Independence. His father, Henry Lee, was a hero of the American Revolution. After falling into debt, however, his father fled the country, leaving Robert to be raised by his mother.

In 1829 Lee graduated second in his class from West Point. During the next 17 years, he became expert in designing defensive military fortifications. His outstanding service in the Mexican War caught the attention of the army's top officers, and in the early 1850s he served a short time as the head of West Point.

As the southern states seceded, Lincoln offered Lee command of Union forces. Although he was opposed to slavery and secession, Lee refused, explaining "I cannot raise my hand against my birthplace, my home, my children." Instead, he resigned from the army and became the top military advisor to Confederate president Jefferson Davis. In May 1862 he took command of the Army of Northern Virginia, a post he held for the rest of the war. After the war Lee served as president of what is now Washington and Lee University in Lexington, Virginia, until his death in 1870 at age 63.

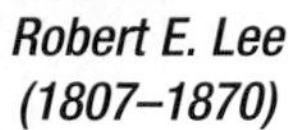

*Robert E. Lee (1807–1870)*

As a commander, Lee earned the loyalty and trust of his troops. "I would follow him onto the battlefield blindfolded," Stonewall Jackson said. Like all great generals, Lee believed in good training and planning. However, he also understood that victory sometimes depends on the willingness to take chances.

## The South Attacks

With McClellan's forces still threatening Richmond, Lee had his opportunity to take a chance. In early June he divided his 55,000-man army, sending several thousand troops to strengthen Stonewall Jackson's forces in western Virginia. The Seven Pines battle had reduced McClellan's army to about 80,000 soldiers. Lee was gambling that the overly cautious McClellan, who was awaiting reinforcements, would not attack Richmond while the Confederate army was weakened.

General Jackson then began to act as though he intended to attack Washington. This tactic caused Lincoln to cancel the order for McClellan's additional troops, keeping them in Washington to protect the Union capital. Jackson then slipped away to join Lee outside Richmond. In late June their combined forces attacked McClellan's larger army in a series of encounters called the Seven Days' Battles. Although the Confederates lost more than 20,000 soldiers, to the Union's nearly 16,000, McClellan decided to retreat.

**The Second Battle of Bull Run** With McClellan having failed, Lincoln turned to General John Pope, who was organizing a new army outside Washington. The President ordered McClellan's troops back to Washington and put Pope in overall command. Lee knew that he must draw Pope's army into battle before McClellan's soldiers joined it. Otherwise, the size of the Union force would be overwhelming.

Lee again divided his army. In late August he sent Jackson's troops north in a sweeping movement around Pope's position. After marching 50 miles in two days, they struck behind Pope's army and destroyed some of his supplies, which were stored at Manassas. Enraged, Pope ordered his 62,000 soldiers into action to smash Jackson. On August 29, while Pope's force was engaged, Lee also attacked it with the main body of the Confederate army.

The battle was fought on virtually the same ground where McDowell had been defeated the year before. Pope met the same fate at this Second Battle of Bull Run. After Pope's defeat, McClellan was returned to command. "We must use what tools we have," Lincoln said in defense of his decision. "If he can't fight himself, he excels in making others ready to fight."

**The Battle of Antietam** With Richmond no longer threatened, Lee decided that the time had come to invade the North. Lee hoped that a victory on Union soil would arouse support in Europe for the South and turn northern public opinion against the war.

In early September 1862, Lee's army bypassed the Union troops guarding Washington and slipped into western Maryland. McClellan had no idea where the Confederates were. Then one of his soldiers found a copy of Lee's orders wrapped around some cigars near an abandoned Confederate camp. Now that he knew the enemy's strategy, McClellan crowed, "If I cannot whip Bobbie Lee, I will be willing to go home."

True to his nature, however, McClellan delayed some 16 hours before ordering his troops after Lee. This gave the Confederate general, who had learned that his plans were in enemy hands, time to prepare for the Union attack. The two armies met at Antietam Creek near Sharpsburg, Maryland, on September 17. Lee had about 40,000 troops, McClellan over 75,000, with nearly 25,000 more in reserve.

Union troops attacked throughout the day, suffering heavy losses. In the first three hours of fighting, some 12,000 soldiers from both sides were killed or wounded. By day's end Union casualties had grown to over 12,000. Lee's nearly 14,000 casualties amounted to more than a third of his army.

The next day the battered Confederates retreated back into Virginia. Lincoln telegraphed McClellan, "Destroy the rebel army if possible." But the ever-cautious general did not take advantage of his opportunity to destroy the Army of Northern Virginia.

The **Battle of Antietam** became the bloodiest day of the Civil War. "God grant these things may soon end and peace be restored," wrote a Pennsylvania soldier after the battle. "Of this war I am heartily sick and tired."

## SECTION 1 REVIEW

### Comprehension

1. *Key Terms* Define: (a) Civil War; (b) First Battle of Bull Run; (c) casualty; (d) war of attrition; (e) shell; (f) canister; (g) Battle of Shiloh; (h) Battle of Antietam.
2. *Summarizing the Main Idea* Why was it clear by the end of 1862 that the Civil War would be a long and bloody struggle ?
3. *Organizing Information* Write the following column headings on a piece of paper: *Union Strategies*, *Confederate Strategies*, *Union Victories*, *Confederate Victories*. Then fill in details from the text in the appropriate column.

### Critical Thinking

4. *Analyzing Time Lines* Review the time line at the start of the section. Choose one battle that you think would have been encouraging for the Confederacy. Explain why you chose that event.
5. *Recognizing Cause and Effect* How did the development of new military technologies affect the Civil War?

### Writing Activity

6. *Writing a Persuasive Essay* In your view, was the North or the South more prepared to fight a war? Write an essay explaining your opinion. Support your ideas with specific examples.

November 1861
The Trent affair

April 1862
Confederate draft law passed

July 1862
Pacific Railroad Act

July 1862
Internal Revenue Act

January 1863
Emancipation Proclamation takes effect

1861 | 1862 | 1863

# 2 Life Behind the Lines

## SECTION PREVIEW

### Objectives

1. Compare the effects of wartime politics on the Confederate and Union governments.
2. Describe the Emancipation Proclamation and its effects, especially on African Americans.
3. List the hardships that befell the North and the South during the war.
4. *Key Terms* Define: draft; recognition; greenback; martial law; Copperhead; writ of *habeas corpus;* Emancipation Proclamation; contraband.

### Main Idea

The Union and Confederate governments struggled to support their armies and care for their citizens. The Union government also moved to abolish slavery.

### Reading Strategy

*Problem Solving* List some possible solutions to the problems that the Union and Confederate governments faced during the war. As you read, take specific notes on how both sides actually responded.

In early 1862 the South faced a crisis. As Grant moved toward Mississippi and McClellan's army threatened Richmond, many Confederate soldiers neared the end of their enlistments. Few seemed ready to reenlist. "If I live this twelve months out, I intend to try mighty hard to keep out [of the army]," pledged one Virginia soldier.

## Politics in the South

The branches and powers of the Confederate government were similar to those of the government of the United States. However, the framers of the Confederate constitution made certain that it recognized states' rights and slavery. These two differences caused difficulties for the South throughout the war.

Like the government of the North, the Confederate government had to persuade individual citizens to sacrifice their personal interests for the common good. Confederate leaders had to find a way to build Southerners' loyalty to their new government. Furthermore, because the South had fewer resources than the North, its war effort depended more on making the best possible use of what it had. Since the southern state governments were strong and sometimes fiercely independent, meeting these objectives would prove difficult.

**Mobilizing for War** Fearing the war would be lost if there were not enough soldiers to fight, General Lee called for a **draft,** or required military service. Opponents of strong central government claimed that the proposal violated the principles the South was fighting for. One Texas senator disagreed with such arguments:

AMERICAN VOICES

> "Cease this child's play. . . . The enemy are in some portions of almost every state in the Confederacy. . . . We need a large army. How are you going to get it? . . . No man has any individual rights, which come into conflict with the welfare of the country."
>
> —Senator Louis Wigfall

*Medals of Honor like this one were awarded to many Civil War soldiers, both white and African American.*

In April 1862 the Confederate congress passed a draft law requiring three years of military service for white men between the ages of 18 and 35. This automatically extended the service of all volunteers for two more years. After the horrible losses at the Battle of Antietam, the upper age for the draft became 45. Later it was raised again to 50. Owners of 20 or more slaves were excused from serving, and so were Southerners wealthy enough to hire a substitute to serve in their place.

The Confederate government took charge of the South's economy. It determined the amount of production of wool, cotton, and leather, and seized control of southern railroads from private owners. Farmers were required to contribute one tenth of their produce to the war effort.

To help raise money for the war, the Confederate congress imposed a tax on personal incomes. The Confederate government also authorized the army to seize male slaves for military labor. Though they were paid a monthly fee for borrowed slaves, planters resented this practice because it disrupted work on their plantations.

**The Impact of States' Rights** A fierce commitment to states' rights worked against the Confederate government and harmed the war effort in many ways. Georgia governor Joseph Brown proclaimed, "I entered into this revolution . . . to sustain the rights of the states . . . and I am *still* a rebel . . . no matter who may be in power."

Many Southerners shared the governor's point of view. Local authorities sometimes refused to cooperate with draft officials. Whole counties in some states were ruled by armed bands of draft-dodgers and deserters. It is estimated that perhaps half of Confederate men eligible for the draft failed to cooperate. "If we are defeated," warned an Atlanta newspaper, "it will be by the people at home."

*In what way was the Confederate government both strong and weak?*

**Seeking Help from Europe** Although the blockade effectively prevented southern cotton from reaching Great Britain and France, Southerners continued to hope for British and French intervention in the war. In May 1861 the Confederate government sent representatives to both nations. Even though the Confederacy failed to gain **recognition,** or official acceptance, as an independent nation, it did receive some help.

Great Britain agreed to allow its ports to be used to build Confederate privateers. One of these vessels, the *Alabama,* captured more than 60 northern merchant ships. In all, 11 British-built Confederate privateers forced most Union shipping from the high seas for much of the war.

Recognition did seem possible for a time in 1862. Napoleon III, the ruler of France, had sent troops into Mexico, trying to rebuild a French empire in the Americas. He welcomed the idea of an independent Confederate States of America on Mexico's northern border. However, France would not give the Confederacy open support without Great Britain's cooperation.

British opinion about the war was divided. Some leaders clearly sympathized with the Southerners. Many believed an independent South would be a better market for British products. Others, however, questioned whether the Confederacy would be able to win the war. The British government adopted a wait-and-see attitude. To get foreign help, the South would have to first prove itself on the battlefield.

## Politics in the North

After early losses to Confederate forces, President Lincoln and his government had to convince some northern citizens that maintaining the Union was worth the sacrifices they were being asked to make. In addition, the federal government found itself facing international crises as it worked to strengthen civilian support for the war.

**Tensions with Great Britain** British talks with the South aroused tensions between Great Britain and the United States. Late in 1861 Confederate president Davis again sent two representatives from the Confederacy to England and France. After evading the Union blockade, John Slidell and James Mason boarded the British mail ship *Trent* and steamed for Europe.

Soon a Union warship stopped the *Trent* in international waters, removed the two Confederates, and brought them to the United States. An outraged British government sent troops to Canada and threatened war unless Slidell and Mason were freed. President Lincoln ordered the release of the Confederates. "One war at a time," he said.

The Union vigorously protested Great Britain's support of the Confederacy. Lincoln demanded $19 billion compensation from

Great Britain for damages done by the privateers, and for other British actions on the South's behalf. This demand strained relations between the United States and Great Britain for nearly a decade after the war.

**Republicans in Control** With southern Democrats out of the United States Congress, the Republicans had little opposition. The Civil War Congresses thus became among the most active in American history. Republicans were able to pass a number of laws during the war that would have a lasting impact on the United States.

Southerners had opposed building a rail line across the Great Plains since Illinois senator Stephen Douglas first proposed it in the early 1850s. In July 1862, however, Congress passed the Pacific Railroad Act with little resistance. The law allowed the federal government to give land and money to companies for construction of a railroad line from Nebraska to the Pacific Coast. The Homestead Act, passed in the same year, offered free government land to people willing to settle on it.

The disappearance of southern opposition allowed Congress to raise tariff rates as well. The tariff became more a device to protect northern industries than to provide revenue for the government. Union leaders turned to other means to raise money for the war.

**Financial Measures** In 1861 the Republican-controlled Congress passed the first federal tax on income in American history. It collected 3 percent of the income of people earning more than $800 a year. The Internal Revenue Act of 1862 imposed taxes on items such as liquor, tobacco, medicine, and newspaper ads. Nearly all these taxes ended when the war was over.

During the war, Congress reformed the nation's banking system. Since 1832, when President Jackson vetoed the recharter of the Second Bank of the United States, Americans had relied on state banks. In 1862 Congress passed an act that created a national currency, called **greenbacks** because of their color. This paper money was not backed by gold, but was declared by Congress to be acceptable for legal payment of all public and private debts.

**Emergency Wartime Actions** Like the government of the Confederacy, the United States government exercised great power during the Civil War. As in the South, efforts focused on raising troops and uniting the nation behind the war effort.

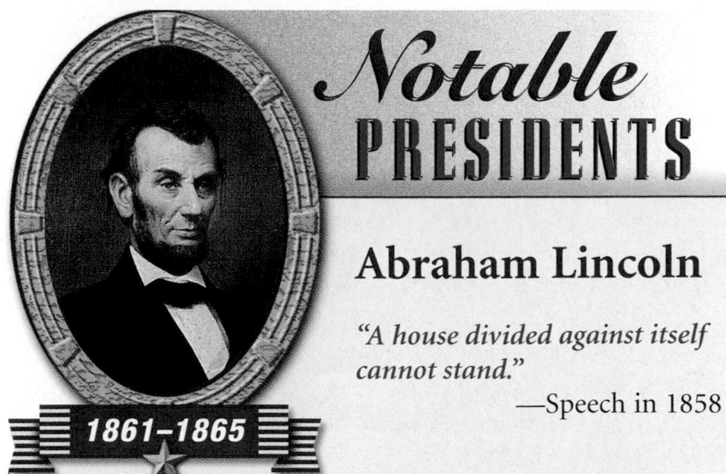


## *Notable* PRESIDENTS

### Abraham Lincoln

*"A house divided against itself cannot stand."*

—Speech in 1858

Abraham Lincoln entered the White House with little training in national politics. Before being elected in 1860, he had been a successful lawyer in Illinois and a member of the House of Representatives for a single term. Nothing, however, could have prepared him for the extraordinary challenges he would face as President.

Lincoln confronted crises on every side. Southern states began seceding from the Union even before he took office. The border states somehow had to be kept in the Union. Many Northerners, while opposing secession, did not want to fight the South, and white Northerners disagreed among themselves about slavery.

Lincoln's actions as President all pointed toward one goal: preserving the Union. He changed commanding generals again and again in a desperate search for one who could defeat the Confederate army. He suppressed freedom of speech and assembly. He issued the Emancipation Proclamation to free the slaves living behind Confederate lines, and in 1863 he called on free blacks to join the Union army. All of these actions brought a torrent of criticism on Lincoln. To some critics he was a power-hungry tyrant; to others he was weak and indecisive.

Along with his commitment to preserving the Union, Lincoln's greatest strengths were his sense of compassion and his ability to express powerful ideas in simple yet moving language. In fact, his words have come to help define the Civil War, from his warning before the war that "A house divided against itself cannot stand" to his hope in 1865 that Americans would face the future "with malice toward none, with charity for all." Assassinated shortly before the war's end, Lincoln would not live to work for the compassionate peace he favored. But he had done more than any other single person to preserve the nation at its time of greatest danger.

#### Connecting to Today

Lincoln is remembered for leading the nation through a time of crisis. His ability to express ideas clearly created support for maintaining a unified nation. ***How important is it that the President be able to rally the people behind a cause? Defend your opinion.***

This cartoon of 1863 echoes Lincoln's warning that "the enemy behind us is more dangerous to the country than the enemy before us." ***Government*** *Explain the symbols in the cartoon.*

Four slave states remained in the Union—Delaware, Maryland, Missouri, and Kentucky. Because of their locations, the continued loyalty of these border states was critical to the Union. Lincoln considered Delaware, where few citizens held slaves, to be secure. In nearby Maryland, however, support for secession was strong. In September 1861 Lincoln ordered that all "disloyal" members of the Maryland state legislature be arrested. This action prevented a vote on secession and assured that Washington would not be surrounded by the Confederacy.

The North needed the loyalty of Kentucky and Missouri in order to keep control of the Ohio and Mississippi rivers. In Missouri, Lincoln supported an uprising to overthrow the pro-Confederate state government. To secure Kentucky, he put the state under **martial law** for part of the war. This is emergency rule by military authorities, during which some Bill of Rights guarantees are suspended. Although Jefferson Davis imposed martial law on parts of the Confederacy, Lincoln is the only United States President ever to exercise this power.

The Union also established a draft. In March 1863 President Lincoln signed a law requiring military service of all white males age 20 to 45. Like the southern law, there were exceptions. To avoid the draft, a Northerner could pay the government $300 or he could hire a substitute to serve in his place.

**Opposition to the War** Riots broke out in the North after the draft law was passed. Mobs of whites in New York City vented their rage at the draft in July 1863. More than 100 people died during four days of destruction. At least 11 of the dead were African Americans, who seemed to be targeted by the rioters.

Although Democrats could not control Congress, some raised their voices in protest against the war. Nicknamed **Copperheads,** after a type of poisonous snake, these Democrats warned that Republican policies would bring a flood of freed slaves to the North. They predicted these freed slaves would take jobs away from whites. Radical Copperheads tried to persuade Union soldiers to desert the army and other Northerners to resist the draft.

To silence the Copperheads and other opponents of the war, Lincoln resorted to extreme measures. He used the army to shut down opposition newspapers and denied others the use of the mails.

In some places Lincoln suspended the **writ of *habeas corpus.*** This is a legal protection requiring that a court determine if a person is lawfully imprisoned. Without it, people can be held in jail for indefinite periods without even being charged with a crime. The Constitution allows suspension of the writ during a rebellion.

More than 13,000 Americans who objected to the Union government's policies were imprisoned without trial during the war. They included newspaper editors and elected state officials, plus southern sympathizers and some who actually did aid the Confederacy. Most Northerners approved of Lincoln's actions as necessary to restore the Union.

## *Emancipation and the War*

While the Copperheads attacked Lincoln for making war on the South, abolitionists and others attacked him for not making it a war to end slavery. As the Union's battlefield casualties mounted, many Northerners began to question whether it was enough to simply restore the nation. Some, including a group in the Republican party called Radical Republicans, wanted the Confederacy punished for causing so much suffering. No punishment could be worse, the Radical Republicans argued, than freeing the slaveholders' "property."

**Lincoln and Slavery** At first, the President resisted pressure to make the abolition of slavery a Union war goal. He insisted that under the Constitution he was bound only to preserve and protect the nation. Lincoln explained this view in a letter to Horace Greeley, an abolitionist newspaper editor:

AMERICAN VOICES "My paramount object in this struggle is to save the Union, and is not to either save or to destroy slavery. If I could save the Union without freeing any slave, I would do it, and if I could save the Union by freeing all the slaves, I would do it; and if I could save it by freeing some and leaving others alone, I would also do that."

—*President Lincoln*

Although Lincoln personally opposed slavery, he did not believe that he had the legal authority to abolish it. He also worried about the effect such an action would have on the loyalty of the border states. However, Lincoln recognized the importance of slavery to the South's war effort. Every slave working in a field or factory freed a white Southerner to fire a gun at Union soldiers. Gradually, he came to regard ending slavery as one more strategy for winning the war.

**The Emancipation Proclamation** In the fall of 1862, as Lee retreated south from Antietam, Lincoln proclaimed that on January 1, 1863, slaves in areas of rebellion against the government would be free. Then, on New Year's Day, 1863, he issued the final **Emancipation Proclamation:**

"I, Abraham Lincoln, President of the United States, by virtue of the power in me vested as Commander-in-Chief, of the Army and Navy of the United States . . . as a fit and necessary war measure for suppressing said rebellion . . . do order and declare that all persons held as slaves within said designated States, and parts of States, are and henceforward shall be free. . . ."

—*The Emancipation Proclamation, January 1863*

**Reaction to the Proclamation** The decree had little direct impact on slavery because it applied only to places that were under Confederate control. Nevertheless, it was condemned in the South and debated in the North. Some abolitionists criticized Lincoln for not having gone far enough. The proclamation did nothing to free people enslaved in the border states, nor did it free slaves living in Confederate areas controlled by Union forces.

Other Northerners, fearing that freed people coming north would cause unemployment, criticized even this limited action. After Lincoln's September announcement, the Democratic party made gains in the congressional elections of November 1862.

The response of black Northerners was much more positive. "We shout for joy that we live to record this righteous decree," abolitionist Frederick Douglass exclaimed. Even if the proclamation brought no immediate end to slavery, it promised that an enslaved people would be free when the North won the war.

Perhaps the most significant reaction occurred in Europe. The abolition movement was strong in England. The Emancipation Proclamation, coupled with news of Lee's defeat at Antietam, ended any real chance that France and Great Britain would intervene in the war.

## *African Americans Fight*

The Emancipation Proclamation had two immediate effects. It inspired southern slaves who heard about it to free themselves by escaping to the protection of Union troops. It also encouraged African Americans to serve in the Union army.

**The Contraband Issue** Southern slaveholders usually fled with their slaves when the Union

Over the course of the Civil War, nearly 180,000 African Americans wore the Union uniform. ***Government*** *How did the Emancipation Proclamation change the role of African Americans in the military?*

army approached. Frequently, however, slaves remained behind or escaped to the safety of nearby Union forces. Believing they had no choice, some Union officers gave these slaves back to slaveholders who demanded return of their "property."

Early in the war, Union general Benjamin Butler devised a legal argument that allowed the Union army to free captured and escaped slaves. During war, one side's possessions may be seized by its enemy. Called **contraband,** these captured items become property of the enemy government. Butler maintained that if slaves were property then they could be considered contraband of war. The Union government, as their new owner, could then let the slaves go.

At first, the army employed these African Americans to build fortifications, drive wagons, and perform countless other noncombat jobs. After the Emancipation Proclamation, however, many enlisted to fight the Confederacy.

**African American Soldiers** When the Civil War began, black volunteers were not allowed to join the Union army. In July 1862, following McClellan's defeats in Virginia, Congress authorized Lincoln to accept African Americans in the army. Several months later, he made the announcement in the Emancipation Proclamation.

Given this encouragement, African Americans rushed to join the fight. By 1865 nearly 180,000 African Americans had enlisted in the Union army. More than half were black Southerners who had been freed from slavery by the fighting. For these soldiers, fighting to help free others who were still enslaved held special meaning. Many African Americans viewed the chance to fight against slavery as a milestone in their history. In total, African Americans composed almost 10 percent of the troops who served the North during the war.

On warships, black and white sailors served together. African American soldiers, however, served in all-black regiments under the command of white officers. Until June 1864 African Americans also earned less pay than white soldiers.

In July 1863, an African American regiment earned a place in history at Fort Wagner, a stronghold that protected the harbor at Charleston, South Carolina. On July 18, the 54th Massachusetts Infantry, commanded by Colonel Robert Gould Shaw, led the attack on the fort. The regiment's charge across a narrow spit of sand cost it nearly half its men. Frederick Douglass's two sons were among the survivors; so was Sergeant William Carney, who became the first African American to earn the Congressional Medal of Honor.

The actions of the 54th Massachusetts demonstrated what Frederick Douglass wrote in his newspaper the following month:

**AMERICAN VOICES** **"Once let a black man get upon his person the brass letters, U.S.; let him get an eagle on his button, and a musket on his shoulder and bullets in his pocket, and there is no power on earth which can deny that he has earned the right to citizenship."**

*—Frederick Douglass*

"All that has been said by orators and poets since the creation of the world in praise of women … would not do them justice for their conduct during the war," said Abraham Lincoln. This woman cared for her children and her soldier husband in a Union camp in 1862. ***Culture** In what other ways did women's lives change during the war?*

## *The Hardships of War*

The Union's changing policies regarding slavery in the South prompted thousands of slaves to escape to freedom. This development hurt the Confederacy in two ways. It depleted the South's labor force, and it provided the North with even greater numerical advantages in the war effort.

The war produced drastic changes in the lives of Northerners and Southerners. With the majority of men off fighting, women on both sides took on new responsibilities. Wives and mothers lived with the fear that every day could bring news of the loss of a loved one. In addition, both sides faced labor shortages, inflation, and other economic problems during the war. By 1863, however, it was clear that the North's greater resources were allowing it to meet these challenges, while the South could not.

**The Southern Economy** Among the problems the Confederacy faced during the war was a food shortage. Invading armies disrupted the South's food-growing regions as well as its production of cotton. In parts of the South not threatened by Union forces, the Confederate draft pulled large numbers of white males out of rural areas. Southern women worked the land, oversaw slaves, and tried to keep farms and plantations operating. However, food production declined in the South as the war progressed.

Many planters made the problem worse by resisting the central government's pleas to shift from raising cotton to growing food crops. While cotton piled up in warehouses, due to the Union blockade, food riots erupted in southern cities. The worst of these occurred in Richmond, where nearly 1,000 women looted bakeries and other shops in April 1863.

Although the Confederacy never was able to provide all the manufactured goods its army needed, southern industry grew during the war. The Confederate government supervised construction of factories to make railroad track, guns and ammunition, and many other items. Women filled many of the jobs in these factories.

The labor shortage and lack of goods contributed to inflation. By late 1862 a bag of salt that cost $2 before the war was selling for $60 in some places. The hardships at home increased desertions in the Confederate army. "We are poor men and are willing to defend our country but our families [come] first," a Mississippi soldier declared.

Conditions at Georgia's Andersonville prison evoked outrage from Northerners and calls for prisoner exchanges. ***Economy*** ***How did the state of the South's economy contribute to the horrible conditions of Confederate prison camps?***

**The Northern Economy** The war hurt industries that depended heavily on southern markets or southern cotton. However, most northern industries boomed. Unlike the Confederacy, the North had the farms and factories to produce nearly everything its army and civilian population needed. War-related industries fared especially well. Philip Armour made a fortune packaging pork to feed Union soldiers. Samuel Colt ran his factory night and day producing guns for the army.

As in the South, when men went off to war, women filled critical jobs in factories and on farms. Many factory owners preferred women employees because they were paid less. This hiring practice kept wages down overall. Prices rose faster than pay during the war.

A few manufacturers made their profits even greater by selling the Union government inferior products: rusty rifles, boats that leaked, hats that dissolved in the rain. Uniforms made from compressed rags quickly fell apart. The soles came off some boots after a few miles of marching.

**Prison Camps** Captured Confederate soldiers were sent to prison camps throughout the North, including Point Lookout in

Maryland and Camp Chase in Ohio. The Ohio Penitentiary also housed some Confederate prisoners. The South's prison camps were located wherever there was room. Andersonville, its most notorious camp, was in a field in Georgia. Richmond's Libby Prison was a converted tobacco warehouse.

The North and South generally treated their prisoners about the same. In most cases officers received better treatment than other prisoners. Andersonville was the exception. Built to hold 10,000 Northerners, it eventually confined nearly 35,000 men in a fenced, 26-acre open area. About 100 prisoners a day died, usually of starvation or exposure. The camp's commander was the only Confederate to be later tried for war crimes. He was convicted and hanged.

*Clara Barton organized an agency to bring relief to wounded soldiers.*

**Improving Medical Conditions** While soldiers faced miserable conditions in prison camps, life was not much better in the battle camps. Health and medical conditions on both sides were frightful. About one in four Civil War soldiers did not survive the war. A Union soldier was three times more likely to die in camp or in a hospital than he was to be killed on the battlefield. In fact, about one in five Union soldiers wounded in battle later died from their wounds. While most doctors were aware of the relationship between cleanliness and infection, they did not know how to sterilize their equipment. Surgeons sometimes went for days without even washing their instruments.

On both sides, thousands of women volunteered to care for the sick and wounded. Government clerk Clara Barton quit her job in order to provide needed supplies and first aid to Union troops in camp and during battle. Known to soldiers as the "angel of the battlefield," Barton continued her service after the war by founding the American Red Cross. Mental health reformer Dorothea Dix volunteered to organize and head the Union army's nursing corps. Some 4,000 women served as nurses for the northern army. By the end of the war, nursing was no longer only a man's profession.

Sanitation in most army camps was nonexistent. Rubbish and rotting food littered the ground. Human waste and heaps of animal manure polluted water supplies. Epidemics of contagious diseases, such as mumps and measles, swept through camps. Sick lists were lengthy. Sometimes only half the troops in a regiment were available for battle.

The United States Sanitary Commission, created in June 1861, attempted to combat these problems. Thousands of volunteers, mostly women, inspected army hospitals and camps. They organized cleanups and provided advice about controlling infection, disease prevention, sewage disposal, and nutrition. Despite these and similar Confederate efforts, about twice as many soldiers on each side died from disease as from the guns of the enemy.

## SECTION 2 REVIEW

### Comprehension

1. *Key Terms* Define: (a) draft; (b) recognition; (c) greenback; (d) martial law; (e) Copperhead; (f) writ of *habeas corpus;* (g) Emancipation Proclamation; (h) contraband.
2. *Summarizing the Main Idea* Give some examples of steps the Confederate and Union governments took to support the war effort.
3. *Organizing Information* Create a web diagram showing the legislation passed by the Republican Congress during the war. Label the center circle *Republican Legislation 1861–1862*. Note three or four pieces of legislation in surrounding circles.

### Critical Thinking

4. *Analyzing Time Lines* Review the time line at the start of the section. Which event on the time line, in your opinion, had the greatest impact on the Civil War?
5. *Determining Relevance* In what ways did the Emancipation Proclamation affect the war?

### Writing Activity

6. *Writing an Expository Essay* Use information from the section to write a one-page essay describing the effects the war had on the economies of the North and the South.

# SKILLS FOR LIFE

**Historical Evidence**

Geography

Graphs and Charts

Critical Thinking

# Using Letters as Primary Sources

When people write letters, they report firsthand about something of interest to themselves. For this reason, letters are a valuable source of historical evidence. Not only do they present factual information about a subject, but they also give clues to the attitudes of people in a particular historical period.

Use the following steps to analyze the historical evidence in the letters on this page.

1. ***Lay the groundwork for analyzing the letters by asking who, when, where, and what.*** (a) What clues do the letters give about the identity of the writers? (b) To whom were the letters written? (c) When were they written? (d) Where were they written? (e) What are the topics of the letters?

2. ***Analyze the information in each letter.*** Study the letters to identify their main points. (a) What specific problems does the writer of letter A describe? (b) What tasks does the writer of letter B perform?

3. ***Study each letter to see what it reveals about conditions and attitudes during the period in which it was written.*** (a) What general difficulties did farm wives face when their husbands were away at war? (b) Summarize what conditions were like for the wounded after Civil War battles. (c) Generalize about the contribution to the war effort made by women during the Civil War.

**TEST FOR SUCCESS**

How do you think the writer of letter A would carry on if her husband did not return from war? Give evidence from the letter to support your answer.

**A**

**Lowndes County, Alabama, June 1, 1862**

Dear husband,

I now take my pen in hand [to] drop you a few lines to let you know that we are all well as common and I am in about the same health that I was when you left. I hopes these lines may find you the same. The boys [her sons] has come home to see me on a furlough [leave from the army] and stayed 10 days. They started back yesterday to the camp. . . . John, my corn is out now and I have not drawed [harvested] any thing yet but hope I will. My crop is nice but Pane [a hired man] has quit and left my crop in bad fix, but the neighbors says they will help us. You said you wanted me to pray for you. As for prayers, I pray for you all the time. I pray for you nearly every breath I draw. . . . Your baby is the prettyest thing you ever saw in your life. She can walk by herself and your little grandson is pretty as pink and grows the fastest in the world. You must come home and see all of your babies and kiss them. I have got the rye cut. . . . Your old mare is gone blind in one eye and something is the matter with one of her feet so that she can't hardly walk. Your hogs and cows is coming on very well, I want you to come home for I want to see you so bad I don't know what to do. I must come to a close by saying I remain your loving wife until death. You must write to me as soon as you get this letter. Goodbye to you.

Lucy Lowe to John P. Lowe

*Adapted from Katherine P. Jones,* Heroines of Dixie, *1955*

**B**

**Gettysburg, Pennsylvania, July 8, 1863**

My Dear Cousin,

I am very tired tonight; have been on the field all day. . . . There are no words in the English language to express the sufferings I witnessed today. The men lie on the ground; their clothes have been cut off them to dress [bandage] their wounds; they . . . have nothing but hardtack [biscuit] to eat only as Sanitary Commissioners, Christian Associations [volunteer workers], and so forth give them. . . . To give you some idea of the extent and numbers of the wounds, four surgeons, none of them whom were idle fifteen minutes at a time, were busy all day amputating legs and arms. I gave to every man that had a leg or arm off a gill [measure] of wine, to every wounded in the Third Division, one glass of lemonade, some bread and preserves and tobacco—as much as I am opposed to the latter. . . . I would get on first rate [remain in good spirits] if they would not ask me to ask to write to their wives; that I cannot do without crying, which is not pleasant to either party.

Cornelia

*Cornelia Hancock,* South After Gettysburg, *1956*

## 1 Confederate Uniform

John Singleton Mosby, a Confederate scout and guerrilla leader, wore this jacket. Mosby and his Partisan Rangers often operated behind enemy lines in Virginia and Maryland.

## 2 Bullet in Shoulder Belt Plate

The soldier who wore this shoulder plate was very lucky. The plate saved his life by stopping a musket bullet.

## 3 Civil War Musket

Many soldiers used a musket, but the rifled musket soon replaced it as the standard weapon. A rifle was more accurate over long distances.

## 4 Bowie Knife

Some Confederate soldiers carried Bowie knives—named after frontiersman Jim Bowie, who died defending the Alamo during the Texas War for Independence in 1836.

## 5 Field Hospital

More soldiers died from disease and from infections caused by wounds than were killed in battle. Field hospitals were ill-equipped to treat the wounded.

## 6 Bottle of Quinine

Many soldiers suffered from the disease of malaria. Quinine relieved some symptoms, but did not cure soldiers of the disease.

7

**Mess Tins**

A soldier carried his own eating implements with him. Most had only a cup, knife, fork, spoon, and metal plate. This more-elaborate mess kit was privately purchased.

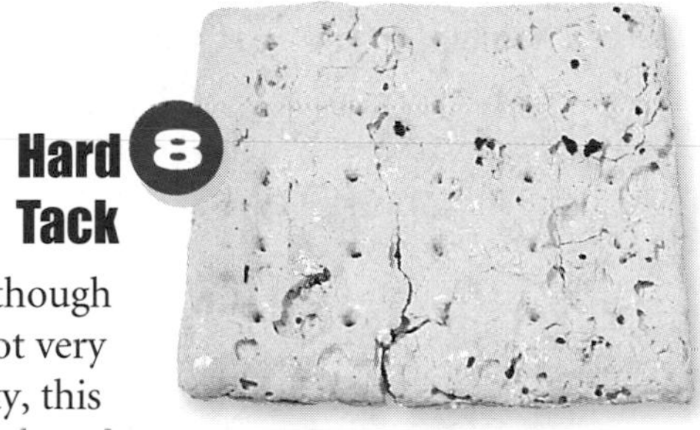

8

**Hard Tack**

Although not very tasty, this chewy bread lasted a long time without spoiling and was easy to carry.

**VIEWING HISTORY**

1. *Summarize* What do the objects and illustrations tell you about the life of the ordinary soldier during the Civil War?

2. *Connecting to Today* Find a monument, museum display, statue, or name of street or highway that is related to the Civil War in your community or some other place and report the following to your class: (a) a description of the site; (b) when it was created; (c) why you think so many communities have a Civil War memorial.

# American ARTIFACTS

FROM EXHIBITIONS AND COLLECTIONS AT THE SMITHSONIAN INSTITUTION'S NATIONAL MUSEUM OF AMERICAN HISTORY

## LIFE AT WAR

When Union and Confederate soldiers set off to war in 1861, both sides expected it to last only a short time. They soon realized that the struggle would not be settled quickly, and that they would have to adapt to long years of war.

As in most wars, much of what the soldiers did was boring or uncomfortable—training for battle, securing food, idling with their fellow soldiers, and marching. Soldiers far preferred these daily activities, however, to the deadly horrors they faced from battle and disease.

Scarcity of clothing was also a problem, especially for the Confederates because of the Union blockade. It was common to see Confederate soldiers barefoot or wearing the blue uniforms taken from Union soldiers killed in battle. *See* 1.

Technological advances changed the way the war was fought. While both sides relied on older weapons such as knives, bayonets, and muskets at the start of the war, rifles became more common as the war progressed. The greater range and accuracy of rifles enabled defenders to cut down attacking troops with terrible efficiency. *See* 2, 3 *and* 4.

Medical care on the battlefield was crude. Surgeons routinely cut off injured arms and legs of wounded soldiers. Without medicines to fight infection, minor wounds often became infected. Diseases like pneumonia and malaria killed more men than guns or cannons. *See* 5 *and* 6.

The armies survived mainly on hard tack, a kind of biscuit that, with bacon and coffee, was the main part of the soldiers' diet. *See* 7 *and* 8.

By the war's end, more than 600,000 people had died—the greatest number of Americans ever to die in a war. Four of every ten men who went off to the Civil War were killed or wounded.

**December 13, 1862** *Battle of Fredericksburg*

**May 1–4, 1863** *Battle of Chancellorsville*

**July 1–3 1863** *Battle of Gettysburg*

**July 4, 1863** *Vicksburg surrenders*

**November 19, 1863** *Lincoln presents Gettysburg Address*

**1863** **1864**

# 3 The Tide of War Turns

## SECTION PREVIEW

### Objectives

1. Analyze the importance of Lee's victories at Fredericksburg and Chancellorsville.
2. Explain how the Battles of Gettysburg and Vicksburg turned the war in the North's favor.
3. Describe the importance of 1863 and the message of the Gettysburg Address.
4. *Key Terms* Define: Battle of Fredericksburg; Battle of Chancellorsville; Battle of Gettysburg; Pickett's Charge; siege; Gettysburg Address.

### Main Idea

Despite southern victories at Fredericksburg and Chancellorsville, the tide of war turned in the summer of 1863, when the North won important battles at Gettysburg and Vicksburg.

### Reading Strategy

*Reinforcing Key Ideas* Write the headings *Gettysburg* and *Vicksburg* on a sheet of paper and take notes about each battle as you read. When finished reading the section, write briefly about why each battle was important in turning the tide of the war.

The Emancipation Proclamation may have renewed enthusiasm for the war among some Northerners, but it had little effect on the battlefield. When General George McClellan delayed in following up on his victory over Robert E. Lee at the Battle of Antietam, Lincoln again removed the general from command.

## Victories for Lee

In November 1862 the President named General Ambrose Burnside to replace McClellan. Sadly for Lincoln, Burnside was better known for his thick whiskers, the origin of the term "sideburns," than for his skills as a military strategist. He soon proved that his poor reputation was justified.

**The Battle of Fredericksburg** Knowing that McClellan had been fired for being too cautious, Burnside quickly advanced into Virginia. His plan was simple—to march his army of some 122,000 men straight toward Richmond. In response, Lee massed his army of nearly 79,000 at Fredericksburg, Virginia, on the south bank of the Rappahannock River. Lee spread his troops along a ridge called Marye's Heights, behind and overlooking the town.

Incredibly, instead of crossing the river out of range of the Confederate artillery, Burnside decided to cross directly in front of Lee's forces. "The enemy will be more surprised [by this move]," he explained. Lee was surprised only by the poor strategy of Burnside's plan.

Union troops poured across the river on specially constructed bridges and occupied the town. Lee let them cross. He knew that his artillery had the area well covered. Lee believed that if Burnside's army attacked, the Confederate forces could easily deal it a crushing defeat.

On December 13, 1862 the **Battle of Fredericksburg** began. Throughout the day Burnside ordered charge after charge into the Confederate gunfire. Some Union army units lost more than half their men. When the fighting ceased at nightfall, the Union had suffered nearly 13,000 casualties. Confederate losses were just over 5,000. A demoralized Burnside soon asked to be relieved of his command.

**The Battle of Chancellorsville** After accepting Burnside's resignation, a worried Lincoln turned to yet another general, Joseph "Fighting Joe" Hooker. The general's plan was to move the Union army around Fredericksburg and attack the Confederates' strong defenses from behind. "May God have mercy on General Lee, for I will have none," Fighting Joe promised.

In late April 1863, Hooker put his plan into action. Leaving about a third of his 115,000-man army outside Fredericksburg, he marched the rest of his troops several miles upriver and slipped across the Rappahannock. Lee soon became aware of Hooker's actions. Confederate cavalry commanded by General J.E.B. "Jeb" Stuart discovered Hooker's force camped about ten miles west of Fredericksburg, near a road crossing called Chancellorsville.

Dividing his forces, Lee sent more than 40,000 Confederate soldiers westward to meet Hooker. About 10,000 troops remained in Fredericksburg. Lee ordered them to build many fires at night, so the enemy across the river would not realize most of the army was gone.

The **Battle of Chancellorsville** began on May 1, 1863. When the Union troops started their march toward Fredericksburg, they suddenly saw Lee's army in front of them. After a brief clash, Fighting Joe ordered them to pull back into the thick woods and build defenses.

The next day, when the Confederates did not attack, Hooker assumed they were in retreat. Instead, Lee had daringly divided his forces a second time. He sent General Stonewall Jackson and 26,000 men on a 12-mile march around the Union army for a late-afternoon attack on its right side. The movement of Jackson's troops was concealed by heavy woods that covered the area.

Again, Hooker was taken by surprise. The only warning was a wave of rabbits and deer that poured into the Union camp moments ahead of the Confederate charge. If darkness had not halted his attack, Jackson would have crushed the Union army.

That night, Jackson and some other officers left the Confederate camp to scout the Union positions for a renewed attack. As they returned, in the darkness some Confederate soldiers mistook them for enemies and opened fire. Three bullets hit Jackson, one shattering his left arm so badly that it had to be amputated.

*The Last Meeting of Lee and Jackson* depicts the two great generals before Lee sends Jackson and his troops to outflank Union forces at Chancellorsville. ***Geography*** ***How did the terrain aid the Confederate plan?***

On May 3, with Stuart now leading Jackson's command, the Confederate army completed its victory. On May 5, Hooker's badly beaten troops withdrew back across the river. Chancellorsville was Lee's most brilliant victory, but it was also his most costly one. On May 10, Jackson died of complications from his wounds. Stonewall Jackson was probably Lee's most brilliant general. His popularity with the troops was exceeded only by Lee's. His death deprived Lee of a man he called his "strong right arm."

**Main Idea CONNECTIONS**

***Why was the death of Stonewall Jackson at the Battle of Chancellorsville a major blow to the Confederate army?***

## *The Battle of Gettysburg*

The crushing defeats at Fredericksburg and Chancellorsville were the low point of the war for the Union. The mood in Washington was dark. Rumors swept the capital that Lincoln would resign as President. Some northern leaders began to talk seriously of making peace with the South. "If there is a worse place than Hell," Lincoln said, "I am in it."

In June 1863 Lee marched his forces northward. The Union blockade and the South's lack of resources were beginning to weaken his army. With all the fighting in Virginia, supplies there had become scarce. Lee hoped to find some in Pennsylvania. More importantly, he

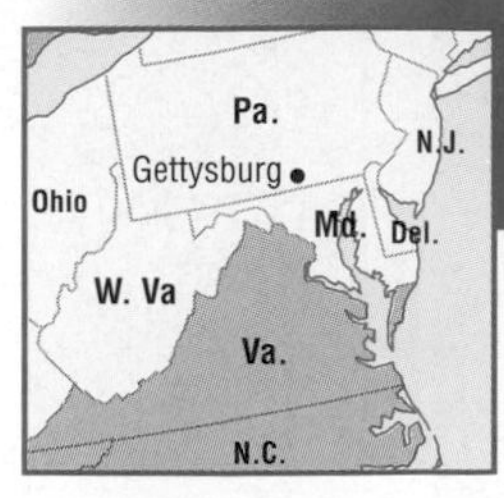

The Battle of Gettysburg was fought over three days. Notice the changes in troop positions over the course of the battle. ***Human-Environment Interaction*** *How did each side attempt to use the terrain to gain an advantage?*

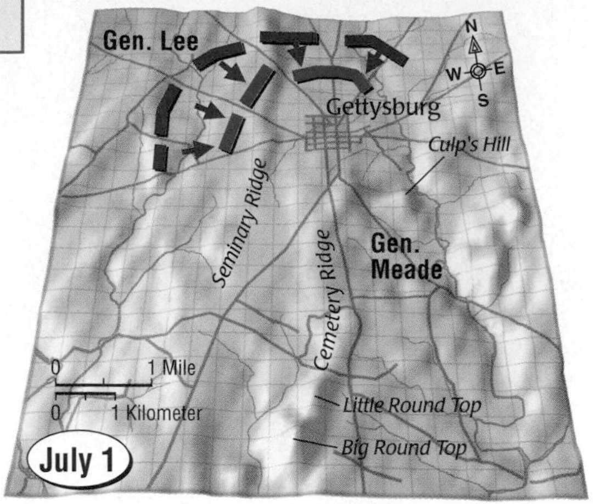


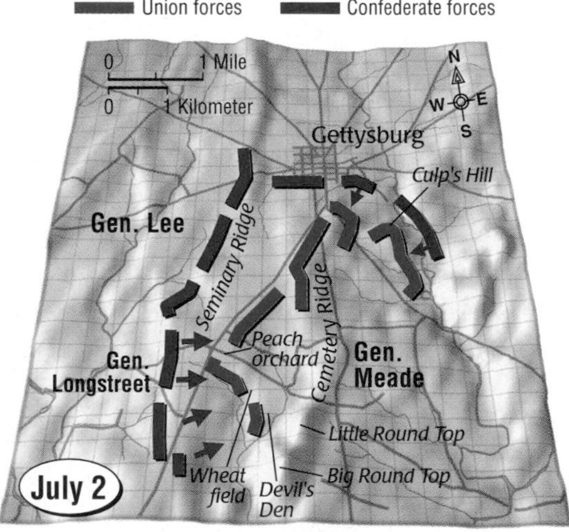


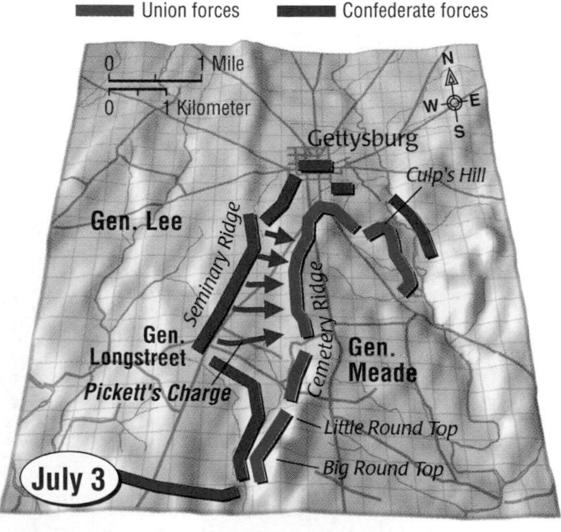


hoped that a major Confederate victory on northern soil would finally push the Union into giving up the war.

As Lincoln prepared to replace Hooker, the Union army moved north, too, staying between the Confederates and Washington. On July 1, some Confederate troops entered the town of Gettysburg, Pennsylvania. Many of them were barefoot, and a supply of shoes was rumored to be stored in the town. There the Confederates encountered a unit of Union cavalry and a fight developed. From this skirmish grew the greatest battle ever fought in North America, the three-day **Battle of Gettysburg.**

**July 1, 1863** Hearing the gunfire coming from Gettysburg, units of both armies rushed to the scene. At first, the Confederates outnumbered the Union forces. Fighting through the day, they pushed the Northerners back onto some hills south of town. Meanwhile, troops on both sides continued to gather. Among the Union soldiers to arrive that night was General George Meade, the new head of the Union army. He had been in command for less than a week.

As units arrived, both armies took up positions on a series of hills. Each army's lines stretched from the outskirts of town, in a southerly direction, for about four miles. The center of the Union line was a long hill called Cemetery Ridge. Another series of hills, called Seminary Ridge, was the center of the Confederate position. Between these ridges was a large field several hundred yards wide.

That evening, Lee discussed his battle plan with General James Longstreet, his second-in-command since Jackson's death. Having won the day's fighting, and fresh from his victory at Chancellorsville, Lee's confidence in his troops was high. He proposed to continue the battle the next day. Longstreet advised against attacking such a strong Union position, but Lee had made up his mind. "The enemy is there," said Lee, pointing to Cemetery Ridge, "and I am going to attack him there." He ordered Longstreet to lead an attack on the southern end of the Union line the next morning.

**July 2, 1863** Although a graduate of West Point, Longstreet preferred more peaceful endeavors. An accountant, he wanted to be in charge of the Confederate army's payroll. Lee made him a field commander instead. "Longstreet is a very good fighter when he . . . gets everything ready," Lee said of him, "but he is so slow."

On this second day of the battle, Longstreet was not ready to attack until about 4:00 P.M. His delays gave Meade the chance to bring up reinforcements. The battle raged into the early evening. Heavy fighting took place in a peach orchard, a wheat field, and a mass of boulders known locally as the Devil's Den.

At one point, some Alabama soldiers noticed that one of the hills in the Union position, called Little Round Top, was almost undefended. They rushed to capture the hill. From it, Confederate artillery could have bombarded the Union lines.

However, Union commanders also had noticed Little Round Top's weakness. About 350 Maine soldiers under Colonel Joshua Chamberlain, a college professor before the war, were ordered to defend the position. They arrived on the hill just before the Alabamans' assault and then held off repeated attacks until they ran out of ammunition. Unwilling to give up, Chamberlain ordered a bayonet charge. The surprised Confederates retreated back down the hill. The Maine soldiers' heroic act likely saved the Union army from defeat. At the end of the day, the Union lines remained intact.

**July 3, 1863** The third day of battle began with a brief Confederate attack on the north end of the Union line. Then the battlefield fell quiet. Finally, in the early afternoon, about 150 Confederate cannons began the heaviest artillery barrage of the war. Some Union generals thought the firing might be to protect a Confederate retreat. However, they were wrong. Lee had decided to risk everything on an infantry charge against the center of the Union position. As he had two days before, Longstreet opposed such a direct attack. Again Lee overruled him.

After a two-hour artillery duel, the Union guns stopped returning fire. Thinking that the Confederate artillery had destroyed the enemy's guns, Longstreet reluctantly ordered the direct attack. Actually, the Union artillery commander had ceased fire only to save ammunition. Now, however, northern soldiers on Cemetery Ridge saw nearly 15,000 Confederates, formed in a line a mile long and three rows deep, coming toward them.

Although this event is known in history as **Pickett's Charge,** General George Pickett was only one of three southern commanders on the field that day. Each led an infantry division of about 5,000 men. As the Confederates marched across about a mile of open ground between the two ridges, the Union artillery resumed firing. Hundreds of canister shells rained down on the soldiers, tearing huge gaps in their ranks. When they closed to within about 200 yards of the Union lines, northern soldiers poured rifle fire into those who remained standing.

Only a few hundred Confederates reached the Union lines—at a bend in a stone wall that became known as the Angle. A survivor described the fighting there:

**AMERICAN VOICES** **"Men fire into each other's faces, not five feet apart. There are bayonet-thrusts, sabre-strokes, pistol-shots; . . . men going down on their hands and knees, spinning round like tops, throwing out their arms, falling; legless, armless, headless. There are ghastly heaps of dead men."**

—*Soldier at Gettysburg*

In about 30 minutes it was over. Scarcely half the Confederate force returned to Seminary Ridge. Lee ordered Pickett to reform his division

Confederate troops in George Pickett's charge at Gettysburg temporarily broke the Union line in the action shown here, at a bend in a stone wall called the Angle. ***Science and Technology*** *How was Pickett's Charge an example of old and new war tactics? How did this combination of warfare result in Confederate defeat?*

In order for Grant to capture Vicksburg, navy gunboats under Commander David Porter had to sail past the city at night under heavy fire. "It was as if hell itself were loose," said one observer. The gunboats survived their mad dash past Vicksburg and linked up with Grant's forces south of the city. ***Geography*** *Why was it important for the Union to capture Vicksburg?*

in case Meade counterattacked. "General Lee, I have no division," Pickett replied.

Pickett's Charge ended the bloodiest battle of the Civil War. Losses on both sides were staggering. The Union army of about 85,000 suffered over 23,000 casualties. Of some 75,000 Southerners, about 28,000 were casualties. For the second time, Lee had lost more than a third of his army. The next day, July 4, the Confederates began their retreat back to Virginia.

## *Vicksburg*

While armies clashed in the East, a Union army in the West struggled to capture the city of Vicksburg, Mississippi. Only this stronghold and a fortress at Port Hudson, Louisiana, prevented the Union from having complete control of the Mississippi River.

Vicksburg seemed safe from attack. It sat on a bluff, high above a sharp bend in the river. From this bluff, Confederate artillery could lob shells at any Union ships that approached the city. In addition, much of Vicksburg was surrounded by swamps. The only approach to the city over dry land was from the east and Confederate forces held that territory.

**Grant Attacks** The Union general who faced these challenges was Ulysses S. Grant. Between December 1862 and April 1863 he made several attempts to either capture or bypass the city. First, he sent General William Tecumseh Sherman and several thousand troops in an unsuccessful attack on Vicksburg from the north. Next he had his army dig a canal across the bend in the river, so Union boats could bypass the city's guns. However, the canal turned out to be too shallow. Then he tried to attack from the north by sending gunboats down another river. This too failed.

An attempt to approach the city through a swampy backwater called Steele's Bayou nearly ended in disaster. The Confederates cut down trees to slow the boats and fired on them from shore. Finally, Sherman's troops had to come and rescue the fleet.

By mid-April 1863, the ground had dried out enough for Grant to try a daring plan. He marched his army down the Louisiana side of the river and crossed into Mississippi south of Vicksburg. Then he moved east and attacked Jackson, the state capital. This drew out the Confederate forces from Vicksburg, commanded by General John Pemberton, to help defend the capital. Before they could arrive, Grant captured Jackson. Then he turned his troops west to fight Pemberton.

On May 16 the two armies clashed at Champion's Hill halfway between Jackson and Vicksburg. Although Grant won another victory, he could not trap Pemberton's army. The Confederates were able to retreat back to Vicksburg's fortifications. In late May, after two more unsuccessful attacks, Grant began a **siege,** a tactic in which an enemy is surrounded and starved in order to make it surrender.

**The Siege of Vicksburg** When Union cannons opened fire on Vicksburg from land and water, a bombardment began that would average 2,800 shells a day. For more than a month, citizens of Vicksburg endured a nearly constant pounding from some 300 guns. The constant schedule of shelling took over everyday life.

Residents dug caves in hillsides, some complete with furniture and attended by slaves. "It was living like plant roots," one cave dweller said. As the siege dragged on, residents and soldiers alike were reduced to eating horses, mules, and dogs. Rats appeared for sale in the city's butcher shops.

By late June, Confederate soldiers' daily rations were down to one biscuit and one piece of bacon per day. On July 4, some 30,000 Confederate troops marched out of Vicksburg and laid down their arms. Pemberton thought he could negotiate the best terms for the surrender on the day that celebrated the Union's independence.

## *The Importance of 1863*

For the North, 1863 had begun disastrously. However, the Fourth of July 1863 was the most joyous Independence Day since the first one 87 years earlier. Thousands of former slaves for the first time could truly celebrate American independence. The holiday marked the turning point of the Civil War.

In the West, Vicksburg was in Union hands. For a time, the people of that city had been sustained by the hope that President Jefferson Davis would send some of Lee's troops to rescue them. But Lee had no reinforcements to spare. His weakened army had begun its retreat into Virginia, never again seriously to threaten Union soil.

Four days later, Port Hudson surrendered to Union forces. The Mississippi River was in Union hands, cutting the Confederacy in two. "The Father of Waters again goes unvexed [undisturbed] to the sea," announced Lincoln in Washington, D.C.

In Richmond there began to be serious talk of making peace. Although the war would continue for nearly two years more, for the first time the end seemed in sight.

## *The Gettysburg Address*

On November 19, 1863, some 15,000 people gathered at Gettysburg. The occasion was the dedication of a cemetery to honor the Union soldiers who had died there just four months before. The featured guest was Edward Everett

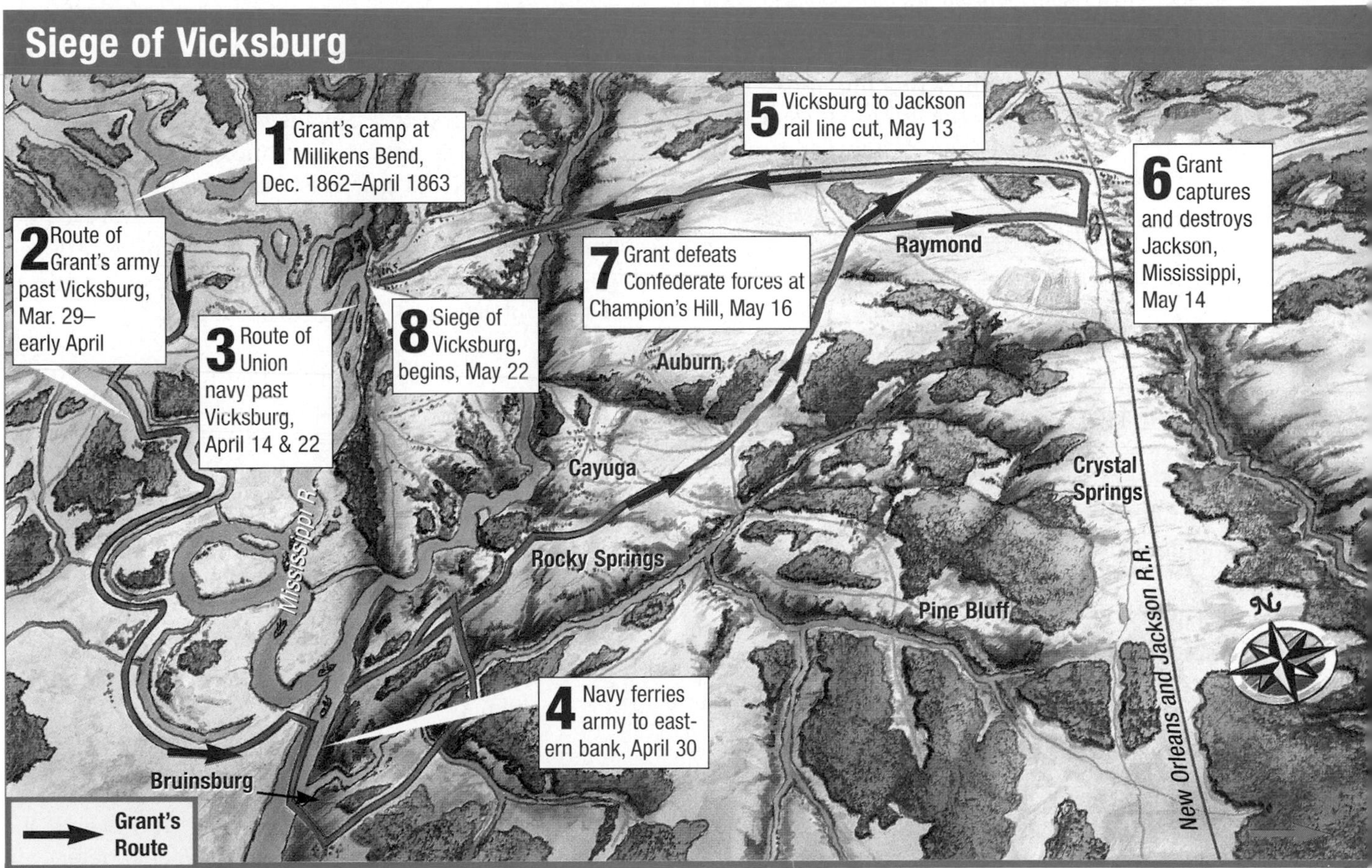

**Siege of Vicksburg**

1 Grant's camp at Millikens Bend, Dec. 1862–April 1863
2 Route of Grant's army past Vicksburg, Mar. 29–early April
3 Route of Union navy past Vicksburg, April 14 & 22
4 Navy ferries army to eastern bank, April 30
5 Vicksburg to Jackson rail line cut, May 13
6 Grant captures and destroys Jackson, Mississippi, May 14
7 Grant defeats Confederate forces at Champion's Hill, May 16
8 Siege of Vicksburg, begins, May 22
Raymond
Auburn
Cayuga
Rocky Springs
Pine Bluff
Crystal Springs
Mississippi R.
New Orleans and Jackson R.R.
Bruinsburg
Grant's Route

Lincoln called capturing Vicksburg "the key" to winning the war. Jefferson Davis considered the city to be "the nailhead that holds the South's two halves together." Grant spent eight months trying to capture it. ***Movement*** *Trace Grant's route on the map and explain the strategy behind it.*

"In times like the present," Lincoln said, "men should utter nothing for which they would not willingly be responsible through time. . . ." ***Government*** ***How do Lincoln's words at Gettysburg represent his goals in the Civil War?***

of Massachusetts, the most famous public speaker of the times. President Lincoln was invited to deliver "a few appropriate remarks" to help fill out the program.

Everett delivered a grand crowd-pleasing speech that lasted two hours. Then it was the President's turn to speak. In his raspy, high-pitched voice, Lincoln delivered his remarks, which became known as the **Gettysburg Address.** In a short, two-minute speech he eloquently explained the meaning of the Civil War. The speech began simply and ended with a statement that redefined the meaning of the United States:

KEY DOCUMENTS

> **"Fourscore and seven years ago our fathers brought forth on this continent, a new nation, conceived in Liberty, and dedicated to the proposition that all men are created equal. . . .**
>
> **[T]hat this nation, under God, shall have a new birth of freedom—and that government of the people, by the people, for the people, shall not perish from the earth."**
>
> —*Lincoln's Gettysburg Address, November 19, 1863*

Lincoln spoke with a wisdom ahead of his time. Most Americans in 1863 did not like his speech. They thought it was too short and simple. But in the years since then, people have come to appreciate that Lincoln's words marked a dramatic new definition of the United States. Freedom and equality no longer belonged to a few, as they had in 1776. They were the right of everyone. Democracy and the Union did not exist to serve the interests of only white men. They existed to preserve freedom for all. Lincoln's Gettysburg Address marked a great milestone in the expansion of liberty to all Americans.

## SECTION 3 REVIEW

### Comprehension

1. *Key Terms* Define: (a) Battle of Fredericksburg; (b) Battle of Chancellorsville; (c) Battle of Gettysburg; (d) Pickett's Charge; (e) siege; (f) Gettysburg Address.
2. *Summarizing the Main Idea* In what ways were the Battles of Gettysburg and the siege of Vicksburg turning points in the Civil War?
3. *Organizing Information* Create a chart that details the major battles discussed in this section. In the first column, write the *names of the battles*. In the next column note the important *Confederate officers* for each battle. In the third column note the *Union officers*, and in the last column write if the battle is considered a *Confederate* or *Union victory.*

### Critical Thinking

4. *Analyzing Time Lines* Review the time line at the start of the section. Write a sentence or phrase that connects each entry to the entry that follows it.
5. *Identifying Central Issues* Explain how the Gettysburg Address redefined the concept of freedom for Americans.

### Writing Activity

6. *Writing an Expository Essay* The events of 1863 are considered to be vital in determining the outcome of the Civil War. Write a one-page essay explaining why. Support your essay with specific examples.

| May 5-6, 1864 | June 3, 1864 | Sept. 2, 1864 | Dec. 21, 1864 | April 9, 1865 | April 14, 1865 |
|---|---|---|---|---|---|
| Battle of the Wilderness | Battle of Cold Harbor | Sherman occupies Atlanta | Sherman captures Savannah | Lee surrenders to Grant at Appomattox | President Lincoln assassinated |

1864 1865 1866

# 4 A New Birth of Freedom

## SECTION PREVIEW

### Objectives

1. Explain Grant's and Sherman's strategies for defeating the South.
2. Summarize the issues and the outcome of the election of 1864.
3. Describe the end of the war and the assassination of President Lincoln.
4. *Key Terms* Define: Battle of the Wilderness; Battle of Spotsylvania; Battle of Cold Harbor; Thirteenth Amendment; guerrilla.

### Main Idea

After years of fighting and countless casualties, the South surrendered in April 1865.

### Reading Strategy

*Arranging Events in Order* As you read, create a time line that lists in order the major events in the section. Beneath each entry write a brief sentence or phrase that connects each event to the entry that follows it.

The Confederates' war strategy for 1864 was a simple one—to hold on. They knew the North would have a presidential election in November. If the war dragged on and casualties mounted, northern voters might replace Lincoln with a President willing to grant the South its independence. "If we can only subsist," wrote an official in the Confederate War Department, "we may have peace."

## Grant Takes Command

President Lincoln understood that his chances for reelection in 1864 depended on the Union's success on the battlefield. In March he summoned Ulysses S. Grant to Washington and gave him command of all Union forces. Grant's plan was to confront and crush the Confederate army and end the war before the November election.

Placing General William Tecumseh Sherman in charge in the West, Grant remained in the East to battle General Lee. He realized that Lee was running short of men and supplies. Grant now proposed to use the North's superiority in population and industry to wear down the Confederates. In the West he ordered Sherman to do the same.

**Battle of the Wilderness** In early May 1864 Grant moved south across the Rapidan River in Virginia with a force of some 120,000 men. Lee had about 65,000 troops. The Union army headed directly toward Richmond. Grant knew that to stop the Union advance, Lee would have to fight. In May and June the Union and Confederate armies clashed in three major battles. This was exactly what Grant wanted.

The fighting began on May 5 with the two-day **Battle of the Wilderness.** This battle occurred on virtually the same ground as the Battle of Chancellorsville the year before.† The two armies met in a dense forest. The fighting was so heavy that the woods caught fire, causing many of the wounded to be

† The Confederate forces felt a sense of repetition when General Longstreet, Lee's second-in-command, was accidentally shot and wounded by his own soldiers only three miles from where Stonewall Jackson had been shot the year before.

burned to death. Unable to see in the smoke-filled forest, units got lost and fired on friendly soldiers, mistaking them for the enemy.

Grant took heavy losses at the Wilderness. However, instead of retreating as previous Union commanders had done after defeats, he moved his army around the Confederates and again headed south. Despite the high number of casualties, Union soldiers were proud that under Grant's leadership they would not retreat so easily.

**Spotsylvania and Cold Harbor** Two days later, on May 8, the Confederates caught up to the Union army near the little town of Spotsylvania Court House. The series of clashes that followed over nearly two weeks are called the **Battle of Spotsylvania.**

The heaviest fighting took place on May 12. In some parts of the battlefield the Union dead were piled four deep. When Northerners began to protest the huge loss of life, a determined Grant notified Lincoln, "I propose to fight it out on this line [course of action] if it takes all summer." Then he moved the Union army farther south.

In early June the armies clashed yet again at the **Battle of Cold Harbor,** just eight miles from Richmond. In a dawn attack on June 3, Grant launched two direct charges on the Confederates, who were behind strong fortifications. Some 7,000 Union soldiers fell in less than an hour.

**The Siege of Petersburg** Unable to reach Richmond or defeat Lee's army, Grant moved his army around the capital and attacked Petersburg, a railroad center south of the city. He knew that if he could cut off shipments of food to Richmond, the city would have to surrender. The attack failed, however.

In less than two months, Grant's army had suffered some 65,000 casualties. The toll had a chilling effect on the surviving Union troops. At Cold Harbor, many soldiers pinned their names and addresses on their uniforms so their bodies could be identified.

Grant then turned to the tactic he had successfully used at Vicksburg. On June 18, 1864, he began the siege of Petersburg. Lee responded by building defenses. While he had lost many fewer men than Grant, it was becoming difficult for Lee to replace all his casualties. He was willing to stay put and wait for the northern election in November.

Grant's stubbornness and Sherman's campaign of total war brought the Civil War to a bloody close. Compare the relative forces of the Union and the Confederacy in the final months of the Civil War. ***Movement*** ***Why do you think Sherman met with little resistance?***

## Final Battles of the Civil War, 1863–1865

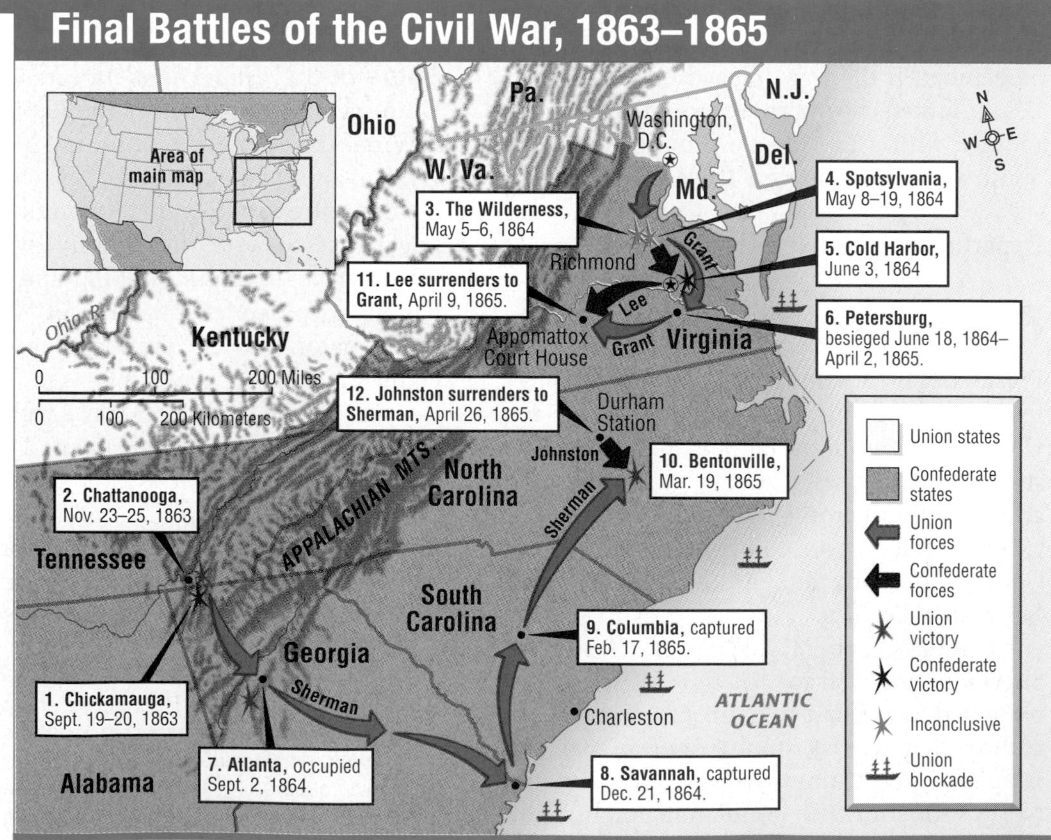

## Sherman in Georgia

**FACT Finder**

**Civil War Casualties**

| | Killed and Mortally Wounded | Dead of Disease | Prisoner-of-War Dead | Wounded | Total Casualties |
|---|---|---|---|---|---|
| **Union** | 110,100 | 224,580 | 30,192 | 275,175 | 640,047 |
| **Confederacy** | 94,000 | 164,000 | 31,000 | 194,026 | 483,026 |
| **Total** | **204,100** | **388,580** | **61,192** | **469,201** | **1,123,073** |

**Source:** *Blood Brothers: A Short History of the Civil War*, by Frank E. Vandiver

***Interpreting Tables*** After four years and more than 10,500 engagements, the Civil War claimed well over a million casualties. ***Science and Technology What was the leading cause of death in the Civil War? What role did science and technology play in the high death tolls of this war?***

As Grant's army advanced against Lee, Sherman began to move south from Chattanooga, Tennessee, to threaten the city of Atlanta. Sherman's strategy was identical to Grant's in Virginia. He would force the main Confederate army in the West to attempt to stop his advance. If the southern general took the bait, Sherman would destroy the enemy with his huge 98,000-man force. If the Confederates refused to fight, he would seize Atlanta, an important rail and industrial center.

**The Capture of Atlanta** Sherman's opponent was General Joseph Johnston, the Confederate commander who had been wounded at the Battle of Seven Pines in Virginia in 1862. Johnston's tactics were similar to Lee's. He would engage the Union force to block its progress. At the same time, he would not allow Sherman to deal him a crushing defeat. In this way, he hoped to delay Sherman from reaching Atlanta before the presidential elections could take place in the North.

Despite Johnston's best efforts, by mid-July 1864 the Union army was just a few miles from Atlanta. Wanting more aggressive action, Confederate president Jefferson Davis replaced Johnston with General James Hood.

The new commander gave Davis—and Sherman—exactly what they wanted. In late July, Hood engaged the Union force in a series of battles. With each clash the southern army lost thousands of soldiers. Finally, with the Confederate forces reduced from some 62,000 to less than 45,000, General Hood retreated to Atlanta's strong defenses. Like Grant at Petersburg, Sherman laid siege to the city. Throughout the month of August, Sherman's forces bombarded Atlanta. In early September the Confederate army pulled out and left the city to the Union general's mercy.

**Sherman Marches to the Sea** "War is cruelty," Sherman once wrote. "There is no use trying to reform it. The crueler it is, the sooner it will be over." It was from this viewpoint that the tough Ohio soldier conducted his military campaigns. Although a number of Union commanders considered Sherman to be mentally unstable, Grant stood by him. As a result, Sherman was fiercely loyal to his commander.

Now, Sherman convinced Grant to permit a daring move. Vowing to "make Georgia howl," in November 1864, Sherman led some 62,000 Union troops on a march to the sea to capture Savannah, Georgia. Before abandoning Atlanta, however, he ordered the city evacuated and then burned.

After leaving Atlanta in ruins, Sherman's soldiers cut a nearly 300-mile long path of destruction across Georgia. The troops destroyed bridges, factories, and railroad lines. They seized and slaughtered livestock. Grain that had recently been harvested for the Confederate troops went to Union soldiers instead.

As the Northerners approached Savannah, the small Confederate force there fled. On December 21 the Union army entered the city without a fight. "I beg to present you, as a Christmas gift, the city of Savannah," read General Sherman's message to Lincoln. For the President, it was the second piece of good news since the November election.

## The Election of 1864

"I am going to be beaten," Lincoln said of his reelection chances in 1864, "and unless some great change takes place, *badly* beaten." In an attempt to broaden Lincoln's appeal, the Republicans dumped Vice President Hannibal Hamlin and nominated Andrew Johnson of

Tennessee to run with the President. Johnson was a Democrat and a pro-Union Southerner.

The Democrats nominated General George McClellan as their candidate. McClellan was only too happy to oppose Lincoln, who had twice fired him. The general was still loved by his soldiers, and Lincoln feared that McClellan would find wide support among the troops. McClellan promised that if elected, he would negotiate an end to the war.

Sherman's capture of Atlanta, however, changed the political climate in the North. Sensing victory, Northerners became less willing to support a negotiated settlement. In November, with the help of ballots cast by Union soldiers, Lincoln won an easy victory, gathering 212 out of a possible 233 electoral votes.

By reelecting Lincoln, voters not only showed their approval of his war policy, but also their increasing acceptance of his stand against slavery. Three months later, in February 1865, Congress joined him in that stand and passed the **Thirteenth Amendment** to the Constitution. It was ratified by the states and became law on December 18, 1865. In a few words, the amendment ended slavery in the United States forever:

KEY DOCUMENTS

**"Neither slavery nor involuntary servitude, except as a punishment for crime whereof the party shall have been duly convicted, shall exist within the United States, or any place subject to their jurisdiction."**

—*Thirteenth Amendment to the Constitution*

As President Lincoln prepared to begin his second term, it was clear to most Northerners that the war was nearly over. In his Second Inaugural Address, in March 1865, Lincoln reflected on the meaning of the previous four years:

KEY DOCUMENTS

**"Both [North and South] read the same Bible and pray to the same God, and each invokes His aid against the other. It may seem strange that any men should dare ask a just God's assistance in wringing their bread from the sweat of other men's faces; but let us judge not that we be not judged. The prayers of both could not be answered. That of neither has been answered fully. The Almighty has His own purposes."**

—*Lincoln's Second Inaugural, March 1865*

## CAUSE AND EFFECT: The Civil War

**CAUSES**

- *Regional differences between the largely industrial North and the agrarian South grow stronger.*
- *The question of slavery in the territories widens the gap between Northern and Southern interests.*
- *The Compromise of 1850 and the Kansas-Nebraska Act inflame passions on both sides of the slavery issue.*
- *An antislavery candidate, Abraham Lincoln, is elected President.*
- *The Lower South secedes to form the Confederate States of America.*
- *The Confederacy attacks Fort Sumter.*

**THE CIVIL WAR**

**EFFECTS**

- *The Union is preserved.*
- *Slavery is abolished.*
- *More than half a million people are dead.*

**Interpreting Charts** Slavery was at the center of the dispute between Northern and Southern interests. The central issue of the Civil War, according to President Lincoln, was the preservation of the Union. In the end, the Union prevailed. ***Government*** ***How did the Civil War resolve the question of slavery? Do you think the war could have ended without a resolution of the issue?***

## *The End of the War*

As Grant strangled Richmond and Sherman prepared to move north from Savannah to join him, Southerners' gloom deepened. President Davis claimed that he had never really counted on McClellan's election, or on a negotiated peace. "The deep waters are closing over us," Mary Chesnut observed in her diary.

**Sherman Moves North** In February 1865 General Sherman's troops left Savannah and headed for South Carolina. As the first state to secede, many Northerners regarded it as the heart of the rebellion. "Here is where the treason began and, by God, here is where it shall end," wrote one Union soldier as the army marched northward.

Unlike Virginia and many other Confederate states, the Carolinas had seen relatively little fighting. Sherman had two goals as he moved toward Grant's position at

Petersburg: to destroy the South's remaining resources and to crush Southerners' remaining will to fight. In South Carolina he did both. The Confederate army could do little but retreat in front of Sherman's advancing force.

South Carolina was treated even more harshly than Georgia. In Georgia, for example, Union troops burned very few of the houses that were in their path. In South Carolina, few houses were spared.

On February 17 the Union forces entered the state capital, Columbia. That night a fire burned nearly half of the city to the ground. Although no one could prove who started the fire, South Carolinians blamed Sherman's troops for the destruction. When the Union army moved into North Carolina, all demolition of civilian property ceased.

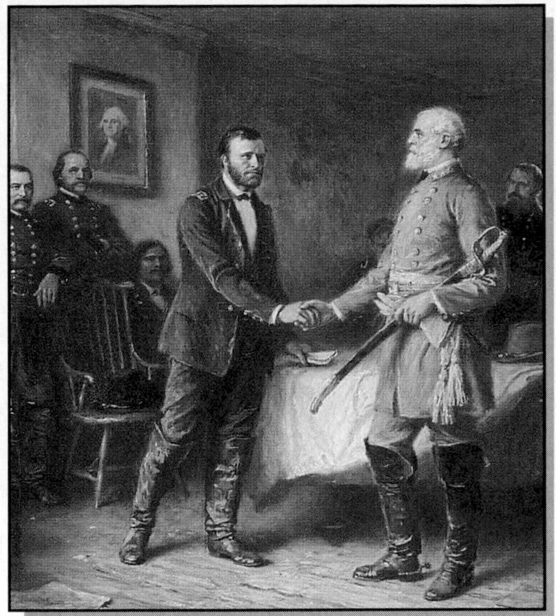

Lee's surrender to Grant was both solemn and civil. ***Government*** ***How would you characterize the terms of the surrender?***

**Surrender at Appomattox** By April 1865, daily desertions had shrunk the Confederate army defending Richmond to less than 35,000 starving men. Realizing that he could no longer protect the city, on April 2 Lee tried to slip around Grant's army. He planned to unite his troops with those of General Johnston, who was retreating before Sherman's force in North Carolina. Lee hoped that together they would be able to continue the war.

Units of General Grant's army tracked the Confederates as they moved west. Each time Lee tried to turn his soldiers south, Grant's troops cut them off. On April 9, Lee's army arrived at the small Virginia town of Appomattox Court House. There the Confederates were surrounded by a much larger Union force. Some of Lee's officers suggested that the army could scatter and continue to fight as **guerrillas**—soldiers who use hit-and-run tactics. Lee rejected this idea, fearing it would bring more devastation to Virginia. Reluctantly he admitted, "There is nothing left for me to do but go and see General Grant, and I would rather die a thousand deaths." He knew the war was over.

That afternoon Lee and Grant met in a private home in the town. General Lee was in his dress uniform, a sword at his side. Grant, wearing his usual private's uniform, was splattered with mud. They briefly chatted about the weather and their service in the Mexican War.

Then Lee asked Grant about the terms of the surrender. These were generous. Southern soldiers could take their horses and mules and go home. They would not be punished as traitors as long as they obeyed the laws where they lived. Grant also offered to feed the starving Confederate army. After the two men signed the surrender papers, they talked for a few more minutes. Then Lee mounted his horse and rode away.

**Main Idea CONNECTIONS**

*Why was Lee finally forced to surrender?*

As news of the surrender spread through the Union army, soldiers began firing artillery salutes. Grant ordered the celebration stopped. He did not want rejoicing at the Southerners' misfortune because, as he pointed out, "the rebels are our countrymen again."

## *Lincoln's Assassination*

A few weeks after Lee's surrender, General Johnston surrendered to Sherman in North Carolina. Throughout May, other Confederate forces large and small also gave up.

Tragically, Abraham Lincoln did not live to see the official end of the war. Throughout the winter of 1864–1865 a group of southern conspirators in Washington, D.C., had worked on a plan to aid the Confederacy. Led by John Wilkes Booth, a Maryland actor with strong southern sympathies, the group plotted to kidnap Lincoln and exchange him for Confederate prisoners of war. After several unsuccessful attempts, Booth revised his plan. He assigned members of his group to kill top Union officials, including General Grant and Vice President Johnson. Booth himself would murder the President.

On April 14, 1865, Booth slipped into the back of the President's unguarded box at

Lincoln's body was displayed in several major cities, such as New York shown here, on its way from Washington, D.C., to its resting place in Springfield, Illinois. ***Culture*** ***Why do you think Lincoln was given such an elaborate and lengthy funeral?***

Ford's Theater in Washington, D.C. Inside, the President and Mrs. Lincoln were watching a play. Booth pulled out a pistol and shot Lincoln in the head. Leaping over the railing, he fell to the stage, breaking his leg in the process. Booth then limped off the stage and escaped out a back alley.

The army tracked Booth to his hiding place in a tobacco barn in Virginia. When he refused to surrender, they set the barn on fire. In the confusion that followed, Booth was shot to death, either by a soldier or by himself.

Mortally wounded, the unconscious President was carried to a boardinghouse across the street from the theater. While doctors and family stood by helplessly, Lincoln lingered through the night. He died early the next morning without regaining consciousness.

In the North, citizens mourned for the loss of the man who had led them through the war. Lincoln's funeral train took 14 days to travel from the nation's capital to his hometown of Springfield, Illinois. As the procession passed through towns and cities, people lined the tracks to show their respect.

Both the North and the South had suffered great losses during the war, but they also both gained by it. They gained an undivided nation, a democracy that would continue to seek the equality Lincoln had promised for it. They also gained new fellow citizens—the African Americans who had broken the bonds of slavery and claimed their right to be free and equal, every one.

## SECTION 4 REVIEW

### Comprehension

1. *Key Terms* Define: (a) Battle of the Wilderness; (b) Battle of Spotsylvania; (c) Battle of Cold Harbor; (d) Thirteenth Amendment; (e) guerrilla.
2. *Summarizing the Main Idea* What strategies did Grant and Sherman use to finally bring victory to the Union?
3. *Organizing Information* Create a flowchart that shows the battles leading up to Lee's surrender at Appomattox. Label the first box *Battle of the Wilderness.* Label the last box *Lee surrenders at Appomattox Court House.*

### Critical Thinking

4. *Analyzing Time Lines* Review the time line at the start of the section. Which event, in your opinion, had the greatest impact on the outcome of the Civil War?
5. *Drawing Conclusions* At the end of the Civil War, General Sherman was called a traitor to the North because of his generosity to the defeated South. Yet many people believe his hatred for the South prompted Sherman's destructive actions in South Carolina. How could the same person be so unforgiving during the war yet generous after it?

### Writing Activity

6. *Writing a Persuasive Essay* In your view, would Lincoln have won the election of 1864 if the South had continued to triumph on the battlefield? Write an essay explaining your opinion. Support it with specific examples.

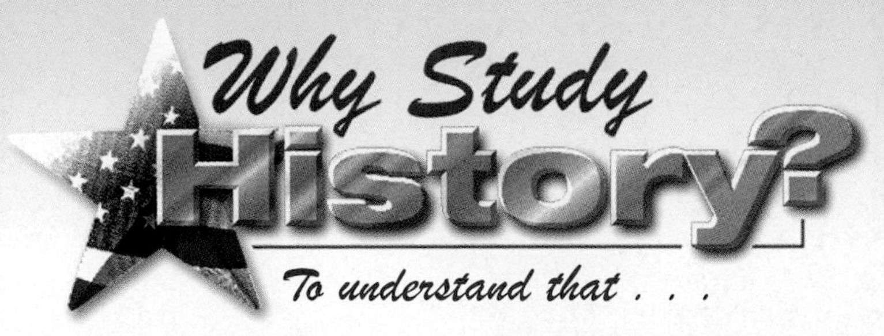


# Americans Remember the Civil War

**More than a century after the Civil War, Americans in both northern and southern states remember that tragic conflict in a variety of ways.**

Confederate and Union soldiers, their rifles drawn, clash in an open field near Sharpsburg, Maryland, on a crisp September day. The battle is not real. It is a reenactment of the Battle of Antietam.

*Battle of Missionary Ridge, Tennessee, in 1863*

Each year thousands of Americans witness or take part in reenactments of famous Civil War battles such as Antietam, Vicksburg, and Gettysburg. Civil War reenactments are staged with historically accurate uniforms and firearms. They are often organized alongside other activities such as parades, talks, and demonstrations of military camp life during the Civil War.

## The Impact Today

The Civil War's enduring power to engage Americans' memory and imagination reflects the impact of the war on the nation. The Civil War pitted American against American, dividing families and causing an enormous amount of death and destruction.

Reenactments are just one way in which Americans remember the conflict. Civil War novels, histories, feature films, and documentaries remain extremely popular among Americans. Towns across the nation have established memorials to Union and Confederate soldiers. Monuments mark almost every Civil War battle site. Literally thousands of Web sites offer information on the conflict.

The oldest intact Civil War monument is a stone cemetery at the Stones River Battlefield near Murfreesboro, Tennessee. It was erected in 1863 to honor a Union brigade led by Colonel William B. Hazen of Ohio. One of the newest monuments, dedicated in 1998, is the African American Civil War Memorial in Washington, D.C. It honors the 235,000 African Americans who fought bravely for freedom. The Gettysburg National Military Park, perhaps the best-known Civil War site, receives more than 1.5 million visitors each year.

## The Impact on You

Research the history of a particular military unit in the Civil War, such as a unit consisting of men from your community or state. Write a report describing when the unit was formed, where it fought, what casualties it suffered, and whether there are any monuments commemorating its achievements.

*Confederate soldiers in a battle reenactment*

# The Shenandoah Valley

*The geographic theme of location explores where a place is, not only in absolute terms but in relation to other places. The location of the Shenandoah Valley affected the way the North and South treated it during the Civil War. What made this valley the site of so many battles?*

A confederate flag and soldier's cap

Great generals study the geography of the land where they are fighting and use it to their advantage. Like geographers, they pay careful attention to location. Because of its location, the Shenandoah Valley played a crucial role in the Civil War.

## Location of the Valley

One of the Southern general Stonewall Jackson's deadliest weapons was a detailed map of the Shenandoah Valley. The Valley is a corridor about 150 miles long and 25 miles wide between the Blue Ridge Mountains and the Alleghenies. Swift and decisive movement was the secret of the Confederate military strategy. Southern armies were able to travel up through the Valley toward the Northern capital of Washington, D.C.

**Great generals study the geography of the land where they are fighting and use it to their advantage.**

As a Union route, the corridor proved less useful. Union armies traveling south through the Valley would end up in the mountains, far away from the Southern capital of Richmond. Eventually, however, Northern armies would devise another tactic.

## The Southern Advantage

As a valley, the Shenandoah formed an excellent corridor for Confederate movement. Its slopes, though forested, were not too steep or rocky for troops on foot or horseback. Furthermore, the Valley Pike, the main road through the Shenandoah, allowed even a large army like that of Confederate general Robert E. Lee to travel rapidly from the heart of Virginia to the borders of the North. And the many gaps in the Blue Ridge mountain chain allowed Southern forces like those led by Stonewall Jackson to duck easily in and out of the Shendandoah Valley as it suited their purposes.

The special characteristics of the Valley also made it valuable to the South for another reason. The population of the Valley was mostly sympathetic to the Confederacy, so Union invaders had to endure constant attacks by armed raiders. Even more helpful to the South were the Valley's splendid pastures and fields, which supplied the Confederate army in Virginia with meat and grain.

## The North Fights Back

Confederate control of the Valley posed an ongoing threat to Union forces. As Union troops marched toward Richmond, Confederate armies would sneak up through the Shenandoah. Union commanders would then have to send part of their troops to defend

Shenandoah Valley and the Civil War

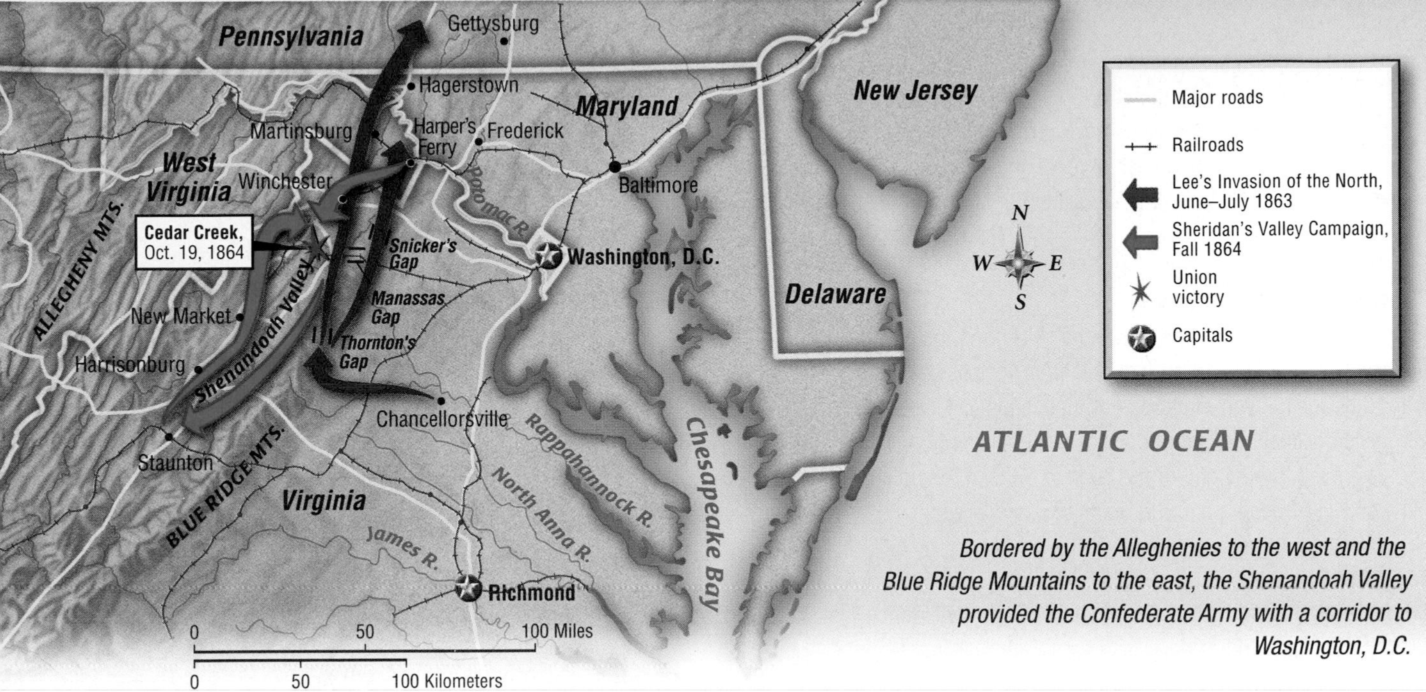


*Bordered by the Alleghenies to the west and the Blue Ridge Mountains to the east, the Shenandoah Valley provided the Confederate Army with a corridor to Washington, D.C.*

Washington, thus diminishing the main part of their army. Hoping to put an end to this, Northern generals repeatedly tried to take control of the Shenandoah during the early years of the war. Even though they did win parts of the Valley at times, they were soon forced to give up their conquests. One key town in the upper Shenandoah Valley, Winchester, changed hands 72 times between 1861 and 1865. The Shenandoah was soon known to Northerners as the "Valley of Humiliation."

## The North Wins the Valley

This was not the end of the story. The commander of Union forces, General Grant, decided in the summer of 1864 that the Southern source of supply had to be shut down once and for all.

He gave these specific instructions to General Phil Sheridan: "Do all the damage to railroads and crops you can. . . . If the war is to last another year, we want the Shenandoah Valley to remain a barren waste."

Sheridan carried out these orders to the letter. In the fall of 1864 he wrote Grant: "The people here are getting sick of the war." Grant answered: "Keep on, and your good work will cause the fall of Richmond."

In the spring of the next year, Grant's words came true. As one Confederate soldier wrote, "There are a good many of us who believe that this shooting match has been carried on long enough. A government that has run out of rations [food for its army] can't expect to do much more fighting."

Early in April 1865, Lee abandoned Richmond and surrendered. In some respects, the war had been lost months before—in the Shenandoah Valley.

## GEOGRAPHIC CONNECTIONS

1. How did the Valley's geographical characteristics help Southerners?
2. Why did Grant want to make the Shenandoah Valley "a barren waste"?

### Themes in Geography

3. *Location* How did the Valley's relative location to Richmond and Washington affect its value to both sides during the war?

# Chapter 2 Review

## Chapter Summary

The major concepts of Chapter 2 are presented below. See also the ***Guide to the Essentials of American History*** or ***Interactive Student Tutorial CD-ROM,*** which contains interactive review activities, time lines, helpful hints, and test practice.

### *Reviewing Main Ideas*

Between the years 1861 and 1865, the North and the South fought a violent Civil War that set neighbor against neighbor and father against son. Hundreds of thousands of Americans were killed or maimed, and property worth billions of dollars was destroyed. By the end of the conflict, African Americans had won their freedom and the Union was preserved.

### *Section 1: From Bull Run to Antietam*

Bloody fighting during the first two years of the Civil War made it clear to both the North and the South that the struggle would be long and difficult.

### *Section 2: Life Behind the Lines*

The Union and Confederate governments struggled to support their armies and care for their citizens. The Union government also moved to abolish slavery.

### *Section 3: The Tide of War Turns*

Despite southern victories at Fredericksburg and Chancellorsville, the tide of war turned in the summer of 1863 when the North won important battles at Gettysburg and Vicksburg.

### *Section 4: A New Birth of Freedom*

After years of fighting and countless casualties, the South surrendered in April 1865.

More than a century after the Civil War, Americans remember that tragic conflict in a variety of ways. People take part in or witness battle reenactments, read novels or histories, watch films and documentaries, and honor the dead at memorials.

## Key Terms

For each of the terms below, write a sentence explaining how it relates to this chapter.

1. Copperhead
2. Pickett's Charge
3. canister
4. siege
5. martial law
6. Thirteenth Amendment
7. Emancipation Proclamation
8. war of attrition
9. Gettysburg Address
10. writ of *habeas corpus*
11. Civil War
12. greenback

## Comprehension

1. What gains did Union forces make in the western part of the Confederacy in the first two years of the Civil War?
2. Briefly summarize Union efforts to capture the southern capital of Richmond in 1861–1863.
3. Why did Lincoln suspend the writ of *habeas corpus*?
4. What laws did the Republican Congress pass during the Civil War to support economic development?
5. Describe the medical and health conditions faced by Union and Confederate soldiers.
6. What was the result of the Battle of Gettysburg?
7. What were the immediate and the long-term effects of Sherman's march to the sea?
8. Briefly describe the events of 1865 that led to Lee's surrender.

## Using Graphic Organizers

On a separate piece of paper, copy the multi-flow map to organize the main ideas of the chapter. On the left side note the causes leading to the Civil War. On the right side note the effects of the Civil War.

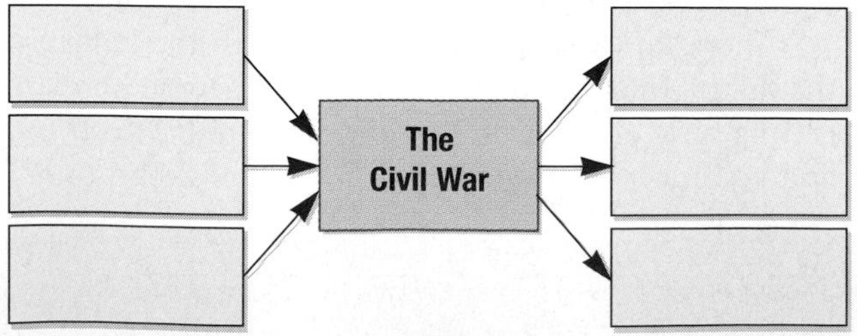

## Analyzing Political Cartoons ▶

1. England and France look on as a pair of combatants fight. Identify the two fighters. (a) What does the figure on the left, labeled "Secession," represent? (b) What does the figure on the right, labeled "The People shall Rule!" represent?
2. What additional threat does the figure on the right face? Explain how you know.
3. What is being trampled? What does it stand for?
4. Identify the political leanings of the cartoonist.

## Critical Thinking

1. ***Applying the Chapter Skill*** Review the Using Letters as Primary Sources skill on page 103. How does the writer of letter B feel about the duties she performs for the soldiers?
2. ***Making Comparisons*** Compare the Union and Confederate military strategies.
3. ***Identifying Alternatives*** What alternatives did President Lincoln have at the start of the Civil War? How might United States history have been different if he had chosen a different course of action?
4. ***Testing Conclusions*** Lincoln came to believe that the Union could not survive if slavery were preserved. Give evidence to support this conclusion.

### INTERNET ACTIVITY

***For your portfolio:***
**CREATE A PHOTO ESSAY**

Access Prentice Hall's *America: Pathways to the Present* site at **www.Pathways.phschool.com** for the specific URLs to complete the activity. Additional resources and related Web sites are also available.

Select a Civil War topic from the links provided at the sites. Choose from the available photographs to create a photographic essay on your topic. Write detailed captions to explain each photograph and its importance in the Civil War. Include an introductory paragraph describing the theme of your photo essay.

### ANALYZING DOCUMENTS ◀▶ INTERPRETING DATA

Turn to the "Civil War Casualties" chart on page 115.

1. Which statement best describes Union deaths due to disease? (a) Twice as many soldiers died from diseases than were killed and mortally wounded. (b) Fewer Union soldiers died from disease than died in prison. (c) Disease killed more Confederate than Union soldiers. (d) More Union soldiers died of disease than were wounded.
2. Which statement best describes the total number of Civil War casualties? (a) Confederate casualties made up the greatest part of the total war casualties. (b) The total number of killed and wounded equaled half the total casualties. (c) Total casualties were split evenly between both sides. (d) Union soldiers made up a greater number of the total casualties.
3. ***Writing*** How do you think the deaths from disease affected soldiers' morale? Explain your opinion.

## Connecting to Today

***Essay Writing*** Read the Gettysburg Address on page 823. Think about how President Lincoln redefined the meaning of the United States in his speech. Then rewrite the Gettysburg Address in your own words, making sure to include a definition of the United States today.

CHAPTER

3

# Reconstruction

## 1865–1877

## CHAPTER FOCUS

This chapter describes Reconstruction, the period following the Civil War, in which efforts were made to rebuild the southern states. In Washington, the nation's leaders argued bitterly over how best to reunify the nation. In the South, meanwhile, African Americans began exercising their newly won freedom, and southerners worked to rebuild the region's economy.

*The* ***Why Study History?*** *page at the end of this chapter explores the connection between black voting rights, which African Americans won during Reconstruction, and black representation in Congress today.*

▲

**VIEWING HISTORY**

Richmond, Virginia, like the South in general, faced an enormous rebuilding task following the Civil War.

***Government*** ***In what ways did the South's political institutions need to be "rebuilt" as well?***

| 1862 | 1863 | 1864 | 1865 | | 1866 |
|---|---|---|---|---|---|
| | **1863** Lincoln's Reconstruction plan | **1864** Wade-Davis Act | **1865** Freedmen's Bureau created | **1865** Civil War ends | **1865** Johnson's Reconstruction plan |

# 1 Presidential Reconstruction

**SECTION PREVIEW**

**Objectives**

1 Describe the condition of the South in the aftermath of the Civil War.
2 Compare the Reconstruction plans of Lincoln and Johnson.
3 Explain how newly freed slaves began to rebuild their lives and how the federal government helped them.
4 *Key Terms* Define: Reconstruction; pardon.

**Main Idea**

During the Reconstruction era, the federal government put forth plans to allow southern states to resume participation in the Union.

**Reading Strategy**

*Organizing Information* As you read, list the main headings of the section in a chart. Beneath each heading, list at least two key facts.

The South was the main battleground of the Civil War and its largest casualty. Hardly a farm or family remained unscarred by the time soldiers began straggling home. A northern journalist described the once-gracious city of Charleston, South Carolina: "A city of ruins, of desolation, of vacant houses, of widowed women, of rotting wharves, of deserted warehouses, of weed-wild gardens, of grass-grown streets."

The federal government's controversial effort to repair the damage to the South and to restore southern states to the Union is known as **Reconstruction.** The Reconstruction program was carried out from 1865 to 1877 and involved four American Presidents.

## The War's Aftermath

At the start of Reconstruction, it was clear that the nation—especially the South—had been changed forever by the war. The changes reached into families and farms.

**The Physical Toll** War had destroyed two thirds of southern shipping and 9,000 miles of railroads. It had devoured farmland, farm buildings, and farm machinery; work animals and one third of all livestock; bridges, canals, and levees; and thousands of miles of roads. Factories, ports, and cities lay smoldering. The value of southern farm property had plunged 70 percent.

**The Human Toll** The Civil War destroyed a generation of young, healthy men—fathers, brothers, and husbands. The North lost 364,000 soldiers, including more than 38,000 African Americans. The South lost roughly 290,000 soldiers, one fifth of its adult white men. One out of three southern men were killed or wounded. Many of the survivors were permanently scarred in mind or body.

In addition, the North's decision to destroy southern homes and property resulted in countless civilian deaths. Children were made orphans; brides became widows.

**Southerners' Hardships** The postwar South was made up of three major groups of people. Each group faced its own hardships and fears.

(1) *Black southerners.* Some 4 million freed people were starting their new lives in a poor region with slow economic activity. As slaves, they had received food and shelter, however

In the final days of the Civil War, Lincoln visited Richmond, Virginia, the captured Confederate capital. In this painting he is shown being greeted by war-weary residents of the city. ***Economics*** ***How does the painting show the damage that Richmond suffered during the war?***

inadequate. Now, after a lifetime of forced labor, many found themselves homeless, jobless, and hungry.

(2) *Plantation owners.* Planters lost slave labor worth about $3 billion. In addition the Captured and Abandoned Property Act of 1863 allowed the federal government to seize $100 million in southern plantations and cotton. With worthless Confederate money, some farmers couldn't afford to hire workers. Others had to sell their property to cover debts.

**Main Idea CONNECTIONS**

*What temporary and permanent changes did the Civil War bring to southern life?*

(3) *Poor white southerners.* Many white laborers could not find work any more because of the new job competition from freedmen. Poor white families began migrating to frontier lands such as Mississippi and Texas to find new opportunities.

**The Changing Plantation** The history of one southern plantation illustrates the complex issues brought about by the war and its aftermath. In 1824, Richard Arnold bought a rice plantation near Savannah, Georgia, which he called White Hall. The Arnolds were among 360,000 white northerners who lived and worked in the South in 1860.

Richard opposed secession. He sold the plantation to his son Thomas, a Confederate supporter, so the Confederacy would not seize it. At the war's end, Richard's northern connections saved White Hall from being seized by the federal government. In 1865 Richard bought White Hall back from Thomas and put him in charge of the rebuilding effort.

The White Hall plantation had suffered considerable damage. But more shocking to Thomas was the attitude of the plantation's freed slaves. They were unreliable, he reported; they refused even to speak to him. Thomas brought in a Union colonel to tell the freedmen that they would be wise to trust Arnold and agree to work for pay. But, Thomas said, one slave spoke up and "said they had made up their minds never to work for me again."

Yet throughout the South, some freed slaves chose to continue working for their former masters. Amos Morel and his wife, Cretia, did stay on to help rebuild the plantation. By the early 1870s, White Hall was one of the largest rice plantations in the South.

## Two Reconstruction Plans

Most southerners accepted the war's outcome and focused on rebuilding their lives. In Washington, however, peacetime launched new battles so fierce that some historians call Reconstruction an extension of the Civil War.

The fall of the Confederacy and the end of slavery raised tough questions. How and when should southern states be allowed to resume their role in the Union? Should the South be punished for its actions, or be forgiven and allowed to recover quickly? Now that black southerners were free, would the races have equal rights? If so, how might those rights be protected? Did the Civil War itself point out a need for a stronger federal government?

At stake were basic issues concerning the nation's political system. Yet it was not even clear which branch of government had the authority to decide these matters.

On these key questions, the Constitution was silent. The Framers had made no provisions for solving the problems raised by the Civil War.

**Lincoln's Plan** With no road map for the future, Lincoln had begun postwar planning as early as December 1863, when he proposed a Ten Percent Plan for Reconstruction. The plan was forgiving to the South:

(1) It offered a **pardon,** an official forgiveness of a crime, to any Confederate who would take an oath of allegiance to the Union and accept federal policy on slavery.

(2) It denied pardons to all Confederate military and government officials and to southerners who had killed African American war prisoners.

(3) It permitted each state to hold a constitutional convention only after 10 percent of voters in the state had sworn allegiance to the Union.

(4) States could then hold elections and resume full participation in the Union.

Lincoln's plan did not require the new constitutions to give voting rights to black Americans. Nor did it "readmit" southern states to the Union, since in Lincoln's view, their secession had not been constitutional.

Lincoln set a tone of forgiveness for the postwar era in his Second Inaugural Address:

KEY DOCUMENTS

> **"With malice toward none; with charity for all; with firmness in the right, as God gives us to see the right, let us strive on to finish the work we are in; to bind up the nation's wounds . . . to do all which may achieve and cherish a just, and a lasting peace, among ourselves, and with all nations."**
>
> —*Lincoln's Second Inaugural Address, March 1865*

Congress, however, saw Lincoln's Reconstruction plan as a threat to congressional authority. The Republican leadership warned that Lincoln "should confine himself to his executive duties—to obey and execute, not make the laws . . . and leave political reorganization to Congress."

Much of Lincoln's opposition came from a group of congressmen from his own party. The group, known as the Radical Republicans, believed that the Civil War had been fought over the moral issue of slavery. Therefore the Radicals insisted that the main goal of Reconstruction should be a total restructuring of society to guarantee black people true equality.

The Radical Republicans viewed Lincoln's plan as too lenient. In July 1864 Congress passed its own, stricter Reconstruction plan, the Wade-Davis Act. Among its provisions, it required ex-Confederate men to take an oath of past and future loyalty and to swear that they had never willingly borne arms against the United States. Lincoln let the bill die in a pocket veto.

Lincoln's hopes came to a violent end less than six weeks after his second inauguration. As discussed in the previous chapter, Lincoln was murdered on April 14, 1865, by John Wilkes Booth. The assassination plunged the nation into grief and its politics into chaos.

**Johnson's Plan** With Lincoln's death, Reconstruction was now in the hands of a one-time slave owner from the South: the former Vice President, Andrew Johnson. Born poor in North Carolina, Johnson grew up to become a tailor. He learned to read and write with the help of his wife and later entered politics in Tennessee as a Democrat.

Johnson had a profound hatred of rich planters and found strong voter support among poor white southerners. He served Tennessee first as governor, then in Congress. Johnson was the only southern senator to remain in Congress after secession. Hoping to attract Democratic voters, the Republican party chose Johnson as Lincoln's running mate in 1864.

When Johnson took office in April 1865, Congress was in recess until December.† During those eight months, Johnson pursued his own plan for the South. His plan, known as Presidential Reconstruction, included these provisions:

(1) It pardoned southerners who swore allegiance to the Union.

(2) It permitted each state to hold a constitutional convention (without Lincoln's 10 percent allegiance requirement).

(3) States were required to void secession, abolish slavery, and ratify the Thirteenth Amendment.

(4) States could then hold elections and resume participation in the Union.

Presidential Reconstruction reflected the spirit of Lincoln's Ten Percent Plan but was more generous to the South. Although officially it denied pardons to all Confederate leaders, in reality Johnson often issued pardons to those who asked him personally. In 1865 alone, he pardoned 13,000 southerners.

**Main Idea CONNECTIONS**

*How did Johnson's Reconstruction plan differ from Lincoln's?*

† Until the mid-1900s, a typical session of the United States Congress lasted only four or five months. Today, Congress remains in session throughout most of the year.

Freedom opened new opportunities for African Americans, such as forming choirs (top left), preaching (above), and getting an education (right). ***Culture* Why do you think northerners volunteered to teach at freedmen's schools?**

## The Taste of Freedom

As politicians debated, African Americans celebrated their new freedom. No longer were they mere property, subject to the whims of white slave owners.

The feeling was overwhelming. "Everybody went wild," said Charles Ames, a Georgia freedman. "We all felt like horses. . . . We was free. Just like that, we was free."

Booker T. Washington, a future leader in black education, was nine years old when the news came: "[W]e were told that we were all free and could go when and where we pleased. My mother, who was standing by my side, leaned over and kissed her children, while tears of joy ran down her cheeks."

**Freedom of Movement** During the war, enslaved people had simply walked away from the plantations upon hearing that a northern army approached. "Right off colored folks started on the move," said James, a freed cowhand from Texas. "They seemed to want to get closer to freedom, so they'd know what it was like—like it was a place or a city."

Many freed people took to the roads looking for family members who had been torn from them by slavery. Not all were successful in finding loved ones, but many joyful reunions did occur. In addition, many couples who had been forbidden to marry under slavery now found each other and got legally married.

**Freedom to Own Land** Black leaders knew that emancipation—physical freedom—was only a start. True freedom would come only with economic independence, the ability to get ahead through hard work.

Freed people urged the federal government to redistribute southern land. They argued that they were entitled to the land that slaves had cleared and farmed for generations.

A Virginia freedman put it this way: "We have a right to the land where we are located. For why? I tell you. Our wives, our children, our husbands, have been sold over and over again to purchase the lands we now locate upon; for that reason we have a divine right to the land."

Proposals to give white-owned land to freedmen got little political support.† Instead, small-scale, unofficial land redistribution took place. For example, in 1871 Amos Morel, the freedman who stayed on at the White Hall plantation, used his wages to buy more than 400 acres of land. He sold pieces to other freedmen and later bought land for his daughter.

† In 1865, Union general William Tecumseh Sherman had set up a land-distribution experiment in South Carolina. He divided confiscated coastal lands into 40-acre plots and gave them to black families. Soon the South buzzed with rumors that the government was going to give all freedmen "forty acres and a mule." Sherman's project was highly successful. However, President Johnson eventually returned much of the land to its original owners, forcing the freedmen out.

**Freedom to Worship** In their struggle to survive, African Americans looked to each other for help. New black organizations arose throughout the South. The most visible were churches. African Americans throughout the South withdrew from racially mixed congregations to form their own churches. They also started thousands of voluntary groups, including mutual aid societies, debating clubs, drama societies, and trade associations.

**Freedom to Learn** Historians estimate that in 1860, 90 percent of black adults were illiterate, partly because many southern states had banned the educating of slaves.

One supporter of black education was Charlotte Forten, a wealthy black woman from Philadelphia. In 1862, after Union troops occupied Port Royal, South Carolina, Forten went there to teach. She observed:

**AMERICAN VOICES** "I never before saw children so eager to learn. Coming to school is a constant delight and recreation to them. . . . Many of the grown people [also] are desirous of learning to read. It is wonderful how a people who have been so long crushed to the earth . . . can have so great a desire for knowledge, and such a capability for attaining it."

—*Charlotte Forten*

Help came from several directions. White teachers, often young women, went south to start schools. Some freed people taught themselves and one another. Between 1865 and 1870, black educators founded thirty African American colleges.

Near the White Hall plantation, two former slaves purchased property in 1870. There they created a center of education and vocational training for African Americans.

**The Freedmen's Bureau** To help black southerners adjust to freedom, Congress created the Freedmen's Bureau in March 1865, just prior to Lincoln's death. It was the first major federal relief agency in United States history.

The Freedmen's Bureau lacked strong support in Congress, and the agency was largely dismantled in 1869. Yet in its short existence the bureau gave out clothing, medical supplies, and millions of meals to both black and white war refugees. More than 250,000 African American students received their first formal education in bureau schools.

For a time, the bureau also distributed confiscated Confederate land to farmers. However, when President Johnson returned these properties to their white owners, black farmers again found themselves landless.

*This child proudly displays clothes and a book furnished by the Freedmen's Bureau.*

## SECTION 1 REVIEW

### Comprehension

1. *Key Terms* Define: (a) Reconstruction; (b) pardon.
2. *Summarizing the Main Idea* How did Johnson's Reconstruction plan differ from Lincoln's?
3. *Organizing Information* Create a chart that describes the challenges faced by three different groups of southerners after the Civil War.

### Critical Thinking

4. *Analyzing Time Lines* Review the time line at the start of the section. Which event on that time line, in your opinion, had the greatest long-term importance? Explain your reasoning.
5. *Determining Relevance* Why was it more difficult for freedmen to exercise their freedom to own land than it was for them to exercise their freedoms to worship or to become educated?

### Writing Activity

6. *Writing a Persuasive Essay* Should the federal government have taken land from white southerners and given it to former slaves? Write an essay in support of or in opposition to this idea.

# SKILLS FOR LIFE

Geography

Graphs and Charts

Historical Evidence

Critical Thinking

# How Maps Show Change over Time

An important task of historians is identifying change over time. One far-reaching change that took place in American life after the Civil War was the breakup of plantations. Maps can show important evidence of such a development.

The historical maps below show the changes to 2,000 acres of land in the post–Civil War South. Use the following steps to identify the changes for which the maps provide evidence.

**1.** ***Identify the location, time period, and subject matter covered by the maps.*** (a) What specific area of land do the maps show, and where is it located? (b) What dates are given on the maps? (c) What physical features do the maps show?

**2.** ***Analyze the key to determine the type of data that it provides.*** Map keys use symbols and colors to illustrate specific data. (a) What do the brown squares represent in the map on the left? (b) What do the green squares represent in the map on the right? (c) How is the symbol for a church distinguishable from the symbol for a schoolhouse?

**3.** ***Analyze the data in the maps.*** Now compare these maps to draw conclusions about the change over time that they indicate. (a) Over what period of time has the change taken place? (b) How has the location of dwellings on the plantation changed during this period? (c) What new buildings have been added? (d) What historical events and trends helped to produce the changes that these maps illustrate?

**TEST FOR SUCCESS**

If the years of the maps were not labeled, would you be able to tell which map showed the plantation in 1860 and which showed the land in 1881? Explain your answer.

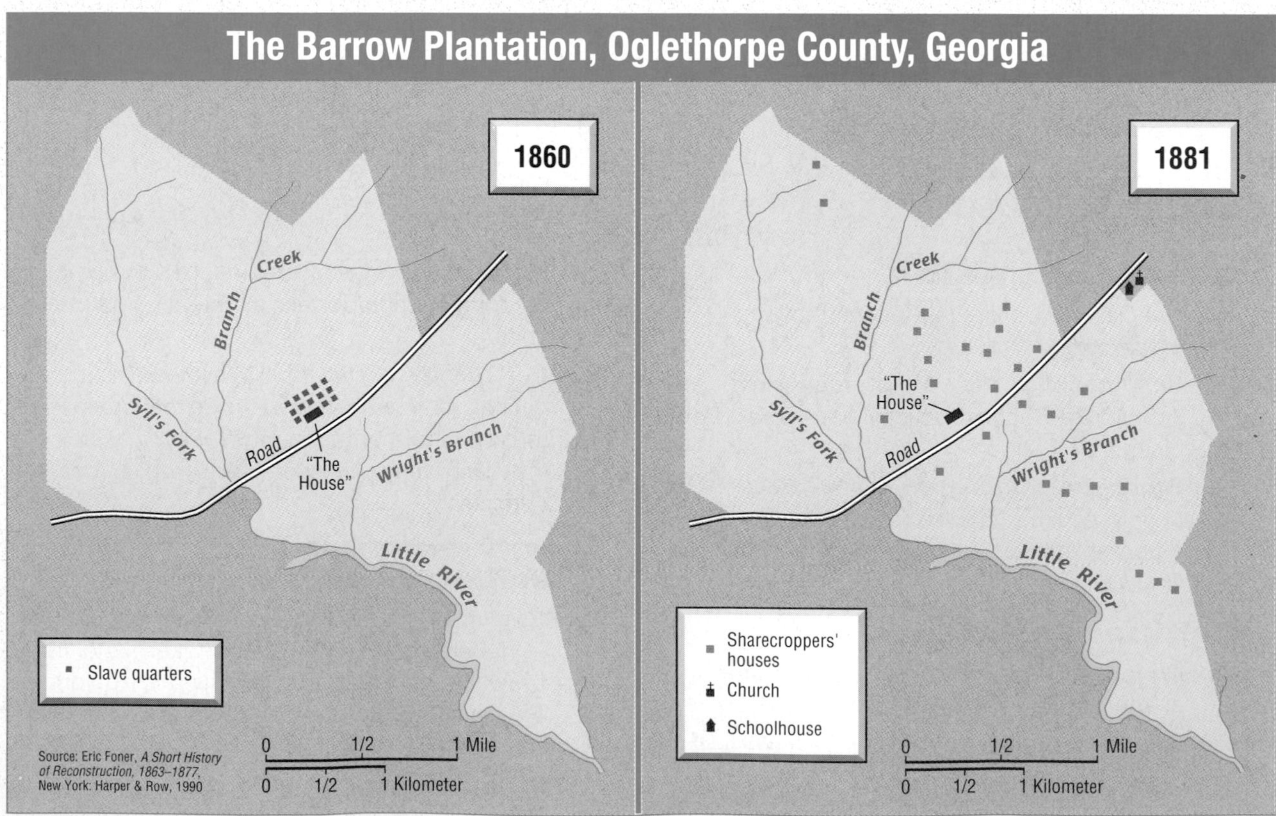

1865
Southern states pass black codes

1867
Radical Reconstruction

1868
President Johnson impeached

1868
Fourteenth Amendment ratified

1870
Fifteenth Amendment ratified

1865 1866 1867 1868 1869 1870

# 2 Congressional Reconstruction

## SECTION PREVIEW

### Objectives

1. Describe the relationship between the black codes and Fourteenth Amendment.
2. Summarize the effects of Radical Reconstruction and of the Fifteenth Amendment.
3. Analyze conditions in the South under Republican government.
4. *Key Terms* Define: black codes; Fourteenth Amendment; civil rights; impeach; Fifteenth Amendment; carpetbagger; scalawag.

### Main Idea

As southern states moved to limit freedmen's rights, Congress took over Reconstruction and passed new laws to protect African Americans' freedom.

### Reading Strategy

*Problem Solving* In the late 1860s, southern states were putting ex-Confederates back in power and trying to keep freedmen in slavelike conditions. List some possible solutions to this problem. As you read, take specific notes on how Congress actually responded.

Black southerners in 1865 faced unseen dangers on the road to freedom. For many African Americans, the initial surge of joy quickly turned to a thousand worrisome questions.

How would freedmen feed and house themselves? Who would take care of the old, the sick, and the orphaned? How could families leave the plantation to seek a better life? Where could they get help in a place where some angry ex-Confederates still carried a gun and a grudge?

## Black Codes

Defeat in war had not changed the fact that white people still dominated southern society. As one white Georgian noted: "[The freedman] has no land; he can make no crops except the white man gives him a chance. . . . He can scarcely get work anywhere but in the rice-fields and cotton plantations. . . . What sort of freedom is that?"

Indeed, one of the main goals of the Civil War, freedoms for enslaved people, was being rolled back. One by one, southern states met Johnson's Reconstruction demands and were restored to the Union. The first order of business in these new, white-run governments was to enact **black codes,** laws that restricted freedmen's rights. The black codes established virtual slavery with provisions such as these:

*Curfews.* Generally, black people could not gather after sunset.

*Vagrancy laws.* Freedmen convicted of vagrancy—that is, not working—could be fined, whipped, or sold for a year's labor.

*Labor contracts.* Freedmen had to sign agreements in January for a year of work. Those who quit in the middle of a contract often lost all the wages they had earned.

*Limits on women's rights.* Mothers who wanted to stay home and care for their families were forced instead to do farm labor.

*Land restrictions.* Freed people could rent land or homes only in rural areas. This forced them to live on plantations.

Southern defiance of Reconstruction enraged northern Republicans in Congress.

They blamed President Johnson for southern Democrats' return to power. Determined to bypass Johnson, Congress used one of its greatest tools: the power to amend the Constitution.

## *Turning Point: Fourteenth Amendment*

In early 1866 Congress passed a Civil Rights Act that outlawed the black codes. Johnson vetoed the measure. As President, Johnson was head of the Republican party. Yet instead of leading congressional Republicans, he was often at odds with them.

As an unelected former Democrat, Johnson had no mandate to govern. A mandate is voter approval of a politician's policies that is implied when he or she wins an election. Lack of a mandate limited Johnson's ability to influence Congress.

Congress overrode the President's veto. Then it took further action. Concerned that courts might strike down the Civil Rights Act, Congress decided to build equal rights into the Constitution. In June 1866 Congress passed the **Fourteenth Amendment,** which was ratified by the states in 1868. The amendment states:

**KEY DOCUMENTS**

> **"All persons born or naturalized in the United States . . . are citizens of the United States and of the State wherein they reside. No State shall make or enforce any law which shall abridge the privileges or immunities of citizens of the United States; nor shall any State deprive any person of life, liberty, or property, without due process of law; nor deny to any person within its jurisdiction the equal protection of the laws. . . ."**
>
> —*Fourteenth Amendment, Section 1*

## TURNING POINT: *The Fourteenth Amendment*

**Ratification of this landmark amendment made possible future victories for American citizens seeking "equal protection of the laws," as the time line below illustrates.**

**1868**
*The Fourteenth Amendment is ratified.*

**1938**
*Congress passes the Fair Labor Standards Act, banning child labor and setting a minimum wage and maximum hours.*

*In the 1960s and beyond, women and minorities sought "equal protection" in jobs, housing, and other areas.*

**1850** **1900** **1950** **2000**

**1920**
*American women gain the right to vote with passage of the Nineteenth Amendment. Photo (left) shows women filling in a map to show states that had approved the amendment.*

**1992**
*Carol Moseley-Braun becomes the first African American woman elected to the United States Senate.*

The full text of the Fourteenth Amendment is on pages 60–61. Its effects have echoed throughout American history, as shown in the time line on the previous page.

## *Radical Reconstruction*

The congressional Republicans who drafted the Fourteenth Amendment consisted of two major groups. One group was the Radical Republicans. Radicals were small in number but increasingly influential. Most Republicans, however, saw themselves as moderates. In politics, a moderate is someone who supports the mainstream views of the party, not the more extreme positions.

Moderates and Radicals both opposed Johnson's Reconstruction policies, opposed the spread of black codes, and favored the expansion of the Republican party in the South. But moderates were less enthusiastic over the Radicals' goal of granting African Americans their **civil rights,** citizens' personal liberties guaranteed by law, such as voting rights and equal treatment. (See Government Concepts at right.) Racial inequality was still common in the North, and moderates did not want to impose stricter laws on the South than those in the North.

**The North Grows Impatient** This reluctance began to dissolve in early 1866, as word spread of new violence against African Americans. In April, the famous Civil War nurse Clara Barton gave graphic testimony in Congress about injured black victims she had treated. During the next three months, white rioters went on rampages against African Americans in Memphis, Tennessee; New Orleans, Louisiana; and New York City. White police joined in the stabbings, shootings, and hangings that killed hundreds.

Despite public outrage against the brutality, Johnson continued to oppose equal rights for African Americans. In the 1866 congressional elections, he gave speeches urging states not to ratify the Fourteenth Amendment. Angry northern voters responded by sweeping Radical Republicans into Congress. Now, Radicals could put their own Reconstruction plans into action.

**Strict Laws Imposed** Calling for "reform, not revenge," Radicals in Congress passed the Reconstruction Act of 1867. Historians note that this was indeed a "radical" act in American history. These are its key provisions:

(1) It put the South under military rule, dividing it into five districts, each governed by a northern general. (See map on the next page.)

(2) It ordered southern states to hold new elections for delegates to create new state constitutions.

(3) It required states to allow all qualified male voters, including African Americans, to vote in the elections.

(4) It temporarily barred southerners who had supported the Confederacy from voting.

(5) It required southern states to guarantee equal rights to all citizens.

(6) It required the states to ratify the Fourteenth Amendment.

**GOVERNMENT CONCEPTS**

***civil rights: the rights to which every citizen is entitled***

▼ **The Historical Context:** The first Civil Rights Act, in 1866, guaranteed citizenship to African Americans. The second, in 1875, guaranteed them equal rights in public places. More fundamentally, in 1868 the Fourteenth Amendment made protection of civil rights part of the Constitution.

▼ **The Concept Today:** Violations of African Americans' civil rights continued and even increased following Reconstruction. Nearly a century later, the civil rights movement of the 1950s and 1960s fought to erase laws that discriminated against African Americans. Today it is illegal to discriminate on the basis of race.

**Congress and the President** The stage was now set for a showdown that pitted Johnson against two powerful Radical Republicans in Congress. Massachusetts Senator Charles Sumner, a founder of the Republican party, was a passionate abolitionist who sought voting rights for black Americans.

In the House, Johnson faced Thaddeus Stevens, a Pennsylvania congressman with a stern face and a personality to match. Stevens led the charge that threatened to bring down Johnson's presidency.

**Main Idea CONNECTIONS**

*What were the main goals of Radical Reconstruction?*

At face value, the contest was a test of wills between the President and his congressional adversaries. Yet it was also a power struggle between the legislative and executive branches of government, a test of the system of checks and balances established by the Constitution.

**A Power Struggle** The crisis began in early 1868, when Johnson tried to fire Secretary of War Edwin Stanton, a Lincoln appointee. Johnson wanted Stanton out because, under the new Reconstruction Act, Stanton, a friend of the Radicals, would preside over military rule of the South.

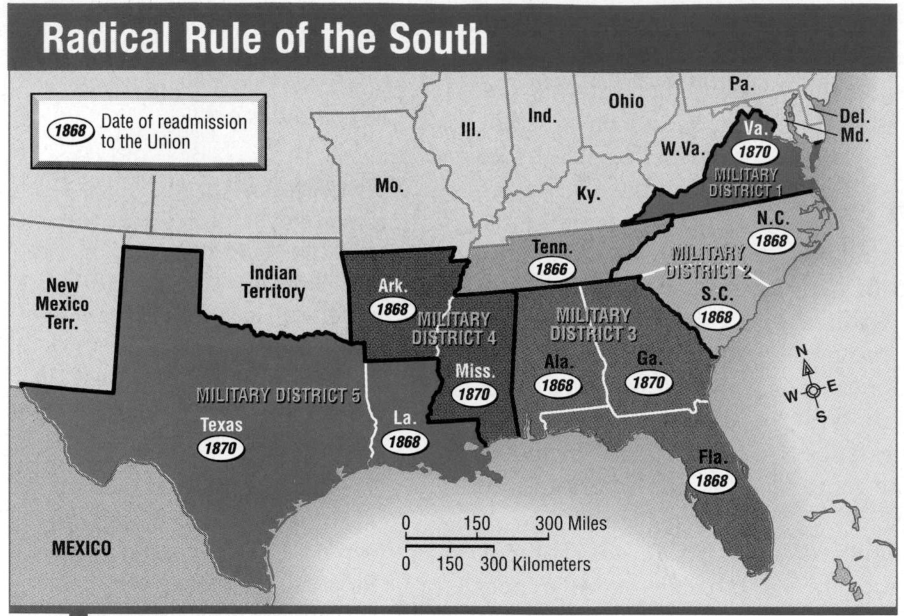


**MAP skills** President Lincoln had hoped to restore southern state governments to "successful operation, with order prevailing and the Union reestablished," by December 1865. Under Radical Republican rule, however, this did not happen for more than a decade. ***Place*** ***Which state was the first to rejoin the Union? Which states rejoined in 1870?***

The firing of Stanton directly challenged the Tenure of Office Act just passed by Congress in 1867. The act placed limits on the President's power to hire and fire government officials.

Under the Constitution, the President must seek Senate approval for candidates to fill certain jobs, such as Cabinet posts. The Tenure of Office Act demanded that the Senate approve the firing of those officials as well, thereby limiting the President's power to create an administration to his own liking. The act also took away the President's constitutional powers as commander in chief of the armed forces.

**Johnson Impeached** Led by the fiery Stevens, the House found that Johnson's firing of Stanton was unconstitutional. On February 24, 1868, House members voted to **impeach** him—to charge him with wrongdoing in office. Johnson became the first President to be impeached.

As called for by the Constitution, in May 1868 the Senate tried President Andrew Johnson for "high crimes and misdemeanors." If two thirds of the senators were to vote for conviction, Johnson would become the first and only President ever removed from office.

The historic vote took place on May 16, 1868. When all the "ayes" and "nays" were counted, Johnson had escaped by the closest of margins: one vote.† The crisis set the precedent that only the most serious crimes, and not merely a dispute with Congress, could remove a President from office.

**Grant Is Elected** President Johnson, as the saying goes, "won the battle but lost the war." He served the remaining months of his term, but with no mandate and no real power. Rejected by the party that had never really embraced him, Johnson went back to Tennessee and regained his Senate seat—as a Democrat.

In the 1868 election, Republicans chose a trusted candidate who was one of their own: the victorious Civil War general, Ulysses S. Grant. In a close race, Grant beat Democrat Horatio Seymour, former governor of New York. Now, Congress and the President were allies, not enemies.

## *The Fifteenth Amendment*

Across the South, meanwhile, freedmen were beginning to demand the rights of citizenship: to vote, to hold public office, to serve on juries, and to testify in court. In a letter to the Tennessee constitutional convention dated January 9, 1865, Nashville freedmen eloquently presented the case for black voting rights:

† All but one senator had declared their votes even before the trial had begun. The lone holdout was Kansas Republican Edmund G. Ross, an opponent of Johnson. His yes vote would have given Radicals the two-thirds majority needed to convict. Despite bribes and threats, Ross insisted on hearing the evidence before deciding. In the end he felt there was insufficient evidence, and he voted with the Democrats and six other Republicans not to convict. For following his conscience, Ross was severely condemned and eventually forced out of office.

**AMERICAN VOICES** "If [freedmen] are good law-abiding citizens, praying for its prosperity, rejoicing in its progress, paying its taxes, fighting its battles, making its farms, mines, work-shops and commerce more productive, why deny them the right to have a voice in the election of its rulers?"

—*The "black citizens of Nashville"*

The letter received no known response. Yet African Americans, and their supporters in Congress, pressed on. (See Comparing Primary Sources on the right.)

In February 1869, at the peak of Radical power, Congress passed the **Fifteenth Amendment** to the Constitution. It stated that no citizen may be denied the right to vote "by the United States or by any State on account of race, color, or previous condition of servitude." Ratified in March 1870, the Fifteenth Amendment was one of the last major pieces of Reconstruction legislation.

The Supreme Court added its weight to the federal Reconstruction effort in 1869. In *Texas v. White,* the Court upheld Congress's right to restructure southern governments. The ruling added new support for federal power over states' rights.

In 1870, with federal troops stationed across the South and with the Fifteenth Amendment in place, southern black men proudly voted. Most voted Republican, while many angry white voters stayed home. The unique situation swept Republicans, including hundreds of freedmen, into public office in the South.

More than 600 African Americans were elected to southern legislatures. Louisiana gained a black governor, P.B.S. Pinchback. Sixteen black men went to Congress. In 1874, Mississippi sent to the Senate a former slave, Blanche Bruce.

## COMPARING PRIMARY SOURCES

### VOTING RIGHTS FOR AFRICAN AMERICANS

The question of whether to extend voting rights to African Americans was hotly debated in the 1860s.

| In Favor of Voting Rights | Opposed to Voting Rights |
|---|---|
| "If impartial suffrage is excluded in rebel States, then every one of them is sure to send a solid rebel representative delegation to Congress, and cast a solid rebel electoral vote. They . . . would always elect the President and control Congress. . . . I am for negro suffrage in every rebel state. If it be just, it should not be denied; if it be necessary, it should be adopted; if it is a punishment to traitors, they deserve it." <br>*—Speech by Thaddeus Stevens, Radical Republican, January 3, 1867* | "Most of the whites are disenfranchised [not legally able to vote] and ineligible for office, whilst the Negroes are [granted] the right of voting. The political power is therefore thrown into the hands of a mass of human beings who, having just emerged from a state of servitude [slavery], are ignorant of the forms of government and totally unfit to exercise this, the highest privilege of a free people." <br>*—Henry William Ravenel, South Carolina planter, journal entry for February 24, 1867* |

***ANALYZING VIEWPOINTS*** **Compare the main arguments made by the two writers.**

## *Blanche K. Bruce*

**AMERICAN BIOGRAPHY** A boy born into slavery in 1841 could expect little more than a life of servitude. Blanche K. Bruce was more fortunate than some. Growing up in Virginia and Missouri, he shared a tutor with his master's son. Bruce later attended Oberlin College in Ohio, until his money ran out.

Bruce then moved to Mississippi and recruited Republicans from among freedmen on the plantations. In 1871 he ran for sheriff of Bolivar County, Mississippi. In a debate, his opponent, a white Democrat, called Bruce "a slave who did nothing but wait on his master."

"It is true that I was a house slave," Bruce replied. "But I freed myself, educated myself, and raised myself up in the world. If my opponent had started out where I did, he would still be there."

Bruce won the sheriff's post, and held other government jobs as well. He worked to ease racial and political tensions, earning respect from Radical and moderate Republicans—even white planters who opposed Reconstruction. In 1874 Bruce won election to the United States Senate.

In Congress Bruce worked to help African Americans. He opposed moves

*Blanche K. Bruce (1841–1898)*

to encourage black people to relocate in the West African country of Liberia. Instead he urged freedmen to stay, get an education, and fight for equality. At his death in 1898, Blanche Bruce was said to be second only to Frederick Douglass as a leader of African Americans.

## *The Republican South*

During Radical Reconstruction, the Republican party was a mixture of people who had little in common but a desire to prosper in the postwar South. This strong bloc of voters included freedmen and two other groups.

*The carpetbag became a symbol of corruption and greed.*

**Carpetbaggers** Northern Republicans who moved to the postwar South became known as **carpetbaggers.** Southerners gave them this insulting nickname, which referred to a type of cheap suitcase made from carpet scraps. The name implied that these northerners had stuffed some clothes into a carpetbag and rushed in to profit from southern misery.

Carpetbaggers were often depicted as greedy men seeking to grab power or make a fast buck. Certainly the trainloads of northerners who disembarked in southern cities included some profiteers and swindlers. Yet historians point out that most carpetbaggers were honest, educated men. They included former union soldiers, black northerners, Freedmen's Bureau officials, businessmen, clergy, and political leaders.

**Scalawags** In the postwar South, to be white and a southerner and a Republican was to be seen as a traitor. Southerners had an unflattering name for white southern Republicans as well: **scalawag,** originally a Scottish word meaning "scrawny cattle." Some scalawags were former Whigs who had opposed secession. Some were small farmers who resented the planter class. Still others were former planters. Many scalawags, but not all, were poor.

Many Southern whites, resenting the power of freedmen, carpetbaggers, and scalawags, criticized the Reconstruction governments as corrupt and incompetent. In reality, Reconstruction legislatures included honest men and dishonest men, qualified politicians and incompetent ones, literate men and a few illiterate ones. Today, most historians agree that these officials were no worse and no better than officials in other regions of the country at this time.

## SECTION 2 REVIEW

### Comprehension

1. *Key Terms* Define: (a) black codes; (b) Fourteenth Amendment; (c) civil rights; (d) impeach; (e) Fifteenth Amendment; (f) carpetbagger; (g) scalawag.
2. *Summarizing the Main Idea* Why did Congress take over Reconstruction, and what policies did it create?
3. *Organizing Information* Create a cause-and-effect chart on Radical Reconstruction.

### Critical Thinking

4. *Analyzing Time Lines* Review the time line at the start of the section. Write a phrase or sentence that connects each entry to the entry that follows it.
5. *Drawing Conclusions* How was the impeachment of Andrew Johnson a test of the nation's system of checks and balances?

### Writing Activity

6. *Writing an Expository Essay* From the perspective of a journalist traveling in the postwar South, write an expository essay describing the effects of Republican government on the region.

1865 Thirteenth Amendment ends slavery

1866 Southern Homestead Act

1872 All southern states have public schools

1872 Rebuilding of southern railroads complete

1865 | 1870 | 1875

# 3 Birth of the "New South"

## SECTION PREVIEW

### Objectives

1. Summarize the post–Civil War changes in southern agriculture.
2. Explain the achievements and limitations of urban and industrial growth in the South.
3. List the beneficial and the harmful ways in which Reconstruction funds were used.
4. *Key Terms* Define: sharecropping; tenant farming; infrastructure.

### Main Idea

Reconstruction transformed the South's economy, as plantations adjusted to the loss of slave labor and the region began to attract investment and industry.

### Reading Strategy

*Formulating Questions* Reread the Main Idea above. Then rewrite it as a question. As you read, take notes that help answer that question.

"No man can work another man's land [without getting] poorer and poorer every year," a black southerner wrote during Reconstruction. One black family in postwar Alabama found this out the hard way.

The Holtzclaw family worked on the cotton farm of a white planter. Every year at harvest time they received part of the cotton crop as payment for their work. But you can't eat cotton, and most years the Holtzclaws' share of the harvest didn't earn them enough money to feed themselves.

Some years the planter gave them nothing at all. So the mother worked as a cook. The father hauled logs at a sawmill for 60 cents a day. The children would wade knee-deep in swamps gathering anything edible. This was not the freedom they had hoped for.

## Changes in Farming

The Holtzclaws were part of an economic reorganization in the "New South" of the 1870s. It was triggered by the ratification of the Thirteenth Amendment in 1865, which ended slavery and shook the economic foundations of the South.

The loss of slave labor raised grave questions for southern agriculture. Would cotton still be king? If so, who would work the plantations? Would freed people flee the South or stay? How would black emancipation affect the poor white laborers of the South? No one really knew.

**Wanted: Workers** Although the Civil War left southern plantations in tatters, the destruction was not permanent. Many planters managed to hang on to their land, and others regained theirs after climbing out of debt.

Planters complained, however, that they couldn't find people willing to work for them. Nobody liked picking cotton in the blazing sun. It seemed too much like slavery. Workers often disappeared to look for better, higher-paying jobs. For instance, railroad workers in Virginia in the late 1860s earned $1.75 to $2.00 a day. Plantation wages came to 50 cents a day at best. Women in the fields earned as little as 6 cents a day.

In simple terms, planters had land but no laborers, while freedmen had their own labor but no land. Out of these needs came new patterns of farming in the South.

*With shovels and pickaxes, workers built railroads that crisscrossed the New South.*

## CAUSE AND EFFECT: Sharecropping and Tenant Farming

**CAUSES**

- *Slavery is abolished.*
- *Small farmers lack capital to buy land.*
- *Planters need a stable work force.*

**SHARECROPPING AND TENANT FARMING**

**EFFECTS**

- *Farmers are caught in a cycle of debt.*
- *Planters and merchants prosper.*
- *Agricultural focus shifts from food crops to cash crops.*

**Interpreting Charts** Whether white or black, most southern farmers remained poor in the years following the Civil War—as did this Florida family (right), thought to be sharecroppers or tenant farmers. The chart (left) shows some of the problems that poor families faced. ***Economics How did farmers get caught in a cycle of debt?***

**Main Idea CONNECTIONS**

*In what ways did Reconstruction change agriculture in the South?*

**Sharecropping** The most common new farming arrangement was **sharecropping.** A sharecropping family, such as the Holtzclaws, farmed some portion of a planter's land. As payment the family was promised a share of the crop at harvest time, generally one third or one half of the yield. The planter usually provided housing for the family.

Sharecroppers worked under close supervision and under the threat of harsh punishment. They could be fined for missing a single workday. After the harvest, some dishonest planters simply evicted the sharecroppers without pay. Others charged the families for housing and other expenses, so that the sharecroppers often wound up in debt at the end of the year. Since they could not leave before paying the debt, these sharecroppers were trapped on the plantation.

**Tenant Farming** If a sharecropper saved enough money, he might try **tenant farming.** Like sharecroppers, tenant farmers did not own the land they farmed. Unlike sharecroppers, however, tenant farmers paid to rent the land, just as you might rent an apartment today. Tenants chose what to plant and when to work. Thus they had a higher social status than sharecroppers.

The Holtzclaws managed to move from sharecropping to tenant farming. They rented 40 acres of land. They bought a mule, a horse, and a team of oxen. William Holtzclaw was a child at the time. "We were so happy at the prospects of owning a wagon and a pair of mules, and having only our father for boss, that we shouted and leaped for joy," he later recalled.

**Effects on the South** Changes in farming during Reconstruction affected the South's economy in several important ways:

*Changes in the labor force.* Before the Civil War, 90 percent of the South's cotton was harvested by slaves. By 1875, white laborers, mostly tenant farmers, picked 40 percent of the crop.

*Emphasis on cash crops.* Sharecropping and tenant farming encouraged planters to grow cash crops, such as cotton, tobacco, and sugar cane, rather than food crops. The South's postwar cotton production soon surpassed prewar levels. As a result of the focus on cash crops, the South had to import much of its food.

*Cycle of debt.* By the end of Reconstruction, rural poverty was deeply rooted in the South, among blacks and whites alike. They remained in a cycle of debt, in which this year's profits went to pay last year's bills. The Southern Homestead Act of 1866 attempted to break that cycle by offering low-cost land to southerners, black or white, who would farm it. By 1874, black farmers in Georgia owned 350,000 acres. Still, most landless farmers could not afford to participate. In the cotton states, only about one black family in 20 owned land after a decade of Reconstruction.

*Rise of merchants.* Tenant farming created a new class of wealthy southerners: the merchants. Throughout the South, stores sprang up around plantations to sell supplies on credit. "We have stores at almost every crossroad," a journalist observed. By 1880 the South had more than 8,000 rural stores.

Some merchants were honest; others were not. Landlords frequently ran their own stores and forced their tenants to buy there at high prices.

After four years of tenant farming, the Holtzclaws watched as creditors carted away everything they owned. "They came and took our corn and, finally, the vegetables from our little garden, as well as the chickens and the pig," Holtzclaw said. The family had no choice but to return to sharecropping.

## Cities and Industry

Southerners who visited the North after the Civil War were astounded at how industrialized the North had become. The need for large-scale production of war supplies had turned small factories into big industries that dominated the North's economy. Industrialization had produced a new class of wage earners. It had ignited city growth and generated wealth. Could all this happen in the South?

Some southern leaders saw a unique opportunity for their region. They urged the South not simply to rebuild its old agricultural economy but to build a new, industrialized one. One of the pro-business voices was Henry Grady, editor of the *Atlanta Constitution.* He called for a "New South" of growing cities and thriving industries.

**The Growth of Cities** Atlanta, the city so punished by Sherman's army, took Grady's advice. Only months after the war, the city was on its way to becoming a major metropolis of the South, as one observer noted:

> **"A new city is springing up with marvelous rapidity. The narrow and irregular and numerous streets are alive from morning till night . . . with a never-ending throng of . . . eager and excited and enterprising men, all bent on building and trading and swift fortune-making."**
>
> —*Visitor to Atlanta, 1865*

A major focus of Reconstruction, and one of its greatest successes, was the rebuilding and extension of southern railroads. By 1872, southern railroads were totally rebuilt and about 3,300 miles of new track laid, a 40 percent increase.

Railroads turned southern villages into towns, and towns into cities. Commerce and population rose not only in Atlanta, but also in Richmond, Nashville, Memphis, Louisville, Little Rock, Montgomery, and Charlotte. On the western frontier, the Texas towns of Dallas, Houston, and Fort Worth were on the rise.

**Limits of Industrial Growth** Despite these changes, Reconstruction did not transform the South into an industrialized, urban region like the North. Most southern factories did not make finished goods such as furniture. They handled only the early, less profitable stages of manufacturing, such as making lumber or pig iron. These items were shipped north to be made into finished products and sold.

Most of the South's postwar industrial growth came from cotton mills. New factories began to spin and weave cotton into undyed fabric. The value of cotton mill production in South Carolina rose from about $713,000 in 1860 to nearly $3 million by 1880. However, the big profits went to northern companies that dyed the fabric and sold the finished product.

Still, the growth of southern industry planted seeds of economic change. For example, Alabama, already the nation's biggest iron producer, would become a major producer of steel.

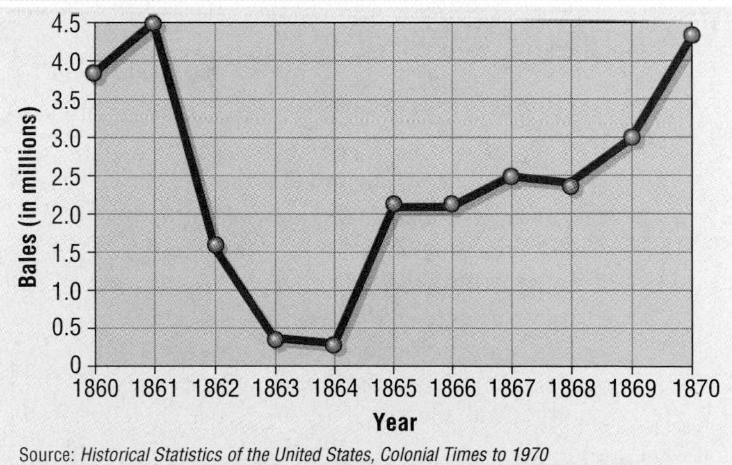

Source: *Historical Statistics of the United States, Colonial Times to 1970*

**Interpreting Graphs** Cotton production was the South's main economic activity until 1930. ***Economics*** ***What accounts for the drop in production in the middle of this chart?***

## *Funding Reconstruction*

The Republicans who led Congress agreed with southern legislatures on the importance of promoting business. The strong conviction that the growth of business would bring better times for everyone was called the "gospel of prosperity." It guided the Reconstruction efforts of Congress and the Reconstruction legislatures throughout the 1870s.

**Raising Money** In a sense, the postwar South was one giant business opportunity. The region's **infrastructure,** the public property and services that a society uses, had to be almost completely rebuilt. That included roads, bridges, canals, railroads, and telegraph lines.

In addition to the rebuilding effort, some states used Reconstruction funds to expand services to their citizens. For instance, following the North's example, all southern states created public school systems by 1872.

Reconstruction legislatures poured money into infrastructure. Some of the money came from Congress and from private investors. The rest, however, was raised by levying heavy taxes on individuals, many of whom were still in deep debt from the war. White southerners, both wealthy and poor, resented this added financial burden.

Spending by Reconstruction legislatures added another $130 million to southern debt. What further angered southerners was evidence that much of this big spending for infrastructure was being lost to corruption.

**Corruption** Today, corruption in government and business is vigorously uncovered and prosecuted. That was not the case a century ago. Government officials in both the North and South regularly used their positions for personal profit.

During Reconstruction, a time of many large and costly government projects, enormous sums of money changed hands rapidly in the form of loans and grants.

The worst cases of fraud involved the railroads. A crooked businessman might bribe a key state senator to win a government contract for construction of a new railroad. The businessman would then collect the construction money, use it for personal investments or even a vacation, then declare bankruptcy. In this way numerous railroads were never built, and millions of dollars raised to rebuild the South evaporated without a trace.

Participants in such schemes included blacks and whites, Republicans and Democrats, southerners and northern carpetbaggers. "You are mistaken if you suppose that all the evils . . . result from the carpetbaggers and negroes," a Louisiana man wrote to a northern fellow Democrat. Democrats and Republicans cooperated "whenever anything is proposed which promises to pay," he observed. The South Carolina legislature even gave $1,000 to the speaker of the House to cover his loss on a horse race!

Not every politician or businessman gave in to temptation. Yet those who did gave Reconstruction a reputation for waste and corruption.

## SECTION 3 REVIEW

### Comprehension

1. *Key Terms* Define: (a) sharecropping; (b) tenant farming; (c) infrastructure.
2. *Summarizing the Main Idea* What effects did Reconstruction have on agriculture and industry in the South?
3. *Organizing Information* Create a diagram to illustrate sharecroppers' cycle of debt. Begin with this entry: "Sharecropper signs one-year contract with planter."

### Critical Thinking

4. *Analyzing Time Lines* Review the time line at the start of the section. Pick one event that was largely successful and one that was not. Write a sentence to explain each of your choices.
5. *Drawing Conclusions* Do you think more Reconstruction money was spent on rebuilding infrastructure, or on housing, jobs, and education for freed people? Explain your answer.

### Writing Activity

6. *Writing an Expository Essay* Write an essay explaining how southern farming changed after the Civil War.

1866
*Ku Klux Klan formed*

1870
*Anti-Klan laws; last states rejoin Union*

1872
*Grant reelected President*

1877
*Hayes wins presidency. Reconstruction ends*

1865 1870 1875 1880

# 4 The End of Reconstruction

## SECTION PREVIEW

### Objectives

1. Assess the impact of racial terrorism on the South.
2. Explain why the Reconstruction period came to an end.
3. List the major successes and failures of Reconstruction.
4. *Key Terms* Define: solid South; Compromise of 1877.

### Main Idea

In the 1870s, white Democrats regained power in the South, and public interest in Reconstruction declined. The program was both a success and a failure.

### Reading Strategy

*Analyzing Cause and Effect* Create a cause-and-effect chart entitled "Why Reconstruction Ended," using the chart in Section 3 as a model. As you read, add information to your chart.

In March 1870 the last southern states were restored to the Union. Yet the United States was still far from united. From 1868 through 1871, groups of white southerners launched a violent backlash against Radical Reconstruction. At the head of the campaign was an organization that started in 1866 as a social club in Tennessee: the Ku Klux Klan, or KKK.

The Klan quickly evolved into a terrorist organization. Klansmen pledged to "defend the social and political superiority" of whites against what they called the "aggressions of an inferior race." The membership consisted largely of ex-Confederate officers and plantation owners who had been excluded from politics. The group also attracted merchants, lawyers, and other professionals. The Klan was supposed to be a "secret society," but in fact most members' identities were well known to their local communities.

## Spreading Terror

During Radical Reconstruction, the Klan sought to eliminate the Republican party in the South by intimidating Republican voters, both white and black. The Klan's long-term goal was to keep African Americans in the role of submissive laborers. This motive still drives Klan activity today.

The Klan's terror tactics varied. Often, horsemen in long robes and hoods appeared suddenly at night, carrying guns and whips. They encircled the homes of their victims, and planted huge burning crosses in their yards. People were dragged from their homes and harassed, tortured, kidnapped, or murdered.

Anyone who didn't share the Klan's goals and hatreds could be a victim: carpetbaggers, scalawags, freedmen who had become prosperous—even those who had merely learned to read. With chilling frequency, black women went to claim the dead bodies of their husbands and sons.

*The Klan left miniature coffins like this, containing written death threats, at the doors of many freedmen and their white supporters.*

**The Federal Response** The violence kindled northern outrage. At President Grant's request, Congress passed a series of anti-Klan laws in 1870 and 1871. The Force Act of 1870 banned the use of terror, force, or bribery to prevent people from voting because of their race. Other laws banned the KKK entirely and strengthened military protection of voters and voting places.

Using troops, cavalry, and the power of the courts, the government arrested and tried thousands of Klansmen. Within a year the KKK was virtually wiped out. Still, the thinly spread federal army could not be everywhere at once. As federal troops gradually withdrew from the South, black suffrage all but ended.

## *Reconstruction Ends*

President Grant, who won reelection in 1872, continued to pursue the goals of Reconstruction, sometimes with energy. However, the widespread corruption in his administration reminded voters of all that was wrong with Reconstruction.

**A Dying Issue** By the mid-1870s, voters had grown weary of Republicans and their decade-long concern with Reconstruction. Historians cite several reasons for this shift:

(1) Reconstruction legislatures taxed and spent heavily, putting southern states into deeper debt.

(2) Reconstruction came to symbolize corruption, greed, and poor government.

(3) As federal troops withdrew from the South, more and more freedmen were prevented from voting, allowing white southerners to regain control of state governments.

(4) White-dominated southern states blocked many federal Reconstruction policies.

(5) Northern voters never fully supported the Radicals' goal of racial equality.

(6) A nationwide economic downturn in 1873 diverted public attention from the movement for equal rights.

The era of Republican control of the South was coming to a close. In 1872 the last ex-Confederates had been pardoned. They combined with other white southerners to form a new bloc of Democratic voters known as the **solid South.** Democrats of the solid South reversed many reforms of the Reconstruction legislatures.

**The Compromise of 1877** Reconstruction politics took a final, sour turn in the presidential election of 1876. Republican Rutherford B. Hayes lost the popular vote to Democrat Samuel Tilden, who had the support of the solid South. The electoral vote, however, was disputed. The map on the left shows the results.

Hayes claimed victory based partly on wins in Florida, Louisiana, and South Carolina. Those states were still under Republican and federal control. Democrats submitted another set of tallies showing Tilden as the winner in those states, and thus in the presidential race.

## Presidential Election of 1876

| Candidate/Party | Electoral Vote | Popular Vote | % Electoral Vote | % Popular Vote |
|---|---|---|---|---|
| Rutherford B. Hayes (Republican) | 185 | 4,034,311 | 50.1 | 48.0 |
| Samuel J. Tilden (Democrat) | 184 | 4,288,546 | 49.9 | 51.0 |
| Peter Cooper (Greenback) | | 75,973 | | 1.0 |
| * States with disputed results | | | | |

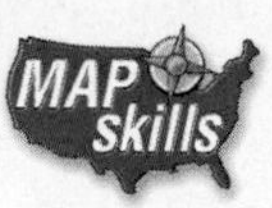


In the tarnished election of 1876, the electoral votes in three states under federal control were disputed, but went to Hayes when he promised to end Reconstruction. ***Location*** *In which states were election results disputed?*

Congress set up a special commission to resolve the election crisis. Not surprisingly, the commission, which included more Republicans than Democrats, named Hayes the victor. However, Democrats had enough strength in Congress to reject the commission's decision.

Finally the two parties made a deal. In the **Compromise of 1877,** the Democrats agreed to give Hayes the victory in the presidential election he had not clearly won. In return, the new President agreed to remove the remaining federal troops from southern states. He also agreed to give huge subsidies to southern railroads. The compromise opened the way for Democrats to regain control of southern politics and marked the end of Reconstruction.

Atlanta, Georgia, rose from the devastation left by the Civil War to become a bustling commercial center, as this 1887 picture shows. ***Government*** ***In what other ways was Reconstruction successful?***

## *Effects of Reconstruction*

Until quite recently, historians saw Reconstruction as a dismal failure, a time simply of corrupt and incompetent government in the South. Today most historians argue that the truth is more complex.

**Successes of Reconstruction** The Reconstruction era included several important accomplishments:

(1) Republicans carried out their two main goals, to rebuild the Union and to help repair the war-torn South.

(2) Reconstruction stimulated economic growth in the South and created new wealth in the North.

(3) The Fourteenth and Fifteenth amendments guaranteed African Americans the rights of citizenship, equal protection under the law, and suffrage. African Americans gained the right to testify in court and to sit on juries.

(4) The Freedmen's Bureau and other organizations helped many black families obtain housing, jobs, and schooling.

(5) Southern states adopted the system of tax-supported, mandatory education practiced in the North. Increased access to education would benefit whites and blacks alike.

**Failures of Reconstruction** Yet the Reconstruction era had a number of failures as well:

(1) As in the era of slavery, most black southerners remained in a cycle of poverty that allowed almost no escape. African Americans still lacked property, economic opportunity, and political power.

(2) After the withdrawal of federal troops from the South, southern state governments and terrorist organizations such as the Ku Klux Klan effectively denied African Americans the right to vote.

(3) Racist attitudes toward African Americans continued, in both the South and the North.

(4) Reconstruction left a lasting bitterness among many white southerners toward the federal government and the Republican party.

(5) While Reconstruction programs resulted in the rebuilding and expansion of southern infrastructure, the region was slow to industrialize. The southern economy continued to emphasize agriculture and to lag far behind the industrialized economy of the North.

(6) Reconstruction did not address concerns of groups such as farmers wanting regulation of railroads, workers seeking safer conditions, and advocates of woman suffrage.

**Main Idea CONNECTIONS**

- ***What trends in the South helped bring about the end of Reconstruction?***
- ***Why do most historians now believe that Reconstruction was not a complete failure?***

**Civil Rights Battles Continue** Members of the women's suffrage movement were angry and disappointed when some Radical Republicans refused to endorse voting rights for women. "Either the theory of our government is false, or women have a right to vote," suffrage worker Lydia Maria Child told the Senate's Radical Republican leader, Charles Sumner, in 1872.

FACT Finder

## Major Reconstruction Legislation

| Date | Legislation | Purpose |
|---|---|---|
| 1865 | 13th Amendment | Abolishes slavery |
| 1865, 1866 | Freedmen's Bureau | Provides services for war refugees and newly freed people |
| 1867 | Reconstruction Acts | Establishes Radical Reconstruction |
| 1868 | 14th Amendment | Defines citizenship; guarantees due process of law and equal protection |
| 1870 | 15th Amendment | Guarantees that voting rights are not denied on the basis of race |
| 1875 | Civil Rights Act | Protects African Americans' rights in public |

**Interpreting Tables** The political cartoon at right shows President Hayes "plowing under" the Reconstruction program. During Reconstruction, the federal government struggled to create a new social and political order in the South. ***Government*** ***What purpose do most of these laws have in common?***

In the decades before the Civil War, women had played prominent roles in the abolitionist movement. During Reconstruction, women's leaders had backed equal rights for African Americans. In both struggles, women pointed out the parallels between the denial of equal rights to blacks and to women. When Reconstruction legislation avoided the issue of women's voting rights, it severed the longtime alliance between abolitionists and the suffrage movement.

For African Americans in the South, Reconstruction's promise of freedom and opportunity would not begin to be realized until the civil rights movement of the 1950s and 1960s. In the words of African American leader W.E.B. du Bois, "The slave went free; stood a brief moment in the sun; then moved back again toward slavery." Or as historian Samuel Eliot Morison concluded, "The North may have won the war, but the white South won the peace."

## SECTION 4 REVIEW

### Comprehension

1. ***Key Terms*** Define: (a) solid South; (b) Compromise of 1877.
2. ***Summarizing the Main Idea*** What were some of the major successes and failures of Reconstruction?
3. ***Organizing Information*** Create a cause-and-effect chart of the events that led to the Compromise of 1877.

### Critical Thinking

4. ***Analyzing Time Lines*** Review the time line at the start of the section. Choose one entry and explain why it was a turning point in the Reconstruction period.
5. ***Identifying Alternatives*** What tactics did some white southerners use to challenge Reconstruction? What might they have done to try to improve Reconstruction governments?

### Writing Activity

6. ***Writing a Persuasive Essay*** In your view, did Reconstruction's successes outweigh its failures? Write an essay explaining your opinion. Support it with specific examples.

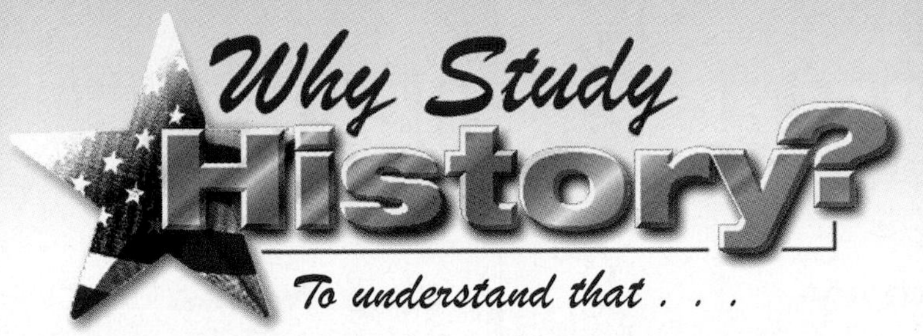


# Congress Represents All Americans

**Although the first African American representatives to Congress were elected during Reconstruction, only in recent years has their number increased substantially.**

*African American congressmen during Reconstruction*

"The right of citizens of the United States to vote shall not be denied or abridged by the United States or by any state on account of race, color, or previous condition of servitude." With ratification of the Fifteenth Amendment in 1870, African Americans won the right to vote. Between 1870 and 1877 sixteen African Americans, including one senator, were elected to Congress.

Many southern whites mobilized against Reconstruction. Through terror and intimidation, the Ku Klux Klan prevented black men from exercising their right to vote. After Reconstruction, the number of black representatives dropped sharply. Only after the civil rights movement secured legal protection of black voting rights in 1965 did the number of black representatives rise again.

## The Impact Today

The number of black representatives rose in the 1990s—in part because several states redrew congressional boundaries to create districts with a large percentage of black voters. Supporters of these "majority-minority districts" see them as a way to give African Americans an equal voice in government. (The percentage of black representatives in Congress is lower than that of African Americans in the population as a whole.) Opponents of the new districts claim that they violate white voters' rights. The Supreme Court has ruled that some of these new districts must be redrawn.

As the number of black representatives has grown, so has the diversity of their views. For example, recent black representatives have disagreed on the degree to which race affects their role in Congress. Democratic senator Carol Moseley-Braun of Illinois, for example, defended government programs that encourage the hiring of minorities. "As a minority," said Moseley-Braun, "I have seen first-hand the benefits" of such programs. By contrast, Republican representative J. C. Watts of Oklahoma stated that he "didn't come to Congress to be a black leader or a white leader but a leader."

*Representative J. C. Watts of Oklahoma*

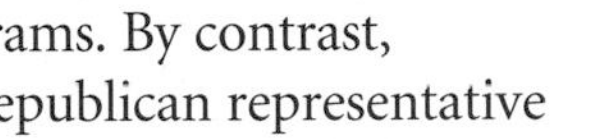

## The Impact on You

Should voters take race into account when choosing a candidate? Write an essay explaining how you, as a future voter, will or will not consider race in elections. As you write your essay, address arguments against your position.

# Chapter 3 Review

## Chapter Summary

CD-ROM REVIEW

The major concepts of Chapter 3 are presented below. See also ***Guide to the Essentials of American History*** or ***Interactive Student Tutorial CD-ROM,*** which contains interactive review activities, time lines, helpful hints, and test practice.

### *Reviewing the Main Ideas*

The end of the Civil War was the beginning of a massive program to repair the South, restructure its economy, reshape its society, and reunite it with the North. Reconstruction forced the nation to grapple with two key issues: the control of southern wealth and political power, and the role and rights of newly freed African Americans.

### *Section 1: Presidential Reconstruction*

Presidents Lincoln and Johnson sought to pardon the South, not to punish it, as freedmen pursued education and jobs.

### *Section 2: Congressional Reconstruction*

Southern defiance of Reconstruction provoked a showdown between President Johnson and Congress and led to major new civil rights laws and Republican control of the South.

### *Section 3: Birth of the "New South"*

Corruption-plagued programs to repair southern war damage brought about limited economic growth.

### *Section 4: The End of Reconstruction*

White southerners undid many Republican reforms, as dwindling northern support brought Reconstruction to an end.

The first African American representatives to Congress were elected during Reconstruction. However, only in recent years has their number increased substantially.

## Key Terms

For each of the terms below, write a sentence explaining how it relates to the post–Civil War period.

1. Reconstruction
2. pardon
3. black codes
4. impeach
5. carpetbagger
6. scalawag
7. sharecropping
8. tenant farmer
9. infrastructure
10. solid South

## Comprehension

1. Name three major problems the South faced at the end of the Civil War.
2. How did Lincoln's plan for Reconstruction compare to Johnson's?
3. How did African Americans try to improve their lives after emancipation?
4. Why did Johnson and Congress clash over Reconstruction?
5. What were the goals of the Fourteenth and Fifteenth amendments?
6. How did Republicans gain control of southern governments?
7. How were Reconstruction legislatures unique in American history?
8. How did the economy of the South change after the Civil War, and in what ways did it remain unchanged?
9. When and why did Reconstruction end?

## Using Graphic Organizers

On a separate sheet of paper, copy the chart below to organize the main ideas of each section in this chapter. Provide at least two supporting details for each main idea.

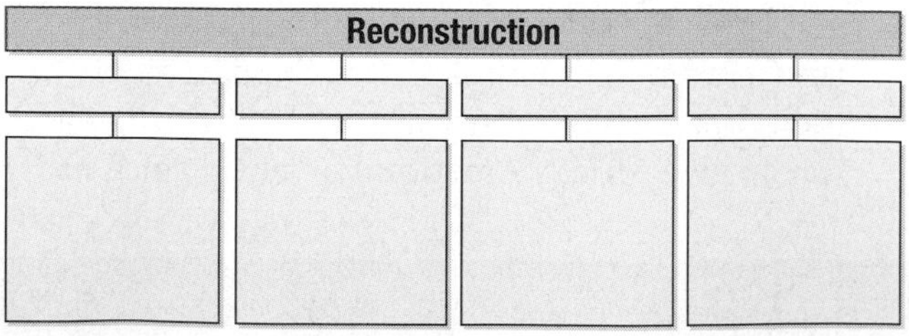

Reconstruction

## Analyzing Political Cartoons ▶

1. This cartoon depicts President Grant riding in a carpetbag. (a) What does Grant represent? (b) What do the soldiers represent? (c) What does the woman represent?
2. State in a sentence or two the message of this cartoon.
3. What was the bias of the cartoonist, and how can you tell?

THE "STRONG" GOVERNMENT 1869–1877.

## Critical Thinking

1. *Applying the Chapter Skill* Evaluate Reconstruction from the point of view of (a) a black sharecropper, (b) an ex-Confederate, (c) a carpetbagger, (d) a Radical Republican.
2. *Identifying Assumptions* Congress accused President Johnson of abusing his presidential powers, and Johnson thought that Congress overstepped its authority in carrying out Radical Reconstruction. What differing assumptions led to these conclusions?
3. *Identifying Central Issues* In what ways was Reconstruction basically a struggle for political power?
4. *Recognizing Ideologies* Why were the strong policies of Radical Reconstruction largely ineffective in changing the attitudes of white southerners toward African Americans?

## INTERNET ACTIVITY

***For your portfolio:***
**PREPARE A REPORT**

Access Prentice Hall's *America: Pathways to the Present* site at **www.Pathways.phschool.com** for the specific URL to complete the activity. Additional resources and related Web sites are also available.

Write a report about Tennessee's Reconstruction experience. Begin by describing Reconstruction in general, then in Tennessee. How did that state's experience differ from Reconstruction elsewhere in the South? How did Reconstruction politics affect Tennessee's African Americans?

## ANALYZING DOCUMENTS ◀ ▶ INTERPRETING DATA

Turn to the "American Voices" quotation in Section 2.

1. Which statement best represents the meaning of the quotation? (a) Freedmen are responsible citizens. (b) Freedmen deserve the right to vote because they earn money for the country. (c) Freedmen deserve the right to vote because they are fulfilling the responsibilities of citizenship. (d) Freedmen deserve to rule themselves.
2. What is the most likely reason the writers never received a response? (a) White Tennesseeans did not want freedmen to vote. (b) White Tennesseans did not want freedmen to become citizens. (c) White Tennesseans thought freedmen should have economic rights, not political rights.
3. *Writing* Do you think the authors emphasized the most important arguments in their letter? Explain your reasoning.

## Connecting to Today

*Essay Writing* Refer to the Turning Point in Section 2. Research and write an essay on one group of Americans today that has benefited from the Fourteenth Amendment. Address these questions: (a) What equal protections have they sought? (b) In the last 50 years, what laws have been passed to grant them equal rights?

# American Heritage®

# My Brush with History

BY DAVID CONYNGHAM

***INTRODUCTION*** The editors of *American Heritage* magazine have selected eyewitness accounts of David Conyngham, an officer in the army of William T. Sherman. Conyngham was also a newspaper correspondent who vividly described his Civil War experiences.

*Union Lieutenant George A. Custer (right) is shown with his friend and prisoner, Confederate Major James Washington.*

*It was no unusual thing* to see our pickets and skirmishers enjoying themselves very comfortably with the rebels, drinking bad whiskey, smoking and chewing worse tobacco, and trading coffee and other little articles. The rebels had no coffee, and our men plenty, while the rebels had plenty of whiskey; so they very soon came to an understanding. It was strange to see these men, who had been just pitted in deadly conflict, trading, and bantering, and chatting, as if they were the best friends in the world. They discussed a battle with the same gusto they would a cock-fight, or horse-race, and made inquiries about their friends, as to who was killed, and who not, in the respective armies. Friends that have been separated for years have met in this way. Brothers who parted to try their fortune have often met on the picket line, or on the battle-field.

I once met a German soldier with the head of a dying rebel on his lap. The stern veteran was weeping, whilst the boy on his knee looked pityingly into his face. They were speaking in German, and from my poor knowledge of the language, all I could make out was, that they were brothers; that the elder had come out here several years before; the younger followed him, and being informed that he was in Macon, he went in search of him, and got conscripted; while the elder brother, who was in the north all the time, joined our army. The young boy was scarcely twenty, with light hair, and a soft, fair complexion. The pallor of death was on his brow, and the blood was flowing from his breast, and gurgled in his throat and mouth, which the other wiped away with his handkerchief. When he could speak, the dying youth's conversation was of the old home in Germany, of his brothers and sisters, and dear father and mother, who were never to see him again.

In those improvised truces, the best possible faith was observed by the men. These truces were brought about chiefly in the following manner. A rebel, who was heartily tired of his crippled position in his pit, would call out, "I say, Yank!"

"Well, Johnny Reb," would echo from another hole or tree.

"I'm going to put out my head; don't shoot."

"Well, I won't."

The reb would pop up his head; the Yank would do the same.

"Hain't you got any coffee, Johnny?"

"Na'r a bit, but plenty of rot-gut."

"All right; we'll have a trade."

They would meet, while several others would follow the example, until there would be a regular bartering mart established. In some cases the men would come to know each other so well, that they would often call out,—

"Look out, reb; we're going to shoot," or "Look out, Yank, we're going to shoot," as the case may be.

Potter House, Atlanta

Blasted by Union artillery fire, the Potter house was one of countless buildings damaged or destroyed by Sherman's forces.

On one occasion the men were holding a friendly reunion of this sort, when a rebel major came down in a great fury, and ordered the men back. As they were going back, he ordered them to fire on the Federals. They refused, as they had made a truce. The major swore and stormed, and in his rage he snatched the gun from one of the men, and fired at a Federal soldier, wounding him. A cry of execration at such a breach of faith rose from all the men, and they called out, "Yanks, we couldn't help it." At night these men deserted into our lines, assigning as a reason, that they could not with honor serve any longer in an army that thus violated private truces. . . .

Our campaign all through Central Georgia was one delightful picnic. We had little or no fighting, and good living. The farm-yards, cellars, and cribs of the planters kept ourselves and animals well stored with provisions and forage. . . .

In passing through the camp one night, I saw a lot of jolly soldiers squatted outside the huts . . . , and between them a table richly stocked with meats and fowls of different kinds, flanked by several bottles of brandy. . . . They thought campaigning in Georgia about the pleasantest sort of life out, and they wondered what would become of the poor dog-gone folks they had left with their fingers in their mouths, and little else to put in them.

Many of our foragers, scouts, and hangers-on of all classes, thought, like Cromwell, that they were doing the work of the Lord, in wantonly destroying as much property as possible. Though this was done extensively in Georgia, it was only in South Carolina that it was brought to perfection. . . .

A planter's house was overrun in a jiffy; boxes, drawers, and escritoires were ransacked with a laudable zeal, and emptied of their contents. If the spoils were ample, the depredators were satisfied, and went off in peace; if not, everything was torn and destroyed, and most likely the owner was tickled with sharp bayonets into a confession where he had his treasures hid. . . . Sorghum barrels were knocked open, bee hives rifled, while their angry swarms rushed frantically about. Indeed, I have seen a soldier knock a planter down because a bee stung him. Hogs are bayonetted, and then hung in quarters on the bayonets to bleed; chickens, geese, and turkeys are knocked over and hung in garlands from the saddles . . . ; cows and calves, so wretchedly thin that they drop down and perish on the first day's march, are driven along, or, if too weak to travel, are shot, lest they should give aid to the enemy.

Should the house be deserted, the furniture is smashed in pieces, music is pounded out of four hundred dollar pianos with the ends of muskets. . . . After all was cleared out, most likely some set of stragglers wanted to enjoy a good fire, and set the house, debris of furniture, and all the surroundings, in a blaze. This is the way Sherman's army lived on the country. They were not ordered to do so, but I am afraid they were not brought to task for it much either.

Source: *Sherman's March Through the South* by David Conyngham, Sheldon & Co., 1865.

### ADDITIONAL READING

**To learn more about the topics discussed in this selection, you might want to read the following books:**

- *For Cause and Comrades: The Will to Combat in the Civil War,* by James M. McPherson (New York: Oxford University, 1997)
- *Marching Through Georgia: The Story of Soldiers and Civilians During Sherman's Campaign,* by Lee B. Kennett (New York: HarperCollins, 1995)
- *Mary Chesnut's Civil War,* edited by C. Vann Woodward (New Haven: Yale University Press, 1981)

# CHAPTER 4 The Expansion of American Industry

## 1850–1900

## CHAPTER FOCUS

*In this chapter you will read about a revolution of new inventions and ideas that transformed the United States after the Civil War. Industrial growth led to more work and wealth for men, women, and business owners. It also led to rising tensions between workers and employers, however.*

*The* **Why Study History?** *page at the end of this chapter explores the connection between today's service economy and the industrial economy that arose in the United States after the Civil War.*

▲ **VIEWING HISTORY**
Citadel Rock looms over the construction of the Union Pacific Railroad through Wyoming Territory in 1868. ***Economics*** ***How was the growth of railroads related to the growth of industry?***

| 1844 | 1856 | 1869 | 1876 | 1880 | 1883 |
|---|---|---|---|---|---|
| *First Morse code telegraph message sent* | *Bessemer process patented* | *Transcontinental railroad completed* | *Bell patents the telephone* | *Edison develops a new light bulb* | *Brooklyn Bridge completed* |

1840 1850 1860 1870 1880 1890

# 1 A Technological Revolution

**SECTION PREVIEW**

**Objectives**

1. Identify some of the changes in people's daily lives in the decades following the Civil War.
2. Describe how advancements in transportation, communication, and electric power affected people and businesses.
3. Explain the effects of the development of the Bessemer process.
4. *Key Terms* Define: patent; productivity; transcontinental railroad; Bessemer process; mass production.

**Main Idea**

In the years after the Civil War, new technology revolutionized American life.

**Reading Strategy**

*Reinforcing Key Ideas* You will be reading about daily life in the United States between 1865 and 1900. As you read, list the ways in which the United States changed in those 35 years.

In the years after the Civil War, the United States developed into an industrial powerhouse. Inventors and scientists, backed by business leaders, created an explosion of inventions and improvements. Their efforts brought about a technological revolution that energized American industry and forever changed people's daily lives.

## Changes in Daily Life

Most Americans today can flip a switch for light, turn a faucet for water, and talk to a friend a thousand miles away just by pressing a few buttons. It is hard for us to imagine life without these conveniences. In 1865, however, daily life was vastly different.

**Daily Life in 1865** Indoor electric lighting did not exist in 1865. Instead, the rising and setting of the sun dictated the rhythm of a day's work. After dark, people lit candles or oil lamps if they could afford them. If they could not, they simply went to sleep, to rise at the first light of dawn.

Imagine summers without the benefits of refrigeration! Ice was available in 1865, but only at great cost. People sawed blocks of ice out of frozen ponds during the winter, packed them in sawdust, and stored them in icehouses for later use.

By modern standards, long-distance communication was agonizingly slow. In 1860, most mail from the East Coast took ten days to reach the Midwest and three weeks to get to the West. An immigrant living on the frontier would wait months for news from relatives in Europe.

*Inventions such as this Singer sewing machine changed daily life for many Americans.*

**Daily Life in 1900** By 1900, this picture of daily life had changed dramatically for millions of Americans. A combination of factors made this change possible.

The post–Civil War years saw tremendous growth in new ideas and inventions. Between 1790 and 1860, the Patent and Trademark Office of the federal government issued just 36,000

This drawing appeared in the April 1890 edition of a journal called *The Woman Inventor.* ***Science and Technology*** ***What does it suggest about women's contributions to the industrial growth of the late 1800s?***

**patents**—licenses to make, use, or sell an invention. In contrast, between 1860 and 1890 500,000 patents were issued for inventions such as the typewriter, sewing machine, and phonograph.

European investors and American business leaders began to invest heavily in new inventions. This combination of American ingenuity and financial backing helped create new industries and expand old ones. By 1900 Americans' standard of living was among the highest in the world. So too was the nation's industrial **productivity**—the amount of goods and services created in a given period of time.

## Railroads Improve Transportation

In 1850 steam-powered ships still provided much of the nation's transportation. Over the following decades, however, improvements in train and track design, plus the construction of new rail lines, gave railroads a big boost.

Before the Civil War most of the nation's railroad tracks were in short lines that connected neighboring cities, mainly in the East. Since there was no standard track width, or gauge, each train could only travel on certain tracks. As a result, goods and passengers often had to be moved to different trains, which caused costly delays. To make matters worse, train travel was dangerous. No system of standard signals existed, and train brakes were unreliable.

**The Transcontinental Railroad** The rail business improved greatly after the Civil War. The key event was the building of the **transcontinental railroad,** a railway extending from coast to coast. The project began in 1862. By this time rail lines already reached from the East Coast to the Mississippi River. Now new rails had to be laid between Omaha, Nebraska, and Sacramento, California.

Government involvement was vital. The project was too big for most private investors, who in any event did not consider building railroads beyond the line of settlement to be profitable. Thus federal government awarded huge loans and land grants to two private companies. The Central Pacific Railroad began laying track eastward out of Sacramento. The Union Pacific Railroad began work toward the west in Omaha.

Most of the workers on the transcontinental railroad were immigrants. Irish workers on the Union Pacific line used pickaxes to dig and level rail beds across the Great Plains at the rate of up to six miles a day. Chinese workers that the Central Pacific had brought to the United States chiseled, plowed, and dynamited their way through the Sierra Nevada mountains.

Finally, after seven years of grueling labor, the two crews approached each other in what is now Utah. On May 10, 1869, at a place called Promontory Point, Central Pacific president Leland Stanford raised his hammer to drive the final, golden spike. A telegraph operator beside the track tapped out a message to crowds throughout the country: "Almost ready now. Hats off. Prayer is being offered. . . . Done!" The nation had its first transcontinental railroad.

**Rail Problems and Solutions** By 1870 railroads could carry goods and passengers from coast to coast, but they still had problems. Trains were often noisy, dirty, and uncomfortable for travelers. The huge engines, spewing smoke and cinders as they thundered through the countryside, aroused fear and distrust.

In spite of the problems, train travel continued to expand and improve. Steel rails replaced iron rails, and track gauges and signals became standardized. Railroad companies also took steps to improve safety. In 1869 George Westinghouse developed more effective air brakes. In 1887 Granville Woods patented a telegraph system for communicating with moving trains, thus reducing the risk of collision.

**Railroads and Time Zones** Scheduling proved to be another problem for railroads. In the 1800s most towns set their clocks independently, according to solar time. When trains started regular passenger service, they had to be "on time." Time differences from town to town created chaos. In 1883 the railroads adopted a national system of time zones to improve

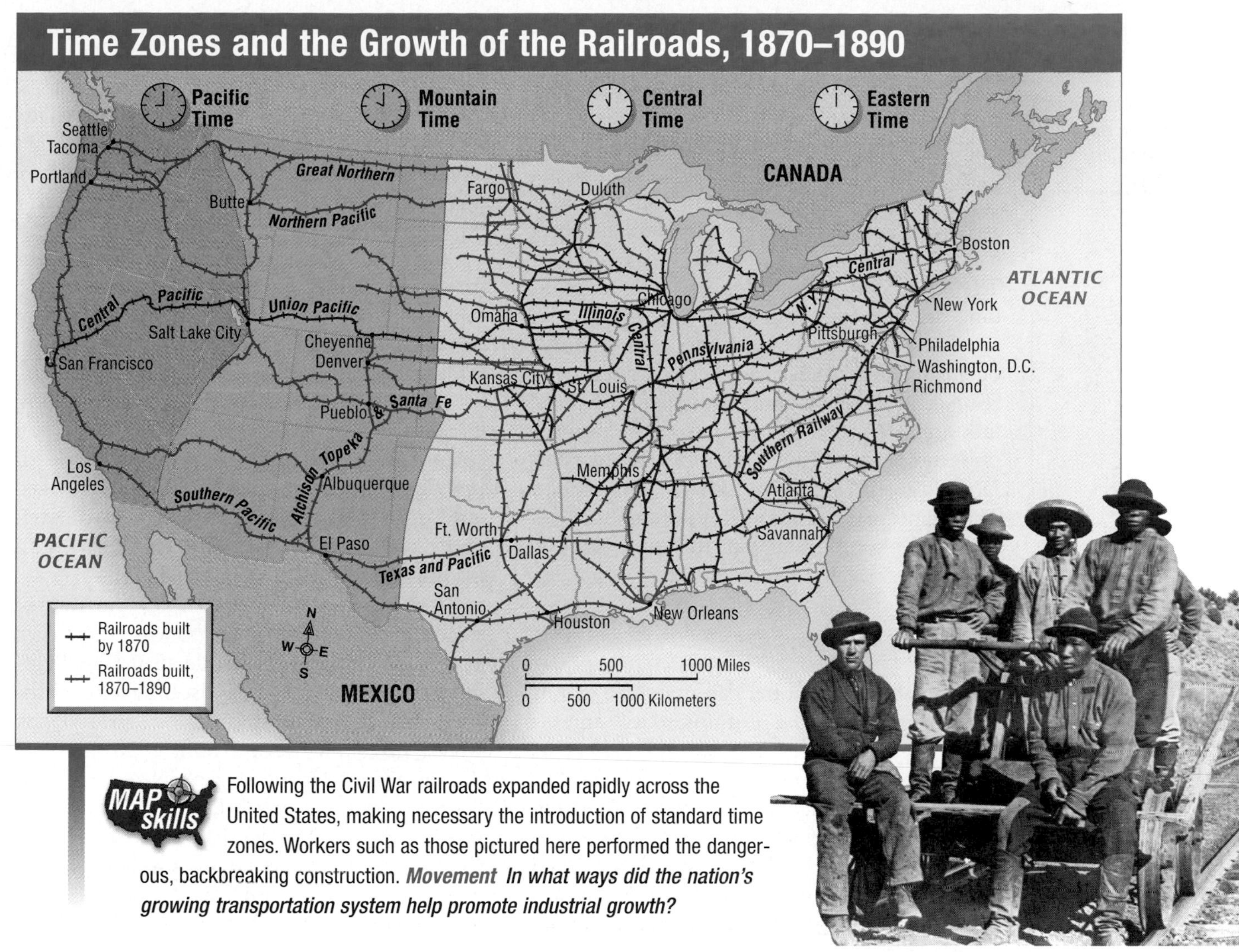


Following the Civil War railroads expanded rapidly across the United States, making necessary the introduction of standard time zones. Workers such as those pictured here performed the dangerous, backbreaking construction. ***Movement*** ***In what ways did the nation's growing transportation system help promote industrial growth?***

scheduling. As a result, clocks in broad regions of the country showed the same time.

Rail improvements such as this made life easier not only for passengers but also for businesses that shipped goods. By the end of the century, some 190,000 miles of rails linked businesses and their customers. Shipping costs dropped enormously. In 1865 shipping a barrel of flour from Chicago to New York cost $3.45. In 1895 it cost just 68 cents.

## *Advances in Communications*

In the late 1800s thousands of people left their homes in Europe and the eastern United States to seek a new life in the West. One of the greatest hardships for these migrants was leaving their loved ones behind. Would they ever hear from family and friends again? By 1900, thanks to many advances in communications, such fears of isolation had diminished.

**The Telegraph** The idea of sending messages over wires had occurred to inventors in the early 1700s. Several inventors actually set up working telegraph systems well before an American, Samuel F. B. Morse, took out a patent on telegraphy.

Morse may not have invented the telegraph, but he perfected it. Morse devised a code of short and long electrical impulses to represent the letters of the alphabet. Using this system, later called Morse code, he sent his first message in 1844. His success signaled the start of a communications revolution.

After the Civil War, several telegraph companies joined together to form the Western Union Telegraph Company. In 1870 Western Union had more than 100,000 miles of wire, over which some 9 million telegraph messages were transmitted. By 1900 the company owned more than 900,000 miles of wire and was sending roughly 63 million telegraph messages a year.

**Main Idea CONNECTIONS**

*How did the telephone revolutionize American life?*

**The Telephone** In 1871 Alexander Graham Bell of Scotland immigrated to Boston, Massachusetts, to teach people with hearing difficulties. After experimenting for several years with an electric current to transmit sounds, Bell patented the "talking telegraph" on March 7, 1876. He had just turned 29. In 1885, Bell and a group of partners set up the American Telephone and Telegraph Company to build long-distance telephone lines.

The earliest local phone lines could connect only two places, such as a home and a business. Soon central switchboards with operators could link an entire city. The first commercial telephone exchange began serving 21 customers on January 28, 1878, in New Haven, Connecticut. That same year President Rutherford B. Hayes had a telephone installed at the White House. By 1900, 1.5 million telephones were in use.

## Electric Power

The blossoming of American inventive genius in the late 1800s had a profound effect on millions of people's lives. For example, scientists began developing new uses for petroleum, including fuels such as gasoline that would help power new machines. Electricity proved to be another productive energy source. It led to many important advances in the nation's industrial development and changed people's eating, working, and even sleeping habits.

**Edison, a Master of Invention** The work of Thomas A. Edison helped make electric power widely available. Born in 1847, Edison grew up tinkering with electricity. While working for a New York company, he improved the stock tickers that sent stock and gold prices to other offices. When his boss awarded him a $40,000 bonus, the 23-year-old Edison left his job and set himself up as an inventor.

In 1876 Edison moved into his "invention factory" in Menlo Park, New Jersey. The young genius, who had never received any formal science training, claimed that he could turn out "a minor invention every ten days and a big thing every six months or so."

Edison's favorite invention, the phonograph, recorded sounds on metal foil wrapped around a rotating cylinder. The first words Edison recorded and then replayed on his phonograph were "Mary had a little lamb." This wondrous machine, introduced in 1877, gained Edison the nickname "Wizard of Menlo Park."

Edison also experimented with electric lighting. His goal was to develop affordable, in-home lighting to replace oil lamps and gaslights. Starting around 1879, Edison and his fellow inventors tried different ways to produce light within a sealed glass bulb. They needed to find a material that would glow without quickly burning up when heated with an electric current.

The team experimented with various threadlike filaments with little success. In 1880 they finally found a workable filament made of bamboo fiber. This filament glowed, Edison said, with "the most beautiful light ever seen."

Other inventors later improved upon Edison's work. Lewis Latimer, the son of an escaped slave, patented an improved method for producing the filament in light bulbs. He worked in Edison's laboratories, where he helped develop new advances in electricity. He later wrote a landmark book about electric lighting.

Until the early 1880s people who wanted electricity had to produce it with their own generator. Hoping to provide affordable lighting to many customers, Edison developed the idea of a central power station. In 1882, to attract investors, Edison built a power plant that lit dozens of buildings in New York City. Investors were impressed, and Edison's idea spread. By 1890 power stations across the country provided electricity for lamps, fans, printing presses, and many other newly invented appliances.

**Westinghouse and Alternating Current** At first Edison used a form of electricity called direct current to transmit power from his stations. Direct current was expensive to generate and could travel only a mile or two.

In 1885 George Westinghouse began to experiment with alternating current, which could be produced and transmitted more cheaply and efficiently. Westinghouse also used a device called a transformer to boost power levels at a station so that electricity could be sent over long distances. Another transformer at a distant substation could reduce power levels as needed. These aspects of Westinghouse's system made home use of electricity practical.

By the early 1890s, investors had used Edison's and Westinghouse's ideas and inventions to create two companies, General Electric and Westinghouse Electric. These companies' products encouraged the spread of the use of electricity. By 1898 nearly 3,000 power stations were lighting some 2 million light bulbs across the land.

**Electricity's Impact on Daily Life** Household use of electric current revolutionized many aspects of daily life. To take but one example, electricity made the refrigerator possible. This invention reduced food spoilage and the need to cut, distribute, and store ice.

Electricity also transformed the world of work and created new jobs. For example, people powered early sewing machines by pushing on a foot pedal. The electric sewing machine, first made in 1889, led to the rapid growth of the ready-made clothing industry. Many of the country's new immigrants, especially women and children, found work making clothing in factories powered by electricity.

Yet the benefits of electricity were not felt equally by all Americans. Rural areas, especially, went without electricity for many decades. Even where electric power was available, many people could not afford the home appliances or other conveniences that ran on electricity.

## *Turning Point: The Bessemer Process*

Through the mid-1800s, the nation depended on iron for railroad rails and the frames of large buildings. But in the 1850s, Henry Bessemer in England and William Kelly in Kentucky independently developed a new process for making steel. In 1856 Bessemer received the first patent for the **Bessemer process.** Steel had long been produced by melting iron, adding carbon, and removing impurities. The Bessemer process made it much easier and cheaper to remove the impurities.

Steel is lighter, stronger, and more flexible than iron. The Bessemer process made possible the **mass production,** or production in great amounts, of steel. As a result, a new age of building began. A majestic symbol of this new age was the Brooklyn Bridge.

**The Brooklyn Bridge** After the Civil War, New York City grew in size as well as population. Many people who worked on the island of Manhattan lived in nearby Brooklyn. The only way to travel between Brooklyn and Manhattan was by ferry across the East River. In winter, ice or winds often shut down the ferry service. Could a bridge high enough to clear river traffic be built across such a large distance? Engineer John A. Roebling, a German immigrant, thought it could.

Roebling designed a suspension bridge with thick steel cables suspended from high towers to hold up the main span. That span,

## TURNING POINT: *The Bessemer Steel Process*

The Bessemer process led to the use of steel in a variety of products, as the time line below indicates.

**1856** *Development of Bessemer process encourages mass production of steel*

**1883** *Brooklyn Bridge completed, using steel cables to suspend a long bridge span*

**1914** *Method developed for producing stainless-steel cutlery*

**1931** *Design of the Empire State Building calls for structural skeleton of steel girders*

**1948** *Steel-belted radial tires introduced*

**1998** *Ultra-light steel frame for autos unveiled*

1850 | 1900 | 1950 | 2000

## exploring TECHNOLOGY *The Brooklyn Bridge*

**The Brooklyn Bridge included two massive towers, one of which is shown being built here. As workers removed earth beneath the tower and piled granite blocks above it, the tower sank into the ground. When completed, the two towers supported the steel cables that in turn held up the span.** ***Science and Technology* *How did the Bessemer process for manufacturing steel make possible the construction of the Brooklyn Bridge?***

arching 1,595 feet above the river, would be the longest in the world. Roebling died shortly after construction of the Brooklyn Bridge began in 1869, so his son Washington took over the project. Washington was disabled in 1872 by a severe attack of decompression sickness ("the bends") while inspecting a foundation deep under the river. Other disasters followed, from explosions and fires to dishonest dealings by a greedy steel-cable contractor.

**A Symbol of American Success** Despite these problems, the Brooklyn Bridge was completed and opened on May 24, 1883. At nightfall crowds gasped as electric light bulbs, which had been strung along the bridge, lit up the darkness and shimmered on the river below. The city celebrated with a magnificent fireworks display. Indeed, the entire United States celebrated, its inventive genius and hard work plainly visible for all the world to see.

## SECTION 1 REVIEW

### Comprehension

1. *Key Terms* Define: (a) patent; (b) productivity; (c) transcontinental railroad; (d) Bessemer process; (e) mass production.
2. *Summarizing the Main Idea* How did Americans' daily lives change between 1865 and 1900?
3. *Organizing Information* Create a chart to describe the major inventions in this section and explain the impact they had on Americans.

### Critical Thinking

4. *Analyzing Time Lines* Review the time line at the start of the section. Which events involved advances in transportation? In communication? In electric power?
5. *Predicting Consequences* What long-term impact do you think the Brooklyn Bridge had on the people of the New York City area?

### Writing Activity

6. *Writing an Expository Essay* Write an essay about the inventiveness of Americans in the last half of the 1800s.

# SKILLS FOR LIFE

**Geography**

**Graphs and Charts**

**Historical Evidence**

**Critical Thinking**

# Using Cross-Sectional Maps

Sometimes it is necessary to use more than one type of map to understand the way a particular piece of land looks. Cross-sectional maps show how an area of land would look if viewed from the side. The cross-sectional map below shows the changes in elevation along the route of the first transcontinental railroad, completed in 1869. These changes in elevation appear on the map as the rising and falling of the bold line. In contrast, physical-political maps show Earth's surface as if viewed from above. The physical political map below gives a bird's-eye view of the vast horizontal distances covered by the railroad.

Snowstorms, floods, and extreme heat all posed great challenges to the workers who built the transcontinental railroad, but the greatest challenges arose from the changes in elevation of the terrain. Follow the steps below to study the cross-sectional map.

**1.** ***Study the region shown on the maps.*** (a) Which landforms on the physical-political map correspond to those on the cross-sectional map? (b) Does the cross-sectional map show the same land area as the political map? Explain.

**2.** ***Analyze the information shown on the cross-sectional map.*** (a) What were the highest and lowest elevations of each railroad route? (b) Where did the sharpest and the most gradual changes occur? (c) Write a paragraph comparing the length and elevation changes of the Central Pacific and Union Pacific routes.

## TEST FOR SUCCESS

Think about the route you follow to school or some other familiar route. Would a cross-sectional map like the one shown below help you explain your route to a stranger? Or would a physical-political map provide all the necessary information? Explain.

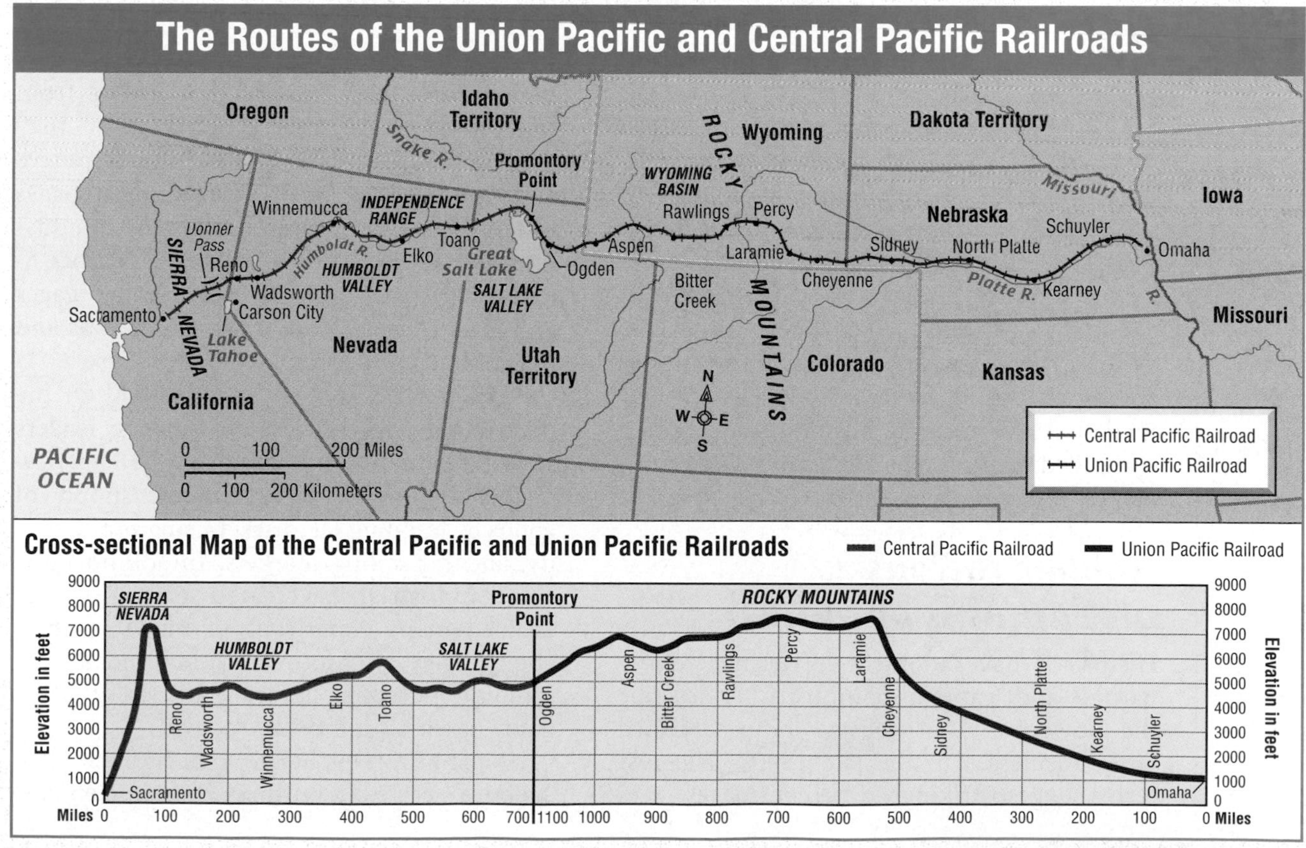

| 1859 | 1870 | 1882 | 1889 | 1890 |
|---|---|---|---|---|
| Titusville oil strike | Standard Oil founded | Standard Oil Trust set up | Carnegie Steel founded | Sherman Antitrust Act passed |

1850 1860 1870 1880 1890

# 2 The Growth of Big Business

**SECTION PREVIEW**

### Objectives

1. Explain why American industrialists of the late 1800s were called both "robber barons" and "captains of industry."
2. Describe the theory of social Darwinism and its connection to big business.
3. Summarize the ways that industrialists gained a competitive edge over rivals, and the effects that big businesses had on American society.
4. *Key Terms* Define: social Darwinism; monopoly; cartel; trust; Sherman Antitrust Act; horizontal consolidation; vertical consolidation; economies of scale; business cycle.

### Main Idea

Big business created wealth for its owners and also for the nation, but it also prompted controversy and concern over its methods.

### Reading Strategy

*Finding Evidence* Read the paragraphs under the heading "Robber Barons or Captains of Industry?" on this page. Look for evidence to support both of these views of industrialists of the late 1800s.

*Industrial growth required the contributions of both workers and business owners, as this illustration suggests.*

The period of invention after the Civil War set the stage for great industrial growth. Still, it would take more than technology to transform the United States. It would take shrewd businesspeople and wealthy investors willing to gamble on new products. Without huge amounts of capital, businesses could not build factories or market their inventions. To succeed, business leaders often combined funds and resources into large companies. Thus was born the age of big business.

## Robber Barons or Captains of Industry?

Historians have adopted the terms "robber barons" and "captains of industry" to describe the powerful industrialists who established large businesses in the late 1800s. The two terms suggest strikingly different images.

"Robber barons" implies that the business leaders built their fortunes by stealing from the public. According to this view, they drained the country of its natural resources and persuaded public officials to interpret laws in their favor. At the same time, these industrialists ruthlessly drove their competitors to ruin. They paid their workers meager wages and forced them to toil under dangerous and unhealthful conditions.

The term "captains of industry," on the other hand, suggests that the business leaders served their nation in a positive way. This view credits them with increasing the supply of goods by building factories, raising productivity, and expanding markets. In addition, the giant industrialists created the jobs that enabled many Americans to buy their new goods. They also founded and funded outstanding museums, libraries, and universities, many of which still thrive today.

Most historians believe that both views of America's early big business contain elements of the truth. For example, consider the story of Andrew Carnegie, one of the United States' first great industrialists.

## Andrew Carnegie

**AMERICAN BIOGRAPHY** Born in Scotland in 1835, Andrew Carnegie knew something about the harsh side of industrialization. His father was a skilled weaver, but the coming of the power loom caused the market for skilled craftsworkers to collapse. Carnegie's family faced hard times. As a result, they immigrated to the United States in 1848, settling near Pittsburgh, Pennsylvania.

*Andrew Carnegie (1835–1919)*

Though he was only 13 years old, Carnegie found work in a cotton mill at $1.20 a week. At age 18 he won the post of secretary to the superintendent in the Pennsylvania Railroad Company. When his boss went to work at the War Department during the Civil War, Carnegie was promoted to his job.

**Captain of the Steel Industry** By the time he was 30, in 1865, Carnegie was making $50,000 a year, and he wanted to invest his wealth. The development of the Bessemer process persuaded Carnegie that steel would soon replace iron in many industries. During the early 1870s, near Pittsburgh, he founded the first steel plants to use the Bessemer process. These holdings would eventually grow into the Carnegie Steel Company, which he established in 1889.

Carnegie's business prospered. This enabled him to cut his prices until he had driven his competitors out of the market. Carnegie soon controlled the American steel industry, from the mines that produced iron ore to the furnaces and mills that made pig iron and steel. He even bought up the shipping and rail lines necessary to transport his products to market.

**Carnegie the Philanthropist** While expanding his business, Carnegie became a major public figure. Through books and speeches, he preached a "gospel of wealth." The essence of his message was simple: People should be free to make as much money as they can. After they make it, however, they should give it away.

By the turn of the century, Carnegie had donated the money for roughly 3,000 free public libraries, supported artistic and research institutes, and set up a fund to study how to abolish war. By the time he died in 1919, Carnegie had given away some $350 million.

Still, not everyone approved of Carnegie's methods. As you will read later in this chapter, workers at his steel plants protested against his company's labor practices. Many others questioned the sincerity of his good works. In reply, Carnegie argued that the success of men like him helped the nation as a whole:

> **"It will be a great mistake for the community to shoot the millionaires, for they are the bees that make the most honey, and contribute most to the hive even after they have gorged themselves full."**
>
> —*Andrew Carnegie*

## Social Darwinism

In statements such as these, Carnegie also suggested that the wealthy were somehow better than other people. This idea, popular in the late 1800s, was based on Charles Darwin's theory of evolution, first published in 1859. According to

### CAUSE AND EFFECT: Growth of Big Business

**CAUSES**

- *Railroad boom lowers the cost of shipping.*
- *New inventions make businesses more efficient.*
- *Nation has rich supply of natural resources.*
- *Small firms merge to form giant companies.*

**GROWTH OF BIG BUSINESS**

**EFFECTS**

- *Steel and oil become giant industries.*
- *Monopolies, cartels, and trusts dominate major industries.*
- *Factory workers face harsh working and living conditions.*
- *Labor unions grow.*

**Interpreting Charts** Technological advances and aggressive business practices combined to form big business. ***Economics*** ***What effects did the growth of big business have on workers?***

**Main Idea CONNECTIONS**

*Why was the government concerned about monopolies?*

Darwin, all animal life had evolved by a process of "natural selection" through which only the fittest survived to reproduce.

A theory soon emerged that applied Darwin's theory to the struggle between workers and employers. Called **social Darwinism,** it held that society should do as little as possible to interfere with people's pursuit of success. If government would stay out of the affairs of business, the theory went, those who were most "fit" would succeed and become rich. Society as a whole would benefit from the success of the fit and the weeding out of the unfit.

Most Americans agreed that the government should not interfere with private businesses. As a result, the government neither taxed businesses' profits nor regulated their relations with their workers.

## Gaining a Competitive Edge

Industrialists used whatever means necessary, fair or unfair, to gain a competitive edge. They paid as little as they could for raw materials, labor, and shipping. Sometimes they sought to take control of their entire industry.

**Monopolies and Cartels** Some companies set out to gain a **monopoly,** or complete control of a product or service. To do this, a business bought its competitors or drove them out of business. Once consumers had no other place to turn for a given product or service, the sole remaining company would be free to raise its prices.

Toward the end of the 1800s, federal and state governments passed laws to prevent certain monopolistic practices. Those laws did not prevent or destroy all monopolies, however. One reason was that political leaders refused to attack the powerful business leaders.

Forming monopolies was not the only way to control an industry. Sometimes industrialists prospered by taking steps to limit competition with other firms. One way was to form a **cartel**—a loose association of businesses that make the same product. Members of a cartel agreed to limit the supply of their product and thus keep prices high.

Neither monopolies nor cartels were foolproof. Monopolies faced the threat of government action, and cartels tended to fall apart during hard economic times. To achieve a more reliable arrangement, Samuel Dodd, a lawyer for oil tycoon John D. Rockefeller, invented yet another strategy.

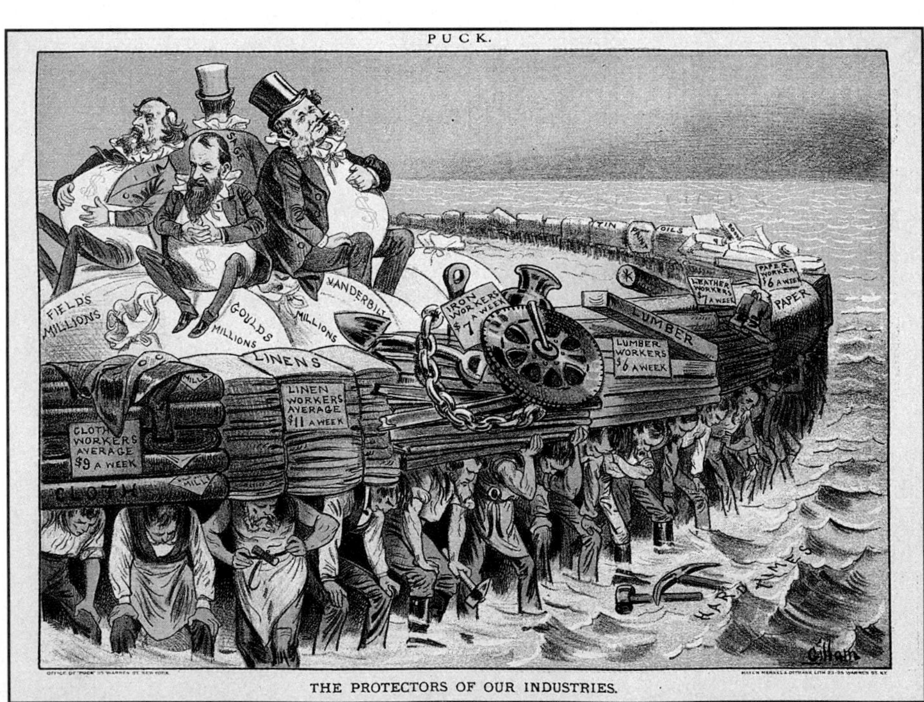

THE PROTECTORS OF OUR INDUSTRIES.

Some Americans were offended by the argument that business leaders protected jobs. ***Economics*** *What does this cartoon suggest about the relationship of workers to business leaders?*

**The Standard Oil Trust** Oil had become a major industry after Edwin L. Drake proved that it could be extracted from the ground through a well. Drake set up his well at Titusville, Pennsylvania, in 1858. A year later he struck oil, and Titusville soon became one of several boom towns in the northwestern part of the state.

Events in Pennsylvania excited John D. Rockefeller. He had become rich from a grain and meat partnership during the Civil War, and he saw the oil business as a way to become even richer. In 1863 Rockefeller built an oil refinery near Cleveland, Ohio. The refinery expanded rapidly. In 1870 Rockefeller and several associates formed the Standard Oil Company of Ohio.

Rockefeller persuaded his railroad friends to give him refunds on part of the cost of transporting his oil. As a result

Vertical Consolidation

Coke fields — purchased by Carnegie
Iron ore deposits — purchased by Carnegie
Steel mills — purchased by Carnegie
Ships — purchased by Carnegie
Railroads — purchased by Carnegie

Carnegie Steel Company — Owns all phases of production

**Interpreting Charts** In the late 1800s large businesses dominated industry. Some companies grew more powerful through horizontal consolidation, in which companies simply bought competitors in their field (above). Other companies grew more powerful through vertical consolidation. By controlling all phases of production, they could lower the costs of making their product and charge less than their competitors (right). ***Economics** What problems might a business face when trying to compete with a company with a vertical monopoly? With a horizontal monopoly?*

of these refunds, Rockefeller could set Standard Oil's prices lower than those of his competitors. As Rockefeller's company sold more oil, he was able to undersell his competitors by charging even less.

Rockefeller soon had enough money to buy out his competitors, but the law stood in his way. State laws prohibited one company from owning the stock of another. This practice reduced competition and therefore "restrained," or held back, free trade.

Samuel Dodd had an idea to get around this ban. In 1882 the owners of Standard Oil and companies allied with it agreed to combine their operations. They would turn over their assets to a board of nine trustees. In return, they were promised a share of the profits of the new organization. The board of trustees, which Rockefeller controlled, managed the companies as a single unit called a **trust.**

In time, 40 companies joined the trust. Because the companies did not officially merge, no laws were violated. Rockefeller's trust, a new kind of monopoly, controlled almost all of the nation's oil-refining capacity.

Trusts proved an effective means of limiting industrial competition. As a result, many Americans began to demand government action to break up these industrial giants. In 1890 Congress responded by passing the **Sherman Antitrust Act.** This law outlawed any combination of companies that restrained interstate trade or commerce.

The act, however, proved ineffective against trusts for nearly 15 years, because the federal government rarely enforced it. Besides, the law's vague wording made it hard to apply in court. The act was applied successfully against labor unions. Federal officials argued that labor unions restrained trade because workers were combining to gain an advantage.

**Methods of Industrial Control** Rockefeller's use of the Standard Oil Trust to create a giant company was an example of **horizontal consolidation.** This method involved bringing together many firms that were in the same business. Other industrialists practiced **vertical consolidation,** or gaining control of the many different businesses that make up all phases of a product's development. Andrew Carnegie used this method in the steel business. He purchased not only steel plants but also the mines that supplied the iron and the railroads that transported the finished products.

By controlling all stages of steel production, Carnegie could lower his costs and drive competitors out of business. He could charge less because of **economies of scale.** That is, as production increases, the cost of each item produced is often lower. As Carnegie Steel expanded, its cost per item went down.

## *Effects on American Society*

Few people truly liked trusts and other large business organizations. In 1873 a New

## Business Cycles

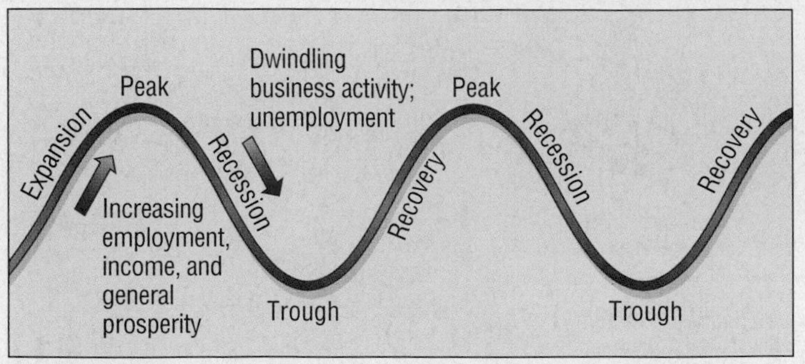


**Interpreting Charts** Although business cycles have no regular intervals, they typically follow the pattern shown above. A recession is a temporary decline in business activity. A prolonged recession is a depression. ***Economics** How did rapid industrial growth result in a depression between 1893 and 1897?*

Englander painted a bleak picture of industrialization:

**AMERICAN VOICES** "It is only too evident that the cause now at work in Lynn may render it rich and prosperous as a city, but with a population of overworked, underpaid hirelings, hopelessly dependent upon employers who act upon the good old rule, the simple plan—that they may take who have the power, and they may keep who can."

—*Resident of Lynn, Massachusetts*

Despite their questionable practices, industrial giants continued to sidestep the law. Politicians did not have the will to crack down on them. After all, these firms contributed mightily to the United States' rising level of wealth. By the turn of the century, such mammoth companies as American Telephone and Telegraph, Swift and Armour, General Electric, Westinghouse, and DuPont were some of America's greatest success stories.

Rapid industrial growth did place strains on the economy. Big businesses sometimes churned out more goods than consumers wanted or could afford. Then they had to lower prices in order to sell their products. To cover their losses, they often cut wages and laid off workers. The resulting shock to the economy could be severe. In 1893, for example, a period of expansion suddenly ended. By the end of the year, nearly 500 banks and more than 15,000 businesses had failed, and the economy sank into a four-year depression.

Economists call such a "boom and bust" period the **business cycle.** One cause of the depression that began in 1893 was a panic. Panics occurred when investors feared that key businesses, heavily in debt, might not be able to repay their loans. Investors rushed to sell stock, stock prices fell, and companies went bankrupt. The resulting unemployment caused widespread misery, especially among workers and their families.

## SECTION 2 REVIEW

### Comprehension

1. *Key Terms* Define: (a) social Darwinism; (b) monopoly; (c) cartel; (d) trust; (e) Sherman Antitrust Act; (f) horizontal consolidation; (g) vertical consolidation; (h) economies of scale; (i) business cycle.
2. *Summarizing the Main Idea* Describe some of the methods that companies used to dominate their markets, and explain why some people questioned those methods.
3. *Organizing Information* Make a two-column chart with columns headed *Robber Baron* and *Captain of Industry*. Now list people, events, and methods from the section in the appropriate column, along with a brief explanation of why each entry appears where it does.

### Critical Thinking

4. *Analyzing Time Lines* Review the time line at the start of the section. Which events could be causes of the Sherman Antitrust Act? Which one event is the likeliest cause? Explain.
5. *Formulating Questions* Write a question that would help you or another reader better understand the information about Andrew Carnegie in this section.

### Writing Activity

6. *Writing a Persuasive Essay* Write an essay in which you explain your agreement or disagreement with the theory of social Darwinism and attempt to convince others to accept your viewpoint.

| 1860 | | | 1880 | | | 1900 |
|---|---|---|---|---|---|---|
| | **1864** Contract Labor Act | **1868** Eight-hour day for government employees | **1881** First time and motion studies of workers | **1887** Major drought ruins many farmers | **1893** Illinois limits child labor | |

# 3 Industrialization and Workers

## SECTION PREVIEW

### Objectives

1. Identify the sources of the growing American work force and the reasons why entire families worked.
2. Describe factory work in the late 1800s.
3. Explain the roles that women and children played in the work force.
4. *Key Terms* Define: piecework; division of labor.

### Main Idea

Industry relied on its laborers, who worked for low wages and often in unsafe factories.

### Reading Strategy

*Predicting Content* Look at the pictures and the main headings in this section. Write a prediction of what life was like for factory workers. As you read, compare your predictions with the information presented in the text.

The United States was ripe for economic prosperity after the Civil War. Its abundant natural resources, inventive minds, and risk-taking entrepreneurs all played central roles in the nation's industrial expansion. This expansion would not have been possible, however, without the millions of workers who toiled in the factories.

## The Growing Work Force

Around 14 million people immigrated to the United States between 1860 and 1900. Most came in the hope of finding work in America's booming industrial centers. During the Civil War, when labor was scarce, the federal government encouraged immigration by passing what has been called the Contract Labor Act. This law, passed in 1864, allowed employers to enter into contracts with immigrants. Employers would pay their cost of passage, and in return, immigrants had to work for a certain amount of time, up to a year. Employers soon began actively recruiting foreign laborers.

In another dramatic population shift, some 8 or 9 million Americans moved to cities during the late 1800s. (See graph at right.) Most of them fled poor economic conditions on the nation's farms. A long drought beginning in 1887, combined with low prices and more competition from foreign wheat producers, left many farm families penniless. Plentiful work in the factories lured the former farmers, as did the faster-paced life of the city.

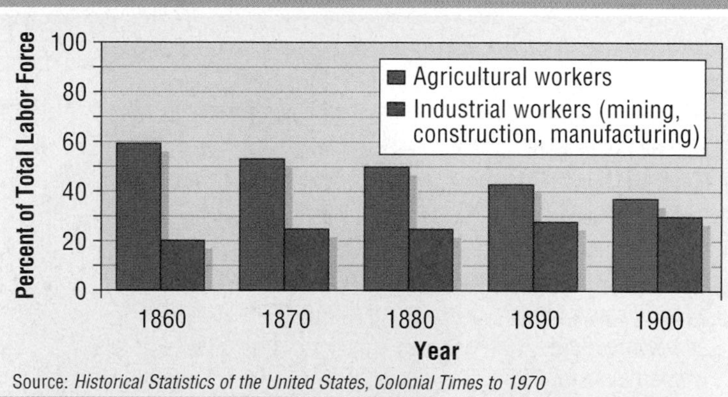

**Interpreting Graphs** The growth of industry in the mid- to late 1800s changed the distribution of the work force. ***Economics*** *Compare the percentage of the labor force engaged in agricultural work with the percentage engaged in industrial work for 1860 and 1900.*

During the 1800s, few African Americans took part in this migration. Although some moved into southern cities, the better job opportunities there were closed to them.

## *Working Families*

For those who labored in the factories, work was a family affair. Every family member worked in some way. Because wages were low, no one person could earn enough to provide for a household.

As a result, children often left school at the age of 12 or 13 to work. Girls sometimes took factory jobs so that their brothers could stay in school. If a mother could not make money working at home, she might take a factory job, leaving her children with relatives or neighbors. If an adult became ill, died, or could not find or keep a job, children as young as 6 or 7 had to bring in cash or go hungry.

In the 1800s needy families were largely on their own. During that century Americans did not believe that government should provide public assistance, except in rare cases. Unemployment insurance, for example, did not exist, so workers received no payments as a result of layoffs or factory closings. The popular theory of social Darwinism held that poverty resulted from personal weakness. Many thought offering relief to the unemployed would encourage idleness.

Families in need relied on private charities. These charities could not afford to help everyone, however. They had limited resources, so only the neediest received the food, clothing, and shelter that charities had to offer.

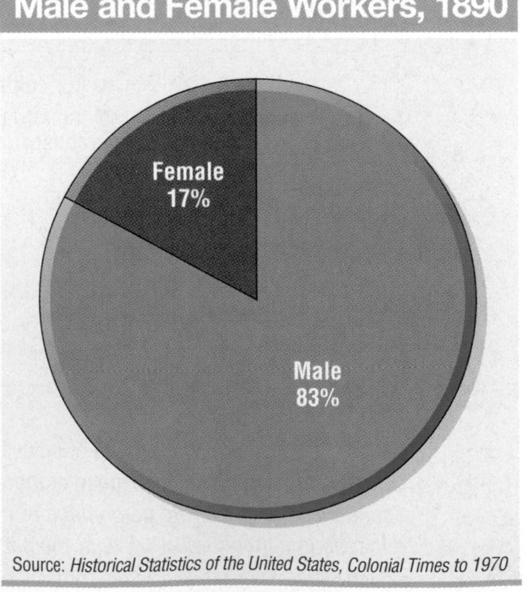


**Interpreting Graphs** In 1890 women formed 17 percent of the labor force. Most of these female workers were unmarried. ***Economics*** ***What obstacles to employment did women industrial workers face?***

## *Factory Work*

By 1860 most states had established a ten-hour workday, yet they rarely enforced it. Thus, most laborers worked twelve hours, six days a week—and even more when they had to meet production goals. An 1868 federal law granted government employees an eight-hour day, but this did not affect private industry. In fact, workers would fight for the eight-hour day well into the 1900s.

In many industries, employers paid workers not by the time worked but by what they produced. Workers received a fixed amount for each finished piece they produced—for example, a few cents for a garment or a number of cigars. This system of **piecework** meant that those who worked fastest and produced the most pieces earned the most money. Piecework favored young and strong workers; older or less able workers suffered.

**Increasing Efficiency** In 1881 Frederick Winslow Taylor set out to improve worker efficiency in the steel plant where he was chief engineer. He began to study the workers, trying to see how much time it took to do various jobs. Then he broke down each task into a number of steps and determined how long each step should take. In the same way he also studied each motion needed in a task. The goal of Taylor's time and motion studies was to get workers to produce more in less time.

Workers hated Taylor's ideas, which imposed an outside control on the way they did their work. They also feared that increased efficiency would result in layoffs or a lower rate of pay for each piece of work.

By the early years of the 1900s, Taylor had used his studies as the foundation of an entire system for the scientific management of workers. In 1911, in his book *The Principles of Scientific Management,* he described his system:

**AMERICAN VOICES** **"The work of every workman is fully planned out by the management at least one day in advance, and each man receives in most cases complete written instructions, describing in detail the task which he is to accomplish, as well as the means to be used in doing the work . . . and the exact time allowed for doing it."**

*—Frederick Winslow Taylor*

John Furguson Weir's painting *Gun Foundry* presents a vivid image of the nation's industrial might. ***Economics* What does the painting suggest about the conditions faced by workers?**

Some employers had their own, unscientific methods of improving efficiency. They simply increased the speed of factory machines or gave each employee more work. Yet they rarely increased workers' pay. The additional workload could endanger workers' health and safety.

**A Strict Work Environment** The routines of factory work differed greatly from those of earlier kinds of work. Factory workers were ruled by the clock, which told them when to start, take any breaks, and stop work. On the farm, in contrast, workers had labored at their own pace.

Less obvious, but equally important, was a change in the relationship between the worker and the product. Craftsworkers traditionally made a product from start to finish, which required them to perform a variety of tasks. Factory workers performed only one small task, over and over, and rarely even saw the finished product. This **division of labor** into separate tasks proved to be efficient, but it took much of the joy out of the work.

Owners seldom visited the factory floor where their workers toiled. Called "hands" or "operatives," the workers were viewed as interchangeable parts in a vast and impersonal machine. One factory manager in 1883 declared, "I regard my people as I regard my machinery. So long as they can do my work for what I choose to pay them, I keep them, getting out of them all I can."

Discipline was strict. To make a profit, factory managers needed to run an efficient operation. Thus they might fine or fire workers for a range of offenses, such as being late or refusing to do a task. Workplaces were not always safe. The noise of the machines was deafening. Lighting and ventilation were poor. Fatigue, faulty equipment, and careless training resulted in frequent fires and accidents. In 1882, the average number of workers killed on the job each week was 675—compared to about 120 today. Despite the harsh conditions, employers suffered no shortage of labor. Factory work offered higher pay and more opportunities than most people could hope to find elsewhere.

## *Working Women and Children*

Employers in industry excluded women from the most-skilled and highest-paying jobs. Of course, not all men had good jobs, either. But factory owners usually assigned women to the operation of simple machines. More complex machines required machinists and engineers. These were almost always men, for only they had access to training in such fields.

Women had almost no chance to advance in factory work. In the garment industry, for example, running the machines that cut large stacks of fabric was defined as a man's job. Typically, women performed only one part of the process of sewing a garment.

In the 1880s, children made up more than 5 percent of the industrial labor force. For many households, children's wages meant the difference between going hungry or having food on the table.

**Main Idea CONNECTIONS**

***Why did women have little chance for advancement in factory work?***

Many children worked under hazardous conditions. The boys at left worked in coal mines. The grime that covers their faces also clogged their lungs, leading to disease. Industrial growth created jobs for African Americans, though opportunities were limited. The men at right were hired for the low-paying job of carrying bricks. White men got the higher-paying jobs as masons. ***Economics Why were so many children put to work?***

Laboring in factories or mines and performing dangerous work was unhealthful for all workers. But it especially threatened growing children. Many children became stunted in both body and mind. In 1892 social reformer Jacob Riis tried to explain the impact of factory work on children in a book titled *Children of the Poor.* Riis wrote that people who spent their whole childhood on the factory floor grew "to manhood and womanhood . . . with the years that should have prepared them for life's work gone in hopeless and profitless drudgery." Thanks to Riis and others, the practice of child labor came under broad attack in the 1890s and early 1900s when states began curbing this practice through legislation†.

† Illinois limited children's time at work to 8 hours a day and 48 hours a week in 1893. By 1912, three fourths of the states had similar laws.

## SECTION 3 REVIEW

### Comprehension

1. *Key Terms* Define: (a) piecework; (b) division of labor.
2. *Summarizing the Main Idea* What made factory work difficult in the late 1800s?
3. *Organizing Information* Create a web diagram to show the two major sources of the growing work force. Use smaller circles to provide details about each of these sources.

### Critical Thinking

4. *Analyzing Time Lines* Review the time line at the start of the section. Which of the events do you think helped factory owners the most? Explain.
5. *Identifying Alternatives* Would the problems faced by women and children in the work force, as described in this section, have been solved by a law banning women and children from working? Explain your answer.

### Writing Activity

6. *Writing an Expository Essay* Write an essay describing the day-to-day life of a typical factory worker in the late 1800s.

1866
National Labor Union organized

1877
Nationwide rail strike

1886
Haymarket Riot

1886
American Federation of Labor organized

1892
Homestead Strike

1894
Pullman Strike

1860 | 1870 | 1880 | 1890 | 1900

# 4 The Great Strikes

## SECTION PREVIEW

### Objectives

1 Summarize the growing gulf between rich business owners and poor workers.
2 List some of the early labor unions and their activities.
3 Describe the causes and outcomes of the major strikes of the late 1800s.
4 *Key Terms* Define: socialism; collective bargaining; scab; anarchist; Haymarket Riot; Homestead Strike; Pullman Strike.

### Main Idea

In the late 1800s workers organized labor unions to improve their wages and working conditions.

### Reading Strategy

*Reinforcing Key Ideas* Make a table with two columns on a sheet of paper. Label one column *Successes* and the other *Failures.* As you read, use the table to keep track of the successes and failures of labor unions.

Industrialization had lowered the prices of consumer goods, but in the late nineteenth century most factory workers did not earn enough to buy them. The successful entrepreneurs of the era had worked hard. Many, like Carnegie, had used their wealth to provide money for good works. Still, in hard times only the poor went hungry. Increasingly, working men and woman took their complaints directly and forcefully to their employers.

## *Gulf Between Rich and Poor*

The 1890 census revealed that the richest 9 percent of Americans held nearly 75 percent of the national wealth. In the best of times, the average worker could earn only a few hundred dollars a year. Many workers resented the extravagant lifestyles of many factory owners.

Poor families had little hope of relief when hard times hit. Some suffered in silence, trusting that tomorrow would be better. Others became politically active in an effort to improve their lives. A few of these individuals were drawn to the idea of socialism, which was then gaining popularity in Europe.

**Socialism** is an economic and political philosophy that favors public (or social) control of property and income, not private control. Socialists believe that society at large, not just private individuals, should take charge of a nation's wealth. That wealth, they say, should be distributed to everyone.

Socialism began in the 1830s as an idealistic movement. Early Socialists believed that people should cooperate, not compete, in producing goods. Socialism then grew more radical, reflecting the ideas of a German philosopher named Karl Marx. In 1848 Marx, along with Friedrich Engels, wrote a famous pamphlet called the *Communist Manifesto.* In it they denounced the capitalist economic system and predicted that workers would one day overturn it.

Most Americans opposed socialism. The wealthy saw it as a threat to their fortunes. Politicians saw it as a threat to public order. Americans in general, including most workers, saw it as a threat to the deeply rooted

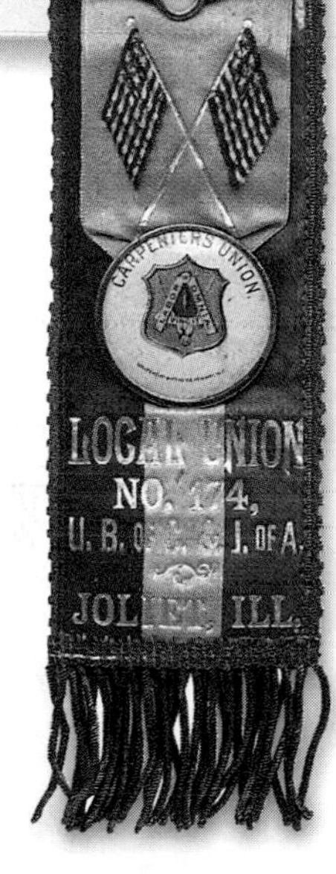


*Workers in many industries formed unions in the late 1800s.*

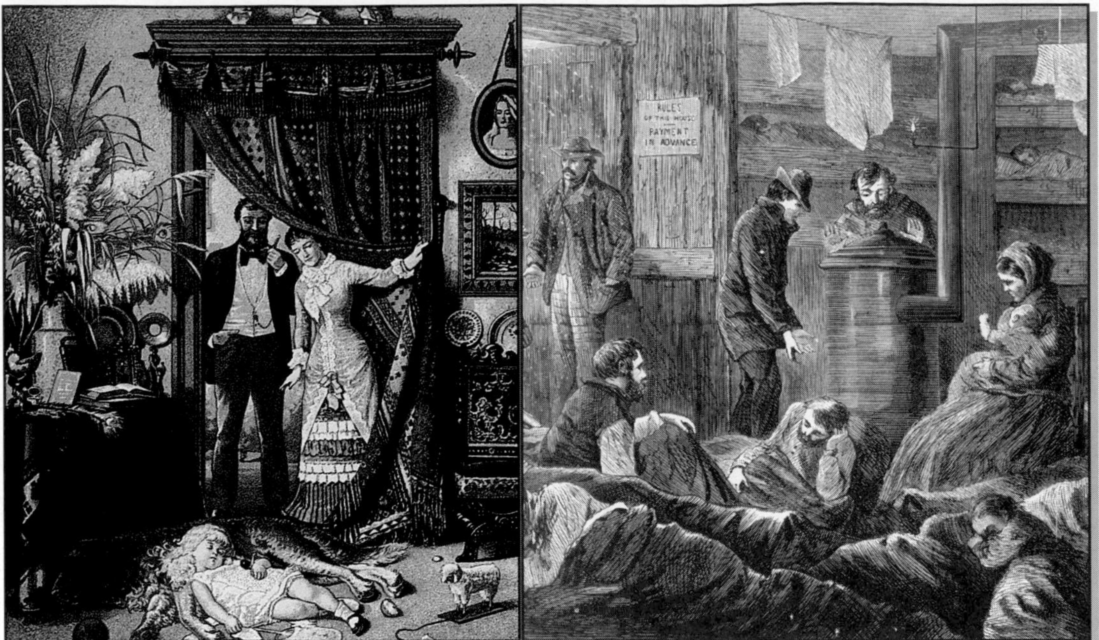


Many workers lived in crowded boardinghouses (far right). Many wealthy industrialists, on the other hand, enjoyed great personal wealth and luxurious comforts (left). ***Economics*** *How did many workers respond to the contrast between the rich and poor?*

American ideals of private property, free enterprise, and individual liberty.

## *The Rise of Labor Unions*

A small percentage of American workers did become Socialists and called for an end to free enterprise. Far more workers, however, chose to work within the system by uniting to form labor unions.

**Early Labor Unions** Workers formed a few local labor unions during the early years of industrialization. These were called trade unions, and they were organized for workers in specific trades. The Federal Society of Journeymen Cordwainers (shoemakers), founded in Philadelphia in 1794, was the strongest of these early unions. Still, it lasted only until 1806, when it was outlawed for engaging in a strike.

Philadelphians took the labor movement to the next level in 1827, when several craft groups joined to form the Mechanics' Union of Trade Societies. This city-wide form of trade union spread quickly to other cities in the East. In 1834 a number of these groups, representing about 21,000 members, organized the National Trades Union. Open to workers from all crafts, the National Trades Union was the first national labor organization. It lasted only a few years before being destroyed by the panic and depression that began in 1837.

**Main Idea CONNECTIONS**

*What was the National Trades Union?*

Strong local unions resurfaced after the Civil War. They began as a way to provide help for their members in bad times, but soon became the means for expressing workers' demands to employers. These demands included shorter workdays, higher wages, and better working conditions.

In the 1860s and 1870s labor activists again began organizing nationally. In Baltimore in 1866 they formed the National Labor Union, representing some 60,000 members. In 1872 this union nominated a candidate for President. It failed, however, to survive a depression that began the following year. Indeed, unions in general suffered a steep decline in membership as a result of the poor economy.

**The Knights of Labor** Another national union, the Noble Order of the Knights of Labor, was formed in Philadelphia in 1869. The Knights hoped to organize all working men and women, skilled and unskilled, into a single union. Membership included farmers and factory workers as well as shopkeepers and office workers. The union actively recruited African Americans, 60,000 of whom joined.

Under the leadership of former machinist Terence Powderly, the Knights pursued broad social reforms. These included equal pay for equal work, the eight-hour day, and an end to child labor. They did not emphasize higher wages as their primary goal.

The leaders of the Knights preferred not to use the strike as a tool. Most members, however, differed with their leadership on this issue. In fact, it was a strike that helped the Knights achieve their greatest strength. In 1885, when unions linked to the Knights forced railroad owner Jay Gould to give up a wage cut, membership quickly soared to 700,000. Yet a series of failed strikes followed, some of them violent. Membership dropped off, and public support for the Knights waned. By the 1890s the Knights had largely disappeared as a national force.

**The American Federation of Labor** A third national union, the American Federation of Labor (AFL), followed the leadership of Samuel Gompers, a London-born cigar maker. Formed in 1886, the AFL had different objectives than the Knights of Labor. The AFL sought to organize only skilled workers in a network of smaller unions, each devoted to a specific craft.

Between 1886 and 1892, the AFL gained some 250,000 members. Yet they still represented only a tiny portion of the nation's total labor force. Few African Americans joined. In theory the AFL was open to African Americans, but local unions often found ways to exclude them from membership. Women, too, were not welcome in the AFL. Gompers opposed the membership of women because he believed that their presence in the work force would drive wages down, as he stated:

AMERICAN VOICES

**"We know to our regret that too often are wives, sisters and children brought into the factories and workshops only to reduce the wages and displace the labor of men—the heads of families."**

—*Samuel Gompers*

Gompers and the AFL focused mainly on issues of workers' wages, hours, and working conditions. This so-called bread-and-butter unionism set the AFL apart from the Knights of Labor. The Knights had sought to help their members through political activity and education. The AFL relied on economic pressure, such as strikes and boycotts, against employers.

Through these tactics the AFL tried to force employers to participate in **collective bargaining,** a process in which workers negotiate as a group with employers. Workers acting as a group had more power than a single worker acting alone. To strengthen its collective bargaining power, the AFL pressed for a "closed shop," a workplace in which only union members would be hired.

## COMPARING PRIMARY SOURCES

### LABOR UNIONS

In 1883 the Senate Committee on Education and Labor held a series of hearings concerning the relationship between workers and management. The committee heard these opposing views about the need for labor unions.

| Testimony of a Labor Leader | Testimony of a Factory Manager |
|---|---|
| "The laws written [by Congress] and now in operation to protect the property of the capitalist and the moneyed class generally are almost innumerable, yet nothing has been done to protect the property of the workingmen, the only property that they possess, their working power, their savings bank, their school, and trades union." —*Samuel Gompers, labor leader* | "I think that . . . in a free country like this . . . it is perfectly safe for at least the lifetime of this generation to leave the question of how a man shall work, and how long he shall work, and what wages he shall get to himself." —*Thomas L. Livermore, manager of a manufacturing company* |

***ANALYZING VIEWPOINTS*** **Compare the main arguments made by the two speakers.**

**The Wobblies** The AFL's policies did not suit all workers. In 1905 in Chicago, 43 groups opposed to the AFL founded the Industrial Workers of the World (IWW), or Wobblies. The IWW, which focused on unskilled workers, was a radical union that included many Socialists among its leadership. A number of IWW strikes were violent on both sides. During World War I, many IWW leaders were convicted of promoting strikes in war-related industries.

**Reaction of Employers** By and large, employers disliked and feared unions. They preferred to deal with employees as individuals instead of in powerful groups. Employers took several measures to stop unions:

(1) They forbade union meetings.

(2) They fired union organizers.

(3) They forced new employees to sign "yellow dog" contracts, in which workers

promised never to join a union or participate in a strike.

(4) They refused to bargain collectively when strikes did occur.

(5) They refused to recognize unions as their workers' legitimate representatives.

In 1902 George F. Baer, the president of a mining company, reflected the opinions of many business leaders when he wrote: "Rights and interests of the laboring man will be protected and cared for—not by the labor agitators, but by the Christian men to whom God has given control of the property interests of the country."

## The Railroad Strike of 1877

The first major case of nationwide labor unrest in the United States occurred in the railroad industry. The strike began on July 14, 1877, when the Baltimore and Ohio Railroad announced a wage cut of 10 percent in the midst of a depression. This was the second wage cut in eight months. Railroads elsewhere imposed similar cuts, along with orders to run "double headers," trains with two engines and twice as many cars as usual. The unusually long trains increased the risk of accidents and the chance of worker layoffs.

Railway workers in Baltimore reacted with violence. Rioting spread rapidly to Pittsburgh, Chicago, St. Louis, and other cities. In Martinsburg, West Virginia, strikers turned back the local militia. President Rutherford B. Hayes sent in federal troops to put down a strike, the first time this had been done in American history.

A week later in Pittsburgh, soldiers fired on rioters, killing and wounding many. A crowd of 20,000 angry men and women reacted to the shootings by setting fire to railroad company property, causing more than $5 million in damage. President Hayes again chose to send in federal troops.

From the 1877 strike on, employers relied on federal and state troops to repress labor unrest. A new and violent era in labor relations had begun.

## Strikes Rock the Nation

From 1881 to 1900 the United States faced one industrial crisis after another. Some 24,000 strikes erupted in the nation's factories, mines, mills, and rail yards during those two decades alone. Three events were particularly violent: the Haymarket Riot and the Homestead and Pullman strikes.

**Haymarket, 1886** On May 1, 1886, groups of workers mounted a national demonstration for an eight-hour workday. "Eight hours for work, eight hours for rest, eight hours for what we will," ran the cry. Strikes then erupted in a number of cities.

On May 3 at Chicago's McCormick reaper factory, police broke up a fight between strikers and scabs. (A **scab** is a negative term for a worker called in by an employer to replace striking laborers. Using scabs allows a company

### Work Stoppages, 1882–1900

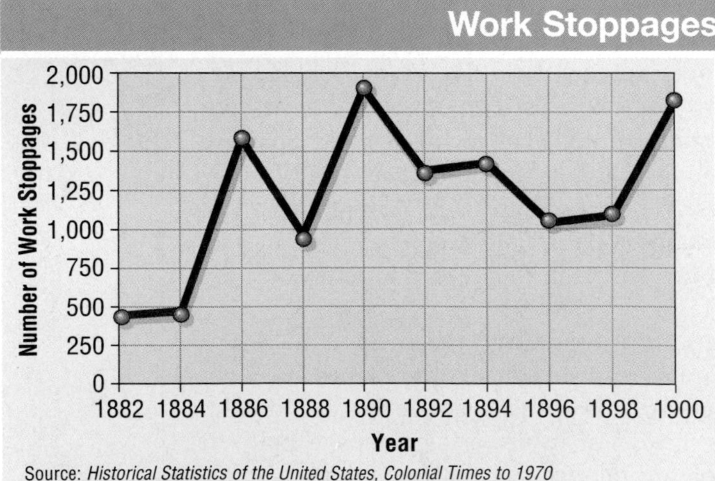


Source: *Historical Statistics of the United States, Colonial Times to 1970*

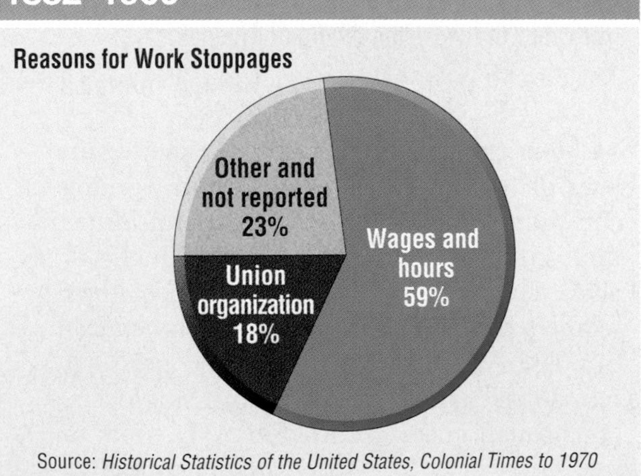


Source: *Historical Statistics of the United States, Colonial Times to 1970*

**Interpreting Graphs** A severe economic depression helped cause a steep decline in union membership in the 1870s. But the 1880s and 1890s saw growth in the number of members and in the number of work stoppages. ***Economics*** ***What were the major reasons for work stoppages in the late 1800s?***

to continue operating and avoid having to bargain with the union.) The police action caused several casualties among the workers.

Union leaders called for a protest rally on the evening of May 4 in Chicago's Haymarket Square. A group of **anarchists,** radicals who violently oppose all government, joined the strikers. Anarchists, such as newspaper editor August Spies, knew how to whip up anger among the workers. He stated:

AMERICAN VOICES "You have endured the pangs of want and hunger; your children you have sacrificed to the factory-lords. In short, you have been miserable and obedient slaves all these years. Why? To satisfy the insatiable greed, to fill the coffers of your lazy thieving master!"

—*August Spies*

The violence of the Haymarket Riot, depicted here, troubled many Americans. ***Culture* Did the incident at Haymarket help or hurt the union cause?**

At the May 4 event someone threw a bomb into a police formation, killing seven officers. In the riot that followed, gunfire between police and protesters killed dozens on both sides. Investigators never found the bomb thrower, yet eight anarchists were tried for conspiracy to commit murder. Four were hanged. Another committed suicide in jail. Governor John P. Altgeld of Illinois decided later that the convictions resulted from public outrage rather than evidence. He pardoned the remaining three anarchists.

To many unionists, the anarchists who took part in the **Haymarket Riot** forever would be heroes. To employers, however, they remained vicious criminals determined to undermine law and order. Much of the American public came to associate unions in general with violence and radical ideas.

**Homestead, 1892** In the summer of 1892, while Andrew Carnegie was in Europe, his partner Henry Frick tried to cut workers' wages at Carnegie Steel. The union at the Carnegie plant in Homestead, Pennsylvania, called a strike.

Frick intended to crush the union. On July 1 he called in the Pinkertons, a private police force known for their ability to break strikes. Under cover of darkness, some 300 Pinkertons moved up the Monongahela River on barges. In a shootout with strikers on shore, several people died and many were wounded.

At first Americans generally sympathized with the striking workers. Then, on July 23, anarchist Alexander Berkman tried and failed to assassinate Frick. Although Berkman was not connected with the strike, the public associated his act with the rising tide of labor violence.

The union admitted defeat and called off the **Homestead Strike** on November 20. Homestead reopened under militia protection. "I will never recognize the union, never, never!" Frick cried. Carnegie believed in unions and accepted their right to strike, as long as no violence took place.†

**Pullman, 1894** Like the strike of 1877, the last of the great strikes also involved the railroad industry. This strike also marked a shift in the federal government's involvement with labor-employer relations.

Sleeping-car maker George Pullman considered himself a caring industrialist. Near Chicago he built a town for his workers that boasted a school, bank, water and gas systems, and comfortable homes. Conditions in the town, however, took a turn for the worse after

† Carnegie Steel (and its successor, U.S. Steel) remained nonunionized until the late 1930s.

Eugene Debs was a successful labor organizer in the late 1800s. Later, Debs would combine his energetic style and his belief in socialism to conduct several unsuccessful presidential campaigns as the leader of the Socialist party. ***Government*** ***Why did the government interfere with the Pullman Strike?***

the Panic of 1893. Pullman laid off workers and cut wages by 25 percent. Meanwhile, he kept rent and food prices in his town at the same levels.

In May 1894 a delegation of workers went to him to protest. In response Pullman fired three of the workers, causing the local union to go on strike. Pullman refused to bargain and instead shut down the plant. The American Railway Union, led by popular labor organizer Eugene V. Debs, called for a boycott of Pullman cars throughout the country. Widespread local strikes followed.

By June 1894 some 120,000 railway workers had joined in the **Pullman Strike.** Debs instructed strikers not to interfere with the nation's mail, but the strike got out of hand. It completely disrupted western railroad traffic, including delivery of the mail.

Railroad owners turned to the federal government for help, and Attorney General Richard Olney came to their rescue. By arguing that the mail had to get through and citing the Sherman Antitrust Act, Olney won a court order forbidding all union activity that halted railroad traffic. Two days later, on July 4, President Grover Cleveland sent in 2,500 federal troops to ensure that strikers obeyed the court order. A week later the strike was over.

The Pullman strike and its outcome set an important pattern. In the years ahead, factory owners appealed frequently for court orders against unions. The federal government regularly approved these appeals, denying unions recognition as legally protected organizations. This official government opposition helped limit union gains for more than 30 years.

## SECTION 4 REVIEW

### Comprehension

1. *Key Terms* Define: (a) socialism; (b) collective bargaining; (c) scab; (d) anarchist; (e) Haymarket Riot; (f) Homestead Strike; (g) Pullman Strike.
2. *Summarizing the Main Idea* Compare the goals and policies of the Knights of Labor and the American Federation of Labor.
3. *Organizing Information* Create a two-column chart to summarize information about the major strikes of the late 1800s.

### Critical Thinking

4. *Analyzing Time Lines* Review the time line at the start of the section. Which national union got started in the midst of a period of great turmoil? Explain.
5. *Making Comparisons* Compare socialism and the labor movement as two different responses to the growing gulf between rich and poor. How did they differ in their proposed solution to the problem?

### Writing Activity

6. *Writing a Persuasive Essay* Write a letter to President Hayes regarding the strike in Martinsburg, West Virginia, in 1877. In your letter, try to persuade the President either to send troops in to stop the strike or to refuse to intervene.

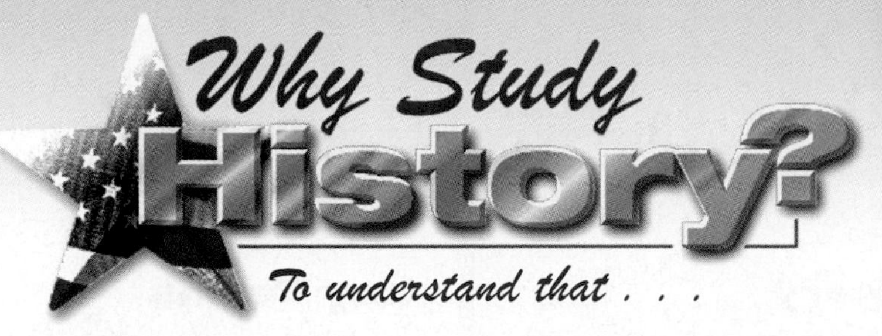


# You Live in a Post-Industrial Society

**A service economy is replacing the industrial economy that arose in the United States in the decades following the Civil War.**

*Factory workers in the late 1800s*

Suppose your great-grandfather worked in a steel mill. Your grandfather worked in a steel mill. Your father works in a computer-repair shop. Why?

Family work histories like the one above are common today. They reflect a historic change in the American economy: the decline of manufacturing and the rise of services. We live, in other words, in a post-industrial age.

## The Impact Today

Services existed even before the rise of industry in the 1800s. In colonial times, people provided such services as shoeing horses, selling cloth, and importing tea. Most Americans, however, lived and worked on farms.

After the Civil War, millions of Americans left farming for factory jobs. Industry powered the nation's economy and employed its workers from the post–Civil War era through most of the twentieth century. It helped create a large and vital middle class and made the United States the world's wealthiest, most powerful economy.

Today the steel, railroad, automotive, and other industries have decreased in economic importance. Meanwhile, the service sector, which includes banking, tourism, food services, recreation, data processing, and health care, has grown enormously. The number of Americans employed in services has more than doubled since 1970. More than 40 million Americans now work in the service sector.

The full impact of the post-industrial age remains to be seen, yet it has already created many changes in our society. More Americans are self-employed. Labor unions have declined. Education and skills have become increasingly important for people seeking jobs. According to some analysts, the loss of manufacturing jobs and the rise of low-paying service jobs (for example, in fast-food restaurants) have widened the gap between rich and poor.

*Workers in a semiconductor factory today*

## The Impact on You

Interview two young or middle-aged adults, perhaps your parents, about their work. Find out what they like and dislike about their jobs. Then interview two older adults. Ask them to explain whether the economy is better or worse today than it was when they were young. Use your interviews to write a feature article about the post-industrial society.

# Chapter 4 Review

## Chapter Summary

The major concepts of Chapter 4 are presented below. See also ***Guide to the Essentials of American History*** or ***Interactive Student Tutorial CD-ROM,*** which contains interactive review activities, time lines, helpful hints, and test practice.

### *Reviewing the Main Ideas*

New technologies such as electric power and the Bessemer process greatly changed American life after the Civil War. Industrialists applied new technologies to create wealth, but most factory workers did not feel that their pay was adequate. To improve their wages and working conditions, workers organized labor unions.

### *Section 1: A Technological Revolution*

In the years after the Civil War, new technology revolutionized American life.

### *Section 2: The Growth of Big Business*

Big business created wealth for owners and also for the country, but it also prompted controversy and concern over its methods.

### *Section 3: Industrialization and Workers*

Industry relied on its laborers, who worked for low wages and often in unsafe factories.

### *Section 4: The Great Strikes*

In the late 1800s workers organized labor unions to improve their wages and working conditions.

A service economy is replacing the industrial economy that arose in the United States after the Civil War. The number of Americans employed in services has more than doubled since 1970.

## Key Terms

For each of the terms below, write a sentence explaining how it relates to the chapter.

1. trust
2. anarchist
3. social Darwinism
4. economies of scale
5. mass production
6. socialism
7. horizontal consolidation
8. vertical consolidation
9. division of labor
10. monopoly
11. business cycle
12. collective bargaining
13. Bessemer process
14. transcontinental railroad

## Comprehension

1. How did new railroads and improvements in railway technology help spur economic growth?
2. Why did increasing the size of companies make sense in the expanding economy of the late 1800s?
3. Why was the Standard Oil Trust formed, and was it successful?
4. How did rapid industrial growth affect the country?
5. Why did most immigrants come to the United States in the late 1800s?
6. What problems did women and children workers face in industrialized America?
7. What steps did employers take to fight labor unions?
8. Which side did the federal government take in the major strikes of the late 1800s? Explain.

## Using Graphic Organizers

On a separate sheet of paper, copy the cause-and-effect flowchart below. In each empty box, write an effect. Add more boxes to show more effects.

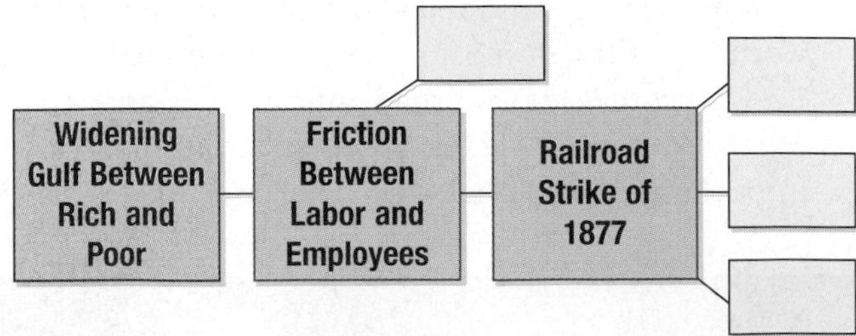

## Analyzing Political Cartoons ▶

1. In the background of this cartoon, a concerned citizen tries to alert Uncle Sam to the dangerous scene in the foreground. (a) What is the snake a symbol of? (b) How do you know? (c) Who is the woman? (d) How do you know?
2. What is the snake doing?
3. What is the cartoon's overall message?

## Critical Thinking

1. ***Applying the Chapter Skill*** Use map resources to plot a route across the Appalachian Mountains, from Raleigh, North Carolina, to Columbus, Ohio. Then draw a cross-sectional map of your route.
2. ***Distinguishing False from Accurate Images*** In your opinion, was Andrew Carnegie more a "captain of industry" or a "robber baron"? Explain.
3. ***Expressing Problems Clearly*** What problems did labor unions have to overcome in order to reach their main goals?
4. ***Making Comparisons*** How have the inventions of the past thirty years changed daily life for you?
5. ***Demonstrating Reasoned Judgment*** Choose two visuals from the chapter and explain why they demonstrate the inequality of labor and business in the late 1800s.

### INTERNET ACTIVITY

***For your portfolio:***
**WRITE AN ARTICLE**

Access Prentice Hall's *America: Pathways to the Present* site at **www.Pathways.phschool.com** for the specific URL to complete the activity. Additional resources and related Web sites are also available.

Explore the links to read about the life and works of Thomas Alva Edison. Write an article describing what you think were Edison's most important inventions and why. In what ways does Edison's career reflect the times in which he lived?

## ANALYZING DOCUMENTS ▶ INTERPRETING DATA

Turn to the Work Stoppages graphs on page 170.

1. Which statement best summarizes the information shown in the graphs? (a) The number of work stoppages fell steadily from 1870 to 1900. (b) The number of work stoppages rose between 1882 and 1900. (c) Work stoppages dropped after 1900. (d) The number of work stoppages fell steadily from 1882 to 1900.
2. What was the main reason for work stoppages in the late 1800s? (a) wages and hours (b) union organization (c) child labor (d) panics
3. ***Writing*** Use the data in the graphs to write a notice inviting workers to a union-organizing meeting. Then create a notice that presents an opposing view to such a meeting.

## Connecting to Today

***Essay Writing*** The Bessemer process helped create what has been termed the "age of steel" in the United States. Is the United States still in the age of steel? If not, how might you describe the present era? Write an essay expressing your view. Include specific examples.

# CHAPTER 5 Looking to the West

## 1860–1900

▲ **VIEWING HISTORY** The prospect of prosperity in the West lured many Americans along the Oregon Trail, as in this 1867 painting by Albert Bierstadt. ***Geography*** ***What does this painting tell you about the journey?***

## CHAPTER FOCUS

*This chapter describes the continued westward expansion in the last decades of the 1800s. Following the Civil War, thousands of settlers poured into the region west of the Mississippi River, looking for land and a place to call their own. Conflicts arose, however, when settlers clashed with Native American peoples living in the newly opened territories.*

*The **Why Study History?** page at the end of this chapter explores the connection between the homesteaders who moved west in the late 1800s and Americans who move in search of new opportunities today.*

| 1862 Morrill Land-Grant Act | 1862 Homestead Act | 1879 "Pap" Singleton leads Exoduster movement | 1890 State of Wyoming gives women right to vote |
|---|---|---|---|

1860 1870 1880 1890

# 1 Moving West

**SECTION PREVIEW**

**Objectives**

1. Explain how settlers acquired land in the West.
2. Describe how settlers worked with each other to overcome the hardships of the West.
3. Describe the experiences of women and African Americans in the West.
4. *Key Terms* Define: Morrill Land-Grant Act; land speculator; Homestead Act; Exoduster.

**Main Idea**

With the encouragement of the federal government, settlers took up the challenges of life in the West.

**Reading Strategy**

*Problem Solving* As you read the section, list possible solutions to the following problems: how to obtain land, how to locate water, how to work prairie sod.

As the nation swelled with new inventions and businesses during the late 1800s, it also expanded across the continent. The story of this expansion is one of rugged frontier families, big businesses, and bold individuals who were willing to take a chance on the unknown.

## Lands for Settlement

By the Civil War, Americans already had settled areas west of the Mississippi and along parts of the West Coast. Following the war, they began filling in the areas in between—the Great Plains, the Pacific Northwest, and the Southwest.

Americans and European immigrants wanted to settle in the West for many reasons. Most hoped for a new start in life. They looked forward to the chance to own a farm and be their own boss, an increasingly difficult goal in the crowded East.

**Big Business Receives Land** Much of the western land to which people were flocking belonged to big businesses. Under the Pacific Railway Acts of 1862 and 1864, the Union Pacific and Central Pacific railroad companies received huge grants of land from the federal government. The original act granted 10 square miles of public land on each side of the track for every mile of track laid.

As settlers flocked to the West, the railroads profited by selling the land to arriving settlers. Especially profitable were the lands close to the tracks, since farmers needed the railroads to transport their goods to the cities.

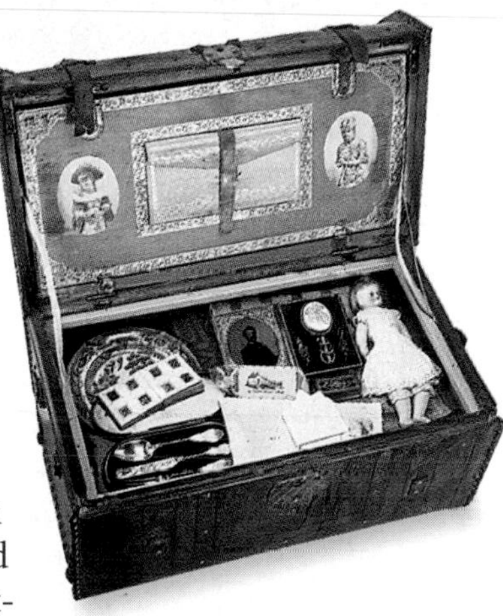

*Only the settlers' most cherished possessions made the trip west.*

**Settling Government Lands** In 1862 the federal government passed two important laws to encourage settlement of the West. The **Morrill Land-Grant Act** of 1862 was created to provide support for state colleges. Under the act, the federal government distributed millions of acres of western lands to state governments. States could then sell the land to fund agricultural "land-grant" colleges. The states sold their land grants at fifty cents an acre to bankers and **land speculators,** people who bought up large areas of land in the hope of later selling it for a profit.

The federal government also gave land directly to settlers through the **Homestead Act,** signed by President Lincoln in 1862. This act offered 160 acres of public land to anyone who met the following requirements:

## exploring TECHNOLOGY A Prairie Homestead, c. 1870

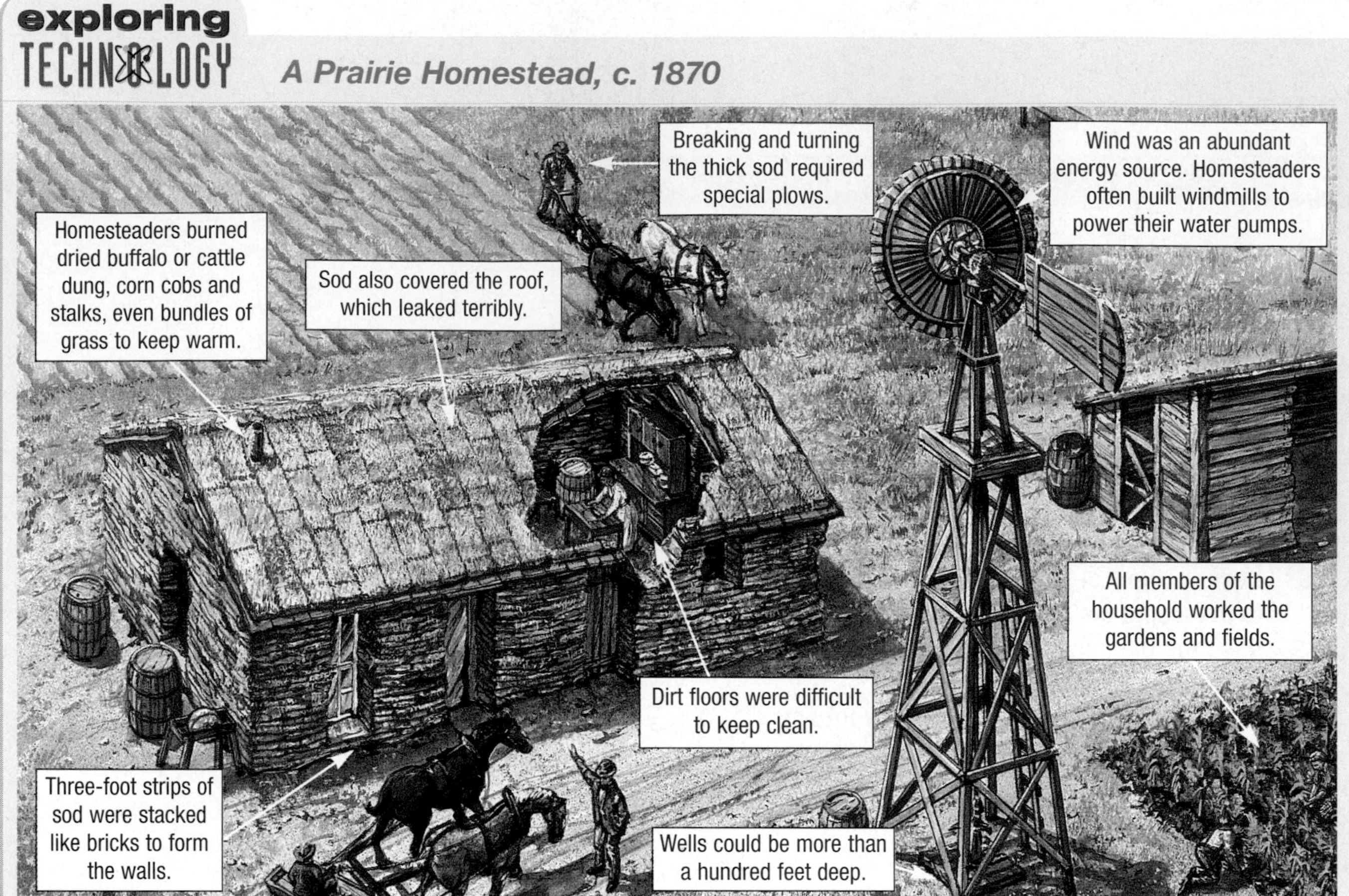


**The geography of the West made homesteading a challenge. Timber was often scarce, so settlers built their first shelters out of the endless expanse of sod. Special plows were required to break through the mass of roots holding the sod together.** ***Science and Technology*** ***What other kinds of technology did homesteaders use to adapt to life on the prairie?***

(1) All applicants had to be at least 21 years of age or the head of a family.

(2) Applicants had to be American citizens or immigrants who had filed for citizenship.

(3) Applicants had to pay a ten-dollar registration fee.

(4) Settlers had to build a house and live on the claim at least six months of the year.

(5) Settlers had to farm the land actively for five consecutive years before they could claim ownership.

By 1900, individual homesteading families had filed 600,000 claims for more than 80 million acres. There were, however, problems with the Homestead Act. Many eager settlers could not meet all of the law's requirements. Others received their claims but were unable to survive economically. Total costs to make a homestead livable could easily reach $1,000, far beyond the reach of many immigrants.

Moreover, most settlers who moved from cities had no farming experience. The tough prairie sod was hard to plow, water was scarce, and the climate ranged from blistering heat to bitter cold. Many farmers gave up before their five years were over.

Fraud was another shortcoming of the Homestead Act. The goal of the act was not simply to distribute land, but to give land to people who would then settle and farm it. Underhanded speculators wheeled portable cabins from plot to plot or built miniature shelters on several plots and then filed phony claims. Land office agents seldom visited the claims, as distances were too great and new claims were being filed daily.

## Settlers Work Together

Even the basic necessities did not come without a struggle for the western settlers. If their claims were not near water, they had to use buckets or cisterns to collect rainwater for drinking, bathing, and cooking. Such open water supplies often carried "prairie fever," or typhoid. A safer source of water could be found underground by digging wells. Until the 1880s, when well-digging machinery became available, digging a well was a difficult and dangerous task.

Working the tough prairie sod also required backbreaking labor. Even after the plowing and planting was done, men often had to spend months away from the homestead earning cash for their families' survival while they waited for their crops to come in. Women, meanwhile, made most of the articles that their families needed, such as clothing, soap, candles, and preserved foods.

In such an unforgiving land, settlers came to rely heavily on each other. Families cooperated in raising houses and barns, sewing quilts, husking corn, and providing many other forms of support.

## African Americans

The majority of settlers who traveled to the West were white. There were, however, thousands of African Americans who moved westward after the Civil War. In many cases they migrated to escape the violence and exploitation that followed Reconstruction. In 1879, Benjamin "Pap" Singleton became the leader of a group of southern African Americans planning a mass "Exodus," similar to the biblical account of the Israelites' flight from Egypt to the promised land. For this reason, these settlers called themselves **Exodusters.**

Life was not easy for the almost 50,000 Exodusters who migrated to western lands. Many came with little money and few possessions. Even after finding work, only a few earned enough to support a homestead. Many resettled farmers lacked experience with the crops, such as wheat and corn, widely grown on the plains. In addition, the Exodusters could not completely escape racial hatred. In spite of these difficulties, Exodusters with farming skills managed to make a living and in general met with better treatment than they had in the South.

## A Frontier for Women

Although most homesteaders went west as families, women were able to file claims on their own. Homesteading alone was, however, an enormous challenge for both women and men.

Even for married women, homesteading often meant long periods of solitude. While many men were away from the homestead earning money, women often stayed behind to prevent squatters from taking the land. (Squatters are people who move onto land that does not belong to them.) Such lonely experiences increased western women's eagerness for opportunities outside the home.

Western women launched an active campaign to gain the vote at the city and state level. They succeeded in making the West a pioneer in granting women's suffrage. In 1887 two Kansas towns, Syracuse and Argonia, passed women's suffrage. Syracuse then elected an all-female town council, and Argonia the nation's first female mayor. Wyoming, which entered the union in 1890, became the first state whose constitution granted women the right to vote.

**Main Idea CONNECTIONS**

*How did western women overcome some of the challenges they faced?*

### SECTION 1 REVIEW

#### Comprehension

1. *Key Terms* Define: (a) Morrill Land-Grant Act; (b) land speculator; (c) Homestead Act; (d) Exoduster.
2. *Summarizing the Main Idea* Describe some of the challenges homesteaders faced and some hardships they endured.
3. *Organizing Information* Create a chart that organizes information about the three federal acts dealing with the distribution of public lands in the West.

#### Critical Thinking

4. *Analyzing Time Lines* Review the time line at the start of the section. Which event, in your opinion, had the greatest long-term impact on the settlement of the West?
5. *Formulating Questions* Based on what you have read, write four questions to ask new homesteaders about their life in the West.

#### Writing Activity

6. *Writing an Expository Essay* Use information from the section to write an essay on the challenges and opportunities women and African Americans found in the West.

**1876** Battle of Little Bighorn

**1877** Nez Percé surrender to U.S. government

**1887** Dawes Act divides Indian lands

**1889** Indian Territory opened for white settlement

**1890** Massacre at Wounded Knee

1870 | 1880 | 1890

# 2 Conflict with Native Americans

## SECTION PREVIEW

### Objectives

1. Summarize the causes and effects of the Indian Wars of the late 1800s.
2. Explain how Indian cultures were weakened by wars and government reforms.
3. Describe the division and settlement of Indian Territory.
4. *Key Terms* Define: reservation; Battle of Little Bighorn; Massacre at Wounded Knee; Dawes Act; boomer; sooner.

### Main Idea

American expansion into the West led to the near destruction of the Native American nations there.

### Reading Strategy

*Outlining Information* Use the headings and subheadings to create an outline of the section. As you read, fill in supporting details.

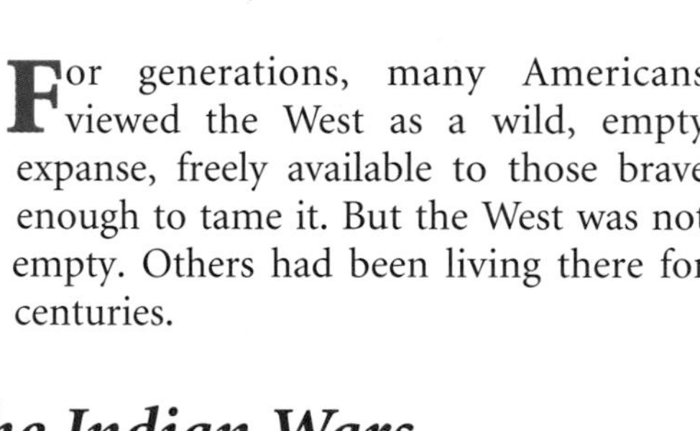

This elaborate feather headdress belonged to a Plains Indian.

For generations, many Americans viewed the West as a wild, empty expanse, freely available to those brave enough to tame it. But the West was not empty. Others had been living there for centuries.

## The Indian Wars

In the 1830s, President Jackson supported the removal of the Cherokee, Choctaw, Creek, Chickasaw, and Seminole peoples living in the East to lands west of the Mississippi. They were crowded into Indian Territory in present-day Oklahoma. By the end of the Civil War, the surviving Native American groups on United States land lived throughout the Great Plains and the West.

**Railroads and Settlers** Following the Civil War, the railroad companies began pushing their way deeper into the West. With each mile of track laid, the Native Americans' chances for survival became bleaker. The Plains soon swarmed with settlers, many of whom felt justified in taking Native American lands. Settlers believed they had a greater right to the land because they improved it by producing more food and wealth than did the Native Americans.

To Native Americans, on the other hand, the oncoming settlers were simply invaders. The Indian peoples wanted to continue to live off their lands as they had been doing, free of the influence of outsiders.

Some Native Americans tried to initiate friendly contacts. Others, however, resisted violently. Many groups, realizing that they were outgunned and outnumbered, eventually signed treaties that sold their lands. These nations accepted federal government demands that they live within **reservations,** or federal lands set aside for Native Americans.

Often these agreements fell apart. One reason was that many had been signed without the full approval of the affected Indian groups. In addition, Native Americans and white settlers had widely different concepts of owning land. When Native Americans signed treaties, they often did not realize that settlers would not let them continue using the land. Isolated acts of violence on both sides set off cycles of revenge and counter-revenge.

**The Final Destruction** One by one, Native American groups fell. (See the map below.) The Navajo and Apache wars began in the Southwest in 1861 and continued on and off for 25 years until the Indians were finally all forced onto reservations, starved, or killed in battle. The Navajo agreed to settle on a reservation in New Mexico in 1865. Some Apache leaders also surrendered between 1871 and 1873, but large numbers of warriors continued their raids on whites until their leader Geronimo surrendered in 1886.

In the 1860s and 1870s, the Cheyenne were devastated. The first blow came in 1864, with Colonel John M. Chivington's massacre of men, women, and children in a peaceful village at Sand Creek in present-day Colorado. Some reports put the number of dead as high as 450. The following year the Cheyenne surrendered their claims and agreed to move to reservations.

The Sioux resisted white expansion as fiercely as any Native American group. The First Sioux War was triggered in 1865 by the federal government's decision to build a road through Sioux lands to connect the East with the mining towns of Bozeman and Virginia City. In response, Sioux warriors ambushed and slaughtered more than 80 soldiers under Captain W. J. Fetterman near Fort Phil Kearny in December 1866.

**Main Idea CONNECTIONS**

*How did the Sioux react to the decision to allow settlers to expand into their territory?*

**Sitting Bull and the Fall of the Sioux**

The First Sioux War ended in 1868, when the Sioux agreed to live on a reservation in the Dakota Territory. In 1875, however, the Second Sioux War began when the federal government allowed miners to go into the Black Hills, in what is now South Dakota, in search of gold. As a result, a number of the Sioux joined Chief Sitting Bull and left their Black Hills reservation.

In June 1876, Lieutenant Colonel George Armstrong Custer was sent to locate and round up the Indians. He moved his cavalry toward the

**Native American Territory and Major Battles, 1860–1890**

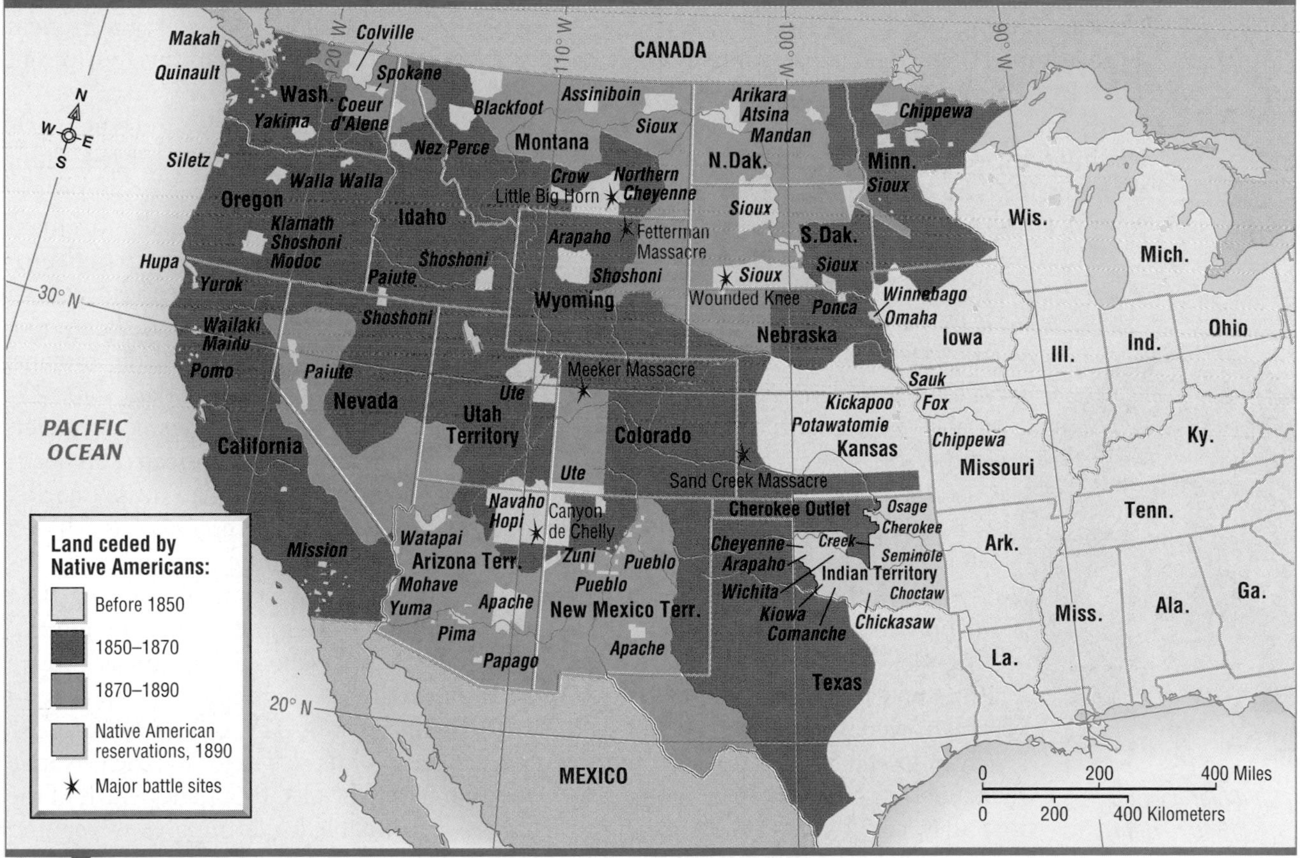

Land ceded by Native Americans:
- Before 1850
- 1850–1870
- 1870–1890
- Native American reservations, 1890
- Major battle sites

Though Native Americans won occasional victories in isolated battles, they were vastly outnumbered by United States troops. ***Location*** *What pattern can you see in the location of the remaining Native American reservations in 1890?*

Little Bighorn River in what is now Montana. There he met a larger-than-expected Sioux force. In the clash that followed—the **Battle of Little Bighorn**—Custer and more than 200 American soldiers were killed. This victory proved to be the Indians' last, as the federal government flooded the region with troops. By the end of 1876, most of the Sioux had returned to their reservations. Sitting Bull escaped to Canada, but returned to a Sioux reservation five years later.

In 1890, following the death of Sitting Bull, soldiers of the Seventh Cavalry tried to arrest a group of the chief's followers who had left their reservation. While the Indians were handing over their weapons in surrender, someone fired a shot. The soldiers then opened fire, killing more than 200 unarmed Sioux (including nearly 70 women and children) in what later became known as the **Massacre at Wounded Knee.**

## Chief Joseph

AMERICAN BIOGRAPHY

The Nez Percé inhabited a large area in the northwest region of the United States. In the 1850s and 1860s, some Nez Percé signed treaties agreeing to sell their lands to the federal government. But the largest group refused. They lived in the Wallowa Valley at the crossroads of present-day Idaho, Oregon, and Washington. As the chief of this group lay dying in 1871, he made his son and successor, Joseph, swear never to sell their homeland.

Fulfilling that promise proved impossible. After pressuring Chief Joseph for five years, General Oliver Otis Howard finally ordered him and his people to leave Wallowa Valley for a reservation in Idaho. Faced with the threat of superior force, Chief Joseph decided that he must give in. Before he could do so, however, a group of Nez Percé youths attacked some settlers who had been accused of stealing Nez Percé horses. The Nez Percé and the United States government were now at war.

Chief Joseph (1840?–1904)

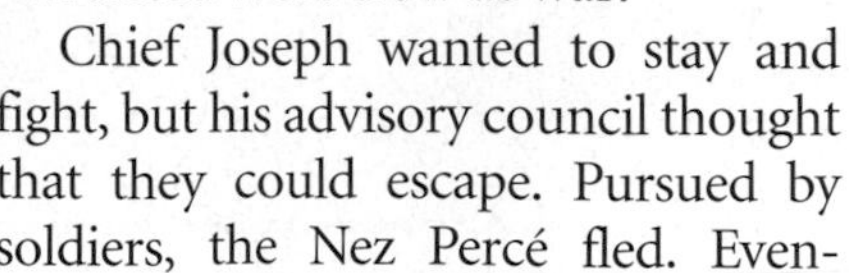

Chief Joseph wanted to stay and fight, but his advisory council thought that they could escape. Pursued by soldiers, the Nez Percé fled. Eventually, Chief Joseph's group reached Montana. Exhausted, they set up camp at Big Hole Basin, but in a surprise raid, American soldiers attacked, killing men, women, and children.

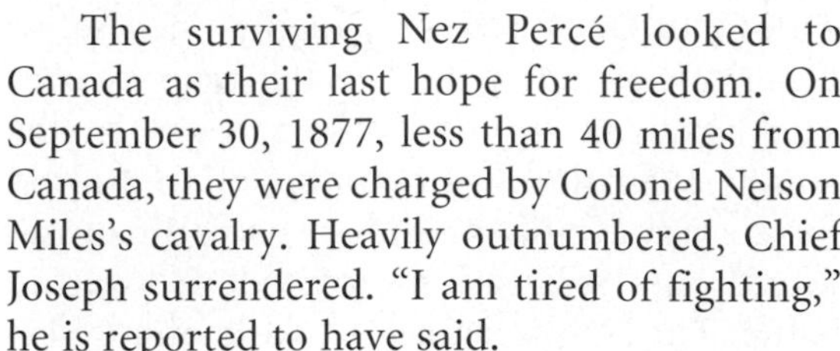

The surviving Nez Percé looked to Canada as their last hope for freedom. On September 30, 1877, less than 40 miles from Canada, they were charged by Colonel Nelson Miles's cavalry. Heavily outnumbered, Chief Joseph surrendered. "I am tired of fighting," he is reported to have said.

The federal government sent Chief Joseph's people to Indian Territory. There, due to heat and malaria, many more Nez Percé died, including all of Joseph's children. In 1885 Chief Joseph and the remaining Nez Percé were permitted to leave for a reservation in present-day Washington State. ■

## Native Cultures Destroyed

As Native Americans lost land and battles to American troops, many aspects of Indian cultures also disappeared. The peoples of the Great Plains, for example, relied on the buffalo for food, clothing, shelter, fuel, and tools. By the 1870s, the great buffalo herds began to disappear. At first the herds were hunted by the railroad companies to feed their workers. Later they were targeted by settlers to clear the range, to satisfy a craze for hides, and even for sport. The federal government encouraged this slaughter as a means to wipe out the Plains peoples' food supply.

Some white Americans found such acts horrifying. Inspired in part by Helen Hunt Jackson's 1881 publication *A Century of Dishonor*, a national "Indian rights" movement arose. Protesting what she saw as the government's broken promises and treaties, Jackson said, "It makes little difference . . . where one opens the record of the history of the Indians; every page and every year has its dark stain."

As sincere as reformers were, however, most believed that Native Americans still needed to be "civilized." Christian missionaries, who ran schools on the reservations, shared this belief. The government supported this opinion and passed a criminal code in 1884 forbidding Indians to practice their religions.

Other reformers sought to break Native American traditions by requiring Indians to farm individual plots. The **Dawes Act** of 1887 gave separate plots of land to each Native American family headed by a male. Much of the land was not suitable for farming, however, and many Native Americans had no interest or experience in agriculture. Many simply sold their lands to speculators. In fact, between 1887 and 1934 the amount of land owned by Native Americans shrank by 65 percent.

## *The Fate of Indian Territory*

For the nearly 70 Indian nations that had been forced into Indian Territory, worse was to come. Following the Civil War, a flood of settlers began to enter the territory. Many were squatters, tempted by the territory's farmland.

Although Native Americans protested and the government tried to stop them, squatters continued to come. Other would-be settlers pressured Congress to allow legal settlement in the territory. In 1889 Congress responded, opening for homesteading nearly 2 million acres in Indian Territory that had not yet been assigned to Native Americans. At noon on April 22, soldiers signaled with their pistols, and hundreds of homesteaders rushed across the border to stake their claims as described:

> **AMERICAN VOICES** "Along the line as far as the eye could reach, with a shout and a yell the swift riders shot out, then followed the light buggies or wagons and last the lumbering prairie schooner and freighters' wagons, with here and there even a man on a bicycle and many too on foot,—above all a great cloud of dust hovering like smoke over a battlefield."
>
> —*Newspaper reporter, 1889*

Within a few hours these settlers, called **boomers,** had staked off hundreds of claims. Oklahoma City had over 10,000 residents by the end of the first day. Many boomers were unhappy to discover that some of the best lands had been reserved by **sooners,** or those people who had sneaked past the government officials earlier to mark their claims.

Under continued pressure from settlers, Congress created the Oklahoma Territory on May 2, 1890. In the following years, the remainder of Indian Territory was opened to settlement.

### COMPARING PRIMARY SOURCES

#### ATTITUDES TOWARD THE ENVIRONMENT

As settlers pushed west, it became clear that they and the Native Americans held different attitudes toward the land.

| In Favor of Respecting the Environment | In Favor of Conquering the Environment |
|---|---|
| "The ground says, the Great Spirit has placed me here to produce all that grows on me, trees and fruit. The same way the ground says, It was from me man was made. The Great Spirit, in placing men on the earth, desired them to take good care of the ground and to do each other no harm." —*Young Chief of the Cayuse, on opposing selling land in Washington Territory, 1855* | "To open the greatest number of mines and extract the greatest quantity of ore, to scatter cattle over a thousand hills, to turn the flower-spangled prairies . . . into wheatfields, . . . to force from nature the most she can be made to yield . . . is preached by Western newspapers as a kind of religion." —*Britain's Lord James Bryce, after visiting the American West in the 1880s* |

***ANALYZING VIEWPOINTS*** **Which of the attitudes expressed above do you think is more common today? Explain.**

## *SECTION 2 REVIEW*

### Comprehension

1. *Key Terms* Define: (a) reservation; (b) Battle of Little Bighorn; (c) Massacre at Wounded Knee; (d) Dawes Act; (e) boomer; (f) sooner.
2. *Summarizing the Main Idea* Describe the pattern of conflict between the United States government and Native Americans.
3. *Organizing Information* Create a chart that organizes information about the devastation of various Native American groups. Include the Navajo, the Apache, the Cheyenne, the Sioux, and the Nez Percé.

### Critical Thinking

4. *Analyzing Time Lines* Review the time line at the start of the section. Select one event and write a paragraph on how it relates to the conquest of the Native Americans.
5. *Expressing Problems Clearly* By what means were Native American cultures destroyed in the late 1800s?

### Writing Activity

6. *Writing a Persuasive Essay* Write a letter to a friend defending or attacking the United States government's decision to open up Indian Territory for settlement. Support your arguments with information from the text.

| 1859 | 1862 | 1867 | 1874 | 1886 |
|---|---|---|---|---|
| *Silver discovered at Nevada's Comstock Lode* | *Congress establishes the Department of Agriculture* | *J. G. McCoy establishes Abilene, Kansas, as a cow town* | *Joseph Glidden invents barbed wire* | *Harsh winter damages cattle industry* |

1859 1869 1879 1889

# 3 Farming, Mining, and Ranching

## SECTION PREVIEW

### Objectives

1. List the changes that transformed farming on the Great Plains.
2. Explain the changing mining industry in the West.
3. Describe the growth and decline of the cattle industry.
4. *Key Terms* Define: dry farming; bonanza farm; placer mining; long drive.

### Main Idea

Modern farming methods, the discovery of mineral deposits, and ranching made the West attractive to many individual settlers and big businesses.

### Reading Strategy

*Reinforcing Main Ideas* Write the following column headings on a piece of paper: *Farming, Mining,* and *Ranching.* As you read, note in the appropriate column how each of these industries had changed by the late 1800s.

*By the late 1800s, machines like these performed many harvesting tasks.*

The pioneers who first settled the West recognized its great potential. Farmers, miners, and ranchers all searched for ways to unlock that potential and make the land fruitful.

## Farming on the Plains

Despite the hopes of many settlers, the Great Plains was not a farmer's paradise. Rainfall was unpredictable, and never enough. The weather swung from one extreme to the other, with summer temperatures exceeding 100°F and winter bringing raging blizzards and bone-chilling cold. Drought and hot winds fed dust storms and prairie fires. Grasshoppers, locusts, and boll weevils ravaged crops and destroyed property.

These challenging conditions weeded out all but the hardiest settlers. But the same inventiveness that had helped spur industrial expansion in the East helped confront such troubles in the West.

**New Technology on the Farm** The dry climate in parts of the West greatly reduced the land's productivity. In response, farmers practiced what is called **dry farming.** This involved techniques such as planting crops that do not require a great deal of water and keeping the fields free of weeds.

Because western farms were very large, farmers welcomed any machines that would save them time and effort. During the 1870s, improvements in farm implements multiplied. Soon farmers were riding behind a plow that made several furrows at once. Other inventions included harrows, equipped with spring teeth to dislodge debris and break up the ground before planting, and automatic drills to spread grain. Steam-powered threshers arrived on the scene by 1875, and cornhuskers and cornbinders by the 1890s.

**Agricultural Knowledge Grows** Congress had established the federal Department of Agriculture in 1862 as part of the Morrill Land-Grant Act. In the 1880s and 1890s, the department gathered statistics on markets, crops, and plant diseases. Government publications helped spread information on new farming techniques, including such topics as crop rotation, hybridization (the crossing of different plants to produce new varieties), and the preservation of water and topsoil.

**The Big Business of "Bonanza" Farms** New machines and farm techniques increased farm output enormously. Owners of large farms now hoped to reap a "bonanza" by supplying food to the growing populations of the East. They began applying to farming the same organizational ideas then taking hold in industry. As one observer noted:

> **"It is no longer left to the small farmer, taking up 160 acres of land, building a log cabin and struggling to secure himself a home. Organized capital is being employed in the work, with all the advantages which organization implies. Companies and partnerships are formed for the cultivation precisely as they are for building railroads, manufactories, etc."**
>
> —Commercial and Financial Chronicle, *1879*

The result was **bonanza farms**—farms controlled by large businesses and managed by professionals. Specializing in single cash crops raised for sale in massive quantities, bonanza farms promised enormous profits to their investors.

The farms' massive output caused problems, however. When the supply of a certain product rose faster than the demand, the market became glutted and prices fell. Such dips in prices were common. To compensate for falling prices, farmers produced ever larger amounts of wheat, but this only made the oversupply problem worse.

**The Problem of Debt** Falling prices contributed to a constant worry for farmers: debt. Once farmers invested in machines, they had to raise only the crop for which the machines were designed. If prices for that crop dipped, farmers could not pay off their debts.

In some cases, land speculation contributed to farmers' debts. Hoping to profit from rising land prices, some farmers bought more land than they could manage. The burden of a heavy mortgage became unbearable when the bottom fell out of the market.

## *Boom and Bust on the Mining Frontier*

"Gold!" Since the California Gold Rush of 1849, this word alone has conjured up the image of lucky prospectors striking it rich. The reality, however, was far more complicated.

**"Pikes Peak or Bust!"** The gold strike at Sutter's Mill, California, in 1848 was the first of several large strikes in the West. In 1859, rumors of gold strikes in the area of Pikes Peak, Colorado, brought on a stampede of wagons with the words "Pikes Peak or Bust!" scrawled on their sides. Also in 1859, a silver strike in Nevada's famed "Comstock Lode" brought on another rush.†

The lure of quick wealth brought people of all colors, ethnic backgrounds, and levels of education into mining towns. Asians, especially men from China who had left railway work, often became miners. While an overwhelming majority of settlers on the mining frontier were men, some women became miners as well.

Miners worked and played hard. Widespread gambling and drunkenness gave mining towns reputations for vice. Actually, most towns settled down quickly. In many cases, the arrival of big mining companies brought stability to the settlement.

*It is unlikely that this man struck it rich panning for gold. Far more successful were those who "mined the miners," or sold goods to the fortune-seekers.*

**Mining Techniques** Miners, working alone or in small groups, searched for metal that was close to the surface. Using a technique called **placer mining,** they shoveled loose dirt into boxes and then ran water over it, causing the heavy minerals to sink to the bottom. Placer mining worked well for finding the loose gold that had washed out of rock and into the streams.

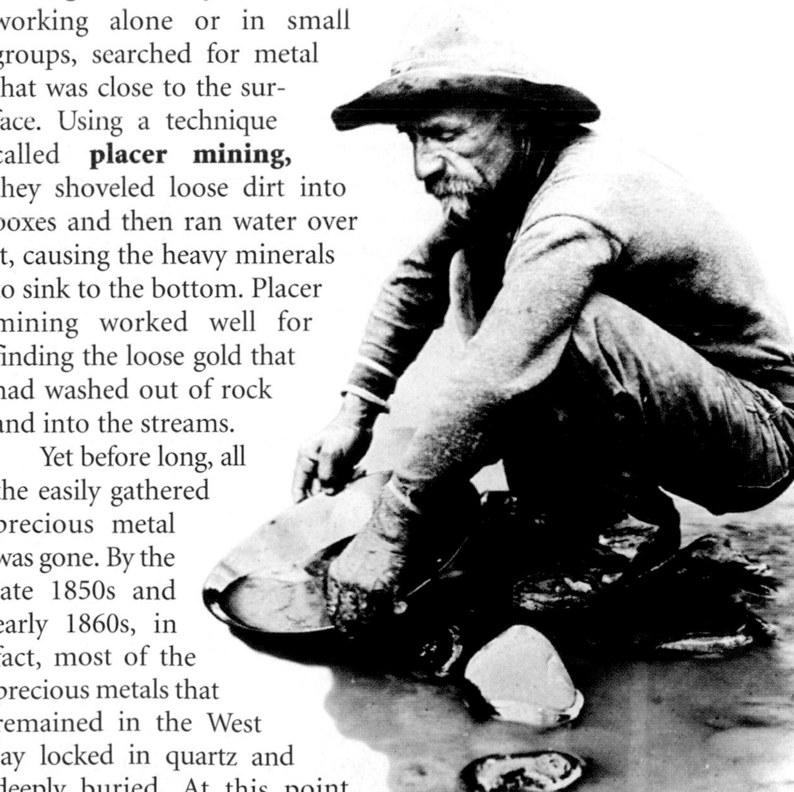

Yet before long, all the easily gathered precious metal was gone. By the late 1850s and early 1860s, in fact, most of the precious metals that remained in the West lay locked in quartz and deeply buried. At this point

† Comstock did not reveal its greatest riches until 1873, when quartz mills and other mining machinery were brought in. From 1859 to 1879 Comstock mines produced $350 million, of which 55 percent was in silver and 45 percent in gold.

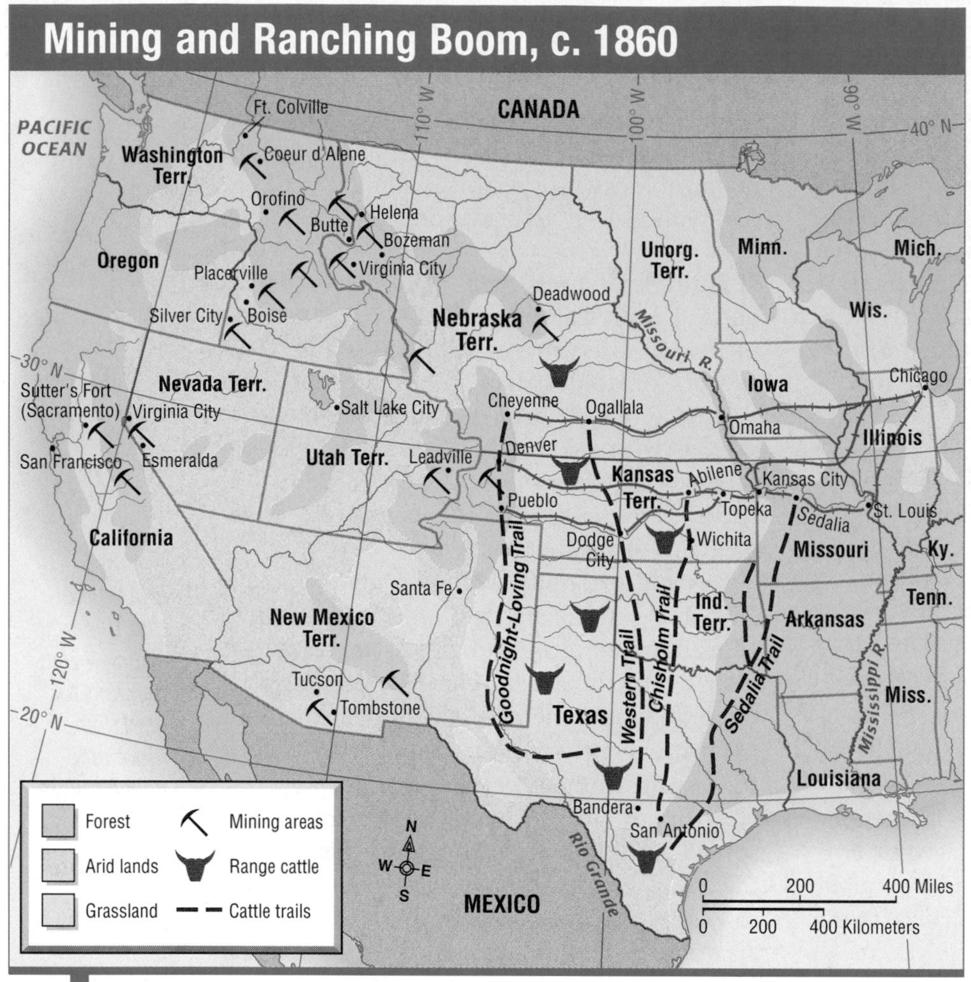


**MAP skills** The mining and ranching boom of the early to mid-1800s was short-lived but intense. In its peak year, the Chisholm Trail alone saw 600,000 head of cattle driven to market. ***Regions*** ***Judging from the map, why do you think the cattle trails followed the routes they did?***

most prospectors straggled home, leaving many mining cities deserted ghost towns.

Large corporations then moved in. Only they could afford the large investments in machinery, mine shafts, and tunnels required to reach these riches. Like so many other industries, mining became the realm of big business.

## *The Cattle Industry*

When American settlers began to arrive in Texas in the early 1800s, they learned the cattle ranching ways of the Mexicans living there. It was not long before Americans had adopted Mexican ranching equipment and dress as their own. Americans also learned from Mexican cattlemen the advantages of raising the hardy Texas longhorn cattle that thrived on the dry, grassy plains.

**Main Idea CONNECTIONS**

*Describe the cattle industry in the late 1800s.*

**Demand Spurs Growth** During the 1860s and 1870s, cattle ranching boomed. The destruction of the buffalo and removal of Native Americans to reservations emptied the land for grazing cattle. The open plains offered a rancher limitless pasture that was free for the taking. At the same time, the growing population of eastern cities drove up the demand for beef. By the end of the Civil War, cattle that sold for $3 to $5 a head in Texas could bring $30 to $50 a head in the meat markets of Chicago and St. Louis.

At first, Texas cattlemen reached these markets by gathering up their herds and driving them northward across the open range. Railroads, however, promised a far easier and faster route to market. In 1867, J. G. McCoy established Abilene, Kansas, on the Hannibal and St. Joe Railroad. The first town built specifically for receiving cattle, it included pens where ranchers held their cattle until they could be shipped out by railroad. Other so-called "cow towns," including Cheyenne in Wyoming Territory and Dodge City and Ellsworth in Kansas, soon sprang up on the rail lines.

**Along the Cattle Trails** A series of routes or trails linked the San Antonio region of Texas with the cow towns to the north. One of the most famous, the Chisholm Trail, ended at Abilene. The Goodnight-Loving Trail followed a twisting route farther west and terminated in Cheyenne.

Managing the **long drive,** or the transporting of cattle from ranges to the cow towns, was the job of the cowboys. The work was neither easy nor pleasant. Pay varied greatly depending on experience. Cowboys braved rough, muddy trails, pounding thunderstorms, and attacks by cattle thieves. Stampedes were another constant danger. Recalled a cowboy after one stampede, "We found 341 dead cattle, two dead horses, one dead cowboy and two more with broken legs after the herd had passed."

As the cattle moved along the trail, two experienced cowboys rode in front of the herd, guiding the animals along the route. Other cowboys rode beside the herd to keep the cattle all together, and still others rode in the dust at the rear, pushing along the stragglers. A cowboy could spend up to 18 hours a day in the saddle and had to be on constant alert.

**Fencing the Open Range** The cattle boom ended in the mid-1880s as a result of several factors. One was Joseph Glidden's 1874 invention of barbed wire, which he claimed was "Light as air. . . . Cheaper than dirt. All steel and miles long. The cattle ain't born that can get through it." Farmers on the Great Plains lacked a supply of trees or rocks with which to build fences. With the invention of barbed wire, farmers could fence their land and keep out grazing cattle that had caused much conflict between farmers and ranchers. Slowly the open range, on which ranchers had freely grazed their huge herds, began to disappear.

Cattlemen contributed to their own downfall by overstocking the market with cattle. They also allowed their herds to overgraze what remained of the range, seriously damaging the prairie grasses. In 1885 beef prices began to fall.

The final death knell sounded with the harsh winter of 1885–1886. Some ranchers lost up to 85 percent of their cattle to freezing temperatures and starvation. That tough winter was followed by a summer of drought that destroyed the grasses and weakened the cattle. The winter of 1886–1887 was even worse than the previous one and wiped out much of the remaining herds. Thousands of individual ranchers, and even many of the larger corporations, were ruined. Cattle ranching survived, but on a much smaller scale and with new breeds of cattle that largely replaced the Texas longhorn.

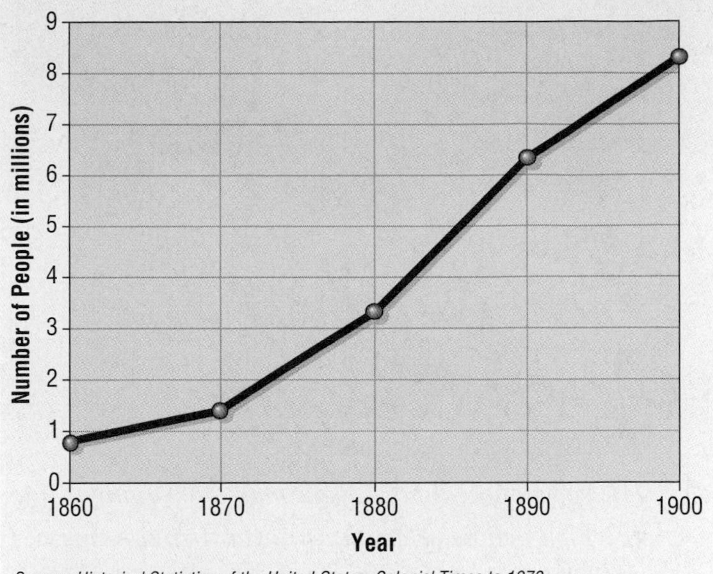


**Interpreting Graphs** The American West saw steady and dramatic population growth during the latter part of the 19th century. ***Geography* What attracted people to the western states?**

## SECTION 3 REVIEW

### Comprehension

1. *Key Term* Define: (a) dry farming; (b) bonanza farm; (c) placer mining; (d) long drive.
2. *Summarizing the Main Idea* What were some of the key developments in farming, mining, and ranching that attracted settlers to the West?
3. *Organizing Information* Create two cause-and-effect charts that organize information about the growth and decline of the cattle industry in the late 1800s.

### Critical Thinking

4. *Analyzing Time Lines* Review the time line at the start of the section. Which entries are related to the decline of the ranching industry?
5. *Identifying Central Issues* Briefly describe the benefits and drawbacks of new farm machinery and farming methods.

### Writing Activity

6. *Writing an Expository Essay* Reread the section "Boom and Bust on the Mining Frontier." Then write a brief essay explaining why most individuals did not "strike it rich" in the mining booms of the late 1800s.

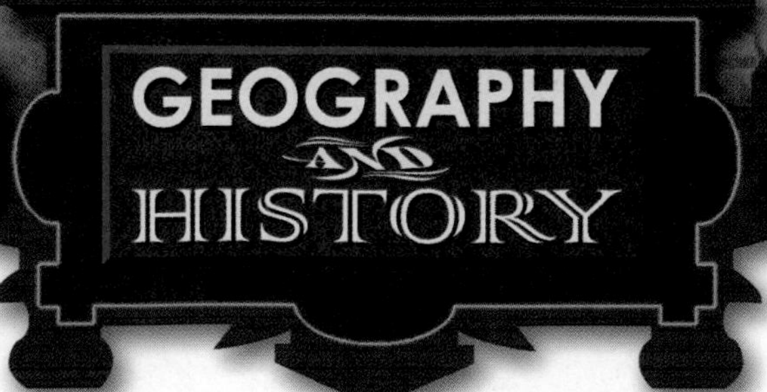


# The End of the Open Range

A cowboy's spur

*The geographic theme of human-environment interaction examines ways in which people affect their natural environment. In the 1800s, conflicts arose between farmers and ranchers over how to use the western plains. Who would win control of the open range?*

How people interact with their environment is largely determined by its natural resources and climate. For instance, if you were a farmer seeking a place to plant crops, you would choose a region with good soil, enough water, and a long growing season. The map on the next page shows land use in the American West today.

Generally, only one land use dominates a region. This is because a single economic activity can use up an area's resources. If there is more than one land use in a place, conflicts may arise. That is what happened when farmers met ranchers on the vast grasslands between the Mississippi River and the Rocky Mountains.

**Free-ranging cattle and cattle being driven to market trampled the farmers' crops. Because the prairie had no trees or stones, there were no materials for fences to keep the cattle out.**

## Ranchers Settle the Plains

Before they were driven from the land, Native Americans hunted great buffalo on the open plains. They knew the value of this rich and expansive land. But until the 1850s, most white settlers from the East hurried right through the plains on their way to the West. Then they discovered the value of the land.

The plains were covered in seemingly limitless grassland. Ranchers soon found that the open range was a perfect place to raise cattle. So began the growth of open-range ranching.

Ranchers were especially attracted to Texas, with its herds of free-roaming longhorns. They fed their cattle on the grass and watered them in the streams and rivers that meandered through the plains. Then they rounded them up for market.

## Railroads Help Ranchers

The ranchers' biggest problem was getting cattle to customers in the Northeast. The long journey could be dangerous. Still, the big demand and the high prices paid for beef convinced cattlemen to take the risk. They found they could drive their cattle several hundred miles north to the railroads. The first of these long drives went from Texas to Sedalia, Missouri, in 1866.

As the miles of railroad extended further west and south, the distance between grazing land and the railroads decreased. "Cow towns" sprang up on the Great Plains next to the rail lines. Ellsworth, Wichita, and Dodge City in Kansas, Cheyenne and Laramie in Wyoming, and other towns processed millions of head of cattle during the late 1870s and early 1880s.

## Farmers Claim the Plains

Ranchers were not the only ones interested in the land. Soon, farmers discovered that beneath the grassy surface of the plains was not sand but as much as six feet of fertile topsoil. This would be excellent land on which to grow crops.

The prairie grasses, however, imprisoned this topsoil with a layer of dense roots called sod. Before land could be farmed, the tough, centuries-old sod had to be broken up. Although "sod busting" required the most advanced and expensive plows, farmers arrived by the thousands, encouraged by the federal government and the railroads to make the plains their home. The railroads could transport the farmers' products to be sold in the Northeast.

Yet all was not well on the plains. Farming and ranching interfered with each other. Free-ranging cattle and cattle being driven to market trampled the farmers' crops. Because the prairie had no trees or stones, there were no materials for fences to keep the cattle out. Barbed wire, introduced in 1874, solved this problem but created another.

## Farmers Win the Range War

Angered by the farmers' attempts to fence off the land, some ranchers started to enclose huge areas of their own. The ranchers' illegal fences sometimes cut farmers off from roads and water supplies. Farmers fought back by cutting the barbed wire and seeking government help. The ranchers fixed their fences and protected them with gunfire.

But even with their fenced ranches, cattlemen were crowded out by the farmers. Farmers could make a living with much less land than cattle ranchers. Because the federal government had a land policy that tried to benefit the largest number of people, it helped the many small farmers more than it helped the few cattle ranchers. Government land-use laws increasingly made open-range ranching impossible. Finally, several years of harsh weather all but destroyed the herds.

### Land Use on the Great Plains

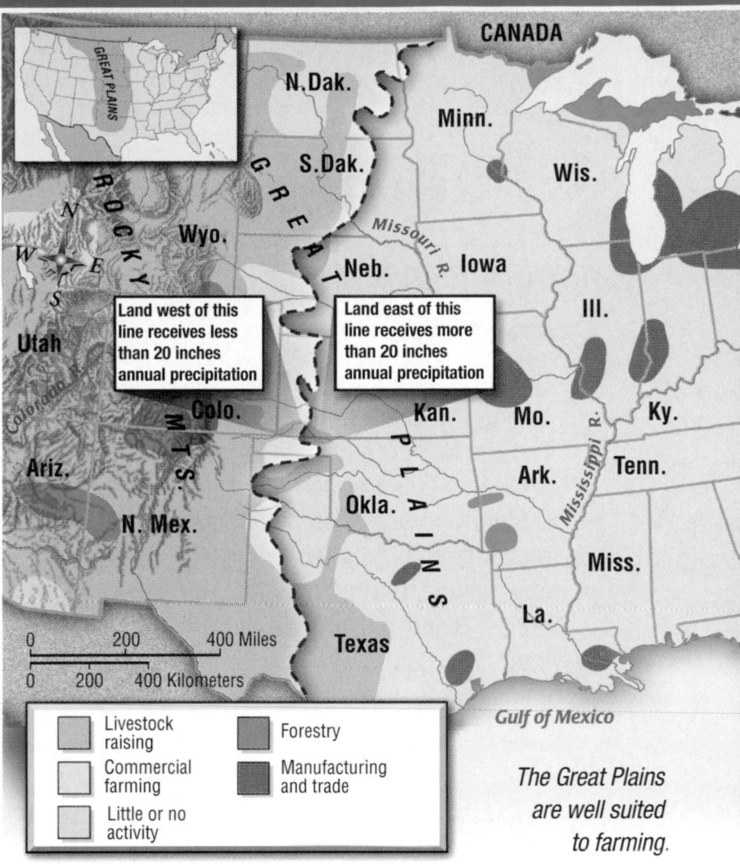


*The Great Plains are well suited to farming.*

1. How did the spread of railroads throughout the South and West help both ranchers and farmers?

2. Before the invention of barbed wire, what problem did the ranchers' cattle cause for the farmers?

### Themes in Geography

3. ***Human-Environment Interaction*** The map shows that the western plains generally receive less than half the rainfall of those parts closest to the Mississippi River. How does this help explain the ways that people interact with and use the land?

| 1873 | 1878 | 1887 | 1887 | 1890 |
|---|---|---|---|---|
| Congress puts nation's currency on a gold standard | Bland-Allison Act | Interstate Commerce Act | Texas Seed bill | Sherman Silver Purchase Act |

1870 1880 1890

# 4 Populism

## SECTION PREVIEW

### Objectives

1. Describe farmers' economic complaints during the late 1800s.
2. List the key organizations formed to protest problems faced by farmers.
3. Understand *populism,* the people behind the movement, and its legacy.
4. *Key Terms* Define: deflation; monetary policy; Bland-Allison Act; the Grange; Interstate Commerce Act; Populist; progressive income tax.

### Main Idea

By the late 1800s, declining incomes for American farmers created fertile ground for a farmers' protest movement.

### Reading Strategy

*Problem Solving* Imagine you are a farmer in the late 1800s. List some of the problems you face and identify some of the organizations that promise to help you.

Farmers in the late 1800s were in trouble. Farm production was up, but so too was debt, as farmers bought expensive new equipment. At the same time, crop prices were down. In 1890 a Congregational minister described the plight of the farmer in this way:

> AMERICAN VOICES "The farmers . . . are the bone and sinew of the nation; they produce the largest share of its wealth; but they are getting, they say, the smallest share for themselves. The American farmer is steadily losing ground. His burdens are heavier every year and his gains are more meager [smaller]."
>
> —*Washington Gladden*

## The Farmers' Complaint

Farmers in the late 1800s were suffering from a long-term decline in crop prices that had begun after the Civil War. Moreover, competition from farmers in other nations had increased. Finally, they complained about the power of big business and the government's refusal to help. Their solution was to unite.

**Farmers and Tariffs** A federal policy of particular concern to farmers was tariffs. Tariffs on imported goods discourage people from buying imports by making them more expensive. Thus, tariffs encourage the sale of goods produced at home.

Americans in the late 1800s were divided on the benefit of tariffs. Industrialists claimed that tariffs protected American factory jobs—and their own profits. However, because tariffs reduced foreign competition, they also encouraged American firms to raise their prices, which was not good for workers.

Tariffs helped farmers in one way: by protecting them against competition from farm imports. But tariffs hurt farmers in two ways. First, they raised the prices of manufactured goods. Second, they prevented foreigners from earning the American currency they needed to buy American crops. Thus, tariffs indirectly reduced the international market for American farm products.

Whenever the government raised tariffs to benefit industry, farmers protested. They saw this high-tariff policy as proof that the government was favoring eastern manufacturers over western farmers. Yet tariffs were not the only concern of the agriculture industry in the late 1800s. The dominant issue for many farmers was "free silver."

**The Money Issue** The value of money is linked to the amount in circulation. If the government increases the money supply, the value of every dollar drops. This drop in value shows up as inflation, a widespread rise in prices on goods of all kinds.

People who borrow money benefit from inflation because the money they pay back to the lender is worth less than the money they borrowed. Inflation also helps people who sell things, such as farm goods, because inflation allows sellers to charge higher prices.

In contrast, if the government reduces the money supply, the value of each dollar becomes greater. This causes **deflation,** or a drop in the prices on goods. People who lend money are helped by deflation because the money they receive in payment of a loan is worth more than the money they lent out.

In the years following the Civil War, the nation's money supply shrank as the federal government took out of circulation the paper money that had been issued during the war. As a result, the nation experienced a prolonged period of deflation.

**Monetary policy,** the federal government's plan for the makeup and quantity of the nation's money supply, thus emerged as a major political issue. Supporters of inflation pushed for an increase in the money supply. Supporters of deflation wanted a "tight money" policy of less currency in circulation.

**Gold bugs** In 1873 the supporters of tight money won a victory. Until that time, United States currency had been on a bimetallic standard. That is, currency consisted of gold or silver coins or United States treasury notes that could be traded in for gold or silver. In 1873, in order to prevent inflation and ensure economic stability, Congress put the nation's currency on a gold standard. This move reduced the amount of money in circulation because the money supply would be limited by the amount of gold held by the government.

Conservative "gold bugs" were pleased. Many of them were big lenders, and they liked the idea of being repaid in currency backed by the gold standard.

**Silverites** "Silverites," mostly silver-mining interests and western farmers, were furious at the nation's move to a gold standard. They claimed that the end of silver as a monetary standard would depress the prices of farm produce. Silverites called instead for free silver—the unlimited coining of silver dollars as a means of increasing the money supply.

The **Bland-Allison Act** of 1878, was, for the silverites, a step in the right direction. This act required the federal government to purchase and coin more silver, increasing the money supply and causing inflation.

Passed by Congress, the Bland-Allison Act was vetoed by President Hayes because he opposed the inflation it would create. Congress then overrode Hayes's

### FACT Finder: Gold Standard vs. Free Silver

| | *Gold Standard* | *Free Silver* |
|---|---|---|
| **Supporters** | Gold Bugs: bankers and wealthy industrialists | Silverites: silver miners, farmers, and debtors |
| **Position** | A gold standard would limit the amount of money in circulation and deflate prices. | The unlimited coinage of silver would increase the money supply and inflate prices. |
| **Benefits** | The economy would be more stable. The wealthy would have protection for their money. | The economy would be stimulated. Farmers would get more money for their goods; debtors would more easily repay loans. |

**Interpreting Tables** One of the biggest concerns of the Populists was the nation's monetary policy. ***Economics*** *Why were farmers supportive of free silver?*

### ECONOMICS CONCEPTS

***monetary policy: the federal government's plan for the size of the nation's money supply***

▼ **The Historical Context:** Farmers in the late 1800s called for an increase in the money supply, which would cause higher prices and thus raise their incomes. Their opponents called for a continued "tight money" policy, in which the money supply is kept low.

▼ **The Concept Today:** The Federal Reserve System, established in 1913, controls the nation's money supply today. Led by its chairman the "Fed" seeks to promote steady economic growth without causing high inflation.

veto. Yet the act had only a limited effect because the Treasury Department refused to buy more than the minimum silver required under the act. The Treasury also refused to circulate the silver dollars that the law required it to mint.

In 1890, Congress passed the Sherman Silver Purchase Act. While not authorizing the free and unlimited coinage of silver that the silverites wanted, it did increase the amount of silver the government was required to purchase every month. The law required the Treasury to buy the silver with notes that could be redeemed for either silver or gold. Yet as people turned in their silver Treasury notes for gold dollars, the gold reserves of the government began to be depleted. To protect the nation's gold supply, President Cleveland oversaw the repeal of the Silver Purchase Act in 1893.

## *Organizing Farmer Protest*

Because farmers lived far from one another and usually relied on their own efforts, they tended not to organize protests against policies that hurt them. In the late nineteenth century, however, farmers began to take advantage of improvements in communication and transportation. They united to form several powerful protest groups.

**The Grange** In 1866 the Department of Agriculture sent Oliver H. Kelley on an inspection tour of southern farms. Disturbed by farmers' isolation, the following year he founded the Patrons of Husbandry, or **the Grange.**

The Grange soon began helping farmers form cooperatives, in which farmers saved money by buying goods in large quantities. The Grange also pressured state legislators to regulate the businesses on which farmers depended—for example, the grain elevators that stored the farmers' crops and the railroads that shipped them. The railroads, which gave better rates to powerful eastern industrialists than unorganized western farmers, received the brunt of farmers' anger.

Although the Grange was popular, by the mid-1870s farmers were turning to other political outlets. A Greenback party, which argued for the circulation of more paper money as a means to cause inflation, elected fourteen members to Congress in 1878. Its power quickly faded, however, as more farmers adopted the free silver position in the currency debate.

**Farmers' Alliances** In the 1880s many farmers joined a network of Farmers' Alliances that were formed around the nation. The alliances launched harsh attacks on monopolies, such as those that controlled the railroads. Alliance lecturer Napoleon B. Ashby accused the nation's millionaires of having made their fortunes by preying upon "the mighty rivers of commerce which the farmers have set flowing."

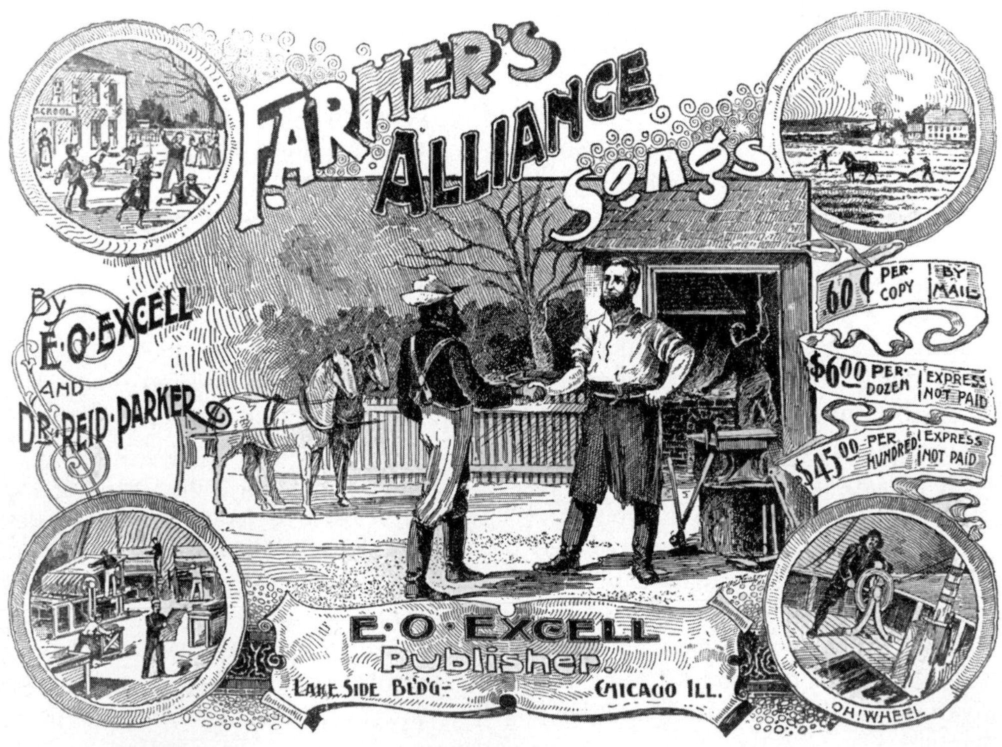


Farmers' Alliances provided an important channel for farmer protest and political action in the late 1800s. This illustration comes from a book of songs for these organizations. ***Culture*** ***What do the images on this songbook cover reveal about the ideals of the Farmers' Alliances?***

The Farmers' Alliance in the South, formed in Texas in the mid-1870s, grew especially powerful.† It emphasized themes that many of the nation's farmers could support: federal regulation of the railroads, more money in circulation, creation of state departments of agriculture, antitrust laws, and farm credit.

Farmer's Alliances held special importance for women, who served as officers and won support for women's political rights. One of the most popular speakers was Kansas lawyer Mary Elizabeth Lease, who bluntly urged farmers to raise "less corn and more Hell!"

African Americans worked through a separate but parallel "Colored Farmers' Alliance." Formed in 1886 in Lovelady, Texas, the group had a quarter of a million members by 1891.

A series of natural disasters gave special urgency to Farmers' Alliance programs. The Mississippi River flooded in 1882. In 1886–1887, twenty-one consecutive months of drought in Texas impoverished 30,000 people. Terrible blizzards, which killed thousands of cattle, struck the West in 1887. The increasingly angry farmers asked, Why was the federal government unwilling to respond to these disasters?

**An Inactive Government** In every election from 1880 to 1892, no candidate won a majority of the popular vote. Only rarely did the President's party command a majority in Congress. Presidents thus lacked the power to take bold action.

In addition, some Presidents were influenced by promises of support from powerful business interests. In return, these Presidents protected American industry, angering many farmers.

The federal government did take some actions. In 1887 Congress passed the Texas Seed bill, which provided seed grain to aid drought victims. But Democratic President Grover Cleveland vetoed the bill, expressing the commonly held view that "though the people support the government, the government should not support the people."

Cleveland did sign the **Interstate Commerce Act** of 1887, a response to the many complaints against the railroad companies. It regulated the prices that railroads charged to move freight between states, requiring the rates to be set in proportion to the distance traveled. The law also made it illegal to give special rates to some customers. While the act did not control the monopolistic practices of the railroads that so angered farmers, it did establish the principle that Congress could regulate the railroads. The act also set up the Interstate Commerce Commission (ICC) to enforce the laws.

Finally, in 1890 President Benjamin Harrison approved the Sherman Antitrust Act. This act was meant to curb the power of trusts and monopolies. But during its first decade, enforcement was lax.

*Mary Elizabeth Lease won fame as a Farmers' Alliance speaker.*

## The Populists

In 1890 the various small political parties associated with the Farmers' Alliances began to enjoy success at the ballot box, especially in the South. In 1891 the Alliances founded the People's party, a new national party that demanded radical changes in federal economic and social policies. The **Populists,** as followers of the new party were known, built their platform around the following issues:

(1) They called for an increased circulation of money.

(2) They urged the unlimited minting of silver.

(3) They supported a **progressive income tax,** in which the percentage of taxes owed increases with income. This would place a greater tax burden on wealthy industrialists and a lesser one on farmers.

(4) They called for government ownership of the country's communications and transportation systems.

(5) In an effort to attract urban support, they endorsed an eight-hour work day. They also opposed the use of Pinkertons, the private police force that had been involved in the bloody Homestead Strike of 1892, as strikebreakers.

*The Populist party grew out of what farmers' protest group?*

Breaking through deeply rooted racial prejudice, Populists sought a united front of African American and white farmers. The poor of both races had a common cause, they argued. As one of the party's leaders explained:

† Hundreds of thousands of farmers joined the Farmers' Alliances. One estimate placed the number of members at close to 3 million.

## Election of 1892

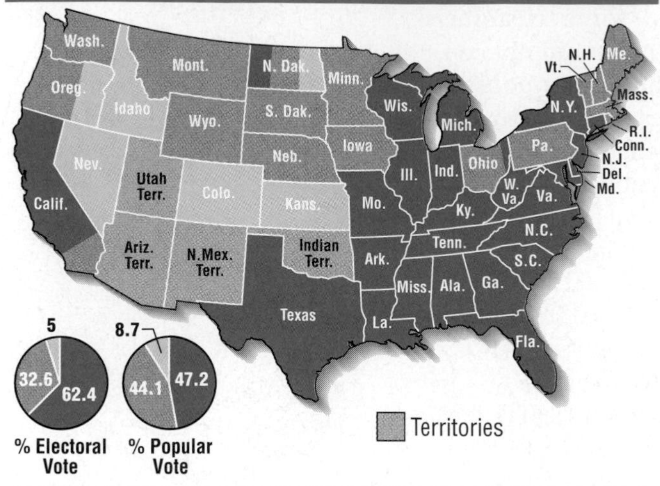


| Candidate/Party | Electoral Vote | Popular Vote |
|---|---|---|
| Grover Cleveland (Democrat) | 277 | 5,554,414 |
| Benjamin Harrison (Republican) | 145 | 5,190,802 |
| James Weaver (People's) | 22 | 1,027,329 |

## Election of 1896

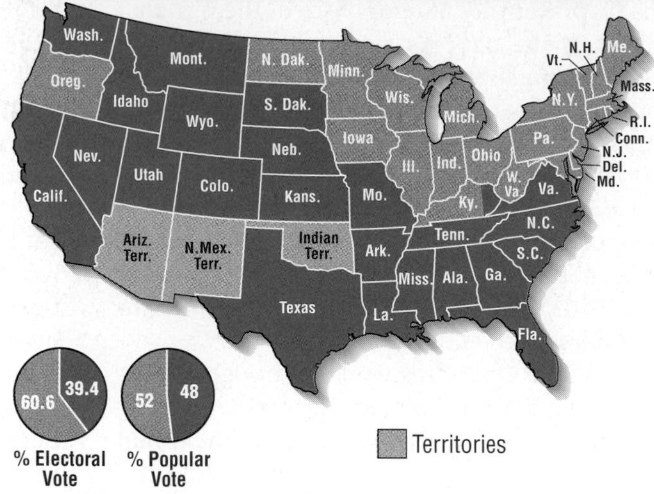


| Candidate/Party | Electoral Vote | Popular Vote |
|---|---|---|
| William McKinley (Republican) | 271 | 7,035,638 |
| William J. Bryan (Democrat) | 176 | 6,497,946 |

In their first presidential election, the People's party ran poorly against both the Democrats and Republicans. In 1896, they shared candidate William Jennings Bryan with the Democrats.
***Regions*** ***What pattern can you identify in the limited success of the Populists in the presidential elections of 1892 and 1896?***

**AMERICAN VOICES** **"Now, the People's Party says to [whites and African Americans], 'You are kept apart that you may be separately fleeced of your earnings. You are made to hate each other because upon that hatred is rested the keystone of the arch of financial despotism [absolute power] which enslaves you both. You are deceived and blinded that you may not see how this race antagonism perpetuates a monetary system which beggars both.'"**

— *Tom Watson*

During the 1892 campaign, populism generated great excitement among its followers. But the party's presidential candidate, Iowan James B. Weaver, won barely a million votes. Democrat Grover Cleveland returned to the presidency.

Back in office, Cleveland alienated labor when he put down the Pullman Strike. He angered farmers with his support for a gold standard and manufacturers when he tried to lower the tariff. The 1893 depression, which had started before he took office, threw millions out of work. When marchers promoting Populist ideas flocked to Washington in 1894, Americans added "hayseed Socialists" to their list of frightening agitators.

## *Bryan's "Cross of Gold"*

Populists saw in Cleveland's troubles the promise of success in the 1896 presidential campaign. In an election that focused mainly on currency issues, the Republicans ran William McKinley on a gold-standard platform. William Jennings Bryan, a former silverite congressman from Nebraska and a powerful speaker, captured the Democratic nomination with an emotional plea for free silver. Using images from the Bible, he stood with head bowed and arms outstretched and cried out at the climax of his speech, "You shall not press down upon the brow of labor this crown of thorns. You shall not crucify mankind upon a cross of gold!" So stunning was Bryan's speech that he captured the nomination of the Populists as well as the Democrats.

The 1896 campaign was one of marked contrasts. Bryan was a whirlwind of activity, traveling all over the country and making speeches at every stop. McKinley ran a more traditional campaign. He remained in his hometown of

Canton, Ohio, greeting visitors and making a few speeches from his front porch.

Despite his best efforts, Bryan lost the election. He carried the Democratic West and South but not one of the urban and industrial midwestern and northern states. In these states, factory workers feared that free silver might cause inflation, which would eat away the buying power of their wages. Thus, despite populism's broad appeal, it could not bridge the ever-widening gap between America's cities and farms. Nor could populism slow America's transition from an agricultural nation to an industrial nation.

This cartoon shows William Jennings Bryan wielding the crown of thorns and cross of gold—Biblical images that he used in a famous speech. ***Culture*** ***Is this cartoon presenting Bryan in a positive or a negative light?***

## Populism's Legacy

By 1897 McKinley's administration had raised the tariff to new heights. In 1900, after gold strikes in South Africa, the Canadian Yukon, and Alaska had added more than $100 million worth of gold to the world's supply, Congress returned the nation to a gold standard. To the surprise of many farmers, crop prices began a slow rise that would last until 1920. The silver movement died, as did populism.

The goals of populism, however, lived on. In the decades ahead, other reformers known as progressives applied populist ideas to urban and industrial problems. In so doing, they launched a new wave of reform that shifted the course of United States history.

## SECTION 4 REVIEW

### Comprehension

1. *Key Terms* Define: (a) deflation; (b) monetary policy; (c) Bland-Allison Act; (d) the Grange; (e) Interstate Commerce Act; (f) Populist; (g) progressive income tax.
2. *Summarizing the Main Idea* By what means did farmers organize to protest and present their views?
3. *Organizing Information* Create a web diagram that presents information about the organizations farmers formed to solve their problems. Label the center circle *Organizing Farmer Protest.* Include at least three organizations in your diagram.

### Critical Thinking

4. *Analyzing Time Lines* Review the time line at the start of the section. Choose one entry and explain how it supported the needs of farmers.
5. *Drawing Conclusions* Populism appealed to people in many parts of the country. How can you explain, then, the failure of the Populist party to win the presidential election of 1896?

### Writing Activity

6. *Writing a Persuasive Essay* Imagine that you are a farmer in the late 1800s. Write a letter to Congress asking for support of economic policies that would help solve some of your problems. Explain how you feel about tariffs and the issues surrounding the gold standard and free silver.

# SKILLS FOR LIFE

**Critical Thinking**

Graphs and Charts

Geography

Historical Evidence

## Drawing Conclusions

Drawing conclusions means reaching an answer or forming an opinion based on information that is suggested but not stated directly. When you read about history or any subject, it is important to be able to draw conclusions. Then you can go beyond what is presented in textbooks and other sources and form new insights about a historical period or event.

Use the following steps and the two passages from the late 1800s that appear on this page to practice drawing conclusions.

**1.** ***Study the facts and ideas that the author presents.*** Read the two passages below, and then answer the following questions about them. (a) What facts does Washington Gladden present to describe the farmers' problems? (b) What factors does Mary Elizabeth Lease cite to explain the farmers' problems as she perceives them?

**2.** ***Make a summary statement as a conclusion about a group of details.*** A statement that summarizes the major points of an argument is one type of conclusion. Clarify each person's position by summarizing the basic information contained in the two passages. Then answer the following questions. (a) From passage A, what can you conclude about the farmers' plight? Would farming be more profitable if farmers worked as hard as laborers? Or, are the farmers' problems beyond their control? (b) From the information in passage B, what can you conclude about the government's response to the problems the farmers are experiencing? Explain your reasoning.

**3.** ***Decide whether or not you can draw a conclusion based on what is stated.*** If an argument does not contain sufficient information, it is possible to jump to a faulty conclusion. Comparing the information in the two passages should raise some questions in your mind. As you answer these questions, you are deciding whether you have enough information to draw conclusions. (a) Given what you read in both passages, what conclusion can you draw about the relationship between farmers and the Populist party? Explain your answer. (b) Based on Lease's ideas in passage B, what conclusion can you draw concerning the ideas of the Populist party and the ideas of the major political parties?

**TEST FOR SUCCESS**

Reread passage A. Based on Gladden's statement, is he concerned or unconcerned about the plight of the farmer?

**Passage A**

"The business of farming has become, for some reasons, extremely unprofitable. With the hardest work and with the sharpest economy, the average farmer is unable to make both ends meet; every year closes with debt, and the mortgage grows till it devours the land. The Labor Bureau of Connecticut has shown, by an investigation of 693 representative farms, that the average annual reward of the farm proprietor of that state for his expenditure of muscle and brain is $181.31, while the average annual wages of the ordinary hired man is $386.36."

*—Washington Gladden, Congregational minister, 1890*

**Passage B**

"The parties lie to us and the political speakers mislead us. We were told two years ago to go to work and raise a big crop, that was all we needed. We went to work and plowed and planted; the rains fell, the sun shone, nature smiled, and we raised the big crop that they told us to. . . . Then the politicians said we suffered from over-production. . . . We want money, land, and transportation. We want the abolition of the national banks, and we want the power to make loans direct from the government. We want the accursed foreclosure system wiped out."

*—Mary Elizabeth Lease, Populist leader*

| 1872 | 1883 | 1893 | 1912 |
|---|---|---|---|
| Congress establishes Yellowstone National Park | "Buffalo Bill" Cody begins his Wild West shows | Historian Frederick Turner develops frontier thesis | Juliette Low founds the American Girl Scouts |

1872 1882 1892 1902 1912

# 5 Frontier Myths

## SECTION PREVIEW

### Objectives

1. Explain why Americans, by 1900, believed that the American frontier no longer existed.
2. Compare the myths and the realities of frontier life.
3. Understand how frontier myths have affected this nation's identity and why they remain important today.
4. *Key Terms* Define: Turner thesis; buffalo soldier; stereotype.

### Main Idea

The story of the "Wild West" has always captured Americans' imagination, but the myths disregard many other experiences that helped shape the nation.

### Reading Strategy

*Reinforcing Key Ideas* As you read, make a list of myths about the American frontier on the left side of a piece of paper. Then, to the right of each myth, write a sentence about the reality of life on the frontier.

As the 1800s came to a close, Americans faced a situation that few could have imagined. After decades of expansion the American frontier seemed to be disappearing. An era of special meaning seemed to be ending. But what, exactly, did the era mean? The answer to that question is surrounded by many myths—and is responsible for many of the nation's most cherished images of itself.

## *The West by 1900*

One by one, areas of the West became United States territories. Residents then wrote constitutions and applied for statehood. A decline in the amount of unorganized territory created the sense that the opportunities of the frontier were fading.

Long before 1900, American observers of the West noticed ominous signs of change. The number of tenant farmers had risen, along with the number of large farms owned by corporations. Many farmers were deep in debt. In 1872 the federal government established Yellowstone National Park to preserve western lands. Located in northwestern Wyoming, southern Montana, and eastern Idaho, the park was the nation's first national park. Despite this step, in 1890 the superintendent of the census announced the end of the frontier. The country's so-called "unsettled area has been so broken into by isolated bodies of settlement," he declared, "that there can hardly be said to be a frontier line."

William F. "Buffalo Bill" Cody became famous by playing up the myths of the American West.

### Turner's Frontier Thesis

In 1893 a young historian named Frederick Jackson Turner delivered a speech in which he claimed that the frontier had played a central role in forming the American character. The West had forced its Anglo-American and European settlers to shed their old ways and adapt, innovate, and invent, he said. To the frontier, Turner claimed, "American intellect owes its striking characteristics." He described these as:

## FACT Finder: The West Joins the Union

| State | Year Admitted |
|---|---|
| California | 1850 |
| Oregon | 1859 |
| Kansas | 1861 |
| Nevada | 1864 |
| Nebraska | 1867 |
| Colorado | 1876 |
| North Dakota | 1889 |
| South Dakota | 1889 |
| Montana | 1889 |
| Washington | 1889 |
| Wyoming | 1890 |
| Idaho | 1890 |
| Utah | 1896 |
| Oklahoma | 1907 |
| New Mexico | 1912 |
| Arizona | 1912 |

**Interpreting Tables** In the late 1800s and early 1900s, one western territory after another achieved statehood. ***Geography*** *Why do you think that the interior of the country was settled later than most of the West Coast?*

KEY DOCUMENTS

**"That coarseness and strength combined with acuteness [keen insight] and inquisitiveness [curiosity]; that practical, inventive turn of mind, quick to find expedients [ways to achieve goals]; . . . that restless, nervous energy; that dominant individualism, working for good and for evil, and withal that buoyancy [liveliness] and exuberance which comes with freedom."**

—*Frederick Jackson Turner*

To Turner, it was the frontier that had produced the highly individualistic, restless, and socially mobile American. Frontier life created Americans who were ready for adventure, bent on self-improvement, and committed to democracy.

**Turner's Critics** The **Turner thesis,** as his view came to be called, made certain assumptions that historians have since modified. Turner defined settlers as whites only and saw no difference in the experiences of women and men. His theory was not a complete picture of frontier life because it did not consider the important contributions African Americans and immigrants from Japan and China made to the West. Nor did Turner consider the impact of settlement on Native American and Spanish-speaking inhabitants.

Turner concentrated on the effects that individuals had on development, but played down the government subsidies and big business investments that were critical to farming, cattle ranching, and mining. Finally, he disregarded the traditions that immigrants had brought from their homelands and used in helping build the nation.

## Frontier Realities

A far more complex view of the West now prevails. This view more accurately reflects the reality of the settlement of the West.

**Diverse Western Settlers** The West did appeal to the restless, adventurous man, but it also appealed to adventurous women. While many women regretted their family's decision to go west, others embraced the more open society and thrived on the frontier.

Still, the West was hardly a land of unlimited opportunity for either men or women. Boom inevitably led to bust, especially when prices fell for the items that settlers produced.

Western settlers were not always eastern whites. Chinese and Japanese settlers farmed the fertile lands of the West Coast. Chinese and African American railway workers went into mining and established businesses in western towns. About 9,000 African Americans worked as cowhands on ranches. Thousands of black Exodusters settled the West. Thousands more African Americans served there as soldiers in the United States Army, most notably in the all-black Ninth and Tenth Cavalry Regiments, which Native Americans named the **"buffalo soldiers."**

**A Limited View of Democracy** Frontier life encouraged certain democratic values. As noted earlier, western states gave women the vote before their eastern counterparts did the same. Yet many settlers rode roughshod over the rights of the Native American peoples they displaced. On the West Coast, white settlers treated Asian immigrants with scorn, isolating them in separate neighborhoods and prohibiting them from owning land.

**The Impact on the Land** Although in the popular mind the settlement of the West meant progress, the costs to the environment were high. Settlers treated the vast natural resources of the West as if they were limitless. Railroad tunnels destroyed mountains. The construction of huge mines scarred the land and leveled forests. Overcultivation eroded fields, and senseless slaughter nearly wiped out the buffalo.

## *Frontier Myths and National Identity*

Despite today's deeper understanding of the history of the American West, frontier myths linger on. Through literature, film, and song, they continue to influence how Americans think about themselves.

**Creating the Myths** The romantic image of the American cowboy began as early as the 1870s, in the dime novels of writers like Edward L. Wheeler. In *Deadwood Dick, The Prince of the Road: or, the Black Rider of the Black Hills,* Wheeler painted a hero who was, at various times, outlaw, miner, gang leader, or cowboy and who dealt out righteous justice against evil.

> **"Mounted upon his midnight steed, and clad in the weird suit of black, he makes an imposing spectacle as he comes fearlessly up. . . .**
>
> **Close up to the side of the coach rides the daring young outlaw, his piercing orbs peering out from the eye-holes in his black mask, one hand clasping the bridle-reins, the other a nickel-plated seven-shooter."**
>
> —*Scene from* Deadwood Dick

Scenes like these kept alive the idea that the West saw little else but stagecoach robberies and killings. Although Wheeler's *Deadwood Dick* was based on a real person, the cowboy of that name was no outlaw. He was an African American named Nat Love. Entering a rodeo contest in a Dakota Territory mining town named Deadwood, Love won several roping and shooting contests. In his autobiography, Love wrote, "Right there the assembled crowd named me 'Deadwood Dick' and proclaimed me champion roper of the Western cattle country."

VIEWING HISTORY Paintings like Frederic Remington's 1902 *The Cowboy* (above) and rodeo stars like Nat Love (right) helped sustain the romanticized image of the American West in the early twentieth century. ***Culture** **How did frontier myths contribute to the national identity?***

In 1883 William F. ("Buffalo Bill") Cody began his Wild West shows, contributing further to frontier myths. These events drew thousands of spectators to steer-roping contests, rodeos, and staged battles between "good" cavalry regiments and "bad" Native Americans.

Writers transformed other real figures from the West, such as Wild Bill Hickok and Calamity Jane, into larger-than-life characters. This is Wheeler again:

> **"Who was that chap?" asked Redburn, not a little bewildered.**
>
> **"That?—why that's Calamity Jane!"**
>
> **"Calamity Jane? What a name."**
>
> **"Yes, she's an odd one. Can ride like the wind, shoot like a sharp-shooter, and swear like a trooper. . . . Owns this coop and two or three other lots in Deadwood; a herding ranch at Laramie; an interest in a paying placer claim [mine] near Elizabeth City, and the Lord only knows how much more."**
>
> **"But it is not a woman?"**
>
> **"Reckon 'tain't nothin' else."**

**Main Idea CONNECTIONS**

*How have the myths of the American West been perpetuated?*

## CAUSE AND EFFECT: Westward Expansion

**CAUSES**

- Big businesses put western land up for sale.
- Morrill Land-Grant Act provides state governments with millions of acres to sell.
- Homestead Act gives land to settlers willing to farm.
- European immigrants, people seeking opportunity, and people fleeing racial prejudice in the East seek land in the West.
- California Gold Rush draws thousands of fortune seekers.

**WESTWARD EXPANSION**

**EFFECTS**

- Violence erupts between settlers and Native Americans.
- Many Native American groups are destroyed or displaced.
- Challenges of prairie farming lead to increased mechanization.
- Bonanza farms and cattle ranching industries develop.
- Frontier myths influence national identity.

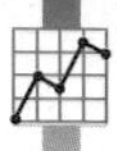

**Interpreting Charts** Westward expansion of the United States changed the human geography of North America. Immigrants, fortune-seekers, and people fleeing racial prejudice soon displaced the original inhabitants of the West. ***Government* *Why do you think the government offered so many incentives to settlers?***

This sketch suggested that a woman had to act masculine and be "mean with a pistol" in order to survive in the West. Thus it helped create one of the several **stereotypes,** or fixed ideas held by people, about the West.

**The "Strenuous Life" of the West** Most stories from the West supported stereotypes about men. The West was the place where a young man could find freedom and opportunity. He could lead a virtuous life and resist the forces of civilization that had made easterners soft. Many writers praised the West for having toughened the bodies and souls of young men. In his histories of the West, future President Theodore Roosevelt urged American men to experience the "strenuous life" of the West before they became too weak from the comforts of modern civilization.

Some male themes also appealed to women. In 1912 Juliette Low founded the American Girl Scouts in part because she feared that civilization had made girls too soft. Praising women homesteaders for their strength and intelligence, she made the scouting techniques of tracking, woodcraft, and wilderness survival the core of her program.

**National Identity** Frontier myths have left permanent marks on the nation's character. How many classic American songs arose from the cowboy era? "Home on the Range," where the buffalo roam, and "Don't Fence Me In" both suggest enduring images of wide-open spaces and freedom from civilization. When Americans hear these songs, they celebrate the richness of their land and the courage of their ancestors.

Reality, however, is much more complex than the myth. It is a balance, for example, between the dream of endless opportunities and the fact that opportunities were not equal for all. Although our image of the West is much simpler and perhaps more heroic than the reality, the myths remain imbedded in the spirit of the nation.

## SECTION 5 REVIEW

### Comprehension

1. *Key Terms* Define: (a) Turner thesis; (b) buffalo soldier; (c) stereotype.
2. *Summarizing the Main Idea* Explain how the myths about the Wild West disregard many other experiences that also helped shape the nation.
3. *Organizing Information* Create a chart that organizes information about the myths and realities of life on the American frontier.

### Critical Thinking

4. *Analyzing Time Lines* Review the time line at the start of the section. Which entry helped to reinforce certain myths about the West in the American imagination?
5. *Identifying Central Issues* What did observers mean when they said that the frontier was "closed" in the late 1800s?

### Writing Activity

6. *Writing a Persuasive Essay* Write a brief essay explaining the Turner thesis and some of the criticisms of it.

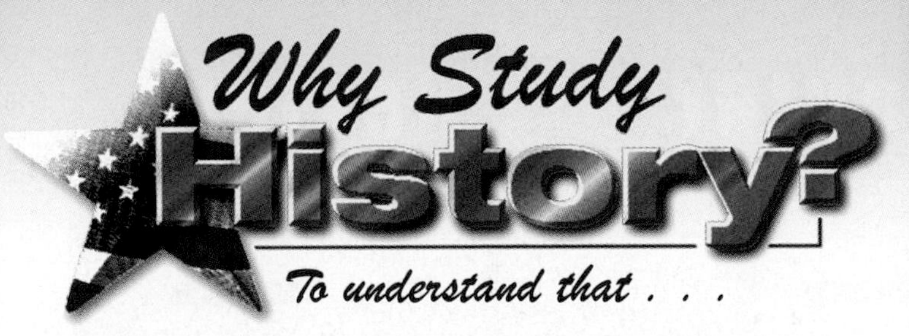


# Americans Are on the Move

**Like the homesteaders who moved west in the late 1800s, many Americans today are seeking opportunity by moving to new places.**

*Family of Nebraska homesteaders in front of their sod house*

Housing developments and shopping malls spring up where cattle once grazed. Country roads are widened into multi-lane highways. Signs of growth such as these have characterized the United States since the 1950s. Since the 1970s, most such growth has occurred in an area that stretches across the nation's southernmost states. Because of its warm and sunny climate, this area has been nicknamed the Sunbelt. Between 1970 and 1980, population in the Sunbelt grew almost twice as fast as in the nation as a whole.

## The Impact Today

Americans have always been on the move. In the mid-1800s thousands headed west to the frontier to build farms or ranches or mine for precious metals.

The shift to the Sunbelt continues the American tradition of migration. Individuals are drawn to the region for various reasons, including a warm climate, low taxes, plentiful jobs, and a low crime rate. Industry and manufacturing have also moved to the Sunbelt from the so-called "Rustbelt," or older industrial areas in the North and Midwest. While many Rustbelt communities have suffered economic hardship as a result of the loss of jobs, this movement has fueled impressive economic growth in the Sunbelt. With growth has come some problems, however, such as strains on public services and increased traffic and pollution.

Growth in the Sunbelt has also affected American politics. The increase in population of Sunbelt states has given the region additional seats in Congress. Between 1970 and 1990, for example, California rose from 43 to 52 representatives in the House of Representatives. The growth of the Sunbelt, a politically conservative region, has helped create a more conservative political climate in the United States.

## The Impact on You

If you were to decide to move to another region of the country, to which region might you move? Choose a state in that region as your destination and find out about its climate and economy. Write a paragraph comparing that state to your current state and describing the advantages and disadvantages that your destination offers.

*New home construction in Texas, part of the growing Sunbelt*

# Chapter 5 Review

## Chapter Summary

The major concepts of Chapter 5 are presented below. See also ***Guide to the Essentials of American History*** or ***Interactive Student Tutorial CD-ROM,*** which contains interactive review activities, time lines, helpful hints, and test practice.

### *Reviewing the Main Ideas*

After the Civil War, Americans accelerated their settlement of lands west of the Mississippi River. Leaving behind the world they knew, adventurous people tried to build new lives on the great frontier. For Native Americans of the West, however, this period was one of defeat and devastation.

### *Section 1: Moving West*

With the encouragement of the federal government, settlers took up the challenges and the hardships of life in the West.

### *Section 2: Conflict with Native Americans*

American expansion into the West led to the near destruction of the Native American nations there.

### *Section 3: Farming, Mining, and Ranching*

Modern farming methods, the discovery of mineral deposits, and ranching made the West attractive to many individual settlers and big businesses.

### *Section 4: Populism*

By the late 1800s, declining incomes for American farmers created fertile ground for a farmers' protest.

### *Section 5: Frontier Myths*

The story of the "Wild West" has always captured Americans' imagination, but the myths disregard many other experiences that also helped shape the nation.

Like the homesteaders who moved west in the late 1800s, many Americans today are seeking opportunity by moving to new places. This mobility has caused a shift in population from older industrial areas in the North and Midwest to an area in the South known as the Sunbelt.

## Key Terms

For each of the terms below, write a sentence explaining how it relates to this chapter.

1. Morrill Land-Grant Act
2. speculator
3. Homestead Act
4. Battle of Little Bighorn
5. boomer
6. squatter
7. bonanza farm
8. long drive
9. deflation
10. monetary policy
11. the Grange
12. buffalo soldier

## Comprehension

1. How did settlers acquire lands in the West?
2. Describe some ways settlers relied on each other.
3. What was the result of the decision to allow settlement in Indian Territory?
4. How did the development of new machines affect farming?
5. Describe several factors that led to the cattle ranching boom of the 1860s and 1870s.
6. Summarize the two opposing arguments in the monetary policy debate of the late 1800s.
7. How did farmers protest their hardships in the late 1800s?
8. What was the message of Frederick Jackson Turner's frontier thesis?

## Using Graphic Organizers

On a separate sheet of paper, copy the tree map organizer on the main ideas about developing the West. Provide at least two supporting details for each main idea.

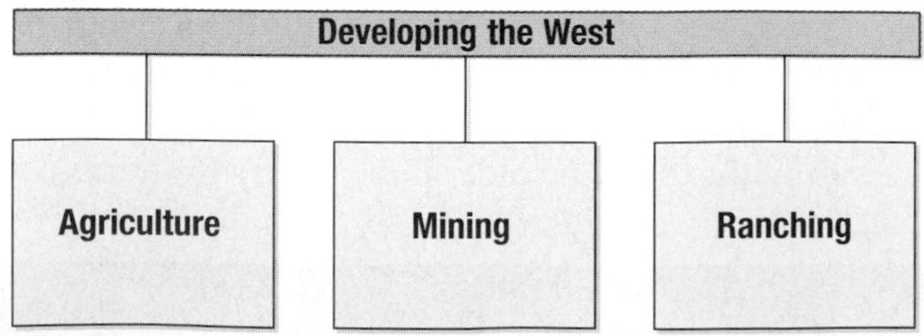

## Analyzing Political Cartoons ▶

1. This hot air balloon holds aloft several Populist figures. (a) How do you know these men are Populists? (b) What is the balloon made of? (c) What does this composition suggest?
2. What is the message of the words on the basket ("Platform of Lunacy")?
3. Analyze the elements of this hot air balloon and state the cartoonist's overall message.

A PARTY OF PATCHES.
Grand Balloon Ascension—Cincinnati, May 20th, 1891.

## Critical Thinking

1. ***Applying the Chapter Skill*** Reread the two passages on page 196. Based on the information in the two passages, what were some of the problems that western farmers faced in the late 1800s?
2. ***Distinguishing False from Accurate Images*** Myths about the frontier led people to believe that the West was a lawless, dangerous place, but one in which everyone could strike it rich. In what ways is this a false image?
3. ***Formulating Questions*** Based on what you have read in the chapter, write three questions to ask farmers about new machinery and farming techniques that helped them farm the Great Plains.
4. ***Recognizing Cause and Effect*** How did settlement in the West contribute to the decline of Native American cultures?

### INTERNET ACTIVITY

***For your portfolio:***
**PREPARE A SUMMARY**

Access Prentice Hall's *America: Pathways to the Present* site at **www.Pathways.phschool.com** for the specific URL to complete the activity. Additional resources and related Web sites are also available.

Read the first-hand account of the Massacre at Wounded Knee. Summarize the events described by Alice Ghost Horse. How old was she at the time of the massacre? How did the soldiers behave before the attack? How did they behave afterward? How did Alice Ghost Horse feel about them?

## ANALYZING DOCUMENTS ◀ INTERPRETING DATA

Turn to the "American Voices" quotation on page 183.

1. Which statement best describes the opening of Indian Territory to settlement? (a) It was an orderly process. (b) Few people took part in settlement of Indian Territory. (c) It was chaotic. (d) All settlers into Indian Territory traveled by foot.
2. What was the most likely reaction of Native Americans to the opening of Indian Territory for settlement? (a) Native Americans welcomed the newcomers. (b) Native Americans felt betrayed by the opening of Indian Territory. (c) Native Americans lobbied Congress to open the territory for settlement. (d) Native Americans moved farther east to avoid settlers.
3. ***Writing*** Do you think the reporter exaggerated the description of the events on the day Indian Territory was opened for settlement? Explain your answer.

## Connecting to Today

***Essay Writing*** Reread the sections on the Populists and the elections of 1892 and 1896 in Section 4. Then research and write an essay on the central platform issues of a political party today. Does the platform represent the interests of a single group or many different groups?

CHAPTER 6

# Politics, Immigration, and Urban Life

## 1870–1915

▲ **VIEWING HISTORY** Immigrants had their hands full as they arrived at Ellis Island to begin a new life in the United States. *Culture* ***What does this photo reveal about their feelings?***

## CHAPTER FOCUS

*This chapter examines political developments around the turn of the century, including issues of political corruption and economic development. It also looks at changes in American cities brought about in part by the influx of immigrants.*

*The* ***Why Study History?*** *page at the end of this chapter analyzes the effects of immigration and immigration policy in the United States today.*

**1877** *Munn* v. *Illinois*

**1881** President Garfield assassinated

**1883** Pendleton Civil Service Act

**1887** Interstate Commerce Act

**1894** Coxey's army marches to Washington, D.C.

**1901** President McKinley assassinated

**1875** | **1885** | **1895** | **1905**

# 1 Politics in the Gilded Age

## SECTION PREVIEW

### Objectives

1. Explain how business influenced politics during the Gilded Age.
2. Describe the government efforts to reform the spoils system and regulate railroads.
3. Explain how the cycle of depression and prosperity hurt the Democrats and helped the Republicans in the 1890s.
4. *Key Terms* Define: Gilded Age; laissez-faire; subsidy; blue law; civil service; Pendleton Civil Service Act; *Munn* v. *Illinois.*

### Main Idea

From 1877 to 1900, national politics was dominated by issues of corruption and reform.

### Reading Strategy

*Structured Overview* Write the following headings from the section on a sheet of paper, leaving room under each: *The Business of Politics; Reforming the Spoils System; Regulating Railroads; Depression to Prosperity.* As you read, list important details under each of these headings.

Many labels have been used to describe the post-Reconstruction era (1877–1900). The most famous is the **Gilded Age,** a term coined by writer Mark Twain. *Gilded* means "covered with a thin layer of gold," and "Gilded Age" suggests that a thin but glittering layer of prosperity covered the poverty and corruption of much of society.

It is an unflattering picture of this era, but it is accurate. This was a golden period for America's industrialists. Their wealth helped hide the problems of immigrants, laborers, and farmers. It also helped cover up the widespread abuse of power in business and government.

## The Business of Politics

The United States faced great challenges as it emerged from Reconstruction. Industrial expansion raised the output of the nation's factories and farms. Some Americans, such as speculators in land and stocks, quickly rose "from rags to riches." At the same time, depressions, low wages, and rising farm debt contributed to discontent among working people.

*Monopolies and trusts control the government in this political cartoon.*

### Laissez-faire Policies

In the late 1800s, businesses operated largely without government regulation. This hands-off approach to economic matters, known by the French phrase **laissez-faire,**† holds that government should play a very limited role in business. Supporters of this strategy maintain that if government does not interfere, the strongest businesses will succeed and bring wealth to the nation as a whole.

In the late 1800s, most Americans accepted this idea in theory. In practice, however, many champions of laissez-faire supported government involvement when it benefited

† The term, meaning "allow to be," may have originated with French economists as early as the 1750s.

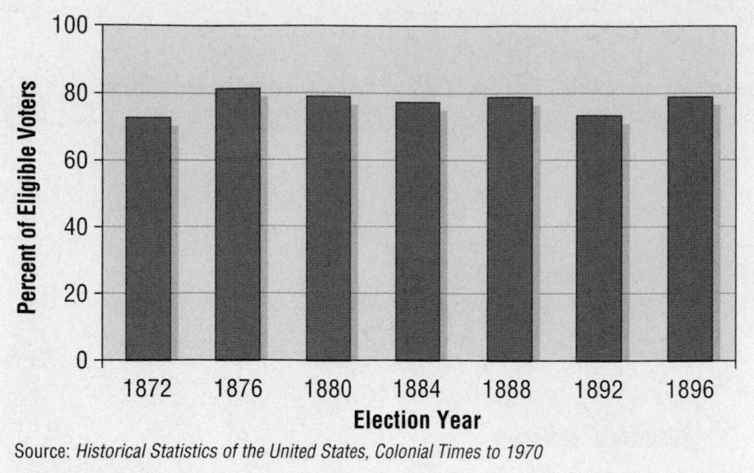


**Interpreting Graphs** Voter turnout was high during the late 1800s compared with later eras. By 1920, it had dropped below 50 percent and has never again risen as high as 65 percent. ***Government** What factors might help explain the high turnout in the late 1800s?*

them. For example, American businesses favored high tariffs on imported goods to encourage people to buy American goods instead. American businesses also willingly accepted government land grants and subsidies. A **subsidy** is a payment made by the government to encourage the development of certain key industries, such as railroads.

Business giants during the Gilded Age supported friendly politicians with gifts of money. Some of these contributions were legal and some were illegal. Between 1875 and 1885, the Central Pacific Railroad reportedly budgeted $500,000 each year for bribes. Central Pacific co-founder Collis P. Huntington explained, "If you have to pay money to have the right thing done, it is only just and fair to do it."

**The Spoils System** American politics also suffered from its reliance on the spoils system, in which elected officials appointed friends and supporters to government jobs, regardless of their qualifications. Introduced by President Jackson in 1829, the system had since flourished. By the Gilded Age, government swarmed with unqualified, dishonest employees.

**Main Idea CONNECTIONS**

*What were the effects of the spoils system?*

The spoils system appealed to many politicians because it ensured them a loyal group of supporters in future elections. Both Democrats and Republicans handed out jobs to pay off the people who had helped them get elected. But the system led to corruption when dishonest appointees used their jobs for personal profit.

**Opposing Political Parties** During the Gilded Age, the Democratic and Republican parties had roughly the same number of supporters. They differed greatly, however, in who those supporters were and in the positions that the parties took on major issues.

Republicans appealed to industrialists, bankers, and farmers. The party was strongest in the North and the upper Midwest and was weak to nonexistent in the South. In general, Republicans favored:

(1) a tight money supply backed by gold;
(2) high tariffs to protect American business;
(3) generous pensions for Union soldiers;
(4) government aid to the railroads;
(5) strict limits on immigration;
(6) enforcement of **blue laws,** regulations that prohibited certain private activities (such as drinking alcoholic beverages on Sundays).

As a rule, the Democratic party attracted those in American society who were less privileged, or at least felt that way. These groups included northern urban immigrants, laborers, southern planters, and western farmers. Claiming to represent the interests of ordinary people, Democrats favored:

(1) an increased money supply backed by silver;
(2) lower tariffs on imported goods;
(3) higher farm prices;
(4) less government aid to big business;
(5) fewer blue laws.

## *Reforming the Spoils System*

Since the two parties had roughly equal strength, presidential candidates needed the votes of almost all members of their party in order to win an election. To avoid offending any of them, candidates generally avoided taking strong stands on controversial issues.

Republicans, especially, whipped up support by "waving the bloody shirt." This meant recalling the bloodshed of the Civil War, a conflict they blamed on the Democrats. This tactic helped Republicans hold on to the presidency for much of the post-Reconstruction era.

Presidents of this period did make some efforts to exercise leadership. Indeed, the Gilded Age witnessed some important reforms in such areas as the spoils system and the railroads.

**Hayes Fights the Spoils System** After his election in 1877, Rutherford B. Hayes surprised many supporters by refusing to use the patronage system. Instead he appointed qualified political independents to Cabinet posts and fired employees who were not needed. By these actions Hayes began to reform the **civil service,** or the government's non-elected workers.

Hayes undertook these reforms without congressional backing, even from members of his own Republican party. He further angered his party on July 11, 1878, when he removed fellow Republican Chester A. Arthur from an important patronage position in New York. Then, with the help of congressional Democrats, he replaced Arthur with one of his own appointments. These moves especially upset Senator Roscoe Conkling, who had used patronage to control the Republican party in New York State.

Hayes had announced at the beginning of his presidency that he would not seek a second term. After his bold attack on the spoils system, he probably could not have won his party's nomination in any case. That attack strengthened the government but also helped weaken the Republicans.

**Garfield's Term Cut Short** As the 1880 presidential election approached, the Republican party was split into three factions. The Stalwarts, followers of Senator Conkling, defended the spoils system. The Half-Breeds, who followed Maine senator James G. Blaine, hoped to reform the spoils system while remaining loyal to the party. Independents opposed the spoils system altogether.

James A. Garfield, a congressman from Ohio, won the party's presidential nomination. Garfield was linked to the Half-Breeds. To balance the ticket, the Republicans chose as their vice-presidential candidate Chester A. Arthur, the New York Stalwart whom Hayes had fired two years earlier.

In the 1880 election Garfield won a narrow victory over the Democratic candidate, General Winfield S. Hancock. Garfield's term was cut short, however, by an assassin's bullet. On July 2, 1881, a mentally unstable lawyer named Charles Guiteau shot Garfield as the President walked through the Washington, D.C., railroad station. When he fired his fatal shot, Guiteau cried out, "I am a Stalwart and Arthur is President now!" Garfield suffered for nearly three months before dying.

It was later revealed that Guiteau, a loyal Republican, had expected to win a job through the spoils system. When Garfield passed him over, Guiteau became so enraged that he decided to murder the President. Guiteau's senseless act caused a public outcry against the spoils system.

**Arthur Ends the Spoils System** Upon Garfield's death, Vice President Chester Arthur became President. Arthur had fought for (and benefited from) patronage in New York. Once in office, however, he urged Congress to support reform of the spoils system. With Garfield's assassination fresh in the nation's mind, President Arthur was able to obtain congressional support for this reform. As a result, the **Pendleton Civil Service Act** became law in 1883.

A GREAT NATION IN GRIEF

*PRESIDENT GARFIELD SHOT BY AN ASSASSIN.*

THOUGH SERIOUSLY WOUNDED HE STILL SURVIVES.

*THE WOULD-BE MURDERER LODGED IN PRISON.*

THE PRESIDENT OF THE UNITED STATES ATTACKED AND TERRIBLY WOUNDED BY A FANATICAL OFFICE-SEEKER ON THE EVE OF INDEPENDENCE DAY—THE NATION HORRIFIED AND THE WHOLE CIVILIZED WORLD SHOCKED—THE PRESIDENT STILL ALIVE AND HIS RECOVERY POSSIBLE.

President Garfield's assassination by a disappointed office seeker roused the nation to the need for reform of the spoils system. ***Government*** *How did President Arthur end the spoils system?*

Powerful Union Pacific Railroad executives are shown here holding a meeting in the lavish surroundings of a private car. ***Government*** *What prompted the government to start regulating the railroad industry?*

The act created a Civil Service Commission, which classified government jobs and tested applicants' fitness for them. It also stated that federal employees could not be required to contribute to campaign funds and could not be fired for political reasons.

**Democrats Take Power** In 1884 the Republicans nominated James G. Blaine, a former Secretary of State and senator from Maine, for President. The Democrats chose Grover Cleveland, former mayor of Buffalo and governor of New York.

Serious issues confronted the nation, such as high tariffs, unfair business practices, and unregulated railroads. Yet the campaign focused mostly on scandals. Had James G. Blaine received railroad stock options in return for favorable votes while he was in Congress? No one could prove it. Had Cleveland fathered a child out of wedlock while a bachelor in Buffalo? Cleveland admitted it was true. Republicans jeered, "Ma, Ma, where's my Pa?" Democrats responded, "Going to the White House, ha, ha, ha!" In spite of his admission, Cleveland won the election, thereby becoming the first Democrat to capture the presidency since 1856.

**Main Idea CONNECTIONS**

*How did Cleveland gain political support?*

Cleveland owed at least some of his success to Republican independents who bolted their party to vote for him. These independents had decided that Blaine was too corrupt to support. An unsympathetic newspaper editor started calling them "Little Mugwumps." (*Mugwump* was an Algonquin word meaning "important chief.") The editor was suggesting that the independents were little men who wanted to be big chiefs. His insult did not keep the Mugwumps from helping to put Cleveland in office.

Cleveland favored tight money policies, so most business interests backed him. Yet not all his policies were pro-business. He opposed high tariffs and took back from the railroads and other interests some 80 million acres of federal land that had been granted to them. In addition, Cleveland supported more government regulation of the powerful railroad companies.

## Regulating Railroads

Railroad regulation had begun in 1869, when Massachusetts investigated charges that railroad companies were overcharging customers. By 1880, about 14 states had railroad commissions to look into complaints about railroad practices. One of those practices was charging more for a short haul than for a long haul over the same track. Others included keeping rates secret and charging different rates to different people for the same service. These practices kept farmers and businesses from predicting their shipping costs.

In 1877 the Supreme Court, in ***Munn* v. *Illinois,*** allowed states to regulate certain businesses within their borders, including railroads. But railroad traffic often crossed state boundaries. Lawyers for the railroads argued that under the Constitution only the federal government could regulate interstate commerce. In 1886, in the *Wabash* case, the Supreme Court agreed. Interstate railroad traffic thus remained unregulated.

Pressure mounted on Congress to curb railroad company abuses. As you read in the last chapter, in 1887 Congress responded by passing the Interstate Commerce Act. The act required that rates be set in proportion to the distance traveled and that rates be made public. It also outlawed the practice of giving special rates to powerful customers. Finally, it set up the nation's first federal regulatory board, the Interstate Commerce Commission (ICC), to enforce the act.

The Interstate Commerce Act failed, however, to give the ICC the power to set railroad rates. Also, to enforce its rulings the ICC had to take the railroads to court. Of the 16 cases involving the ICC that came before the Supreme Court between 1887 and 1905, the Court ruled against the ICC 15 times.

## *Depression to Prosperity*

Boosted by vigorous industrial growth, American business generally grew during the late 1880s and into the 1890s. But in 1893 a depression struck, and prosperity did not return until around 1900. These ups and downs made the economy the hottest political issue of this period.

**Focus on Tariffs** Cleveland lost the 1888 election to Republican Benjamin Harrison. The campaign had focused on tariffs. Cleveland favored a minor reduction in tariffs, while Harrison wanted an increase. Harrison's position won him plenty of business support and, ultimately, the presidency.

Among President Harrison's achievements was the signing of the Sherman Antitrust Act in 1890, described earlier. Like the Interstate Commerce Act, however, this seemingly bold action failed to curb the power of the largest corporations until well after the turn of the century.

Meanwhile, Harrison made good his campaign promise to business by approving a huge tariff increase in 1890. He also supported legislation on behalf of special business interests. Although he was thought to be conservative with public funds, Harrison dipped deep into the Treasury to award huge new pensions to dependents of Civil War soldiers.

These actions would later damage the economy, and they did not help Harrison in the election of 1892. Many new immigrants had swelled the ranks of the Democratic party. Campaigning again for lower tariffs, Grover Cleveland was returned to the presidency.

**Cleveland's Second Term** Cleveland's second term started badly. Thanks in part to the drained treasury, a panic hit the country in 1893. This began a four-year depression, the worst yet in American history. Millions of workers lost their jobs or had their wages slashed, yet the government offered no help.

In 1894 Jacob S. Coxey, a wealthy Ohio quarry owner who had become a Populist, demanded that government create jobs for the unemployed. Coxey called on unemployed workers to march on the nation's capital. "We will send a petition to Washington with boots on," he declared.

Many small "armies" started out on the protest march, but only Coxey's army reached Washington. Police arrested him and a few others for illegally carrying banners on the Capitol grounds and for trampling the grass. A song sung by Coxey's supporters mocked the government for worrying more about its lawns than its citizens. It was sung to the tune of "The Star-Spangled Banner":

**AMERICAN VOICES** **"Oh, say, can you see, by the dawn's early light
That grass plot so dear to the hearts of us all?
Is it green yet and fair, in well-nurtured plight,
Unpolluted by the Coxeyites' hated foot-fall?
Midst the yells of police, and swish of clubs
through the air,
We could hardly tell if our grass was still there.
But the green growing grass does in triumph
yet wave,
And the gallant police with their buttons of brass
Will sure make the Coxeyites keep off the grass."**

—*Anonymous*

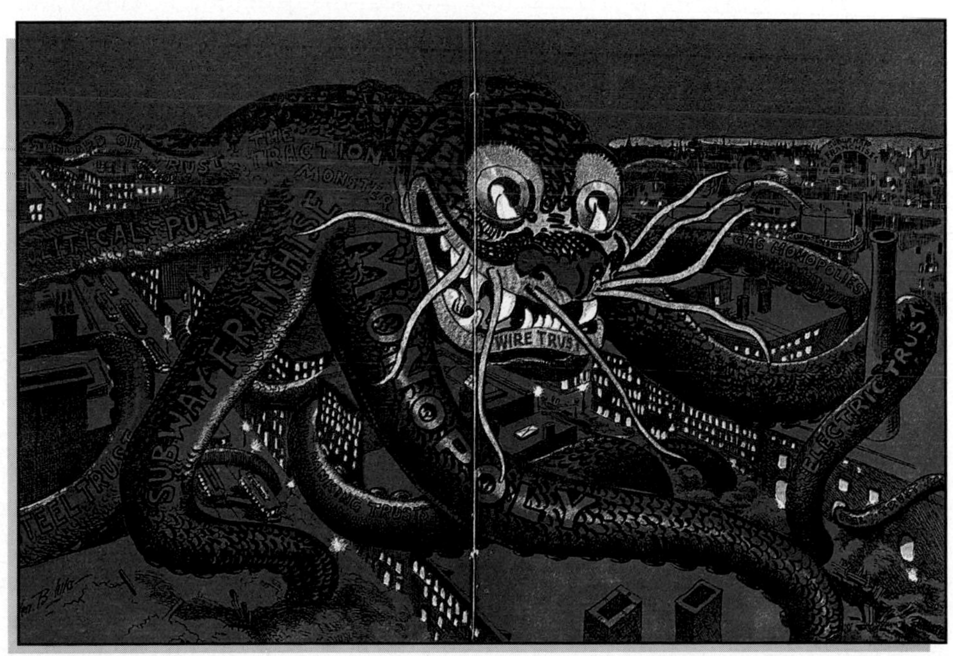

One cartoonist saw trusts and monopolies as a monstrous octopus. ***Government*** *How successful was Harrison in curbing the power of trusts?*

Coxey's original "army" of around 100 men was joined by an additional 400 or so men as it made its way to Washington, D.C. ***Government How effective was Coxey's protest?***

In his second term Cleveland managed to anger not only the unemployed but almost everyone else. In 1893 he upset farmers by repealing the Sherman Silver Purchase Act, which had become law just three years before. He enraged unions when he sent federal troops to Chicago during the Pullman strike of 1894.

By the time of his party's convention in 1896, Cleveland had turned many fellow Democrats against him. Hence, the President failed to win his party's nomination.

**McKinley Wins in 1896** The Populists had emerged as a political power during the economic hard times of the early 1890s and had made gains in the 1894 elections. But in 1896 William Jennings Bryan, presidential candidate of the Populists and Democrats, lost to the Republican, William McKinley, who was supported by urban workers and the middle class.

President McKinley oversaw passage of a new tariff and strengthening of the gold standard. These actions brought Republicans an even more decisive victory against Bryan in 1900. As the economy began to climb out of the 1890s depression, Republicans claimed credit with their slogan "A Full Dinner Pail."

McKinley did not live long enough to enjoy the effects of the returning prosperity. On September 6, 1901, McKinley went on a tour of the Pan-American Exposition in Buffalo, New York. There a mentally ill anarchist named Leon Czolgosz shot the President as he greeted the public. McKinley died a few days later.

## SECTION 1 REVIEW

### Comprehension

1. *Key Terms* Define: (a) Gilded Age; (b) laissez-faire; (c) subsidy; (d) blue law; (e) civil service; (f) Pendleton Civil Service Act; (g) *Munn* v. *Illinois.*
2. *Summarizing the Main Idea* How did several Presidents reform the spoils system?
3. *Organizing Information* Draw a flowchart to show the sequence of events related to the regulation of railroads.

### Critical Thinking

4. *Analyzing Time Lines* Review the time line at the start of the section. Decide whether you agree or disagree with the following statement: "The federal government's passage of legislation to regulate railroads paved the way for states to enact their own laws." Explain your answer.
5. *Recognizing Cause and Effect* Big businesses sought political influence by making large contributions to "friendly" politicians. How do you think these politicians voted on tariff legislation? Why?

### Writing Activity

6. *Writing an Expository Essay* Write an essay exploring how economic issues affected the outcome of presidential elections during the Gilded Age.

| 1882 | 1886 | 1892 | 1907 | 1910 | 1913 | 1921 |
|---|---|---|---|---|---|---|
| *Chinese Exclusion Act* | *Statue of Liberty erected* | *Ellis Island immigration center opened* | *Gentlemen's Agreement signed* | *Angel Island immigration center built* | *Webb Alien Land Law enacted* | *Immigration Restriction Act* |

**1882** — **1892** — **1902** — **1912** — **1922**

# 2 People on the Move

## SECTION PREVIEW

### Objectives

1. Describe the experiences of immigrants in the late 1800s and early 1900s.
2. Compare immigration from Europe, Asia, and Mexico.
3. Explore the experiences of two typical immigrants.
4. *Key Terms* Define: steerage; quarantine; Chinese Exclusion Act; segregation; Gentlemen's Agreement; alien.

### Main Idea

Millions of immigrants, representing many different cultures, arrived in the United States during the late 1800s and early 1900s.

### Reading Strategy

*Formulating Questions* Write down several questions you might ask about the experiences of immigrants around 1900. As you read, note answers to your questions.

It was sometimes said that America's streets were paved with gold. This myth held a grain of truth for the millions of immigrants who left a life of utter poverty behind. They came to America because it offered, if not instant wealth, then at least the chance to improve their lives. Some immigrants did get rich here, through hard work and determination. Many more managed to carve out a decent life for themselves and their families. For these immigrants, the chance to come to the United States was indeed a golden opportunity.

## The Immigrant Experience

In the late 1800s, people in many parts of the world were on the move from farms to cities and from one country to another. Immigrants from around the globe were fleeing crop failures, shortages of land and jobs, rising taxes, and famine. Some were also escaping religious or political persecution.

**Immigrants' Hopes and Dreams** The United States received a huge portion of this global migration. In 1860 the resident population of the United States was 31.5 million people. Between 1865 and 1920, close to 30 million additional people entered the country.

*Millions of immigrants brought their belongings and their dreams to the United States in the late 1800s.*

Some of these newcomers dreamed of getting rich, or at least of receiving free government land through the Homestead Act. Others yearned for personal freedoms. In America, they had heard, everyone could go to school, young men were not forced to serve long years in the army, and citizens could freely take part in a democratic government.

**Crossing the Ocean** In the late 1800s, steam-powered ships could cross the Atlantic Ocean in two to three weeks. By 1900, on more powerful steamships, the crossing took just one week. Even this brief journey, however, could be difficult, especially for those who could not afford cabins. Most immigrants traveled in **steerage,** a large open area beneath the ship's deck. Steerage offered limited toilet

These arrivals on Ellis Island contemplate a bewildering yet promising future in their new homeland.

facilities, no privacy, and poor food, but the fare was relatively cheap.

Crossing the vast Pacific Ocean took much longer, but the arrangements were similar. Passengers traveled in steerage, with few comforts. Where a person came from, however, could make a difference in the conditions aboard ship. Immigrants from Japan, whose power in the world was growing, often received better treatment than those from China, which at that time was a weak country.

**Arriving in America** Information about the number and origins of the nation's immigrants is not precise. Officials often misidentified the origins of immigrants. About one third of them were "birds of passage." These were usually young, single men who worked for a number of months or years and then returned home.

Historians estimate that about 10 million immigrants arrived between 1865 and 1890. Most came from northern European countries: about 2.8 million from Germany, another 1.8 million from Great Britain, and nearly 1.4 million from Ireland.

In the 1890s, the pattern of immigration shifted dramatically. Most new immigrants came from the countries of southern and eastern Europe and the Middle East. Between 1890 and 1920 about 10 million Italians, Greeks, Slavs, Eastern Europeans, Russian Jews, and Armenians arrived. Around 3.8 million immigrants came from Italy alone. From Russia came another 3 million.

Until the 1880s, decisions about whom to allow into the country were left to the states. In 1882 the federal government began excluding certain categories of immigrants. In 1891 the Office of the Superintendent of Immigration was formed to determine who was fit for life in America and who was not.

Immigrants entered through several ports. European newcomers might come through Boston, Philadelphia, or Baltimore. Asians might enter through San Francisco or Seattle. Yet more than 70 percent of all immigrants came through New York City, the "Golden Door."

## Immigrants from Europe

Throughout most of the 1800s, immigrants arriving in New York entered at the Castle Garden depot, near the southern tip of Manhattan. In 1892, the federal government opened a huge reception center for steerage passengers on Ellis Island in New York Harbor, near where the Statue of Liberty had been erected in 1886. The statue, a gift from France, celebrated "Liberty Enlightening the World." It became a symbol of the United States as a place of refuge and hope.

**Physical Exams** In 1892 the federal government required all new immigrants to undergo a physical examination. Those that were found to have a contagious disease such as tuberculosis faced **quarantine,** a time of isolation to prevent the spread of a disease. They could even be deported. People with trachoma, an eye disease common among immigrants, were automatically sent back to their country.

Fiorello La Guardia, who later became mayor of New York City, worked as an interpreter at Ellis Island. "It was harrowing to see families separated," he remembered in the book *The Making of an Insurgent:*

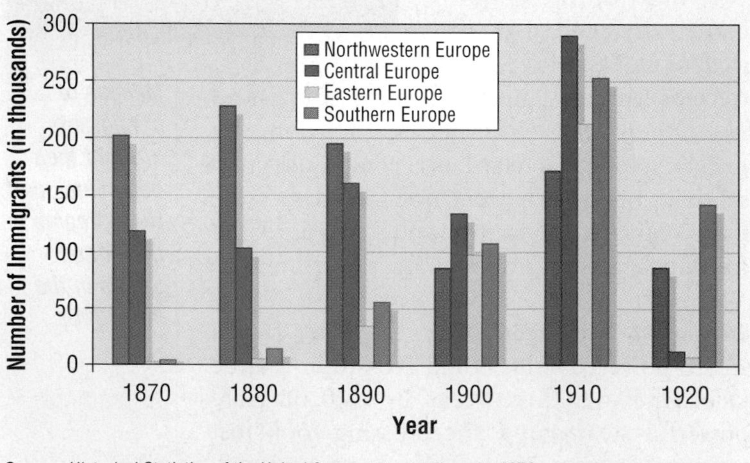

**Interpreting Graphs** The greatest number of immigrants came from Europe. ***Geography*** ***Name the region from which most European immigrants came for each year shown.***

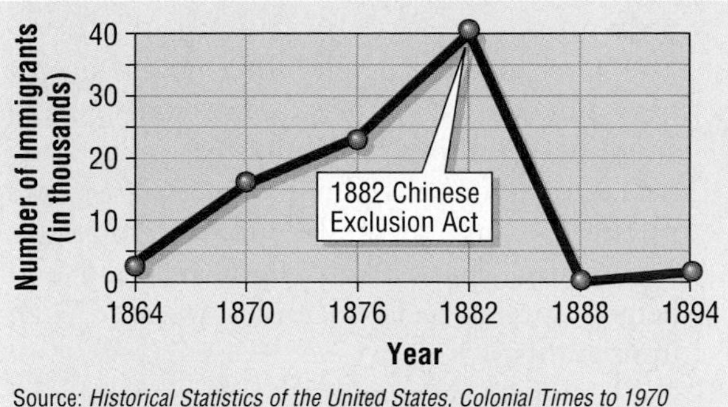


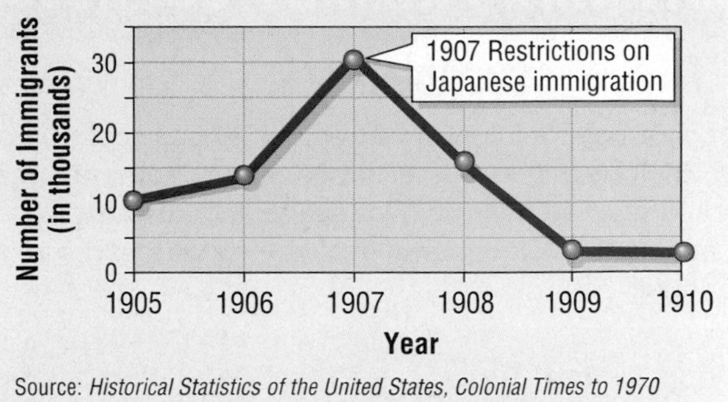

**Interpreting Graphs** Anti-Asian pressure groups used both economic and pseudo-scientific justification to limit Asian immigration to the United States. ***Diversity* *What effect did the 1882 Chinese Exclusion Act and the 1907 restrictions on Japanese immigration have on immigration?***

**AMERICAN VOICES** **"Sometimes, if it was a young child who suffered from trachoma, one of the parents had to return to the native country with the rejected member of the family. When they learned their fate, they were stunned. They . . . had no homes to return to."**

—*Fiorello La Guardia*

After their physicals, immigrants showed their documents to officials and then collected their baggage. If they had the address of friends or relatives, they headed off to find them. Those who were on their own had a harder time. Criminals hung around ports with fake offers of lodgings and jobs, stealing money and baggage from the unwary.

**Where Immigrants Settled** Immigrants often sought to live in communities established by previous settlers from their homelands. These communities formed not only in ports of entry, such as New York and Boston, but also in inland cities. In this way, large settlements of Poles and Italians grew in Buffalo, Cleveland, Detroit, and Milwaukee. A diverse group of immigrants found a home in Chicago, a growing port, railroad hub, and industrial center. Some immigrants continued on to mining towns of the West. Only 2 percent went to the South, an area that offered newcomers few jobs.

Once settled, immigrants looked for work. When jobs were scarce, employers (many of whom were immigrants themselves) took advantage of the newcomers. They paid them less than other workers and paid the women even less than the men. Female seamstresses, for example, did the same job as male tailors, working up to 14 hours a day, 6 days a week, but earning only half as much as the men.

## *Immigrants from Asia*

Most of the immigrants who entered the United States through West Coast ports came from Asia. Chinese and Japanese formed the largest groups by far. Culturally, Asians differed greatly from both Americans and Europeans, and those differences made them targets of suspicion and even hostility. Often as a result, Asian immigrants found that the path to acceptance was especially difficult.

*Chinese immigrants brought distinctive styles and customs to the United States.*

**Chinese Excluded** In the mid-1800s, American railroad companies recruited about a quarter of a million Chinese workers. Thousands of them helped build the transcontinental railroad, completed in 1869.

Like the indentured servants of the colonial era, the Chinese were required

## COMPARING PRIMARY SOURCES

### CULTURAL TIES

Many people held opinions on how immigrants could best adjust to their new lives in the United States. Some thought they should give up their own language and customs as quickly as possible. Others thought they should hold on to their heritage.

#### Breaking Cultural Ties

"We wanted to be Americans so quickly that we were embarrassed if our parents couldn't speak English. My father was reading a Polish paper. And somebody was supposed to come to the house. I remember sticking it under something. We were that ashamed of being foreign."

*—Louise Nagy, a Polish immigrant, 1913*

#### Preserving Cultural Ties

"We ate the same dishes, spoke the same language, told the same stories, [as in Syria]. . . . To me the colony [neighborhood] was a habitat so much like the one I had left behind in Syria that its home atmosphere enabled me to maintain a firm hold on life in the face of the many difficulties which confronted me in those days."

*—Abraham Ribahny, on his neighborhood in New York, 1893*

*ANALYZING VIEWPOINTS* **Compare the statements of the two speakers.**

**Main Idea CONNECTIONS**

*Why did Chinese immigrants face hostility?*

to work for their companies until they had paid the cost of their passage and upkeep. Many Chinese immigrants paid their debts, settled down, and began to work in other fields, often side by side with white Americans and European immigrants. Those occupations included mining, farming, fishing, factory work, food preparation, and laundering.

In this way the Chinese contributed to their new country, but that often was not enough to earn the respect of white society. Like many European immigrants, the Chinese tended to live in their own ethnic communities, such as the Chinatown section of San Francisco. Living in such communities was not only more comfortable for them but also safer, for it helped them avoid expressions and acts of hostility from non-Asian neighbors.

American Labor unions fought hard to exclude Chinese immigrants. Because the Chinese accepted low wages, they affected the rates of pay of all workers. The unions maintained that if Chinese laborers kept pouring into California, wage rates there would continue to drop.

Other groups claimed the Chinese simply were not worthy of being Americans. Using scientific-sounding but faulty reasoning, anti-Asian movements claimed that Asians were physically and mentally inferior to white Americans. These claims both reflected and helped spread racist attitudes toward Asian immigrants.

Congress responded to the demands of unions and others by passing the **Chinese Exclusion Act** in 1882. The act prohibited Chinese laborers from entering the country. It did not, however, prevent entry by those who had previously established residence or who had family already living in the United States. The act was renewed in 1892 and 1902 and then made permanent. It was not repealed until 1943.

In 1910 the federal government built an immigration center on Angel Island in San Francisco Bay, similar to the center on Ellis Island in New York Harbor. There immigrants underwent a lengthy examination. Besides having to pass medical checks, the Chinese newcomers also had to prove that they should not be excluded.

**Japanese Restricted** Many of the earliest Japanese to immigrate to the United States came from Hawaii. They had migrated to Hawaii to work on sugar plantations, and when the United States obtained Hawaii in 1898, a number of Japanese saw an opportunity for a better life in America.

By 1920 some 200,000 Japanese had arrived through West Coast ports. Most Japanese settled in the Los Angeles area, and soon they were producing a large percentage of southern California's fruits and vegetables. Mainly involved in private business, the Japanese did not compete with union laborers as the Chinese had. Still, labor unions and the political leaders who supported them fought to stop Japanese immigration.

More than economic motives were at work, for some acts reflected prejudice against Asians generally. In 1906, for example, the San Francisco school board ruled that all Chinese, Japanese, and Korean children should attend a separate school. The Japanese government condemned this **segregation,** or forced separation, claiming it violated an 1894 treaty that gave Japanese citizens the right to enter the

United States freely. The issue threatened to become an international crisis.

In response, President Theodore Roosevelt reached a compromise with Japanese officials in 1907. Named the **Gentlemen's Agreement** because it was not an official government document, the compromise called on San Francisco to end its school segregation and Japan to stop issuing passports to laborers.

Anti-Japanese feeling, however, did not subside. In 1913 California passed the Webb Alien Land Law, which banned **alien** (noncitizen) Asians from owning farmland.

## *Immigration from Mexico*

In 1902 Congress passed the Newlands National Reclamation Act to promote the irrigation of southwestern lands. Over the next decade, irrigation turned millions of acres of desert into fertile farmland across Texas, Arizona, New Mexico, and California.

The new farmland meant new jobs in the sparsely populated Southwest. Employers hired Mexican laborers to work on farms as well as in mines. Roughly 50,000 Mexicans headed north between 1900 and 1910. The Mexican Revolution, which began in 1910, increased the flow north over the next decade.

When the United States entered World War I in 1917, demand increased sharply for laborers to grow and harvest food and mine the copper, coal, and other vital minerals needed for the war effort. Around a million Mexicans, 10 percent of Mexico's population, came to the United States during this decade.

When the Immigration Restriction Act of 1921 limited immigration from Europe and Asia, labor shortages again drew Mexicans across the border. By 1925 Los Angeles had the largest Spanish-speaking population of any North American city outside of Mexico.

## *Two Immigrant Portraits*

Facts and figures tell only a part of the story of immigration in the United States. The drama behind the figures is best revealed in the accounts of ordinary people, whose lives and experiences reflect the struggles and triumphs of living day to day in a new land.

**Sadie Frowne, Polish Immigrant** Sadie Frowne's early years in her native Poland were happy. Her mother kept a grocer's shop and worked in the fields with her husband. Sadie helped out with chores whenever she could. When Sadie was 10, however, her father died.

Unable to support themselves, Sadie and her mother looked to the United States, where they hoped to build a new life. Sadie's aunt, who lived in New York City, collected donations to pay for their passage to America.

In 1898, 13-year-old Sadie and her mother made the 12-day Atlantic crossing:

**AMERICAN VOICES** **"There were hundreds of other people packed in with us, men, women and children, and almost all of them were sick. . . . We thought we should die, but at last the voyage was over, and we came up and saw the beautiful bay and the big woman with the spikes on her head and the lamp that is lighted at night in her hand."**

—*Sadie Frowne*

In New York Sadie worked as a live-in servant. Her mother found a job as a garment worker. Tragedy then struck again when Sadie's mother contracted a fatal case of tuberculosis, a disease then raging through the crowded neighborhoods of New York City.

Now she would have to support herself. Sadie landed a new job as a skirt maker, earning $4 for a six-day week. She rented a room with another young woman for $1.50 a week.

By keeping her expenses down, Sadie was now able to set aside a dollar a week for "clothing and pleasure" and another dollar for savings. She went to school at night to learn English. She also worked to improve her sewing skills, found a better job, and moved to a nicer place in Brooklyn.

With constant work, sacrifice, and determination, Sadie was living out the dream of millions of immigrants. It was a dream of simple comforts, modest prosperity, and the chance for a better life.

*Treasured items from home, such as this stuffed bear and set of spoons, helped provide a link between an immigrant's old life and new.*

**Take Eto, Japanese Picture Bride** Tameji Eto came to the United States from Japan in 1904. After working as a farmhand he became a foreman for the Pacific Coast Railroad Company. He earned enough to lease land for his own farm.

Japanese picture brides, such as these women in traditional dress, looked with both hope and apprehension to life in a new land with new husbands they had never met. ***Culture*** ***What other social challenges do you think new immigrants faced in the United States?***

Tameji began to think of settling down and starting a family. Because few Japanese women had immigrated to the United States, Tameji's thoughts turned to Take, the sister of one of his school friends back in Japan. He wrote her family to ask permission to marry her.

Nineteen-year-old Take had no memory of Tameji. Yet her parents insisted that she agree to the arranged marriage, and Take accepted the proposal. Clutching Tameji's photograph, her only means of identifying her future husband, she sailed for the United States.

On board ship, Take met other "picture brides," women whose marriages had been arranged through the exchange of photographs across the Pacific Ocean. Like her companions, Take spent the voyage trying to adapt to strange foods and wondering about her future.

After her arrival and a 10-day quarantine for an eye infection, Take finally met Tameji. Luckily, he looked like his picture, "straight and tall with lots of hair," and he also seemed kind. Together they set out for Tameji's land in the frontier town of Grand Arroyo, California.

For Take the frontier life posed a challenge, but one she accepted. She later told one of her eight children that farming the semiarid California land "was not easy, but it was my future as well as [Tameji's], and I wanted to be a part of it. Father never demanded I work so hard. I did it because it was necessary and I wanted to."

The Etos' hard work paid off, and by 1919 they had enough money to buy their own farm. Because of the Webb Alien Land Law, however, they had to buy land under the name of a white friend. After some difficult years, the farm did well. Take cared for her children and cooked for a farm crew of 40 to 50 men. Finally, after 15 years of hard work, the Etos could afford a journey back to Japan to see their parents and tell them of their success in America.

## SECTION 2 REVIEW

### Comprehension

1. *Key Terms* Define: (a) steerage; (b) quarantine; (c) Chinese Exclusion Act; (d) segregation; (e) Gentlemen's Agreement; (f) alien.
2. *Summarizing the Main Idea* Where did various groups of immigrants settle once they had entered the United States?
3. *Organizing Information* Create a Venn diagram to compare the experiences of European, Asian, and Mexican immigrants.

### Critical Thinking

4. *Analyzing Time Lines* Review the time line at the start of the section. How do the entries reflect varying attitudes toward immigration?
5. *Drawing Conclusions* Why do you think steamships have a steerage area for immigrants?

### Writing Activity

6. *Writing a Persuasive Essay* Write a letter that Sadie Frowne or Take Eto might have written to persuade a relative in her former homeland that she did the right thing by coming to the United States.

| 1871 Great Chicago Fire | 1877 Reconstruction ends; segregation begins to rise | 1885 Nation's first skyscraper built, in Chicago | 1890 Jacob Riis's How the Other Half Lives | 1897 First subway opens in Boston |
|---|---|---|---|---|

1870 — 1880 — 1890 — 1900

# 3 The Challenge of the Cities

## SECTION PREVIEW

### Objectives

1. Explain why people left farms for cities in the late 1800s and early 1900s.
2. Describe some of the new developments that helped cities grow.
3. Describe urban living conditions and the results of city growth.
4. *Key Terms* Define: suburb; tenement; ghetto; restrictive covenant; political machine; graft.

### Main Idea

Millions of people moved into the cities, creating new growth and new challenges.

### Reading Strategy

*Reading for Evidence* As you read, find evidence to support the following statement: "The arrival of large numbers of newcomers, from both within and outside the nation, radically changed the face of the nation's cities."

While millions of immigrants from around the world were settling in the cities of the United States, growing numbers of Americans were moving there, too. Between 1880 and 1920, 11 million Americans left behind the economic hardship of their farms and headed for the opportunities of the cities. This migration within the country, combined with the new immigration, brought explosive growth to the nation's urban centers.

## From Farms to Cities

Women and men alike took part in the migration from rural to urban America. As factories produced more of the goods that farm women had once made, the need for women's labor on farms declined. In addition, as new machines replaced manual labor on many farms, the need for male farmhands shrank. The result was a striking shift in the nation's population. Between 1880 and 1910, the percentage of the nation's population living on farms fell from 72 to 54 percent.

Many African Americans took part in this internal migration. In 1870 fewer than a half million of the nation's 5 million African Americans lived outside the South. But after Reconstruction ended in 1877, segregation and acts of racial violence against African Americans increased. By 1890, partly as a result of these pressures, another 150,000 black southerners had left the South, and many rural African Americans had moved into nearby cities. Then, in the 1910s, the boll weevil destroyed cotton crops and floods ruined Alabama and Mississippi farmlands. These disasters drove several hundred thousand more African Americans out of the South, mostly to northern cities.

*Cities like Chicago, pictured on this postcard, grew upward and outward in the late 1800s.*

## How Cities Grew

The arrival of large numbers of newcomers, from both within and outside the nation, radically changed the face of the nation's cities. Between 1865 and 1900 many features of modern city life, both good and bad, first appeared—from subways and skyscrapers to smog and slums.

VIEWING HISTORY Growing cities lured migrants from within the United States as people left rural areas to find work. This woman found a job as a porter in a subway, itself a product of urban expansion. ***Geography*** *How did transportation change city settlement patterns?*

Before the Civil War, cities were small in area, rarely extending more than 3 or 4 miles across. Most people lived near their workplace, and they walked wherever they had to go. The introduction of public, horse-drawn carriages that traveled on rails began to change this pattern. Introduced in 1832 in New York City, they allowed people who could afford the fares to move outside the cities. Those people made their homes in the **suburbs,** or residential communities surrounding the cities.

Later in the 1800s, motorized methods of transportation made commuting much easier and speeded suburban growth. The first elevated trains, built in 1868 in New York, allowed commuters to bypass the congested streets. Cable cars, introduced in San Francisco in 1873, allowed quick access to the city's steep hills. Electric trolleys, first used in Richmond, Virginia, in 1888, replaced horse-drawn cars and reached even farther into the suburbs. Subway trains first appeared in Boston in 1897. Finally, the automobile, invented in 1893 and mass-produced beginning in the 1910s, guaranteed that expansion into the suburbs would continue.

**Main Idea CONNECTIONS**

*In what ways did cities grow in the late 1800s, and why?*

Cities grew upward as well as outward. Before the Civil War, buildings stood no more than five stories high. Yet as urban space became scarce, buildings were made taller and taller. To build these mammoth structures, engineers relied on the strength of Bessemer steel girders.

To reach the upper floors, people relied on the speed and efficiency of elevators. In 1853 Elisha Graves Otis, an American, invented a safety device that made passenger elevators possible. The first one went into operation four years later. The first skyscraper, Chicago's Home Insurance Company Building, appeared in 1885. Ten stories tall, it was built with a framework of iron and steel and had four passenger elevators.

As cities expanded, specialized areas emerged within them. Banks, financial offices, law firms, and government offices located in one central area. Retail shops and department stores located in another. Industrial, wholesale, and warehouse districts formed a ring around the center of the city.

## *Urban Living Conditions*

Some urban workers moved into housing built especially for them by mill and factory owners. The rest found apartments wherever they could. Many middle-class residents who moved to the suburbs left empty buildings behind. Owners converted these buildings into multifamily units for workers and their families.

Speculators also built many **tenements,** low-cost apartment buildings designed to house as many families as the owner could pack in. A group of dirty, run-down tenements could transform an area into a slum.

**Conditions in the Slums** Before long, because of poverty, overcrowding, and neglect, the old residential neighborhoods of cities gradually declined. Trees and grass disappeared beneath the new, cheaply built tenements. Hundreds of people were crammed into spaces meant for a few families. Soot from coal-fired steam engines and boilers made the air seem dark and foul even in daylight. Open sewers attracted rats and other disease-spreading vermin.

In 1905 journalist Eleanor McMain quoted a university student who described a block of tenements in the Italian district of New Orleans as "death traps, closely built, jammed together, with no side openings. Twenty-five per cent of the yard space is damp and gloomy. . . . Where the houses are three or more rooms in depth, the middle ones are dark, without outside ventilator. . . . There is no fire protection whatever."

Fire was a constant danger in cities. With tenement buildings so closely packed together, even a small fire could quickly consume a neighborhood. Once a fire started, it leaped easily from roof to roof. As a result, most large cities had major fires during this period.

Chicago experienced one of the most devastating: the Great Chicago Fire of 1871. Nobody knows for sure what started it, but before it was over, 18,000 buildings had burned, leaving some 250 people dead and 100,000 homeless.

Property damage estimates reached $200 million, the equivalent of $2 billion today. A similar fire in Boston the following year caused the equivalent of nearly $1 billion damage.

Contagious diseases, including cholera, malaria, tuberculosis, diphtheria, and typhoid, thrived in crowded tenement conditions. Epidemics, such as the yellow fever that swept through Memphis, Tennessee, in the late 1870s and through New Orleans, Louisiana, in the early 1900s, took thousands of lives. Children were especially vulnerable to disease. In New York City, in one district of tenements, 6 out of 10 babies died before their first birthday.

**Ghettos** Some urban neighborhoods became **ghettos,** areas in which one ethnic or racial group dominated. Many newly arrived immigrants chose to live near others of their ethnic group because of the comfort of familiar language and traditions. These ethnic communities strongly reflected the culture of the homeland. In 1904 Emily Dinwiddie, a tenement-house inspector, wrote a joyful description of Philadelphia's "Little Italy:"

**"The black-eyed children rolling and tumbling together, the gaily colored dresses of the women and the crowds of street vendors all give the neighborhood a wholly foreign appearance."**

—*Emily Dinwiddie*

Dinwiddie's delight with the neighborhood did not lessen her distress at the slum conditions and poverty that she saw.

Other ghettos formed when ethnic groups isolated themselves, often because of threats from whites. San Francisco's Chinatown had well-known street boundaries: "From Kearny to Powell, and from California to Broadway," recalled one resident. "If you ever passed them and went out there, the white kids would throw stones at you."

Still other urban ghettos resulted from **restrictive covenants.** These were agreements among homeowners not to sell real estate to certain groups of people. Covenants often prevented African Americans, Mexicans, Asian Americans, and Jews from buying land or houses in the better neighborhoods.

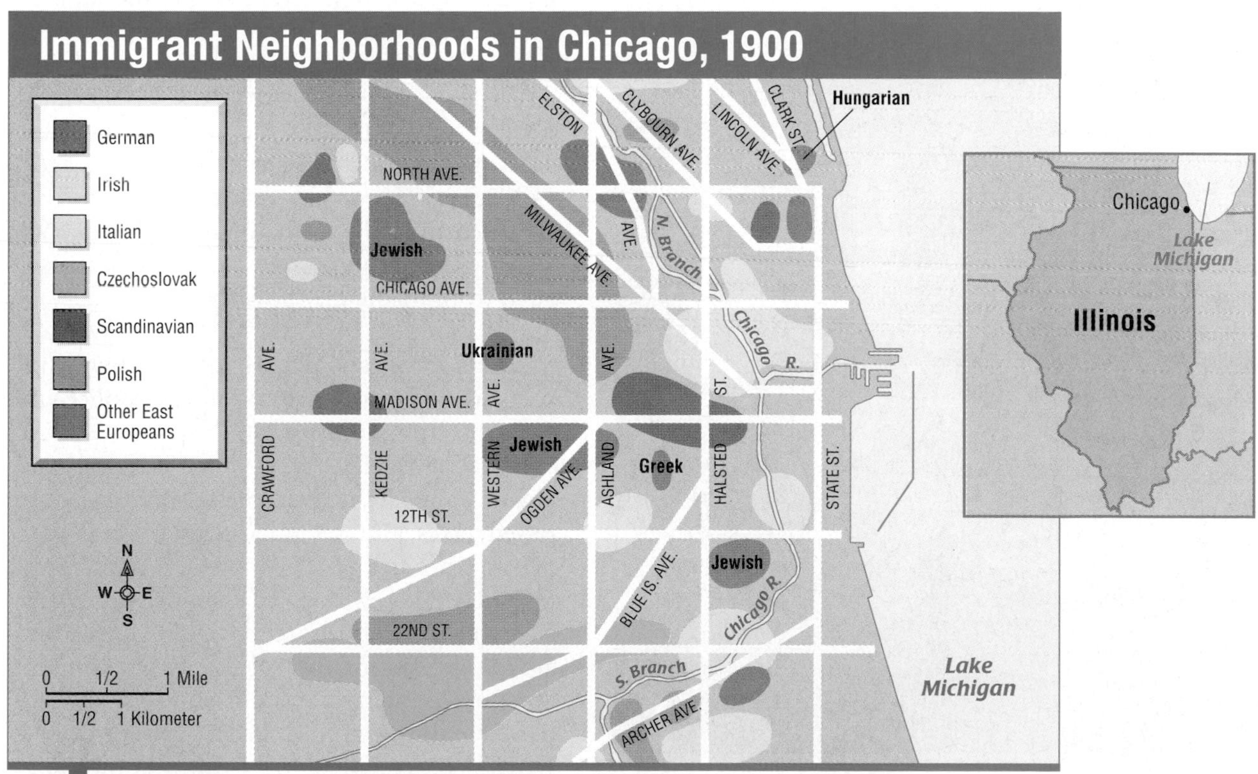


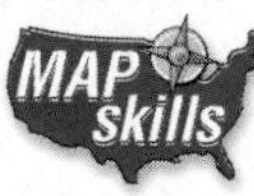


As this map of Chicago shows, immigrants often settled in communities that had been established by others from their homeland, creating ethnic neighborhoods within cities. ***Place*** *What advantages and disadvantages might ethnic neighborhoods have offered their residents?*

## Jacob Riis

AMERICAN BIOGRAPHY Some reformers worked to improve the lives of the urban poor. One was Jacob Riis. A native of Denmark, Riis had boarded a steamship bound for America in 1870 at the age of 21 and settled in New York City. There he personally experienced the dreadful conditions in which many new Americans lived.

Riis held various jobs before he landed a position as a police reporter in 1873. Riis honed his writing skills while covering New York's Lower East Side, a tenement slum bursting with immigrant families. He worked for the New York *Tribune* from 1877 to 1888 and the New York *Evening Sun* from 1888 to 1899.

*Jacob Riis (1849–1914)*

While still a reporter at the *Sun*, Riis began writing books about what he had seen. In *How the Other Half Lives*, published in 1890, Riis exposed the horrors of tenement life to a shocked American public. Hoping to generate public support for reform of the tenement "system," he painted a bleak picture of New York's future:

> AMERICAN VOICES **"Today three-fourths of [New York's] people live in the tenements. . . . We know now that there is no way out; that the 'system' that was the evil offspring of public neglect and private greed has come to stay, a storm-centre forever of our civilization. Nothing is left but to make the best of a bad bargain."**
>
> —*Jacob Riis,* How the Other Half Lives, *1890*

In order to document his reporting, Riis mastered the new technology of flash photography. Drawings based on those photographs appeared in his books, and he showed the actual photographs of overcrowded rooms and run-down buildings in his lectures on the plight of immigrants. As a result of Riis's work, New York State passed the nation's first meaningful laws to improve tenements.

This photograph by Jacob Riis shows the kind of cramped, unsafe apartments in which many immigrants were forced to live. ***Government** How did city governments address the problems of urban living conditions?*

## The Results of City Growth

Some city residents could avoid urban problems simply by leaving the cities. The middle and upper classes began moving to the suburbs in the late 1800s. As a result, the gap between the well-to-do and the poor widened.

A few cities preserved areas for the most wealthy residents near the city center. These areas include Boston's Beacon Hill, Chicago's Gold Coast, and San Francisco's Nob Hill. Often, people living in these neighborhoods also owned country estates and were quite isolated from the nearby poverty.

**Political Divisions** Rapid urban growth put pressure on city officials to improve police and fire protection, transportation systems, sewage disposal, electrical and water service, and health care. To deliver these services, cities raised taxes and set up offices to deal with people's needs.

Increased revenue and responsibilities gave city governments more power. Competition among groups for control of city government grew more intense. Some groups represented the remaining middle and upper classes. Others represented new immigrants and workers.

**The Rise of Political Bosses** Out of these clashing interests, the **political machine** was born. This was an unofficial city organization designed to keep a particular party or group in power and usually headed by a single, powerful "boss." Sometimes the boss held public office. More often he handpicked others to run for office and then helped them win.

Political machines worked through the exchange of favors. Machines used an army of ward leaders, each of whom managed a city district, to hand out city jobs and contracts to residents of their ward and do other favors for them. In return, those residents supported the machine's candidates on election day. Similarly, individuals or companies wanting a favor from the city could get it by first paying some money to the machine. **Graft,** or the use of one's job to gain profit, was a major source of income for the machines.

Many people blamed the success of political machines on the large number of urban immigrants. They charged that immigrants, poorly educated and with little experience in democracy, were being taken advantage of by corrupt politicians. Immigrants tended to support political machines, because they helped poor people at a time when neither government nor private industry would.

Cincinnati's George B. Cox, a former saloon owner, was an unusual example of a fairly honest political boss. A Republican, in 1879 he won election to the city council. In true machine fashion he used this post to guarantee election victories and business contracts for the party faithful. But he also worked with local reformers to improve the quality of police officers and city services.

Perhaps the most notorious boss was William Marcy Tweed. "Boss" Tweed controlled Tammany Hall, the political club that ran New York City's Democratic party. Once Tweed and his pals gained access to the city treasury in 1870, they used various illegal methods to plunder it, including padding bills and submitting false receipts.† Tweed also used his power to persuade businesses to pay him for nonexistent services. Through countless such instances of fraud and graft, the Tweed ring amassed many millions of dollars.

*Cartoonist Thomas Nast illustrated "The 'Brains'" of Boss Tweed in 1871.*

The brilliant political cartoons of German immigrant Thomas Nast helped bring Tweed down by exposing his methods to the public. Convicted of crimes in 1873, Tweed eventually died in jail. Under new leaders, however, Tammany Hall dominated New York politics for another half century.

† Urban disasters, such as the great fires in Chicago and Boston, pointed out the need for better city government. Galveston, Texas, demolished by a hurricane in 1900, completely restructured its government under a commission to run the major municipal agencies. Other cities hired professional managers.

## SECTION 3 REVIEW

### Comprehension

1. *Key Terms* Define: (a) suburb; (b) tenement; (c) ghetto; (d) restrictive covenant; (e) political machine; (f) graft.
2. *Summarizing the Main Idea* What were living conditions like for new immigrants in cities?
3. *Organizing Information* Make a graphic organizer that shows the different reasons that people moved from farms to cities.

### Critical Thinking

4. *Analyzing Time Lines* Review the time line at the start of the section. In 1890 Jacob Riis published his book *How the Other Half Lives.* Which other event in the time line most directly relates to the theme of Riis's book? Explain.
5. *Demonstrating Reasoned Judgment* Do you think that the political machine helped or hurt cities overall? Explain.

### Writing Activity

6. *Writing an Expository Essay* Describe the inventions and developments that helped cities grow both outward and upward.

# SKILLS FOR LIFE

**Graphs and Charts**

**Geography**

**Historical Evidence**

**Critical Thinking**

## Reading Tables and Analyzing Statistics

Statistical tables present large amounts of numerical data clearly and concisely. The patterns suggested by statistics must be carefully analyzed, however, and their sources evaluated for reliability. Statistics should be verified by other historical evidence. Use the following steps to read and interpret the data below.

**1.** ***Determine what type of information is presented and decide whether the source is reliable.*** The title of the table and the labels for the rows and columns tell you what information is presented. The source is usually found below the table. (a) What is the table's title? (b) How many decades are covered? (c) What is the source of the statistics in the table? (d) Can the data be used as historical evidence?

**2.** ***Read the information in the table.*** Note that the table provides the total number of immigrants for each region for a given five-year period. (a) Between 1871 and 1875, how many immigrants came from Asia? (b) Between 1881 and 1885, which region provided the largest number of immigrants? The smallest?

**3.** ***Find relationships among the statistics.*** You can use the data in this table to compare the immigrant populations from different regions or to trace changes in one region's immigration pattern over time. (a) Which region had the largest total number of immigrants between 1871 and 1920? (b) During which decade did the region called The Americas show the sharpest drop in number of immigrants? (c) Which region in the table showed the largest increase in number of immigrants from 1871 to 1920?

**4.** ***Use the data in the table to draw conclusions.*** Between 1891 and 1900 the unemployment rate in the United States averaged 10.5 percent. Between 1901 and 1910, it averaged 4.5 percent. Using the data in the table, what conclusions can you draw about the relationship between the unemployment rate and the immigration rate for those time periods?

### TEST FOR SUCCESS

Imagine that you are preparing a report on immigration during this period. What kinds of information would you look for in the table to make your report more interesting?

**Estimated Number of Immigrants to the United States, by Region, 1871–1920**

| | North-western Europe | Central Europe | Eastern Europe | Southern Europe | Asia [1] | The Americas [2] | Africa | Oceania |
|---|---|---|---|---|---|---|---|---|
| **1871–1875** | 858,325 | 549,610 | 15,580 | 37,070 | 65,727 | 193,354 | 205 | 6,312 |
| **1876–1880** | 493,866 | 254,511 | 24,052 | 39,248 | 58,096 | 210,690 | 153 | 4,602 |
| **1881–1885** | 1,193,819 | 1,128,528 | 63,443 | 120,297 | 60,432 | 403,977 | 331 | 4,406 |
| **1886–1890** | 1,131,844 | 729,967 | 157,749 | 211,399 | 7,948 | 22,990 | 526 | 8,168 |
| **1891–1895** | 745,433 | 762,216 | 251,405 | 314,625 | 19,255 | 14,734 | 163 | 2,215 |
| **1896–1900** | 392,907 | 432,363 | 270,421 | 389,608 | 51,981 | 24,238 | 187 | 1,750 |
| **1901–1905** | 761,527 | 1,121,234 | 711,546 | 1,050,721 | 115,941 | 63,774 | 1,829 | 6,134 |
| **1906–1910** | 807,020 | 1,365,530 | 1,058,024 | 1,260,424 | 127,626 | 298,114 | 5,539 | 6,890 |
| **1911–1915** | 652,189 | 1,027,138 | 978,931 | 1,137,539 | 123,719 | 528,098 | 5,847 | 6,126 |
| **1916–1920** | 201,304 | 23,276 | 33,547 | 322,640 | 68,840 | 615,373 | 2,596 | 7,301 |

[1] No record of immigration from Korea prior to 1948. [2] No record of immigration from Mexico for 1886 to 1893.
Source: *Historical Statistics of the United States*

| 1869 | 1874 | 1882 | 1889 | 1893 | 1894 |
|---|---|---|---|---|---|
| Prohibition party founded | Woman's Christian Temperance Union founded | New York Charity Organization Society formed | Hull House founded | Anti-Saloon League founded | Immigration Restriction League formed |

1865 1875 1885 1895

# 4 Ideas for Reform

**SECTION PREVIEW**

### Objectives

1. Describe the efforts in the late 1800s to control immigration and personal behavior.
2. Explain how different movements helped the needy.
3. *Key Terms* Define: nativism; temperance movement; prohibition; vice; social gospel movement; settlement house.

### Main Idea

A variety of groups worked to improve social, economic, and political conditions in the cities.

### Reading Strategy

*Reinforcing Key Ideas* Write down these headings: *Controlling Immigrants* and *Helping the Needy.* As you read, list under the correct heading strategies used to reform cities.

In 1890 New York City had as many Italians as the city of Naples, Italy, and as many Germans as Hamburg, Germany. It had twice as many Irish as Dublin, Ireland, and twice as many Jews as Warsaw, Poland. Other cities around the country also attracted large numbers of immigrants. The many Americans migrating from the countryside boosted urban populations further. This steady stream of people to the cities brought serious problems that needed solutions.

## Controlling Immigration and Behavior

Many Americans linked all the problems of the cities to the new immigrants. By controlling immigrants, they hoped to restore what they believed was a past of purity and virtue. Groups were formed to pursue this goal. Some sought to keep immigrants out, while others wanted to control their behavior.

**Nativism** In the 1850s the Know-Nothing party had gained many followers by vowing to restrict immigration. Thirty years later this policy of **nativism,** or favoring native-born Americans over immigrants, reappeared. The rise of immigrants to positions of power in the cities helped provoke this new wave of antiforeign bias. Passage of the Chinese Exclusion Act in 1882 showed how politically effective the new nativists were.

Nativists did not oppose only Asian immigration. The American Protective Association, a nativist group founded in 1887, also targeted immigrants in general. It called for the teaching of only American culture and the English language in schools and demanded tighter rules on citizenship and employment of aliens.

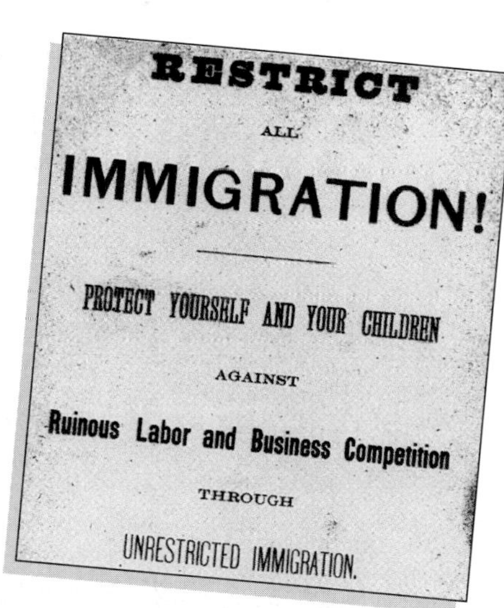


*This 1885 brochure reflects the fear that hiring immigrants would lower wages.*

Nativists won a victory in 1885, when Congress repealed the Contract Labor Act. Passed in 1864, the law had allowed employers to recruit foreign laborers. Even after the law's repeal, however, employers often illegally brought in foreign workers to replace striking

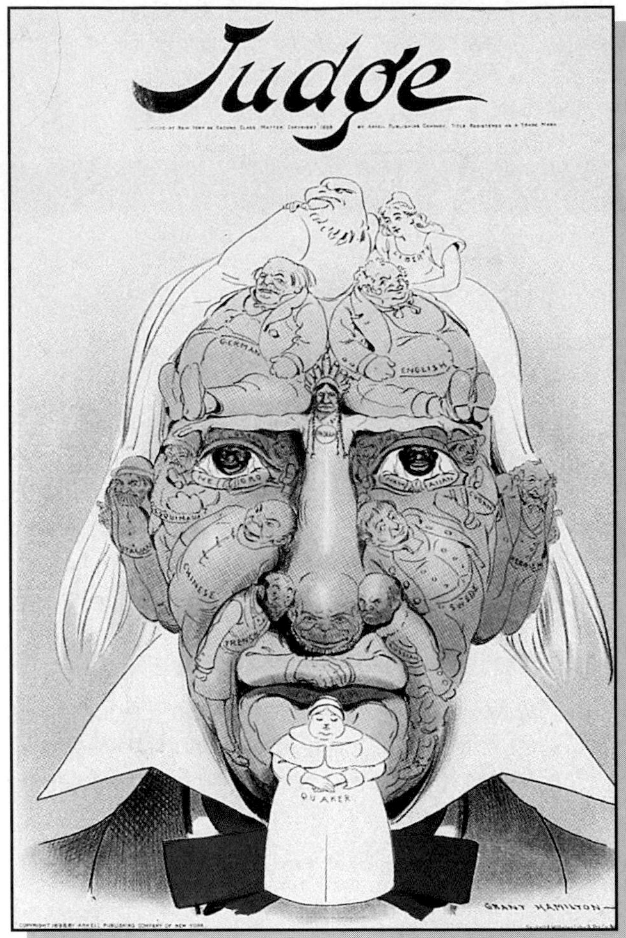

The caption on this cartoon reads "Uncle Sam is a man of strong features." ***Diversity*** ***What does the cartoon suggest about the artist's view of immigration?***

employees. Such actions only heightened nativist feelings among workers.

**Main Idea CONNECTIONS**

*How did some Americans want to change the customs of immigrants?*

There were nativists among the wealthy as well. The Immigration Restriction League was organized in 1894 by some recent graduates of Harvard College. The League hoped to exclude immigrants considered unfit by forcing them to pass literacy tests. Its main targets were immigrants from southern and eastern Europe, whose cultures differed greatly from those of League members.

**Prohibition** Like nativism, another movement begun before the Civil War saw a revival later in the 1800s: the **temperance movement,** an organized campaign to eliminate alcohol consumption. Three groups dominated the new temperance movement: the Prohibition party, founded in 1869, the Woman's Christian Temperance Union, founded in 1874, and the Anti-Saloon League, founded in 1893. These groups opposed drinking on the grounds that it led to personal tragedies. They supported **prohibition,** a ban on the manufacture and sale of alcoholic beverages.

Prohibition groups also opposed drinking because of what they saw as the links among saloons, immigrants, and political bosses. Immigrant men often used saloons as social clubs, where they could relax and also pick up information about jobs. Prohibitionists believed that saloons undermined public morals. Some prohibitionists even claimed that saloons formed the center of a movement to take over the United States.

"Foreign control or conquest is rapidly making us un-Christian, with immorality throned in power," one prohibitionist wrote in 1908. Had foreigners used "armies and fleets," he declared, they could not have achieved greater control.

**Purity Crusaders** As cities grew, drugs, gambling, prostitution, and other forms of vice became big business. **Vice** (immoral or corrupt behavior) was not unique to the cities. But large urban populations made vice highly visible and very profitable. Then as now, many residents fought to rid their communities of unwholesome and illegal activities.

"Purity crusaders" led the way. In 1873 Anthony Comstock founded the New York Society for the Suppression of Vice. The following year he won passage of a law that prohibited sending obscene materials through the United States mail. Material deemed obscene included descriptions of methods to prevent unwanted pregnancy. For decades the Comstock Law, as it came to be known, slowed the distribution of information about birth control.

Other purity crusaders attacked urban political machines, saying that machine-controlled police forces profited from vice. Police were known to demand payment from gamblers, for example, in return for ignoring illegal activities.

On occasion, purity crusaders joined forces with other reformers to run for public office. By campaigning on an anti-vice platform, some succeeded in throwing machine candidates out of office. Usually the political machines regained power in later elections by mocking the self-righteous tone of many purists and by arguing that morality was a personal issue.

## Helping the Needy

Another group of reformers, moved by social conscience or religious idealism, preferred to improve society by helping the needy. They argued that prosperous Americans should fight poverty and improve unwholesome social conditions in cities.

**The Charity Organization Movement** In 1882 Josephine Shaw Lowell founded the New York Charity Organization Society (COS). The COS tried to make charity a scientific enterprise. Members kept detailed files on those who received help. In this way COS leaders could more easily determine how to serve their clients. Yet keeping detailed files also allowed COS leaders to distinguish between the poor whom they considered worthy of help and those whom they deemed unworthy. This attitude sometimes led to unkind treatment of the needy.

Some charity reformers interfered in the lives of immigrants. One clergyman who worked in a southern Italian neighborhood claimed that social workers burst into homes of immigrant women. There they "upset the usual routine of their lives, opening windows, undressing children, giving orders not to eat this and that, not to wrap babies in swaddling clothes."

Many COS members wanted immigrants to adopt American, middle-class standards of child-raising, cooking, and cleaning. They did not care how strange these customs seemed to people with different cultural backgrounds. This disturbed some immigrants, but others were grateful for the advice and assistance.

**The Social Gospel Movement** In the 1880s and 1890s, urban churches began to provide social services for the poor who now surrounded them. They also tried to aim prohibition and purity campaigns in new directions. Instead of blaming immigrants for drinking, gambling, and other behaviors, the churches sought to treat the misfortunes that drove people into such activities.

Soon a social reform movement developed within religious institutions. Called the **social gospel movement,** it sought to apply the gospel (teachings) of Jesus directly to society and focused on the gospel ideals of charity and justice, especially by seeking labor reforms. In 1908, followers of such views formed the Federal Council of the Churches of Christ. This organization supported improved living conditions and a larger share in the national

Some reformers focused their efforts on helping immigrants adjust to life in the United States. This immigrant is learning English. ***Culture* *What else is she learning?***

wealth for all workers. Other religious organizations, including some Jewish synagogues, adapted the social gospel ideal for themselves.

**The Settlement Movement** Thousands of young, educated women and men put the social gospel into practice in an innovative reform program called the settlement movement. These young reformers would move into a house in the midst of a poor neighborhood. From this **settlement house,** a kind of community center, they offered social services.

The settlement movement had begun in Britain. Its founders believed that simply giving money to the poor never really helped them. In order to find out what would be most helpful, social workers had to live in poor neighborhoods. There they could witness the effects of poverty firsthand.

In 1889, inspired by the British settlement movement, Jane Addams and Ellen Gates Starr bought the rundown Charles Hull mansion in Chicago. They repaired it and opened its doors to their immigrant neighbors. At first, Starr and Addams simply wanted to get to know them, offering help when needed. Soon they began anticipating and responding to the needs of the community as a whole.

Over the decades that followed, Addams and Starr turned Hull House into a center of community activity. At Hull House, neighbors

Reformers offered help to newcomers by watching over their children while they worked. ***Economics*** ***What other services did settlement houses offer?***

Settlement houses like Hull House sprang up across the country. Each was unique. The Henry Street Settlement, founded by Lillian Wald on New York's Lower East Side, was originally a nurses' settlement. Wald's plan was to develop a system to offer home care to the poor. Its programs soon expanded to resemble many of those at Hull House. Missionaries, too, founded settlement houses, in part to gain converts but also to apply the social gospel in practical ways.

By 1910 there were more than 400 settlement houses. Most were supported by donations and staffed by volunteers or people willing to work for low wages and free room and board. Hundreds of college graduates, especially women excluded from other professions, became settlement workers. Except for leaders, such as Addams and Wald, most workers spent only a few years in these jobs. Many moved on to professional careers in social work, education, or government.

could attend cultural events, take classes, or display exhibits of crafts from their home countries. The settlement set up child-care centers, playgrounds, clubs and summer camps for boys and girls; employment and legal-aid bureaus; and health-care clinics. It also launched investigations of city economic, political, and social conditions. These actions laid the foundation for many later reforms.

They moved on, but few ever forgot their settlement experience. "I don't know that my attitude changed," wrote one former settlement worker, "but my point of view certainly did, or perhaps it would be more true to say that now I have several points of view." By helping its workers see social issues in new ways, the settlement houses energized the reform movement while improving the lives of the urban poor.

## SECTION 4 REVIEW

### Comprehension

1. *Key Terms* Define: (a) nativism; (b) temperance movement; (c) prohibition; (d) vice; (e) social gospel movement; (f) settlement house.
2. *Summarizing the Main Idea* How did Prohibition groups and purity crusaders differ from charity, social gospel, and settlement movements?
3. *Organizing Information* Create a two-column chart listing the key urban problems and the solutions offered by various reform groups.

### Critical Thinking

4. *Analyzing Time Lines* Review the time line at the start of the section. How are the entries for 1869, 1874, and 1893 related?
5. *Demonstrating Reasoned Judgment* How might the anti-immigrant arguments of wealthy nativists have differed from those of less-wealthy nativists?

### Writing Activity

6. *Writing a Persuasive Essay* Write a letter to the editor (around 1910) about the need for government or private funding to set up a settlement house. Show why such programs help strengthen communities.

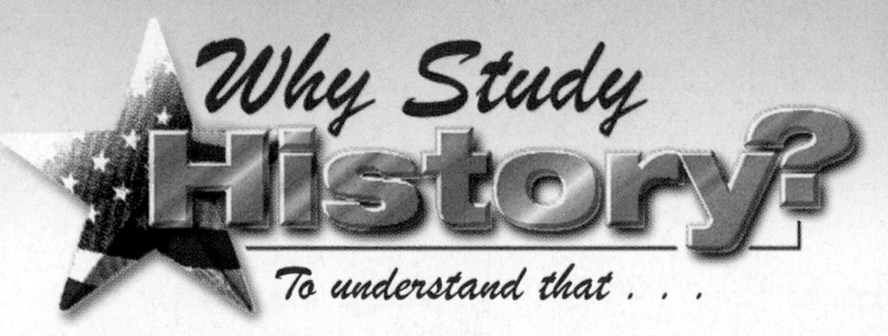


# Immigration Continues Today

**Since the great surge of immigration in the late 1800s and early 1900s, millions of people from dozens of nations have moved to the United States.**

*Family of immigrants arriving at Ellis Island in 1905*

Look around your classroom. What ethnic and racial backgrounds are reflected in the faces of your classmates? Listen to conversations on the streets of a large city. You may hear people speaking languages such as Spanish, Vietnamese, French, Russian, and Japanese.

The United States has always benefited from the intelligence and hard work of its immigrants. Yet some Americans have felt threatened by the continued arrival of immigrants and have called for measures to restrict immigration.

## The Impact Today

More than 20 million people came to the United States between 1890 and 1920. Some Americans viewed this surge of immigration as a threat to their way of life. Most Americans at that time were of northern and western European ancestry, and an increasing share of the new immigrants came from eastern and southern Europe, China, and Japan.

In the 1920s, widespread fear of foreigners prompted Congress to pass laws limiting immigration, especially from countries outside northern and western Europe. These laws set quotas, or numerical limits, on the number of immigrants allowed from certain countries.

This country-based quota system remained in effect until 1965. A new immigration law in that year established broader quotas of 120,000 immigrants from the Western Hemisphere, 170,000 from the Eastern Hemisphere, and 20,000 from any one nation.

Immigration policy continues to be debated and revised. The Immigration Act of 1990 raised the overall immigration quota. Laws passed in 1986 and 1996 sought to halt the tide of illegal immigration, for example by toughening the penalties for smuggling people into the country. Many Americans call for additional changes in immigration policy. Some want to reduce the immigration quotas dramatically. Others just want to make immigration laws fair.

## The Impact on You

Do you think immigration is good or bad for the United States? Make a list of its benefits and drawbacks. Write a "law" on immigration, based on your views. Specify the various elements of your law and explain how they should be enforced.

*Family of newly naturalized American citizens*

# Chapter 6 Review

## Chapter Summary

The major concepts of Chapter 6 are presented below. See also ***Guide to the Essentials of American History*** or ***Interactive Student Tutorial CD-ROM,*** which contains interactive review activities, time lines, helpful hints, and test practice.

### *Reviewing the Main Ideas*

During the Gilded Age, powerful and unregulated businesses amassed great wealth with the help of corrupt politicians. The economic boom attracted millions of immigrants to the United States. Most of them settled in cities, which led to overcrowding and other problems. Reformers worked to improve conditions in the cities.

### *Section 1: Politics in the Gilded Age*

From 1877 to 1900, national politics was dominated by issues of corruption and reform.

### *Section 2: People on the Move*

Millions of immigrants, representing many different cultures, arrived in the United States during the late 1800s and early 1900s.

### *Section 3: The Challenge of the Cities*

Millions of people moved into the cities, creating new growth and new challenges.

### *Section 4: Ideas for Reform*

A variety of groups worked to improve social, economic, and political conditions in the cities.

Since the big waves of immigration around the turn of the century, millions more immigrants have come to America, raising new controversies about immigration policy.

## Key Terms

For each of the terms below, write a sentence explaining how it relates to this chapter.

1. suburb
2. graft
3. political machine
4. Chinese Exclusion Act
5. prohibition
6. steerage
7. laissez-faire
8. tenement
9. civil service
10. nativism
11. Gilded Age
12. segregation
13. settlement house
14. ghetto
15. blue law

## Comprehension

1. How did business influence politicians during the Gilded Age?
2. What problems did the spoils system create?
3. Why did so many people want to come to the United States in the late 1800s and early 1900s?
4. Starting in the 1890s, where did large numbers of immigrants come from?
5. How did slums develop in cities?
6. What were the advantages and disadvantages of political machines for urban residents?
7. What actions did nativists take to restrict immigration?
8. How did the settlement movement seek to help the needy?

## Using Graphic Organizers

On a large sheet of paper, copy the web diagram below. Add as many connecting circles as you need, and fill them with information from the chapter.

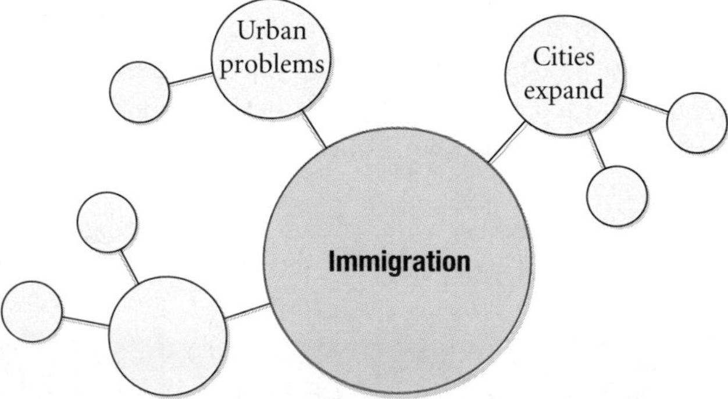

## Analyzing Political Cartoons ▶

1. This scene shows a strength contest once popular at fairs. The goal was to test one's strength in an attempt to ring the bell at the top of the column. Examine the scene. Who are the contestants?
2. Examine the game. (a) What are the contestants hitting? (b) What is the bell? (c) What is the mallet?
3. Read the caption. Describe the cartoonist's message in a brief paragraph.

*Try Your Strength, Gents!*
*The Harder You Hit It, The Higher It Goes.*

## Critical Thinking

1. *Applying the Chapter Skill* Look back at the table on the Skills for Life page. World War I was fought between 1914 and 1918. How does the table reflect the influence of the war on immigration to the United States?
2. *Drawing Inferences* What character trait did President Rutherford B. Hayes exhibit by his actions regarding the spoils system? Explain your answer.
3. *Drawing Conclusions* What conclusion can you draw from the fact that Tammany Hall dominated New York City politics for more than 50 years?
4. *Predicting Consequences* What might have been the effect if the United States had adopted all the ideas of the nativists?

### INTERNET ACTIVITY

***For your portfolio:***
**CREATE A DIARY ENTRY**

Access Prentice Hall's *America: Pathways to the Present* site at **www.Pathways.phschool.com** for the specific URL to complete the activity. Additional resources and related Web sites are also available.

Study the photographs of immigrants arriving at Ellis Island. How did people arrive? Where did they come from? What did they do at Ellis Island? Select a country of origin and create a fictional diary entry recounting an immigrant's experience at Ellis Island.

### ANALYZING DOCUMENTS ▶ INTERPRETING DATA

Turn to the map titled "Immigrant Neighborhoods in Chicago, 1900," in Section 3.

1. Which group formed the largest immigrant neighborhood in Chicago at this time? (a) Polish (b) German (c) Italian (d) Irish
2. Which group seemed to be concentrated in just one distinct neighborhood? (a) Jewish (b) Scandinavian (c) Czechoslovak (d) German
3. *Writing* Write a tour guide to the immigrant neighborhoods of Chicago. In the guide, describe the route that visitors might take to explore the main ethnic neighborhoods.

## Connecting to Today

*Essay Writing* Today, the Democratic and Republican parties both try to appeal to the large American middle class. Write an essay comparing and contrasting the major parties of today with those in the Gilded Age. Be sure to address this question: Did all levels of society have a political voice in both eras?

# CHAPTER 7 Daily Life in the Gilded Age

## 1870–1915

## CHAPTER FOCUS

*This chapter describes social and cultural changes that took place in society in the period following Reconstruction through the early 1900s. While education expanded and new forms of entertainment were invented, many people in society resisted changes, especially in the status of African Americans and women.*

*The **Why Study History?** page at the end of this chapter explores the connection between the surge in educational opportunities in the late 1800s and the role of education today.*

▲ **VIEWING HISTORY** These spectators are enjoying the thrill of race car driving at the Indianapolis Motor Speedway. ***Culture* What role did sports and entertainment play in the Gilded Age?**

| 1881 | 1895 | 1905 | 1910 |
|---|---|---|---|
| Tuskegee Institute founded | Booker T. Washington delivers Atlanta Exposition speech | W.E.B. Du Bois establishes Niagara Movement | Nearly 60 percent of American children attend school |

1870 1880 1890 1900 1910

# 1 The Expansion of Education

## SECTION PREVIEW

### Objectives

1. List reasons why public schools expanded during the late 1800s.
2. Describe the higher education opportunities that were available after the Civil War.
3. Examine the views of W.E.B. Du Bois on civil rights and education for African Americans.
4. *Key Terms* Define: literacy; assimilation; philanthropist; Niagara Movement.

### Main Idea

Education was a lofty goal that was out of reach for most nineteenth-century Americans. As the century came to a close, however, more and more Americans gained the opportunity to learn.

### Reading Strategy

*Reinforcing Main Ideas* As you read the section, make a list of examples of how educational opportunities expanded between 1870 and 1910.

Americans had long understood that a democratic society functioned best when its citizens could read and write. By the late 1800s, however, an education had become more than just a worthy goal. For a growing number of Americans, it was a necessary first step toward economic and social success. In recognition of this fact and in response to public demand, educational opportunities expanded.

## *The Growth of Public Schools*

By the time of the Civil War, more than half of the nation's white children were attending the nation's free public schools. Because most children had to help their families earn a living, however, many left school at an early age. A high school diploma was still the exception. In 1870, only 2 percent of all 17-year-olds graduated from high school. An even lower percentage of students went on to college.

The vast majority of American children attended school for only a few years and acquired only basic skills. As industries grew after the Civil War, young people came to realize that they needed more than basic skills to advance in life. Parents began pressuring local governments to increase school funding and lengthen the school year. At the same time, reformers pressured state governments to limit child labor.

By 1900, 31 states had laws that required children between the ages of 8 and 14 to attend school. Although unevenly enforced, these laws had a powerful effect. By 1910 nearly 60 percent of American children attended school, with more than a million students in high school.

**Immigrants and Education** Many immigrants placed a high value on American public education. In the mid-1890s, the Russian immigrant father of author Mary Antin was proud to send his children to a Boston public school, convinced "there was no surer way to their advancement and happiness."

One of the most important functions of the public schools was to teach literacy skills. **Literacy** is the ability to read and write. For many immigrants, learning to read and write English was an important achievement in their

## Illiteracy in the United States, 1870–1920

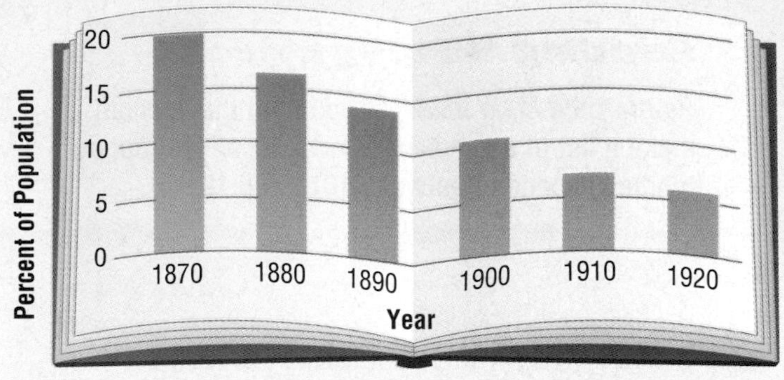


Source: *Historical Statistics of the United States, Colonial Times to 1970*

**Interpreting Graphs** The expansion of education meant more students in classrooms, such as this one in Nebraska in 1895. ***Culture*** ***How do the illiteracy figures above show the success of the push for expanding education?***

quest to succeed in the United States. Adults attended school at night to learn English and civics, which they needed to qualify for citizenship.

Beyond teaching basic literacy skills, public schools also played a role in assimilating immigrants into the American way of life. **Assimilation** is the process by which people of one culture become part of another culture. Public school teachers taught their students about American standards of thrift, patriotism, and hard work. Students also learned how to cook traditional American foods and play American games like baseball. As a result of their schooling, many immigrant children became Americanized.

Some parents resisted Americanization. Fearing that their children would forget their heritage, many parents sent their children to religious schools where they could learn their own cultural traditions in their native languages. For example, Polish parents in Chicago in the early 1900s sent their children to Roman Catholic schools. There, Polish history and religion were taught in Polish, and American history, bookkeeping, and algebra were taught in English.

Of course, the process of Americanization was not a one-way street. The contact between Americans and newer immigrants, both in public schools and in the wider society, allowed for a constant sharing of cultural traditions. As immigrants shared customs and habits from their homelands, they enriched their new country and helped to redefine American culture itself.

**Uneven Support for Schools** Though state and local government support for education was expanding, not everyone benefited equally. This is because most schools throughout the country were segregated. Compared to white schools, schools for African Americans received far less money. Writing of her upbringing in Durham, North Carolina, in the 1910s, civil rights activist Pauli Murray remembered vividly the contrast between "what we had and what the white children had." She noted:

**AMERICAN VOICES** **"We got the greasy, torn, dog-eared books; they got the new ones. They had field day in the city park; we had it on a furrowed, stubby hillside. They got wide mention in the newspaper; we got a paragraph at the bottom. . . . We came to know that whatever we had was always inferior."**

—*Pauli Murray*

Mexican Americans in parts of the Southwest and many Asians in California were also sent to separate schools that were less well funded than those for white children. In 1900, only a small percentage of Native American children were receiving any formal schooling at all.

## *Higher Education Expands*

Between 1880 and 1900, more than 250 new American colleges and universities opened to train people in the skills needed by a growing industrial economy. Wealthy Americans often endowed, or gave money or property to, institutions of higher learning. For example, in 1885 Leland Stanford, the entrepreneur who had helped build the transcontinental railroad, and his wife, Jane Lathrop Stanford, founded Stanford University in memory of their son. John D. Rockefeller made donations to the University of Chicago that eventually totaled $40 million.

With the opening of these new schools, college enrollment more than doubled between 1890 and 1910. Even with this growth in enrollment, however, only a small percentage of Americans went to college. In the 1890s annual family incomes averaged under a thousand dollars and parents were hard-pressed to meet college costs. A few less fortunate but gifted students won scholarships or worked their way through college.

By 1915 some middle-income families began to aspire to and attain college educations for their children. The availability of advanced education would distinguish the United States from other industrialized countries.

**Women and Higher Education** After the Civil War, some women called for greater educational opportunities. In response, educators and **philanthropists,** people who give donations to worthy causes, established private women's colleges with high academic standards. The first was New York's Vassar College, which opened in 1865.

Pressure also increased on men's colleges in the 1880s and 1890s to admit women. Rather than do so, some schools founded separate institutions for women that were related to the men's schools. Tulane University in Louisiana became the only major southern university to take this step when it established Sophie Newcomb College in 1886. Shortly thereafter, Columbia in New York opened Barnard (1889), Brown in Rhode Island started Pembroke (1891), and Harvard University in Massachusetts established Radcliffe (1879).

Opportunities for men and women to study together—coeducation—also increased. A number of religiously based colleges, including Oberlin, Knox, Antioch, Swarthmore, and Bates, had been coeducational since long before the Civil War. In the postwar years, they were joined by institutions such as Cornell. Boston University announced in 1873 that it welcomed women not only as students but also as professors.

Because most scholarships went to men, women had a harder time obtaining a college education. Even those who could afford the cost faced prejudice against educating women.

**Main Idea CONNECTIONS**

*What factors led to the expansion of higher education?*

The women in this 1880 Smith College chemistry class were among the first to benefit from new higher education opportunities. ***Culture*** *What obstacles did women face in seeking higher education?*

## Bachelor's Degrees Conferred, 1870–1920

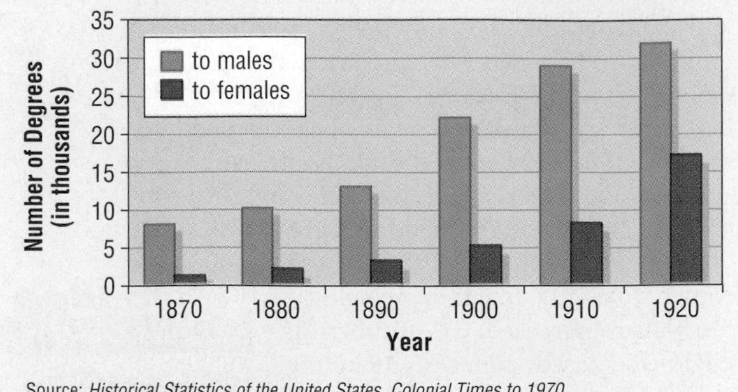


Source: *Historical Statistics of the United States, Colonial Times to 1970*

**Interpreting Graphs** The number of women earning bachelor's degrees rose dramatically between 1870 and 1920. Even by 1920, however, nearly twice as many degrees were earned by male students. ***Culture*** *In what ways was the call for women's access to higher education answered?*

Parents feared that college made daughters too independent or "unmarriageable" or brought them in contact with unacceptable friends. When Martha "Minnie" Carey Thomas finally persuaded her Quaker father to allow her to take the Cornell University entrance exams, he said to her, "Well, Minnie, I am proud of thee, but this university is an awful place to swallow thee up."

Women had to struggle to gain access to most state-funded institutions. For example, in 1863 the coeducational University of Wisconsin required women to stand until all male students had found seats. After 1867 Wisconsin directed women into a "Female College." In 1873, however, when women refused to attend segregated classes, the university was forced to reestablish coeducation.

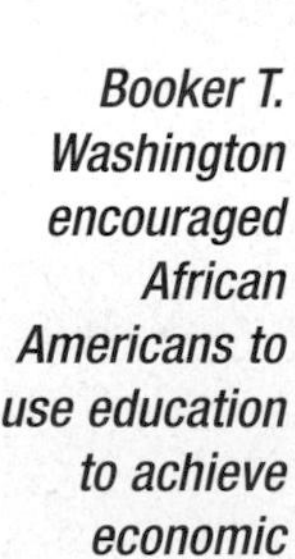

*Booker T. Washington encouraged African Americans to use education to achieve economic success.*

### African Americans and Higher Education

African Americans also had to fight prejudice in institutions of higher learning. A few colleges, such as Oberlin, Bates, and Bowdoin, did accept blacks. Most did not. In 1890 only 160 African Americans were attending white colleges.

Many more were studying at the nation's African American institutions. Several predominantly black colleges, including Atlanta, Fisk, Hampton Institute, and Howard, were founded through the efforts of the American Missionary Association. Wilberforce University, incorporated in 1856 in Ohio, is the nation's oldest private African American school. By 1900, more than 2,000 students had graduated from 34 African American colleges.

Schools founded for African Americans after the Civil War generally accepted both women and men. The number of women attending remained small, however, because most of the scholarships went to men. Anna Julia Cooper, an Oberlin graduate who later became an educator, estimated that there were only 30 black women studying in college in the United States in 1891.

**Booker T. Washington** Among the black college graduates was Booker T. Washington. Born into slavery in 1856, Washington began his studies at Hampton Institute in Virginia in 1872. His education there inspired him to spend his life promoting the growth of a similar institution, Tuskegee Institute, which he founded in Alabama in 1881.

Washington taught his students the skills and attitudes that he thought would help them succeed in society. Washington told his students to temporarily put aside their desire for political equality and instead to focus on building economic security by gaining vocational skills. He urged them to prepare for productive, profitable work and to bring their intellect "to bear upon the everyday practical things of life, upon something that is needed to be done, and something which they will be permitted to do in the community in which they reside." African Americans could win white acceptance eventually, he predicted, by succeeding economically.

Washington spelled out his ideas in a speech he delivered in 1895 at the Atlanta Exposition:

**AMERICAN VOICES**

**"To those of my race who depend on bettering their condition . . . I would say: 'Cast down your bucket where you are'—cast it down . . . in agriculture, mechanics, in commerce, in domestic service, and in the professions. . . . No race can prosper till it learns that there is as much dignity in tilling a field as in writing a poem. . . . In all things that are purely social we can be as separate as the fingers, yet one as the hand in all things essential to mutual progress."**

*—Booker T. Washington*

In addition to appealing to many African Americans, Washington's ideas relieved those whites who worried that educated African Americans would seek more equality within society. Whites began to consult him on all issues concerning race relations. President Theodore Roosevelt invited Washington to the White House in 1901. Washington's autobiography, *Up From Slavery* (1901), became a classic, and he became a dominant force in the African American community.

## *W.E.B. Du Bois*

**AMERICAN BIOGRAPHY** W.E.B. Du Bois led the next generation of African Americans in a different direction. Born in Massachusetts, Du Bois graduated from Tennessee's Fisk University and then in 1895 became the first African American to earn a Ph.D. from Harvard. Du Bois taught economics, history, and sociology at Atlanta University and in 1905 helped found the **Niagara Movement.** This was a group of African Americans that called for full civil liberties, an end to racial discrimination, and recognition of human brotherhood.

Du Bois rejected Washington's message, which he mockingly called the Atlanta Compromise. Instead, Du Bois argued that the brightest African Americans had to step forward to lead their people in their quest for political and social equality and civil rights. He urged those future leaders to seek an advanced liberal arts education rather than a vocational education as Washington promoted. Only when they had developed "intelligence, broad sympathy, knowledge of the world that was and is, and of the relation of men to it," he wrote, would they be equipped to lead "the Negro race."

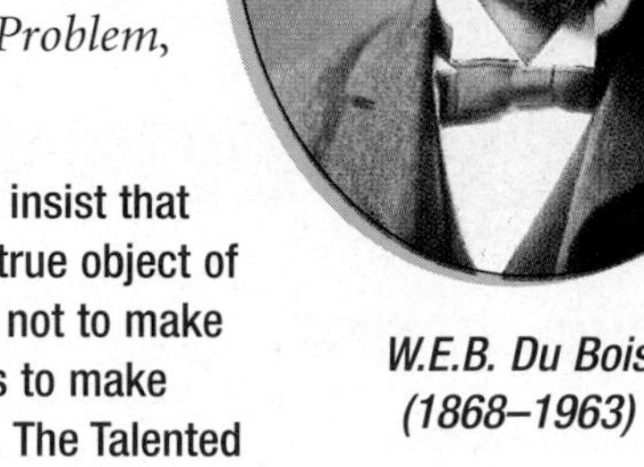

*W.E.B. Du Bois (1868–1963)*

In a collection of articles published in 1903 called *The Negro Problem*, Du Bois wrote:

**AMERICAN VOICES** "I insist that the true object of all true education is not to make men carpenters, it is to make carpenters men. . . . The Talented Tenth of the Negro race must be made leaders of thought and missionaries of culture among their people. No others can do this work and Negro colleges must train men for it."

— *W.E.B. Du Bois*

In writings such as *The Souls of Black Folk*, Du Bois urged blacks not to define themselves as whites saw them. Instead, he insisted that they take pride in both their African and their American heritages.

In 1910 Du Bois left his teaching post at Atlanta University to work as publications director at the National Association for the Advancement of Colored People (Section 3). He would remain associated with the NAACP for many years, becoming perhaps the best-known black leader of the first half of the twentieth century. ■

## SECTION 1 REVIEW

### Comprehension

1. *Key Terms* (a) literacy; (b) assimilation; (c) philanthropist; (d) Niagara Movement.
2. *Summarizing the Main Idea* Give examples of how educational opportunities expanded between 1870 and 1910.
3. *Organizing Information* Make a list of reasons why public schools expanded during the late 1800s.

### Critical Thinking

4. *Analyzing Time Lines* How did Washington's ideas, as portrayed in his speech at Atlanta, differ from the ideas of Du Bois and the members of the Niagara Movement?
5. *Drawing Inferences* Why do you think education was so important to many immigrants?

### Writing Activity

6. *Writing an Expository Essay* Write an essay outlining the higher education opportunities that were available after the Civil War.

| 1884 | 1891 | 1899 | 1903 |
|---|---|---|---|
| *Mark Twain publishes* The Adventures of Huckleberry Finn | *Basketball invented* | *Scott Joplin composes "Maple Leaf Rag"* | The Great Train Robbery *released* |

1884 — 1894 — 1904

# 2 New Forms of Entertainment

## SECTION PREVIEW

### Objectives

1. Describe the popular amusements that emerged in the late 1800s.
2. Summarize the influence of African American musical styles on mass culture.
3. *Key Terms* Define: vaudeville; yellow journalism; ragtime.

### Main Idea

New forms of entertainment and sports emerged during the late 1800s.

### Reading Strategy

*Formulating Questions* Before you read, write a question about each heading in the section. As you read, look for answers to these questions.

*Basketball and other sports were popular forms of recreation at the turn of the century.*

In rural America, time spent in play was considered time wasted. Only after the harvest was in or during special celebrations would rural people allow themselves to enjoy leisure activities at family and community gatherings. These activities tended to be free, with people providing their own food and music.

In contrast, factory laborers worked by the clock. After long hours on the job, they wanted fun things to do. A commercial recreation industry emerged to meet the need for inexpensive entertainment for all Americans.

## *Popular Amusements in the Late 1800s*

Of all the places where working people gathered in the late 1800s, saloons were the most popular. Denver (population 133,859) had nearly 500 saloons by 1900; New York City (population 3,437,202) had an estimated 10,000. Besides providing entertainment, saloons served as places for forging neighborhood and ethnic ties and political alliances. Most saloon customers were men. Women preferred to attend dance halls and cabarets, where they could watch musical shows and dance the latest dances.

Trolley parks—amusement parks built at the ends of trolley lines—were popular with the whole family. Moving pictures also appeared during this era. *The Great Train Robbery*, released in 1903, was a huge success and demonstrated very clearly the profits that could be made from movies. By 1908 the nation had 8,000 nickelodeons, theaters set up in converted stores or warehouses that charged a nickel admission. They showed slapstick comedies and other films to as many as 200,000 people daily.

**Vaudeville** Live theatrical performances also attracted large crowds in this era. **Vaudeville,** a type of inexpensive variety show that first appeared in the 1870s, was the most popular. Vaudeville performances consisted of comic sketches based on ethnic or racial humor, song-and-dance routines, ventriloquists, jugglers, and trapeze artists.

Vaudeville was strictly for the family. Theater owners insisted on keeping everything on a "high plane of respectability and moral cleanliness." A "Notice to Performers" posted on the backstage wall of a prominent vaudeville house in 1899 warned:

**AMERICAN VOICES** **"Such words as Liar, Slob, Son-of-a-Gun, Devil . . . and all other words unfit for the ears of ladies and children, also any reference to questionable streets, resorts, localities, and bar-rooms, are prohibited under fine of instant discharge."**

—*"Notice to Performers"*

Baseball was a well-established spectator sport by 1886, when the picture of this team was taken. ***Geography*** *Why was commercial recreation largely an urban phenomenon?*

**Sports** As leisure time expanded in the late 1800s, sporting events also became a favorite pastime. Boxing and horse racing were widely enjoyed spectator sports, but baseball was by far the most popular.

By 1860, groups such as firefighters, police officers, and teachers had formed baseball clubs in many American cities. When audiences for these games grew, entrepreneurs enclosed fields and charged admission. Teams formed into leagues and began to play championship games. In 1869 the nation's first true professional team, the Cincinnati Red Stockings, was formed. By the 1870s the sport's best players were paid. The most popular leagues included Native American and white immigrant players. African Americans were included only for a short time. After their exclusion, even the best African Americans had to play in segregated leagues until the late 1940s.

What Americans loved most about baseball was the speed, daring, and split-second timing of the game. Pitcher Christy Mathewson commented, "The American public wants its excitement rolled up in a package and handed out quickly." Baseball fulfilled that desire.

Two other games also took hold of the American public during the late 1800s. Football emerged as a popular American game when Walter Camp began adapting the European game of rugby during the 1880s. Basketball, the only major sport of exclusively American origin, was invented in 1891. A physical education instructor, Dr. James Naismith of Springfield, Massachusetts, invented the game to keep athletes fit during winter.

Women, too, took up sports. Ice-skating had long been a favorite recreation of women. The national bicycling fad of the late 1800s also became popular among women. Bicycling required practical clothing, and so brought about changes in women's clothing styles. "For muscle-play, freedom is the first requisite," a doctor advised in an 1896 article entitled "Bicycling for Women: The Puzzling Question of Costume." Women athletes abandoned corsets, which wrapped tightly around their torsos and restricted breathing. Women's involvement in sports also led to the popularity and acceptance of shirtwaists (ready-made blouses) that were tucked into shorter or split skirts.

**Main Idea CONNECTIONS**

*What impact did the emergence of sports have on women?*

Women students also played basketball. Assuming that stiff competition and hard physical exertion were unhealthy for women, recreation specialists devised less demanding rules for them. Women athletes also learned gymnastics and swam, although society's strict dress codes required them to wear black cotton stockings under short dresses or bloomers.

**Newspapers** For city residents, newspapers always had been a vital source of information. In the late 1800s, they became a popular form of entertainment as well. Taking advantage of new typesetting machinery that allowed printers to set whole lines of type quickly, publishers created larger and more interesting

Newspapers such as the *Chicago Daily News* offered readers both information and entertainment. Magazines also expanded in this era, assisted by lowered postal rates. ***Culture*** *What is "yellow journalism"?*

publications. They introduced new features, such as comics, sports sections, Sunday editions, women's pages, stories "hot off the wires," and graphic pictures.

Between 1870 and 1900, newspaper circulation soared from 2.6 to 15.1 million copies a day. Competing heatedly with one another, publishers urged reporters to discover fresh news sources and lurid details of murders, vice, and scandal—anything to sell more papers. Such "sensational" news coverage came to be called **yellow journalism,** a reference to the yellow ink used in a popular comic strip of the era.

Several publishers became national figures. Hungarian-born Joseph Pulitzer, who owned the *St. Louis Post-Dispatch* and in 1883 bought the *New York World,* hoped to "expose all fraud and sham, fight all public evils and abuses." Californian William Randolph Hearst used his father's gold-mining millions to put out the even more sensational *New York Journal.*

Yellow journalism troubled many people. Critics charged that the "yellow press" intruded into private lives, invented facts, and sensationalized the ordinary with exaggeration.

**Magazines and Popular Fiction** It was also during the late 1800s that magazines came into wide circulation. This increase in circulation resulted in part from a law passed by Congress in 1879 lowering the postal rates for periodicals. Some of the popular magazines included *McClure's, Cosmopolitan,* and *Munsey's.*

Many of the stories that appeared weekly or monthly in popular magazines were written to appeal to the dreams and aspirations of American readers. The main character in Horatio Alger's *Ragged Dick,* which appeared in magazines in 1867 and the following year as a book, embodied the American dream of rising from "rags to riches" through cheerfulness, honesty, and hard work. *Ragged Dick* and other stories reminded the working poor of the seemingly boundless opportunities available to them in the nation's industrial cities.

Other writers, including Samuel Langhorne Clemens (whose pen name was Mark Twain), chose to write about the more corrupt side of industrialization and Gilded Age politics. Twain's novel *The Gilded Age,* written with his neighbor Charles Dudley Warner, began a trend that continued into the twentieth century of using the novel as a vehicle for social protest.

In addition to political writings, Twain is known for his classic American tales of youthful adventure and life along the Mississippi River. These include *The Adventures of Tom Sawyer* (1876), and *The Adventures of Huckleberry Finn* (1884). Twain's descriptions of the Mississippi and his humor captivated his audiences' hunger for information about distant parts of the country.

Like Twain, popular writers during the late 1800s were admired for their ability to describe the people and places of specific regions of the United States with great color and detail. While Sarah Orne Jewett wrote about the people of Maine and many of New England's disappearing traditions, Bret Harte described the excitement of the California Gold Rush. Other "local color" writers included George Washington Cable, Joel Harris, and Kate Chopin in the South, Edward Eggleston in Indiana, and O. Henry, who wrote about both Texas and New York City.

## African American Influence

As the entertainment culture expanded, it absorbed many forms of African American art.

In the process, the culture also transformed African American culture in order to meet the tastes of white audiences.

**The Negro Spiritual** In 1871 nine Fisk University students went on a singing tour to raise money for their struggling school. When the Fisk Jubilee Singers began to concentrate solely on spirituals, or African American religious folk songs, they excited such interest that triumphal tours of the United States, England, and Europe resulted. Britain's Queen Victoria was so impressed that she had a group portrait of them painted.

In the process of making the spiritual acceptable to white audiences, the Fisk group and others like it transformed the musical form. It acquired characteristics of the European musical tradition with which whites were familiar. This new spiritual became identified as an American art form, as opposed to a purely African American one.

**Minstrel Shows** Other forms of African American culture were also absorbed into the white entertainment world. The minstrel show began when white actors discovered they could captivate audiences with exaggerated imitations of African American music, dance, and humor. The shows perpetuated racist stereotypes, generally portraying African Americans as foolish imitators of a white culture they could not understand.

White actors in minstrel shows performed in "blackface"—that is, they blackened their faces and hands and painted on wide grins. African Americans also performed in minstrel shows, as minstrel jobs were often the only stage work they could get.

**Ragtime and Jazz** A type of music known as **ragtime** originated among black musicians playing in saloons in the South and Midwest in the 1880s. Consisting of melodies with shifting accents over a steady, marching-band beat, it became a rage in the 1890s. Ragtime composer Scott Joplin, who came from St. Louis, Missouri, became famous for his "Maple Leaf Rag" composed in 1899.

*The music of ragtime composer Scott Joplin remains popular today.*

Jazz grew out of the vibrant musical culture of New Orleans, a city with a popular marching-band tradition. After the Civil War, African American bands experimented with new styles of playing, including "raggy" rhythms and call-and-response forms in which singers or instruments respond to a single leader. They also played jazzed-up versions of familiar melodies, such as hymns or the mournful "blues" songs of southern sharecroppers.

New Orleans jazz styles from the 1890s slowly worked their way northward through towns along the Mississippi River. By 1915, thanks in part to the success of the phonograph, jazz and the dances associated with it were becoming a national passion.

## SECTION 2 REVIEW

### Comprehension

1. *Key Terms* (a) vaudeville; (b) yellow journalism; (c) ragtime.
2. *Summarizing the Main Idea* Describe some of the new forms of entertainment that emerged in the late 1800s.
3. *Organizing Information* Make a chart describing the three forms of African American music that were absorbed into the mass culture in the late 1800s.

### Critical Thinking

4. *Analyzing Time Lines* Review the time line at the start of the section. What categories of popular entertainment are included?
5. *Drawing Inferences* What role do you think compulsory education played in bringing about a larger market for newspapers, magazines, and novels?

### Writing Activity

6. *Writing an Expository Essay* Write an essay explaining how the growth of cities helped make possible the growth of entertainment and recreation.

## Early Baseball

Many songs, such as the polka tune shown on this sheet music cover, celebrated the heroes of baseball. Fans of Georgetown University's baseball team dyed the ball (in the mitt) dark blue and painted in the score to honor their team's victory over Yale in 1899.

1

## Football at the Turn of the Century

This football card shows that players wore much less protection than modern players. The only protection came from padded pants (also worn by some basketball players of the time), which protected players from bruises.

## Women Cyclists

5

By the 1890s women had joined the bicycle craze and entered into this active, public sport. On this 1870 bicycle, the pedals connect directly to the front wheels at the axle. The introduction of a chain and foot brakes in the 1890s made pedaling much easier and gave the cyclist more control.

## Ice Skating

A common winter sport before the 1800s, ice skating became a "mania" in the 1860s.

## 4 Skiing

Skiing began in Norway in the mid-1800s when the addition of bindings made it possible for skiers to turn and jump. Norwegian immigrants then brought the sport to Minnesota, from where it spread to other snowy areas in the United States.

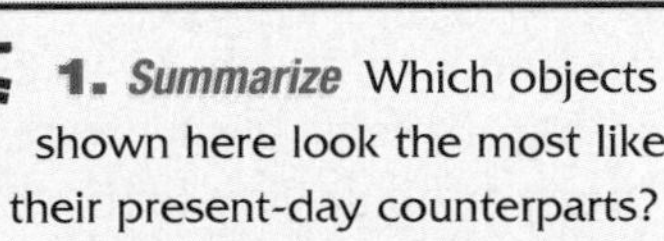

**VIEWING HISTORY**

1. ***Summarize*** Which objects shown here look the most like their present-day counterparts?

2. ***Connecting to Today*** Think about the role of sports today. Then write an editorial on one of the following topics: (a) how participating in sports can benefit people; (b) whether professional athletes should be seen as role models; (c) whether girls and women currently have enough opportunities to participate in sports.

# THE GROWTH OF SPORTS

Fun for fun's sake was the new way of thinking at the turn of the twentieth century. The great rise in sports reflected the changes sweeping across America. The nation's growing wealth and workers' demands allowed for more leisure time than ever before. Also, while Americans had earlier shunned activities that did not create wealth or improve character, it was now morally acceptable to pursue interests for simple enjoyment.

Sporting became a form of recreation as well as entertainment. Baseball and skating became widely popular. The game of American football grew out of rugby and soccer. Collegians developed a new set of rules, such as the system of downs and the position of quarterback. Baseball achieved its status as the great American pastime in the last third of the 1800s. In 1903 the first World Series was played. *See* 1 *and* 2.

Sports provided year-round entertainment, even in colder parts of the country. Ice skating grew in popularity with the introduction of low-priced, store-bought skates. Skiing came to the United States from Scandinavia, and in later decades would become widely popular with the creation of the ski tow. *See* 3 *and* 4.

Sports engaged women as well as men. Before the late 1800s, outdoor sports activities for women were limited. But women's steady struggle for legal and political rights advanced their freedom. For example, in the bicycling fad of the late 1800s, many women no longer wore restrictive clothing. The athletic demands of riding a bicycle required more practical apparel. This angered many people, but neither an opinion nor a peculiar piece of clothing would stop the enthusiasts. *See* 5.

American men and women would continue to ride, play, and swim their way through the twentieth century. Sports were here to stay. They had become a necessary part of life, one that contributed to health and quality of life.

**1883** Supreme Court overturns Civil Rights Act of 1875

**1896** Plessy v. Ferguson

**1908** Race riots in Springfield, Illinois

**1909** NAACP founded

1880 | 1890 | 1900 | 1910

# 3 The World of Jim Crow

**SECTION PREVIEW**

### Objectives

1 List the means by which African Americans were discriminated against after Reconstruction.
2 Describe how African Americans responded to discrimination.
3 *Key Terms* Define: poll tax; grandfather clause; Jim Crow; *Plessy* v. *Ferguson;* lynching; National Association for the Advancement of Colored People (NAACP).

### Main Idea

African Americans found their hopes dashed in the years after Reconstruction. Yet many not only resisted discrimination, but achieved success in spite of the obstacles placed before them.

### Reading Strategy

*Organizing Information* As you read this section, make a list of the methods white society used to prevent African Americans from achieving equality.

Within a few years after the end of Reconstruction in the 1870s, African Americans began to see many of their newly won freedoms disappear. In the South, black Americans were prevented from voting and were subjected to segregation laws and random violence. Discrimination was also widespread in the North.

## Post-Reconstruction Discrimination

*African American voters faced intimidation at the polls.*

Booker T. Washington's belief that white Americans would accept hard-working African Americans into equal citizenship was proving too optimistic. Some southern whites, who in the past had used slavery to repress African Americans, now turned to other vicious methods of oppression.

**Voting Restrictions** In many southern communities, whites were concerned that African Americans would gain too much political power by exercising their right to vote. As a result, southern states used several tactics during the 1890s to deny the vote to blacks. Some southern states began to require voters to own property and to pay a **poll tax,** or special fee, before they could vote. Both of these requirements were beyond the financial reach of most African Americans. Voters also had to demonstrate minimum standards of knowledge by passing literacy tests. These tests were specifically designed to keep African Americans from voting. In fact, blacks were often given much more difficult tests than whites.

To ensure that the literacy tests did not keep too many whites from voting, some states passed special laws. These laws exempted men from certain voting restrictions if they themselves had voted, or had ancestors who had voted, prior to black suffrage. African Americans, therefore, were not exempted from the literacy tests. Such laws are examples of **grandfather clauses.** A grandfather clause is a passage in a piece of legislation that exempts a group of people from obeying a law provided they met certain conditions before that law was passed.

**Segregation** During this period many states also instituted a system of legal segregation that further degraded African Americans. This system was called **Jim Crow,** after a minstrel song-and-dance routine.

Although Jim Crow laws usually are associated with the South, they first appeared in the 1830s, when Massachusetts allowed railroad companies to separate black and white passengers. It was in the South, however, that Jim Crow became firmly established. Jim Crow laws began to appear in the South a few years after the end of Reconstruction and were solidly in place by 1900.

Jim Crow dominated almost every aspect of daily life by the early 1900s. The laws required the separation of blacks and whites in schools, parks, public buildings, hospitals, and on transportation systems. African Americans and whites could not use the same water fountains or public toilets. They could not sit in the same sections of theaters. Facilities designated for blacks were almost always inferior.

***Plessy* v. *Ferguson*** With its rulings, the Supreme Court upheld many of the Jim Crow laws. In 1883 the Court overturned the Civil Rights Act of 1875, which had guaranteed African American rights in public places. According to the Supreme Court, the Fourteenth Amendment could not prevent private organizations from discriminating against individuals.

Perhaps the greatest setback to African American equality came with the Court's establishment of the "separate-but-equal" doctrine with the case of ***Plessy* v. *Ferguson*** in 1896. In this case, African American Homer Plessy argued that his right to "equal protection of the laws" was violated by a Louisiana law that required separate seating for white and black citizens on public railroads. In its decision, the Court held that segregation was legal as long as the separate facilities provided for blacks were equal to those provided to whites. The Fourteenth Amendment, the Court stated, was "not intended to give Negroes social equality but only political and civil equality."† The ruling in *Plessy* proved hard to enforce, and African American schools and other facilities in the South were rarely if ever made equal.

FACT *Finder*

## Adoption of Voting Restrictions in the South, 1889–1908

| *Year* | *Poll Tax* | *Literacy Test* | *Property Test* | *Grand-father Clause* | *Other** |
|---|---|---|---|---|---|
| 1889 | FL | | | | TN, FL |
| 1890 | MS, TN | MS | | | MS |
| 1891 | | | | | AR |
| 1892 | AR | | | | |
| 1893 | | | | | AL |
| 1894 | | | | | SC, VA |
| 1895 | SC | SC | | | SC |
| 1896 | | | | | |
| 1897 | | | | | LA |
| 1898 | LA | LA | LA | LA | |
| 1899 | | | | | NC |
| 1900 | NC | NC | NC | NC | |
| 1901 | AL | AL | AL | AL | |
| 1902 | VA, TX | VA | VA | | VA |
| 1903 | | | | | TX |
| 1904 | | | | | |
| 1905 | | | | | |
| 1906 | | | | | |
| 1907 | | | | | |
| 1908 | | GA | GA | GA | GA |

*Registration, multiple-box, secret ballot, understanding clause
Source: *The American Record: Images of the Nation's Past*, Volume Two, edited by William Graebner and Leonard Richards

**Interpreting Tables** As shown above, southern states began to adopt discriminatory voting laws in the late 1800s. Though the laws varied in their techniques, the effect was always the same—African Americans were denied the vote. ***Government*** ***Which states had the widest variety of voting restrictions?***

**Violence** The worst feature of the post-Reconstruction decline in conditions for African Americans was **lynching.** The term refers to a mob's illegal seizure and execution of a person. Between 1882 and 1892, an estimated 1,200 black people were lynched. Sometimes the victims were suspected criminals. Often

† Segregated public facilities were permitted until *Plessy* was overturned by the *Brown* v. *Board of Education* case in 1954, which stated that separate facilities were inherently unequal.

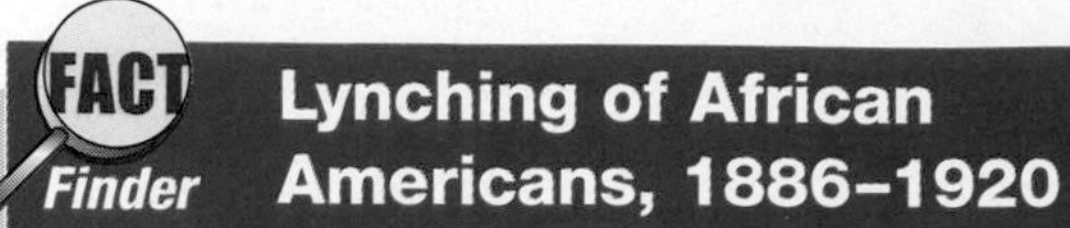


**Lynching of African Americans, 1886–1920**

| Years | Number of Persons Lynched |
|---|---|
| 1886–1890 | 392 |
| 1891–1895 | 639 |
| 1896–1900 | 493 |
| 1901–1905 | 407 |
| 1906–1910 | 345 |
| 1911–1915 | 279 |
| 1916–1920 | 275 |

Source: *Historical Statistics of the United States, Colonial Times to 1970*

**Interpreting Tables** Violence against African Americans was an alarmingly frequent phenomenon in the late 1800s. In spite of vocal protests, mobs had killed more than 3,000 African Americans by the 1920s. ***Government*** *Why do you think lynch mobs were rarely pursued or caught?*

they were merely individuals who were unlucky enough to be in the wrong place at the wrong time. The seizure sometimes included a mock trial, torture, and even mutilation, before the victim was hanged and riddled with bullets. Those who carried out these horrors were rarely pursued or caught, much less punished. Although most lynchings took place in the South, African Americans in the North were sometimes lynched as well.

**Main Idea CONNECTIONS**

*How did some African Americans respond to legal segregation in the South?*

**Conditions in the North Decline** Many African Americans, though realizing that life in the North was far from perfect, moved there in part to escape legal segregation. What they found instead was de facto discrimination, or discrimination "in fact" instead of by law. Northern schools, housing, and employment were effectively segregated.

As many African Americans moved north, they began to compete with white Americans and recent immigrants for work in the industrial cities. Whites' fears of racial equality erupted in the form of race riots in 1900 in New York City and in 1908 in Springfield, Illinois. The Springfield riot was touched off when authorities refused to release a black prisoner charged with rape to a crowd of white citizens. After learning that the prisoner had been secretly transferred to another city, a mob of several thousand white citizens attacked, looted, and burned black businesses and homes and killed two elderly African Americans. The Illinois state militia gained control of the mob only after two days.

## *African Americans Resist Discrimination*

As conditions for African Americans deteriorated, black leaders began to seek new approaches to race problems. For example, Bishop Henry M. Turner of the African Methodist Episcopal church advocated black pride and emigration to Africa. Others criticized Booker T. Washington for his silence on such issues as lynching. Such attacks ignored Washington's quiet support for legal cases against segregation and his financial support for civil rights and black businesses.

As you read in Section 1, a number of outspoken African Americans came together under the leadership of W.E.B. Du Bois in 1905 to denounce all discrimination. Meeting in Niagara Falls, Ontario, Canada, they vowed never to accept "inferiority," bow to "oppression," or apologize "before insult." "We do not hesitate to complain, and to complain loudly and insistently," they warned.

The Niagara Movement, as this group came to be called, gained only about 400 members and won few victories. After the 1908 Springfield race riot, however, its members joined with concerned white citizens to discuss solutions to the conflict between the races.

**The NAACP** Mary White Ovington, a white social worker who had worked in black neighborhoods, was among the concerned individuals. She helped organize a national conference on the "Negro Question" to be held on Lincoln's birthday in 1909. Niagara Movement leaders attended. This event marked the founding of the **National Association for the Advancement of Colored People (NAACP).**

By 1914 the NAACP had 50 branches and 6,000 members. Its magazine, *Crisis*, edited by Du Bois, reached more than 30,000 readers. The organization worked primarily through the courts. It won its first major victory when the Supreme Court declared grandfather clauses in voting restriction laws unconstitutional in 1915. In the decades ahead, the NAACP would remain a vital force in the fight for civil rights.

**African American Achievement** African American mutual aid and benefit societies also multiplied in this period. Social workers and church groups founded settlement houses in black neighborhoods. The Young Men's and Young Women's Christian Associations developed separate recreational and guidance programs for African American youth. The National Urban League, founded in 1911, improved job opportunities and housing for blacks.

Also during this period, African American intellectuals began to publish literature, history, and groundbreaking sociological studies. Black-owned businesses appeared everywhere. To help them, Booker T. Washington founded the National Negro Business League in 1900. By 1907 it had 320 branches.

In 1912 Madam C. J. Walker spoke at the annual meeting of the Negro Business League. She was a notable example of African American achievement at the turn of the century. Born Sarah Breedlove, Walker came from a family of ex-slaves and sharecroppers. Her first seven years were spent on a Louisiana cotton plantation. Then, after the death of her parents, she moved to Vicksburg, Mississippi, to work as a servant. She later moved to St. Louis, where she worked for 17 years laundering clothes.

"I got myself a start by giving myself a start," Walker would later say. She did so by developing her own preparations to style the hair of African American women. Walker moved to Denver, Colorado, in 1905, where she married C. J. Walker, a newspaper sales agent. There she set up a prosperous mail-order business for her hair products. She also established a chain of beauty parlors and training schools. By 1916 her company claimed 20,000 employees.

Her business was a great success and Walker moved to Harlem, in New York City, an area that had begun to attract African American residents. Her Harlem town house and later her estate in Irvington-on-Hudson, New York, became gathering places for the country's African American leaders. Walker supported black welfare, education, and civil rights work with large contributions. She also made many speeches for the antilynching drives of the NAACP and for African American women's organizations. "The girls and women of our race must not be afraid to take hold of business endeavor," she said in her 1913 speech to the Negro Business League. "I want to say to every Negro woman present, don't sit down and wait for the opportunities to come. . . . Get up and make them!"

*George Washington Carver rose from slavery to become an important agricultural scientist. He is most famous for his work on peanuts.*

## SECTION 3 REVIEW

### Comprehension

1. *Key Terms* Define: (a) poll tax; (b) grandfather clause; (c) Jim Crow; (d) *Plessy* v. *Ferguson;* (e) lynching; (f) National Association for the Advancement of Colored People (NAACP).
2. *Summarizing the Main Idea* List some of the methods that white society used to discriminate against African Americans after Reconstruction.
3. *Organizing Information* Make a graphic organizer showing the actions African Americans took in response to discrimination.

### Critical Thinking

4. *Analyzing Time Lines* Review the time line at the start of the section. Which two events on the time line represent actions taken by African Americans to combat discrimination?
5. *Expressing Problems Clearly* How did the Supreme Court's decision in *Plessy* v. *Ferguson* contribute to the denial of African American rights?

### Writing Activity

6. *Writing an Expository Essay* Write an expository essay outlining three methods used by white society to restrict black voting rights.

# SKILLS FOR LIFE

**Historical Evidence**

**Critical Thinking**

**Graph & Chart**

**Geography**

# Reading a Political Cartoon

Political cartoons can tell you a great deal about the past. For many years, cartoonists have tried to influence public feeling about important issues. To do so, they use visual images to exaggerate or highlight certain details about the facts. This is one reason why cartoons often can make a point more strongly than words alone can.

Study the cartoon below, published in 1892. Ask yourself what point about Jim Crow laws the cartoonist was trying to make. Then answer the following questions.

**1.** ***Identify the symbols used in the cartoon.*** Cartoons often use symbols, visual images that stand for some other idea or event. For example, a skull and crossbones is a commonly used symbol for death. A dove is a symbol for peace. To understand a cartoon, you must be able to identify the symbols it uses.

Decide what the symbols in this cartoon are. (a) What is the figure on the left holding in his right hand? What are the men on the right holding? (b) What is the building at the right meant to be? (c) Based on these symbols, what groups do these people represent?

**2.** ***Analyze the meaning of the symbols.*** Use your reading of this chapter and the cartoon to decide what the symbols refer to. (a) What do the signs on the building say? (b) What practice is being referred to in this cartoon?

**3.** ***Interpret the cartoon.*** Draw conclusions about the cartoonist's point of view. (a) What do you think the cartoonist thought of Jim Crow laws? Give evidence to support your answer. (b) How is the cartoonist trying to influence the public's attitude toward the practice? (c) How does the cartoonist portray the white figures? Is this a sympathetic portrayal?

**TEST FOR SUCCESS**

Locate a political cartoon in a newspaper or news magazine. Use the steps on this page to identify and analyze any symbols used in the cartoon and to interpret and identify the central issue of the cartoon.

THE POLITICAL PINKERTONS

**1873** *Association for the Advancement of Women is founded*

**1874** *Woman's Christian Temperance Union is formed*

**1890** *General Federation of Women's Clubs and the National American Woman Suffrage Association are formed*

**1896** *Rural free delivery begins*

1870 | 1880 | 1890 | 1900 | 1910

# 4 Women in the Late 1800s

## SECTION PREVIEW

### Objectives

1. Describe the debate over women's equality in the late 1800s.
2. List ways in which women's work in the home changed in the late 1800s.
3. Describe women's work outside the home during the late 1800s.
4. *Key Terms* Define: department store; rural free delivery; mail-order catalog.

### Main Idea

Changes in women's lives, including new jobs, new educational opportunities, and new roles in the home, fueled a debate on the proper role of women in society at the turn of the century.

### Reading Strategy

*Reinforcing Main Ideas* As you read this section, look for evidence to support the following statement: "Although much had changed in women's lives by the turn of the century, much had stayed the same."

"Women hain't no business a votin'," pronounced Josiah Allen, a fictional creation of the popular turn-of-the-century humorist Marietta Holley. "They had better let the laws alone, and tend to their housework. The law loves wimmin and protects 'em." Replied his wife, Samantha, "If the law loves wimmin so well, why don't he give her as much wages as men get for doin' the same work?"

## *The Debate over Women's Equality*

Most Americans around 1900 would have known exactly what Samantha and Josiah were arguing about. They would have called it *the woman question,* a wide-ranging debate about the social role of women that grew out of several major developments of the era.

For women like Samantha Allen, the woman question boiled down to a few key demands: Women should be able to vote. They should be able to control their own property and income, and they should have access to higher education and professional jobs.

Women's rights advocates were countered by those who insisted that giving women economic and political power would upset the social order. Some argued that allowing women any public roles would destroy their femininity.

What was the reality of women's lives at the turn of the century? Women worked in most sectors of the economy and in many areas of public life. Their work at home continued to be essential. At the same time a small number of women were earning advanced degrees and entering professions. Others were building voluntary organizations that took leading roles in reforming education, labor relations, public health, and other areas of society.

*New technologies, such as this washing machine, helped ease women's housekeeping burdens.*

New technology reduced the time many women spent performing household chores. New responsibilities as household consumers, as suggested in the ad above, emerged along with these changes. ***Economics*** ***In what ways were women engaged in the economy at the end of the 19th century?***

## Women's Work in the Home

As they had for centuries, women continued to perform most of the jobs in the home. Thanks to the era's technological revolution, some aspects of this work became less time-consuming. However, women still had much to do. In households that could not afford the benefits of technology, housework continued to be strenuous. Many homes were without indoor plumbing. Even as late as 1917, only one quarter of American homes had electricity. Though technology was not available to all people, it did free many women to pursue wage work, careers, and voluntary activity.

By 1900, fewer women were making their own bread or butchering and preserving their own meat. The number of foods available in tin cans increased fourfold between 1870 and 1880. Few women produced their family's clothing from start to finish anymore. Instead, they began to shop for these items at stores and through the mail.

Growing urban populations, an abundance of manufactured goods, public transportation, and electric lighting led to the development of **department stores.** Department stores are retail establishments that carry a wide variety of goods. Unlike small general stores, which carried only a few items at high prices, department stores could offer their customers lower prices because they were able to buy larger quantities from manufacturers. Some of the earliest department stores included Marshall Field in Chicago, which opened in 1865, and Macy's in New York City, which opened in 1858.

Of course, farming families in rural areas of the Midwest also wanted access to manufactured items at low prices. Despite the protests of local shopkeepers, the United States Post Office began offering **rural free delivery** (RFD) in 1896 to any group of farmers who petitioned their congressman. By 1905, the Post Office was delivering mail on over 32,000 RFD routes. This free service gave farm families access to big-city goods through the use of **mail-order catalogs,** or printed materials advertising a wide range of goods that could be purchased by mail. Two of the largest mail-order companies were Montgomery Ward and Sears, Roebuck and Company. Both of these companies worked hard to gain their customers' trust by offering money-back guarantees.

## Working Outside the Home

In 1870 nearly two million women and girls, or one in every eight over the age of 10, worked outside the home. Women worked in each of the 338 occupations listed in the United States census. Most of these working women were single. In the decades that followed, however, a rising proportion of married women would go to work.

Most single female workers were between the ages of 16 and 24. Employers assumed they would leave upon marriage and rarely gave them supervisory jobs or advanced training. They also paid women \$3 to \$5 a week less than men—about 30 to 60 percent less—on average.

Domestic work was an important source of income for many women. In 1900 about one in fifteen American homes employed live-in servants. Most were women from foreign countries or African Americans. Working from dawn to dusk, six-and-a-half days a week, these women cooked, cleaned, washed, ironed, and cared for children. Many supported their own families who lived elsewhere.

American society accepted the stereotype that women did not have the mental capacity for professional training. In 1873 retired Harvard Medical School professor Edward H. Clarke warned in his famous book *Sex in Education* that young women could not engage in studying and learning while at the same time retaining "uninjured health and a future secure from [sickness], hysteria, and other derangements of the nervous system."

Three years before Clarke made this warning, the United States had 525 physicians, 67 ministers, and 5 lawyers who were women. Still, most Americans believed that for women, careers and married life did not go together. Self-supporting women were allowed to train for professions but were discouraged from entering fields that put them in competition with men. Women professionals found opportunities mostly in women's colleges and hospitals.

**Volunteering for a Larger Role in Society** Women in both the North and South had performed important voluntary service during the Civil War. Afterward, there was an explosion of interest among many women in voluntary associations.

Women joined these organizations primarily for intellectual and social reasons. They studied subjects of common interest, gave talks on selected topics, or heard lectures by distinguished guests. Some organizations, such as the New England Woman's Club, founded in 1868, pursued specific causes such as temperance and girls' education. Others worked to establish new libraries and playgrounds. African American club women in Atlanta studied a national adult education program. The Chicago Woman's Club read Karl Marx's writings and other theoretical works.

**Main Idea CONNECTIONS**

***Describe the prevailing attitudes toward women's work outside the home in the late 1800s.***

Whatever their focus, clubs gave women invaluable experience in speaking, writing, and financial skills. They helped women increase their self-confidence and take their first steps toward public life.

As the number of clubs for women increased, the idea of joining them into national associations took hold. In 1873 the Association for the Advancement of Women came into being, and in 1890 the General Federation of Women's Clubs was formed. These groups took on increasingly ambitious projects, including suffrage and the correction of political abuses. In doing so, they joined with other groups founded to pursue specific reforms, such as the Woman's Christian

During this era, more women moved out of the home and into the workplace. Some, such as the telephone operators at left, worked in the new industries that came with industrialization. ***Economics*** ***Why did employers routinely deny young women supervisory jobs or advanced training?***

## COMPARING PRIMARY SOURCES

### EQUALITY FOR WOMEN

Americans debated the social, political, and economic roles of women in the late 1800s and early 1900s.

| For Women's Rights | Against Women's Rights |
|---|---|
| "These things the women want to do and be and have are not in any sense masculine. They do not belong to men. They never did. They are departments of our social life, hitherto monopolized [until now controlled] by men." —*Charlotte Perkins Gilman, "Are Women Human Beings?"* Harper's Weekly, *May 25, 1912* | "So I say deliberately that the so-called woman movement is an attempt to escape the function of woman, a revolt against the fact that woman is not a man. . . . It is a rising against nature. It is a revolt against God." —*Dr. Cyrus Townsend Brady, from a sermon given October 17, 1915* |

***ANALYZING VIEWPOINTS*** **Summarize the arguments presented in the excerpts above.**

Temperance Union, formed in 1874, and the National American Woman Suffrage Association, formed in 1890. This last group would carry the cause of women's suffrage to victory some 30 years later.

**New Women, New Ideas** During this period of change, women struggled to agree on a proper focus for their activities. By the early 1900s, the woman question had grown to include a number of issues besides economic and political rights.

One issue was the question of lifestyle: How should women dress and behave? As more women entered the work force or went to college, they took this matter into their own hands. In search of more convenient hair styles, they began to shorten their hair. They raised hemlines and wore skirts and blouses that were more suited to their new activities. The New England Woman's Club even opened a store where women could buy the new styles of clothing.

Courting and marriage customs also changed. For example, instead of entertaining a man at home, many women now went out on dates without supervision. "New women," as they were sometimes called, still hoped to marry. Yet they seemed to have higher expectations of fulfillment in marriage. As a result, the divorce rate rose from one in twelve in 1900 to one in nine by 1916. Many married "new women" began to push for the legalized spread of information about birth control, a campaign led by New York nurse Margaret Sanger. Such developments were shocking to more traditional Americans.

What was the consensus among women on the woman question? Though the majority agreed with the principle of greater rights, most women still saw domestic fulfillment as their chief goal. The right to vote was another matter. The issue of the vote prompted huge numbers of women to support the suffrage movement in some way. Soon the vote would be the one issue on which women from many walks of life would unite.

## SECTION 4 REVIEW

### Comprehension

1. *Key Terms* Define: (a) department store; (b) rural free delivery; (c) mail-order catalog.
2. *Summarizing the Main Idea* What arguments were used by those Americans who did not want to expand women's roles in the economy and society in the late 1800s?
3. *Organizing Information* List the main characteristics of women's work outside the home in this period.

### Critical Thinking

4. *Analyzing Time Lines* Review the time line at the beginning of this section. What do the organizations on this time line represent?
5. *Determining Relevance* How did the growth in women's employment and volunteer activity outside the home support the demands by women for greater political and social roles?

### Writing Activity

6. *Writing an Expository Essay* Write an essay detailing some of the ways women benefited from membership in clubs.

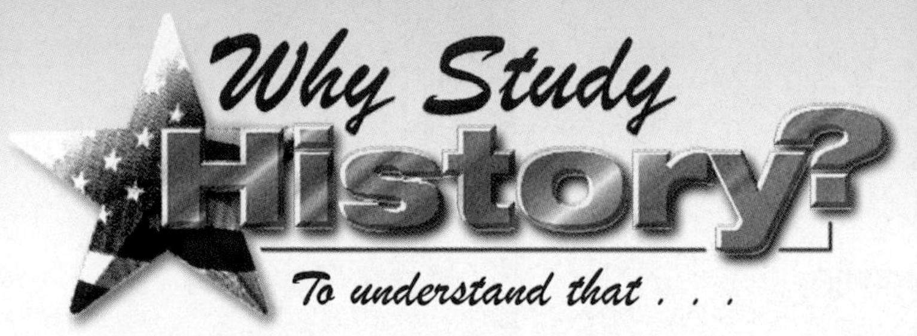


# Education Is the Key to Success

**Educational opportunity in the United States surged in the late 1800s. Today a good education is the gateway to economic success.**

*North Dakota classroom around 1910*

What are your plans after high school? Will you work for a while to earn money for college? Go straight on to school? Take any job you can find? Times have changed since the late 1800s, when fewer than 10 percent of Americans graduated from high school. Today, more than 80 percent of Americans are high school graduates.

Recent statistics show that a good education has become an economic necessity, leading to higher wages and more stable employment. Between 1970 and 1994, for example, the hourly earnings of workers without college degrees declined. Hourly earnings of workers with college degrees rose. In 1998, the unemployment rate of high school dropouts was almost twice the rate for high school graduates and more than three times the rate for college graduates. A 1998 survey by the Bureau of Labor Statistics found that nearly 20 percent of high school dropouts ages 16 to 24 were unemployed.

## The Impact Today

In preparing for life after high school, young people have many options. Some students take Advanced Placement courses in history, chemistry, calculus, or other subjects. By doing well on an Advanced Placement examination, high school students can get credit for introductory college courses.

Some students take courses in auto mechanics, bookkeeping, secretarial work, or other trades. Many high school students receive valuable on-the-job training through summer or part-time jobs.

A number of special programs help students prepare for work or further academic study after high school. For example, a government-sponsored program called Job Corps gives disadvantaged youth the academic, vocational, and social training that they need to obtain good jobs. Summer study programs, such as the Institute for the Academic Advancement of Youth at Johns Hopkins University, introduce students to the academic workload they can expect in college.

## The Impact on You

Think about educational programs, work or apprenticeship programs, and other activities that might help you prepare for life after high school. Formulate a five-year plan for achieving your goals. You might ask guidance counselors, teachers, and librarians for help.

*High school student learning auto repair*

# Chapter 7 Review

## Chapter Summary

The major concepts of Chapter 7 are presented below. See also ***Guide to the Essentials of American History*** or ***Interactive Student Tutorial CD-ROM,*** which contains interactive review activities, time lines, helpful hints, and test practice.

### *Reviewing the Main Ideas*

Between 1870 and 1915, more children began to attend school, and college became an attainable goal for a growing number of students. A recreation industry, which borrowed heavily from African American culture, also emerged. Yet some segments of society refused to grant African Americans and women an equal chance at success.

### *Section 1: The Expansion of Education*

Education was a lofty goal that was out of reach for most nineteenth-century Americans. As the century came to a close, however, more and more Americans gained the opportunity to learn.

### *Section 2: New Forms of Entertainment*

New forms of entertainment and sports emerged during the late 1800s.

### *Section 3: The World of Jim Crow*

African Americans found their hopes dashed in the years after Reconstruction. Yet many not only resisted discrimination, but achieved success in spite of the obstacles placed before them.

### *Section 4: Women in the Late 1800s*

Changes in women's lives, including new jobs, new educational opportunities, and new roles in the home, fueled a debate on the proper role of women in society at the turn of the century.

Educational opportunity surged in the late 1800s. Today education is the gateway to economic success. A number of special programs help students prepare for work or further academic study after high school.

## Key Terms

For each of the terms below, write a sentence explaining how it relates to this chapter.

1. literacy
2. assimilation
3. philanthropist
4. vaudeville
5. yellow journalism
6. Niagara Movement
7. poll tax
8. grandfather clause
9. rural free delivery
10. ragtime
11. NAACP
12. Jim Crow

## Comprehension

1. Why did public schools gain more students in the late 1800s?
2. In what ways were the experiences of women and African Americans similar with regard to higher education?
3. What entertainment was available to enjoy during the late 1800s?
4. Where and how did ragtime and jazz originate?
5. How did the NAACP and the National Urban League help African Americans during the early 1900s?
6. What was the Supreme Court's ruling in *Plessy* v. *Ferguson*?
7. What methods were used to prevent African Americans from voting?
8. Describe how women achieved greater social equality by the early 1900s.

## Using Graphic Organizers

On a separate sheet of paper, copy the tree map to organize information about the expansion of education. Fill in at least two main idea statements for each heading.

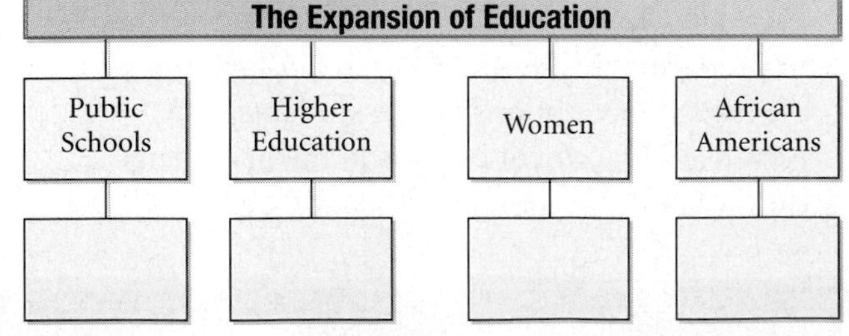

## Analyzing Political Cartoons ▶

1. Read the words at the top of the cartoon. To what government do they refer?
2. Identify the figures. (a) What does each figure represent? (b) How do you know?
3. Analyze the woman on the right. (a) Why is she shackled? (b) Why is she appealing to the man on the left? (c) What is the purpose of representing the woman in the middle as supporting the woman on the right?
4. Read the words at the bottom of the cartoon. Explain the cartoonist's message.

## Critical Thinking

1. ***Applying the Chapter Skill*** Locate a political cartoon in a newspaper or weekly news magazine. Identify and analyze the meanings of the symbols in the cartoon and then write a statement summarizing the cartoon's main point.
2. ***Making Comparisons*** As greater numbers of people sought entertainment during the late 1800s, a commercial recreation industry emerged. How are the types of activities available today similar to the types of activities available during the late 1800s?
3. ***Expressing Problems Clearly*** Jim Crow required the segregation of whites and African Americans. Aside from the fact that facilities for African Americans were inferior, how might segregation have harmed African Americans?

### INTERNET ACTIVITY

***For your portfolio:***
**WRITE AN ESSAY**

Access Prentice Hall's *America: Pathways to the Present* site at **www.Pathways.phschool.com** for the specific URL to complete the activity. Additional resources and related Web sites are also available.

Read about the life of African American entrepreneur Sarah Breedlove (Madam C. J.) Walker. How does her life and work exemplify the social changes of the era in which she lived?

### ANALYZING DOCUMENTS ◀ ▶ INTERPRETING DATA

Turn to the graph of illiteracy in the United States in Section 1.

1. In which year were illiteracy rates the highest? (a) 1870 (b) 1880 (c) 1890 (d) 1920
2. Which of the following statements best summarizes the information in this graph? (a) Few people were able to read and write in the late 1800s. (b) About 10 percent of the United States population was illiterate in 1900. (c) During the period from 1870 to 1920, illiteracy rates dropped in the United States. (d) Literacy was an important requirement for citizenship in the United States.
3. ***Writing*** Write an essay in which you describe some of the likely causes for a decrease in illiteracy in the United States between 1870 and 1920.

### Connecting to Today

***Making Comparisons*** During the 1890s local storekeepers protested rural free delivery by the Post Office because they feared competition from mail-order businesses that offered a greater variety of goods at lower prices. Describe the challenges faced by local storeowners today. How are they similar to the challenges faced by local storekeepers in the 1890s?

**American Heritage®**

# My Brush with History

BY AN AFRICAN AMERICAN WOMAN IN THE SOUTH

***INTRODUCTION*** The editors of *American Heritage* magazine have selected this account, published in 1902 and written by an unnamed African American woman living in the South. In it she described the world of Jim Crow—the daily frustrations and humiliations that African Americans had to endure as they struggled to build successful lives.

*I am a colored woman, wife and mother.* I have lived all my life in the South, and have often thought what a peculiar fact it is that the more ignorant the Southern whites are of us the more vehement they are in their denunciation of us. They boast that they have little intercourse with us, never see us in our homes, churches or places of amusement, but still they know us thoroughly.

They also admit that they know us in no capacity except as servants, yet they say we are at our best in that single capacity. What philosophers they are! The Southerners say we Negroes are a happy, laughing set of people, with no thought of tomorrow. How mistaken they are! The educated, thinking Negro is just the opposite. There is a feeling of unrest, insecurity, almost panic among the best class of Negroes in the South. In our homes, in our churches, wherever two or three are gathered together, there is a discussion of what is best to do. Must we remain in the South or go elsewhere? Where can we go to feel that security which other people feel? Is it best to go in great numbers or only in several families? These and many other things are discussed over and over. . . .

I know of houses occupied by poor Negroes in which a respectable farmer would not keep his cattle. It is impossible for them to rent elsewhere. All Southern real estate agents have "white property" and "colored property." In one of the largest Southern cities there is a colored minister, a graduate of Harvard, whose wife is an educated, Christian woman, who lived for weeks in a tumble-down rookery because he could neither rent nor buy in a respectable locality.

*Educated African Americans were often restricted to low-paying jobs.*

Many colored women who wash, iron, scrub, cook or sew all the week to help pay the rent for these miserable hovels and help fill the many small mouths, would deny themselves some of the necessaries of life if they could take their little children and teething babies on the cars to the parks of a Sunday afternoon and sit under trees, enjoy the cool breezes and breathe God's pure air for only two or three hours; but this is denied them. Some of the parks have signs, "No Negroes allowed on these grounds except as servants." Pitiful, pitiful customs and laws that make war on women and babes! There is no wonder that we die; the wonder is that we persist in living.

Fourteen years ago I had just married. My husband had saved sufficient money to buy a small home. On account of our limited means we went to the suburbs, on unpaved streets, to look for a home, only asking for a high, healthy locality. Some real estate agents were "sorry, but had nothing to suit," some had "just the thing," but we discovered on investigation that they had "just the thing" for an unhealthy pigsty. Others had no "colored property." One agent said that he had what we wanted, but we should have to go to see the lot after dark, or walk by and give the place a casual look; for, he said, "all the white people in the neighborhood would be down on me." Finally, we bought this lot. When the house was being built we went to see it. Consternation reigned. We had ruined his neighborhood of poor people; poor as we, poorer in manners at least. The people who lived next door received the sympathy of their friends. When we walked on the street (there were no sidewalks) we were embarrassed by the stare of many unfriendly eyes.

Laundry day in Birmingham, Alabama

*In the Jim Crow South, even laundry services were segregated by race.*

Two years passed before a single woman spoke to me, and only then because I helped one of them when a little sudden trouble came to her. Such was the reception, I a happy young woman, just married, received from people among whom I wanted to make a home. Fourteen years have now passed, four children have been born to us, and one has died in this same home, among these same neighbors. Although the neighbors speak to us . . . , not one woman has ever been inside of my house, not even at the times when a woman would doubly appreciate the slightest attention of a neighbor. . . .

White agents and other chance visitors who come into our homes ask questions that we must not dare ask their wives. They express surprise that our children have clean faces and that their hair is combed. . . .

We were delighted to know that some of our Spanish-American heroes were coming where we could get a glimpse of them. Had not black men helped in a small way to give them their honors? In the cities of the South, where these heroes went, the white school children were assembled, flags waved, flowers strewn, speeches made, and "My Country, 'tis of Thee, Sweet Land of Liberty," was sung. Our children who need to be taught so much, were not assembled, their hands waved no flags, they threw no flowers, heard no thrilling speech, sang no song of their country. And this is the South's idea of justice. Is it surprising that feeling grows more bitter, when the white mother teaches her boy to hate my boy, not because he is mean, but because his skin is dark? I have seen very small white children hang their black dolls. It is not the child's fault, he is simply an apt pupil. . . .

Source: Anonymous, *Independent* magazine, 1902.

### ADDITIONAL READING

**To learn more about the topics discussed in this selection, you might want to read the following books:**

- *The Crucible of Race: Black/White Relations in the American South Since Emancipation,* by Joel Williamson (New York: Oxford University Press, 1984)
- *The Souls of Black Folk,* by W.E.B. Du Bois (New York: Library of America, 1986)
- *Trouble in Mind: Black Southerners in the Age of Jim Crow,* by Leon Litwak (New York: Alfred A. Knopf, 1998)
- *Up from Slavery,* by Booker T. Washington (New York: Oxford University Press, 1995)

# unit TWO

# The United States on the Brink of Change

## 1890–1920

*The industrial boom at the turn of the century had far-reaching effects. It created serious problems that inspired a reform movement known as progressivism. It also led the United States to join the scramble for new territories as it searched for new markets. Both the ambitions of the imperialists and the ideals of the progressives contributed to the nation's growing role as a world power. This role eventually drew the United States into the horrors of World War I.*



### UNIT THEMES

**Foreign Relations** Pursuit of new markets and territory fueled United States expansion.

**Culture** Progressive reformers sought governmental solutions to the problems that resulted from rapid industrialization.

**Science and Technology** New forms of weaponry and warfare contributed to a devastating stalemate in World War I.

**EVENTS IN THE UNITED STATES**

**1890** *National American Woman Suffrage Association formed*

**1898** **Turning Point:** *The Spanish-American War (p. 265)*

**1899** *John Hay announces Open Door Policy*

**1904** *Roosevelt Corollary to the Monroe Doctrine*

| Presidents | Cleveland | Harrison | Cleveland | McKinley |
|---|---|---|---|---|

**1885** **1890** **1895** **1900**

**EVENTS IN THE WORLD**

**1895**
- *Japan defeats China in Sino-Japanese War*
- *Cubans rebel against Spanish rule*

**1900** *Boxer Rebellion breaks out in China*

**VIEWING HISTORY** New York City's docks were teeming with activity in the early 1900s. Spurred by an economic boom, the United States reached across the Atlantic Ocean in its quest to become an economic and political world power. ***Geography*** ***How did expansion overseas draw the United States into international conflicts?***

- **1906** *Upton Sinclair publishes* The Jungle
- **1913** *Sixteenth and Seventeenth amendments ratified*
- **1914** *Panama Canal completed*
- **1917** *United States declares war on Germany*
- **1918** *Wilson announces Fourteen Points*
- **1920** *Nineteenth Amendment ratified*

T. Roosevelt | Taft | Wilson

1905 | 1910 | 1915 | 1920

- **1905** *Japan defeats Russia in Russo-Japanese War*
- **1914** *World War I begins*
- **1917** *Russian Revolution*
- **1918** *Germany surrenders*
- **1919** *League of Nations formed*

*Suffrage poster*

CHAPTER

# Becoming a World Power

## 1890–1913

## CHAPTER FOCUS

*This chapter describes the years when the United States grew to be a world power. Growth in American industry pushed business and political leaders to look for new markets abroad. Some Americans, inspired by grand dreams of an empire, pursued new territory as well.*

*The* **Why Study History?** *page at the end of this chapter explores the connection between United States participation in world affairs in the early 1900s and its role in the global community today.*

▲

**VIEWING HISTORY**
Edward Moran captured the triumph of the Great White Fleet in his 1899 painting *Return of the Conquerors.* ***Foreign Relations*** ***Why did the United States expand its influence overseas?***

| 1867 | 1875 | 1881 | 1884 | 1890 |
|---|---|---|---|---|
| *United States buys Alaska and annexes Midway Islands* | *United States signs trade agreement with Hawaii* | *Congress establishes Naval Advisory Board* | *American businessman granted long-term lease in Costa Rica* | *Alfred Mahan publishes* The Influence of Sea Power Upon History |

1865 | 1875 | 1885 | 1895

# 1 The Pressure to Expand

## SECTION PREVIEW

### Objectives

1. Explain some of the reasons for the growth of imperialism around the world.
2. Summarize the American view regarding imperialism prior to 1890.
3. *Key Terms* Define: imperialism; nationalism; annex; banana republic.

### Main Idea

In the late 1800s, as European nations took over vast areas in Africa and Asia, American leaders looked to expand American influence abroad.

### Reading Strategy

*Reinforcing Main Ideas* As you read, create a list of the pressures that led the United States to adopt a policy of political and economic expansion overseas.

By the late 1800s, the industrialists, inventors, and workers of the United States had built a powerful industrial economy. But the overproduction of food and goods led to financial panic and depression. Labor and farmers protested their plight, helping to convince business and political leaders that the United States must secure new markets abroad. Some people also began to believe that the United States had a duty to carry democratic values and Christianity to others around the globe.

## Growth of Imperialism

Meanwhile, as the maps on the next page show, Europe had reached new heights in its quest for territories to rule. The late 1800s marked the peak of European imperialism, with much of Africa and Asia under foreign domination. Under **imperialism,** stronger nations attempt to create empires by dominating weaker nations—economically, politically, culturally, or militarily.

**Why Imperialism Grew** Several factors accounted for the burst of imperialistic activity in the late 1800s.

(1) *Economic factors.* The growth of industry in Europe created an increased need for natural resources, such as rubber and petroleum. Manufacturing nations also required new markets in which to sell their manufactured goods.

*Businesses, such as this fruit grower, eagerly sought new markets abroad.*

(2) *Nationalist factors.* Competition among European nations for large empires was the result of **nationalism,** or devotion to one's nation. For example, when France acquired colonies in West Africa in the late 1800s, rival nations Great Britain and Germany seized lands nearby to stop French expansion.

(3) *Military factors.* Advances in military technology produced European armies and navies that were far superior to those in Africa and Asia. Also, Europe's growing navies required bases around the world for taking on fuel and supplies.

(4) *Humanitarian factors.* Humanitarian and religious goals spurred on imperialists. Colonial officials, doctors, and missionaries believed they had a duty to spread the blessings of Western civilization, including its law, medicine, and Christian religion.

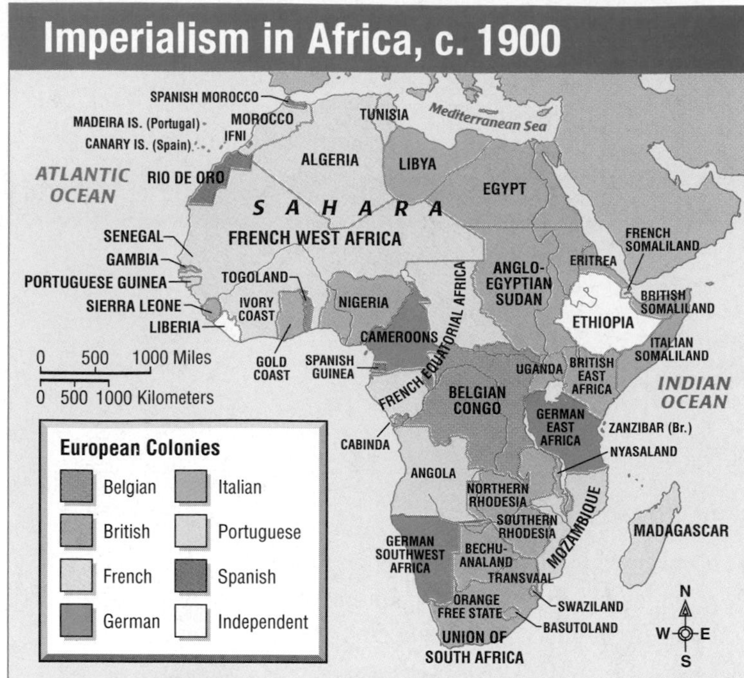


**MAP skills** By 1900, European imperialist nations controlled vast amounts of territory in Africa. ***Place*** ***Which African nations retained their independence from imperialist control?***

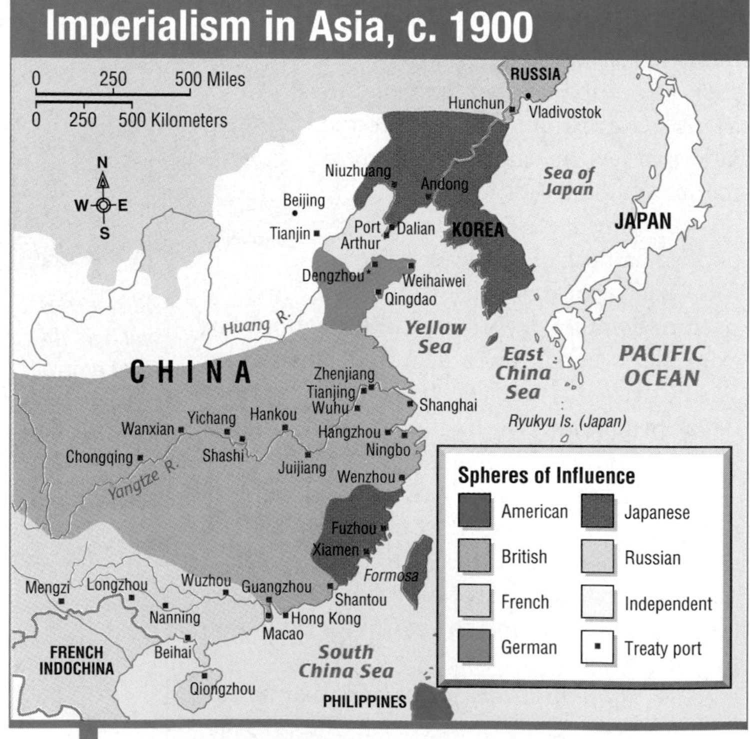


**MAP skills** The United States and Japan joined European nations in exerting economic control, or "spheres of influence," in Asian nations. ***Location*** ***Where was the American sphere of influence?***

**Europe Leads the Way** Improved transportation and communication made it easier for Great Britain, France, and Russia, all with long imperialist traditions, to extend their grip to far-flung lands. Great Britain, in particular, acquired so much new territory around the globe that the saying "The sun never sets on the British Empire" became popular. Competition for new territory grew even more intense when Germany, unified in 1871, seized colonies in Africa and Asia.

By 1890 the United States was eager to join the competition for new territories. Supporters of expansion denied that the United States sought to **annex** foreign lands. (To annex is to join a new territory to an existing country.) Yet annexation did take place.

## *The United States and Imperialism*

In his Farewell Address in 1796, President George Washington had advised Americans to "steer clear of permanent alliances" with other countries. For the next century, Americans generally followed Washington's advice. The nation's rapid economic growth along with the settlement of the West left the United States with little interest in foreign affairs.

There were instances, however, when Americans "looked outward." In 1866, for example, Secretary of State Seward sent 50,000 troops to the Mexican border after France placed an emperor on the Mexican throne. In the face of this army, the French abandoned their colonial venture. Then, in 1867, Seward bought Alaska from Russia. Most Americans ridiculed the venture. Seward, they said, was buying "walrus-covered icebergs" in a "barren, worthless, God-forsaken region." Seward, however, waged a successful campaign to educate the nation about Alaska's rich resources. In the end, the Senate ratified the purchase, and the United States took possession of "Seward's Folly."

Americans also showed their interest in the Pacific. In 1853 an American fleet led by Commodore Matthew C. Perry sailed into Tokyo Bay and convinced Japan to open trade relations with the United States. By the 1860s the United States and several European countries had signed a series of treaties that allowed for expanded trade with China.

Now the United States government wanted control of some Pacific islands to use as refueling and repair stations for its naval vessels. To this end, Seward annexed the uninhabited

Midway Islands in 1867. Eight years later the United States government signed a treaty with Hawaii. This agreement allowed Hawaiians to sell sugar in the United States duty free, as long as they did not sell or lease territory to any foreign power.

By the 1890s, American attitudes toward foreign affairs had changed. A debate arose over what foreign policy would best serve the United States. Some argued that the country should continue to avoid foreign entanglements. Others offered a variety of reasons for increased American involvement in international affairs.

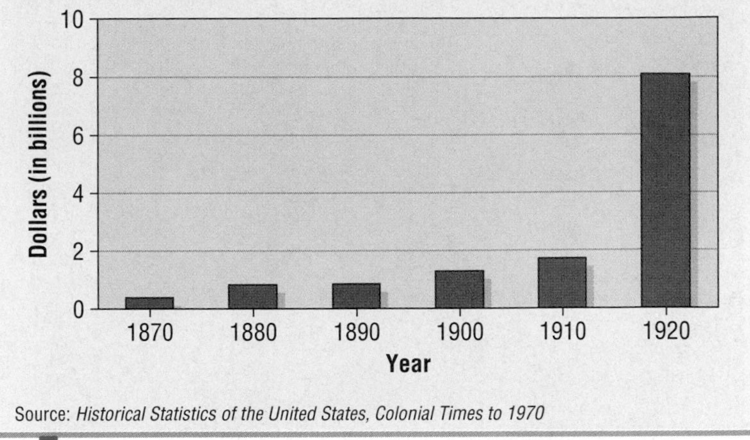


**Interpreting Graphs** The expansion of American businesses into international markets in the late 1800s and early 1900s led to the rapid rise in U.S. exports during this period. ***Economics* By how much did U.S. exports increase between 1870 and 1920?**

**Promoting Economic Growth** A chief argument in favor of expansion was economic. By the late 1800s, Americans simply could not consume all of the food and other goods that their nation produced. In 1890, James G. Blaine, Secretary of State under President Harrison, summarized the situation as follows:

> **AMERICAN VOICES** **"We have developed a volume of manufactures which, in many departments, overruns the demands of the home market. . . . Our great demand is expansion . . . of trade with countries where we can find profitable exchanges."**
>
> —*James G. Blaine*

Many business leaders agreed that the economic problems of the nation could only be solved by expanding its markets. For this reason, they threw their support behind expansionist policies. Some American businesses already dominated international markets. In the 1880s and 1890s, firms such as Rockefeller's Standard Oil and American Telephone and Telegraph had all became popular internationally. So had products such as McCormick farm machinery, Singer sewing machines, Kodak cameras, and Sherwin-Williams paint.

Other American business leaders had gone a step further and invested directly in the economies of other countries. In some cases their investments gave them political influence in those countries. In Central America, for example, an American named Minor C. Keith provided financial services to the Costa Rican government. In return, in 1884 he won long-term leases for lands and railroad lines. By 1913 Keith's United Fruit Company not only exported 50 million bunches of bananas a year to the United States, but also dominated the governments and economies of Costa Rica, Guatemala, and Honduras. As a result, some people began to refer to the Central American nations as **banana republics.**

**Protecting American Security** Lobbyists who favored a strong United States Navy formed a second force pushing for expansion. By the 1880s, United States warships left over from the Civil War were rusting and rotting. Naval officers joined with business interests to convince Congress to build modern steam-powered, steel-hulled ships to protect overseas trade.

The most influential of these officers was Captain (later Admiral) Alfred T. Mahan. In his 1890 book, *The Influence of Sea Power Upon History, 1660–1783,* Mahan argued that the nation's economic future hinged on gaining new markets abroad. In his view, the United States needed a powerful navy to protect these markets from foreign rivals.

> **Main Idea CONNECTIONS**
>
> *Why did Alfred T. Mahan think it was necessary for the United States to build a strong navy?*

Influenced by supporters of an expanded navy, Congress established a Naval Advisory Board in 1881. The board pushed to increase the navy's budget. Two years later, Congress authorized the building of three cruisers and two battleships, including the U.S.S. *Maine.* Finally, the Naval Act of 1890 called for the construction of more battleships, gunboats, torpedo boats, and cruisers. By 1900, the United States had one of the most powerful navies in the world. The expanded fleet suggested that the United

As this 1901 political cartoon suggests, the United States relied on the principles of the Monroe Doctrine to block European involvement in Latin America. ***Foreign Relations*** ***How did expansion of trade lead to the expansion of the United States Navy?***

States was willing and able to confront an enemy on the open sea.

**Preserving American Spirit** A third force for expansion consisted of people who feared that the United States was losing its vitality. Among them were Massachusetts senator Henry Cabot Lodge, historian Frederick Jackson Turner, and a rising young politician from New York named Theodore Roosevelt. Worried that the closing of the frontier would sap the nation's energy, they argued that a quest for empire might restore the country's pioneer spirit.

These and other leaders of the day also drew on the doctrine of social Darwinism to justify the takeover of new territories, just as they had done earlier to defend the conquest of Native Americans. In the opinion of respected leaders such as Congregationalist minister Josiah Strong and Indiana senator Albert J. Beveridge, the civilizations produced by Anglo-Saxon and Teutonic (Germanic) peoples were superior to the societies they conquered.

Thus, social Darwinists believed that expansionism was not only this nation's destiny but a noble pursuit as well, for it introduced Christianity and modern civilization to other peoples around the world. It is important to remember that this was an era before scientific studies showed that no racial or national group is superior to any other.

**Public Opinion Leans Toward Expansion** Gradually public opinion warmed to the idea of expansionism. Most Americans did not see themselves as potential rulers of oppressed foreign peoples, but they did want new markets abroad and favorable trade relations. What they soon discovered was that political and military entanglements tended to follow. The United States would find itself in difficult, bloody, and painful foreign conflicts.

## SECTION 1 REVIEW

### Comprehension

1. *Key Terms* Define: (a) imperialism; (b) nationalism; (c) annex; (d) banana republic.
2. *Summarizing the Main Idea* Why did United States policymakers feel the need to secure new markets abroad in the late 1800s?
3. *Organizing Information* Create a web diagram that describes the major arguments for American expansionism. Label the center circle *Arguments for Expansionism.* Include supporting details in at least three surrounding circles.

### Critical Thinking

4. *Analyzing Time Lines* Review the time line at the start of the section. Which event, in your opinion, best reflects American expansionist policies?
5. *Drawing Conclusions* What factors aided European imperialism in the late 1800s?

### Writing Activity

6. *Writing an Expository Essay* Research and write a brief essay tracing the history of American expansionism before 1880. Be sure to include specific examples of expansionism in your essay.

| 1891 | 1895 | 1898 | 1898 | 1899 |
|---|---|---|---|---|
| *United States demands compensation from Chile* | *United States demands Britain acknowledge Monroe Doctrine* | *U.S.S. Maine explodes in Havana harbor* | *Congress approves annexation of Hawaii* | *John Hay publishes Open Door Policy* |

1891 1893 1895 1897 1899

# 2 The Spanish-American War

**SECTION PREVIEW**

### Objectives

1. Describe the ways in which the United States took advantage of several incidents in Latin America to reaffirm the Monroe Doctrine.
2. Analyze the events leading up to and following the Spanish-American War.
3. Identify the areas after the war where the United States gained influence and new territories.
4. *Key Terms* Define: arbitration; jingoism; sphere of influence; Open Door Policy.

### Main Idea

A swift American victory in the Spanish-American War confirmed the nation's status as a world power, but it left some people arguing over how to govern newly acquired territories.

### Reading Strategy

*Organizing Information* Create a two-column chart entitled *United States Foreign Policy.* In the left-hand column, list countries where the United States pursued expansionist policies. In the right-hand column list the effects of United States policies.

Those in the United States who dreamed of expansion looked to three main areas of the world in the late 1800s: Latin America, the islands of the Pacific, and China. In the 1890s, the United States established a pattern of intervention in these three areas that changed its status in world politics. In the process of expanding and becoming a world power, however, the United States increasingly found itself in conflict with other nations.

## Involvement in Latin America

American expansionists paid close attention to the political and economic actions of countries in the Western Hemisphere. During the 1890s, the United States played an active role in several diplomatic and military conflicts in Latin America.

**United States in Latin America** In 1891 an angry Chilean mob attacked a group of American sailors on shore leave in Valparaíso. They killed two Americans and injured seventeen others. The United States government reacted strongly, forcing Chile to pay $75,000 to the families of those sailors who were killed or injured. Two years later, when a rebellion threatened the friendly republican government of Brazil, President Cleveland ordered naval units to Rio de Janeiro to protect United States shipping interests. This show of force broke the back of the rebellion.

In the third and most important incident of the era, the United States confronted the nation then considered the most powerful in the world, Great Britain. Since the 1840s, Britain and Venezuela had disputed ownership of a piece of territory located at the border between Venezuela and British Guiana. In the 1880s, the dispute intensified when rumors surfaced of mineral wealth in this border area. President Cleveland's Secretary of State, Richard Olney, demanded in July 1895 that Britain acknowledge the Monroe Doctrine and submit the boundary dispute to **arbitration.** (Arbitration is the settlement of a dispute by a person chosen

**FACT Finder**

**Morning Journal Sales**

| Date | Amount |
|---|---|
| 1895 | 30,000 |
| 1897 | 400,000 |
| 1898 | 1,000,000 |

Source: *American Heritage,* February 1957

**Interpreting Tables** Sale of William Randolph Hearst's *Morning Journal* soared in 1898 thanks to sensational stories before and during the Spanish-American War. ***Culture How did yellow journalism influence U.S. participation in the Spanish-American War?***

to listen to both sides and come to a decision.) The British government replied that the doctrine had no standing in international law.

Eventually Britain backed down and agreed to arbitration. Concerned about the rising power of Germany in Africa, the British government realized that it needed to stay on friendly terms with the increasingly powerful United States.

### The Cuban Rebellion

By the mid-1890s the United States had not only reaffirmed the Monroe Doctrine, it had also forced the world's most powerful nation to bow to its will. Events in Cuba soon paved the way for a far more spectacular display of American power.

An island nation off the coast of Florida, Cuba first rebelled against Spain in 1868. After ten years of fighting the rebels, Spain finally put in place a few meager reforms to appease the Cuban people. In 1895, after the island's economy had collapsed, Cubans rebelled again.† This time Spain sent 150,000 troops and its best general, Valeriano Weyler, to put down the rebellion. In a desperate attempt to prevent civilians from aiding the rebels, Weyler instituted a policy of "reconcentration." He forced hundreds of thousands of Cubans into guarded camps. The prisoners, including women, children, and the elderly, lived in miserable conditions with little food or sanitation. Over two years, disease and starvation killed an estimated 200,000 Cubans.

Cuban exiles living in the United States, led by the journalist José Martí, urged the United States to intervene. Both Presidents Cleveland and McKinley refused. They were unwilling to spend the money that intervention would require and feared the United States would be saddled with colonial responsibilities it could not handle. Frustrated, Cuban guerrillas turned to the one tactic they knew would attract the United States government's attention: the destruction of American sugar plantations and mills in Cuba. As a result, business owners increased their pressure on the government to act.

Demands for United States intervention in Cuba also came from an unexpected source—American newspapers. In the 1890s a fierce competition for readers broke out between two New York City newspapers, the *New York World* and the *New York Morning Journal.* Both newspapers reported exaggerated and sometimes false stories about the events in Cuba in order to increase circulation. The battle pitted the *World*'s established publisher, Joseph Pulitzer, against a newcomer to the city, the *Journal*'s William Randolph Hearst.

## William Randolph Hearst

**AMERICAN BIOGRAPHY** Hearst, the son of a gold-mining tycoon, grew up in California. His first venture into newspaper publishing came in 1887, when he took control of the *San Francisco Examiner,* a faltering paper owned by his father. Hearst used a combination of investigative reporting and sensationalist stories to increase circulation. His methods turned the struggling paper around, and within two years he was showing a profit.

*William R. Hearst (1863–1951)*

In 1895 Hearst expanded his efforts into the New York City market when he bought the *New York Morning Journal.* He set about improving the paper by luring experienced journalists from other papers, including the *World.* Hearst used a variety of other techniques to increase the *Journal*'s circulation, including printing sensational crime stories, using illustrations and vivid headlines to draw in the reader, and lowering the price to one penny.

Newspaper publishers Hearst and Pulitzer both took advantage of the horrifying stories coming from Cuba about the "Butcher"

† A Spanish decision to impose increased taxes and to restrict trade was responsible for the collapse of the Cuban economy.

Weyler and his barbed-wire concentration camps. Their sensational headlines and stories, known as yellow journalism, whipped up the American public in favor of the rebels. The intense burst of national pride and the desire for an aggressive foreign policy that followed came to be known as **jingoism.** The name came from a line in a British song of the 1870s: "We don't want to fight, yet by Jingo! if we do, We've got the ships, we've got the men, and got the money too."

Hearst went on to serve briefly in the United States House of Representatives. He continued to expand his publishing empire, acquiring newspapers in cities throughout the country. By 1935 he owned 28 major newspapers, 18 magazines, and several radio stations and news services. Although the era of rabid yellow journalism declined following the turn of the century, the innovations of Hearst and his competitors continue to influence journalism today. ■

## *Turning Point: The Spanish-American War*

The stories printed in newspapers such as the *Journal* strengthened American sympathy for the Cuban rebels. Slowly the demand for United States intervention began to build.

**Steps to War** Early in 1898 riots erupted in Havana, the capital of Cuba. In response, President McKinley moved the battleship U.S.S. *Maine* into the city's harbor to protect American citizens and property. A few weeks later, in early February 1898, United States newspapers published a letter stolen from the Spanish ambassador to Washington, Dupuy de Lôme. The de Lôme letter, which described McKinley as "weak and a bidder for the admiration of the crowd," caused an outcry in the United States.

Then, on February 15, an explosion sank the *Maine,* killing more than 250 American sailors. Even though the blast probably had been caused by a fire that set off ammunition, an enraged American public blamed the Spanish for the disaster and called for war. Still, McKinley hesitated.

On the other side of the world, the people of another of Spain's last remaining possessions, the Philippine Islands, also were rebelling. In the view of Theodore Roosevelt, then Assistant Secretary of the Navy, the Philippines could become a key base from which the United States might protect its Asian trade. On February 25, while his boss, the Secretary of the Navy, was out of the office, Roosevelt cabled naval commanders in the Pacific to prepare for military action against

## TURNING POINT: *The Spanish-American War*

**As you can see from the time line, after the Spanish-American War the United States became involved in many foreign conflicts, some thousands of miles from home.**

**1898** *The United States enters the Spanish-American War.*

**1941** *After Japan bombs Pearl Harbor, the United States enters World War II against the Axis.*

**1964** *Congress passes the Gulf of Tonkin Resolution, authorizing the use of American military force in the war in Vietnam.*

**1900** | **1925** | **1950** | **1975** | **2000**

**1917** *After a time of neutrality, the United States reacts against German submarine warfare by entering World War I on the side of the Allies.*

**1950** *After North Korea's invasion of South Korea, President Truman calls on American troops to defend South Korea.*

**1991** *The United States and its allies free Kuwait from Iraqi occupation in the Gulf War.*

Spain. When President McKinley discovered what Roosevelt had done, he ordered most of the cables withdrawn, but he made an exception in the case of the cable directed to Admiral George Dewey. Dewey was told to attack the Spanish fleet in the Philippines if war broke out with Spain.

Late in March, in a final attempt at a peaceful solution, McKinley sent a list of demands to Spain. These included compensation for the *Maine,* an end to the concentration camps, a truce in Cuba, and Cuban independence. Eager to find a peaceful settlement to the crisis, Spain accepted most of the American demands. Still, McKinley decided he could not resist the growing cries for war. On April 11, he sent a war message to Congress. A few days later, rallying to the cry of "Remember the *Maine*!" Congress recognized Cuban independence and authorized force against Spain.

**"A Splendid Little War"** The war's first action took place, not in Cuba, but in the Philippines as shown on the map on this page. On May 1, 1898, Admiral Dewey launched a surprise attack on Spanish ships anchored in Manila Bay, destroying Spain's entire Pacific fleet in just seven hours. In Cuba, meanwhile, United States warships quickly bottled up Spain's Atlantic fleet in the harbor at Santiago.

American army troops gathered in Tampa, Florida, to prepare for an invasion of Cuba. The group that received the most publicity was the 1st Volunteer Cavalry, known as the Rough Riders. Its leader, Theodore Roosevelt, had resigned his position as Assistant Secretary of the Navy and recruited an eclectic group of volunteers that included cowboys, miners, policemen, and college athletes. On July 1, 1898, Roosevelt led the Rough Riders in a charge up San Juan Hill, which became the most famous incident of the war. Several units of African American troops also performed superbly in the land war. A white soldier later wrote the *Washington Post* that "if it had not been for the Negro cavalry, the Rough Riders would have been exterminated."

The Spanish fleet made a desperate attempt to escape Santiago harbor on July 3. In the ensuing battle, the United States Navy sank every Spanish ship, setting off wild Independence Day celebrations back in the United States.

It had all seemed quite simple. Although 2,500 Americans had died in the short war, fewer than 400 died in battle. The remainder

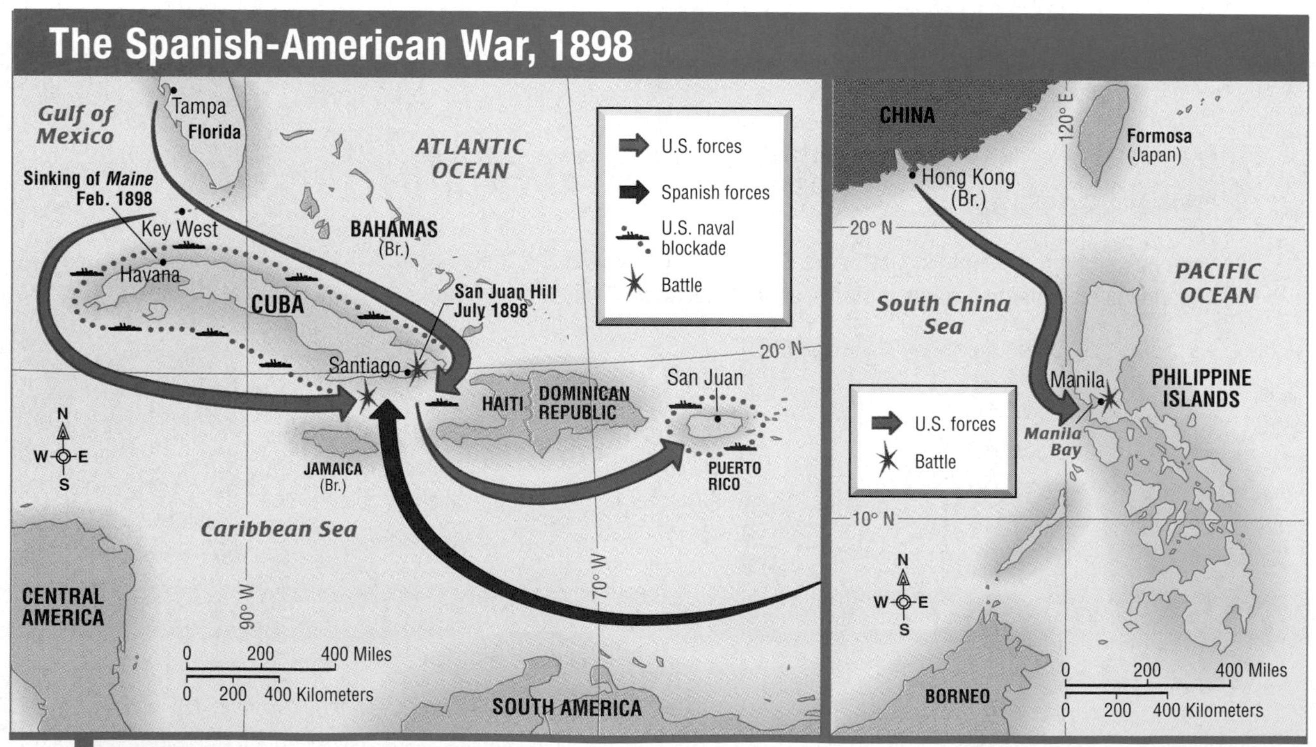


**MAP skills** Although the Spanish-American War was fought in two locations on opposite sides of the world, the United States defeated Spain in just nine weeks. ***Location*** ***At what specific sites were the major battles of the war fought?***

Filipinos were encouraged by the United States to fight Spain for independence, only to find themselves under U.S. domination following the Spanish-American War. Filipino civilians suffered extremely high casualty rates during the three-year war between the United States and the Philippines. ***Economics What economic motive did the United States have to take over the Philippines?***

died from food poisoning, yellow fever, malaria, and inadequate medical care. Future Secretary of State John Hay captured the public mood when he wrote his friend Teddy Roosevelt that it had been "a splendid little war."

## After the War

The United States signed the Treaty of Paris with Spain in December 1898. In the treaty the Spanish government recognized Cuba's independence. In return for a payment of $20 million, Spain also gave up the Philippines, Puerto Rico, and the Pacific island of Guam to the United States. These became "unincorporated" territories of the United States, which meant that their residents would not become American citizens.

**Dilemma in the Philippines** Although many Americans supported the treaty, others were deeply troubled by it. How could the United States become a colonial power without violating the nation's most basic principle—that all people have the right to liberty? Forced to justify this departure from American ideals, President McKinley explained that rebels in the Philippines were on the edge of war with one another and that the Filipino people were "unfit for self-government." If the United States did not act first, moreover, European powers might seize the islands. After a heated debate, the Senate ratified the treaty in February 1899.

Filipino rebels had fought with American troops in the war against Spain with the expectation that victory would bring independence. But when rebel leader Emilio Aguinaldo issued a proclamation in January 1899 declaring the Philippines a republic, the United States ignored him. Mounting tensions between the rebel forces and American soldiers finally erupted into war in February. In the bitter three-year war that followed, 4,200 Americans were killed and 2,800 more wounded. Fighting without restraint—and sometimes with great brutality—American forces killed some 16,000 Filipino rebels and as many as 200,000 Filipino civilians. Occasional fighting continued for years. The Philippines did not gain complete independence until 1946.

**The Fate of Cuba and Puerto Rico** Supporters of Cuban independence had attached an amendment, called the Teller Amendment, to Congress's 1898 war resolution against Spain. The document promised that the United States would not annex Cuba. Yet American involvement in Cuba did not end with the victory over Spain. In order to protect American business interests in the chaotic environment

**Main Idea CONNECTIONS**

*Why did the United States continue to intervene in Cuba after the Spanish-American War?*

that followed the war, President McKinley installed a military government in Cuba led by General Leonard Wood. The military government would rule for three years. This government organized a school system and restored economic stability. It also established a commission led by Major Walter Reed of the Army Medical Corps that found a cure for the deadly disease yellow fever.

In 1900 the military government authorized the Cubans to begin to draft a constitution. The new constitution was modeled on the United States Constitution and did not allow for continued American involvement in Cuba. The United States government, however, insisted that the Cubans include provisions outlined in a document called the Platt Amendment. The Platt Amendment stipulated that the Cuban government could not enter any foreign agreements, must allow the United States to establish two naval bases on the island, and must give the United States the right to intervene whenever necessary. The Platt Amendment remained in force until 1934.

Unlike Cuba, Puerto Rico did not become independent. In an attempt to stem a growing independence movement, the United States government granted Puerto Ricans United States citizenship in 1917.

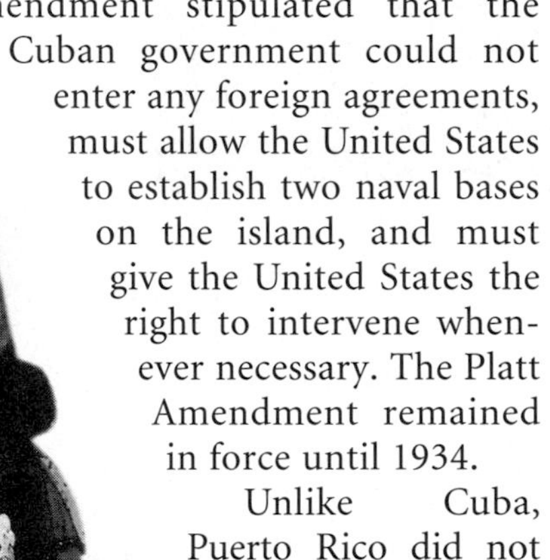

Queen Liliuokalani was Hawaii's last monarch. By the time she came into power, Hawaii was already dominated by U.S. business concerns. ***Economics*** ***What finally caused the fall of Hawaii's monarchy?***

## *Other Gains in the Pacific*

The United States government was intervening in other parts of the Pacific at the same time that the Spanish-American War was brewing. This intervention eventually brought about changes in the American relationship with Hawaii, Samoa, and China.

**Annexation of Hawaii** Hawaii had become increasingly important to United States business interests in the late 1800s. In 1887 Hawaii and the United States renewed a trade treaty that allowed Hawaiian sugar to be sold duty free in the United States. Hawaii also leased Pearl Harbor to the United States as a fueling and repair station for naval vessels. That same year, white Hawaiian-born planters forced the Hawaiian king, Kalakaua, to accept a new constitution that, in effect, gave them control of the government.

When the king died in 1891, his sister Liliuokalani came to the throne. A strong nationalist, Queen Liliuokalani opposed United States control of the islands and sought to reduce the power of foreign merchants. In 1893, with the help of the United States Marines, pineapple planter Sanford B. Dole removed Queen Liliuokalani from power. In addition he proclaimed a republic and requested that Hawaii be annexed by the United States.

When William McKinley was elected President, he supported the annexation. "We need Hawaii just as much and a good deal more than we did California. It is manifest destiny," McKinley said in early 1898. After briefly considering whether the Hawaiian people wished to be annexed, Congress was swayed by arguments that the United States needed naval stations in Hawaii in order to be a world power. In 1898 Congress approved the annexation of Hawaii.

**Samoa** The Polynesian islands of Samoa represented another possible stepping-stone to the growing trade with Asia. Back in 1878, the United States had negotiated a treaty with Samoa offering protection in return for a lease on Samoa's fine harbor at Pago Pago. When Britain and Germany began competing for control of these islands in the 1880s, tension between these European powers and the United States almost led to war. Eventually the three nations arranged a three-way protectorate of Samoa in 1889. The withdrawal of Great Britain from Samoa in 1899 left Germany and the

United States to divide up the islands. A year after the annexation of Hawaii, the United States had acquired the harbor at Pago Pago as well.

Competition for trade in China led to Secretary Hay's Open Door Policy. ***Foreign Relations*** ***According to this cartoon, who holds the "key" to China's open door?***

**An Open Door to China** China's huge population and its vast markets were increasingly important to American trade by the late 1800s. But the United States was not the only nation interested in China. Countries such as Russia, Germany, Britain, France, and Japan were seeking **spheres of influence,** or areas of economic and political control, in China. In 1899 John Hay, President McKinley's Secretary of State, wrote notes to the major European powers trying to persuade them to keep an "open door" to China. He wanted to ensure through his **Open Door Policy** that the United States would have equal access to China's millions of consumers. Hay's suggestions met with a cool response from the other countries.

Meanwhile, many Chinese resented foreign influence of any kind. A secret society called the Righteous and Harmonious Fists (the western press called them "Boxers") started a rebellion in the spring of 1900 that led to the massacre of 300 foreigners and Christian Chinese. Although the European powers eventually defeated the Boxers, Secretary Hay feared that these imperialist nations would use the rebellion as an excuse to seize more Chinese territory. Thus, he issued a second series of Open Door notes. These notes reaffirmed the principle of open trade in China and made an even stronger statement about the intention of the United States to preserve it.

## SECTION 2 REVIEW

### Comprehension

1. *Key Terms* Define: (a) arbitration; (b) jingoism; (c) sphere of influence; (d) Open Door Policy.
2. *Summarizing the Main Idea* What actions led to the Spanish-American War?
3. *Organizing Information* Create a flowchart that organizes information about the events that led the United States into war with Spain. Begin your chart with *1895: Cuban Rebellion flares after economic collapse* and end with *December 1898: United States signs treaty with Spain.*

### Critical Thinking

4. *Analyzing Time Lines* Review the time line at the start of the section. Pick one event where the United States intervened in another country and explain why this event was typical of United States foreign policy.
5. *Recognizing Cause and Effect* Describe how the 1895 dispute between the United States and Great Britain reaffirmed the validity of the Monroe Doctrine.

### Writing Activity

6. *Writing a Persuasive Essay* Write an essay that supports or refutes the following statement: *United States expansionist policies in the Pacific earned the nation new territories and increased its influence in the region.*

# SKILLS FOR LIFE

Geography

Graphs and Charts

Historical Evidence

Critical Thinking

# Using a Time Zone Map

Until the late 1800s, communities around the world calculated local time by the sun. When railroads began providing rapid long-distance train service between many communities—each with its own version of local time—this method began to cause scheduling nightmares.

In 1884 delegates from 27 nations met in Washington, D.C., to discuss the problem. They eventually agreed on a system of worldwide standard time. Under this system, the world is divided into 24 time zones, shown by colored bands on the map below. Time is the same throughout each zone.

The Prime Meridian, which passes through Greenwich, England, at 0° longitude, is the starting point for calculating the time in each zone. The International Date Line —located in the Pacific Ocean at 180° longitude—is where the date changes. The calendar date to the east of this line is one day earlier than that to the west.

Use the following steps to read the time zone map below.

**1.** ***Study the information on the map.*** The numbers at the bottom of the map indicate the number of hours each time zone differs from Greenwich time at the Prime Meridian. For example, a value of +3 means that the time in that zone is three hours later than Greenwich time; –3 means it is three hours earlier. The numbers at the top of the map provide examples of how this system works. (a) If it is 12:00 noon, Greenwich time, what time is it in Moscow? In Denver? (b) If it is 2:00 P.M. in Abidjan, Côte d'Ivoire, what time is it in the zone labeled +7? In the zone labeled –4?

**2.** ***Compare the time in your zone with other zones around the world.*** Find your time zone on the map. (a) If it is 1:00 A.M. in the time zone where you live, what time is it in Karachi, Pakistan? In Guangzhou, China? (b) If it is 12:00 noon in São Paulo, Brazil, what time is it where you live? (c) If it is 9:00 P.M. on Wednesday where you live, what time and day is it in Brisbane, Australia?

**TEST FOR SUCCESS**

If you flew west from Cairo, Egypt, to Lima, Peru, how many hours forward or back would you have to set your watch?

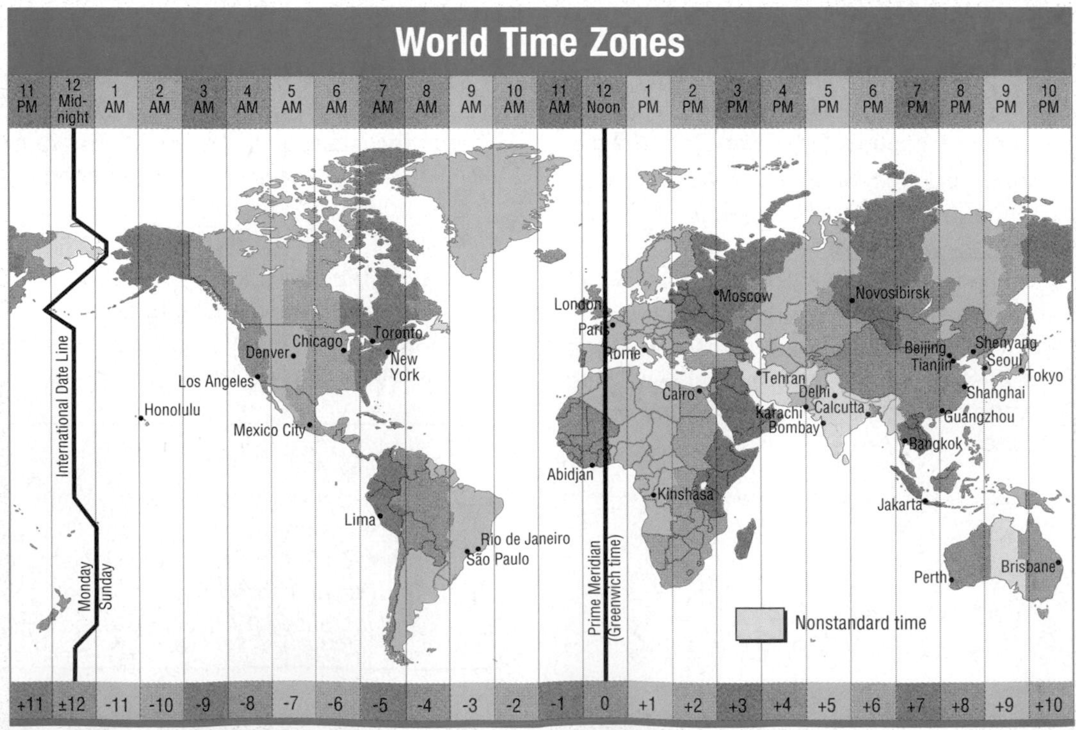

1901
*Theodore Roosevelt becomes President when William McKinley is assassinated*

1904
*President Roosevelt issues Roosevelt Corollary to the Monroe Doctrine*

1904
*Construction begins on Panama Canal*

1905
*Roosevelt mediates settlement of Russo-Japanese War*

1908
*William Howard Taft elected President*

1900 1902 1904 1906 1908

# 3 Expansion Under Roosevelt and Taft

**SECTION PREVIEW**

### Objectives

1 Explain why the United States built the Panama Canal and the impact that it had.
2 Compare American foreign policy in the early 1900s in Latin America and in Asia.
3 Describe President Taft's use of "dollar diplomacy," including its legacy as an American foreign policy.
4 *Key Terms* Define: concession; Roosevelt Corollary; dollar diplomacy.

### Main Idea

President Theodore Roosevelt conducted a vigorous foreign policy that suited the new status of the United States as a world power. Although President William Howard Taft continued Roosevelt's policies, he preferred a more subtle approach to influencing other nations.

### Reading Strategy

*Formulating Questions* Reread the Main Idea above. Then rewrite it as two questions. As you read the section, take notes that help answer the questions.

By 1900 the United States had emerged as a genuine world power. It controlled several overseas territories and had a large and vigorous economy. These circumstances contributed to William McKinley's decisive victory in the presidential election of 1900. One year later McKinley was dead, cut down by an assassin's bullet. Theodore Roosevelt, McKinley's Vice President, was now President. The new President developed a foreign policy to support the nation's new role in the world. Under his leadership, the United States continued to intervene in the affairs of countries that were of economic and strategic interest to the nation.

## The Panama Canal

The Spanish-American War brought home to Americans the need for a shorter route between the Pacific and Atlantic oceans. A canal built across Central America would link the Atlantic and Pacific oceans, making global shipping much faster. It would also allow the United States Navy to move quickly from one ocean to the other in time of war.

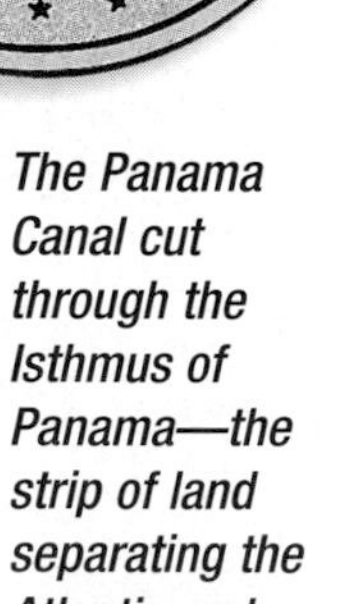


*The Panama Canal cut through the Isthmus of Panama—the strip of land separating the Atlantic and Pacific oceans.*

**Building the Canal** The Isthmus of Panama was an ideal location for such a route. At that time Panama was a province of the South American nation of Colombia. In 1879 a French company headed by Ferdinand de Lesseps had bought a 25-year **concession** from Colombia to build a canal across Panama. (A concession is a grant for a piece of land in exchange for a promise to use the land for a specific purpose.) Defeated by yellow fever and severe mismanagement, the company abandoned the project 10 years later. It offered its

## Cross Section of the Panama Canal Zone

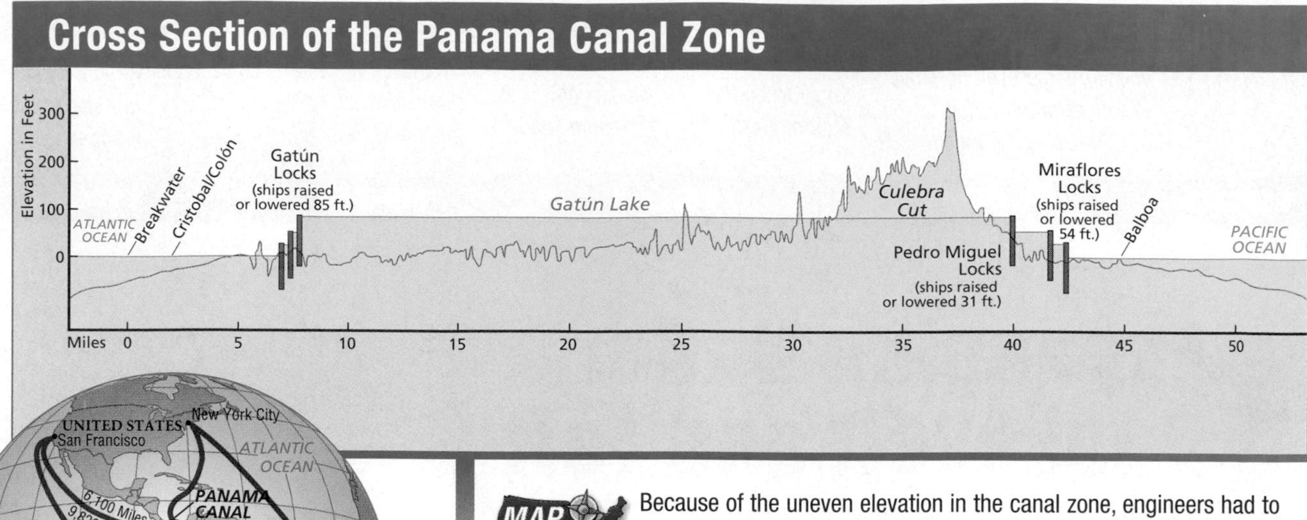


**MAP skills** Because of the uneven elevation in the canal zone, engineers had to design a series of locks (above) to raise and lower the ships so that they could pass through the canal. Compare the sea route from New York City to San Francisco (left) with and without the canal. ***Movement* By how many miles did the Panama Canal reduce the journey?**

remaining rights to the United States for $100 million. When the price fell to $40 million, Congress passed the Spooner Act in 1902 that authorized the purchase of the French assets. The act required that the United States work out a treaty with Colombia for a lease on the land.

Treaty negotiations went nowhere. Colombia was waiting for the French concession to expire in 1904 so that it could offer the isthmus at a higher price. Roosevelt was enraged by this attempt by Colombian "bandits" to "rob" the United States. He secretly made it clear to Philippe Bunau-Varilla, an official with the French company, that the United States would not interfere if the company organized a Panamanian revolution against Colombia.

**Main Idea CONNECTIONS**

*Why did President Roosevelt secretly support the revolution in Panama?*

The revolt took place in November 1903 with United States warships waiting offshore to provide support for the rebels. The United States immediately recognized an independent Panama and became its protector. In return, Panama ratified the Hay–Bunau-Varilla Treaty in February 1904. The treaty gave the United States a permanent grant of a 10-mile-wide strip of land for a Canal Zone. The United States had complete sovereignty over this zone. The Panamanians received $10 million.

Construction of the canal began in 1904. To complete this mammoth task, workers were brought in from several countries. Many of them had no construction experience whatsoever. After receiving proper training, the workers surpassed all expectations. They finished the canal in 1914, six months ahead of schedule and $23 million under budget.

**Reaction to the Canal** Roosevelt's opponents did not appreciate the methods he had used to secure the Canal Zone. A newspaper published by William Hearst commented, "Besides being a rough-riding assault upon another republic over the shattered wreckage of international law . . . it is a quite unexampled instance of foul play in American politics."

Most Americans, however, approved of President Roosevelt's actions in Panama. They were convinced that the canal was vital to national security and prosperity. Two years after leaving office, Theodore Roosevelt gave a speech at the University of California at Berkeley in which he justified his methods:

**AMERICAN VOICES** **"If I had followed traditional, conservative methods I would have submitted a dignified State paper of probably 200 pages to Congress and the debates on it would have been going on yet; but I took the Canal Zone and let Congress debate; and while the debate goes on the canal does also."**

—*Theodore Roosevelt*

Despite its success as a link between the Atlantic and Pacific, the Panama Canal left a long heritage of ill will among Latin Americans toward the United States. In recognition of the illegal means used to acquire the Canal Zone, Congress voted to pay $25 million to Colombia in 1921, after TR had died.

## *Foreign Policy in the Early 1900s*

In 1901 Roosevelt reminded an audience at the Minnesota State Fair of an old African proverb: "Speak softly and carry a big stick; you will go far." In his view, the "big stick" was the United States Navy. Indeed, the threat of military force allowed Roosevelt to conduct an aggressive foreign policy.

**The Roosevelt Corollary** In December 1904, Roosevelt issued a message to Congress that became known as the **Roosevelt Corollary** to the Monroe Doctrine. Roosevelt began this corollary, or extension of a previously accepted idea, by denying that the United States wanted any more territory.

**KEY DOCUMENTS** "It must be understood that under no circumstances will the United States use the Monroe Doctrine as a cloak for territorial aggression. We desire peace with all the world, but perhaps most of all with the other peoples of the American continent. . . . It is always possible that wrong actions toward this nation . . . may result in our having to take action to protect our rights; but such action will not be taken with a view to territorial aggression."

—*Roosevelt Corollary to the Monroe Doctrine, Theodore Roosevelt, 1904*

The United States wanted only "to see neighboring countries stable, orderly, and prosperous," he said. But if the countries engaged in activities harmful to the interests of the United States or if their governments collapsed, inviting intervention from stronger nations, then the United States would be forced to exercise "an international police power." In other words, the United States government would intervene to prevent intervention from other powers. This was the central point of the Roosevelt Corollary.

The first test of the Roosevelt Corollary concerned the small Caribbean island republic of Santo Domingo (now the Dominican

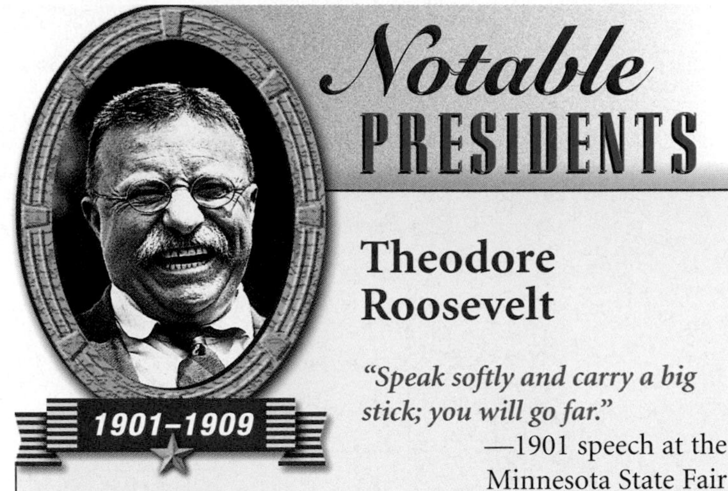


## *Notable* PRESIDENTS

### Theodore Roosevelt

*"Speak softly and carry a big stick; you will go far."*
—1901 speech at the Minnesota State Fair

Born into a wealthy New York family, Theodore Roosevelt had asthma as a child, but at his father's insistence he overcame it with rigorous physical exercise. "TR" developed a stocky body, a fighter's toughness, and a love for strenuous living.

As a Republican politician in New York in the 1880s, TR called for a larger government role in the economy, a stand that made him leader of the Progressives. TR believed in honest as well as active government. During a six-year term on the U.S. Civil Service Commission, he enforced the merit system. TR later attacked corruption as head of the New York City Police Board.

In 1897 TR was appointed Assistant Secretary of the Navy. There he built up a two-ocean fleet and urged a tougher American foreign policy. When the Spanish-American War was declared in 1898, TR, though nearly 40 and with poor eyesight, demanded to see combat. He organized the "Rough Riders" and led them on a famous charge up Cuba's San Juan Hill.

The war made TR a national hero. Returning to New York, he won the governorship in 1898. Two years later President McKinley chose TR as his running mate. (Conservative New York Republicans, unhappy at TR's Progressive policies, were not sorry to see him leave New York.) In 1901 McKinley was assassinated. Roosevelt became, at age 42, the nation's youngest President to that time.

TR saw the presidency as a "bully pulpit," or a wonderful stage from which to win public support for his brand of strong leadership. His economic policies included regulating big business and encouraging labor unions. His foreign policies reflected the "big stick" approach described in the quotation above. TR was also a vocal conservationist, acting to preserve the nation's natural resources and wildlife. Most importantly, TR's boldness and constant activity helped create the modern image of the President.

#### Connecting to Today

Do you think that American foreign policy today should be guided by the principle of "speak softly and carry a big stick"? Explain your answer.

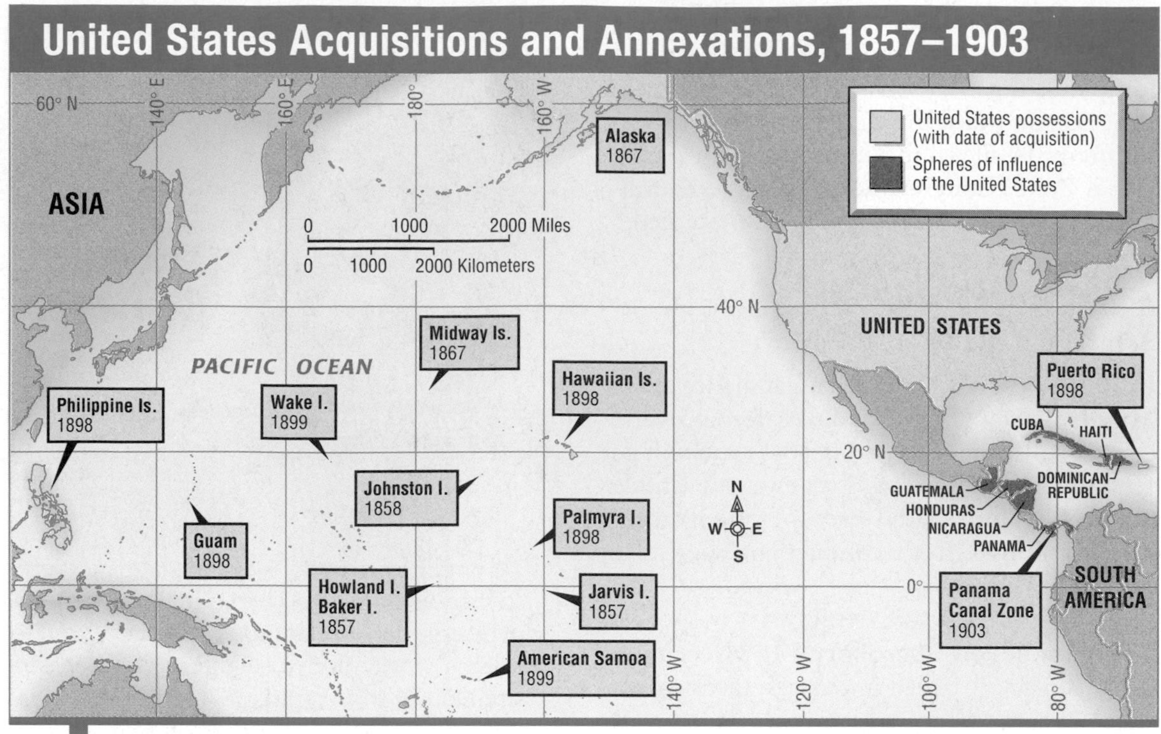


**MAP skills** Between 1857 and 1903, the United States acquired many new territorial possessions around the globe. ***Location*** ***Why do you think so many of these new possessions were islands located in the Pacific Ocean?***

Republic). When the island went bankrupt, European nations threatened to intervene to collect their money. Roosevelt moved quickly to establish American supervision of customs collections. Bankers in the United States took over the country's finances and paid its European debt. Roosevelt's actions were initially blocked by Congress. The President was able to get around congressional opposition by creating an executive agreement with Santo Domingo's president.

Under Roosevelt, United States intervention in Latin America became common. This development angered many Latin Americans. Congress also was displeased with Roosevelt's single-handed foreign policies that seemed to strengthen the President's powers while weakening their own.

Published after the announcement of the Roosevelt Corollary, this political cartoon depicts Teddy Roosevelt as the world's police officer, using his "big stick" to maintain order and stability in Latin America. ***Foreign Relations*** ***How did Roosevelt justify U.S. interventions in Latin America?***

**Roosevelt as Peacemaker** In Asia, the President's chief concern was to preserve an "open door" to trade with China. In order for this to happen, Roosevelt believed that both Japan and Russia had to be kept in check. In 1904 the two nations went to war. Roosevelt feared that a Japanese victory would upset the balance of power in Asia. Working in secret through friends in the diplomatic corps, the President looked for a way to end the war.

In 1905 Roosevelt mediated a peace agreement to the Russo-Japanese War. He invited delegates from the two nations to Portsmouth, New Hampshire, where he persuaded Japan to be satisfied with small grants of land and control over Korea instead of a huge payment of money. He also secured a promise from Russia to vacate Manchuria, which remained part of China. Roosevelt succeeded in keeping trade in China open to all nations. His role as mediator won him the Nobel Peace Prize.

## *Taft and Dollar Diplomacy*

William Howard Taft, elected to the presidency in 1908, was not as aggressive as Roosevelt in pursuing foreign policy aims. A distinguished lawyer from Ohio, Taft had served as Roosevelt's Secretary of War and had headed the commission that governed the Philippines.

Taft's main foreign policy goals were to maintain the open door to Asia and preserve stability in Latin America. As for the rest, he preferred "substituting dollars for bullets." By this he meant maintaining orderly societies abroad by increasing American investment in foreign economies. Although some of Taft's contemporaries mocked his approach, calling it **dollar diplomacy,** Taft himself later used this term with pride.

Although President William Howard Taft shared Teddy Roosevelt's policy goals, he adopted a less aggressive approach to foreign policy. ***Foreign Relations*** ***What was Taft's dollar diplomacy?***

Dollar diplomacy did not succeed as well as Taft had hoped. Although it increased the level of United States financial involvement abroad, the results were not always profitable. For example, when Taft's Secretary of State, Philander Knox, persuaded bankers from the United States to invest in railroad projects in China and Manchuria, Russia and Japan united in an effort to block the influence of the Americans. In addition, many United States investments in China were lost when the country's government collapsed in revolution in 1911.

Dollar diplomacy also created enemies in Latin America, especially in the Caribbean and Central America, where local revolutionary movements opposed American influence. Although the United States reached new heights as an international power under Roosevelt and Taft, anti-colonialism abroad and anti-imperialism at home provided a growing check to further expansion.

### SECTION 3 REVIEW

#### Comprehension

1. *Key Terms* Define: (a) concession; (b) Roosevelt Corollary; (c) dollar diplomacy.
2. *Summarizing the Main Idea* How was President Taft's dollar diplomacy both similar to and different from the approach to foreign policy taken by Theodore Roosevelt?
3. *Organizing Information* Create a chart that compares information about American foreign policy in the early 1900s. Label one column *Latin America* and the other *Asia.* In each column describe American foreign policy in general terms. Provide at least one example to support your description.

#### Critical Thinking

4. *Analyzing Time Lines* Review the time line at the start of the section. Choose one entry and explain how it is an example of American foreign policy in the early 1900s.
5. *Identifying Central Issues* How did the United States secure the rights to build a canal through Panama?

#### Writing Activity

6. *Writing an Expository Essay* Write a brief essay explaining President Taft's main foreign policy goals. Include his plan for accomplishing these goals.

# The Panama Canal

*The geographic theme of place explores how physical and human characteristics make one environment different from another. On a world map it is hard to see these characteristics. The Isthmus of Panama, for example, seems a thread of land. But up close, it is miles wide, formed of violent rivers, dense forests, and towering mountains. How did these characteristics and others affect the effort to build the canal?*

Workers digging the Panama Canal

Three factors affected the building of the Panama Canal. First, engineers had to decide where the canal should be located. Second, they had to cope with environmental hazards to workers. Finally, massive amounts of earth had to be moved to complete the project. The canal was to become the greatest engineering accomplishment of its era.

> **The canal was to become the greatest engineering accomplishment of its era.**

## Cutting Across the Continental Divide

When the construction team arrived in Panama in 1904, the end points of the canal already had been decided. The canal would begin at Colón on the Atlantic Ocean side and end close to Panama City on the Pacific Ocean side, as the map on the next page shows.

Two major obstacles impeded its path, however. One was the Continental Divide, a ridge across Central America that separates rivers that flow west from rivers that flow east. A decision was made to cut through the Divide. Engineers soon realized that some of the work had already been done. In the 1880s, a French company trying to build a canal had scooped out 19 million cubic yards of dirt and rock from the Divide near Culebra. At the time, no one would have guessed that this excavation, the Culebra Cut, would require digging another 96 million cubic yards before it was finished.

## Taming the Chagres River

The other geographic obstacle was the wild and unpredictable Chagres River. It had to be tamed if the canal was to be built.

Taming the river had been a challenge for ages. The French had never really solved the problem. The American solution was to "drown" it.

Drowning the river meant that a huge earthen dam would be laid across the river valley at Gatún (see map opposite). This section of the Chagres would then overflow, creating the largest artificial lake in the world at that time. The Chagres would become the only river in the world to cross a continental divide and flow into two oceans at once.

From the entrance at Colón Harbor, ships using the new canal would sail 7 miles up a channel and ascend through three locks to a height of 85 feet above sea level. Then they would cross the new and sprawling Gatún Lake for 24 miles, pass through the 9 miles of the Culebra Cut, and descend by one lock to a smaller lake about 1 mile long. Another set of two locks would bring them to sea level and the final 8-mile leg of the canal to the open Pacific.

## An Environmental Problem Solved

While engineers were wrestling with the location of the canal, army physician William Gorgas wrestled with an environmental hazard that threatened workers: the mosquito. Medical science had learned only a few years before that two of the deadliest tropical diseases, yellow fever and malaria, were transmitted by mosquitoes.

The secret of mosquito control, Gorgas found, was to cover, destroy, or drain every place where mosquitoes could lay their eggs. This meant every tank, jar, hollow, and puddle, indoors or out, had to be covered. Dividing the cities on the canal route into districts, he assigned an inspector to check every house on a daily basis for uncovered or standing water. He also gave orders that any pools that could not be drained were to be covered with a film of oil or kerosene.

Gorgas's methods wiped out yellow fever before the end of 1905. Malaria, which was carried by a tougher mosquito, was not eliminated, but was much reduced.

*Panama Canal Zone*

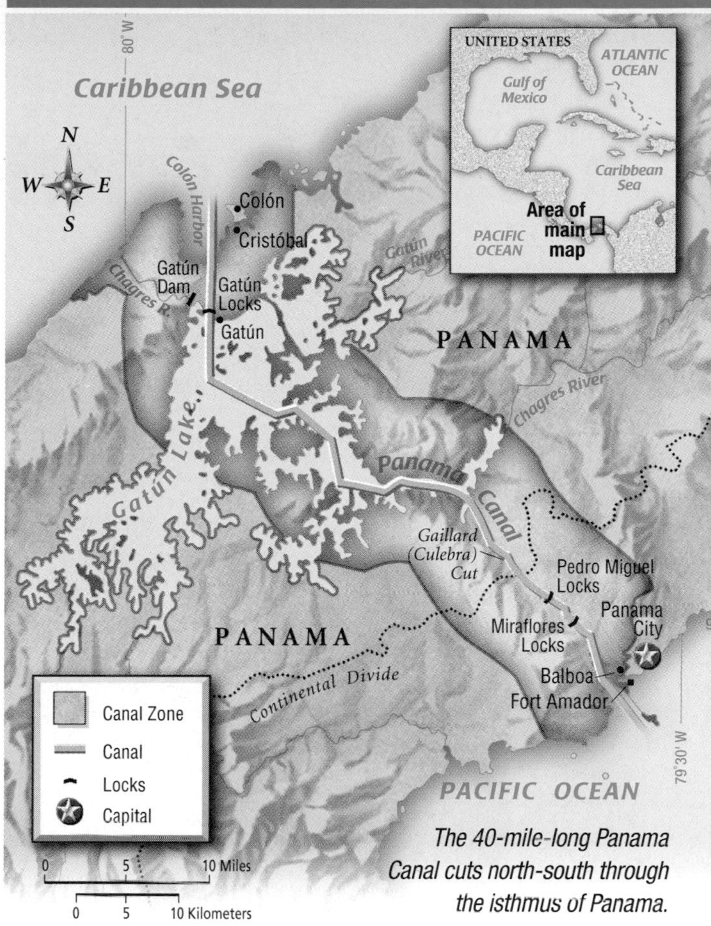


The 40-mile-long Panama Canal cuts north-south through the isthmus of Panama.

## Solving Problems of Movement

When it came to actually digging the canal, the chief engineer, John F. Stevens, viewed the project as a simple problem of movement: dirt—lots of it—had to be moved. As an experienced builder of railroads, he knew that the cheapest, fastest way to move anything on land was by railroad.

Within a week after his arrival, the new chief engineer had ordered double tracks laid. To get the dirt from the ditch to the train cars, Stevens brought in monster steam shovels. President Theodore Roosevelt, on an inspection visit to Panama, wrote, "Now we have taken hold of the job. . . . The huge steam shovels are hard at it, scooping huge masses of rock and gravel and dirt." The shovels were so efficient they filled five hundred trains with debris every day.

The highly efficient railway system could not solve another problem, however. Panama could not provide enough supplies to keep tens of thousands of workers fed and busy. Thus, ships traveled frequently between Colón and the United States. Ships brought in workers as well, some 45,000 of them, from 97 different nations. By 1914, the geographic obstacles had been overcome and the "big ditch" was completed.

1. What two problems of movement did the building of the canal entail, and how were they solved?
2. How did Dr. Gorgas change the environment of Panama, and what effect did his work have?

### Themes in Geography

3. *Place* Describe how engineers solved one geographical problem in locating the canal.

| 1895 | | 1905 | | | 1915 |
|---|---|---|---|---|---|
| | **1898** *Anti-Imperialist League established* | | **1907** *Roosevelt sends the "Great White Fleet" on trip around the world* | **1910** *Boy Scouts formed in the United States* | **1914** *Construction of the Panama Canal is completed* |

# 4 Debating America's New Role

## SECTION PREVIEW

### Objectives

1. Describe the main arguments raised by the anti-imperialists.
2. Explain why imperialism appealed to many Americans.
3. Understand how imperialism made the United States both welcome and unpopular around the world.
4. *Key Terms* Define: racism; compulsory; Great White Fleet.

### Main Idea

After the Spanish-American War, the debate intensified over whether it was appropriate for the United States to build an empire.

### Reading Strategy

*Outlining Information* Skim the section and use the headings and subheadings to create an outline. As you read the section, fill in supporting details.

This 1870 weathervane shows pride in the United States' new role as a world power.

Before the Spanish-American War, United States citizens were already debating the consequences of an expanded role in world affairs. Walter Gresham, President Cleveland's Secretary of State in 1894, cautioned against "the evils of interference in affairs that do not specially concern us." Until the annexation of the Philippines in 1898, however, most citizens supported overseas involvement.

## The Anti-Imperialists

After the annexation, opposition to imperialism grew. In November 1898, opponents of United States policy in the Philippines established the Anti-Imperialist League. Most of its organizers were well-to-do professionals. They included editor E. L. Godkin, Democratic politician William Jennings Bryan, settlement house leader Jane Addams, and novelist Mark Twain.

**Moral and Political Arguments** The anti-imperialists used a variety of arguments to support their position. The strongest of these were moral and political in nature. Expansionist behavior, the anti-imperialists asserted, was a rejection of the nation's foundation of "liberty for all." As one prominent Republican and former senator explained in 1899:

AMERICAN VOICES

> "We regret that it has become necessary in the land of Washington and Lincoln to reaffirm that all men, of whatever race or color, are entitled to life, liberty, and the pursuit of happiness."
>
> —*Carl Schurz*

Other anti-imperialists argued that the United States already had enough difficulties at home and should not take on more responsibilities. Finally, anti-imperialists noted that imperialism threatened the nation's democratic foundations. The large standing armies that were employed to bring other nations under American control could be used just as easily to crush dissent at home.

**Racial Arguments** Other anti-imperialists saw **racism** at work in imperialism. Racism is a belief that differences in character or intelligence are due to one's race. Many Americans of this period believed that people of Anglo-Saxon heritage were superior to other races. The public officials who developed the country's policies shared these sentiments.

African Americans were at first torn about imperialistic issues. As United States citizens, they wanted to support their country. But they recognized the racism that underlay imperialism. A leader of the A.M.E. Zion Church had this to say in 1899:

> **AMERICAN VOICES** "Had the Filipinos been white and fought as bravely as they have, the war would have been ended and their independence granted a long time ago."
>
> —*Bishop Alexander Walters*

Although most southern Democrats also opposed imperialism, they did so for different reasons. Many southern politicians feared the effects of having to absorb more people of different races into the United States. Consequently, southern Democrats led the movement in the Senate against ratifying the treaty with Spain after the Spanish-American War. A number of anti-imperialists outside the South also opposed imperialist policies because of the fear that they would encourage people of different racial backgrounds to move to the United States.

**Economic Arguments** Finally, anti-imperialists raised economic objections to expansionist policies. In the view of these thinkers, it was not a good time for the United States to expand. First, expansion involved too many costs. Maintaining the necessary armed forces required more taxation, debt, and possibly even **compulsory,** or required, military service.

Samuel Gompers raised another concern. He argued that laborers coming to the United States from annexed territories would compete with American workers for jobs. Since these immigrants would work for lower wages, their presence would drive all wages down.

## *Imperialism's Appeal*

Despite the strength of these arguments, imperialism maintained a powerful hold on the American imagination. Some people looked to a new frontier abroad to keep Americans from losing their competitive edge. The director of the census had declared the frontier "closed" in the 1890 census. Imperialism offered a new kind of frontier for American expansion.

**Main Idea CONNECTIONS**

*What was the connection between imperialism and the closing of the American frontier?*

The growth and popularity of youth scouting programs during this period shows that many Americans shared a "frontier mentality." Sir Robert Baden-Powell, an army officer of the

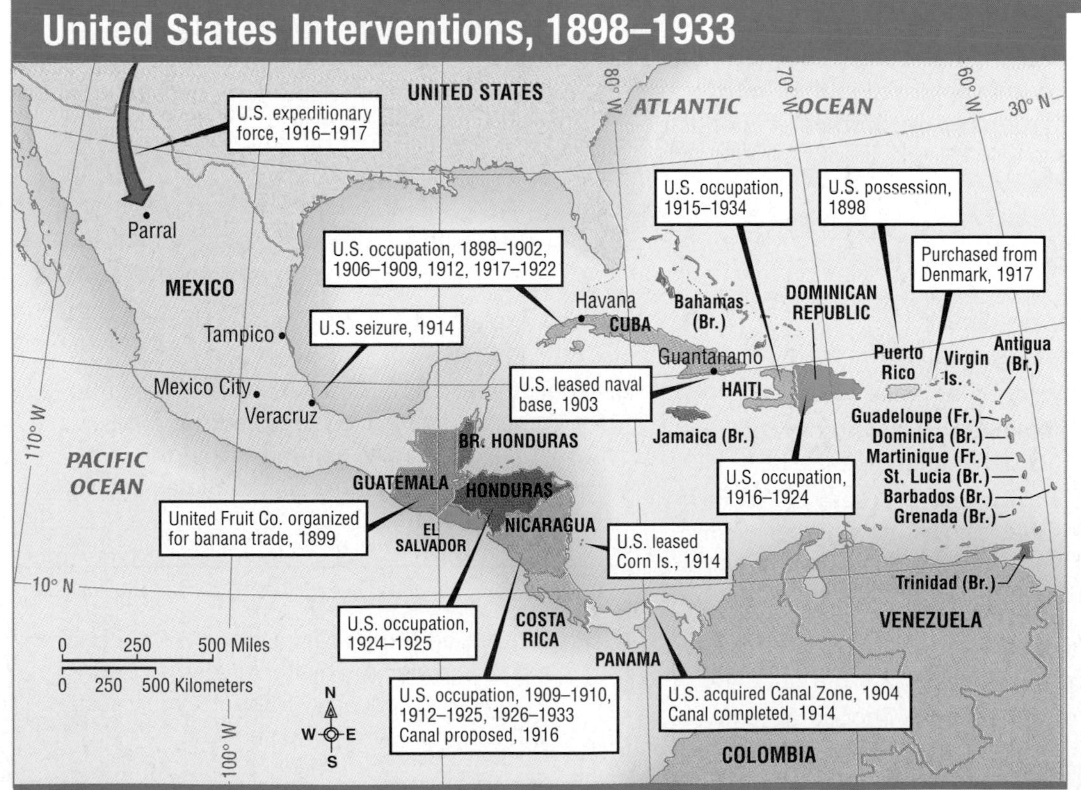

This map shows how frequently the United States intervened in the affairs of Latin American countries in the early 1900s. The United States government defended these interventions as necessary for the protection of the nation's economic and political interests. ***Place*** *What form did most of these interventions take?*

## COMPARING PRIMARY SOURCES

### IMPERIALISM

The Spanish-American War heightened the debate between imperialist and anti-imperialist factions at home.

**Anti-Imperialist**

"We assume that what we like and practice, and what we think better, must come as a welcome blessing to Spanish-Americans and Filipinos. This is grossly and obviously untrue. They hate our ways. They are hostile to our ideas. Our religion, language, institutions, and manners offend them."

*—William G. Sumner, Yale University professor, in an 1898 speech*

**Pro-Imperialist**

"Think of the tens of thousands of Americans who will invade mine and field and forest in the Philippines when a liberal government, protected and controlled by this republic, if not the government of the republic itself, shall establish order and equity there!"

*—Albert J. Beveridge, leading imperialist and later United States senator, in an 1898 speech*

***ANALYZING VIEWPOINTS*** **Which of the viewpoints do you think best represents the political ideals of liberty and equality on which the United States was founded?**

British Empire, had used scouting techniques (tracking, woodcraft, and wilderness survival) to great success in a battle in South Africa. A few years after he returned to Britain as a war hero, Baden-Powell founded the Boy Scout movement. Scouting appeared in the United States in 1910 and soon became immensely popular.

Many people were swayed by the practical advantages of imperialism. They agreed with the economic arguments that emphasized the need to gain access to foreign markets. Others embraced the strategic reasons for expansion.

In December 1907 Roosevelt sent part of the United States Navy on a cruise around the world. The trip was designed to demonstrate the nation's impressive naval power to the world. The **Great White Fleet,** as the gleaming white ships were called, made a big impression everywhere it sailed. For American citizens, the fleet clearly showed the benefits of having a powerful navy.

## *Two Sides of Imperialism*

Having begun a pattern of international involvement, shown on the map on the previous page, the United States discovered that these actions frequently took on a life of their own. In the Caribbean and Central America, for example, the United States often had to defend governments that were unpopular with local inhabitants. In Latin America, the cry "Yankee, Go Home!" began to be heard. Even before the Panama Canal was completed in 1914, Panamanians began to complain that they suffered from discrimination.

On the other hand, other countries—even those fearful about maintaining their independence—began to turn to the United States for help. Both welcomed and rejected, the United States would spend the rest of the century trying to decide the best way to reconcile its growing power and national interests with its relationships with other nations.

## *SECTION 4 REVIEW*

### Comprehension

1. *Key Terms* Define: (a) racism; (b) compulsory; (c) Great White Fleet.
2. *Summarizing Main Ideas* Name some of the major arguments of the anti-imperialists.
3. *Organizing Information* Create a two-column chart that shows how imperialism made the United States both welcome and unpopular around the world.

### Critical Thinking

4. *Analyzing Time Lines* Review the time line at the start of the section. Choose an entry and explain why it reflects the debate over America's new role.
5. *Identifying Assumptions* Based on the arguments they used against imperialism, what kind of role do you think the anti-imperialists believed the United States should play in world affairs?

### Writing Activity

6. *Writing an Expository Essay* Write a brief essay explaining why imperialism appealed to many Americans. Support your essay with examples from the section.

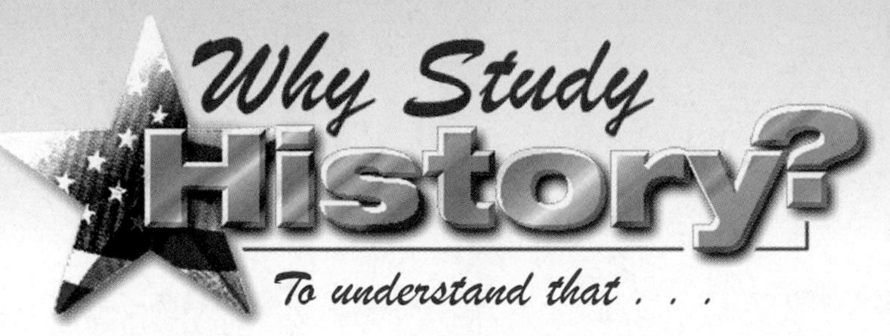


# Your Nation Is a World Power

Since the Spanish-American War, the United States has played an increasingly active role in events around the world.

*Teddy Roosevelt and the Rough Riders, 1898*

"U.S. Air Assault Pounds Iraq." "U.S. Peacekeepers Arrive in Bosnia." "U.S. Food Shipments Reach North Korea." Headlines such as these reflect the extent of American involvement in distant parts of the world, as well as the many different types of involvement. As the United States has grown into a world power, its participation in world affairs has increased dramatically.

## The Impact Today

In 1796 President George Washington warned Americans against involvement with foreign nations. For roughly a century American leaders heeded Washington's advice, avoiding foreign entanglements as much as possible.

That policy ended in the 1890s. The Spanish-American War marked the beginning of a more active foreign policy, in which the United States participated in foreign conflicts and acquired overseas territories, such as the Philippines.

American overseas involvement became especially widespread after the end of World War II in 1945. For the next half-century the United States and the Soviet Union, the world's two most powerful nations, fought a cold war for influence in Europe, Africa, Asia, and Latin America. To fight communism in other nations, the United States supplied large amounts of economic and military aid. American military forces fought large, costly wars in Korea and Vietnam and intervened in other nations such as the Dominican Republic and Grenada.

The cold war ended in the early 1990s with the collapse of the Soviet Union. Still, the United States remains committed to an active international role. In 1991, for example, American military forces liberated Kuwait from Iraqi occupation. Two years later, American troops went to Bosnia as part of a United Nations peacekeeping force aimed at ending the ethnic conflict raging there. The United States has assisted former Communist nations in their transition to democratic governments and market economies. Finally, the United States has played a leading role in international efforts to expand trade and promote economic growth around the world.

## The Impact on You

What guidelines should American leaders use in deciding whether to become involved in the affairs of other countries? Discuss the issue with your classmates, friends, and family. Then write a "policy statement" outlining your conclusions about United States involvement abroad.

*Marine comforts a Somali child during an American relief effort in 1992*

# Chapter 8 Review

## Chapter Summary

The major concepts of Chapter 8 are presented below. See also ***Guide to the Essentials of American History*** or ***Interactive Student Tutorial CD-ROM,*** which contains interactive review activities, time lines, helpful hints, and test practice.

### *Reviewing the Main Ideas*

By the 1890s, farms and factories in the United States were producing more than the nation could consume. Soon, many business and political leaders began to pursue new markets abroad. Inspired by dreams of an empire, some Americans pushed for new territory as well. American expansion caused some citizens to raise doubts about the morality of imperialism.

### *Section 1: The Pressure to Expand*

In the late 1800s, as European nations took over vast areas in Africa and Asia, American leaders looked to expand American influence abroad.

### *Section 2: The Spanish–American War*

A swift American victory in the Spanish-American War confirmed the nation's status as a world power, but it left some people arguing over how to govern newly acquired territories.

### *Section 3: Expansion Under Roosevelt and Taft*

President Theodore Roosevelt conducted a vigorous foreign policy that suited the new status of the United States as a world power. Although President William Howard Taft continued Roosevelt's policies, he preferred a more subtle approach to influencing other nations.

### *Section 4: Debating America's New Role*

After the Spanish-American War, the debate intensified over whether it was appropriate for the United States to build an empire.

Since the 1890s, the United States has played an active role in world affairs. On numerous occasions, Americans have provided military and economic aid to countries in need.

## Key Terms

For each of the terms below, write a sentence explaining how it relates to this chapter.

1. annex
2. Open Door Policy
3. Great White Fleet
4. Roosevelt Corollary
5. imperialism
6. sphere of influence
7. nationalism
8. dollar diplomacy
9. jingoism
10. banana republic

## Comprehension

1. Briefly explain the arguments of Alfred T. Mahan, Henry Cabot Lodge, and Albert J. Beveridge regarding expansionism.
2. Describe how the 1895 dispute between the United States and Great Britain reaffirmed the Monroe Doctrine.
3. Why did the American public favor war with Spain in 1898?
4. What was the Open Door Policy, and why was it important for the United States?
5. Describe Theodore Roosevelt's approach to foreign policy.
6. How did the Roosevelt Corollary affect United States policy in Latin America?
7. Explain President Taft's policy of dollar diplomacy.
8. Explain why anti-imperialists believed that imperialism betrayed basic American principles.

## Using Graphic Organizers

On a separate sheet of paper, copy the multi-flow map to show the causes and effects of American expansion during the late 1800s and early 1900s. Provide at least three causes and three effects.

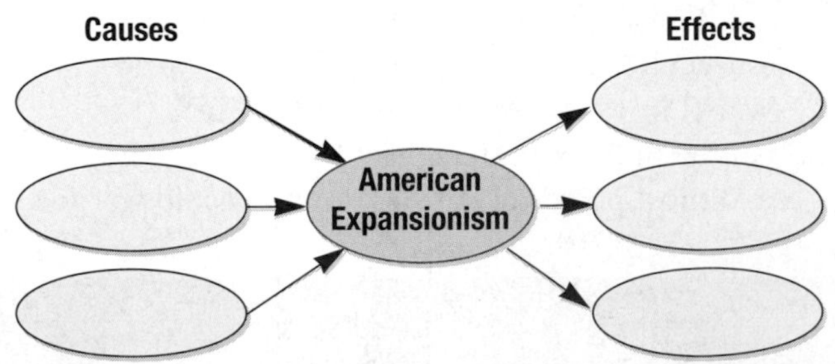

## Analyzing Political Cartoons ▶

1. The caption to this 1904 political cartoon was: "HIS 128th BIRTHDAY. 'Gee but this is an awful stretch!'" (a) Whose birthday is it? (b) How do you know? (c) What is the "awful stretch" referring to? (d) How do you know?
2. What is the cartoonist's view on United States imperialism?

## Critical Thinking

1. *Applying the Chapter Skill* Review the time zone map on page 270. Name two cities on the map that are in the same time zone as New York City.
2. *Identifying Central Issues* How did the popular philosophy of social Darwinism make it easier for some Americans to embrace imperialist policies in the late 1800s?
3. *Drawing Conclusions* During the late 1800s, the press fanned the flames of the Spanish-American War by publishing sensational stories about Spanish cruelties in Cuba. On what current issues has the press played a major role in influencing public opinion?
4. *Distinguishing Fact from Opinion* President McKinley's Secretary of State, John Hay, referred to the Spanish-American War as "a splendid little war." Can you think of any Americans, in addition to anti-imperialists, who might disagree with Hay?

### INTERNET ACTIVITY

***For your portfolio:***
**CREATE A TIME LINE**

Access Prentice Hall's *America: Pathways to the Present* site at **www.Pathways.phschool.com** for the specific URL to complete the activity. Additional resources and related Web sites are also available.

Read the biography of William Howard Taft and create a time line of his career. Write a paragraph summarizing Taft's professional life. How would you characterize his career? What do you consider his most important achievement? What did Taft consider his most important achievement?

## ANALYZING DOCUMENTS ◀ INTERPRETING DATA

Turn to the "American Voices" quotation on page 272.

1. Theodore Roosevelt is suggesting that his policies made it (a) impossible to build the canal. (b) possible to return Panama to Colombia. (c) easier to build the canal. (d) necessary to submit a State paper to Congress.
2. What is the most likely reason Roosevelt felt he had to justify his policies regarding the Panama Canal even after he left office? (a) Colombia was asking for the return of the Canal Zone. (b) Anti-imperialists were complaining about his high-handed methods. (c) Panama was asking for more money. (d) Congress was considering returning the land to Panama.
3. *Writing* Do you think Roosevelt's argument justifies his actions? Explain your reasoning.

## Connecting to Today

*Essay Writing* The United States still intervenes in foreign countries when its interests are threatened. Write a letter to the editor of a newspaper in which you argue either for or against an interventionist foreign policy. Research recent examples of United States actions in foreign countries and use them to support your arguments.

CHAPTER 9

# The Era of Progressive Reform

## 1890–1920

▲

**VIEWING HISTORY**

These women cheer the passage of the Nineteenth Amendment, which extended the vote to women. *Government* ***What other lasting reforms originated in the Progressive Era?***

## CHAPTER FOCUS

At the turn of the century, a spirit of reform known as progressivism took hold of many Americans. Less a united movement than a loose collection of informal alliances among reform groups, progressivism targeted the challenges of an urban, industrialized nation.

*The* **Why Study History?** *page at the end of this chapter explores the rise of volunteer organizations during the Progressive Era and community service activities today.*

1879
*Henry George writes* Progress and Poverty

1888
*Edward Bellamy writes* Looking Backward

1899
*National Consumers' League founded*

1906
*Upton Sinclair publishes* The Jungle

1870 1880 1890 1900 1910

# 1 The Origins of Progressivism

## SECTION PREVIEW

### Objectives

1. Describe the new reform ideas that took hold at the turn of the century.
2. Summarize the methods muckrakers used to bring about reforms.
3. List the goals that most progressive reformers had in common.
4. *Key Terms* Define: municipal; injunction; home rule; muckraker; Progressive Era; social welfare program.

### Main Idea

At the end of the 1800s, many citizens recognized the need to solve problems resulting from rapid industrialization and urban growth. The appearance of many reform movements caused historians to refer to the period as the Progressive Era.

### Reading Strategy

*Organizing Information* As you read the section, create a list of the reforms that Progressives worked to bring about.

During the last part of the 1800s, rapid industrialization had contributed to the growth of the nation's cities, population, and wealth. This growth had come at a cost, however. Unemployment, unsafe working conditions, and political corruption continued to plague the nation. Many citizens realized that private efforts to address these issues, such as charity and settlement houses, were inadequate. Some argued that the government needed to become more involved in solving the nation's problems.

## *New Reform Ideas*

The 1880s and 1890s were filled with lively debates about how to reform society. The ideas of journalists Henry George and Edward Bellamy were among the most popular. Socialists, labor leaders, and city government reformers also had many followers.

**Two Leading Reformers** In 1879 Henry George wrote *Progress and Poverty* in an effort to explain why poverty continued to flourish in such an advanced civilization. George concluded that poverty arose because some people bought and held on to land until its price went up. This practice, known as speculation, prevented others from using the land productively.

To solve this problem, George proposed that the government charge landowners a single tax on the value of the land itself. In the past, landowners had been taxed on improvements to the land, such as houses and cultivation. A single tax would make speculation in land less attractive by increasing the cost of holding land without using it. George's ideas had a powerful effect. "Single-tax" clubs sprang up everywhere. In 1894, club members from Iowa, Ohio, Minnesota, and Pennsylvania migrated to Fairhope, Alabama, to establish a single-tax colony.

In 1888 newspaper editor Edward Bellamy published *Looking Backward.* In this novel a man undergoes hypnosis in 1887 and wakes up in the year 2000. Upon waking, the man finds the United States transformed. In place of harsh working conditions, poverty, and political corruption, he finds a country where the government has taken over the largest companies. In the novel, the government has also reorganized the companies with the goal of meeting human needs rather than making profits. Wrote Bellamy:

**AMERICAN VOICES** "In a word, the people of the United States concluded to assume the conduct of their own business, just as . . . years before they had assumed the conduct of their own government."

—*Edward Bellamy,* Looking Backward

Bellamy's novel was a phenomenal best seller. In response to its ideas, hundreds of "Nationalist" clubs formed.

**Socialists** Bellamy's views were related to the widely discussed ideas of socialism. Socialism is an economic and political philosophy favoring public or government control of property and income. Many American socialists in this era wanted to end the capitalist system, distribute wealth more equally, and nationalize American industries. They wished to do so through the ballot box, not through revolution. In 1901 they formed the Socialist Party of America. By 1912 the party had won more than 1,000 **municipal,** or city government, offices.

**The Labor Movement** Like members of the Socialist party, some union members also hoped for fundamental economic change. Unions, however, focused their efforts on the goals of reducing hours and gaining better wages and working conditions.

The union movement grew in the 1890s, but only slowly. Employers discouraged union membership, preferring to deal with individual workers. If unions were successful despite this discouragement, business leaders could count on courts to issue **injunctions,** or court orders, prohibiting workers from going on strike.

**Municipal Reform** The spirit of reform was also felt within city governments. Municipal reformers opposed the influence of political bosses. They argued that only a civil service system based on merit instead of favors would keep political appointees out of important jobs enforcing labor laws. Reformers also worked for **home rule,** a system by which cities exercise a limited degree of self-rule. Home rule allowed cities to escape from domination by state governments, which often were controlled by political machines or rural interests.

Municipal reformers sometimes appeared naive in their belief that they could abolish corruption. Some of them also held negative views of immigrants, whom they felt were

In spite of the obstacles facing unions, the International Ladies Garment Workers Union (ILGWU) formed in 1900. After a strike in 1909, which included 20,000 New York City women garment workers, the ILGWU won the right to bargain collectively, or negotiate contracts with employers. ***Economics How did businesses prevent workers from striking?***

responsible for many city problems. Still, their ideas formed an important element of the era's spirit of reform.

This cartoon shows that TR himself was willing to wield the muckrake to attack difficult problems. Here, TR tries to clean up the nation's meatpacking industry. ***Culture*** *How did muckrakers use the media to advance reform?*

## *The Muckrakers*

Many reformers at the turn of the century worked to bring about change in a systematic manner. Relying heavily on scientific data and expert testimony, they first investigated issues of concern, such as slum or sweatshop conditions. Next, they publicized the results of their investigations. Readers could then put pressure on legislators to pass and enforce new laws. Women's clubs and charitable groups provided a key means of increasing support for reform and pressuring officials to take action.

Journalists also alerted the public to wrongdoing in politics and business. Theodore Roosevelt called such writers **muckrakers.** He took the term *muckraker* from John Bunyan's 1678 book *Pilgrim's Progress,* in which one of the characters was too busy raking filth on Earth to lift his eyes to heaven. While Roosevelt approved of legitimate exposure of wrongdoing, he condemned those who "earn their livelihood by telling . . . scandalous falsehoods about honest men."

Despite Roosevelt's criticism, the muckrakers included many respected writers who identified and exposed real abuses. Lincoln Steffens exposed political corruption in St. Louis and other cities. Ida Tarbell revealed the abuses committed by the huge Standard Oil trust. *The Jungle,* a novel by Upton Sinclair published in 1906, described the horrors of the meatpacking industry. Publication of the book led to the creation of a federal meat inspection program. Wrote Sinclair of the nation's filthy canneries:

**AMERICAN VOICES** "It seemed they must have agencies all over the country, to hunt out old and crippled and diseased cattle to be canned. . . . It was stuff such as this that made the 'embalmed beef' that had killed several times as many United States soldiers as all the bullets of the Spaniards [in the Spanish-American War]."

—*Upton Sinclair,* The Jungle

## *The Goals of the Progressives*

Americans read the muckrakers' novels and newspaper accounts with enthusiasm. Whether angered or sickened by what they read, many Americans were inspired to take action by joining reform organizations. Many of these new reform movements had their roots in earlier reform groups. These included nativists, prohibitionists, purity crusaders, charity reformers, social gospel adherents, settlement house workers, and Populists. Because all these groups were working to bring about "progress" in society, historians refer to the period from about 1890 to 1920 as the **Progressive Era.**

Unlike the socialists and some other reformers, most Progressives did not support sweeping economic and political changes. Many deeply feared the violence of revolution. Most Progressives were Americans of average wealth. They did not want to lose the high standard of living and personal liberty that democracy and a free-enterprise system had given them. Instead Progressives wanted to free the existing government of corruption so that it could be more efficient in an expanded role as guardian of workers and the poor.

Workers of all ages had little protection against workplace hazards—and few benefits when accidents befell them on the job. The fate of injured or killed workers aroused public sympathy and demands for reform. ***Government*** ***Why did Progressives push for social welfare programs?***

**An Expanded Role for Government** Many Progressives also argued that government must play a larger role in regulating economic activity. This regulation would prevent businesses from treating workers and competing companies unfairly. Progressives opposed government control of businesses, except for those companies that supplied essential services such as water, electricity, and transportation. They wanted most businesses to operate independently—provided they took workers' needs into account.

**Main Idea CONNECTIONS**

*Why did many Progressives argue that government must play a larger role in regulating economic activity?*

Progressives also believed that government ought to increase its responsibility for human welfare, or well-being. Workers had little protection against low wages, unemployment, or workplace hazards. Progressives proposed that government protect workers from such circumstances. They also wanted government to develop more **social welfare programs,** which would help ensure a basic standard of living for all Americans. These programs included unemployment, accident, and health insurance. Some also favored a social security system that would aid the disabled and the elderly. Progressives expected that government would rely on experts and scientists to plan efficient programs, which professionals, not politicians, would manage.

**Women Work for Reforms** As social worker Jane Addams explained in a 1910 *Ladies' Home Journal* article, women had a special interest in the reform of American society:

> **AMERICAN VOICES** **"Women who live in the country sweep their own dooryards and may either feed the refuse [trash] of the table to a flock of chickens or allow it innocently to decay in the open air and sunshine. In a crowded city quarter, however, if the street is not cleaned by the city authorities no amount of private sweeping will keep the tenement free from grime; if the garbage is not properly collected and destroyed a tenement house mother may see her children sicken and die of diseases."**
>
> —*Jane Addams*

In short, Addams argued that women in cities could not care for their families without government help. Progressive women did not all agree on how to reform society. Many focused on outlawing alcohol; others on reforming conditions in the workplace. Whatever their focus, many women agreed that they needed the right to vote. The cause of women's suffrage was important to many Progressives.

Because women and their children were workers, labor issues were also important to progressive women. Florence Kelley became a leader in the work for labor reform. She came from a prominent Pennsylvania family. Her father, William Darrah Kelley, was a fifteen-term member of Congress. Her great-aunt, Sarah Pugh, had a strong influence on her. An abolitionist and suffragist, Pugh had once refused to use cotton and sugar because slave labor produced them.

After completing her education at Cornell University in New York, and at the University of Zurich in Switzerland, Kelley became a resident in Jane Addams's Hull House in Chicago. When federal officials asked Addams to investigate labor conditions in the neighborhood, Addams recommended Kelley for the job. "Hull House was . . . surrounded in every direction by home work carried on under the sweating system," Kelley wrote later. "From the age of eighteen months few children able to sit in high chairs at tables were safe from being required to pull basting threads." Once, Kelley reported, a public official who was supposed to visit a sweatshop refused to enter, fearing contamination from one of the many diseases, such as tuberculosis, that raged through the tenements at that time.

Largely through her efforts, in 1893 Illinois passed a law prohibiting child labor, limiting working hours for women, and regulating sweatshop conditions. The governor put Kelley in charge of enforcing it. She became so frustrated by the district attorney's refusal to prosecute cases that she earned a law degree in order to take legal action herself.

In 1897 a new governor replaced Kelley as factory inspector with a political friend who did nothing to enforce the 1893 law. It was this experience that drew Kelley into municipal reform. Kelley believed that a civil service system would keep unqualified political appointees out of important regulatory jobs.

Kelley also served as general secretary of the National Consumers' League (NCL). The NCL was organized in 1899 to unite local consumers' leagues. Through the leagues, women investigated the conditions under which goods were made and sold. They also encouraged consumers to purchase goods only at shops that did not employ children or require overtime. Leagues insisted that factories obey state factory inspection laws. Later they insisted that they pay a minimum wage. Under Kelley's leadership, the NCL spearheaded national movements to outlaw child labor and protect workers, especially women. When criticized over this issue, Kelley would ask why "seals, bears, reindeer, fish, wild game in the national parks, buffalo" and numerous other creatures were worthy of government protection, "but not the children of our race and their mothers."

Kelley's legacy lasted long after her death in 1932. In 1954 Supreme Court justice Felix Frankfurter said that Florence Kelley "had probably the largest single share in shaping the social history of the United States during the first thirty years of this century."

*Florence Kelley*

**Resistance to Progressive Reforms** To protect vulnerable citizens, Progressives backed increased levels of government control over people's lives. They thought government should have some say in housing, health care, and even in the content of the movies people watched. This aspect of progressivism aroused resistance, often among the very people Progressives hoped to help. For example, Progressives saw child labor laws as critical to social progress. Employers who relied on cheap child labor, however, opposed the laws. In addition, poor families who could not survive without sending their children to work also objected. Such disputes added to the perception that Progressives were insensitive to the poor.

## SECTION 1 REVIEW

### Comprehension

1. ***Key Terms*** Define: (a) municipal; (b) injunction; (c) home rule; (d) muckraker; (e) Progressive Era; (f) social welfare program.
2. ***Summarizing the Main Idea*** Summarize the diverse goals of the progressive reformers.
3. ***Organizing Information*** Create a chart with two columns, one labeled *Problem* and the other labeled *Progressive Solution.* Complete the chart using information from this section.

### Critical Thinking

4. ***Analyzing Time Lines*** Review the time line at the start of the section. How does each of the events on this time line reflect the spirit of the Progressive Era?
5. ***Recognizing Ideologies*** What beliefs about the role of government lay at the heart of the Progressive Era?

### Writing Activity

6. ***Writing a Persuasive Essay*** Write a letter to the editor of a 1905 newspaper arguing why it is important for the paper to publish the muckrakers' articles.

SKILLS FOR LIFE

Critical Thinking

Geography

Graphs and Charts

Historical Evidence

# Testing Conclusions

Testing conclusions means checking statements or opinions to see whether or not they are supported by known data. Data that are known to be valid can be used as criteria for testing a conclusion. If the data support the conclusion, then you have reason to believe that the conclusion is sound. Use the following steps to test the validity of conclusions.

**1.** ***Study the conclusions to recognize the type of data that is necessary to verify them.*** If supporting data are provided, decide if they are useful for testing the conclusions. Read the conclusions at right, examine the data in the tables, and answer the following questions: (a) Upon what information are the conclusions based? (b) Is there a relationship between the conclusions and the evidence provided?

**2.** ***Decide on the criteria by which the conclusions could be tested.*** Some conclusions are based upon trends and must be tested against data that cover a period of time. Other conclusions are more specific and may need exact data for verification. (a) Does Conclusion 1 deal with a trend or with a specific point in time? (b) Would data covering a period of time be needed to support Conclusion 2?

**3.** ***Test the conclusions by comparing them with the data.*** Decide if the data support or contradict the conclusions and whether additional information is needed to determine the validity of some conclusions. (a) Do the facts support or contradict Conclusion 3? (b) Do you agree with Conclusion 4?

**Conclusions:**

1. The twenty-year period between 1900 and 1920 saw a steady and significant growth in union membership.

2. By 1920, union workers earned more money than nonunion workers while working fewer hours.

3. In terms of a percent of the work force, more workers were union members in 1910 than in 1920.

4. The reason why the vast majority of workers did not join labor unions in the early 1900s was that work stoppages led to pay stoppages and decreased earnings.

**TEST FOR SUCCESS**

According to the data, is the following conclusion valid or not? "In 1900 builders claimed more union members than any other industry."

**Work Force and Labor Union Membership**

| Year | Total Workers | Total Union Membership | Percentage of Work Force in Unions |
|---|---|---|---|
| 1900 | 29,073,000 | 868,000 | 3.0 |
| 1910 | 37,371,000 | 2,140,000 | 5.7 |
| 1920 | 42,434,000 | 5,048,000 | 11.9 |

**Union Membership by Industry**

| Year | Building | Textiles | Public Service |
|---|---|---|---|
| 1900 | 153,000 | 8,000 | 15,000 |
| 1910 | 459,000 | 21,000 | 58,000 |
| 1920 | 888,000 | 149,000 | 161,000 |

**Average Union and Nonunion Hours and Earnings in Manufacturing Industries**

| | Union | | Nonunion | |
|---|---|---|---|---|
| Year | Weekly Hours | Hourly Earnings | Weekly Hours | Hourly Earnings |
| 1900 | 53.0 | $0.341 | 62.1 | $0.152 |
| 1910 | 50.1 | $0.403 | 59.8 | $0.188 |
| 1920 | 45.7 | $0.884 | 53.5 | $0.561 |

Source: *Historical Statistics of the United States, Colonial Times to 1970*

| 1902 | 1905 | 1908 | 1911 | 1913 | 1913 |
|---|---|---|---|---|---|
| *United Mine Workers strike over low wages* | *United States Forest Service established* | *Muller v. Oregon* | *Triangle Shirtwaist Factory fire* | *Sixteenth and Seventeenth amendments ratified* | *Department of Labor formed* |

**1900** — **1910** — **1920**

# 2 Progressive Legislation

## SECTION PREVIEW

### Objectives

1. Describe urban reforms that took place during the Progressive Era.
2. Summarize the reforms made in state government that gave voters more power.
3. List the reforms that took place at the federal level.
4. *Key Terms* Define: direct primary; initiative; referendum; recall; holding company.

### Main Idea

Because of public demand, local, state, and federal legislatures enacted a number of progressive reforms in the early 1900s.

### Reading Strategy

*Organizing Information* As you read this section, create a chart listing the major progressive reforms made at the local, state, and federal levels.

Public demand for change led to a tremendous amount of legislation in the early 1900s. Reform took place at all levels of government—city, state, and federal.

## Urban Reforms

Many of the earliest progressive reforms were made at the city level. Cities were home to most of the settlement workers, club members, and professionals who were pushing many of the reforms. Thus, they were on hand to maintain the pressure for change.

**Attacking the Bosses** Political machines and bosses sustained heavy criticism during the Progressive Era. For the most part, they were able to survive such attacks. New York City provides a good example. In 1896 Columbia University president Seth Low ran for mayor, supported by municipal reformers. To help his campaign against Tammany Hall's ward bosses, settlement houses sent children out to post handbills in their neighborhoods. Low lost the election, but he tried again in 1901 and won. But the Tammany Hall machine returned to power in the next election. Over the following decades, New York voters switched back and forth between reformers and old political bosses.

In some cities, voter support for reforms prompted machine politicians to work with reformers. Together they registered voters, improved city services, established public health programs, and enforced tenement codes. Such alliances brought about astonishing improvements in urban life in some places.

**Cities Take Over Utilities** Reformers made efforts to regulate or dislodge the monopolies that provided city utilities such as water, gas, and electricity. Reform mayors Hazen S. Pingree of Detroit (1889–1897), Samuel M. "Golden Rule" Jones of Toledo (1897–1904), and Tom Johnson of Cleveland (1901–1909) pioneered city control or ownership of utilities. City control provided residents with more affordable services. By 1915, nearly two out of three cities had some form of city-owned utilities.

**Providing Welfare Services** Some reform mayors led movements for city-supported welfare services. Hazen Pingree provided public baths, parks, and a work-relief program.

Women workers crowd the floor of this Progressive Era factory. ***Economics* Why did Florence Kelley consider labor issues to be women's issues?**

"Golden Rule" Jones opened playgrounds, free kindergartens, and lodging houses for the homeless. "Nobody has a right to rule anybody else," he once said. In his view, all people would be good if social conditions were good.

## State Reforms

Some governors and state legislators also were active in promoting progressive reforms. Governors Robert "Battling Bob" La Follette in Wisconsin and Hiram Johnson in California, among others, introduced reforms to give voters a more direct voice in government. They also worked for reforms in the workplace.

**Main Idea CONNECTIONS**

*Why did Progressive reformers want to give voters more power?*

**More Power to Voters** Progressive reformers believed they could put an end to corruption in government by limiting the power of party bosses and politicians. One way to do this was to give voters more direct say in lawmaking and in choosing candidates. Five important gains were made by voters during the Progressive Era:

(1) *Direct Primaries.* Throughout the country, party leaders had long handpicked who would run for office. By 1904 Governor La Follette had instituted a **direct primary** in Wisconsin. A direct primary is an election in which voters cast ballots to select nominees for upcoming elections. By 1916 all but three states had direct primaries.

(2) *The Seventeenth Amendment.* In 1904 Oregon began allowing voters, rather than the state legislature, to choose their United States senator. By 1913 more than enough states were electing their senators in this way to ratify the Seventeenth Amendment to the Constitution. This amendment allows for the popular election of senators.

(3) *Initiative.* Many states also passed laws allowing citizens to use an **initiative** process. Through this process, citizens can propose new laws by obtaining a certain percentage of voters' signatures on a petition. Once the required number of signatures is gathered, the proposed law is then placed on the ballot in the next election.

(4) *Referendum.* The **referendum** process also gave voters a more direct role in legislation. Using this process, citizens may demand via petition that a law passed by the legislature be "referred" to voters for their approval or rejection.

(5) *Recall.* The **recall** procedure gave voters the ability to remove public officials from office before the next election.

**Reforms of the Workplace** Workplace tragedies also led to demands for reform. Late in the afternoon on Saturday, March 25, 1911, a match or cigarette ignited a fire on the eighth floor of the Triangle Shirtwaist Company in New York City. Because many of the exit doors were locked to prevent employee theft, 146 people died in the blaze.

The horror of the Triangle fire roused the public to action. The day after the tragedy, the Women's Trade Union League and the Red Cross formed a committee to improve fire safety standards. The committee called on the city to appoint fire inspectors, to make fire drills compulsory, and to unlock and fireproof exits.

Motivated in part by this disaster, state reformers also worked toward ending unsafe working conditions. Some states established labor departments to provide information and dispute-resolution services to employers and employees. Other states developed workers' accident insurance programs and compensation systems. By 1920 all but five states had taken steps to make it easier for workers to collect payment for workplace accidents.

Government efforts to control working conditions met legal opposition at every turn. In the case of *Lochner* v. *New York* (1905), for example, the Supreme Court struck down a law setting maximum hours for bakers. The law was declared void on the ground that it was "an illegal interference with the rights of individuals . . . to make contracts."

After this setback, reformers tried to convince the courts that government had to control conditions to protect women. This approach worked. In the 1908 case of *Muller* v. *Oregon,* the United States Supreme Court upheld an Oregon law that limited hours for women laundry workers to ten hours a day.

Labor reformers were successful on some other fronts as well. By 1907 the National Child Labor Committee had convinced some thirty states to abolish child labor. Child labor was often defined as employment of children under age 14. Minimum wage legislation for women and children also made headway, with Florence Kelley leading a national campaign. After Massachusetts adopted a minimum wage in 1912, eight other states followed.

## Federal Reforms

A number of important progressive reforms were also made at the federal level. Beginning with Theodore Roosevelt, the White House became a powerful voice for change.

**Theodore Roosevelt's "Square Deal"** As President, Theodore Roosevelt was determined to use his powers vigorously. He got his chance in May 1902, when the United Mine Workers called a strike to protest their low wages. As winter approached and mine owners continued to refuse to talk to the union, TR decided to intervene. Lacking coal, the nation would be without a key source of heating fuel.

Roosevelt insisted that both sides submit to arbitration, in which an impartial third party decides on a legally binding solution. To encourage mine owners to accept this step, TR threatened to use the army to seize and operate the mines. In 1903 arbitrators granted the miners a 10 percent raise and reduced their hours from 10 to 9. They did not grant official recognition of their union, however. When Roosevelt called this a "square deal" for both sides, the phrase became a slogan of his presidency.

After his reelection in 1904, Roosevelt urged Congress to pass laws to regulate the food and drug industries and the railroads. In 1906 the Hepburn Act authorized the Interstate Commerce Commission to limit rates if shippers complained of unfair treatment. Also in 1906 the Pure Food and Drug Act and the Meat Inspection Act required accurate labeling of ingredients, strict sanitary conditions, and a rating system for meats.

**Antitrust Activism** Although the Sherman Antitrust Act in 1890 was in place as a check on big business, it had never been vigorously enforced. Reversing this trend, Roosevelt's Attorney General used the act to sue the Northern Securities Company. Northern Securities was a holding company. A **holding company** buys up stocks and bonds of smaller companies. In doing so, it creates a monopoly. Northern Securities had brought about a slight dip in railroad rates by forming such a monopoly. But in 1904 the government convinced the Supreme Court that the company was in violation of the Sherman Act. The Court dissolved the company.

By the time Roosevelt had completed his second term in 1909, the government had filed 42 antitrust actions. The beef trust, Standard Oil, and the American Tobacco Company were either broken up or forced to reorganize. TR was not antibusiness. He did not wish to destroy trusts that he deemed "good," or not harmful to the public. But he believed that they should be supervised and controlled.

**Protecting the Environment** Roosevelt also urged Congress to extend the earlier steps that

This 1904 political cartoon compared Standard Oil to an octopus with a stranglehold on government. ***Economics*** *What was TR's attitude toward monopolies?*

FACT Finder

## Progressive Era Legislation

| Date | Legislation | Purpose |
|---|---|---|
| 1890 | Sherman Antitrust Act | Outlawed monopolies and practices that result in restraint of trade, such as price fixing. |
| 1902 | National Reclamation Act | Created to plan and develop irrigation projects. |
| 1905 | United States Forest Service | Created to manage the nation's water and timber resources. |
| 1906 | Hepburn Act | Required railroads to obtain permission from the Interstate Commerce Commission before raising rates. |
| 1906 | Pure Food and Drug Act | Outlawed interstate transportation of impure or diluted foods and the deliberate mislabeling of foods and drugs. |
| 1906 | Meat Inspection Act | Required federal inspection of meat processing to ensure sanitary conditions. |
| 1913 | Department of Labor | Cabinet department created to protect and promote the welfare and employment of working people. Began with four existing bureaus, including the Children's Bureau. |
| 1913 | 16th Amendment | Gave Congress the power to levy an income tax. |
| 1913 | 17th Amendment | Provided for the direct election of senators. |
| 1916 | National Park Service | Created to take over the administration of the nation's parks. |
| 1919 | 18th Amendment | Prohibited the manufacture and sale of liquor. (Repealed in 1933.) |
| 1920 | Women's Bureau | Created within the Department of Labor to promote the status of working women. |

**Interpreting Tables** Progressive reform touched many aspects of life, including business, natural resources, labor, and consumer protection. ***Government*** *Which reforms required constitutional amendments?*

had been taken to protect the nation's natural environment and resources. For example, at the urging of explorers and nature writers such as John Wesley Powell and John Muir, Congress had established Yellowstone in Wyoming as the nation's first national park in 1872. In 1890 Yosemite in California was also established as a national park. Presidents Harrison and Cleveland preserved some 35 million acres of forest land.

Now, in the early 1900s, the federal government called in experts to develop a policy for land and water use based on scientific data. In 1905 Roosevelt named Gifford Pinchot, a forester, to head a new United States Forest Service. At Pinchot's recommendation, TR set aside more than 200 million acres of land for national forests, mineral reserves, and water projects. The National Reclamation Act, passed in 1902, set aside money from the sale of public lands to fund the construction of irrigation systems in arid states.

**A New Labor Department** In response to pressure from women's clubs and labor organizations, in 1912 the government established a Children's Bureau. The following year, the Department of Labor was added as a new Cabinet department. A Women's Bureau was formed in 1920. These two bureaus, both part of the Department of Labor, supported legislation that would benefit women and children. Julia Lathrop and Mary Anderson, the heads of these bureaus, became the first female bureau heads at the federal level.

**New Constitutional Amendments** Like the Seventeenth Amendment ratified in the same year, progressive reformers fought for the ratification of the Sixteenth Amendment in 1913. The Sixteenth Amendment authorized Congress to collect income taxes. Prior to this amendment, the government relied on income from tariffs. Progressives argued that tariffs pushed up the prices of goods purchased by

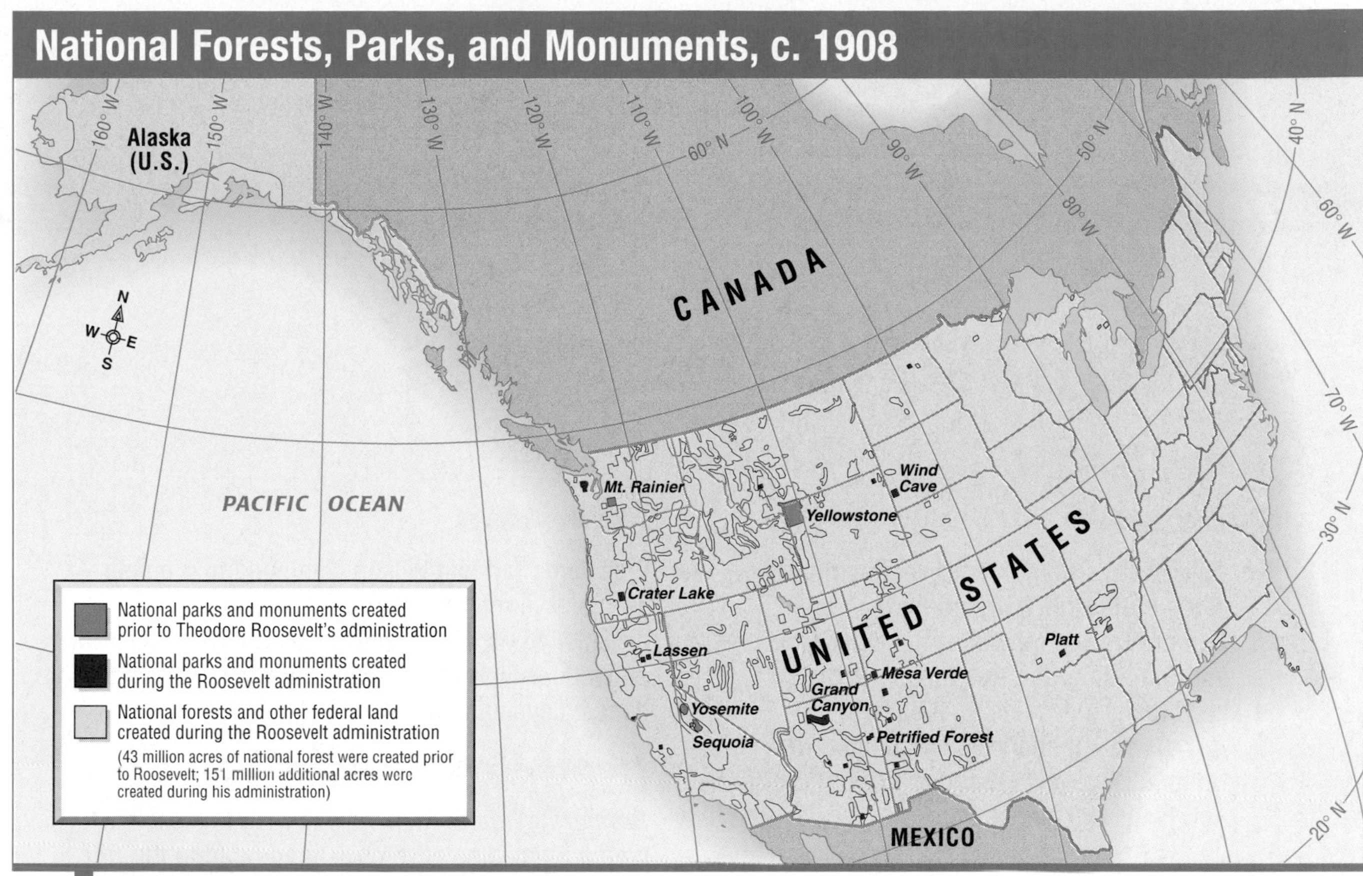


**MAP Skills** TR was convinced that "vigorous action must be taken" to save the nation's natural environment. ***Location*** ***What do you notice about the location of the nation's parks, monuments, and forests?***

the working poor. In contrast, the Sixteenth Amendment allowed the government to derive more of its income from the wealthy.

The Eighteenth Amendment was also pushed forward by progressive reformers and was ratified in 1919. The amendment made it illegal for Americans to make, sell, or import liquor. Although not all Progressives favored prohibition, many thought it would protect society from the poverty and violence associated with drinking. As you will read, this amendment proved to be controversial.

## SECTION 2 REVIEW

### Comprehension

1. *Key Terms* Define: (a) direct primary; (b) initiative; (c) referendum; (d) recall; (e) holding company.
2. *Summarizing the Main Idea* Briefly describe the progressive reforms that were made at the city, state, and federal levels.
3. *Organizing Information* Create a diagram showing the changes that gave voters a more direct role in democracy.

### Critical Thinking

4. *Analyzing Time Lines* Which events on the time line are related to labor reforms?
5. *Testing Conclusions* Provide evidence to support the conclusion that progressivism was not a single, unified movement.

### Writing Activity

6. *Writing a Persuasive Essay* Write a letter to city officials in New York asking for specific workplace reforms.

**1908** *Taft elected President*
**1910** *Ballinger-Pinchot Affair*
**1912** *Wilson elected President*
**1913** *Federal Reserve system established*
**1914** *Clayton Antitrust Act*
**1916** *Wilson reelected President*

**1905** **1910** **1915** **1920**

# 3 Progressive Presidents

**SECTION PREVIEW**

### Objectives

1 Describe the major controversies that took place during Taft's presidency.
2 Summarize the results of the election of 1912 and the role of the Bull Moose party.
3 List Wilson's policies as President.
4 *Key Terms* Define: conservationist; New Nationalism; New Freedom; Clayton Antitrust Act; Federal Reserve system.

### Main Idea

Presidents Taft and Wilson continued to promote progressive reforms. Some Progressives were dissatisfied with Taft's policies and formed their own party. Roosevelt ran as the Progressive party's presidential candidate in 1912.

### Reading Strategy

*Organizing Information* As you read this section, create a time line of reforms made during the Taft and Wilson presidencies.

*William H. Taft*

Progressivism had always been a series of informal alliances among like-minded reform groups. In 1912, however, a number of progressive reformers created their own political party. Though this party did not win the presidential election that year, its ideas continued to hold the attention of American voters and politicians.

## *Taft's Presidency*

The day after his election in 1904, Theodore Roosevelt announced he would not seek another presidential term. As the campaign of 1908 neared, Roosevelt handpicked his Secretary of War, William Howard Taft, to be the next Republican presidential nominee. On the Democratic side, William Jennings Bryan tried for a third and last time to win the office. Taft won easily.

President Taft had pledged to carry on TR's progressive program. He fulfilled that promise. Taft pursued some 90 antitrust cases and supported numerous other reforms. As President, however, Taft had neither Roosevelt's energy nor strength of personality. He gave in to the Republican "old guard," which resisted many progressive programs. One such issue in which Taft compromised on his support for progressivism was tariff reduction. Progressives favored lowering tariffs because higher tariffs hurt consumers and favored business. Taft's failure to reduce tariffs angered Progressives in his own party. As a result, a faction of Progressives who disliked Taft's policies developed within the Republican party.

**The Ballinger-Pinchot Affair** A party crisis in 1910 only worsened matters for Taft. Taft compromised on yet another important progressive cause when he ignored the protests of **conservationists.** (Conservationists are people concerned with the care and protection of natural resources.) Taft's Secretary of the Interior, Richard A. Ballinger, allowed a private group of business people to obtain several million acres of Alaskan public lands. The lands contained rich coal deposits. Roosevelt's appointee to head the Forest Service, Gifford Pinchot, felt that Ballinger had shown special preference to the purchasing group. When Pinchot protested to a congressional committee, Taft fired him.

Upset over Taft's handling of the affair, the progressive faction within the Republican party rebelled against him. They joined with Democrats in a vote to investigate Ballinger. Although never found guilty of wrongdoing, Ballinger eventually resigned.

The progressive faction also took action against the Republican old guard. Because the old guard controlled the House Rules Committee, they had been able to block much reform legislation.† In 1910, the progressive faction amended the House rules so that the powerful old guard member and House Speaker, Joseph G. Cannon, would no longer appoint the committee. Instead the committee would be elected by the House. In addition, the Speaker of the House was barred from serving on the committee.

In spite of his respectable record on progressive issues, Taft's presidency became entangled in controversy and conflict with Congress. ***Government*** ***What does this cartoon suggest about TR's reaction to Taft's difficulties?***

**The Midterm Elections of 1910** Following Taft's election in 1908, Roosevelt had set off on a long hunting trip to East Africa. On his trip home from Africa, Roosevelt was hailed as a hero throughout Europe. He returned to the United States to a wildly cheering crowd in New York and a storm of protest against Taft. At first Roosevelt remained silent. Soon, however, he could not resist entering the political battle between Taft and the Progressives. Roosevelt began speaking in support of progressive candidates in the 1910 midterm elections. He called for more federal regulation of business, welfare legislation, and progressive reforms. He favored stronger workplace protections for women and children, income and inheritance taxes, direct primaries, and the initiative, referendum, and recall. TR called this program the **New Nationalism.**

Republicans lost seats in the election while Democrats captured a majority in the House of Representatives. Progressive Democrats and Republicans dominated the Senate. By early 1912 Roosevelt announced that he would oppose Taft for the Republican presidential nomination.

**Taft's Record** Taft did not have a bad record on progressive causes. He had reserved more public lands and brought more antitrust suits in four years than TR had in seven. He also had supported the Children's Bureau, the Sixteenth and Seventeenth amendments, and the Mann-Elkins Act of 1910. This act gave the Interstate Commerce Commission the power to regulate telephone and telegraph rates. In the end, however, Taft never gained the full support of the progressive Republicans.

## *The Election of 1912*

Roosevelt and Taft both vied for the Republican presidential nomination at the party's Chicago convention in 1912. Taft, who controlled the central party machinery, won the nomination handily. Charging Taft's group with fraud, the Progressives marched out vowing to form their own party. In August they held their own convention and formed the Progressive party with Roosevelt as their

**Main Idea**

***Why did Progressives form their own party in 1912?***

† The House Rules Committee decides whether or not, and under what conditions, a bill will be taken up by the House.

FACT Finder

## Presidential Election of 1912

| Candidate and Party | Popular Vote | Percent | Electoral Vote |
|---|---|---|---|
| Woodrow Wilson/Democrat | 6,296,547 | 41.8 | 435 |
| Theodore Roosevelt/Progressive | 4,118,571 | 27.4 | 88 |
| William H. Taft/Republican | 3,486,720 | 23.2 | 8 |
| Eugene V. Debs/Socialist | 900,672 | 6.0 | — |
| Eugene Chafin/Prohibition | 206,275 | 1.4 | — |
| Arthur E. Reimer/Socialist Labor | 28,750 | 0.8 | — |

**Interpreting Tables** In the 1912 election, progressive ideas played a part in the platforms of the Democrats, Progressives, Republicans, and Socialists. ***Government*** *What would have happened if TR had not run and Taft had received TR's votes?*

candidate. California's progressive crusader, Hiram Johnson, was TR's running mate. When TR was asked about his physical readiness for a campaign, he said, "I feel fit as a bull moose!" The Bull Moose party became the nickname of the Progressive party.

*The new Progressive party took the Bull Moose as its symbol.*

**The Bull Moose Party** The Bull Moose platform included tariff reduction, women's suffrage, more regulation of business, and an end to child labor. The platform also called for an eight-hour workday, a federal workers' compensation system, and the popular election of senators. Many women joined the party and campaigned for progressive candidates. In those states where women had already won the right to vote, women ran for state and local offices.

TR ran a vigorous campaign that became legendary. During one speech in Milwaukee, Roosevelt was shot by a would-be assassin. Despite bleeding from a chest wound, Roosevelt continued to speak for an hour and a half before seeking medical aid. "It takes more than this to kill a bull moose," he said as he showed the crowd his bloodstained shirt.

**A Four-Way Election** Four men sought the presidency in 1912. Taft was the Republican candidate. Roosevelt represented his Bull Moose Progressives. Labor leader Eugene V. Debs ran on the Socialist ticket. Woodrow Wilson, governor of New Jersey, headed the Democratic ticket. Like Roosevelt, Wilson ran on a reform platform. Unlike Roosevelt, he criticized both big business and big government. As part of his **New Freedom** policy, he promised to enforce antitrust laws without threatening free economic competition.

Despite gaining only about 42 percent of the popular vote, Wilson won the election. This was in part because the Republican vote was split between Roosevelt and Taft. The Democrats also took control of both houses of Congress.

## *Wilson's Policies as President*

As the governor of New Jersey, Wilson had acquired a reputation as a reformer. As he explained during the 1912 campaign, "We used to think . . . that all that government had to do was to put on a policeman's uniform, and say, 'Now don't anybody hurt anybody else.'" But life in the early 1900s had become so complex that Wilson believed government had to "step in and create new conditions."

Government did "step in" in 1914 when Congress passed the **Clayton Antitrust Act** to strengthen the Sherman Antitrust Act of 1890. The Clayton Act spelled out specific activities big businesses could not do. For example, the act stated that companies could not use contracts to prevent their buyers from purchasing goods from their competitors. The Clayton Act also stated that members of unions could not be "held or construed to be illegal combinations in restraint of trade under the antitrust laws." The act lent further support to unions by making strikes, peaceful picketing, and boycotts legal. As a result, courts were prevented from issuing injunctions unless union activities led to "irreparable injury to property."

With the Clayton Act passed, the government was now committed to regulating business. To help in this task, Wilson and the Congress created a Federal Trade Commission (FTC) in 1914. Its purpose was to set up fair trade laws and to enforce antitrust laws. The FTC could punish companies by issuing "cease and desist orders" if they followed unfair business practices.

**The Federal Reserve System** Wilson also lowered many tariffs and instituted major financial reforms. In 1913 he helped establish the **Federal Reserve system,** which reorganized the federal banking system as follows:

1. The system created eight to twelve regional Federal Reserve Banks throughout the country. All national banks were required to become members of these banks. The Federal Reserve Banks were the central banks for their districts. Member banks stored some of their capital and their cash reserves at the Federal Reserve Bank in their district.

2. All of the Federal Reserve Banks were supervised by a Federal Reserve Board appointed by the President.

3. Each of the regional Federal Reserve Banks allowed member banks to borrow money to meet short-term demands. This helped to prevent bank failures that occurred when large numbers of depositors withdrew funds during an economic panic. Such bank failures could cause widespread job loss and misery.

4. The system also created a new national currency known as Federal Reserve notes. This allowed the Federal Reserve to expand or contract the amount of money in circulation according to business needs.

Another Wilson financial reform was the establishment of the Federal Farm Loan Board in 1916. This board and a system of Farm Loan Banks made loans available to farmers. Farmers could borrow money for five to forty years at rates lower than those offered by commercial banks.

Wilson was less active in social justice legislation. He allowed his Cabinet officers to extend the Jim Crow practice of separating the races in federal offices. This was a practice that had begun under Taft. Wilson also opposed a constitutional amendment on women's suffrage because his party platform had not endorsed it.

**Brandeis to the Supreme Court** Early in 1916 Wilson nominated progressive lawyer Louis D. Brandeis to the Supreme Court. Born in 1856 in Louisville, Kentucky, Brandeis was known for his brilliance and for fighting many public causes. His work earned him the name "the people's lawyer."

Brandeis supported Wilson in 1912 and advised him during the campaign. When Wilson nominated him to the Supreme Court, the action drew a storm of protest. Opponents, who included former President Taft, accused Brandeis of being too radical. Anti-Semitism also played a part in opposition to Brandeis. He was the first Jewish Supreme Court nominee. Nevertheless, Brandeis won his seat on the Court and served with distinction until 1939. His appointment marked the peak of progressive reform at the federal level.

This 1916 Wilson campaign truck publicizes Wilson's record during his first term as President. ***Government*** ***Which of his policies contributed most to Wilson's reelection?***

***Wilson projected a winning attitude with this presidential campaign button.***

**Wilson Wins a Second Term** Wilson ran for reelection in 1916. By then, progressivism had lost some of its appeal. TR did not want to run again. Instead, he endorsed Wilson's Republican opponent, Charles Evans Hughes, a former governor of New York and Supreme Court justice. The campaign was dominated by debate over the war then raging in Europe. Wilson won a narrow victory by promising to keep the country out of war.

## *The Limits of Progressivism*

By the mid-1910s, Progressives could take pride in the many changes they had helped bring about. They had redefined the role of

President Roosevelt met with Booker T. Washington at the White House in 1901. ***Government*** ***What was Roosevelt's record on African American rights?***

government in business and politics. There were limits to what they had accomplished, however. For example, Progressives focused primarily on the problems of cities. They did little to address the plights of tenant and migrant farmers and of nonunionized workers in general. Some supported immigration restriction and literacy tests.

In addition, many Progressives supported the government's imperialistic policies abroad. Just as they believed in their ability to uplift the slums in American cities, they favored the "civilizing" of undeveloped nations.

**African Americans and Progressivism** What seems progressive to one class, race, or region might seem regressive, even repressive, to another. For example, many African Americans felt ignored by Progressives. Only a tiny group of Progressives, those who helped found the NAACP, concerned themselves with the worsening race relations of the era. Although Roosevelt invited Booker T. Washington to the White House in 1901, he did little else to support African American rights during his presidency. At the 1912 Progressive party convention, Roosevelt declined to seat African American delegates from the South for fear of alienating white southern supporters. In addition, some white southern Progressives who favored the women's vote did so for racist reasons. They realized that the white vote would double if suffrage passed. African Americans, on the other hand, would fall further behind because of their lower population and the effectiveness of voting restrictions in the South.

**The End of Progressivism** In August 1914, war broke out in Europe, and many nations began to assemble troops and supplies. Americans worried about how long they could remain uninvolved in the European conflict. Soon, calls to prepare for war drowned out calls for reform in the United States. By the end of 1916 the reform spirit had sputtered out, but the drive for women's suffrage remained.

## SECTION 3 REVIEW

### Comprehension

1. *Key Terms* Define: (a) conservationist; (b) New Nationalism; (c) New Freedom; (d) Clayton Antitrust Act; (e) Federal Reserve system.
2. *Summarizing the Main Idea* In what areas did President Taft back away from progressive reform? What happened when he did this?
3. *Organizing Information* Wilson and Roosevelt both favored progressive reforms. Use the table on page 298 to determine what percentage of American voters voted for the two progressive candidates in 1912.

### Critical Thinking

4. *Analyzing Time Lines* Review the time line at the start of the section. How are the second and third events on the time line related?
5. *Identifying Central Issues* Based on the actions he took as President, summarize Wilson's view of the proper role of government.

### Writing Activity

6. *Writing an Expository Essay* Write an essay describing some of the ways in which the goals of the Progressives were limited.

| 1890 | 1900 | 1910 | 1913 | 1920 |
|---|---|---|---|---|
| **1890** *National American Woman Suffrage Association (NAWSA) formed* | **1900** *Carrie Chapman Catt leads NAWSA* | | **1913** *Alice Paul and Lucy Burns lead a suffrage rally in Washington, D.C.* | **1920** *Nineteenth Amendment ratified* |

# 4 Suffrage at Last

## SECTION PREVIEW

### Objectives

1 List some of the efforts Susan B. Anthony and other women made in their quest to win suffrage at the turn of the century.
2 Summarize the different strategies that suffragists used to win the vote.
3 Analyze the factors that led to a final victory for the suffragists.
4 *Key Terms* Define: civil disobedience; National American Woman Suffrage Association (NAWSA); Congressional Union.

### Main Idea

While demonstrating their skills as organizers and activists, women finally won the right to vote with the ratification of the Nineteenth Amendment in 1920.

### Reading Strategy

*Reinforcing Main Ideas* As you read this section, list and briefly describe the methods women used to win the right to vote.

American women activists first formally demanded the right to vote in 1848 at a meeting in Seneca Falls, New York. Their struggle for suffrage and other rights continued throughout the second half of the century. One of the leaders in the fight was Susan B. Anthony.

## *Susan B. Anthony*

AMERICAN BIOGRAPHY Like her father, a Quaker abolitionist, Susan B. Anthony was a crusader. Throughout her life she worked for radical change. In her thirties Anthony fought to give women a stronger voice in the temperance movement. She also joined the fight to abolish slavery. From 1856 to 1861 she served as an agent of the American Anti-Slavery Society. Following the Civil War, Anthony demanded that women be given the same rights as African Americans under the Fourteenth and Fifteenth amendments. Although this effort failed, Anthony continued her tireless campaign for women's rights as head of the National Woman Suffrage Association. In 1872 she led a group of women to the polls in Rochester, New York, where she insisted on voting. Anthony was arrested for this act of civil disobedience. (**Civil disobedience** is a nonviolent refusal to obey a law in an effort to change the law.) While Anthony awaited her trial, she set out on a highly publicized lecture tour. During one of these lectures she asserted:

*Susan B. Anthony (1820–1906)*

"The preamble of the Federal Constitution says: 'We, the people of the United States. . . .' It was we, the people; not we, the white male citizens; nor yet we, the male citizens; but we, the whole people, who formed the Union. And we formed it, not to give the blessings of liberty, but to secure them; not to the half of ourselves and the half of our posterity, but to the whole people—women as well as men."

—*Susan B. Anthony*

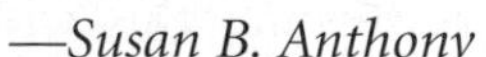

## COMPARING PRIMARY SOURCES

### THE NINETEENTH AMENDMENT

In the early 1900s, the debate over women's suffrage heated up.

| Pro-Women's Suffrage | Anti-Suffrage |
|---|---|
| "The great doctrine of the American Republic that 'all governments derive their just powers from the consent of the governed' justifies the plea of one-half of the people, the women, to exercise the suffrage. The doctrine of the American Revolutionary War that taxation without representation is unendurable justifies women in exercising the suffrage." —*Robert L. Owen, senator from Oklahoma, 1910* | "In political warfare, it is perfectly fitting that actual strife and battle should be apportioned [given out] to man, and that the influence of woman, radiating from the homes of our land, should inspire to lofty aims and purposes those who struggle for the right. I am thoroughly convinced that woman can in no better way than this usefully serve the cause of political betterment." —*Grover Cleveland,* Ladies' Home Journal, *October 1905* |

***ANALYZING VIEWPOINTS*** **Summarize the arguments presented in the primary sources above.**

Although Anthony was convicted at her trial, she refused to pay the $100 fine. In 1890 veteran leaders of the suffrage movement, including Anthony, Elizabeth Cady Stanton, and Lucy Stone, were joined by a younger generation of leaders in forming the **National American Woman Suffrage Association (NAWSA).** Anthony served as president of NAWSA from 1892 until 1900. ■

## *Suffrage at the Turn of the Century*

By the time of NAWSA's founding, women had won many rights. For example, married women could now buy, sell, and will property. Yet legal efforts to win suffrage had failed. Perhaps more troubling to suffrage workers were the widely held attitudes about women and their proper social roles. When lawyer Myra Bradwell of Chicago was denied a state license to practice law in 1869, she took her case to the Supreme Court. In *Bradwell* v. *Illinois* (1873), the Court upheld the denial, reaffirming the "wide difference in the respective spheres and destinies of man and woman." Although Illinois had given Bradwell her license by 1890, most Americans believed that woman's proper sphere remained the home, not the workplace.

By 1900, however, growing numbers of women were demanding the vote. Some were participating in voluntary organizations that were investigating social conditions. These women were publicizing their findings, suggesting reforms, lobbying officials, and monitoring enforcement of new laws. Working women were becoming more active in unions, picketing, and getting arrested. To many of these women, it seemed ridiculous to deny women the vote.

As the suffrage movement became more energetic, an antisuffrage movement mobilized. People opposed to women's suffrage made two basic arguments. The first was that women were powerful enough without the vote. The second was the old notion that giving women the vote would blur the distinctions between the sexes and make women more masculine. Suffrage opponents also included liquor interests, who assumed that women voters would quickly establish prohibition.

## *Suffragist Strategies*

Suffragists followed two paths toward their goal. One path was to press for a constitutional amendment. The most commonly used method of amending the Constitution required two thirds of each house of Congress to pass a measure. The measure then had to be ratified by three fourths of the state legislatures.

The other path pursued by suffragists was to get individual states to permit women to vote. At first this approach was more successful, especially in the western states. There, survival on the frontier required the combined efforts of men and women and encouraged a greater sense of equality.

Pushing for a federal amendment proved the more difficult approach. The first amendment introduced in Congress in 1868 stalled. In 1878 suffragists introduced a new amendment that adopted the wording of suffrage leader Susan B. Anthony:

KEY DOCUMENTS **"The right of citizens of the United States to vote shall not be denied or abridged by the United States or by any state on account of sex."**

—*The Nineteenth Amendment*

With this language, the proposed amendment received its first committee hearing. Elizabeth Cady Stanton described the chair of the committee, Senator Wadleigh of New Hampshire, as a picture of "inattention and contempt." "He stretched, yawned, gazed at the ceiling, cut his nails, sharpened his pencil, changing his occupation and position every two minutes."

Stalled again, the bill was not debated until 1887. It was then defeated in the Senate by a vote of 16 for, 34 against, and 26 absent. Supporters reintroduced the "Anthony Amendment," as the bill came to be called, every year until 1896. Then it disappeared, and did not resurface again until 1913.

**The Movement Strengthens in the 1910s** At the turn of the century, the idea of votes for women had become more acceptable. The suffrage movement, however, was at a low point. New leadership and new techniques were desperately needed to give it momentum.

One of these new leaders was Carrie Chapman Catt. Catt was a former high school principal and superintendent of schools in Mason City, Iowa. A talented speaker and organizer, she headed NAWSA from 1900 to 1904, and then again after 1915. As head of NAWSA, Catt insisted on close, precinct-by-precinct political work.

Alice Paul also emerged as a leader in the women's suffrage movement. She had experienced the aggressive English suffrage movement while she was a student in England. In January 1913, she and a friend, Lucy Burns, took over the NAWSA committee that was working on congressional passage of the federal suffrage amendment.

Two months later, the two women had organized a parade of 5,000 women in Washington, D.C. The parade took place on the day before Woodrow Wilson's inauguration. It drew so much attention that no crowd greeted Wilson when he arrived at the train station. After this success, Paul transformed her committee into a new organization, the **Congressional Union (CU).**

**A Split in the Movement** Following Paul's action, a split occurred within the suffrage movement. Paul's CU called for an aggressive, militant campaign for the constitutional amendment. She planned to enter different states, bypass the suffrage organizations there, and set up new ones.

The leadership of NAWSA did not agree with Paul's plan. In February 1914 they expelled her group from the organization. The CU went on to stage militant protests. They demonstrated in front of the White House, burned copies of President Wilson's speeches and even a life-size dummy made to look like Wilson. CU members were sent to prison for their demonstrations, where they went on hunger strikes to protest prison conditions. NAWSA condemned the CU, not their treatment.

**Main Idea CONNECTIONS**

*How did NAWSA and the CU differ in their strategies for winning women's suffrage?*

Meanwhile, NAWSA's state suffrage campaigns continued. Hopes had centered on winning the vote in four eastern states, New York, Pennsylvania, Massachusetts, and New Jersey. In 1915 the suffrage campaigns failed in all four states. At that point, Catt was reinstated as NAWSA president and was given free rein to bring about victory. Out of this challenge came her "Winning Plan."

Colorful parades became a favorite technique of suffragists in the 1910s. Suffragists in this 1912 parade in New York City offered a suffrage "plank" for political party platforms. ***Culture*** *What caused the split in the suffrage movement?*

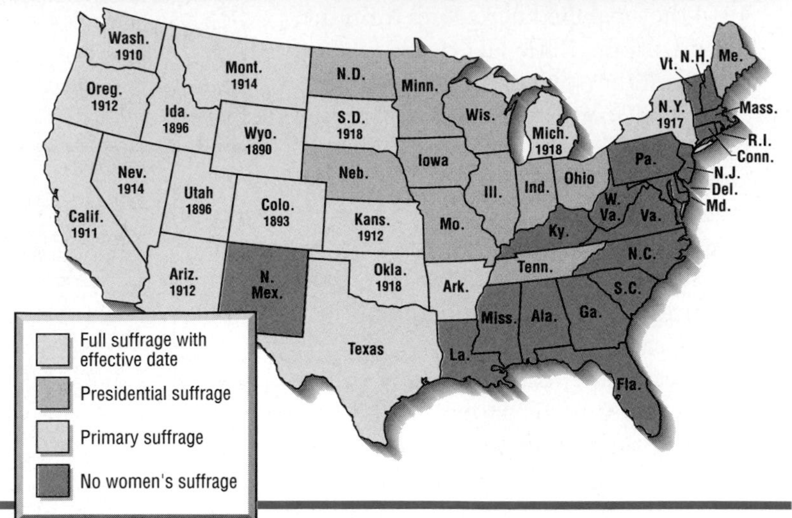


MAP skills Women's suffrage was already in place in many states by the time the Nineteenth Amendment was ratified. ***Location*** ***What pattern do you notice in the locations of states that did and did not pass suffrage at the state level?***

This plan consisted of developing a large group of full-time leaders to work in "red-hot" campaigns for six years. In addition, NAWSA decided to focus on getting Congress to propose the federal amendment.

By 1917, NAWSA had 2 million members. It was the largest voluntary organization in the country. In the fall, New York State finally voted for women's suffrage.

**Impact of World War I** The United States entered World War I in April 1917. Women hastened to do their patriotic duty by volunteering for ambulance corps and medical work and by taking on jobs left by men. Arguments of separate spheres for women and men were forgotten during wartime. In addition, Congress adopted the Eighteenth Amendment prohibiting the sale of liquor. As a result of this action, liquor interests no longer had reason to fight suffrage.

## *The Final Victory for Suffrage*

In 1918 Congress formally proposed the suffrage amendment. Its members finally succumbed to the political forces of states that had passed suffrage and to the unrelenting work of NAWSA. They also had been keenly embarrassed and disturbed by the treatment the women of Paul's CU had received in jail. After the amendment was proposed in Congress the ratification battle began. It would end on August 24, 1920, when Tennessee became the necessary thirty-sixth state to ratify the suffrage amendment.

As Carrie Chapman Catt commented when the exhausting fight was all over, "It is doubtful that any man . . . ever realized what the suffrage struggle came to mean to women. . . . It leaves its mark on one, such a struggle." The Nineteenth Amendment marked the last major reform of the Progressive Era.

### *SECTION 4 REVIEW*

#### Comprehension

1. *Key Terms* Define: (a) civil disobedience; (b) National American Woman Suffrage Association (NAWSA); (c) Congressional Union.
2. *Summarizing the Main Idea* What were the two main strategies of the suffrage movement during the late 1800s and early 1900s?
3. *Organizing Information* Make a list of the events that finally led to victory in the fight for women's suffrage.

#### Critical Thinking

4. *Analyzing Time Lines* Review the time line at the start of the section. How many years passed between the formation of NAWSA and the ratification of the Nineteenth Amendment?
5. *Recognizing Ideologies* Recall what you have read about the reasons for the passage of suffrage in the West and at the national level. In the end, what seemed to "prove" women's fitness to vote?

#### Writing Activity

6. *Writing an Expository Essay* Write an essay describing the major accomplishments of Susan B. Anthony.

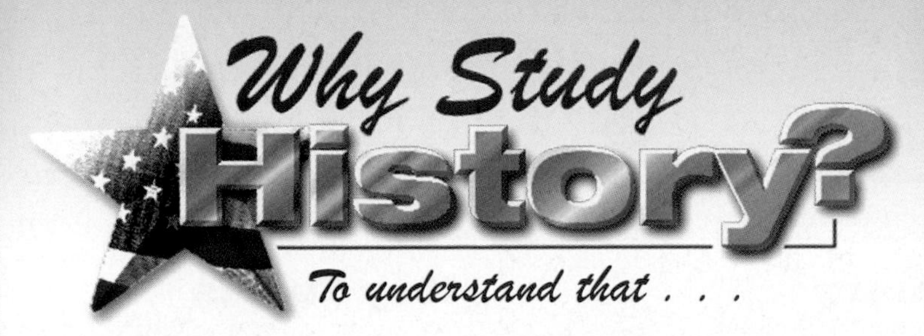


# You Can Make a Difference

**The spirit of progressive reform remains alive today in the volunteer community service activities performed by Americans of all ages.**

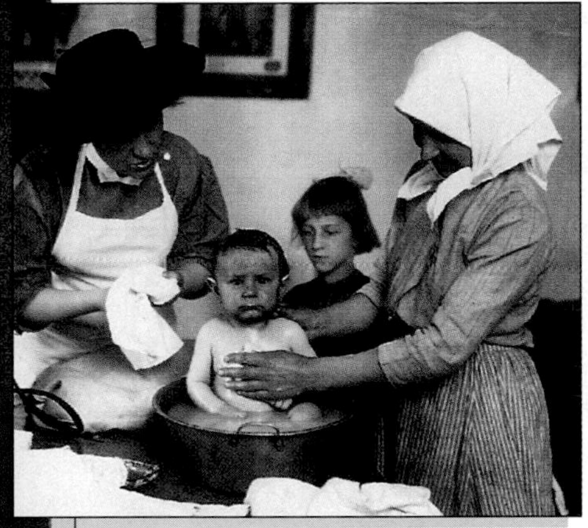

*Nurse visiting an immigrant household around 1915*

A youth group in Cape Cod, Massachusetts, adopts a stretch of highway and keeps it litter-free. High school cheerleaders in Houston, Texas, organize an aluminum can drive to fund a Mother's Day luncheon in a local nursing home. A support group made up of teens in San Francisco serves dinner at a local soup kitchen.

In urban and rural communities throughout the United States, millions of Americans participate regularly in some form of volunteer service. They are taking steps to tackle such important and difficult problems as hunger, illiteracy, pollution, and poverty.

## The Impact Today

Reformers of the Progressive Era targeted issues such as child labor, women's suffrage, workplace hazards, poverty, and political corruption. Great progress has been made on some of these issues. Others, such as corruption and poverty, remain a concern. In addition, problems such as cleanup of hazardous waste have emerged as major issues since the Progressive Era. Today individual volunteers, along with various private, public, and non-profit organizations, have mobilized to address both old and new issues.

Young Americans play a vital role as volunteers. Millions of youths participate in the volunteer programs of Youth Service America (YSA). Founded in 1986, this alliance of organizations works to build healthy communities and foster citizenship through volunteerism. YSA includes more than 100 organizations, representing more that 15 million young Americans.

Each year YSA observes National Youth Service Day, when young people kick off a year-long commitment to volunteer service and meet new friends engaged in a common cause. The day includes activities such as planting gardens, picking up roadside litter, and delivering meals to senior citizens.

## The Impact on You

Choose one problem in your community that troubles you—for example, homelessness, air or water pollution, substance abuse, or toxic waste disposal. Discuss the problem with family, friends, and neighbors to get ideas for dealing with it. Write a one-page proposal for a volunteer service project that you would like to create to address the problem you chose.

*Teenage volunteer tutoring a young student*

# Chapter  Review

## Chapter Summary

The major concepts of Chapter 9 are presented below. See also ***Guide to the Essentials of American History*** or ***Interactive Student Tutorial CD-ROM,*** which contains interactive review activities, time lines, helpful hints, and test practice.

### *Reviewing the Main Ideas*

Progressive reformers at the turn of the century worked to meet the challenges of an urban, industrialized society. In spite of opposition, Progressives were able to redefine government's role in American life, and to enact such lasting reforms as women's suffrage.

### *Section 1: The Origins of Progressivism*

At the end of the 1800s, many citizens recognized the need to solve problems resulting from rapid industrialization and urban growth. The appearance of many reform movements caused historians to later refer to the period as the Progressive Era.

### *Section 2: Progressive Legislation*

Because of public demand, local, state, and federal legislatures enacted a number of progressive reforms in the early 1900s.

### *Section 3: Progressive Presidents*

Presidents Taft and Wilson continued to promote progressive reforms. Some Progressives were dissatisfied with Taft's policies and formed their own party. Roosevelt ran as the Progressive party's presidential candidate in 1912.

### *Section 4: Suffrage at Last*

While demonstrating their skills as organizers and activists, women finally won the right to vote with the ratification of the Nineteenth Amendment in 1920.

The spirit of progressive reform remains alive today in the volunteer community service activities performed by Americans of all ages. Millions of Americans participate regularly in some form of volunteer service.



## Key Terms

Use each of the terms below in a sentence that shows how it relates to the chapter.

1. Federal Reserve system
2. injunction
3. home rule
4. social welfare program
5. direct primary
6. initiative
7. referendum
8. recall
9. Clayton Antitrust Act
10. holding company
11. conservationist
12. New Nationalism
13. New Freedom

## Comprehension

1. What did Progressives see as good about the United States? What did they want to reform?
2. What were the typical methods of progressive reformers?
3. Summarize progressive reforms at the municipal and state levels.
4. Briefly describe progressive reforms at the national level.
5. What were the successes and failures of the Taft presidency?
6. Why did progressivism come to an end?
7. Where did campaigns to achieve suffrage first meet with success?
8. How did the Congressional Union and the National American Woman Suffrage Association differ in their strategies?

## Using Graphic Organizers

On a separate sheet of paper, copy the tree map below to organize information about progressive legislation at the city, state, and national levels. In the lower boxes, fill in examples of city, state, and federal reforms.

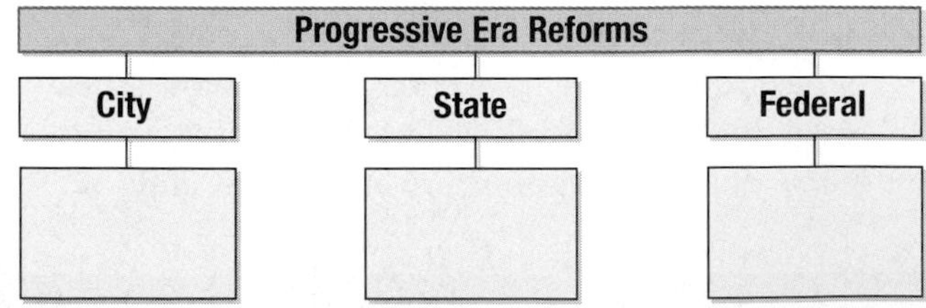

## Analyzing Political Cartoons ▶

1. Examine the images in the cartoon. (a) What is the woman holding? (b) What does it represent? (c) In what manner is she holding it?
2. Notice the woman's clothing. What point is the cartoonist trying to make with her clothing?
3. What is the "delusion" referred to in the cartoon?

## Critical Thinking

1. ***Applying the Chapter Skill*** Based on the election results in 1912, is it reasonable to conclude that most Americans favored some amount of progressive reform? Explain.
2. ***Identifying Central Issues*** What was the Clayton Antitrust Act and why was it important to progressive reformers?
3. ***Expressing Problems Clearly*** What was the purpose of the Federal Reserve system?
4. ***Demonstrating Reasoned Judgment*** Progressives were sometimes criticized for being insensitive to the needs of the poor. Do you think that this criticism was justified?
5. ***Identifying Central Issues*** What does the fate of Taft's presidency suggest about the nature of the presidency and presidential leadership?

## INTERNET ACTIVITY

***For your portfolio:***
**WRITE AN ESSAY**

Access Prentice Hall's *America: Pathways to the Present* site at **www.Pathways.phschool.com** for the specific URLs to complete the activity. Additional resources and related Web sites are also available.

Use the links provided to read biographies of famous suffragists and a time line of the women's rights movement. Write an essay describing the suffrage movement. Who were suffragists? How would you characterize the suffrage movement? How did it differ from other struggles for liberty?

## ANALYZING DOCUMENTS ▶ INTERPRETING DATA

Turn to the map of women's suffrage on page 304.

1. Which of the following states had given women full suffrage prior to the passage of the Nineteenth Amendment? (a) Iowa (b) North Dakota (c) Colorado (d) Kentucky.
2. Which of the following statements best summarizes the information on the map?
(a) States throughout the nation refused to grant women suffrage.
(b) Many states in the West had granted women full suffrage prior to passage of the Nineteenth Amendment.
(c) Many states in the Southeast had granted women full suffrage prior to passage of the Nineteenth Amendment. (d) States in the Midwest generally supported full suffrage for women.
3. ***Writing*** What factors contributed to the granting of full suffrage to women in the western states?

## Connecting to Today

Florence Kelley led a campaign to investigate labor conditions in the United States. Consumers pressured owners to comply with laws. Today, similar work is being done on an international level. Conduct research and write a brief essay on one or more of the groups monitoring international labor issues.

CHAPTER

# 10 The World War I Era

## 1914–1920

**VIEWING HISTORY**
United States infantrymen charge out of their trench and into battle in this 1918 photograph.
***Foreign Relations* Why had the United States been reluctant to join the World War?**

## CHAPTER FOCUS

*This chapter discusses the World War I era, during which much of Europe became embroiled in conflict. Despite American reluctance, powerful forces pulled the nation into battle. With the end of the war, President Wilson sought a peace treaty and a new international organization to prevent world-wide conflict from ever happening again.*

*The* ***Why Study History?*** *page at the end of this chapter explores the connection between the advances in weaponry during World War I and the continued horrors of modern warfare.*

| June 28, 1914 | July 28, 1914 | August 1, 1914 | August 4, 1914 |
|---|---|---|---|
| Assassination of Archduke Francis Ferdinand | Austria-Hungary declares war on Serbia | Germany declares war on Russia | Britain declares war on Germany |

1914 — 1915

# 1 The Road to War

## SECTION PREVIEW

### Objectives

1. Identify the main causes of World War I.
2. Describe how the conflict expanded to draw in much of Europe.
3. Describe the American response to the war in Europe.
4. *Key Terms* Define: militarism; mobilization; Central Powers; Allies; stalemate; autocrat.

### Main Idea

As World War I began and then expanded to much of Europe, the United States remained neutral.

### Reading Strategy

*Formulating Questions* Rewrite the Main Idea above as a question. As you read the section, write down answers to your question.

On June 28, 1914, Archduke Francis Ferdinand and his wife Sophie made a state visit to Sarajevo, the capital of Bosnia. Bosnia was a new province within the Austro-Hungarian Empire, and Francis Ferdinand was heir to the empire's throne.

That morning a bomb thrown by a terrorist bounced off the archduke's car and exploded, injuring two officers in another car. Unfazed, Francis Ferdinand attended a state ceremony and then rode to the hospital to see the wounded officers. Gavrilo Princip, a second terrorist, just 19 years old, happened to spot the car as it slowly moved down a narrow street. He pulled out his pistol and shot the archduke and his wife to death.

Princip, a Bosnian nationalist, believed that Austria-Hungary had no right to rule Bosnia. Little did he know that his act of terrorism would have such grave consequences.

## Causes of World War I

The assassination of Archduke Francis Ferdinand ignited what was called the Great War, later known as World War I. But the main causes of the war existed well before 1914. Those causes included imperialism, militarism, nationalism, and alliances.

(1) *Imperialism.* A great scramble for colonies took place in the late 1800s. European powers rushed to beat each other to the remaining uncolonized areas of the world, particularly in Africa and China. This surge of imperialism sharpened rivalries within Europe. Japan joined the roster of colonial powers when it won the Sino-Japanese War in 1895 and acquired Korea, Taiwan, and territory on China's mainland.

(2) *Militarism.* By the early 1900s in Europe, diplomacy had taken a back seat to **militarism.** This policy involved aggressively building up a nation's armed forces in preparation for war. Under this policy the military gained more authority. The great powers of Europe—Austria-Hungary, France, Germany, Great Britain, and Russia—all engaged in militarism. Their endless planning for war made war much more likely.

*Soldiers in World War I wore gas masks to protect against poison gas, a horrible new weapon introduced in the war.*

(3) *Nationalism.* Two kinds of nationalism contributed to World War I. The first was the tendency for countries such as the great powers to act in their own national interest. When such action went against the national interest of another nation, warfare could result. The second kind of nationalism occurred in countries with diverse populations. In such countries the longing of an ethnic minority for independence often led to violence.

(4) *Alliances.* A complicated system of alliances developed among the nations of Europe during the late nineteenth century. Designed to bolster each nation's security, the alliances bound the great powers to come to each other's aid in the event of attack. In 1914 the fragile balance of power that had kept the peace for decades led its creators into war.

## The Conflict Expands

At the time of the assassination, Bosnia was the focal point of a nationalist dispute between Austria-Hungary, which had recently annexed Bosnia, and its neighbor Serbia. Convinced that Serbia was behind the assassination, Austria-Hungary used the event as an excuse to crush its small enemy. On July 28, 1914, Austria-Hungary declared war on Serbia.

This declaration of war set off a chain reaction that worked its way through Europe's complex web of alliances. On July 29, Russia, as Serbia's protector, began **mobilization**—the readying of troops for war. Germany, Austria-Hungary's chief ally, demanded that Russia stop mobilizing. Russia refused. At that point, Russia's ally, France, began to ready its troops, as did Germany.

On August 1, Germany declared war on Russia. Germany's military leaders had long prepared for this day. Their country lay between France to the west and Russia to the east. To avoid being trapped by advancing French and Russian armies, Germany had developed a first-strike strategy. Known as the Schlieffen Plan, it called for a quick sweep through France to knock the French out of the war. Then the German army would concentrate on Russia.

Germany put the plan into action. To reach France as fast as possible, the German army had to pass through Belgium. To Germany's dismay, this invasion brought Great Britain, Belgium's protector, into the conflict on August 4. Germany had hoped that Britain, with its powerful navy, would stay neutral.

One week after the war started, all the great powers of Europe had been drawn into it. The conflict divided them into two sides. Germany and Austria-Hungary made up the **Central Powers.** Russia, France, Serbia, and Great Britain were called the **Allies.**

**Stalemate** Each side felt confident of swift victory. Six weeks, experts said, and it would all be over. The experts were wrong. Relatively equal in size and strength, the two sides reached a bloody **stalemate,** a situation in which neither side is able to gain the advantage.

In earlier wars a forceful offense led by a heroic cavalry often was enough to secure victory in battle. Now defensive forces could use modern firepower, such as machine guns and long-range artillery, to stop such advances. In September 1914 the German army, following the Schlieffen Plan, advanced to within 30 miles of Paris. There, at the river Marne, a combined French and British force stopped their progress. Both sides then dug in.

Holed up in lines of muddy, rat-infested trenches, the two sides faced each other across an empty "no-man's land." For months each side tried to reach the other's lines to destroy or at least push back the enemy. But neither side

**European Alliances in World War I**

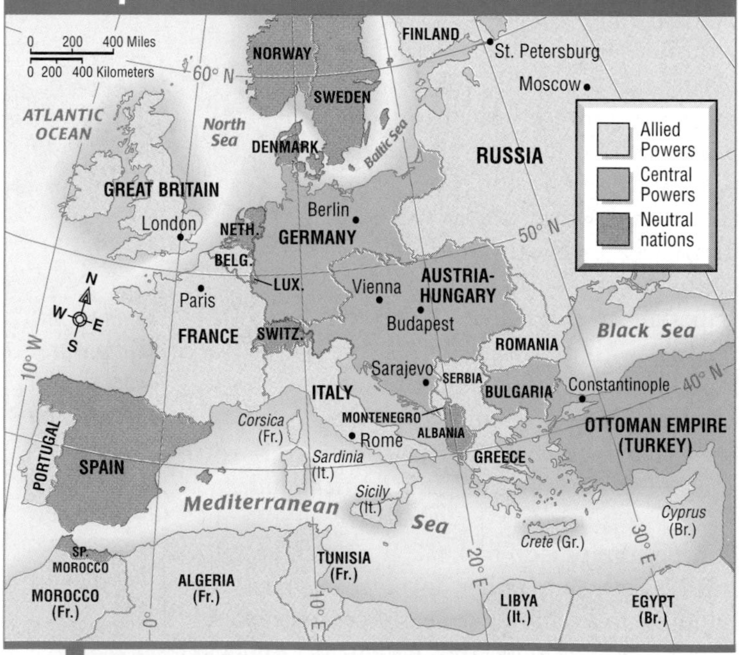

MAP skills Before the war, Europe was a land of empires and alliances. When Austria-Hungary declared war on Serbia, much of the continent was drawn into the conflict. ***Location*** ***Based on this map, which side, if any, had a geographical advantage in the war? Explain.***

was able to gain more than a few miles, and that only at appalling human cost.

Meanwhile, an Austrian army captured Belgrade, the Serbian capital. Combined German and Austro-Hungarian forces pushed the Russian lines back. At the end of 1914, the Ottoman Empire, centered in what is now Turkey, entered the war on the side of the Central Powers. In the spring of 1915, Italy joined the Allies.

**Modern Warfare** In 1914 the youth of Europe had marched off to fight, eager for a chance to be heroic. They came up against new killing machines of amazing efficiency. Ripped apart by machine guns, hand grenades, or artillery shells, and choked by poison gases, soldiers found that heroism came at a ghastly price.

If soldiers charging across no-man's land toward the enemy survived the artillery shells that rained down upon them, the enemy's machine guns, firing 450 rounds a minute, mowed them down. The generals, unaccustomed to the new weaponry, repeatedly gave the order to attack. That strategy, however, produced only a mounting pile of dead infantry. In the Battle of the Somme in 1916, for example, the British suffered some 20,000 deaths in a single day of combat.

Morale sank. Desperate, the armies began using any tactic available. Erasing the distinction between soldier and civilian, they burned fields, killed livestock, and poisoned wells. They tunneled under the no-man's land to plant bombs below enemy trenches. German submarines torpedoed any ship they believed to be carrying arms to the Allies. A British naval blockade slowly starved the German people. None of these tactics brought a quick end to the conflict.

Trench warfare ranged from crudely dug foxholes (above) to a series of elaborate trenches stretching for miles. Trench networks allowed armies to fire on the enemy, obtain supplies and reinforcements, and take cover from enemy fire. ***Science and Technology** How did trench warfare contribute to a stalemate in World War I?*

## The American Response

Newspapers in the United States had recorded the march toward war in bold headlines. "Austria Declares War, Rushes Vast Army into Serbia; Russia Masses 80,000 Men on Border."

Americans read the news with mounting alarm. How could all these great countries of beauty and culture be at war with one another?

Some Americans felt personally involved. More than a third of the nation's 92 million people were first- or second-generation immigrants. They still identified with their old countries. About a quarter of these were German American, and another eighth were Irish American. Both of these groups felt hostility toward Great Britain because of past conflicts and the current war in Europe. For this reason, they favored the Central Powers over the Allies.

Most Americans, however, opposed the Central Powers. One reason was Kaiser Wilhelm, the ruler of Germany. The Kaiser, or emperor, was an **autocrat**—a ruler with unlimited power. Also, Americans saw the Germans as a people of frightening militarism and cold-blooded efficiency. Reporters who had rushed to Belgium in August 1914 to witness the German advance toward France fueled this view. Richard Harding Davis described the event for New York *Tribune* readers as "not men marching, but a force of nature like a tidal wave, an avalanche, or a river flooding its banks."

**Main Idea CONNECTIONS**

*What were the reactions in the United States to the outbreak of World War I?*

**American Neutrality** Trade strongly influenced the American position on the war. Between 1897 and 1914 United States commercial investments overseas had increased fivefold, from $700 million to $3.5 billion. Now German submarines and a British naval

This "peace ship" journeyed to Europe in 1915 with hopes of ending the war. Suffragist and social reformer Jane Addams, second from the left in the front row, joined the delegation. ***Foreign Relations*** *How did the peace movement differ from the preparedness movement?*

blockade of the North Sea were putting those investments at risk. To protect the investments, President Wilson on August 4, 1914, officially proclaimed the United States a neutral country. The American government protested the actions of both sides and tried to act as peacemaker.

**The Preparedness Movement** American business leaders welcomed the proclamation of neutrality. Still, those who had strong commercial ties to Great Britain urged that the United States get ready for war. Their watchword was "preparedness." They wanted their country to be in a position to aid Great Britain if necessary. In December 1914 preparedness supporters organized a National Security League to "promote patriotic education and national sentiment and service among people of the United States."

By the late summer of 1915, the movement's leaders had persuaded the government to set up camps to train American men for combat. By the summer of 1916, Wilson had worked out an agreement with Congress for large increases in the armed forces.

**The Peace Movement** When World War I broke out, a peace movement also swung into gear. Its members consisted primarily of former Populists, Midwest progressives, and social reformers.

Women were particularly active in the movement. On August 29, 1914, suffragists dressed in black and carrying a banner of a dove marched down New York City's Fifth Avenue. In November 1915 a group of female and male social reformers founded the American Union Against Militarism.

Congress also included some peace advocates. They insisted on paying for preparedness through a tax on the makers of arms and through higher income taxes. Claude Kitchin, member of Congress from North Carolina, predicted that when people discovered "that the income tax will have to pay for the increase in the army and navy, . . . preparedness will not be so popular with them as it now is." Congress did increase taxes, but the preparedness movement remained strong.

## SECTION 1 REVIEW

### Comprehension

1. *Key Terms* Define: (a) militarism; (b) mobilization; (c) Central Powers; (d) Allies; (e) stalemate; (f) autocrat.
2. *Summarizing the Main Idea* What was the main reason that the United States stayed neutral at the start of World War I?
3. *Organizing Information* Create a cause-and-effect chart that shows why World War I started and what some of its effects were.

### Critical Thinking

4. *Analyzing Time Lines* Review the time line at the start of the section. What clue suggests to you that the major powers expected the crisis between Austria-Hungary and Serbia to lead to war?
5. *Checking Consistency* The alliance system in Europe in 1914 was designed to maintain peace. Yet it seemed to make the conflict worse once the fighting began. Explain this apparent inconsistency.

### Writing Activity

6. *Writing a Persuasive Essay* Write an essay in which you express your support for the preparedness movement. Persuade your readers that the United States has no choice but to be ready to go to war.

# SKILLS FOR LIFE

**Critical Thinking**

**Historical Evidence**

**Geography**

**Graphs and Charts**

## Identifying Alternatives

Identifying alternatives means finding one or more possible solutions to a problem. In the previous section, you read about the conflict in the United States over how to react to the war raging in Europe. The passages on this page make the case for two responses the United States might have made. Passage A presents the views of then President Woodrow Wilson, as stated in August 1914. Passage B, which was published in January 1915, presents the thoughts of former President Theodore Roosevelt.

Use the following steps to identify and analyze the alternatives presented in the passages.

**1.** ***Identify the nature of the problem under discussion.*** Before you can identify alternative solutions to a problem, you must understand what the problem is. (a) What is the issue that both passages address? (b) Does each passage present the same approach to the problem?

**2.** ***Identify the solutions proposed in the two passages.*** (a) What does Passage A suggest is the proper response of the United States to the war raging in Europe? (b) How does Passage B propose that the United States respond to the war? (c) In what ways are these two viewpoints similar or different?

**3.** ***Evaluate the potential effectiveness of each view.*** Consider the strengths and weaknesses of each proposal. For example, you might ask the following questions about Passages A and B: (a) What difficulties do you see in Wilson's suggestion that the United States not judge the actions of other nations? (b) What might happen if the United States acts in a "disinterested" way, as Wilson suggests? (c) Does Roosevelt make clear what he means when he refers to a nation that "does ill"? (d) Does Roosevelt explain the basis by which nations should be judged "highly civilized" or "well behaved"?

**4.** ***Consider other alternatives.*** Recall the nature of the problem under discussion. Then, using insights you gained above, think of other possible solutions. Ask: (a) What should be the goal of the United States in responding to the war in Europe? (b) What steps are most likely to achieve that goal?

### TEST FOR SUCCESS

Do you think President Wilson or President Roosevelt would have been the first to declare war on a nation that provoked the United States? Explain your answer, based on Passages A and B.

**A**

*"My thought is of America. . . . [T]his great country of ours . . . should show herself in this time of peculiar trial a nation fit beyond others to exhibit the fine poise of undisturbed judgment, the dignity of self-control, the efficiency of dispassionate* [unemotional] *action; a nation that neither sits in judgment upon others nor is disturbed in her own counsels and which keeps herself fit and free to do what is honest and disinterested and truly serviceable for the peace of the world."*

Woodrow Wilson, *Appeal for Neutrality,* August 19, 1914

**B**

*"Our true course should be to judge each nation on its conduct, unhesitatingly to antagonize every nation that does ill [at the point] it does ill, and equally without hesitation to act. . . .*

*One of the greatest of international duties ought to be the protection of small, highly civilized, well-behaved and self-respecting states from oppression and conquest by their powerful military neighbors. . . .*

*I feel in the strongest way that we should have interfered, at least to the extent of the most emphatic diplomatic protest and at the very outset—and then by whatever further action was necessary—[when Germany invaded Belgium]."*

Theodore Roosevelt, *America and the World War,* 1915

| May 1915 | March 1916 | November 1916 | February 1917 | March 1917 | April 1917 |
|---|---|---|---|---|---|
| Lusitania sunk | Sussex sunk | Wilson reelected | Germany resumes unrestricted submarine warfare; Zimmermann note | Russian Revolution; City of Memphis, Illinois, and Vigilancia sunk | United States declares war on Germany |

1915 1916 1917 1918

# 2 The United States Declares War

**SECTION PREVIEW**

### Objectives

1. Describe German submarine tactics during World War I.
2. Identify events that moved the United States toward war.
3. *Key Terms* Define: U-boat; Sussex pledge; filibuster; Zimmermann note; Russian Revolution.

### Main Idea

German submarine warfare helped push the United States into World War I.

### Reading Strategy

*Organizing Information* Imagine that you are a member of Congress in 1917. You must decide whether the United States should go to war against Germany and the other Central Powers. As you read the section, list the events that influence your decision.

*This German poster urged U-boats on their mission. The translation is, "Submarine: come out!"*

From 1915 to 1917 friction between the United States and Germany increased. The preparedness movement continued to gain support in the United States, and the pressure to join in the war intensified. Ultimately, actions by the Central Powers pushed Congress and the President into entering the war on the side of the Allies.

## German Submarine Warfare

One action that provoked angry calls for war in the United States was the German use of submarine warfare. This tactic was effective militarily, but it cost the Germans dearly in terms of American public opinion.

The German **U-boat,** short for *Unterseeboot,* or submarine, was a terrifying new weapon that changed the rules of naval warfare. Passenger and merchant ships had no defense against the submarine, which could go undetected nearly anywhere in the ocean. Submarine attacks depended on the element of surprise. Unlike other naval ships, U-boats issued no warning to their targets. This struck many Americans as uncivilized.†

The British encouraged such anti-German feelings. Shortly after the war began, the British cut the transatlantic cable connecting Germany and the United States. All news of the European front henceforth flowed through London. Its pro-Allied bias helped shape the opinion of the people in the United States in favor of punishing Germany for its use of the submarine.

American public opinion of the Germans sank even lower on May 7, 1915, when a U-boat sighted the *Lusitania,* a British passenger liner, in the Irish Sea. Suspecting correctly that the ship carried weapons for the Allies, the U-boat fired on the liner. Eighteen minutes later the *Lusitania* disappeared beneath the waves along with its almost 1,200 passengers. Included among the dead were 128 Americans, who had

† Americans did not react the same way to the British blockade of Germany, even though it threatened freedom of the seas and was slowly starving the German people. They generally thought that such a blockade was reasonable during wartime. In contrast, German attempts to break the blockade with submarines seemed unfair.

NOTICE!

TRAVELLERS intending to embark on the Atlantic voyage are reminded that a state of war exists between Germany and her allies and GreatBritian and her allies; that the zone of war includes the waters adjacent to the British Isles; that, in accordance with formal notice given by the Imperial German Government, vessels flying the flag of Great Britian, or of any of her allies, are liable to destruction in those waters and that travellers sailing in the war zone on ships of Great Britian or her allies do so at their own risk.

IMPERIAL GERMAN EMBASSY,

WASHINGTON, D. C., APRIL 22, 1915.

American public opinion was extremely critical of Germany and its use of U-boats. The cartoon (right) suggests that Germany felt no remorse for the loss of American lives. Germany, however, did warn travelers—including passengers of the *Lusitania*—to stay out of the war zone (left). ***Foreign Relations*** *What does this cartoon suggest about Wilson's response to the sinking of the* **Lusitania?**

boarded the *Lusitania* in spite of German warnings to stay off British ships. Nevertheless, the American press went wild over what they called Germany's act of "barbarism."

Wilson urged patience. He demanded that Germany stop its submarine warfare and make payments to the victims' families. Germany's reply that the ship carried small arms and ammunition did not quiet American anger. Wilson sent a second, stronger note of protest. In response, Germany promised to stop sinking passenger ships without warning, as long as the ship's crew offered no resistance to German search or seizure.

Still, U-boats continued to torpedo Allied ships. On March 24, 1916, a German submarine sank the *Sussex,* a French passenger steamship. The United States threatened to cut diplomatic ties to Germany. In what came to be called the **Sussex pledge,** the German government again promised that U-boats would warn ships before attacking.

The series of demands and broken promises that led up to the Sussex pledge frustrated Wilson. He could not threaten force without entering the war. During this time, however, Wilson did embrace the concept of preparedness. He also authorized New York bankers to make a huge loan to the Allies. American neutrality was beginning to weaken.

## Moving Toward War

In the presidential election of 1916, Wilson ran on the slogan "He kept us out of war." The Republicans, who nominated Supreme Court justice Charles Evans Hughes, criticized Wilson for not taking a stronger stand against Germany. American voters gave Wilson a narrow victory.

Germany soon tested Wilson's patience. On February 1, 1917, Germany violated the Sussex pledge by resuming unrestricted submarine warfare. German strategists knew that it might bring the United States into the war. But they felt fairly confident that they could defeat Britain and win the war before American entry could make a difference.

Germany's action dashed Wilson's hope of maintaining freedom of the seas—and American neutrality. On February 3 the United States broke off diplomatic relations with Germany. Wilson asked Congress for permission to arm American merchant ships.

**Main Idea CONNECTIONS**

*What was the impact of Germany's unrestricted submarine warfare?*

*President Woodrow Wilson reluctantly led the nation into World War I.*

**The Zimmermann Note** In the Senate, a group of antiwar senators tried to prevent action on Wilson's request by using a **filibuster.** (A filibuster is a tactic in which senators take the floor, begin talking, and refuse to stop talking to prevent a vote on a measure.) While this was taking place, the British revealed the contents of an intercepted German telegram. In the note Arthur Zimmermann, Germany's foreign secretary, made a secret offer to Mexico.

> **"We shall endeavor to keep the United States neutral. In the event of this not succeeding, we make Mexico a proposal of alliance. . . : Make war together, make peace together, . . . and . . . Mexico is to reconquer the lost territory in Texas, New Mexico, and Arizona."**
>
> —*Arthur Zimmermann*

Neither Wilson nor Mexico took the **Zimmermann note** seriously. Its release, however, scored another public relations victory for Great Britain. The United States edged closer to war.

**Revolution in Russia** By early 1917 Russia already had suffered enormous casualties in the war: more than 1.5 million killed, roughly 2.5 million taken prisoner, and millions more wounded. Austrian and German forces had advanced deep into Russian territory. Poorly fed and miserably equipped, the Russians fell back farther and farther into their interior.

Then, in March 1917, Czar Nicholas II, Russia's autocratic leader, was forced to give up power. The Russian monarchy was replaced with a republican government. This **Russian Revolution** elated the prowar faction in the United States. Concern over being allied with the czar had helped slow the nation's move toward entry into the war. The fall of the czar removed a last stumbling block to a full American commitment to the Allies.

**The War Resolution** Between March 16 and March 18, Germany sank the United States ships *City of Memphis, Illinois,* and *Vigilancia.* On March 20 Wilson's Cabinet voted unanimously for war. Casting the issue in idealistic terms, Wilson told Congress on April 2 that "the world must be made safe for democracy." He stated:

> AMERICAN VOICES **"It is a fearful thing to lead this great peaceful people into war, the most terrible and disastrous of all wars, civilization itself seeming to be in the balance. But the right is more precious than peace."**
>
> —*Woodrow Wilson*

A war resolution passed 82 to 6 in the Senate and 373 to 50 in the House. On April 6, 1917, the President signed it.

## SECTION 2 REVIEW

### Comprehension

1. *Key Terms* Define: (a) U-boat; (b) Sussex pledge; (c) filibuster; (d) Zimmermann note; (e) Russian Revolution.
2. *Summarizing the Main Idea* Why did German submarine warfare upset Americans so much?
3. *Organizing Information* Create a flowchart that shows the events leading up to American entrance into World War I. Charts might consist of a series of boxes connected by arrows.

### Critical Thinking

4. *Analyzing Time Lines* Review the time line at the start of the section. Which event do you think most directly caused the United States to declare war on Germany? Explain.
5. *Identifying Alternatives* Consider the causes that brought the United States into World War I. What would the United States have had to do to avoid the conflict altogether? For what reasons did the United States not take such steps?

### Writing Activity

6. *Writing a Persuasive Essay* Choose one of the events that led to American involvement in World War I. Imagine that the event has just taken place. Write an essay to try to persuade the President and Congress that the United States should enter the war now, based on that one event.

| May 1917 | June 1917 | March 1918 | June 1918 | August 1918 | November 1918 |
|---|---|---|---|---|---|
| *Selective Service Act; Convoy system put in place* | *American troops arrive in France* | *Russia exits war* | *Battle of Château-Thierry* | *Allied counteroffensive* | *Cease-fire ends fighting* |

1917 — 1918 — 1919

# 3 Americans on the European Front

## SECTION PREVIEW

### Objectives

1. Describe how the United States prepared to take part in World War I.
2. Explain how American troops helped turn the tide of the war.
3. Describe the war's end and its costs.
4. *Key Terms* Define: Selective Service Act; American Expeditionary Force; convoy; armistice; genocide.

### Main Idea

American troops helped the Allies defeat the Central Powers in World War I.

### Reading Strategy

*Predicting Content* Create a list of this section's boldface headings and subheadings. Under each one, write a one-sentence prediction of what the content will be. Then check your predictions against the actual text.

By the time the United States entered the war in April 1917, the Allies desperately needed replacement troops. In June, President Wilson agreed to send a small force to Europe under the command of General John J. Pershing. A veteran of the Spanish-American War, the general had also taught for a time at West Point. Pershing would need all his experience and skills to lead the American forces against a determined German army.

## *Preparing for Action*

Despite the success of the preparedness movement, in April 1917 the United States was far from ready to send an army to the European front. Instead, a cautious Congress sent naval support, supplies, arms, and $3 billion in loans. The token force of 14,500 men led by General Pershing served mainly to boost Allied morale. After landing in France, Pershing realized that he needed more troops. He recommended that the army should number 1 million men by 1918 and 3 million the year after that.

**Draftees and Volunteers** When the United States entered World War I, the armed forces had only 120,000 enlisted men and 80,000 National Guardsmen. In May 1917 Congress passed a **Selective Service Act,** authorizing a draft of young men for military service.

During the Civil War the draft had sparked riots. Now, however, the general feeling that this would be the "war to end all wars" resulted in wide acceptance of the program. By November 1918 more than 24 million men had registered for the draft. From those, a lottery picked 3 million draftees to serve in the war. Volunteers and National Guardsmen made up the remainder of what was called the **American Expeditionary Force** (AEF).

*In 1917 American soldiers marched off to war, carrying items such as this shaving kit.*

Among the Americans who served their country were thousands of women. Some 11,000 women volunteered to serve in uniform as nurses, drivers, and clerks. Another 14,000 women served abroad, as civilians

Denied combat opportunity by the United States, these New York National Guardsmen fought with the French as the 369th Infantry Regiment. Though facing combat for the first time, they performed with such skill and bravery that they were awarded the French Croix de Guerre. ***Diversity*** ***Why do you think African Americans suffered discrimination in the armed forces?***

American and Allied units fought separately, but a further division existed within the American ranks. The more than 300,000 African Americans who volunteered or were drafted into service were kept apart from white troops. Though many African Americans fought with distinction and nearly 4,000 died or were wounded, most never saw combat. The marines refused to accept African Americans altogether, and the navy used them for minor tasks only. The army, too, used African Americans mostly for manual labor.

These assignments distressed many African Americans. The 369th Infantry Regiment, who came to be known as the Harlem Hell Fighters, was especially eager to fight. Its members persuaded their white officers to loan the regiment to the French, who integrated the regiment into the French army. Because of their distinguished service, the entire regiment received France's highest combat medal, the Croix de Guerre.

working for the government or for private agencies.

**The Convoy System** In addition to building a fighting force, the War Department had to worry about transporting its troops overseas. In April 1917 alone, German U-boats had sunk more than 400 Allied and neutral ships.

Starting in May 1917 all merchant and troop ships traveled in a **convoy.** A convoy consisted of a group of unarmed ships surrounded by a ring of destroyers, torpedo boats, and other armed naval vessels. The torpedo boats were specially equipped to track and destroy submarines. Between April and December 1917, merchant marine losses dropped by half.

**American Soldiers in Europe** From the time the AEF arrived in France in June 1917, Pershing kept them independent of the Allied armies. In Pershing's view the Allies had become too accustomed to defensive action. He wanted to save his men's strength for offensive moves.†

† American infantrymen were called *doughboys.* This term originated during the Civil War in reference to the dumpling-shaped buttons on Union infantry uniforms.

## *Turning the Tide of War*

As American involvement in the war expanded, a major development occurred within the alliance. In November 1917 followers of Vladimir Lenin, called Bolsheviks, violently overthrew Russia's government. Lenin had been living in Switzerland and had promised to make peace with Germany if he ever gained control in Russia. For this reason Germany had helped arrange his return to Russia in April 1917. By November, Lenin had taken over the country.

Lenin made peace with Germany on March 3, 1918. Russia's exit from the war freed the Germans from the two-front war they had been forced to fight. From March through May 1918, German forces turned all their energies toward pounding the French and British lines. They finally broke through, and by June 3 were about 50 miles from Paris.

**Americans Save Paris** American forces came to the rescue. Marching out from Paris, the men received this word from their leader, Brigadier

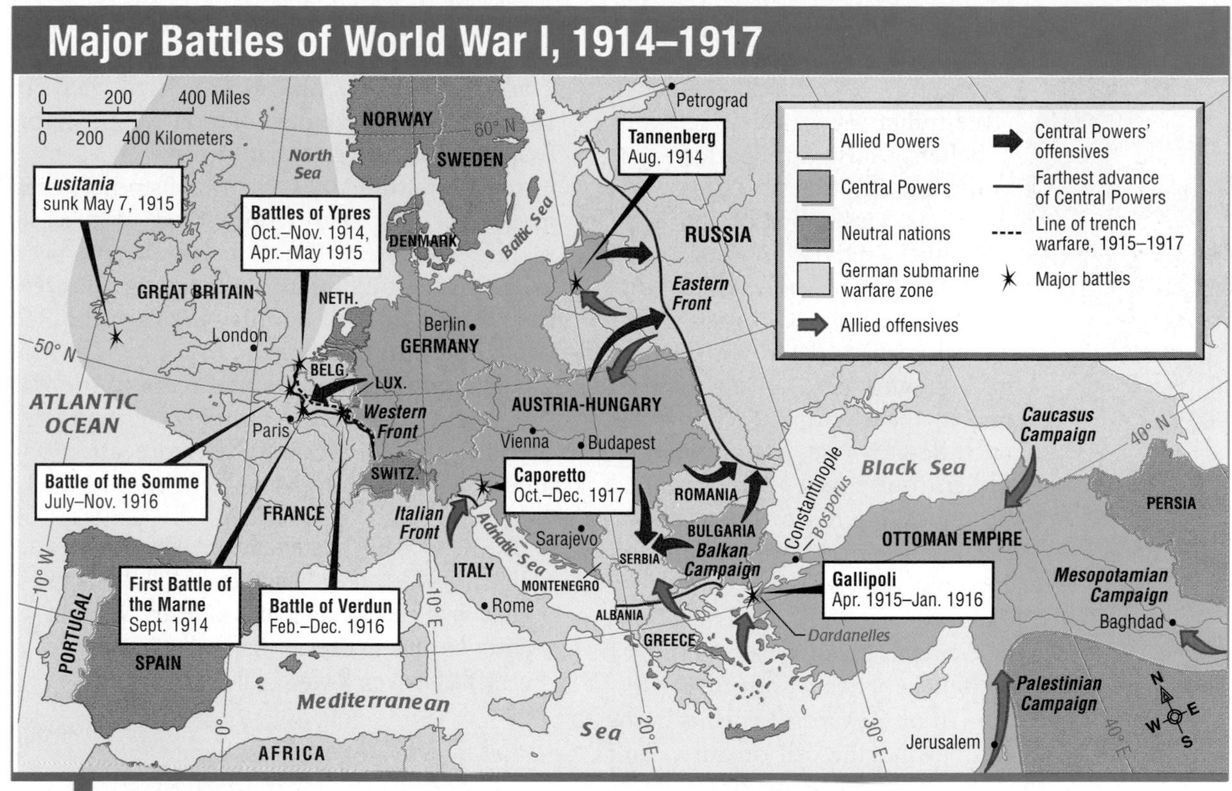


**MAP skills** After the Germans advanced through Belgium, the French prevented them from capturing Paris in the First Battle of the Marne. The war, however, was far from over. A deadly stalemate ensued. ***Location*** ***Locate the line of trench warfare. What was its strategic value? Why didn't it extend across Switzerland?***

General James G. Harbord: "We dig no trenches to fall back on. The Marines will hold where they stand." At the battle of Château-Thierry in early June, they did just that. At a loss of over half of their troops, they helped the French save Paris, blunted the edge of the German advance, and began to turn the tide of the war.

**Allied Counterattack** After turning back the Germans outside Paris, the Allies took heart. Using a new weapon, the tank, which could cross trenches and roll through barbed wire, they began to break the German lines. On August 8 at the battle of Amiens, the Allied armies stopped the German advance once and for all.

On August 11, German general Erich von Ludendorff sensed that the end was near. He advised Kaiser Wilhelm to seek a peace settlement. The Allies, however, insisted on total surrender. In September some 500,000 American troops, assisted by 100,000 French, began to hit the final German strongholds. In the battle of St. Mihiel, the first major military effort entirely in American hands, General Pershing and his troops ousted the Germans from a long-held position. Soon after, the German army was in full retreat.

The Allies also began to use airplanes to drop bombs. Aerial dogfights already had taken place. Each side had its "aces," such as the American captain Eddie Rickenbacker, who downed 26 enemy fighters. Now Colonel Billy Mitchell organized a fleet of over 1,400 bomb-carrying planes. Although not very effective at first, bombing raids would become a devastating weapon in the future.

**Main Idea CONNECTIONS**

*What were some of the military innovations introduced during World War I?*

## *Corporal Alvin York*

**AMERICAN BIOGRAPHY** The final Allied assault, the Meuse-Argonne Offensive, began on September 26, 1918. Over a million AEF troops began the drive to expel the Germans from France and cut their supply lines. Many acts of heroism shone during these final months. But the bravery of Corporal Alvin York stood out above the rest.

Born in 1887, York grew up in the mountains of Tennessee, where he learned to shoot by hunting wild turkeys. York did not volun-

Corporal Alvin York (1887–1964)

teer to fight. In fact, he applied to be classified a conscientious objector, someone who refuses to serve in the military because of religious beliefs. His application was denied, and he was drafted.

As a member of the 82nd Infantry Division, York took part in the Meuse-Argonne Offensive. On October 8 his patrol tried to destroy a German machine-gun nest, losing half its men in the attempt. Facing heavy machine-gun fire, the remaining soldiers took cover. York continued the attack on his own, killing 25 machine-gunners with his rifle and pistol and capturing 132 German soldiers.

When a general asked about his exploits, York replied, "General, I would hate to think I missed any of them shots; they were all at pretty close range—50 or 60 yards." For his heroism above and beyond the call of duty, York received the Congressional Medal of Honor as well as the French Croix de Guerre.

## Ending the War

The Allies pressed on against their enemy. The German commanders begged for peace, still hoping to dictate some terms. The Allies refused. By the time the **armistice,** or cease-fire, came, the Kaiser had fled to Holland. On November 11, 1918, the guns finally fell silent.

More than 50,000 American soldiers died in battle, and many more died of disease, mainly influenza. The toll would have been even greater but for the efforts of volunteer nurses serving their country through the Red Cross and other agencies.

The physical and mental scars of the war ran deep. Corporal Elmer Sherwood of Indiana, just 21 years old, wrote after one bloody battle in August 1918:

AMERICAN VOICES **"Hundreds of bodies of our brave boys lie on Hill 212, captured with such a great loss of blood. We will never be able to explain war to our loved ones back home even if we . . . live and return."**

—*Corporal Elmer Sherwood*

American losses were tiny compared with those suffered by the Europeans. The total death toll of 8 million soldiers and sailors is only an estimate. Still, this figure averages out to more than 5,000 soldiers killed on each day of the war. Germany, Austria-Hungary, Russia, and France all suffered more than a

## Major Battles of World War I, 1917–1918

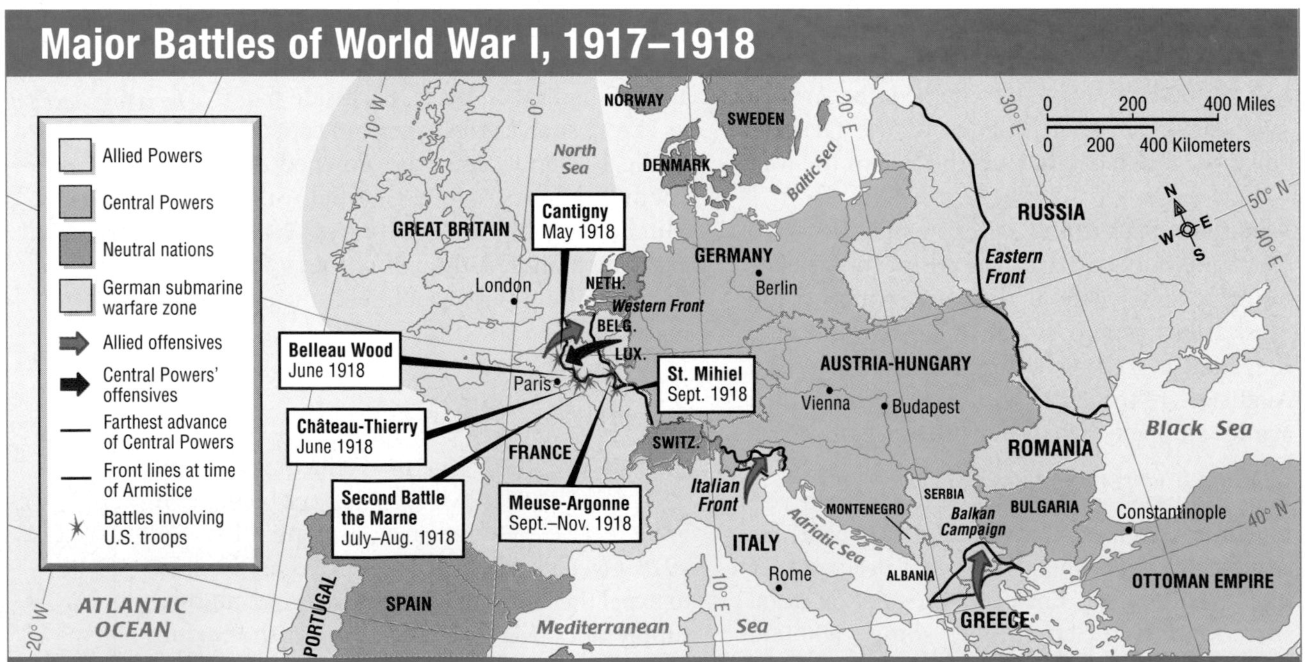


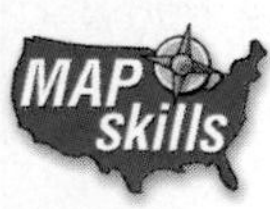
In 1917 the United States entered the war, providing the Allies with both economic and military support. ***Location*** ***Why was the fighting concentrated on the western fronts by 1917–1918?***

## exploring TECHNOLOGY World War I Tank

The tank was another new weapon introduced in World War I. It was designed to cross rough terrain and trenches while remaining invulnerable to enemy fire. Tanks were used to launch assaults in advance of foot troops. *Science and Technology How was the tank a response to trench warfare?*

million war dead. Just under 900,000 British troops died. While most of the fighting and dying took place in Europe, there were battles in the Middle East and Africa as well.

The terrible slaughter extended beyond the battlefields. Millions of civilians died during and immediately after the fighting, from starvation, disease, or war-related injuries. These deaths included hundreds of thousands of Armenian civilians. In a campaign of **genocide,** or the organized killing of an entire people, Ottoman forces deported and murdered Armenians, whom they suspected of disloyalty to the government. The killings of Armenians would continue into the early 1920s.

## SECTION 3 REVIEW

### Comprehension

1. *Key Terms* Define: (a) Selective Service Act; (b) American Expeditionary Force; (c) convoy; (d) armistice; (e) genocide.
2. *Summarizing the Main Idea* What role did American troops play in World War I?
3. *Organizing Information* Create a chart with three headings: *Preparing for Action, Turning the Tide,* and *Ending the War*. Fill in the chart with important details from the section.

### Critical Thinking

4. *Analyzing Time Lines* Review the time line at the start of the section. How long did it take for the American Expeditionary Force to make a significant impact on the course of the war? Explain.
5. *Drawing Inferences* Long after Pershing's American Expeditionary Force arrived in Europe, French soldiers were still asking, "Where are the Americans?" Why do you think they asked that question?

### Writing Activity

6. *Writing an Expository Essay* Write an essay focusing on the number of war deaths suffered by the main combatants in World War I.

| February 1917 Literacy test for immigrants | June 1917 Espionage Act | August 1917 Lever Food and Fuel Control Act | September 1917 Police raids against IWW members | May 1918 Sedition Act |
|---|---|---|---|---|

1917 — 1918 — 1919

# 4 On the Home Front

## SECTION PREVIEW

### Objectives

1 Explain how the government financed the war and managed the wartime economy.
2 Describe how efforts to enforce loyalty led to hostility and repression.
3 Describe how the lives of Americans on the home front changed during the war.
4 *Key Terms* Define: Liberty Bond; price controls; rationing; daylight saving time; sedition; vigilante.

### Main Idea

Americans and their government took extraordinary steps at home to support the war effort.

### Reading Strategy

*Reading for Evidence* As you read, look for evidence to support the following statement, which appears on this page: "Waging war required many sacrifices at home." On a sheet of paper, list as many kinds of sacrifices described as you can.

The U.S. government used posters to whip up sentiment against the "Huns"—the Germans.

Waging war required many sacrifices at home. Despite the efforts of the preparedness movement, the American economy was not ready to meet the demands of modern warfare. In this era, war required huge amounts of money and personnel. As President Wilson explained, now "there are no armies . . . ; there are entire nations armed."

## Financing the War

The government launched a vigorous campaign to raise money from the American people. It started offering **Liberty Bonds,** special war bonds sold to support the Allied cause. Like all bonds, they could later be redeemed for the original value of the bonds plus interest. Secretary of the Treasury William Gibbs McAdoo had the idea for Liberty Bonds. By selling war bonds to enthusiastic Americans, McAdoo raised more than $20 billion. This allowed the United States to loan more than $10 billion to the Allies during and just after the war.

Responding to the slogan "Every Scout to Save a Soldier," Boy Scouts and Girl Scouts set up booths on street corners and sold bonds. The government hired popular commercial artists to draw colorful posters and recruited famous screen actors to host bond rallies. An army of 75,000 "four-minute men" gave brief (four-minute) speeches before movies, plays, and school or union meetings to persuade audiences to buy bonds.

## Managing the Economy

The government also called on industry to convert to the production of war goods. In 1918 Wilson won authority to set up a huge bureaucracy to manage this process. Business leaders flocked to Washington to take up posts in thousands of new agencies. Because they gave their service for a token salary, they were called "dollar-a-year" men and women.

**New Agencies** A War Industries Board, headed by financier Bernard Baruch, oversaw the nation's war-related production. The board had far-reaching powers. It doled out raw materials, told manufacturers what and how much to produce, and even fixed prices.

A War Trade Board licensed foreign trade and punished firms suspected of dealing with the enemy. A National War Labor Board, set up in April 1918 under former President Taft, worked to settle any labor disputes that might hinder the war effort. (Labor leader Samuel Gompers promised to limit labor strife in war-production industries.) A separate War Labor Policies Board, headed by Harvard law professor Felix Frankfurter, set standard wages, hours, and working conditions in the war industries. Labor unions won limited rights to organize and bargain collectively.

**Regulating Food and Fuel Consumption** In August 1917 Congress passed the Lever Food and Fuel Control Act. This act gave the President the power to manage the production and distribution of foods and fuels vital to the war effort.

Using the slogan "Food will win the war," the government began regulating food consumption. Under the leadership of engineer and future President Herbert Hoover, the Food Administration worked to increase agricultural output and reduce waste. Hoover had the power to impose **price controls,** a system of pricing determined by the government, on food. He also could have begun a system of **rationing,** or distributing goods to consumers in a fixed amount. But he opposed both these approaches. Hoover hoped instead that voluntary restraint and increased efficiency would accomplish the Food Administration's goals.

Women played a key role in Hoover's program. Writing to women in August 1917, he preached a "Gospel of the Clean Plate." He appealed:

**AMERICAN VOICES** **"Stop, before throwing any food away, and ask "Can it be used?" . . . Stop catering to different appetites. No second helpings. Stop all eating between meals. . . . One meatless day a week. One wheatless meal a day. . . . No butter in cooking: use substitutes."**

—*Herbert Hoover*

"The American woman and the American home," Hoover concluded, "can bring to a successful end the greatest national task that has ever been accepted by the American people." Eager to take part in the war effort, women across the country responded to this patriotic challenge.

The Lever Food and Fuel Control Act also created an agency called the Fuel Administration. It sponsored gasless days to save fuel. This agency also began the practice of **daylight saving time**—turning clocks ahead one hour for the summer. This new policy increased the number of daylight hours available for activities. In this way daylight saving time lessened the need for artificial light, which lowered fuel consumption.

**Main Idea CONNECTIONS**

*In what way did the Fuel Administration agency help in the war effort?*

**A Progressive Victory?** Thanks to the war, some hopes of progressive-era reformers had come to pass. Government now regulated American economic life to an extent most progressives had never dreamed possible. When regulation spilled over into more private areas of life, however, some progressives wondered if the growth in public power had gone too far.

In addition, to the dismay of all progressives, regulation had not lessened the power of the corporate world. Indeed, during the war the influence of business leaders grew, the government relaxed its pursuit of antitrust suits, and corporate profits tripled.

## *Enforcing Loyalty*

News and information also came under federal control during World War I. The government imposed censorship on the press and banned some publications from the mails.

In 1917 George Creel, a Denver journalist and former muckraker, was made head of the Committee on Public Information. His job was to rally popular support for the war. Creel's office coordinated the production of short films, pamphlets explaining war aims, and posters selling recruitment and Liberty Bonds.

**Fear of Foreigners** As in all wars, the fear of espionage, or spying, was widespread. A few months after the sinking of the *Lusitania,* a staff member of the German embassy left his briefcase on an American train. In it were plans for weakening pro-Allied sentiment and disrupting the American economy.

The government feared that secret agents might try to undermine the war effort by destroying transportation or communication networks. The possibility of such acts of sabotage put the government on alert. It also generated calls for restrictions on immigration.

The National Security League, having won its battle for preparedness, began to preach "100 Percent Americanism." Early in 1917 the League got Congress to pass, over Wilson's veto, a literacy test for immigrants. This test excluded those who could not read English or some other language. As it turned out, relatively few immigrants failed the test. Still, the test set the stage for a vigorous revival of nativism.

**"Hate the Hun!"** Once the United States declared war, alertness for spies approached hysteria. The war also spurred a general hostility toward Germans. People began calling them Huns, in reference to an Asiatic people who brutally invaded Europe in the fourth and fifth centuries. German composers and musicians were banned from symphony concerts. German measles became "liberty measles," and a hamburger (which was named after Hamburg, a German city) became a "liberty sandwich."

Yet it was a mob of Americans who showed brutality and hatred in April 1918, when they lynched German-born citizen Robert Prager near St. Louis. Despite his German heritage, Prager had in fact tried to enlist in the navy. His lynching was but one of numerous wartime attacks on people of German descent.

"I am afraid we are going to have a good many instances of people roughly treated on very slight evidence of disloyalty," wrote Secretary of War Newton Baker. Indeed, as this 1917 photograph shows, anti-German feeling in the United States led to the arrest of many citizens of German descent. ***Government*** *How did government policies such as the Sedition Act contribute to nativist hatred?*

**Repression of Civil Liberties** In his message to Congress in 1917, calling for war on Germany, Wilson had claimed that the United States would be fighting for liberty and democracy. His claim offended those who suffered from wartime restrictions on their civil liberties.

In that same war message Wilson warned that disloyalty would be "dealt with with a firm hand of stern repression." Accordingly, Congress in 1917 passed the Espionage Act, which made it illegal to interfere with the draft. The Espionage Act was amended in 1918 by the Sedition Act. (**Sedition** is speech or actions that encourage rebellion.) The Sedition Act made it illegal to obstruct the sale of Liberty Bonds or to discuss anything "disloyal, profane, scurrilous, or abusive" about the American form of government, the Constitution, or the army and navy.

The government pursued more than 1,500 prosecutions and won more than 1,000 convictions. Socialist and former presidential candidate Eugene Debs drew a ten-year jail sentence for criticizing the American government and business leaders and urging people to "resist militarism."

**Controlling Political Radicals** Socialists such as Debs argued that the war was merely a quarrel among imperialist capitalists. This view became a rallying point for antiwar sentiment. In the elections of 1917 in New York, Ohio, and Pennsylvania, socialists made impressive gains.

The radical labor organization Industrial Workers of the World (IWW) also gained new supporters. Its membership of western miners, migrant farm workers, and other unskilled laborers supported the IWW's goal of overthrowing capitalism.

The views of socialists and the IWW distressed moderate labor leaders like Samuel Gompers, who had pledged union cooperation with the war effort. The police hounded the IWW. Raids in September 1917 led to the conviction of nearly 200 members in trials held in Illinois, California, and Oklahoma. Groups of **vigilantes,** citizens who take the law into their own hands, lynched and horsewhipped others.

## Changing People's Lives

American patriotism and war fever made military styles and activities more acceptable at home. Scouting programs for boys and girls, involving military-style uniforms, marching, and patriotic exercises, grew in popularity. Military drill became part of many school programs. By the summer of 1918, all able-bodied males in colleges and universities became army privates, subject to military discipline.

**Social Mobility for Minorities and Women** Americans turned away from military styles and activities after the war. But other social changes had more lasting effects. The war cut off the flow of immigrants from Europe, and the armed forces took many young men out of the labor pool. Businesses, especially war-related industries, suddenly needed workers. These wartime conditions propelled some people into higher paid jobs. Factories that used to discriminate against African Americans and Mexican Americans now actively recruited them.

The African Americans who left the South to work in northern factories added to a steady stream of migrants that had started in the late 1800s. The stream turned into a flood during the war, when some 500,000 African Americans joined what came to be called the Great Migration.

Wage-earning women, too, benefited from the diminished work force. Some women found jobs on farms, thanks to organizations such as the Women's Land Army. Others moved into jobs previously closed to them, such as telegraph messenger, elevator operator, and letter carrier. A few earned management positions.

As a result of the war, about 400,000 women joined the industrial work force for the first time. In 1917 a speaker for the Women's Trade Union League proclaimed, "At last, after centuries of disabilities and discrimination, women are coming into the labor and festival of life on equal terms with men." Such pronouncements, while premature, celebrated what seemed like a major social change.



*The IWW gained strength during World War I. It also became the target of the government's effort to control political radicals.*

**Prohibition Finally Passes** In 1917 the temperance movement was almost a century old. In that year Congress proposed the Eighteenth Amendment to the Constitution, which made it illegal to manufacture, sell, or transport alcoholic beverages in the United States. Members of Congress backed the Eighteenth Amendment in part to show patriotism during wartime. The production of alcohol used a lot of grain, which was now needed to make the bread to feed people at home and overseas. The states ratified the Prohibition Amendment in 1919.

## SECTION 4 REVIEW

### Comprehension

1. *Key Terms* Define: (a) Liberty Bond; (b) price controls; (c) rationing; (d) daylight saving time; (e) sedition; (f) vigilante.
2. *Summarizing the Main Idea* What special powers did new government agencies have over industry and labor during the war?
3. *Organizing Information* Create a chart to show the steps the government took to finance the war, manage the economy, and boost Americanism.

### Critical Thinking

4. *Analyzing Time Lines* Review the time line at the start of the section. Which event do you think did the most to change Americans' lives? Explain.
5. *Demonstrating Reasoned Judgment* Do you think the Sedition Act was a good way to deal with critics during wartime? Explain.

### Writing Activity

6. *Writing a Persuasive Essay* Write an essay in the form of a speech for one of the "four-minute men." Before you begin, decide who your audience is and craft your speech to persuade that audience to buy war bonds.

## Plow 2

Sharecropping farmers walked behind a mule-drawn plow like this one to break the land.

## 1 Handmade Doll

Cash-poor African Americans made or grew much of what they used in the South. This doll had its own handmade cradle and blankets.

## 3 Store Owner's Record Book

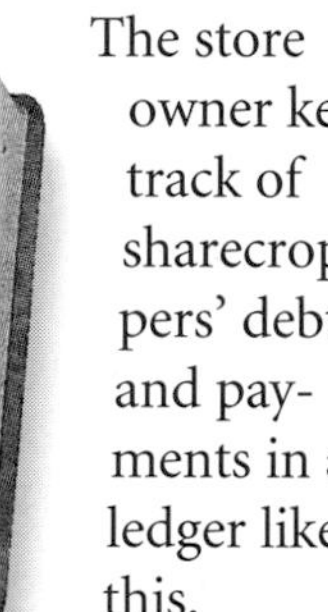

The store owner kept track of sharecroppers' debts and payments in a ledger like this.

## 4 Home Schooling

In the South, African American parents frequently served as their children's teachers.

## 5 Suitcase and Bibles

African American families could only bring a limited number of items with them on their journey northward.

6

### World War I Soldiers

Many African Americans learned about race relations in other countries when they served as soldiers during World War I. This was the first time most African Americans had traveled more than a few miles from home.

### Job Opportunities

7

Industries expanded for wartime production during World War I, and many workers were drafted into the armed forces. Thus job opportunities for African Americans rose sharply during the war.

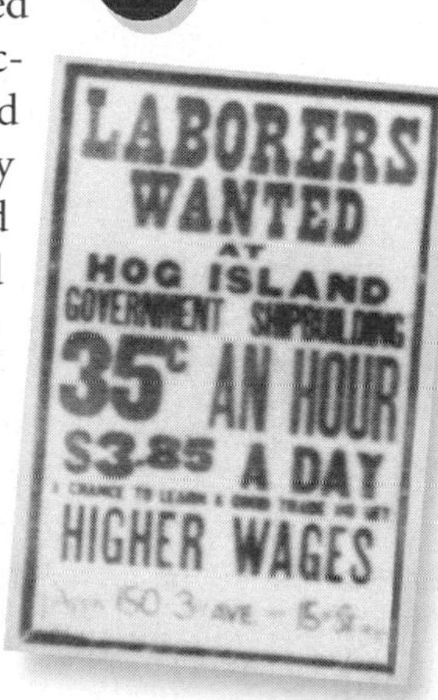


**VIEWING HISTORY**

1. ***Summarize*** What do the objects tell you about daily life for African Americans in the South and in the North?

2. ***Connecting to Today*** Think about the reasons people migrate today. Are they similar or different from the reasons of African Americans during the Great Migration? Report the following to your class: (a) a current example of a migration; (b) whether you think that migrating always changes life for the better.

American ARTIFACTS

FROM EXHIBITIONS AND COLLECTIONS AT THE SMITHSONIAN INSTITUTION'S NATIONAL MUSEUM OF AMERICAN HISTORY

## AFRICAN AMERICANS' GREAT MIGRATION

The African American poet Margaret Walker called the South "Sorrow home." Perhaps this sentiment was shared by African Americans as they began their "Great Migration" north. Beginning in 1915, hundreds of thousands of African Americans packed up their bags, eager to take advantage of northern opportunities and leave behind the poverty and discrimination of the Jim Crow South. This move would change both the lives of the migrants and the history of race relations in the North.

Life had not been easy in the South. More than two thirds of African Americans were sharecropping farmers who paid landowners a part of their crops in exchange for rent of their land. Farming was backbreaking work for the whole family, and rarely did sharecroppers earn enough money for more than survival. Most fell deeper and deeper in debt to landlords, landowners, and store owners. *See* 1, 2, *and* 3.

African Americans in the South had to rely on their own efforts to get by. Since schools for African Americans were few in number and poorly funded, many children were taught at home instead. The hope that conditions would be better in the North led many African Americans to pack their few possessions and head north. *See* 4 *and* 5.

World War I created new opportunities. For one thing, scores of African Americans served in Europe, bringing home new ideas about race relations and civil rights. In addition, job opportunities grew in the North. African Americans streamed north to fill many of the openings. While leaving their homes would not be easy, African Americans believed a better way of life awaited them. *See* 6 *and* 7.

| January 1918 | January 1919 | June 1919 | March 1920 | April 1921 | July 1921 |
|---|---|---|---|---|---|
| *Wilson announces Fourteen Points* | *Paris Peace Conference opens* | *Versailles Treaty signed* | *Senate refuses to ratify Versailles Treaty* | *Reparations Commission announces German debt to Allies* | *United States declares formal end to war* |

1918 1919 1920 1921 1922

# 5 Global Peacemaker

**SECTION PREVIEW**

### Objectives

1. Describe how Wilson's vision for peace fared during the Paris Peace Conference.
2. Explain the main points of the peace treaty and describe Wilson's efforts to gain approval for the treaty.
3. Describe the difficult adjustments many Americans had to make after the war.
4. *Key Terms* Define: Fourteen Points; self-determination; spoils; League of Nations; reparations; Versailles Treaty.

### Main Idea

When the fighting ended in Europe, President Wilson pressed for a treaty that would bring peace to the postwar world.

### Reading Strategy

*Reinforcing Key Ideas* As you read, take notes on how the Versailles Treaty was created and why the United States Senate refused to ratify it.

On January 8, 1918, President Wilson stood before the Congress of the United States. The war had not ended, yet Wilson talked about peace. He hoped that the world could "be made safe for every peace-loving nation which, like our own, wishes to live its own life, determine its own institutions, be assured of justice and fair dealing by the other peoples of the world as against force and selfish aggression."

## *Wilson's Vision for Peace*

Wilson's program for reaching these goals came to be called the **Fourteen Points,** for the number of provisions it contained. Wilson's first point called for an end to entangling alliances, a key cause of the war. He wrote:

KEY DOCUMENTS "Open covenants of peace, openly arrived at, after which there shall be no private international understandings of any kind but diplomacy shall proceed always frankly and in the public view."

—*Woodrow Wilson*

The remaining provisions of the Fourteen Points dealt with a variety of issues related to keeping the peace after the war. They included removal of trade barriers among nations and the reduction of armaments. Wilson also sought the protection of the right of Austria-Hungary's ethnic groups to **self-determination,** or the power to make decisions about one's own future.

Wilson hoped that these points would form the basis of peace negotiations. Germany assumed they would. At first, the Allies appeared to cooperate. But it soon became obvious that Wilson's colleagues did not share his idealism. After a while, the Fourteen Points began to unravel.

## *The Paris Peace Conference*

In January 1919 an international peace conference was held in Paris. Wilson decided to head the United States delegation. With the exception of one elderly diplomat, Republican Henry White, he chose not to name any other senior Republicans to the group.

## FACT Finder: World War I Casualties

| | Allies | Central Powers |
|---|---|---|
| **Military Battle Deaths** | 4,889,000 | 3,132,000 |
| **Military Wounded** | 12,809,000 | 8,420,000 |
| **Total Casualties** | *17,698,000* | *11,552,000* |

**Interpreting Tables** The postwar years would find nations coping with the huge number of casualties. ***Foreign Relations*** *How might the casualty figures have influenced the peace plan?*

When Wilson arrived in Paris, Parisians threw flowers in his path and greeted the American President as a conquering hero. Wilson claimed that he was not interested in the **spoils,** or rewards, of war. That is, he did not expect the United States to gain any territory taken from the war's losers. His only goal was to establish a permanent agency to guarantee international stability. As Wilson had declared two years earlier, "There must be not a balance of power, but a community of power; not organized rivalries, but an organized common peace."

**Wilson Forced to Compromise** All would not go Wilson's way. First, the Allies were interested in spoils. In particular, they wanted to divide up Germany's colonies. The French wanted more. Determined never to be invaded again, they pressed for the total humiliation if not destruction of Germany.

Russia, although absent from the conference, was on everyone's mind. In March 1918 civil war had erupted there. British, French, and American forces had become involved in the civil war on the side of Lenin's opponents. Would Lenin's government survive? Would it present a set of war claims? As it turned out, Lenin's government held on to power, and it refused to claim any spoils of war. Russia would, in fact, sign a Treaty of Friendship and Cooperation with Germany in 1922.

From the start of the Paris Peace Conference, Wilson was forced to compromise on the principles outlined in the Fourteen Points. He had to give up, for example, the idea of respecting the rights of native peoples in Germany's colonies. He finally agreed that the Allied powers could simply take over the colonies.

**The League of Nations** Wilson did, however, convince the other powers to postpone further discussion of Germany's fate and move directly to his ideas for global security. After 10 days of hard work, he produced a plan for the **League of Nations,** an organization in which the nations of the world would join together to ensure security and peace for all members. Wilson then left for home, hoping to persuade Congress and the nation to accept his plan.

For Wilson, the heart of his proposal for the League of Nations was Article 10 of the plan. This provision pledged members of the League to regard an attack on one as an attack on all. Since the League would not have any military power, the force of the article was moral only. Nevertheless, 39 Republican senators or senators-elect signed a statement rejecting it.

The peace process helped lead to the transformation of the map of Europe. ***Location*** *In what ways does this map of Europe differ from the map on page 310?*

## COMPARING PRIMARY SOURCES

### LEAGUE OF NATIONS

The debate over joining the League of Nations often hinged on the effect that joining would have on American sovereignty or independence.

| In Favor of Joining the League of Nations | Opposed to Joining the League of Nations |
|---|---|
| "The United States will, indeed, undertake . . . to 'respect and preserve as against external aggression the territorial integrity and existing political independence of all members of the League,' and that engagement constitutes a very grave and solemn moral obligation. But it is a moral, not a legal, obligation, and leaves our Congress absolutely free to put its own interpretation upon it." *—President Woodrow Wilson, testifying before the Foreign Relations Committee, August 19, 1919* | "Shall we go there, Mr. President, to sit in judgment, and in case that judgment works for peace join with our allies, but in case it works for war withdraw our cooperation? How long would we stand as we now stand, a great Republic commanding the respect and holding the leadership of the world, if we should adopt any such course?" *—Senator William Borah (Idaho), testifying in the Senate, November 19, 1919* |

***ANALYZING VIEWPOINTS*** **On what basis does each speaker support or oppose American entry into the League?**

They feared that the article could be used to drag the United States into unpopular foreign wars.

## *The Peace Treaty*

In March 1919 Wilson returned to the peace conference. The Big Four—Britain, France, Italy, and the United States—dominated the proceedings. Though the Allies accepted Wilson's plan for the League of Nations, opposition to the League from Congress and many Americans had weakened Wilson's position at the conference.

French premier Georges Clemenceau took advantage of that weakness to demand harsh penalties against Germany. Wilson feared that these demands would lead to future wars, but he could not get Clemenceau to budge.

**Main Idea CONNECTIONS**

*What factors forced Wilson to compromise on his plans at the Paris Peace Conference?*

Wilson also had to compromise elsewhere. Self-determination for the peoples of Austria-Hungary proved hard to apply. As the map on the previous page shows, the conference created the new nations of Czechoslovakia and Yugoslavia. Their borders were drawn with the ethnic populations of the region in mind. But these arrangements failed even then to resolve all ethnic tensions.†

Wilson had more luck opposing the demands of Vittorio Orlando, Italy's prime minister. Italy claimed several pieces of territory formerly controlled by Austria-Hungary. Wilson and the other Allied leaders refused to support Italy's claims. Because of his failure at the peace conference, Orlando had to resign as prime minister.

**War Guilt and Reparations** Wilson met his greatest defeat when he gave in to French insistence on German war guilt and financial responsibility. The French wanted to cripple Germany. The demands of the British, led by David Lloyd George, supported the French goal. They insisted on billing Germany for **reparations,** or payment from an enemy for economic injury suffered during a war. In 1921 a Reparations Commission ruled that Germany owed the Allies $33 billion, an amount far beyond its ability to pay. As Wilson had feared, Germany never forgot or forgave this humiliation.

**Signing the Treaty** The Allies presented the treaty to the Germans on May 7, 1919. Insisting that the treaty violated the Fourteen Points, the Germans at first refused to sign it. They soon gave in, however, when threatened with a French invasion. On June 28 the great powers signed the treaty at Versailles, the former home of French kings, outside of Paris. Thus, the treaty is known as the **Versailles Treaty.**

## *Seeking Approval at Home*

On July 8, treaty in hand, Wilson returned home to great acclaim. But many legislators had doubts. Some senators opposed the treaty because it included American commitment to the League of Nations. These senators were called the "irreconcilables," because they could not be reconciled to, or made to accept, the treaty. Irreconcilables argued that joining the League would weaken American independence.

Senator Henry Cabot Lodge, chair of the Foreign Relations Committee, led another group called the "reservationists." This group wanted to impose reservations, or restrictions,

† In the early 1990s these same ethnic tensions would contribute to the breakup of the two nations.

on American participation in the League. In particular they wanted a guarantee that the Monroe Doctrine would remain in force. Wilson's point that compliance with League decisions was "binding in conscience only, not in law," failed to persuade them.

**Wilson Tours the Country** Determined to win grass roots support for the League, Wilson took to the road in September. In 23 days he delivered three dozen speeches. After this tremendous effort, he suffered a stroke that paralyzed one side of his body. He would remain an invalid, isolated from his Cabinet and visitors, for the rest of his term.

During his illness, Wilson grew increasingly inflexible. Congress would have to accept the treaty and the League as he envisioned it, or not at all. In November 1919 the Senate voted on the treaty with Lodge's reservations included. The vote was 39 for, 55 against. When the treaty came up without the reservations, it went down again, 38 to 53. In the face of popular dismay at this outcome, the Senate reconsidered the treaty in March 1920, but once again the treaty failed to win approval.

**A Formal End to Hostilities** On May 20, 1920, Congress voted to declare the war officially over. Steadfast to his principles, Wilson vetoed it. Finally, on July 2, 1921, another joint resolution to end the war passed. By that time a new President, Warren G. Harding, was in office, and he signed it. Congress ratified separate peace treaties with Germany, Austria, and Hungary that October.

## *Difficult Postwar Adjustments*

The war spurred the United States economy, giving a big boost to American businesses. The United States was now the world's largest creditor nation. In 1922 a Senate debt commission calculated that European countries owed the United States $11.5 billion.

The return to peace caused problems for the country at large, however. By April 1919 about 4,000 servicemen a day were being mustered out of the armed forces. But nobody had devised a plan to help returning troops merge back into society. The federal agencies that controlled the economy during the war had abruptly canceled war contracts. As a result, jobs proved scarce.

The women who had taken men's places in factories and offices also faced readjustment. Late in 1918, Mary Van Kleeck, head of the Women in Industry Service, reported that "the question heard most frequently was whether women would now retire from industry." Many women did, either voluntarily or because they were fired.

**Postwar Gloom** Many artists and intellectuals in the United States entered the postwar years with a sense of gloom or disillusionment. They expressed their feelings in books, paintings, and other artistic works. Social reformers experienced similar emotions. They had been encouraged by the government-business collaboration during the war. For most of them, the end of the war marked the end of an era of optimism.

**GOVERNMENT CONCEPTS**

***checks and balances:** the system, established by the Constitution, that enables each of the three branches of the federal government to check the other branches*

▼ **The Historical Context** After President Wilson signed the Versailles Treaty, the treaty went to the Senate. There, a two-thirds vote in favor of the treaty was needed for American acceptance of the treaty to become official. The Senate, however, failed to approve the treaty.

▼ **The Concept Today** Many people complain today that the branches of government should work together more and check each other less. Yet the system of checks and balances helps keep government responsible to the voters.

**CAUSE AND EFFECT: World War I**

**CAUSES**

- *Imperialism leads to international rivalries, particularly within Europe.*
- *Nationalism between and within countries intensifies.*
- *Military buildup in Europe intensifies.*
- *Europe develops a complicated system of alliances.*
- *Archduke Francis Ferdinand of Austria-Hungary is assassinated.*
- *Austria-Hungary declares war on Serbia.*

**WORLD WAR I**

**EFFECTS**

- *Map of Europe is redrawn.*
- *League of Nations is formed.*
- *United States economy is boosted.*
- *United States suffers post-war disillusionment.*

**Interpreting Charts** The assassination of Francis Ferdinand was the spark that ignited the powder keg of imperialism, nationalism, and alliances that began a world war. ***Foreign Relations*** *Why was Congress opposed to the League of Nations?*

A federal employment service kept jobs filled during the war. After the war, it had to cope with thousands of returning soldiers. *Economics Why were jobs scarce?*

Others felt the postwar gloom as well. The enthusiasm that had greeted the start of the Great War had faded by war's end. The realities of trench warfare, death, and destruction hit many people very hard. Alice Lord O'Brian, a military post exchange director from Buffalo who was twice decorated, expressed the views of many who were directly involved in the war. She stated:

**AMERICAN VOICES** "We all started out with high ideals. . . . [A]fter being right up here almost at the front line . . . I cannot understand what it is all about or what has been accomplished by all this waste of youth."

—*Alice Lord O'Brian*

**African American Troops at Home** Like white troops, black soldiers came home to a hero's welcome. When they went to find jobs, however, the reception was different.

W.E.B. Du Bois, editor of the NAACP's magazine, the *Crisis,* had supported the war. In July 1918 he had written, "Let us, while this war lasts, forget our special grievances and close our ranks . . . with our white citizens and the allied nations that are fighting for democracy." A year later, after more lynchings of African Americans, including some still in uniform, his message became defiant. "This country of ours, despite all its better souls have done and dreamed, is yet a shameful land," he wrote in May 1919. "It lynches. . . . It steals from us. . . . It insults us. . . . We return. We return from fighting. We return fighting."

Du Bois's views heralded a new era in the struggle for equality. The entire nation was on the threshold of a stormy era—the 1920s.

## SECTION 5 REVIEW

### Comprehension

1. *Key Terms* Define: (a) Fourteen Points; (b) self-determination; (c) spoils; (d) League of Nations; (e) reparations; (f) Versailles Treaty.
2. *Summarizing the Main Idea* What kind of impact did President Wilson's ideas make at the Paris Peace Conference?
3. *Organizing Information* Create a web diagram to organize information about the peace-making efforts after World War I.

### Critical Thinking

4. *Analyzing Time Lines* Review the time line at the start of the section. Which event best summarizes the results of Wilson's peace efforts? Explain.
5. *Drawing Inferences* Why did the Fourteen Points fail as a basis of peace negotiations?

### Writing Activity

6. *Writing a Persuasive Essay* Write an essay about the treatment of African Americans after the war. Compare the way black soldiers should have been treated with the way they were treated. Persuade your readers that despite the mistreatment, the struggle for equality will continue.

Why Study History?

To understand that . . .

# Modern Warfare Poses Grave Dangers

**The horrors of modern warfare unleashed by World War I remain a threat to peoples around the world. Today's dangers include chemical and biological weapons.**

*World War I soldier with protective gas mask*

The weapons of World War I, such as the machine gun and chemical weapons, turned the battlefields of Europe into vast killing grounds. World War I also blurred the distinction between soldier and civilian, as troops razed enemy towns, burned fields, and poisoned water supplies. Since World War I, nations have invented even more lethal weapons, increasing the potential for destruction and the risk to civilians — even those living far from the battlefield.

## The Impact Today

About 90,000 of the more than 8 million soldiers who died in World War I were poisoned or asphyxiated by chemical weapons, such as chlorine gas and mustard gas. Thousands more suffered lasting injuries. The impact of chemical weapons was so horrifying that, in the Geneva Protocol of 1925, nations outlawed the use of chemical and biological weapons in war.

Since the Geneva Protocol a number of nations have stockpiled chemical and biological weapons that could be used in war. During the Iran-Iraq War in the 1980s, Iraq unleashed chemical weapons on Iranian soldiers and Kurdish civilians. Thousands were killed or wounded.

Many nations have signed treaties to stop the proliferation, or spread, of chemical and biological weapons. For example, the 1972 Biological Weapons Convention prohibits the development and use of biological weapons. In addition, the 1997 Chemical Weapons Convention bans the production, stockpiling, transfer and use of chemical weapons.

Despite international efforts, chemical and biological weapons continue to pose a worldwide threat. In 1995, a radical Japanese group released sarin gas in the Tokyo subway system, killing several people and injuring thousands. The incident served as a warning that lethal agents of modern warfare can be deployed by terrorists against unsuspecting civilian populations.

## The Impact on You

Look for newspaper or magazine articles about international efforts to limit nuclear, chemical, or biological weapons. Write a one-page "policy paper" in which you summarize these efforts and present your own ideas about how nations should work together to reduce the risk that these weapons will be used.

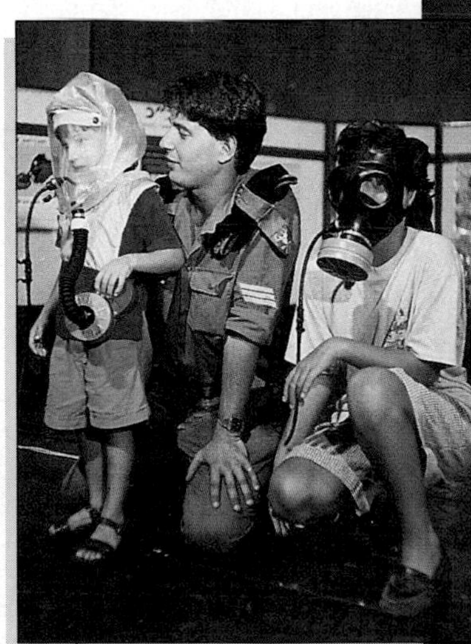

*Civil defense training for Israeli children*

# Chapter 10 Review

## Chapter Summary

The major concepts of Chapter 10 are presented below. See also ***Guide to the Essentials of American History*** or ***Interactive Student Tutorial CD-ROM,*** which contains interactive review activities, time lines, helpful hints, and test practice.

### *Reviewing the Main Ideas*

World War I began in 1914 as a European war. The United States remained neutral. After German submarine warfare drew the Americans into the war in 1917, United States troops, supplies, and loans helped the Allies defeat the Central Powers. President Wilson hoped to devise a peace treaty that would eliminate the main causes of war.

### *Section 1: The Road to War*

As World War I began and then expanded to much of Europe, the United States remained neutral.

### *Section 2: The United States Declares War*

German submarine warfare helped push the United States into World War I.

### *Section 3: Americans on the European Front*

American troops helped the Allies defeat the Central Powers in World War I.

### *Section 4: On the Home Front*

Americans and their government took extraordinary steps at home to support the war effort.

### *Section 5: Global Peacemaker*

When the fighting ended in Europe, President Wilson pressed for a treaty that would bring peace to the postwar world.

The horrors of modern warfare unleashed by World War I continue to haunt the world. Despite efforts by the international community to stop the use of chemical and biological weapons, they pose a worldwide threat.

## Key Terms

For each of the terms below, write a sentence explaining how it relates to the chapter.

1. Liberty Bond
2. Allies
3. convoy
4. American Expeditionary Force
5. militarism
6. Versailles Treaty
7. Zimmermann note
8. U-boat
9. armistice
10. sedition
11. Central Powers
12. League of Nations
13. Fourteen Points
14. stalemate

## Comprehension

1. What were the main causes of World War I?
2. What were the reactions in the United States to the outbreak of the war in Europe?
3. Why did the United States declare war on Germany?
4. Name some of the military innovations introduced during World War I.
5. How did American troops help turn the tide of the war on the battlefield?
6. Why and how did the government try to control the economy at home?
7. What was the American reaction to the Versailles Treaty and to the League of Nations?

## Using Graphic Organizers

On a separate sheet of paper, copy the cause-and-effect flowchart to organize the main ideas of the chapter. Fill in each box with the appropriate effect. Remember that effects sometimes also become causes.

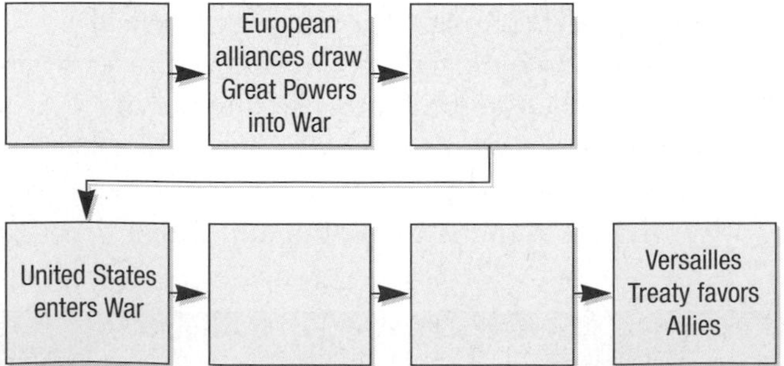

## Analyzing Political Cartoons ▶

1. Analyze the images in this 1919 cartoon. (a) Who is the man? (b) What does the little boy represent? (c) How do you know?
2. Who does the man in the cartoon want the "child" to play with?
3. Why does the "child" want to "play by himself"?
4. Explain the meaning of the cartoon.

*THE CHILD WHO WANTED TO PLAY BY HIMSELF.* *President Wilson: "Now come along and enjoy yourself with the other nice children. I promised that you'd be the life and soul of the party."*

## Critical Thinking

1. ***Applying the Chapter Skill*** The United States chose to go to war with Germany in 1917 largely because of continued German submarine attacks on neutral shipping. Identify alternative solutions to this problem of U-boat attacks. Discuss your alternative in a written proposal to President Wilson.
2. ***Predicting Consequences*** What might have happened on the European front if General Pershing had decided to mix the American troops in with the Allied armics instead of keeping them independent?
3. ***Demonstrating Reasoned Judgment*** Do you think women played a key role in World War I? Why or why not?
4. ***Expressing Problems Clearly*** It is often said that Woodrow Wilson won World War I but then "lost the peace." Explain your understanding of this statement.

### INTERNET ACTIVITY

***For your portfolio:***
**CREATE A GRAPH**

Access Prentice Hall's *America: Pathways to the Present* site at **www.Pathways.phschool.com** for the specific URL to complete the activity. Additional resources and related Web sites arc also available.

Use the statistics provided at the site to create a bar graph of the financial costs of World War I.

### ANALYZING DOCUMENTS ▶ INTERPRETING DATA

Turn to the Exploring Technology diagram of a tank on page 321.

1. Tank crews felt secure against rifle fire because of the tank's (a) pressed-steel track plate. (b) armor plating. (c) commander. (d) 105-horsepower, six-cylinder engine.
2. The tank was able to cross battlefield trenches and barbed wire because of its (a) pressed-steel track plate. (b) armor plating. (c) 57-mm pedestal-mounted guns. (d) Lewis machine guns.
3. ***Writing*** Imagine that you were part of a tank crew at the front during World War I. Write a letter to your family describing your tank and what warfare is like from the inside of a tank.

## Connecting to Today

***Essay Writing*** Compare the ability of the United States to be a peace-maker today with its ability after the war. What characteristics does it take for a country to serve as a peacemaker? Does the United States have those characteristics today? Did it have them in Wilson's time?

# American Heritage®

# My Brush with History

BY A WORLD WAR I PILOT

***INTRODUCTION*** The psychological stresses of modern warfare were felt not only by soldiers in the trenches but also by those who fought in the skies overhead. The passage below, selected by the editors of *American Heritage* magazine, is from the diary of an unknown pilot in World War I.

***We've lost a lot of good men.*** It's only a question of time until we all get it. I'm all shot to pieces. I only hope I can stick it. I don't want to quit. My nerves are all gone and I can't stop. I've lived beyond my time already.

It's not the fear of death that's done it. I'm still not afraid to die. It's this eternal flinching from it that's doing it and has made a coward out of me. Few men live to know what real fear is. It's something that grows on you, day by day, that eats into your constitution and undermines your sanity. I have never been serious about anything in my life and now I know that I'll never be otherwise again. But my seriousness will be a burlesque for no one will recognize it.

Here I am, twenty-four years old, I look forty and I feel ninety. I've lost all interest in life beyond the next patrol. No one Hun will ever get me and I'll never fall into a trap, but sooner or later I'll be forced to fight against odds that are too long or perhaps a stray shot from the ground will be lucky and I will have gone in vain. Or my motor will cut out when we are trench strafing or a wing will pull off in a dive. Oh, for a parachute! The Huns are using them now. I haven't a chance, I know, and it's this eternal waiting around that's killing me. I've even lost my taste for liquor. It doesn't seem to do me any good now. I guess I'm stale. Last week I actually got frightened in the air and lost my head. Then I found ten Huns and took them all on and I got one of them down out of control. I got my nerve back by that time

*Since few pilots had parachutes, aerial "dogfights" in World War I were often fatal to the loser.*

and came back home and slept like a baby for the first time in two months. What a blessing sleep is! I know now why men go out and take such long chances and pull off such wild stunts. No discipline in the world could make them do what they do of their own accord. I know now what a brave man is. I know now how men laugh at death and welcome it. I know now why Ball went over and sat above a Hun airdrome and dared them to come up and fight with him. It takes a brave man to even experience real fear. A coward couldn't last long enough at the job to get to that stage. What price salvation now?

War is a horrible thing, a grotesque comedy. And it is so useless. This war won't prove anything. All we'll do when we win is to substitute one sort of Dictator for another. In the meantime we have destroyed our best resources. Human life, the most precious thing in the world, has become the cheapest. After we've won this war by drowning the Hun in our own blood, in five years' time the sentimental fools at home will be taking up a collection for these same Huns that are killing us now and our fool politicians will be cooking up another good war. Why shouldn't they? They have to keep the public stirred up to keep their jobs and they don't have to fight and they can get soft berths for their sons and their friends' sons. To me the most contemptible cur in the world is the man who lets political influence be used to keep him away from the front. For he lets another man die in his place.

The worst thing about this war is that it takes the best. If it lasts long enough the world will be populated by cowards and weaklings and their children. And the whole thing is so useless, so unnecessary, so terrible! . . .

The devastation of the country is too horrible to describe. It looks from the air as if the gods had made a gigantic steam roller, forty miles wide and run it from the coast to Switzerland, leaving its spike holes behind as it went. . . .

I've lost over a hundred friends, so they tell me—I've seen only seven or eight killed—but to me they aren't dead yet. They are just around the corner, I think, and I'm still expecting to run into them any time. I dream about them at night when I do sleep a little and sometimes I dream that some one is killed who really isn't. Then I don't know who is and who isn't. I saw a man in Boulogne the other day that I had dreamed I saw killed and I thought I was seeing a ghost. I can't realize that any of them are gone. Surely human life is not a candle to be snuffed out. . . .

Source: *Anonymous, War Birds: Diary of an Unknown Aviator,* Doran, 1926.

### ADDITIONAL READING

**To learn more about the topics discussed in this selection, you might want to read the following books:**

- *The Canvas Falcons: The Men and the Planes of World War I,* by Stephen Longstreet (New York: Barnes & Noble Books, 1995)
- *The First World War: A Complete History,* by Martin Gilbert (New York: Henry Holt, 1994)
- *The Last Days of Innocence: America at War, 1917–1918,* by Meirion and Susie Harries (New York: Random House, 1997)
- *The Penguin Book of First World War Poetry,* edited by Jon Silkin (New York: Penguin Books, 1981)

***More than 8 million soldiers died in World War I, making it the costliest war in history to that time.***

WWI Cemetery

unit THREE

# Boom Times to Hard Times

## 1919–1938

*Optimism and faith in business and technology characterized the United States in the 1920s. That faith was shattered with the stock market crash of October 1929. The fragile prosperity of the decade quickly gave way to a period of severe economic distress known as the Great Depression. In the election of 1932, voters chose Franklin Delano Roosevelt as the President to lead them out of hard times.*



### UNIT THEMES

**Culture** The nation underwent a change in manners and morals during the 1920s.

**Economics** The stock market crash of 1929 resulted in a worldwide economic depression.

**Government** FDR's New Deal forged a new link between the government and the economy.

**EVENTS IN THE UNITED STATES**

**1919**
- *Red scare*
- *Palmer raids*

**1924** *Teapot Dome scandal*

**1927** *Sacco and Vanzetti executed*

**1929** *Stock market crashes*

Presidents: Wilson | Harding | Coolidge

1915 — 1920 — 1925

**EVENTS IN THE WORLD**

**1920** *Adolf Hitler helps form Nazi party in Germany*

**1923** *Hitler fails in attempted coup*

**1929** *The term apartheid is introduced in South Africa*

**VIEWING HISTORY** During the Great Depression, poverty and suffering were constant traveling companions to families like the one above, who were forced to move from town to town in search of work. ***Culture* How did the Great Depression change both the government and society?**

FDR campaign button

**1931** *Scottsboro Boys convicted*

**1932** *Turning Point: The Election of 1932* *(p. 397)*

**1933** *Prohibition repealed*

**1935** *Social Security Act passed*

**1939** *Supreme Court outlaws sit-down strike*

Hoover | F. D. Roosevelt

1930 | 1935 | 1940

**1931** *Japanese troops occupy Manchuria*

**1933** *Hitler and the Nazis take over Germany*

**1935** *Italy invades Ethiopia*

**1937** *Japan launches a full-scale war against China*

CHAPTER

# 11 The Twenties

## 1920–1929

## CHAPTER FOCUS

*This chapter explores the decade of the 1920s. More than just a time between two world wars, the 1920s literally set in motion much of modern America. Cars hit the roads. Business boomed. Radios crackled. Hemlines moved up. The nation moved to the new sound of jazz, while the tiny town of Hollywood gave the world motion pictures.*

*The **Why Study History?** page at the end of this chapter explores the connection between generational differences of the 1920s and those of today.*

▲

**VIEWING HISTORY**

*Sixth Avenue Elevated at Third Street, 1928,* by John Sloan, captures the high spirits of the 1920s. ***Culture* How does this painting show changing social morals?**

**1919** *Red scare; Palmer raids; widespread labor strikes*

**1920** *Harding elected President*

**1923** *Harding dies; Coolidge takes office*

**1924** *Teapot Dome scandal uncovered; Coolidge wins election*

**1927** *Sacco and Vanzetti executed*

**1928** *Kellogg-Briand Pact; Hoover elected President*

**1915** **1920** **1925** **1930**

# 1 A Republican Decade

## SECTION PREVIEW

### Objectives

1. Analyze the causes and effects of the red scare and the labor strikes of 1919.
2. Describe key features of the Republican administrations of the 1920s.
3. Compare the Harding and Coolidge presidencies.
4. *Key Terms* Define: communism; red scare; isolationism; disarmament; quota; Teapot Dome scandal; Kellogg-Briand Pact.

### Main Idea

Republican administrations of the 1920s pursued pro-business economic policies and an isolationist foreign policy.

### Reading Strategy

*Creating an Outline* Copy the headings in this section. As you read, write down at least two key points under each heading.

Warren G. Harding "looks like a President," said a political friend promoting the handsome, silver-haired Ohio senator for the Republican nomination in 1920. Harding sounded like a President, too. He had a deep voice and dignified speaking style and impressed people as honest and kind.

Yet Harding's speeches often left people wondering what his views were. One Democrat called Harding's speeches "an army of pompous phrases moving across the landscape in search of an idea."

Yet voters got the message when Harding declared that America needed "not heroism but healing, not nostrums [fake cures] but normalcy." In a nation weary of war abroad and sacrifice at home, the mere promise of "normalcy" gave Harding a landslide victory over Democrat James Cox and his running mate, Franklin D. Roosevelt.

## The Red Scare

"Normalcy" appealed to Americans in 1920 because the times seemed anything but normal. Having suffered through World War I, Americans were soon caught up in events both in faraway Russia and at home that convinced many people that the United States was threatened by political violence.

**The Russian Revolution** In March 1917 Russia's absolute ruler, Czar Nicholas II, lost his popularity as a result of a series of tragically poor decisions, including leading his country into World War I. The war brought devastating casualties and severe food shortages. With riots in the streets and the army too weak to protect him, Nicholas was forced to abdicate.

*What events in Russia caused concern among war-weary Americans?*

After months of upheaval, a revolutionary named Vladimir I. Lenin saw his opportunity. With such slogans as "End the war! All land to the peasants!" Lenin and his followers, referred to as the Bolsheviks, took power November 6, 1917. The new Bolshevik government put all privately owned farms, industries, land, and transportation under government ownership.

In early 1918, civil war engulfed the nation. Lenin's forces were called the "Reds." His opponents, the "Whites," included former landowners, government officials, and army leaders. Britain, France, Japan, and the United States, whose investments in Russia had been seized by Bolsheviks, backed the Whites.

After two bloody years, millions of deaths, and widespread destruction, the Reds triumphed in 1920. In time their new nation became known as the Union of Soviet Socialist Republics (USSR), or the Soviet Union.

Lenin made **communism** the official ideology of the Soviet Union. As practiced in the Soviet Union, communism meant the following:

(1) The government owned all land and property.

(2) A single political party controlled the government.

(3) Individuals had no rights that the government was bound to respect.

(4) The government vowed to stir up revolutions in other countries and spread communism throughout the world.

The Communist system was openly hostile to American beliefs and values, such as capitalism, private ownership of land and business, and First Amendment freedoms. As early as 1919 a **red scare,** an intense fear of communism and other extreme ideas, gripped the United States. Americans called for known Communists to be jailed or driven out of the country.

The case of Sacco and Vanzetti inspired much protest, including this piece of folk art. ***Government*** *Why did the artist include a plea for a fair trial?*

**Schenck v. U.S.** A 1919 Supreme Court decision seemed to some people to justify jailing Communists. During World War I, a war opponent named Charles Schenck had mailed letters to men who were drafted, urging them not to report for duty. He was convicted of breaking the Espionage Act, a wartime law aimed at spies and people who opposed the war. He appealed the case, claiming that he was only exercising his right to speak freely.

In the Court's written opinion, Justice Oliver Wendell Holmes, Jr., said that the government was justified in silencing free speech when there is a "clear and present danger" to the nation. He compared what Schenck had done to shouting "Fire!" in a crowded theater, which would cause a dangerous panic.

**The Palmer Raids** As the red scare heightened, the United States government began a campaign to identify and root out groups whose activities posed a "clear and present danger" to the country. In 1919 the Justice Department, headed by Attorney General A. Mitchell Palmer, set up a special force to conduct raids and arrest suspected "subversives" (people trying to subvert, or overthrow, the government). Palmer's targets included Communists, socialists, and anarchists.

Palmer's force jailed thousands of people. Most had been born overseas. Many were innocent of any crime. More than 500 immigrants were deported, or sent back to their homelands, although they had not been convicted of any crime.

Palmer received strong support at first. The army's chief of staff urged that those deported be sent away on "ships of stone with sails of lead," and popular preacher Billy Sunday suggested that a firing squad would save money on ships.

The red scare reached such a fever that in January 1920 the New York State Assembly voted to expel five members who were socialists. Yet the five had been legally elected and had broken no rules or laws. People were outraged that the assembly had ignored the public's right to elect whomever they wanted.

**Sacco and Vanzetti** The red scare played a part in one of the most controversial events in United States history. The story began on April 15, 1920, when gunmen robbed and killed the guard and paymaster of a shoe factory in South Braintree, Massachusetts. A few weeks later, police arrested two Italian immigrants in connection with the crime.

One, Nicola Sacco, was a shoemaker, while the other, Bartolomeo Vanzetti, was a fish peddler. Both were carrying guns when they were arrested, and Sacco's was the same model used in the crime. Yet many Americans suspected that the real reason the two men were accused of the crime was that they were immigrants. The case drew international attention and controversy.

Sacco and Vanzetti were soon convicted and sentenced to die. Their case was appealed to higher courts again and again for years, but their conviction was upheld.† In 1927, Sacco and Vanzetti were electrocuted.

**Union Membership and Work Stoppages, 1916–1920**

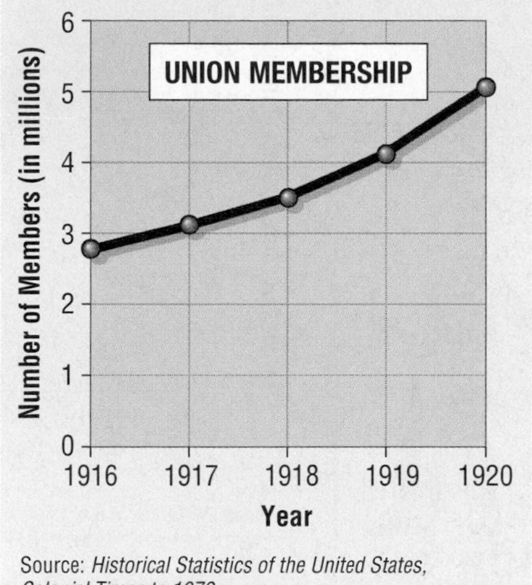


Source: *Historical Statistics of the United States, Colonial Times to 1970*

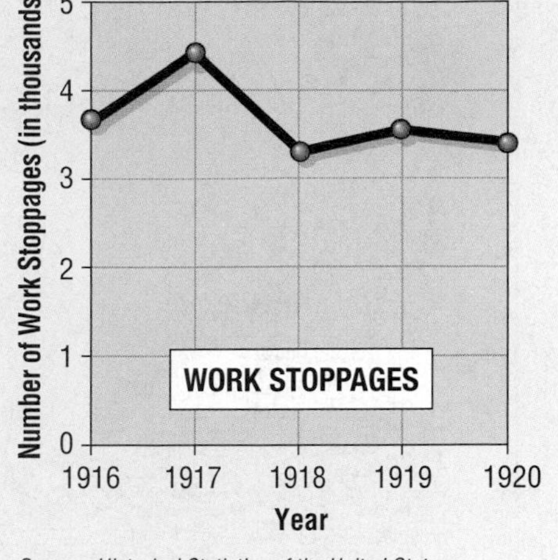


Source: *Historical Statistics of the United States, Colonial Times to 1970*

**Interpreting Graphs** The post–World War I years were stormy ones for labor and business. The number of annual strikes was high and union membership was on the rise. ***Economics** Based on this information, how would you summarize the condition of organized labor in 1920?*

## *Labor Strikes*

One cause of the red scare was a wave of labor unrest in 1919. Many Americans were convinced that Communists were behind the strikes. Most of the unrest, however, had a simpler cause. In early 1919 food prices and rents shot up, and by 1920 the cost of living was more than double prewar levels.

**The Boston Police Strike** Boston police officers had not received a pay increase since the start of World War I. In the fall of 1919, they decided they had had enough of sacrifice. When 19 officers were fired for union activity, the whole force voted to strike.

With police off the job, rioting soon broke out in Boston. Massachusetts governor Calvin Coolidge called out the state guard. "There is no right to strike against the public safety by anybody, anywhere, anytime," Coolidge said. The future President gained national attention for his firm response to the strike.

† Investigators in 1961 reexamined Sacco's gun and found that it was indeed the murder weapon, although it had never been proven that it was Sacco who fired the gun. On the 50th anniversary of the executions, August 23, 1977, Massachusetts governor Michael Dukakis decreed that Sacco and Vanzetti had not received their right to a fair trial.

**Steel and Coal Strikes** Meanwhile, steelworkers in Gary, Indiana, and several other cities struck in 1919. Claiming that the strike was the work of Communists, the United States Steel Corporation used force to break it. The corporation's private police force killed 18 strikers and beat hundreds more.††

Another strike in that troubled fall of 1919 took place in the coal fields. The United Mine Workers of America (UMW) had made a no-strike agreement during the war, but they claimed the agreement ended with the armistice. The government claimed the agreement was still in effect. When the workers struck for a shorter work week and better pay, Attorney General Palmer got a court to order strikers back to work. Although the UMW canceled the strike, it did manage to get its workers a raise.

After hitting its high point in 1919, strike activity declined during the 1920s, as the economy boomed and wages rose. Union membership dropped during 1921 and 1922, and did not grow again through the rest of the decade.

†† A follow-up investigation produced the "Report on the Steel Strike of 1919," which helped limit working hours in the steel industry.

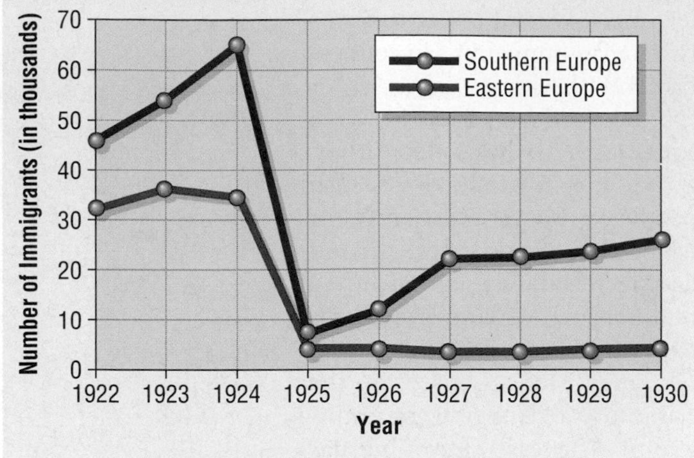


Source: *Historical Statistics of the United States, Colonial Times to 1970*

**Interpreting Graphs** The 1921 cartoon at left satirized American immigration restriction. ***Government Describe the effect of Harding's immigration policies on the number of immigrants from eastern and southern Europe as shown by the graph above.***

## *Republican Leadership*

Strikes, arrests, revolution overseas—such events frightened Americans in the 1920s, and they turned to the Republican party to maintain stability. In a remarkable solidifying of its power, the Republican party dominated all three branches of government. Republican Presidents Warren G. Harding, Calvin Coolidge, and Herbert Hoover served from 1921 to 1933. Republicans held the majority in Congress during this time. In addition, Supreme Court decisions of the era reflected the influence of its new Chief Justice, former President William Howard Taft, appointed by Harding in 1921.

Republican leaders of this generation were united in basic goals and ideals. They favored business, and many of them were in fact businessmen. They wanted social stability, believing that it promoted economic growth.

## *The Harding Presidency*

President Harding took office as the red scare and the labor strikes were beginning to subside. In that respect, the country did seem to be getting back to "normalcy."

Harding made some wise Cabinet appointments. The able administrator (and future President) Herbert Hoover became Secretary of Commerce. Treasury Secretary Andrew Mellon was one of the nation's most powerful businessmen. Under Harding and his Republican successors, Mellon shaped the economic policies of the 1920s. However, Harding showed terribly poor judgment in many of his appointments, giving jobs to friends, some of whom were incompetent and dishonest. These decisions would eventually overwhelm his presidency and his life.

### Isolationism

Harding's foreign policy reflected Americans' postwar desire for a return to **isolationism,** a policy of avoiding political or economic alliances with foreign countries. Hence Harding made no further attempt to join the League of Nations.

Yet the President did support efforts to find ways of preventing future wars. He called for **disarmament,** a program in which the nations of the world would voluntarily give up their weapons. In 1921 Harding convened the Washington Conference, at which several major nations signed treaties limiting the size of their navies.

In 1922 Congress, with Harding's support, passed the Fordney-McCumber Tariff, which raised rates on a number of imports. It especially discouraged imports that competed with goods made by new American industries, such as china, toys, and chemicals.

### Limiting Immigration

As Americans became more isolationist, they also became more nativist.

As you have read, nativism is a movement favoring native-born Americans over immigrants. It had first appeared in the 1800s, but after World War I it grew stronger, for several reasons:

(1) Many Americans believed that people from foreign countries could never be fully loyal to the United States.

(2) Nativists, who were mostly Protestants, had long disliked immigrants who were Catholics, Orthodox Christians, or Jews.

(3) Americans often blamed the problems of cities, such as slums and corruption, on the immigrants who lived in them.

(4) Workers feared immigrants might take their jobs away from them.

(5) Nativists argued that some immigrants came from the most unstable parts of Europe, where World War I had started. They believed that these immigrants might hold or might adopt dangerous political ideas.

When immigration rose sharply after World War I, nativist reaction was swift. In 1921, at Harding's request, and again in 1924, Congress passed laws restricting immigration. The laws limited annual immigration to 350,000 people and set up a **quota,** or numerical limit, on immigrants from each foreign nation. The laws set low quotas for immigrants from southern and eastern European countries, including Italy, Poland, and Russia. Asian immigration was banned altogether.

**The Teapot Dome Scandal** At the start of 1923, the economy was bouncing back from wartime disruptions, and the President enjoyed strong popularity. Within months, however, Harding was dead.

In the months before his death, major corruption scandals in Harding's administration were coming to light. There was no evidence that the President was involved in the scandals. In fact, Harding became terribly disturbed when he heard of the scandals, and the strain may have contributed to his death, from heart problems, on August 2, 1923.

By 1924 the extent of the corruption in Harding's administration had become known. One official had stolen government funds. Others had taken bribes in return for help getting contracts approved or laws passed. Several other officials were also accused of wrongdoing, and two committed suicide.

The worst Harding scandal came to be known as the **Teapot Dome scandal.** In 1921 and 1922, Harding's Secretary of the Interior, Albert B. Fall, secretly gave oil drilling rights on government oil fields in Elk Hills, California, and Teapot Dome, Wyoming, to two private oil companies. In return, Fall received more than $300,000 in illegal payments and gifts disguised as loans. He later went to jail for his role in the scandal.

## *The Coolidge Presidency*

Vice President Calvin Coolidge was visiting his parents in Vermont on August 3, 1923, when word arrived of Harding's death. At 2:30 A.M., by the light of a kerosene lamp, Coolidge's father, a justice of the peace, administered to him the oath of office of President of the United States.

*The Democrats in 1924 tried to use public anger over the Teapot Dome affair to defeat the Republicans, as this campaign artifact shows.*

Coolidge was still widely respected for his actions as governor of Massachusetts. He had played no part in the Harding scandals. In fact, one Democrat said that Coolidge's "great task was to restore the dignity and prestige of the Presidency when it had reached the lowest ebb in our history." After finishing Harding's term, Coolidge ran in the 1924 election, defeating Democrat John W. Davis and Progressive Robert M. La Follette with the slogan "Keep cool with Coolidge."

Coolidge had a reputation as a skilled public speaker, but in private he was a man of few words. Someone said of him that "he could be silent in five languages."†

**Laissez Faire** In one sentence, Coolidge summed up a major theme of the Republican decade: "The business of the American people is business." The best that the government could do, he believed, was not to interfere with the growth of business. This laissez-faire business policy helped fuel the tremendous economic boom of the 1920s. As part of his laissez-faire policy, Coolidge tried to make the federal government smaller. For example, when war veterans won a bonus payment from Congress, he vetoed the bill on the grounds

**Main Idea CONNECTIONS**

*What policies did Republican leaders pursue in the 1920s?*

† Many funny anecdotes grew up around "Silent Cal," as he was called. His wife, Grace, told the story of a young woman who sat next to Coolidge at a dinner party. The woman told Coolidge that she had bet that she could get him to say at least three words. Without looking at her, the President said, in his typically dry wit: "You lose."

Calvin Coolidge, shown here with a saxophone, was known for his support of big business. ***Economics*** ***What does this cartoon say about big business's reaction to his policies?***

that the government could not afford it. (Congress overrode his veto in 1924.)

Coolidge's effort to have government do less drew criticism from those who saw it as a failure to take action. The noted newspaper columnist Walter Lippmann said:

**AMERICAN VOICES** **"Mr. Coolidge's genius for inactivity is developed to a very high point. It is a grim, determined, alert inactivity, which keeps Mr. Coolidge occupied constantly."**

*—Columnist Walter Lippmann, 1926*

**Continued Isolationism** Coolidge continued the isolationist policies of Harding. He left most foreign policy up to his Secretary of State, Frank B. Kellogg.

In 1928, isolationism led to an unusual treaty worked out by Kellogg and French Foreign Minister Aristide Briand. Under the **Kellogg-Briand Pact,** 15 nations agreed not to use the threat of war in their dealings with one another. More than 60 nations eventually joined the pact. The Kellogg-Briand Pact seemed to be a good idea, but it was unrealistic and unworkable because it had no provisions for enforcement. By 1941, many of the nations that had signed the pact were at war.

## *The Election of 1928*

As Coolidge neared the end of his first full term, he was asked about his political plans. "I do not choose to run for President in 1928," was his brief and famous reply. In his place, Republicans nominated Herbert Hoover. During and after World War I, Hoover had won respect for programs he ran in Europe to ease hunger. He had held Cabinet posts under Harding and Coolidge.

Hoover's main opponent was Alfred E. Smith of New York, a popular Democratic governor and the first Roman Catholic to be nominated for President. Americans hoped that what they called the "Coolidge prosperity" would continue under Hoover. They elected him by a large margin, about 21.4 million to 15 million.

## *SECTION 1 REVIEW*

### Comprehension

1. *Key Terms* Define: (a) communism; (b) red scare; (c) isolationism; (d) disarmament; (e) quota; (f) Teapot Dome scandal; (g) Kellogg-Briand Pact.
2. *Summarizing the Main Idea* What were the main goals of the Republican administrations of the 1920s?
3. *Organizing Information* Create two cause-and-effect charts, one on the red scare and one on the labor strikes of 1919.

### Critical Thinking

4. *Analyzing Time Lines* Refer to the time line at the start of the section. Which entries show a return to "normalcy," as Harding put it, and which indicate political or social upheaval? Explain your answers.
5. *Recognizing Ideologies* What beliefs did Harding and Coolidge share? In what ways did their presidencies differ?

### Writing Activity

6. *Writing a Persuasive Essay* From the perspective of a writer living during the 1920s, write a persuasive essay about events connected to the red scare. Urge your readers either to (a) support ongoing efforts to arrest suspected subversives or (b) protest the hysteria of the red scare.

| 1927 | 1927 | 1929 | 1929 | 1929 | 1930 |
|---|---|---|---|---|---|
| American companies spend $3.2 billion on advertising | Ford introduces the Model A | Value of electrical appliances reaches $2.3 billion | Nearly $2 billion spent on roads and bridges | Value of top 200 companies reaches $81 billion | Americans own more than 23 million cars |

1927 1928 1929 1930

# 2 A Business Boom

## SECTION PREVIEW

### Objectives

1. Describe how the growth of a consumer economy changed American life.
2. Explain how Henry Ford made automobiles affordable for average Americans.
3. Explain why American businesses boomed in the 1920s.
4. *Key Terms* Define: consumer economy; installment plan; assembly line.

### Main Idea

During the 1920s, new products and Americans' power to purchase them grew rapidly, producing a decade of enormous business growth.

### Reading Strategy

*Recognizing Cause and Effect* As you read, make a list of factors that caused a business boom in the 1920s.

Forget malls and food courts. Until the 1920s, you couldn't even find a shopping center. Food was not "fast." Billboards did not line the highways because there were no highways, few cars, and relatively few advertisements.

Then came the 1920s, a decade that gave birth to much of modern America. In Kansas City, the nation's first shopping center opened, giving consumers a more convenient way to shop. The first fast-food chain, A & W Root Beer, began selling burgers and soft drinks. Advertising became big business in the 1920s, with companies spending an amazing $3.2 billion on ads in 1927. And in Michigan, a young man named Ford was building an automobile empire. This was no ordinary decade.

## A Consumer Economy

Despite a year or so of uncertainty after World War I, the United States economy made a rapid adjustment. The rise in incomes that had begun during the war had resumed by 1920. Between 1914 and 1926, average wages rose more than 28 percent. The number of millionaires in the United States more than doubled in the same period. The main cause of this growth was the development of the **consumer economy,** one that depends on a large amount of buying by consumers—individuals who use (or "consume") products. During the 1920s, a consumer economy developed rapidly in the United States.

**Buying on Credit** Until the 1920s, Americans generally paid cash for anything they bought. Borrowing money for any purchase but a house or land was considered unthrifty, even immoral. During the 1920s, the nation eagerly adopted a new way to buy goods. Instead of paying the full price at once, consumers arranged to pay on an **installment plan,** a system that lets customers make partial payments (installments) at set intervals over a period of time until the total debt is paid. Installment plans fueled the growth of the consumer economy.

Installment plans encouraged people to buy who otherwise would not, even though they had to pay interest charges ranging from 11 to 40 percent. By 1929, Americans were using the installment plan to buy 60 percent of all cars, 70 percent of furniture, 80 percent of vacuum

*Electrical appliances changed the nature of housework.*

**exploring TECHNOLOGY** *The Model T Production Plant*

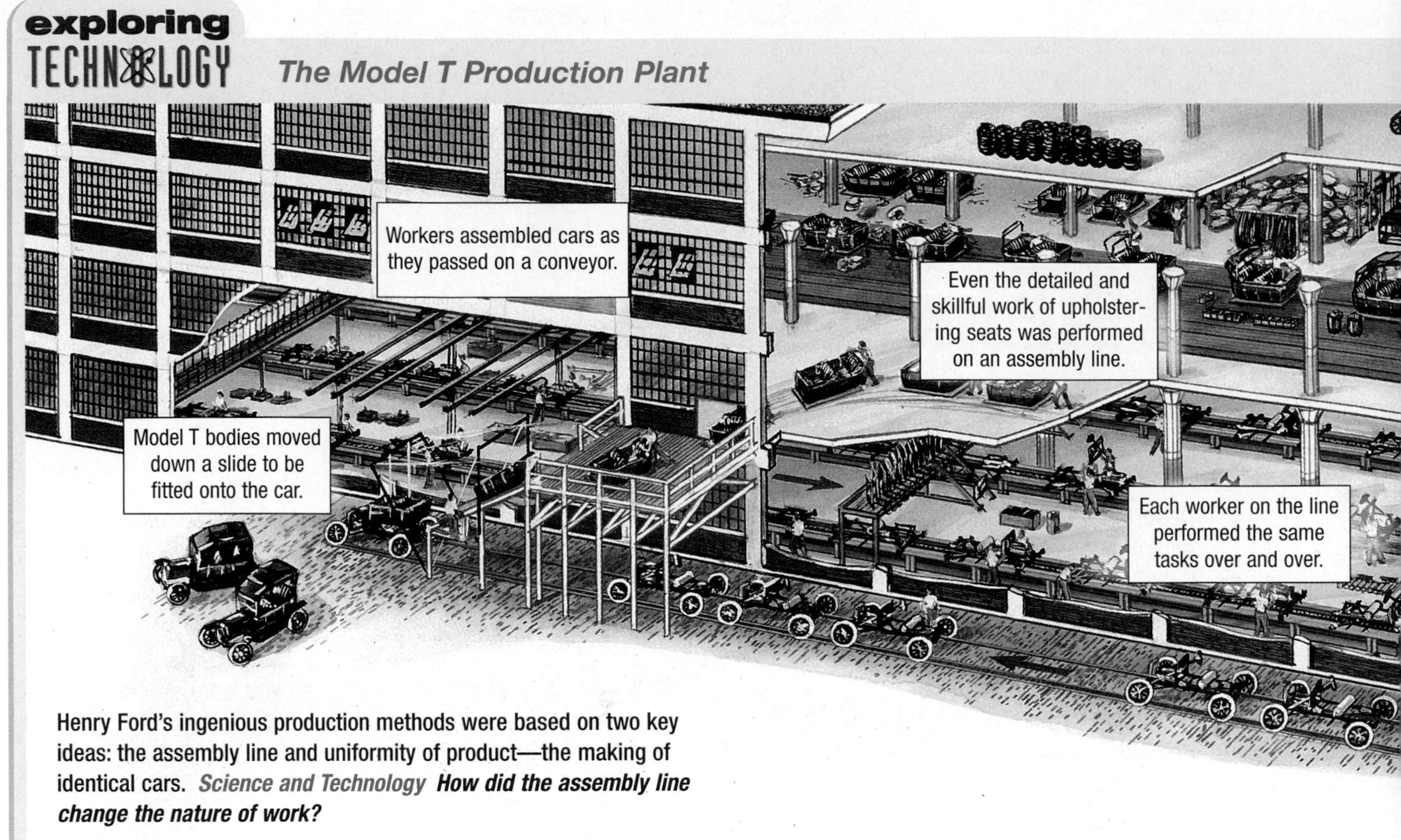


Henry Ford's ingenious production methods were based on two key ideas: the assembly line and uniformity of product—the making of identical cars. *Science and Technology* ***How did the assembly line change the nature of work?***

cleaners, radios, and refrigerators, and 90 percent of sewing machines and washing machines.

**Electric Power** These new power-hungry appliances created a surge in the demand for electricity. Between 1913 and 1927, the number of electric power customers more than quadrupled. The number of people who had electric lights jumped from 16 percent to 63 percent in about the same time.

Though the cities were gaining electric power rapidly, the countryside was not. The cost of running electric lines to scattered farming communities was simply too high. By 1925, for example, only 4 percent of American farms were connected to a power plant. Still, many farm families used wind-powered generators to bring handy new electric products to their remote homes.

**Main Idea CONNECTIONS**

*What caused the increased demand for electric power in the 1920s?*

The growth of General Electric Company illustrates how the increasing use of electricity went hand in hand with the boom in consumer sales. General Electric was formed in 1892 to take over Thomas Edison's electric light business. During the 1920s, the company grew dramatically on sales of a variety of household electrical appliances. It also sold electric motors and other products for industry. Between 1919 and 1929, the value of electrical products of this kind more than doubled, from nearly $1 billion to $2.3 billion. General Electric rode this wave of consumer buying to become one of the world's largest companies.

**New Products to Buy** Among the products General Electric offered were electric toasters, ovens, sewing machines, coffee pots, irons, and vacuum cleaners. Other companies, too, offered a vast array of goods, from telephones to cosmetics. Some of these were updated versions of products that had been around for centuries. Others had never been seen before.

## *Ford and the Automobile*

Another product that was invented in the 1890s but became available to the mass market in the 1920s was the automobile. Charles and Frank Duryea of Springfield, Massachusetts, developed a model in 1892, and several other inventors soon followed their lead. Over the

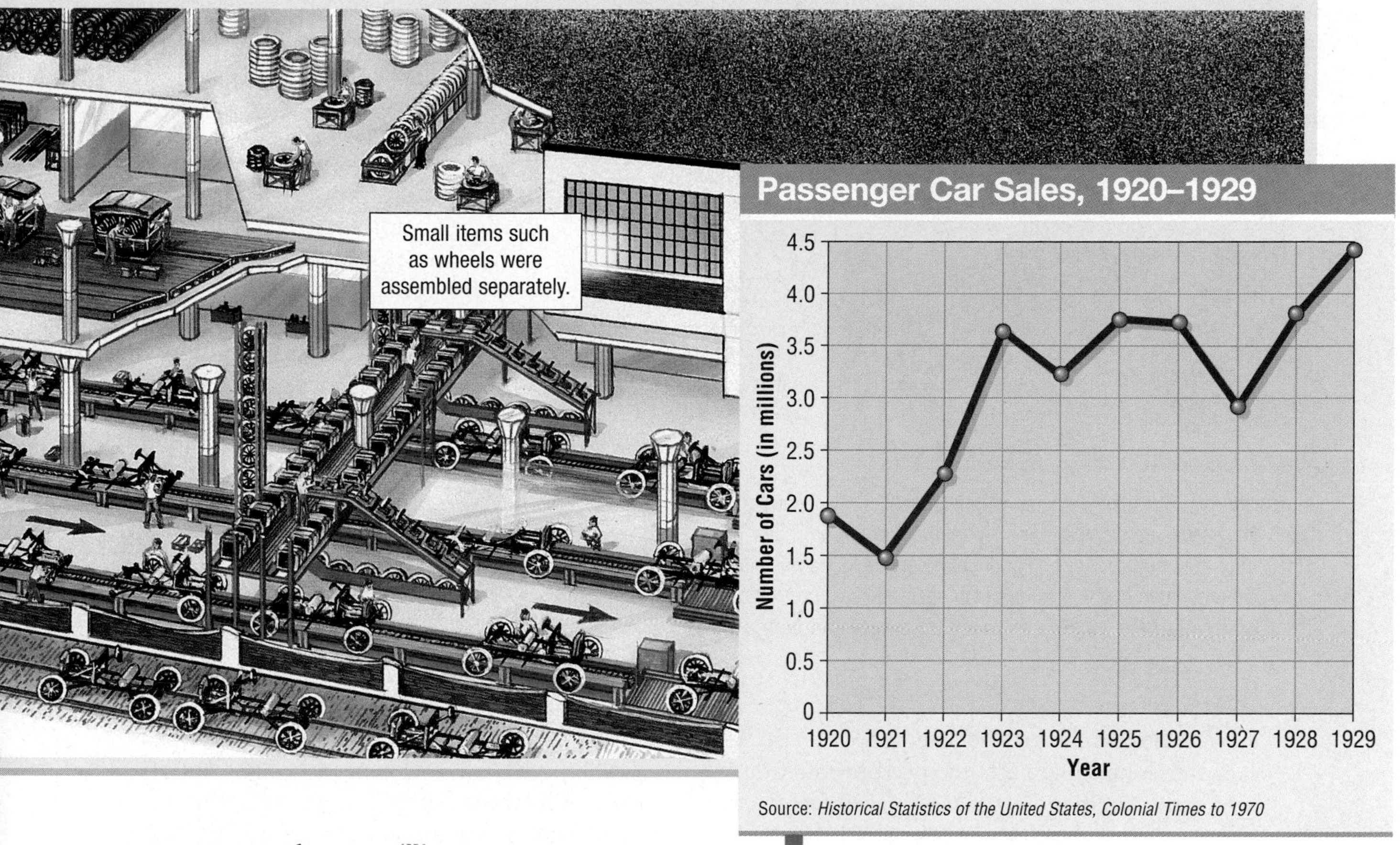


**Interpreting Graphs** Use of the assembly line made the growth of the automobile industry possible. ***Economics*** ***What was the overall trend in car sales during the 1920s?***

next 28 years, about 8 million cars were put on the road. Yet in the ten years after that, during the 1920s, the number of registered cars rose by over 15 million. Much of this rapid growth was due to the efforts of the legendary businessman Henry Ford.

**Ford and the "Model T"** Ford was born on a Michigan farm during the Civil War, the son of Irish immigrants. Early in life he showed a skill with machines. In the late 1880s, he worked as an engineer with a lighting company in Detroit. In his spare time he began inventing a "horseless carriage." In 1896 Ford perfected his first version of the lightweight, gas-powered car, which he called the "quadricycle." He soon sold it to get the money to build a better one. By 1903, he had started his own automobile company. Only a few years later, in 1908, Ford sold 30,000 of an improved type that he called the Model T.

**Ford's Assembly Line** In those days, 30,000 was a huge number of cars. Yet Ford had even bigger dreams. He wanted to "democratize the automobile," producing even more cars and selling them at prices ordinary people could afford. This goal was what set him apart from all other car makers and made him one of the most influential people of the century.

To achieve his goal, he adapted for his factories the revolutionary assembly line, shown in the Exploring Technology feature above. An **assembly line** is a manufacturing process in which each worker does one specialized task in the construction of the final product. In the past, an individual worker might build an entire product, such as a gun. In the automobile business, that process would have been inefficient since each worker would have to master hundreds of tasks. On an assembly line, however, one worker might install windshields on all the cars. Another might mount the tires, or weld a certain part in place, or apply the paint.

Ford did not invent the assembly line, but he made it more efficient: Ford's assembly line moved while the workers stayed in place, instead of having the workers move from

## The Impact of the Automobile

*The automobile industry had an enormous impact on related industries during the 1920s. Petroleum producers in particular had a difficult time meeting demand as Americans took to the road.*

**Interpreting Diagrams** The automobile industry not only affected related industries, but created new ones as well. Manufacturers of batteries, spark plugs, and other auto parts supplied car components. Service industries such as filling stations and mechanic shops soon became necessities. ***Economics What role did the prosperity of the 1920s play in the automobile industry?***

vehicle to vehicle. The assembly line also used interchangeable parts to speed production. At Ford's Highland Park, Michigan, factory, the assembly line spit out a Model T every 24 seconds. Between 1908 and 1927, Ford built half of the automobiles produced in the entire world, more than 15 million cars.

By making large numbers of identical automobiles in an identical way, Ford could take advantage of economies of scale. The more automobiles he made, the less each one cost. In 1914, the first year his assembly line was in full swing, his company sold Model T's at $490 each. This was almost half of what a car had cost in 1910. The following year he actually dropped the price to $390.

**Main Idea CONNECTIONS**

*How was Ford able to make cars affordable to many Americans?*

Ford's cars were identical. He joked that his customers could get their Model T's in any color they liked, as long as it was black. However, other car makers realized that the American public wanted different colors and styles of cars. When General Motors introduced its low-priced Chevrolet in several colors, Ford lost many customers. Not until 1928 did he introduce a choice of colors in a new automobile, the Model A.

Ford's success, however, came partly from vertical consolidation, controlling the businesses that make up phases of a product's development. Ford boasted that he could take a load of raw ore on Monday morning and sell it as a car 52 hours later on Wednesday afternoon. The ore came from Ford's own iron mines and was forged in his own blast furnaces and steel mills, which were fired by coal from his 16 coal mines. Wood used in the car came from his 700,000 acres of forests, rubber from his plantations in Brazil, glass for windshields from his own glassworks. He shipped materials over his own railroad and his own fleet of ships. Nearly all the tools used in his factories were made in his own shops. Furthermore, this entire empire was built with his own money.

**A Complex Businessman** Like the empire he ran, Ford was a complex man. He had both good qualities and personal failings. For example, he won praise in 1914 for introducing a $5-a-day pay rate for many of his workers. This was double what other factories paid at the time. Yet he was not always generous. He ruled his company harshly, and used violence to fight unions. Though he showed genius in giving millions of Americans a car they could afford, he stubbornly refused to keep up with their changing tastes. By 1936 the Ford Motor Company had slipped to third place in the car business.

Critics of his system claimed the assembly line was hard on the workers. Ford admitted that work on the assembly line would be boring to him, but insisted that his employees enjoyed it. In his 1922 autobiography he stated:

**AMERICAN VOICES**

> **"Probably the most monotonous task in the whole factory is one in which a man picks up a gear with a steel hook, shakes it in a vat of oil, then turns it into a basket. . . . Yet the man on that job has been doing it for eight solid years . . . and he stubbornly resists every attempt to force him into a better job!"**
>
> —*Henry Ford,* My Life and Work, *1922*

Another of Ford's failings was his contempt for history, which he described as "bunk," or nonsense. Because he did not understand the past, he could not understand the present. He sailed a rented ocean liner across the Atlantic in 1915 and made a hopeless effort to talk Europe out of fighting World War I. In 1920, he used his own newspaper, the *Dearborn Independent,* to blame Jews for the world's problems. However, in 1927, after being sued for slander, he apologized for these attacks and sold the paper.

## *Industrial Growth*

Through Ford's genius, automobile making became the nation's biggest single manufacturing industry in the 1920s. By the late twenties, cars were using 15 percent of America's steel, 80 percent of its rubber, half its glass, 65 percent of its leather upholstery, and 7 billion gallons of its gasoline every year.

Thousands of new businesses arose to serve automobile travel, including garages, car dealerships, motels, campgrounds, gas stations, and restaurants. Truck lines began hauling the nation's freight, and motorized buses traveled new routes through both countryside and city. About 3.7 million people were employed directly or indirectly because of the automobile industry by 1929. In that year the nation spent nearly $2 billion to build and maintain its roads and bridges.

Other industries were growing, too. Under Republican laissez-faire policies, which limited the government's regulation of business, the value of the nation's businesses took off. Between 1919 and 1929 the 200 top American companies nearly doubled their value, which rose from $43 billion to $81 billion.

Interestingly, the power of monopolies declined even while American business was getting bigger. Rapid business expansion opened up new opportunities for competitors to the giant monopolies of the 1800s.

*Route 66, begun in the mid-1920s, linked urban and rural communities between Chicago and Los Angeles.*

The United States Steel Corporation is a good example. When created by the powerful banker J. P. Morgan in 1901, it controlled about 60 percent of the steel business. By 1930, it had grown enormously. Yet its competitors also grew, and in that year United States Steel controlled only about 39 percent of the steel business.

Likewise, the companies that had once made up the Standard Oil Trust grew with the demand for oil products during the 1920s. Even so, by 1930 they controlled only about half of the nation's oil business.

Besides the automobile, steel, oil, and electrical industries, other businesses that boomed during the 1920s were the publishing, motion picture, and machine-making industries. People seemed eager to prove that the business of the United States truly was business.

### SECTION 2 REVIEW

#### Comprehension

1. ***Key Terms*** Define: (a) consumer economy; (b) installment plan; (c) assembly line.
2. ***Summarizing the Main Idea*** Write a paragraph summarizing the main reasons for the business boom of the 1920s.
3. ***Organizing Information*** Create a cause-and-effect chart on the growth of car production in the 1920s.

#### Critical Thinking

4. ***Analyzing Time Lines*** Refer to the time line at the start of the section. Choose three entries and explain how they influenced modern American life.
5. ***Recognizing Ideologies*** From what you read about Henry Ford, what conclusions can you draw about what he believed in and valued?

#### Writing Activity

6. ***Writing a Persuasive Essay*** Write a newspaper column that might have appeared in the late 1920s. Explain why the government's laissez-faire approach to the economy seems to be working. Support your case with statistics from this section.

# SKILLS FOR LIFE

**Critical Thinking**

Geography

Graphs and Charts

Historical Evidence

# Analyzing Advertisements

Advertisements offer important evidence of the consumer goods and services that were promoted during a historical period. Ads often hold clues to widely held ideas, attitudes, and values. However, when using advertisements as historical evidence, keep in mind that ads can reflect what advertisers want people to value and desire, rather than representing the reality for most of the consumers of the time.

By the 1920s, the "what-it-is, what-it-does" type of advertising was giving way to "situational" ads. These ads depicted not only the products but also the ways in which those products might increase personal satisfaction or enhance the lives of typical consumers.

One such ad from the 1920s is shown here. Use the following steps to analyze it.

**1.** ***Identify the subject of the ad.*** (a) What product or service does it promote? (b) What facts about the product does the ad provide? (c) What issue does this advertisement use to appeal particularly to men? To women?

**2.** ***Analyze the advertisement's reliability as historical evidence.*** (a) Do you think the people depicted in the ad represent typical consumers of the 1920s? Explain. (b) What is the unstated message that the advertiser is using in this case to persuade people to buy the product?

**3.** ***Study the ad to learn more about the historical period.*** (a) What social or cultural values are promoted in the advertisement? (b) In general, do you think advertisements reflect consumers' desires for products or create the desire for such products? Explain.

**TEST FOR SUCCESS**

Think of a modern advertisement you've seen for a specific product such as a car, a food, or a type of running shoe. Use the steps shown here to analyze the ad.

1924
Women governors elected in Wyoming and Texas

1926
Ederle becomes first woman to swim English Channel

1927
Lindbergh makes first nonstop transatlantic flight

1927
Babe Ruth sets baseball's home-run record

1924 1926 1928 1930

# 3 Society in the 1920s

## SECTION PREVIEW

### Objectives

1. Describe changes in women's attitudes and roles in society during the 1920s.
2. Analyze the causes for population changes in American cities and suburbs.
3. Identify some of the heroes of the 1920s and explain their popularity.
4. *Key Terms* Define: flapper; demographics; barrio.

### Main Idea

The 1920s was a time of rapid social change, in which women, in particular, adopted new lifestyles and attitudes. Amid these changes many Americans admired heroes who embodied old-fashioned values.

### Reading Strategy

*Formulating Questions* Write down three questions you might ask to help you better understand the social changes of the 1920s.

After the war ended and the nation prospered, the manners and attitudes of Americans were bound to change. A symbol of this shift was the **flapper.** The term described a new type of woman: young, rebellious, fun loving, and bold. One author depicted the flapper this way:

AMERICAN VOICES "Breezy, slangy, and informal in manner; slim and boyish in form; covered in silk and fur that clung to her as close as onion skin; with carmined [vivid red] cheeks and lips, plucked eyebrows and close-fitting helmet of hair; gay, plucky and confident."

—*Preston Slosson,* The Great Crusade and After, *1930*

## *Women's Changing Roles*

Actually, the flapper represented only a tiny number of American women. Yet the symbol had a wide impact on fashion and manners. More than anything else, it stood for a longing to make a break with the past.

**The Flapper Image** Women of the 1920s preferred shorter dresses than those of their mothers. Hemlines rose from 6 inches above the ground in 1919 to knee-length or even higher by 1927. Dresses and blouses became much simpler. Amazingly, between 1913 and 1928, the average amount of fabric used to make a woman's outfit shrank from 19.5 yards to just 7 yards.

Women also discarded other symbols of the past. While their mothers had worn their hair long, young women "bobbed," or cut short, their hair. Even the hat they preferred, the tight-fitting cloche, matched their helmet-shaped haircuts. They also began wearing makeup, which had once been considered a sign of immorality.

Women's manners changed along with their appearance. Before the 1920s, women rarely smoked or drank in public. By the end of the decade, many women were doing both. Between 1918 and 1928 the number of cigarettes produced in the United States more than doubled. Though men were smoking

*Flappers defined a whole new style of dress.*

more, too (many switching from cigars and pipes to cigarettes), a big part of the increase was due to the new woman smoker.

**Women Working and Voting** Despite the power of the flapper image, large numbers of young people did not rebel against traditions. While many women had their hair bobbed and wore shorter skirts, some adopted the new styles because they were more convenient, not because they admired the flapper lifestyle.

**Main Idea CONNECTIONS**

*What types of social change did many women experience in the 1920s?*

Convenience was an issue for women who were moving into office, sales, service, and some professional jobs during the 1920s. Generally only single women could get jobs, and even then they held them only until they were married. If married women did go to work, they usually had to quit if they became pregnant.

For this and other reasons, employers seldom trained women for higher positions or paid them on the same scale as men. Women in leadership positions were few. Many hospitals refused to hire women doctors, and many law firms rejected women lawyers.

Like the situation of women at work, women's status in politics changed little. Although as of 1920 women could vote in national elections, they seldom did. One estimate suggested that only about 35 percent of all women voters went to the polls. When they did, their votes did not change politics as much as suffragists had hoped. In national elections especially, women voted in patterns similar to men. They seemed to have a noticeable impact, however, in local elections.

Still, women did begin to seek and win state and national political office. Jeannette Rankin of Montana had begun the trend when she was elected to the House of Representatives in 1916, becoming the first woman to serve in either house of Congress. Miriam A. Ferguson from Texas and Nellie Tayloe Ross of Wyoming, both wives of former governors, were elected governors themselves in 1924. By 1928, there were 145 women in 38 state legislatures. Thus, although women did not increase their political power as quickly as suffragists had hoped, they did lay a foundation for future participation in government.

To celebrate the passage of the Nineteenth Amendment in 1920, Alice Paul adds the "ratification star" to the flag of the National Woman's Party. ***Culture*** *Why do you think more women did not turn out to vote in the early 1920s?*

## *Cities and Suburbs*

The 1920s saw demographic as well as social changes. **Demographics** are the statistics that describe a population, such as data on race or income. The major demographic change of the 1920s was a movement away from the countryside. During the decade some 6 million people moved from rural areas to the cities.

**African Americans in the North** As you read earlier, the passage of Jim Crow laws, as well as new job opportunities in the North, produced the Great Migration of blacks from the South to northern cities from the late 1800s through World War I. The industrial boom you read about in Section 2 further encouraged this demographic shift.

Throughout the early 1900s, jobs for African Americans in the South had been scarce and low-paying. Many factory jobs simply were closed to them. As industries expanded production during the 1920s, many new job opportunities opened up for African Americans in the North. In 1860, 93 percent of all African Americans lived in the South. By 1910, this had dropped very little, to 89 percent. By 1930, it had fallen far more, to 80 percent.

Yet the North was no promised land. African American factory workers often faced

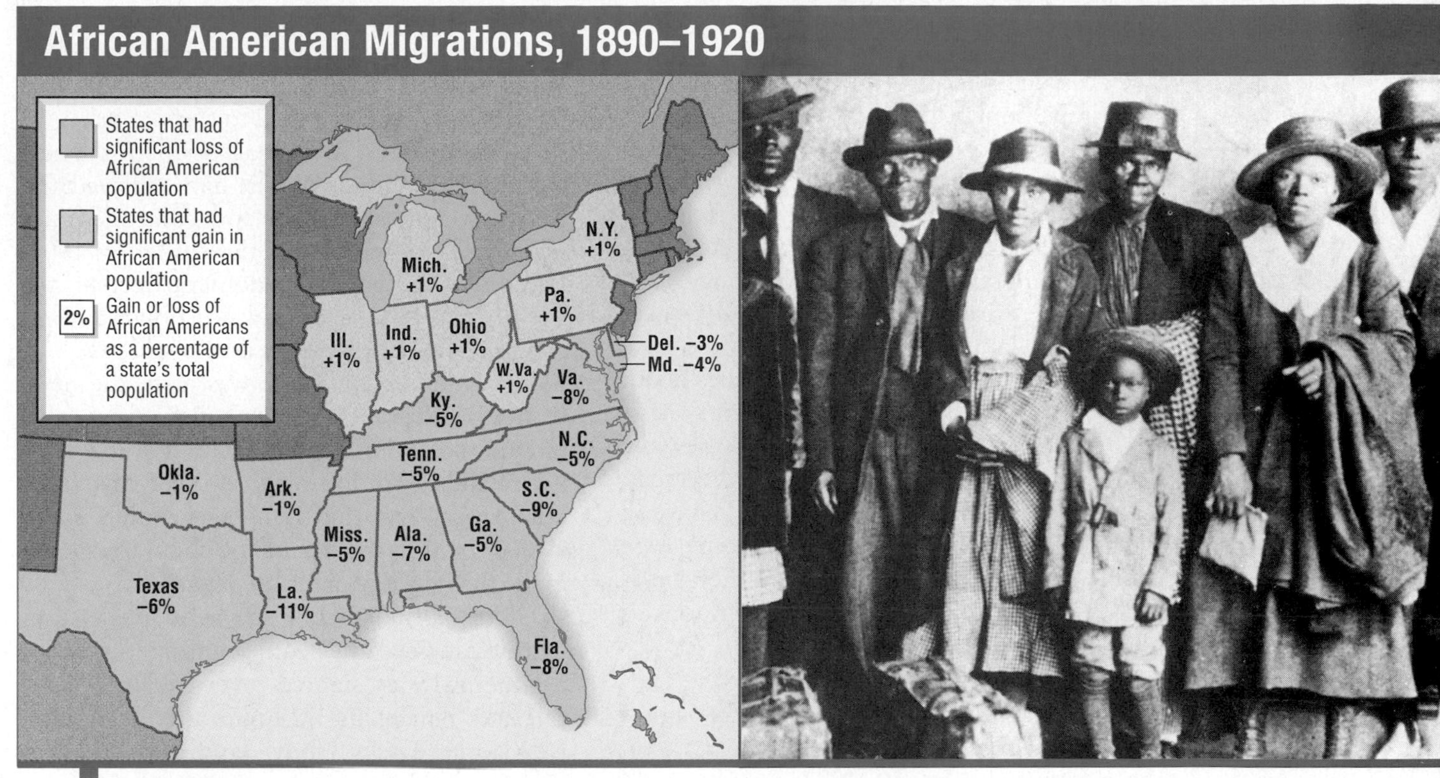


MAP skills The migration of African Americans from the South to the North helped alter the populations of both regions. This family moved from the rural South to settle in Chicago in 1912. ***Movement* Which states lost the largest percentages of their black populations?**

anger and hatred from whites, who feared that migrants threatened their jobs and wages. African American women often had to work as household help for whites, at wages that kept them trapped in poverty.

**Other Migration** As you read, the nation's immigration laws were tightened in the 1920s. As the number of immigrants from Europe decreased, employers turned to immigrants from Mexico and Canada to fill low-paying jobs. The new immigration quotas did not apply to nations in the Americas.

In the West, Mexicans supplied this labor, migrating across the border to work on the farms of California and the ranches of Texas. In the Northeast, Canadians from the French-speaking province of Quebec traveled south to work in the paper mills, potato fields, and forests of New England and New York.

The migrants also took jobs in the cities. Los Angeles, for example, became a magnet for Mexicans and developed a distinct **barrio,** or Spanish-speaking neighborhood. New York also attracted Spanish-speakers—Puerto Ricans migrating in the hope of a better life in the United States.

**Growth of the Suburbs** One result of the movements of Americans in the 1920s was a huge increase in the size of American suburbs. Some suburban growth had taken place earlier, as cities built transportation systems that used electric trolleys, or railway cars, that ran on rails laid in or along streets. The trolleys allowed people to get from the suburbs to jobs and stores in the city quickly and cheaply.

When automobiles were introduced, electric trolleys lost passengers. Between 1916 and 1926, about 2,500 miles of trolley track were abandoned. Yet the loss of trolleys did not slow the growth of suburbs.

About 80 percent of the old trolley routes were soon replaced by bus lines. By the middle of the 1920s, about 70,000 buses were operating throughout the United States. The automobile extended transportation lines even farther.

New York City is a good example of demographic change during the 1920s. The number of residents decreased in Manhattan, the heart of the city. Meanwhile, one of the city's suburbs, Queens, saw its population double.

## American Heroes

The changing morals of the 1920s made many Americans hungry for the values of an earlier era. Their memories of the senseless brutality of World War I remained strong. In America's cities, they saw people indulging in behavior that had always been connected with immorality—smoking, drinking, wearing revealing clothing and bright makeup. The newspapers of the time were filled with sensational headlines about crimes and sins of every description.

**Main Idea CONNECTIONS**

*Why did Americans seem to long for heroes during the 1920s?*

It was no wonder, then, that the nation became fascinated with heroes, especially those who seemed to have all the virtues of the good old days. Some were sports stars. Others were experts in new fields such as aviation. None became as famous as "Lucky Lindy."

**"Lucky Lindy"** The sky was drizzling rain at Roosevelt Field on Long Island, New York, on the morning of May 20, 1927. A 25-year-old Minnesotan, Charles Lindbergh, climbed into the cockpit of his specially built plane, the *Spirit of St. Louis,* and revved the engine. He had not slept much, but he did not dare wait any longer. Two other teams were waiting on the airfield, hoping to be the first to fly nonstop from New York to Paris. The prize was $25,000, and Lindbergh was determined to capture it.

In those days, flying was an infant science. Orville and Wilbur Wright had achieved the first powered, sustained, and controlled airplane flight only two decades earlier, in 1903. Radio and navigation equipment were primitive at best. Lindbergh had no copilot and no computer to fly his plane so he could rest.

The minute his plane was aloft, the news flashed by telegraph and telephone to news desks around the nation. Americans everywhere took notice and began to wait eagerly for news. The newspapers fed this hunger, printing some 27,000 columns of information about Lindbergh in the first few days after his departure.

After a brutal flight over the Atlantic Ocean, battling icy weather and fighting off sleep, Lindbergh was sighted over Ireland, then England. Finally, 33 1/2 hours after he had left New York, "Lucky Lindy" landed safely in an airfield outside Paris.

America went wild with celebration. Lindbergh was brought home on a Navy cruiser, given the Congressional Medal of Honor, and honored with parades in every state in the nation.

VIEWING HISTORY

Charles Lindbergh, pictured here with his *Spirit of St. Louis,* not only inspired the nation but also fostered the development of commercial aviation. ***Culture*** ***Why was the nation so hungry for heroes?***

Yet despite this frenzy of hero-worship, Lindbergh remained modest and calm. He refused offers of millions of dollars in publicity fees. Fame and applause could not spoil him. To millions of Americans, Lindbergh was proof that the solid moral values of the old days lived on in the heartland of America.

**Amelia Earhart** Lindbergh's feat inspired later flyers, including Amelia Earhart, who in 1932 flew across the Atlantic alone. Three years later Earhart flew solo from Hawaii to California, a challenge that had resulted in the deaths of many aviators before her. In 1937, however, attempting to fly around the world, she disappeared somewhere in the Pacific Ocean.

**Heroes of Sports** In general, the 1920s were a time when Americans began to enjoy sports as never before. A highly publicized fight between boxers Jack Dempsey and Georges Carpentier in 1921 broke the record for ticket sales, taking in $1 million. Dempsey won the fight to become the heavyweight champion of the world and a new American hero.

Of all the heroes of the era, none generated more excitement than baseball legend George Herman "Babe" Ruth. Known as "the Sultan of Swat," Babe Ruth set records in hitting, pitching, and outfielding that stood for decades.

During his career, with the Boston Red Sox and then with the New York Yankees, Ruth hit 714 home runs, a record that was unbroken for nearly 40 years. In 1927 the champion enthralled Americans by setting the legendary record of 60 home runs in a 154-game season.

*Tennis star Helen Wills and boxing champion Jack Dempsey*

Women, too, excelled in sports. For example, Gertrude Ederle smashed record after record in women's freestyle swimming. In the Olympic Games of 1924 she won a gold medal. In 1928 she became the first woman to swim the 35-mile-wide English Channel. Her time beat the men's record by nearly two hours.

Besides being eager spectators, more Americans began participating in sports. With more leisure time and with the mobility of automobiles, people took up golf, tennis, swimming, and other types of recreation.

## SECTION 3 REVIEW

### Comprehension

1. *Key Terms* Define: (a) flapper; (b) demographics; (c) barrio.
2. *Summarizing the Main Idea* In what ways did Americans react to the changing social values of the 1920s?
3. *Organizing Information* Make a tree map entitled *Women in the 1920s.* On the first level, create categories labeled *Changes in Lifestyles, Women at Work,* and *Women in Politics.* Then fill in facts under each of these categories.

### Critical Thinking

4. *Analyzing Time Lines* Refer to the time line at the start of the section. Choose three entries and explain the significance of each.
5. *Recognizing Cause and Effect* How did the business boom of the 1920s affect the nation's demographics?

### Writing Activity

6. *Writing an Expository Essay* Write a magazine article titled "The Roaring Twenties." Describe some of the trends and people who gave the 1920s this name.

| 1920 | 1922 | 1923 | 1924 | 1925 | 1926 |
|---|---|---|---|---|---|
| *Nation's first commercial radio station begins operation* | *Claude McKay's* Harlem Shadows | *Duke Ellington begins jazz career in New York City* | *George Gershwin's* Rhapsody in Blue | *F. Scott Fitzgerald's* The Great Gatsby | *Ernest Hemingway's* The Sun Also Rises |

**1920** **1922** **1924** **1926**

# 4 Mass Media and the Jazz Age

## SECTION PREVIEW

### Objectives

1. Analyze the impact of the growth of the nation's mass media.
2. Identify some of the major figures of the Jazz Age and other artistic figures of the 1920s.
3. Show how the Lost Generation and the Harlem Renaissance influenced American culture.
4. *Key Terms* Define: mass media; Jazz Age; Lost Generation; Harlem Renaissance.

### Main Idea

Radio, movies, and jazz were some of the new forms of information, entertainment, and the arts that began in the 1920s. The decade was an especially creative period for music, art, and literature.

### Reading Strategy

*Organizing Information* As you read, write down facts that will help you to define what the Jazz Age was. Then use your notes to write a one-sentence definition.

*Lillian Gish worked in silent films and "talkies."*

Before 1900, few outside of Los Angeles had even heard of the dusty little suburb northwest of the city. It had been built by a prohibitionist, who hoped it would remain a dry town, free of drinking and bad behavior.

In the early 1900s, however, filmmakers moved into the little town. They were attracted by its sunny climate, its variety of landscapes from desert to snowy mountains, and the large work force available in the area.

Movies made the little town big. In time, its main avenue became a strip of expensive shops and bars. Stars drove the streets in luxurious imported cars, trailed by reporters.

By the 1920s, the whole nation knew about it. In fact, the whole world knew about it. Dusty little Hollywood had grown up.

## The Mass Media

Hollywood's new fame reflected a major trend of the 1920s. Before that time, the United States had been largely a collection of regional cultures. Interests, tastes, and attitudes varied widely from one region to another. The majority of people simply did not travel about much, talk to those in other regions, or even read much of the same news as others.

The 1920s changed all that. Films, nationwide news gathering, and the new industry of radio broadcasting produced a truly national culture. Print and broadcast methods of communicating information to large numbers of people are known as the **mass media.**

**Movies** From their beginnings in the 1890s, motion pictures had been a wildly popular mass medium, and through the 1920s, people just kept coming. Between about 1910 and 1930, the number of theaters rose from about 5,000 to about 22,500. During the later part of the decade, the nation's theaters showed movies to roughly 90 million Americans each week—at a time when the total population was less than 125 million. Movie making had become the fourth largest business in the country.

These growth figures are even more amazing in view of the fact that before 1927, movies

## FACT Finder: Growth of the Mass Media, 1920–1930

| | |
|---|---|
| Newspapers | Between 1920 and 1930 daily newspaper circulation rose from 27,791,000 to 39,589,000—an increase of 42%. |
| Motion Pictures | Between 1922 and 1930 the number of people attending motion pictures rose from 40 million per week to 90 million per week—an increase of 125%. |
| Radios | Between 1920 and 1930 the number of households with radios, like the one at right, rose from 20,000 to 13,750,000—an increase of 68,650%. |

Source: *Historical Statistics of the United States, Colonial Times to 1970*

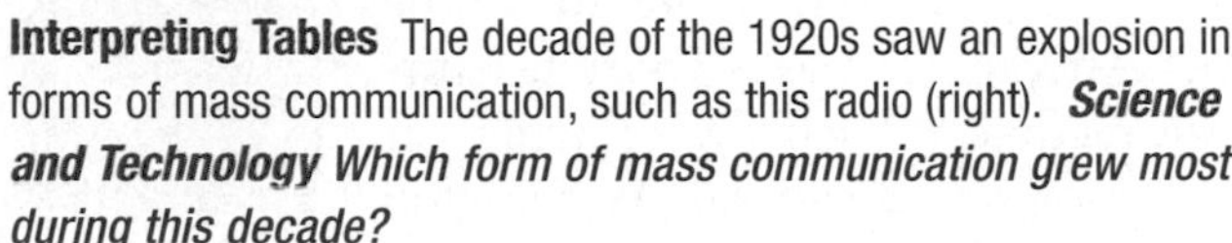

**Interpreting Tables** The decade of the 1920s saw an explosion in forms of mass communication, such as this radio (right). ***Science and Technology** Which form of mass communication grew most during this decade?*

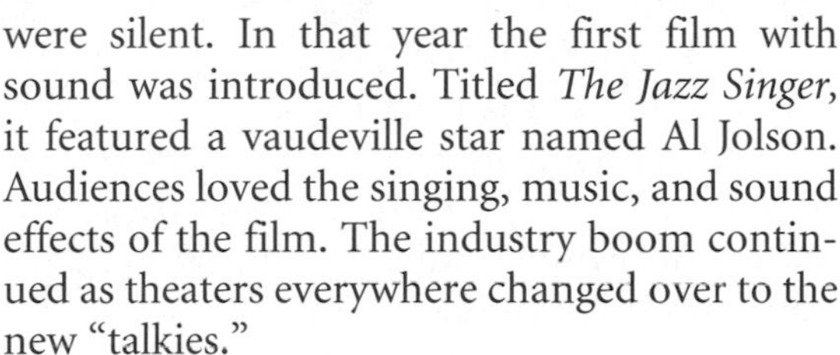

were silent. In that year the first film with sound was introduced. Titled *The Jazz Singer,* it featured a vaudeville star named Al Jolson. Audiences loved the singing, music, and sound effects of the film. The industry boom continued as theaters everywhere changed over to the new "talkies."

**Newspapers** Americans followed the off-screen lives of their favorite stars in another mass medium, the newspaper. During the 1920s newspapers increased both in their size and in the number of readers. In 1900, a hefty edition of *The New York Times* totaled only 14 pages. By the mid-1920s, however, newspapers even in mid-sized American cities were totaling more than 50 pages a day, and Sunday editions were enormous. In fact, the use of newsprint roughly doubled in the United States between 1914 and 1927.

Although newspapers were getting bigger, the number of them was declining. Between 1914 and 1929, several thousand newspapers and magazines went out of business in the United States. Often, newspaper chains owned by a single individual or company bought up established papers and merged them. Between 1923 and 1927, the number of chains doubled, and the total number of newspapers they owned rose by 50 percent.

William Randolph Hearst, the legendary publisher of the *San Francisco Examiner* and the *New York Journal,*† gained control of newspapers in more than 20 cities. As newspapers became a mass medium, people shared the same information, read about the same events, and were influenced by the same ideas and fashions. Thus newspapers helped create a common culture.

**Radio** As a mass medium, radio barely existed until the 1920s. Before that time, only about 20,000 Americans had radio sets, all homemade. As an experiment, in 1920 Frank Conrad of the Westinghouse Company in East Pittsburgh tried sending recorded music and baseball scores over the radio. The response was so great that Westinghouse began broadcasting programs on a regular basis. Soon the nation had its first radio station operating as a for-profit business, Pittsburgh's KDKA.

**Main Idea CONNECTIONS**

*What social changes were brought about by the mass media?*

The growth of radio was tremendous. By 1922 more than 500 stations were on the air, and Americans were eagerly buying radios to listen to them. To reach more people, networks

† Hearst's life and quest for power were the basis for one of the most popular motion pictures ever, Orson Welles's 1941 classic *Citizen Kane.*

such as the National Broadcasting Company (NBC) linked many individual stations together. Each station in the network played the same programming. Soon much of the country was listening to the same jokes, commercials, music, sports events, religious services, and news. Other companies imitated NBC, building networks of their own. Thus radio became a medium for the masses.

## The Jazz Age

Radio combined with the great African American migration to the cities to produce another highlight of the 1920s—a music called jazz. This music features improvisation, a process by which musicians make up music as they are playing it rather than relying completely on printed scores. It also has a type of off-beat rhythm called syncopation.

**Jazz Arrives** Jazz grew out of African American music of the South, especially ragtime and blues. By early in the 1900s, bands in New Orleans were playing the new mix of styles, and many radio listeners began hearing the new sound for the first time in the 1920s. Soon jazz became a nationwide craze. Younger people in particular loved to dance to the new music. By 1929, a survey of stations showed that two thirds of all radio air time was devoted to jazz.

Jazz won over even Americans who had been horrified by it at first. It seemed to sum up the character of the decade. The great symphony conductor Leopold Stokowski declared that jazz was "an expression of the times, of the breathless, energetic, superactive times in which we are living." It was no surprise that the 1920s came to be called the **Jazz Age.**

*Jazz music, played on phonographs like this one, lay at the heart of a dramatic change in fashion, manners, and morals.*

**The Jazz Clubs** One of hottest places to listen to jazz was Harlem, a district on the northern end of New York City. By one count, Harlem had some 500 jazz clubs. About a dozen clubs gave shows mostly for white visitors, including the Cotton Club, Connie's Inn, and the Saratoga Club.

Nearly all the great jazz musicians played in the Harlem clubs at one time or another. The Jelly Roll Morton Band had a smooth, modern sound. Louis "Satchmo" Armstrong improvised brilliant solos on his trumpet or sang soulful tunes. One of the best remembered jazz musicians to play in Harlem, however, was "the Duke" himself—Duke Ellington.

## Duke Ellington

AMERICAN BIOGRAPHY

Edward Kennedy Ellington was born in Washington, D.C., in 1899. His father worked as a butler but later became a blueprint maker for the navy. The Ellingtons were able to keep up a middle-class life in a time when doing so was especially difficult for African Americans.

"Duke," as Ellington was called, showed talent at both drawing and piano from an early age. At 17 he was supporting himself by playing in clubs in Washington at night and painting signs during the day. Although he was offered a scholarship at the Pratt Institute of Fine Arts in New York City, he turned it down in favor of continuing his musical career.

*Duke Ellington (1899–1974)*

In 1923, jazz musician Fats Waller persuaded Ellington and several of his musician friends to move to New York. They formed a band and soon landed a job at the Hollywood Club in the downtown area. This band, under various names and in one form or another, continued to play with Ellington until his death in 1974.

In the 1920s, he worked with superb jazz musicians such as Bubber Miley on trumpet, "Tricky Sam" Nanton on trombone, and Sonny Greer on drums. Later Billy Strayhorn joined as an assistant arranger.

Though Ellington was an excellent pianist, his greatest genius was as a bandleader, arranger, and composer. For some 50 years, Ellington's music and his band's music seemed one and the same.

For example, even though "Take the A Train," the band's theme song, was written by Strayhorn, most people associate it with Ellington. Yet Ellington was also a brilliant composer in his own right, writing at least a thousand pieces in his long career, including music for concerts, broadway shows, films, and operas.

Ellington's music lives on today. His old recordings are still available, and new artists continually rework such great tunes as "Mood Indigo," "Solitude," "In a Sentimental Mood," "Blue Harlem," and "Bojangles." Even a century after his birth, among jazz musicians the Duke is still the king. ■

Edward Hopper painted this lonely scene, called *Automat,* in 1927. The Automat was a popular restaurant chain in which one could purchase a snack or a meal from a vending machine and eat it at a table. ***Culture What does the painting suggest about Hopper's view of the society of the times?***

## *Other Artists*

The jazz spirit ran through all the arts of the 1920s. People spoke of "jazz poetry" and "jazz painting." Its strongest effect, of course, was on other forms of music. Composer George Gershwin, the son of Russian immigrants, won overnight success in 1924 with his *Rhapsody in Blue.* Composed for jazz bandleader Paul Whiteman, this piece was first played by Whiteman's orchestra and throbbed with jazz rhythms. Yet it was not quite jazz and not quite symphony. Instead it was a magical blend of the two.

**Painting** Like jazz musicians, American painters of the 1920s did not shy away from taking the pulse of American life. Painters such as Edward Hopper and Rockwell Kent showed the nation's rougher side, from cities to coal mines, from the streets to the barrooms.

By contrast, a young artist named Georgia O'Keeffe painted natural objects such as flowers, animal bones, and landscapes. Yet her simple images always suggest something greater than themselves. A range of hills, for example, seem almost to shudder with life. O'Keeffe continued to paint until her death in 1986 at the age of nearly 100.

**Literature** Several writers, too, began fruitful careers during the 1920s. Muckraking novelist Sinclair Lewis attacked American society with savage irony. His targets included the small town (in *Main Street,* 1920), the prosperous conformist (*Babbit,* 1922), the medical business (*Arrowsmith,* 1925), and dishonest ministers (*Elmer Gantry,* 1927). Lewis refused a Pulitzer Prize in 1926, but he did win (and accept) the Nobel Prize for Literature in 1930, the first such award to go to an American.

Another writer destined for the Nobel Prize was playwright Eugene O'Neill. In a career stretching from the 1920s into the 1950s, he wove dark, poetic tragedies out of the material of everyday American life. Until his time, most American theaters had shown only European plays or light comedies. The power of O'Neill's work proved to the public that the American stage could achieve a greatness rivaling that of Europe.

## *The Lost Generation*

One set of writers during the 1920s gained the name the **Lost Generation,** because of their belief that they were lost in a greedy, materialistic world that lacked moral values. Many of these writers and thinkers flocked to Greenwich Village, part of Manhattan, in New York City. (For decades afterward, Greenwich Village would remain a cultural center for bohemians, or rebels against conventional lifestyles.)

*F. Scott Fitzgerald and his wife, Zelda Sayre, lived the life of the Lost Generation.*

VIEWING HISTORY

Writers Langston Hughes (far left) and Zora Neale Hurston (top left) helped make Harlem a leading artistic center. Jazz singer Bessie Smith (bottom left) helped fill jazz nightspots in the North (above). Harlem was also a vital social hub in the 1920s. ***Culture*** ***Why do you think Harlem became the center of a literary awakening in the 1920s?***

Others became expatriates, or people who live outside their homeland. Discontent with American society of the 1920s, they left the country to live in Paris, or other parts of Europe thought to be more intellectually stimulating.

The most prominent writers of the Lost Generation were John Dos Passos, Archibald MacLeish, Hart Crane, e. e. cummings, Ernest Hemingway, and F. Scott Fitzgerald. Hemingway wrote of the Lost Generation in his 1926 novel *The Sun Also Rises.* His novels and short stories are read today for their direct, simple style.

F. Scott Fitzgerald was both part of the Lost Generation and part of the flapper world. In fact, some people believe Fitzgerald had a part in creating flapper culture with his novel *This Side of Paradise*, published in 1920. His 1925 masterpiece, *The Great Gatsby*, focused on the wealthy, sophisticated Americans of the Jazz Age. Not surprisingly, this Lost Generation writer found the rich to be self-centered and shallow.

After Hemingway made the term "Lost Generation" famous, it was taken up by the flappers. They liked to imagine themselves as rebels against the culture of their time, living a life both fast and dangerous. As their motto they took the words of a popular poet of the day, Edna St. Vincent Millay:

AMERICAN VOICES

**"My candle burns at both ends;**
**It will not last the night;**
**But ah, my foes, and oh, my friends—**
**It gives a lovely light!"**

—*Edna St. Vincent Millay,*
*"First Fig," 1920*

## *The Harlem Renaissance*

For African Americans, the cultural center of the United States increasingly was New York City's Harlem. The number of African Americans living in Harlem grew from 50,000 in 1914 to about 200,000 in 1930. Not just a national center for jazz, Harlem also became the home of an

African American literary awakening of the 1920s known as the **Harlem Renaissance.**

James Weldon Johnson emerged as a leading writer of the Harlem group. Johnson lived in two worlds, the political and the literary. As executive secretary of the NAACP, he led the group during an active time in its history, while pursuing a writing career that inspired younger members of the Harlem group. His most famous work, *God's Trombones* (1927), is a collection of sermons in rhythmic verse modeled after the style of traditional black preaching.

Alain Locke's 1925 book *The New Negro* celebrated the blossoming of African American culture. Locke noted that both African and American heritage could be enriching, not conflicting.

Zora Neale Hurston came to New York as a young actress, became an anthropologist, and gained fame as a Harlem writer with her poignant novel *Their Eyes Were Watching God* (1937). Dorothy West, another accomplished writer, tackled the dual themes of being black and being a woman.

The leading poets of the Harlem Renaissance were Claude McKay and Countee Cullen. McKay produced a large body of work, including *Harlem Shadows* (1922), and was a voice of protest against the sufferings of African Americans in white society.

The gifted Cullen is best known for his 1925 collection of poems called *Color*. He was also responsible for bringing to light the talents of the Harlem writers by collecting many of their works into *Caroling Dusk: An Anthology of Verse by Negro Poets* (1927).

The Harlem writer perhaps most studied today is Langston Hughes, a poet, short story writer, journalist, and playwright whose career stretched into the 1960s. Hughes spoke with a clear, strong voice about the joys and difficulties of being human, being American, and being black:

**"I, too, sing America.**
**I am the darker brother.**
**They send me to eat in the kitchen**
**When company comes,**
**But I laugh,**
**And eat well,**
**And grow strong. . . .**

**Tomorrow,**
**I'll be at the table**
**When company comes.**
**Nobody'll dare**
**Say to me,**
**"Eat in the kitchen,"**
**Then.**

**Besides,**
**They'll see how beautiful I am**
**And be ashamed—**

**I, too, am America."**

—*Langston Hughes,*
*"I, Too," 1926*

**Main Idea CONNECTIONS**

***What themes did Harlem writers deal with in their works?***

## SECTION 4 REVIEW

### Comprehension

1. *Key Terms* Define: (a) mass media; (b) Jazz Age; (c) Lost Generation; (d) Harlem Renaissance.
2. *Summarizing the Main Idea* What types of cultural changes took place in the United States during the 1920s?
3. *Organizing Information* Create a web diagram with the label *Mass Media* in the center circle. Fill out the diagram to show the various media that developed during the 1920s and some effects these media had on American life.

### Critical Thinking

4. *Analyzing Time Lines* Refer to the time line at the start of the section. Choose two people listed on the time line and explain why each was important to the Jazz Age.
5. *Analyzing Documents* Reread the poem above. (a) In a sentence, state the message of the verse. (b) How does it express the spirit of the Harlem Renaissance?

### Writing Activity

6. *Writing an Expository Essay* Write an essay describing the spirit of the Jazz Age. Use supporting details from the section.

1

**Duke Ellington**

Duke Ellington, pictured on the sheet music of one of his famous compositions, became one of America's greatest composers.

3

**Flapper's Dress and Beads**

Flapper clothes were a must for doing the newest dances to jazz music.

2

**Dizzy Gillespie's Trumpet**

Dizzy Gillespie, whose bent horn distinguished him from other trumpet players, pioneered the modern jazz and bebop styles. His career began in the 1930s and spanned seven decades.

4

**Hymie Shertzer**

The well-known saxophonist worked with many bands as well as in recording studios and in radio.

5

**Shertzer's Saxophone**

The saxophone was invented in Europe in 1840 but never became a popular orchestral instrument. Musicians like Shertzer, however, made the sax's smooth, easily blended sound one of the major voices of the jazz band.

FROM EXHIBITIONS AND COLLECTIONS AT THE SMITHSONIAN INSTITUTION'S NATIONAL MUSEUM OF AMERICAN HISTORY

# THE GROWTH OF JAZZ

Today rock or hip hop might be your musical choice, but in the 1920s and 1930s, jazz shook the walls of dance clubs. Have you heard of Duke Ellington? Dizzy Gillespie? Benny Goodman? They were just a few of the musicians whose trumpets, saxophones, and clarinets blended to create one of music's most popular styles—jazz. *See* **1** *and* **2**.

One reason for jazz's popularity was that its offbeat, spontaneous rhythms reflected the lively spirit of the generation. Young people hungry for expression flocked to the dance halls. The flapper with her jazz-style clothes became a symbol of what came to be known as the Jazz Age. The short dresses and fake jewelry were new and daring, shocking many in the older generations. *See* **3**.

Jazz exploded across the American music scene during a time of great excitement and change. Americans' notions of art and literature were expanding as artists experimented with new forms of expression. A surge in mass media—movies and newspapers—made information available to more people. Radio had just begun broadcasting, allowing people to hear the same styles of music across the nation. *See* **4** *and* **5**.

Jazz had its roots in the African American music of the South. Yet as its popularity grew, jazz crossed racial boundaries. Black jazz artists like Duke Ellington, Count Basie, and Jimmie Lunceford became very popular among white as well as black audiences. White artist Benny Goodman's 1936 quartet that included African American musicians Lionel Hampton and Teddy Wilson was the first popular racially mixed jazz group. *See* **6** *and* **7**.

Jazz musicians developed their own styles and signatures. Today, these styles are part of the American culture. Few musical movements have withstood the test of time like jazz. Just ask any fan.

## 6 Benny Goodman's Clarinet

Known as the "King of Swing," Goodman began his jazz career in 1923. His "big band" helped make jazz popular with white audiences, but he preferred small groups. Goodman was also a classical performer who made recordings with leading symphony orchestras.

## 7 1920s Jazz Band

This band, which was photographed in St. Louis, is unidentified. The band played New Orleans-style jazz.

1. ***Summarize*** What do the objects tell you about the growth of jazz?
2. ***Connecting to Today*** Think about the music of today. How does it compare to that during the 1920s and 1930s? Prepare an oral report for your class in which you explain whether you think that today's music will withstand the test of time, as jazz has.

| 1919 | 1920 | 1922 | 1925 | 1925 |
|---|---|---|---|---|
| Race riots in Chicago and other cities | Prohibition takes effect | Anti-lynching law fails to pass in Congress | Scopes trial | Marcus Garvey's "Back to Africa" movement ends |

1918 1920 1922 1924 1926

# 5 Cultural Conflicts

## SECTION PREVIEW

### Objectives

1. Analyze the effects of Prohibition.
2. Summarize the main issue in the Scopes trial.
3. Explain why an increase in racial tensions occurred following World War I.
4. *Key Terms* Define: bootlegger; speakeasy; fundamentalism; Scopes trial.

### Main Idea

Rapid social change after World War I caused conflicts among people with differing beliefs and values.

### Reading Strategy

*Problem Solving* As you read, list types of conflicts that divided Americans during the 1920s. Note ways these problems could have been eased.

Prohibition forced many beer companies to find new beverages to brew, as these labels show.

Prohibition of all alcoholic beverages became the law of the land when the Eighteenth Amendment to the Constitution took effect on January 16, 1920. Yet for many people, life went on as usual, including for President Harding, as the daughter of former President Theodore Roosevelt witnessed:

AMERICAN VOICES "Though violation of the Eighteenth Amendment was a matter of course in Washington, it was rather shocking to see the way Harding disregarded the Constitution he was sworn to uphold. . . . There were always, at least before the unofficial dinners, cocktails in the upstairs hall outside the President's room. . . .

One evening . . . a friend of the Hardings asked me if I would like to go up to the study. . . . No rumor could have exceeded the reality. . . . Trays with bottles containing every imaginable brand of whiskey stood about. . . ."

—*Alice Roosevelt Longworth,* Crowded Hours, *1933*

## Prohibition

The Volstead Act, the law passed by Congress in 1919 to enforce the Eighteenth Amendment, was ignored most of all in the cities of the East Coast. A 1924 report showed Kansans obeying the law at a rate of about 95 percent and New Yorkers at a rate of only about 5 percent. Thus Prohibition sharpened the contrast between urban and rural moral values during the 1920s.

**Bootlegging** Americans who defied the Volstead Act had to get their liquor, beer, and wine from somewhere. A new type of criminal now came along to supply Americans with alcohol: the bootlegger.

In the old days, **bootleggers** merely had been drinkers who hid flasks of liquor in the leg of their boots. Now the term was used to describe suppliers of illegal alcohol. Some bootleggers smuggled whiskey from the Caribbean or Canada. Others operated stills—devices that made alcohol from corn, grain, potatoes, or other fruit and vegetable sources.

Many bootleggers' customers were owners of **speakeasies,** illegal bars that flourished in the cities. Entrance to the speakeasies was restricted. A heavy gate usually blocked the door, to be opened only when customers showed a membership card or were recognized by a guard.

**Organized Crime** In several cities, criminals formed large, efficient organizations that controlled the distribution of alcohol. Individuals or gangs who tried to compete were run out of town or murdered. The streets of American cities became a battleground, as gangsters fought for control with machine guns and sawed-off shotguns.

Successful bootleggers often expanded into other illegal activities, including gambling, prostitution, and a highly profitable business called racketeering. In the typical "racket," local businesses were forced to pay a fee for "protection." Those who refused to pay might be gunned down or their businesses blown to bits. In one period of a little more than a year, 157 bombs were set off by racketeers in Chicago. Terrified citizens went along with the gangsters' demands. The supporters of Prohibition had never dreamed that their ideals would bear such evil fruit.

**Al Capone** The most notorious of the gangster organizations was in Chicago. There, bootlegging had added immense wealth to an already successful gambling, prostitution, and racketeering business that reached into nearly every neighborhood, police station, and government office.

In 1925 a young crime boss murdered his way to the top of Chicago's organized crime network. He was Al Capone, nicknamed "Scarface."

Capone was a ruthless criminal with a talent for avoiding jail. With so much money at his disposal ($60 million a year from bootlegging alone), Capone found it easy to buy the cooperation of police and city officials. Politicians, even judges, took orders from him.

The government fought back with improved law enforcement. The Federal Bureau of Investigation (FBI), headed by J. Edgar Hoover, became a dedicated, independent force against organized crime during the 1920s.

For years, Capone managed to slip out of any charges brought against him. Finally, in 1931 he was convicted of tax evasion and sent to prison. Bootlegging, however, remained a problem until Prohibition was ended in 1933.

## COMPARING PRIMARY SOURCES

### THE EIGHTEENTH AMENDMENT

Violations of Prohibition led Congress to hear testimony on whether the Eighteenth Amendment should be repealed.

**In Favor of Repeal**

"I will concede that the saloon was odious [offensive], but now we have delicatessen stores, pool rooms, drug stores, millinery shops, private parlors, and 57 other varieties of speakeasies selling liquor and flourishing."

*—Representative Fiorello La Guardia of New York, 1926*

**Against Repeal**

"Instead of lowering our standards, we urge that the law be strengthened. . . . The closing of the open saloon . . . has resulted in better national health; children are born under better conditions, homes are better, and the mother is delivered from the fear of a drunken husband."

*—Ella A. Boole, president of the National Woman's Christian Temperance Union, 1926*

***ANALYZING VIEWPOINTS*** **Compare the main arguments made by the two speakers.**

Chicago gangster Al Capone (left) confers with his lawyer in this 1929 photo. ***Government*** *How was the government finally able to put Capone away?*

William Jennings Bryan (right) and Clarence Darrow (left) faced off on the issue of evolution in Dayton, Tennessee, in 1925. ***Government*** *What was the constitutional issue at the heart of the matter?*

## *Issues of Religion*

In addition to prohibition, an issue that highlighted the differences between urban and rural Americans was evolution. Specifically, should public schools teach the Biblical version of the creation of humans or the theory of evolution? The problem touched off a debate that continues to this day.

**Fundamentalism** Before the teaching of evolution became an issue, many Americans were already uneasy with changes in society. During the early part of the century, challenges to traditional beliefs came from several directions:

(1) Science and technology were taking a larger role in everyday life and thought.

(2) War and the widespread problems of modern society were causing more people to question whether God existed or took an active role in human affairs.

(3) Some scholars were saying that the Bible was a document written by humans and contained contradictions and even historical inaccuracies.

**Main Idea CONNECTIONS**

*What social changes of the early 1900s did some Americans find disturbing?*

In response to these challenges, religious traditionalists published a series of 12 pamphlets called *The Fundamentals.* They stated a set of beliefs that have since come to be called **fundamentalism.** In addition to traditional Christian ideas about Jesus Christ, fundamentalists argued that the Bible was inspired by God and cannot contain contradictions or errors. They declared that the Bible is literally true and that every story in it actually took place as described.

Fundamentalism gained tremendous attention in the 1920s. The most famous fundamentalist preacher of the times was Billy Sunday. His series of more than 300 revivals attracted an estimated total attendance of 100 million. Another popular preacher of the time was Aimee Semple McPherson. Founder of the Angelus Temple, she owned her own radio station and skillfully used the power of mass media in her work.

**Evolution and the Scopes Trial** Fundamentalists were deeply disturbed by several ideas that were gradually gaining acceptance. One of these, the theory of evolution, stated that human beings and all other living species developed over time from simple life forms.

Fundamentalists denounced the evolution theory, saying it contradicted the history of creation as stated in the Bible. They worked for the passage of laws to prevent public schools from teaching evolution.

When Tennessee passed such a ban, a science teacher named John T. Scopes challenged it as unconstitutional and decided to test the law in the courts. He asked a friend to file suit against him for teaching evolution. Thus began the case popularly known as the **Scopes trial.**

The case became a battle between two of the country's greatest lawyers. William Jennings Bryan, a fundamentalist and former presidential candidate, volunteered to prosecute Scopes.

Lawyer Clarence Darrow, agreeing with Scopes's view of the issue as a constitutional one, volunteered for the defense. Darrow had won fame for defending political and labor activists such as Eugene V. Debs.

The trial took place in the small town of Dayton, Tennessee, in the withering heat of July 1925. In this new era of mass media, journalists swarmed around the courthouse, telegraphing some 2 million words of reporting to their papers over the ten days of the trial. This was the first trial ever broadcast over American radio.

At one level, the case was a simple one. Scopes readily admitted he had taught the subject, and the jury found him guilty and fined him $100.† But there were more complex issues at stake, including the clash between modern beliefs and traditional values of the country.

The dramatic climax of the case came when Darrow put Bryan himself on the stand to testify as an expert on the Bible. Under Darrow's intense questioning, Bryan admitted that even he did not interpret all of the Bible literally.

Fundamentalists saw Bryan as a martyr for their cause, especially when, exhausted from the grueling battle, he died just a few days after the trial. Modernists saw Darrow as a defender of science and reason.

Although the trial was seen as a setback for fundamentalism, the movement remained active. In later decades it would grow in membership and strength.

## Racial Tensions

Another clash of the 1920s had to do with race. The Great Migration of African Americans to the North in the early 1900s had been triggered not only by the growth of jobs in the North, but also by an increase in violence against African Americans in the South. Sadly, many black migrants found that they could not escape prejudice by moving north.

**Violence against African Americans** In what became known as the "Red Summer," race riots erupted in about 25 cities nationwide during the summer of 1919. The bloodiest of the riots occurred in Chicago, where the African American population more than doubled between 1910 and 1920. This increase led to overcrowded neighborhoods and heightened tensions between blacks and whites.

***Why did racial tensions increase after World War I?***

The violence was touched off when a nine-year-old black boy, swimming at a beach on Lake Michigan, accidentally floated into a "whites only" area. Several whites threw stones at him, and the boy drowned. Furious blacks accused the whites of killing him, and fighting broke out.

The riot spread through the city. For 13 days, parts of Chicago were without law and order. By the end, some 23 African Americans and 15 whites were dead, another 537 people wounded, and 1,000 blacks left homeless. Similar violence broke out in 1919 in Omaha, Tulsa, and Washington, D.C.

Racial violence was also directed against individuals. During the 1920s, the lynchings of the Jim Crow era continued. Many of these new crimes were the work of an old enemy of racial harmony, the Ku Klux Klan.

***This 1920s Klan poster leaves no doubt about the Ku Klux Klan's view on immigration.***

**Revival of the Klan** During Reconstruction, President Grant's campaign against the Klan had largely eliminated it. However, in 1915 a former Methodist circuit preacher from Atlanta, Colonel William J. Simmons, revived the organization. By 1922, the Klan membership had grown to about 100,000. By 1924, it was roughly 4 million. The new Klan was no longer a southern organization. In fact, the state with the greatest number of Klansmen was Indiana.

During the early 1920s, Klan members carried out many crimes against African Americans, Catholics, Jews, immigrants, and others. They rode by night, beating, whipping, even killing their victims, terrorizing blacks and whites alike. Then, in 1925, the head of the Klan in Indiana was sentenced to life imprisonment for assaulting a girl who later poisoned herself. The nation was finally shocked into action, and police began to step up enforcement. By 1927, Klan activity had diminished once again.

† The Tennessee Supreme Court later threw out Scopes's fine on the grounds that it was too high. Thus the Scopes case could not be used to make an appeal to a higher court to test Tennessee's law against teaching evolution. The law remained in force until 1967, but no other teachers were prosecuted.

Marcus Garvey (right) is shown here at a Universal Negro Improvement Association equal rights parade. Although his Black Star project ended in disgrace, Garvey received a pardon from President Coolidge before completing his five-year jail sentence. ***Culture*** ***Why do you think Garvey sought to bolster self-esteem among African Americans?***

**Fighting Discrimination** Increasing violence against African Americans rallied the efforts of the National Association for the Advancement of Colored People (NAACP). During the 1920s, the NAACP worked in vain to pass federal anti-lynching laws. A proposed law passed the House of Representatives in 1922, but died in the Senate. Nevertheless, because of improved law enforcement at the state level, lynchings gradually decreased to ten per year in 1929.

During the 1920s, the NAACP also worked to protect African Americans' right to vote, but again it had only limited success. A Texas law establishing a separate primary election for whites was declared unconstitutional. Yet African Americans in the South still could not gain the political power they deserved in a true democracy.

**The Garvey Movement** Some African Americans, frustrated by continued violence and discrimination, dreamed of a new homeland where they could live in peace. The leader of this movement was an African American named Marcus Garvey.

Garvey had come to New York from his native Jamaica in 1916 to establish a new headquarters for his Universal Negro Improvement Association (UNIA). The UNIA sought to build up African Americans' self-respect and economic power. Its message of racial pride attracted a large number of followers.

Garvey urged African Americans to return to "Motherland Africa." He gathered $10 million for a steamship line (the "Black Star") that would take his followers back to the motherland. In 1925, however, Garvey was jailed on fraud charges, and the UNIA collapsed. Still, Garvey's ideas remained an inspiration to later "black pride" movements.

## SECTION 5 REVIEW

### Comprehension

1. *Key Terms* Define: (a) bootlegger; (b) speakeasy; (c) fundamentalism; (d) Scopes trial.
2. *Summarizing the Main Idea* Why did divisions emerge within American society during the 1920s?
3. *Organizing Information* Create a cause-and-effect chart on Prohibition.

### Critical Thinking

4. *Analyzing Time Lines* Refer to the time line at the start of the section. Which events do you think had a lasting impact on society, and which did not? Explain your answer.
5. *Making Inferences* How might the participation of African Americans in World War I have influenced the racial tensions that emerged just after the war?

### Writing Activity

6. *Writing an Expository Essay* From the perspective of a writer in the 1920s, write an essay that explains the key issues in the Scopes trial. Base your analysis on the facts in this section.

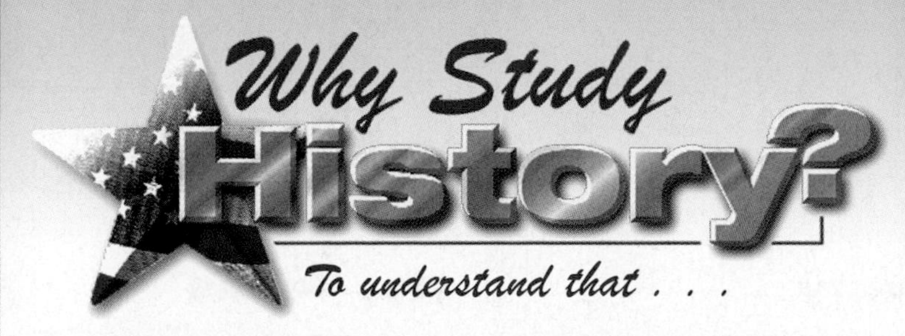


# The Generation Gap Is Not New

**Today, as in the 1920s, the American youth culture is markedly different from that of the older generation.**

Slang terms, clothing styles, musical tastes—these are areas in which young people traditionally set themselves apart from their parents and grandparents. To many older Americans, the pastimes and attitudes of youth are sad proof that the nation's morals have decayed. Yet a "generation gap" has divided older and younger people for centuries, and society has always managed to survive.

*Jazz record from the 1920s*

## The Impact Today

In the 1920s such trends as short skirts and jazz music troubled some Americans. Today an increasing number of Americans are disturbed by the rise in obscene language and sexual and violent images in popular music, movies, television, and the Internet. These aspects of youth culture have prompted calls for government, schools, and parents to regulate these undesirable influences.

Public and private institutions have heeded the call. For example, many school systems have decided to adopt dress codes or school uniforms to promote order and decrease violent behavior. Television networks have adopted a coding system that indicates the content of programs and their appropriateness for younger audiences.

How many Americans support actions such as these? A clear majority of those interviewed in one nationwide poll approved of greater restrictions on television programming, as well as on the lyrics to popular songs. A whopping 93 percent of interviewees favored stricter parental supervision of different forms of youth entertainment.

Some Americans, however, caution that restrictions on entertainment could go too far and become a form of censorship. These people often point out that, while every generation has its rebellions, most young people grow up to be responsible adults.

## The Impact on You

Ask five people in your community to evaluate the following statement: "Warning labels on popular music and television coding systems are needed to protect young people from harmful influences and ideas." Decide what you think. Then write an editorial for your school newspaper that explains your point of view. Your editorial should deal with the arguments raised by the five people you interviewed.

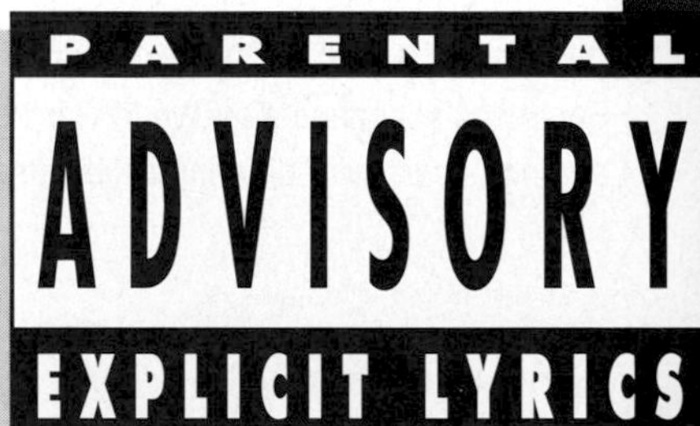


*Warning label placed on CDs with explicit lyrics*

# Chapter 11 Review

## Chapter Summary

The major concepts of Chapter 11 are presented below. See also ***Guide to the Essentials of American History*** or ***Interactive Student Tutorial CD-ROM,*** which contains interactive review activities, time lines, helpful hints, and test practice.

### *Reviewing the Main Ideas*

The 1920s was a decade of rapid business growth under the postwar laissez-faire policies of three Republican Presidents. The 1920s brought social change as well, including new freedoms for women, a blossoming of the arts, and the effects of Prohibition.

### *Section 1: A Republican Decade*

Republican administrations of the 1920s pursued pro-business economic policies and an isolationist foreign policy.

### *Section 2: A Business Boom*

During the 1920s, new products and Americans' power to purchase them grew rapidly, producing a decade of enormous business growth.

### *Section 3: Society in the 1920s*

The 1920s was a time of rapid social change, in which women, in particular, adopted new lifestyles and attitudes. Amid these changes many Americans admired heroes who embodied old-fashioned values.

### *Section 4: Mass Media and the Jazz Age*

Radio, movies, and jazz were some of the new forms of information, entertainment, and the arts that began in the 1920s. The decade was an especially creative period for music, art, and literature.

### *Section 5: Cultural Conflicts*

Rapid social change after World War I caused conflicts among people with differing beliefs and values.

Today, as in the 1920s, the American youth culture is markedly different from that of the older generation.

## Key Terms

Use each of the terms below in a sentence that shows how it relates to the chapter.

1. bootlegger
2. communism
3. Jazz Age
4. installment plan
5. fundamentalism
6. Teapot Dome scandal
7. flapper
8. assembly line
9. mass media

## Comprehension

1. (a) What events of 1919 caused the red scare? (b) How did the government respond?
2. (a) What events brought disgrace upon the Harding presidency? (b) How did Coolidge restore respect to the office?
3. How did a decade of Republican government affect the economy?
4. Describe the impact of Henry Ford on American business and society.
5. In what ways did the role of women change during the 1920s?
6. What types of demographic change occurred during the 1920s?
7. What was the Lost Generation? What trends in society did they find troubling?
8. What themes and experiences did the writers of the Harlem Renaissance explore?
9. What long-term effects did Prohibition produce?
10. What divisions in American society were reflected in the Scopes trial?

## Using Graphic Organizers

On a separate sheet of paper, copy the chart below. In each box write a sentence summarizing information from the chapter.

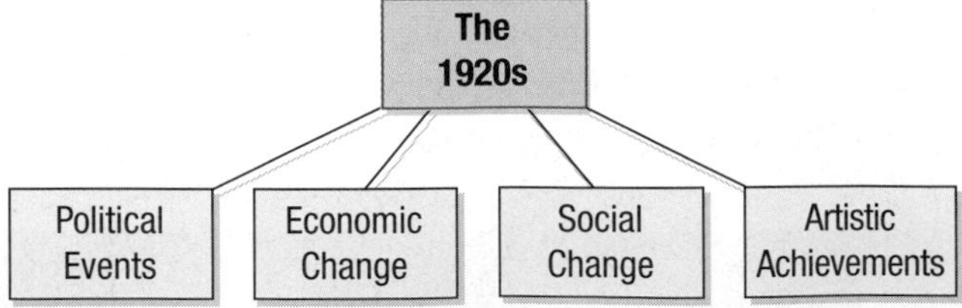

## Analyzing Political Cartoons ▶

1. This cartoon appeared in 1924. (a) Who was President in 1924? (b) What were the big news items regarding the presidential administration in 1924?
2. Describe the scene in the cartoon. What is it satirizing?
3. Why are Cabinet members for sale?

## Critical Thinking

1. ***Applying the Chapter Skill*** Turn to the vacuum cleaner ad on page 347. From what you know about the changing attitudes of young women of the 1920s, why might this ad have appealed to them?
2. ***Demonstrating Reasoned Judgment*** Explain the meaning of this statement: "For many African Americans, migration to the North was a mixed success."
3. ***Recognizing Ideologies*** What beliefs and fears helped fuel the red scare? Were those fears justified? Explain your reasoning.
4. ***Drawing Conclusions*** What connection might there have been between the mass media and the flapper image?

## INTERNET ACTIVITY

***For your portfolio:***
**WRITE AN ESSAY**

Access Prentice Hall's *America: Pathways to the Present* site at **www.Pathways.phschool.com** for the specific URL to complete the activity. Additional resources and related Web sites are also available.

Read about the cycles of nativism in American history and a Boston journalist's perspective on the continuing effects of the Sacco and Vanzetti trial. What factors contribute to nativism? What are the dangers of nativism? Write an essay exploring these questions, using the Sacco and Vanzetti case as an example.

## ANALYZING DOCUMENTS ◀ ▶ INTERPRETING DATA

Turn to the excerpt from the poem "First Fig" in Section 4.

1. Which of the following best expresses the meaning of the first line? (a) She feels bright. (b) She stays up all night. (c) She is religious. (d) The pace of her life is dangerously fast.
2. Which of the following best expresses the meaning of the last line? (a) Her lifestyle is exciting while it lasts. (b) She feels bright and lovely. (c) Her friends and foes approve of her lifestyle. (d) Her life is quiet.
3. ***Writing*** Why do you think the flappers thought of this poem as their motto? Why do think the writer herself disapproved of this interpretation?

## Connecting to Today

***Essay Writing*** Write an essay that addresses this statement: "The 1920s laid the foundation for today's society." Use examples from the economy and from society.

CHAPTER

# 12 Crash and Depression

## 1929–1933

## CHAPTER FOCUS

*This chapter examines the events leading to the crash of the stock market in 1929 and the economic disaster it unleashed: the Great Depression. The chapter looks at how the Depression took its toll and how Americans learned to cope with it.*

*The **Why Study History?** page at the end of this chapter explores the connection between investing in the stock market in 1929 and investing in it today.*

▲
**VIEWING HISTORY**
The effects of the Great Depression show on the weary faces of this homeless Oklahoma family.
*Economics* ***What evidence does this photo give of the depth of their poverty?***

| 1927 | 1928 | 1929 | 1929 | 1929 |
| --- | --- | --- | --- | --- |
| Coolidge vetoes farm relief bill | Hoover elected President | Home building falls by 25 percent | 200 companies own nearly half of all industry | In October, value of stocks climbs to $87 billion |

1927 — 1928 — 1929

# 1 The Economy in the Late 1920s

**SECTION PREVIEW**

**Objectives**

1. Explain why the economy appeared to be healthy in the 1920s.
2. Explain why, in reality, the economy was headed into danger.
3. *Key Terms* Define: welfare capitalism; speculation; buying on margin.

**Main Idea**

During the 1920s, rising wealth and a booming stock market gave Americans a false sense of faith in the economy. In fact, there were signs that the economy was in trouble.

**Reading Strategy**

*Outlining Information* Use the headings and subheadings in this section to help you create an outline. As you read, add two key facts under each subheading.

The mood of most Americans in the late 1920s was optimistic, and with good reason. Medical advances had greatly reduced deaths from whooping cough, diphtheria, and other serious diseases. Since 1900 the number of infant deaths had declined, and life expectancy had lengthened more than 10 years, to 59 years for men and 63 years for women.

The brightest hopes seemed to come from the economy. In his final message to Congress, President Calvin Coolidge said that the country could "regard the present with satisfaction and anticipate the future with optimism." His successor, Herbert Hoover, predicted that "poverty will be banished from this nation."

## Economy Appears Healthy

When Coolidge chose not to run in 1928, Hoover won easily, benefiting from years of prosperity under the Republicans. A self-made millionaire, Hoover was widely admired for the way he had organized food relief in Europe during and after World War I. He had also been an effective Secretary of Commerce for Presidents Harding and Coolidge. People expected that the good times would get even better under Hoover.

**"Wonderful Prosperity"** As Hoover took office, the United States economy seemed to be in fine shape. In 1925, the market value of all stocks was $27 billion. Over the next few years, it soared. In 1928 alone, stock values rose by almost $11.4 billion. Because the stock market was widely regarded as the nation's economic weathervane, *The New York Times* could describe the year as one "of unprecedented advance, of wonderful prosperity." By early October 1929, stock values hit $87 billion.

Working people seemed to have prospered in the post–World War I period. Since 1914, the value of workers' wages had risen more than 40 percent. Although certain industries were troubled, and some workers lost jobs to assembly-line machinery, unemployment averaged below 4 percent. Even critics of capitalism made optimistic predictions:

*During the 1920s, catalogs brimming with exciting new goods tempted consumers to buy on credit.*

This car advertisement from the late 1920s reflects the apparent prosperity and optimism of those years. ***Economics*** ***In what other ways was prosperity apparent in the late 1920s?***

> **AMERICAN VOICES** "Big business in America is producing what the Socialists held up as their goal: food, shelter and clothing for all. You will see it during the Hoover administration."
>
> *—Journalist Lincoln Steffens, 1928*

**"Everybody Ought to Be Rich"** People had unusually high confidence in the business world during the 1920s. For some, business success became almost a religion. One of the decade's best-selling books was *The Man Nobody Knows* (1925). Written by Bruce Barton, an advertising executive, it told the biblical story of Jesus' life in business terms. Barton portrayed Jesus as a managerial genius who "picked up twelve men [a reference to Jesus' 12 apostles, or followers] from the bottom ranks of business and forged them into an organization that conquered the world."

Similarly, Americans trusted the advice of corporate leaders such as John J. Raskob. In a 1929 article, "Everybody Ought to Be Rich," he stated that savings of only $15 a week over 20 years could bring a $400-a-month income from investments. "I am firm in my belief," Raskob said, "that anyone not only can be rich, but ought to be rich."

**Main Idea CONNECTIONS**

*Why did Americans have so much confidence in the economy in the 1920s?*

The three Republican Presidents of the 1920s equated the interests of the nation with the interests of business. Although people in the late 1920s were wildly buying stocks with borrowed money, the Hoover administration did little to discourage such borrowing.

**Welfare Capitalism** Following the violent labor strikes of 1919, the postwar economy stabilized, and during the 1920s organized labor lost members. To keep the unions weak, many companies launched strategies to meet some of their workers' needs without demands from unions. This new approach to labor relations was known as **welfare capitalism.** Employers raised wages and provided benefits such as paid vacations, health plans, and even English classes for recent immigrants.

## *Economic Danger Signs*

Despite the apparent prosperity, all was not well. Only later did many people recognize the warning signs of an unsound economy.

**Uneven Prosperity** Despite some stock market success stories, it was mainly the rich who got richer. Huge corporations rather than small businesses dominated industry. In 1929, 200 large companies controlled 49 percent of American industry.

Similarly, a small proportion of families held most of the nation's personal wealth. (See the graph on the next page.) In 1929, the richest Americans—24,000 families, or just 0.1 percent of the population—had incomes of more than $100,000. They also held 34 percent of the country's total savings.

By contrast, 71 percent of individuals and families earned less than $2,500 a year. Nearly 80 percent of all families had no savings. Many people earned so little that almost everyone in a family, including children, had to work just to get by.

**Buying on Credit** Another sign of trouble was an increase in personal debt. In the 1920s assembly-line production made consumer items more affordable and available. People bought radios, vacuum cleaners, refrigerators, and other exciting new products, whether or not they could afford them.

Traditionally, Americans feared debt and postponed buying goods until they had the cash to pay for them. Now, however, installment plans made expensive items irresistible.

**Playing the Stock Market** Fed by the optimism of the age, a "get-rich-quick" attitude prevailed during the 1920s. The dizzying climb of stock prices encouraged widespread **speculation,** the practice of making high-risk investments in hopes of getting a high gain.

Before World War I only the wealthy played the stock market. Now, the press reported stories of ordinary people who had made fortunes. Small investors entered the market, often with their life savings. To attract less-wealthy investors, stockbrokers encouraged a practice called **buying on margin.** It allowed investors to purchase a stock for only a fraction of its price (10 to 50 percent) and borrow the rest.

Brokers charged high interest and could demand payment of the loan at any time. But if the stock price went up, borrowers could sell at a price high enough to pay off loan and interest charges and still make money.

**Too Many Goods, Too Little Demand** By the late 1920s, the country's warehouses held piles of unbought consumer goods. Wages had risen, but people still could not afford to buy goods as fast as the assembly lines turned them out.

Although the stock market kept rising, overproduction caused some industries to slow in the late 1920s. The automobile industry, which had helped create American prosperity, slumped after 1925. Industries that depended on it—steel, rubber, and glass—also declined. Housing construction fell by 25 percent between 1928 and 1929.

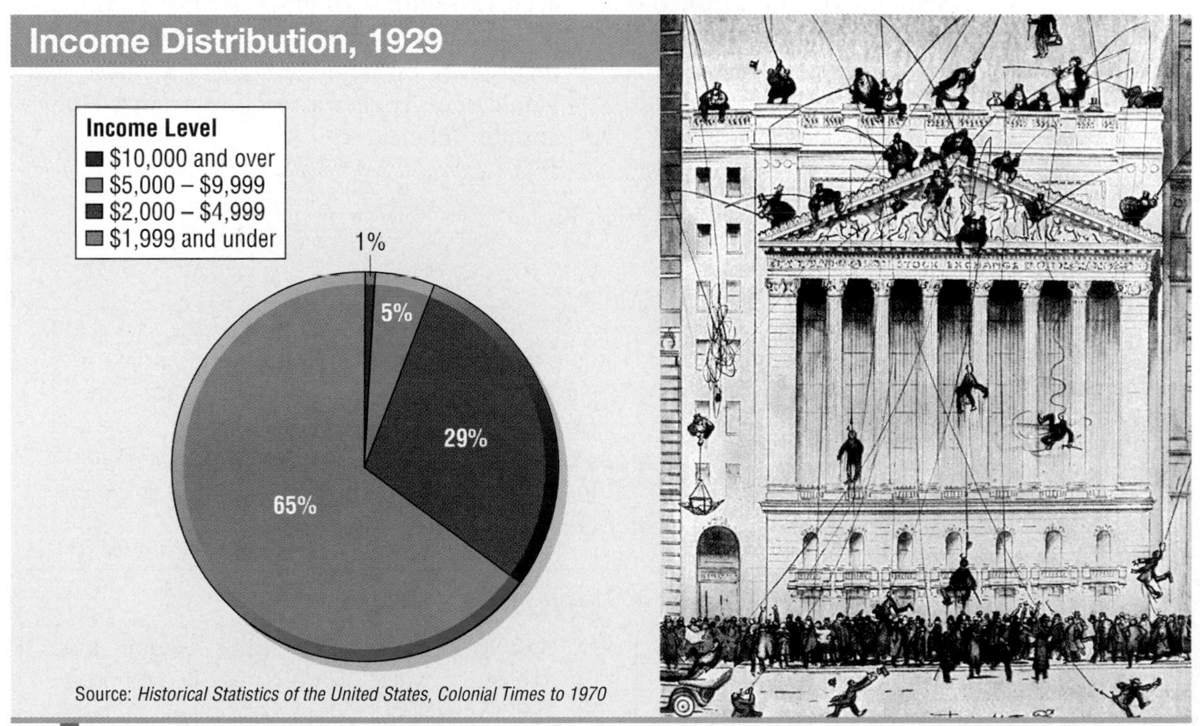


**Interpreting Graphs** The circle graph (left) shows how unevenly the country's wealth was distributed in the 1920s. At right, greedy stockbrokers fish for new clients from the top of the New York Stock Exchange. ***Economics*** *What percentage of American families earned less than $2,000 a year in 1929?*

Farm families faced hard times in the 1920s. Many had to watch as their homes, land, and animals were sold at auction. ***Economics*** ***Why were farmers struggling economically?***

**Trouble for Farmers** For some sectors of the farm economy, the 1920s brought not prosperity but devastation. Farm prices had stayed high during the war and just afterward. But when the wartime demand ended, prices, especially for wheat and cotton, plummeted. During the good times, many farmers had purchased the new tractors and other machinery now available. This allowed them to put more land under cultivation, so they bought more land as well.

Falling farm prices made farmers unable to repay their debts for land and machinery. Rural banks suffered when loans were not repaid, and about 6,000 banks went out of business.

Congress responded with the McNary-Haugen farm relief bill, a measure designed to increase the price farmers received for their crops. Congress passed the bill twice, in 1927 and 1928, but each time President Coolidge vetoed it, believing that it was not the government's job to provide such assistance.

Farmers continued to suffer. "We were in the Depression before 1929, we just didn't call it that," recalled a rural Tennessean.

**Trouble for Workers** Life remained exceedingly hard for many factory workers as well. While companies grew wealthy, most laborers still worked long hours for low wages. Conditions were especially bad in coal mines and southern textile mills. In the rayon mills of Elizabethton, Tennessee, for instance, women worked 56-hour weeks, earning 16 to 18 cents an hour—about $10 a week.

To some observers, these factors—uneven wealth, rising debt, stock speculation, overproduction, and the hardships of farmers and workers—clearly signaled trouble in the economy. In 1928, Belle Moskowitz, who had managed Al Smith's losing presidential campaign that year, predicted that "growing unemployment, business depression, or some false step" would soon trigger a reaction against Hoover and his policies.

## SECTION 1 REVIEW

### Comprehension

1. *Key Terms* Define: (a) welfare capitalism; (b) speculation; (c) buying on margin.
2. *Summarizing the Main Idea* Why did Americans unwisely trust the economy in the 1920s?
3. *Organizing Information* Create a web diagram to show the reasons that Americans in the 1920s had confidence in the health of the economy.

### Critical Thinking

4. *Analyzing Time Lines* Review the time line at the start of this section. (a) Which entries indicate a booming economy? (b) Which indicate signs of trouble? Explain your reasoning. *Note:* Some may fit both (a) and (b).
5. *Identifying Supporting Details* List five signs that the economy was in danger. Explain your choices.

### Writing Activity

6. *Writing a Persuasive Essay* Assume the role of the writer of a business column in a 1920s newspaper. Write an essay to persuade your readers either (a) to take advantage of the money-making opportunities in the booming economy, or (b) to show caution in their investments and avoid speculation.

| 1929 | 1929 | 1929 | 1931 | 1932 | 1933 |
|---|---|---|---|---|---|
| (Sept. 3) Stock market reaches all-time high of 381 points | (Oct. 24) Black Thursday | (Oct. 29) Black Tuesday | Ford shuts down Detroit factories | One fourth of work force is unemployed | Money in 9 million savings accounts has been wiped out |

1929 1930 1931 1932 1933

# 2 The Stock Market Crash

## SECTION PREVIEW

### Objectives

1. Outline the key events of the stock market's Great Crash of 1929.
2. Analyze the effects of the Crash.
3. List the main causes of the Great Depression.
4. *Key Terms* Define: Dow Jones Industrial Average; Black Tuesday; Great Crash; business cycle; Great Depression; Gross National Product (GNP).

### Main Idea

In October 1929 panic selling caused the United States stock market to crash. The crash led to a worldwide economic crisis called the Great Depression.

### Reading Strategy

*Arranging Events in Order* Copy the time line above on a separate sheet of paper. As you read, add more information to the time line. Make notes on how one event led to the next.

In early 1928 the **Dow Jones Industrial Average,** an average of stock prices of major industries, had climbed to 191. By Hoover's inauguration day, March 4, 1929, it had risen another 122 points. On September 3, the Dow Jones Average reached an all-time high of 381.

## The Market Crashes

The rising stock market dominated the news. Keeping track of prices became almost as popular as counting Babe Ruth's home runs. Eager, nervous investors filled brokerage houses to catch the latest news coming in on the ticker tape. Prices for many stocks soared far above their real value in terms of the company's earnings and assets.

**Black Thursday** After the peak in September, stock prices fell slowly. Some brokers began to call in loans, but others continued to lend even more. One bank official assured the nervous public: "Although in some cases speculation has gone too far, . . . the markets generally are now in a healthy condition."

When the stock market closed on Wednesday, October 23, the Dow Jones average had dropped 21 points in an hour. The next day, Thursday, October 24, worried investors began to sell, and stock prices fell. Investors who had bought General Electric stock at $400 a share sold it for $283 a share.

Ticker-tape machines delivered investors both good and bad news about their stocks.

Again, business and political leaders told the country not to worry. Another banking executive said that only a nation as rich as the United States could "withstand the shock of a $3 billion paper loss on the Stock Exchange in a single day without serious effects to the average citizen." Hoover maintained that the nation's business "is on a sound and prosperous basis."

**Black Tuesday** To stop the panic, a group of bankers pooled their money to buy stock. This action stabilized prices, but only for a few days.

**From Riches to Ruin** It took time for people to recognize the extent of the disaster caused by the Crash. One wealthy Bostonian who lost heavily in the market wrote in his diary, "The profit in my little book melted yesterday to seven thousand. It is probably nil [nothing] today. . . . My dreams of a million—where are they?"

For people whose entire wealth did not depend on the stock market, life went on much as before, with perhaps a few cutbacks. Others, including wealthy families, lost everything. Brokers and banks called in their loans, but people did not have cash to pay them.

As stock market prices fell, the ticker tape could not report market activity fast enough. Nervous investors crowded into Wall Street, hoping to hear the latest news. ***Economics*** ***Why did President Hoover believe the economy could weather the stock market crash?***

## ECONOMICS CONCEPTS

***business cycle:*** ***the periodic growth and contraction of a nation's economy***

- **The Historical Context:** The Crash of 1929 brought an abrupt end to the economic expansion of the 1920s and ushered in the Great Depression. Following the Crash, political leaders debated whether to fight the Depression through higher government spending or to rely on the natural operation of the business cycle to restore prosperity.
- **The Concept Today:** The American economy continues to alternate between periods of higher growth and periods of slower growth, or contraction. The federal government, through its policies on taxing, spending, and the money supply, seeks to prevent shocks to the economy such as the Crash of 1929.

By Monday prices were falling again. Investors all over the country raced to get their money out of the stock market. On October 29, known as **Black Tuesday,** a record 16.4 million shares were sold, compared with the average 4 million to 8 million shares a day earlier in the year.

This collapse of the stock market is known as the **Great Crash.** Despite efforts to halt it, the Crash continued beyond Black Tuesday. By November 13, the Dow Jones average had fallen from its September high of 381 to 198.7. Overall losses totaled $30 billion. The Great Crash was part of the nation's **business cycle,** periods in which the economy grows, then contracts. (See the Economics Concepts feature above.)

## *The Crash Affects Millions*

By 1929, about 4 million people out of a population of 120 million had invested in the stock market. They were the first to suffer from the Crash, but it soon affected millions who had never owned a single share of stock.

The Crash triggered a much wider, long-term crisis called the **Great Depression,** a severe economic decline that lasted from 1929 until the United States' entry into World War II in 1941. The Great Depression was felt throughout the United States, causing millions of Americans to lose their jobs, farms, and homes. The Depression had a ripple effect, producing economic turmoil throughout the world for years.

**Impact on Workers and Farmers** As income and profits fell, American factories began to close. Thousands of workers lost their jobs or had their pay cut. In August 1931 Henry Ford shut down his Detroit automobile factories, putting at least 75,000 people out of work.

In some European countries, workers had government unemployment insurance, but the United States had no such program. By 1932 more than 12 million people were unemployed, about a quarter of the labor force (see graph on the next page). Others worked only part-time or had their wages cut. The **Gross National Product (GNP)**—the total value of goods and services a country produces annually—was $103 billion in 1929. By 1933 it was only $56 billion.

## Economic Impact of the Great Depression

Source: *Historical Statistics of the United States, Colonial Times to 1970*

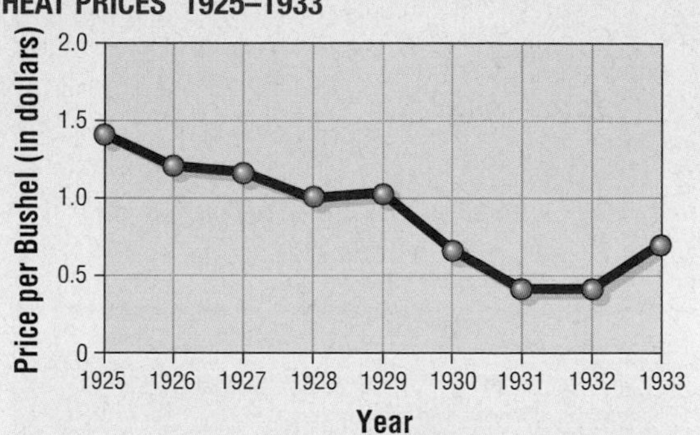


Source: *Historical Statistics of the United States, Colonial Times to 1970*

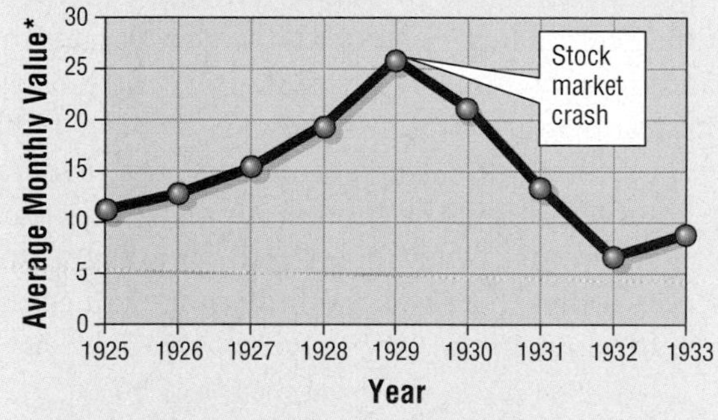


*Based on Standard and Poor's index of common stocks
Source: *Historical Statistics of the United States, Colonial Times to 1970*

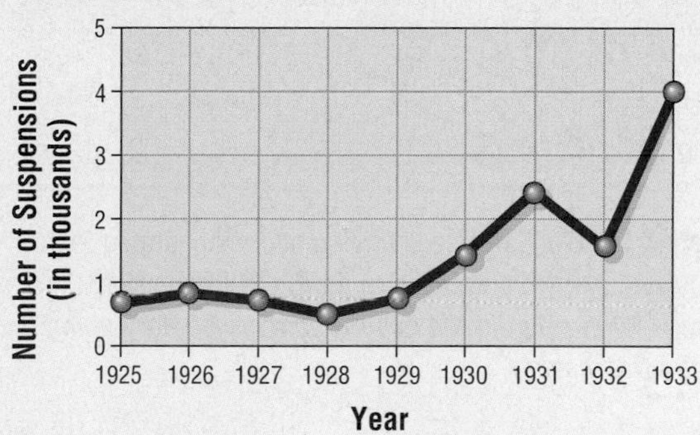


Source: *Historical Statistics of the United States, Colonial Times to 1970*

**Interpreting Graphs** The stock market crash caused a series of economic disasters. It hastened the fall of farm prices, added millions of people to the ranks of the unemployed, and forced the government to suspend the activity of thousands of banks. ***Economics* *Roughly how many workers became unemployed between 1929 and 1933?***

The effects of the Crash spread. Restaurants and other small businesses closed because customers could no longer afford to go to them. Once-wealthy families dismissed household workers. Farm prices, already low, fell even more, bringing final disaster to many families. In 1929, a bushel of wheat had sold for $1.04; in 1932 it brought a mere 38 cents. (See graph above.) Cotton dropped from 17 to 6.5 cents a pound.

**Banks Close** Unpaid farm loans already had ruined many rural banks. Now city banks were in trouble. Banks exist on the interest they earn from lending out their deposits. They assume that not everyone will claim their deposits at once. After the stock market crash, people with loans to repay as well as nervous depositors rushed to withdraw their money.

Thousands of banks closed their doors when they could not return their depositors' money. In just a few years, more than 5,500 banks failed. By 1933, the money from 9 million savings accounts had vanished.

**Impact on the World** By the 1930s, international banking, manufacturing, and trade had made nations interdependent. When the world's leading economy fell, the global economic system began to crumble.

After World War I, the United States had insisted that France and Britain, its wartime allies, repay their war debts. At the same time, Congress kept import taxes high, making it hard for European nations to sell goods in the United States. With economies weakened by the war and little chance of selling goods in the United States, the Allies had to rely on Germany's reparations payments for income.

As long as United States companies invested in Germany, reparations payments continued. But with the Depression, investments fell off. German banks failed, Germany suspended reparations, and the Allies in turn stopped

## CAUSE AND EFFECT: The Great Depression

**CAUSES**

- *The 1920s economy is out of balance.*
- *Americans are increasingly in debt.*
- *Speculation is on the rise.*
- *Overproduction slows industrial growth.*
- *The federal government introduces a tight-money policy in order to control credit.*
- *The stock market crashes in October 1929.*

**THE GREAT DEPRESSION**

**EFFECTS**

- *Millions of workers lose their jobs.*
- *Gross National Product falls dramatically.*
- *Many banks fail.*
- *Increased poverty leads to health and social problems.*
- *Global economy suffers.*

**Interpreting Charts** Carefree spending and exaggerated faith in the nation's economy contributed to the Great Depression. ***Economics* What role did the government's monetary policy play in the Depression?**

paying their debts. Europeans no longer could afford to buy American-made goods. Thus the American stock market crash started a downward cycle in the global economy.

## Causes of the Depression

The stock market crash of 1929, though devastating to investors, was only the final push that toppled the fragile structure of the American economy. Deeper problems were the real underlying causes of the Great Depression.

**Overspeculation** During the 1920s, speculators bought stocks with borrowed money, then pledged those stocks as collateral to buy more stocks. *Collateral* is an item of value that a borrower agrees to forfeit to the lender if the borrower cannot repay a loan. Brokers' loans went from under $5 million in mid-1928 to $850 million in September 1929. The stock market boom was based on borrowed money and optimism instead of real value.

**Government Policies** Mistakes in monetary policy were also to blame. During the 1920s the Federal Reserve system, which regulates the amount of money in circulation, cut interest rates to spur economic growth. Then in 1929, worried about overspeculation, the Federal Reserve limited the money supply to discourage lending. After the Crash, however, this meant that there was too little money in circulation to help the economy recover.

**An Unstable Economy** Overall, the seemingly prosperous economy lacked a firm base. National wealth was unevenly distributed, with the most money in the hands of a few families who tended to save or invest rather than buy goods. Industry produced more goods than most consumers wanted or could afford. Farmers and many workers had not shared in the economic boom. The unevenness of the 1920s prosperity made rapid recovery impossible.

## SECTION 2 REVIEW

### Comprehension

1. *Key Terms* Define: (a) Dow Jones Industrial Average; (b) Black Tuesday; (c) Great Crash; (d) business cycle; (e) Great Depression; (f) Gross National Product.
2. *Summarizing the Main Idea* What were the causes and effects of the stock market crash of 1929?
3. *Organizing Information* Use the information in the four charts on the previous page to create a web diagram. Show the effects of the Depression on unemployment, wheat prices, stock prices, and bank closings.

### Critical Thinking

4. *Analyzing Time Lines* Review the time line at the start of this section. Find examples of the financial impact and the social impact of the Great Crash of 1929.
5. *Analyzing Cause and Effect* Why do you think the Great Depression had such a huge impact on economies in other countries?

### Writing Activity

6. *Writing an Expository Essay* It is the day after Black Tuesday. Write a newspaper article explaining to readers what happened to the economy in the past week.

| 1930s | 1931 | 1931 | 1932 | 1935 |
|---|---|---|---|---|
| *Dust storms ruin farms in the Great Plains* | *Scottsboro* | *Homeless in New York City number about 15,000* | *About 56 percent of African Americans are unemployed* | *Dorothea Lange begins project to photograph migrant farmers* |

**1930 1931 1932 1933 1934 1935**

# 3 Social Effects of the Depression

**SECTION PREVIEW**

### Objectives

1. Describe the spread of poverty during the Great Depression.
2. Identify Dorothea Lange.
3. Define the social problems caused by poverty in the 1930s and explain how people struggled to survive.
4. *Key Terms* Define: Hooverville; Dust Bowl.

### Main Idea

Most people were not immediately affected by the 1929 stock market crash. But by the early 1930s, wage cuts and growing unemployment brought widespread suffering and discrimination.

### Reading Strategy

*Reinforcing Main Ideas* As you read, list examples of how the Great Depression affected different parts of American society.

Not everyone felt the impact of the Great Crash immediately. Many Americans thought the Depression that followed would not last. For them, reality hit in 1931 or 1932.

As hard times spread to all levels of society, a song from a 1932 Broadway revue became a theme song of the times:

**AMERICAN VOICES** "Once I built a railroad, made it run,
Made it race against time.
Once I built a railroad, now it's done.
Brother, can you spare a dime?"

## Poverty Spreads

Imagine that the bank where you had a savings account suddenly closed. Your money was gone. Or your parents lost their jobs and could not pay the rent or mortgage. One day you came home to find your furniture on the sidewalk—you had been evicted.

People at all levels of society faced these situations. Professionals and white-collar workers, who had felt more secure than laborers, suddenly were laid off with no prospects of finding another job. Those whose savings disappeared found it hard to understand why banks no longer had the money they had deposited for safekeeping.

**"Hoovervilles"** The hardest hit were those at the bottom of the economic ladder. Some unemployed laborers, unable to pay their rent, moved in with relatives. Others drifted. In 1931, census takers estimated the homeless in New York City alone at 15,000.

Homeless people sometimes built shanty towns, with shacks of tar paper, cardboard, or scrap material. These shelters of the homeless came to be called **Hoovervilles,** mocking the President, whom people blamed for the crisis.

A woman living in Oklahoma visited one Hooverville: "Here were all these people living in old, rusted-out car bodies," she noted. "There were people living in shacks made of orange crates. One family with a whole lot of kids were living in a piano box."

*The number of people without jobs rose dramatically after the Crash.*

Makeshift huts served as homes for the homeless and unemployed in this New York City Hooverville.
***Economics*** *What group of people was hardest hit by the Depression?*

**Farm Distress** Farm families suffered as low food prices cut their income. When they could not pay their mortgages, they lost their farms to the banks, which sold them at auction. In the South, landowners expelled tenant farmers and sharecroppers. In protest against low farm prices, farmers dumped thousands of gallons of milk and destroyed other crops. These desperate actions shocked a hungry nation.

**The Dust Bowl** For thousands of farm families in the Midwest, the harsh conditions of the Depression were made even more extreme by another major crisis of the decade. This one was not economic, but environmental. It was the **Dust Bowl,** a region in the Great Plains where drought and dust storms took place for much of the 1930s. (See the Geography and History feature following this section.)

Low farm prices and terrible weather caused many families to sell their farms or see them taken away. More than 440,000 people left Oklahoma during the 1930s. Nearly 300,000 people left Kansas. Thousands of families in Oklahoma, Texas, Kansas, and other southwestern Plains states migrated to California. Many found work on California's farms as laborers. About 100,000 of the Dust Bowl migrants headed to cities, such as Los Angeles, San Francisco, and San Diego.

One woman was there to witness their arrival, and to tell their story to the rest of America. She was photographer Dorothea Lange.

## *Dorothea Lange*

"The camera is an instrument that teaches people how to see without a camera," said photographer Dorothea Lange. In the 1930s and for all time, Lange taught the nation to see the realities of the Depression in the faces of suffering Americans.

Born in New Jersey in 1895, Lange decided at a young age to be a photographer. In 1918 Lange opened a portrait studio in San Francisco and did a prosperous business photographing wealthy clients.

Beyond the windows of her studio, she could see the spreading effects of the Depression: jobless men in worn-out shoes; hungry babies; desperate mothers. She thought about the vast difference "between what I was working on in the printing frames [in the studio] and what was going on in the street."

So she took to the streets, becoming a photojournalist of sorts, long before there was such a term. Lange drew on her experience in making portraits. She could put her subjects at ease, working quietly and respectfully, in the bread lines and the soup kitchens and along the waterfronts.

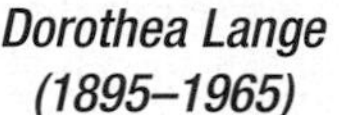
*Dorothea Lange (1895–1965)*

Lange's first exhibition, in 1934, landed her an assignment to photograph the hundreds of migrant workers streaming into California from the Dust Bowl. Lange's photographs showed the world the desperation and bravery of whole families reduced to picking peas in the sun and sleeping in cars or makeshift shelters.

The pictures stirred public attention and helped win aid for the workers. Lange's work also captured the attention of the Farm Security Administration (FSA), an agency set up by Hoover's successor, President Franklin Delano Roosevelt, to help farmers recover from the Depression. In 1935 Lange became one of several photographers hired by the FSA to document the lives of migrant farmers.

Lange worked for the FSA until 1939. Her most famous photograph, "Migrant Mother" (1936), shown on the Unit opener, has become a symbol of the Depression. The face of the undernourished mother displays a numbness to her destitute surroundings in a peapickers' camp; a profound worry for her shy children who huddle around her; and yet, a certain determination to pull through it all.

"She told me her age, that she was thirty-two," Lange recalled. "She said that they had been living on frozen vegetables from the surrounding fields and the birds that the children killed. She had just sold the tires from her car to buy food. There she sat in that lean-to tent with her children huddled around her, and seemed to know that my pictures might help her. . . ."

Lange's work helped bring about the creation of government migrant camps. Her work also inspired John Steinbeck's Depression-era novel *The Grapes of Wrath.*

Lange went on to document the sufferings and mistreatment of other Americans until her death in 1965. But she will be forever linked in people's minds to the 1930s, and the human courage that she made a part of the nation's permanent record. ■

## *Poverty Strains Society*

As the Depression wore on, it took a serious physical and psychological toll on the entire nation. Unemployment and fear of losing a job caused great anxiety. People became depressed; many considered suicide, and some did take their own lives.

**Impact on Health** "No one has starved," President Hoover declared, but some did, and thousands more went hungry. Impoverished people who could not afford food or shelter got sick more easily. Children suffered most from the long-term effects of poor diet and inadequate medical care.

"All last winter we never had a fire except about once a day when Mother used to cook some mush or something," one homeless boy recalled. "When the kids were cold they went to bed. I quit high school, of course."

"White Angel Breadline" is one of Dorothea Lange's most famous photographs. ***Culture*** ***What effect did her photographs have on the general public?***

Poverty was especially hard on sharecroppers in the South who had to live in improvised camps after being evicted from their farms by landowners. ***Economics* How did increased poverty lead to a decline in health?**

In the country, people grew food and ate berries and other wild plants. In cities, they sold apples and pencils, begged for money to buy food, and fought over the contents of restaurant garbage cans. Families who had land planted "relief gardens" to feed themselves or to barter food for other items.

**Stresses on Families** Living conditions declined as families moved in together, crowding into small houses or apartments. The divorce rate dropped because people could not afford separate households. People gave up even small pleasures like an ice cream cone or a movie ticket.

Men who had lost jobs or investments often felt like failures because they could no longer provide for their families. If their wives or children were working, men thought their own status had fallen. Many were embarrassed to be seen at home during normal work hours. They were ashamed to ask friends for help.

Women faced other problems. Those who depended on a husband's paycheck worried about feeding their hungry children. Working women were accused of taking jobs away from men.

Even in the better times of the 1920s, Henry Ford had fired married women. "We do not employ married women whose husbands have jobs," he explained. In the Depression, this practice became common. In 1931, the American Federation of Labor endorsed it. Most school districts would not hire married women teachers, and many fired those who got married.

Many women continued to find work, however, because poor-paying jobs such as domestic service, typing, and nursing were considered "women's work." The greatest job losses of the Depression were in industry and other areas that had seldom hired women.

**Discrimination Increases** Hard economic times put groups of Americans in competition with one another for a shrinking number of jobs. This produced a general rise in suspicions and hostilities against minorities. African Americans, Hispanics, and in the West, Asian Americans, all suffered as white laborers began to demand the low-paying jobs typically filled by these minorities.

African Americans continued to leave the South, although not as many as in the 1920s. They had jobs such as janitors or baggage carriers in northern cities, but soon lost even those jobs to whites. Black unemployment soared—about 56 percent of black Americans were out of work in 1932. Photographer Gordon Parks, who rode the trains to Harlem, later wrote:

**AMERICAN VOICES** **"To most blacks who had flocked in from all over the land, the struggle to survive was savage. Poverty coiled around them and me with merciless fingers."**

—*Photographer Gordon Parks*

Because relief programs discriminated against African Americans, black churches and organizations like the National Urban League gave private help. The followers of a Harlem evangelist known as Father Divine opened soup kitchens that fed thousands every day.

Discrimination increased for African Americans in the South. Some white southerners declared openly that blacks had no right to a job if whites were out of work. African Americans were denied civil rights such as access to education, voting, and health care. Lynchings increased.

Hispanics and Asian-Americans lost not only their jobs but also their country. Thousands were deported—even those born in America.

The justice system often ignored the rights of minority Americans. In March 1931, near Scottsboro, Alabama, nine black youths who had been riding the rails were arrested and accused of raping two white women on the train. Without being given the chance to hire a defense lawyer, eight of the nine were quickly convicted by an all-white jury and sentenced to die.

The case of the "Scottsboro boys" was taken up, and sometimes exploited, by northern groups, most notably the Communist party. The party helped supply legal defense and organized demonstrations, which, in the end, helped overturn the convictions.

*"If they come to take my farm, I'm going to fight. I'd rather be killed outright than die by starvation," said one Depression-era farmer. Although farm families were hard hit by the Depression, the fighting spirit represented by this quotation was seen across the country.*

## *Stories of Survival*

A generation of Americans would live to tell their grandchildren how they survived the Depression. Wilson Ledford first felt the effects of the Depression in March 1930 when he was 15, living in Chattanooga, Tennessee, with his mother and younger sister. Ledford looked after the family horse and cow, chopped wood for the fireplace, tended the garden that provided family food, and raised corn to feed the animals:

**AMERICAN VOICES** **"We had to raise most of what we ate since money was so scarce. . . . Sometimes I plowed for other people when I could get the work. . . . I got 15 cents an hour for plowing, and I furnished the horse and plow."**

—*Wilson Ledford*

Nothing was wasted. Ledford's mother kept chickens and traded eggs at the store for things they could not raise. Overalls cost 98 cents; shoes were $2. She bought a pig for $3 and raised it for meat, and made jelly from wild blackberries. Despite the family's own poverty, she gave extra milk and butter to "some poor people, a woman with three small children who lived in a one-room shack with a dirt floor."

Ledford never got to high school, "as survival was more important." In the summers of 1932 and 1933, Ledford hauled ice, working "12 hours a day, six days a week, and made $3.00 a week."

Later Ledford bought a truck to haul coal, cotton, and oranges, then worked nights in a woolen mill while carrying ice during the day. Finally, "I got a call from Chickamauga Dam and I went to work there. That was a good job working on the dam. I made 60 cents an hour. Times were better by then, but did not start booming until World War II started."

## SECTION 3 REVIEW

### Comprehension

1. ***Key Terms*** Define: (a) Hooverville; (b) Dust Bowl.
2. ***Summarizing the Main Idea*** How did the effects of the Great Crash widen into a deeper economic crisis?
3. ***Organizing Information*** Create a cause-and-effect chart showing the impact of poverty on Americans.

### Critical Thinking

4. ***Analyzing Time Lines*** Review the time line at the start of the section. Choose two items and explain how they were related to the Great Depression.
5. ***Analyzing Primary Sources*** In your own words, rewrite the American Voices quotation by photographer Gordon Parks.

### Writing Activity

6. ***Writing an Expository Essay*** In what ways was Dorothea Lange important to her time and to people in future generations? Write an essay addressing this question. Include supporting details from this section.

# The Dust Bowl

*The geographic theme of regions examines the characteristics that set one area apart from others. Between 1933 and 1940, so much earth blew out of the central and southern Great Plains that the region became known as the Dust Bowl. What factors contributed to this environmental disaster?*

A migrant worker and her children

The Great Plains is called "America's breadbasket." Deep, fertile soils, a long growing season, and flat land give it its farming advantage. But the region has always experienced severe weather. Hot and humid tropical air masses come from the Gulf of Mexico. Cold polar air masses rush southward from above the Arctic Circle. When these air masses collide, powerful storms with fierce updrafts are created.

The complex root systems of the grasslands had protected the land from the weather. But as you will see, drought and human interaction during the 1930s created a near disaster.

**The drought and winds persisted for more than seven years, bringing ruin to farmers.**

### Farmers Plow the Plains

It was the dryness of the region that early settlers noticed first. For this reason, maps in the early 1800s referred to the Great Plains as the Great American Desert. By the late 1800s, however, farmers discovered an important truth about the Great American Desert. When there was water, the Great Plains was one of the world's best farming regions.

The soil of the Great Plains looked promising, but early farmers in the region faced a major obstacle. The soil was protected by a thick layer of grasses with roots that were difficult to cut. Breaking the roots required expensive steel plows and months of hard labor. Yet, from the time that hard winter wheat was first introduced in central Kansas in the mid-1870s, farmers in the plains sank their plow blades into the sod and turned it over to make wheat fields.

### Wheat Replaces Grassland

In the early years of the twentieth century, wheat brought good prices, and farmers continually increased the acres of plowed land by getting rid of native grasses. In 1917 prices rose with the great demand caused by World War I. The price increases stimulated an even greater rush to plow more land to grow wheat. "Plant more wheat! Wheat will win the war!" was the slogan. By 1919, farmers had plowed under nearly 4 million acres of grassland. Though the war was over, the big plow-up continued.

It was new technology that allowed so much land to be plowed. Plowing with tractors allowed farmers to turn over far more acres in a day than they ever could have without those machines. When prices for wheat began to fall in the early 1920s, farmers responded by growing even more wheat. In the five years between 1925 and 1930 alone, more than 5 million additional acres of grassland disappeared,

## The Dust Bowl

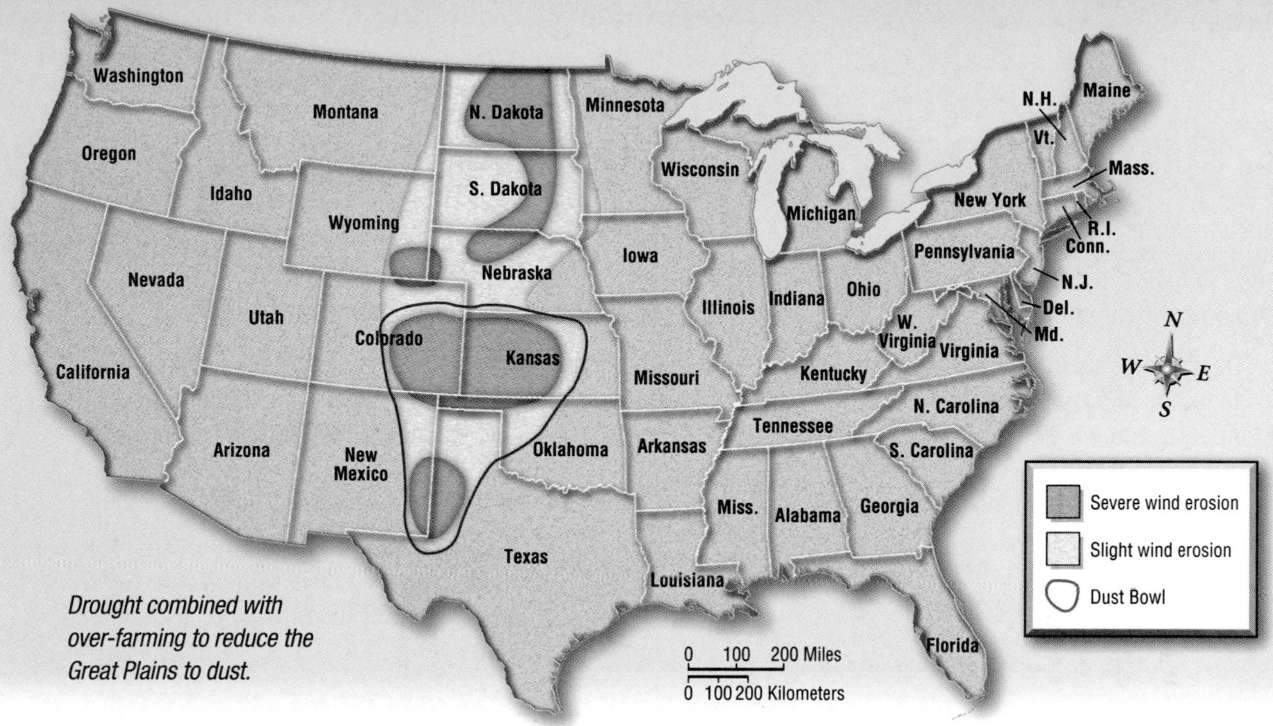


*Drought combined with over-farming to reduce the Great Plains to dust.*

converted to wheat fields by the relentless plow blades. But this conversion came with a cost.

### *Causes of Dust Storms*

In the early 1930s, the dust storms began. Farmers said they were the result of the severe drought that would last through the decade. While drought was a major factor in creating the Dust Bowl, it was not the only factor. Farming practices also contributed.

As long as there was a thick layer of prairie grasses to protect the topsoil, severe weather could not harm the land. However, when farmers plowed the land, they stripped the soil of its natural protection. Winds picked up the dark, nutrient-rich topsoil and carried it eastward, sometimes for hundreds of miles, leaving behind barren, shifting dunes of grit and sand. The map above shows the extent of soil erosion across the plains.

### *People Lose their Farms*

The most severe storms of the dry years were called "black blizzards." Time after time, dirt was sucked up and dropped by the ton over states and cities to the east. The dirt darkened the sky in New York City and Washington, D.C. It stained the snows of New England red and dropped on ships hundreds of miles off the Atlantic Coast. The drought and winds persisted for more than seven years, bringing ruin to farmers.

The combination of terrible weather and low prices for farm products caused about 60 percent of Dust Bowl families to lose their farms. Relief did not come until the early 1940s, when the rains finally arrived and World War II drove farm prices up.

**1.** (a) What features of land and climate make the Great Plains a good farming region? (b) What features make it a poor farming region?

**2.** What caused the black blizzards of the 1930s?

#### Themes in Geography

**3.** *Regions* How did farmers destroy the region's natural protection against severe weather?

**1931** Al Capone convicted of tax evasion

**1931** Empire State Building, world's tallest, opens

**1933** Twenty-first Amendment repeals Prohibition

**1933** Former President Coolidge dies

1931 | 1932 | 1933

# 4 Surviving the Great Depression

## SECTION PREVIEW

### Objectives

1. Describe ways in which Americans pulled together to survive the Depression.
2. Analyze the signs of social change in the 1930s.
3. *Key Term* Define: Twenty-first Amendment.

### Main Idea

Americans survived the Great Depression with determination and even humor. They helped one another, looked for solutions, and waited for the hard times to pass.

### Reading Strategy

*Problem Solving* If you had lived during the Depression, what might you have done to get by? As you read, make a list of the strategies that helped Americans to survive.

*This "kind-hearted woman" symbol drawn on a fence post meant that the family inside would offer handouts to a needy passer-by.*

No one who lived through the Great Depression ever forgot it. Long after the economy rebounded, the "Depression generation," even those who recovered enough to live a very comfortable life, would continue to pinch pennies as if financial ruin were just around the corner. Many Americans avoided buying on credit, instead saving for years to pay cash for needed items. Others even stuffed money under their mattresses rather than trust their life savings to banks.

## Americans Pull Together

Not all the memories of the Depression were bad or despairing, as one reporter noted:

> **"The great majority of Americans may be depressed. They may not be well pleased with the way business and government have been carried on, and they may not be at all sure that they know exactly how to remedy the trouble. They may be feeling dispirited. But there is one thing they are not, and that is—beaten."**
>
> —*Journalist Gerald W. Johnson, 1932*

People pulled together to help each other. Tenant groups formed to protest rent increases and evictions. In some farm communities, people agreed to keep bids low when foreclosed farms were auctioned. Buyers then returned the farms to their original owners.

People helped those they saw as worse off than themselves. One woman remembered:

> **"There were many beggars, who would come to your back door, and they would say they were hungry. I wouldn't give them money because I didn't have it. But I did take them in and put them in my kitchen and give them something to eat."**
>
> —*Depression survivor Kitty McCulloch*

McCulloch also gave one beggar a pinstripe suit belonging to her husband, who, she explained, already had three others.

**Seeking Political Solutions** As bad as conditions were, there were no widespread calls for radical political change. In Europe, economic problems brought riots and political upheaval, but in the United States most citizens trusted the democratic process to handle the problems. As one writer wryly observed at the time:

> **AMERICAN VOICES** **"Ten million unemployed continue law-abiding. No riots, no trouble, no multi-millionaires cooked and served with cranberry sauce, alas."**
>
> —*Writer William Saroyan, 1936*

For some Americans, however, radical and reform movements offered new solutions to the country's problems, promising a fairer distribution of wealth. The Communist party had about 14,000 members, mainly intellectuals and labor organizers. In the 1932 election, the Communist candidate polled just over 100,000 votes. Socialists, who called for gradual social and economic changes rather than revolution, did better. Their presidential candidate, Norman Thomas, won 881,951 votes in 1932, about 2.2 percent of the total vote.

Voting figures and party membership do not reflect the notable interest in radical and reform movements in the 1930s. Those who were part of those movements remember the decade as a high point of cooperation among different groups of Americans—students, workers, writers, artists, and professionals of all races. They worked together for social justice in cases such as that of the Scottsboro Boys.

**Depression Humor** For the most part, Americans gritted their teeth and waited out the hard times. Jokes and cartoons kept people laughing through their troubles. The term "Hooverville" was at first a joke. People who slept on park benches huddled under "Hoover blankets"—old newspapers. Empty pockets turned inside out were "Hoover flags." When Babe Ruth was criticized for requesting a salary of $80,000, higher than Hoover's, he joked, "I had a better year than he did."

People fought despair by laughing at it. In 1929 humorist Will Rogers quipped, "When Wall Street took that tail spin, you had to stand in line to get a window to jump out of." A cartoon that showed two men jumping out of a window arm-in-arm was captioned "The speculators who had a joint account."

## *Signs of Change*

Looking back, we know that the Great Depression largely came to an end with the United States' entry into World War II in 1941. Americans suffering through the Depression, of course, had no idea when the hard times would end. They looked for signs of change, and even in the early 1930s there were some.

**Prohibition Is Repealed** In February 1933, just 14 years after it passed the Eighteenth Amendment banning the sale of alcoholic beverages, Congress passed the **Twenty-first Amendment,** repealing Prohibition. The amendment was ratified by the end of the year.

Some people, including President Hoover, regretted the end of the ban, but most welcomed repeal as an end to a failed social experiment and as a curb on gangsters who profited from bootlegging. Control of alcohol returned to the states, eight of which chose to continue the ban on liquor sales.

**The Empire State Building** For many, a dramatic symbol of hope was the new Empire State Building, begun in 1930. John J. Raskob, the developer of the gleaming new skyscraper, won the race to build the world's tallest building.

Showing the darker side of Depression humor, an end-of-the-year cartoon in *Life* magazine summed up the hopes and disasters of 1929. ***Culture*** *Why did Americans use humor to fight their despair?*

Despite the economic hardships of the 1930s, American architects raced to build the world's tallest building. Workers like the man shown above looked out over New York City as they labored to complete the Empire State Building. ***Culture How was the Empire State Building a symbol of hope?***

Some 2,500 to 4,000 people worked on its construction on any given day. The cost of the construction was about $41 million (including land). Because of the Depression, projected building costs were cut in half.

The 102-story Empire State Building soared 1,250 feet into the sky and was topped with a mooring mast for blimps. The building's 67 elevators, traveling 1,000 feet per minute, brought visitors to its observation deck. On the first Sunday after it opened in 1931,† more than 4,000 people paid a dollar each to make the trip.

**The End of an Era** By 1933, it was clear that an era was ending. One by one, symbols of the 1920s faded away. In 1931 organized crime gangster Al Capone was at last brought down, convicted of tax evasion and sent to prison. Baseball legend Babe Ruth retired in 1935. The Depression-era labor policies of automaker Henry Ford, once admired for his efficiency, made him labor's prime enemy.

In 1932 the nation was horrified when the infant son of aviation hero Charles Lindbergh and Anne Morrow Lindbergh was kidnapped and murdered. Somehow this tragedy seemed to echo the nation's distressed condition and its fall from the energy and heroism of the 1920s. Finally, in January 1933, Calvin Coolidge, the frugal former President who presided over the freewheeling prosperity of the 1920s, died.

† On May 1, President Hoover pressed a button in Washington, D.C., and officially turned on the building lights, illuminating the New York skyline.

## SECTION 4 REVIEW

### Comprehension

1. *Key Term* Define: Twenty-first Amendment.
2. *Summarizing the Main Idea* To what extent did Americans' attitudes and outlook help them survive the Depression?
3. *Organizing Information* Make a web diagram showing ways that people worked to overcome the hardships of the Depression.

### Critical Thinking

4. *Analyzing Time Lines* Review the time line at the start of this section. Choose two items and explain why they seemed to signal changing times.
5. *Analyzing Primary Sources* Explain the quotation from William Saroyan. What does it suggest about people's fears during the Depression?

### Writing Activity

6. *Writing an Expository Essay* In a time of crisis, the building of an expensive skyscraper such as the Empire State Building might have been seen as wasteful. Instead, many Americans found it inspiring. What might account for this view of the project?

# Distinguishing False from Accurate Images

Distinguishing false from accurate images means examining widely held beliefs about a person, a thing, or an event to determine whether or not those beliefs are based in fact. When studying history, you may uncover source materials such as newspaper and magazine articles that use stereotypes or that put forth misleading ideas. Learning to recognize the differences between false and accurate images will help you to reach your own conclusions about a statement.

The letter excerpted below was written to President Herbert Hoover during the early years of the Depression. Practice distinguishing between false and accurate images by using the following steps.

**1.** ***Summarize the main message of the passage.*** The first step in evaluating a piece of information is to understand what its central message is. Read the excerpt at right and answer the following question: What is the main point of the letter?

**2.** ***Look for generalizations and overstatements in the passage.*** Generalizations are broad and oversimplified statements about people, events, or issues that are presented as being accurate in all cases. Overstatements exaggerate or stretch the truth. These techniques often signal claims that are unsupported by facts and, therefore, may indicate the use of false images. (a) What generalizations can you find in the letter? (b) What overstatements or unsupported claims do you find?

**3.** ***Look for supporting facts or evidence.*** Accurate statements are usually backed up by statistics, quotations, or other verifiable evidence. Facts can be fabricated and used in misleading ways, however, so always check them for accuracy. (a) What verifiable facts, if any, are given in the letter below? (b) Based on the use of facts in the letter, what can you conclude about the accuracy of its message?

**TEST FOR SUCCESS**

(a) What false images were created about the United States economy prior to the Great Crash? (b) Write an accurate statement about the economy at that time, based on verifiable evidence given in Section 2.

Annapolis, Maryland
September 10, 1931

My dear Mr. Hoover,

In these days of unrest and general dissatisfaction, it is absolutely impossible for a man in your position to get a clear and impartial view of the general conditions of things in America today. But, of this fact I am very positive, that there is not five per cent of the poverty, distress, and general unemployment that many of your enemies would have us believe. It is true, that there is much unrest, but this unrest is largely caused . . . by the excessive prosperity and general debauchery through which the country has traveled since the period of the war. The result being that in three cases out of four, the unemployed [person] is looking for a very light job at a very heavy pay, and with the privilege of being provided with an automobile if he is required to walk more than four or five blocks a day.

National Relief Director, Walter S. Gifford, and his committee are entirely unnecessary at this time, as it has a tendency to cause communities to neglect any temporary relief to any of their people, with the thought of passing the burden on to the National Committee. . . .

. . . Believe me to be one of your well wishers in this ocean of conflict.

Yours sincerely,
W. H. H.

| 1930 | 1930 | 1932 | 1932 | 1932 |
|---|---|---|---|---|
| Construction begins on Boulder Dam | Congress passes Hawley-Smoot tariff | Hoover sets up Reconstruction Finance Corporation | Bonus Army protesters forced out of Washington | Franklin Delano Roosevelt elected President |

**1930** **1931** **1932**

# 5 The Election of 1932

## SECTION PREVIEW

### Objectives

1 Outline Hoover's responses to the Great Depression.
2 Explain what Roosevelt meant when he offered Americans a "new deal."
3 Explain why the 1932 election was a turning point in United States history.
4 *Key Terms* Define: Hawley-Smoot tariff; Bonus Army.

### Main Idea

As the Depression worsened, people blamed Hoover and the Republicans for their misery. The 1932 presidential election brought a sweeping victory for Democrat Franklin D. Roosevelt and a new direction for American government.

### Reading Strategy

*Compare and Contrast* As you read, make notes about Hoover's policies and his style of governing. Do the same for Roosevelt. Then compare the key characteristics of these two candidates in the 1932 election.

For a few months after the stock market crash, President Hoover, along with business leaders, insisted that the key to recovery was confidence. Hoover blamed the Great Depression on "world-wide economic conditions beyond our control"—not on problems in the United States economy.

## *Hoover's Limited Strategy*

Taking Hoover's advice, business and government leaders tried to maintain public confidence in the economy. Even as factories closed, Hoover administration officials insisted that conditions would improve soon.

**Voluntary Action Fails** Hoover believed that voluntary controls by United States businesses were the best way to end the economic crisis. He quickly organized a White House conference of business leaders and got their promise to maintain wage rates. At first, many firms did keep wages up. By the end of 1931, however, companies were quietly cutting workers' pay.

Hoover held rigidly to this principle of voluntary action. A shy man, he was successful in business but inexperienced in politics. He could not make his plan attractive to the American people. After a year of misery, they began to blame him and the Republicans for the crisis.

**The Government Acts** As the hardships continued and criticisms increased, Hoover took a more active approach. To create jobs, the government spent more on new public buildings, roads, parks, and dams. Boulder Dam (later renamed Hoover Dam) was begun in 1930. A President's Emergency Committee on Employment advised local relief programs.

Trying to protect domestic industries from foreign imports, in 1930 Congress passed the **Hawley-Smoot tariff,** the highest import tax in history. The tariff backfired. European countries raised their own tariffs, bringing a sudden slowdown in international trade. Hoover suspended the Allies' payments of their war debts, but Europe's economies grew weaker.

In 1932, Hoover set up the Reconstruction Finance Corporation (RFC), which gave government credit to banks so that they could extend loans. The RFC reflected the theory that prosperity at the top would help the economy as a whole. To many people, however, it seemed that the government was helping bankers while ordinary people went hungry.

Some government efforts helped, but not enough. Hoover wanted state and local governments to handle relief, but their programs never had enough money. Despite the RFC, banks continued to fail.

**Hoover's Unpopularity Grows** Many people blamed Hoover, not always fairly, for their problems. Hoover argued that direct federal relief would destroy people's self-respect and create a large bureaucracy. His refusal to help brought bitter public reaction and negative publicity. Although his World War I relief work had made him the "Great Humanitarian," Hoover's attitude toward Depression relief made him seem cold and hard-hearted.

While people went hungry, newspapers showed a photograph of him feeding his dog on the White House lawn. People booed when he said such things as "Our people have been protected from hunger and cold."

Private charities and local officials could not meet the demands for relief as Hoover wanted. Finally, in 1932, Hoover broke with tradition and let the RFC lend the states money for unemployment relief. But it was too little and too late.

As the Depression deepened, some economists backed the ideas of British economist John Maynard Keynes. He said that massive government spending could help a collapsing economy and encourage more private spending. This economic theory was not yet widely accepted, however.

**Veterans March on Washington** A low point for Hoover came in the summer of 1932, when 20,000 jobless World War I veterans and their families encamped in Washington, D.C. The **Bonus Army,** as they called themselves, wanted immediate payment of a pension bonus that had been promised for 1945. The House of Representatives agreed, but the Senate said no. Most of the Bonus Army then went home, but a few thousand stayed, living in shacks.

Although the bonus marchers were generally peaceful, a few violent incidents prompted Hoover to call in the army. General Douglas

## COMPARING PRIMARY SOURCES

### FIGHTING THE DEPRESSION

Sharp philosophical differences characterized the presidential campaign of 1932.

**Against Drastic Measures**

"We are told by the opposition that we must have a change, that we must have a new deal. It is not the change . . . to which I object but the proposal to alter the whole foundations of our national life which have been built through generations of testing and struggle."

*—Herbert Hoover, speech at Madison Square Garden, October 31, 1932*

**For Drastic Measures**

"I have recounted to you in other speeches, and it is a matter of general information, that for at least two years after the Crash, the only efforts made by the [Hoover administration] to cope with the distress of unemployment were to deny its existence."

*—Franklin D. Roosevelt, campaign address, October 13, 1932*

***ANALYZING VIEWPOINTS*** **Compare the statements made by the two candidates.**

MacArthur's troops set fire to the Bonus Army camps after driving out the protesters. ***Culture*** *Why do you think the government's response to the Bonus Army hurt Hoover at election time?*

## Election of 1932

| Candidate/Party | Electoral Vote | Popular Vote | % Electoral Vote | % Popular Vote |
|---|---|---|---|---|
| Franklin D. Roosevelt (Democrat) | 472 | 22,821,857 | 88.9 | 57.4 |
| Herbert Hoover (Republican) | 59 | 15,761,841 | 11.1 | 39.7 |
| Minor parties | | 1,160,615 | | 2.9 |

Franklin D. Roosevelt and the Democratic party won the popular vote in 1932 as well as a huge margin of electoral votes.
*Location* ***Which states' electoral votes did Hoover win?***

MacArthur decided to use force to drive the marchers out of Washington. Armed with bricks and stones, the Bonus Army veterans faced their own country's guns, tanks, and tear gas. Many people were injured. Hoover was horrified, but he took responsibility for MacArthur's actions. In the next election, the lingering image of this ugly scene would help defeat him.

## A "New Deal" for America

"I pledge myself to a new deal for the American people," announced presidential candidate Franklin Delano Roosevelt as he accepted the Democratic party's nomination at its Chicago convention in July 1932. Delegates cheered, and an organ thundered out the song "Happy Days Are Here Again."

The Republicans, in June, had again named Hoover. As the presidential campaign took shape, the differences between the two candidates became very clear.

In Franklin and Eleanor Roosevelt, the Democrats had a remarkable political couple to bring them victory. Franklin, nicknamed "FDR" by the press, was born in 1882. He graduated from Harvard University and took a job in a law firm, although his main interest was politics. He was elected twice to the New York State Senate before becoming Assistant Secretary of the Navy in President Woodrow Wilson's administration.

In 1920, FDR ran for Vice President but lost. The following summer, he came down with polio and never walked without help again. He spent much of the 1920s recovering at Warm Springs, Georgia, but kept up his political interests.

Eleanor Roosevelt, a niece of Theodore Roosevelt, was born in 1884 into a wealthy family. She married her distant cousin Franklin in 1905. During the 1920s, in New York State, Eleanor worked for public housing legislation, state government reform, birth control, and better conditions for working women. By 1928, when FDR was persuaded to run for governor of New York, Eleanor was an experienced political worker and social reformer.

After FDR's success as governor of New York (1929–1932), his supporters believed him ready to try for the presidency. With his broad smile and genial manner, he represented a spirit of optimism that the country badly needed.

Unlike Hoover, FDR was ready to experiment with governmental roles. Though from a wealthy background, he had genuine compassion for ordinary people, in part because of his disability. He was also moved by the great gap between the nation's wealthy and the poor.

As governor of New York, he had worked vigorously for Depression relief. In 1931, he set up an unemployment commission and a relief administration, the first state agencies to aid the poor in the Depression era. When, as a presidential candidate, FDR promised the country a "new deal," he had similar programs in mind.

## *Turning Point: The Election of 1932*

Hoover, the incumbent candidate for President, summed up the choice that voters had in 1932:

> **AMERICAN VOICES** **"This campaign is more than a contest between two men. . . . It is a contest between two philosophies of government."**
>
> —*President Herbert Hoover, October 1932*

This statement also accurately describes the long-term impact of the 1932 presidential election. It was a historic battle between those who believed that the federal government could not and should not try to fix people's problems, and those who felt that large-scale problems such as the Depression required the government's help. The election would have an enormous effect on public policy for decades to come. (See the Turning Point time line below.)

Still arguing for voluntary aid to relieve the Depression, Hoover attacked the Democratic platform. If its ideas were adopted, he said, "this will not be the America which we have known in the past." He sternly resisted the idea of giving the national government more power.

Roosevelt, by contrast, called for "a reappraisal of values" and controls on business:

> **AMERICAN VOICES** **"I feel that we are coming to a view through the drift of our legislation and our public thinking in the past quarter century that private economic power is . . . a public trust as well."**
>
> —*Franklin Delano Roosevelt, 1932*

While statements like this showed FDR's new approach, probably any Democratic candidate could have beaten Hoover in 1932. Even longtime Republicans deserted him. A reserved man by nature, Hoover became grim and isolated. He gave few campaign speeches. Crowds jeered his motorcade.

## TURNING POINT: *The Election of 1932*

**The election of FDR launched an era of greater government involvement in social welfare programs, an era that would last until the 1980s.**

**1932**
*Roosevelt is elected President after promising "a new deal for the American people."*

**1980**
*Reagan is elected President on a pledge to cut social welfare spending.*

**1996**
*Federal welfare reform gives states control over welfare programs.*

**1925** | **1950** | **1975** | **2000**

**1935**
*Social Security Act is passed, providing aid to retired workers, dependent mothers and children, and others.*

**1965**
*Federal medical aid programs for the elderly (Medicare) and the poor (Medicaid) are established under Johnson.*

This *New Yorker* cover drawing of FDR's inauguration clearly shows how people saw Roosevelt, the new President, in contrast with Hoover. ***Culture* *Why did voters so overwhelmingly favor FDR?***

FDR won the presidency by a huge margin of 7 million popular votes. (See the map on page 396.) Much of his support came from groups that had begun to turn to the Democrats in 1928: urban workers, coal miners, and immigrants of Catholic and Jewish descent. Some people did not vote *for* Roosevelt as much as they voted *against* Hoover and the Republican policies.

On a rainy day in 1933, FDR stood before a Depression-weary crowd and took the oath of office of President of the United States. As reporter Thomas Stokes observed, a stirring of hope moved through the crowd when Roosevelt said, "This nation asks for action and action now."

Phrases like this foreshadowed a sweeping change in the style of presidential leadership and government response to its citizens' needs. Ultimately, such changes altered the way many Americans viewed their government and its responsibilities.

In the depths of the Great Depression, many Americans had to give up cherished traditional beliefs in "making it on their own." They turned to the government as their only hope. Thus, as you will read in the next chapter, the Roosevelt years saw the beginning of many programs that changed the role of the government in American society.

The words of FDR's Inaugural Address gave much of the country renewed hope:

**KEY DOCUMENTS** **"So first of all let me assert my firm belief that the only thing we have to fear is fear itself."**

*—First Inaugural Address, President Franklin Delano Roosevelt, 1933*

Having overcome fear in his own life many times, Roosevelt spoke with conviction and confidence, reassuring a frightened nation.

## SECTION 5 REVIEW

### Comprehension

1. ***Key Terms*** Define: (a) Hawley-Smoot tariff; (b) Bonus Army.
2. ***Summarizing the Main Idea*** How did Hoover's failures bring victory for Roosevelt?
3. ***Organizing Information*** Make a chart listing the measures Hoover enacted to ease the Depression. For each, describe the outcome.

### Critical Thinking

4. ***Analyzing Time Lines*** Review the time line at the start of this section. Choose three items and describe the impact of each.
5. ***Distinguishing False from Accurate Images*** Do you think the criticisms of Hoover were justified, or might the Depression have brought failure for any President? Explain your reasoning.

### Writing Activity

6. ***Writing an Expository Essay*** Take the position of a reporter covering FDR's inaugural speech. Write a newspaper essay describing what the President said and analyzing the changes he will bring to American government.

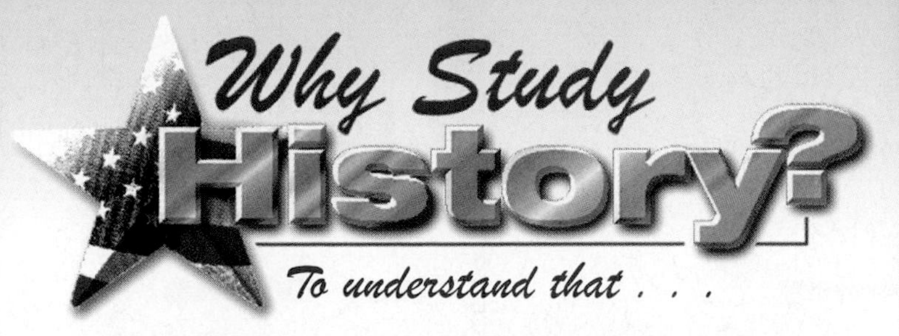


# Investing Involves Risk

**Today, as in the 1920s, an increasing number of Americans with various incomes are investing their money in the stock market.**

*Traders watch the ticker tape in 1929*

In the 1980s, a group of women friends in Illinois pooled their money to share the risks and rewards of investing. They outlined their investment strategies, and their extraordinary results, in a book titled *The Beardstown Ladies.* Though doubts arose over the accuracy of their figures, the Beardstown Ladies inspired many Americans who were eager for financial reward to pool their own money in investment clubs.

## The Impact Today

Before the stock market crash of 1929, most Americans were optimistic about the nation's economic strength. Not only did the wealthy invest huge amounts of money in the stock market, but small investors were entering the market in greater numbers. In 1929 about 10 percent of American households owned stocks.

For years after the 1929 crash, most Americans were wary of investing their hard-earned money in stocks. As recently as the early 1980s, only 25 percent of households held stock.

In the 1990s a new mood of optimism, similar to that of the 1920s, gripped the nation. As the stock market enjoyed several years of spectacular gains, many Americans chose to invest their savings in stocks or mutual funds. Some hoped to get rich quickly, but most had a longer-term goal: saving money for their retirement. The number of households owning stocks or mutual funds rose from about 32 percent in 1989, to about 49 percent in 1998.

The stock market boom of the 1990s was accompanied by a surge in the formation of investment clubs. Today the National Association of Investors Corporation, a nonprofit organization of clubs and individual investors, includes more than 37,000 clubs. Investment clubs on the Internet are popular, too. Some, like the Pioneer Online Investment Club, meet and conduct business entirely online. Members of other online clubs meet face to face, using World Wide Web sites as links to investment resources.

## The Impact on You

*In 1998, the Beardstown Ladies follow stock prices in the newspaper*

Set up an imaginary investment club with three classmates. First, study the financial pages of newspapers or magazines and work together to choose four or five stocks of companies to invest in. "Buy" 100 shares of each. Write down the date of purchase, the price paid, and the symbol for each company. Keep track of your stocks, recording each day the changes in price and your profit or loss. At the end of two weeks, calculate how much money you made—or lost.

# Chapter 12 Review

## Chapter Summary

The major concepts of Chapter 12 are presented below. See also ***Guide to the Essentials of American History*** or ***Interactive Student Tutorial CD-ROM,*** which contains interactive review activities, time lines, helpful hints, and test practice.

### *Reviewing the Main Ideas*

The prosperity of the 1920s disguised an economy in danger. The stock market crashed in October 1929, destroying millions of dollars of wealth and triggering the Great Depression. Hoover's unpopular policies brought FDR to power and his activist approach to government.

### *Section 1: The Economy in the Late 1920s*

During the 1920s, rising wealth and a booming stock market gave Americans a false sense of faith in the economy. In fact, there were signs that the economy was in trouble.

### *Section 2: The Stock Market Crash*

In October 1929, panic selling caused the United States stock market to crash. The Crash led to a worldwide economic crisis called the Great Depression.

### *Section 3: Social Effects of the Depression*

Most people were not immediately affected by the Great Crash. But by the early 1930s, wage cuts and unemployment brought widespread suffering and discrimination.

### *Section 4: Surviving the Great Depression*

Americans survived the Great Depression with determination and even humor. They helped one another, looked for solutions, and waited for the hard times to pass.

### *Section 5: The Election of 1932*

As the Depression worsened, people blamed Hoover and the Republicans for their misery. The 1932 election was a sweeping victory for Democrat Franklin D. Roosevelt and a new direction for American government.

Today, as in the 1920s, an increasing number of Americans are investing their money in the stock market.



## Key Terms

For each of the terms below, write a sentence explaining how it relates to the Great Depression.

1. Twenty-first Amendment
2. Bonus Army
3. speculation
4. Hooverville
5. Black Tuesday
6. Great Crash
7. Dust Bowl
8. Hawley-Smoot tariff
9. Dow Jones Industrial Average
10. business cycle
11. Great Depression
12. buying on margin
13. Gross National Product (GNP)
14. welfare capitalism

## Comprehension

1. Name three problems that plagued farmers during the 1920s and 1930s.
2. Why was President Hoover criticized for his handling of the Depression?
3. How did overspeculation in the stock market endanger the economy?
4. Why was the election of 1932 a turning point in the nation's history?
5. What were the immediate and the long-term effects of the Great Crash?
6. How did the Depression affect minorities?
7. What was welfare capitalism, and why did companies adopt this approach in the 1920s?
8. What did Americans do to try to help one another during the Depression?

## Using Graphic Organizers

On a separate sheet of paper, copy the chain-of-events chart below and fill in the empty boxes.

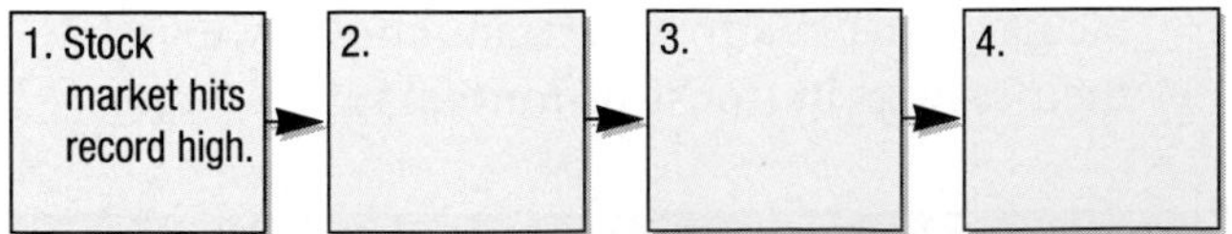

## Analyzing Political Cartoons ▶

1. This political cartoon appeared in 1931. Who is the figure in the center of the cartoon?
2. What is the crowd doing?
3. What is the cartoonist's attitude toward Hoover's handling of the Depression?

## Critical Thinking

1. ***Applying the Chapter Skill*** Study the cover of the *New Yorker* magazine in Section 5. (a) What point is the cartoonist trying to make? (b) Do you think the characterization of these two men is fair and accurate? Explain your reasoning.
2. ***Identifying Assumptions*** Why do you think so many Americans of various incomes engaged in dangerous speculation on the stock market during the 1920s?
3. ***Drawing Conclusions*** How did the government's response to the Bonus Army help ruin Hoover's presidency?
4. ***Recognizing Ideologies*** How did the political ideologies of Hoover and Roosevelt affect their decision making?
5. ***Analyzing Primary Sources*** What did one farmer mean when he said, "We were in the Depression before 1929, we just didn't call it that"?

### INTERNET ACTIVITY

***For your portfolio:***
**CREATE A DIARY ENTRY**

Access Prentice Hall's *America: Pathways to the Present* site at **www.Pathways.phschool.com** for the specific URLs to complete the activity. Additional resources and related Web sites are also available.

Read the first-hand accounts of people who traveled illegally by railroad to find work during the Depression. Create a fictional diary entry of one such hobo. Why did you leave home? Where did you go? What people did you meet and what experiences did you have along the way?

### ANALYZING DOCUMENTS ▶ INTERPRETING DATA

Turn to the series of four graphs in Section 2.

1. About how many banks suspended their business in 1933?
   (a) about 2,000 (b) about 2,300
   (c) about 1,500 (d) about 4,000
2. Which of the following statements best summarizes the data on the unemployment graph?
   (a) The numbers of unemployed people peaked in 1929.
   (b) Unemployment was low in 1925. (c) Unemployment increased dramatically between 1929 and 1933. (d) Unemployment decreased after 1933.
3. ***Write*** Imagine you are a wheat farmer. Write a letter to the President describing your situation. Use specific data from the graph in your letter.

## Connecting to Today

***Essay Writing*** Reread the Turning Point feature in Section 5. Address the following question in an essay: What evidence can you find today of the effects of the election of 1932?

CHAPTER

# 13 The New Deal

## 1933–1938

▲ **VIEWING HISTORY** Campaigning for President in 1932, Franklin Roosevelt shakes hands with a miner in Elm Grove, West Virginia. ***Government How did the New Deal attempt to fight the Depression?***

## CHAPTER FOCUS

*This chapter describes the New Deal, a series of programs designed by Franklin Roosevelt to help Americans during the Depression. The New Deal promised to change the relationship between the government and the economy. Critics of the program noted that many people were left out and that the Depression continued. Still, the New Deal left permanent marks on American political, social, and cultural life.*

*The **Why Study History?** page at the end of this chapter explores the connection between the creation of the Social Security program and its impact on life today.*

| 1933 FDR takes office | 1933 Emergency Banking Act | 1933 Federal Emergency Relief Administration (FERA) set up | 1935 Second New Deal launched | 1935 Wagner Act passed | 1935 Social Security Act passed | 1936 FDR wins second term |
|---|---|---|---|---|---|---|

1933 — 1934 — 1935 — 1936

# 1 Forging a New Deal

## SECTION PREVIEW

### Objectives

1. Identify the programs FDR created to restore the nation's hope, and explain the role of Eleanor Roosevelt.
2. Identify key New Deal personnel, and explain why the New Deal faltered.
3. Describe the Second New Deal and how the voters responded to it in the 1936 election.
4. *Key Terms* Define: New Deal; hundred days; public works program; Tennessee Valley Authority (TVA); Second New Deal; Wagner Act; Social Security system.

### Main Idea

President Roosevelt sought to end the Depression through the programs of the New Deal.

### Reading Strategy

*Structured Overview* Write two column headings on a sheet of paper: *New Deal* and *Second New Deal.* As you read, list details from the section in the appropriate column and note the significance of each detail.

When Franklin Roosevelt took office in 1933, he had big plans for the country. He had already promised "a new deal for the American people," and he kept his word. The **New Deal** became his program of relief, recovery, and reform aimed at combating problems caused by the Depression.

Even Roosevelt himself, however, was not sure exactly how the New Deal would work. Nevertheless, the new President's personality and willingness to experiment won him the support of the American people.

## Restoring the Nation's Hope

Shortly after FDR took office, World War I veterans staged a second Bonus March on Washington. This time, the new administration provided campsites for the veterans. Even more astounding, Eleanor Roosevelt paid them a visit.

When she walked up to a group of marchers, "They looked at me curiously and one of them asked my name and what I wanted," she recalled. By the time she left an hour later, the veterans were waving and calling out, "Good-by and good luck to you!" The First Lady later told reporters how polite the marchers had been. By this act she both soothed popular fears about renewed radical agitation and demonstrated the new administration's approach to unrest.

*The National Recovery Administration (NRA) was one of many new agencies combating the Depression.*

FDR also soothed the public. In his Inaugural Address of March 4, 1933, he told Americans, "The only thing we have to fear is fear itself." The first Sunday after taking office, Roosevelt spoke to the nation over the radio in the first of what became regular "fireside chats." His easy manner and confidence made people feel better.

**The First Hundred Days** In campaigning for the White House, FDR had promised "bold, persistent experimentation." No one knew exactly what that experimentation would include, only that someone was going to do something. As reporter Arthur Krock noted,

## Franklin Delano Roosevelt

*"The only thing we have to fear is fear itself."*

—First Inaugural Address

Courage in times of crisis was perhaps Franklin Roosevelt's greatest strength and most powerful legacy. His first crisis was personal rather than political. In 1921 Roosevelt was stricken with polio, which paralyzed his legs and threatened to destroy what had been a promising political career. (Roosevelt had been the Democratic vice-presidential candidate the year before.)

Refusing to quit, Roosevelt returned to politics. In 1928 he ran for governor of New York. Despite his paralysis, which meant he had to be helped or even carried onto podiums to speak, Roosevelt campaigned energetically and won the election. Four years later he ran for President. In a campaign dominated by the gloom of the Great Depression, Roosevelt's confidence helped bring him victory.

As President, Roosevelt fought the Great Depression through what he called "bold, persistent experimentation." "It is common sense to take a method and try it," he explained. "If it fails, admit it frankly and try another. But above all, try something." This commitment to government action gave the American people much-needed hope.

Roosevelt showed a similar commitment as commander in chief during World War II. After the attack on Pearl Harbor in 1941, Roosevelt rallied a shocked nation and oversaw the creation of the greatest military force in history. Elected President for a record fourth time in 1944, Roosevelt died in April 1945, just months before the victorious end of the war.

Roosevelt had plenty of faults, and plenty of critics. Yet as this nation's leader in the two great battles of the twentieth century—the Great Depression and World War II—Franklin Roosevelt's place in American history is secure.

### Connecting to Today

Should government programs to help the elderly and the poor be temporary responses to crises such as the Great Depression, or should they be permanent? Defend your position.

Washington "welcomes the 'New Deal,' even though it is not sure what the New Deal is going to be."

From his inauguration in March through June 1933, a period known as the **hundred days,** FDR pushed program after program through Congress to provide relief, create jobs, and stimulate economic recovery. He based some of these programs on the work of federal agencies that had controlled the economy during World War I. Former Progressives figured prominently, inspiring New Deal legislation or administering programs.

**Closing the Banks** FDR's first step was to restore public confidence in the nation's banks. On March 5, 1933, he ordered all banks to close for the next four days. He then pushed Congress to pass the Emergency Banking Act, which they did on March 9. The act authorized the government to inspect the financial health of all banks.

Many Americans had been terrified by the prospect of losing all their savings in a bank failure. By his actions FDR hoped to assure the American people that their banks would not fail. Indeed, government inspectors found that most banks were healthy, and two thirds had reopened by March 15.

After the brief "bank holiday," Americans regained confidence in the banking system. They began at last to put more money back into their accounts than they took out. This allowed banks to make loans that would help stimulate the economy. In June Congress increased confidence further by establishing a Federal Deposit Insurance Corporation (FDIC) to insure bank deposits up to $5,000.

**Providing Relief and Creating Jobs** FDR's next step was to help overburdened local relief agencies. He persuaded Congress in May to establish a Federal Emergency Relief Administration (FERA), which sent funds to these agencies. Harry Hopkins directed this agency. He was in office barely two hours before he had given out $5 million.

Hopkins professed a strong belief in helping people find work:

**AMERICAN VOICES** "Give a man a dole [handout], and you save his body and destroy his spirit. Give him a job and pay him an assured wage and you save both the body and the spirit."

—*Harry Hopkins*

To help people who were out of work, the FERA also put federal money into **public works programs,** government-funded projects to build public facilities. One of these programs, set up in November 1933, was the Civil Works Administration (CWA). The CWA gave jobs building or improving roads, parks, airports, and other facilities to the unemployed. The CWA was a tremendous morale booster to its 4 million employees. As a former insurance salesman from Alabama remarked, "When I got that [CWA identification] card, it was the biggest day in my whole life. At last I could say, 'I've got a job.'"

FDR believed strongly in conservation of the environment. For this reason the Civilian Conservation Corps (CCC) was his favorite program. Established by an act of Congress in March 1933, the CCC put more than 2.5 million young, unmarried men to work restoring and maintaining forests, beaches, and parks.

CCC workers earned only $1 a day, but they lived in camps free of charge and received food and medical care as well as job training. Thanks to Eleanor Roosevelt's intervention, from 1934 to 1937 the CCC funded similar programs for young women, though only 8,500 women took part.

Public works programs also helped Native Americans. John Collier, FDR's commissioner of Indian Affairs, used New Deal funds and Native American workers to build schools, hospitals, and irrigation systems. Native Americans also benefited from the Indian Reorganization Act of 1934, which ended the sale of tribal lands begun under the Dawes Act (1887) and restored ownership of some lands to Indian groups.

VIEWING HISTORY This CCC worker is planting seedlings in Montana. The CCC gave young people jobs and preserved the nation's natural resources. ***Economics** What long-term benefits did workers derive from working in the CCC?*

**A Helping Hand to Business** The sharp decline of industrial prices in the early 1930s had caused many business failures and much unemployment. The National Industrial Recovery Act (NIRA) of June 1933 sought to bolster those prices. The NIRA established the National Recovery Administration (NRA), an agency that set out to balance the unstable economy through sensible planning.

This planning took the form of industry-wide codes that would spell out fair practices. The codes regulated wages, working conditions, production, and even prices. They also set a minimum wage and gave organized labor collective bargaining rights. These rights allowed workers to negotiate as a group with employers. NRA officials wrote some of the codes, and they negotiated the details of some codes with the affected businesses. But many codes were drawn up by the largest companies in an industry, which pleased businesses but drew criticism from other people.

For a brief time, the codes stopped the tailspin of industrial prices. But by the fall of 1933, when higher wages went into effect, prices rose, too. Consumers stopped buying. The cycle of rising production and falling consumption returned, and many more businesses failed. Businesses soon complained that the codes were too complicated and that control by the NRA was too rigid.

**Main Idea CONNECTIONS**

*Why did the codes implemented by the NRA fail to balance the unstable economy?*

The best part of the NIRA may have been its Public Works Administration (PWA). Directed by Secretary of the Interior Harold Ickes, the PWA launched projects ranging from the Grand Coulee Dam on the Columbia River in the state of Washington, to the causeway connecting Key West to the Florida mainland, to New York City's Triborough Bridge.

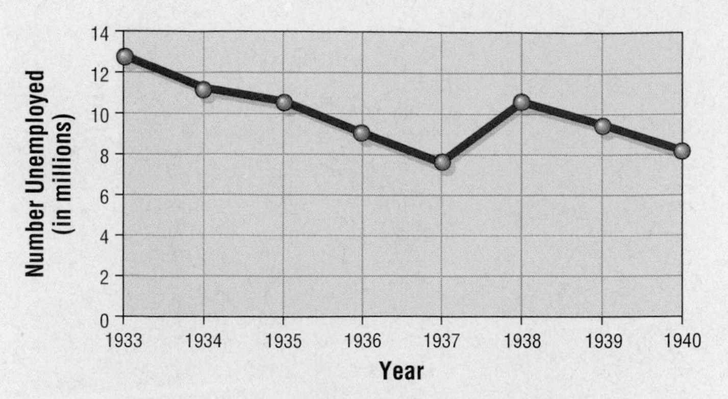


**Interpreting Graphs** One of Roosevelt's greatest challenges during the hundred days was combating unemployment. ***Economics*** ***By how much did unemployment decline between 1933 and 1937?***

The Federal Securities Act, passed in May 1933, required companies to provide information about their finances if they offered stock for sale. To provide further protection against economic downturns, Congress also reformed the stock market. The next year Congress set up the Securities and Exchange Commission (SEC) to regulate the stock market. The SEC was given the power to tell companies what information must be included in their financial statements. Congress also gave the Federal Reserve Board power to regulate the purchase of stock on margin—a practice that had contributed heavily to the crash of 1929.

**Saving Homes and Farms** Many middle-income homeowners were having trouble paying their mortgages. The Home Owners' Loan Corporation (HOLC) refinanced, or reshaped the terms of, mortgages to make the payments more manageable. Between June 1933 and June 1936, the HOLC made about one million low-interest loans.

Many farmers were losing their homes and their land because of the low prices they received for their products. An Agricultural Adjustment Administration (AAA), set up in May 1933, tried to raise farm prices through subsidies, or government financial assistance. The AAA used proceeds from a new tax to pay farmers not to raise certain crops and animals. Lower production, it was hoped, would raise prices.

Under this program some farmers plowed under growing crops. Many Americans could not understand how the federal government could encourage the destruction of food while so many were hungry.

**The TVA** One public works project proved especially popular. The **Tennessee Valley Authority (TVA),** created in May 1933, helped farmers and created jobs in one of the country's least developed regions. By reactivating a hydroelectric power facility started during World War I, the TVA provided cheap electric power, flood control, and recreational opportunities to the entire Tennessee River valley, as shown on the map on the next page.

## *New Deal Personnel*

FDR surrounded himself with eager and hardworking advisers. Some, like Harry Hopkins and Harold Ickes, went directly into his Cabinet or headed one of the new agencies. Others, such as Raymond Moley, Adolf A. Berle, and Rexford G. Tugwell, were part of a so-called brain trust, an informal group of intellectuals who helped devise policies.

For the first time a woman held a Cabinet post. Frances Perkins became Secretary of Labor, a job she held until 1945. Perkins successfully pressed for laws that would help wage earners as well as the unemployed. Perkins was one of more than two dozen women who held key New Deal positions.

FDR's administration broke new ground by hiring African Americans to more than a hundred policy-making posts. One of Roosevelt's key appointees, Mary McLeod Bethune, held the highest position of any African American woman in the New Deal. Bethune was a former elementary school teacher, a college president, and the founder of the National Council of Negro Women. She entered government service with a reputation as one of the country's most influential spokespersons for African American concerns.

Appointed director of the Division of Negro Affairs of the National Youth Administration in 1936, Bethune advised FDR on programs that aided African Americans. In the process she increased her level of influence. She forged a united stand among black officeholders by organizing a Federal Council on Negro Affairs. This unofficial group, known as the black cabinet, met weekly to hammer out priorities and to increase African American support for the New Deal.

New Deal projects included the Grand Coulee Dam, the California Central Valley Water Project, and the Tennessee Valley Authority, or TVA. The TVA linked industry, agriculture, forestry science, and flood prevention. ***Human-Environment Interaction** To how many states did the TVA provide service?*

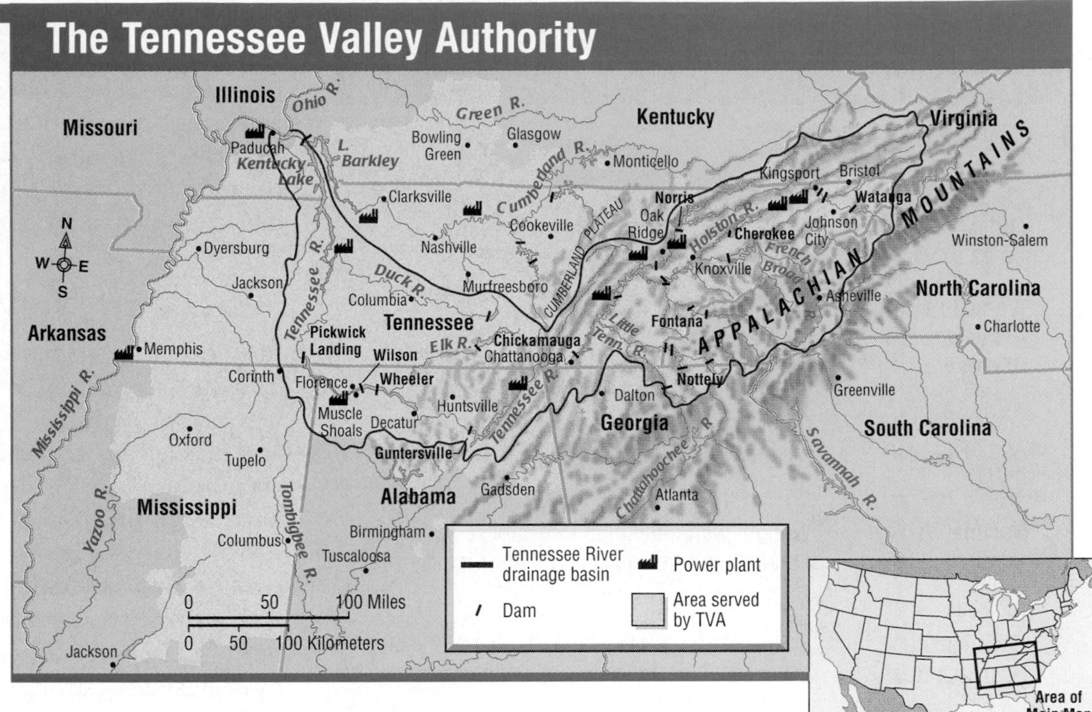


## *Eleanor Roosevelt*

**AMERICAN BIOGRAPHY** Among FDR's most important colleagues was his wife, Eleanor Roosevelt. She threw herself into supporting the New Deal and traveled widely for her husband, whose disability made traveling difficult. She reported to him on conditions in the country and on the effects his programs were having.

Eleanor Roosevelt, a niece of Theodore Roosevelt, was born in New York City on October 11, 1884. A member of a wealthy family, Eleanor attended private schools. In 1905 she married her distant cousin Franklin, and they had six children.

During World War I Eleanor Roosevelt joined the war effort as a volunteer, aiding soldiers passing through New York City. After the war she expanded her volunteer work, involving herself with social and political reforms. In 1922 she became a member of the Women's Trade Union League and also began active service in the New York State Democratic party.

After helping FDR win the presidency, Eleanor Roosevelt began to reshape the position of First Lady. She toured the country in place of her husband, visiting coal mines, sewing rooms, and housing projects. Back in the White House she held her own press conferences for women correspondents. She gave lectures and in 1935 started a newspaper column called "My Day," in which she drummed up support for the New Deal.

*Eleanor Roosevelt (1884–1962)*

At times, Mrs. Roosevelt took stands that embarrassed her husband. For example, in 1938 she attended a Birmingham, Alabama, meeting of the Southern Conference for Human Welfare, an interracial group. She knew she was expected to obey local Jim Crow laws that required African Americans and whites to sit in separate parts of the auditorium. In protest she sat in the center aisle, between the divided races. Her act received wide publicity, and no one missed its symbolism.

Eleanor Roosevelt's activities troubled some Americans. In their view a First Lady should act only as a gracious hostess at state dinners. Gradually, however, the public got used to her unconventional style, and many came to admire her for her enthusiasm, humanity, and idealism. ■

## *The New Deal Falters*

The zeal and energy with which New Dealers attacked the Depression pleased most observers. But when the new programs failed to bring

## Some New Deal Agencies

FACT Finder

| Agency | Purpose |
|---|---|
| Civilian Conservation Corps (CCC) | Provided jobs to young, unmarried men (and, later, women) to work on conservation and resource development projects. |
| Works Progress Administration (WPA) | Gave the unemployed work in building construction and arts programs. |
| Public Works Administration (PWA) | Sponsored massive public works projects such as dams and hydroelectric plants. |
| National Recovery Administration (NRA) | Worked with industries to establish codes outlining fair business and labor practices. |
| National Labor Relations Board (NLRB) | Enforced provisions of the Wagner Act, which included the right to collective bargaining and other union rights |
| Federal Deposit Insurance Corporation (FDIC) | Insured bank deposits up to $5,000. |
| Securities and Exchange Commission (SEC) | Regulated the stock market and protected investors from dishonest trading practices. |
| Agricultural Adjustment Administration (AAA) | Attempted to raise farm prices by paying farmers to lower farm output. |
| Social Security Administration (SSA) | Provided old-age pensions, disability payments, and unemployment benefits. |

**Interpreting Tables** New Deal zeal created dozens of federal agencies. ***Government*** ***How did these agencies aim to help both the nation and individuals?***

about significant economic improvement, criticism began to mount. Many worried about the increasing power that New Deal agencies were giving to the federal government. Former President Hoover warned against "a state-controlled or state-directed social or economic system. . . . That is not liberalism; it is tyranny," he said.

FDR also found his programs under attack by the Supreme Court. In 1935 the Court declared the NIRA unconstitutional because it gave the President lawmaking powers and regulated local, rather than interstate, commerce. The following year, the Court ruled that the tax that funded AAA subsidies to farmers was also unconstitutional. Two of the most important elements of the New Deal had crumbled. It was time to reassess.

## A Second New Deal

Most of the public remained behind Roosevelt. The midterm elections of 1934 showed overwhelming nationwide support for FDR's administration. In 1935 he launched a new, even bolder burst of legislative activity. Some have called this period the **Second New Deal.** In part, it was FDR's response to critics who said he was not doing enough for ordinary Americans. The Second New Deal included more social welfare benefits, stricter controls over business, stronger support for unions, and higher taxes on the rich.

**New and Expanded Agencies** New agencies attacked joblessness even more aggressively than before. The Works Progress Administration (WPA), an agency set up in 1935 and lasting eight years, provided work for more than 8 million citizens. The WPA constructed or improved more than 20,000 playgrounds, schools, hospitals, and airfields and supported the creative work of many artists and writers. (See Section 3.)

The Second New Deal responded to the worsening plight of agricultural workers. The original AAA had ignored many of the farm workers who did not own land. In the Southwest, for example, Mexican American farm workers struggled to survive. Many of these migrant workers were forced to return to Mexico. Others tried to form unions, causing fierce resistance from farmer associations. In the South, landlords had accepted the AAA subsidies, taken land out of production, and left tenants and sharecroppers to fend for themselves.

In May 1935 Rexford Tugwell set up a Resettlement Administration that loaned money to owners of small farms and helped resettle tenants and sharecroppers on productive land. In 1937 a Farm Security Administration (FSA) replaced Tugwell's agency. It loaned more than $1 billion to farmers and set up camps for migrant workers.

**New Labor Legislation** Labor unions had liked the NIRA provision known as 7a, which granted them the right to organize and bargain collectively. When the NIRA was declared unconstitutional, however, workers began to demand new legislation to protect their rights.

In July 1935 Congress responded. It passed a National Labor Relations Act, called the **Wagner Act** after its leading advocate, New York senator Robert Wagner. The Wagner Act legalized practices allowed only unevenly in the past. These included collective bargaining and closed shops, which are workplaces open only to union members. It also outlawed spying on union activities and blacklisting, a practice in which employers agreed not to hire union leaders. The act set up a National Labor Relations Board (NLRB) to enforce its provisions. In 1938 a Fair Labor Standards Act banned child labor and established a minimum wage for all workers covered under the act.

**Social Legislation** In 1935 Congress also passed the Social Security Act. The act established a **Social Security system** to provide security, in the form of regular payments, to people who could not support themselves. This system offered three types of insurance:

(1) *Old-age pensions and survivors' benefits.* Workers and their employers paid equally into a national insurance fund. Retired workers or their surviving spouses were eligible to start receiving Social Security payments at age 65. The act did not cover farm and domestic workers until amended in 1954.

(2) *Unemployment insurance.* Employers with more than eight employees funded this provision by paying a tax. The government distributed the money to workers who lost their jobs. States administered their own programs, with federal guidance and financial support.

(3) *Aid for dependent children, the blind, and the physically disabled.* The federal government sent money grants to the states to help support needy individuals in these categories.

The Social Security system, though harshly criticized, helped millions of beneficiaries feel more secure. Its success has helped inspire numerous other social welfare programs.

*The Social Security Act provided a variety of benefits to many retired, disabled, and unemployed workers.*

## *The 1936 Election*

No one expected the Republican presidential candidate of 1936, Kansas governor Alfred M. Landon, to beat FDR. But few predicted the extent of FDR's landslide. FDR carried every state except Maine and Vermont, winning 523–8 in the electoral college.

FDR's landslide victory showed that most Americans supported the New Deal. Yet the New Deal still had many critics with their own sizable followings.

### SECTION 1 REVIEW

#### Comprehension

1. ***Key Terms*** Define: (a) New Deal; (b) hundred days; (c) public works program; (d) Tennessee Valley Authority (TVA); (e) Second New Deal; (f) Wagner Act; (g) Social Security system.
2. ***Summarizing the Main Idea*** What was the first major step FDR took to combat the Depression, and how did it help?
3. ***Organizing Information*** Create a flowchart to describe FDR's actions during the hundred days.

#### Critical Thinking

4. ***Analyzing Time Lines*** Review the time line at the start of the section. From these events, which personality trait do you think describes FDR better: reckless or fearless? Explain.
5. ***Making Comparisons*** Compare the success of the early New Deal programs and the Second New Deal. Explain why those first programs faltered and how the Second New Deal gave FDR a boost in the 1936 election.

#### Writing Activity

6. ***Writing an Expository Essay*** Write an essay about New Deal personnel as if it were the 1930s. In the essay either support or oppose FDR's choice of advisers, including his wife and the government officials named in the section.

| 1932 | 1934 | 1934 | 1935 | 1937 |
|---|---|---|---|---|
| Huey Long's Share-the-Wealth program | American Liberty League founded | EPIC clubs formed in California | Wealth Tax Act | FDR's Court-packing scheme |

1932 1934 1936 1938

# 2 The New Deal's Critics

**SECTION PREVIEW**

### Objectives

1. Identify which Americans received only limited benefits from the New Deal.
2. Describe how politicians and demagogues criticized the New Deal.
3. Explain FDR's Court-packing scheme.
4. *Key Terms* Define: American Liberty League; demagogue; nationalization.

### Main Idea

A variety of critics pointed out the shortcomings of the New Deal as well as its potential for restricting individual freedom.

### Reading Strategy

*Formulating Questions* Scan the section and note the main headings. Turn each main heading into a question. As you read, answer the questions that you have created.

Franklin Roosevelt's success at the polls in 1936 suggests complete approval of his New Deal. Indeed, many Americans benefited from the relief programs. Letters thanking the President poured into the White House. One writer said, "There ain't no other nation in the world that would have sense enough to think of WPA and all the other A's."

Yet the New Deal inspired its share of critics, too. Another letter writer said, "If you could get around the country as I have and seen the distress forced upon the American people, you would throw your darn NRA and AAA, and every other . . . A into the sea."

## The Limits of the New Deal

For all its successes, the New Deal fell short of many people's expectations. The Fair Labor Standards Act, for example, covered fewer than one quarter of all gainfully employed workers. It set the minimum wage at 25 cents an hour, which was well below what most covered workers already made. New Deal agencies also were generally less helpful to women and minority groups than they were to white men.

**Women** Many aspects of New Deal legislation put women at a disadvantage. The NRA codes, for example, permitted lower wages for women's work in almost a quarter of all cases. In relief and job programs, men and boys received strong preference. Jobs went to male "heads of families," unless the men were unable to work.

No New Deal provision protected domestic service, the largest female occupation. In 1942 an African American domestic worker in St. Louis pleaded with the President to ask employers, the "rich people," to "give us some hours to rest in and some Sundays off and pay us more wages." Working 14-hour days, she earned only $6.50 per week. A brutally honest official wrote back to her:

> **AMERICAN VOICES** "State and Federal labor laws, which offer protection to workers in so many occupations, have so far not set up standards for working conditions in domestic situations. There is nothing that can be done . . . to help you and others in this kind of employment."
>
> —*Roosevelt administration official*

This picture, taken at a relief center in Louisville, Kentucky, highlights the struggle of African Americans to overcome both the Depression and the effects of prejudice. ***Culture*** ***How does this photograph reflect the racial discrimination that was part of the New Deal relief programs?***

**African Americans** Federal relief programs in the South, including public works projects, reinforced racial segregation. As a rule African Americans were not offered jobs at a professional level. They were kept out of skilled jobs on dam and electric power projects, and they received lower pay than whites for the same work. Because the Social Security Act excluded both farmers and domestic workers, it failed to cover nearly two thirds of working African Americans.

African Americans in the North had not supported FDR in 1932, but by 1936 they had joined his camp. Often the last hired and first fired, they had experienced the highest unemployment rates of any group during the Depression. For this reason those who did gain employment appreciated many of the New Deal programs.

Yet the New Deal did nothing to end discriminatory practices in the North. The employment of only whites in white-owned businesses in black neighborhoods was especially troubling. In the absence of help from the federal government, African Americans took matters into their own hands. Protesters picketed and boycotted such businesses with the slogan "Don't shop where you can't work."

The early Depression had seen an alarming rise in the number of lynchings. The federal government again offered no relief. In 1935 and 1938 bills to make lynching a federal crime went down to narrow defeat. NAACP head Walter White recalled in 1948 that FDR had given this explanation for his refusal to support these measures:

**AMERICAN VOICES** **"Southerners, by reason of seniority rule in Congress, are chairmen or occupy strategic places on most of the Senate and House committees. If I come out for the anti-lynching bill now, they will block every bill I ask Congress to pass to keep America from collapsing. I just can't take that risk."**

—*Franklin Roosevelt*

Of course, Roosevelt's record had much that African Americans could applaud. He appointed more African Americans to policy-making posts than any President before him. The Roosevelts also seemed genuinely concerned for the fate of African Americans. These factors help to explain FDR's wide support among black voters.

## *Political Critics*

African Americans may have supported FDR. But many others, with widely differing political views, criticized the New Deal.

**New Deal Does Too Much** A number of Republicans, in Congress and elsewhere, opposed Roosevelt. They knew something had to be done about the Depression, but they believed that the New Deal went too far.

These critics included many wealthy people, who regarded FDR as their enemy. Early in the New Deal, they had disapproved of programs such as the TVA, which they considered to be socialistic. The Second New Deal gave them even more to hate, as FDR pushed through a series of higher taxes aimed at the rich. One of these was the Revenue Act of 1935, also known as the Wealth Tax Act. This act raised the tax rate on individual incomes over $50,000 and also increased rates on the income and profits of corporations.

**Main Idea CONNECTIONS**

*Why did many wealthy Americans oppose the New Deal?*

The Social Security Act also aroused political opposition. Some of FDR's enemies claimed that it penalized successful, hardworking people. Others saw the assignment of Social Security numbers as the first step toward a militaristic, regimented society. They predicted that soon people would have to wear metal dog tags engraved with their Social Security numbers.

Uncle Sam is being restrained by New Deal agencies and policies created by FDR to fight the Depression. Note the flock of blue eagles—symbols of the NRA. ***Economics*** *What complaints did critics have with the New Deal?*

A group called the **American Liberty League,** founded in 1934, spearheaded much of the opposition to the New Deal. It was led by former Democratic presidential candidate Alfred E. Smith, the National Association of Manufacturers, and business figures such as John J. Raskob and the Du Pont family.

The league charged the New Deal with limiting individual freedom in an unconstitutional, "un-American" manner. To them, programs such as compulsory unemployment insurance smacked of "Bolshevism," referring to the political philosophy of the founders of the Soviet Union.

**New Deal Does Not Do Enough** Many Progressives and Socialists also attacked the New Deal. But these critics accused FDR's programs of not providing enough help.

In 1934 muckraking novelist and Socialist Upton Sinclair ran for governor of California on the Democratic ticket. His platform, "End Poverty in California" (EPIC), called for a new economic system in which the state would take over factories and farms. EPIC clubs formed throughout the state, and Sinclair won the primary. Terrified, opponents used shady tactics to discredit Sinclair. They produced fake newsreels showing people who spoke with a Russian accent praising Sinclair. Associated unfairly with communism, Sinclair lost the election.

The New Deal had only limited success in eliminating poverty. This helped lead to a revival of progressivism in Minnesota and Wisconsin. Running for the United States Senate, Wisconsin Progressive Robert La Follette, Jr., argued that "devices which seek to preserve the unequal distribution of wealth . . . will retard or prevent recovery." His brother, Philip, also took a radical stand, calling for the redistribution of income. Philip's ideas persuaded the state Socialist party to join his Progressives after he won the Wisconsin governorship in 1934.

## *Other Critics*

Some New Deal critics were **demagogues**—leaders who manipulate people with half-truths, deceptive promises, and scare tactics. One such demagogue was Father Charles E. Coughlin (CAWG-lin), a dynamic speaker who used the radio to broadcast his message. Throughout the 1930s the so-called Radio Priest held listeners spellbound from his studio in Detroit. In 1934 Father Coughlin's weekly broadcasts reached an audience estimated at more than 10 million people.

Coughlin achieved popularity even though he sometimes contradicted himself. One time he advocated the **nationalization,** or conversion to government ownership, of banks and the redistribution of their wealth. Another time he defended the sanctity of private property, which includes banks. At first he supported FDR and the New Deal. Later he denounced them, through his radio show and the organization he formed in 1934 called the "National Union for Social Justice."

Coughlin's attacks on FDR grew increasingly reckless. In 1936 he called him Franklin "Double-crossing" Roosevelt and described him as a "great betrayer and liar."

By the end of the 1930s, Coughlin was issuing openly anti-Jewish statements. He also began showering praise on Adolf Hitler and Benito Mussolini, two menacing leaders who were then rising to power in Europe. Coughlin's actions alarmed many Americans and he lost some of his support. In 1942 Roman Catholic officials ordered him to stop broadcasting his show.

Huey Long was a different type of demagogue. A country lawyer, he won the governorship of Louisiana in 1928 and became a United States senator in 1932. Unlike many other southern Democrats, Long never used racial attacks to build a base of power. Instead, he worked to help the underprivileged, improving education, medical care, and public services. He also built an extraordinarily powerful and ruthless political machine in his home state.

Originally a supporter of FDR, Long broke with him early in the New Deal. "Unless we provide for redistribution of wealth in this country, the country is doomed," he said. While in the Senate, Long developed a program called "Share-the-Wealth." In 1932 he submitted a proposal to limit individual income to $1 million and inheritance to $5 million. The government would take the rest through taxes. In 1934 he devised a plan to give every American family a minimum $5,000 "homestead allowance" and a minimum annual income of $2,000.

Long's program for helping all Americans achieve wealth attracted many followers. His success helped push FDR to propose new taxes on wealthy Americans in the Second New Deal. Meanwhile, Long himself began to eye the presidency. But in September 1935 the son-in-law of one of Long's political enemies shot and killed him.

Long and Coughlin never seriously threatened FDR or the New Deal. But their popularity warned Roosevelt that if he failed to solve the nation's problems, he risked losing popular support.

## COMPARING PRIMARY SOURCES

### THE NEW DEAL

FDR's promise to improve life for all Americans with a New Deal did not win approval from all quarters.

#### In Favor of the New Deal

"Roosevelt is the only President we ever had that thought the Constitution belonged to the pore [poor] man too. . . . Yessir, it took Roosevelt to read in the Constitution and find out them folks way back yonder that made it was talkin' about the pore man right along with the rich one. I am a Roosevelt man."

*—Testimony by mill worker George Dobbin, 1939. Collected in* These Are Our Lives, *Federal Writers Project of the Works Progress Administration (1939).*

#### Opposed to the New Deal

"All the prosperity he had brought to the country has been legislated and is not real. Nothing he has ever started has been finished. My common way of expressing it is that we are in the middle of the ocean like a ship without an anchor. No good times can come to the country as long as there is so much discrimination practiced. . . . I don't see much chance for our people to get anywhere when the color line instead of ability determines the opportunities to get ahead economically."

*—Testimony by Sam T. Mayhew, 1939. Collected in* Such As Us *(1978)*

***ANALYZING VIEWPOINTS*** **Compare the main arguments made by the two speakers.**

## *The Court-Packing Scheme*

Roosevelt received criticism not only for his programs, but also for his actions. No act aroused more opposition than his attempt to "pack" the Supreme Court.

Throughout the early New Deal the Supreme Court had caused FDR his greatest frustration. The Court had invalidated the NIRA, the AAA, and many state laws from the progressive era. In February 1937 FDR proposed a major court reform bill.

The Constitution had not specified the number of Supreme Court justices. Congress had last changed the number in 1869. But by Roosevelt's time, the number nine had become well established. Arguing that he merely wanted to lighten the burden of the aging justices, FDR asked Congress to pass his reform bill. The legislation would have enabled him to appoint as many as six additional justices, one for each justice over 70 years of age. Most people understood Roosevelt's real intention. He wanted to "pack" the Court with judges favorable to the New Deal.

Negative reaction came swiftly from all sides. Critics blasted the President for trying to inject politics into the judiciary. They warned Congress not to let him undermine the sacred constitutional principle of separation of powers.

With several dictators ruling in Europe, the world seemed already to be tilting toward tyranny. If Congress let FDR reshape the Supreme Court, critics worried, the United States might start heading down the same slope. Sam E. Roberts of Kansas, in a letter to his representative in Congress, expressed the fears of many:

**GOVERNMENT CONCEPTS**

***separation of powers:* *the separation of powers within the federal government among the legislative, executive, and judicial branches***

- **The Historical Context:** One of the many arguments made against President Roosevelt's 1937 proposal to expand the Supreme Court was that it would weaken the separation of powers. Roosevelt, his critics stated, was trying to undermine the independence of the judicial branch of the federal government.
- **The Concept Today:** Conflicts between the President and the Supreme Court, as well as other conflicts between different branches of government, continue to occur today. Yet all three branches retain their independent powers.

AMERICAN VOICES **"Our liberty is much more important than any whim of the President's. He might be a kind dictator himself, but after the stage is set the next President might be a Hitler or Mussolini."**

—*Sam E. Roberts*

California's aging senator Hiram W. Johnson echoed the views of many legislators:

AMERICAN VOICES **"Shall the Congress make the Supreme Court subservient to [subject to] the presidency? The implications of this are so grave and far-reaching, I can do but one thing, and that is, . . . oppose this extraordinary legislation."**

—*Senator Hiram W. Johnson*

FDR was forced to withdraw his reform bill. He also suffered political damage. Many Republicans and Southern Democrats united against further New Deal legislation. This alliance remained a force for years to come.

FDR did wind up with a Court that tended to side with him. Some older justices retired, allowing FDR to appoint justices who favored the New Deal. Even earlier, however, the Court had begun to uphold measures from the Second New Deal, including the Wagner Act. The Court may have been reacting to public opinion, or it may have decided that those measures were better thought out and more skillfully drafted than earlier ones.

## SECTION 2 REVIEW

### Comprehension

1. *Key Terms* Define: (a) American Liberty League; (b) demagogue; (c) nationalization.
2. *Summarizing the Main Idea* Why did people criticize FDR and the New Deal?
3. *Organizing Information* Create a Venn diagram to compare the demands of the Progressives, Father Coughlin, and Huey Long.

### Critical Thinking

4. *Analyzing Time Lines* Review the time line at the start of the section. Were most criticisms of FDR's programs aimed at the Second New Deal? Explain.
5. *Drawing Conclusions* Why did women and African Americans benefit less from the New Deal than white men?

### Writing Activity

6. *Writing a Persuasive Essay* Write an essay about FDR's court reform bill. Defend one side of the issue in your essay.

SKILLS FOR LIFE

Critical Thinking

Geography

Graphs and Charts

Historical Evidence

# Distinguishing Fact from Opinion

When you read historical materials such as speeches, letters, and diaries, you will find that their authors express both facts and opinions. A fact is something that can be proved to be true by checking an encyclopedia or other source. An opinion is a judgment that reflects beliefs or feelings.

To determine the soundness of an author's ideas, you need to be able to distinguish between fact and opinion. The ability to do so will help you evaluate what you read and reach your own conclusions about historical events.

Read the excerpt criticizing the New Deal from a speech by Herbert Hoover at the Republican National Convention in 1936. Use the following steps to distinguish between fact and opinion in the speech.

**1.** ***Determine which statements are facts.*** Remember that facts can be verified in other sources. (a) For what reason is Hoover's first statement, about the Supreme Court, easily recognizable as a fact? (b) Choose two other statements of fact in the excerpt. Explain how you might prove that each statement is a fact.

**2.** ***Determine which statements are opinions.*** Sometimes authors signal opinions with phrases such as "I believe" or "I think," but often they do not. Other clues that indicate opinions are sweeping generalizations and emotion-packed words. (a) What indicates that the final sentence of the first paragraph is an opinion rather than a fact? (b) Choose two other statements of opinion, and explain what tells you that they are opinions.

**3.** ***Evaluate opinions as you read.*** Generally, an opinion is more reliable when an author gives facts to support it. (a) How does Hoover support his opinion that many New Deal acts "were a violation of the rights of men and of self-government"? (b) Does he present any facts to support his statement that the Congress has "abandoned its responsibility"? (c) In your opinion, how good a job has Hoover done in supporting his opinions? Explain your answer.

**TEST FOR SUCCESS**

Write a paragraph about some aspect of the New Deal. Include in your paragraph one opinion based on facts and one opinion that is unreliable.

"The Supreme Court has reversed some ten or twelve of the New Deal major enactments. Many of these acts were a violation of the rights of men and of self-government. Despite the sworn duty of the Executive and Congress to defend these rights, they have sought to take them into their own hands. That is an attack on the foundations of freedom.

More than this, the independence of the Congress, the Supreme Court, and the Executive are pillars at the door of liberty. For three years the word 'must' has invaded the independence of Congress. And the Congress has abandoned its responsibility to check even the expenditures [spending] of money. . . .

We have seen these gigantic expenditures and this torrent of waste pile up a national debt which two generations cannot repay. . . .

Billions have been spent to prime the economic pump. . . .We have seen the frantic attempts to find new taxes on the rich. Yet three-quarters of the bill will be sent to the average man and the poor. He and his wife and his grandchildren will be giving a quarter of all their working days to pay taxes. Freedom to work for himself is changed into a slavery of work for the follies of government. . . .

We have seen the building up of a horde of political officials. We have seen the pressures upon the helpless and destitute to trade political support for relief. Both are a pollution of the very fountains of liberty."

—*Herbert Hoover, excerpted from*
American Ideals Versus the New Deal

| 1935 | 1935 | 1936 | 1937 | 1937 | 1939 |
|---|---|---|---|---|---|
| WPA begins to fund projects in the arts | CIO created | Sit-down strike at GM's Flint, Michigan, auto plants | Republic Steel strike | Economic recession begins | Supreme Court outlaws sit-down strike |

1935 1937 1939

# 3 Last Days of the New Deal

## SECTION PREVIEW

### Objectives

1. Explain what caused the recession of 1937.
2. Identify labor union triumphs resulting from the New Deal.
3. Describe the effects of the New Deal in terms of culture and lasting achievements.
4. *Key Terms* Define: national debt; revenue; coalition; sit-down strike.

### Main Idea

The New Deal had a lasting effect on many aspects of American life.

### Reading Strategy

*Reading for Evidence* As you read, look for evidence to support the claim on this page that the New Deal led to "some profound changes in American life."

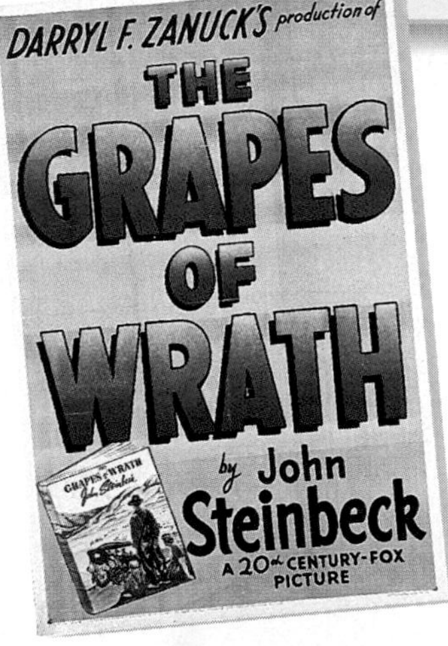


*The Depression era produced many lasting works of art, including the novel* The Grapes of Wrath.

The New Deal attacked the Great Depression with a barrage of programs that affected nearly every American. The New Deal did not end the nation's suffering, but it did lead to some profound changes in American life. Voters began to expect a President to formulate programs and solve problems. People accepted more government intervention in their lives, and laborers demanded more changes in the workplace.

## The Recession of 1937

The New Deal did not put an end to the Depression, but its massive government spending did lead to some economic improvement. The improvement did not last long, however, as the economy collapsed again in August 1937. Industrial production fell, as did employment levels.

The new Social Security tax was partly to blame for this recession. The tax came directly out of workers' paychecks, through payroll deductions. Americans now had less money in their pockets, so they bought fewer goods.

Americans also had less money because FDR had cut way back on expensive programs such as the WPA. The President had become distressed at the rising **national debt.** This is the total amount of money the federal government has borrowed and has yet to pay back. The government borrows when its **revenue,** or income, does not keep up with its expenses. To fund the New Deal, the government had to borrow massive amounts of money. As a result, the national debt rose from $21 billion in 1933 to $43 billion by 1940.†

After 1937 Harry Hopkins and others persuaded FDR to expand the WPA and other programs that had been slashed. Joblessness and misery slowly decreased. Still, hard times lasted until well into the 1940s.

## Unions Triumph

The New Deal changed the way Americans thought about labor unions. The Wagner Act

† The national debt is different from the federal budget deficit. The deficit is the shortfall between the amount of revenue the government takes in and the amount it spends.

**Interpreting Graphs** The New Deal was paid for by huge increases in government spending. Because of yearly federal deficits, the national debt expanded greatly during the Depression. ***Economics*** ***In which year was the deficit the greatest? The lowest?***

provided federal protection for the activities of labor unions, making unions more attractive to workers. Union membership rose from about 3 million in 1933 to 10.5 million by 1941, a figure representing 11.3 percent of the nonagricultural work force. By 1945 some 36 percent were unionized, the high-water mark for unions in the United States.

**A New Labor Organization** Activism by powerful union leaders helped increase membership. The cautious and craft-based American Federation of Labor (AFL) had done little to attract unskilled industrial workers during its half-century of existence. In 1935 United Mine Workers president John L. Lewis joined with representatives of seven other AFL unions to try to change this situation. They created a Committee for Industrial Organization (CIO) within the AFL.

Although the AFL did not support its efforts, the CIO sought to organize the nation's unskilled workers. It sent organizers into steel mills, auto plants, and southern textile mills and welcomed all workers. The AFL suspended the CIO unions in 1936.

Nevertheless, two years later the CIO had 4 million members. In November 1938 this **coalition,** or alliance of groups with similar goals, changed its name to the Congress of Industrial Organizations. John L. Lewis became its first president. The aim of this coalition of industrial unions was to challenge conditions in industry, and their main tool was the strike.

**An Era of Strikes** The Wagner Act legalized collective bargaining and told management it had to bargain in good faith with certified union representatives. But the act could not force a company to accept union demands. Although the Wagner Act was designed to bring about industrial peace, in the short run it led to a wave of spectacular strikes.

Many of these work stoppages took the form of **sit-down strikes,** in which laborers stopped work but refused to leave the workplace. Supporters outside then organized picket lines. Together, the strikers and the picket lines prevented the company from bringing in scabs, or substitute workers.

The first sit-down strikes took place in early 1936 at three huge rubber-tire plants in Akron, Ohio. The success of the sit-downs led to similar strikes later in the year at several General Motors (GM) auto plants. The most famous began December 31, 1936. In this strike, laborers associated with the United Auto Workers (UAW) occupied GM's main plants in Flint, Michigan.

GM executives turned off the heat and blocked entry to the plants so that the workers could not receive food. They also called in the police against

**Main Idea CONNECTIONS**

*In what sense did labor triumph in the 1930s?*

*John L. Lewis*

The successful sit-down strike at the Fisher body plant during the winter of 1936–1937 (above) demonstrated the effectiveness of the new work stoppage technique. Here, workers guard a window during the strike. ***Economics*** ***How did sit-down strikes differ from other strikes?***

the picketers outside. Violence erupted. The wife of a striker then grabbed a bullhorn and urged other wives to join the picketers.

Women later organized food deliveries to supply the strikers, set up a speakers' bureau to present the union's position to the public, and formed a Women's Emergency Brigade to take up picket duty. Governor Frank Murphy of Michigan and President Roosevelt refused to use the militia against the strike. By early February General Motors had given in.

Not all strikes were as successful. Henry Ford continued to resist unionism. In 1937 at a Ford Motor Company plant near Detroit, his men beat UAW officials when the unionists tried to distribute leaflets. Walter Reuther, a beating victim and future president of the UAW, later testified about the incident:

**AMERICAN VOICES** **"They picked me up about eight different times and threw me down on my back on the concrete. While I was on the ground they kicked me in the face, head, and other parts of my body. . . . I never raised a hand."**

—*Walter Reuther*

Like Ford, the Republic Steel Company refused to sign with steelworkers' unions until war loomed in 1941. At one strike against Republic Steel on May 30, 1937, Chicago police killed 10 picketers and injured another 84. This Memorial Day tragedy showed that labor, despite its triumphs, still faced many challenges. Another sign came in the form of a Supreme Court ruling. In 1939 the Court outlawed the sit-down strike as being too potent a weapon and an obstacle to negotiation.

## New Deal's Effects on Culture

Artists created enduring cultural legacies for the nation during the Depression. They were aided by federal funds allocated by Congress to support the popular and fine arts.

**Literature** Several works of literature destined to become classics emerged during this period. One example is Pearl Buck's novel *The Good Earth* (1931), a saga of peasant struggle in China. In 1936 Tennessee writer James Agee and photographer Walker Evans lived for a few weeks with sharecropper families in Alabama. Together they produced a masterpiece of nonfiction literature, *Let Us Now Praise Famous Men* (1941). John Steinbeck wrote *The Grapes of Wrath* (1939), a powerful tale about Dust Bowl victims who travel to California in search of a better life. In 1937 folklorist Zora Neale Hurston published *Their Eyes Are Watching God,* a novel about a strong-willed African American woman and the Florida town in which she lived.

**Radio and Movies** The new medium of radio became a major source of entertainment for most American families. In particular, comedy shows peaked in the 1930s, producing stars such as Jack Benny, Fred Allen, George Burns, and Gracie Allen. The first daytime dramas, called soap operas because soap companies often sponsored them, emerged in this period. These 15-minute stories, designed to provoke strong emotional responses, were meant to appeal to women who remained at home during the day. Symphony music and opera also flourished on the radio.

By 1933 the movies had recovered from the initial setback caused by the early Depression. Americans needed an escape from hard times, and the movies gave it to them—in Technicolor. This entertainment was not free, like radio broadcasts, but it was affordable. For a quarter, customers could see a double feature (introduced in 1931) or take the whole family to a drive-in theater (introduced in 1933). Federal agencies used motion pictures to publicize their work. The Farm Security Administration, for example, produced documentaries of American agricultural life.

Some Hollywood studios concentrated on optimistic films about common people who triumphed over evil, such as Warner Brothers' *Mr. Smith Goes to Washington* (1939). Comedies were very popular, too. In this era the zany Marx Brothers produced such comic classics as *Monkey Business* (1931) and *Duck Soup* (1933).

The greatest box-office hits, however, transported Americans out of the gloom of Depression into a happier time. The *Wizard of Oz,* released in 1939, allowed viewers to escape to a whole different world. Moviegoers flocked to musicals that featured large orchestras and exquisitely choreographed dance numbers with dancers in luxurious costumes.

No one understood the needs of Depression-era audiences better than Walt Disney, whose Mickey Mouse cartoons delighted moviegoers everywhere. Disney also released the classic cartoon *Snow White and the Seven Dwarfs* (1937) in this period.

**The WPA and the Arts** FDR believed that the arts were not luxuries that people should give up in hard times. For this reason he earmarked WPA funds to support unemployed artists, musicians, historians, theater people, and writers. The Federal Writers' Project, established in 1935, assisted more than 6,000 writers, including Richard Wright, Saul Bellow, Margaret Walker, and Ralph Ellison. Historians with the project surveyed the nation's local government records, wrote state guidebooks, and collected life stories from about 2,000 former slaves.

Other projects supported music and the visual arts. The Federal Music Project started community symphonies and organized free music lessons. It also sent music specialists to lumber camps and small towns to collect and preserve a fast-disappearing folk heritage.

The Federal Art Project, begun in 1935, put more than 10,000 artists to work. They painted some 2,000 murals, mainly in public buildings. They also produced about 100,000 other paintings, 17,000 sculptures, and many other works of art.

The Federal Theatre Project, directed by Vassar College professor Hallie Flanagan, was the most controversial. Flanagan used drama to create awareness of social problems. Her project launched the careers of many actors, playwrights, and directors who later became famous, including Burt Lancaster, Arthur Miller, John Houseman, and Orson Welles.

Accusing the Federal Theatre Project of being a propaganda machine for international communism, the House Un-American Activities Committee (HUAC) investigated the project in 1938 and 1939. In July 1939 Congress killed the project's appropriation.

Government support for the arts led to many lasting works, including this mural painted by Thomas Hart Benton in 1930 for the New School of Social Research in New York City. Audrey McMahon, New York Director of the WPA, said: "We did the best we could, and that best was very good." ***Culture*** *In what ways can art be considered a necessity, and not a luxury?*

## *Lasting New Deal Achievements*

The New Deal did not completely vanish when the Depression ended. Its accomplishments continued in many forms. This legacy ranges from physical monuments that dot the American landscape to towering political and social achievements that still influence American life.

**Public Works and Federal Agencies** Many New Deal bridges, dams, tunnels, public buildings, and hospitals stand to this day. These durable public works are visible reminders of this extraordinary period of government intervention in the economy.

Some of the federal agencies from the New Deal era have also endured. The Tennessee Valley Authority remains a model of government planning. The Federal Deposit Insurance Corporation still guarantees bank deposits. The Securities and Exchange Commission continues to monitor the workings of the stock exchange. And in rural America, farmers still plant according to federal crop allotment strategies.†

**Social Security** Few people today seriously question the place of the Social Security system in American society. Social Security, however, has had many critics. You read about some of these critics in Section 2. Others attacked Social Security because, at first, payments were very low.

For a long time the system discriminated against women. It assumed, for example, that the male-headed household was typical. A mother could lose benefits for her children if a man, whether providing support for her or not, lived in her house. Women who went to work when their children started school rarely stayed in the work force long enough or earned high enough wages to receive the maximum benefits from the system.

**A Legacy of Hope** Of all of its achievements, perhaps the New Deal's greatest was to restore a sense of hope. People poured out their troubles to the President and First Lady. Eleanor and Franklin Roosevelt received thousands of letters daily in the late Depression era. Every letter contained a story of continued personal suffering. In their desperation people looked to their government for support. Indeed, government programs did mean the difference between survival and starvation for millions of Americans.

By the end of the 1930s, the event that would ultimately bring a lasting economic recovery to the United States was set in motion on the battlefields of Europe. Several years would pass before that recovery reached the United States. When it did arrive, it came in the form of another tremendous test of American character: world war.

† These strategies were put in place to conserve soil and reduce acreage after the Supreme Court struck down AAA crop-reduction plans.

## SECTION 3 REVIEW

### Comprehension

1. *Key Terms* Define: (a) national debt; (b) revenue; (c) coalition; (d) sit-down strike.
2. *Summarizing the Main Idea* How did the Wagner Act affect labor unions in the United States?
3. *Organizing Information* Create a four-column chart to show how the New Deal affected the *economic*, *political*, *social*, and *cultural* aspects of American life.

### Critical Thinking

4. *Analyzing Time Lines* Review the time line at the start of the section. Which event do you think did the most to undercut the period of labor triumph?
5. *Testing Conclusions* FDR's advisers concluded that certain actions were needed to combat the recession of 1937. What action did they advise, and were they proved right or wrong? Explain.

### Writing Activity

6. *Writing an Expository Essay* Write an essay that examines the legacy of the New Deal. In your essay, suggest which aspects of that legacy you think have been positive for the country and which have been negative.

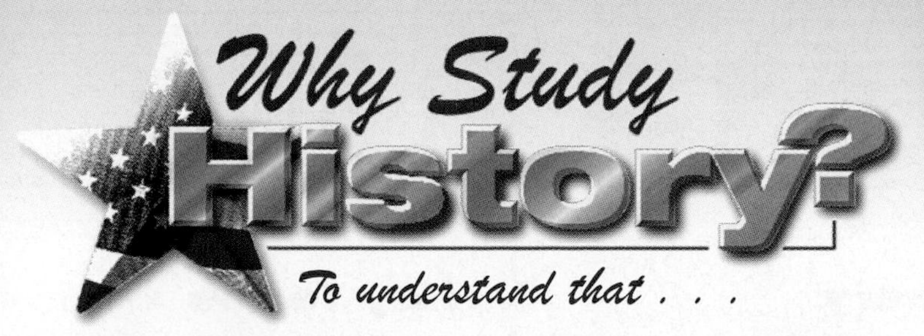


# Americans Depend on Social Security

**Since its creation in 1935, the Social Security system has been an important safety net for millions of older Americans.**

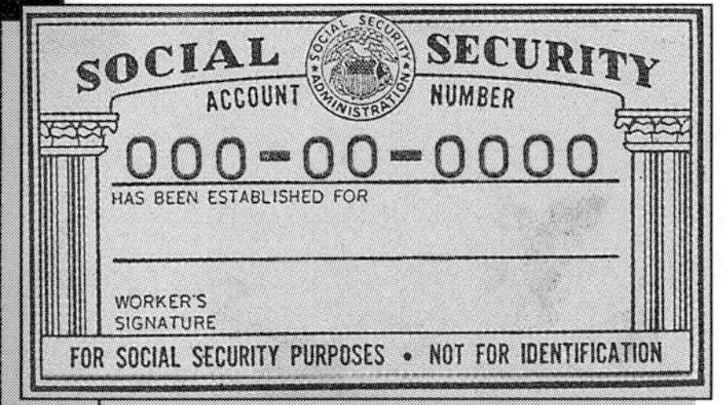


*Sample Social Security card with individual account number*

Few of us expect to work for the rest of our lives. Instead we plan to retire at a certain age, such as 65 or 70, and enjoy more free time—visiting relatives, traveling, learning new hobbies. Yet when jobs end, paychecks end too. Meanwhile, expenses for groceries, clothing, housing, gasoline, and health care remain. How do retired Americans pay their bills?

## The Impact Today

The New Deal included a Social Security system to provide old-age pensions for retired workers. Social Security, one of the most popular programs run by the federal government, allows Americans to retire with a basic income. It also provides benefits for disabled workers and for the wives, husbands, and children of deceased workers. For many Americans, Social Security is their prime source of income.

Together, the federal government and working Americans finance the Social Security system. Unfortunately, as the retirement-age population of the United States has grown, so too has the cost of the program. Since 1970 the number of Social Security recipients has increased from about 26 million to more than 40 million. In the same period, the cost of the program has shot up from around $30 billion to more than $300 billion.

The population of working Americans is not growing quickly enough to fund continued increases in Social Security spending. At some point after the year 2000, in fact, the amount paid to retirees will exceed the amount collected to finance the program. Social Security will become an unsupportable burden unless something is done.

Many solutions to the problem have been proposed. They include raising the retirement age, cutting annual increases in Social Security benefits, raising the taxes that finance Social Security, and paying Social Security benefits only to people who earn less than a certain amount of money. There are also proposals to supplement or replace Social Security with a system of individual retirement accounts. While Americans disagree over specific solutions, they do agree that retired Americans should be able to live in dignity and comfort.

## The Impact on You

Interview your parents and other adults to get their ideas on how to solve the Social Security problem. (You may ask their opinion of the ideas listed above.) Make a table showing possible solutions and the pros and cons of each. Then write a one-page report explaining which solution you support and why.

*Many older Americans rely on Social Security*

# Chapter 13 Review

## Chapter Summary

The major concepts of Chapter 13 are presented below. See also ***Guide to the Essentials of American History*** or ***Interactive Student Tutorial CD-ROM,*** which contains interactive review activities, time lines, helpful hints, and test practice.

### *Reviewing the Main Ideas*

In the 1930s Franklin Roosevelt introduced the New Deal, a set of programs aimed at ending the Great Depression. Some critics attacked the New Deal because they thought it went too far and others because they thought it did not go far enough. The New Deal did not end the Depression, but it did have a lasting effect on American life.

### *Section 1: Forging a New Deal*

President Roosevelt sought to end the Depression through the programs of the New Deal.

### *Section 2: The New Deal's Critics*

A variety of critics pointed out the shortcomings of the New Deal as well as its potential for restricting individual freedom.

### *Section 3: Last Days of the New Deal*

The New Deal had a lasting effect on many aspects of American life.

Since its creation in 1935, Social Security has been an important safety net for millions of Americans. A growing population of retirees, however, has placed a great strain on Social Security funding. The government is considering several solutions to the problem.

## Key Terms

Use each of the terms below in a sentence that shows how it relates to the chapter.

1. New Deal
2. demagogue
3. sit-down strike
4. Social Security system
5. nationalization
6. Tennessee Valley Authority (TVA)
7. national debt
8. Second New Deal
9. hundred days
10. Wagner Act

## Comprehension

1. Why did FDR begin the New Deal by closing the nation's banks?
2. How did the National Industrial Recovery Act aim to help businesses?
3. What did the 1936 election reveal about voters' attitudes toward the New Deal?
4. What were some of the limitations of the New Deal?
5. What was the main criticism of the New Deal by the American Liberty League?
6. Why did President Roosevelt attempt to "pack" the Supreme Court?
7. What factors led to the recession of 1937?
8. What permanent changes took place for labor unions as a result of the New Deal?

## Using Graphic Organizers

On a separate sheet of paper, copy the tree map to organize the main ideas of the chapter. Then fill in the empty boxes with at least three important supporting details. Details for *Hundred Days* and *Second New Deal* might focus mainly on programs. Provide a variety of *Criticisms* and *Legacies.*

## Analyzing Political Cartoons ▶

1. Examine the images in this New Deal era cartoon.
   (a) Who is the magician?
   (b) What is the rabbit that he is pulling out of the hat?
2. What does the caption "Old Reliable" mean?
3. Summarize the cartoon's message in a single sentence.

## Critical Thinking

1. *Applying the Chapter Skill* Suppose you could use these three sources for a report on the 1936 election: (a) a speech by Alfred M. Landon, (b) a political encyclopedia, (c) Franklin Roosevelt's diary for 1936. Which source would you turn to for verifiable facts about the 1936 election? Why? Which sources would you turn to for opinions? Why?
2. *Identifying Central Issues* Do you think that the New Deal was a success or a failure? Explain, citing information from the chapter.
3. *Demonstrating Reasoned Judgment* Do you agree with the way Eleanor Roosevelt carried out the role of First Lady, or do you think she should have acted differently? Explain.

### INTERNET ACTIVITY

**For your portfolio:**
**WRITE AN ARTICLE**

Access Prentice Hall's *America: Pathways to the Present* site at **www.Pathways.phschool.com** for the specific URL to complete the activity. Additional resources and related Web sites are also available.

Read about the New Deal support of the arts and view a sampling of the artwork. Write an article about the art programs of the New Deal in general and a single medium or theme in the arts during this period in detail. What were the goals of the arts at this time? Were they achieved?

### ANALYZING DOCUMENTS ▶ INTERPRETING DATA

Turn to the "Tennessee Valley Authority" map on page 407.

1. Which section of the country was affected most by the TVA?
   (a) Northeast (b) Midwest
   (c) Southwest (d) Southeast
2. Which Tennessee city had four dams and two power plants within 25 miles of it? (a) Kingsport
   (b) Nashville (c) Oak Ridge
   (d) Chattanooga
3. *Writing* By the late 1930s the TVA was well established. Write an interview that might have taken place between a reporter and a farmer, homeowner, banker, or some other person living in the region affected by the TVA. Introduce the interview by reviewing the purpose of the TVA project.

### Connecting to Today

*Essay Writing* Some politicians still favor large government programs as a way to eliminate social and economic problems. Choose a present-day problem. Write an essay either supporting or opposing the use of a New Deal kind of approach to solving it.

# American Heritage®

## My Brush with History

BY TOM FLEMING

***INTRODUCTION*** Both the boom times of the 1920s and the hard times of the 1930s produced numerous heroes and other celebrities. Thanks to advances such as radio, these national heroes were familiar to Americans all across the country. Seeing one in person was an experience that average Americans long remembered.

In the passage below, Tom Fleming recalls the "bright autumn afternoon" of October 1, 1932. On that day Fleming, then a young boy, saw three of the best-known Americans of the period: the President, the man who would become the next President, and the greatest baseball player of his era.

Babe Ruth

*Like every American boy in the twenties and thirties,* I revered Babe Ruth as the greatest name in baseball. What made him come alive for me was a genuine American League baseball that my father brought home after one of his trips to New York. Ruth had fouled it off, and Dad had jumped up and caught it one-handed. "Just for you," he said. That was at Yankee Stadium, the "House that Ruth built."

Of course, I wanted to see Babe Ruth play too, but this wasn't easy. Dad and I were Cub fans. Ruth was an American Leaguer with the Yankees, so when they came to Chicago, they played the White Sox in Comiskey Park on the South Side.

In the fall of 1932 it became clear that Babe would be coming to Wrigley Field (the Cubs and Yankees had reached the World Series). It was beyond expectation that I would actually get to see those games; I hoped that perhaps I could sneak into the coach's office in the high school locker room and catch a few plays on his radio before the bell rang for afternoon classes.

One evening in September Dad came home in an unusually buoyant mood. I was doing a jigsaw puzzle at the family game table in the den. I watched him take off his suit coat and drape it deliberately over the back of his desk chair. As he unbuttoned his vest, he leaned forward and took a small envelope from his inside coat pocket.

Inside the envelope was a pair of tickets to the October 1 home opener of the World Series—the Cubs and the Yankees at Wrigley Field.

"Now you can see Babe Ruth," he said.

Our beloved Wrigley Field had been transformed for the Series, with red, white, and blue bunting draped everywhere. Temporary stands had been set up in the outfield to accommodate the huge crowd. Our seats were only six rows back from the playing field on the left-field side, between the end of the Cubs' dugout and third base.

"There's your man," Dad said, pointing to left field as we settled in. Sure enough, there he was warming up with his teammates—the Bambino, the Sultan of Swat, the Colossus of

Clout—Babe Ruth, all six feet two inches and 215 pounds of him.

When the players left the field, the announcer introduced President Hoover, who was in the stands for the big game. The applause was scattered, and I was shocked to hear boos. (As a Boy Scout I thought you didn't do such a thing to a President.) When Governor Franklin D. Roosevelt was introduced, there was much more applause and fewer boos. Both men were on the campaign trail for the presidential election coming up that November. If I had been politically conscious, I would have known right then that Mr. Hoover was in trouble, for it seemed most fans felt Hoover wasn't having nearly as good a year as Ruth.

Charlie Root took the mound for the Cubs. He was in trouble from the first pitch. With the first two Yankees on base on a walk and a throwing error by the shortstop Billy Jurges, Ruth lumbered up to the plate. He promptly did what he was famous for—lofted one of his patented homers out to the center field seats.

The Cubs lifted our hearts with some good hitting, especially from Kiki Cuyler, but they never seemed to get real control of the game. The score was 4 to 4 when Ruth stepped into the box at the top of the fifth inning.

How lucky we were to be on the third-base side. As a left-handed batter, Ruth faced us, and we could see his every move and gesture. Root was very careful. After each strike the Babe raised his right arm, showing one finger for a strike, then two, to keep the stands posted on the duel between him and the pitcher. The crowd reacted wildly. When the count stood at 2 and 2, Ruth stepped back a bit and then pointed grandly to the outfield, making a big arc with his right hand.

Dad poked me in the ribs.

"Look at him point, son! Look at him point! He's calling a home run!"

The very air seemed to vibrate. I held my breath, digging my fingernails into my palms.

Ruth stepped back into the batter's box, ready for Root's next pitch. It came in knee-high, and the Babe connected solidly with his great swing. The crowd let out a volcanic, spontaneous gasp of awe. Everybody knew it was gone, gone, gone as it soared high and out over the center-field score board for one of the longest homers ever hit out of Wrigley Field.

The Babe started his trip around the bases. When he rounded second and came toward us, we saw a triumphant smile on his face. Past third, he leaned over and pointed into the Cub dugout. I can only guess what he said to the Cub bench jockeys, although I probably wouldn't have known all the words then.

Root and Hartnett, the Cub battery, later denied that Ruth had called his shot or pointed. I guess that as great competitors they didn't want to give Ruth any more luster than he already had. Dad and I knew that Babe Ruth had pointed though. The Yankees went on to win, 7 to 5, and four of their runs were provided by Babe Ruth. That was the Sultan of Swat at his greatest.

As we were leaving the ballpark, a loud siren wailed just below us, and we rushed over to the ramp railing to see what was going on. Below was the big white touring car of the city greeter, and beside him on the back seat was Governor Roosevelt—gray felt hat and cigarette holder at the jaunty angle cartoonists loved to draw. For a brief moment my eyes locked with his as he looked up at the people lining the railing.

At that moment I realized I was seeing a new star about to enter a more serious arena. That day was a capsule of life. I passed from my boyhood interests to those of the greater game of politics on that bright autumn afternoon of October 1, 1932.

Source: *American Heritage* magazine, November 1990.

### ADDITIONAL READING

**To learn more about the topics discussed in this selection, you might want to read the following books:**

- *Babe Ruth: His Life and Legend,* by Kal Wagenheim (Maplewood, N.J.: Waterfront Press, 1990)
- *Baseball: An Illustrated History,* narrative by Geoffrey C. Ward, based on a filmscript by Geoffrey C. Ward and Ken Burns (New York: Alfred A. Knopf, 1994)
- *FDR: The New York Years, 1928–1933,* by Kenneth S. Davis (New York: Random House, 1985)
- *The Life of Herbert Hoover,* by George H. Nash (New York: W.W. Norton, 1983)

unit FOUR

# Hot and Cold War

## 1939–1960

*Many Americans were determined to stay out of another European conflict, but Japan's attack on Pearl Harbor ended the debate on American entry into World War II. After the war, the nation barely had time to enjoy its hard-won peace before a "cold war" developed between the United States and the Soviet Union. The state of international tension and the threat of nuclear destruction cast a long shadow across the postwar era.*



### UNIT THEMES

**Foreign Relations** German, Italian, and Japanese aggression in the 1930s led to global warfare.

**Culture** Cold war tensions raised popular fears of Communist infiltration into American society and government.

**Diversity** Following World War II, African Americans began to push harder for civil rights.

**EVENTS IN THE UNITED STATES**

**1941** *Japan attacks Pearl Harbor*

**1942** *Internment of Japanese Americans*

**1944** *D-Day invasion*

**1947** *Truman Doctrine*

**1948** *Turning Point: The Marshall Plan (p. 493)*

Presidents: F. D. Roosevelt

1935 — 1940 — 1945

**EVENTS IN THE WORLD**

**1939** *Germany invades Poland*

**1941** *Germany invades USSR*

**1945** *Germany and Japan surrender*

**1949** *Communists take over China*

**VIEWING HISTORY** The government used powerful images—such as the illustration on this "Buy War Bonds" poster—to encourage Americans on the home front to make their own contributions to the war effort. **Culture** ***How did World War II affect American culture and America's role in world affairs?***

*Army Medal of Honor*

**1950** *Korean War begins*

**1954** Brown *v.* Board of Education

**1955** *Montgomery bus boycott begins*

**1956**
- *Interstate Highway Act*
- *Supreme Court outlaws segregation on buses*

Truman | Eisenhower

**1950** **1955** **1960**

**1954** *Vietnamese win independence*

**1957** *USSR launches* Sputnik

**1959** *Castro overthrows Cuban dictatorship*

**1960** *USSR shoots down U.S. spy plane*

CHAPTER

# 14 World War II

## 1939–1945

### CHAPTER FOCUS

This chapter describes World War II, in which the United States and the other Allies battled aggression in Europe, northern Africa, and Asia. A Japanese attack on Pearl Harbor brought an end to the hope that the United States could remain neutral. Once involved, America fully committed its material and human resources to the global conflict.

The **Why Study History?** page at the end of this chapter explores the connection between the Holocaust and the continued threat of genocide today.

▲

**VIEWING HISTORY**

American troops plunge into action on the French shore of Normandy in 1944.

**Foreign Relations** **What finally caused the United States to enter into World War II?**

| 1933 | 1935 | 1938 | 1939 | 1941 |
|---|---|---|---|---|
| Adolf Hitler becomes dictator of Germany | Italy invades Ethiopia | Germany annexes Austria and the Sudetenland | Germany invades Poland | Japan attacks Pearl Harbor |

1933 1935 1937 1939 1941

# 1 Prelude to Global War

## SECTION PREVIEW

### Objectives

1. Explain how Fascist and Nazi aggression led to war in Europe.
2. List the reasons that made Japan eager to build an empire.
3. Describe the American response to the war in Europe and explain how the Japanese attack on Pearl Harbor pulled the United States into the war.
4. *Key Terms* Define: totalitarian; fascism; Axis Powers; appeasement; *blitzkrieg;* Allies; Lend-Lease Act.

### Main Idea

Depressed economic conditions and a desire to build powerful nations led to the rise of dictators in Germany and Italy and eventually to a second global conflict.

### Reading Strategy

*Organizing Information* Create a concept map by drawing five large circles on a piece of paper and labeling each circle with a heading from the section. Add supporting information in smaller circles and draw lines connecting them to the large circles.

Throughout the 1930s the Depression kept a tight grip on the American economy. While Americans faced personal hardship and political upheaval at home, conditions in other countries were even worse. The United States watched warily as dictators in Europe and Asia sought to solve their nations' problems by extending their power at the expense of other nations.

## *Fascism and Nazism*

Throughout the 1920s and 1930s brutal dictators came to power in Europe. In Germany, Italy, and the Soviet Union **totalitarian** governments controlled every aspect of life. These governments used terror to suppress individual rights and to silence all forms of opposition.

Germany's Adolf Hitler and Italy's Benito Mussolini based their governments on a philosophy called **fascism.** Fascism places the importance of the nation above the value of the individual. Hitler and Mussolini focused on the need to rebuild Germany and Italy.

Unlike communism, which calls for all society to jointly own the nation's means of production, fascism allows private business. According to Communist theory, conflicts between workers and owners will not exist in a Communist society, because the workers are the owners. In a Fascist system such conflicts are resolved by the government's power. Under both systems, however, the result is the same. Individual rights and freedoms are lost as everyone works for the benefit of society and the nation.

*The official Nazi emblem, the swastika, became a symbol of terror in World War II.*

**Mussolini Controls Italy** Benito Mussolini had fought and been wounded in World War I. Along with many other Italians, Mussolini felt his country had been shortchanged in the peace settlement after the war. In 1919 he joined with other dissatisfied war veterans to organize the revolutionary Fascist party.

Calling himself *Il Duce* ("the leader"), Mussolini organized Fascist groups throughout Italy. He relied on gangs of Fascist thugs, called Blackshirts because of the way they dressed, to terrorize and bring under control those who opposed him. By 1922 Mussolini had become such a powerful figure that when he threatened to march on Rome, the king panicked and appointed him prime minister.

Mussolini and the Fascists swiftly attempted to deal with the political and economic problems that had plagued Italy since World War I. Claiming that efficiency and order were necessary to restore the nation's greatness, they suspended elections, outlawed all other political parties, and soon established a dictatorship.

"The Country Is Nothing Without Conquest," proclaimed a Fascist slogan. In October 1935 Mussolini put those words into practice by invading Ethiopia. The Ethiopians resisted fiercely, but by March 1936 the East African nation was in Italian hands.

**Hitler Rules Germany** While Mussolini was gaining control in Italy, a discontented Austrian painter was rising to power in Germany. Like Mussolini, Hitler had been wounded while serving in World War I. He, too, was enraged by the outcome of the war and by the terms of the peace settlement.

In 1919 Hitler joined a small political party which soon took the name National Socialist German Workers' party, or Nazi party. His powerful public-speaking abilities quickly made him a leader. In November 1923, with some 3,000 followers, Hitler tried to overthrow the German government. Authorities easily crushed the uprising. Although Hitler was sentenced to five years in prison, he was confined for only nine months.

*Adolf Hitler spoke with a charismatic passion that electrified audiences.*

Most of Hitler's time in prison was devoted to writing the first volume of an autobiography titled *Mein Kampf* ("My Struggle"). In it Hitler outlined the Nazi philosophy, his views of Germany's problems, and his plans for the nation. According to *Mein Kampf*, Germany had been weakened by certain groups who lived within its borders. He was highly critical of the nation's Jewish population, which he blamed for Germany's defeat in World War I.

In *Mein Kampf*, Hitler proposed strengthening the nation's military and expanding its borders to include Germans living in other nations. He also called for purifying the so-called Aryan "race" (blond, blue-eyed Germans) by removing from Germany those groups he considered undesirable. In time, removal came to mean the mass murder of millions of Jews and other peoples.

Saddled with huge debts because of World War I, Germany suffered high unemployment and massive inflation during the 1920s. In the early 1930s, the effects of the Great Depression further ravaged the German people. Hitler and the Nazis promised to stabilize the country, rebuild the economy, and restore the empire that had been lost.

Because of such promises, Hitler gradually won a large following. By January 1933 the Nazi party was the largest group in the *Reichstag* (the German parliament) and Hitler became head of the German state. He soon silenced his opposition, suspended civil liberties, and convinced the *Reichstag* to give him dictatorial powers. Hitler then took for himself the title *Der Führer,* or "the leader."

## Europe Goes to War

Like Mussolini, Hitler saw expansion as a way to bolster national pride. He also longed to return Germany to a dominant position in the world. On March 9, 1936, German troops moved into the Rhineland, a region in western Germany along the borders of France and Belgium. The Treaty of Versailles, signed after World War I, had expressly excluded German military forces from the region. The invasion of the Rhineland was an enormous gamble for Hitler because it clearly violated the Versailles Treaty. In addition, the German army was not yet ready to fight. Had Britain or France threatened to attack, Hitler later admitted, he would have withdrawn his forces. However, neither nation resisted him.

Also in 1936, Hitler signed an alliance with the Italian dictator, Mussolini. This created what Mussolini called an "axis" between Rome and Berlin, the capitals of the two nations. Germany and Italy, joined later by Japan, became known as the **Axis Powers.**

**The German Empire Grows** Encouraged by his success in the Rhineland, in March 1938 Hitler sent German troops into the neighboring nation of Austria and annexed it. When Britain and France protested, he was defiant. German-Austrian affairs were the concern of only the German people, he said.

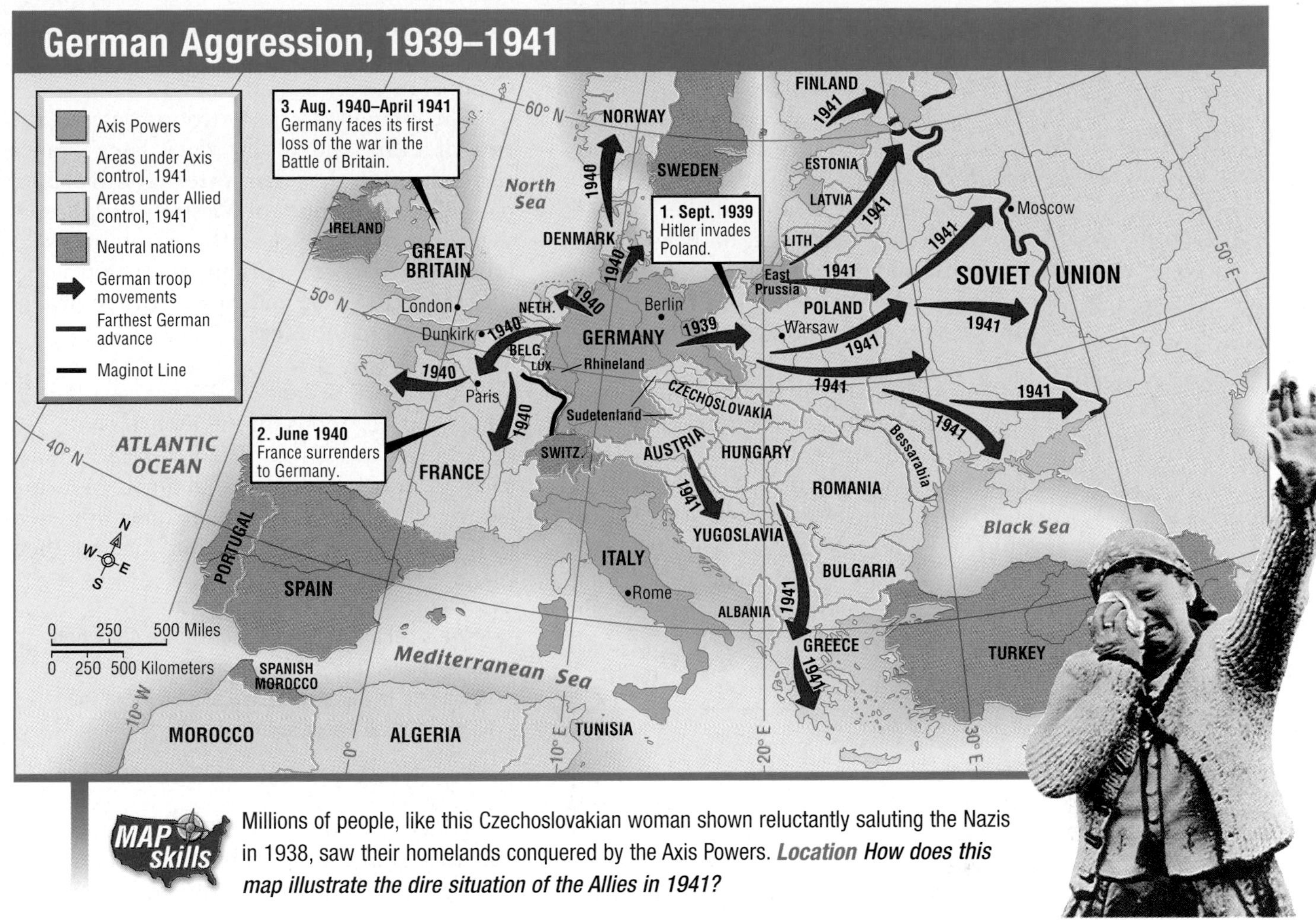


**MAP skills** Millions of people, like this Czechoslovakian woman shown reluctantly saluting the Nazis in 1938, saw their homelands conquered by the Axis Powers. ***Location*** ***How does this map illustrate the dire situation of the Allies in 1941?***

Several months later, Hitler demanded the Sudetenland, a region of western Czechoslovakia with a heavily German population. In an effort to avoid war, representatives from England, France, Germany, and Italy met in Munich, Germany, in September 1938. Britain and France followed a policy of **appeasement,** or giving in to someone's demands in order to keep the peace. Neither country was prepared for war, and the peoples of both countries had not forgotten the awful costs of World War I. At the Munich Conference, therefore, Britain and France agreed to let Hitler have the Sudetenland, hoping that his appetite for territory would be satisfied. "Britain and France had to choose between war and dishonor," said Winston Churchill, a member of Parliament, of this action. "They chose dishonor. They will have war."

Churchill's prophecy came true. In March 1939, only six months after occupying the Sudetenland, Hitler annexed the rest of Czechoslovakia. British and French leaders warned him that any further German expansion risked war. On March 31, 1939, they formally pledged their support to Poland, agreeing to come to its aid if invaded by Germany. By now, however, Hitler was unconcerned about such threats. After signing a treaty with the Soviet Union so that he would face no threat from the east, Hitler invaded Poland on September 1, 1939. Two days later Britain and France declared war on Germany.

***Blitzkrieg* and *Sitzkrieg*** In invading Poland, the German military unveiled a tactic called ***blitzkrieg,*** or "lightning war." Tanks, artillery, and soldiers, moving by truck instead of on foot, rapidly struck deep into enemy territory before the foe had time to react. Using this tactic, German troops overran Poland in less than a month. In mid-September, under the terms of his agreement with Hitler, Stalin attacked and seized eastern Poland for the Soviet Union.

> **Main Idea CONNECTIONS**
> *Describe Germany's strategy for overwhelming its enemies.*

After Poland fell, the war entered a quiet period. The Germans labeled the lull the *sitzkrieg,* or "sit-down war." For the next several months German troops sat and watched French forces on the Maginot Line, a massive system of defenses that France had built along its border with Germany. The American press called this "the phony war."

On April 9, 1940, the phony war came to an end as Hitler launched an attack on Denmark and Norway. Then, on May 10, German troops moved around the Maginot Line and launched a *blitzkrieg* on Belgium, the Netherlands, and France. All three countries were quickly overwhelmed.

In the face of this savage German attack, British forces in France retreated to the coastal city of Dunkirk. There, over a nine-day period in late May and early June, one of the greatest rescues in the history of warfare took place. While other troops fought to slow the advancing Germans, some 900 vessels were hastily assembled. The makeshift fleet consisted mainly of tugboats, yachts, and other small private craft. Braving merciless attacks by the *Luftwaffe* (the German air force), they carried nearly 340,000 soldiers across the English Channel to Great Britain.

On June 14, German troops entered the city of Paris and a few days later France surrendered. In less than three months Hitler had conquered most of Western Europe. Of the **Allies,** the name given those countries who fought the Axis, Great Britain now stood alone. (The United States and Soviet Union would eventually join the Allies.)

**The Battle of Britain** As France was falling, Hitler massed troops on the French coast. His next target was Great Britain, just 20 miles away across the English Channel. Winston Churchill, now Britain's prime minister, pledged that the British would defend their island at all costs:

> **"We shall fight on the beaches, we shall fight on the landing grounds, we shall fight in the fields and in the streets, we shall fight in the hills; we shall never surrender."**
>
> —*Winston Churchill*

Hitler turned to the *Luftwaffe* to destroy Britain's ability and will to resist. In what became known as the Battle of Britain, he launched the greatest air assault the world had yet seen. As many as 1,000 planes a day rained bombs on Britain. Although its Royal Air Force (RAF) was greatly outnumbered, RAF pilots sometimes flew six and seven missions a day, inflicting heavy losses on the attackers. "Never in the field of human conflict was so much owed by so many to so few," said Churchill, praising the courageous resistance of the RAF.

The British people were equally brave. In December 1940, German bombing of London started some 1,500 fires, setting the center of the city ablaze. Despite the massive losses, the British people held on to their will to fight. By the end of 1941, when the German raids had ended, some 20,000 Londoners had been killed and roughly 73,000 injured.

London's St. Paul's Cathedral (above) survived while surrounding buildings were reduced to rubble during the bombing. The cathedral became a powerful symbol of Britain's spirit of defiance. ***Culture How did this spirit help defeat the*** **Luftwaffe*****?***

## *Japan Builds an Empire*

Many Japanese were as unhappy with their situation in Asia in the 1920s as Italians and Germans were with their status in Europe. Located on a chain of small islands, Japan lacked sufficient raw materials and markets for its industries. It also needed land to support its

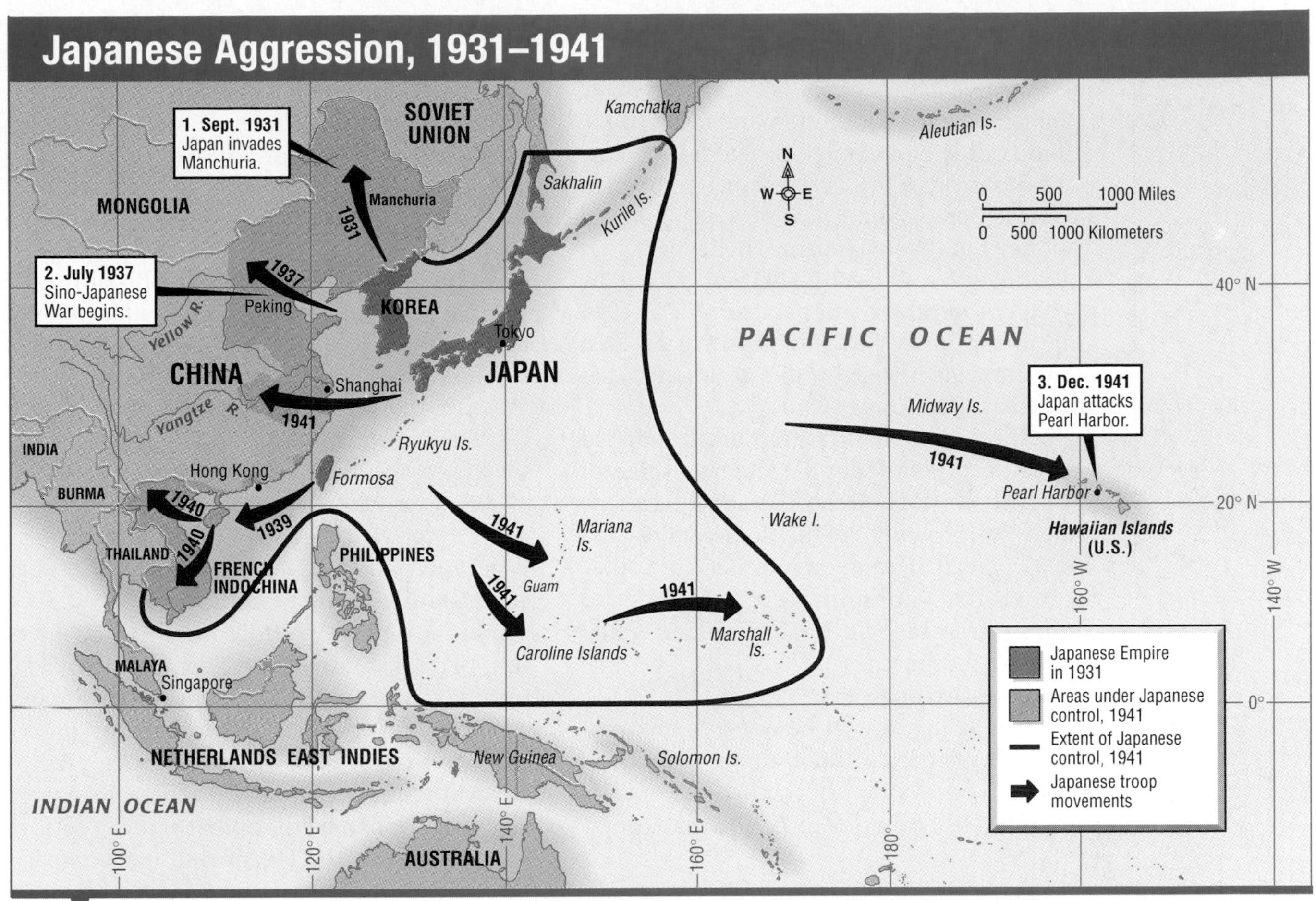


**MAP skills** The Japanese were as eager as the Germans and Italians to build an empire. **Location** *Judging from this map, what regions appear to be in the greatest danger of being attacked next by Japan?*

growing population. For these reasons, some Japanese were eager to establish an empire.

Discontent spread after 1930, as the Great Depression added to Japan's economic woes. Yet world leaders and most Japanese were shocked in 1931, when Japan's army seized Manchuria, a mineral-rich region in northern China. During the next five years, the deepening Depression gave Japan's military a powerful voice in its government. In 1937 Japan resumed its aggression in China. Despite American help, the Chinese army of General Jiang Jieshi (jyawng jeh SHEE) was no match for the invaders.† An ongoing battle between Jiang's army and the Communist guerrilla fighters led by Mao Zedong contributed to the weakness of China. By 1940 the Japanese controlled most of eastern China.

Japan next set its sights on Southeast Asia and the Dutch East Indies. First, it became an ally of Germany and Italy in the Tripartite Pact of September 1940. Then in April 1941 the Japanese signed a neutrality pact with the Soviet Union. The stage was now set for Japan to challenge the Europeans and Americans for supremacy in Asia.

## The American Response

American officials watched Japan's actions in Asia with growing concern. In 1938 President Franklin D. Roosevelt began a naval buildup in the Pacific. The following year he moved the American Pacific Fleet from San Diego, California, to Pearl Harbor in the Hawaiian Islands.

**America Remains Neutral** Americans did not want to fight a war in Asia any more than they did in Europe. Most remained

† In earlier textbooks, this name is spelled Chiang Kai-shek. A newer method of spelling Chinese names with Roman letters is used today.

disillusioned by World War I. They had fought to make the world safe for democracy, but now questioned whether their actions had made any difference. In addition, many believed the nation already had enough problems at home, as the American economy remained trapped in the Great Depression. These people supported a policy of isolationism, believing that American interests would be best served by staying out of other nations' quarrels. In 1940 some isolationists formed the America First Committee. At its height, this group attracted more than 800,000 members.

In the mid-1930s, Congress had responded to isolationist sentiment by passing a series of Neutrality Acts. These laws declared that the United States would withhold weapons and loans from all nations at war. Further, they required that nonmilitary goods sold to nations at war be paid for in cash and transported by the purchaser. This policy became known as "cash and carry."

Believing that war in Europe was unavoidable, Roosevelt tried without success to get these restrictions eased. After the war began, Congress passed the Neutrality Act of 1939. This law permitted Britain and France to purchase weapons on a cash-and-carry basis. A later amendment allowed American merchant ships to transport these purchases to Britain. Yet loans and purchases on credit remained illegal.

**American Involvement Grows** German aggression scared many Americans. Roosevelt was thus gradually able to offer Britain more help. In September 1940 he traded 50 old destroyers to Britain in return for permission to build bases on British territory in the Western Hemisphere.

That same month, Congress authorized the first peacetime draft in the nation's history. The Selective Service Act required all males ages 21 to 36 to register for military service. From this pool a limited number of men were selected to serve a year in the army.

In November 1940 Roosevelt won reelection to a third term as President. His easy victory encouraged him to push for greater American involvement in the war. In January 1941 he proposed to provide war supplies to Great Britain without any payment in return. Roosevelt explained the policy to the American people through the use of a simple comparison: if your neighbor's house is on fire, you don't sell him a hose. You lend it to him and take it back after the fire is out.

Congress responded by passing the **Lend-Lease Act** in March 1941, which authorized the President to aid any nation whose defense he believed was vital to American security. Roosevelt immediately began sending aid to Britain, and the United States became, as FDR had said in a speech in 1940, "the great arsenal of democracy."

## *Japan Attacks Pearl Harbor*

Soon after France fell to the Germans, the Japanese demanded control of French colonies in Indochina. In mid-1941 Japanese forces occupied the region. In response, Roosevelt froze Japanese financial assets in the United States and cut off all trade with Japan. For the next few months, leaders in both nations looked for ways to avoid war.

American diplomats in Tokyo, eager to avoid a confrontation, urged the President to compromise. They warned that pushing the Japanese would result in war. Some of Roosevelt's advisers at home, however, called for a tough stance. The government had cracked secret Japanese codes and had

**Pearl Harbor, December 7, 1941**

Ships sunk
Ships damaged
Ships undamaged
East Loch
Raleigh
Utah
Ford Island
Nevada
Arizona
Vestal
Tennessee
Maryland
West Virginia
Oklahoma
U.S. Naval Air Station
California
Helena
Oglala
Southeast Loch
U.S. Naval Station
Honolulu
St. Louis
Pennsylvania
Shaw
Downes
Cassin
U.S. Naval Station
Pearl Harbor
Pearl Harbor Naval Shipyard
N W E S
0 1/4 1/2 Mile
0 1/4 1/2 Kilometers
Hawaiian Islands
Kauai
Niihau
Oahu
Molokai
Pearl Harbor
Lanai
Maui
Hawaii
0 100 Miles
0 100 Kilometers

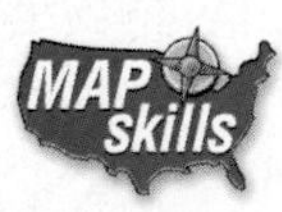


The Japanese attack on Pearl Harbor was surprising and swift. *Location Where did the Japanese inflict the most damage?*

been intercepting messages. American officials knew that Japan was planning to seize more territory.

In October 1941, General Hideki Tojo, who supported war with the United States, became prime minister of Japan. Yet Roosevelt still hoped for peace. He proposed to his advisers that trade could be resumed if Japan halted any further troop movements. On November 25, the American government learned that a Japanese fleet was moving toward Southeast Asia. The United States demanded that Japan withdraw from all conquered territory and from its Tripartite Pact with Germany and Italy.

Even as this tough message was being sent, a second Japanese fleet of 6 aircraft carriers and more than 20 other ships was under way. Japan's leaders had decided that their goals in Asia could not be achieved as long as the American fleet remained in Hawaii. That threat had to be destroyed.

Shortly after 7:00 A.M. on December 7, an American army radar operator on the Hawaiian island of Oahu reported to his headquarters that planes were headed toward him. The only officer on duty that Sunday morning decided they were American. "Don't worry about it," the officer told the radar operator, as he hung up the phone. Less than an hour later more than 180 Japanese warplanes streaked overhead. Most of the Pacific Fleet lay at anchor in Pearl Harbor, crowded into an area less than three miles square.

Japanese planes bombed and strafed (attacked with machine-gun fire) the fleet and the airfields nearby. By 9:45 it was over. In less than two hours some 2,400 Americans had been killed and nearly 1,200 wounded. Nearly 300 American warplanes were damaged or destroyed; 18 warships had been sunk or heavily damaged, including 8 of the fleet's 9 battleships. Japan lost just 29 planes.†

The attack on Pearl Harbor stunned the American people. Calling December 7, 1941, "a date which will live in infamy," Roosevelt the next day asked Congress to declare war on Japan:

**KEY DOCUMENTS**

> **"Hostilities exist. There is no blinking at the fact that our people, our territory, and our interests are in grave danger. With confidence in our armed forces—with the unbound determination of our people—we will gain the inevitable triumph—so help us God."**
>
> —*Franklin D. Roosevelt*

Three days later, Germany and Italy declared war on the United States. For the second time in the century, Americans were part of a world war. Their contributions would make the difference between victory and defeat for the Allies.

---

† The Japanese did not achieve their main goal, which was to destroy the three aircraft carriers that were part of the American fleet. Two of the carriers, accompanied by the fleet's heavy cruisers, were at sea during the attack. The third was undergoing repairs in California.

## SECTION 1 REVIEW

### Comprehension

1. *Key Terms* Define: (a) totalitarian; (b) fascism; (c) Axis Powers; (d) appeasement; (e) *blitzkrieg;* (f) Allies; (g) Lend-Lease Act.
2. *Summarizing the Main Idea* What steps did Italy, Germany, and Japan take in the mid-1930s to extend their power?
3. *Organizing Information* Create a flow map to show how German and Italian aggression led to war. Begin with *October 1935: Italy invades Ethiopia* and end with *September 1939: England and France declare war on Germany.*

### Critical Thinking

4. *Analyzing Time Lines* Review the time line at the start of the section. Which entry was responsible for bringing the United States into World War II?
5. *Recognizing Cause and Effect* What were some of the reasons behind Japan's desire to build an empire in Asia?

### Writing Activity

6. *Writing an Persuasive Essay* Write a letter to President Roosevelt that expresses support for or opposition to the Lend-Lease Act.

| Sept. 1942 | Nov. 1942 | July 1943 | June 1944 | Dec. 1944 | May 1945 |
|---|---|---|---|---|---|
| Battle of Stalingrad begins | British win decisive victory at El Alamein in Egypt | American troops attack Sicily | D-Day invasion of Western Europe begins | Battle of the Bulge begins | Germany surrenders |

1942 1944 1946

# 2 The Road to Victory in Europe

## SECTION PREVIEW

### Objectives

1. Identify the various groups of Americans who mobilized to fight the war.
2. Understand how the Allied decision to begin fighting in North Africa and Italy affected war efforts in the Soviet Union.
3. Show how the Allied invasion of Western Europe led to the end of the war in Europe.
4. *Key Terms* Define: Atlantic Charter; GI; Battle of Stalingrad; carpet bombing; D-Day; Battle of the Bulge; Yalta Conference.

### Main Idea

To secure victory in Europe, the Allies waged war in North Africa, Western Europe, and the Soviet Union between 1941 and 1945.

### Reading Strategy

*Formulating Questions* Skim the section and write down the main headings. Then rewrite each heading as a question. As you read, note the answers to your questions.

*Fatigues were standard wear for American soldiers.*

In August 1941, unknown to the rest of the world, two warships quietly lay at anchor off the coast of Newfoundland. Aboard were Prime Minister Winston Churchill and President Franklin Roosevelt. Both men believed the United States would soon be allied with Britain in war, and they were meeting to agree on the war's goals. The two leaders pledged "a peace that will afford all nations the means of dwelling in safety inside their own boundaries." Roosevelt and Churchill put this and other principles into writing in the **Atlantic Charter.** The agreements reached at this meeting would form the basis for the United Nations.

## *Americans Mobilize for War*

As the United States prepared for war, thousands of American men received official notices to enter the army or navy. After the bombing of Pearl Harbor, tens of thousands more volunteered to serve. Roosevelt shared his vision of what these troops would be asked to fight for:

> AMERICAN VOICES "We look forward to a world founded upon four essential freedoms. The first is freedom of speech and expression. . . . The second is freedom of every person to worship God in his own way. . . . The third is freedom from want [need]. . . . The fourth is freedom from fear."
>
> —*Franklin D. Roosevelt*

**The GI War** World War II greatly changed the lives of the men and women who were uprooted from home and sent far away to fight for freedom. The 16 million Americans who served as soldiers, sailors, and aviators made their way through distant deserts, jungles, swamps, turbulent seas, and forbidding skies. For those on the front lines, the war was often a desperate struggle just to stay alive.

American soldiers called themselves **GIs,** after the "Government Issue" stamp that appeared on all shoes, clothes, weapons, and other equipment provided by the military. While the "four freedoms" and the Atlantic Charter may have defined the goals of the United States in the war, most GIs served for more personal reasons. As soldiers fought in filthy foxholes overseas, they dreamed of home and a cherished way of life. When asked what he was fighting for, a young marine on the Pacific front replied, "What I'd give for a piece of blueberry pie."

**Diversity in the Armed Forces** Americans from all ethnic and racial backgrounds fought during World War II. Among these were more than 300,000 Mexican Americans. Most enlisted in the army. Mexican American troops fought to defend the Philippines, served in the North African campaign, and took part in the D-Day invasion of France in 1944.

Some 25,000 Native Americans also served in the army and other branches of the military. The marines recruited about 300 Navajos to serve as radio operators. They developed a code based on their language that the Japanese could not break when they eavesdropped on marine radio transmissions. The "code talkers," as they became known, provided a vitally important secure communications link in several key battles in the Pacific.

Although Japanese Americans were not accepted into the armed forces until early 1943, thousands volunteered to fight. Many came from the camps where tens of thousands of Japanese Americans were detained during the war. Eventually more than 20,000 Japanese Americans fought in the United States armed services. Most were Nisei, or citizens born in the United States of Japanese immigrant parents. The all-Nisei 442nd Regimental Combat team won so many commendations for bravery while fighting in Europe that it became the most decorated military unit in American history.

African American troops also played an important role in the war. Nearly a million African Americans volunteered or were drafted to serve in the military. At first, most black troops were limited to support roles. However, black leaders pushed to get African Americans into combat. By late 1942, faced with mounting casualties, military authorities reluctantly gave in.

Like Japanese American troops, African Americans fought in segregated units. The African American 761st Tank Battalion captured 30 major towns from the Germans in a grueling 183-day campaign. The Army Air Force 99th Fighter Squadron, known as the Black Eagles,

## COMPARING PRIMARY SOURCES

### INTEGRATION OF THE ARMED FORCES

Discussion about desegregating the armed forces during World War II aroused strong feelings on both sides. Below are two viewpoints.

**In Support of Integration**

"Though I have found no Negroes who want to see the United Nations lose this war, I have found many who, before the war ends, want to see the stuffing knocked out of white supremacy. . . . If freedom and equality are not vouchsafed [granted] the peoples of color, the war for democracy will not be won. . . . We demand the abolition of segregation and discrimination in . . . [all] branches of national defense."

*—A. Philip Randolph, African-American labor and civil rights leader, November 1942*

**In Opposition to Integration**

"In this hour of national crisis, it is much more important that we have the full-hearted co-operation of the thirty million white southern Americans than that we satisfy the National Association for the Advancement of Colored People. . . . If they be forced to serve with Negroes, they will cease to volunteer; and when drafted, they will not serve with that enthusiasm and high morale that has always characterized the soldiers and sailors of the southern states."

*—W. R. Poage, Texas state representative, 1941*

***ANALYZING VIEWPOINTS*** **What arguments does each side use to support its viewpoint?**

To defeat the Japanese in the Pacific, United States Marines had to keep their strategies from the enemy. Navajo code talkers like these allowed the Allies to stay one step ahead of the Japanese. ***Diversity** How else did the armed forces benefit from diversity?*

**exploring TECHNOLOGY** World War II Submarine

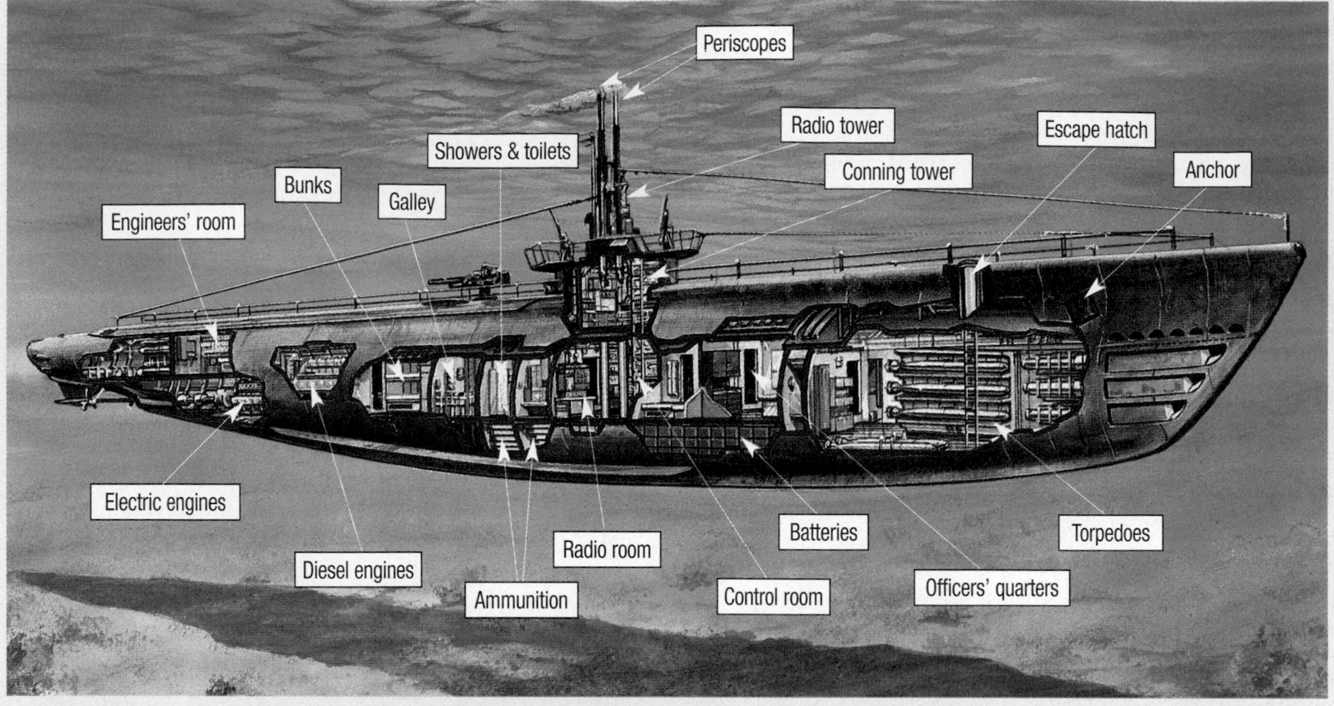


Both the Germans and the Allies used subs to attack enemy merchant convoys. The Allies used asdic, a form of echo-location, to detect enemy subs. ***Science and Technology*** *How does one development in war technology often lead to another?*

shot down more than 110 enemy planes over Italy. In late 1944, when heavy casualties in Europe forced the army to accept African Americans into white combat units, nearly 5,000 additional black volunteers stepped forward.

**Women in the Armed Forces** Not all soldiers were men. By the war's end, roughly 350,000 American women had volunteered for military service. Faced with a personnel shortage, officials were willing to use women in almost all areas except combat. About 13,000 women marines worked as clerks, typists, airfield control tower operators, mechanics, photographers, and drivers. Another 10,000 women served in the Coast Guard.

Some 1,200 WASPs (Women Air Force Service Pilots) ferried planes around the country and towed practice targets for antiaircraft gunners. The Navy had a similar organization, the WAVES (Women Accepted for Volunteer Emergency Service). One quarter of the 86,000 WAVES served in naval aviation. With nearly 100,000 officers and enlisted personnel, the Women's Army Corps (WAC) was the largest of the women's military groups. The WAC's commander, Colonel Oveta Culp Hobby, led more people than many army generals.

**Main Idea CONNECTIONS**

*Describe the roles that women played during World War II.*

## *Fighting in North Africa and Italy*

When the United States entered the war in 1941, the situation was critical. London and other major British cities had suffered heavy damage during the Battle of Britain. The Germans' *blitzkrieg* had extended Nazi control across most of Europe. In North Africa a German army led by General Erwin Rommel, known as the "Desert Fox" for his shrewd tactics, was equally successful. Many people feared that Germany could not be stopped.

**The Battle of the Atlantic** At sea a desperate struggle developed in the effort to keep German submarines from isolating Great Britain. To deliver the food and supplies that the British needed, merchant ships formed convoys. American warships often served as escorts. The Germans countered with groups of as many as 30 submarines, called wolf packs, that carried out coordinated attacks on the convoys. After the United States entered the war, the Battle of the Atlantic spread as German submarines began attacking merchant ships off the American coast.

Although Allied warships used sonar (underwater sound equipment) to locate and attack submarines, the wolf packs were highly effective. In the Atlantic they sank nearly 175 ships in June 1942 alone.

**The North Africa Campaign** Since August 1940, a British army had been battling Italian and German troops in North Africa. In November 1942 the British, under General Bernard Montgomery, won a decisive victory at El Alamein in Egypt. The Germans began to retreat west. A few days later, British and American troops commanded by American general Dwight D. Eisenhower landed in Morocco and Algeria and quickly pushed eastward. In May 1943 the two Allied armies came together in Tunisia, trapping Rommel's forces. Despite Hitler's instructions to fight to the death, nearly 240,000 Germans and Italians surrendered.

Churchill and Roosevelt met once again in January 1943, this time at Casablanca, Morocco. At this Casablanca Conference they planned strategy for fighting much of the rest of the war. The decision was made to continue concentrating Allied resources on Europe before trying to win the war in the Pacific. Churchill and Roosevelt also agreed to accept only the unconditional surrender of Italy, Germany, and Japan.

**The Invasion of Italy** In July 1943, American troops under General George S. Patton attacked Sicily, just south of the Italian mainland. When the island fell in just 38 days, Mussolini was overthrown. In September, as

## Allied Advances in Europe and Northern Africa, 1942–1945

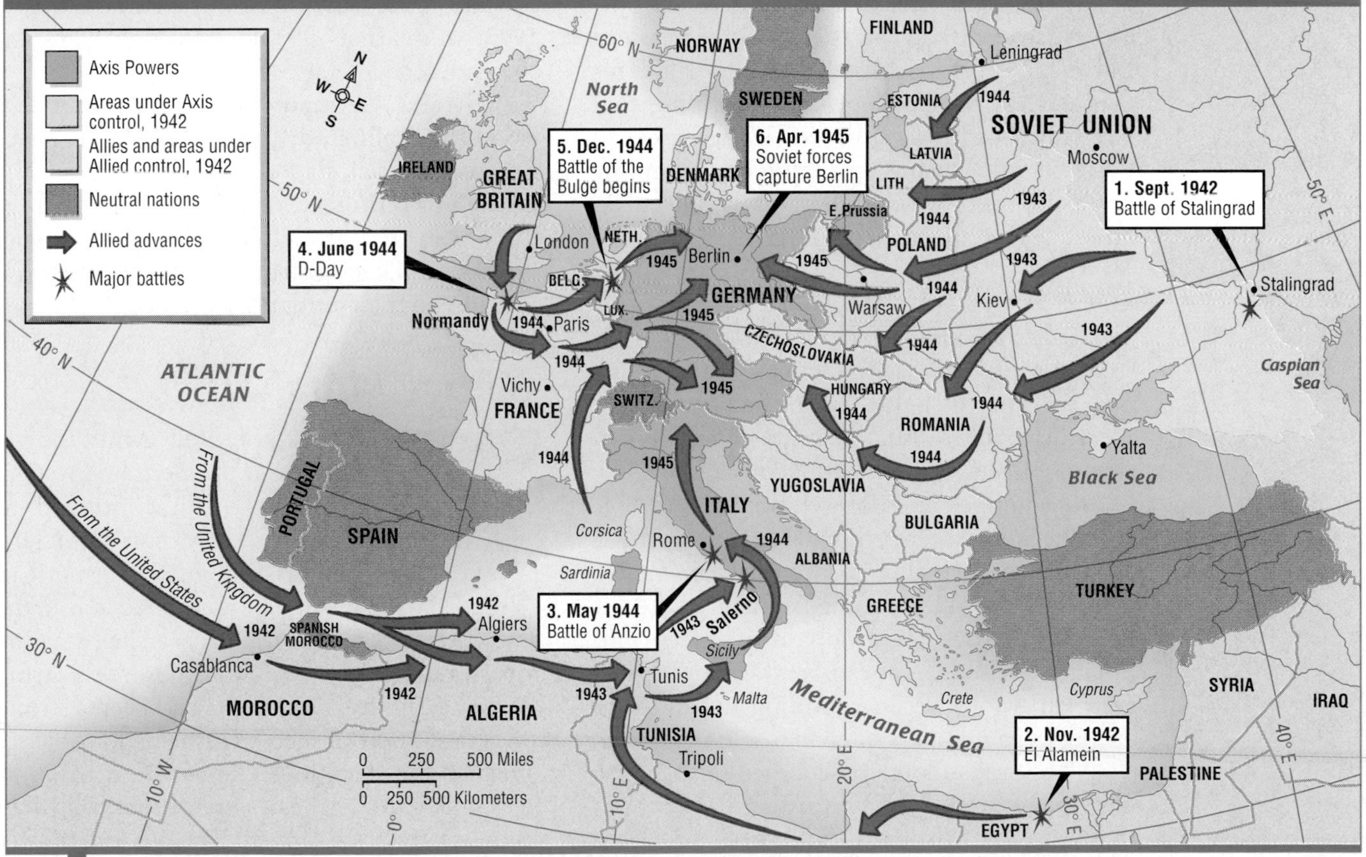

Axis Powers
Areas under Axis control, 1942
Allies and areas under Allied control, 1942
Neutral nations
Allied advances
Major battles

1. Sept. 1942 Battle of Stalingrad
2. Nov. 1942 El Alamein
3. May 1944 Battle of Anzio
4. June 1944 D-Day
5. Dec. 1944 Battle of the Bulge begins
6. Apr. 1945 Soviet forces capture Berlin

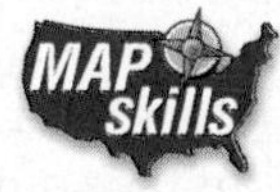


Axis Powers controlled most of Europe by the time the United States entered the war in 1941.
***Location*** *What geographic advantage did the United Kingdom have over other European nations that helped protect it from German aggression?*

Allied troops threatened the rest of Italy, its new government surrendered.

German troops in Italy, however, continued to resist, blocking roads and destroying bridges as they retreated up the Italian peninsula. By November, German defenses stiffened and the Allied advance stalled. In January, to get it moving again, an Allied force landed behind the German lines at Anzio, just south of Rome. For the next four months Allied soldiers fought to move more than a few miles beyond the beach. Before they finally broke through German defenses in May 1944, some 72,000 American soldiers had been killed or wounded.

After winning the Battle of Anzio, the Allies quickly captured Rome. However, many more months of heavy fighting were required before the Germans in northern Italy finally surrendered in April 1945. The Americans suffered nearly 190,000 casualties during the Italian campaign. German losses approached half a million troops.

## War in the Soviet Union

Meanwhile, as the Allies battled their way across northern Africa and southern Europe, an epic struggle had been developing in eastern Europe. As early as 1924 Hitler had called for conquest of the Soviet Union, claiming that Germany needed *lebensraum* (living space) to the east. After losing the Battle of Britain, he broke his pact with Stalin and launched an attack against the Soviet Union.

**The Germans Advance, 1941–1942** In June 1941, nearly 3.6 million German and other Axis troops poured across the length of the Soviet border, from the Baltic Sea in the north to the Black Sea in the south. The nearly 3 million Red Army soldiers opposing this onslaught were poorly equipped and not well trained.

The Soviets were unprepared for the intensity and the brutality of the German attack. The *Luftwaffe* quickly gained control of the air, and German ground troops drove deep into Soviet territory. In lands they occupied, German troops began rounding up and executing large numbers of civilians.

The Soviets adopted a scorched earth policy, destroying everything useful to the enemy as they retreated. In the meantime, Stalin asked Roosevelt for help through the Lend-Lease program. However, Congress blocked this request for many months. American aid did not begin to flow until June 1942.

By that summer, German armies threatened major cities deep inside the Soviet Union. Stalin desperately urged his allies to launch an attack on Western Europe. He believed such an attack would take pressure off the Soviet Union's Red Army in the east by forcing Hitler to divide his forces. Churchill, however, hesitated to make such a risky invasion. At Casablanca he persuaded Roosevelt instead to invade Italy, which he called the "soft underbelly" of Europe. The Soviets would have to confront the bulk of the German army on their own.

**The Battle of Stalingrad** The Red Army decided to make its stand at Stalingrad, a major industrial railroad center. In mid-September 1942 the Germans began a campaign of bombing and shelling that lasted more than two months. The Soviets took up positions in the rubble that remained of Stalingrad and engaged the advancing German troops in bitter house-to-house fighting.

In mid-November, taking advantage of the harsh Russian weather, Soviet forces counterattacked and surrounded the German army. In late January, the Red Army launched a final assault on the freezing enemy. On January 31, 1943, more than 90,000 surviving Germans surrendered.

In all, Germany lost some 330,000 troops at Stalingrad; the Soviet Union never released official data on its casualties. The **Battle of Stalingrad** was the turning point of the war in the east. After their victory, Soviet forces began a long struggle to regain the territory lost to the Germans.

## George Marshall

AMERICAN BIOGRAPHY

As the Red Army slowly forced the German invaders back, Stalin continued to push for the long-promised invasion of Western Europe. Everyone assumed that American George Marshall would be appointed to lead the assault once it finally began. Marshall was the top American general and Roosevelt's Army Chief of Staff. In addition, he had been a strong voice in support of such an invasion long before others were willing to back it.

Thus, the Allies were shocked when Roosevelt instead tapped Dwight Eisenhower to lead the invasion. Marshall was so important to the overall war effort, the President said in explaining his decision, that he would not sleep well if the general were out of the country.

George Marshall
(1880–1959)

A graduate of Virginia Military Institute, Marshall had served in France during World War I, where he aided in planning major Allied victories. Promotions were slow after the war, however, until Marshall came to Washington, D.C. There he became Deputy Chief of Staff in 1938 and was named to the army's top job just a year later.

As Army Chief of Staff, Marshall pushed the President to prepare for war by strengthening the army. Soon after America's entry into World War II, Marshall called for an invasion of Western Europe. He opposed Churchill's plan to focus on North Africa and Italy first. Churchill later credited Marshall with being "the true organizer of [the Allies'] victory."

After the war ended in 1945, Marshall resigned. However, President Harry Truman quickly called him back to public service. As Secretary of State, Marshall launched a massive effort to rebuild postwar Europe. Today that program is known as the Marshall Plan. For this work Marshall received the Nobel Peace Prize in 1953. ■

## *The Invasion of Western Europe*

At every conference of Allied leaders after the United States entered the war, Marshall pushed for an attack on the German forces occupying France. Allied planes were already bombing Germany. In late 1943 the British finally agreed to go along with Marshall's proposal to launch a land invasion as well.

**The Air War** The RAF had begun bombing Germany in 1940. However, the *Luftwaffe* quickly forced the British to give up daylight missions for safer but less accurate nighttime raids. When the Germans started to target cities during the Battle of Britain, the RAF responded in kind. It abandoned attempts to pinpoint targets and developed a technique called **carpet bombing,** in which large numbers of bombs were scattered over a wide area. German cities suffered heavy damage as a result.

Allied bombing of Germany had intensified after the United States entered the war. In the spring of 1943 the bombing campaign was stepped up yet again in order to soften Germany for the planned Allied invasion. By 1944 British and American commanders were conducting coordinated air raids—American planes bombing by day and the RAF by night. At its height, some 3,000 planes were involved in this campaign.

**Preparation for Invasion** A massive buildup of troops began in southern England as American, British, and Canadian forces were joined by Polish, Dutch, Belgian, and French troops. In response, the Germans strengthened their defenses along the French coastline. As they waited for the invasion to begin, German soldiers added machine-gun emplacements, barbed wire fences on beaches, land and water mines, and underwater obstructions.

**D-Day** Shortly after midnight on June 6, 1944, the largest landing by sea in history began as some 4,600 invasion craft and warships slipped out of their harbors in southern England. As the ships crossed the English Channel, about 1,000 RAF bombers pounded German defenses at Normandy. Meanwhile,

General Dwight Eisenhower (left) commanded many Allied initiatives in Europe, including the D-Day landing at Normandy in 1944. ***Geography*** ***Why was Hitler expecting the main thrust of the invasion to be at Calais, and not Normandy?***

some 23,000 airborne British and American soldiers, in a daring nighttime maneuver, were dropped behind enemy lines.

At dawn on **D-Day,** the code name for the day the invasion began, Allied warships in the channel began a massive shelling of the coast. Some 1,000 American planes continued the RAF's air bombardment. Then around 150,000 Allied troops and their equipment began to come ashore along 60 miles of Normandy coast.

Despite the advice of his generals to launch a counterattack, Hitler hesitated. He feared a larger invasion at the narrowest part of the English Channel near Calais. Nevertheless, German resistance at Normandy was fierce. At Omaha Beach, the code name for one landing site, the Allies suffered some 2,000 casualties.

In spite of the heavy casualties of D-Day, within a week a half million men came ashore. By late July the Allied force in France numbered some 2 million troops.

**The Battle of the Bulge** Bitter fighting followed as the Allies broke through German defenses at Normandy and pushed across France. In late August 1944, American troops liberated Paris. British and Canadian forces freed Brussels and Antwerp in Belgium a few days later. In mid-September, a combined Allied force attacked the Germans occupying Holland. At about the same time, Americans crossed the western border of Germany.

The Nazis fought desperately to defend their homeland. After reinforcing the army with thousands of additional draftees, some as young as 15, they launched a counterattack in Belgium and Luxembourg in December 1944. This battle came to be known as the **Battle of the Bulge.**

As the German attack overwhelmed the American forces and pushed them back, many small units became cut off from the rest of the army. The soldiers of these isolated units fought gallantly. From his headquarters near Paris, Eisenhower ordered more troops to the scene. The most spectacular of these reinforcement actions was carried out by General Patton. In just a few days he moved his entire army of 250,000 soldiers from western France to help stop the German advance.

The Battle of the Bulge was the largest battle in Western Europe during World War II and the largest ever fought by the United States Army. It involved some 600,000 GIs, of whom about 80,000 were killed, wounded, or captured. German losses totaled about 100,000 troops. After this battle, most Nazi leaders recognized that the war was lost.

## CAUSE AND EFFECT: World War II

**CAUSES**

- *Fascism takes hold in Italy and Germany.*
- *Germany invades the Rhineland and annexes Austria and Czechoslovakia.*
- *Germany invades Poland.*
- *Japan aggressively builds an empire in Asia.*

**WORLD WAR II**

**EFFECTS**

- *Europe and Japan are left in ruins.*
- *Two thirds of Europe's Jewish population is killed.*
- *The United States and the Soviet Union emerge as world powers.*
- *The cold war begins.*

**Interpreting Charts** Foreign aggression on both sides of the world erupted into global war. ***Foreign Relations*** ***How was the world changed by the end of the war?***

# War Ends in Europe

In March 1945, as Allied bombers continued to hammer German cities, American ground forces crossed the Rhine River and advanced toward Berlin from the west. Meanwhile, the Soviets pushed into Germany from the east.

**The Soviets Advance** The fighting between German and Soviet forces from 1941 to 1945 was the greatest conflict ever fought on a single front. At any given time it involved more than 9 million troops. The costs of this struggle were horrific. The 13.6 million Soviet and 3 million German military killed accounted for more than two thirds the total dead for all World War II. Current research in records in the former Soviet Union places the total of Soviet civilian and military deaths at 27 million.

After the hardships their nation had endured, Soviet leaders considered the capture of Berlin, Germany's capital, a matter of honor. In late April 1945 the Soviets fought their way into Berlin. They found a city more than 80 percent destroyed by Allied bombing.

While some Soviet troops attacked Berlin, other elements of the Red Army continued to drive west. On April 25, they met American troops at the Elbe River.

**Germany Surrenders** In Berlin, Hitler had refused to take his generals' advice to flee as the Soviets closed in on the city. Instead he fulfilled a vow he had made in 1939: "I shall stand or fall in this struggle. I shall never survive the defeat of my people." On May 1, the German government announced that Hitler had committed suicide. A few days later, on May 8, 1945, Germany surrendered.

American soldiers rejoiced and civilians celebrated V-E Day (Victory in Europe Day) at home as the war in Europe came to an end. The war was not over yet, however, as Japan was still to be defeated.

A United States soldier and Russian soldier (left and right) share a moment of camaraderie after meeting at the Elbe River in April 1945. ***Foreign Relations*** ***How did Soviet assaults in 1945 help end the war?***

**The Yalta Conference** In February 1945, two months before the fall of Berlin, Roosevelt, Churchill, and Stalin met at Yalta, a city in the Soviet Union near the Black Sea. The purpose of the **Yalta Conference** was to plan for the postwar world. The leaders agreed to split Germany into four zones, each under the control of one of the major Allies. The city of Berlin, which would lie in the Soviet zone, would be similarly divided. Stalin promised to allow elections in the nations his army liberated from the Germans. He also promised to enter the war against Japan soon after Germany surrendered.

The agreements at Yalta were only partially fulfilled. Stalin refused, for example, to honor his promise for free elections. Roosevelt and Churchill were accused of not doing enough to prevent Soviet domination of Eastern Europe. The issue of Eastern Europe would be at the heart of the problems that later arose between the Soviet Union and the Western Allies.

## SECTION 2 REVIEW

### Comprehension

1. *Key Terms* Define: (a) Atlantic Charter; (b) GI; (c) Battle of Stalingrad; (d) carpet bombing; (e) D-Day; (f) Battle of the Bulge; (g) Yalta Conference.
2. *Summarizing the Main Idea* What events helped turn the tide of war in favor of the Allies?
3. *Organizing Information* Create a four-column chart on a sheet of paper. Label the columns *1942, 1943, 1944,* and *1945*. In each column list the major battles and events in the European and North African theaters of war for that year.

### Critical Thinking

4. *Analyzing Time Lines* Review the time line at the start of the section. Explain how the Allied decision to delay an invasion of Western Europe and fight instead in North Africa and Italy affected war efforts in the Soviet Union.
5. *Checking Consistency* Why do you think Americans who were denied full rights at home were eager to take part in the war against fascism?

### Writing Activity

6. *Writing an Expository Essay* Joseph Stalin repeatedly asked the Allies to invade Western Europe in order to take the pressure off the Soviet Union. Write an essay convincing the Allied leaders to support this plan, or write a reply explaining why the invasion had to be delayed.

| May 1942 | June 1942 | Feb. 1943 | June 1944 | Feb. 1945 | Aug. 1945 |
|---|---|---|---|---|---|
| *Battle of the Coral Sea* | *Battle of Midway* | *Japanese abandon Guadalcanal* | *Americans capture Mariana Islands* | *Land invasion at Iwo Jima* | *Atomic bomb dropped on Hiroshima* |

1942 1944 1946

# 3 The War in the Pacific

## SECTION PREVIEW

### Objectives

1. Summarize the Japanese advance in the Pacific in 1941 and 1942 and describe Allied victories that turned the tide of the war.
2. Describe the Allied struggle for the Pacific islands, including Iwo Jima and Okinawa.
3. Describe the Manhattan Project and its effect in bringing an end to the war.
4. *Key Terms* Define: Bataan Death March; Battle of the Coral Sea; Battle of Midway; Battle of Guadalcanal; *kamikaze;* Battle of Iwo Jima; Battle of Okinawa; Manhattan Project.

### Main Idea

Fierce fighting and heavy casualties characterized the war in the Pacific Ocean as the Allied forces struggled to turn back Japanese advances.

### Reading Strategy

*Organizing Information* Sketch a map that shows the areas where fighting took place in the Pacific Ocean. As you read the section, mark the major battle sites on your map. Also note who won each battle.

The bombing of Pearl Harbor was only the first of several Japanese offensives across the Pacific. Just hours after the attack on Pearl Harbor, Japanese warplanes based in China hit Clark Field, the main American air base in the Philippine Islands. (American troops had occupied the Philippines since the Spanish-American War in 1898.) The American planes sat neatly parked along the runways at Clark Field. As Japanese planes swept over the airfield, strings of bombs fell toward their targets. Planes and buildings were blown to pieces. Returning to their base, the Japanese attackers rejoiced over their success. Many were puzzled, however. They asked, What was the matter with the enemy? Didn't the Americans know the war had started?

## *The Japanese Advance, 1941–1942*

Although news of Pearl Harbor had reached Douglas MacArthur, the commanding general, the Americans at Clark Field had not expected an immediate attack. About half of General MacArthur's air force was destroyed as it sat on the ground.

Within days, a large Japanese force landed in the Philippines. MacArthur withdrew most of his troops to the Bataan Peninsula on Manila Bay. There he set up defenses, hoping the navy would be able to evacuate his army to safety.

**The Philippines Fall** For some four months, American and Filipino troops held out on the Bataan Peninsula. In March, realizing the situation was hopeless, President Roosevelt ordered MacArthur to escape to Australia. The general was reluctant to abandon his soldiers to the Japanese, but promised,"I shall return."

When the peninsula's gallant troops surrendered to Japanese forces in early April, about 2,000 soldiers and nurses escaped to the fortified island of Corregidor in Manila Bay. Joining the fort's defenders, they fought on for another month. The holdouts survived nearly constant Japanese bombing and artillery barrages by living in the rock tunnels of the fortress. Finally, running low on ammunition and food, over 11,000 Americans and Filipinos surrendered on May 6, 1942.

As the Bataan Peninsula fell, some 76,000 Filipinos and Americans became prisoners of war. Japanese soldiers split the prisoners into groups of 500 to 1,000 and marched them some 60 miles to a railroad. Those who survived the ordeal were shipped to prison camps where they were held for the rest of the war. However, already weakened from weeks without enough food or medicine, at least 10,000 prisoners died during the 6- to 12-day march. Many were executed by the guards when they could not keep up.

Word of what became known as the **Bataan Death March** did not reach America until three years later, when three soldiers escaped from their prison camp. After the war the general blamed for organizing the march was one of six Japanese executed for war crimes.

**The War at Sea** As Japanese forces spread across the Pacific, the battered American navy fought desperately to stop them. In May 1942, a largely American naval group halted a Japanese advance by engaging a superior enemy fleet in the Coral Sea, northeast of Australia. The **Battle of the Coral Sea** was the first naval combat carried out entirely by aircraft. The enemy ships never came within sight of one another. Planes launched from the aircraft carriers bombed and strafed the enemy forces more than 70 miles away.

The costs of the five-day battle were high. Both sides lost more than half their aircraft. The American aircraft carrier *Lexington* was destroyed, and the *Yorktown* was badly damaged. But one Japanese carrier sank, another lost most of its planes, and a third was put out of action. Militarily the battle was probably a draw. However, it prevented the Japanese from establishing the bases they needed to bomb Australia, thus blocking the invasion of that nation.

## *Allied Victories Turn the Tide*

While the Soviets resisted German advances and the Allies prepared to invade North Africa, two critical battles took place in the Pacific. Midway Island, near Hawaii, and Guadalcanal, in the western Pacific near the Coral Sea, were small but strategic islands. In mid-1942, the battles for these islands changed the course of the war in the Pacific.

**The Battle of Midway** Despite his success at Pearl Harbor, Japanese admiral Isoroku Yamamoto believed that American naval power still held the key to victory or defeat in Asia. He hoped to destroy what remained of the Pacific Fleet by luring it into battle at Midway Island, northwest of Hawaii. Yamamoto committed a large part of Japan's navy to his plan. He correctly believed that American admiral Chester Nimitz would use all his resources to protect Midway, which was vital to the defense of Hawaii.

The **Battle of Midway** erupted on June 4, 1942. Like the action in the Coral Sea, it was fought entirely from the air. The American planes found the Japanese carriers at a vulnerable time—the Japanese were still loading bombs onto their planes. The Americans swiftly demolished three of four Japanese carriers as bombs stacked up on their decks exploded in the attack. The fourth was destroyed trying to escape. The sinking of these carriers, plus the loss of some 250 planes they carried, was a devastating blow to Japanese naval power. After the Battle of Midway, Japan was unable to launch any more offensive operations.

**Main Idea CONNECTIONS**

*Why was the Battle of Midway an important victory for the Allies?*

**The Battle of Guadalcanal** The victory at Midway allowed the Allies to take the offensive in the Pacific. Their first goal was to capture Guadalcanal in the Solomon Islands. When more than 11,000 marines landed on

This eerie scene of Guadalcanal, painted by Kerr Eby, is called *Ghost Trail.* ***Geography*** *What was the geographical challenge of the Battle of Guadalcanal?*

the island in August 1942, some 2,200 Japanese fled into the jungle. Months of fighting followed. By November the American navy controlled the waters around Guadalcanal.

The **Battle of Guadalcanal** provided the marines with their first taste of jungle warfare. As they slogged through swamps, forded rivers, and hacked through tangles of vines, they frequently encountered enemy units. The marines made easy targets for Japanese snipers hidden in the underbrush or in the tops of palm trees. When Japan's forces finally slipped off the island in February 1943, their withdrawal went undetected until the marines discovered their empty boats on the beach.

## *Struggle for the Islands*

From Guadalcanal, American forces began island-hopping, a strategy of selectively attacking or bypassing specific enemy-held islands. The Japanese fiercely defended their positions. Both sides suffered heavy casualties before the Allies won the war in 1945.

**Island-Hopping in the Pacific** In 1943 and 1944 the Allies pushed north from Australia and west across the central Pacific. As forces under General MacArthur and Admiral William Halsey leapfrogged through the Solomon Islands, other Americans led by Admiral Nimitz began a similar campaign in the Gilbert Islands. After seizing the island of Tarawa, Nimitz used it to launch bombing raids on Japan's bases in the Marshall Islands. By February 1944, these attacks had crippled Japanese air power. This allowed Nimitz's forces to seize Kwajalein and Eniwetok at the northwest end of the island group.

From the Marshalls, Nimitz captured parts of the Mariana Islands in June. American long-range bombers were able to reach Japan from this location. By the end of 1944, American planes were dropping tons of explosives on Japanese cities.

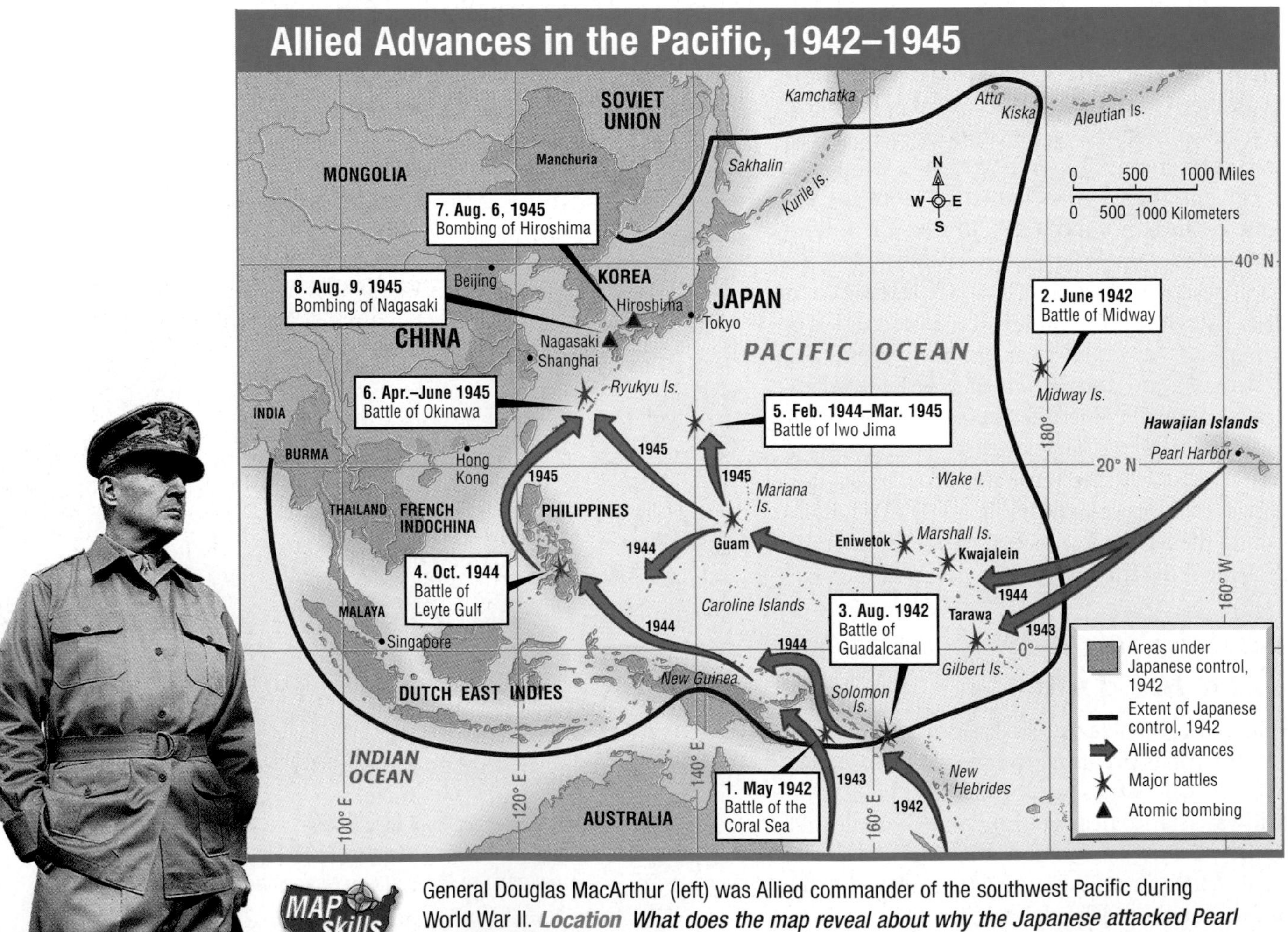


General Douglas MacArthur (left) was Allied commander of the southwest Pacific during World War II. ***Location*** *What does the map reveal about why the Japanese attacked Pearl Harbor in 1941?*

**The Philippines Campaign** As American forces pushed forward in the summer of 1944, military planners decided to bypass the Philippine Islands. MacArthur vigorously opposed this strategy, claiming that the United States had an obligation to free the Filipino people. The general's arguments convinced Roosevelt, who reversed the decision.

In mid-October, some 160,000 American troops invaded the Philippine island of Leyte. After the beach was secure, General MacArthur dramatically waded ashore from a landing craft. As news cameras recorded the historic event, MacArthur proclaimed, "People of the Philippines, I have returned."

While American troops fought their way inland, the greatest naval battle in world history developed off the coast. More than 280 warships were engaged during the three-day Battle of Leyte Gulf. The Japanese high command directed nearly every warship still afloat to attack the enemy. This battle saw the first use of ***kamikazes,*** or suicide planes.† Japanese pilots deliberately crashed their aircraft, which were heavily loaded with bombs, into their targets. Despite this tactic, the Japanese were badly beaten and their navy was virtually destroyed.

Japanese land forces continued to resist, however. In the more than two months it took American troops to control Leyte, some 80,000 Japanese defenders were killed. Fewer than 1,000 Japanese surrendered. The battle for Manila, the Philippines' capital city, on the island of Luzon, was equally hard fought. The nearly month-long struggle left most of Manila in ruins and some 100,000 Filipino civilians dead. Not until June 1945 were the Philippines securely in Allied hands.

## Iwo Jima and Okinawa

The **Battle of Iwo Jima** was one of the bloodiest of the war. The struggle for this tiny volcanic island, less than 700 miles from Japan, was both long and intense. The island's steep rocky slopes were honeycombed with caves and tunnels. More than 600 guns, many encased in concrete bunkers, were protected by the natural terrain. In November 1944, American bombers, based in the recently conquered Marianas, began to pound Iwo Jima from the air. For 74 days American planes and warships poured nearly 7,000 tons of bombs and more than 20,000 shells onto Iwo Jima's defenders.

In mid-February 1945, marines stormed the beaches from the ships offshore. They encountered furious resistance from the Japanese. After three days of combat, the marines had advanced only about 700 yards inland. Eventually nearly 110,000 American troops were involved in the campaign. Although fewer than 25,000 Japanese opposed the Americans, it took almost a month for the marines to secure the island. The enemy fought virtually to the last defender. Only 216 Japanese were taken prisoner.

The American forces suffered an estimated 25,000 casualties in capturing this 14-square-mile island. Twenty-seven Medals of Honor were awarded for actions on Iwo Jima, more than in any other single operation of the war. Admiral Nimitz described the island as a place where "uncommon valor was a common virtue."

The **Battle of Okinawa,** fought from April to June 1945, was equally bloody. Nearly 100,000 defenders occupied this island, which was little more than 350 miles from Japan itself. The Japanese troops on Okinawa knew they were the last obstacle to an Allied invasion of the Japanese home islands. Many had pledged to fight to the death to prevent their homeland from falling.

The American and British force amassed at Okinawa was second in size only to the

### World War II Deaths

| Country | Military Deaths | Civilian Deaths | Total Deaths |
|---|---|---|---|
| **Axis** | | | |
| Germany | 3,250,000 | 2,350,000 | 5,600,000 |
| Italy | 226,900 | 60,000 | 286,900 |
| Japan | 1,740,000 | 393,400 | 2,133,400 |
| **Allies** | | | |
| France | 122,000 | 470,000 | 592,000 |
| Great Britain | 305,800 | 60,600 | 366,400 |
| United States | 405,400 | — | 405,400 |
| Soviet Union | 11,000,000 | 6,700,000 | 17,700,000 |

Source: *World War II: A Statistical Survey*, by John Ellis

**Interpreting Tables** Accurate death tolls are hard to determine, and figures vary widely. Scholars do not dispute, however, the horrific human cost of the war. ***Culture Which nation suffered the greatest human loss?***

† The term *kamikaze* means "divine wind" and refers to a typhoon which reputedly saved Japan in 1281 by destroying a Mongol fleet that was sailing to invade the islands.

Normandy invasion in Europe. Some 1,300 warships and more than 180,000 combat troops were gathered to drive the enemy from the island. Japanese pilots flew nearly 2,000 *kamikaze* attacks against this fleet. On the island, defenders made equally desperate *banzai* charges—attacks designed to kill as many of the enemy as possible while dying in battle.

One GI described the long, hard-fought campaign to take Okinawa:

**AMERICAN VOICES** **"Our attack pattern was: barrage a hill with bombs and shells, move up the foot soldiers, hold it against counterattacks, fight down the reverse slope, then start on the next one. We would attack during the day, dig in for the night—not for sleep, but for safety. A hole was never deep enough when the Japanese started their barrage. And then, at night, they would come, a screaming banzai or a single shadow."**

—*An American GI at Okinawa*

In June, when the Japanese resistance finally ended after almost three months, only 7,200 defenders remained to surrender. For American forces, nearly 50,000 casualties made the Battle of Okinawa the costliest engagement of the Pacific war. At long last, however, the way was open for an invasion of Japan.

## *The Manhattan Project*

After the grueling battles at Iwo Jima and Okinawa, American soldiers began to prepare themselves for the invasion of Japan. They knew how costly such an invasion would be. Unknown to them, however, work was nearly done on a bomb that would make the invasion unnecessary.

The story begins in August 1939, when President Roosevelt received a letter from Albert Einstein, a brilliant Jewish physicist who had sought refuge in America from the Nazis.† In his letter, Einstein suggested that an incredibly powerful new type of bomb could be built. He hinted that the Germans were already at work on such a weapon. Roosevelt, concerned that Germany not develop this weapon first, organized the top secret **Manhattan Project** to develop such a bomb.

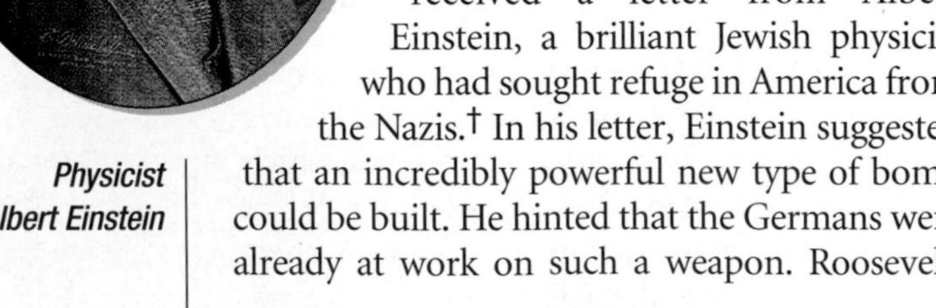

*Physicist Albert Einstein*

Scientists had already succeeded in splitting the nucleus of the uranium atom. However, to make an atomic bomb they had to create a controlled chain reaction. In such a reaction, particles released from the splitting of one atom would cause another atom to break apart, and so on. The theory was that the energy released when so many atoms were split would produce a massive explosion. In 1942, Enrico Fermi, a scientist who had left Fascist Italy, accomplished such a chain reaction in a laboratory at the University of Chicago.

On July 16, 1945, Manhattan Project scientists field-tested Fermi's work. In the desert of New Mexico they detonated the world's first atomic bomb. With a blinding flash of light, the explosion blew a huge crater in the earth and shattered windows some 125 miles away. As he watched, J. Robert Oppenheimer, who headed the building of the bomb, remembered the words of the *Bhagavad Gita,* the Hindu holy book: "Now I am become Death, the destroyer of worlds."

**The Decision to Drop the Bomb** Once the bomb was ready, the question became whether to use it. Other courses of action existed for bringing an end to the war. Allied planners had already worked out plans for a massive invasion of Japan. However, Japanese resistance to an attack on their home islands was expected to be even greater than it had been in the rest of the Pacific.

A naval blockade or continued conventional bombing could also help defeat Japan. A demonstration of the new weapon on some deserted island might show the Japanese the atomic bomb's awesome power. Some diplomats believed that Japan might give up more quickly if the United States softened its insistence on an unconditional surrender.

An advisory group of scientists, military leaders, and government officials, called the Interim Committee, formed in the spring of 1945. The committee members debated these ideas and many others. In the end, they found themselves unwilling to recommend any of the alternatives. The heavy American casualties at Iwo Jima and Okinawa were a factor in the committee's support for using the bomb.

Although the recommendation was unanimous, many other scientists who had worked

† Albert Einstein is also famous for the development of the theory of relativity that linked energy and matter in the now well-known formula $E=mc^2$.

on the bomb's development disagreed with the Interim Committee's endorsement of its use. The final decision, however, rested with the President. That burden fell on Harry S. Truman, President for barely three months after Roosevelt's sudden death in April 1945. Truman had no difficulty making up his mind. He considered the bomb to be a military weapon and had no doubt that it should be used. Despite the controversy that later arose over whether the bombing was justified, Truman never regretted his decision. "You should do your weeping at Pearl Harbor," he said to his critics in 1963.

**Japan Surrenders** On August 6, 1945, an American plane dropped an atomic bomb on Hiroshima, a city in southern Japan and the site of a large army base. No one knows for sure how many people were killed. The official Japanese estimate is that 140,000 died in the explosion or within a few months from burns or radiation poisoning. Thousands of others survived, but with horrible burns. Some 90 percent of the city's buildings were damaged or totally destroyed. A Hiroshima resident described the scene after the bombing as follows:

> **"Wherever you went, you didn't bother to take the roads. Everything was flat, nothing was standing, no gates, pillars, walls, or fences. You walked in a straight line to where you wanted to go. Practically everywhere you came across small bones that had been left behind."**
>
> —*Hiroshima survivor*

A moment before the bomb code-named "Little Boy" leveled Hiroshima, the American GI above would have been standing in the midst of a thriving city. ***Science and Technology*** ***How was the atomic bomb different from other war technology?***

Three days later a second bomb, dropped on Nagasaki, produced similar devastation, disfigurement, and death. The Japanese people were stunned by these developments. On August 14, the government of Japan accepted the American terms for surrender. The next day Americans celebrated what appeared to be the end of the war. The formal surrender agreement was signed on September 2, 1945, in a ceremony aboard the U.S.S. *Missouri* in Tokyo Bay. The long and destructive war had finally come to an end.

## SECTION 3 REVIEW

### Comprehension

1. ***Key Terms*** Define: (a) Bataan Death March; (b) Battle of the Coral Sea; (c) Battle of Midway; (d) Battle of Guadalcanal; (e) *kamikaze;* (f) Battle of Iwo Jima; (g) Battle of Okinawa; (h) Manhattan Project.
2. ***Summarizing the Main Idea*** Which two battles changed the course of the war in the Pacific?
3. ***Organizing Information*** Use information from the section to create a chart that identifies the Allied successes in the Pacific from 1943 to 1945.

### Critical Thinking

4. ***Analyzing Time Lines*** Review the time line at the start of the section. Write a sentence or phrase that connects each entry to the one that follows it.
5. ***Identifying Alternatives*** What were some of the alternatives to dropping the atomic bomb on Japan?

### Writing Activity

6. ***Writing an Expository Essay*** Write a brief essay that explains why the Japanese were able to advance through the Pacific so easily in 1941 and 1942. Also note how the Allies succeeded in changing the momentum of the war.

# SKILLS FOR LIFE

**Historical Evidence**

Critical Thinking

Geography

Graphs and Charts

# Examining Photographs

Photographs are a form of visual evidence that can provide valuable information about an event or historical period. They show what people or places in recent history looked like and can document momentous occasions. Photographers, however, like other observers of events, have their own points of view. Therefore, you must analyze their photographs carefully.

By their choice of subject, lighting, and camera angle, photographers can influence what is seen and how it is perceived. They may choose to photograph a scene that strikes them as interesting, dramatic, or revealing but that, in reality, is not typical or representative. Photographers may also distort the appearance of objects in their pictures to create an illusion or convey a particular mood. By making these choices, photographers affect what may be learned from their pictures.

The photograph below, taken by Joe Rosenthal, is one of the most famous photographs taken during World War II. The photograph shows victorious United States Marines hoisting the American flag on the Pacific island of Iwo Jima. Use the following steps to analyze and evaluate the photograph.

1. ***Study the photograph to identify the subject.*** Look at the photograph as a whole, then study the details. (a) What do you see in the picture? (b) What broad subject does the photograph seem to illustrate? (c) Was the photograph likely taken before, during, or after a battle? Explain.

2. ***Analyze the reliability of the photograph as a source of information.*** (a) What mood or emotion is captured in this photograph? (b) What aspects of the photograph capture this mood? (c) Is it significant that this photo is in black and white, not color? Explain. (d) What role does the photographer play in shaping this image? What choices might he have made before taking the picture?

3. ***Study the photograph to learn more about the historical period.*** Refer to the photograph and what you have read about World War II to answer the following questions. (a) How might Americans back home have reacted to this photograph? (b) What can photographs such as this one contribute to knowledge of an event that written sources cannot?

**TEST FOR SUCCESS**

From what you have read in this chapter about the fighting in the Pacific islands during World War II, do you think this photograph presents a realistic picture of the war? Explain.

| 1935 | 1937 | 1938 | 1942 | 1943 | 1944 | 1945 |
|---|---|---|---|---|---|---|
| Nazis pass the Nuremberg Laws | Jewish businesses forcibly "Aryanized." | Kristallnacht violence results in destruction of Jewish synagogues and businesses | The "final solution" announced at Wannsee Conference | Warsaw ghetto uprising | Roosevelt creates the War Refugee Board | Allied troops liberate concentration camps |

1935 1940 1945

# 4 The Holocaust

## SECTION PREVIEW

### Objectives

1. Explain how persecution of Jews and other minorities increased in Germany under the Nazis during the 1930s.
2. Describe how the Nazis carried out their plans for genocide.
3. *Key Terms* Holocaust; anti-Semitism; concentration camp; *Kristallnacht;* Wannsee Conference; death camp; War Refugee Board.

### Main Idea

During World War II, the Nazis carried out a brutal plan that resulted in the deaths of 6 million Jews and millions of other victims.

### Reading Strategy

*Arranging Events in Order* As you read the section, create a time line of the events related to the Holocaust. Write a sentence to describe each event.

When Adolf Hitler came to power in 1933, he set about implementing the Nazi philosophy outlined in his book *Mein Kampf.* Chief among his goals was the removal of so-called "non-Aryans," in particular the Jews.

No persecution of Jews in world history equals the extent and brutality of the **Holocaust,** Nazi Germany's systematic murder of European Jews. In all, some six million Jews, about two thirds of Europe's Jewish population, had been massacred by the end of World War II. Some five to six million other people also died in Nazi captivity.

## The Start of Persecution

Theories that European peoples, so-called Aryans, were superior to Middle Eastern peoples called Semites had developed in Germany in the mid-1800s. (Semitic peoples include Arabs, Ethiopians, and other Middle Eastern and North African groups, as well as Jews.) Although these theories were rejected by all responsible scholars at the time, others used them to justify continued persecution. By the 1880s **anti-Semitism** had come to mean hostility toward Jews. When the Nazi party gained control of Germany's government in 1933, anti-Semitism became the official policy of the nation.

Nazis singled out Jews for persecution by forcing them to wear yellow Stars of David like this one.

**The Nazis Take Action** Under Nazi rule, German citizens were encouraged to stop patronizing Jewish businesses. In 1935, the Nazis passed the Nuremberg Laws, stripping Jews of their German citizenship and forbidding marriage between Jews and non-Jews.

In 1937 and 1938 the Nazis began a program to "Aryanize" Jewish businesses. They required Jews to register their property and dismissed Jewish employees and managers. Jewish doctors were banned from treating non-Jews. All German people had to carry identity cards. The Nazi government marked Jews' cards with a red letter "J" and gave all Jews new middle names—"Sarah" for women and "Israel" for men. This practice made it easier for the police to identify Jews.

When the Nazis came to power, they organized the SA, a police unit charged with silencing opposition to the Nazis. Later, Hitler formed the SS, an elite guard that became the private army of the Nazi party. In addition, a Secret

VIEWING HISTORY

Above, a Jewish shopkeeper sweeps up shop windows left shattered by *Kristallnacht.* At right, the "J" stamp on this girl's identification paper identifies her as Jewish. ***Government** In what other ways did the Nazis organize the persecution of Jews?*

State Police, or Gestapo, was formed to identify and pursue those people who did not follow the new laws of the Nazi regime. Political enemies were thrown into hastily built "camps" in empty warehouses and factories guarded by SS troops.

Typically, **concentration camps** are places where prisoners of war and political prisoners are confined, usually under harsh conditions. However, the Nazi camps soon held many other people considered by them to be "undesirable," including the homeless, homosexuals, Jehovah's Witnesses, and persons with mental and physical disabilities. By the late 1930s, Gypsies were also being imprisoned.

***Kristallnacht*** Organized attacks on Jews began in early 1938, after Hitler's annexation of Austria. On the night of November 9–10, 1938, Nazi thugs throughout Germany and Austria looted and destroyed Jewish stores, houses, and synagogues. The incident became known as ***Kristallnacht*** ("Night of the Broken Glass"), referring to the broken windows of the Jewish shops. Mass arrests of Jews followed.

**Refugees Seek an Escape** From 1933 through 1937 about 130,000 Jews fled Germany. The Nazis encouraged this emigration because it helped to achieve their plan. At first, most refugees merely moved to other European nations. As the numbers grew, however, Jews began to go to Palestine, Latin America, and the United States.

Responding to calls for the United States to take action, President Roosevelt called for an international conference to discuss the growing numbers of Jewish refugees. However, the Evian Conference, held in France in July 1938, failed to deal with the situation. With the exception of the Dominican Republic, none of the 29 nations represented, including the United States, was willing to ease its immigration laws.

## *From Murder to Genocide*

In 1939, the invasion of Poland brought some 2 million Jews under German control. In Warsaw over 350,000 Jews, about 30 percent of the Polish capital's population, were rounded up and confined in less than 3 percent of the city's area. The Warsaw ghetto was sealed off by a wall topped with barbed wire. Guards prevented movement between the ghetto and the rest of the city. Hunger, overcrowding, and a lack of sanitation brought on disease. The death rate soared as Jews were placed in ghettos throughout Poland and Eastern Europe.

**The *Einsatzgruppen*** Special forces called the *Einsatzgruppen,* or mobile killing units, were sent to Poland in 1939. There they systematically murdered members of Poland's upper class, along with intellectuals, priests, and influential Jews. In 1941 the *Einsatzgruppen* carried out Hitler's orders to eliminate Communist political leaders and Jews during the invasion of the Soviet Union.

While Hitler accepted mass murder by firing squad as appropriate for a war zone, he felt the method was not suitable for nations already conquered. In January 1942, government officials met at the **Wannsee Conference** outside Berlin to announce a plan for what one Nazi leader called the "final solution to the Jewish question." The plan called for establishing a number of special concentration camps in rural areas of Germany and elsewhere. There, the genocide, or deliberate destruction of Europe's Jewish population, was to be carried out.

**The Death Camps** In 1941 the Nazis had begun experimenting on Jews and Soviet prisoners of war to determine the most efficient way of killing people. They chose a poison gas, called Zyklon B, to be administered in specially designed chambers disguised as showers. In December 1941 a "model" operation was opened in western Poland. On the first day, some 2,300 Jews were killed.

Eventually the Nazis built six camps in Poland. Unlike the earlier concentration camps, where prisoners were forced to perform hard labor, these **death camps** existed only for mass murder. Jews were crammed into trains and transported to these extermination centers. Most Jews did not know where they were going when they boarded the trains.

On arrival at the camps, prisoners were organized into a line and quickly inspected. The elderly, most women with children, and those who looked too weak to work were herded into gas chambers and killed. Guards forced prisoners to carry the dead to the crematoria, where the bodies were burned in huge ovens.

Those who escaped immediate death at the extermination camps endured almost unbearable conditions. Men and women alike had their heads shaved and a registration number tattooed on their arms. Given only one set of clothes, prisoners were interned in crowded, unheated barracks. There were no bathrooms or beds. Food was usually a thin, foul-tasting soup made with rotten vegetables. Diseases swept through the camps and claimed many who were weakened by harsh labor and the lack of food. Periodic "selections" took place where the weak and ill were sent to the gas chamber.

The number of people killed in the labor and death camps is staggering. About 43,000 prisoners perished at Germany's Buchenwald labor camp, between 1937 and 1945. However, this number pales in comparison to the genocide at Auschwitz, a death camp in Poland. There, more victims were murdered than anywhere else—as many as 1.5 million people, some 90 percent of them Jews.

**Fighting Back** Some Jews, both in and outside the camps, fiercely resisted the Nazis. In April 1943, the Warsaw ghetto revolted against deportation to the death camp Treblinka. For some 27 days about 700 Jews armed with little more than pistols and homemade bombs held out against more than 2,000 Germans with tanks.

Revolts also erupted in the camps themselves. In August 1943, rioting Jews damaged Treblinka so badly that it had to be closed. Escape was the most common form of resistance, however. Most attempts failed, but a few people managed to bring word of the death camps to the outside world.

**Main Idea CONNECTIONS**

*What were conditions like in the camps?*

**Rescue and Liberation** American newspapers showed little interest in the Holocaust during the war years. In addition, the Jewish community in the United States was ineffective in rousing the government to take action toward rescuing Jews. Immigration quotas were not raised and existing quotas for Jews were not filled.

Finally, in January 1944, over the objection of the State Department, Roosevelt created the

**FACT Finder** **Estimated Jewish Losses in the Holocaust**

| *Country* | *Estimated Minimum Loss* | *Percentage of Initial Jewish Population Lost* |
|---|---|---|
| Poland | 2,900,000 | 88–91% |
| Soviet Union | 1,000,000 | 33–36% |
| Hungary | 550,000 | 67–69% |
| Romania | 271,000 | 44–47% |
| Czechoslovakia | 146,150 | 71% |
| Lithuania | 140,000 | 83–85% |
| Germany | 134,500 | 24–25% |
| Netherlands | 100,000 | 71% |
| France | 77,320 | 22% |
| Latvia | 70,000 | 77–78% |
| Greece | 60,000 | 78–87% |
| Yugoslavia | 56,200 | 72–81% |
| Austria | 50,000 | 27% |
| Belgium | 28,900 | 44% |
| Italy | 7,680 | 17% |

**Interpreting Tables** The horror of the Holocaust touched many nations. ***Culture* *Which country do you think was most altered by the Holocaust?***

The haunted faces of these starving prisoners reflect the horrors they experienced in a concentration camp in Ebensee, Austria. ***Foreign Relations*** *How did camp liberation lead to the Nuremberg Trials?*

**War Refugee Board** (WRB) to try to help people threatened with murder by the Nazis. In a short time, its programs helped save some 200,000 lives. With WRB funding, for example, Swedish diplomat Raoul Wallenberg rescued thousands of Hungarian Jews by issuing them special Swedish passports. Wallenberg disappeared into Soviet-controlled Eastern Europe after the war. After he disappeared, Congress made Wallenberg an honorary U.S. citizen for his humanitarian war work.

A WRB effort to bring Jews to America was less successful. Some 1,000 refugees were held at an army camp in Oswego, New York, but Roosevelt would not expand the program.†

As Allied armies advanced in late 1944, the Nazis abandoned concentration camps outside Germany and moved their prisoners to camps on German soil. In May 1945, as Germany collapsed, camp guards fled and American troops for the first time were able to witness the horrors of the Holocaust. A young soldier described the conditions he discovered as he entered the barracks at Buchenwald:

**AMERICAN VOICES** **"The odor was so bad I backed up, but I looked at a bottom bunk and there I saw one man. He was too weak to get up; he could just barely turn his head. . . . He looked like a skeleton; and his eyes were deep set. He didn't utter a sound; he just looked at me with those eyes, and they still haunt me today."**

*—Leon Bass, American soldier*

Sickened by the death camps, in November 1945 the Allies placed 24 leading Nazis on trial for crimes against humanity. At the Nuremberg Trials 12 of them received the death sentence. More significant than the number of convictions, the trials established an important principle—the idea that individuals were responsible for their own actions. No longer could war criminals escape punishment by saying they were only "following orders."

† A larger rescue was carried out by a single individual. Oskar Schindler was a Nazi industrialist who purposely employed some 1,300 Jews in his factories in Poland and Czechoslovakia. Their jobs saved them from being shipped to the gas chambers.

## SECTION 4 REVIEW

### Comprehension

1. *Key Terms* Define: (a) Holocaust; (b) anti-Semitism; (c) concentration camp; (d) *Kristallnacht;* (e) Wannsee Conference; (f) death camp; (g) War Refugee Board.
2. *Summarizing the Main Idea* What was the Holocaust?
3. *Organizing Information* Create a web diagram that organizes information about Nazi persecution of Jews and others in Germany during the 1930s. In the center circle write *Nazi Persecution Grows.* Include at least four supporting details in the surrounding circles.

### Critical Thinking

4. *Analyzing Time Lines* Review the time line at the start of the section. Explain how the first entry made it easier for the third to take place.
5. *Identifying Central Issues* How did the Nazis implement their plans for genocide?

### Writing Activity

6. *Writing an Expository Essay* Several survivors of the Nazi concentration camps wrote books describing their experiences in the camps. Research and write an essay that relates the story of one survivor.

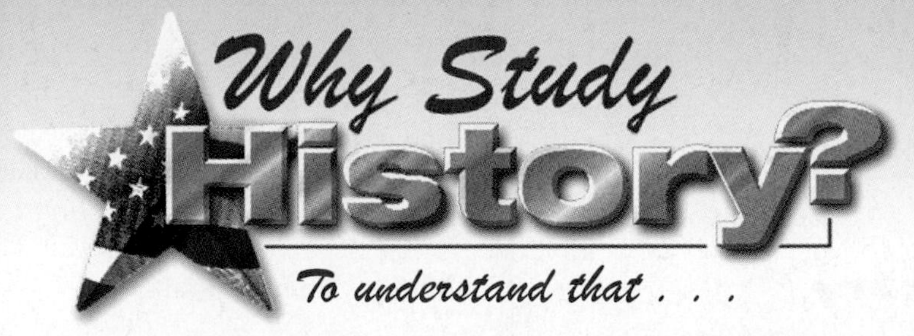


# Genocide Has Happened Again

**The threat of genocide did not end with the defeat of Nazi Germany. It continues to deserve worldwide attention today.**

*Nazis rounding up Jewish families*

Entire families tortured to death. Children beaten savagely. Elderly men and women shot and buried in mass graves. In this chapter you read about the horrors of the Holocaust. Nazi Germany murdered an estimated 6 million Jews, as well as some 5 to 6 million Slavs, gypsies, Communists, homosexuals, and disabled people. Only the Allies' conquest of Germany stopped the mass killing.

In this century, and even in your own lifetime, there have been other mass murders. Between 1915 and 1923, for example, hundreds of thousands of Armenians were killed by the Turkish government. In Cambodia in the 1970s, the Communist Khmer Rouge government killed an estimated 1 million people. In 1994, Hutu soldiers and civilians in the African nation of Rwanda slaughtered at least 1 million men, women, and children of a rival tribe, the Tutsi.

Genocide was also committed during a civil war in Bosnia between 1992 and 1995. The war, fueled by long-standing ethnic and religious hatreds, claimed the lives of roughly 200,000 Bosnian Muslims, Serbs, and Croats.

## The Impact Today

International laws and tribunals have condemned genocide and punished those who take part in it. In 1948, the United Nations declared genocide a crime under international law. A number of Nazis charged with "crimes against humanity" were tried and executed at the Nuremberg Trials. (Only a fraction, however, of those who participated in the killing were prosecuted.) More recently, there have been efforts to bring to trial those who committed atrocities in the Bosnian war.

Unfortunately, prosecuting war criminals cannot bring back their victims or mend the lives of loved ones who survived them. Only changes in peoples' attitudes toward others can ensure that genocide will never happen again.

*Rwandan refugees fleeing violence*

## The Impact on You

Brainstorm with your classmates to create a list of places in the world where serious racial, ethnic, or religious hatreds exist today. Try to find out the history behind these conflicts by doing library research. Think of ways that people in those places could help ease the hatreds. Write a short essay on what individuals can do to create greater understanding among different peoples.

# Chapter 14 Review

## Chapter Summary

The major concepts of Chapter 14 are presented below. See also the ***Guide to the Essentials of American History*** or ***Interactive Student Tutorial CD-ROM,*** which contains interactive review activities, time lines, helpful hints, and test practice.

### *Reviewing the Main Ideas*

German, Italian, and Japanese aggression in the 1930s led to war in Europe and Asia. Many Americans hoped that the United States could remain neutral. They quickly changed their minds after Japan bombed the American naval base at Pearl Harbor. At the end of the war, people around the world reacted in horror as they discovered the full extent of Nazi Germany's attempt to destroy the Jews of Europe.

### *Section 1: Prelude to Global War*

Depressed economic conditions and a desire to build powerful nations led to the rise of dictators in Germany and Italy and eventually to a second global conflict.

### *Section 2: The Road to Victory in Europe*

To secure victory in Europe, the Allies waged war in North Africa, Western Europe, and the Soviet Union between 1941 and 1945.

### *Section 3: The War in the Pacific*

Fierce fighting and heavy casualties characterized the war in the Pacific Ocean as the Allied forces struggled to turn back Japanese advances.

### *Section 4: The Holocaust*

During World War II, the Nazis carried out a brutal plan that resulted in the deaths of 6 million Jews and millions of other victims.

The threat of genocide did not end with the defeat of Nazi Germany. It continues to deserve worldwide attention today. Despite international laws condemning genocide, other mass killings have taken place in the twentieth century.



## Key Terms

For each of the terms below, write a sentence explaining how it relates to this chapter.

1. Lend-Lease Act
2. Battle of Midway
3. Holocaust
4. Axis Powers
5. concentration camp
6. Yalta Conference
7. *Kristallnacht*
8. totalitarian
9. GI
10. Allies
11. D-Day

## Comprehension

1. How did Hitler come to power in Germany?
2. How did the United States support the Allies with economic aid while staying out of the fighting?
3. Why did Japan attack Pearl Harbor?
4. What contribution did Native Americans make to the American military effort?
5. What events in Europe and the Pacific helped turn the tide in favor of the Allies?
6. What was the D-Day operation?
7. Why did the United States not have to invade Japan to end the war?
8. What was Hitler's "final solution"?

## Using Graphic Organizers

On a separate piece of paper, copy the flowchart to organize information about the events of World War II. Add additional boxes if you need to. Begin your chart with the entry *1939: Germany invades Poland.* End with *May 1945: Germany surrenders; August 1945: Japan surrenders.*

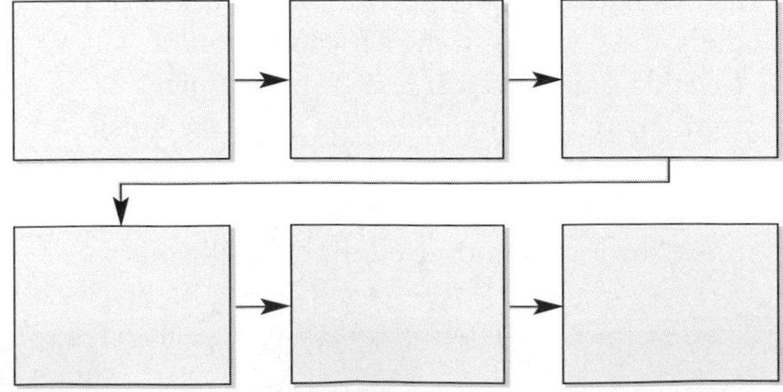

## Analyzing Political Cartoons ▶

1. Analyze the images in the cartoon. (a) What do the two figures in the bed represent? (b) How do you know? (c) Who is the third figure joining them?
2. What is the common interest the three figures share?
3. Why is the "unexpected guest" joining the other two by circumstance?

## Critical Thinking

1. *Applying the Chapter Skill* Turn to the photo on page 454. What can you learn about the Holocaust from this photograph?
2. *Expressing Problems Clearly* The Soviet Union fought on the Allied side during World War II, yet soon after became a bitter enemy of the United States. Give evidence to show that the seeds of conflict between the United States and the Soviet Union were already present during World War II.
3. *Demonstrating Reasoned Judgment* World War II propaganda influenced the way many Americans viewed the Japanese. List two reasons for American hostility toward the Japanese.
4. *Predicting Consequences* If Britain and France had not adopted a policy of appeasement, would Adolf Hitler have been as successful as he was in overrunning Europe?

### INTERNET ACTIVITY

***For your portfolio:***
**CREATE A GRAPH**

Access Prentice Hall's *America: Pathways to the Present* site at **www.Pathways.phschool.com** for the specific URL to complete the activity. Additional resources and related Web sites are also available.

Create a bar graph showing the number of casualties the United States suffered in the Revolutionary War, the Civil War, World War I, and World War II. Which war claimed the most casualties? Why do you think this is so?

## ANALYZING DOCUMENTS ◀ ▶ INTERPRETING DATA

Turn to the "American Voices" quotation on page 448.

1. Which phrase best describes the American campaign on Okinawa? (a) long and hard fought (b) easy (c) completely safe (d) over in one day
2. According to the description of the fighting, you can infer that the terrain on Okinawa was (a) flat and sandy. (b) heavily wooded. (c) rocky. (d) hilly.
3. **Writing** Write a brief paragraph describing how you think the GIs felt during the long nights on Okinawa.

## Connecting to Today

*Essay Writing* The horrible slaughter of six million Jews during the Holocaust is an example of genocide. Research and write an essay on a more recent case where one group tried to carry out a campaign of genocide against another ethnic group. In your essay, include the global community's reactions to the killings.

# CHAPTER 15 World War II at Home

## CHAPTER FOCUS

*As war raged in Europe, the United States government faced the enormous challenge of mobilizing American businesses and civilians to help win the war. The government launched a massive campaign to remind people to conserve, participate, and sacrifice.*

*The* **Why Study History?** *page at the end of this chapter explores the connection between women's work during World War II and their work today.*

**VIEWING HISTORY**
Men and women work side by side to produce war planes in this 1944 illustration from *The Saturday Evening Post.* ***Culture How did the war change life at home?***

| 1941 | 1942 | 1943 | 1943 |
|---|---|---|---|
| OPA sets limits on prices and rents | Income taxes are raised to finance war | FDR creates Office of War Mobilization | United Mine Workers call several strikes |

1941 | 1942 | 1943 | 1944

# 1 The Shift to Wartime Production

## SECTION PREVIEW

### Objectives

1. Explain how American businesses mobilized for war.
2. Summarize how World War II affected the American work force.
3. List the methods the government used to finance the war.
4. *Key Terms* Define: Office of War Mobilization; Liberty ship; wildcat strike; war bond; deficit spending.

### Main Idea

At the beginning of World War II, the government mobilized industries and workers to produce materials for the war.

### Reading Strategy

*Formulating Questions* Before you read this section, look at the illustrations and then write one question for each of the main headings. Answer the questions as you read.

Supplying goods to the Allied forces at the start of World War II helped boost the American economy. The country began to emerge from the Depression as a result of this production. Industries were eager to start making cars, refrigerators, and washing machines again, and consumers were eager to buy them. For the sake of the war effort, however, the American economy soon had to convert full time to making war equipment.

## *Mobilizing the Economy for War*

President Roosevelt understood that the outcome of the war ultimately depended on America's ability to produce enough bombers, tanks, uniforms, and other war materials. The war had destroyed many factories in Europe, cutting down the other Allies' production. Japan's conquests in the Pacific cut off supplies of rubber, oil, and tin.

**The Government Steps In** To meet the demand, FDR knew that the government would have to coordinate the production of American businesses. Even before Pearl Harbor, new government agencies were dealing with the war economy. In April 1941, an executive order established the Office of Price Administration (OPA). Its job was to keep shortages from sending up prices and rents and causing inflation. Later the OPA oversaw rationing of scarce resources.

*Many advertisements linked their products to wartime patriotism.*

The War Production Board (WPB) was set up in January 1942 to direct the conversion of peacetime industries to those that made war goods. It quickly halted the production of hundreds of civilian consumer goods, from cars to lawn mowers to bird cages. The armed forces gave out contracts and scheduled production, but the WPB set priorities and allocated raw materials.

As the war went on, dozens of other agencies were set up to deal with war production, labor questions, and scarce resources. To

## Passenger Car and Military Aircraft Production, 1939–1946

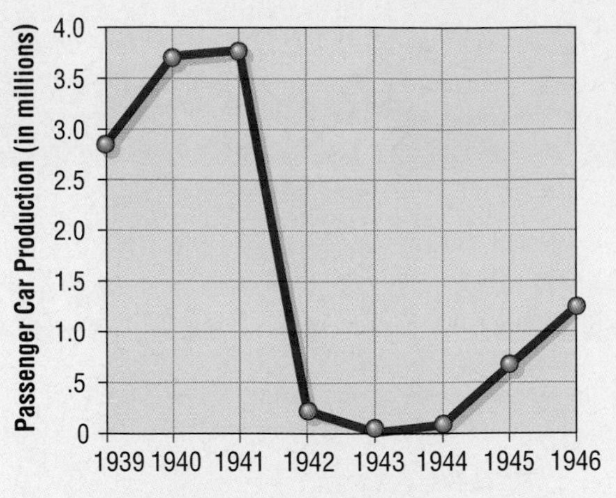


Source: *Miracle of World War II: How American Industry Made Victory Possible,* by Francis Walton

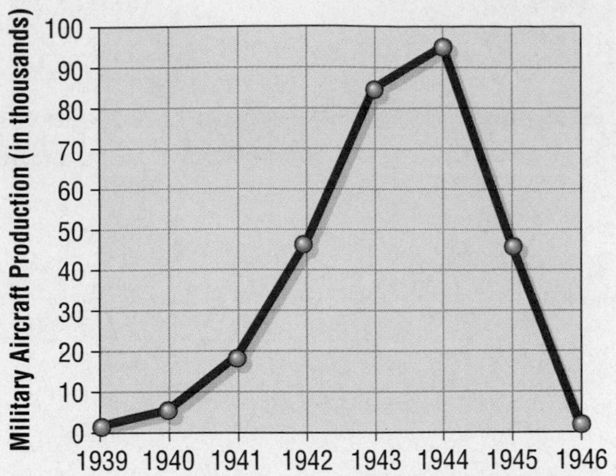


Source: *Historical Statistics of the United States, Colonial Times to 1970*

**Interpreting Graphs** Many industries were converted to military production during World War II. ***Economics*** ***What overall trends in auto production and military aircraft production do these graphs show?***

centralize those agencies, in May 1943 the President organized a superagency, the **Office of War Mobilization.** James F. Byrnes, a longtime member of Congress and close presidential adviser, headed it. Working from a makeshift office in the White House, Byrnes had such broad authority that he was often called the "assistant president." Some people said that Byrnes ran the country while FDR ran the war.

Welder Benny Chan gives the "V for Victory" sign. ***Culture*** ***Why was patriotism linked to industry?***

**Industries Convert** As production of consumer goods stopped, factories converted to war production. Shirt factories made mosquito netting. Typewriter plants made machine guns. On February 1, 1942, after the last cars rolled off the assembly lines, workers began converting automobile factories to produce bombers. The OPA took over the 500,000 new cars in stock. During the war years, it carefully rationed out cars to people who really needed them, such as country doctors.

In addition to converting plants, the Ford Motor Company built a huge new factory to make B-24 Liberator bombers, using the assembly-line techniques used for cars. When the Willow Run plant, near Ann Arbor, Michigan, opened in 1942, it was the largest factory space in the world. The assembly line stretched for a mile across what was once a flat meadowland. Willow Run had production problems at first, but by late 1943 it was building 340 planes a month.

Entrepreneurs in other industries also revolutionized production. Henry J. Kaiser introduced mass production techniques to shipbuilding and set production speed records. Instead of building a ship from the keel up,

Kaiser's engineers built sections of the ship in different parts of the shipyard. As huge cranes brought in the finished sections, welders put them together. The Kaiser shipyards also speeded up operations with crews that specialized in making one part, such as bows or bulkheads (walls).

The vessels that made Kaiser famous were called **Liberty ships** (though other shipyards also built them). They were large, sturdy merchant ships that usually carried supplies or troops, but were sometimes converted to hospital ships or other uses. In 1941 it took an average of 150 days to build one Liberty ship. As the war went on, Kaiser shipyards cut building time to an average of 46 days and even set a record of 4 days.

**New Business Approaches** War production demanded new approaches to business. As Secretary of War Henry L. Stimson put it, "If you are going to try to go to war, or to prepare for war, in a capitalist country, you have to let business make money out of the process." To guarantee profits, the government established the "cost-plus" system for military contracts. The military paid development and production costs, plus a percentage of costs as profit. Pride and patriotism also provided industry leaders with motivation. Factories with good production records could fly pennants bearing the Army-Navy "E" for Excellent.

Thousands of business executives went to Washington to work in the new government agencies that were coordinating war production. As government employees, they received a token "dollar-a-year" salary, while remaining on their own companies' payrolls.

Some entrepreneurs found profitable new markets for their products during the war. Robert Woodruff, head of Coca-Cola, declared in December 1941: "We will see that every man in uniform gets a bottle of Coca-Cola for five cents wherever he is and whatever it costs [the company]." By the time the war was over, American troops had drunk 5 billion bottles of Coca-Cola. At the same time, Woodruff's company had established a future "army" of civilian consumers, those who had enjoyed the drink while in uniform.

**The "Great Arsenal of Democracy"** In December 1940, Franklin Roosevelt had told Americans that the country must become "the great arsenal of democracy." In each year of war, the United States raised its production goals for military materials, and each year it met them. By the middle of 1945, the nation had produced (in rounded numbers) 300,000 airplanes; 80,000 landing craft; 100,000 tanks and armored cars; 5,600 merchant ships (including about 2,600 Liberty ships); 6 million rifles, carbines, and machine guns; and 41 billion rounds of ammunition.

VIEWING HISTORY Kaiser's Liberty ship *Robert E. Peary* (above) was built in a matter of days. The government urged Americans to help protect these ships from enemy attack (right). ***Economics*** *How was Kaiser able to produce ships so fast?*

**Main Idea CONNECTIONS**

*What did Franklin Roosevelt mean when he said that America must be the "great arsenal of democracy"?*

## *The Wartime Work Force*

War production benefited workers, too, ending the massive unemployment of the 1930s.

## Unemployment and Weekly Earnings, 1940–1945

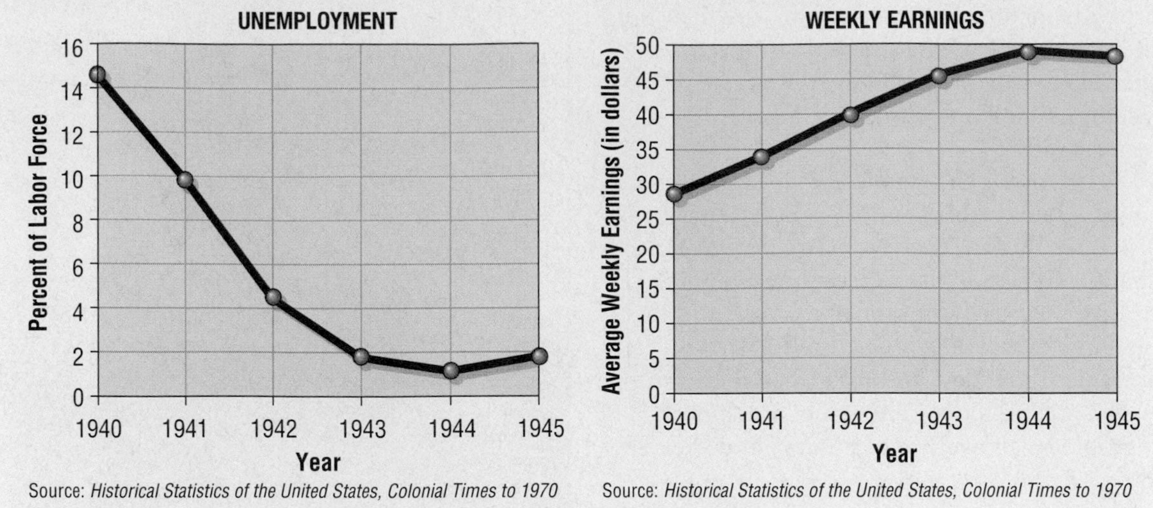


**Interpreting Graphs** War mobilization had a positive effect on the labor force.
***Economics By how much did unemployment fall between 1940 and 1945? By how much did average weekly wages increase during the same period?***

As the graphs above show, by 1943 unemployment had fallen dramatically. Average weekly wages in manufacturing, adjusted for inflation, rose by more than 50 percent between 1940 and 1945.

With more people working, union membership rose. Between 1940 and 1941, the number of workers belonging to unions increased by 1.5 million. Union membership continued to rise sharply once the United States entered the war. It went from 10.5 million in 1941 to 14.8 million in 1945.

Two weeks after the attack on Pearl Harbor, labor and business representatives agreed to refrain from strikes and "lockouts"—a tactic in which an employer keeps employees out of the workplace to avoid meeting their demands. As the cost of living rose during the war, however, the no-strike agreement became hard to honor. The government continually had to remind citizens of the importance of the agreement. A construction company superintendent recalled what happened during the building of a military base in New Jersey:

> **AMERICAN VOICES** "They started at one time to develop a strike there, and some big guy from the Pentagon came down, and he just laid the cards on the table: 'There'll be no strikes.' Everybody kind of buckled down, and we finished the thing in record time."
>
> —*Leonard Williamson*

Still, the number of strikes rose sharply between 1942 and 1943, and it continued to rise in the last two years of the war. Some of the strikes were **wildcat strikes**—that is, they were organized by the workers themselves and not endorsed by the unions.

The most serious troubles with union labor were in the coal mines. There, John L. Lewis, head of the United Mine Workers union, called strikes on four occasions in 1943. Lewis and the miners watched industry profits soar while their wages stayed the same. They demanded a pay raise to compensate for the rising cost of living. Secretary of the Interior Harold L. Ickes finally negotiated an agreement with Lewis. Meanwhile, Congress passed the Smith-Connally Act in June 1943, limiting future strike activity.

## *Financing the War*

Wartime production was so vital that the United States government was willing to spend whatever was necessary. Federal spending increased from $8.9 billion in 1939 to $95.2 billion in 1945. The Gross National Product (GNP) more than doubled in that time. Overall, the cost to the federal government between 1941 and 1945 was about $321 billion—ten times as much as World War I.

Higher taxes paid for about 41 percent of the cost of the war. The Revenue Act of 1942 increased the number of Americans who paid income taxes from 13 million to 50 million people. It also introduced the idea of withholding income taxes from people's paychecks, known as "pay-as-you-go." Income tax rates went up gradually during the war years, reaching a high of 94 percent for the richest taxpayers. Extra taxes were also levied on corporate profits and consumer goods.

The government borrowed the rest of the money from banks, private investors, and the public. Starting in 1941, the Treasury Department launched bond drives to encourage Americans to buy **war bonds,** government savings bonds that financed the war. Movie stars and war heroes urged the public to "buy bonds." Even schoolchildren brought their dimes or quarters to school each week, buying defense stamps that would eventually add up to the price of a bond. Total war bond sales brought in about $186 billion.

During the Depression, British economist John Maynard Keynes had argued for **deficit spending**—government spending of borrowed money—to get the economy moving. Many other economists believed the economy would recover if government left it alone. There was some deficit spending in the 1930s, but government borrowing skyrocketed during World War II. Deficit spending turned the economy around overnight, bringing wartime prosperity. It also created a huge national debt that caused economic problems later.

This war bond poster used powerful images to convince people to buy war bonds. ***Economics*** *How else did the government raise money to pay for the war?*

## SECTION 1 REVIEW

### Comprehension

1. *Key Terms* Define: (a) Office of War Mobilization; (b) Liberty ship; (c) wildcat strike; (d) war bond; (e) deficit spending.
2. *Summarizing the Main Idea* What steps did the government take to mobilize industries and labor for war production?
3. *Organizing Information* Create a web diagram to organize the different types of actions taken by government and business to convert the American economy into a wartime economy.

### Critical Thinking

4. *Analyzing Time Lines* Review the time line at the start of the section. Choose one entry and explain its consequences.
5. *Formulating Questions* Imagine that you are a government planner in 1942. Draw up a list of "nonessential" civilian goods that will be rationed or not produced at all.

### Writing Activity

6. *Writing a Persuasive Essay* You are making a speech at a bond drive, trying to persuade people to buy war bonds. Write a draft of the speech you will give.

1941 OPA begins rationing auto tires

1941 Birthrate begins to rise from Depression levels

1942 Popular movies such as Casablanca combine patriotism and entertainment

1943 Point rationing begins

1943 All-American Girls' Softball League begins

1940 | 1942 | 1944

# 2 Daily Life on the Home Front

## SECTION PREVIEW

### Objectives

1. Describe some features of American popular culture during World War II.
2. Explain how shortages and controls affected everyday civilian life.
3. List some of the ways the government enlisted public support for the war.
4. *Key Terms* Define: Office of War Information; victory garden.

### Main Idea

As the war economy brought both prosperity and shortages, the government worked to keep Americans at home involved in the war effort.

### Reading Strategy

*Formulating Questions* Before you read, rewrite each of this section's main headings in the form of a question. Look for answers to the questions as you read.

*Low traffic speeds helped save on fuel and rubber.*

The daily life of most Americans during World War II was filled with constant reminders of the war. Nearly everyone had a relative or friend in the military, and people closely followed war news on the radio. The war uprooted families, too. Many soldiers' wives and children moved in with relatives. Other people moved to new places to take defense jobs. Although the wartime economy gave many people their first extra cash since the Depression, shortages and rationing limited what people could buy. Books, movies, and sports provided a chance to escape wartime worries. At the same time, many Americans of all ages took part in the war effort by buying bonds or recycling paper and tin.

## Wartime Popular Culture

Americans' morale was quite high as wartime spending ended the Depression. In 1941, about 24 percent of all American families had incomes of less than $1,000 a year. By 1945, new jobs created by the war brought that figure below 20 percent. One measure of people's optimism was an increase in the birthrate. The population grew by 7.5 million between 1940 and 1945, nearly double the rate of growth for the 1930s. The postwar "baby boom" that extended through the 1950s really began during World War II.

As the wartime economy expanded, many Americans suddenly found themselves earning more money than they needed for basic necessities. They were eager to spend this extra income on new cars, trucks, or home appliances. Since war production made those goods unavailable, they looked for other ways to spend their money.

**Books and Movies** People bought and read more books and magazines. The new Pocket Books company, founded by Robert de Graff in 1939, developed a market for small-size paperback books. De Graff believed that more Americans would read if books were less expensive, more widely available, and easy to carry. He published paperback versions of recent bestsellers at just 25 cents. In only two months,

34,000 copies of the first Pocket Book, Dale Carnegie's *How to Win Friends and Influence People,* were sold. Soldiers carried Pocket Books with them into combat. When the war was over, the market for paperbacks continued to grow.

Millions of Americans—about 60 percent of the population—also went to the movies every week. Hollywood, too, was doing its part for the war effort, making movies for both soldiers and civilians. Director Frank Capra, for example, who was known for warm-hearted comedies, made a series of films for the army called *Why We Fight.* Many wartime films were love stories, adventure tales, or light comedies that took audiences' minds off the serious business of war. Others, such as *Casablanca,* added themes of patriotism and confidence in an Allied victory. Movie newsreels also boosted patriotism.

With high spirits and money to spend, Americans on the home front were eager for entertainment. Pete Gray, a one-armed outfielder (above), did his part for the war effort by playing for the St. Louis Browns and giving the "troops" at home a lift. ***Culture* *Why were Americans so eager for diversions?***

**Baseball** Although more than 4,000 of the 5,700 major and minor league baseball players were in the military services, Americans still flocked to baseball games during the war. Ball clubs had to scramble to find other players. To fill their rosters, some placed want ads in newspapers:

> **AMERICAN VOICES** "If you are a free agent and have previous professional experience, we may be able to place you to your advantage on one of our clubs. We have positions open on our AA, B, and D classification clubs. If you believe you can qualify for one of these good baseball jobs, tell us about yourself."
>
> —Sporting News, *February 25, 1943*

For the first time, women had a chance to play ball professionally. In 1943 Philip Wrigley founded the All-American Girls' Softball League, which became the All-American Girls' Baseball League in 1945. Women who played for teams such as the Rockford (Illinois) Peaches and the South Bend (Indiana) Blue Sox had to attend charm school and wear impractical skirted uniforms. They put up with such difficulties to play the sport they loved. Their games drew hundreds of fans.

**Popular Music** As in World War I, many popular songs encouraged hope and patriotism. Frank Loesser's "Praise the Lord and Pass the Ammunition" was based on a widely told story about a navy chaplain who took over an anti-aircraft gun at Pearl Harbor after the gunners had been killed. "There's a Star-Spangled Banner Waving Somewhere" was a best-selling record in 1942.

**Main Idea CONNECTIONS**

*How did movies, sports, and songs help the war effort?*

Other ballads, like "I'll Be Seeing You" and "You'd Be So Nice to Come Home To," reflected people's longing for loved ones who were far away. In the 1942 film *Holiday Inn,* Bing Crosby sang Irving Berlin's song "White Christmas." It quickly became a sentimental favorite, both for soldiers overseas and for civilians at home.

## *Shortages and Controls*

Although they had money to spend, Americans lived with shortages throughout the war. Some familiar consumer items were simply unavailable "for the duration." Metal to make zippers or typewriters was used for guns, and rubber for girdles went into tires for army trucks. Nylon

## FACT Finder: Government Controls on Wartime Economy

| Agency or Program | Function |
|---|---|
| Rationing (1941) | Limited consumption of goods such as rubber, gasoline, sugar, meat, butter, and cheese. |
| Fair Employment Practice Committee (1941) | Established to end racial discrimination in war production industries and government employment. |
| Office of Price Administration (1942) | Limited prices on all nonfarm commodities. Controlled rents in defense areas. |
| National War Labor Board (1942) | Used mediation and arbitration to settle labor disputes in defense industries. |
| Revenue Act of 1942 | Raised the number of people who paid income taxes from 13,000,000 to 50,000,000 and raised the tax rate of the wealthiest Americans. |
| Labor Disputes Act (Smith-Connally Anti-Strike Act) (1943) | Gave the President more power to seize war production plants threatened by labor disputes. Made illegal any attempts to strike at plants the government had seized. |

**Interpreting Tables** The government took firm control of the economy to keep the war effort afloat. ***Culture How did these government controls affect people's attitude toward the war?***

made parachutes instead of stockings. To save cloth, government regulations changed fashions. Men's suits no longer had vests, patch pockets, or trouser cuffs. Women's skirts were cut shorter and narrower.

People got used to the shortages. Not only were great amounts of food being sent to the military, but supplies of some imported foods were cut off. Sugar, for example, became scarce when the Philippines, the major source of American imports, fell to the Japanese. Many shipping lanes were closed, making it hard to bring in tropical fruits or Brazilian coffee.

Worried that shortages would cause price increases, the government used tough measures to head off inflation. Early in the war, the Office of Price Administration (OPA) was given authority to freeze rents and prices. In December 1941, the OPA began rationing, or distributing, auto tires. The goal of rationing was a fair distribution of scarce items.

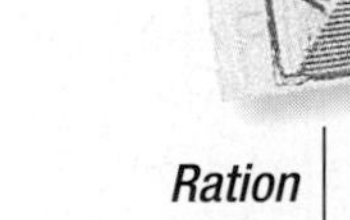

*Ration stamps*

Beginning in 1943, the OPA assigned point values to items such as sugar, coffee, meat, butter, canned fruit, and shoes. Consumers were issued ration books of coupons worth a certain number of points for categories of food or clothing. Once they had used up their points, they could not buy any more of those items until they got new ration books or traded coupons with neighbors. One young woman who grew up in California during the war remembered her mother's gatherings to trade coupons:

**AMERICAN VOICES** **"My mother and all the neighbors would get together around the dining-room table, and they'd be changing a sugar coupon for a bread or a meat coupon. It was like a giant Monopoly game. It was quite exciting to have all the neighbors over and have this trading and bargaining. It was like the New York Stock Exchange. This was our social life."**

—*Sheril Cunning, as quoted in* "The Good War" *by Studs Terkel*

Gasoline for cars was rationed, too, on the basis of need. Signs asked, "Is this trip necessary?"

## *Enlisting Public Support*

The government understood the need to maintain morale. It tried to create a sense of patriotism and participation in the war effort, while convincing citizens to accept rationing and to conserve precious resources. The **Office of War Information** was set up in June 1942 to work with magazine publishers, advertising agencies, and radio stations. It hired writers and artists to create patriotic posters and ads.

One unexpectedly popular idea was the **victory garden.** Shortly after the Japanese attack on Pearl Harbor, the Secretary of Agriculture suggested that families could plant home gardens to make up for the farm produce sent to feed the soldiers. Soon people in cities and suburbs were planting tomatoes, peas, and radishes in backyards, empty parking lots, and playgrounds. By 1943, victory gardens were producing about one third of the country's fresh vegetables.

The war became a part of everyday life in many ways. Periodically, people drew their shades for nighttime "blackouts," which tested their readiness for possible bombing raids. Men too old for the army joined the Civilian Defense, wearing their CD armbands as they tested air-raid sirens. Women knit scarves and socks or rolled bandages for the Red Cross.

Shortages produced efforts to recycle scrap metal, paper, and other materials. In one drive, people collected tin cans, pots and pans, razor blades, old shovels, and even old lipstick tubes. In Virginia, volunteers raised sunken ships from the James River; in Wyoming they took apart an old steam engine to use the parts. At home, people were asked to save kitchen fats because the glycerin could be used to make powder for bullets or shells. Some historians have questioned whether the items collected were ever really used in the war. Whether they were or not, the collection drives kept adults and children actively involved in the war effort.

"Play your part." "Conserve and collect." "Use it up, wear it out, make it do or do without." These slogans echoed throughout the United States and reminded people on the home front of their part in the war.

Children, too, did their part for the war effort. These boys in New York City used their powers of persuasion—and noise-making—to urge their neighbors to contribute to an aluminum drive. ***Economics*** ***How did the government handle the shortages of consumer items?***

## SECTION 2 REVIEW

### Comprehension

1. *Key Terms* Define (a) Office of War Information; (b) victory garden.
2. *Summarizing the Main Idea* What direct effects did wartime shortages have on the everyday lives of Americans at home?
3. *Organizing Information* Create a web diagram showing the ways in which civilians on the home front had to interact with the government and government agencies during World War II.

### Critical Thinking

4. *Analyzing Time Lines* Review the time line at the start of the section. Identify the events that you think would have come to an end once the war was over.
5. *Identifying Assumptions* What did the government hope to achieve by such efforts as scrap metal drives?

### Writing Activity

6. *Writing a Persuasive Essay* How could you motivate a group of people to organize a scrap metal drive? Write an editorial for your community newspaper in which you persuade people to organize and cooperate in the war effort.

## 1 Wartime Posters

At work, on the street, at the movies, these posters reminded people that their way of life depended on the outcome of the war. The posters used images of happy families to personalize the war and stir up even more support for the war effort.

## 2 Hitler and Uncle Sam

This button used gallows humor to ask everyone to "pull" together to win the war. The need to put aside disagreements among Americans was a common wartime message.

## 3 Dogs for Defense

The armed forces needed dogs to sniff out explosives, and for many other tasks. Citizens who donated dogs to the military could proudly wear this button.

## 4 Victory Button

The letter "V, " for victory, was the most common symbol of the war effort. Many businesses used the V and the American flag to send a patriotic and promotional message.

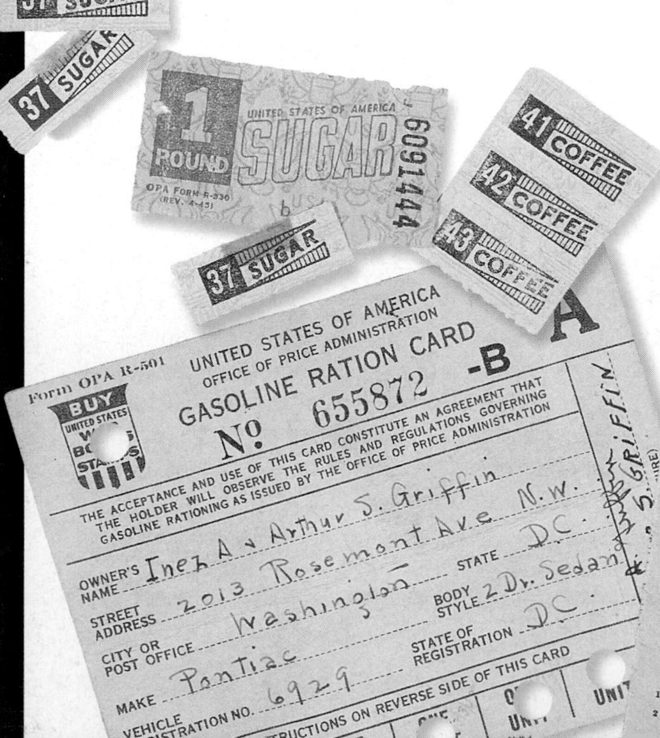


## 5 Ration Cards and Stamps

Notice the initials OPA, which stood for Office of Price Administration. This agency distributed the ration books and also had the authority to set prices for items in short supply.

From Exhibitions and Collections at the Smithsonian Institution's National Museum of American History

# ON THE HOME FRONT

During World War II, colorful posters papered the windows of American businesses. Pleas rang out across the radio, urging Americans to sacrifice and band together. Everywhere there were reminders that the nation was in a life-or-death struggle against totalitarian dictatorships. *See* 1 *and* 2.

Every life was affected by the war. If you didn't have a family member in the armed forces, you knew someone—a neighbor or friend—who was serving in the armed forces or working in a defense plant. Even the family dog was a possible recruit. The army used dogs as sentries on the battlefront and in other ways. *See* 3.

The steady stream of patriotic messages kept Americans focused on the job at hand—putting individual disagreements aside to work together for the good of the country. People showed their support by wearing victory buttons, marked by the letter "V." *See* 4.

Supporting the war effort also meant putting up with shortages. The government rationed certain items that were scarce or needed by the armed forces. Ration books restricted things like gasoline and sugar. Conserving and recycling were also necessary. The recycling effort included hundreds of everyday products. *See* 5 *and* 6.

In addition to working hard, Americans contributed their own money to pay for the war effort. They did this by purchasing war savings bonds. Savings bonds gave thousands of Americans a personal and financial stake in the outcome of the war. *See* 7.

6

**Label on Milk Bottle**

This label conveyed the message that conserving resources was every American's patriotic duty.

7

**Sleeve for U.S. War Bonds**

The government borrowed an incredible $135 billion from individual Americans to finance the war effort.

**Viewing History**

1. *Summarize* What do the objects tell you about daily life during the war?

2. *Connecting to Today* In peacetime as well as wartime, government and other organizations conduct public relations campaigns to persuade people to support some policy or change their behavior. Report on the following to your class: (a) examples of recent campaigns; (b) what, in your view, makes such campaigns successful or unsuccessful.

| 1942 | 1942 | 1944 |
|---|---|---|
| *"Rosie the Riveter" becomes a symbol for women war workers* | *National War Labor Board backs "equal pay for equal work"* | *Number of women working exceeds 19 million* |

1940 — 1942 — 1944

# 3 Women and the War

## SECTION PREVIEW

### Objectives

1. Explain why new kinds of jobs opened up for women in World War II.
2. Compare the benefits and problems that women workers experienced.
3. Describe what happened to women workers at the end of the war.
4. *Key Terms* Define: Rosie the Riveter; seniority.

### Main Idea

During World War II, more American women went to work in nontraditional, war-industry jobs, but they were discouraged from keeping those jobs after the war ended.

### Reading Strategy

*Outlining Information* As you read this section, create an outline that includes the headings from the section. Fill in at least two main ideas for each heading.

*The motto of the women's Auxiliary Reserve Pool (ARP) during World War II was Prepared and Faithful.*

A popular song in 1942 told the story of a fictional young woman called **Rosie the Riveter,** who worked in a defense plant while her boyfriend Charlie served in the marines. The government used images of Rosie the Riveter in posters and recruitment films of the 1940s to attract women to the work force.

The government image of Rosie was young, white, and middle class. Patriotism was her main motive for taking a war job—she wanted to do her part on the home front while her boyfriend was fighting. In reality, American women of all ages and ethnic and economic backgrounds went to work in the wartime economy. Patriotism was only one of many reasons they took new and different jobs.

## Changes for Working Women

Before the war, most women who worked for wages were single and young. Even during the hard times of the Depression, most people disapproved of married women working—that is, holding paying jobs outside the home. Social disapproval was reinforced by the fear that working women would take jobs away from unemployed men. According to a poll taken in 1936, 82 percent of Americans believed that a married woman should not work if her husband had a job. Nonetheless, by 1940 more than 15 percent of all married women were working.

**New Kinds of Jobs** Except for teaching and nursing, few women entered professional careers. They often had to take low-paying jobs such as sales clerks or household servants. Women with factory jobs usually worked in industries that produced clothing, textiles, and shoes, while men dominated the higher-paying machinery, steel, and automobile industries. Almost everywhere, women earned less than men.

Like World War I, World War II brought women into different parts of the work force. As men were drafted into the armed forces, many factory jobs fell vacant. News of these better-paying job openings attracted women who were working in traditional women's jobs. They moved into manufacturing, particularly the defense industries. Like the fictional Rosie, women worked in airplane plants and shipyards as riveters, steelworkers, and welders.

These women welders at the Kaiser shipyard in Richmond, California, are working on the Liberty ship *S.S. George Washington Carver.* ***Economics*** *How did wartime job recruitment change the kinds of jobs women filled?*

**Recruiting Women Workers** Still there was a labor shortage. To fill those jobs, the Office of War Information launched a recruitment campaign. It was aimed at women who normally would not have considered working outside the home: older and married women.

Posters and advertisements told women that it was their patriotic duty to work for their country. "An American homemaker with the strength and ability to run a house and raise a family . . . has the strength and ability to take her place in a vital War industry," one ad declared. As a result of this campaign, the number of working women rose by almost one third, from 14.6 million in 1941 to about 19.4 million in 1944. (See the graph on the next page.) Women at one point made up about 35 percent of the total civilian labor force.

The campaign brought married women workers into the labor force. They soon accounted for almost three quarters of the increase. For the first time in American history, they outnumbered single working women. More than 2 million women over the age of 35 found jobs, and by the end of the war, half of all women workers were over age 35.

## Benefits of Employment

Despite their resistance in the past, employers were usually pleased to have women workers during the war. Some of their reasons seem misguided today. Employers assumed, for instance, that women could do simple, repetitious tasks more effectively than men. They thought that women were better suited for certain welding jobs because they could squeeze into smaller places.

**Women and Work** On the whole, women were pleased to be employed. The money they earned made a difference in their lives. For example, Josephine McKee, a Seattle mother of nine who worked at the Boeing Aircraft Company, was able to pay off debts from the Depression. Leola Houghland, also from Seattle, used her shipyard earnings to pay for her family's home.

Other women found the work more interesting and challenging than what they had done before. Evelyn Knight left a job as a cook to work in a navy yard. She explained, "After all, I've got to keep body and soul together, and I'd rather earn a living this way than to cook over a hot stove." Many women took jobs for patriotic reasons. One rubber plant worker declared, "Every time I test a batch of rubber, I know it's going to help bring my three sons home quicker."

Women were eager to prove that they could do whatever their jobs required. Beatrice Morales Clifton, a mother of four, had never worked outside the home. At first, she found that other workers at Lockheed Aircraft in

**Main Idea CONNECTIONS**

*What benefits did women experience as a result of wartime employment?*

Los Angeles resented working women. Her confidence grew, however, as she mastered one skill after another:

AMERICAN VOICES "I felt proud of myself and felt good [because] I had never done anything like that. I felt good that I could do something, and being that it was war, I felt that I was doing my part. I went from 65 cents to $1.05 [an hour]. That was top pay. It felt good and, besides, it was my own money. I could do whatever I wanted with it."

—*Beatrice Morales Clifton*

Clifton left her wartime job after the war, then returned to Lockheed in 1951. By the time she retired in 1978, she was a supervisor for about 50 other workers.

**Jobs for African Americans** Black women had long worked in greater proportion than white women. Generally, though, only domestic work such as cleaning and child care was open to them. When they applied for defense jobs, African American women often faced both gender prejudice and racial discrimination. Some women fought back. Through lawsuits and other forms of protest, African American women improved their chances in the work force. Between 1940 and 1944, the proportion of African American women in industrial jobs increased from 6.8 percent to 18 percent. The number working in domestic service dropped from 59.9 percent to 44.6 percent.

**Labor Force, 1940–1945**

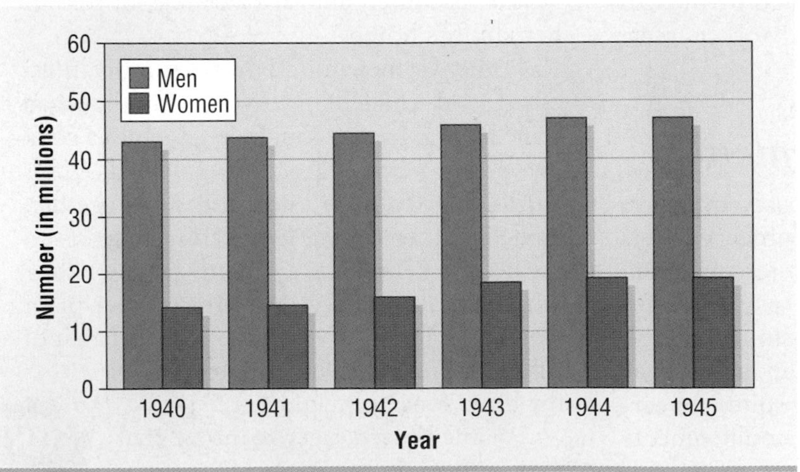

**Interpreting Charts** Wartime production created a demand for workers, both male and female. ***Economics*** ***Compare the overall trend in women's employment during World War II with the ratio of women to men in the labor force during the war.***

## *Problems for Working Women*

In spite of the benefits of working, women faced a number of problems in the workplace. Some faced hostile reactions from other workers, particularly in jobs previously held only by men. Many managers were uneasy about mixing the sexes, and so set up strict rules. General Motors, for example, fired male supervisors and female employees found "fraternizing," or socializing with one another.

Working women also worried about leaving their children alone. More than half a million women with children under the age of 10 worked during the war, and day-care centers were scarce. Even when care was available, most women preferred to have family members or friends care for their children. This often required making complicated arrangements. Women were encouraged to work, but at the same time they continued to also be responsible for their children and their homes.

Women also earned much less than men doing the same jobs. The National War Labor Board declared in the fall of 1942 that women who performed "work of the same quality and quantity" as men should receive equal pay. This policy was widely ignored. Women began at the bottom, with the lowest-paying jobs. Because they had less **seniority,** or status that is derived from length of service, they commonly advanced more slowly. Their wages reflected these patterns. At the Willow Run plant in 1945, women earned a yearly average of $2,928, compared with $3,363 for men. Conditions improved toward the end of the war, but the gap never disappeared.

## *After the War*

The government drive to bring women to defense plants assumed that when the war was over, women would leave their jobs and return home. War work was just "for the duration." While many women wanted to continue working at the war's end, the pressures to return home were intense. Returning servicemen expected to get their jobs back. They also longed

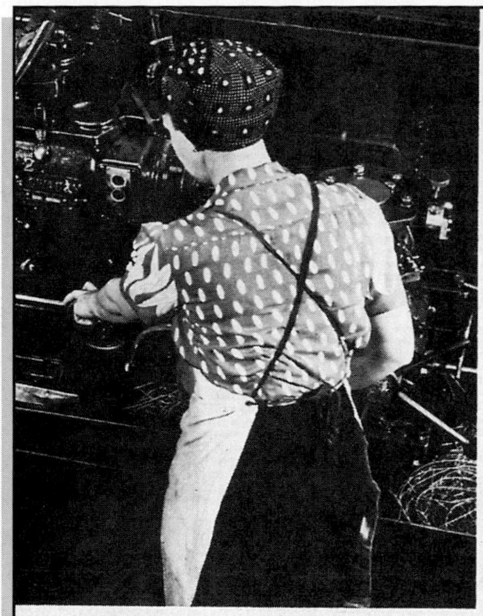

Sisters under the apron—Yesterday's war worker becomes today's housewife.

**What's Become of Rosie the Riveter?**

Government campaigns aimed at women did an about-face once the war was over. Posters such as this one tried to persuade women to give up their factory jobs and return to full-time homemaking. ***Culture*** ***Why were women being urged out of the work force?***

to return to the kind of family life they had known before the war. A new campaign by industrialists and government officials now encouraged women to leave their jobs. Articles in women's magazines changed their emphasis after the war, too. They focused on homemaking, cooking, and child care, starting a trend that would continue into the 1950s and 1960s.

As the economy returned to peacetime, twice as many women as men lost factory jobs. Some women were tired of their defense jobs, which in many cases were not very fulfilling once the wartime sense of urgency ended. They looked forward to returning home. Others, however, had discovered new satisfactions in the workplace that made them want to keep on working. As one woman stated, "For the first time in their lives, they worked outside the home. They realized that they were capable of doing something more than cook a meal." Some women also continued to work part time to bring in additional income.

## SECTION 3 REVIEW

### Comprehension

1. *Key Terms* Define: (a) Rosie the Riveter; (b) seniority.
2. *Summarizing the Main Idea* How did employment patterns for women change during World War II?
3. *Organizing Information* Make a two-column chart comparing the benefits of war work for women with the problems and disadvantages they faced. Label one column *Benefits,* the other *Drawbacks and Problems*.

### Critical Thinking

4. *Analyzing Time Lines* Review the time line at the start of the section. Choose one event and relate it to present-day conditions for working women.
5. *Recognizing Bias* Although women workers were recruited during the war, once it ended they were pressured to leave their jobs and return to domestic work. What underlying beliefs does this series of events suggest?

### Writing Activity

6. *Writing a Persuasive Essay* How would you prepare an all-male work force to accept women workers? Write a short guide that will convince the workers to accept the newcomers as equals.

# SKILLS FOR LIFE

**Critical Thinking**

**Geography**

**Graphs and Charts**

**Historical Evidence**

# Identifying Assumptions

Identifying assumptions means recognizing the unstated beliefs that may underlie a statement or action. An assumption is an idea that a person takes for granted as true. In fact, it may prove either true or false, but in order to determine the accuracy of an assumption, you must first be able to recognize it as such.

Editorials, opinion pieces, and illustrations frequently contain many assumptions. Magazine covers, such as the one shown here, are often excellent sources of information about public attitudes toward historical events. At the same time, illustrations may be drawn in such a way that they also reveal assumptions of the artist.

By the time artist Norman Rockwell's portrayal of "Rosie the Riveter" appeared on the cover of *The Saturday Evening Post* in 1943, American women by the thousands were already making history. They were working in nontraditional factory jobs, assembling ships and airplanes for the country's war effort.

To examine the accuracy of the image portrayed in this illustration, use the following steps to identify and evaluate the assumptions on which it may be based.

**1.** ***Determine the subject of the cover illustration.*** Study the illustration carefully and answer the following questions. (a) What is the woman in the illustration doing? (b) Who is "Rosie the Riveter" supposed to represent? (c) What general subject or issue does the illustration address? (d) What is the overall message of the illustration?

**2.** ***Define the artist's point of view.*** To help determine if the artist is presenting a particular viewpoint, answer the following questions. (a) What seems to be the artist's purpose in creating this illustration? (b) How would you describe the artist's attitude toward the subject? (c) What aspects of the illustration clearly express this point of view? (d) Are there any elements in the illustration that seem to contradict each other? If so, what might the artist be trying to convey through these contradictions?

**3.** ***Identify the assumptions on which the artist's viewpoint is based and decide whether they are valid.*** To help decide if the artist's assumptions can be supported by facts, answer the following questions. (a) What assumptions, if any, does the artist make about the nature of the work performed by the woman in the illustration? Does the artist make any assumptions about why she holds this job? (b) What assumptions, if any, does the artist make about the women who work in nontraditional jobs? (c) Can any aspects of a person's physical appearance, such as clothes or posture, be reliably linked to his or her occupation? Explain. (d) How can you find out if the artist's apparent assumptions are valid?

## TEST FOR SUCCESS

Choose an advertisement from a current magazine and analyze it by determining (a) the assumptions made by the advertiser about the audience for this product; (b) the purpose of the ad; and (c) the artist's or photographer's point of view.

| 1941 | 1942 | 1942 | 1943 | 1945 |
|---|---|---|---|---|
| Executive Order 8802 outlaws race discrimination in war plants | FDR authorizes the internment of Japanese Americans | CORE is founded to work for racial equality | Race riots in Detroit, New York, and Los Angeles | Japanese Americans are released from internment camps |

1941 1942 1943 1944 1945

# 4 The Struggle for Justice at Home

**SECTION PREVIEW**

### Objectives

1. Describe the kinds of discrimination that African Americans faced and the steps they took to counter them.
2. Compare the experiences of Mexican Americans and Native Americans at home during World War II.
3. Explain why Japanese Americans were interned during the war.
4. *Key Terms* Define: "Double V" campaign; Nisei; internment camp.

### Main Idea

While the war brought new job opportunities for some racial and ethnic minorities, Japanese Americans were the victims of widespread intolerance.

### Reading Strategy

*Organizing Information* As you read, create a graphic organizer including information about the experiences of African Americans, Mexican Americans, Native Americans, and Japanese Americans during the war.

President Roosevelt, in his 1942 Columbus Day speech, expressed the need to overcome bigotry for the sake of the wartime effort: "In some communities employers dislike to hire women. In others they are reluctant to hire Negroes. We can no longer afford to indulge such prejudice."

In fact, the war did bring greater opportunities for some groups of Americans. Nevertheless, racial and ethnic prejudices did not disappear during the war years. Instead, the pressures of wartime made some of those injustices more obvious. Japanese Americans in particular faced hardship and hostility because of Japan's part in the war.

## Discrimination Continues Against African Americans

When the war began, the struggle to end discrimination against African Americans had been under way for decades. Yet the Jim Crow system, which established the strict legal separation of the races, was still strong in the South. The North had fewer laws enforcing segregation. In reality, however, African Americans in the North faced discrimination in employment, education, and housing.

**Economic Discrimination** African American unemployment was high in 1941, with one out of five potential workers jobless. Even government agencies set up to help workers during the Depression honored employers' requests for "whites only." Such attitudes allowed old patterns to continue.

During the 1940s, more than 2 million African Americans migrated from the South to cities in the North. (See the map on the next page.) They found new job opportunities but also encountered new problems. Segregation severely limited the houses and apartments where African Americans were welcome. In addition, many could not afford good housing. As a result, many ended up living in urban ghettos, neighborhoods where members of a minority group are concentrated. A survey taken in 1941 showed that 50 percent of all African American homes were substandard, versus only 14 percent of white homes.

*The "Double V" campaign urged victory over enemies overseas and over racial discrimination at home.*

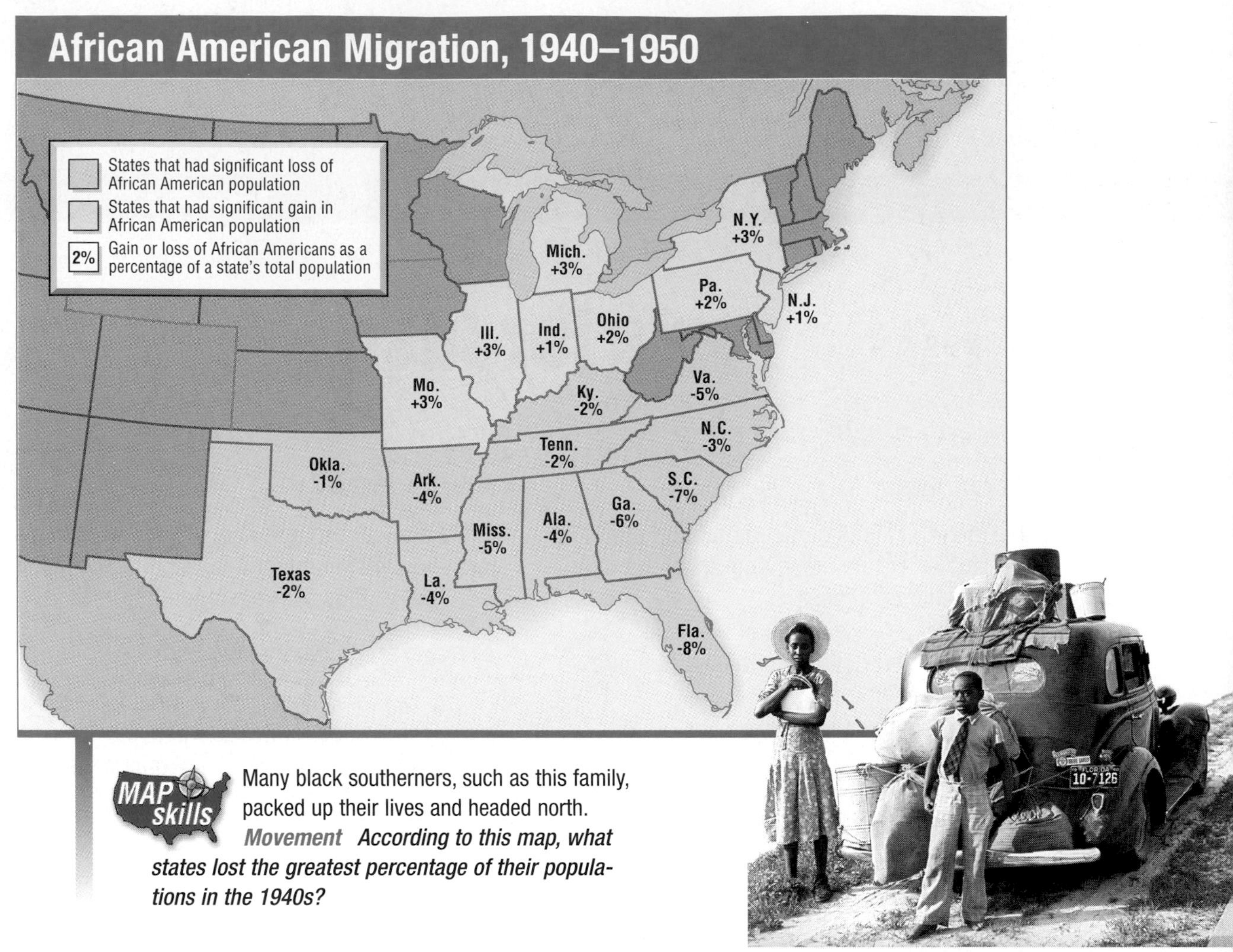


**MAP skills** Many black southerners, such as this family, packed up their lives and headed north. *Movement* ***According to this map, what states lost the greatest percentage of their populations in the 1940s?***

To make things worse, white workers and homeowners often feared and resented the newcomers in their workplaces and neighborhoods. In some places, resentments escalated into violence and riots. In June 1943, riots in Detroit killed 34 people and did millions of dollars worth of damage. Later that summer, riots broke out in New York City.

**Soldiers and Segregation** Even in the American military, where men were risking their lives for their country, white and African American troops were strictly segregated. At home, an army uniform was no block to prejudice. Alexander J. Allen, who worked for the Baltimore Urban League during the war, remarked, "It made a mockery of wartime goals to fight overseas against fascism only to come back to the same kind of discrimination and racism here in this country." In Kansas, for instance, the owner of a lunch counter refused to serve a group of African American GIs. One of them told this story:

**AMERICAN VOICES** **"'You know we don't serve coloreds here,' the man repeated. . . .We ignored him, and just stood there inside the door, staring at what we had come to see—the German prisoners of war who were having lunch at the counter. . . .We continued to stare. This was really happening. It was no jive talk. The people of Salina would serve these enemy soldiers and turn away black American GIs."**

—*Lloyd Brown*

**Divided Opinions** In a 1942 poll, six out of ten whites felt that black Americans were satisfied with existing conditions and needed no new opportunities. Government attitudes mirrored this lack of concern. Franklin Roosevelt was not willing to disrupt the war effort to promote social equality. "I don't think, quite frankly," he said in late 1943, "that we can bring about the millennium [a period of human perfection] at this time."

African Americans, however, worked for change on their own. *The Pittsburgh Courier*, an African American newspaper, launched a **"Double V" campaign.** The first V was for victory against the Axis powers, the second for victory in winning equality at home.

Another step was the founding of the Congress of Racial Equality (CORE) in Chicago in 1942. CORE believed in using nonviolent techniques to end racism. In May 1943 it organized its first sit-in at a restaurant called the Jack Spratt Coffee House. Groups of CORE members, including at least one African American, filled the restaurant's counter and booths. They refused to leave until everyone was served. The sit-in technique ended Jack Spratt's discriminatory policies and quickly spread to CORE groups in other cities. These efforts paved the way for later civil rights actions.

*This man protested outside a Chicago milk company in 1941.*

## *A. Philip Randolph*

AMERICAN BIOGRAPHY

While organized labor won better working conditions for many people in the early 1900s, many unions did not accept African American members. Through two world wars, A. Philip Randolph worked to overcome that discrimination. He made a place for black Americans in the labor movement.

While working his way through college in New York and later as a ship's waiter, Randolph began work as a union organizer. He also entered politics and became a lecturer. Starting in 1925, Randolph gradually won recognition for the Brotherhood of Sleeping Car Porters, a railway union. At the time, most railroad maids and porters were African Americans. For years, railway companies had stopped them from unionizing. The new union won its first major victory in 1937, getting higher wages and cuts in working hours and travel requirements.

Even as war production grew, many factories still turned away African Americans. To protest, Randolph planned a massive march on Washington for July 4, 1941. Worried about the effect on national unity, President Roosevelt tried to talk Randolph out of the march. Finally, on June 25, 1941, the President signed Executive Order 8802 and Randolph called off the march. The order opened jobs and job training programs in defense plants to all Americans "without discrimination because of race, creed, color, or national origin." The order also created the Fair Employment Practices Committee (FEPC) to hear complaints about job discrimination in defense industries and government. Though this law was weakly enforced, it was still a beginning.

*A. Philip Randolph (1889–1979)*

After the war, Randolph continued as a labor leader. He became a vice president of the combined AFL and CIO labor union in 1955. When the civil rights movement got under way, the march that Randolph had wanted to hold years before finally took place. In August 1963, he directed the March on Washington, D.C. There, more than 200,000 people gathered to call for jobs and freedom. Randolph, then 74 years old, stood beside Martin Luther King, Jr., as King gave his famous "I Have a Dream" speech.

**Main Idea CONNECTIONS**

*How did the wartime economy benefit Mexican Americans?*

## Mexican Americans

Like African Americans, both Mexican American citizens and Mexicans working in the United States faced discrimination during the war. On the other hand, the wartime economy brought Mexican Americans new job opportunities in defense industries. By 1944, about 17,000 had jobs in the Los Angeles shipyards, where none had worked three years before. Mexican Americans also found jobs in shipyards and aircraft factories elsewhere in California and in Washington, Texas, and New Mexico. Some headed for other war production centers such as Detroit, Chicago, Kansas City, and New York.

**The Bracero Program** In agriculture, a shortage of farm laborers led the United States to seek help from Mexico. In 1942 an agreement between the two nations provided for transportation, food, shelter, and medical care for thousands of *braceros* (Spanish for "workers"), Mexican farm laborers brought to work in the United States. Between 1942 and 1947, more than 200,000 braceros worked on American farms and, occasionally, in other industries. The program brought a rise in the Latino population of Los Angeles and other cities in southern California. Many lived in Spanish-speaking neighborhoods called *barrios.* Crowded conditions and discrimination caused tensions to rise within the *bracero* communities.

**Zoot Suit Riots** In the 1940s some young Mexican Americans in the Los Angeles barrio began to wear a style known as the "zoot suit." It had a long draped jacket and baggy pants with tight cuffs. "Zoot-suiters" often wore a slicked-back "ducktail" haircut. This look offended many people, especially sailors who came to Los Angeles on leave from nearby military bases. Groups of sailors roamed the streets looking for "zoot-suiters," whom they beat up and humiliated for looking "un-American." One Spanish newspaper, *La Opinión*, urged the Mexican American youths not to respond with more violence, but some took revenge on the sailors when they could.

Early in June 1943, the street fighting turned into full-scale riots. Local newspapers usually blamed Mexican Americans for the violence. Police often arrested the victims rather than the sailors who had begun the attacks. Army and navy officials finally intervened, restricting soldiers' off-duty access to Los Angeles.

Mexican American "zoot-suiters" were the targets of attacks in 1943, but they themselves were often blamed by police for the violence. ***Diversity*** ***Why do you think soldiers and police were set against zoot-suiters?***

## Native Americans

The war also changed the lives of Native Americans. About 25,000 Native Americans joined the armed forces (as you read in the previous chapter). Many others migrated to urban centers to work in defense plants. Roughly 23,000 Native Americans worked in war industries around the country.

Life in the military or in the cities was a new experience for Native Americans who had lived only on reservations. They had to adapt quickly to white culture. At the end of the war, those who had moved away often did not return to reservation life. For some, the cultural transition brought a sense of having lost their roots.

## Japanese Americans

Japanese Americans suffered the worst discrimination during the war. In late 1941, they were a tiny minority in the United States, numbering only 127,000 (about 0.1 percent of the entire population). Most lived on the West Coast, where prejudice against them had always been strong. About two thirds of the Japanese Americans were **Nisei,** or people born in the United States of parents who had emigrated from Japan. Although they were native-born citizens, they still often met hostility from their white neighbors.

Hostility grew into hatred and hysteria after Japan attacked Pearl Harbor. Rumors flew about sabotage on the West Coast. The press increased people's fears with headlines such as "Jap Boat Flashes Message Ashore" and "Japanese Here Sent Vital Data to Tokyo." Americans were left with the feeling that Japanese spies were everywhere.

At assembly centers for Japanese Americans, tags with family identification numbers were attached to each piece of luggage and likewise to each family member. Permitted to take only a few possessions with them, many were forced to abandon what they could not carry or sell. ***Government*** *Why do you think the Supreme Court failed to uphold the rights of Japanese Americans?*

**Japanese Relocation** As a result of these fears and prejudices, the government decided to remove all "aliens" from the West Coast. On February 19, 1942, President Roosevelt signed Executive Order 9066. It authorized the Secretary of War to establish military zones on the West Coast and remove "any or all persons" from such zones. For a few months, foreign-born Italians and Germans were also told to move away from the coast, but those orders were soon changed. The War Relocation Authority was then set up to move out everyone of Japanese ancestry—about 110,000 people, both citizens and noncitizens. They would go to **internment camps** in remote areas inland. (Internment means confinement, especially during wartime.)†

Relocation took place so fast that Japanese Americans had little time to secure their property before they left. Many lost their businesses, farms, homes, and other property. Henry Murakami, a resident of California, remembers losing the $55,000 worth of fishing nets that had been his livelihood:

> **AMERICAN VOICES** **"When we were sent to Fort Lincoln [in Bismarck, North Dakota] I asked the FBI men about my nets. They said, 'Don't worry. Everything is going to be taken care of.' But I never saw the nets again, nor my brand-new 1941 Plymouth, nor our furniture. It all just disappeared. I lost everything."**
>
> —*Henry Murakami*

Japanese Americans had no idea where they were going when they boarded the buses for the internment camps. Monica Sone, who lived in Seattle, imagined her camp would be "out somewhere deep in a snow-bound forest, an American Siberia. I saw myself plunging chest deep in the snow, hunting for small game to keep us alive." She and her family packed their winter clothes, only to end up in Camp Minidoka, on the sun-baked prairie of central Idaho where the normal July temperature is about 90 degrees Fahrenheit.

All the internment camps were in desolate areas, with wooden barracks covered with tar paper. Inside the barracks, families had a room equipped with only cots, blankets, and a light bulb. People had to share toilet, bathing, and dining facilities. Barbed wire and armed guards surrounded the camps.

**Legal Challenges** A few Japanese Americans challenged the internment policy in the courts. Four cases eventually reached the Supreme Court, which ruled that the wartime relocation was constitutional. In one case, California resident Fred Toyosaburo Korematsu, a defense-plant worker, was arrested for refusing

† Similar fears swept Canada, which interned Japanese Canadians.

## COMPARING PRIMARY SOURCES

### INTERNMENT OF JAPANESE AMERICANS

The forced internment of Japanese Americans produced strong feelings on both sides of the issue. Two views are given below. How does each of these viewpoints address the issue of constitutional rights?

| For Internment | Against Internment |
|---|---|
| "It is a fact that the Japanese navy has been reconnoitering [investigating] the Pacific Coast .... It is [a] fact that communication takes place between the enemy at sea and enemy agents on land. The Pacific Coast is officially a combat zone: some part of it may at any moment be a battlefield. Nobody's constitutional rights include the right to reside and do business on a battlefield." —*Walter Lippmann, American columnist, February 12, 1942* | "Racial discrimination in any form and in any degree has no justifiable part whatever in our democratic way of life. . . . All residents of this nation are kin in some way by blood or culture to a foreign land. Yet they are primarily and necessarily a part of . . . the United States [and are] . . . entitled to all rights and freedoms guaranteed by the Constitution." —*Supreme Court Justice Frank Murphy's dissenting opinion,* Korematsu *v.* United States, *1944* |

***ANALYZING VIEWPOINTS*** **What different assumptions does each of these writers make about Japanese Americans on the West Coast?**

to report to a relocation center. Korematsu appealed, saying his civil rights had been violated.

The Supreme Court ruled in *Korematsu* v. *United States* (1944) that the decision was not based on race. The majority opinion said that "the military urgency of the situation demanded that all citizens of Japanese ancestry be segregated from the West Coast temporarily." The dissenting opinion, however, labeled the policy "an obvious racial discrimination."

Early in 1945, Japanese Americans were allowed to leave the camps. Some returned home and resumed their lives, but others found that they had lost nearly everything. As time passed, many Americans came to believe that the internment had been a great injustice. In 1988 Congress passed a law awarding each surviving Japanese American internee a tax-free payment of $20,000. More than 40 years after the event, the United States government also officially apologized.

**Nisei Soldiers** Despite injustices against the Japanese Americans, more than 20,000 of them served in the armed forces. About 1,200 of the Japanese Americans who volunteered did so from relocation centers. Many other volunteers came from Hawaii, where there had been no internment.

The 442nd Regimental Combat Team was made up entirely of Japanese Americans. Fighting in France and Germany, its soldiers won more medals for bravery than any other unit in United States history.

## *SECTION 4 REVIEW*

### Comprehension

1. *Key Terms* Define: (a) "Double V" campaign; (b) Nisei; (c) internment camp.
2. *Summarizing the Main Idea* Did the wartime economy make workplace discrimination worse or just create more of it?
3. *Organizing Information* Make a tree-map chart comparing and contrasting the wartime experiences of the four different ethnic and racial groups discussed in this section.

### Critical Thinking

4. *Analyzing Time Lines* Review the time line at the start of the section. Which of those events do you think had the greatest impact on conditions for minorities after the war? Write a short paragraph explaining your choice.
5. *Recognizing Bias* The government acted more harshly against Japanese Americans than against people of Italian and German ancestry. Why do you think this discrimination occurred?

### Writing Activity

6. *Writing a Persuasive Essay* Imagine that you are an adviser to Franklin D. Roosevelt and have been asked to give the President your opinion about A. Philip Randolph's idea for a protest march. Are you in favor of or against the march? Write a memo to FDR persuading him that your opinion is right.

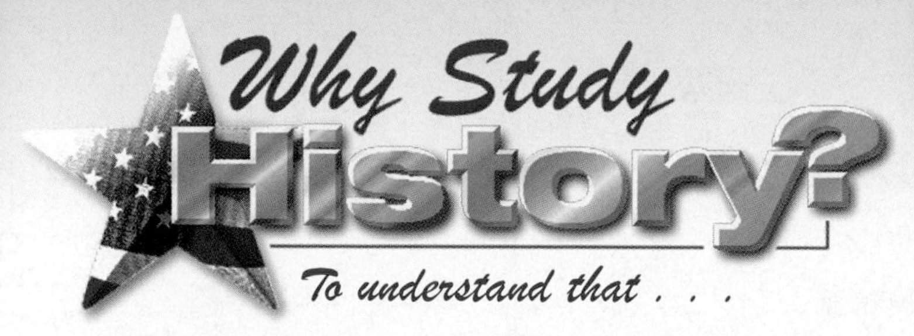


# Most Women Are in the Work Force

**Working women in the United States today are facing some of the same challenges that confronted working women during World War II.**

The alarm clock rings at 5:30 A.M. Ann Bogar makes breakfast and packs lunches for her husband and children before leaving the house at 6:15. Bogar is an executive assistant in an oil and gas company based in Houston, Texas.

Millions of American women like Bogar begin each weekday by preparing breakfast and helping children get ready for school. They also work outside the home—as teachers, bankers, lawyers, secretaries, doctors, computer programmers, sales associates, rabbis or ministers, waitresses, or business executives.

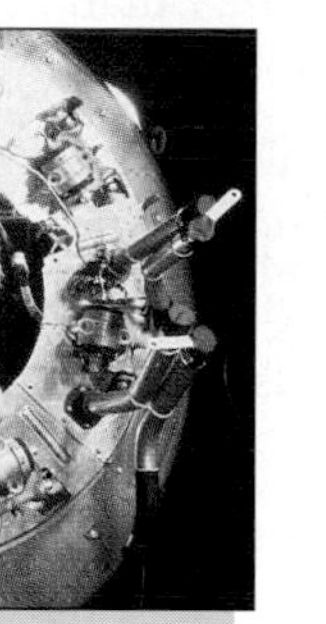

*Woman assembling aircraft during World War II*

## The Impact Today

During World War II, about 6 million American women joined the work force. They took jobs in factories and offices to help the war effort and replace the men who were fighting overseas. After the war, most women returned to their jobs as homemakers—some by choice, others as a result of pressure by government and industry. Still, women's work experience helped shape the expectations of later generations.

In 1940 only about 15 percent of married women worked outside the home. Today more than 60 percent do. Many women work to meet the challenges and reap the rewards of a career. Others work out of necessity, to help meet the living expenses of their families.

In the 1940s, working women earned significantly less money than men who performed the same jobs. Although women have made strides toward greater economic equality, they still experience wage discrimination. In 1999, full-time women wage and salary earners earned 76 percent of men's median weekly earnings. This wage gap exists for women at all educational levels. Even female college graduates earn roughly 16 percent less than their male peers.

Women make up about 61 percent of employees in the nation's top 500 companies but only 2.4 percent of corporate executives. Why? In seeking to move up the corporate ladder, many women encounter a "glass ceiling" of gender-based barriers to advancement. Women often start in areas such as personnel and staff support, which do not generally lead to top management positions. Also, there are few women executives to act as sponsors to younger women, helping them to rise in the corporation. An important challenge for American corporations is to ensure that women have equal opportunity for advancement.

*Office worker*

## The Impact on You

Create a typical daily schedule that shows the responsibilities of two working parents. You can base this schedule on your own family or that of a neighbor. Your schedule should show what each parent's typical day is like and how the parents divide household responsibilities.

# Chapter 15 Review

## Chapter Summary

The major concepts of Chapter 15 are presented below. See also ***Guide to the Essentials of American History*** or ***Interactive Student Tutorial CD-ROM,*** which contains interactive review activities, time lines, helpful hints, and test practice.

CD-ROM REVIEW

### *Reviewing the Main Ideas*

Wartime production ended the Depression, bringing prosperity and high employment. As factories stopped producing consumer goods and converted to making military equipment, government programs worked to keep popular support behind the war effort. War jobs brought new opportunities for women and members of most minorities, but discrimination continued.

### *Section 1: The Shift to Wartime Production*

At the beginning of World War II, the government mobilized industries and workers to produce materials for the war.

### *Section 2: Daily Life on the Home Front*

As the war economy brought both prosperity and shortages, the government worked to keep Americans at home involved in the war effort.

### *Section 3: Women and the War*

During World War II, more American women went to work in nontraditional, war-industry jobs, but they were discouraged from keeping their jobs after the war ended.

### *Section 4: The Struggle for Justice at Home*

While the war brought new job opportunities for some racial and ethnic minorities, Japanese Americans were the victims of widespread intolerance.

Working women today face many of the same challenges that confronted working women during World War II. Today about 61 percent of married women work outside the home.

## Key Terms

For each of the terms below, write a sentence explaining how it relates to the chapter.

1. Liberty ship
2. wildcat strike
3. war bond
4. deficit spending
5. rationing
6. Office of War Mobilization
7. Office of War Information
8. victory garden
9. "Double V" campaign

## Comprehension

1. How did World War II end the Depression?
2. What changes did American businesses make at the start of the war?
3. In what two ways did the government finance war costs and war production?
4. What were the responsibilities of the Office of Price Administration?
5. Name five items that were in short supply during the war. How did these shortages affect people at home?
6. What changes took place in the kinds of jobs women held before and during World War II?
7. Describe some of the benefits that women got from war work.
8. What strategies did African Americans use to gain equal rights during World War II?
9. What attitudes led to the internment of Japanese Americans during World War II?

## Using Graphic Organizers

On a separate sheet of paper, copy the tree-map organizer below. Using your own words, fill in the main ideas for each category.

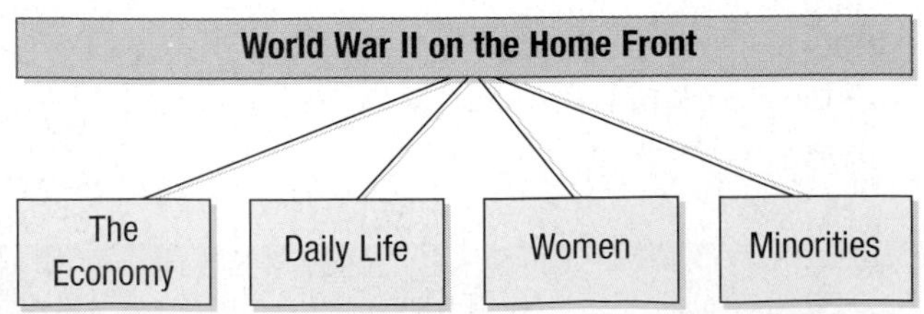

## Analyzing Political Cartoons ▶

1. What does the woman in the cartoon symbolize?
2. What is the significance of her having her own "man-size" pay?
3. What point does the man's speech make?
4. Examine both figures. What message is conveyed by the woman's huge size and the man's clothing?

## Critical Thinking

1. ***Applying the Chapter Skill*** What assumptions did employers and society as a whole make about the women who took new jobs during World War II? How were these like or unlike those that were made about "Rosie the Riveter"?
2. ***Perceiving Cause-Effect Relationships*** Why were there shortages of sugar, coffee, and tropical fruits during World War II?
3. ***Drawing Conclusions*** Why did Americans generally accept rationing, bond drives, and other government programs to involve them in the war effort?
4. ***Predicting Consequences*** How might the changes that the war brought for African Americans have affected the later civil rights movement?

### INTERNET ACTIVITY

***For your portfolio:***
**CREATE A DIARY ENTRY**

Access Prentice Hall's *America: Pathways to the Present* site at **www.Pathways.phschool.com** for the specific URLs to complete the activity. Additional resources and related Web sites are also available.

Read several interviews with women who experienced life on the home front in World War II. Create a fictional diary entry of a week in the life of one such woman. Choose a typical week or a week during which a major event happened. How did the war affect the lives of the people at home?

### ANALYZING DOCUMENTS ◀▶ INTERPRETING DATA

Turn to the map on page 476.

1. One of these statements about this map is *not* true. Which is it? (a) Every state in the South lost population in the wartime migration. (b) Florida, Georgia, and South Carolina lost the greatest percentage of their populations. (c) Every state in the industrial Northeast gained population in the African American migration.
2. Which statement best reflects the information shown on this map? (a) African Americans moved mainly to northern industrial areas. (b) Wartime job opportunities were available to African Americans throughout the United States. (c) West Coast war industries did not draw African Americans.
3. ***Writing*** In one paragraph, summarize the events shown by this map and what they meant for African Americans.

## Connecting to Today

***Essay Writing*** Choose one of the groups whose wartime experiences are discussed in Section 4. Then research and write an essay about the changes that have taken place in that group's position in American society in the 50-plus years since World War II.

CHAPTER

# 16 The Cold War

## 1945–1960

Ben Shahn

## CHAPTER FOCUS

*This chapter examines the post–World War II hostility between the United States and the Soviet Union that played out in large and small conflicts across the globe.*

*The **Why Study History?** page at the end of this chapter explores the connection between defense spending before and after the cold war.*

▲

**VIEWING HISTORY**

Artist Ben Shahn's 1945 painting entitled *Reconstruction* portrays the rebuilding process after World War II. ***Culture*** ***What feelings does the artist seem to depict?***

**1945**
*Yalta Conference (February); UN founded (April); FDR dies, Truman becomes President (April); Potsdam Conference (July)*

**1946**
*Stalin predicts triumph of communism (February); Churchill gives iron curtain speech (March); Kennan article on containment (July)*

**1947**
*Truman Doctrine*

**1945** | **1946** | **1947**

# 1 Origins of the Cold War

**SECTION PREVIEW**

### Objectives

1. Explain why 1945 was a critical year in international relations and how it was followed by conflicting postwar goals.
2. Describe how the Soviet Union tightened its control over Eastern Europe.
3. Identify the iron curtain and how it led to containment policy and the Truman Doctrine.
4. *Key Terms* Define: satellite nation; iron curtain; cold war; containment; Truman Doctrine.

### Main Idea

At the end of World War II, conflicting goals for Europe led to growing hostility between the United States and the Soviet Union.

### Reading Strategy

*Arranging Events in Order* As you read, make a list of events that led to the development of the cold war. List the date of each event. Then, arrange them in chronological order.

"I know you will not mind my being brutally frank when I tell you that I can personally handle Stalin," President Roosevelt told Winston Churchill during World War II. "He thinks he likes me better, and I hope he will continue to." By 1944, Roosevelt was so sure of Stalin's cooperation that he began calling the Soviet dictator "Uncle Joe."

A Roosevelt adviser later wrote that the President did not have "any real comprehension of the great gulf that separated [their] thinking." Churchill, however, clearly understood the situation. "Germany is finished," he told an adviser. "The real problem is Russia. I can't get the Americans to see it."

## 1945—A Critical Year

The wartime cooperation between the United States and the Soviet Union was a temporary arrangement. The two nations had a history of bad feelings following the Russian Revolution. During the revolt, President Wilson had dispatched American troops to Russia to support anti-Communist resistance. The United States did not recognize the legal existence of the Soviet government until 1933.

As wartime allies, the Soviets disagreed bitterly with their American and British partners over battle tactics and postwar plans. As the end of the war approached, relations grew increasingly tense.

**Differences at Yalta** In February 1945, Roosevelt met with Stalin and Churchill at Yalta

*Churchill, Roosevelt, and Stalin, (left to right) met at Yalta to discuss postwar Europe.*

At its birth, the United Nations was hailed by President Harry Truman as "a victory against war itself." In this photograph, Truman and representatives from other member nations look on as Secretary of State Edward Stettinius signs the UN charter in June 1945. ***Government*** ***Why do you think Congress agreed to United States membership in the United Nations, even though it had not supported the League of Nations?***

to work out the future of Germany and Poland. They agreed on the division of Germany into American, British, French, and Soviet occupation zones. (Later, the American, French, British zones were combined to create West Germany. The Soviet zone became East Germany.) Roosevelt and Churchill rejected Stalin's demand that Germany pay the Soviet Union $10 billion in war damages.

Roosevelt pressed Stalin at Yalta to declare war on Japan. The atomic bomb had not yet been tested, and the President wanted Soviet help if an invasion of Japan became necessary.

Poland proved the most difficult issue to address at Yalta. The Red Army had occupied that country and supported the Communist-dominated government. Stalin opposed the return of Poland's prewar government. Historically, Poland was an invasion route into Russia. The Polish government, Stalin insisted, must be sympathetic to Soviet security needs.

The meeting stalled until Stalin agreed on elections to let Poles choose their own type of government. Disputes over Poland would continue to strain American-Soviet relations.

**The United Nations** One item on which the leaders all agreed at Yalta was creation of the United Nations (UN), a new international peacekeeping organization. The League of Nations, founded after World War I, had failed largely because the United States refused to join. This time, policymakers got congressional support for the UN.

In April 1945, delegates from 50 nations met in San Francisco to adopt a charter, or statement of principles, for the UN. The charter stated that members would try to settle their differences peacefully. It vowed to try to stop wars from starting and to end those that did break out.

All member nations belonged to the UN's General Assembly. Representatives of 11 countries sat on a Security Council. The United States, the Soviet Union, Great Britain, France, and China had permanent seats on the council and a veto over proposed policies.

**Truman Takes Command** Roosevelt never lived to see his dream of the United Nations fulfilled. On April 12, 1945, just two weeks before the UN's first meeting, the President died while resting at Warm Springs, Georgia. Although he was in poor health and noticeably tired, his unexpected death shocked the nation. No one was more surprised than Vice President Harry S. Truman, who suddenly found himself President.

Few Vice Presidents have been less prepared to become President. While he had spent 10 years in Congress, Truman had been Vice President for just 82 days. Roosevelt had never involved him in major foreign policy discussions. Truman at first adopted FDR's willingness to compromise with the Soviets. But before long his attitude hardened.

**The Potsdam Conference** Truman's first meeting with Stalin came in July 1945 in the Berlin suburb of Potsdam. The Allies continued to debate the issues that had divided them at Yalta, including the future of Germany and of Poland. Stalin renewed his demand for war payments from Germany, and Truman insisted on the promised Polish elections.

At Potsdam, Truman got word that the atom bomb had been tested in New Mexico. Hoping to intimidate Stalin, Truman told him that America had a new weapon of extraordinary force. Stalin, who already knew of the bomb from Soviet spies, simply nodded and said that he hoped it would be put to good use. Stalin's casual manner hid his concern over America's new strategic advantage.

## *Conflicting Postwar Goals*

Shortly after Truman took office he scolded Soviet Foreign Minister Vyacheslav Molotov for the Soviet Union's failure to allow Polish elections. Molotov was offended by Truman's bluntness. "I have never been talked to like that in my life," Molotov protested. "Carry out your agreements and you won't get talked to like that," Truman snapped.

**The American View** Tensions over Poland illustrated American and Soviet leaders' differing views of the world. Americans had fought to bring democracy and economic opportunity to the conquered nations of Europe and Asia. The United States hoped to see these goals achieved in the postwar world. An economically strong and politically open world also served American interests by providing markets for its products.

**The Soviet View** After losing more than 20 million people during the war and suffering widespread destruction, the Soviet Union was determined to rebuild in ways that would protect its own interests. One way was to establish **satellite nations,** countries subject to Soviet domination, on the western borders of the Soviet Union. These governments would be friendly to Communist goals.

Stalin thus refused to cooperate with new agencies such as the World Bank and the International Monetary Fund, intended to help build strong, capitalist economies. Instead, he installed or supported totalitarian Communist governments in Eastern Europe.

**Main Idea CONNECTIONS**

***How did American and Soviet goals for postwar Europe differ?***

## *Soviets Tighten Their Hold*

The Soviet Union quickly gained control over Eastern European nations freed from the Nazis. The promised elections in Poland did not take place for nearly two years. Meanwhile, Poland's Soviet-installed government eliminated all political opposition.

**Albania and Bulgaria** In Albania, Communist guerrilla forces had driven out the Germans by 1944. When elections were held the following year, all anti-Communist leaders had been silenced. Soviet troops rolled into Bulgaria in 1944, and the Communists secured their hold on the country by 1948.

### A Divided Europe

This map shows the nations controlled by Communist and non-Communist countries. After World War II, the Soviet Union was highly concerned about protecting its national security. ***Location*** *How does this map illustrate the policy pursued by the Soviet Union to protect itself from its non-Communist rivals in Europe?*

VIEWING HISTORY

Winston Churchill (left) is shown making the 1946 speech in which he introduced the idea of the iron curtain. In the cartoon (right), United States Secretary of State James Byrnes is portrayed as a determined suitor. ***Foreign Relations*** ***Whom is he courting? How does the cartoonist rate his chances of success?***

**Czechoslovakia** The Czechs desperately tried to hold on to their democratic multiparty political system. The Communist candidate won 40 percent of the vote in free elections in 1946, but Communist repression in neighboring nations weakened the Czech Communists' popularity. They plotted to take power, therefore, by replacing all non-Communist police officers with party members. By 1948 Czechoslovakia was a Soviet satellite nation.

**Hungary and Romania** After Communist candidates lost elections in Hungary in late 1945, Soviet troops remained in that country and demanded Communist control of the police. The arrest of anti-Communist leaders allowed the Communists to win new elections held in 1947. The Red Army also stayed in Romania, and in 1945 the Soviets forced the Romanian king to name a Communist as prime minister. Less than two years later, the prime minister forced the king to resign.

**East Germany** While the Western Allies wanted a strong, rebuilt Germany at the center of Europe, Stalin was determined that the Germans would never threaten his nation again. He established national control of all East German resources and installed a brutal totalitarian government there. In 1949, under the Communist government, the country became known as the German Democratic Republic.

**Finland and Yugoslavia** Two other countries managed to maintain a degree of independence from the Soviet Union. Finland signed a treaty of cooperation with the Soviets in 1948. The treaty required Finland to remain neutral in foreign affairs but allowed it to manage its domestic affairs. In Yugoslavia, Communists gained control in 1945 under the leadership of Josip Broz, better known as Tito. A fiercely independent dictator, Tito refused to take orders from Stalin, who unsuccessfully tried to topple him in 1948. For the next three decades Tito would pursue his own brand of communism relatively free from Soviet interference.

## *The Iron Curtain*

In a February 1946 speech, Stalin predicted the ultimate triumph of communism over capitalism. Yet he knew that it would be years before the Soviets were strong enough militarily to directly confront the United States.

In the meantime, Stalin called on Communists to spread their system by other means. He soon established Cominform, a Soviet agency intended to direct the activities of Communist parties throughout the world.

The month after Stalin's speech, Winston Churchill responded. Although he had recently been defeated for reelection as prime minister by Clement Attlee, Churchill remained a powerful voice of opposition to the Soviet Union. Speaking at Westminster College in Fulton, Missouri, he condemned the division of Europe that Stalin had already accomplished:

**KEY DOCUMENTS** **"From Stettin in the Baltic to Trieste in the Adriatic, an iron curtain has descended across the Continent. Behind that line lie all the capitals of . . . Central and Eastern Europe. . . . The Communist parties, which were very small in all these Eastern States of Europe, have been raised to preeminence and power far beyond their numbers and are seeking everywhere to obtain totalitarian control. . . . This is certainly not the Liberated Europe we fought to build up. Nor is it one which contains the essentials of permanent peace."**

—*"Iron Curtain" speech, Winston Churchill, March 5, 1946*

In his speech, Churchill called on Americans to help keep Stalin from closing the **iron curtain** of Communist domination and oppression around any more nations.

These two speeches set the tone for the **cold war,** the competition that developed between the United States and the Soviet Union for power and influence in the world. For nearly 50 years, until the collapse of the Soviet Union in 1991, the cold war was characterized by political and economic conflict and military tensions. The rivalry stopped just short of a "hot" war—a direct military engagement—between the two competing nations. However, United States military forces did engage in combat in other nations in efforts to defeat Soviet-supported uprisings and invasions.

## Containment

In a secret telegram to the State Department in early 1946, George Kennan, a top American diplomat stationed in Moscow, analyzed Soviet behavior and policy. Like Stalin, Kennan saw the Soviet Union's weaknesses. Soon thereafter, he publicized his observations in an anonymous magazine article.

Soviet policies show "no real faith in the possibility of a permanently happy coexistence of the Socialist and capitalist worlds," Kennan warned. The Soviets believed the triumph of communism was inevitable. Therefore, Kennan concluded:

**AMERICAN VOICES**

> **"[The Soviet Union] cannot be easily defeated or discouraged by a single victory on the part of its opponents . . . but only by intelligent long-range policies . . . no less steady in their purpose . . . than those of the Soviet Union itself. In these circumstances, it is clear that the main element of any United States policy toward the Soviet Union must be that of a long-term, patient but firm and vigilant containment of Russian expansive tendencies."**
>
> —*American diplomat George Kennan, article in* Foreign Affairs *magazine, July 1947*

From Kennan's analysis, the policy of **containment** emerged. This policy recognized the possibility that Eastern Europe was already lost to communism. It called for the United States to resist Soviet attempts to form Communist governments elsewhere in the world.

### CAUSE AND EFFECT: The Cold War

**CAUSES**

- *United States and USSR clash over the postwar administration of Poland.*
- *USSR's totalitarian government is increasingly at odds with Western ideals.*
- *Stalin pledges to ensure the survival of the Soviet system, while Churchill urges the West to oppose it.*

**THE COLD WAR**

**EFFECTS**

- *United States adopts a policy to "contain" communism.*
- *Truman Doctrine offers U.S. aid to countries opposing communism.*
- *NATO and Warsaw Pact are formed.*
- *Fear of communism at home leads to a climate of suspicion in American culture.*

**Interpreting Charts** The cold war affected life in the United States, as people began to fear communism within the nation. ***Foreign Relations*** ***What effect did the cold war have on United States foreign policy?***

**Main Idea CONNECTIONS**

*What was the policy of containment?*

Critics saw containment as too moderate an approach to Soviet-American relations. They called for action to push the Communists out of Eastern Europe, Russia, and anywhere else. Kennan, however, argued that the Soviet system "bears within it the seeds of its own decay" and would eventually crumble. Thus, although containment remained controversial, it became the cornerstone of America's cold war foreign policy.

## The Truman Doctrine

President Truman soon had a chance to apply the policy of containment. Since 1945 the Soviet Union had been making threats against Turkey. Stalin wanted control of the Dardanelles, a narrow strait in Turkey that would give Soviet ports on the Black Sea access to the Mediterranean. In addition, a civil war had broken out in nearby Greece in the closing days of the war. There Communists fought to overthrow the government that had returned to power after the Axis invaders withdrew.

Still suffering from the economic devastation of WWII, Britain announced in February

*President Truman was named Man of the Year by* Time *in 1949.*

1947 that it could no longer afford to provide aid to Greece and Turkey. The British suggested that the United States take over responsibility for defending the region. Undersecretary of State Dean Acheson reported that at that moment Great Britain "handed the job of world leadership, with all its burdens and all its glory, to the United States."

State Department officials developed a plan to provide American aid to Greece and Turkey. To head off congressional opposition, Acheson warned of grave dangers if the United States failed to act. "Only two great powers remain in the world," he observed, "the United States and the Soviet Union."

In March 1947, in a speech before a joint session of Congress, Truman called on the United States to take a leadership role. In a statement of principles known as the **Truman Doctrine,** he established another major policy that guided American actions in the cold war.

**KEY DOCUMENTS**

**"Nearly every nation must choose between alternative ways of life. The choice is too often not a free one. One way of life is based upon the will of the majority. . . . The second way of life is based upon the will of a minority forcibly imposed upon the majority. . . . I believe that it must be the policy of the United States to support free peoples who are resisting attempted subjugation [conquest] by armed minorities or by outside pressures. I believe that we must assist free peoples to work out their own destinies in their own way."**

*—Truman Doctrine, speech by President Harry S. Truman to Congress, March 12, 1947*

Responding to Truman's plea, Congress approved $400 million in aid for Greece and Turkey. In addition, the United States soon established military bases in both countries.

During the next four decades, the Truman Doctrine and the policy of containment continued to guide United States foreign policy. These principles would lead the United States into controversial involvements in "hot" and "cold" conflicts around the world.

## SECTION 1 REVIEW

### Comprehension

1. *Key Terms* Define: (a) satellite nation; (b) iron curtain; (c) cold war; (d) containment; (e) Truman Doctrine.
2. *Summarizing the Main Idea* How did postwar hostility develop between the United States and the Soviet Union?
3. *Organizing Information* Create a time line to show how the Soviets tightened their hold on Eastern Europe.

### Critical Thinking

4. *Analyzing Time Lines* Refer to the time line at the start of the section. Why was 1945 a crucial year in history?
5. *Drawing Conclusions* What effects do you think the Stalin and Churchill speeches of 1946 had on American public opinion?

### Writing Activity

6. *Writing an Expository Essay* How did the idea of containment and the Truman Doctrine affect cold war policy?

# SKILLS FOR LIFE

**Critical Thinking**

Geography

Graphs and Charts

Historical Evidence

## Recognizing Cause and Effect

History is more than a list of events; it is a study of relationships among events. Recognizing cause and effect means examining how one event or action brings about others. If you can understand how events or ideas relate to and affect each other, you can begin to formulate workable solutions to problems.

Follow the steps below to practice recognizing cause and effect.

**1.** ***Identify the two parts of a cause-effect relationship.*** A cause is an event or action that brings about an effect. As you read, look for key words that signal a cause-effect relationship. Words such as *because, due to,* and *on account of* signal causes. Words such as *so, thus, therefore,* and *as a result* signal effects. Read statements A through C at right, and answer the following questions. (a) Which statements contain both a cause and an effect? (b) Which is the cause and which is the effect in each statement? (c) What words, if any, signal the cause-effect relationship?

**2.** ***Remember that an event can have more than one cause and more than one effect.*** Several causes can lead to one event. So, too, can a single cause have several effects. Read statement D at right, and respond to the following. (a) Find an example of a cause that has more than one effect. (b) Find an example of an effect that has more than one cause.

**3.** ***Understand that an event can be both a cause and an effect.*** A cause can lead to an effect, which in turn can be the cause of another event. In this way, causes and effects can form a chain of related events. You can diagram the following statements to show such a chain: The United States feared Soviet expansion in Europe. →The United States began a military buildup. →The Soviet Union began a military buildup. →An arms race between the two countries began. Now read statement D below. Draw a diagram showing the chain of related events.

### TEST FOR SUCCESS

Use the information in the preceding section under the heading "The Soviet View" to write a statement in one or two sentences that shows cause and effect.

## Statements

**A** Because President Roosevelt believed that postwar cooperation with the Soviet Union was necessary, he viewed Stalin as a partner—if not an ally—in formulating a peace.

**B** Unlike Roosevelt, President Truman was persuaded by advisers that the Soviet Union would become a "world bully" after the war. As a result, he adopted a "get tough" policy whose aim was to block any possibility of Soviet expansion.

**C** The Soviets, for their part, believed that the United States was intent on global domination and meant to encircle the Soviet Union with anti-Communist states.

**D** Due to mounting distrust between the United States and the Soviet Union, each power came to view the postwar peace negotiations as an opportunity to test the other's global objectives. Thus, negotiating the status of Poland became the first such test. Other tests included the plans for former German satellite states and the policies for the occupation of Germany. Each power regarded its own positions in these negotiations as essentially defensive, but each viewed the other's stances as aggressive and expansionist. Together these tests and stances produced the cold war, an armed and dangerous truce that lasted for 45 years.

| 1947 | 1948 | 1948 | 1948 | 1949 | 1953 | 1955 |
|---|---|---|---|---|---|---|
| Hollywood Ten hearings | Marshall Plan enacted | Berlin airlift begins | HUAC probes Hiss spy case | Communists take China; Soviets test atom bomb; NATO created | Rosenbergs executed for spying | Warsaw Pact created |

1947 — 1951 — 1955

# 2 The Cold War Abroad and at Home

## SECTION PREVIEW

### Objectives

1. Explain how the Marshall Plan, the Berlin airlift, and the creation of NATO helped achieve American goals in postwar Europe.
2. Assess the impact of two Communist advances on American foreign policy.
3. Summarize the effects of the cold war on American life.
4. *Key Terms* Define: Marshall Plan; Berlin airlift; North Atlantic Treaty Organization (NATO); collective security; Warsaw Pact; HUAC; Hollywood Ten; blacklist; McCarran-Walter Act.

### Main Idea

As the cold war intensified, American policy focused on rebuilding and unifying Western Europe. At home, emotionally charged spy cases raised fears of Communist infiltration into American society and government.

### Reading Strategy

*Organizing Information* As you read, list major challenges the United States faced in its efforts to oppose communism. Then describe the solutions carried out.

Truman's decision to send aid to Turkey and Greece was only a down payment on rebuilding Europe. World War II had devastated the continent to a degree never before seen. About 21 million people had been made homeless. In Poland, some 20 percent of the population had died. Nearly 1 of every 5 houses in France and Belgium had been damaged or destroyed. Across Europe, industries and transportation were in ruins. Agriculture suffered from the loss of livestock and equipment. In France alone, damage equaled three times the nation's annual income.

## *Turning Point: The Marshall Plan*

American policymakers were determined not to repeat the mistakes of the post–World War I era. This time the United States would help restore the war-torn nations so that they might create stable democracies and achieve economic recovery. The Truman Doctrine was one of two fundamental shifts in postwar foreign policy intended to fulfill these goals. The other was the **Marshall Plan,** which called for the nations of Europe to draw up a program for economic recovery from the war. The United States would then support the program with financial aid.

The plan was unveiled by Secretary of State George C. Marshall in 1947. The Marshall Plan responded to the concern of American policymakers that Communist parties were growing stronger across Europe, and the Soviet Union might intervene to support more of these movements. The plan also reflected the belief that United States aid for European economic recovery would create strong democracies and open new markets for American goods.

Marshall described his plan in a speech at Harvard University in June 1947:

**"It is logical that the United States should do whatever it is able to assist in the return of normal economic health in the world, without which there can be**

no political stability and no assured peace. Our policy is directed not against any country or doctrine but against hunger, poverty, desperation, and chaos. Its purpose should be the revival of a working economy in the world so as to permit the emergence of political and social conditions in which free institutions can exist.”

—*Marshall Plan speech at Harvard University by Secretary of State George C. Marshall, June 5, 1947*

The Soviet Union was invited to participate in the Marshall Plan, but it refused the help and pressured its satellite nations to do so as well. Soviet Foreign Minister Vyacheslav Molotov called the Marshall Plan a vicious American scheme for using dollars to “buy its way” into European affairs. In fact, Soviet leaders did not want outside scrutiny of their country's economy. Seventeen Western European nations joined the plan: Austria, Belgium, Denmark, France, Greece, Iceland, Ireland, Italy, Luxembourg, the Netherlands, Switzerland, Norway, Portugal, Sweden, Turkey, the United Kingdom, and West Germany.

In 1948 Congress approved the Marshall Plan, which was formally known as the European Recovery Program. Over the next four years, the United States sent some $13 billion in grants and loans to Western Europe. The region's economies were quickly restored, and the United States gained strong trading partners in the region.

**Main Idea CONNECTIONS**

*What was the purpose of the Marshall Plan?*

## *The Berlin Airlift*

One of the nations that benefited from the Marshall Plan was West Germany. By 1948 American, British, and French leaders had become convinced that Stalin was not going to allow the reunification of Germany. Therefore the Western Allies prepared to merge their three occupation zones to create the Federal Republic of Germany, or West Germany.

## TURNING POINT: *The Marshall Plan*

**Since the announcement of the Marshall Plan, the United States has sent economic help to countries facing a variety of challenges.**

**1948**
*The Marshall Plan provides aid to Western Europe.*

**1961**
*President Kennedy creates the Peace Corps, a program of volunteers to help developing nations.*

**1997**
*The United States sends food shipments to North Korea to help ease a severe famine.*

**1940** | **1960** | **1980** | **2000**

**1973**
*United States sends famine relief to Bangladesh after its bloody war for independence.*

**1992**
*The United States begins helping Russia's transition to a market economy.*

## Partitioning of Berlin, 1949

After the partitioning of Berlin (above), the Soviet Union blockaded West Berlin. Rather than risk a military engagement, Truman responded by ordering an airlift (top) to bring supplies to the city. ***Movement* Why did Stalin blockade West Berlin?**

The western part of Berlin, which lay in the Soviet zone, was to become part of West Germany. The Soviets responded in 1949 by forming the German Democratic Republic, or East Germany.

Capitalist West Berlin and Communist East Berlin became visible symbols of the developing cold war struggle between the Soviet Union and the Western powers. Hundreds of thousands of Eastern Europeans left their homes in Communist-dominated nations, fled to East Berlin, and then crossed into West Berlin. From there they booked passage to freedom in the United States, Canada, or Western Europe.

Stalin decided to close this escape route by forcing the Western powers to abandon West Berlin. In June 1948, when a dispute developed over using West German money in that city, the Soviets used it as an excuse to block Allied access to West Berlin. All shipments to the city through East Germany were banned. The blockade threatened to create severe shortages of food and other supplies needed by the 2.5 million people in West Berlin.

Truman did not want to risk starting a war by using military force to open the transportation routes. Nor did he want to give up West Berlin to the Soviets. Instead Truman began the **Berlin airlift,** moving supplies into West Berlin by plane. During the next 15 months, British and American military aircraft made more than 200,000 flights to deliver food, fuel, and other supplies. At the height of the Berlin airlift, nearly 13,000 tons of goods arrived in West Berlin daily.†

The Soviets finally gave up the blockade in May 1949, and the airlift ended the following September. By this time the Marshall Plan had

† In May 1998, a reunified Germany celebrated the 50th anniversary of the Berlin airlift. President Bill Clinton and German Chancellor Helmut Kohl participated in the ceremonies. They honored the courage of the pilots, who had showered the city with food, medicine, and even chocolate, and the city's residents, who endured a frightening year at the center of superpower conflict.

helped achieve economic stability in the capitalist nations of Western Europe, including West Germany. Berlin, however, remained a focal point of East-West conflict.

## *NATO*

In the early postwar period, the international community pinned its hopes on the United Nations to protect nations and maintain world peace. However, the Soviet Union's frequent use of its veto power in the Security Council prevented the UN from effectively dealing with a number of postwar problems.

This development soon made it clear that Western Europe would have to look beyond the UN in protecting itself from Soviet aggression. In 1946 Canadian Foreign Minister Louis St. Laurent proposed creating an "association of democratic peace-loving states" to defend Western Europe against attack by the Soviet Union.

American officials expressed great interest in St. Laurent's idea. Truman was determined that the United States not return to pre–World War II isolationism. The Truman Doctrine and the Marshall Plan soon demonstrated his commitment to making America a leader in postwar world affairs.

Yet Truman did not want the United States to be the only nation in the Western Hemisphere pledged to defend Western Europe from the Communists. For this reason, Canada's role in any proposed organization became vital to American support.

In April 1949, Canada and the United States joined Belgium, Britain, Denmark, France, Iceland, Italy, Luxembourg, the Netherlands, Norway, and Portugal to form the **North Atlantic Treaty Organization (NATO).** Member nations agreed that "an armed attack against one or more of them . . . shall be considered an attack against them all."†

†NATO provided the model for similar alliances with nations in other parts of the world. In 1954, the United States joined Britain, France, Australia, New Zealand, Pakistan, the Philippines, and Thailand in creating the Southeast Asia Treaty Organization (SEATO). Five years later, the United States joined an existing alliance of Britain, Iran, Pakistan, and Turkey to form the Central Treaty Organization (CENTO). These regional alliances and other collective security arrangements became key elements of America's policy of containment.

### COMPARING PRIMARY SOURCES

#### JOINING NATO

In the late 1940s, debates took place in Congress and in the press over whether the United States should join the North Atlantic Treaty Organization (NATO).

**For Joining NATO**

"From now on, no one will misread our motives or underestimate our determination to stand in defense of our freedom. . . . The greatest obstacle that stands in the way of complete recovery [from World War II] is the pervading and paralyzing sense of insecurity. The treaty is a powerful antidote to this poison. . . . With this protection afforded by the Atlantic Pact, Western Europe can breathe easier again."

*—Texas Senator Tom Connally, chairman of the Foreign Relations Committee, 1949*

**Against Joining NATO**

"This whole program in my opinion is not a peace program; it is a war program. . . . We are committing ourselves to a policy of war, not a policy of peace. We are building up armaments. We are undertaking to arm half the world against the other half. We are inevitably starting an armament race. . . . The general history of armament races in the world is that they have led to war, not to peace."

*—Ohio Senator Robert A. Taft, 1949*

***ANALYZING VIEWPOINTS*** **Compare the main arguments made by the two senators.**

This principle of mutual military assistance is called **collective security.** Having dropped its opposition to military treaties with Europe for the first time since the Monroe Doctrine, the United States became actively involved in European affairs.

In 1955, the Soviet Union responded to the formation of NATO. It created the **Warsaw Pact,** a military alliance with its satellite nations in Eastern Europe.

## *Communist Advances*

In 1949, two events heightened American concerns about the cold war. The first was President Truman's terrifying announcement that the Soviet Union had successfully tested an atomic bomb. Then, just a few weeks later, Communist forces took control of China.

**The Soviet Atomic Threat** "We have evidence that within recent weeks an atomic explosion occurred in the USSR," Truman told

**FACT Finder** **NATO and Warsaw Pact Members, 1955**

| | | |
|---|---|---|
| ***NATO*** | | |
| Belgium | Italy | United Kingdom |
| Canada | Luxembourg | United States |
| Denmark | Netherlands | Greece |
| France | Norway | Turkey |
| Iceland | Portugal | West Germany |
| ***Warsaw Pact*** | | |
| USSR | Czechoslovakia | Poland |
| Albania | East Germany | Romania |
| Bulgaria | Hungary | |

**Interpreting Tables** After World War II, the world began squaring off again. Alliances formed between non-Communist nations and between Communist nations. ***Foreign Relations Why did Western Europe feel that the United Nations was inadequate to protect against Soviet aggression?***

reporters in September 1949. The news jolted Americans. New York, Los Angeles, and other American cities now risked the horrible fate of Hiroshima and Nagasaki.

Truman's response to the Soviet atomic threat was to forge ahead with a new weapon to maintain America's nuclear superiority. In early 1950, he gave approval for development of a hydrogen, or thermonuclear, bomb, which was many times more destructive than the atomic bomb. The first successful thermonuclear test occurred in 1952, reestablishing the United States as the world's leading nuclear power.

At about the same time, Truman organized the Federal Civil Defense Administration. The new agency flooded the nation with posters and other information about how to survive a nuclear attack. These included plans for building bomb shelters and instructions for holding air raid drills in schools. Privately, however, experts ridiculed these programs as almost totally ineffective. Not until the late 1950s did civil defense truly become a federal government priority.

**China Falls to the Communists** The struggle between China's government and Communist revolutionaries had been a long one. It began in the 1920s, after the Chinese government under Jiang Jieshi began to imprison and kill Communists. Mao Zedong and a handful of other Communist leaders escaped to southern China. From there they organized poor, discontented rural peasants and started a civil war.

During World War II, Mao and Jiang grudgingly cooperated to resist the invading Japanese. The war enabled Mao to strengthen his forces, and by its end his army had grown to about 700,000. Mao also launched popular political, social, and economic reforms in the regions he controlled.

As World War II drew to a close, the fighting between the Communists and government forces resumed in China. The Truman administration at first provided economic and military assistance to Jiang. Despite this aid, by 1947 Mao's forces had occupied much of China's countryside, and its northern cities had begun to come under their control.

When Jiang asked for more American help, Truman and his advisers concluded that Mao's takeover of China probably could not be prevented. Instead they decided to focus on saving Western Europe from Soviet domination.

In early 1949 China's capital of Peking (now Beijing) fell to the Communists. A few months later, Mao proclaimed the creation of the People's Republic of China. The defeated Jiang and his followers withdrew to the island of Taiwan, off the Chinese mainland. There they continued as the Republic of China, claiming to be the legitimate government of the entire Chinese nation. With American support, the Republic of China also held on to China's seats in the UN's General Assembly and Security Council.

Many Americans viewed the "loss of China" as a stain on the record of the Truman administration. It led to calls from members of Congress and others for greater efforts to protect the rest of Asia from communism. It also caused some Americans to suspect the loyalties of those involved in making military and foreign policy.

## *The Cold War at Home*

Throughout the Great Depression, tens of thousands of Americans had joined the Communist party, which was a legal organization. Many were desperate people who had developed serious doubts about the American capitalist system, partly because of the economic collapse of the 1930s. Others were intellectuals who were attracted to Communist ideals. After World War II, however, improved economic times, as well as the increasing distrust of Stalin, caused many people to become disappointed with communism.

Most American Communists quit the party, but some of these citizens remained members, whether active or not. Now, as a new red scare began to grip America, their pasts came back to haunt them.

During the presidencies of Truman and his successor, Dwight D. Eisenhower, concern about the growth of world communism raised fears of a conspiracy to overthrow the government, particularly when a number of spies were caught and tried. These fears launched an anti-Communist crusade that violated the civil liberties of many Americans. Anyone who had ever had Communist party ties and many who had never even been Communists were swept up in the wave of persecutions.

## Early Cold War Crises, 1944–1950

| Year | Crisis | Significance |
|---|---|---|
| 1944–1948 | Poland, Albania, Bulgaria, Czechoslovakia, Hungary, Romania, and East Germany become Soviet satellite nations. | Communist power grows with the Soviet Union's domination of Eastern Europe. |
| 1948–1949 | Soviet Union blockades West Berlin. Truman initiates Berlin airlift to supply the city with food, fuel, and other necessities. | Tensions increase between the United States and the Soviet Union, with Berlin a focal point of East-West conflict. |
| | Soviet Union develops nuclear weapon technology. | The United States no longer has the upper hand in weapons technology. |
| | China falls to Communist dictator Mao Zedong. | China is no longer the "anchor" of democracy in Asia. |

**Interpreting Tables** A series of early cold war crises stepped up demands on the government to deal effectively with the spread of communism. ***Foreign Relations*** ***Why was the fall of China to communism seen as a crisis?***

**The Loyalty Program** As the Truman administration pursued its containment policy abroad, government officials launched programs to root out any element of communism that might have infiltrated the United States. Exposure of a number of wartime spy rings in 1946 increased Americans' anxiety. (In recent years, evidence of Soviet infiltration has come to light. It is known, for instance, that Soviet spies gathered information on the United States nuclear program that helped the USSR advance its own atomic development.)

When Republicans made big gains in the 1946 congressional elections, Truman worried that his rivals would take political advantage of the loyalty issue. To head off this possibility, he began his own investigation, establishing a federal employee loyalty program in 1947.

Under this program, all new employees hired by the federal government were to be investigated. In addition, the FBI checked its files for evidence of existing government employees who might be engaged in suspicious activities. Those accused of disloyalty were brought before a Loyalty Review Board.

While civil rights were supposed to be safeguarded, in fact those accused of disloyalty to their country often had little chance to defend themselves. Rather than being innocent until proven guilty, they found that the accusation alone made it difficult to clear their names.

The Truman program examined several million government employees, yet only a few hundred were actually removed from their jobs. Still, the loyalty program added to a climate of suspicion taking hold in the nation.

**HUAC** As the Loyalty Review Board carried out its work, Congress pursued its own loyalty program. The House Un-American Activities Committee, referred to as **HUAC,** had been established in 1938 to investigate disloyalty on the eve of World War II. Now it began a postwar probe of Communist infiltration of government agencies and, more spectacularly, a probe of the Hollywood movie industry.

Claiming that movies had tremendous power to influence the public, in 1947 HUAC charged that numerous Hollywood figures had Communist leanings that affected their filmmaking. In fact, some Hollywood personalities were or had been members of the Communist party. Others in the industry had openly supported various causes and movements with philosophical similarities to communism.

***Why did Truman create a loyalty program?***

With government encouragement, Hollywood had also produced some movies favorable to the Soviet Union and its people. This had been during the war, when the United States and the Soviet Union had been allies.

Many stars protested HUAC's attitude and procedures. Actor Frederic March asked Americans to consider where it all could lead:

> **AMERICAN VOICES** "Who's next? . . . Is it you, who will have to look around nervously before you can say what's on your mind? . . . This reaches into every American city and town."
>
> —*Actor Frederic March, 1947*

**The Hollywood Ten** In September and October 1947, HUAC called a number of Hollywood writers, directors, actors, and producers to testify. They were a distinguished lot, responsible for some of Hollywood's best films of the previous decade.

Facing the committee, celebrities who were accused of having radical political associations had little chance to defend themselves. The committee chairman, Republican representative J. Parnell Thomas of New Jersey first called witnesses who were allowed to make accusations based on rumors and other flimsy evidence. Then the accused were called.

Over and over the committee asked, "Are you now or have you ever been a member of the Communist party?" When some attempted to make statements, they were denied permission.

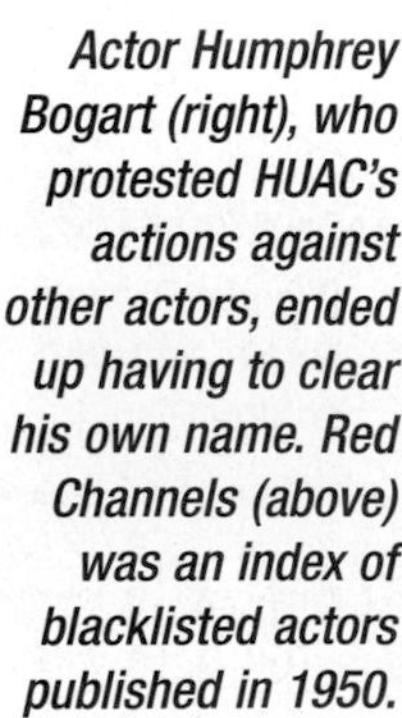

*Actor Humphrey Bogart (right), who protested HUAC's actions against other actors, ended up having to clear his own name. Red Channels (above) was an index of blacklisted actors published in 1950.*

Invoking their Fifth Amendment rights, 10 of the accused declined to answer the committee's questions. The **Hollywood Ten** were cited for contempt of Congress and served jail terms ranging from six months to a year.

The HUAC investigations had a powerful impact on filmmaking. Nervous motion picture executives denounced the Hollywood Ten for having done a disservice to their industry. The studios compiled a Hollywood **blacklist,** a list of people whom employers agree not to hire. Many other entertainment figures were added to the blacklist simply because they seemed subversive or they opposed the idea of a blacklist. The list included actors, screenwriters, directors, and broadcasters.

In the past, Hollywood had been willing to make movies on controversial subjects such as racism and anti-Semitism. Now studios resisted all films dealing with social problems and concentrated on pure entertainment.

**The McCarran-Walter Act** While HUAC carried out its work, Democrat Pat McCarran headed a Senate hunt for Communists in the movie industry, labor unions, the State Department, and the UN. Senator McCarran became convinced that the most disloyal Americans were immigrants from Communist-dominated parts of the world.

At his urging, in 1952 Congress passed the **McCarran-Walter Act.** This law established a quota system for each country, discriminating against potential immigrants from Asia and Southern and Central Europe. President Truman vetoed McCarran's bill, calling it "one of the most un-American acts I have ever witnessed in my public career." Congress, however, passed the bill over the President's veto.

**Spy Cases Inflame the Nation** Two famous spy cases helped fuel the suspicion that a conspiracy within the United States was aiding the Communists overseas in their military and political successes. In 1948, HUAC investigated Alger Hiss, who had been a high-ranking State Department official before he left government service. Whittaker Chambers, a former Communist who had become a successful *Time* magazine editor, accused Hiss of having been a Communist in the 1930s. Hiss denied the charge and sued Chambers for slander. Chambers then went one step further and declared that Hiss had been a Soviet spy.

Too much time had passed for the spying charge to be pressed. After two trials, Hiss was

VIEWING HISTORY

Demonstrators (right) show the depth of anti-Communist feeling in the post-war period. Ethel and Julius Rosenberg, (above) were the first U.S. civilians to be executed for espionage. ***Culture*** *How did spy cases affect Americans' perception of a Communist threat in society?*

convicted of perjury for lying in the slander case. In 1950 he went to prison for four years.

Not all Americans were convinced he was guilty, and for many years thereafter the Hiss case was hotly debated. For most people, however, the case seemed to prove that there was a real Communist threat in the United States.

Several months after Hiss's conviction, Julius and Ethel Rosenberg, a married couple who were members of the Communist Party, were accused of passing atomic secrets to the Soviets during World War II. After a highly controversial trial, the Rosenbergs were convicted of espionage and executed in 1953. The case was another event that inflamed anti-Communist passions and focused attention on a possible internal threat to the nation's security.

Like the Hiss case, the Rosenbergs' convictions were debated for years afterward. Careful work by historians in once-classified American records and in secret Soviet records opened at the end of the cold war indicate that both Alger Hiss and Julius Rosenberg were guilty.

## SECTION 2 REVIEW

### Comprehension

1. *Key Terms* Define: (a) Marshall Plan; (b) Berlin airlift; (c) NATO; (d) collective security; (e) Warsaw Pact; (f) HUAC; (g) Hollywood Ten; (h) blacklist; (i) McCarran-Walter Act.
2. *Summarizing the Main Idea* What events abroad and at home in the late 1940s and early 1950s helped raise Americans' fears of communism?
3. *Organizing Information* Construct a cause-and-effect chart showing the origins and impact of the Truman Doctrine.

### Critical Thinking

4. *Analyzing Time Lines* Refer to the time line at the start of the section. How was 1949 a key year in the development of the cold war?
5. *Determining Relevance* How does America's pre–World War II isolationism relate to a discussion of the Marshall Plan, the Berlin airlift, and NATO?

### Writing Activity

6. *Writing a Persuasive Essay* Did Americans have reason for concern about Communist infiltration of government and society? Consider the events going on in the world.

| 1950 | 1950 | 1953 | 1956 | 1957 | 1957 | 1960 |
|---|---|---|---|---|---|---|
| Korean War begins | McCarthy launches anti-Communist campaign | Soviet Union tests hydrogen device | Suez crisis | Eisenhower Doctrine | Soviet Union launches Sputnik satellite | U-2 incident |

1950 — 1955 — 1960

# 3 The Cold War Expands

**SECTION PREVIEW**

### Objectives

1 Describe General Douglas MacArthur and his role in the Korean War.
2 Analyze the effects of Senator Joseph McCarthy's anti-Communist campaign.
3 Trace the development of the cold war and the arms race in the 1950s.
4 *Key Terms* Define: Korean War; 38th parallel; domino theory; arms race; brinkmanship; ICBM; *Sputnik;* U-2 incident.

### Main Idea

During the 1950s, the cold war spread to new locations around the world. At home, a senator's anti-Communist crusade ruined many people's careers but ultimately failed.

### Reading Strategy

*Outlining Information* Copy the headings in this section on a sheet of paper. As you read, add two or three key facts under each heading to create an outline.

Koreans hoped their nation would be restored after Japan withdrew. However, in 1945 the Allies agreed to divide the nation temporarily into a Soviet-occupied northern zone and an American-occupied southern zone. Soon a pro-American government formed in South Korea and a Communist regime in North Korea. Occupying forces withdrew from both zones in 1948 and 1949.

In June 1950, the **Korean War** broke out when North Korean troops streamed across the **38th parallel,** the latitude line dividing the two nations, aiming to reunite Korea by force. Because the USSR was boycotting the Security Council at the time to protest the exclusion of Communist China, the UN was able to act. It called on its members to defend South Korea.

## Douglas MacArthur

AMERICAN BIOGRAPHY

A hero of two world wars and a strong anti-Communist, General Douglas MacArthur was Truman's choice to lead the UN forces in Korea. For MacArthur, the command capped a long, distinguished, and controversial career.

General Douglas MacArthur (1880–1964)

The son of an army officer, MacArthur graduated from the United States Military Academy at West Point in 1903 at the top of his class. He was cited seven times for bravery in World War I and by 1918, at age 38, had attained the rank of general. After serving in the Philippines during the 1920s, he returned to the United States in 1930 to become Army Chief of Staff.

At the start of World War II President Roosevelt appointed MacArthur to be commander of American forces in Asia. From this post he organized the defense of the Philippines and, later, the three-year island-hopping campaign against the Japanese in the Pacific.

As virtual dictator of Japan during the postwar occupation period, MacArthur was responsible for establishing Western democracy there and for creating Japan's new democratic constitution. He was less successful in implementing democracy in South Korea, where he also commanded American occupation forces. There MacArthur supported South Korean president Syngman Rhee, despite Rhee's brutal elimination of his opponents.

Although a hero to those he commanded and to much of the American public, MacArthur was disliked by many political leaders, who viewed him as overly ambitious. MacArthur, in turn, had little respect for either Roosevelt or Truman, both of whom he viewed as soft on communism. His attitude made MacArthur an anti-Communist hero. Yet his characteristic contempt for anyone with authority over him led him to take actions that undermined his otherwise brilliant career. ■

## The Korean War

Despite his difficult personality, MacArthur was an excellent military strategist, and he developed a bold plan to drive the invaders from South Korea. With Soviet tanks and air power, the North Koreans had swept through South Korea in just weeks. Only a small part of the country, near the port city of Pusan, remained unconquered.

**Main Idea CONNECTIONS**

*In what way was the Korean War a cold war conflict?*

MacArthur suspected that the North Koreans' rapid advance had left their supply lines stretched thin. He decided to strike at this weakness. After first sending forces to defend Pusan, in September 1950 he landed troops at Inchon in northwestern South Korea, and attacked enemy supply lines from behind.

MacArthur's strategy worked. Caught between UN forces in the north and south, and with their supplies cut off, the invaders fled back across the 38th parallel. UN troops pursued them northward. American and South Korean leaders began to boast of reuniting Korea under South Korean control. Such talk alarmed the Chinese Communists, who had been in power less than a year and who did not want a pro-Western nation next door.

As UN troops approached North Korea's border with China, the Chinese warned them not to advance any farther. MacArthur ignored the warning. On November 24, 1950, the general announced his "Home by Christmas" offen-

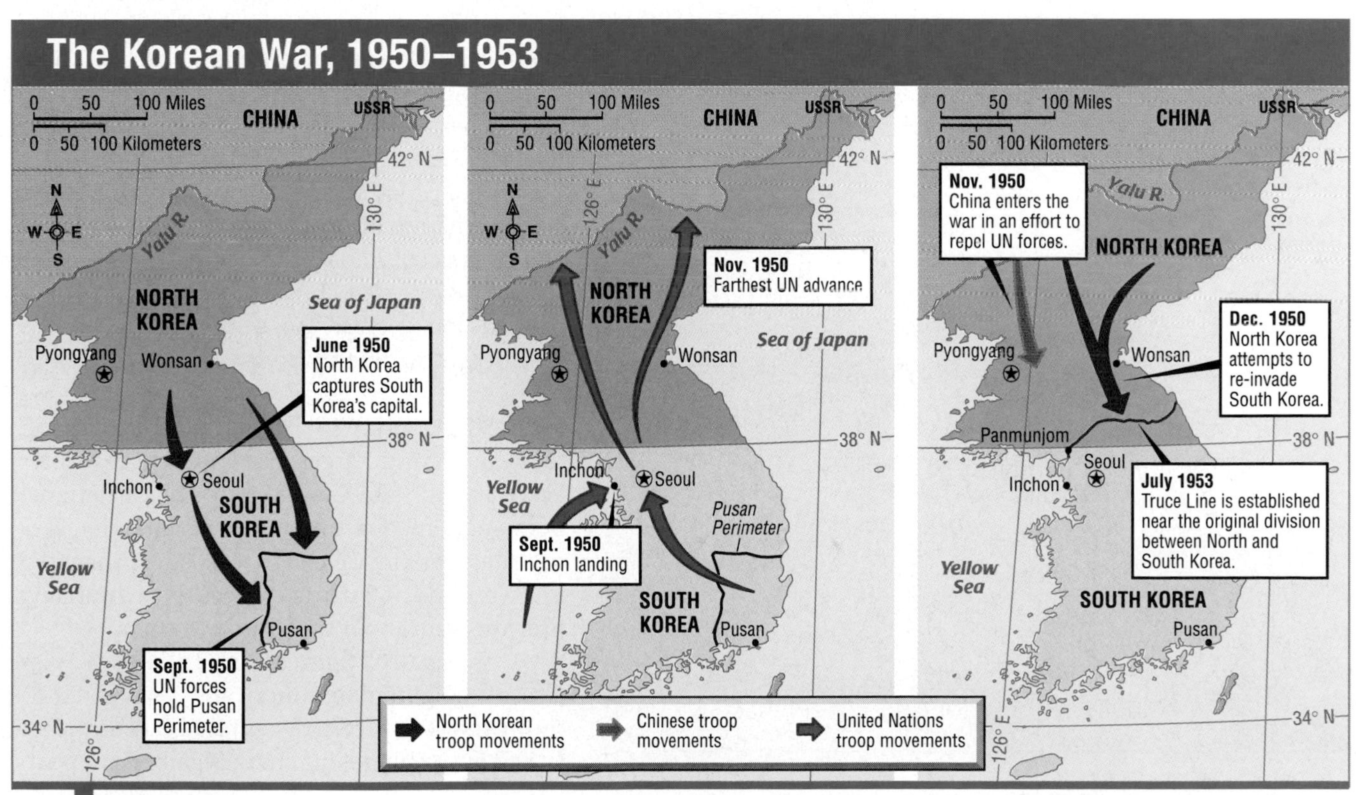


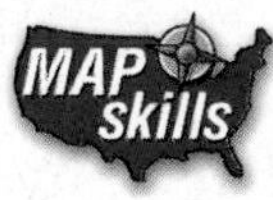


These maps show the back-and-forth nature of the fighting in the Korean War. ***Movement*** ***Examine the maps and the movements of the UN troops. Why do you think China entered the war when it did?***

sive, designed to drive the enemy across the North Korean border at the Yalu River into China and end the war.

Chinese troops poured across the Yalu to take the offensive. The Chinese and North Koreans pushed the UN forces back into South Korea. A stalemate developed.

MacArthur favored breaking the stalemate by opening a second front in the war. He urged that the Chinese opposition forces of Jiang Jieshi on the island of Taiwan be returned to the mainland to attack the Chinese Communists. Truman opposed this strategy, fearing it could lead to a widespread war in Asia.

Unable to sway Truman, MacArthur sent a letter to House Minority Leader Joseph Martin in March 1951, attacking the President's policies. Martin made the letter public. On April 11, Truman fired MacArthur for insubordination.

MacArthur returned home to a hero's welcome. In an address to a joint session of Congress on April 19, he made an emotional farewell:

**AMERICAN VOICES** **"Since I took the oath at West Point, the hopes and dreams [of youth] have all vanished. But I still remember the refrain of one of the most popular barracks ballads of that day, which proclaimed most proudly that old soldiers never die, they just fade away. And like the old soldier of that ballad, I now close my military career and just fade away, an old soldier who tried to do his duty as God gave him the light to see that duty. Good-bye."**

*—General Douglas MacArthur, speech to Congress, April 19, 1951*

Once tempers cooled, MacArthur did, in fact, fade from view, and Truman was able to keep the war limited. However, the struggle dragged on for over two more years. Finally, a truce was signed in 1953, leaving Korea divided at almost exactly the same place as before the war, near the 38th parallel.

The Korean War caused enormous frustration at home. Americans wondered why about 55,000 of their soldiers had been killed and 103,000 wounded for such limited results. They wondered if their government was serious about stopping communism.

More than 5.8 million military personnel and more than 1.6 million draftees served in the Korean War. ***Culture*** ***Why were Americans frustrated by the outcome of the war?***

## The McCarthy Era

The events in Asia seemed to many Americans to support sensational charges made in 1950 by Republican senator Joseph McCarthy of Wisconsin. During a speech in Wheeling, West Virginia, McCarthy held up a paper that he claimed was a list of 205 known Communists in the State Department.

In fact, McCarthy's list was nothing more than the names of people still in their jobs, who had been accused of disloyalty under Truman's federal employee loyalty program. When pressed for details, the senator reduced the number from 205 to 57.

**McCarthy's Rise to Power** McCarthy soon took on larger targets. He attacked former Secretary of State George Marshall, a national hero and a man of unquestioned integrity, saying he was involved in "a conspiracy so immense and an infamy so black as to dwarf any previous venture in the history of man."

Communist aggression in Korea was already heightening Americans' fear of communism when McCarthy aired his accusations. In this atmosphere, his charges gained support.

**McCarthy's Fall** In early 1954, McCarthy charged that even the army was full of Communists. Finally, political and military leaders decided that he had to be stopped.

Meanwhile, army officials charged McCarthy with seeking special treatment for an aide who had been drafted. As charges and countercharges flew between McCarthy and the army, the senator's subcommittee voted to investigate the claims.

The Army-McCarthy hearings began in late April 1954. Democrats asked that the hearings be televised, hoping that the public would see McCarthy for what he was. Ever eager for publicity, the senator fell into the trap by agreeing to the coverage. For the next several weeks, Americans remained riveted to their TVs. Most were horrified by McCarthy's bullying tactics and baseless allegations.

By the time the hearings ended in mid-June, the senator had lost even his most hard-core supporters. The Senate condemned him for his reckless actions. Unrepentant, the senator charged his accusers with being tools of the Communists. However, he no longer had credibility. Although McCarthy remained in the Senate, his power was gone. He died three years later, a broken man.

Eventually this second red scare, much like the one that followed World War I, subsided. But the nation was damaged by the era's suppression of free speech and open, honest debate.

VIEWING HISTORY The comic book at right shows how the media capitalized on peoples' fears. Above, Army counsel Joseph Welch (seated at table) listens in disgust to Senator McCarthy as he discusses Communist infiltration into the army. ***Government*** ***What finally led to McCarthy's downfall?***

## The Cold War in the 1950s

When Republican and World War II hero Dwight Eisenhower succeeded Truman as President in 1953, American cold war policy entered a new phase. Eisenhower's Secretary of State, John Foster Dulles, was a harsh anti-Communist who considered winning the cold war to be a moral crusade. Dulles believed Truman's containment policy was too cautious. Instead, he called for a policy to roll back communism where it had taken hold.

As a military leader, Eisenhower recognized the risks of confronting the Soviets. He acted as a brake on Dulles's more extreme views. Eisenhower realized that the United States could not intervene in the affairs of the Soviet Union's Eastern European satellite nations. So when East Germans revolted in 1953, and Poles and Hungarians in 1956, the United States kept its distance as Soviet troops crushed the uprisings.

Eisenhower understood that any other response risked war with the Soviet Union. He wanted to avoid that at all costs. Thus the policy of containment remained in effect during the 1950s.

**Southeast Asia** In July 1953, Eisenhower fulfilled a campaign promise to bring the Korean War to an end. He was aided in this effort by the sudden death of Stalin in March and by the rapid rise of more moderate Soviet leaders.

Meanwhile, another conflict had developed. This one was in Vietnam, a French colony in Southeast Asia that had fallen to Japan during World War II. Just after the Japanese surrender in 1945, Ho Chi Minh, head of the Vietnamese Communist party, had declared the colony's independence. France rejected Ho's declaration and sent troops to reassert its authority in Vietnam. An ugly war began to unfold.

Eisenhower subscribed to what became known as the **domino theory.** This belief held that if one country fell to the Communists, its neighbors soon would follow, like a toppling row of dominos. By 1954 the United States was providing substantial military aid to support France in its Southeast Asian war.

After a major defeat in May 1954, France withdrew its forces. An international conference divided Vietnam, like Korea, into a

Following the 1948 war, the new state of Israel controlled most of what had once been Palestine. **Regions** ***What regions were still held by Palestinians after the 1948 war?***

Communist north and anti-Communist south. The United States provided aid to South Vietnam but resisted greater involvement. That course would change in the 1960s.

**The Middle East** The cold war was also played out in the historic tensions of the Middle East. Britain and France were given control over much of this region after World War I. The British area included Palestine, a region on the Mediterranean coast and biblical home of the Jewish people.

In the 1930s, anti-Semitism in Germany and Eastern Europe forced many Jews to seek safety in Palestine. Calls for a Jewish state followed. In 1947 the British turned the question over to the UN, which called for the creation of two states in the area, one Jewish and one Arab. In May 1948 the Jews in Palestine proclaimed the new nation of Israel. (See map above.)

*How did the cold war affect the Middle East?*

Conflict soon erupted between Israel and its Arab neighbors, who also viewed Palestine as their ancient homeland. The United States supported Israel. The Soviet Union generally backed the Arab opposition.

While supporting Israel, the United States worked to prevent oil-rich Arab nations from falling under the influence of the Soviet Union. In 1952, a nationalist leader gained control in Iran. The next year the United States Central Intelligence Agency (CIA) organized his overthrow and restored to power the pro-American Shah of Iran.

The next cold war clash in the Middle East was the Suez crisis of 1956. When Egypt's ruler, Gamal Abdel Nasser, sought Soviet support, America and Great Britain cut off their aid. Nasser responded by seizing the British-owned Suez Canal, a vital waterway that passed through Egypt and allowed Middle East oil to reach Europe via the Mediterranean.

In late 1956, British and French forces attacked Egypt to regain control of the canal. Reacting to Soviet threats of "dangerous consequences," Eisenhower persuaded his NATO allies to withdraw from Egypt, which retained control of the canal.

Eisenhower then acted to combat further Soviet influence in the Middle East. In January 1957, the President announced the Eisenhower Doctrine. This policy stated that the United States would use force "to safeguard the independence of any country or group of countries in the Middle East requesting aid against [Communist-inspired] aggression." Eisenhower used his doctrine in 1958 to justify landing troops in Lebanon to put down a revolt against its government.

**Latin America** The cold war likewise affected Latin America. Since the mid-1920s, the United States had exercised control over the economies of some 10 Latin American nations. In Central America, United States troops had invaded Nicaragua and Honduras to prop up leaders who supported American interests.

After World War II, the United States became concerned about the possible spread of communism to other Latin American nations, especially where American companies had large investments. In 1947, the United States signed the Rio Pact, a regional defense alliance with 18 other nations in the Western Hemisphere. The following year the United States led the way in forming the Organization of American States (OAS) to increase cooperation among the nations of the hemisphere.

In 1954 the CIA helped overthrow the government of Guatemala on the grounds that its leaders were sympathetic to radical causes. The CIA takeover restored the property of an American corporation, the United Fruit Company, which had been seized by the Guatemalan government. Such actions fueled a Soviet perception that America was escalating the cold war.

In 1958 another crisis began as revolutionary leader Fidel Castro overthrew the corrupt Cuban dictator Fulgencio Batista. Batista, who fled the country on January 1, 1959, had ties to American organized crime. Yet Eisenhower would not support Castro after the CIA reported that his movement had been infiltrated by Communists.

When Castro seized American property in Cuba, Eisenhower responded by cutting diplomatic ties and halting exports to the island. Castro then turned to the Soviet Union for economic and military aid, which it would rely on for the next three decades.

## The Arms Race

Throughout the 1950s the United States and the Soviet Union waged an increasingly intense struggle for world leadership. Whenever one side appeared to be gaining the upper hand in the cold war, the other would respond with new programs and policies. Nowhere was this competition more dangerous than in the **arms race,** the struggle to gain weapons superiority.

**The Growth of Nuclear Arsenals** In August 1953, less than a year after the United States exploded its first thermonuclear device, the Soviet Union successfully tested a hydrogen device of its own. In part to publicize that the United States still led in nuclear technology, in December 1953 Eisenhower announced an Atoms for Peace Plan at the United Nations. The President's proposal called for the world's nations to work together under UN supervision to find peaceful uses for nuclear technology. The Soviet Union, which did not want to give the UN any of its nuclear material, refused to participate.

At the same time, Eisenhower stepped up the American weapons development program to counter the new Soviet nuclear threat. Between 1954 and 1958 the United States conducted 19 hydrogen bomb tests at Bikini Island in the Pacific.

The first of these explosions, in March 1954, was over 750 times more powerful than the atomic bomb that was dropped on Nagasaki in World War II. Japanese fishermen some 90 miles from the blast suffered severe radiation burns, and residents of an island nearly 200 miles away had to be evacuated. The test chillingly revealed that nuclear war could threaten the entire world with radioactive contamination.

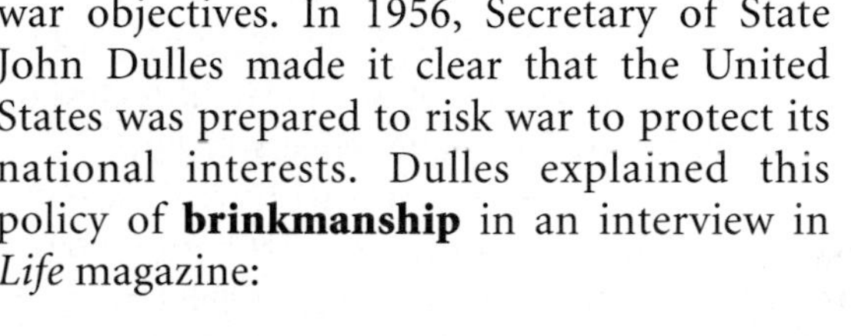

*A 1959* Newsweek *illustration showed Soviet leader Khrushchev (left) and Eisenhower (right) using arms to maintain a balance of power.*

**Brinkmanship** American policymakers used the fear of nuclear war to achieve their cold war objectives. In 1956, Secretary of State John Dulles made it clear that the United States was prepared to risk war to protect its national interests. Dulles explained this policy of **brinkmanship** in an interview in *Life* magazine:

**U.S. Defense Spending, 1940–1960**

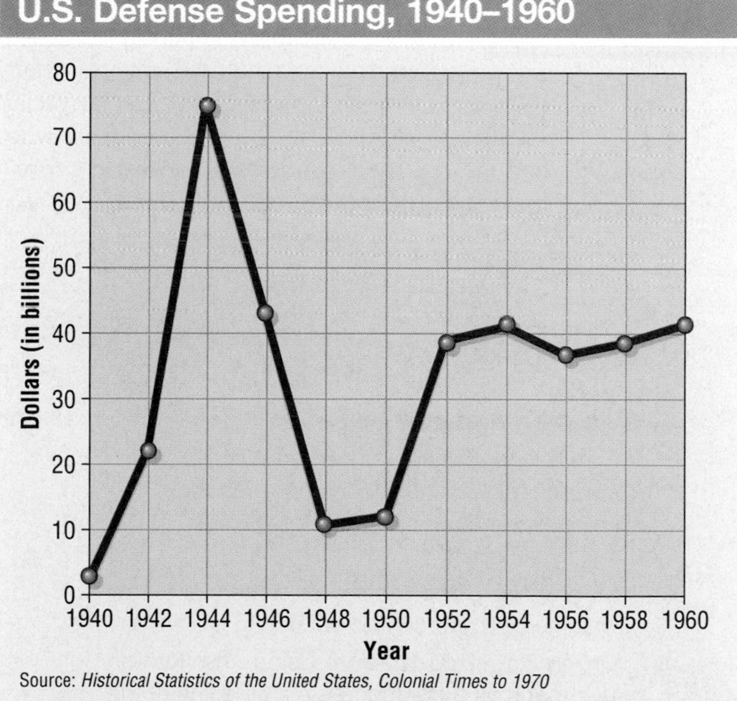



Source: *Historical Statistics of the United States, Colonial Times to 1970*

**Interpreting Graphs** The competition for world leadership led to an arms race between the United States and the Soviet Union. ***Government*** ***Describe the pattern of American defense spending in the post–World War II era. What was the cause of the sharpest rise?***

**"The ability to get to the verge without getting into the war is the necessary art. If you cannot master it, you inevitably get into war. If you try to run away from it, if you are scared to go to the brink, you are lost."**

—*Secretary of State John Foster Dulles, interview in* Life *magazine, 1956*

Many Americans agreed with the reaction of Illinois senator Adlai Stevenson: "I am shocked that the Secretary of State is willing to play Russian roulette with the life of our nation." Still, the Eisenhower administration employed the policy a number of times.

**Cold War in the Skies** To carry hydrogen bombs to their targets, American military planners relied mainly on the United States Air Force. Unable to match this strength, the Soviets instead focused on long-range rockets known as intercontinental ballistic missiles, or **ICBMs,** as their primary delivery system.

**Main Idea CONNECTIONS**

*Why did the launch of* Sputnik *shock Americans?*

Americans also worked to develop ICBMs. However, in part because of its dependence on conventional air power, the United States lagged behind the Soviet Union in missile development.

The size of this technology gap became startlingly apparent in 1957, when the Soviets used one of their rockets to launch ***Sputnik,*** the first artificial satellite to orbit Earth. Most Americans, who had viewed their country as the world's foremost scientific power, were mortified.

Worse yet, the United States' own satellite and rocket, rushed to the launching pad before it was ready, came crashing to the ground. Another fear prompted by *Sputnik* was the realization that the rocket used to launch it could also carry a hydrogen bomb to American shores.

In May 1960, the Soviet military again demonstrated its capabilities by shooting down an American spy plane over Soviet territory with a guided missile. The plane, called a U-2, flew more than 15 miles high. At such altitudes, American officials had assumed that the spy planes were immune to attack. The **U-2 incident** shattered this confidence.

One of the legacies of the cold war was the creation of what Eisenhower called a "permanent armaments industry of vast proportions." He warned that the existence of this "military-industrial complex," employing millions of Americans and having a financial stake in war-making, could become a threat to peace:

**"Our arms must be mighty, ready for instant action. . . . We recognize the imperative need for this development. Yet we must not fail to comprehend its grave implications. . . . [In] government, we must guard against the acquisition of unwarranted [unnecessary] influence, whether sought or unsought, by the military-industrial complex. The potential for the disastrous rise of misplaced power exists and will persist."**

—*Farewell Address, President Dwight D. Eisenhower, January 17, 1961*

## SECTION 3 REVIEW

### Comprehension

1. *Key Terms* Define: (a) Korean War; (b) 38th parallel; (c) domino theory; (d) arms race; (e) brinkmanship; (f) ICBM; (g) *Sputnik;* (h) U-2 incident.
2. *Summarizing the Main Idea* Where and how was the cold war carried out during the 1950s?
3. *Organizing Information* Using the Korean War maps as a guide, create a time line of the major events of the war.

### Critical Thinking

4. *Analyzing Time Lines* Refer to the time line at the start of the section. Choose three entries and summarize their causes and effects.
5. *Determining Relevance* What overstatements did Senator McCarthy make in his accusations about Communists?

### Writing Activity

6. *Writing an Expository Essay* Trace the development of the arms race in the 1950s. What effect did the policy of brinkmanship have on the arms race?

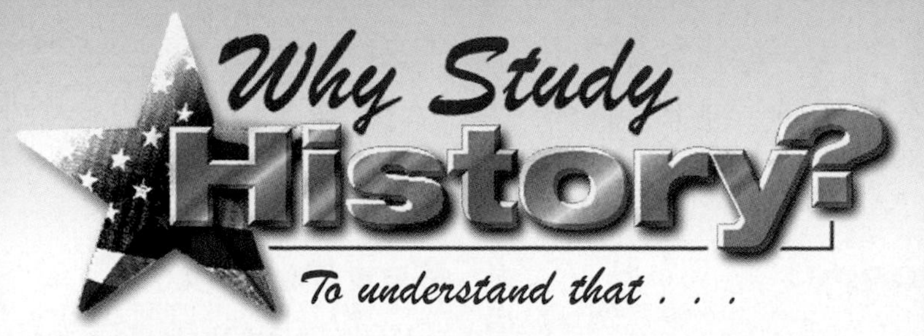


# Defense Spending Affects You

High defense spending in recent decades has had a major impact on American society that continues to this day.

*Bomber assembly line, 1950s*

In 1971, one Huey helicopter cost the United States as much as 66 units of low-income housing. In 1998, the estimated cost of one B-2 Stealth bomber was roughly half the yearly expenses of the National Park Service. The more that the nation spends on weapons, the less it has available for domestic needs. Yet, while many Americans support cuts in defense spending, others warn of the military risks and economic consequences.

## The Impact Today

During the cold war, as you have read, the United States sought to contain communism around the world. To achieve this goal, the United States devoted a high proportion of the federal budget to defense. Billions of dollars were spent building weapons, training troops, and establishing military bases.

In 1950, the United States spent approximately $13 billion on defense, which amounted to a little less than one third of the federal budget. By 1961, defense spending had soared to $47 billion, or roughly one half of the total budget. Many Americans became concerned. In 1961, outgoing President Dwight Eisenhower warned the nation about the "military-industrial complex," or the growing alliance of business and military leaders who worked together to keep defense spending high.

Defense spending continued to increase in dollar amounts in the 1970s, 1980s, and early 1990s. At the same time, it slowly declined as a percentage of the total federal budget, averaging about 25 percent between 1975 and 1990.

Since the collapse of the Soviet Union in 1991, American defense spending has decreased significantly as a percentage of the federal budget. Today defense spending represents only about 16 percent of the total budget. This is the lowest percentage since before World War II.

Cutting defense spending can create problems. For example, the United States must maintain the military strength it needs not only to defend itself but also to meet its commitments to other nations. In addition, high defense spending produces jobs. In 1971, the Pentagon employed 3.8 million workers, including men and women in the armed forces. An additional 2.2 million people worked in defense-related private industries. Although these numbers have decreased in recent years, millions of Americans still owe their jobs to defense spending.

## The Impact on You

Imagine that you have been assigned to write an editorial on future defense spending. What information would you need before deciding whether defense spending should increase, decrease, or remain the same? List five questions that you would want to research.

*Ceremony at closing of army base, 1996*

# Chapter 16 Review

## Chapter Summary

The major concepts of Chapter 16 are presented below. See also ***Guide to the Essentials of American History*** or ***Interactive Student Tutorial CD-ROM,*** which contains interactive review activities, time lines, helpful hints, and test practice.

### *Reviewing the Main Ideas*

After World War II, the United States and the Soviet Union entered a period of intense hostility known as the cold war. The conflict was mostly indirect, taking place in countries where the two superpowers competed for influence and in a nuclear arms race. The cold war inflamed anti-Communist fears and suspicions at home.

### *Section 1: Origins of the Cold War*

At the end of World War II, conflicting goals for Europe led to growing hostility between the United States and the Soviet Union.

### *Section 2: The Cold War Abroad and at Home*

As the cold war intensified, American policy focused on rebuilding and unifying Western Europe. At home, emotionally charged spy cases raised fears of Communist infiltration into American society and government.

### *Section 3: The Cold War Expands*

During the 1950s, the cold war spread to new locations around the world. At home, a senator's anti-Communist crusade ruined many people's careers but ultimately failed.

High defense spending in recent decades has had a major impact on American society that continues to this day.

## Key Terms

Use each of the terms below in a sentence that shows how it relates to the chapter.

1. domino theory
2. *Sputnik*
3. Truman Doctrine
4. U-2 incident
5. Hollywood Ten
6. cold war
7. iron curtain
8. Berlin airlift
9. containment
10. NATO
11. HUAC
12. Marshall Plan
13. brinkmanship
14. satellite nation
15. blacklist
16. Warsaw Pact

## Comprehension

1. How did Germany come to be a divided nation?
2. Who were Alger Hiss and the Rosenbergs?
3. Why were NATO and the Warsaw Pact created?
4. What events led to the Berlin airlift?
5. Describe the rise and fall of Senator Joseph McCarthy.
6. What were the Potsdam and Yalta conferences?
7. Who was Douglas MacArthur, and what is his historical significance?
8. What was the importance of the Iron Curtain speech?

## Using Graphic Organizers

Using information from the chapter, fill in the ovals to identify the causes and effects of the cold war.

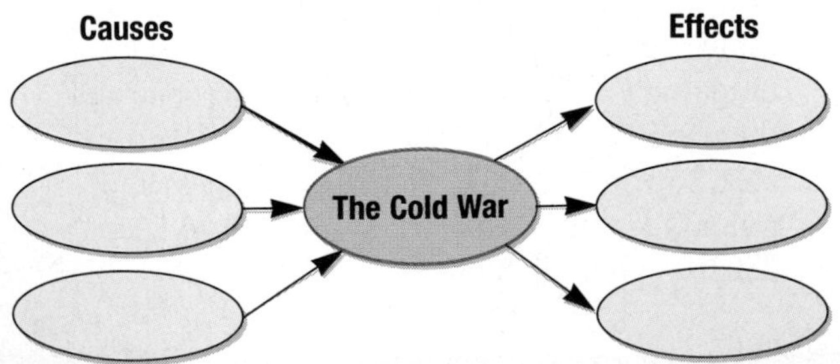

## Analyzing Political Cartoons ▶

1. Examine the images in this 1949 cartoon. (a) What is the flame that the man is about to douse? (b) What does it represent?
2. (a) What does the man represent? (b) How do you know?
3. What is the cartoonist's message?

## Critical Thinking

1. ***Reviewing the Chapter Skill*** Write a cause-and-effect statement about the Korean War.
2. ***Arranging Events in Order*** List three or four major events that preceded Churchill's declaration that an "iron curtain" had divided Europe.
3. ***Recognizing Ideologies*** How did differing ideologies lead to the development of the cold war?
4. ***Analyzing Primary Sources*** Reread the Key Documents quotation from Eisenhower at the end of Section 3. Restate the main point in your own words.

## INTERNET ACTIVITY

***For your portfolio:***
**PREPARE A SUMMARY**

Access Prentice Hall's *America: Pathways to the Present* site at **www.Pathways.phschool.com** for the specific URL to complete the activity. Additional resources and related Web sites are also available.

Read about the history and organization of the United Nations. Choose one branch or suborganization of the United Nations and prepare a summary of the work carried out by that branch.

## ANALYZING DOCUMENTS ◀ ▶ INTERPRETING DATA

Turn to the excerpt from the Truman Doctrine at the end of Section 1.

1. What was the main purpose of Truman's speech? (a) to frighten the Soviet government (b) to make clear how the United States would respond to Communist aggression (c) to win congressional approval of the containment policy (d) to expand the cold war.
2. Who did Truman promise to help? (a) subjugated minorities (b) armed resistance movements (c) majorities whose freedom was threatened (d) all of the above.
3. ***Writing*** Do you think the Truman Doctrine would be a good model for conducting American foreign policy today? Why or why not?

## Connecting to Today

***Essay Writing*** Since the breakup of the Soviet Union and the end of the cold war around 1991, relations between the United States and Russia have changed. Research and write an essay explaining the changes. Compare American and Russian goals today. Do you think Russia is still a threat to American interests?

CHAPTER 17

# The Postwar Years at Home

## 1945–1960

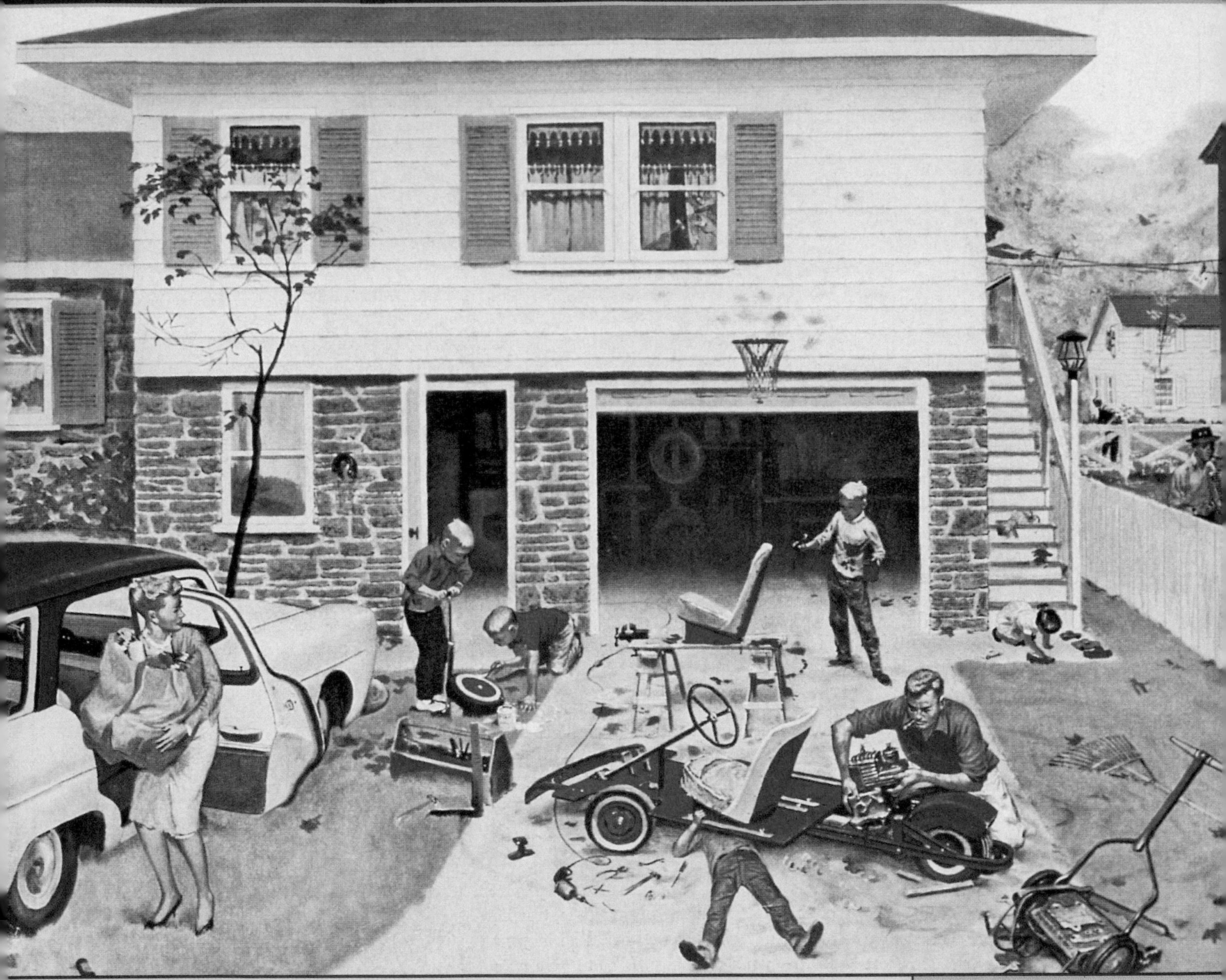

VIEWING HISTORY This image of 1950s suburban life is on the cover of a 1958 issue of *The Saturday Evening Post.* **Culture What does this picture tell you about life in the United States in the 1950s?**

## CHAPTER FOCUS

This chapter describes the years following World War II, during which time Americans began to enjoy the benefits of their new standing as a military and economic superpower. While not all groups shared in the prosperity, most Americans now were able to buy the homes, cars, and other items that they had once only dreamed of owning.

The **Why Study History?** page at the end of this chapter explores the connection between President Truman's efforts to provide health care to Americans and the continued demands on the health care industry today.

**1944** *GI Bill offers veterans low-interest loans and a college education*

**1947** *Invention of the transistor allows computer industry to grow*

**1954** *Dr. Jonas Salk successfully tests polio vaccine*

**1955** *AFL and the CIO merge*

**1956** *Interstate Highway Act provides money for an interstate highway system*

**1944** **1950** **1956**

# 1 The Postwar Economy

## SECTION PREVIEW

### Objectives

1 Understand that following World War II, rapid economic growth encouraged businesses to reorganize.

2 Describe how technological advances transformed life in the United States.

3 Explain how changes in the working lives of Americans influenced the growth of suburbs, highways, and consumer credit.

4 *Key Terms* Define: per capita income; conglomerate; franchise; transistor; baby boom; GI Bill.

### Main Idea

The American Dream, characterized by a home in the suburbs and a car in the garage, came true for many people in the postwar years.

### Reading Strategy

*Reading for Evidence* Note the statement below that, after the war, the United States "embarked on one of its greatest periods of economic expansion." As you read the section, look for evidence to support this statement.

When American soldiers returned from the battlefields, they wanted to put the horrors of the war behind them and enjoy the comforts of home. During the war, when most items were rationed or not produced at all, many people had simply put their money into savings. Now most Americans were eager to acquire everything the war—and before that, the Depression—had denied them.

## Businesses Reorganize

During the postwar years, the United States embarked on one of its greatest periods of economic expansion. The gross national product (GNP) more than doubled, jumping from $212 billion in 1945 to $504 billion in 1960. **Per capita income,** the average income per person, increased from $1,526 to $2,788.

Major corporate expansion accompanied economic growth. In the 1950s a few huge firms dominated many industries. General Motors, Ford, and Chrysler overshadowed all competitors in the automobile industry; General Electric and Westinghouse enjoyed similar positions in the electrical business. Giant corporations, fearful after the Great Depression of investing all their resources in a single business, became **conglomerates.** (A conglomerate is a large corporation that owns many smaller companies that produce entirely different goods and services.) They reasoned that if one area of the economy failed, their investments in another area would be safe. International Telephone and Telegraph, for example, purchased Avis Rent-a-Car, Sheraton Hotels, Hartford Fire Insurance, and Continental Baking.

*In the economic boom of the 1950s, the United States developed an automobile-centered culture.*

At the same time, another kind of expansion took place. In 1954 Ray Kroc, who sold milkshake machines called Multimixers, was amazed when two brothers who owned a restaurant in San Bernardino, California, ordered their tenth Multimixer. With ten

*This sign at the original fast-food restaurant in San Bernardino, California, advertised the McDonald brothers' mass-produced hamburgers.*

machines, the restaurant could make 50 milkshakes at once. Because of the restaurant's fast, efficient service and its prime location along a busy highway, it was enjoying great success. Intrigued by the possibilities, Kroc purchased the two brothers' idea of assembly-line food production. He also acquired the name of the brothers' restaurant: McDonald's. Kroc built a nationwide chain of fast-food restaurants. Others quickly saw the benefits in selling **franchises,** or the right to open a restaurant using a parent company's brand name and system, to other eager entrepreneurs. Hundreds of other restaurant franchises followed.

The franchise system flourished in the 1950s. It worked so well that it was applied to other kinds of businesses, such as clothing stores and automobile muffler shops. The system's advantage lay in the fact that an individual with only a few thousand dollars could own a small business that enjoyed the support of a multimillion-dollar parent company. With the growth of the franchise system, unique stores with ties to the local community were replaced by nationwide chains that were the same everywhere in the country.

## Technology Transforms Life

Developments in technology spurred industrial growth. Rushing to keep up with demand, businesses produced hundreds of new and improved products, such as dishwashers and gas-powered lawnmowers, that would save the consumer time and money. Eager Americans filled their homes with the latest inventions.

**Television** In the 1950s Americans fell in love with television. Developed in the 1930s, television became enormously popular after World War II. By 1953 two thirds of all American families owned TVs.

In 1955 the average American family watched television four to five hours a day. Children grew up on such programs as *Howdy Doody* and *The Mickey Mouse Club.* Teenagers danced to the rock-and-roll music played on *American Bandstand,* a predecessor of today's MTV. Other viewers followed situation comedies like *I Love Lucy* and *Father Knows Best.*

Three large networks controlled television programming. They raised the money to broadcast their shows by selling advertising time. Television commercials constantly bombarded Americans with advertisements for the latest consumer products. Companies got their money's worth from advertising dollars; millions of viewers were persuaded to buy the items they saw on television commercials.

**The Computer Industry** Television was not the only machine that changed American culture. Wartime research led to the development of ever more powerful calculators and computers. During the 1950s, American businesses reached out to embrace the computer industry. Grace Hopper, a research fellow at Harvard University's computation laboratory, pioneered the creation of the software that runs computers. She also introduced the term *debugging,* which was born when she removed a moth caught in a relay switch that had caused a large computer to shut down. Today the term means "ridding a computer program of errors."

In 1948 scientists at Bell Telephone Laboratories invented the **transistor,** a tiny circuit device that amplifies, controls, and generates electrical signals. The transistor could do the work of a much larger vacuum tube, but took up less space. Because of the transistor, giant machines that once filled whole rooms could now fit on a desk. Calculations that had taken hours could now be computed in fractions of a second. The Census Bureau purchased one of the first computer systems to tally the 1950 census.

**Households with Televisons, 1950–1960**

Number of Households (in millions)
0 5 10 15 20 25 30 35 40 45 50
1950 1951 1952 1953 1954 1955 1956 1957 1958 1959 1960
Year

Source: *Historical Statistics of the United States, Colonial Times to 1970*

**Interpreting Graphs** Notice how many households acquired televisions during the 1950s. ***Economics*** *How do you think television influenced economics?*

**Nuclear Power** An entirely new industry, the generation of electrical power through the use of atomic energy, resulted from the research that had produced the atomic bomb. In 1956 film producer Walt Disney voiced Americans' hopes and fears about atomic power in his book and film *Our Friend the Atom.* Disney began with a story about a fisherman who found a sealed bottle. When the fisherman opened the bottle, a genie escaped and threatened to kill him. The fisherman got the genie back into the bottle and would only open it again when the genie promised to grant him three wishes. "The story of the atom is like that tale." Disney explained:

AMERICAN VOICES

> **"The fable . . . has a happy ending; perhaps our story can, too. Like the Fisherman we must bestir our wits [think carefully before we act]. We have the scientific knowledge to turn the Genie's might into peaceful and useful channels."**
>
> —*Walt Disney*

The next year, navy captain Hyman G. Rickover oversaw the development of the first commercial nuclear power plant in Shippingport, Pennsylvania. The new plant promised the peaceful use of atomic energy that Walt Disney had imagined.

**Advances in Medicine** Americans also found hope in developments made in medicine. In 1954, Dr. Jonas Salk and Dr. Thomas Francis conducted a successful field test of a vaccine to prevent one of the most feared diseases—poliomyelitis. Before the vaccine, the disease, known commonly as polio, killed or disabled more than 20,000 children in the United States every year. Salk's injected vaccine, together with an oral version developed later by Dr. Albert Sabin, effectively eliminated the threat of polio.

Research in the development of drugs that could fight bacterial infections had been under way long before the start of World War II. By 1944, advances in the production of antibiotics, such as penicillin, saved countless lives. During the 1950s, doctors discovered other antibiotics effective against penicillin-resistant bacteria.

Doctors who had served during the war saving the lives of wounded soldiers came home to a new era of surgical advances. They made great strides in the growing specialty of heart surgery. Lessons learned in war allowed doctors to operate to correct heart defects.

These Chicago-area commuters display the conformity that has come to characterize the 1950s. ***Culture*** ***What role did the changes in the economy play in the growing uniformity of the culture?***

## *Changes in the Work Force*

In earlier years, most Americans made a living as blue-collar workers, or those who produce goods. After the war, however, new machines performed many of the jobs previously done by people. By 1956 a majority of all American workers held white-collar jobs, in which they no longer produced goods but instead performed services for others, working at counters or in offices.

The growth of the service industry had a great effect on the lives of Americans. The new white-collar workers felt encouraged by the working conditions they found: clean, bright offices. But they soon realized that office jobs had drawbacks as well. Work in large corporations was often impersonal. White-collar workers had little connection with the products that their companies made. Employers might pressure employees to dress, think, and act alike. Sociologist C. Wright Mills had this scathing comment: "When white-collar people get jobs, they sell not only their time and energy but their personalities as well."

For those who kept their blue-collar jobs, working conditions and wages improved during the 1940s and 1950s. During this period, workers in

**Main Idea CONNECTIONS**

***How did the growing service industry affect the lives of Americans?***

some unions won important gains, such as guaranteed cost-of-living increases. By 1955 nearly 33 percent of the total labor force in the United States was unionized. In that year, the two largest unions, the American Federation of Labor (AFL) and the Congress of Industrial Organizations (CIO) merged. The AFL-CIO, a new and more powerful organization, remains a major force today.

## Suburbs and Highways

With so many people working and making a better living than ever before, the **baby boom** that had begun during World War II continued. The birthrate, which had fallen to 19 births per 1,000 people during the Depression, soared to more than 25 births per 1,000 in its peak year of 1957.

Levitt and other developers offered not just houses, but entire communities. ***Culture*** ***What were the benefits and drawbacks of Levittowns?***

**Moving to the Suburbs** Growing families retreated from aging cities and sought new houses in suburbs that ringed the urban areas. World War II veterans enjoyed the benefits of the Servicemen's Readjustment Act of 1944, commonly known as the **GI Bill,** which gave them low-interest mortgages to purchase their new homes.†

Developers like William J. Levitt began to cater to the demand for housing. Levitt built new communities in the suburbs, pioneering mass-production techniques in home building. He bought precut and preassembled materials and built houses in just weeks instead of months. Proud of his creations, Levitt gave his name to the new towns. Soon there was a Levittown in New York, another in Pennsylvania, and a third in New Jersey. Others adopted Levitt's techniques, and new communities sprang up all over the United States.

For the first time, average Americans could easily afford to buy their own home. While most fully enjoyed life in their new houses, others complained that the developments all looked too much alike. Folk singer Malvina Reynolds expressed her distaste for the new communities with these words from "Little Boxes," a popular song of the era:

> Little boxes on the hillside
> Little boxes made of ticky-tacky
> Little boxes on the hillside
> Little boxes all the same.
> There's a green one and a pink one
> And a blue one and a yellow one
> And they're all made out of ticky-tacky
> And they all look just the same.

**Cars and Highways** Suburban growth brought with it other changes. Stores began to move from cities to shopping centers located in

### Birth Rate, 1930–1960

Live Births (per 1,000 people): 0, 5, 10, 15, 20, 25

Year: 1930, 1935, 1940, 1945, 1950, 1955, 1960

Source: *Historical Statistics of the United States, Colonial Times to 1970*

**Interpreting Graphs** A healthy postwar economy encouraged people to have larger families. ***Culture*** ***What was the difference in the birth rate between 1945 and 1955?***

†Nearly half of all eligible veterans took advantage of another provision in the GI Bill that offered money for college tuition.

the suburbs. Americans, at the same time, depended more on automobiles and less on public transportation. To meet the demand, auto makers started introducing new car designs every year. People eagerly awaited the unveiling of the latest models. During the 1950s American auto makers produced up to 8 million new cars each year.

Growth in the car industry created a need for more and better roads. The 1956 Interstate Highway Act provided $26 billion to build an interstate highway system more than 40,000 miles long. The project provided a national web of new roads and allowed for the evacuation of major cities in the event of nuclear attack.

The car culture inspired the development of many new businesses. Americans, especially teenagers, flocked to drive-in movies and restaurants. Families, encouraged by car advertisements that urged them to "See the USA," headed off on vacations at national parks, seaside resorts, and amusement parks.

## Consumer Credit Debt, 1946–1960

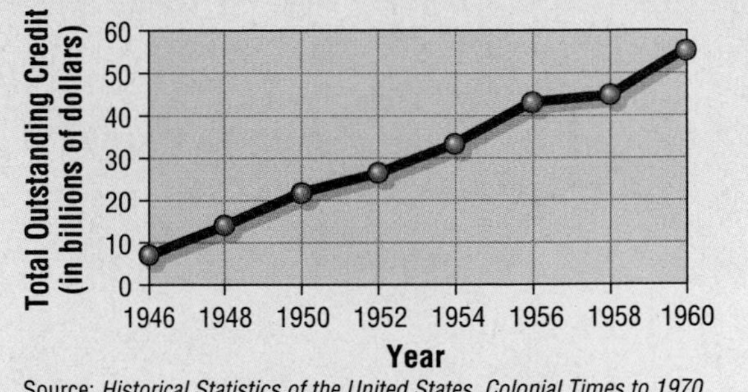


Source: *Historical Statistics of the United States, Colonial Times to 1970*

**Interpreting Graphs** Consumer debt included far more than just credit card debt. The consumer credit debt shown in this graph includes installment payments, home loans, and other loans as well as credit card debts. ***Economics By how much did consumer credit debt increase between 1946 and 1960?***

## *The Growth of Consumer Credit*

Eager to cash in on the increasing number of cars on the road, gasoline companies began offering credit cards to loyal customers. These cards allowed people to charge gas purchases when they were on the road. Americans found the cards easy and convenient to use.

After years of depression and war, Americans willingly went into debt to purchase the products they wanted. (See the graph on this page.) Lending agencies picked up the credit card idea and made borrowing easy. The Diner's Club credit card appeared in 1950, followed at the end of the decade by the American Express card, and then by the BankAmericard (later called Visa).

Advertisers persuaded consumers that only by buying new products could they attain status and success. Americans responded by using their credit to purchase washing machines, vacuum cleaners, and television sets. The United States had become, in the words of economist John Kenneth Galbraith, "the affluent society."

## *SECTION 1 REVIEW*

### Comprehension

1. *Key Terms* Define: (a) per capita income; (b) conglomerate; (c) franchise; (d) transistor; (e) baby boom; (f) GI Bill.
2. *Summarizing the Main Idea* How did the growth of the United States economy after World War II help many people achieve the American Dream?
3. *Organizing Information* Create a two-column chart that shows how conglomerates and the franchise system changed the American economy after World War II.

### Critical Thinking

4. *Analyzing Time Lines* Review the time line at the start of the section. In your opinion, which entry had the greatest impact on American society in the postwar years?
5. *Identifying Central Issues* What technological advances had an important impact on Americans in the decade after World War II?

### Writing Activity

6. *Writing a Persuasive Essay* Changes in the workplace influenced the growth of suburbs, highways, and consumer credit. Write an ad convincing people to move to the suburbs, buy a car, or apply for a credit card.

GEOGRAPHY AND HISTORY

# The Suburban Explosion

*The geographic theme of location explores where a place is, not only in absolute terms but in relation to other places. After World War II, American cities rapidly expanded outward as people moved into the suburbs—places defined by their location near cities. What factors contributed to this suburban explosion?*

A 1950s game piece reflects the suburban ideal.

In the decades following World War II, the location of people's homes and jobs changed. Millions of people moved to the suburbs, leveling the land, building homes, highways and stores. The suburbs that housed them soon became major centers for shopping, working, and recreation. But this change did not come without a price.

> **In 1956, the nation's first enclosed, climate-controlled shopping center opened. The suburban mall became increasingly popular for suburban consumers.**

## The Expansion of Waterfront Centers

In the 1700s, the largest cities in the United States were commercial centers located on waterfronts. This was because goods and people could travel more easily and quickly over water than on land. Workplaces in these cities were clustered near the waterfront, with homes located nearby, so people could walk between home and work.

In the decades before and after the Civil War, railroads grew, cutting paths outward from these waterfront centers. The compact, circular-shaped cities began to expand. Small residential communities sprouted around railroad stations situated six or more miles from the central cities. These small communities provided quiet settings and appealing neighborhoods for those who could afford to make the daily rail trips to and from their jobs in the city.

## People Leave the Cities

After the late 1880s, electric-powered streetcar lines reached into the surrounding countryside. This enabled even more urban residents to move out of city centers. Many of the homes they built were bigger and had more land around them.

By the time the United States entered World War I in 1914, some of the larger cities extended ten miles out from their centers, where most people still worked and shopped. Streetcar lines did not extend as far in some directions as in others, and thus the overall shape of the cities was star-like.

## Relocation After World War II

During the Great Depression and World War II, most Americans put their desire for better surroundings on hold. Once the war ended, however, millions of people returned to the nation's cities, where they married, had children in record numbers, and then began to search for bigger homes. Also, in the first decade after the war ended, the number of automobiles owned by city dwellers increased dramatically.

Housing in cities filled quickly. Because many veterans now owned automobiles, they had more options as to where they might live. Now they could consider living in locations outside cities.

The GI Bill made money readily available for housing. The result was construction at a rate unprecedented in the nation's history. Between 1947 and 1965, at least 1.25 million new houses were built each year, with more than one half of those in the suburbs.

## The Growth of Edge Cities

In 1956 the federal government established an interstate highway system to connect major cities. In addition to highways radiating out from city centers, engineers constructed "beltways" that circled cities at distances of six to twenty miles from the core. But as people moved to the suburbs, they found it inconvenient to travel back into the city for things they needed. In 1956, the nation's first enclosed, climate-controlled shopping center opened. The suburban mall became increasingly popular for suburban consumers.

A major reason for the success of the mall was that people could easily get to it from the freeway. Such mall locations were also ideal sites for offices, factories, service providers, and other businesses. These businesses were grouped in low buildings located on either side of heavily traveled freeways and streets. All this new construction formed what journalist Joel Garreau called the "edge city."

The rapid growth of edge cities was not without its problems. As suburbs became more densely settled, pollution, crime, and other problems that had plagued the central cities began to creep in. Of greatest concern to the people who worked, shopped, and lived in edge cities was the increasing traffic congestion. The easy access that attracted people to the suburbs was becoming a memory. Urban observers today wonder how new forms of transportation will change the geography of American cities.

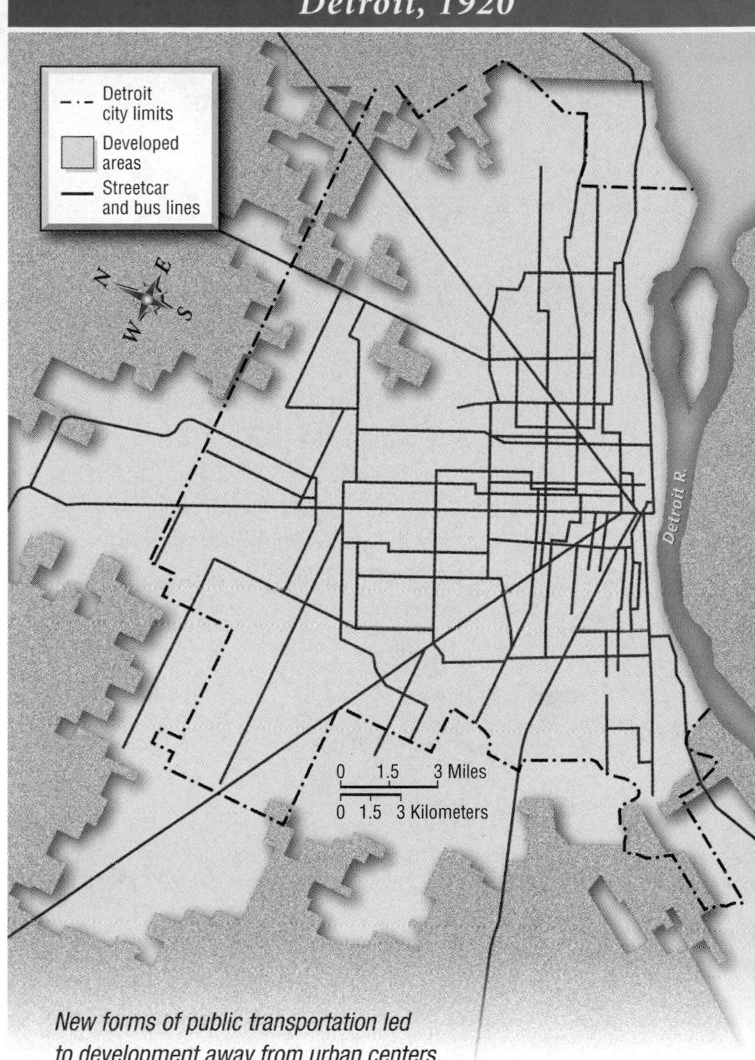

New forms of public transportation led to development away from urban centers.

## GEOGRAPHIC CONNECTIONS

1. Choose three forms of transportation mentioned in the passage and describe how each affected the growth of cities.
2. What factors contributed to the boom in suburban housing construction after World War II?

### Themes in Geography

3. *Location* The earliest large cities were located on waterfronts. How might new changes in transportation affect the location of cities?

**1946** *Dr. Spock publishes* The Common Sense Book of Baby and Child Care

**1953** *Alan Freed begins playing rock and roll on a Cleveland, Ohio, radio station*

**1955** *The film* Rebel Without a Cause *released*

**1957** *Jack Kerouac publishes his best-selling novel* On the Road

**1945** | **1950** | **1955** | **1960**

# 2 The Mood of the 1950s

## SECTION PREVIEW

### Objectives

1. Explain why most Americans valued comfort and security during the 1950s.
2. Describe the expectations about the proper roles for men and women in society.
3. Identify some ways in which people challenged conformity during the 1950s.
4. *Key Terms* Define: rock and roll; beatnik.

### Main Idea

After World War II, many Americans were blessed with wealth, success, and leisure. Conformity seemed the order of the day, although some groups made it their business to avoid the popularly accepted lifestyles of the 1950s.

### Reading Strategy

*Reinforcing Main Ideas* Write two headings on a piece of paper: *Conformity* and *Nonconformity.* As you read the section, note relevant information in the appropriate column. Then write a sentence explaining whether conformity or nonconformity was more prevalent in the 1950s than in American life today.

*The hula-hoop craze was one of many 1950s fads.*

Most Americans were comfortable during the 1950s. They valued security over adventure, reflecting the mood of a nation still recovering from years of depression and war. They applauded the apparent harmony that minimized differences between individuals and groups in the United States. Compromise, rather than conflict, was the way disagreements could be settled. People wanted to enjoy their newly won prosperity and provide even better opportunities for their children.

## Comfort and Security

In the past, sociologist David Riesman observed, Americans had valued individuality. Now most preferred to conform. Riesman cited *Tootle the Engine,* a children's story in the popular Little Golden Book series. Tootle, a young train engine, found it was more fun to play in the fields than it was to stay on the tracks. His fellow citizens in "Engineville" worked hard to break him of the habit. Tootle finally absorbed the lesson of his peers: "Always stay on the track no matter what." The story, Riesman believed, was a powerful parable for the young people of the 1950s.

**Youth Culture** Some called the youth of the 1950s the "silent generation." The silent generation seemed to have little interest in the problems and crises of the larger world. The strong economy allowed more young people to stay in school rather than leave early to find a job. With more leisure time, some teenagers appeared to devote their energies to organizing parties and pranks, joining fraternities and sororities, and generally pursuing entertainment and fun.

American businesses seized the opportunity to market products directly to this youth culture. Advertisements and movies helped to build an image of what it meant to be a teenager in the 1950s. The girls were shown in bobby socks and poodle skirts and the boys in letter sweaters. These images created a greater sense of conformity in style.

**A Resurgence in Religion** In the 1950s Americans, who had drifted away from religion in earlier years, flocked back to their churches or synagogues. The new interest in religion was a response in part to the cold-war struggle against "godless communism." Some looked to religion to find hope in the face of the threat of nuclear war.

Evidence of the newfound commitment to religion was everywhere. In 1954 Congress added the words "under God" to the Pledge of Allegiance, and the next year it required the phrase "In God We Trust" to appear on all American currency. Like other aspects of American life, religion became more commercial. Those in need could call Dial-a-Prayer for the first time, and new slogans such as "The family that prays together stays together" became commonplace. Evangelists used radio and television to carry their messages to more people than ever before. By the end of the 1950s, 95 percent of all Americans felt linked to some formal religious group.

## *Billy Graham*

AMERICAN BIOGRAPHY

One evangelist who gained a wide following in the 1950s was Billy Graham. Born in Charlotte, North Carolina, William Franklin Graham, Jr., was the son of a prosperous dairy farmer. After declaring his faith as a teenager, Graham attended fundamentalist institutions in Tennessee and Florida. In 1939 he was ordained as a Southern Baptist minister. He continued his education at Wheaton College in Illinois, graduating in 1943.

After leaving Wheaton, Graham joined Youth for Christ, an organization founded to minister to young soldiers during World War II. Following the war, his reputation grew as a result of appearances at tent revivals and at Youth for Christ rallies in the United States and Europe.

Thousands of Americans flocked to hear Graham preach at large-scale crusades, or tours, in major cities throughout the United States. In 1949, Graham gained widespread recognition at a crusade in Los Angeles, California. Originally scheduled to last for three weeks, the crusade was extended as crowds filled the tent every night for more than eight weeks. More crusades followed, with a 1957 meeting in New York City's Madison Square Garden lasting for 16 weeks.

*Billy Graham (b.1918)*

Graham's direct style of speaking made religion accessible, and he became known as fundamentalism's chief spokesperson. In addition to his televised crusades, Graham published his sermons and started the magazine *Decision.* He has also written 18 books. Graham's prominence continued to grow and he was a frequent guest at the White House. In 1996, he was awarded the Congressional Gold Medal. ■

## *Men's and Women's Roles*

Americans in the post–World War II years were keenly aware of the roles that they were expected to play as men and women. Men were supposed to go to school and then find jobs to support wives and children. Theirs was the public sphere, the world away from home where they earned money and made important political, economic, and social decisions. Men of this time often judged themselves and others by what they could buy with the money they earned.

**Main Idea CONNECTIONS**

*How did the traditional role of women in the 1950s support the ideals of postwar America?*

Women in the 1950s were expected to play a supporting role for their husbands' lives in the public sphere. They kept house, cooked meals, and raised children. Many women had enjoyed working outside the home during World War II and were reluctant to give up good jobs. But many young couples wanted to start families, and most Americans at that time expected mothers to stay at home with their children. Moreover, there were no day-care centers. In 1947 *Life* magazine recorded women's frustration in a photo essay titled "The American Woman's Dilemma."

By the 1950s the dilemma seemed solved. Most middle-class women settled into the demands of raising children and maintaining their suburban homes. In 1956 *Life* produced a special edition on women that carried a very different message from the issue of nine years before. In a story titled "Busy Wife's Achievements," *Life* profiled Marjorie Sutton, a happy housewife who had married at the age

*The "happy housewife" portrayed in the 1950s media looked glamorous as she used state-of-the-art appliances to cook and clean.*

of 16, had four children, and now kept busy with the PTA, Campfire Girls, and charity causes. She served as "home manager, mother, hostess, and useful civic worker," and even found time to exercise twice a week "to help preserve her size 12 figure."

The pediatrician Dr. Benjamin Spock assured American families that mothers should stay home with their young children. In *The Common Sense Book of Baby and Child Care,* published in 1946 and still selling today (in revised form), he advised a mother to remain with her children if she wanted them to grow up stable and secure. Adlai Stevenson, Democratic candidate for President in 1952 and 1956, reinforced this message when he told a group of female college students that "the assignment for you, as wives and mothers, you can do in the living room with a baby in your lap or in the kitchen with a can opener in your hand."

In 1963 Betty Friedan published an explosive critique of the 1950s' ideal of womanhood. Friedan had graduated with top honors from Smith College in 1942, but had given up her career as a journalist to become a full-time homemaker and mother. In her book *The Feminine Mystique,* Friedan lashed out at the culture that denied creative roles to women:

> **AMERICAN VOICES** **"It was unquestioned gospel [in the 1950s] that women could identify with nothing beyond the home—not politics, not art, not science, not events large or small, war or peace, in the United States or the world, unless it could be approached through female experience as a wife or mother or translated into domestic detail!"**
>
> —*Betty Friedan,* The Feminine Mystique

Millions of women, Friedan charged, were frustrated with their roles in the 1950s.

The situation was not as simple as Friedan claimed, however. In fact, more women than ever before—many of them married with children—held paying jobs in the 1950s. Besides the satisfaction of earning their own money, women wanted to be able to buy the items that were part of the media image of "the good life"—automobiles, electric appliances, and so on. In 1950, 24 percent of all married American women had jobs; by 1960 the figure had risen to 31 percent. Married women with jobs had first begun to outnumber unmarried women with jobs near the end of World War II; in the postwar years, the gap grew even larger. The graph at left shows these trends.

**Female Labor Force, 1950–1960**

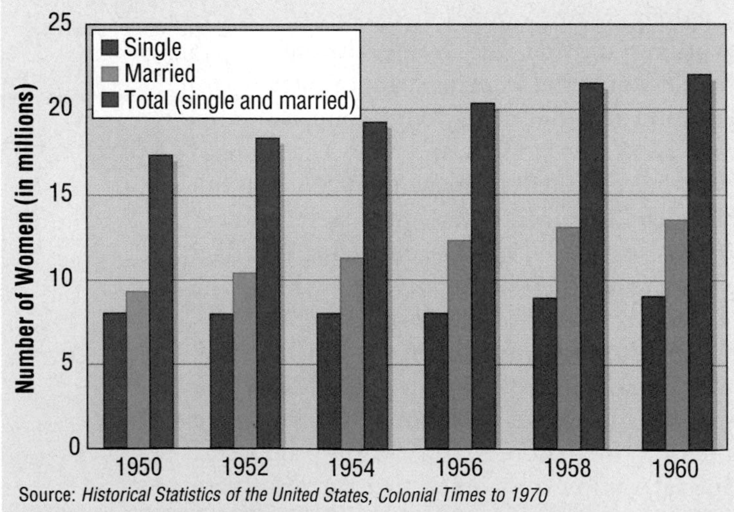


**Interpreting Graphs** More and more women continued to join the labor force throughout the 1950s. ***Culture According to the graph, what change was taking place in the female labor force?***

## *Challenges to Conformity*

Occasionally, challenges to 1950s society erupted. Some young people rejected the values of their parents and felt misunderstood and alone. A few films, such as *Rebel Without a Cause,* released in 1955, captured these feelings of alienation. The movie's young star, James Dean, became a teen idol and a film legend.

Holden Caulfield, the main character in J. D. Salinger's 1951 novel, *The Catcher in the Rye,* was troubled by the hypocrisy of the "phonies" he saw at boarding school and in the world around him. Throughout the book, Holden struggles to preserve his own integrity despite the fierce pressure to conform. Many readers could relate to this experience.

Young people sought a style they could call their own. In 1953, Alan Freed, a radio disc jockey in Cleveland, Ohio, began playing a new type of music that had grown out of the rhythm-and-blues tradition. He called this new music **rock and roll.** Teenagers across the nation quickly became fans of the driving beat and simple melodies that characterized rock and roll. They rushed to buy records of their favorite performers, such as Chuck Berry, Bill Haley and the Comets, and Little Richard.

One of the most popular rock-and-roll singers was Elvis Presley. Presley's performances showcased his flamboyant style and good looks. He attracted hordes of screaming teenage girls everywhere he went. Presley released many records that became huge hits, including "Don't Be Cruel," "Hound Dog," and "Heartbreak Hotel." Many adults disliked the new music, fearing it would cause a rise in immorality. Despite some efforts to ban rock concerts and keep records out of stores, rock and roll's popularity soared.

Members of the "Beat Generation," called **beatniks,** launched a different kind of challenge. Beatniks, some of them writers, some artists, some simply participants in the movement, stressed spontaneity and spirituality instead of apathy and conformity. They challenged traditional patterns of respectability and shocked other Americans with their more open sexuality and their use of illegal drugs.

Author Jack Kerouac, the spiritual leader of the beatniks, gathered with others in coffee houses in San Francisco, California, to share ideas and experiences. The unconventional Kerouac typed his best-selling novel *On the Road*, published in 1957, on a 250-foot roll of paper. The novel's lack of standard punctuation and paragraph structure was meant to reflect an open approach to life. One of Kerouac's friends, Allen Ginsberg, used the unstructured and chaotic style of the Beat Movement to write his powerful and moving poem "Howl."

## COMPARING PRIMARY SOURCES

### ROCK-AND-ROLL MUSIC

When the defiant beat of rock and roll burst onto the American scene in the mid-1950s, few people remained impartial about its sound or its impact.

**Opposed to Rock and Roll**

"Rock 'n' roll . . . is sung, played and written for the most part by [mentally deficient] goons and by means of its almost imbecilic repetition and sly, lewd, in plain fact, dirty lyrics . . . it manages to be the [warlike] music of every sideburned delinquent on the face of the earth."

—*Singer Frank Sinatra,* The New York Times, *January 12, 1958*

**In Favor of Rock and Roll**

"If my kids are home at night listening to my radio program, and get interested enough to go out and buy records and have a collection to listen to and dance to, I think I'm fighting delinquency."

—*Radio disc jockey Alan Freed,* The New York Times, *January 12, 1958*

***ANALYZING VIEWPOINTS*** **What does each viewpoint above say about the relationship between rock music and delinquency?**

## SECTION 2 REVIEW

### Comprehension

1. *Key Terms* Define: (a) rock and roll; (b) beatnik.
2. *Summarizing the Main Idea* In what aspects of American life was conformity most visible during the period between 1945 and 1960?
3. *Organizing Information* Use information from the section to create a web diagram that shows ways in which Americans expressed the values of comfort and security.

### Critical Thinking

4. *Analyzing Time Lines* Review the time line at the start of the section. Choose one event that you think best illustrates the mood of the 1950s. Explain why you chose that entry.
5. *Identifying Central Issues* What social and economic roles were men and women expected to play in the 1950s?

### Writing Activity

6. *Writing an Expository Essay* Research and write a brief essay on a person or group of people that challenged conformity in the 1950s. You might want to write on a rock-and-roll artist, a movie star, or a writer involved in the Beat Movement.

# SKILLS FOR LIFE

**Historical Evidence**

Graphs and Charts

Geography

Critical Thinking

## Evaluating Magazine Advertisements

Magazine advertisements can be a rich and colorful source of evidence about the past. Because popular weekly or monthly magazines are aimed at a broad audience, advertisements frequently reflect a society's prevailing attitudes and values. Remember, though, that every ad also reflects the purpose of the company whose products are being advertised—namely, to sell its products. Therefore, an ad may present a slanted or false view of the desirable American life, designed to make consumers want to buy certain products.

Use the following steps to evaluate the advertisement at right, which appeared in the *Saturday Evening Post* in April 1958.

**1.** ***Identify the nature of the advertisement.*** Carefully review the entire advertisement, then answer the following questions. (a) What is the point of this advertisement? What does it encourage readers to do? (b) What company created this ad? What product does the company make? (c) What other products are shown in the ad? (d) Who do you think is the intended audience for the advertisement?

**2.** ***Study the advertisement to evaluate the underlying messages it contains.*** Look closely at the image in the ad. (a) What things seem to make the people shown in the advertisement happy? (b) Does this ad suggest a preference for suburban life or city life? Explain why you think so.

**3.** ***Study the advertisement to learn more about the historical period.*** Use the information in the ad to help you answer the following questions. (a) Based on what you see in this ad, how closely linked were happiness and material wealth in the minds of many Americans in the 1950s? (b) Would everyone in the 1950s have been able to afford to buy the items shown in the ad? (c) Are your conclusions consistent with what you already know about the United States in the 1950s? Explain.

### TEST FOR SUCCESS

What does this ad suggest is the "good life" toward which Americans should strive?

**2,350 prizes worth over $100,000**

**No jingles to write . . . no boxtops to mail!**

**Get in on the celebration** of the birth of a wonderful new Wheaties! All you do is write your name and address and mail in accordance with the easy Sweepstakes rules. For Sweepstakes rules see the specially marked New Wheaties "Sweepstakes" packages in your store, or write to General Mills, Inc., Dept. 185, 623 Marquette Avenue, Minneapolis 2, Minnesota.

**Four Great Weekly Drawings**

**Each week New Wheaties is giving away 306 Prizes!**

**1st PRIZE**—16-Ft. Glasspar Del Mar Cabin Cruiser with Johnson Super Sea-Horse V-50 Outboard Motor.

**5 2nd PRIZES**—Aircap Master-Ride Power Mower.

**50 3rd PRIZES**—Coleman Pak-Table with 4 folding chairs.

**50 4th PRIZES**—Cronco Port-O-Rator Cooler.

**100 5th PRIZES**—Sportcraft Official Badminton Set.

**100 6th PRIZES**—Full case of Hormel Dairy Brand Franks.

Weekly Drawings Will Be Held On

**APRIL 21 • APRIL 28 • MAY 5 • MAY 12**

After each drawing, all entries are saved and added to the following week's entries. Thus, every entry you send in has a chance to win a wonderful prize in any or all of the remaining weekly drawings! In addition, all entries received by 8 A.M. May 19, 1958, are eligible for the mammoth Grand Prize Drawing! So enter early and often! Subject to Federal, State and local laws.

**LOOK FOR THIS SPECIAL SWEEPSTAKES PACKAGE!**

**NEW WHEATIES takes your taste outdoors** Take the "ho-hum" out of breakfast. Try the new taste that shows you how good whole wheat can really be. Big, golden flakes, radiant-crisped clean through to *stay* crackling crisp in milk. Chock-full of the food value whole wheat's famous for. *Your* family would enjoy the New Wheaties tomorrow morning!

**GIANT GRAND PRIZE DRAWING ON MAY 19, 1958**

All entries received by 8 A.M. on May 19, 1958, are eligible for:

**1st Grand Prize — $10,000 IN CASH!**

**Plus one each of every other prize in the Sweepstakes!**

- 16-Ft. Glasspar Del Mar Cabin Cruiser with Johnson Super Sea-Horse V-50 Outboard Motor.
- Aircap Master-Ride Power Mower.
- 5½ H.P. Johnson Sea-Horse Outboard Motor.
- Boy's or Girl's Roadmaster Jet Pilot Bicycles.
- Coleman Pak-Table with 4 folding chairs.
- Wilson: Patty Berg, or Sam Snead Golf Club Set.
- South Bend Spin Cast® Rod, Reel and Line Set.
- 8-Ft. Doughboy Splasher Pool.
- Cronco Port-O-Rator Cooler.
- Royal Chef Charcoal Brazier.
- Sportcraft Official Badminton Set.
- Full case of Hormel Dairy Brand Franks.
- Year's Supply of New Radiant-Crisp Wheaties (120 12-oz. packages).

Plus Year's Supply of Hormel Prime Choice Steaks—(Choice of a deluxe gift box of 8 New York Cut or 12 Tenderloins each week for 52 weeks).

1125 Other Grand Prizes!

**75 2nd PRIZES**—Johnson Sea-Horse 5½ H.P. Outboard Motors.

**100 3rd PRIZES**—Wilson Golf Club Sets (3 woods, 5 irons, your choice of Patty Berg or Sam Snead Models).

**100 4th PRIZES**—Roadmaster Jet Pilot Bicycles (Your choice of boy's or girl's model).

**200 5th PRIZES**—8-Ft. Doughboy Splasher Pools.

**400 6th PRIZES**—South Bend Spin Cast® Rod, Reel and Line Sets.

**200 7th PRIZES**—Royal Chef Charcoal Braziers.

**50 8th PRIZES**—Year's Supply of New Radiant-Crisp Wheaties (120 12-oz. packages).

General Mills

NEW "*Breakfast of Champions*"

**1946** *The government eases economic controls and prices soar*

**1947** *Congress passes Taft-Hartley Act*

**1948** *Truman wins upset victory in presidential election*

**1952** *Republicans capture the White House and both houses of Congress*

**1958** *Congress passes National Defense Education Act*

1946 — 1952 — 1958

# 3 Domestic Politics and Policy

## SECTION PREVIEW

### Objectives

1. Describe Truman's domestic policies as outlined in his Fair Deal.
2. Describe how Truman won the election of 1948.
3. Explain the highlights of Dwight Eisenhower's Republican presidency.
4. *Key Terms* Define: Taft-Hartley Act; modern republicanism; National Defense Education Act.

### Main Idea

Presidents Harry S. Truman and Dwight D. Eisenhower used two very different styles of leadership to meet the challenges they faced during the postwar period.

### Reading Strategy

*Problem Solving* Evaluate how Presidents Truman and Eisenhower handled domestic affairs. As you read, note positive and negative points about the administration of each President. Then write a brief analysis of each President and use them to give each a grade.

The 1950s were a conservative time politically as well as culturally. Most Americans pressured the government to help maintain the nation's newly won prosperity. Democrat Harry S. Truman first struggled with the problems of reconversion to a peacetime economy, then fought for a reform program blocked repeatedly by Congress. Republican Dwight D. Eisenhower took a more low-key approach to the presidency. His genial, reassuring manner made him one of the most popular Presidents in the years following World War II.

## Truman's Domestic Policies

Harry Truman wanted to follow in Franklin Roosevelt's footsteps, but he often appeared ill-prepared for the presidency. He seemed to have a scattershot approach to governing, offering a new batch of proposals in every speech. People wondered where his focus lay.

**Moving to a Peacetime Economy** Truman's first priority was reconversion—the social and economic transition from wartime to peacetime. Soldiers wanted to return home, and politicians were flooded with messages that warned, "No boats, no votes." Truman responded quickly and got most soldiers home by 1946.

*This sign, which sat on Truman's desk, expressed both his responsibility and authority.*

Lifting the economic controls that had kept wartime inflation in check proved a more difficult challenge. Most Americans had done without consumer goods during World War II. Now they wanted those goods, and they wanted them right away. The government eased the controls in July 1946, and prices soared almost 25 percent. One political cartoonist quipped that prices had gone "Over the moon!" Since wages failed to keep up with prices, many people still could not enjoy the fruits of their years of sacrifice.

In some ways, the economic issues facing the United States at the end of World War II were similar to those at the end of World War I. Workers demanded wage increases that they had forgone for the sake of the war effort. In 1946, 4.6 million workers went on strike, more than ever before in the United States. Strikes hit the automobile, steel, electrical, coal, and railroad industries and affected nearly everyone in the country.

**Main Idea CONNECTIONS**

*Why did Truman oppose labor's demand for higher wages?*

Though Truman agreed that workers deserved high wages, he thought that their demands were inflationary. He feared that such increases would push the prices of goods still higher. In his view, workers failed to understand that big wage increases might destroy the health of the economy.

In the spring of 1946, a railroad strike caused a big disruption in the economy. In response, Truman asked Congress for the power to draft the striking workers into the army. He would then be able to order them as soldiers to stay on the job. Truman's request was soundly rejected by the Senate.

Truman's White House took other steps against labor as well. When John L. Lewis and his United Mine Workers defied a court order against a strike, the Truman administration asked a judge to serve Lewis with a contempt of court citation. The court fined Lewis $10,000 and his union $3.5 million.

Congress went even further than Truman. In 1947 it passed the **Taft-Hartley Act.** This act allowed the President to declare an 80-day cooling-off period when strikes hit industries that affected the national interest. During this period, strikers had to return to work while the government conducted a study of the situation. Reflecting the widespread anti-Communist feelings gripping the United States at the time, the measure also required union officials to sign non-Communist oaths. Furious union leaders complained bitterly about the measure, and Truman vetoed it. Congress, however, passed the act over Truman's veto.

**Truman's Fair Deal** Truman had supported Roosevelt's New Deal, and now, playing on the well-known name, he devised a program he called the Fair Deal. The Fair Deal extended the New Deal's goals.

Truman agreed with FDR that government needed to play an active role in securing economic justice for all American citizens. As the war ended, he introduced a 21-point program that included legislation designed to promote full employment, a higher minimum wage, greater unemployment compensation for workers without jobs, housing assistance, and a variety of other items. Over the next ten weeks, Truman added more proposals to the Fair Deal. By early 1946 he had asked for a national health insurance program and legislation to control atomic energy.

Truman ran into tremendous political opposition in Congress. A coalition of conservative Democrats and Republicans opposed him at every turn. They rejected the majority of the Fair Deal initiatives, passing only the Employment Act of 1946. In this act they created a Council of Economic Advisers to advise the President.

As the 1946 midterm elections approached, Truman seemed little more than another bungling bureaucrat. Some people commented, "You just sort of forget about Harry until he makes another mistake." Others adapted a well-known saying: "To err is Truman." Truman's support in one poll dropped from 87 percent just after he assumed the presidency to 32 percent in November 1946. The results of the 1946 elections reflected many people's feelings that

Harry S. Truman became the first President ever to campaign in Harlem, the heart of New York City's African American population. ***Government*** *How did Truman's support of civil rights cause a split in the Democratic party?*

Truman was not an effective leader. Republicans won majorities of both houses of Congress.

The 80th Congress battered the President for the next two years. Under the leadership of the conservative Republican senator Robert A. Taft of Ohio, commonly known as "Mr. Republican," the Republican party did whatever it could to reduce the size and the power of the federal government, to decrease taxes, and to block Truman's liberal goals.

## *The Election of 1948*

Truman decided to seek another term as President in 1948. He had no reason to expect victory, however, because even in his own party, his support was disintegrating. The southern wing of the Democratic party, protesting a moderate civil rights plank in the party platform, split off from the main party. These segregationists formed the States' Rights, or Dixiecrat, party and nominated Governor J. Strom Thurmond of South Carolina for President.

Meanwhile, the liberal wing of the Democratic party deserted Truman to follow Henry Wallace, who headed the Progressive party ticket. Wallace had been Franklin Roosevelt's second Vice President, and many Democrats believed that he was the right person to carry out the measures begun by Roosevelt. Most recently Wallace had served as Truman's Secretary of Commerce. Wallace had resigned, however, because he did not support Truman's cold war policies.

Running against Republican Thomas E. Dewey, governor of New York, Truman crisscrossed the country by train. He campaigned not so much against Dewey as against the Republican Congress, which the President repeatedly mocked as the "do-nothing" 80th Congress. Truman's campaign style was electrifying. In off-the-cuff speeches, he challenged all Americans: "If you send another Republican Congress to Washington, you're a bigger bunch of suckers than I think you are." "Give 'em hell, Harry," the people yelled as Truman got going. And he did.

Among other things, Truman vehemently attacked Congress's farm policy. In the past, a federal price-support program permitted farmers to borrow money to store surplus crops until someone bought the produce. Recently, however, Congress had failed to provide additional storage bins, just as a good harvest loomed on the horizon. Truman told the farmers:

***The* Chicago Daily Tribune *was so certain of Truman's defeat that it printed this erroneous edition before the votes were tallied.***

**AMERICAN VOICES** **"The Republican Congress has already stuck a pitchfork in the farmers' backs. . . . When you have to sell your grain below the support price because you have no place to store it, you can thank this same Republican Congress."**

—*Harry Truman*

On election day, although virtually all experts and polls picked Dewey to win, Truman scored an astounding upset. With this victory, he stepped out of FDR's shadow to claim the presidency in his own right.

Truman looked forward to a chance to push further for his legislative goals. Over the next four years, however, the Fair Deal scored only occasional successes. Instances of corruption among federal officials further hurt Truman's image.

After at first toying with the idea, Truman decided not to run for reelection in 1952. Instead, the Democrats chose Adlai Stevenson, governor of Illinois, as their presidential candidate.

## *Dwight Eisenhower and the Republican Approach*

Running against Stevenson for the Republicans was Dwight Eisenhower, former commander-in-chief of the Allied forces, president of Columbia University, and head of NATO. As a public figure, Eisenhower's approach to politics differed from that of Harry Truman. Whereas Truman was a scrappy fighter, Ike—as the people affectionately called Eisenhower—had always been a talented diplomat. During World

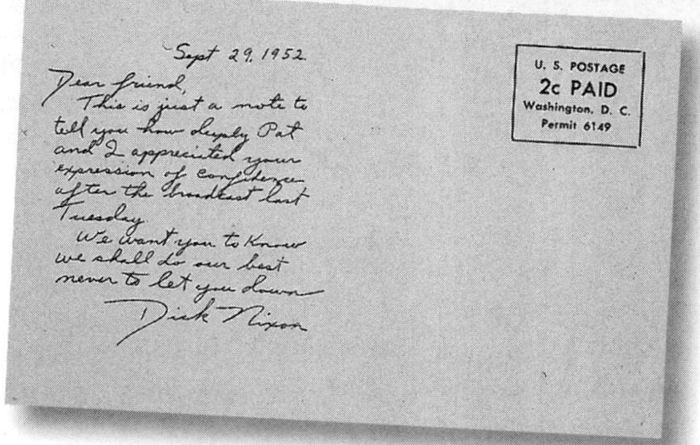

Sept 29, 1952

Dear friend,
This is just a note to tell you how deeply Pat and I appreciated your expression of confidence after the broadcast last Tuesday.
We want you to know we shall do our best never to let you down—
Dick Nixon

U. S. POSTAGE
2c PAID
Washington, D. C.
Permit 6149

Richard Nixon thanked the voters who had shown their support after his "Checkers" speech with this postcard. ***Culture*** ***What image of Nixon does this photograph promote?***

War II, Eisenhower forged agreements among Allied military commanders. His easy-going charm gave Americans a sense of security.

By 1952 Americans across the land chanted, "I Like Ike." The Republicans devised a "$K_1C_2$" formula for victory, which focused on three problems: Korea, communism, and corruption. Eisenhower promised to end the Korean War, and the Republican party guaranteed a tough approach to the Communist challenge. Eisenhower's vice-presidential running mate, Californian Richard M. Nixon, hammered on the topic of corruption in government.

***The "I Like Ike" message was seen everywhere in 1952, even on cosmetics containers.***

**The Checkers Speech** In spite of his overwhelming popularity, Eisenhower's candidacy hit a snag in September 1952. Newspapers accused Richard Nixon of having a special fund, set up by rich Republican supporters. "Secret Nixon Fund!" and "Secret Rich Man's Trust Fund Keeps Nixon in Style Beyond His Salary," screamed typical headlines. In fact, Nixon had done nothing wrong, but the accusation that he had received illegal gifts from political friends was hard to shake.

Soon, cries arose for Eisenhower to dump Nixon from the ticket. Eisenhower decided to allow Nixon to save himself, if he could. On September 23, Nixon went on television to explain the situation in his own words. He emotionally denied wrongful use of campaign funds. Nixon also gave a detailed account of his personal finances. In response to the charge that he was living above his means, he described his wife, Pat, as wearing a "good old Republican cloth coat."

The emotional climax of the speech came when Nixon admitted that he had, in fact, received one gift from a political supporter:

**AMERICAN VOICES** **"It was a little cocker spaniel dog. . . . Black and white spotted. And our little girl—Tricia, the 6-year-old—named it Checkers. And you know the kids love that dog and I just want to say this right now, that regardless of what they say about it, we're going to keep it."**

*—Richard Nixon*

At the end of his speech, Nixon requested that the American people contact the Eisenhower campaign to register their opinions as to whether or not he should stay on the Republican ticket. People from all across the nation called, wired, and wrote to Eisenhower, demanding that Nixon continue as his running mate. Nixon had turned a political disaster into a public relations bonanza.

Support for Eisenhower continued to grow through the fall. Democratic candidate Adlai Stevenson never had a chance. Ike got 55 percent of the popular vote and swept into office with a Republican Congress as well.

**Eisenhower as President** Ike's natural inclination was to work behind the scenes. One writer has described his style as the "hidden hand." "I am not one of those desk-pounding types that likes to stick out his jaw and look like he is bossing the show," Eisenhower said. Critics misinterpreted his apparent lack of leadership, joking about an Eisenhower doll—you wound it up and it did nothing. Eisenhower defended his approach, declaring:

**AMERICAN VOICES** "Now, look, I happen to know a little about leadership. I've had to work with a lot of nations, for that matter, at odds with each other. And I tell you this: you do not lead by hitting people over the head. . . . I'll tell you what leadership is. It's persuasion—and conciliation—and education—and patience. It's long, slow tough work. That's the only kind of leadership I know or believe in—or will practice."

*—Dwight Eisenhower*

The American people approved of Ike's style. In 1956, Eisenhower once again faced Stevenson and easily won reelection. This time he gathered an even greater margin of victory, with almost 58 percent of the vote. The Democrats, however, retained control of Congress in the 1956 election.

**Modern Republicanism** In domestic matters, Eisenhower was determined to slow the growth of the federal government. He also wanted to limit the President's power and increase the authority of Congress and the courts. Eisenhower was not, however, interested in completely reversing the New Deal.

Ike's priorities included cutting spending, reducing taxes, and balancing the budget. He called this approach to government "dynamic conservatism" or **modern republicanism.** He intended to be "conservative when it comes to money, liberal when it comes to human beings."

In the tradition of past Republican Presidents such as Coolidge and Hoover, Eisenhower favored big business. His Cabinet was composed mostly of successful businessmen, plus one union leader. Critics charged that the Cabinet consisted of "eight millionaires and a plumber." For Secretary of Defense he chose Charles E. Wilson, former president of General Motors, who claimed that "what was good for our country was good for General Motors, and vice versa."

Modern republicanism sought to encourage and support corporate America. It transferred control of about $40 billion worth of offshore oil lands from the federal government to the states so that the states could lease oil rights to corporations. The administration worked to end government competition with big business.

Ike's attempt to balance the budget backfired. His cuts in government spending caused the economy to slump. When that happened, tax revenues dropped, and the deficit grew larger instead of smaller. Economic growth, which

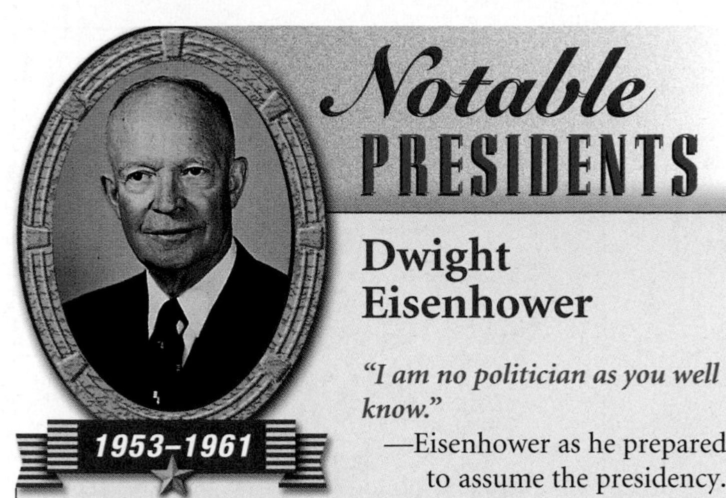


## *Notable* PRESIDENTS

### Dwight Eisenhower

*"I am no politician as you well know."*

—Eisenhower as he prepared to assume the presidency.

Born in Texas in 1890, Dwight Eisenhower grew up in Abilene, Kansas. After high school he attended the U. S. Military Academy at West Point and began a long and distinguished military career. That career peaked during World War II when Eisenhower, as supreme commander of the Allied Expeditionary Force, oversaw the D-Day landings in France and the final defeat of Germany. After the war Eisenhower served as Army Chief of Staff, president of Columbia University, and then head of NATO, the North Atlantic Treaty Organization.

Though "Ike" had no formal political experience, both major parties courted him as a presidential candidate because of his enormous wartime prestige. In 1952 he ran as a Republican and won a landslide victory in the general election. His wide grin, folksy manner, and proven leadership abilities gained him support around the country.

Eisenhower helped bring peace by negotiating a truce in 1953 that ended the fighting in Korea. He was a strong defender of American interests abroad, yet he also feared that high military spending would harm the economy. Thus Eisenhower endorsed a military strategy of relying on nuclear weapons, rather than more costly conventional armies, in conflicts around the world.

At home, Eisenhower generally favored restraint in government actions and spending. He did, however, strongly support the Interstate Highway Act of 1956, which created a nationwide network of roads. Also, in 1957 Eisenhower sent federal troops to enforce school desegregation in Little Rock, Arkansas.

Eisenhower's critics sometimes complained about his low-key approach to the presidency and blamed him for lacking strong leadership. Yet he provided the nation with stability and reassurance during a dangerous period of the cold war.

#### Connecting to Today

How might experience as a military leader help a President? Can you think of any ways in which such experience might not be helpful? Explain.

"Wonder Why We're not Keeping Pace?"

The author of this cartoon blamed U.S. government and education for the nation's failure to keep pace with Soviet technology. ***Government*** *What steps did the government take to improve American education?*

had averaged 4.3 percent between 1947 and 1952, fell to 2.5 percent between 1953 and 1960. The country suffered three economic recessions during Eisenhower's presidency, from 1953 to 1954, from 1957 to 1958, and again from 1960 to 1961.

Despite occasional economic troubles, Eisenhower helped maintain a mood of stability in America. He also underscored the basic commitment the government had made during the New Deal to ensure the economic security of all Americans. For example, in 1954 and 1956 Social Security was extended to make eligible 10 million additional workers. In 1955 the minimum wage was raised from 75 cents to one dollar an hour.

**Meeting the Technology Challenge** When the Soviet Union launched *Sputnik* in 1957, as described in the previous chapter, many Americans feared a nuclear attack would soon follow. Others grew concerned that the United States was losing its competitive edge. In response, less than a year later Congress passed and President Eisenhower signed into law the **National Defense Education Act** of 1958. The measure was designed to improve science and mathematics instruction in the schools so that the United States could meet the scientific and technical challenge from the Soviet Union. The act provided millions of dollars in low-cost loans to college students and significant reductions in repayments if they ultimately became teachers. The federal government also granted millions to state schools for building science and foreign language facilities.

## SECTION 3 REVIEW

### Comprehension

1. ***Key Terms*** Define: (a) Taft-Hartley Act; (b) modern republicanism; (c) National Defense Education Act.
2. ***Summarizing the Main Idea*** How did Truman's and Eisenhower's approaches to the role of the federal government in solving domestic problems differ?
3. ***Organizing Information*** Create a web diagram that organizes information about Eisenhower's policies known as modern republicanism. In the center circle write *Eisenhower's Modern Republicanism.* Include details from the section for at least five surrounding circles.

### Critical Thinking

4. ***Analyzing Time Lines*** Review the time line at the start of the section. Choose one event that relates to domestic policies or politics in the postwar years and write a paragraph explaining why you think that event was important to the nation.
5. ***Expressing Problems Clearly*** What was the main problem that President Truman faced in the election of 1948?

### Writing Activity

6. ***Writing a Persuasive Essay*** Reread the section on the Checkers speech. Then write a letter to President Eisenhower either in support of or opposition to keeping Richard Nixon on the Republican ticket. Include specific examples to support your opinion.

**1946** *Truman appoints Committee on Civil Rights*

**1947** *Jackie Robinson is first African American to play major league baseball*

**1948** *Truman orders desegregation of armed forces*

**1954** Brown v. Board of Education of Topeka, Kansas

**1955** *Bus boycott begins in Montgomery, Alabama*

**1956** *Supreme Court declares segregation on buses illegal*

1946 | 1951 | 1956

# 4 Demands for Civil Rights

**SECTION PREVIEW**

### Objectives

1. Describe the progress made in the struggle for equality during the Truman years.
2. Understand such highlights of the 1950s as the *Brown* decision, the Montgomery bus boycott, and the confrontation in Little Rock.
3. Describe how other minorities began to follow the example set by the African American movement.
4. *Key Terms* Define: *Brown* v. *Board of Education of Topeka, Kansas;* Montgomery bus boycott; integration.

### Main Idea

Following World War II, African Americans began to push harder in the civil rights movement and brought about significant results.

### Reading Strategy

*Formulating Questions* Reread thc main idea above. Then rewrite it as a question. As you read the section, write down possible answers to your question.

Before and during World War II, African Americans were not treated as equals by a large portion of American society. After the war, however, the campaign for civil rights began to accelerate. Millions of people believed that the time had come to demand that the nation live up to its creed that all are equal before the law.

## *The Struggle for Equality*

The story of the postwar struggle for racial equality begins with President Truman. While holding in private many of the racial prejudices he had learned growing up in the South, Truman recognized that as President he had to take action. In a letter to a friend, he wrote, "I am not asking for social equality, because no such things exist, but I am asking for equality of opportunity for all human beings."

**Truman's Actions** Truman had publicly supported civil rights for many years. In September 1946 he met with a group of African American leaders to discuss the steps that needed to be taken to achieve their goals. They asked Truman to support a federal antilynching law, abolish the poll tax as a voting requirement, and establish a permanent board to prevent discriminatory practices in hiring. Congress refused to address any of these concerns, so in December 1946, Truman appointed a biracial Committee on Civil Rights to look into race relations. This group produced a report demanding action on the concerns listed above. In addition they also recommended that a permanent civil rights commission be established.

WITH TRUMAN for CIVIL RIGHTS

*This 1948 campaign button proclaimed Truman's commitment to civil rights.*

Once more Congress failed to act. In July 1948 Truman took action and banned discrimination in the hiring of federal employees. He also ordered an end to segregation and discrimination in the armed forces. Real change came slowly, however. Only with the onset of the Korean War in 1950 did the armed forces make significant progress in ending segregation.

After his brilliant first season with the Brooklyn Dodgers, Jackie Robinson was featured on baseball cards such as the one above, issued in 1951. ***Diversity*** ***How did Robinson's career serve the cause of civil rights?***

**Jackie Robinson** The battle against racial segregation was taken up not only in the military but on the professional baseball diamond as well. For years, major league baseball had refused to allow African Americans to participate, forcing them to play in the separate Negro Leagues. In the mid-1940s, Branch Rickey, the general manager of the Brooklyn Dodgers, decided to challenge the ban.

Rickey selected an athlete named Jackie Robinson to be the first African American to break the color line. Robinson had grown up in Pasadena, California, and attended the University of California in Los Angeles. In college Robinson earned letters in football, basketball, baseball, and track.

Robinson had a record of standing up against racial injustice. While he was in the army during World War II, a bus driver had snarled at him, "Get in the back where you belong or there'll be trouble." Robinson knew that buses on the army post were not segregated, so he stood his ground. Although he had not broken any rules, Robinson had to undergo a court-martial before clearing his name.

**Main Idea CONNECTIONS**

***What was the principle behind the Supreme Court's ruling in* Brown v. Board of Education*?***

The mental toughness that Robinson acquired from such experiences and his ability to rise above the injustices he encountered served him well during his baseball career. In August 1945, Branch Rickey called Robinson into his office and told the ballplayer of his plan to integrate baseball. Then, in a calculated move to test how Robinson would respond to the pressure he was likely to face, Rickey acted the part of those who might try to discourage him. He roared insults at Robinson and threatened him with violence. "Mr. Rickey," Robinson finally said, "do you want a ballplayer who's afraid to fight back?" Rickey answered, "I want a player with guts enough not to fight back."

Robinson played first for the Montreal Royals, a minor league team, during the 1946 season. Then in 1947 he joined the Brooklyn Dodgers, becoming the first African American to play in the major leagues. Despite many instances of prejudice, Robinson behaved with dignity and had a sparkling first season. He was named Rookie of the Year in 1947. In 1949 he was voted the league's most valuable player. Just as important, Robinson fostered pride in African Americans around the country and opened the way for other African Americans to follow him into professional sports.

## Brown *v.* Board of Education

Perhaps the greatest civil rights victory in the early postwar period took place in the courts. For years the NAACP had tried to get the 1896 *Plessy* v. *Ferguson* decision overturned. That decision held that segregation of the races in public institutions and accommodations was constitutional as long as facilities were "separate but equal." In practice, that was rarely—if ever—the case.

In 1951 Oliver Brown sued the Topeka, Kansas, Board of Education to allow his 8-year-old daughter Linda to attend a school that only white children were allowed to attend. She passed the school on her way to the bus that took her to a distant school for African Americans. After appeals, the case reached the Supreme Court. There a lawyer named Thurgood Marshall argued on behalf of Brown and against segregation in America's schools.

On May 17, 1954, in ***Brown* v. *Board of Education of Topeka, Kansas,*** the Supreme Court issued its historic ruling. It declared unanimously that "separate facilities are inherently unequal." The "separate but equal" doctrine was no longer permissible in public education.† President Eisenhower, who privately disagreed with the *Brown* ruling, said only that "the Supreme Court has spoken and I am sworn to uphold the constitutional processes in this country; I will obey." A year later, the Court ruled that local school boards should move to desegregate "with all deliberate speed."

† The Supreme Court's decision struck down laws in Kansas, Delaware, South Carolina, and Virginia that required or allowed separate schools for blacks and whites.

## The Montgomery Bus Boycott

In 1955 the nation's attention shifted from the courts to the streets of Montgomery, Alabama. In December Rosa Parks, a seamstress who had been secretary of the Montgomery NAACP for 12 years, took a seat in the middle section of a bus, where both African Americans and whites usually were allowed to sit. When a white man got on at the next stop and had no seat, however, the bus driver ordered Parks to give up hers. She refused. Even when threatened with arrest, she held her ground. At the next stop, police seized her and ordered her to stand trial for violating the segregation laws.

Civil rights leaders in Montgomery quickly met and, after Jo Ann Robinson of the Women's Political Council (WPC) suggested the idea, decided to organize the **Montgomery bus boycott.** The plan called for African Americans to refuse to use the entire bus system until the bus company agreed to change its segregation policy. Robinson and other members of the WPC wrote and distributed leaflets announcing the boycott. Martin Luther King, Jr., the 26-year-old minister of the Baptist church where the original boycott meeting took place, eventually became the spokesperson for the protest movement. He proclaimed:

**"There comes a time when people get tired . . . tired of being segregated and humiliated, tired of being kicked about by the brutal feet of oppression. We have no alternative but to protest."**

—*Martin Luther King, Jr.*

The morning of the first day of the boycott, King walked the streets of Montgomery. He was anxious to see how many African Americans would participate. Here are excerpts from his account of that morning:

**"During the rush hours the sidewalks were crowded with laborers and domestic workers, many of them well past middle age, trudging patiently to their jobs and home again, sometimes as much as twelve miles. They knew why they walked, and the knowledge was evident in the way they carried themselves. And as I watched them I knew that there is nothing more majestic than the determined courage of individuals willing to suffer and sacrifice for their freedom and dignity."**

—*Martin Luther King, Jr.*

These participants in the Montgomery bus boycott seemed not to mind getting a little wet as they walked to work. ***Culture* How did the boycott demonstrate the effectiveness of applying economic pressure to promote social change?**

Over the next year, 50,000 African Americans in Montgomery walked, rode bicycles, or joined car pools to avoid the city buses. Despite losing money, the bus company refused to change its policies. Finally, the Supreme Court ruled that bus segregation, like school segregation, was unconstitutional.

The Montgomery bus boycott produced a new generation of leaders in the African American community, particularly Martin Luther King, Jr. In addition, it introduced nonviolent protest as a means of achieving equality for minority groups in the United States.

## Resistance in Little Rock

The protests in Montgomery, as well as the ruling in *Brown* v. *Board of Education,* caused many southern whites to react with fear and angry resistance. The worst confrontation came at Central High School in Little Rock, Arkansas. Just before the start of the 1957 school year, Governor Orval Faubus declared that he could not keep order if he had to enforce **integration,** or the bringing together of different races. He posted Arkansas National Guard troops at the school who turned away nine African American students.

Eisenhower could no longer avoid the issue of segregation. Faubus's actions were a direct

African American students like Elizabeth Ekford of Little Rock, Arkansas, had to endure the insults of white students who disagreed with the Court's *Brown* v. *Board* decision. ***Government* *What finally forced Eisenhower to support desegregation?***

challenge to the Constitution and to his own authority as President. Eisenhower acted by placing the National Guard under federal command. With paratroopers and other soldiers on guard in Arkansas to protect the nine students, the long, slow process of school integration began.

## Other Voices of Protest

African Americans were not the only group to demand equal rights after World War II. Mexican Americans, for instance, also worked for their rights. In one case a funeral home in Texas refused to bury Felix Longoria, a Mexican American war hero. Protests in the Mexican American community over the refusal led to the soldier's burial in Arlington National Cemetery in Washington, D.C. Groups like the Community Service Organization and the Asociación Nacional México-Americana found that peaceful protest could slowly bring about some of the results Mexican Americans desired.

Native Americans faced a unique situation. The federal government managed the reservations where most Native Americans lived in terrible poverty. In 1953, however, the government adopted a new approach, known as "termination," which sought to eliminate reservations altogether. The goal of the policy was to assimilate Native Americans into the mainstream of American life.

Termination met with resistance. In time the federal government discarded the termination policy. Yet the problems of the Native Americans remained: poverty, discrimination, and little real political representation. For Native Americans, the civil rights advances of the 1950s were mere tokens of the real gains that were needed.

## SECTION 4 REVIEW

### Comprehension

1. *Key Terms* Define: (a) *Brown* v. *Board of Education of Topeka, Kansas;* (b) Montgomery bus boycott; (c) integration.
2. *Summarizing the Main Idea* What avenues of protest did civil rights activists use in their struggle?
3. *Organizing Information* Create a flowchart that organizes information about the events that took place in Little Rock, Arkansas.

### Critical Thinking

4. *Analyzing Time Lines* Review the time line at the start of the section. Chose one entry and explain how it was a result of increased demands for equality from African Americans following World War II.
5. *Identifying Central Issues* How did Mexican Americans and Native Americans assert their rights in the 1950s?

### Writing Activity

6. *Writing an Expository Essay* Use information from the section to create a poster that explains the issues in *Brown* v. *Board of Education* or describes the Montgomery bus boycott.

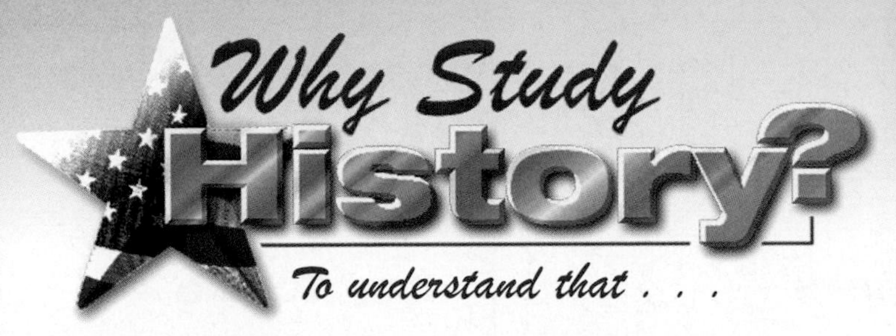


# Health Care Is a Growing Concern

**Providing quality health care, an issue during President Truman's administration, remains an important challenge for the United States.**

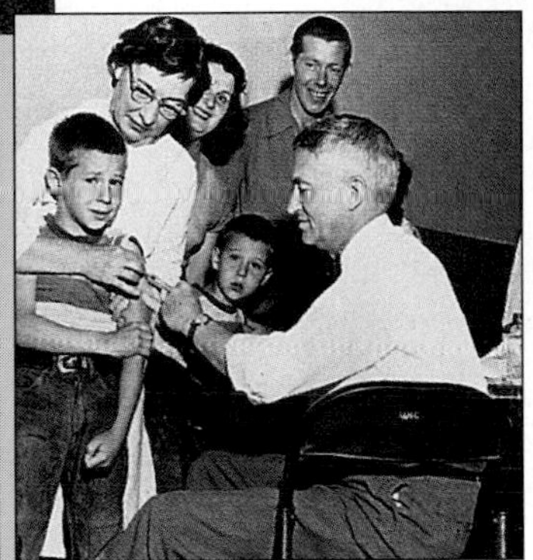
*First polio vaccine is given in 1955*

A house in the suburbs, a two-car garage, a television set, a refrigerator, and a washing machine—these items were a part of the American Dream in the 1950s. Thanks to improvements in medicine, good health care also became available to many more Americans. New operations extended the lives of people with heart disease, for example, and millions of Americans benefited from newly developed antibiotics and other medicines.

## The Impact Today

In 1950, the average life expectancy of Americans was about 67 years. By 2000, it had increased to about 76 years. The change occurred partly from advances in health care and greater access to quality care. In the 1950s and afterward, Americans began to expect better and more affordable health care.

Yet as the demand for health care increased, the costs soared. Between 1960 and 1998, total health care costs in the United States grew from $27 billion to more than $1 trillion. As health care became more expensive, the number of Americans too poor to afford health insurance grew. By 1999 an estimated 43 million Americans lacked health insurance.

For many years, most Americans received health care under insurance plans for which they, or their employers, paid. Traditional "fee for service" insurance allowed individuals to choose their own doctors. It also gave health care providers flexibility in treating patients.

In recent years, efforts to reduce health care costs have prompted the rise of "managed care" plans like health maintenance organizations (HMOs). These organizations seek to "manage" health care closely to keep costs down.

Today roughly 150 million Americans are enrolled in managed-care plans. Many are unhappy with their plans, however. In a 1997 study, three fifths of those surveyed said that managed care causes doctors to spend less time with patients and makes it harder to get specialized care. Only one fourth of the people surveyed believed that managed-care plans make health care more affordable. Thus, many Americans question whether managed care can provide quality care at a lower cost.
Other critics, focusing on the large number of Americans without health insurance, are calling for an effort to provide health care for all Americans.

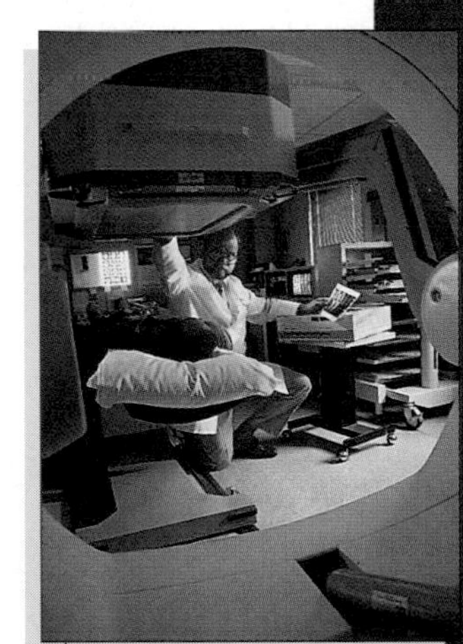
*New medical technology is beneficial but expensive*

## The Impact on You

Ask your parents, grandparents, or other adults what type of health care plans they have. Ask how satisfied they are with their health care and why. Then write three paragraphs giving the pros and cons of each plan.

# Chapter 17 Review

## Chapter Summary

The major concepts of Chapter 17 are presented below. See also ***Guide to the Essentials of American History*** or ***Interactive Student Tutorial CD-ROM,*** which contains interactive review activities, time lines, helpful hints, and test practice.

### *Reviewing the Main Ideas*

Americans had dreamed of peace and prosperity through 16 grueling years of economic depression and world war. After the war, they embraced a wide array of technological developments that promised to make their lives easier, and they relished the chance to live more comfortably than their parents had. Minorities began to speak more loudly for equality of civil rights.

### *Section 1: The Postwar Economy*

The American Dream, characterized by a home in the suburbs and a car in the garage, came true for many people in the postwar years.

### *Section 2: The Mood of the 1950s*

After World War II, many Americans were blessed with wealth, success, and leisure. Conformity seemed the order of the day, although some groups made it their business to avoid the popularly accepted lifestyles of the 1950s.

### *Section 3: Domestic Politics and Policy*

Presidents Harry S. Truman and Dwight D. Eisenhower used two very different styles of leadership to meet the challenges they faced during the postwar period.

### *Section 4: Demands for Civil Rights*

Following World War II, African Americans began to push harder in the civil rights movement and brought about significant results.

Providing quality health care, an issue during Harry Truman's administration, remains an important challenge for the United States. Yet as the demand for care increases, the costs also soar.

## Key Terms

Use each of the terms below in a sentence that shows how it relates to the chapter.

1. Taft-Hartley Act
2. conglomerate
3. GI Bill
4. beatnik
5. integration
6. baby boom
7. modern republicanism
8. rock and roll
9. National Defense Education Act
10. Montgomery bus boycott

## Comprehension

1. How did the conglomerate and the franchise system change the American economy after World War II?
2. What factors contributed to suburban development from 1945 to 1960?
3. Give examples showing how the media fostered expectations about the proper role of women.
4. What challenges to the rigid expectations of the period arose in the 1950s?
5. What problem did Harry Truman face as the nation converted to a peacetime economy after World War II?
6. What were Dwight Eisenhower's goals for the presidency? How successful was he in achieving these goals?
7. How did African Americans use the courts and nonviolent protest in their battle for equality?

## Using Graphic Organizers

On a separate sheet of paper, copy the web diagram to organize information about the culture and politics of postwar America. Provide at least six supporting details in the surrounding circles.

## Analyzing Political Cartoons ▶

1. A cartoonist drew this view of suburban life in 1952. (a) What is most striking about this community? (b) What do you know about such communities?
2. Read the caption. What is the cause of the woman's dilemma?
3. What is the cartoonist saying about life in a 1950s suburb?

*"I'm Mrs. Edward M. Barnes. Where do I live?"*

## Critical Thinking

1. ***Applying the Chapter Skill*** Review the Evaluating Magazine Advertisements skill on page 522. Find an advertisement in a modern magazine that shows a family and evaluate it to see if it reveals information about life in the United States today.
2. ***Recognizing Cause and Effect*** In what ways did the Depression and World War II contribute to the postwar economic boom of the 1950s?
3. ***Demonstrating Reasoned Judgment*** Which technological advance of the 1950s—atomic energy, computers, or television—do you think has had the most far-reaching impact on the way Americans live? Explain why you think so.
4. ***Identifying Central Issues*** What was the principle behind the Supreme Court's ruling in *Brown* v. *Board of Education*?

### INTERNET ACTIVITY

***For your portfolio:***
**CREATE A DIARY ENTRY**

Access Prentice Hall's *America: Pathways to the Present* site at **www.Pathways.phschool.com** for the specific URL to complete the activity. Additional resources and related Web sites are also available.

Follow the links to learn about Harry S. Truman by looking at the photographs and reading some of his campaign speeches. Then write a diary entry from Truman's point of view about life during the 1948 campaign. What issues was Truman concerned about? How did people respond to Truman?

### ANALYZING DOCUMENTS ▶ INTERPRETING DATA

Turn to the "Birth Rate, 1930–1960" graph on page 514.

1. After what year did the birth rate rise higher than its 1930 level? (a) 1940 (b) 1945 (c) 1955 (d) 1960
2. According to the graph, the birth rate was the lowest in (a) 1930. (b) 1935. (c) 1945. (d) 1960.
3. ***Writing*** Research and write a brief essay describing the impact of the baby boom generation on American culture.

## Connecting to Today

***Essay Writing*** Reread the section on pages 519–520 that describes the *Life* photo essay. Then write the text for a *Life* photo essay about a working mother's life today. Include activities from a typical working mother's day.

# American Heritage®

# My Brush with History

BY ROBERT RODDEWIG

***INTRODUCTION*** In the passage below, Robert Roddewig, a sailor on the battleship U.S.S. *Missouri* in the final months of World War II, describes a terrifying experience in the waters near Japan. As you read, think about the responsibilities that Roddewig had despite his young age.

*The year was 1945.* As an eighteen-year-old eligible for the draft, I had enlisted in the Navy before graduation from high school in Davenport, Iowa. After boot camp and radio school, at Farragut, Idaho, I was assigned to the staff of Adm. William F. "Bull" Halsey aboard the *Missouri,* an *Iowa*-class battleship.

I felt honored to pull duty as a staff member with a four-star admiral. Halsey usually selected the *New Jersey,* another *Iowa*-class ship, but the *Jersey* had steamed stateside for some badly needed maintenance and repair. The *Missouri* got the call.

Battleship "Missouri"

*Launched in 1944, the* Missouri *was nearly 900 feet long and had a crew of 1,900.*

There were seven radio transmitting-and-receiving stations aboard the *Missouri,* and I usually spent my four hours handling routine communications among ships of the fleet. I had been onboard several weeks and had not even seen the admiral. Then I was transferred to the radio station just behind the ship's bridge. I would be copying coded messages from several military shore stations. When decoded, these transmissions would help our meteorologists map weather conditions over possible Japanese bombing targets. I quickly came to realize the importance of my work. The safety of our carrier pilots might well depend upon the accuracy and thoroughness of the radiomen on duty behind the bridge.

To obtain weather information I usually copied station NPG Honolulu or an Army station from Andrews Air Force Base on Guam. These were clear stations with little interference of any kind. But station KCT from Vladivostok, U.S.S.R., was different.

If our planes were to raid the Japanese islands of Hokkaidō or Honshū, we needed the weather report from KCT. The Japanese, knowing this, constantly jammed the KCT frequency with music, loud laughter, foreign languages—anything and everything to drown out the signal. It required keen concentration to find our signal and stay on it while totally ignoring all the "trash."

One evening I was copying KCT with the usual Japanese garbage jamming my frequency. I had my eyes closed, and I was concentrating totally on that faint but distinctive signal: Dit dah dit. I automatically hit the R key on the typewriter (or mill, as the Navy called it). Dah dit dit dit, B. Dit dit dit, S.

Then a loud voice behind me asked, "Are they jamming our station?"

"Yes, sir," I replied, my concentration broken. I hit the space bar of the mill several times to indicate missed letters. I found the signal once again.

"Are you able to copy it?" The voice again. I hit the space bar several more times before finding my signal once more. "Will you be able to get enough for us?" And the space-bar routine again. But this time I blurted out, "Shut up!"

When the transmission was complete, I pulled the message from my machine. Wondering if the blank spaces would ruin our mapmaking effort, I turned in my seat—and looked up at four stars on each lapel of a brown shirt. I had just met Admiral Halsey.

Oh my …, I thought. I was an insignificant radioman, third class, and I had told an admiral to shut up.

At nineteen years my life would end. I would be fortunate to get a court-martial for insubordination along with a dishonorable discharge from the Navy.

"Sir, are you the one I told to 'shut up'?"

This tough-looking admiral was standing there with arms folded and legs apart in a mild inverted Y, brown naval field cap pulled to his brow, jaw jutting menacingly with lips pressed firmly together. I could see now why they called him Bull Halsey.

"Yes, lad," he blared.

"I apologize, sir. I did not know it was you. I have no excuse, sir."

The admiral broke his stance and began to pace the floor. "Lad," he bellowed, "when I come into this radio shack and speak to you while you are on that radio, you do not tell me to shut up! Do you understand?"

His voice boomed like the nine 16-inch guns attached to the ship's three main turrets.

"Yes, sir, I understand." I was frozen at attention and, I am certain, tears were welling in my eyes.

Then, stopping in front of me and looking me straight in the eye, he went on in a very calm and friendly voice. "If I or anyone else ever bothers you while you are on that radio, you do not tell them to shut up. What you tell them is to stay out of here and that's an order. Do you understand, lad?"

I could only look at him and stammer, "Yes, sir."

We saluted. Admiral Halsey went on his way. I never met him again.

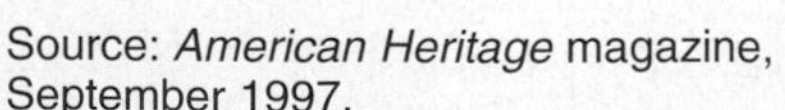
Source: *American Heritage* magazine, September 1997.

*General Douglas MacArthur called Admiral Halsey the "greatest fighting admiral" of World War II.*

## ADDITIONAL READING

**To learn more about the topics discussed in this selection, you might want to read the following books:**

- *Battleship Missouri,* by Valerie Drogues (New York: Crestwood House, 1994)
- *Combined Fleet Decoded: The Secret Story of American Intelligence and the Japanese Navy During World War II,* by John Prados (New York: Random House, 1995)
- *Eagle Against the Sun: The American War with Japan,* by Ronald H. Spector (New York: Free Press, 1985)
- *The Two-Ocean War: A Short History of the United States Navy in the Second World War,* by Samuel Eliot Morison (Boston: Little, Brown, 1963)

unit FIVE

# The Upheaval of the Sixties

## 1960–1975

*When John F. Kennedy became President in 1961, many Americans felt a sense of optimism. Buoyed by the promise of change, African Americans pushed hard to claim their civil rights. The civil rights movement also inspired women, Latinos, Native Americans, and others to seek equality. Although great strides were made in the 1960s, the hope that began this turbulent decade was shattered by a series of assassinations, a wave of urban riots, and a controversial war in Southeast Asia.*



### UNIT THEMES

**Government** President Lyndon Johnson pushed through Congress the most ambitious social program since FDR's New Deal.

**Culture** A mood of change and protest characterized the 1960s.

**Foreign Relations** Attempts to stop the spread of communism led to costly foreign entanglements.

**EVENTS IN THE UNITED STATES**

**1962** *Cuban missile crisis*

**1963** *President Kennedy assassinated*

**1964** Turning Point: *Civil Rights Act* *(p. 577)*

**1966** *National Organization for Women formed*

**1968** *Martin Luther King, Jr., assassinated*

Presidents | Kennedy | Johnson

**1960** **1965**

**EVENTS IN THE WORLD**

**1961** *Berlin wall built*

**1963** *South Vietnam leader Diem assassinated*

**1966** *Chinese Cultural Revolution*

**1967** *Six-Day War in Middle East*

**1968** *Tet Offensive in Vietnam*

**VIEWING HISTORY** Civil rights workers march toward a better future in this 1965 voter registration drive in Selma, Alabama. ***Culture*** ***Why were such public demonstrations so successful in bringing about change?***

**1970**
*Environmental Protection Agency established*

**1972**
*Gloria Steinem founds MS. magazine*

**1973**
- *Vietnam peace agreement signed*
- *Roe v. Wade decision*

Nixon

**1970** — **1975**

**1971**
*India and Pakistan go to war*

**1972**
*Martial law declared in Philippines*

**1975**
*Fall of South Vietnam*

*1969 Woodstock music festival poster*

# CHAPTER 18 The Kennedy and Johnson Years

## 1961–1969

### CHAPTER FOCUS

*A spirit of optimism energized the United States during the early 1960s. John F. Kennedy, the youngest President ever elected, focused on cold war politics. His successor, Lyndon B. Johnson, rallied the Congress and the country behind the most ambitious social program since the New Deal of the 1930s.*

*The **Why Study History?** page at the end of this chapter explores the connection between government assistance to the poor during the Kennedy and Johnson years and today.*

▲ **VIEWING HISTORY**
President John F. Kennedy delivers an inspiring address at his inauguration.
***Government*** ***What were Kennedy's plans for the country?***

| 1960 | 1961 | 1962 | 1962 | 1963 |
|---|---|---|---|---|
| John F. Kennedy elected President | Alan Shepard becomes first American to travel in space | John Glenn becomes first American to orbit Earth | Michael Harrington publishes *The Other America* | President Kennedy assassinated |

1960 — 1962 — 1964

# 1 The New Frontier

## SECTION PREVIEW

### Objectives

1 Describe the election of 1960 and its outcome.
2 Summarize Kennedy's domestic programs.
3 Explain Americans' reaction to President Kennedy's assassination.
4 *Key Terms* Define: mandate; New Frontier; Warren Commission.

### Main Idea

Before his assassination in 1963, President John F. Kennedy proposed a number of domestic programs to improve the economy and to address issues of inequality, including poverty and civil rights. Most of Kennedy's proposals were defeated in Congress.

### Reading Strategy

*Reinforcing Main Ideas* As you read the section, create a list of the programs that Kennedy proposed.

On September 26, 1960, millions of Americans turned on their televisions to watch as two presidential candidates squared off in the country's first televised debate. The two candidates were Republican Richard Nixon (Eisenhower's Vice President) and Democrat John F. Kennedy. With studio lights glaring, Nixon appeared tired and hot. Kennedy, in contrast, looked polished and relaxed. He had hired consultants to help him with makeup and clothes. This debate and the three that followed had a major impact on the outcome of the election. The debates also changed forever the role that television would play in American politics.

## The Election of 1960

Kennedy, a Massachusetts Democrat who had served in the United States House of Representatives and Senate, faced serious obstacles in his quest for the presidency. He was only forty-three years old, and many questioned whether he had the experience needed for the nation's highest office. In addition, Kennedy was a Roman Catholic, and no Catholic had ever been elected President. Kennedy put an end to the religion issue when he won the primary in the largely Protestant state of West Virginia. With that hurdle behind him, he campaigned hard, with promises to spur the sluggish economy.

During the last years of the Eisenhower administration, the Gross National Product (GNP) had grown very slowly. In addition, the economy had suffered several recessions. During the campaign, Kennedy proclaimed that it was time to "get America moving again."

In the election, Kennedy won by an extraordinarily close margin.† Though the electoral vote was 303 to 219, Kennedy won by only 120,000 popular votes out of more than 34 million cast. If but a few thousand voters in Illinois or Texas had cast ballots for Nixon, the Republicans would have won. As a result of

† Although the youngest person ever to be elected President, Kennedy was not the youngest ever to hold the office. Theodore Roosevelt, who became President when McKinley was assassinated, was the youngest to hold the office.

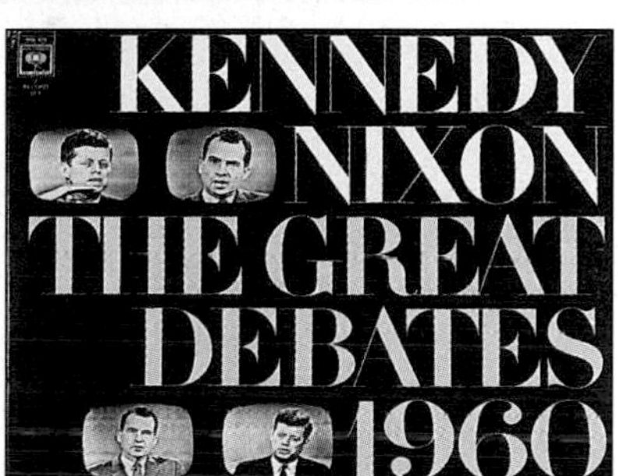


*Presidential candidates Richard Nixon and John F. Kennedy squared off in a series of televised debates in 1960.*

Jacqueline and John F. Kennedy dazzled the nation with their beauty, youth, and glamour. ***Government Why was Kennedy's administration later nicknamed Camelot?***

this razor-thin victory, Kennedy entered office without a strong **mandate.** A mandate is a set of wishes expressed to a candidate by his or her voters. Without such a mandate, Kennedy would have difficulty pushing his more controversial measures through Congress.

No matter how slim his margin of victory, Kennedy was now President. In ringing phrases he declared in his Inaugural Address:

KEY DOCUMENTS

**"Let the word go forth from this time and place, to friend and foe alike, that the torch has been passed to a new generation of Americans, born in this century, tempered by war, disciplined by a hard and bitter peace. . . . And so, my fellow Americans, ask not what your country can do for you; ask what you can do for your country."**

—*John F. Kennedy,* Inaugural Address

The new administration was buoyant, energetic, and full of optimism. Jacqueline Kennedy, the President's wife, charmed the country with her grace. Nobel Prize winners visited the White House. The Kennedys and their friends loved to play touch football on the lawn or take long hikes.

The administration, which seemed full of idealism and youth, later earned the nickname "Camelot" after a 1960 Broadway musical. The musical portrayed the legendary kingdom of the British King Arthur. Arthur dreamed of transforming medieval Britain from a country in which "might makes right," or the strong always get their way, into one where power would be used to achieve right.

## *Kennedy's Domestic Programs*

In a speech early in his administration, Kennedy said that the nation was poised at the edge of a **New Frontier.** The name stuck and was used to describe Kennedy's proposals to improve the economy, give aid to the poor, and breathe new life into the space program.

**The Economy** Concerned about the continuing recession, Kennedy hoped to work with the business community to restore prosperity to the nation. Often, however, he faced resistance from executives who were suspicious of his plans. The worst fears of business leaders were realized in the spring of 1962. When the U.S. Steel Company announced that it was raising the price of steel by $6 a ton, other firms did the same. Worried about inflation, Kennedy called the price increase unjustifiable and charged that it showed "utter contempt for the public interest." He ordered a federal investigation into the possibility of price-fixing. Under that pressure, U.S. Steel and the other companies backed down. Business leaders remained angry, and the stock market fell in the steepest drop since the Great Crash of 1929.

On the larger issue of ending the economic slump, Kennedy proposed cutting taxes. In 1963 the President called for a $13.5 billion cut in taxes over three years. The measure would reduce government income and create a budget deficit at first. Kennedy believed, however, that the extra cash in taxpayers' wallets would stimulate the economy and bring added tax revenues in the end. The tax-cut proposal was soon bottled up in a congressional committee and stood little chance of passage.

**Combating Poverty and Inequality** Kennedy also was eager to take action against poverty and inequality. In his first two years in office, Kennedy hoped that he could help the poor simply by stimulating the economy. In 1962 author Michael Harrington described the situation of the poor in his book, *The Other America.* Harrington's book revealed that while many Americans were enjoying the prosperity of the

1950s, a shocking one fifth of the population was living below the poverty line. Kennedy began to believe that direct aid to the poor was necessary.

Despite his concern, Kennedy rarely succeeded in pushing legislation through Congress. Kennedy's ambitious plans for federal aid for education and medical care for the aged both failed. Kennedy did succeed, however, in raising the minimum wage and passing the Housing Act of 1961. This act provided $4.9 billion for urban renewal. Congress also approved the Twenty-Fourth Amendment to go to the states for ratification. This amendment outlawed the poll tax, which was still being used in five southern states to keep poor African Americans from voting.

**The Space Program** Kennedy was more successful in his effort to breathe life into the space program. Following the Soviet Union's launch of *Sputnik* in 1957, numerous government agencies and industries had been working furiously with NASA, the National Aeronautics and Space Agency, to place a manned spacecraft in orbit around Earth. As part of the Mercury program, seven test pilots were chosen to train as astronauts in 1959. Government spending and the future of NASA seemed uncertain, however, when a task force appointed by Kennedy recommended that NASA concentrate on exploratory space missions without human crews.

All of this changed in April 1961. The Soviet Union announced that Yuri Gagarin had become the first human to travel in space and had circled Earth on board the Soviet spacecraft *Vostok*. Gagarin's flight rekindled Americans' fears that the United States was falling behind the Soviet Union.

Twenty-three days later, on May 5, 1961, the United States made its own first attempt to send a person into space. Astronaut Alan Shepard made a 15-minute suborbital flight that reached an altitude of 115 miles. Though this flight did not match the orbital flight of the Soviets, its success did convince Kennedy to move forward. On May 25, Kennedy issued a bold challenge to the nation. He said the United States "should commit itself to achieving the goal, before this decade is out, of landing a man on the moon."†

Both the nation and the government accepted the challenge, and funding for NASA was increased. Less than a year later, on February 20, 1962, John Glenn successfully completed three orbits around Earth and landed in the Atlantic Ocean near the Bahamas. Later that year Kennedy spoke at Rice University in Houston, Texas:

**Federal Funding of NASA, 1950–1965**

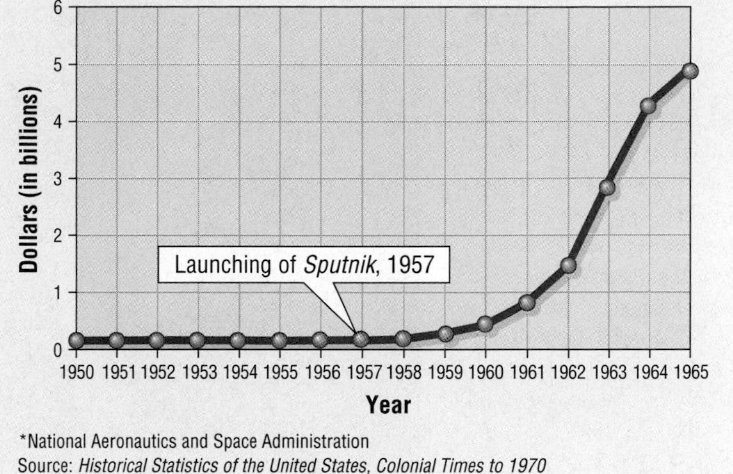


*National Aeronautics and Space Administration
Source: *Historical Statistics of the United States, Colonial Times to 1970*

**Interpreting Graphs** NASA grew out of the National Advisory Committee for Aeronautics, which was established in 1915. Alarmed by the launching of *Sputnik*, in 1958 Congress authorized the new federal agency to promote the research and development of air and space. ***Economics*** ***How does the graph illustrate the influence of the Soviet Union's* Sputnik *on United States policy?***

**Main Idea CONNECTIONS**

***Why did Kennedy's space program succeed while most of his other domestic programs did not?***

**AMERICAN VOICES** **"We set sail on this new sea because there is new knowledge to be gained, and new rights to be won, and they must be won and used for the progress of all people. . . . [O]nly if the United States occupies a position of preeminence can we help decide whether this new ocean will be a sea of peace or a new, terrifying theater of war."**

—*John F. Kennedy*

## Kennedy Is Assassinated

On November 22, 1963, as Kennedy looked ahead to reelection the following year, he traveled to Texas to mobilize support. Texas Governor John Connally and his wife Nelly met Kennedy and his wife at the airport in Dallas. Together they rode through the streets of Dallas in an open limousine. Thousands of supporters lined the route of the motorcade. Suddenly shots rang and bullets struck both Connally and the President. While Connally

† For the remainder of the decade, succeeding NASA flights brought the country closer and closer to its goal. On July 20, 1969, United States astronaut Neil Armstrong became the first person to set foot on the moon.

A sad and solemn-looking Lyndon Johnson is sworn in as President aboard Air Force One shortly after President Kennedy's assassination. A grief-stricken Jacqueline Kennedy (right) looks on. ***Culture*** *What was the nation's reaction to Kennedy's death?*

was only wounded, President Kennedy was pronounced dead soon after his arrival at a nearby hospital. The country was shattered. Millions of Americans remained glued to their television sets for the next four days as the impact of the tragedy sank in.

Shortly after Kennedy's death, a commission headed by Chief Justice Earl Warren was formed to investigate the crime. The prime suspect in Kennedy's assassination was Lee Harvey Oswald, a former marine and supporter of Cuba's Fidel Castro. Two days after Kennedy's assassination, Oswald was transferred from one jail to another. While the nation watched on television, Dallas nightclub owner Jack Ruby stepped through the crowd of reporters and fatally shot Oswald. After months of investigation, the **Warren Commission** declared that Oswald had worked alone in shooting the President. Since then, however, some people have argued that Oswald was involved in a larger conspiracy, and that he was killed in order to protect others who had helped plan Kennedy's murder.

Lyndon Johnson, who had also traveled to Dallas with Kennedy, took the presidential oath of office on board Air Force One just ninety minutes after Kennedy's death. Johnson went on to make good use of the spirit of hope and the desire for change that Kennedy had inspired. He saw enacted much of the legislation that his predecessor had tried to push through Congress.

## SECTION 1 REVIEW

### Comprehension

1. *Key Terms* Define: (a) mandate; (b) New Frontier; (c) Warren Commission.
2. *Summarizing the Main Idea* What were some of the successes and failures of Kennedy's domestic policies?
3. *Organizing Information* Create a time line of the major events in the space program between 1959 and 1962.

### Critical Thinking

4. *Analyzing Time Lines* Review the time line at the start of the section. How did President Kennedy respond to Michael Harrington's book, *The Other America?*
5. *Drawing Inferences* Why was the Kennedy administration nicknamed "Camelot"? How did the dream of Camelot end?

### Writing Activity

6. *Writing an Expository Essay* Write an essay describing the role of television in the election of 1960 and its role today.

# SKILLS FOR LIFE

**Historical Evidence**

Critical Thinking

Geography

Graphs and Charts

## Exploring Oral History

Oral history is made up of people's verbal accounts and recollections of former times and events. As historical evidence, it is one of the oldest and most universal methods by which people have acquired information about the past.

Today, historians preserve oral history by interviewing people and recording their words on audio- or videotape or in written transcripts. Historians may gather oral history at the time an event takes place or at some later date, perhaps years or even decades later.

Historians often seek out oral histories because they give a unique perspective on the past. Oral histories are a type of primary source and therefore are more valuable to historians than secondary sources. Oral histories record not only facts about the past, but also people's opinions, feelings, and impressions—all important to a historian in putting together a picture of the past.

The excerpt at right is taken from a 1983 interview with John Lewis, an Atlanta city council member, on the twentieth anniversary of President Kennedy's death. In 1963 Lewis was chairperson of the Student Nonviolent Coordinating Committee and one of the leaders of the civil rights March on Washington.

Read the oral account at right and then use the following steps to analyze its content.

**1.** ***Identify the nature of the oral account.*** (a) Who was interviewed? (b) When did the interview take place? (c) What was Lewis's attitude toward Kennedy at the time of his death? (d) Did that attitude change in any way over time?

**2.** ***Determine the reliability of the evidence.*** (a) How might Lewis's role in the events being recollected affect his interpretation of those events? (b) How might events after Kennedy's death have affected the account? (c) What do Lewis's views reveal about his political perspective?

**3.** ***Study the evidence to learn more about the historical event.*** (a) What impact does Lewis think Kennedy's presidency had on government policy and the nation? (b) What can you learn about Kennedy's presidency from Lewis's account?

**TEST FOR SUCCESS**

Why must historians be cautious when using oral history accounts as resources?

### An Interview with John Lewis: Remembering President Kennedy's Assassination

"I was living in Atlanta then, but I had gone back to Nashville for a trial. I was getting into a car to go to the Nashville airport when I heard it on the radio. And to me, it was the saddest moment in my life. I had grown up to love and to admire President Kennedy. I remember crying on the plane.

I saw him as a sort of guy that listened. Sincere. Caring. People argue and say that he didn't really do anything. But he did listen, and during that period from 1961 to 1963, I'll tell you, I think probably for the first time in modern American history, we felt, "Well, we have a friend in the White House." On some things we disagreed. We'd call them up and argue and debate with them on some issue, and we said a lot of different things, and sometimes it was harsh. But we saw the Kennedy administration during that period as a sympathetic referee in the whole struggle for civil rights.

His campaign had created a sense of hope, a sense of optimism for many of us. When someone asked him about the civil rights sit-ins that year, he said, 'By sitting down, these young people are standing up for the very best in American tradition.'"

—*Newsweek,* November 28, 1983

| 1962 | 1963 Johnson becomes President | 1964 Johnson elected President | 1965 Immigration Act of 1965 | 1966 Miranda v. Arizona |
|---|---|---|---|---|

# 2 The Great Society

**SECTION PREVIEW**

**Objectives**

1. Describe Johnson's path to the White House.
2. List some of the programs and effects of Johnson's Great Society.
3. Identify some of the landmark cases handed down by the Supreme Court under Chief Justice Earl Warren.
4. *Key Terms* Define: Great Society; Volunteers in Service to America (VISTA); Medicare; Medicaid; Immigration Act of 1965; Miranda rule; apportionment.

**Main Idea**

The goals of Johnson's Great Society program were to improve the economy, education, and the environment, as well as to offer government assistance to the poor.

**Reading Strategy**

*Organizing Information* As you read, create a chart describing the key elements of Johnson's Great Society program.

*Lyndon Johnson used his forceful personality to forge a Great Society.*

Speaking to the nation for the first time after John F. Kennedy's death, President Johnson expressed his grief at the loss. "All I have," he declared in this address, "I would have given gladly not to be standing here today." He went on to convey his determination to carry on where the slain President had left off. Johnson's theme was "Let us continue." Once in office, he used all the talents he had developed as Senate Majority Leader to push through Congress an extraordinary program of reforms on domestic issues.

## LBJ's Path to the White House

Lyndon B. Johnson arrived in the United States House of Representatives in 1937 as a New Deal Democrat from Texas. In 1948 he won a seat in the Senate, but only by a tiny margin of 87 votes. He was promptly dubbed "Landslide Lyndon"—a nickname that stuck for the rest of his career. In the Senate, Johnson demonstrated both his talent and his ambition by winning leadership posts. In the six years from 1954 to 1960, he became famous for his ability to work within the political system to accomplish his goals.

When Johnson's bid for the Democratic nomination failed in 1960, he accepted Kennedy's invitation to run for the vice presidency. Once elected, however, Johnson was frustrated with the powerlessness of the office. He was also unhappy being away from Congress, where he had been so effective. Then came the assassination, and suddenly he was President.

## Building the Great Society

Like LBJ, Congress was aware that the American people needed some action that would heal the wound caused by the loss of their President. Swift passage of Kennedy's civil rights (see the next chapter) and tax-cut bills followed. Soon Johnson branched out and sought laws to aid public education, provide medical care for the elderly, and eliminate poverty. By the spring of 1964, he had begun to use the phrase ***Great Society*** to describe his goals. In a speech at the University of Michigan in May 1964, he told students:

AMERICAN VOICES **"Your imagination, your initiative, and your indignation will determine whether we build a society where progress is the servant of our needs, or a society where old values and new visions are buried under unbridled [unrestrained] growth. For in your time we have the opportunity to move not only toward the rich society and the powerful society, but upward toward the Great Society."**

—*Lyndon B. Johnson*

**The Election of 1964** Johnson's early successes paved the way to a true landslide victory over Republican Barry Goldwater in the election of 1964. Goldwater, a senator from Arizona, held conservative views that seemed radical to many Americans. For example, he opposed civil rights legislation, and he believed that military commanders should be allowed to use nuclear bombs as they saw fit on the battlefield. The Johnson campaign took advantage of voters' fears of nuclear war. They aired a television commercial in which a little girl's innocent counting game turned into the countdown for a nuclear explosion. Johnson received 61 percent of the popular vote and an overwhelming 486 to 52 tally in the Electoral College. Democratic majorities were established in both houses of Congress: 295 Democrats to 140 Republicans in the House of Representatives and 68 to 32 in the Senate. Landslide Lyndon now had the mandate to move ahead even more aggressively.

**The Tax Cut** Like Kennedy, Johnson believed that a budget deficit could be used to improve the economy. Not everyone agreed. To gain conservatives' support for Kennedy's tax-cut bill, which was likely to bring about a deficit, Johnson also agreed to cut government spending. Once that was done, the measure passed and worked just as planned. When the tax cut went into effect, the Gross National Product (GNP) rose 7.1 percent in 1964, 8.1 percent in 1965, and 9.5 percent in 1966. The deficit, which many people feared would grow, actually shrank. This was because the revival of prosperity generated new tax revenues. Unemployment fell, and inflation remained in check.

**The War on Poverty** Next, LBJ pressed for the antipoverty program that Kennedy had begun to consider. In his 1964 State of the Union message Johnson vowed, "This administration today, here and now, declares unconditional war on poverty in America." The Economic Opportunity Act, passed in the summer of 1964, was created to combat several causes of poverty including illiteracy, unemployment, and inadequate public services. Almost $950 million was set aside to fund 10 separate programs, including work training programs and **Volunteers in Service to America (VISTA).** VISTA sent volunteers to help people in poor communities. The act also gave the poor a voice in defining housing, health, and education policies in their own neighborhoods.

**Main Idea CONNECTIONS**

*What was the Economic Opportunity Act of 1964?*

**Aid to Education** Johnson was equally successful in his effort to provide funds for education. He endorsed the Elementary and Secondary Education Act to provide aid to states based on the number of children from low-income homes. That money, totalling $1.3 billion, would be distributed to public as well as private schools, including parochial schools. When the Education Act was passed, Johnson signed it into law in the small Texas school he had attended as a child. The graph below shows federal aid to schools from 1959 to 1972.

**Federal Dollars to Public Schools, 1959–1972**

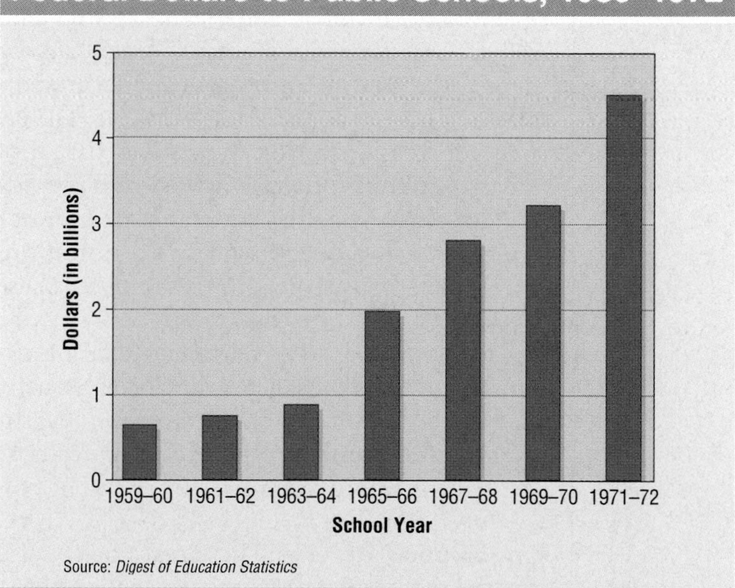


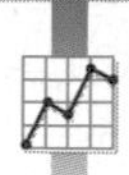

**Interpreting Graphs** Congress passed President Johnson's Elementary and Secondary Education Act in 1965. ***Economics How does the graph illustrate the overall effect of this legislation?***

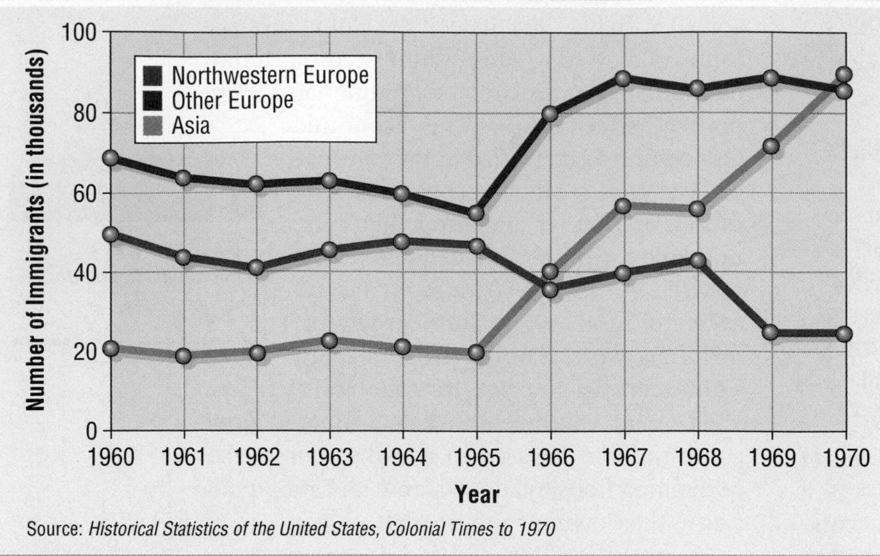

**Interpreting Graphs** Congress eased the strict restrictions on immigration with the more generous Immigration Act of 1965. ***Diversity** On which group of immigrants did this legislation have the greatest effect?*

**Medicare and Medicaid** Johnson also focused attention on the increasing cost of medical care. Twenty years before, Harry Truman had proposed a medical assistance plan as part of his Fair Deal program. It had never been passed into law. Johnson used his leadership skills to push two new programs through Congress, Medicare and Medicaid. **Medicare** provided hospital and low-cost medical insurance for most Americans age 65 and older. "No longer will older Americans be denied the healing miracle of modern medicine," Johnson declared. "No longer will illness crush and destroy the savings that they have so carefully put away." **Medicaid** provided low-cost health insurance for poor Americans of any age who could not afford their own private health insurance. These broad-based health care programs were the most important pieces of social welfare legislation since the passage of the Social Security Act in 1935. They demonstrated the government's commitment to provide help to those Americans who needed it.

**Immigration Reform** The Great Society also revised the immigration policies that had been in place since the 1920s. The immigration laws passed in 1921 and 1924 had set quotas, or numerical limits, for each foreign nation. The laws set low quotas for immigrants from southern and eastern Europe and banned Asian immigration altogether. The **Immigration Act of 1965** eliminated the quotas for individual countries and replaced them with more flexible limits. These included 170,000 people from the Eastern Hemisphere and 120,000 from the Western Hemisphere.† Family members of United States citizens were exempted from the quotas, as were political refugees. In the 1960s approximately 350,000 immigrants entered the United States each year; in the 1970s the number rose to more than 400,000 a year.

## *Earl Warren*

Earl Warren earned his law degree at the University of California, Berkeley, and went on to serve as district attorney and then attorney general in California. While serving as the governor of that state, Warren ran as the Republican candidate for Vice President in 1948. Warren left his office as governor of California when he was appointed Chief Justice of the United States by President Eisenhower in 1953. Warren served as Chief Justice until he retired in 1969.

Under Earl Warren, the Supreme Court took action to overturn many old laws and court rulings and to establish new legal precedents. For example, just one year after Warren's appointment, the Court outlawed segregation in public schools with its decision in *Brown* v. *Board of Education* (1954). (See the previous chapter.) In 1965 the Court struck down a Connecticut law that prohibited the use of birth control. In another area, the Court ruled that religious prayer in public schools was unconstitutional according to the First Amendment principle of separation of church and state. In yet another significant decision, the Court decreed that obscenity laws could not restrict material that might have some "redeeming social value." Many of the Court's other far-reaching decisions were made in the areas of criminal procedure and legislative apportionment.

† The 1965 law did place a maximum of 20,000 immigrants from any one country.

**Criminal Procedure** Earl Warren and other members of the Supreme Court were concerned with safeguarding the constitutional rights of the individual against the power of the state. In particular, the Warren Court handed down several decisions protecting the rights of persons accused of crimes.

The case of *Mapp* v. *Ohio* (1961) established the exclusionary rule, which stated that evidence seized illegally could not be used in a trial. The court's decision in *Gideon* v. *Wainwright* (1963) ruled that suspects in criminal cases who could not afford a lawyer had the right to free legal aid. In the case of *Escobedo* v. *Illinois* (1964), the justices stated that accused individuals had to be given access to an attorney while being questioned.

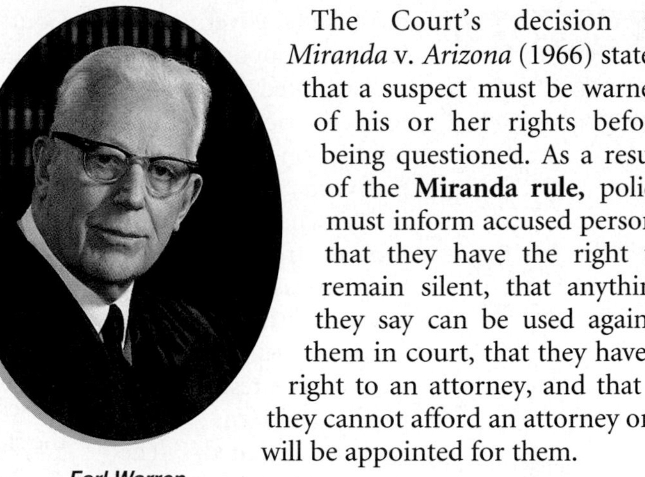

*Earl Warren (1891–1974)*

The Court's decision in *Miranda* v. *Arizona* (1966) stated that a suspect must be warned of his or her rights before being questioned. As a result of the **Miranda rule,** police must inform accused persons that they have the right to remain silent, that anything they say can be used against them in court, that they have a right to an attorney, and that if they cannot afford an attorney one will be appointed for them.

**Congressional Reapportionment** The Warren Court also handed down a series of decisions having to do with **apportionment,** or the distribution of a legislative body's seats among electoral districts. At the time that Warren came to the Court,

## FACT Finder: Great Society Legislation, 1964–1966

| *Legislation* | *Purpose* |
|---|---|
| Economic Opportunity Act, 1964 | Created to combat causes of poverty such as illiteracy and unemployment. |
| Volunteers in Service to America (VISTA), 1964 | Sent volunteers to help people in poor communities and set up community action programs to give the poor a voice in defining local housing, health, and education policies. |
| Medicare, 1965 | Provided hospital and low-cost medical insurance for most Americans age 65 and older. |
| Medicaid, 1965 | Provided low-cost health insurance for poor Americans of any age who could not afford their own private health insurance. |
| Elementary and Secondary Education Act of 1965 | Provided education aid to states based on the number of children from low-income homes. |
| Immigration Act of 1965 | Eliminated strict quotas for individual countries and replaced them with more flexible limits. |
| The Department of Housing and Urban Development (HUD), 1965 | Established to oversee the nation's housing needs and to develop and rehabilitate urban communities. HUD also provided money for rent supplements and low-income housing. |
| The National Foundation of the Arts and Humanities, 1965 | Offered grants to artists and scholars. |
| Water Quality Act, 1965; Clean Water Restoration Act, 1966 | Brought about water and air quality standards and provided funding for environmental research. |
| The National Traffic and Motor Vehicle Safety Act, 1966 | Established safety standards for all vehicles to protect consumers. |

**Interpreting Tables** Great Society legislation addressed a wide range of topics. ***Economics*** *Which legislation attempted to combat poverty?*

## GOVERNMENT CONCEPTS

***judicial review:* *the power of federal courts to decide whether laws are constitutional***

- **The Historical Context:** The Supreme Court first assumed the power to decide whether laws were constitutional in the case of *Marbury* v. *Madison* (1803). In the 1950s and 1960s the Supreme Court made a number of major rulings that overturned state laws in such areas as school segregation and apportionment of congressional districts. Critics charged that the Supreme Court was interfering in questions that the U.S. Constitution declared should be decided by legislatures.
- **The Concept Today:** While specific Supreme Court decisions still cause controversy, Americans generally accept the Court's right to judge the constitutionality of state and federal laws. In recent years the membership and rulings of the Supreme Court have been more conservative than during the 1960s.

most state governments had not reapportioned or redistributed their electoral districts to reflect population shifts. Over the years, many people in the United States had moved from rural to urban areas. Because the electoral districts were not redrawn, rural citizens were overrepresented and urban citizens were underrepresented. The Warren Court's decision in the case of *Baker* v. *Carr* (1962) declared that congressional districts had to be apportioned on the basis of "one person, one vote." This decision prevented the party in power from drawing district lines in unfair ways to give themselves more votes.† In *Reynolds* v. *Sims* (1964) the Supreme Court held that state legislative districts not based on the "one person, one vote" formula violated the equal protection clause of the Fourteenth Amendment.

Many of the Warren Court's decisions were controversial. Some people argued that the justices had gone too far in their "loose construction" of the Constitution. The opponents hoped to see more conservative judges appointed to the Court so that the new rulings could be overturned. ■

## *Effects of the Great Society*

At first the Great Society seemed enormously successful. Opinion polls taken in 1964 after Johnson introduced his vision of the Great Society showed him to be more popular than Kennedy had been at a comparable point in his presidency. Pressed by Johnson, Congress had passed Kennedy's tax-cut bill early in 1964, and the state of the economy improved.

Soon, however, criticisms began to surface. New programs raised expectations, and disillusionment followed when not all demands could be met. Some Americans complained that too many of their tax dollars were being spent on poor people. Other critics argued that Great Society programs put too much authority in the hands of the federal government. Despite such criticisms, the number of people living in poverty in the United States was cut in half during the 1960s and early 1970s.

Michael Harrington, who wrote about poverty in his book *The Other America,* argued that the amount of money the government spent was not nearly enough. He wrote, "What was supposed to be a social war turned out to be a skirmish and, in any case, poverty won." Before long it was a war in Southeast Asia that began to consume the resources that Johnson had hoped to spend on his programs at home.

† Today each of the 435 seats in the United States House represents an average of 665,000 persons.

## *SECTION 2 REVIEW*

### Comprehension

1. *Key Terms* Define: (a) Great Society; (b) Volunteers in Service to America (VISTA); (c) Medicare; (d) Medicaid; (e) Immigration Act of 1965; (f) Miranda rule; (g) apportionment.
2. *Summarizing the Main Idea* Summarize the goals of Johnson's Great Society.
3. *Organizing Information* Create a graphic organizer listing and describing the Warren Court cases relating to protecting the rights of the accused.

### Critical Thinking

4. *Analyzing Time Lines* Review the time line at the start of the section. Why do you think Johnson won the election in 1964?
5. *Demonstrating Reasoned Judgment* Do you think Johnson's Great Society programs were a success? Why or why not?

### Writing Activity

6. *Writing an Expository Essay* Write an essay outlining Johnson's qualities as an effective legislator.

| 1961 | 1961 | 1961 | 1961 | 1962 | 1963 | 1965 |
|---|---|---|---|---|---|---|
| Peace Corps established | Kennedy announces the Alliance for Progress | Bay of Pigs invasion | Berlin Wall erected | Cuban Missile Crisis | Limited Nuclear Test Ban Treaty signed | United States involvement in Vietnam intensifies |

1961 — 1963 — 1965

# 3 Foreign Policy in the Early 1960s

**SECTION PREVIEW**

### Objectives

1. Describe the United States' role in the Bay of Pigs invasion.
2. Analyze the events leading to the building of the Berlin Wall and the Cuban Missile Crisis.
3. Outline the goals of Kennedy's Alliance for Progress and the Peace Corps.
4. Summarize Johnson's foreign policy.
5. *Key Terms* Define: Bay of Pigs invasion; Berlin Wall; Cuban Missile Crisis; Limited Test Ban Treaty; Alliance for Progress; Peace Corps.

### Main Idea

President Kennedy acted boldly in response to a series of dramatic cold war crises in Cuba and Berlin. Johnson continued many of Kennedy's foreign policies.

### Reading Strategy

*Formulating Questions* Before you read the section, write one question for each of the main headings. As you read, look for answers to those questions.

In his Inaugural Address, Kennedy proclaimed that the United States would do anything to uphold freedom throughout the world:

KEY DOCUMENTS

> "Let every nation know, whether it wishes us well or ill, that we shall pay any price, bear any burden, meet any hardship, support any friend, oppose any foe to assure the survival and the success of liberty."
>
> —*John F. Kennedy,* Inaugural Address

As President at the height of the cold war between the Soviet Union and the United States, Kennedy spoke boldly. Three crises during Kennedy's short time in office gave him the opportunity to prove that he would also act boldly.

## The Bay of Pigs Invasion

Kennedy's first serious foreign crisis arose in Cuba, an island approximately 90 miles off the Florida coast. The United States had worried about Cuba ever since revolutionary Fidel Castro had seized power. Castro had overthrown the United States-backed dictator Fulgencio Batista in 1959. Some Cubans had supported Castro because he promised to improve the lives of poor people. Castro claimed that the poor were being exploited by wealthy Cubans and by United States companies operating in Cuba.

Once in power, Castro had taken over private property, including property owned by United States corporations in Cuba. The United States broke diplomatic relations with Cuba and refused to accept Castro as the country's legitimate leader. When Castro developed ties to the Soviet Union, United States officials began to fear that he could become a model for revolutionary upheaval throughout Latin America.

After Kennedy became President, he learned of a plan that President Eisenhower had approved in 1960. Under this plan, the Central Intelligence Agency (CIA) was training

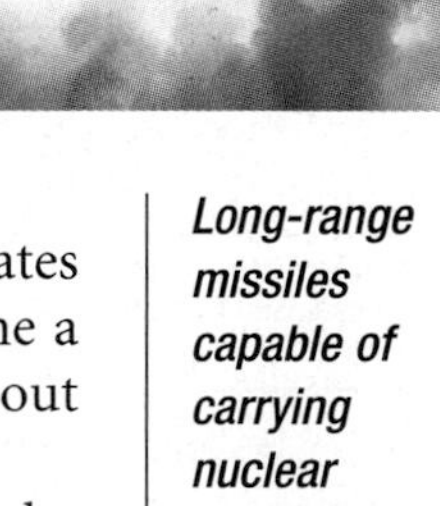

*Long-range missiles capable of carrying nuclear explosives heightened cold war tension.*

Cuban opponents of Castro. The training took place in Guatemala, a nearby Central American country. When it was complete, the Cubans planned to invade Cuba. Kennedy and his advisers expected that the Cuban people would use the opportunity to help overthrow Castro.

Resistance to the plan soon surfaced, however. When Senator J. William Fulbright, Democratic chairman of the Foreign Relations Committee, learned of the scheme, he called it an "endless can of worms." In a memorandum to the President, he declared:

**AMERICAN VOICES** **"To give this activity even covert [secretive] support is of a piece with the hypocrisy and cynicism for which the United States is constantly denouncing [condemning] the Soviet Union in the United Nations and elsewhere. This point will not be lost on the rest of the world—nor on our own consciences. . . . The Castro regime is a thorn in the flesh; but it is not a dagger in the heart."**

— *Senator J. William Fulbright*

Despite such reservations and those of some military leaders, Kennedy accepted the advice of the CIA, Joint Chiefs of Staff, and Secretary of Defense. He reluctantly pushed ahead.

The **Bay of Pigs invasion,** depicted in the map below, took place on April 17, 1961. It was a total disaster. An air strike failed to destroy Cuba's air power. Castro was therefore able to stop the United States-backed troops from coming ashore. When advisers urged Kennedy to use United States planes to provide air cover for the 1,500 Cuban soldiers, he refused. Rather than continue a hopeless effort, he chose simply to accept defeat.

The United States lost a great deal of prestige in the disastrous attack. To begin with, the invasion was clumsy and incompetent. Furthermore, the nation's support of an effort to overthrow another nation's government was exposed to the world. The United States faced anger from other countries in Latin America for violating agreements not to interfere in the Western Hemisphere. European leaders, who had high hopes for the new President, were concerned about the kind of leadership he planned to provide.

## Bay of Pigs Invasion, 1961

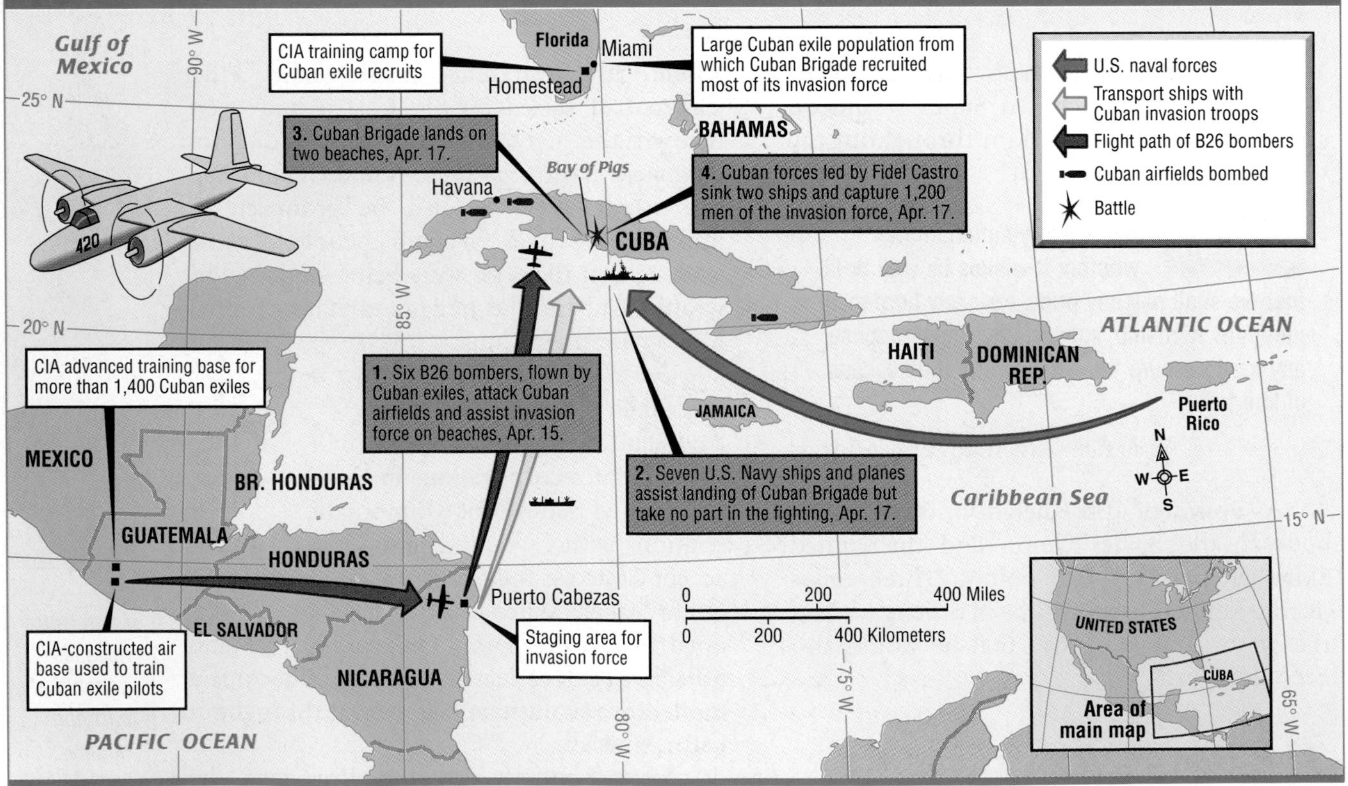

Gulf of Mexico
90° W
25° N
CIA training camp for Cuban exile recruits
Florida
Miami
Homestead
Large Cuban exile population from which Cuban Brigade recruited most of its invasion force
U.S. naval forces
Transport ships with Cuban invasion troops
Flight path of B26 bombers
Cuban airfields bombed
Battle
3. Cuban Brigade lands on two beaches, Apr. 17.
BAHAMAS
Bay of Pigs
4. Cuban forces led by Fidel Castro sink two ships and capture 1,200 men of the invasion force, Apr. 17.
Havana
420
CUBA
85° W
20° N
ATLANTIC OCEAN
CIA advanced training base for more than 1,400 Cuban exiles
1. Six B26 bombers, flown by Cuban exiles, attack Cuban airfields and assist invasion force on beaches, Apr. 15.
HAITI
DOMINICAN REP.
JAMAICA
Puerto Rico
MEXICO
BR. HONDURAS
2. Seven U.S. Navy ships and planes assist landing of Cuban Brigade but take no part in the fighting, Apr. 17.
Caribbean Sea
N
W
E
S
15° N
GUATEMALA
HONDURAS
Puerto Cabezas
0 200 400 Miles
0 200 400 Kilometers
EL SALVADOR
Staging area for invasion force
CIA-constructed air base used to train Cuban exile pilots
NICARAGUA
75° W
UNITED STATES
CUBA
Area of main map
65° W
80° W
PACIFIC OCEAN

This map traces the ill-fated Bay of Pigs invasion authorized by President Kennedy in 1961. **Location** *How does the map show why the United States would want to maintain friendly governments in Latin American nations?*

## The Berlin Crisis

Upset by the failure at the Bay of Pigs, Kennedy was now even more determined to respond firmly to growing Communist threats. When Soviet leader Nikita Khrushchev took action again to increase Soviet power, Kennedy responded boldly.

This time the issue was Germany. After World War II, the Allies had divided Germany into zones. The United States, Great Britain, the Soviet Union, and France each controlled one sector of the country. While the original intention was that the zones would be temporary, the lines had hardened as cold war tensions increased among the former Allies. In time the western regions had been combined into one, creating the nation of West Germany. The sector controlled by the Soviet Union became East Germany. The city of Berlin, although located completely inside East Germany, had also been divided among the World War II victors.

The Soviet effort to cut off access to Berlin in 1948 had failed as a result of President Truman's successful Berlin airlift. Now the Soviets made another effort to resolve problems in Berlin on their own terms. They demanded a peace treaty that would make the division of the city permanent. Their goal was to cut off the large flow of East Germans who frequently escaped to West Germany, particularly through Berlin.

Kennedy feared that the Soviet effort in Germany was part of a larger plan to take over the rest of Europe. Kennedy's first conversation with Khrushchev in Vienna, Austria, in June 1961 went poorly. When Khrushchev made a public ultimatum regarding Germany, Kennedy felt bullied by the Soviet leader.

Upon returning home, Kennedy decided to show the Soviets that the United States would not be intimidated. He asked Congress for a huge increase of more than $3 billion for defense. He doubled the number of young men being drafted into the armed services, and he called up reserve forces for active duty. At the same time, he sought over $200 million for a program to build fallout shelters across the country. He argued that the United States had to be prepared if the crisis led to nuclear war.

Kennedy appeared on television to tell the American people that West Berlin was "the great testing place of Western courage and will, a focal point where our solemn commitments . . . and Soviet ambitions now meet in basic confrontation." The United States, he said, would not be pushed around: "We do not want to fight—but we have fought before."

The Berlin Wall began as a series of concrete and barbed wire barriers. Over the years it grew into a heavily fortified wall separating West Berlin from East Berlin over a stretch of 28 miles. It also extended for 75 miles around West Berlin, separating it from the rest of East Germany. ***Foreign Relations*** ***Why was the Berlin Wall an appropriate symbol of the cold war?***

The Soviets responded by building a wall in Berlin beginning in August 1961. The **Berlin Wall** became a somber symbol of the cold war. Still, by stopping the flow of East Germans to the West, the Soviet Union had found a way to avoid a showdown over East Berlin. Although the immediate crisis was over, the tensions of the cold war continued. Standing near the Berlin Wall in June 1963, Kennedy spoke to a cheering crowd saying that the United States "will risk its cities to defend yours because we need your freedom to protect ours." He concluded his speech with the rousing words, "*Ich bin ein Berliner.*" I am a Berliner.

**Main Idea CONNECTIONS**

***How did President Kennedy respond to Khrushchev's ultimatum regarding Germany?***

## The Cuban Missile Crisis

Kennedy had a chance to restore his prestige in another crisis with Cuba. The Soviet Union, disturbed by the attempted invasion at the Bay of Pigs, had pledged to support Cuba. On October 16, 1962, photographs taken from a United States spy plane revealed that the Soviets were building missile bases on Cuban soil. Khrushchev may have been trying to bolster Soviet power by positioning missiles so close to the United States. The missiles did not alter the overall strategic balance between the United States and the Soviet Union. The Soviets could already inflict serious damage on the United States from bases within their own country. Nevertheless, Kennedy was convinced that the missiles in Cuba presented a direct challenge to which he must respond.

The President quickly convened his top advisers in a series of secret meetings. His brother Robert, serving as the nation's Attorney General, argued against an air strike to knock out the missiles. It seemed, he said, too much like the Japanese attack on Pearl Harbor that had started World War II. President Kennedy ordered United States forces on full alert. Bombers and missiles were armed with nuclear weapons. The fleet was ready to move. Soldiers were prepared to invade Cuba at a moment's notice.

Kennedy's advisers in the National Security Council realized the danger of the situation. Throughout this **Cuban Missile Crisis,** nuclear warheads on both sides were poised and ready for use. At one point former Secretary of State Dean Acheson joined the deliberations and declared that the United States had to knock out the Soviet missiles. He was then asked what would happen next. His response points out the very real danger of a local conflict escalating, or expanding, into a widespread war:

*Acheson:* I know the Soviet Union well. I know what they are required to do in the light of their history and their posture around the world. I think they will knock out our missiles in Turkey.

*An NSC Adviser:* Well, then what do we do?

*Acheson:* I believe under our NATO treaty . . . we would be required to respond by knocking out a missile base inside the Soviet Union.

*Another Adviser:* Then what do they do?

*Acheson:* That's when we hope that cooler heads will prevail, and they'll stop and talk.

After preparing the armed forces, Kennedy went on television on Monday, October 22, to tell the public about the missiles. During the

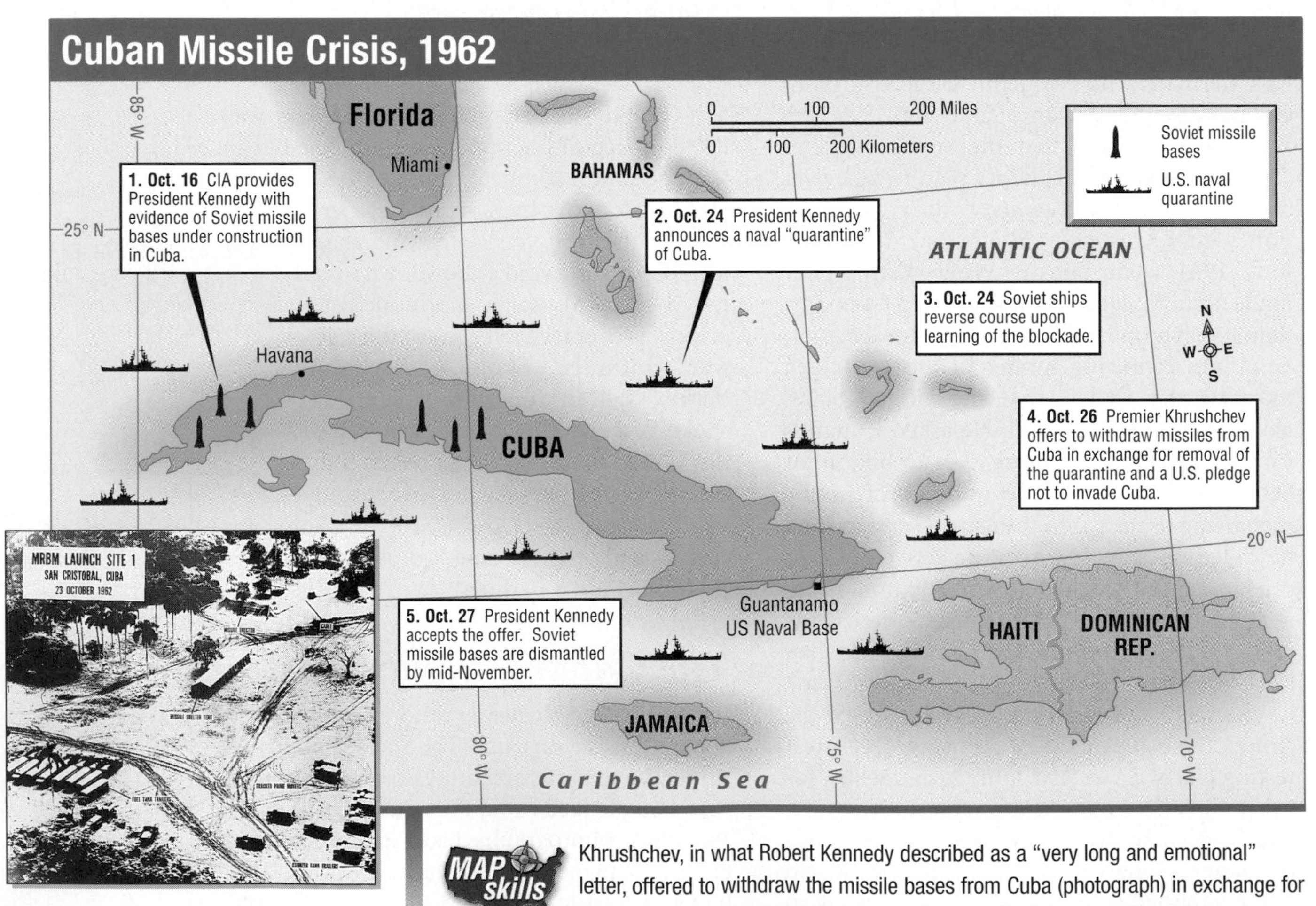


MAP skills Khrushchev, in what Robert Kennedy described as a "very long and emotional" letter, offered to withdraw the missile bases from Cuba (photograph) in exchange for assurances that the United States would not invade Cuba. ***Location*** ***What advantages and disadvantages would the missile bases have given the Soviet Union?***

**exploring TECHNOLOGY** *1960s Bomb Shelter*

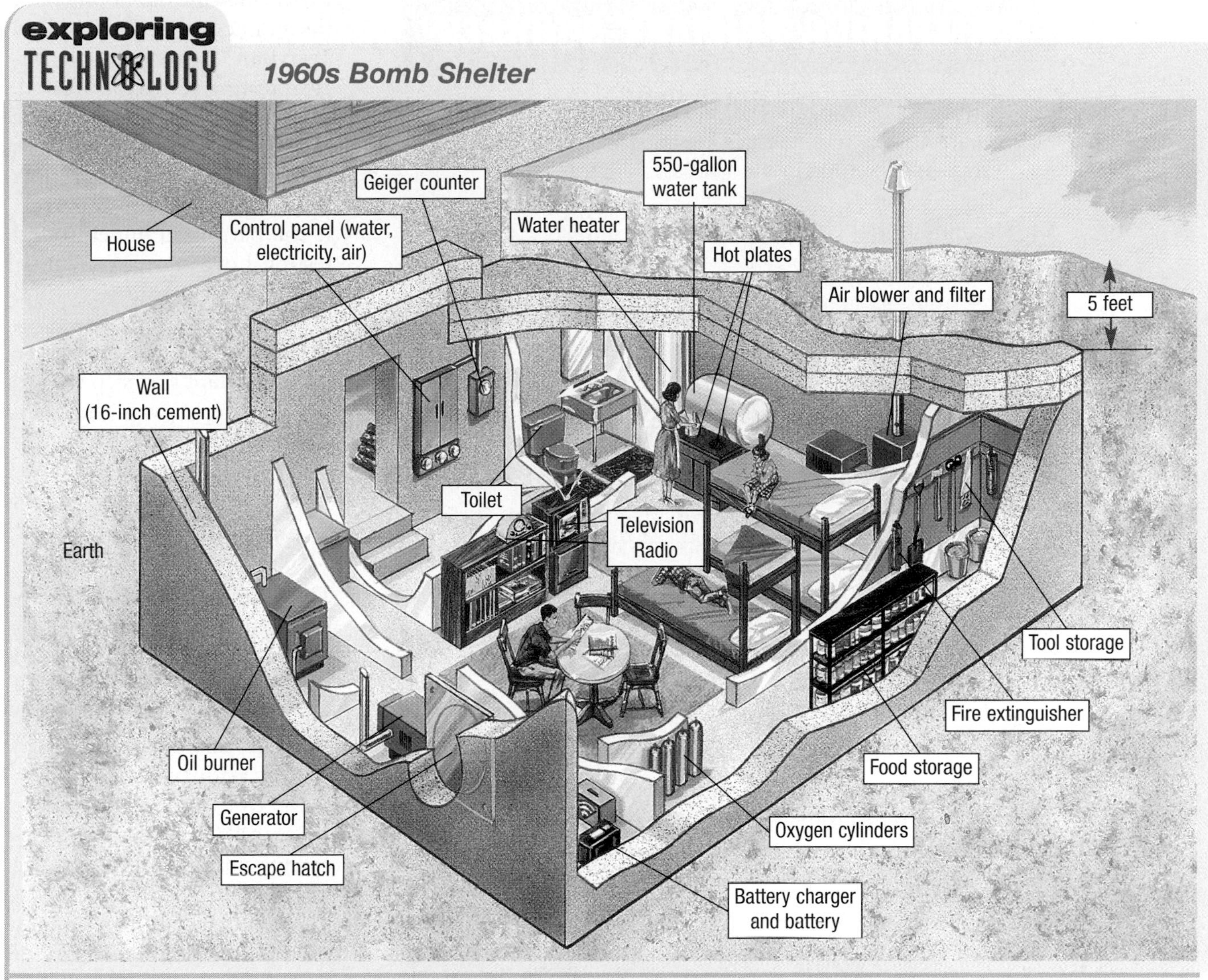


After an atomic explosion, radioactive particles attach themselves to dust in the atmosphere, which continues to rain down upon the earth for as long as two weeks. Many Americans hoped they could survive a nuclear war in a basement fallout shelter. In the shelter shown above, an air filter protects people from breathing radioactive dust, and a Geiger counter tells them when the radioactivity outside has returned to a safe level. ***Foreign Relations*** ***How were bomb shelters a symbol of the cold war era?***

speech he demanded that the Soviets remove the missiles. The United States, he said, would not shrink from the risk of nuclear war. He then announced that he had authorized a naval "quarantine" around Cuba. The quarantine would prevent the Soviets from transporting more missiles to Cuba. Kennedy was careful not to call the action a "blockade," because a blockade is an act of war.

For the next two days the two most powerful nations in the world stood teetering on the brink of disaster. The naval quarantine was put into effect on Wednesday, October 24. United States forces were ready to respond as soon as the line was crossed. On October 25 a Soviet ship crossed the line and was stopped by the Navy. Because it was carrying only oil it was allowed to proceed. At the same time several other Soviet ships were headed toward Cuba. To everyone's great relief, the Soviet ships suddenly reversed their direction. Khrushchev had called the ships back, though work on the missile sites inside Cuba continued.

On October 26 Khrushchev sent Kennedy a long letter in which he pledged to remove the missiles if Kennedy promised that the United States would end the quarantine and stay out of Cuba. A second letter delivered the next day demanded that the United States remove its missiles from Turkey in exchange for the

## COMPARING PRIMARY SOURCES

### THE COLD WAR

The United States and its allies continued to battle against Communist expansion in the 1960s.

**For Civility in the Cold War**

"The issues called the cold war . . . must be met with determination, confidence, and sophistication. . . [C]hannels of communication should be kept open. . . . Our discussion, public or private, should be marked by civility; our manners should conform to our own dignity and power and to our good repute throughout the world."

*Secretary of State Dean Rusk in a speech at the University of California, Berkeley, California, March 20, 1961*

**For Aggressiveness in the Cold War**

"[I]t is really astounding that our government has never stated its purpose to be that of complete victory over the tyrannical forces of international communism. . . . And we need an official act, such as the resumption of nuclear testing, to show our own peoples and the other freedom-loving peoples of the world that we mean business."

*Senator Barry Goldwater of Arizona in an address to the United States Senate, July 14, 1961*

***ANALZYING VIEWPOINTS*** **What strategy did each of the speakers want to pursue during the cold war?**

withdrawal of Soviet missiles in Cuba. The United States accepted the terms of the first note and ignored the second. With that, the crisis was over. As Secretary of State Dean Rusk observed to President Kennedy, "We have won a considerable victory. You and I are still alive."

In the Cuban Missile Crisis, the world was closer than ever before to nuclear war. Far more powerful hydrogen bombs had replaced the first atomic weapons, and this was the closest the superpowers had come to using them. For a time, Kennedy emerged from the confrontation as a hero. He had stood up to the Soviets and shown that the United States would not be pushed around. His reputation, and that of the Democratic party, improved. This popular support helped with mid-term congressional elections just weeks away.

The Cuban Missile Crisis did lead to a number of efforts to reduce the risk of nuclear war. Once the confrontation was over, Kennedy and Khrushchev established a "hot line" between their two nations to allow for immediate discussion in the event of a future crisis. In the summer of 1963, they also signed the first nuclear treaty since the development of the atomic bomb. The **Limited Test Ban Treaty** banned nuclear testing above the ground. By doing so it eliminated the radioactive fallout that was threatening to contaminate human, animal, and plant life. It still permitted underground testing, however, and scientists continued to create bigger and bigger bombs. Nonetheless, as Kennedy noted, the treaty was, "an important first step toward peace, a step toward reason, a step away from war."

## *The Alliance for Progress*

The Limited Test Ban Treaty reflected Kennedy's hopes for a peaceful and better world. So too did his establishment of the **Alliance for Progress** in 1961. In addition to his bold stands against communism, Kennedy tried to promote "peaceful revolution" in developing countries around the world. Through his efforts, Kennedy hoped to encourage countries to ally themselves with the democratic countries of the West rather than with the Soviet Union.

To counter pro-Communist revolutionary movements, the United States wanted to help countries in Latin America, Asia, and Africa. To do so, Kennedy believed that modern transportation and communication systems and stable governments sympathetic to the United States were necessary. Two months after taking office, Kennedy called on all the people of the Western Hemisphere to join in a new Alliance for Progress or *Alianza para Progreso.* The Alliance would be a vast cooperative effort to satisfy the basic needs of the North, Central, and South American people for homes, work, land, health, and schools.

The task was a huge undertaking. The administration pledged $20 billion from the United States over ten years. The money would be spent to promote economic development and social reform and to sidetrack revolution before it occurred. All citizens in the Western Hemisphere, Kennedy declared, had "a right to social justice," and that included "land for the landless, and education for those who are denied education." Soon, however, Latin Americans began to question the benefits of the Alliance. Some viewed it simply as a tool of the United States to stop the spread of communism. Because of such doubts, the Alliance for Progress never lived up to Kennedy's expectations.

## The Peace Corps

Kennedy's hope for a world in which nations worked together peacefully to solve problems was also reflected in his establishment of the Peace Corps in 1961. This new program would send volunteers abroad as educators, health workers, and technicians to help developing nations around the world.

Paul Cowan was typical of many **Peace Corps** volunteers. After graduating from college in 1963, he worked in the civil rights movement tutoring African American children in Maryland. In 1965 Cowan and his wife, Rachel, joined the Peace Corps and prepared to work in South America. After a training program at the University of New Mexico, they went to the city of Guayaquil in Ecuador to do community development work. Their job was to raise the standard of living in poor areas and to work with local governments to provide services such as garbage removal and clean water. Today Peace Corps volunteers throughout the world continue to work for Kennedy's vision of a peaceful world.

## Johnson's Foreign Policy

The Alliance for Progress and the Peace Corps, while worthwhile efforts, could not erase the tensions of the cold war. When Johnson came to the presidency in 1963, he too faced threats of Communist expansion.

**The Dominican Republic** In 1965 Johnson heard that the military-backed government in the Dominican Republic, a Caribbean nation close to Cuba, had been attacked by rebels. Johnson feared that the disruption might endanger United States citizens living there. Arguing (wrongly, it turned out) that Communist elements were causing the disruption, Johnson sent 22,000 marines to the Dominican Republic. Their presence tipped the balance away from the rebels.

Peace Corps volunteers live alongside the citizens of the countries which they are sent to, doing the same work, eating the same food, and speaking the same language. This Peace Corps volunteer (left) is teaching sewing skills to women in Sri Lanka. ***Culture*** ***How does the Peace Corps contribute to Kennedy's vision of a peaceful world?***

President Johnson often felt annoyed when problems in Latin America took his attention away from domestic policy. **Location** *In the context of the cold war, why did United States leaders consider it important to maintain a strong presence in this part of the world?*

## Latin America, 1965

Within a few months a provisional government backed by the United States was put in place. Elections were held the following year.

**Vietnam** Johnson's administration was also deeply involved in the ongoing conflict between Communist North Vietnam and non-Communist South Vietnam in Southeast Asia. (You will read about this war in an upcoming chapter.) Like Kennedy, Johnson was determined to prevent the spread of communism. By 1963 about 16,000 military advisers were already in South Vietnam. The United States was also contributing economic aid to the South Vietnamese government. Johnson opposed more direct United States involvement in the war in his 1964 campaign for President. Before long, he could not tolerate simply letting the Communists take over South Vietnam. During 1965, American involvement in the conflict deepened as more and more troops and money were sent to prop up the South Vietnamese government.

## SECTION 3 REVIEW

### Comprehension

1. *Key Terms* Define (a) Bay of Pigs invasion; (b) Berlin Wall; (c) Cuban Missile Crisis; (d) Limited Test Ban Treaty; (e) Alliance for Progress; (f) Peace Corps.
2. *Summarizing the Main Idea* Was President Johnson's approach to foreign affairs similar to or different from Kennedy's? Explain your answer.
3. *Organizing Information* Create a time line of events leading up to and during the Cuban Missile Crisis.

### Critical Thinking

4. *Analyzing Time Lines* Review the time line at the start of this section. Why was the Berlin Wall built in 1961?
5. *Determining Relevance* Why do you think Kennedy established the Alliance for Progress and the Peace Corps?

### Writing Activity

6. *Writing an Expository Essay* Write an essay outlining the basic events leading up to and during the Bay of Pigs invasion.

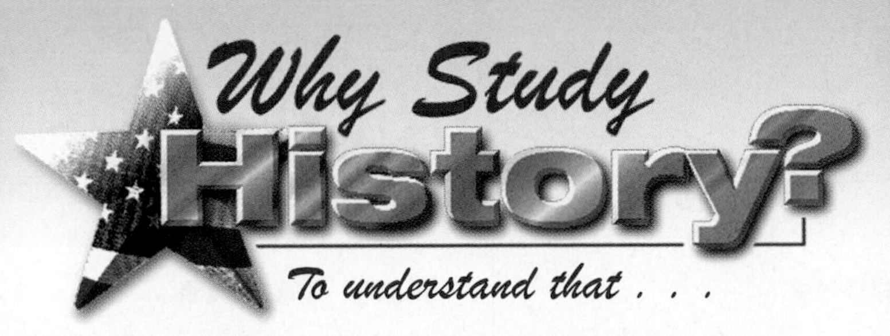


# Welfare Remains a Controversial Issue

**Many Americans' views on social welfare programs have changed in the decades since President Johnson declared his war on poverty.**

*President Johnson passing out Medicare checks, 1968*

Low-income preschoolers attend Head Start to ensure that they will be ready for grade school. VISTA volunteers live and work on Indian reservations and among the homeless to help poor people help themselves. These images of social welfare programs date from the 1960s, when the federal government launched a massive effort to help poor, elderly, and disabled Americans.

Today discussions of social welfare programs bring different images to many Americans' minds. Many Americans worry that the programs are not fighting poverty effectively. Why have Americans' views on social welfare changed?

## The Impact Today

For a number of years, the Great Society programs initiated by President Johnson distributed aid to poorer Americans. Between 1970 and 1992, federal spending on social welfare programs increased dramatically, from about $1.5 billion to $1.3 trillion. Tens of millions of Americans received some form of assistance through programs such as Medicare and Medicaid, Head Start, food stamps, school lunches, low-income housing assistance, job training, and Aid to Families with Dependent Children.

By the 1980s, however, many Americans were angry about the large amounts of money spent on federal anti-poverty programs. Critics argued that federal spending had created a cycle of dependency in which generations of poor families chose to remain on public assistance rather than become self-sufficient.

Presidents Reagan and Bush shared this view. In the 1980s and early 1990s, they persuaded Congress to make cuts in Medicare and Medicaid, federal pensions, food stamps, and government-guaranteed home mortgages.

President Clinton promised to "end welfare as we have known it." Congress called for sweeping reforms as well. In 1996 Clinton signed the Personal Responsibility and Work Opportunity Reconciliation Act. This new welfare law made dramatic cuts in spending. It set a lifetime limit of five years of receiving welfare benefits and required welfare recipients to work in exchange for help.

Supporters of the welfare reform law saw the "welfare to work" provision as a way to encourage individual effort. Critics pointed out that many welfare recipients are single mothers who have no safe place to leave their children while at work. The full effects of the law will not be known for years.

## The Impact on You

In your view, what responsibility, if any, does the government have toward the unemployed? (For example, should the government support people until they find work? Should it provide public jobs when other jobs are unavailable?) Present your conclusions in an essay. Give reasons to support your views.

*Participant in state "welfare to work" program*

# Chapter 18 Review

## Chapter Summary

CD-ROM REVIEW

The major concepts of Chapter 18 are presented below. See also ***Guide to the Essentials of American History*** or ***Interactive Student Tutorial CD-ROM,*** which contains interactive review activities, time lines, helpful hints, and test practice.

### *Reviewing the Main Ideas*

Kennedy's New Frontier program and Johnson's Great Society program both aimed at bringing about domestic reforms in education, the economy, and poverty. The foreign policies of both Presidents were largely influenced by the dynamics of the cold war.

### *Section 1: The New Frontier*

Before his assassination in 1963, President John F. Kennedy proposed a number of domestic programs to improve the economy and to address issues of inequality, including poverty and civil rights. Most of Kennedy's proposals were defeated in Congress.

### *Section 2: The Great Society*

The goals of Johnson's Great Society program were to improve the economy, education, and the environment, as well as to offer government assistance to the poor.

### *Section 3: Foreign Policy in the Early 1960s*

President Kennedy acted boldly in response to a series of dramatic cold war crises in Cuba and Berlin. Johnson continued many of Kennedy's foreign policies.

Americans' views on social welfare have changed since President Johnson declared war on poverty. Some Americans argue that instead of ending poverty, federal spending created a cycle of dependence.

## Key Terms

For each of the terms below, write a sentence explaining how it relates to this chapter.

1. mandate
2. New Frontier
3. Great Society
4. Medicare
5. Medicaid
6. Immigration Act of 1965
7. Miranda rule
8. apportionment
9. Limited Test Ban Treaty
10. Peace Corps
11. Alliance for Progress

## Comprehension

1. Explain why the Kennedy administration was compared to the Broadway musical *Camelot.*
2. What domestic programs did Kennedy propose?
3. Why was Kennedy's domestic program largely unsuccessful?
4. What actions were taken to investigate Kennedy's assassination?
5. What domestic programs did Johnson propose?
6. Describe three landmark decisions handed down by the Supreme Court under Earl Warren.
7. What were some of the consequences to the United States of the failed Bay of Pigs invasion?
8. Describe the Berlin Crisis of 1961.
9. Why did Kennedy establish the Peace Corps?
10. What was Johnson's approach to foreign policy?

## Using Graphic Organizers

On a separate sheet of paper, copy the tree map below. Fill in at least two facts or main ideas for each of the headings on the tree.

| Foreign Policy, 1961–1962 | | |
|---|---|---|
| Bay of Pigs | Berlin Crisis | Cuban Missile Crisis |
| | | |

## Analyzing Political Cartoons ▶

1. This cartoon was printed in November 1962. Examine the figures. (a) Who is the man on the left? (b) Who is the man on the right? (c) What are they trying to do?
2. Examine the box. What does the monster represent?
3. What is the overall message of the cartoon?
4. What event do you think inspired the cartoon?

## Critical Thinking

1. *Applying the Chapter Skill* Interview an adult who remembers Kennedy's assassination. Ask him or her to describe their reaction to the news as well as the impact of the assassination on the nation.
2. *Making Comparisons* Describe the programs you would implement if you were to create a Great Society today. In what ways would they be similar to the programs of Johnson's Great Society?
3. *Predicting Consequences* How did the beliefs of Presidents Kennedy and Johnson about the spread of communism influence their foreign policy decisions?
4. *Drawing Inferences* In what ways did the Warren Court help to uphold the principle that a person is "innocent until proven guilty"?

### INTERNET ACTIVITY

***For your portfolio:***
**WRITE AN ARTICLE**

Access Prentice Hall's *America: Pathways to the Present* site at **www.Pathways.phschool.com** for the specific URL to complete the activity. Additional resources and related Web sites are also available.

Write an article on Lyndon Johnson's presidency. Analyze the "American Covenant" portion of Lyndon Johnson's 1965 Inaugural Address. Identify the issues Johnson refers to in each paragraph. Then identify the Great Society policies or programs that address each issue. How did Johnson attempt to fulfill the American Covenant? Why did he say that America must end its isolationism?

### ANALYZING DOCUMENTS ▶ INTERPRETING DATA

Turn to the graph of immigration on page 548.

1. In which year did the number of immigrants from Asia equal about 40,000? (a) 1960 (b) 1965 (c) 1966 (d) 1967
2. Which of the following groups experienced the greatest increases in immigration between 1965 and 1970? (a) Asians (b) Northwestern Europeans (c) Other Europeans (d) North Americans
3. *Writing* How did the Immigration Act of 1965 affect overall immigration to the United States? How did it reflect the other liberal reforms of the era?

### Connecting to Today

*Identifying Central Issues* Although the cold war has ended, the threat of nuclear war remains. Conduct research to learn more about nuclear disarmament and nuclear proliferation in the post-cold war era.

# CHAPTER 19 The Civil Rights Movement

## 1954–1968

## CHAPTER FOCUS

*This chapter examines the civil rights movement of the 1960s, the historic battle to desegregate America and win equal treatment for African Americans. Challenged by violent opposition and internal divisions, the civil rights movement nonetheless won significant victories on the road to freedom.*

*The **Why Study History?** page at the end of this chapter explores how far the United States has come in achieving racial equality, and how far the nation still has to go.*

▲ **VIEWING HISTORY**
Civil rights leader Martin Luther King, Jr. (center) leads a protest march from Selma to Montgomery, Alabama, in 1965. ***Culture*** ***Describe the attitude of the marchers.***

| 1954 | 1955 | 1957 | 1960 |
|---|---|---|---|
| *Brown v. Board of Education strikes down "separate but equal"* | *Bus boycott in Montgomery, Alabama, begins* | *Southern Christian Leadership Conference founded* | *Student Nonviolent Coordinating Committee founded* |

**1954** **1956** **1958** **1960**

# 1 Leaders and Strategies

## SECTION PREVIEW

### Objectives

1. Explain how the activities of existing civil rights organizations laid the groundwork for the movement of the 1960s.
2. Describe the philosophy that Martin Luther King, Jr., brought to the movement.
3. Explain why some students formed their own civil rights organization.
4. *Key Terms* Define: interracial; Congress of Racial Equality (CORE); Southern Christian Leadership Conference (SCLC); nonviolent protest; Student Nonviolent Coordinating Committee (SNCC).

### Main Idea

The civil rights movement of the 1960s consisted of many separate groups, whose leaders and methods differed while sharing the same goal of securing equal rights for all Americans.

### Reading Strategy

*Problem Solving* Civil rights workers faced violence, even death, from opponents of change. List techniques you might use when confronted with this problem. Then read on to see what actually happened.

The civil rights movement of the 1950s and 1960s was a grassroots effort of ordinary citizens determined to end racial injustice in the United States. Although no central organization directed the movement, several major groups formed to share information and coordinate civil rights activities. Each of the groups described in this section had its own goals, priorities, and strategies. In different ways, they all helped to focus the energies of thousands of Americans committed to securing civil rights for all citizens.

## Laying the Groundwork

Although the civil rights movement spread nationwide in the 1960s, the struggle had been going on for decades. World War II spotlighted much of the racism that existed throughout the United States.

In the postwar era, several landmark events occurred as both African Americans and white Americans reacted against obvious injustices in the South. These events set the stage for the civil rights battles of the 1960s.

As you read previously, one turning point was the Supreme Court's 1954 decision in the Topeka, Kansas, case of *Brown* v. *Board of Education.* The Court's ruling struck down the doctrine of "separate but equal" that had kept African Americans in segregated—and usually inadequate—public schools. Despite resistance, the integration of public schools moved forward from then on.

*Civil rights marchers drew the nation's attention to issues of racial equality.*

**NAACP** Behind the case of *Brown* v. *Board of Education* was the National Association for the Advancement of Colored People (NAACP), one of the oldest civil rights organizations in the United States. In 1909, a number of people

In a 1955 meeting in Atlanta, Georgia, NAACP leaders met with African American leaders from southern states to discuss the *Brown* v. *Board of Education* ruling. Seated at the table (second from left) is Thurgood Marshall, NAACP chief counsel. ***Government*** ***What was the goal of the NAACP?***

**Main Idea CONNECTIONS**

*What approach did the NAACP take toward ending discrimination?*

associated with the Niagara Movement founded this **interracial** organization, one with both African Americans and white Americans as members.

The NAACP worked to secure full legal equality for all Americans and to remove barriers that kept them from voting. W.E.B. Du Bois, a prominent African American scholar, was a founding member. He summarized the NAACP's goals in a memo to the organization's board of directors:

> **AMERICAN VOICES** "The main object of this association is to secure for colored people, and particularly for Americans of Negro descent, free and equal participation in the democracy of modern culture. This means the clearing away of obstructions to such participation, effort toward fitting these people for this participation, and it means also the making of a world democracy in which all men may participate."
>
> —*W.E.B. Du Bois*

Du Bois, who was the first African American to receive a doctoral degree from Harvard University, served as director of publicity and research. He also edited the NAACP magazine, *Crisis*.

From the start, the NAACP focused on challenging the laws that prevented African Americans from exercising their full rights as citizens. The group worked for new laws and brought lawsuits.

In the 1920s and 1930s, lynching was still a threat to African Americans, particularly in the South. Working to end such violence, the NAACP succeeded in getting two anti-lynching bills passed by the House of Representatives in the 1930s. Southern leaders in the Senate prevented the bills from becoming law, but the NAACP kept the issue of lynching in the public eye.

The NAACP was more successful in its lawsuits that challenged segregation laws. In the 1920s and 1930s, it had won a number of legal battles in the areas of housing and education. The *Brown* decision on school segregation was another major legal victory.

The NAACP appealed mainly to educated, middle- and upper-class African Americans and some liberal white Americans. It emphasized achieving legal equality for all races. Critics, however, charged that it was out of touch with the basic issues of economic survival faced by many African Americans.

**National Urban League** One organization that took on the economics issue was the National Urban League, founded in 1911. It sought to assist people moving to major American cities. It helped African Americans moving out of the South find homes and jobs and made sure that they received fair treatment at work.

Urban League workers looked for migrant families on ship docks and at train stations. They placed them in apartments they had inspected. They also insisted factory owners and union leaders teach African American workers the skills that could lead to better jobs.

**CORE** Founded by pacifists in 1942, the **Congress of Racial Equality (CORE)** was dedicated to bringing about change through peaceful confrontation. It, too, was interracial, with both African American and white members. During World War II, CORE had organized demonstrations against segregation in cities including Baltimore, Chicago, Denver, and Detroit.

In the years after World War II, CORE director James Farmer worked without pay in order to keep the organization alive. The growing interest in civil rights in the 1950s gave him a new base of support and allowed him to turn CORE into a national organization. It would play a major role in the confrontations that lay ahead.

## The Philosophy of Nonviolence

The successful Montgomery bus boycott led to the founding of a new and significant civil rights organization. In 1957 Martin Luther King, Jr., and other African American clergymen organized the **Southern Christian Leadership Conference (SCLC).** SCLC introduced the concept of **nonviolent protest,** a peaceful way of protesting against policies. Nonviolent protesters did not resist even when attacked by opponents.

In its first official statement, SCLC set out this principle:

AMERICAN VOICES

> **"To understand that nonviolence is not a symbol of weakness or cowardice, but as Jesus demonstrated, nonviolent resistance transforms weakness into strength and breeds courage in the face of danger."**
>
> —*SCLC statement*

SCLC shifted the focus of the civil rights movement to the South. Earlier organizations had been dominated by northerners. Now southern African American church leaders moved into the forefront of the struggle for equal rights. Among them, Martin Luther King, Jr., became a national figure.

## Martin Luther King, Jr.

AMERICAN BIOGRAPHY

When the Montgomery bus boycott began, Martin Luther King, Jr., was a young, small-town Baptist preacher. Within a few years he would become one of the most loved and admired—and also one of the most hated—people in the United States. King became not only a leader in the African American civil rights movement but also a symbol of nonviolent protest for the entire world.

Born in Atlanta, Georgia, in 1929, King grew up amid all the symbols of southern segregation—separate schools, stores, churches, and public places. Though he had white playmates as a child, that ended when he reached school age. King's father, Martin Luther King, Sr., and his grandfather were both prominent and respected Baptist preachers. He was raised with a sense of personal pride and dignity that went beyond the limitations of segregation.

Even in high school, young Martin was an inspiring and eloquent public speaker. Graduating early from high school, he went to Morehouse College in Atlanta. He earned a divinity degree at Crozer Theological Seminary in Pennsylvania, then a doctorate in theology at Boston University in 1955. There he met and married Coretta Scott.

On the night of April 26, 1960, burning crosses—the symbol of the Ku Klux Klan—appeared in the front yards of many African American residents of Atlanta. Above, Martin Luther King, Jr., calmly removes a cross from his lawn as his young son looks on. ***Culture** How did King move to the forefront of the civil rights movement?*

## COMPARING PRIMARY SOURCES

### Integrating Schools

In parts of the Deep South, the battle for equal rights continued to be fought at the nation's schoolhouse doors each September, long after the Supreme Court ordered schools to desegregate in 1954.

| For School Integration | Against School Integration |
|---|---|
| "Nearly nine years have elapsed since the Supreme Court ruled that state laws requiring or permitting segregated schools violate the Constitution. . . . Since that time it has become increasingly clear that neither violence nor legalistic measures will be tolerated as a means of thwarting court-ordered desegregation." *—President John F. Kennedy, message to Congress, February 28, 1963* | "I draw the line in the dust and toss the gauntlet before the feet of tyranny and I say segregation today, segregation tomorrow, segregation forever." *—Alabama governor George Wallace, Inaugural Address, January 14, 1963* |

***ANALYZING VIEWPOINTS*** **How do these two speeches, made about a month apart, reflect the divisions in the country?**

It was at Morehouse College that Martin Luther King, Jr., was first influenced by the beliefs of Mohandas K. Gandhi. Gandhi had been a leader in India's long struggle to gain independence from Great Britain, which finally succeeded in 1947.

Gandhi preached a philosophy of nonviolence as the only way to achieve victory against much stronger foes. Those who fought for justice must peacefully refuse to obey unjust laws, Gandhi taught. They must remain nonviolent, regardless of the violent reactions such peaceful resistance might provoke. The tactic required tremendous poise and courage.

*Martin Luther King, Jr. (1929–1968)*

King's first job as pastor was in Montgomery, Alabama. Though only 27 years old, he was chosen to lead the year-long boycott of the city's segregated bus system that began in December 1955.

Once the Montgomery boycott ended, King began training volunteers for what they might expect in the months ahead. Films, songs, and skits showed Gandhi's activities and demonstrated the success of passive resistance in India. Bus boycotters were advised to follow 17 rules for maintaining a nonviolent approach as they prepared to ride newly desegregated vehicles through the South. These are some of those rules:

**AMERICAN VOICES** **"Pray for guidance and commit yourself to complete nonviolence in word and action as you enter the bus. . . .**
**Be loving enough to absorb evil and understanding enough to turn an enemy into a friend. . . .**
**If cursed, do not curse back. If pushed, do not push back. If struck, do not strike back, but evidence love and goodwill at all times. . . .**
**If another person is being molested, do not arise to go to his defense, but pray for the oppressor and use moral and spiritual force to carry on the struggle for justice. . . . Do not be afraid to experiment with new and creative techniques for achieving reconciliation and social change. . . .**
**If you feel you cannot take it, walk for another week or two [rather than ride the bus]."**

*—Leaflet distributed in black churches*

For his role in the Montgomery boycott, King gained national prominence. For the next 11 years, he would play a key role in almost every major civil rights event. His work earned him the Nobel Peace Prize in 1964.

King's opponents would attack him physically and verbally, and he would often go to jail for his beliefs. Death threats were frequent. As King had sometimes predicted, he did not live to see the success of the movement. He was assassinated in Memphis, Tennessee, in April 1968, at the age of 39.† King's accused killer, a white southerner named James Earl Ray, was convicted in 1969 and sentenced to 99 years in prison. ††

† To honor the slain leader, Congress voted to make King's birthday a federal holiday beginning in 1986. It is observed on the third Monday of January each year.

†† Ray confessed to the crime, but three days later retracted his story. In the 1990s the King family, convinced that Ray was not the killer and hoping to find the real one, supported his attempt to have the case reopened. Ray died in prison in 1998. Later that year the Justice Department began a review of the case.

## *SNCC Breaks Away*

Nonviolent protest was a practical strategy in the civil rights struggle. It also represented a moral philosophy.

"To accept passively an unjust system is to cooperate with that system; thereby the oppressed become as evil as the oppressor," King said. "Noncooperation with evil is as much a moral obligation as is cooperation with good." King's message was that African Americans would ultimately win. At the same time, his philosophy of nonviolence won the support of many white Americans for the growing movement for change.

An offshoot of SCLC took a somewhat different approach. The **Student Nonviolent Coordinating Committee,** usually known as **SNCC** (pronounced "snick"), was originally part of SCLC. It began in 1960 at a meeting in Raleigh, North Carolina, for students active in the struggle. SCLC executive director Ella Baker thought that the NAACP and SCLC were not keeping up with the demands of young African Americans. She wanted to give them a way to play an even greater role in the civil rights movement.

More than 200 students showed up for the first SNCC meeting. Most came from southern communities, but some northerners attended as well.

Baker delivered the opening address. "The younger generation is challenging you and me," she told the adults present. "They are asking us to forget our laziness and doubt and fear, and follow our dedication to the truth to the bitter end."

Martin Luther King spoke next to the young audience, calling the civil rights movement "a revolt against the apathy and complacency of adults in the Negro community. . . ."

At the end of the meeting, the participants organized a temporary coordinating committee. A month later, student leaders met with Baker and other SCLC and CORE leaders and voted to maintain their independence from other civil rights groups. By the end of the year, the Student Nonviolent Coordinating Committee was a permanent and separate organization. It was interracial at first, though that changed in later years.

SNCC filled its own niche in the American civil rights movement. It gave young activists a chance to make decisions about priorities and tactics. It also shifted the focus of the civil rights movement away from church leaders alone. SNCC also sought more immediate change, while most of the older organizations were committed to gradual change.

One of SNCC's most influential leaders was Robert Moses, a former mathematics teacher in Harlem. As the civil rights movement developed, he wanted to be involved. He first went to work for SNCC in Atlanta, and later headed for Mississippi to encourage other African American students to come to SNCC meetings.

*Impatient for change, young NAACP members founded their own activist group, SNCC.*

Police arrested SNCC member Eddie Brown at a 1962 protest in Albany, Georgia. ***Culture*** ***How do Brown's actions reflect the philosophy of nonviolent protest?***

Anne Moody and her family suffered terribly because of her civil rights activities. ***Diversity** What niche did SNCC fill in the civil rights movement?*

While Martin Luther King, Jr., spoke with eloquence and passion, Moses was more soft spoken. He took time to gather his thoughts, and then he spoke slowly. Todd Gitlin, a white student activist leader, later noted that Moses was loved and trusted "precisely because he seemed humble, ordinary, accessible."

Gitlin went on to describe Moses's style of oratory:

> **AMERICAN VOICES** **"He liked to make his points with his hand, starting with palm downturned, then opening his hand outward toward his audience, as if delivering the point for inspection, nothing up his sleeve. The words seemed to be extruded [thrust forth], with difficulty, out of his depths. What he said seemed earned. . . . To teach his unimportance, he was wont [accustomed] to crouch in the corner or speak from the back of the room, hoping to hear the popular voice reveal itself."**
>
> —*Todd Gitlin*

One young civil rights worker faced resistance from a most difficult source: her own family. Anne Moody joined the NAACP in college in Mississippi and worked with CORE and SNCC. She endured humiliation, physical violence, and jailing for her participation in civil rights protests. But the toughest test came when her brother was beaten and nearly lynched in her hometown of Centreville, Mississippi. The local sheriff warned that Moody should never return home. Her frightened mother begged her to stop her civil rights work, and her sister angrily told her that her work was threatening the life of every African American in Centreville. Still, Moody continued. She was one of many who would sacrifice deeply for her beliefs.

## SECTION 1 REVIEW

### Comprehension

1. *Key Terms* Define: (a) interracial; (b) Congress of Racial Equality (CORE); (c) Southern Christian Leadership Conference (SCLC); (d) nonviolent protest; (e) Student Nonviolent Coordinating Committee (SNCC).
2. *Summarizing the Main Idea* What events of the 1940s and 1950s laid the groundwork for the civil rights movement of the 1960s?
3. *Organizing Information* Make a two-column chart showing the prominent civil rights organizations working in the early 1960s and their goals and/or characteristics.

### Critical Thinking

4. *Analyzing Time Lines* Review the time line at the start of the section. How would you explain the long gap in time between the founding of the NAACP and the start of CORE and SCLC?
5. *Making Comparisons* In what important ways did SNCC and its goals differ from the SCLC?

### Writing Activity

6. *Writing an Expository Essay* As a student in the 1960s you have been asked to help organize a local chapter of SNCC. Write an agenda for organizing such a group, explaining how you would recruit members and work for change.

SKILLS FOR LIFE

**Historical Evidence**

Critical Thinking

Graph & Chart

Geography

# Using Autobiography and Biography

Autobiography and biography are two major sources of evidence about a historical period. An autobiography is an account of a person's life as written by that person. A biography is an account of a person's life written by someone else.

Both sources offer clues—revealed in the narrative—of what society was like at the time the person lived. As well as describing the person's life, an autobiography or biography also describes the kind of conditions under which people lived, how they reacted to those conditions, and the attitudes and values prevailing at that time.

An autobiography can be especially helpful in capturing a moment in time because it is a firsthand account. But both autobiography and biography must be judged on their reliability. How objective is the writer about the facts presented? Do the facts seem colored by the writer's desire to cast the person profiled in a good or bad light? Or do the facts seem straightforward and believable?

Use the following steps to analyze an excerpt from *And the Walls Came Tumbling Down*, by Ralph Abernathy. Abernathy was a civil rights leader who worked with Martin Luther King, Jr., in organizing the Montgomery bus boycott and who later founded SCLC with King.

**1.** ***Identify the kind of account and the subject of the profile.*** (a) Is the excerpt from an autobiography or a biography? How can you tell? (b) What events is Abernathy describing? How can you tell?

**2.** ***Analyze the source's reliability as historical evidence.*** (a) How well acquainted is the writer with the facts he describes? (b) What is his point of view toward them? (c) How accurate do you judge his report to be? Explain.

**3.** ***Search for clues that tell what the historical period was like.*** (a) What groups are in conflict and why? (b) What can you learn about the level of violence that exists in some parts of society? (c) What is the attitude of certain whites to the struggle? (d) What is the attitude of the African Americans involved?

**TEST FOR SUCCESS**

What are the advantages and the drawbacks of using autobiography as a historical reference source?

> "Though we knew that our people could follow the path of nonviolence while in control of themselves, we also knew that in moments of sudden anger almost anybody could be tempted to strike back—and one injured policeman could nullify the work of weeks. So we took particular care to teach our people to count to ten before they responded in any way to verbal or physical abuse.
>
> We also showed them how to march along bent over, elbows guarding their stomachs and hands covering their ears and temples. We devised this technique for use in the event that we were bombarded with rocks and bottles while demonstrating. We also taught a modified version of the same maneuver for use while being beaten with fists or billy clubs.
>
> Then, too, we told everyone to go limp when anyone laid hands on them during an arrest. In the first place, it signaled to the arresting officer that he would encounter no active resistance; hence there was no need for excessive force. But equally important, a limp body was harder to handle, took more time to haul into a paddy wagon, and therefore limited the efficiency of the police. . . .
>
> It is surprising how many of the situations we would later face were actually anticipated and discussed in these Saturday workshops. By the time we reached the end of our years together, Martin and I had seen people assaulted with fists, clubs, bottles, and rocks and were moved by the manner in which they endured such abuse. Almost without exception they behaved exactly as we taught them to behave. They protected themselves from the full force of blows, but they didn't strike back, even when their lives were endangered; and for the most part they replied with courtesy and charity."
>
> —And the Walls Came Tumbling Down,
> *the Rev. Ralph David Abernathy, 1989*

**1960** CORE holds lunch counter sit-ins

**1961** Freedom Riders challenge segregation on interstate buses

**1962** James Meredith enrolls at University of Mississippi

**1963** Protests in Birmingham

**1963** King writes "Letter from the Birmingham Jail"

1960 | 1961 | 1962 | 1963

# 2 The Struggle Intensifies

## SECTION PREVIEW

### Objectives

1. Describe the goals of sit-ins and Freedom Rides and the reactions they provoked.
2. Summarize civil rights protests in Albany, Georgia, and at "Ole Miss."
3. Explain how violence against protesters in Birmingham affected attitudes throughout the nation.
4. *Key Terms* Define: sit-in; Freedom Ride; Albany Movement.

### Main Idea

The tactics of nonviolent protest, including sit-ins and boycotts, challenged segregation and brought change, but also generated violent confrontations.

### Reading Strategy

*Analyzing Outcomes* As you read, make a list of the civil rights protests mentioned and their outcomes. Write a sentence summarizing the effectiveness of these protests.



*This protester picketed a restaurant in Georgia.*

"We Shall Overcome," sang civil rights protesters. As they had anticipated, angry white segregationists met many peaceful protests with violence. But the civil rights protesters remained committed to nonviolence.

## Sit-Ins Challenge Segregation

As you read in a previous chapter, the Congress of Racial Equality (CORE) created the **sit-in** in 1943 to desegregate the Jack Spratt Coffee House in Chicago. In this technique, a group of CORE members simply sat down at a segregated lunch counter or other public place. If they were refused service at first, they simply stayed where they were.

This tactic was a popular form of protest in the early 1960s. It often worked because it forced business owners to decide between serving the protesters or risking a disruption and loss of business. In some places, sit-ins brought strong reactions. John Lewis, a SNCC activist, participated in sit-ins in Nashville, Tennessee, in 1960s. He remembered the experience:

> AMERICAN VOICES
>
> "It was a Woolworth in the heart of the downtown area, and we occupied every seat at the lunch counter, every seat in the restaurant. . . . A group of young white men came in and they started pulling and beating primarily the young women. They put lighted cigarettes down their backs, in their hair, and they were really beating people.
>
> In a short time police officials came in and placed all of us under arrest, and not a single member of the white group, the people that were opposing our sit-in, was arrested."
>
> —*John Lewis*

Soon thousands of students were involved in the sit-in campaign, which gained the support of SCLC. Martin Luther King, Jr., told students that arrest was a "badge of honor." In 1961, some 70,000 students participated in sit-ins, and 3,600 served time in jail. The protests began a process of change that could not be stopped.

Signs like the one at the right were clear indications of how institutionalized segregation was in the South. Above, John Salter, Jr., Joan Trumpauer, and Anne Moody (left to right) held a sit-in at a Jackson, Mississippi, lunch counter in May 1963. A hostile crowd registered their response by mocking and pouring food on the three activists. ***Economics* Why was the sit-in often a successful tactic?**

## The Freedom Rides

In *Boynton* v. *Virginia* (1960), the Supreme Court expanded its earlier ban on segregation on interstate buses. As a result, bus station waiting rooms and restaurants that served interstate travelers could not be segregated, either.

In 1961 CORE, with aid from SNCC, organized and carried out the **Freedom Rides.** They were a tactic designed to test whether southern states would obey the Supreme Court ruling and allow African Americans to exercise the rights newly granted to them.

**Violence Greets the Riders** The first Freedom Ride departed Washington, D.C., on May 4, 1961. Thirteen freedom riders, both blacks and whites, boarded an interstate bus heading south. (See the map of the route on the next page.) At first the group encountered only minor conflicts. In Atlanta the group split into two buses headed for the Deep South. It was there that the trip turned dangerous.

In Anniston, Alabama, a heavily armed white mob met the first bus at the terminal. The bus attempted to flee. CORE director James Farmer described what happened next:

AMERICAN VOICES **"Before the bus pulled out, however, members of the mob took their sharp instruments and slashed tires. The bus got to the outskirts of Anniston and the tires blew out and the bus ground to a halt. Members of the mob had boarded cars and followed the bus, and now with the disabled bus standing there, the members of the mob surrounded it, held the door closed, and a member of the mob threw a firebomb into the bus, breaking a window to do so. Incidentally, there were some local policemen mingling with the mob, fraternizing with them while this was going on."**

—*James Farmer*

The riders escaped before the bus burst into flames, but many were beaten by the mob as they stumbled out of the vehicle, choking on the smoke. They had anticipated trouble, since they meant to provoke a confrontation. However, the level of violence took them by surprise.

As a result of the savage response, Farmer considered calling the project off. SNCC leaders, though, begged to go on. Farmer warned, "You know that may be suicide." Student activist Diane Nash replied, "If we let them stop us with violence, the movement is dead! . . .

The Freedom Riders left Washington, D.C., for New Orleans, Louisiana, to test southern compliance with desegregation laws.
*Movement Through how many states did they pass? What kinds of opposition did they face?*

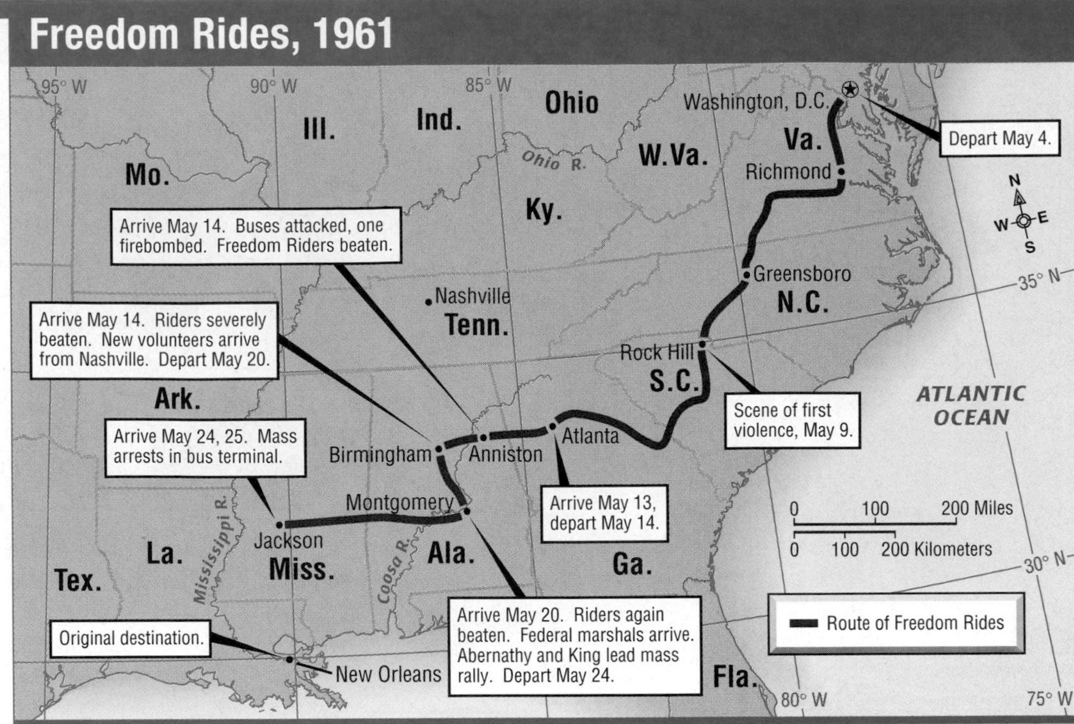


Your troops have been badly battered. Let us pick up the baton and run with it."

**National Reactions** Photographs of the smoldering bus in Anniston, horrified the country. Burke Marshall, the Assistant Attorney General who headed the Justice Department's Civil Rights Division, was astonished "that people—presumably otherwise sane, sensible, rational—would have this kind of reaction simply to where people were sitting on a bus."

The violence intensified in Birmingham and Montgomery. Upon their arrival in Jackson, Mississippi, the riders met no mobs but were arrested immediately. New volunteers arrived to replace them and were also arrested, This first Freedom Ride died out in Jackson, but about 300 Freedom Riders continued the protest throughout that summer. Attorney General Robert Kennedy had at first been reluctant to lend federal support to the protest, but now he sent federal marshals to protect the Freedom Riders.

Kennedy took further measures. He pressured the Interstate Commerce Commission to issue a ruling prohibiting segregation in all interstate transportation—trains, planes, buses. The Justice Department sued local communities that did not comply.

On May 14, 1961, a group of white men in Anniston, Alabama, attacked a busload of Freedom Riders. They tossed a bomb into the bus and beat the fleeing activists. Local hospitals refused to treat the wounded Freedom Riders.
***Government*** *How did the federal government respond?*

## *The Albany Movement*

In October 1961, a group of black Americans in Albany, Georgia, known as the **Albany Movement,** began a year-long campaign of protest marches. They called for desegregation of bus terminals and talks with white community leaders. Martin Luther King, Jr., went to Albany to help. His presence inspired many blacks to join, yet it irritated some local civil rights leaders, who resented outside involvement.

The Albany police chief, Laurie Pritchett, kept police violations of civil rights out of public view. His tactic of "nonviolent opposition" to the protests deprived the Albany Movement of the nationwide sympathy that the Freedom Riders had gained. The movement largely fizzled out by the end of 1962.

## Integration at "Ole Miss"

In September 1962, James Meredith, a black Air Force veteran, fought a personal battle for equal rights. Meredith was a student at Jackson State College but wanted to transfer to the all-white University of Mississippi, known as "Ole Miss." After being turned down on racial grounds, Meredith got legal help from the NAACP.

The Supreme Court upheld Meredith's claim. Mississippi governor Ross Barnett declared that Meredith could not enroll, whatever the Court said. Barnett personally blocked the way to the admissions office.

The issue became a standoff between the governor and the Justice Department. Crowds of angry white protesters destroyed vehicles bringing marshals to campus. As violence erupted on campus, tear gas covered the grounds. Two bystanders were killed and hundreds of people hurt. Finally, President Kennedy sent army troops to restore order, and federal marshals escorted Meredith to class.

## Clash in Birmingham

Elsewhere, civil rights leaders looked for chances to protest segregation nonviolently. The Rev. Fred Shuttlesworth, head of the Alabama Christian Movement for Human Rights, in Birmingham, invited Martin Luther King, Jr., to visit the city in April 1963. Birmingham's population was 40 percent African American, but King had called it "the most segregated city in the country." Victory there could be a model for resistance.

King planned boycotts of downtown stores and attempts to integrate local churches. Business leaders, fearing disruptions and lost sales, tried to negotiate with Shuttlesworth to call off the plan, without success.

When reporters wanted to know how long King planned to stay, he drew on a biblical story and told them he would remain until "Pharaoh let his people go." Birmingham police commissioner Eugene "Bull" Connor, a determined segregationist, replied, "I got plenty of room in the jail."

Mississippi's Lieutenant Governor, Paul Johnson (left), is shown reviewing a court order admitting James Meredith (right) to the University of Mississippi. Johnson disobeyed the court order and refused to admit Meredith. ***Government*** ***To what lengths did the government have to go in order to force Mississippi to comply with the Court's decision?***

**Main Idea CONNECTIONS**

*How did local police often treat nonviolent protesters?*

**From Birmingham Jail** The campaign began nonviolently with protest marches and sit-ins. City officials declared that the marches violated a regulation prohibiting parades without a permit. Connor arrested King and other demonstrators. When a group of white clergy criticized the campaign as an ill-timed threat to law and order by an "outsider," King responded from his cell.

In his "Letter from the Birmingham Jail," King defended his tactics and his timing:

**KEY DOCUMENTS**

**"Frankly, I have yet to engage in a direct-action campaign that was 'well timed' in the view of those who have not suffered unduly from the disease of segregation. For years now I have heard the word 'Wait!' It rings in the ear of every Negro with piercing familiarity. This 'Wait!' has almost always meant 'Never.'"**

—*"Letter from the Birmingham Jail," Martin Luther King, Jr., 1963*

Police in Birmingham, Alabama, used high-powered hoses to break up civil rights marches in 1963. Television coverage of this brutal treatment of peaceful demonstrators prompted widespread sympathy for the movement. ***Government*** *How did the Birmingham crisis end?*

After more than a week, King was released on bail. Soon after, he made a difficult decision: to let children join the campaign. Though dangerous, it would test the conscience of the Birmingham authorities and the nation.

As they marched with the adults, "Bull" Connor arrested more than 900 of the children. Police used high-pressure fire hoses, which could tear the bark from trees, on the demonstrators. They also brought out trained police dogs that attacked marchers' arms and legs. When protesters fell to the ground, policemen beat them with clubs and took them off to jail.

**The Nation Watches** Television cameras brought the scenes of violence to people across the country. Even those unsympathetic to the civil rights movement were appalled.

As reporter Eric Sevareid observed, "A newspaper or television picture of a snarling police dog set upon a human being is recorded in the permanent photo-electric file of every human brain."

In the end, the protesters won. A compromise arranged by Assistant Attorney General Burke Marshall led to desegregation of city facilities and fairer hiring practices. An interracial committee was set up to aid communication.

The success of the Birmingham marches was just one example that proved the effectiveness of nonviolent protest. Sometimes the technique did not work, or worked only slowly. Nevertheless, nonviolent protest as a means to social change had earned itself a place of honor in the history of civil rights in the United States.

## SECTION 2 REVIEW

### Comprehension

1. *Key Terms* Define: (a) sit-in; (b) Freedom Ride; (c) Albany Movement.
2. *Summarizing the Main Idea* How did the violent response to the Freedom Rides and the Birmingham boycott aid the civil rights movement?
3. *Organizing Information* Create a web diagram with *Nonviolent Protest* at the center, showing events and examples of this technique.

### Critical Thinking

4. *Analyzing Time Lines* Review the time line at the start of the section. Write a sentence that explains the broader effect of each event.
5. *Identifying Alternatives* If student protesters had not chosen nonviolent protest, what other options might they have used, for example, in ending lunch-counter segregation?

### Writing Activity

6. *Writing a Persuasive Essay* In May 1961, an article in *The New York Times* urged the Freedom Riders to call off their plans, saying, "Non-violence that deliberately provokes violence is a logical contradiction." Write an essay explaining why you agree or disagree with this opinion.

| 1963 | 1964 | 1964 | 1965 | 1965 |
|---|---|---|---|---|
| King delivers "I Have a Dream" speech | Freedom Summer voter registration drives | Congress passes Civil Rights Act | March from Selma to Montgomery, Alabama | Congress passes Voting Rights Act |

1963 — 1964 — 1965

# 3 The Political Response

## SECTION PREVIEW

### Objectives

1. Analyze how President Kennedy's policies on civil rights changed between 1961 and 1963.
2. Describe the political impact of the March on Washington.
3. Summarize the progress in civil rights made under Lyndon Johnson.
4. *Key Terms* Define: March on Washington; cloture; Civil Rights Act of 1964; Voting Rights Act of 1965.

### Main Idea

Continuous civil rights protests in the 1960s gradually made politicians respond to public opinion and move forward with strong civil rights legislation.

### Reading Strategy

*Analyzing Cause and Effect* As you read, analyze how effective the civil rights movement was by making a list of all the major cause-and-effect relationships you can find.

As a senator from Massachusetts, Kennedy had voted for civil rights measures but never actively pushed the issue. During his presidential campaign, however, Kennedy had sought and won many African American votes with bold rhetoric. In 1960 he proclaimed, "If the President does not himself wage the struggle for equal rights—if he stands above the battle—then the battle will inevitably be lost."

## Kennedy on Civil Rights

In October 1960, just weeks before the election, Senator Kennedy had a chance to make a powerful gesture of goodwill toward African Americans. Martin Luther King, Jr., had been arrested in Alabama and sentenced to four months of hard labor. His family feared for his life in the prison camp. Kennedy called King's wife, Coretta Scott King, and offered his help. Robert Kennedy then persuaded the Alabama sentencing judge to release King on bail.

Word of the Kennedys' actions raced through the black community. Many switched their votes from Nixon to Kennedy. The votes were crucial in Kennedy's slim margin of victory.

Once in office, however, Kennedy moved slowly on issues such as fair housing. He did not want to alienate southern Democratic senators whose votes he needed on foreign policy issues. Yet, Kennedy did appoint a number of African Americans to prominent positions.

The violent response to the Freedom Rides in 1961 embarrassed the President when he met with Soviet leader Nikita Khrushchev. Observers around the world watched the brutality in Birmingham early in 1963. Aware that he had to respond, Kennedy spoke to the American people on television:

**AMERICAN VOICES** "We preach freedom around the world, and we mean it, and we cherish our freedom, here at home, but are we to say to the world, and much more importantly, to each other that this is a land of the free except for the Negroes? . . . The time has come for this nation to fulfill its promise."

—*President John F. Kennedy, television address*

*Students demanded leadership from President Kennedy.*

VIEWING HISTORY "Jobs and Freedom" was the official slogan of the March on Washington in 1963. Thousands turned out to show their support for the civil rights movement. ***Government*** ***Why was President Kennedy at first opposed to the march?***

Earlier in his term, Kennedy had proposed a modest civil rights bill. After the crisis in Birmingham, he introduced a far stronger one. It would prohibit segregation in public places, ban discrimination wherever federal funding was involved, and advance school desegregation. Powerful southern segregationists in Congress, however, kept the bill from coming up for a vote.

## The March on Washington

To focus national attention on Kennedy's bill, civil rights leaders proposed a march on Washington, D.C. Kennedy feared it would alienate Congress and might cause racial violence. Yet when he could not persuade organizers to call off the march, he gave it his support.

The **March on Washington** took place in August 1963. More than 200,000 people came from all over the country. Labor leader A. Philip Randolph directed the march. Participants included religious leaders and celebrities, such as writer James Baldwin, entertainer Sammy Davis, Jr., and baseball player Jackie Robinson.

**Main Idea CONNECTIONS**

*What was the purpose of the March on Washington?*

The march was peaceful and orderly. After many songs and speeches, Martin Luther King, Jr., delivered what was to become his best-known address. With power and eloquence, he spoke to all Americans:

**KEY DOCUMENTS**

> **"I have a dream that one day this nation will rise up and live out the true meaning of its creed, 'We hold these truths to be self-evident, that all men are created equal.' I have a dream that one day on the red hills of Georgia, sons of former slaves and the sons of former slave owners will be able to sit down together at the table of brotherhood. . . . I have a dream that my four little children will one day live in a nation where they will not be judged by the color of their skin, but by the content of their character. . . . When we allow freedom to ring, when we let it ring from every village and every hamlet, from every state and every city, we will be able to speed up that day when all of God's children, black men and white men, Jews and Gentiles, Protestants and Catholics, will be able to join hands and sing in the words of the old Negro spiritual: 'Free at last. Free at last. Thank God Almighty, we are free at last.'"**
>
> —*"I Have a Dream" speech, Martin Luther King, Jr., August 28, 1963*

## Johnson on Civil Rights

The new President, Lyndon Johnson, was a Texan who had voted against civil rights measures early in his congressional career. As Senate majority leader, however, he had worked successfully to get a civil rights bill passed in 1957. Now Johnson used his political skills to pass Kennedy's bill. In his first public address, he told Congress and the country that nothing "could more eloquently honor President Kennedy's memory than the earliest possible passage of the civil rights bill."

After the House of Representatives passed the bill, civil rights opponents in the Senate started a lengthy filibuster, exercising their right of unlimited day-and-night debate. Johnson finally enlisted his former colleague, Republican minority leader Everett Dirksen, to support the rarely used procedure called **cloture**—a three-fifths vote to limit debate and call for a vote. In June 1964 the Senate voted for cloture. Soon after, the bill passed with support from both Democrats and Republicans.

## *Turning Point: The Civil Rights Act*

The **Civil Rights Act of 1964** had an impact in many areas, including voting, schools, and jobs. It gave the Justice Department authority to act vigorously in school segregation and voting rights cases. The law's major sections (called "titles") included these provisions:

(1) Title I banned the use of different voter registration standards for blacks and whites.

(2) Title II prohibited discrimination in public accommodations, such as motels, restaurants, gas stations, theaters, and sports arenas.

(3) Title VI allowed the withholding of federal funds from public or private programs that practice discrimination.

(4) Title VII banned discrimination on the basis of race, sex, religion, or national origin by employers and unions. †

(5) Title VII also created the Equal Employment Opportunity Commission (EEOC) to investigate charges of job discrimination.

† A last-minute change, which was meant to make it harder for the bill to pass, changed the wording of Title VII to forbid sex discrimination as well as racial discrimination in employment. When the 1964 Civil Rights Bill passed anyway, it was the first law to call for equal hiring opportunities for women.

## TURNING POINT: *The Civil Rights Act of 1964*

**Following the Civil Rights Act of 1964, other federal laws and Supreme Court decisions dealt with the issue of discrimination.**

**1964**
*Civil Rights Act of 1964 outlaws discrimination in a variety of areas*

**1968**
*Civil Rights Act of 1968 bans discrimination in housing*

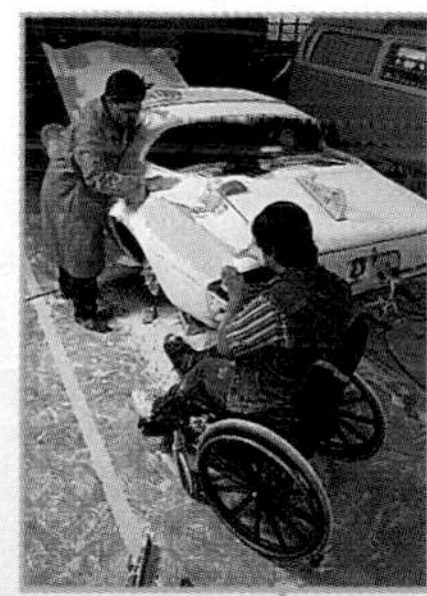

**1990**
*Americans with Disabilities Act guarantees disabled Americans equal opportunity in employment and public accommodations*

1960 | 1970 | 1980 | 1990 | 2000

**1967**
*Age Discrimination in Employment Act prohibits job discrimination against people age 40 or older*

**1978**
*In the Bakke case, the Supreme Court rules that race may be a factor (though not the only one) in school application decisions*

**1995**
*In the Adarand case, the Supreme Court limits government in giving preferences to minority groups*

## FACT Finder — Major Civil Rights Protests, 1954–1965

| Year | Event | Outcome |
|---|---|---|
| 1954 | *Brown* v. *Board of Education* | Supreme Court ruled that separate educational facilities for whites and African Americans are inherently unequal. |
| 1955–1956 | Montgomery Bus Boycott | Bus company was forced to desegregate its buses. Martin Luther King, Jr., emerged as an important civil rights leader. |
| 1961 | Freedom Rides | Interstate Commerce Commission banned segregation in interstate transportation. |
| 1963 | James Meredith sues University of Mississippi for admission | Supreme Court upheld Meredith's right to enter the all-white institution. |
| 1963 | Protest marches in Birmingham, Alabama | Violence against peaceful demonstrators shocked the nation. Under pressure, Birmingham desegregated public facilities. |
| 1963 | March on Washington | More than 200,000 people demonstrated in an impressive display of support for civil rights. |
| 1965 | Selma March | State troopers attacked marchers. Johnson used federal force to protect route from Selma to Montgomery, and thousands joined march. |

***Interpreting Tables*** The visibility of civil rights protests led to advances in civil rights on both the local and national level. ***Culture What did most of these protests have in common?***

Over the years, the Civil Rights Act of 1964 has helped millions of Americans and affected the nation's political and business life. The lasting impact of the legislation is shown in the Turning Point feature on the previous page.

*Fannie Lou Hamer*

**Freedom Summer** Even with a strong new law, change came slowly. Protests continued, and segregationists often answered them with violence. In 1964, leaders of the major civil rights groups organized a voter registration drive in Mississippi. About a thousand African American and white volunteers, mostly college students, joined in what came to be called Freedom Summer. Many white Mississippians were already angry about the new Civil Rights Act. The Ku Klux Klan held rallies to intimidate the volunteers.

Soon three young civil rights workers were reported missing: James Chaney, Andrew Goodman, and Michael Schwerner. Later in the summer, FBI agents found their bodies buried in a new earthen dam a few miles from where their burned-out station wagon had been found. These three murders were only part of the turbulence reported that summer. Civil rights leaders also reported 80 mob attacks. Volunteers were beaten up and a few wounded by gunfire. About a thousand were arrested. African American churches and homes were burned or firebombed.

**The Democratic Convention** Newly registered Mississippi voters, along with members of SNCC, organized the Mississippi Freedom Democratic party (MFDP). The MFDP sent delegates to the Democratic National Convention in the summer of 1964. The delegates argued that they, not politicians from the segregated party organization, were the rightful representatives.

One delegate was Fannie Lou Hamer, who had lost her job on a cotton plantation when she tried to register to vote. She told the convention about her experiences in one voter drive:

AMERICAN VOICES

> **"I began to scream, and one white man got up and began to beat me on my head and tell me to 'hush.' . . . All of this on account we want to register, to become first class citizens. [If] the Freedom Democratic Party is not seated now, I question America."**
>
> —*Fannie Lou Hamer*

The MFDP rejected an offer by President Johnson to seat two MFDP delegates of his choosing and to change the rules for the 1968 convention to eliminate discrimination. Johnson was reelected in a landslide in 1964, but he knew he had to do something about the issue of voting rights.

**The Selma March** Many black southerners still had trouble obtaining one basic right: voting. In Selma, Alabama, police and sheriff's deputies were arresting people just for standing in line to register to vote. To call attention to the voting rights issue, King and other leaders decided to organize a protest march. They would walk from Selma to the state capital, Montgomery, about 50 miles away.

As the marchers set out on a Sunday morning in March 1965, armed state troopers on horseback charged into the crowd with whips, clubs, and tear gas. TV pictures of the attack again shocked many viewers. In response, President Johnson put the Alabama National Guard under federal control. He sent them, along with federal marshals and army helicopters, to protect the march route. When the Selma marchers started out again, supporters from all over the country flocked to join. By the time the march reached Montgomery, the ranks had swelled to about 25,000 people.

**The Voting Rights Act** Reacting to Selma, Johnson also went on national television, promising a strong new law to protect voting rights. Raising his arms, Johnson repeated, "And . . . we . . . shall . . . overcome!" That summer, despite another filibuster, Congress passed the **Voting Rights Act of 1965.**

Under the act, federal officials could register voters in places where local officials were blocking registration by African Americans. The act also effectively eliminated literacy tests and other barriers. In the year after the law passed, more than 400,000 African Americans registered to vote in the Deep South.

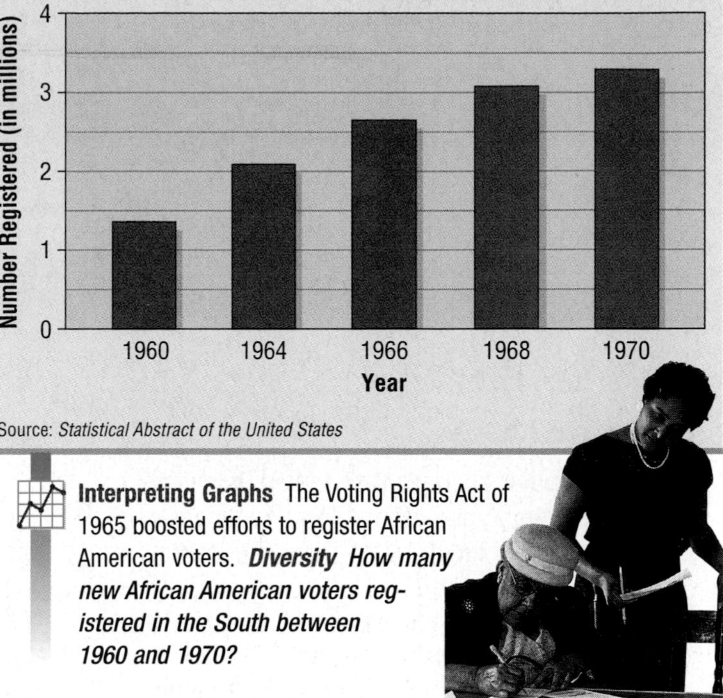


**Interpreting Graphs** The Voting Rights Act of 1965 boosted efforts to register African American voters. ***Diversity** How many new African American voters registered in the South between 1960 and 1970?*

**Legal Landmarks** Together, the Civil Rights Act of 1964 and the Voting Rights Act of 1965 created an entirely new voting population in the South. That meant that more black Americans would be elected to political office. Another legal landmark was the Twenty-fourth Amendment to the Constitution, ratified in 1964. It barred the use of the poll tax in federal elections.

For some African Americans new laws were not nearly enough. Impatient with the slow pace of progress, they were ready to listen to more militant leaders.

## SECTION 3 REVIEW

### Comprehension

1. *Key Terms* Define: (a) March on Washington; (b) cloture; (c) Civil Rights Act of 1964; (d) Voting Rights Act of 1965.
2. *Summarizing the Main Idea* What events forced both Kennedy and Johnson to move ahead with civil rights legislation?
3. *Organizing Information* Create a two-column chart comparing the provisions of the Civil Rights Act and the Voting Rights Act.

### Critical Thinking

4. *Analyzing Time Lines* Review the time line at the start of the section. Explain how each event is related to the one after it.
5. *Tracing Cause and Effect* How did President Johnson's previous experience in Congress help to achieve passage of the Civil Rights Act?

### Writing Activity

6. *Writing an Expository Essay* Write a short news story explaining the reasons for the March on Washington.

| 1962 | 1963 | 1964 | 1965 | 1966 | 1968 | 1968 |
|---|---|---|---|---|---|---|
| | **1963** Baldwin's The Fire Next Time | **1964** King receives Nobel Peace Prize | **1965** Malcolm X assassinated; riots in Watts | **1966** Black Panther party organized | **1968** King assassinated | **1968** Kerner Commission reports on civil disorders |

1962 · 1964 · 1966 · 1968

# 4 The Challenge of Black Power

## SECTION PREVIEW

### Objectives

1. Compare the ways that James Baldwin, Malcolm X, and other African Americans expressed anger at the pace of progress toward civil rights.
2. Explain the principles and tactics used by advocates of black power.
3. Summarize the legacy of the civil rights movement.
4. *Key Terms* Define: Nation of Islam; black nationalism; black power; de jure segregation; de facto segregation.

### Main Idea

Gains in civil rights came so slowly that some African Americans rejected nonviolence, calling for black power and more militant actions.

### Reading Strategy

*Outlining Information* On a separate sheet of paper, copy the headings and subheadings in this section. As you read, add at least two key facts under each subheading to create on outline.

*Author James Baldwin wrote movingly of the black experience.*

The passage of two civil rights acts represented enormous progress. Over time, African Americans would use these statutes to win court battles that would tear down segregation. But in the meantime, African Americans still faced economic and social discrimination. Many were angry at this slow pace of change.

In 1964, Martin Luther King, Jr., whom the world admired for nonviolent protest, won the Nobel Peace Prize. Yet some Americans in the civil rights movement questioned his approach.

The movement was becoming deeply divided. Younger leaders rejected the ideas of both nonviolence and integration with white society. The simmering anger of many African Americans against continuing injustices was reflected in more militant rhetoric, sometimes exploding into urban riots.

## James Baldwin

In 1963, in the bestseller *The Fire Next Time,* writer James Baldwin told how generations of oppression and suffering had set African Americans apart but had also made them stronger. Now, he said, African Americans were tired of promises. Their anger was ready to erupt. As Baldwin put it, "the Negro himself no longer believes in the good faith of white Americans—if, indeed, he ever could have."

Baldwin's essays and novels were powerful descriptions of the African American experience that touched both black and white Americans deeply. He was a strong voice for the civil rights movement. In *Notes of a Native Son* (1955), Baldwin wrote about the damaging effects of segregation in the United States. He recounted "the Negro's past, of . . . death and humiliation; fear by day and night; fear as deep as the marrow of the bone; doubt that he was worthy of life, since everyone around him denied it. . . ."

## Malcolm X

Outside the mainstream civil rights movement, more militant political leaders emerged. The best known was Malcolm X, born Malcolm Little in Omaha, Nebraska, in 1925. His father, a Baptist minister who spread the "back-to-Africa" message of Marcus Garvey, died when Little was a child. Growing up in ghettos in Detroit, Boston, and New York, Little turned to crime. At age 20, he was arrested for burglary and served seven years in prison. While in jail he joined the **Nation of Islam,** a group often called the Black Muslims. Viewing white society as oppressive, it preached black separation and self-help.

**Black Nationalism** The Nation of Islam was founded in 1933 in Chicago by Elijah Muhammad. He taught that Allah (the Muslim name for God) would bring about a "Black Nation," a union among all nonwhite peoples. According to Elijah Muhammad, one of the keys to self-knowledge was knowing one's enemy. For him, the enemy of the Nation of Islam was white society.

Members of the Nation of Islam did not seek change through political means but waited for Allah to create the Black Nation. In the meantime, they tried to lead righteous lives and worked hard to become economically self-sufficient.

Released from prison in 1952, Malcolm Little changed his name to Malcolm X. (The other name, he said, came from slaveowners.) He spent the next 12 years as a minister of the Nation of Islam, winning followers with his fiery speeches. He spread the ideas of **black nationalism,** a belief in the separate identity and racial unity of the African American community.

**Opposition to Integration** Malcolm X disagreed with both the tactics and the goals of the early civil rights movement. He called the March on Washington the "Farce on Washington," and voiced his irritation at "all of this non-violent, begging-the-white-man kind of dying . . . all of this sitting-in, sliding-in, wading-in, eating-in, diving-in, and all the rest." Instead of preaching brotherly love, he rejected ideas of integration. Asking why anyone would want to join white society he noted:

**AMERICAN VOICES**

"No sane black man really wants integration! No sane white man really wants integration! No sane black man really believes that the white man ever will give the black man anything more than token integration. No! The Honorable Elijah Muhammad teaches that for the black man in America the only solution is complete separation from the white man. . . . The American black man should be focusing his effort toward building his own businesses, and decent homes for himself. As other ethnic groups have done, let the black people, wherever possible, however possible, patronize their own kind, hire their own kind, and start in those ways to build up the black race's ability to do for itself. That's the only way the American black man is ever going to get respect."

—*Malcolm X*

**Main Idea CONNECTIONS**

*Why did black nationalists such as Malcolm X believe the civil rights desegregation movement was doomed to fail?*

Malcolm X and Elijah Muhammad came to disagree about many things, including political action. In 1964 Malcolm X left the Nation of Islam and formed his own religious organization, called Muslim Mosque, Inc. He

Elijah Muhammad (left) called African Americans "the lost-found Nation of Islam in the wilderness of North America." Malcolm X (right) was a leading minister of the Nation of Islam until 1964. ***Diversity*** *How did black nationalism differ from other civil rights activism?*

Members of the Black Panthers marched through the streets of New York City in 1968 to protest the trial of Huey P. Newton. Newton had been convicted of voluntary manslaughter in the death of a police officer. His conviction was later overturned. ***Economics*** ***What efforts did the Black Panthers make to improve the quality of life in black communities?***

then made a pilgrimage (a religious journey) to Mecca, the holy city of Islam in Saudi Arabia.

Seeing millions of Muslims of all races worshipping together peacefully had a profound effect on Malcolm X. It changed his views about separatism and hatred of white people. When he returned, he was ready to work with other civil rights leaders and even with white Americans on some issues. It seemed as if Malcolm X might become one of the leaders in a unified civil rights movement. His change of heart, however, earned him some enemies.

A month later, in February 1965, he was shot to death at a rally in New York. Three members of the Nation of Islam were charged with the murder.

Malcolm X's message of black nationalism lived on. He particularly influenced younger members of SNCC, the Student Nonviolent Coordinating Committee.

## *The Black Power Movement*

One SNCC leader who heard Malcolm's message was Stokely Carmichael. Born in Trinidad, in the West Indies, in 1941, Carmichael came to the United States at the age of 11 and was soon involved in protests. At Howard University in Washington, D.C., he and other students took over the Washington chapter of SNCC.

As Carmichael rose to SNCC leadership, the group became more militant. After being beaten and jailed for his participation in demonstrations, he was tired of nonviolent protest. He called on SNCC workers to carry guns for self-defense. He wanted to make the group exclusively black, rejecting white activists.

The split in the civil rights movement became obvious in June 1966. At a protest march in Greenwood, Mississippi, while King's followers were singing, "We Shall Overcome," Carmichael's supporters drowned them out with "We Shall Overrun." Then Carmichael, just out of jail, jumped into the back of an open truck to challenge the moderate leaders:

**AMERICAN VOICES**

**"This is the twenty-seventh time I have been arrested, and I ain't going to jail no more! . . . The only way we gonna stop them white men from whuppin' us is to take over. We been saying freedom for six years—and we ain't got nothin.' What we gonna start saying now is 'black power!'"**

—*Stokely Carmichael, public address, June 1966*

As he repeated "We . . . want . . . black . . . power!" the audience excitedly echoed the new slogan. Carmichael's idea of **black power** called on African Americans "to unite, to recognize their heritage, to build a sense of community . . . to begin to define their own goals, to lead their own organizations and support those organizations."

**The Black Panthers** In the fall of 1966, a new militant political party, the Black Panthers, was formed by activists Bobby Seale and Huey Newton. The Panthers wanted African Americans to lead their own communities. They demanded that the federal government rebuild the nation's ghettos to make up for years of neglect. Newton repeated the words of Chinese Communist leader Mao Zedong: "Power flows from the barrel of a gun." Though the Panthers had violent encounters with police, they also set up community programs such as day-care centers and free breakfast programs.

Black power gave rise to the "Black is beautiful" slogan, fostering racial pride. It also led to a serious split in the civil rights movement. More radical groups like SNCC and the Black Panthers moved away from the NAACP and other more moderate organizations.

**Riots in the Streets** The early civil rights movement focused on battling **de jure segregation,** racial separation created by law. Changes in the law, however did not address the tougher issue of **de facto segregation,** the separation caused by social conditions such as poverty. De facto segregation was a fact of life in most American cities, not just in the South. (See map below right.)

There were no "whites only" signs above water fountains in northern cities, yet discrimination continued in education, housing, and employment. African Americans were kept out of well-paying jobs, job training programs, and suburban housing. Inner-city schools were run-down and poorly equipped.

Residents of ghetto neighborhoods viewed police officers as dangerous oppressors, not upholders of justice. James Baldwin remarked that a white police officer in one of these neighborhoods was "like an occupying soldier in a bitterly hostile country." Eventually, frustration and anger boiled over into riots and looting. In 1964, riots ravaged Rochester, New York; New York City; and several cities in New Jersey.

One of the most violent riots occurred in the Los Angeles neighborhood of Watts. On August 11, 1965, police in Watts pulled over a 21-year-old black man for drunken driving. At first the interaction was friendly among the police, the suspect, and a crowd of Watts residents that had gathered. When the suspect resisted arrest, however, one police officer panicked and began swinging his riot baton. The crowd was outraged, and the scene touched off six days of rioting.

Thousands of people filled the streets, burning cars and stores, stealing merchandise, and sniping at firefighters. When the national guard and local police finally gained control, 34 people were dead and more than a thousand were injured.

Violence spread to other cities in 1966 and 1967. Cries of "Burn, baby, burn" replaced the gentler slogans of the earlier civil rights movement.

Another serious blow to believers in nonviolence was the assassination of Martin Luther King, Jr., in 1968 (which you will read about in a later chapter). Sorrow and anger again caused riots across the country.

A concerned federal government set up a special National Advisory Commission on Civil Disorders, headed by former Illinois Governor Otto Kerner, to investigate. In 1968 the Kerner Commission report declared flatly that the riots were an explosion of the anger that had been smoldering in the inner-city ghettos. It declared that "our nation is moving toward two societies, one black, one white—separate and unequal."

*One result of the civil rights movement was the wearing of ethnic African clothing as a symbol of black pride.*

## *Legacy of the Movement*

At times, both black and white Americans wondered whether real progress in civil rights was possible. Many young activists felt frustrated and discouraged when the movement failed to bring changes quickly. Lyndon Johnson was devastated by the violence that

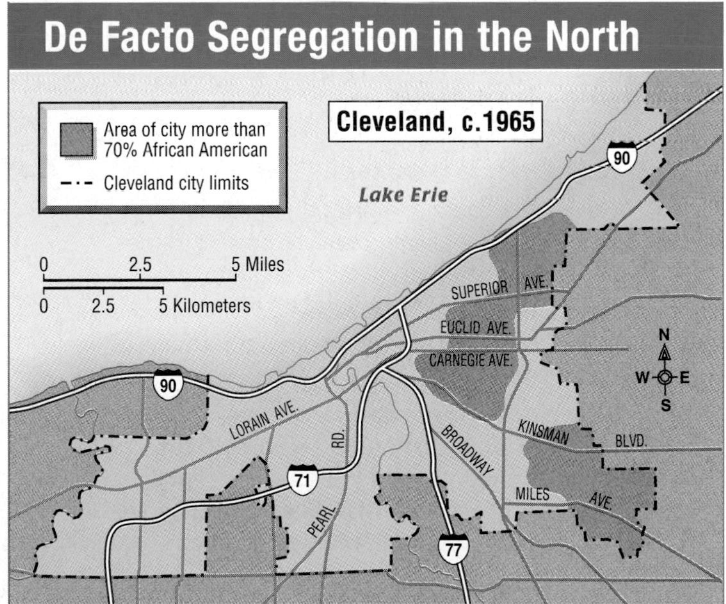


MAP skills This map shows the areas of Cleveland, Ohio, with the highest concentrations of African Americans in the mid-1960s. ***Place*** ***What social and economic factors may have contributed to this pattern of settlement?***

The rallying cry "Burn, Baby, Burn" became a nightmarish reality in the streets of Los Angeles in 1965. After firefighters quenched the flames in buildings all over Watts, crowds of looters moved in to carry off the spoils. ***Culture*** ***What set off the Watts riot?***

exploded near the end of his presidency. "How is it possible," he asked, "after all we've accomplished?" Still, the measures passed by his administration had brought tremendous change. Segregation was now illegal. Because of voter registration drives, thousands of African Americans could now vote. The power they wielded changed the nature of American political life.

Between 1970 and 1975, the number of African American elected officials rose by 88 percent. Black mayors were elected in Atlanta, Detroit, Los Angeles, and Newark, N.J. Others served in Congress and state legislatures. In 1966 Barbara Jordan became the first African American elected to the Texas state Senate since Reconstruction. Six years later she was elected to the United States Congress. Jordan noted what made the movement necessary:

**AMERICAN VOICES**

> **"The civil rights movement called America to look at itself in a giant mirror. . . . Do the black people who were born on this soil, who are American citizens, do they really feel that this is the land of opportunity, the land of the free? . . . America had to say no."**
>
> —*Texas Representative Barbara Jordan*

Trying to change the answer to that question spurred the civil rights movement. It was the first step toward making the United States a fairer society for all.

## SECTION 4 REVIEW

### Comprehension

1. ***Key Terms*** Define: (a) Nation of Islam; (b) black nationalism; (c) black power; (d) de jure segregation; (e) de facto segregation.
2. ***Summarizing the Main Idea*** What was the lasting impact of the civil rights movement of the mid-1960s?
3. ***Organizing Information*** Create a two-column chart to compare the basic ideas of the leaders discussed in this section. Put people's names in the left column, with summaries of their ideas in the right column.

### Critical Thinking

4. ***Analyzing Time Lines*** Review the time line at the start of the section. Choose three events and explain how each played a part in the division of the civil rights movement.
5. ***Distinguishing Fact from Opinion*** Malcolm X once said that for African Americans, "the only solution is complete separation from the white man." Explain the factors that make this statement either a fact or an opinion.

### Writing Activity

6. ***Writing a Persuasive Essay*** Black nationalists believed that African Americans should establish communities separate from white society. Do you think this was a desirable goal? Explain.

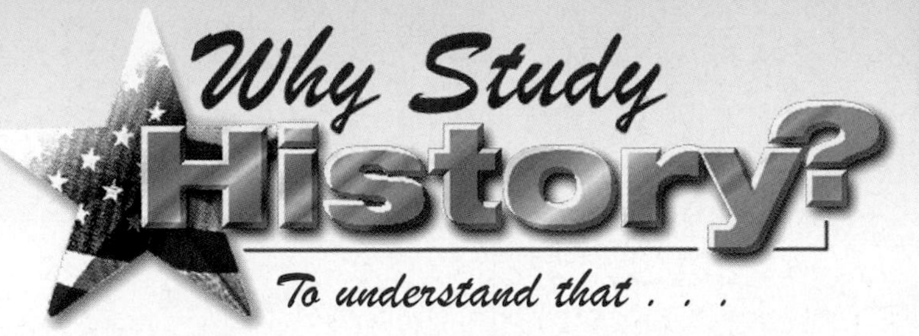


# You Can Help Achieve Racial Equality

**In years following the civil rights movement, the United States has made progress toward equal access to education and jobs.**

*James Meredith, who integrated the University of Mississippi in 1962*

The civil rights movement of the 1960s achieved tremendous victories in ending legal discrimination based on race. Are there segregated public schools in your community? No. Today public schools educate boys and girls of any race in the same classrooms. Are there segregated public hospitals in your community? No. African American and white physicians treat patients of different races side by side.

Still, the United States is not a colorblind society. Much remains to be done to ensure that all American children have the opportunity to realize their dreams.

## The Impact Today

Since the civil rights movement, many African Americans have achieved a higher standard of living. In 1970 only 10 percent of black families had incomes above $50,000 dollars per year. In 1993, the figure had risen to nearly 18 percent. Greater educational opportunities, the result of school integration, helped create these economic gains. In 1960 only about 20 percent of African Americans age 25 or older had completed high school. A mere 3 percent had finished four years of college. By 1994 those numbers had increased to 73 percent and 13 percent, respectively.

Affirmative action policies have also created greater opportunities for African Americans. Affirmative action gives preference to racial minorities in such areas as job hiring and college admissions. Almost all institutions doing business with or receiving funds from the federal government have practiced affirmative action since the 1960s. Many private institutions and businesses have also adopted affirmative action policies.

Affirmative action has been controversial from the beginning. Many Americans argue that giving preference to some groups amounts to "reverse discrimination" that is unfair to other groups. In recent years, opponents of affirmative action have mobilized to eliminate it. For example, in 1996, California voters passed Proposition 209, which outlaws racial preferences in education and employment. The law has dramatically affected admissions to schools in the University of California system. At one school, African American acceptance fell by 66 percent two years after Proposition 209 was passed.

Supporters of affirmative action fear that laws like Proposition 209 will worsen racial inequality. Opponents of affirmative action claim that outlawing all racial preferences is the only way to achieve true racial equality.

*Racially mixed campus in New York State*

## The Impact on You

Do you think affirmative action is a good way to achieve racial equality? Discuss the issue with your classmates. Then generate lists of arguments for and against affirmative action.

# Chapter 19 Review

## Chapter Summary

The major concepts of Chapter 19 are presented below. See also ***Guide to the Essentials of American History*** or ***Interactive Student Tutorial CD-ROM,*** which contains interactive review activities, time lines, helpful hints, and test practice.

### *Reviewing the Main Ideas*

In the early 1960s, new groups and new leaders emerged in the fight for civil rights for African Americans. Continuing pressure from those groups, plus growing public sympathy, forced political action and the passage of strong new legislation. Though Martin Luther King, Jr., and his supporters carried on nonviolent protest, other African Americans took a more militant position.

### *Section 1: Leaders and Strategies*

The civil rights movement of the 1960s consisted of many separate groups whose leaders and methods differed while sharing the goal of securing equal rights.

### *Section 2: The Struggle Intensifies*

The tactics of nonviolent protest, including sit-ins and boycotts, challenged segregation and brought change, but also generated violent confrontations.

### *Section 3: The Political Response*

Continuous civil rights protests in the 1960s gradually made politicians respond to public opinion and move forward with strong civil rights legislation.

### *Section 4: The Challenge of Black Power*

Gains in civil rights came so slowly that some African Americans rejected nonviolence, calling for Black Power and more militant actions.

In the years following the civil rights movement, the United States has made progress toward equal access to education and jobs. Yet much remains to be done to ensure that all American children have the opportunity to realize their dreams.

## Key Terms

For each of the terms below, write a sentence explaining how it relates to this chapter.

1. interracial
2. black nationalism
3. de jure segregation
4. sit-in
5. Freedom Ride
6. cloture
7. Civil Rights Act of 1964
8. Voting Rights Act of 1965
9. de facto segregation

## Comprehension

1. Name two groups that were working for African Americans' rights *before* the 1960s. What did they accomplish?
2. What new approach did Martin Luther King, Jr., bring to the civil rights movement? What was the inspiration for his philosophy?
3. What happened during a typical sit-in?
4. What were the goals of the Freedom Rides?
5. What was Johnson's role in passing civil rights legislation?
6. What events spurred the passage of the Voting Rights Act?
7. What were the beliefs of the Nation of Islam?
8. How did Malcolm X's pilgrimage to Mecca change his thinking?
9. What major changes occurred in the civil rights movement in the mid-1960s?

## Using Graphic Organizers

On a separate sheet of paper, copy the tree map below. Fill in the boxes with major protests and descriptions of their outcomes. Each section of the tree map should focus on one event or tactic of nonviolent protest, such as sit-ins.

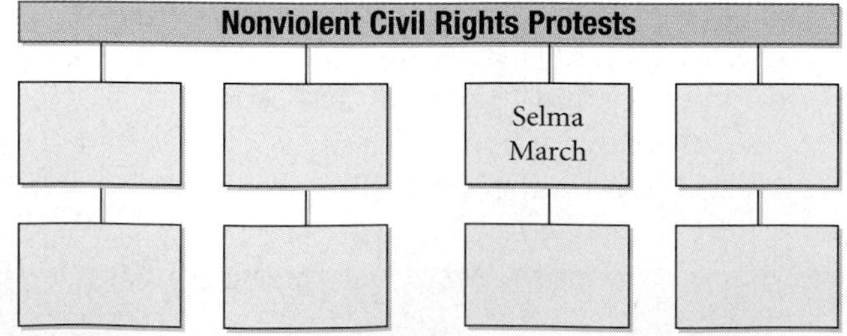

## Analyzing Political Cartoons ▶

1. Examine both panels of the cartoon. What does the man represent?
2. (a) What does the first pit represent? (b) What does the second pit represent?
3. What is the man's overall goal, and what obstacles does he face?
4. What point is the cartoonist trying to make?

## Critical Thinking

1. *Applying the Chapter Skill* Reread the excerpt on the Skills for Life page. (a) Why was Ralph Abernathy a reliable source for information about the civil rights movement? (b) How might his association with Martin Luther King, Jr., have affected his point of view toward those events?
2. *Analyzing Cause and Effect* Why did the violent reactions of segregationists to nonviolent protests such as the Freedom Rides actually help those protests become more effective?
3. *Formulating Questions* Make a list of three to five questions that you could ask a student activist from the 1960s in order to find out his or her reasons for taking part in the civil rights movement.
4. *Drawing Conclusions* Voter registration drives greatly increased African Americans' political power in the South. What are the potential results of increased political influence for a certain group?

### INTERNET ACTIVITY

***For your portfolio:***
**WRITE AN ESSAY**

Access Prentice Hall's *America: Pathways to the Present* site at **www.Pathways.phschool.com** for the specific URL to complete the activity. Additional resources and related Web sites are also available.

Use the links provided to read about Martin Luther King, Jr., and the civil rights movement. Write an essay on a particular aspect of King's life or the civil rights movement.

## ANALYZING DOCUMENTS ◀▶ INTERPRETING DATA

Turn to the excerpt from King's "I Have a Dream" speech in Section 3.

1. Which of the following phrases best *summarizes* King's dream? (a) that Americans of all religions will be free at last (b) that all Americans will achieve true equality and freedom (c) that African Americans will form a brotherhood (d) that children will not be judged by their color.
2. King hopes that his dream will be fulfilled (a) in the long run. (b) in his children's lifetime. (c) in the 20th century. (d) today.
3. *Writing* King said that he hoped the nation would "live out the true meaning" of the statement "all men are created equal." Write two or three paragraphs that explain what you think is the meaning of that phrase.

## Connecting to Today

*Essay Writing* Reread the list of provisions of the 1964 Civil Rights Act in Section 3. Research current newspapers and news magazines. Then write an essay showing how these laws and regulations have affected American life and politics today.

CHAPTER 20

# Other Social Movements

## 1960–1975

## CHAPTER FOCUS

This chapter describes the social revolution of the 1960s and early 1970s. The civil rights movement of the 1960s spurred other groups, such as women, Latinos, Asian Americans, and Native Americans, to work for their own goals of equality. Activists adapted civil rights tactics to launch movements to protect the environment and to improve the quality and safety of consumer goods.

*The* ***Why Study History?*** *page at the end of this chapter explores the connection between social activists of the 1960s and early 1970s and activists today who are working to secure rights for victims of crimes.*

▲ **VIEWING HISTORY**
The first Earth Day rallies helped bring environmental issues to the public's attention. ***Culture*** ***What other social movements were competing for the nation's attention?***

| 1963 | 1966 | 1971 | 1972 | 1973 |
|---|---|---|---|---|
| Betty Friedan publishes The Feminine Mystique | National Organization for Women formed | National Women's Political Caucus organized | Gloria Steinem founds Ms. magazine | Roe v. Wade decision |

1962 · 1966 · 1970 · 1974

# 1 The Women's Movement

**SECTION PREVIEW**

### Objectives

1. Summarize the background of the women's movement and analyze the impact of the civil rights movement on it.
2. Describe how feminist leaders organized groups to advocate for women's rights and explain the impact of feminism.
3. Understand that the feminist movement was opposed by some who wanted to preserve traditional roles.
4. *Key Terms* Define: feminism; National Organization for Women (NOW); *Roe* v. *Wade;* Equal Rights Amendment (ERA).

### Main Idea

Encouraged by the gains of the civil rights movement, a women's movement arose in an effort to end discrimination based on gender.

### Reading Strategy

*Organizing Information* Write the following three column headings on a piece of paper: *Social Conditions for Women in the 1950s, Steps Taken by Feminists to Change Conditions,* and *Opposition to the Feminist Movement.* As you read the section, note relevant information in the appropriate column.

The African American struggle for civil rights made other groups aware of other inequalities in American life. Women, though not a minority in numbers, recognized that certain aspects of society placed them at a disadvantage. They became determined to elevate their status.

The quest for women's rights was not new to the nation's history. In the late 1800s, particularly, women had worked for the right to vote and for equality in education and in jobs. The term **feminism** first came into recorded use in 1895 as a word to describe the theory of political, economic, and social equality of men and women. Feminists were those who believed in or acted on behalf of this theory.

## Background of the Women's Movement

The women's movement of the 1960s sought to change aspects of American life that had been accepted for decades. Mainstream society expected women to put home and family first. The stereotype of women in the 1950s placed them in the home, married and raising children. During and after World War II, however, more and more women entered the labor force. By the beginning of the 1960s, about half of all women held jobs.

*The new women's movement chose symbols of power to represent its cause.*

In addition, an increasing number of women were going to college. In 1950 only 25 percent of all Bachelor of Arts degrees were earned by women. Twenty years later, in 1970, it was 41 percent. Better-educated women had high hopes for the future, but often were discouraged by the discrimination they faced when they looked for jobs or tried to advance in their professions. Many people thought it was appropriate for young women who entered the work force to leave after only a few years in order to start families. In many cases, employers were reluctant to invest training in women because they were not expected to stay on the job for very long. Other employers

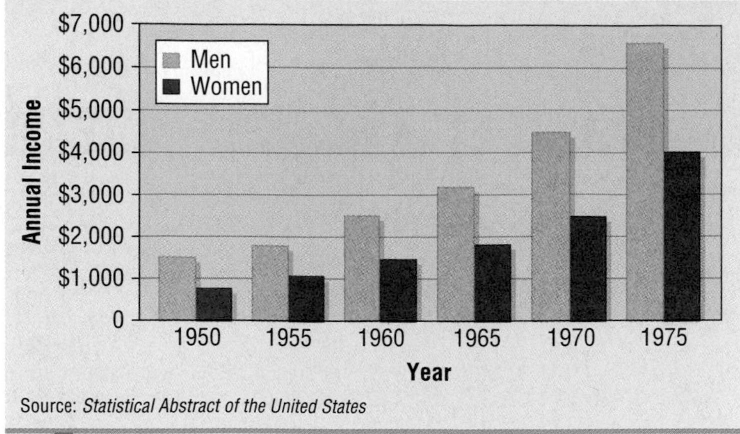


**Interpreting Graphs** Women's incomes continued to lag behind men's earnings, partly because many low-paying fields were traditionally considered "women's work." ***Economics Did the gap increase or decrease between 1950 and 1975?***

completely denied women job opportunities for which they were qualified because they believed that home and family should be a woman's only responsibility.

Women who did enter the work force often found themselves underemployed, performing jobs and earning salaries below their abilities. Working women earned less than working men doing similar or even identical jobs. In 1963, women, on average, were paid only 63 cents for each dollar that men earned. By 1973 this figure had dropped to 57 cents. The graph above shows median incomes of men and women from 1950 to 1975. This financial inequality created a growing sense of frustration among women and led to demands for change.

**Main Idea CONNECTIONS**

*How did women's salaries compare to men's salaries?*

## The Impact of the Civil Rights Movement

While social conditions set the scene for the women's movement, the civil rights movement provided a model for techniques and an inspiration for action. Black and white women joined in the struggle for civil rights and gained valuable skills from their work in the movement.

As they worked to bring racial discrimination to an end, many women in the civil rights movement were discouraged. They were expected to make coffee and do clerical work while men made most of the policy decisions. Frustrated over their assigned roles, they applied the techniques they had learned in the civil rights movement to address their own concerns.

The civil rights movement also provided women with legal tools to fight discrimination. One important piece of legislation was the 1964 Civil Rights Act.

Originally, the section of the act called Title VII prohibited discrimination based on race, religion, or national origin. When Congress debated the bill, however, some opponents of civil rights added an amendment to outlaw discrimination on the basis of gender. This action was a strategy to make the entire bill look ridiculous, so that it would fail in the final vote. To the dismay of its opponents, both the amendment and the bill passed. The new Civil Rights Act now had a provision that gave women a legal framework to fight discrimination.

Even with the added boost of the new legislation, progress took time. Women soon discovered that the Equal Employment Opportunity Commission (EEOC) set up by the bill did not take women's discrimination claims seriously. Nevertheless, Title VII would be tremendously important as the women's movement gained strength.

## Women's Groups Raise Consciousness

As the 1960s unfolded, women began to meet together to compare experiences. Women civil rights workers met to look for ways in which they could play a larger role in the struggle. Soon they went beyond politics, exploring other aspects of their lives. The growing movement drew women who were active in other forms of protest and reform. They included student radicals, opponents of the draft, and workers for welfare rights and other social issues.

Another important influence was Betty Friedan's 1963 book *The Feminine Mystique.* Friedan described the cultural patterns that prevented women from achieving their full potential. Many readers recognized what she called "the problem that has no name"—the disillusionment that came from trying to be the perfect wife and mother, the only roles for women that society valued.

**Women Form Support Groups** Meeting in kitchens and living rooms, women in consciousness-raising groups began to talk about their lives in new ways. One participant, Nancy Hawley, a community activist in Boston, Massachusetts, was troubled by patterns she saw in her work. "Though many of us were working harder than the men," she noted, "we realized we were not listened to and often ignored."

Throughout the country, growing numbers of women recognized the negative attitudes directed toward them. In New Orleans, Louisiana, civil rights activist Cathy Cade mentioned that her boyfriend had made fun of her for going to a "women's meeting." Others in her group told stories of being teased or ridiculed for coming to a women's group. Such lack of support outside the group made their bond stronger within the group. As Cade put it:

> **AMERICAN VOICES** **"One thing became clear: that in the black movement I had been fighting for someone else's oppression and now there was a way that I could fight for my own freedom, and I was going to be much stronger than I ever was."**
>
> —*Cathy Cade*

Betty Friedan voiced many women's feelings in her influential book *The Feminine Mystique.* ***Culture*** ***What was "the problem that has no name"?***

In San Francisco, California, Mimi Feingold, also a veteran of the civil rights and draft resistance movements, felt the same sense of exhilaration at her group's first meeting:

> **AMERICAN VOICES** **"It was something that we had all been waiting for, for a long time. It was a really liberating experience for all of us. . . . This was finally permission to look at our own lives and talk about how unhappy we were."**
>
> —*Mimi Feingold*

**Women Organize NOW** In 1966 a small group of women decided to form an organization to pursue their goal of achieving equality with men. These women were frustrated that existing women's groups were unwilling to pressure the Equal Employment Opportunity Commission to take women's grievances more seriously. Twenty-eight professional women, including Betty Friedan, established the **National Organization for Women (NOW).** Their goal was "to take action to bring American women into full participation in the mainstream of American society now."

NOW sought fair pay and equal job opportunities. It attacked the "false image of women" in the media, such as advertising that used sexist slogans or photographs. In one such ad in the 1960s, for example, an oven manufacturer asked, "Can a woman ever feel right cooking on a dirty range?" In so doing the ad reinforced the popular notion that a woman's sole contribution was to be a homemaker. NOW also called for more balance in marriages, with men and women sharing parenting and household responsibilities. A year after NOW was founded, it had 1,000 members. Only four years later some 15,000 women had joined.

For some women, NOW seemed too extreme; for others it was not extreme enough. Some saw NOW—and the women's

Women from different backgrounds shared their stories in informal meetings and found they had common experiences. ***Culture*** ***What role did consciousness-raising groups play in the feminist movement?***

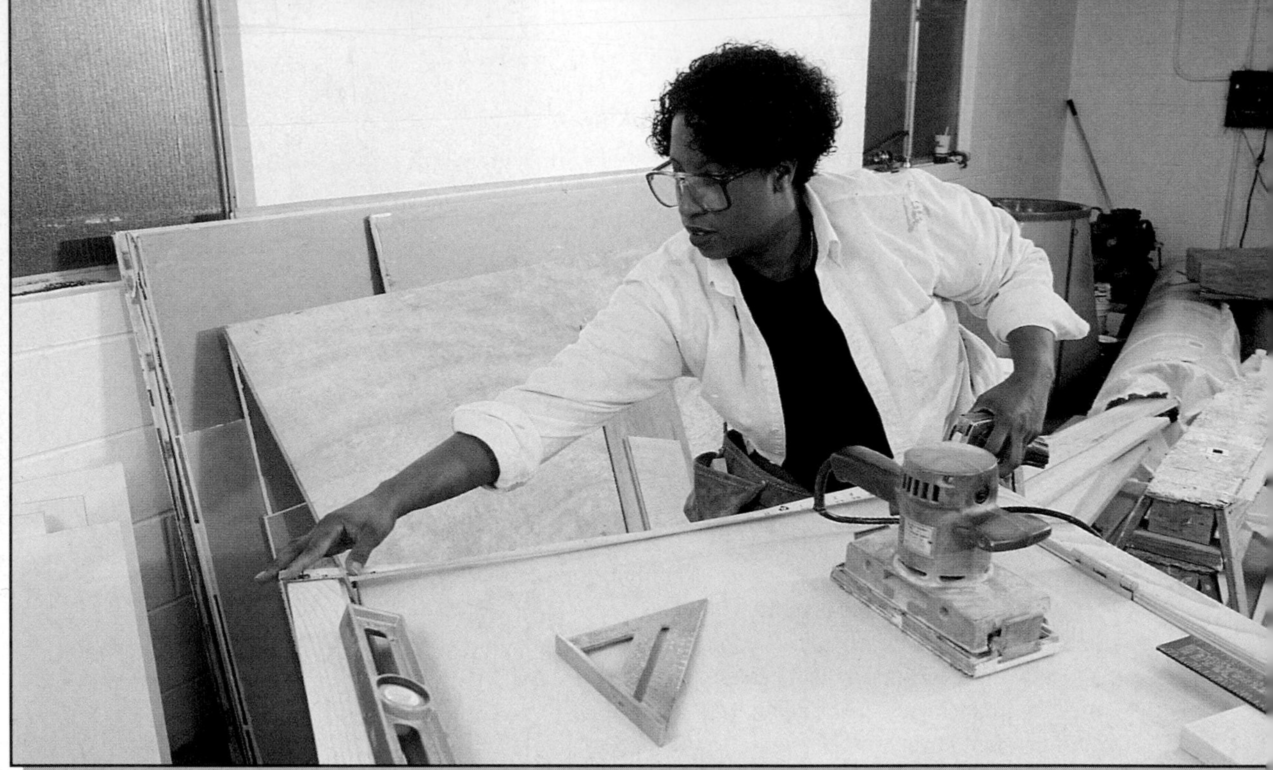

Changing attitudes expanded job opportunities for women by allowing them to work in traditionally male fields. ***Culture*** *How was this changing attitude reflected in higher education?*

movement in general—as mainly for the benefit of white, middle-class women. Nonetheless, NOW served as a rallying point in the movement to end sex discrimination and to promote equality for all women.

## *The Impact of Feminism*

The women's movement came of age in the early 1970s. Songs helped to express the energy of the struggle. In 1971 pop singer Helen Reddy recorded a song that was soon broadcast on radio stations around the country. Delivered in the ringing, forceful style of an anthem, Reddy's hit song proclaimed:

> I am woman, hear me roar
> In numbers too big to ignore,
> And I know too much to go back
> and pretend. . . .
> Yes, I've paid the price
> But look how much I gained.
> If I have to, I can do anything.
> I am strong, I am invincible,
> I am woman.

Reddy's lyrics reflected a sense of women's self-confidence and a strength that drove the movement on.

*This cover from the first edition of* Ms. *magazine shows the many roles women had to fill.*

**Literary Impact** Books and magazines likewise promoted the cause. *Our Bodies, Ourselves,* a handbook published by a women's health collective in Boston, encouraged women to understand their own health issues. It sold 200,000 copies in the first several years after its publication and three million by 1990. In 1972 journalist Gloria Steinem and several other women founded *Ms.* magazine. Devoted to feminist issues, *Ms.* provided women with viewpoints that were decidedly different from those in *Good Housekeeping, Ladies' Home Journal,* and other women's magazines of the day. All 300,000 copies of the preview issue sold out in eight days. Only one year later, *Ms.* had nearly 200,000 subscribers. While not all readers considered themselves feminists, the magazine familiarized them with the arguments and issues of the women's movement.

**A Shift in Attitudes** Slowly the women's movement brought a shift in attitudes. For example, a survey of first-year college students revealed a significant change in career goals. In 1970, men interested in fields such as business, law, engineering, and medicine outnumbered women by eight to one. Five years later, the margin had dropped to three to one. More women entered law school and medical school. They were finally admitted to military academies and trained as officers. In 1971 the National Women's Political Caucus was formed to expand women's participation in politics. By working from within the system, women were able to gain broader support for the goals of the women's movement.

Many women did not actively participate or support the women's movement. Still, most agreed with NOW's goal to provide women with better job opportunities. Many were also pleased to see that the women's movement brought with it a greater recognition of issues important to women. These concerns included the need for child-care facilities, shelters for homeless women, more attention to women's health concerns, and increased awareness of harassment.

Despite many shared concerns, the women's movement continued to be divided as to its goals. In 1972 *Time* magazine observed, "The aims of the movement range from the modest, sensible amelioration [betterment] of the female condition to extreme and revolutionary visions." Radical feminists emphasized the need to end male domination, sometimes rejecting men, marriage, and childbearing. Other women rejected the strong opinions of the radicals, fearing they would cause a split in the women's movement.

***Roe* v. *Wade*** One issue that had the potential to divide the movement was abortion. NOW and other groups worked to reform the laws governing a woman's decision to choose an abortion instead of continuing an unwanted pregnancy. Many states outlawed or severely restricted access to abortion. Women who could afford to travel to another state or out of the country could usually find legal medical services, but poorer women often turned to abortion methods that were not only illegal but unsafe.

A landmark social change came in 1973, when the Supreme Court legalized abortion in the controversial ***Roe* v. *Wade*** decision. The justices based their decision on a constitutional right to personal privacy and struck down state regulation of abortion in the first three months of pregnancy. However, the ruling still allowed states to restrict abortions during the later stages of pregnancy. The case was, and remains, highly controversial, with radical thinkers on both sides of the argument.

**The Equal Rights Amendment** Many women also took part in the campaign for a change to the Constitution that would make discrimination on account of sex illegal. In 1972 Congress passed the **Equal Rights Amendment (ERA)** to the Constitution:

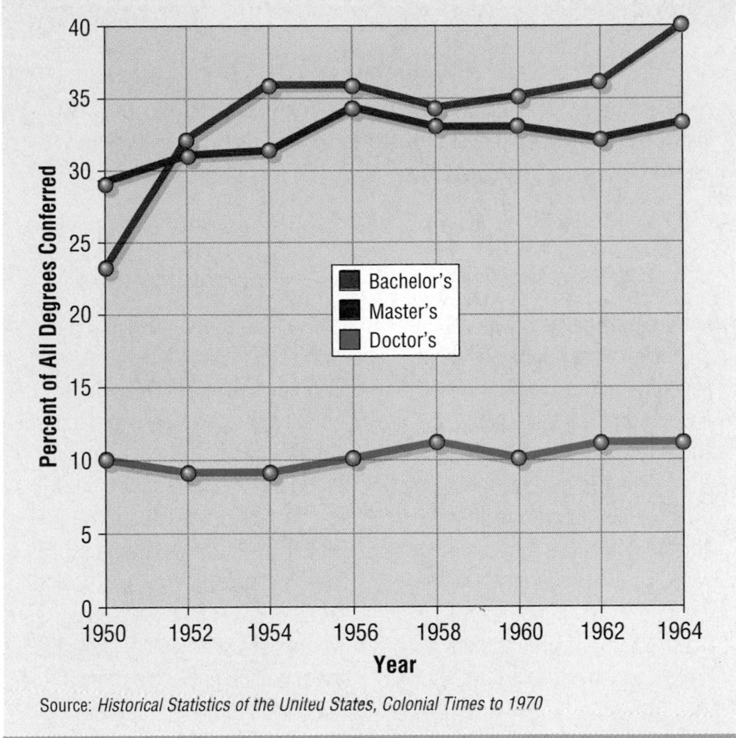


**Interpreting Graphs** As women's educational levels rose, so did their expectations of good jobs and fair salaries. ***Diversity*** ***At which degree level—bachelor's, master's, or doctoral—did women gain the least?***

**KEY DOCUMENTS**

> **"Equality of rights under the law shall not be denied or abridged by the United States or by any State on account of sex."**
>
> —*Equal Rights Amendment, 1972*

To become law, the amendment had to be ratified by thirty-eight states. Thirty states complied quickly, then a few others, and approval at first seemed certain. Strong opposition surfaced, however, and the struggle for ratification limped along until 1982 and then died.

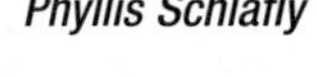
*Phyllis Schlafly*

## *Opposition to the Women's Movement*

Conservative political activist Phyllis Schlafly led a national campaign to block ratification of the ERA, saying:

## COMPARING PRIMARY SOURCES

### ON WORKING MOTHERS

In the early years of the women's movement, experts on both sides voiced their opinions in the debate over the issue of working mothers.

| In Favor of Working Mothers | Opposed to Working Mothers |
|---|---|
| "At the present time, one can say anything—good or bad—about children of employed mothers and support the statement by some research finding. But there is no definitive evidence that children are less happy, healthy, adjusted, because their mothers work. The studies that show working women to be happier, better, more mature mothers do not get much publicity." <br>—*Betty Friedan,* The Feminine Mystique, *1963* | "To work or not to work? Some mothers have to work to make a living. Usually their children turn out all right, because some reasonably good arrangement is made for their care. But others grow up neglected and maladjusted. . . . It doesn't make sense to let mothers go to work making dresses in a factory or tapping typewriters in an office, and have them pay other people to do a poorer job of bringing up their children." <br>—*Benjamin Spock, M.D.,* Baby and Childcare, *1957 edition, first published in 1945* |

***ANALYZING VIEWPOINTS*** **What argument does each author use to support his or her opinion?**

**AMERICAN VOICES** **"It won't do anything to help women, and it will take away from women the rights they already have, such as the right of a wife to be supported by her husband, the right of a woman to be exempted from military combat, and the right . . . to go to a single-sex college."**

—*Phyllis Schlafly*

Women already had legal backing for their rights, Schlafly argued. ERA supporters contested Schlafly's charges about the supposed effects of the ERA, such as coed bathrooms and the end of alimony. Such arguments prevented the ERA from being ratified within the time limit.

Schlafly was not alone in her opposition. Many men at first were hostile to the feminist movement, which became known as "women's liberation" or "women's lib." Nor were all women sympathetic. Some responded by stressing their desire to remain at home and raise children and voicing their satisfaction with traditional roles.

Some African American women felt that combatting racial discrimination was more important than battling sex discrimination. In 1974, NOW's African American president Aileen Fernandez acknowledged that "Some black sisters are not sure that the feminist movement will meet their current needs."

Many working-class women felt removed from the movement, too. They believed they were being encouraged to give up homemaking in order to take up the unpleasant paid labor their husbands endured.

## SECTION 1 REVIEW

### Comprehension

1. *Key Terms* Define: (a) feminism; (b) National Organization for Women (NOW); (c) *Roe* v. *Wade;* (d) Equal Rights Amendment (ERA).
2. *Summarizing the Main Idea* Name at least three ways in which women tried to fight discrimination.
3. *Organizing Information* Create a web diagram that shows the issues supported by organized women's groups such as NOW. Write *Issues Supported by the Women's Movement* in the center circle. Include at least six supporting details in circles surrounding the center circle.

### Critical Thinking

4. *Analyzing Time Lines* Review the time line at the start of the section. In your opinion, which event had the greatest impact on the women's movement? Explain your reasoning.
5. *Identifying Assumptions* What beliefs prompted many women to join the women's movement in the 1960s?

### Writing Activity

6. *Writing an Expository Essay* Research and write an essay about the opposition to the women's movement. Focus your essay on the battle to stop the ratification of the ERA.

# SKILLS FOR LIFE

**Critical Thinking**

Graphs and Charts

Historical Evidence

Geography

## Recognizing Bias

Recognizing bias means being aware of information and ideas that are one-sided or that present only a partial view of a subject. Knowing how to recognize bias is important because this skill helps you to better understand not only historical events, but also current issues. Campaign speeches, debates on controversial topics, and opinions expressed in the media all contain elements of bias. The ability to spot bias will help you analyze information.

Bias often is attached to issues that have emotional impact. One such issue is the women's movement, which questions the role of women in American life. Both of the excerpts on this page were taken from articles written during the women's movement in the late 1960s and early 1970s. Use the following questions to help you determine whether either of these writings is biased.

**1.** ***Decide whether or not the excerpt presents only one side of an issue while suggesting it covers all sides.*** Writing from a single viewpoint signals imbalance—and bias. Read both passages and then answer the following questions. (a) What is the overall message of each excerpt? (b) Which presents only one side of the issue while suggesting that it presents a complete picture?

**2.** ***Determine whether the issue as described is supported by opinions or verifiable facts.*** Sometimes what appear to be facts are actually opinions disguised as facts. (a) Which details presented in the excerpts can be checked for accuracy? (b) Are any opinions presented as though they were facts? Give an example from the excerpts.

**3.** ***Examine the excerpts for hidden assumptions or generalizations that are not supported by facts.*** What hidden assumptions or generalizations do you find in Excerpt A? Excerpt B?

### TEST FOR SUCCESS

Analyze the excerpts below for bias. Which excerpt is the least biased? Explain your answer.

**A**

"What do black women feel about Women's Lib? Distrust. It is white, therefore suspect. They don't want to be used again to help somebody gain power—a power that is carefully kept out of their hands. They look at white women and see them as the enemy—for they know that racism is not confined to white men. . . . The faces of those white women hovering behind that black girl at the Little Rock school in 1957 do not soon leave the retina of the mind."

—*Toni Morrison,*
*"What the Black Woman Thinks About Women's Lib,"*
The New York Times Magazine, *August 22, 1971*

**B**

"The 14th and 15th amendments, written in 1868 and 1870, said: 'All persons born or naturalized in the U.S. are citizens and have the right to vote.'

Susan B. Anthony, considering herself to be a person, registered and voted in 1872. She was arrested, brought to trial, convicted of the crime of voting—because she was a woman, and the word *persons* mentioned in our Constitution did not mean women. . . . If she were alive today, Susan B. Anthony might vote, but she would still see 1000 legal discriminations against women upon various state statute books. . . .

The solution of the problem of giving women 100 per cent protection of the Constitution . . . is the adoption of the Equal Rights for Women Amendment which reads: *Equality of rights under law shall not be denied or abridged by the United States or by any state on account of sex."*

—*Marjorie Longwell,*
*"The American Woman—Then and Now,"*
Delta Kappa Gamma Magazine, *Fall 1969*

1959
*Hawaii becomes a state*

1967
*Cesar Chavez organizes boycott of grapes*

1968
*Mexican American students protest inferior quality schools*

1970
*La Raza Unida formed*

1959 — 1965 — 1971

# 2 Ethnic Minorities Seek Equality

## SECTION PREVIEW

### Objectives

1. Describe the Latino population.
2. Explain how Cesar Chavez and others protested discrimination.
3. Describe the ways in which Asian Americans fought against racial discrimination and made economic and political gains in the 1960s and 1970s.
4. *Key Terms* Define: Latino; migrant farm worker; United Farm Workers (UFW); Japanese American Citizens League (JACL).

### Main Idea

Inspired by the civil rights movement, Latinos and Asian Americans launched their own movements to overcome discrimination.

### Reading Strategy

*Outlining Information* Skim the section and use the headings and subheadings to create an outline. As you read, fill in appropriate details in your outline of the section.

Inspired by the civil rights and women's movements, other ethnic and racial groups began to fight for equality during the 1960s and 1970s. In May 1970, journalist Rubén Salazar predicted the future of the Chicano movement in Los Angeles, California. "We are going to overthrow some of our institutions," he said. "But in the way Americans have always done it: through the ballot, through public consensus. That's a revolution." Three months later, Salazar was killed when rioting broke out after police tried to stop a Chicano anti-Vietnam War demonstration. Although Salazar was not an activist, after his death he became a martyr to the movement.

## The Latino Population

People whose family origins are in Spanish-speaking Latin America, or **Latinos,** come from many places. They share the same language and some elements of culture. But whether they come from Puerto Rico, Cuba, Mexico, or other parts of the Americas, Latinos often have been seen as outsiders. They have been denied equal opportunities in many aspects of life, including employment, education, and housing.

In the late 1960s and early 1970s, more and more people arrived from Central America and South America. Between 1970 and 1980, census figures for people "of Spanish origin" rose from 9 million to 14.6 million. Specific groups tended to settle in certain areas. Cubans moved to Florida, Puerto Ricans moved to the Northeast, and Mexicans moved to the West and Southwest.

Mexican Americans, often known as Chicanos, always have been the most numerous Latinos in the United States. In the 1960s, they began to organize against discrimination in education, jobs, and the legal system, leading to *el Movimiento Chicano*—the Chicano movement.

**Cultural Identity** Activists began encouraging pride in Mexican American culture and its dual heritage from Spain and the ancient cultures of Mexico. In 1967 Rodolfo "Corky" Gonzales, a Denver, Colorado, activist, wrote a long poem that raised Mexican Americans' self-awareness nationwide. *Yo Soy Joaquin* ("I am Joaquin") expresses the importance of cultural identity. It begins:

> I am Joaquin
> lost in a world of confusion
> caught up in the whirl of a gringo [white] society,
> confused by the rules,
> scorned by attitudes,
> suppressed by manipulation
> and destroyed by modern society.

Gonzales' claim was that the Anglos—white, English-speaking non-Latinos—had undermined Mexican Americans' control over their lives through economic pressure and through institutions such as the schools, the Roman Catholic Church, and the media.

**Education** Schools in the barrios, or Latino neighborhoods, were crowded and run-down, with high dropout rates. In March 1968, 10,000 Mexican American students walked out of five such Los Angeles high schools to protest their unequal treatment. Students in other parts of California, and in Colorado and Texas, followed their example. Students demanded culturally sensitive courses, better facilities, and Latino teachers and counselors.

**Fact Finder — United Farm Workers Achievements**

| | |
|---|---|
| ***Financial*** | • First collective bargaining agreements between workers and growers<br>• First contracts requiring hiring out of union halls<br>• First pension plan for retired farm workers<br>• First functioning credit union for farm workers<br>• Extension of unemployment compensation for farm workers |
| ***Health and Safety*** | • First union contracts requiring rest periods, clean drinking water, hand washing facilities, and protection against exposure to pesticides<br>• First comprehensive union health benefits for farm workers and their families<br>• First union contracts regulating safety and sanitary conditions of farm labor camps<br>• Abolition of the crippling short-handled hoe<br>• Extension of disability and workers' compensation to farm workers |

**Interpreting Tables** Labor activists Cesar Chavez and Dolores Huerta founded the United Farm Workers Association (UFWA) in Fresno, California, in 1962. ***Economics What do you view as the UFWA's most important achievement, and why?***

## *Cesar Chavez*

**AMERICAN BIOGRAPHY** The students were not, however, the only people protesting in the Latino community. Throughout the 1960s organizers struggled to unite Latino farm workers. Cesar Chavez, founder of the United Farm Workers, became a hero to millions of Americans, both Latino and Anglo. He was born in Yuma, Arizona, where his family had farmed for three generations. During the Great Depression, they lost their adobe farmhouse because they could not afford the taxes. Relocating to California, they made their living as **migrant farm workers,** moving from farm to farm to provide the labor needed to plant, cultivate, and harvest crops. Chavez later remembered how his family fostered a powerful sense of independence:

*Cesar Chavez (1927–1993)*

> **AMERICAN VOICES** **"I don't want to suggest we were that radical, but I know we were probably one of the strikingest families in California, the first ones to leave the fields if anyone shouted "Huelga!" — which is Spanish for *Strike!*"**
>
> —*Cesar Chavez*

As he grew up among farm workers, Chavez came to believe that unions offered the best opportunity to gain bargaining power and resist employers' economic power. Migrant farm workers were some of the most exploited workers in the country. They had to spend long hours doing backbreaking work for little pay. In the 1960s Chavez began to organize Mexican field hands into what became the **United Farm Workers (UFW).** He and a group of loyal followers went from door to door and field to field. By 1965 the union had 1,700 members.

The UFW's first target was the grape growers of California. Chavez, like Martin Luther King, Jr., believed in nonviolent action. In 1967, when growers refused to grant more pay, better working conditions, and union recognition, Chavez organized a successful nationwide consumer boycott of grapes picked on nonunion farms. Later boycotts of lettuce and other crops also won consumer support.

**Main Idea CONNECTIONS**

*What methods did Cesar Chavez use to gain rights for migrant farm workers?*

Chavez's efforts created many angry enemies and even brought him death threats. He responded by saying:

**AMERICAN VOICES** **"It's not me who counts, it's the Movement. And I think that in terms of stopping the Movement—this one or other movements by poor people around the country—the possibility is very remote. . . . The tide for change now has gone too far."**

— *Cesar Chavez*

In 1975 California passed a law that required collective bargaining between growers and union representatives. Workers now had a legal basis to ask for better working conditions. Chavez's efforts not only made him a national hero but also brought migrant farm workers into the movement for civil rights.

## *Other Latino Protests*

Mexican Americans had other heroes, too. Some formed organizations that took a militant approach, while others used political action. In

Mexico's northern neighbors, California and Texas, receive the majority of immigrants from Mexico. This mural in Los Angeles illustrates Mexican American pride. ***Culture*** *How did Chicano activists use their cultural heritage in the Chicano movement?*

1961 voters in San Antonio, Texas, elected Henry B. González to Congress. Another Texan, Elizo "Kika" de la Garza, went to the House of Representatives in 1964, while Joseph Montoya of New Mexico was elected to the Senate.

New political groups formed to support Latino interests. For example, José Angel Gutiérrez brought together Latino groups in Crystal City, Texas, leading to the formation of the political party *La Raza Unida* in 1970. The new party worked for better housing and jobs and backed Latino political candidates.

Another leader, Reies López Tijerina, argued that the Anglo culture had stolen the Chicanos' land and heritage. To call attention to broken treaties, in 1966 his *Alianza Federal de Mercedes* (Federal Alliance of Land Grants) marched on the New Mexico state capital, Santa Fe.

At about the same time, the Mexican American Legal Defense and Educational Fund (MALDEF) was founded. It has provided legal aid to help Mexican Americans defend their rights and encouraged Mexican American students to become lawyers.

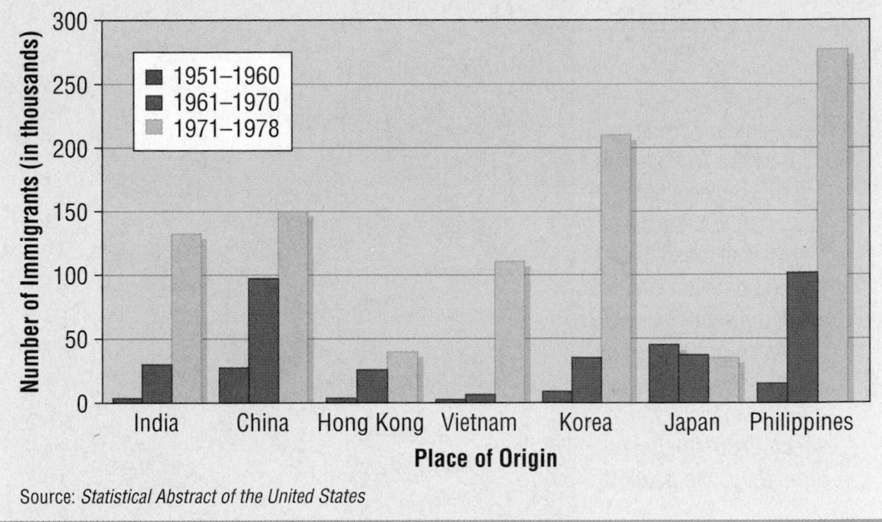

**Interpreting Graphs** Patterns of immigration from Asia changed dramatically in the 1950s, 1960s, and 1970s. ***Diversity*** ***From which two countries came the greatest number of people in the 1950s? In the 1970s?***

## *Asian Americans Fight Discrimination*

Ever since their arrival in the United States, Americans of Chinese and Japanese ancestry have faced racial discrimination. Prejudice against Japanese Americans reached a peak during World War II, while the Communist takeover of China in 1949 influenced attitudes toward Chinese Americans. Still, the years after the war brought many hopeful and positive changes for Asian Americans.

**Japanese Americans After the War** A major issue for Japanese Americans was compensation for the losses they had suffered during their wartime internment in the 1940s. As previously discussed, Japanese American citizens living along the West Coast were forced to relocate to internment camps. The government had feared that they were a risk to American security following Japan's attack on Pearl Harbor. Not only had their lives been disrupted, but they had lost hundreds of millions of dollars in homes, farms, and businesses. The main voice for Japanese Americans, the **Japanese American Citizens League (JACL),** in 1948 won passage of the Japanese American Claims Act. Under the act, Congress eventually paid relatively small amounts for property losses.†

About two thirds of Japanese Americans who had been relocated returned to the Pacific Coast. Others moved to cities east of the Rockies. Their new communities were more a part of mainstream society than the prewar *nihonmachis*—"Japantowns"—had been.

**Economic Changes** Although Asian Americans as a group were well educated, in 1960 they earned less than white Americans. In California, for example, for each $51 a white male was paid, a Chinese man would earn $38 and a Japanese man, $43. College graduates faced prejudice in attempting to move into management jobs.

As a group, Asian Americans in the 1960s and 1970s made economic gains faster than other minorities. Nonetheless, they still faced

† The United States did not officially apologize for the losses and injuries suffered by interned Japanese Americans until 1988. In that year Congress passed legislation that provided some monetary compensation to the approximately 60,000 surviving Japanese Americans who had been interned.

These girls are celebrating Hawaii's new status as the nation's fiftieth state in 1959. Statehood for Hawaii created, for the first time, a state in which most voters were of Asian or part-Asian ancestry. ***Diversity* How did Hawaii's statehood affect Asian Americans throughout the nation?**

discrimination and relied on the example of the civil rights movement to push for gains. Some Chinese American community activists in the 1970s asked for federal help in overcoming problems of unemployment, health, and language barriers. The 1970s also saw an increase in immigration from other Asian countries, especially Korea, India, and Vietnam, as illustrated by the graph on the previous page.

**Political Representation** In 1959 Asian Americans' self-image took a major step forward with the granting of statehood to Hawaii. The new state sent Hiram Leong Fong, a Chinese American, to the Senate, and Daniel K. Inouye, a Japanese American, to the House of Representatives. Other Asian American lawmakers have since been elected to various positions in local and state governments as well as in the federal government.

## SECTION 2 REVIEW

### Comprehension

1. *Key Terms* Define: (a) Latino; (b) migrant farm worker; (c) United Farm Workers (UFW); (d) Japanese American Citizens League (JACL).
2. *Summarizing the Main Idea* What were the main movements launched by Latinos and Asian Americans to overcome racial discrimination?
3. *Organizing Information* Create a two-column chart to organize information about Latino and Asian American protests. Label the two vertical columns *Latinos* and *Asian Americans.* Label the two horizontal rows *Reasons for Protest* and *Results of Protest.*

### Critical Thinking

4. *Analyzing Time Lines* Review the time line at the start of the section. Choose one entry and explain its role in expanding the rights of Latinos or Asian Americans.
5. *Identifying Central Issues* What role did Cesar Chavez play in the Chicano struggle for equal rights?

### Writing Activity

6. *Writing a Persuasive Essay* Write a pamphlet urging consumers to support the grape boycott organized by Cesar Chavez and the United Farm Workers.

1968
American Indian Movement (AIM) formed

1969
Occupation of Alcatraz begins

1972
Congress passes Indian Education Act

1973
AIM takes over reservation at Wounded Knee

1975
Indian Self-Determination and Education Assistance Act passed

1968 | 1972 | 1976

# 3 Native American Struggles

## SECTION PREVIEW

### Objectives

1. Describe the unique problems Native Americans faced.
2. Summarize the roots of Native American activism.
3. Understand how Native Americans confronted the government with protests and legal challenges to win more self-determination.
4. *Key Terms* Define: American Indian Movement (AIM); autonomy.

### Main Idea

Native Americans in the 1960s also took their cue from the civil rights movement to work to improve their living conditions.

### Reading Strategy

*Formulating Questions* Write the main headings from the section on a piece of paper. Formulate at least two questions for each heading and look for answers to your questions as you read the section.

Native Americans made up another minority group that was inspired by the civil rights movement to seek equality and control over their own lives. Shifting government policies had caused Native Americans great suffering over the years. Activists began using legal challenges and direct action to reach their goals.

## Native Americans Face Unique Problems

As the original inhabitants of North America, Native Americans occupied a unique social and legal position. Although Indian cultures and languages varied among peoples, white society viewed them as one group. By 1871 the United States no longer recognized Indian nations as independent powers. It did not, however, extend Native Americans full citizenship.

From the 1800s on, government agencies limited self-government for Native Americans and often worked to erase their traditional lifestyles. Not until the Snyder Act of 1924 was citizenship granted to all Native Americans born in the United States. After 1924 Native Americans were recognized as citizens of both the United States and their own nations or tribal groups.

A Sioux woman joins a protest against federal policies for Native Americans.

As a whole, Native Americans have routinely been denied equal opportunities. Many states refused to give them the vote until pushed by Native American communities. It was not until 1948 that Arizona and New Mexico granted Indians the right to vote. Native Americans have higher rates of unemployment, alcoholism, and suicide, as well as a shorter life expectancy, than white Americans. Many communities have suffered from poverty and poor living conditions. Like other nonwhite groups, Native Americans have been the victims of centuries-old stereotypes reinforced by the images in movies and other media.

Native Americans also have had some grievances unique to their situation. Dennis Banks, a Chippewa, explained why he became an activist:

**AMERICAN VOICES** "It was a question of this government being responsible to me, and not seeing to it that I had an opportunity to lead a decent life, or to own a piece of land, or to find a good job, like they had promised my ancestors in all these treaties. They broke all of those promises. They stole everything from them and wrecked their way of life—which was a good way."

—*Dennis Banks*

## Roots of Native American Activism

An important part of the Native Americans' way of life was their ties to the land and what it stood for. "Everything is tied to our homeland," declared D'Arcy McNickle, a Native American anthropologist, in 1961. Yet, many years after pioneers first moved onto Native American territory, state and federal governments continued to take over traditional tribal lands. Protecting what was left became a major goal of Native Americans.

Native Americans living on reservations, like the Navajo reservation above, suffer a rate of poverty far higher than that of the rest of the United States. ***Economics*** *What are some of the historical reasons behind this poverty?*

**Land Claims** A government project in New York State triggered one early protest. According to rights originally granted in a 1794 treaty, the Seneca Nation owned the land on its Allegany reservation. The federal government, however, wanted to build a dam there as part of a flood control project. The Kinzua Dam would affect 10,000 acres of hunting and fishing land, as well as homes and sacred sites.

In 1956 Congress held hearings, which did not include the Seneca, and appropriated funds for the dam. After legal appeals failed, the Seneca in 1961 went to President John Kennedy to ask that the project be halted. The President supported the government claim to the lands, and the dam was built. After construction was completed, Congress agreed to pay $15 million in damages to the Seneca, but this did not restore the land.

Other Native Americans responded to this decision by bringing lawsuits for violations of treaty rights and failure to make promised payments. Court rulings supported many claims. For example, in 1967 the Court of Claims ruled that the federal government had forced the Seminole to give up Florida lands in 1823 for an unreasonably low price. The court directed the government to pay more to the Seminole community.

**The American Indian Movement** One of the primary activist movements was started in Minneapolis in 1968 by Dennis Banks and George Mitchell, both Chippewa. At a meeting of 250 people representing 20 Native American organizations, Banks set forth the goals: "Let's get a new organized effort going, a new coalition that will fight for Indian treaty rights and better conditions and opportunities for our people."

The new organization came to be called the **American Indian Movement (AIM).** It originally focused on the special problems of Native Americans living in cities. Following the example of militant black groups, AIM set up Native American patrols to monitor street activity. It also began survival schools to encourage racial and cultural pride in young people. Eventually AIM's goals broadened to include the protection of Native American legal rights. They began to fight for **autonomy,** or self-government, with respect to local matters, especially natural resources on Native American lands. They also sought the restoration of lands that they believed had been illegally taken from them.

AIM leader Dennis Banks leads a protest march in South Dakota. Mount Rushmore looms in the background as a powerful symbol of the changes wrought on America by white Americans of European descent. ***Government*** ***How did the federal government respond to Native American activism?***

Many people, both white and Native American, criticized AIM's militant approach. On the group's second anniversary, however, Banks repeated its goals:

AMERICAN VOICES **"The government and churches have demoralized, dehumanized, massacred, robbed, raped, promised, made treaty after treaty, and lied to us. . . . We must now destroy this political machine that man has built to prevent us from self-determination."**

—*Dennis Banks*

## Confronting the Government

To call attention to issues long ignored, Native Americans staged several standoffs with the federal government. In 1972, demonstrators protesting the violation of treaties between the United States and various Indian groups formed the Broken Treaties Caravan. They traveled to Washington, D.C., and occupied the Bureau of Indian Affairs' offices for six days. Other protests were even more dramatic.

**The Occupation of Alcatraz** In 1969, seventy-eight protesters from several Native American groups landed on Alcatraz, an island in San Francisco Bay on which stood an abandoned federal prison. They claimed the 13-acre rock under the terms of the Fort Laramie Treaty of 1868, which allowed male Native Americans to file homestead claims on federal lands.

Others joined the group, planning to turn the deserted island into an educational and cultural center. In March 1970, author Vine Deloria, Jr., a Standing Rock Sioux, wrote hopefully about the project in *The New York Times:*

AMERICAN VOICES **"By making Alcatraz an experimental Indian center operated and planned by Indian people, we would be given a chance to see what we could do toward developing answers to modern social problems. . . . Perhaps we would not succeed in the effort. . . . It just seems to a lot of Indians that this continent was a lot better off when we were running it."**

—*Vine Deloria, Jr.*

VIEWING HISTORY Echoes of history surrounded the Sioux village of Wounded Knee, where AIM members, led by Russell Means (left) and others, protested past and present federal government actions against Native Americans. ***Government*** ***Why did AIM take issue with the federal government?***

The occupation failed. Federal marshals eventually removed the last protesters after a year and a half. But the episode succeeded in drawing national attention to Native American grievances.

**Confrontation at Wounded Knee** An even more dramatic confrontation came in 1973 at the Oglala Sioux village of Wounded Knee, South Dakota. There, in 1890, the army's Seventh Cavalry had massacred more than 200 Sioux men, women, and children.

The Pine Ridge reservation around the village was one of the country's poorest, with half its families living on welfare. In February 1973, AIM leaders Russell Means and Dennis Banks and some 200 AIM members took over the village. AIM refused to leave the reservation until the United States government agreed to investigate the treatment of Indians and the poor conditions on the reservation. AIM members also demanded that the United States review 371 treaties they said the government had broken over the years.

**Main Idea CONNECTIONS**

*What did AIM leaders demand during their confrontation at Wounded Knee?*

Other Native American leaders came out in support of the occupation. Onondaga Chief Oren Lyons, speaking for the Iroquois, said:

**AMERICAN VOICES** **"We support the Oglala Sioux Nation or any Indian Nation that will fight for its sovereignty. . . . The issue here at Wounded Knee is the recognition of the treaties between the United States Government and the sovereign nations that were here before."**

— *Onondaga Chief Oren Lyons*

Federal marshals and FBI agents surrounded the village, allowing only occasional shipments of supplies. From time to time, gunfire broke out. As the siege went on, agents arrested some 300 people, including news reporters and outside supporters.

The standoff finally came to an end in May, when AIM agreed to surrender their weapons and leave the reservation. In exchange, the government consented to reexamine treaty rights. During the siege, two AIM members had been killed and about a dozen people hurt, including two federal marshals.

**Government Response** Native American activism brought some responses from the government. The Kennedy and Johnson administrations in the 1960s tried to bring jobs and income to some reservations by encouraging industries to locate there. They also encouraged the leasing of reservation lands to energy and development corporations. But many Native Americans worried about the effects of these projects on the land. In the 1970s, the Navaho, Crow, Northern Cheyenne, and others sought to renegotiate or cancel many of the leases.

Pressure by Indians also led to their inclusion in Great Society programs dealing with housing, health, and education. Government agencies made resources available and let Native Americans plan and run their own programs and, in some places, their own schools.

A number of laws passed in the 1970s favored Native American rights. The Indian Education Act of 1972 gave parents and tribal councils more control over schools and school programs. The Indian Self-Determination Act of 1974 upheld Native American autonomy and let local leaders administer federally supported social programs for housing and education.

Native Americans also continued to win legal battles to regain land, mineral, and water rights. For example, in 1971 the Alaska Federation of Natives was given $1 billion and 40 million acres of land. In 1970, after rejecting a cash settlement, the Taos in New Mexico won back Blue Lake, a religious shrine, as well as 48,000 acres of land.

Wearing traditional ceremonial dress, George Crows Fly High and Martha Grass seek a meeting with Supreme Court justices. ***Government** What sorts of issues did Native American groups seek to settle in the courts?*

## SECTION 3 REVIEW

### Comprehension

1. ***Key Terms*** Define: (a) American Indian Movement (AIM); (b) autonomy.
2. ***Summarizing the Main Idea*** How did the African American civil rights movement influence the tactics of Native American groups?
3. ***Organizing Information*** Create a web diagram that organizes information about the various Indian protests and legal challenges. In the center circle write *Native Americans Seek Equality Through Protest.* Provide details in surrounding circles.

### Critical Thinking

4. ***Analyzing Time Lines*** Review the time line at the start of the section. Choose one entry and explain its significance in the struggle for Native American rights.
5. ***Expressing Problems Clearly*** What problems were typical of Native American communities in the 1960s?

### Writing Activity

6. ***Writing an Expository Essay*** Write a brief essay about the goals of the American Indian Movement. Be sure to include answers to the following questions: How did AIM try to achieve its goals? In your opinion, was the group successful? Why or why not?

| 1962 | 1966 | 1970 | 1970 | 1972 | 1974 |
|---|---|---|---|---|---|
| Rachel Carson publishes Silent Spring | National Traffic and Motor Vehicle Safety Act | First Earth Day celebrated on April 22 | Environmental Protection Agency established | Congress passes Clean Water Act | Nuclear Regulatory Commission established |

1962 1966 1970 1974

# 4 The Environmental Movement

## SECTION PREVIEW

### Objectives

1. Describe the efforts begun in the 1960s to protect the environment.
2. Explain how the government has tried to balance economic development with environmental protection.
3. Understand that a movement for consumers' rights grew out of other protest movements of the 1960s.
4. *Key Terms* Define: Nuclear Regulatory Commission (NRC); Environmental Protection Agency (EPA); Clean Air Act; Clean Water Act.

### Main Idea

The mood of protest in the 1960s energized movements to preserve the environment and to ensure the safety of consumer products.

### Reading Strategy

*Reading for Evidence* The text below states that the efforts of environmentalists and consumerists "brought lasting changes in public attitudes and public policy." As you read the section, look for evidence to support this statement.

*People showed their support for the environmental movement by wearing buttons such as this one.*

In the 1960s and the early 1970s, the mood of protest surrounding the civil rights movement inspired several other movements. Environmentalists demanded actions that would preserve and restore the earth's environment and resources. Consumer advocates used proven protest techniques to ensure that industry would be accountable to their customers and workers. These efforts brought lasting changes in public attitudes and public policy.

## Protecting the Environment

Like the women's movement, the environmental movement of the 1960s had roots in the American past. In the late 1890s and early 1900s, Progressives had worked to make public lands and parks available for the people. New Deal programs of the 1930s included tree-planting projects in an effort to put people back to work—and to conserve forests and farmlands. The modern environmental movement, however, stemmed even more directly from the work of one woman.

**Rachel Carson** Marine biologist Rachel Carson grew up wanting to become a writer. Her mother taught her to appreciate nature and encouraged Carson's growing interest in zoology. In the 1930s and 1940s Carson combined her talents and began to write about scientific subjects for general audiences. In 1951 she published *The Sea Around Us,* which was an immediate bestseller and won the National Book Award. This book, and her next, *The Edge of the Sea,* made her famous as a naturalist. A main theme in Carson's work was the notion that human beings are part of nature. Furthermore, she believed that humans carried a great responsibility because they had the power to change the environment. Her most influential book, *Silent Spring,* warned against the abuse of that power.

In *Silent Spring,* published in 1962, Carson attacked the use of chemical pesticides, particularly DDT. She argued that DDT had increased agricultural productivity but killed various plants and animals along with the insect pests that were its target. She stated:

**AMERICAN VOICES** **"The most alarming of all man's assaults upon the environment is the contamination of air, earth, rivers, and sea with dangerous and even lethal materials. This pollution is for the most part irrecoverable. . . . In this now universal contamination of the environment, chemicals are the sinister and little-recognized partners of radiation in changing the very nature of the world."**

—*Rachel Carson in* Silent Spring

VIEWING HISTORY Disturbed by the changes she saw in the environment, biologist Rachel Carson sounded a trumpet call to action in her book *Silent Spring,* inspiring others to join a strong environmental movement. ***Science and Technology*** ***According to Carson's book, how was science and technology working against the public interest?***

As Carson explained, chemicals sprayed on crops entered into living organisms and moved from one to another in a chain of poisoning and death. Specifically, the lingering effects of DDT threatened to destroy many species of birds and fish, including the national symbol, the bald eagle.

*Silent Spring* caused a big stir. The chemical industry fought back vigorously, arguing that Carson confused the issues and left readers "unable to sort fact from fancy." The public was not persuaded by this attack. So great was national concern that a special presidential advisory committee was appointed. It called for continued research and warned against the widespread use of pesticides. Eventually DDT was banned in the United States, and other chemicals were controlled more strictly. (For more information about the impact of *Silent Spring,* see the "Geography and History" feature that follows this section.)

It was not only DDT that worried people. They became more conscious of poisonous fumes in the air, oil spills on beaches, and toxic wastes buried in the ground. In the mid-1960s, President Lyndon Johnson addressed environmental concerns as part of the Great Society. Johnson hoped for "an environment that is pleasing to the senses and healthy to live in." Environmental legislation was part of his broader reform program.

**Nuclear Power** During the 1960s, concern about the overuse of nonrenewable resources, such as oil and gas, had encouraged the development of nuclear power plants built to generate electricity. Many people considered nuclear plants to be better than coal-burning plants because they caused less air pollution. Nuclear plants, however, produced steam that was then discharged into local waterways. The steam raised water temperatures, killing fish and plant life.

*Environmental activists battled for a variety of issues in the 1960s, including the banning of nuclear power.*

People were also worried about the possibility of nuclear plant accidents. People feared that in the event of an accident, radioactivity would be released into the air, causing serious damage to all plant and animal life in the surrounding area. In response to these fears, the government created the **Nuclear Regulatory Commission (NRC)** in 1974. The NRC became responsible for overseeing the use of nuclear materials in civilian life. Its chief goal was to ensure that nuclear power plants and facilities were operated safely.

Concern about Earth and its resources prompted Earth Day rallies and mass clean-up activities. ***Geography*** *What earlier efforts at environmental protection produced the new environmental movement?*

**Public Response** Besides Rachel Carson, other scientists were alarmed by environmental problems. They too began to publicize their concerns. For example, in his 1971 book *The Closing Circle,* biologist Barry Commoner warned about rapid increases in pollution.

Grassroots environmental movements sprang up in many places as a result of increased awareness. Groups supporting conservation efforts and opposing actions such as the building of new nuclear plants gained attention. In 1969, Senator Gaylord Nelson of Wisconsin announced plans to hold a national day of discussion and teaching about the environment. The following year, on April 22, 1970, Americans celebrated the first Earth Day. Organizers stressed the important role Americans could play in improving awareness of environmental issues and bringing an end to environmental damage. Earth Day would become a yearly observance. Its aim was to heighten concern for the environment, to increase awareness about environmental issues, and to clean up pollution and litter.

**Main Idea CONNECTIONS**

*How did Americans respond to the environmental concerns of scientists?*

**Government Actions** The efforts of environmentalists helped spur the federal government to create a new agency that would set and enforce national pollution-control standards. In 1970, President Nixon established the **Environmental Protection Agency (EPA).** The EPA was formed by combining existing federal agencies concerned with air and water pollution.

One of the EPA's early responsibilities was to enforce the **Clean Air Act.** Passed by Congress in 1970 in response to public concerns about air pollution, the Clean Air Act was designed to control pollution caused by industries and car emissions. The EPA forged an agreement with car manufacturers to install catalytic converters (devices that convert tailpipe pollutants to less dangerous substances) in cars to reduce harmful emissions.

In 1972 the EPA gained further responsibilities when Congress enacted the **Clean Water Act** to regulate the discharge of industrial and municipal wastewater. The act also provided for grants to build better sewage-treatment facilities. As the nation's watchdog against polluters, the EPA continues to monitor and reduce air and water pollution. It regulates the disposal of solid waste and the use of pesticides and toxic substances.

## Balancing Jobs and the Environment

Efforts to clean up and preserve the environment did not come without a cost. Many industry leaders worried that the new regulations would be confusing to follow and overly costly to businesses. They raised concerns that the increased costs associated with cleaning up the air and water would result in the loss of jobs. Government and industry worked to balance the demands of economic development and environmental protection.

The development of oil fields in Alaska provides an example of how the government tried to achieve this balance. Construction began in 1974 on an 800-mile long pipeline designed to carry oil across the frozen landscape to ice-free ports in the southern part of Alaska. Growth in the oil industry created new jobs and expanded revenues for the state.

Development brought with it increased concern over the welfare of the Alaskan wilderness and the rights of native Alaskans. The Alaska Native Claims Settlement Act of 1971 set aside millions of acres of land for the state's native groups, to be used partly for conservation purposes. In 1978 and again in 1980 additional land was added to the state's protected conservation areas.

## The Consumer Movement

The consumer movement was yet another outgrowth of the 1960s protests. It too had earlier roots. The Pure Food and Drug Act of 1906, for example, was one early effort to maintain standards and protect the public. In the 1960s and early 1970s, however, the consumer movement grew far stronger and larger.

Attorney Ralph Nader spearheaded the new consumer effort. Nader had been a serious activist all his life. While a student at Princeton University in the early 1950s, Nader protested the spraying of campus trees with DDT. His interest in automobile safety began at Harvard Law School. In 1964 Daniel Patrick Moynihan, then Assistant Secretary of Labor, hired Nader as a consultant on the issue of automobile safety regulations.

**FACT Finder** **Major Environmental Legislation, 1964–1976**

| Year | Legislation | Description |
|---|---|---|
| 1964 | Wilderness Act | Designated lands to be maintained and preserved for public enjoyment. |
| 1966 | Rare and Endangered Species Act | Established protection for rare, endangered, and threatened plants and animals. |
| 1970 | Environmental Protection Agency | Created as an independent federal agency to administer the laws that affect the environment. |
| 1970 | Clean Air Act | Instituted a research and development program to prevent and control air pollution. |
| 1972 | Clean Water Act | Established regulations for preventing urban and industrial water pollution. |
| 1974 | Resource Conservation and Recovery Act | Established guidelines for storage and/or disposal of existing hazardous waste. |
| 1974 | Safe Drinking Water Act | Established guidelines for safe drinking water. |
| 1976 | Toxic Substance Control Act | Enacted to regulate the commercial manufacture, processing, and distribution of chemical substances. |

**Interpreting Tables** The government responded to environmental activism by enacting a series of legislation, including the formation of the Environmental Protection Agency. ***Government*** *How do these acts affect both individuals and industry?*

Attorney and consumer activist Ralph Nader shed a light on consumer health and safety issues not seen since the Progressive era. ***Government*** ***What was the government's response to Nader's accusations against the auto industry?***

The government report Nader wrote soon became a book, *Unsafe at Any Speed: The Designed-in Dangers of the American Automobile.* It began:

> **AMERICAN VOICES** **"For over half a century the automobile has brought death, injury, and the most inestimable sorrow and deprivation to millions of people. . . . [T]his mass trauma began rising sharply four years ago reflecting new and unexpected ravages by the motor vehicle. A 1959 Department of Commerce report projected that 51,000 persons would be killed by automobiles in 1975. That figure will probably be reached in 1965, a decade ahead of schedule."**
>
> —*Ralph Nader in* Unsafe at Any Speed

Like the muckrakers of the Progressive era, Nader drew attention to the facts with passionate arguments. He called many cars "coffins on wheels," pointing to dangers such as a tendency to flip over. The industry, he charged, knowingly continued to build over one million cars before confronting the safety problems.

Nader's book was a sensation. In 1966 he testified before Congress about automobile hazards. That year, Congress passed the National Traffic and Motor Vehicle Safety Act. The *Washington Post* noted that, "Most of the credit for making possible this important legislation belongs to one man—Ralph Nader. . . . A one-man lobby for the public prevailed over the nation's most powerful industry."

Nader broadened his efforts and investigated the meatpacking business, helping to secure support for the Wholesome Meat Act of 1967. He next looked into consumer problems in other industries. Scores of volunteers, called "Nader's Raiders," signed on to help. They turned out report after report on such issues as the safety of products such as baby food and insecticides and inspired consumer activism. As ordinary Americans began to stand up for their rights, consumer protection offices began to respond to their many complaints.

## SECTION 4 REVIEW

### Comprehension

1. *Key Terms* Define: (a) Nuclear Regulatory Commission (NRC); (b) Environmental Protection Agency (EPA); (c) Clean Air Act; (d) Clean Water Act.
2. *Summarizing the Main Idea* In what ways were the environmental and consumer movements similar to other protest movements of the 1960s and 1970s?
3. *Organizing Information* Create a cause-and-effect chart on the consumer movement. Be sure to include how the movement began, by whom it was led, and some of its effects.

### Critical Thinking

4. *Analyzing Time Lines* Review the time line at the start of the section. Explain how the first entry caused one of the later entries to occur.
5. *Recognizing Cause and Effect* Describe how Rachel Carson's *Silent Spring* initiated the environmental movement.

### Writing Activity

6. *Writing a Persuasive Essay* Balancing jobs and the environment often involves tradeoffs. Research and write an essay in support of or in opposition to the development of oil fields in the Alaskan wilderness.

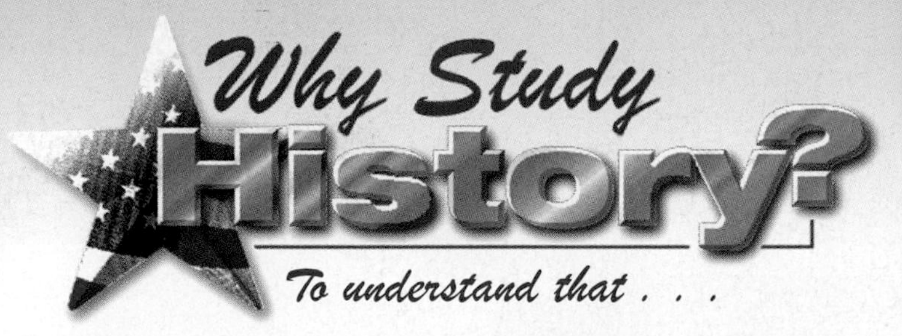


# Crime Victims Have Rights

**A social movement of recent years has been the effort to secure fair treatment for crime victims and to protect potential victims.**

Les Thomas shakes his head as he reads the news. A convicted sex offender has been paroled after only three years in jail. Thomas believes that the nation's courts pay more attention to the rights of people accused of committing crimes than to the rights of their victims. Many Americans share Thomas's viewpoint. They are demanding that judges and legislators get tough on crime.

*Women's rights march, 1970s*

## The Impact Today

Social activists in the 1960s and early 1970s sought equal rights for people who suffered discrimination because they were born into a particular group—for example, women. Today many Americans are mobilizing to secure rights for the millions of people who are victims or potential victims of crime. According to FBI figures, nearly 14 million crimes were committed in the United States in 1995 alone.

New laws have helped protect crime victims' rights. One such law allows crime victims to speak in court during the sentencing portion of trials. In this way, victims can influence the punishment of their offenders.

Victims' rights has also become a constitutional issue. By 1998, victims' rights amendments had been added to 27 state constitutions. President Clinton endorsed a victims' rights amendment to the United States Constitution in 1996.

Alongside the victims' rights movement, a movement has emerged to protect potential victims of sexual assault. In 1994, public outrage over the murder of Megan Kanka, a seven-year-old New Jersey girl, led to the passage of a law popularly known as Megan's Law. It requires that law enforcement officials and communities in New Jersey be notified when a convicted sex offender moves into the area.

A number of states passed similar laws. Congress followed suit in 1996, requiring law enforcement agencies in all 50 states to notify schools, day-care centers, and parents about the presence of sexual offenders in the community.

Laws designed to protect victims and potential victims have drawn some criticism. Most criticism focuses on whether such laws violate the rights of people accused of committing crimes.

## The Impact on You

List the rights that you believe crime victims should have. Then examine the Fourth, Fifth, Sixth, and Eighth amendments to the Constitution. Consider whether your list of rights violates the rights listed there. Finally, write an essay on how best to ensure victims' rights in a free society.

*Demonstration in support of Megan's Law*

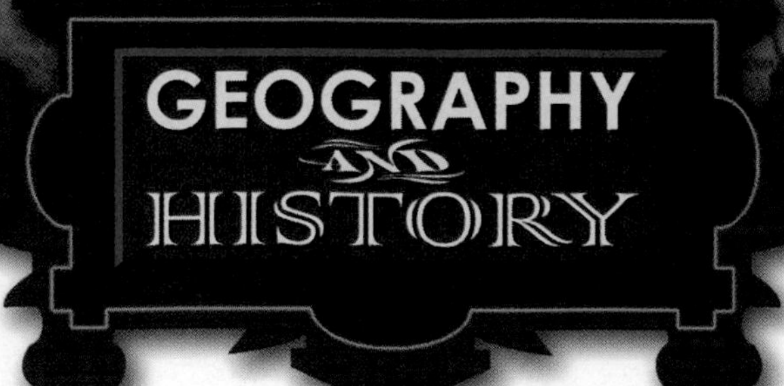


# The Environmental Movement

*The geographic theme of human-environment interaction examines ways in which people affect their natural environment. Rachel Carson's book* Silent Spring *blamed the disappearance of songbirds from America's towns and cities on the widely used pesticide DDT. Why did Carson's book have such an impact?*

The book that launched the environmental movement

The publication of *Silent Spring* in 1962 is usually described as a landmark event in the history of the environmental movement. Author Rachel Carson planted an important concept in the public's mind: that humans are a part of a living ecological system, not outside of or dominant over it.

> Progress in science and technology that made humans' lives easier might have unintended outcomes.

## Humans and the Environment

Until the 1960s, most Americans believed that humans should use nature for their own ends. Science was seen as a tool for this use.

However, scientists had long been interested in the concept that people, plants, and animals all depend on one another to survive. Progress in science and technology that made humans' lives easier might have unintended outcomes. Cars, for example, enabled people to live outside the cities in which they worked. Yet cars caused pollution. By the end of the 1960s, cars and trucks were the source of more than half the air pollution in the United States.

Like cars, insecticides had both positive and negative consequences. Scientists began to weigh the environmental costs of insecticides, such as DDT, against their proven benefits in fighting insects. Chemical companies and the agricultural lobbies, however, favored continued use of DDT.

## The Use of DDT

For many years, DDT had been used by large-scale commercial farmers. Many American farm crops had come originally from Europe and Asia, bringing their own insect pests with them. By the early 1900s, farmers were ready to use any easy-to-use, inexpensive method to kill insects that gobbled up corn, wheat, and other crops.

Farmers turned enthusiastically to chemical insecticides, but many of these poisons contained metals such as lead or arsenic that were deadly to humans. DDT, which was apparently not toxic to humans even in massive doses, seemed like a wonderful solution.

## New Research

By the 1960s, however, new research findings caused some people to question the assumption that humans

## A Shift in Public Opinion: The Environment

***"Which of these problems would you like to see government devote most of its attention to in the next two years?"*** **– Gallup poll question**

| | Percent of Public Mentioning Item | | |
|---|---|---|---|
| ***Issue*** | ***1965*** | ***1970*** | ***Five-Year Change*** |
| Reducing amount of crime | 41 | 56 | +15% |
| Reducing pollution of air and water | 17 | 53 | +36% |
| Improving public education | 45 | 31 | -14% |
| Helping people in poor areas | 32 | 30 | -2% |
| Conquering "killer" diseases | 37 | 29 | -8% |
| Improving housing, clearing slums | 21 | 27 | +6% |
| Reducing racial discrimination | 29 | 25 | -4% |
| Reducing unemployment | 35 | 25 | -10% |
| Improving highway safety | 18 | 13 | -5% |
| Beautifying America | 3 | 5 | +2% |

Source: *The Politics of Environmental Concern*, by Walter A. Rosenbaum

should freely exploit nature. Rachel Carson brought some of that new research to light.

In *Silent Spring*, Carson pointed out that DDT not only poisoned insects, but also killed birds that ate the poisoned insects. She based her book on observations of the negative effect of DDT caused by massive spraying in American urban areas in an attempt to protect Dutch Elm trees from insect pests. As it turned out, DDT remained in the ecosystem long after it had destroyed insect pests. It built up in the fatty tissues of birds and fish that ate the poisoned insects, and its long-term effects could be fatal. In birds, for example, DDT weakened shell formation so that young birds did not hatch. Predator birds high in the food chain, such as hawks and eagles, reached the crisis stage first because they ate smaller birds, fish, and rodents containing DDT. The more food the birds ate, the higher their concentration of DDT became.

### The Environmental Movement

After the publication of *Silent Spring*, a growing public awareness of the theme of interaction between humans and the environment led to a national environmental movement. The movement continued to grow throughout the 1960s, partly because of court cases against the use of DDT brought by the Environmental Defense Fund, one of many activist groups. At the close of the decade, the movement won official government recognition with the founding of the Environmental Protection Agency in 1970.

*Silent Spring* sparked a debate that in 1972 resulted in the banning of almost all uses of DDT in the United States. Even more significantly, by questioning the belief that nature exists for the benefit of humanity, Carson and other scientists and historians helped introduce a new ideology. Within a decade, environmentalism grew from something that interested only a small number of geographers and scientists to a nationwide movement embraced by a majority of citizens.

1. Why were American crops such as wheat and corn susceptible to insect pests?
2. How did farmers' use of DDT affect other parts of the environment?

**Themes in Geography**

3. ***Human-Environment Interaction*** How did the belief that humans should use the natural world for their own ends change during the 1960s?

# Chapter 20 Review

## Chapter Summary

CD-ROM REVIEW

The major concepts of Chapter 20 are presented below. See also ***Guide to the Essentials of American History*** or ***Interactive Student Tutorial CD-ROM,*** which contains interactive review activities, time lines, helpful hints, and test practice.

### *Reviewing the Main Ideas*

Change. Upheaval. Action. These words describe the social revolution of the late 1960s and early 1970s. The 1960s civil rights movement breathed new life into other issues. Women, Latinos, Asian Americans, and Native Americans adapted civil rights tactics to achieve their own goals of equality. Similar tactics helped launch movements to protect the environment and improve the quality and safety of certain consumer goods.

### *Section 1: The Women's Movement*

Encouraged by the gains of the civil rights movement, a women's movement arose in an effort to end discrimination based on gender.

### *Section 2: Ethnic Minorities Seek Equality*

Inspired by the civil rights movement, Latinos and Asian Americans launched their own movements to overcome discrimination.

### *Section 3: Native American Struggles*

Native Americans in the 1960s also took their cue from the civil rights movement to work to improve their living conditions.

### *Section 4: The Environmental Movement*

The mood of protest in the 1960s energized movements to preserve the environment and to ensure the safety of consumer products.

In recent years social activists have worked to secure fair treatment of victims of crime. New laws have been passed to protect crime victims' rights, and many states have added victims' rights amendments to their constitutions.

## Key Terms

Use each of the terms below in a sentence that shows how it relates to the chapter.

1. Equal Rights Amendment (ERA)
2. United Farm Workers (UFW)
3. autonomy
4. Environmental Protection Agency (EPA)
5. feminism
6. migrant farm worker
7. Latino
8. Clean Air Act
9. National Organization for Women (NOW)
10. American Indian Movement (AIM)

## Comprehension

1. What were some of the goals of NOW?
2. What opposition did the women's movement encounter?
3. What role did Cesar Chavez play in the Chicano struggle for equal rights?
4. What positive changes did the years after World War II bring for Asian Americans?
5. Why did Native American activists confront the federal government?
6. Describe some of the tactics used by the American Indian Movement.
7. How did people show their support for the environmental movement?
8. What were two of the targets of Ralph Nader's consumer movement?

## Using Graphic Organizers

On a separate piece of paper, copy the tree map to organize information about some of the major protest movements in the 1960s and 1970s. Provide at least two supporting details describing each movement.

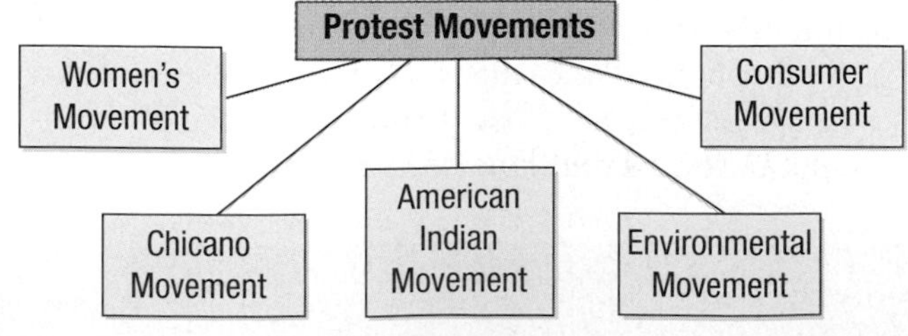

## Analyzing Political Cartoons ▶

1. Examine the images in the cartoon. What do the ships represent?
2. Who are the people, and what do they represent?
3. Explain the humor in the dialogue, and the serious point it is making.

## Critical Thinking

1. ***Applying the Chapter Skill*** Review the Recognizing Bias skill on page 595. Then turn to the quote by author Vine Deloria, Jr., on page 603. Are any opinions presented as though they were facts? Give an example from the excerpt.
2. ***Drawing Conclusions*** During the 1960s and 1970s, Cesar Chavez's United Farm Workers organized buyer boycotts of grapes, lettuce, and other produce. Explain the purpose of these boycotts.
3. ***Demonstrating Reasoned Judgment*** Think of a local concern that affects your community, for example, the need for increased recycling in your neighborhood. Following the examples of any of the activists you have read about in the chapter, such as Gloria Steinem, Cesar Chavez, Rachel Carson, or Ralph Nader, what could you do to champion your cause?

## INTERNET ACTIVITY

***For your portfolio:***
**Prepare a Report**

Access Prentice Hall's *America: Pathways to the Present* site at **www.Pathways.phschool.com** for the specific URLs to complete the activity. Additional resources and related Web sites are also available.

Read about Rachel Carson and prepare a report about her efforts to warn people about the dangers of pesticides. How was Carson's book *Silent Spring* received? Who opposed her findings? What was Carson's legacy to the environmental movement?

## ANALYZING DOCUMENTS ◀ ▶ INTERPRETING DATA

Turn to the first "American Voices" quotation on page 603.

1. Which of the following was one of AIM's goals as expressed by Dennis Banks? (a) to join the government (b) to make no changes to Native American lifestyles (c) to make radical changes in order to gain self-determination (d) to enter into a new treaty with the government
2. How did Banks suggest that AIM achieve its goals? (a) through peaceful demonstration (b) by destroying the political machine built by the government and churches (c) by joining churches (d) by ignoring the problem
3. ***Writing*** Do you think Banks's speech would have been successful at persuading other people to join AIM in their efforts? Explain why or why not.

## Connecting to Today

***Essay Writing*** Earth Day, first celebrated in 1970, is still observed every year. Research and write an essay on some of the most recent Earth Day activities in or near your community. Then create a list of activities you could plan to celebrate the next Earth Day.

CHAPTER

# 21 The Vietnam War and American Society

## 1960–1975

## CHAPTER FOCUS

The Vietnam War was one of the most tragic events of the cold war. Hundreds of thousands of soldiers served in Vietnam, and billions of dollars were spent on the war effort. Over time, many Americans questioned the extent of United States involvement in this faraway conflict. In this chapter you will read about the war and other issues that caused deep divisions within American society.

The *Why Study History?* page at the end of this chapter explores the connection between the use of a military draft during the Vietnam War and the all-volunteer military forces in existence today.

▲

**VIEWING HISTORY**
American soldiers like this one endured extreme fighting conditons in Vietnam. *Foreign Relations* ***Why were American soldiers sent to fight in Vietnam?***

| 1955 | 1961 | 1963 | 1964 | 1965 | 1968 |
|---|---|---|---|---|---|
| *Diem becomes president of South Vietnam* | *Kennedy takes office* | *Military coup overthrows Diem* | *Gulf of Tonkin Resolution* | *War in Vietnam escalates* | *Tet Offensive* |

1955 1960 1965 1970

# 1 Deepening American Involvement

**SECTION PREVIEW**

### Objectives

1. Describe the background events leading up to war between North and South Vietnam.
2. Describe the Vietnam policies of President Kennedy and Robert McNamara.
3. Explain how President Johnson changed the course of the war.
4. *Key Terms* Define: Geneva Conference; Viet Cong; Gulf of Tonkin Resolution; escalation; Ho Chi Minh Trail; Tet Offensive.

### Main Idea

The United States entered the Vietnam War to defeat Communist forces threatening South Vietnam.

### Reading Strategy

*Structured Overview* Write the following column headings on a sheet of paper: *Background of the War, Kennedy's Vietnam Policy, Johnson's War.* As you read the section, take notes in the appropriate column.

American involvement in Vietnam began during the early years of the cold war. It ended in defeat and disappointment more than twenty years later.

## Background of the War

Vietnam had a history of nationalism that extended back nearly 2,000 years. The Vietnamese spent much of that time resisting attempts by neighboring China to swallow their small country. In the 1800s France established itself as a new colonial power in Vietnam, and it met similar resistance.

After World War II Ho Chi Minh, a nationalist who sympathized with Communist ideas, led the Vietnamese independence movement. He aroused his people's nationalism in order to repel the French. Policymakers in the United States, however, saw Ho merely as a Communist, and therefore an enemy.

While France and Vietnam fought, an international conference met in Geneva, Switzerland. Representatives of Ho Chi Minh, Vietnamese emperor Bao Dai, Cambodia, Laos, France, the United States, the Soviet Union, China, and Britain discussed the situation in Indochina. After the French defeat at Dien Bien Phu in May 1954, the conference tried to settle the conflict.

As a result of the **Geneva Conference,** Vietnam was divided into two separate nations in July 1954. Ho Chi Minh controlled northern Vietnam. Ngo Dinh Diem, a former official in Bao Dai's government, became the premier of southern Vietnam. Diem, who had lived in exile in the United States, gained the backing of the United States. In 1955, Diem became the president and declared South Vietnam a republic. Thus began United States involvement in the Vietnam War. The war lasted from 1955 to 1975 and was fought to protect South Vietnam from being taken over by Communists.

The Geneva agreements provided for elections to be held in 1956 to unify the country. South Vietnam refused to support this part of the agreement, and the United States government backed this decision. The elections never took place.

*The fates of three nations—Vietnam, the United States, and France—became interwoven in the struggle for control over Vietnam.*

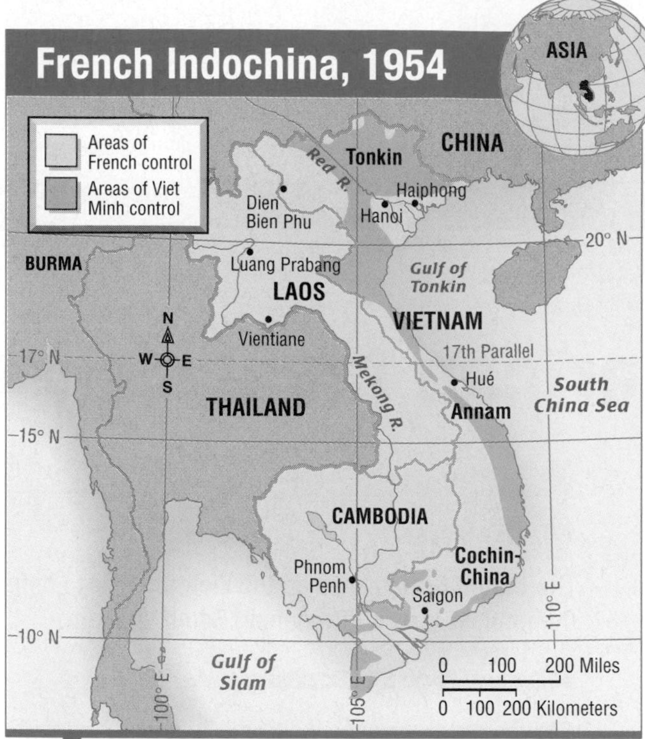


**MAP skills** Events in Southeast Asia caught the attention of the United States in 1954, as France struggled to maintain control in this region. ***Regions*** ***Where was the largest region of Viet Minh (Ho Chi Minh's) control?***

## Kennedy's Vietnam Policy

President Eisenhower pledged his support to Diem's South Vietnamese government. In 1960 he provided some 675 United States military advisers to assist in the struggle against the North. When President Kennedy took office in 1961, he did even more. Kennedy was determined to prevent the spread of communism at all costs. This meant strengthening and protecting the government that the United States had helped create in South Vietnam.

Kennedy sent Vice President Lyndon Johnson to Vietnam to assess the situation there. Diem told him that if South Vietnam was to survive, it would need even more aid. In response, Kennedy increased the number of American military advisers to Vietnam. By the end of 1963, that number had grown to more than 16,000.

Military aid by itself could not ensure success. Diem lacked support in his own country. He imprisoned people who criticized his government and filled many government positions with members of his own family. United States aid earmarked for economic reforms went instead to the military and into the pockets of corrupt officials.

In addition, Diem launched an unpopular program to move peasants from their ancestral lands to "strategic hamlets." These government-run farming communities were intended to isolate the peasants from Communist influences seeping into South Vietnam.

In addition, Diem was a Catholic in a largely Buddhist country. When Diem insisted that Buddhists obey Catholic religious laws, serious opposition developed. In June 1963 a Buddhist monk burned himself to death. Photographs showing his silent, grisly protest appeared on the front pages of newspapers around the world. Other monks followed the example, but their martyrdom did not budge Diem.

Kennedy finally realized that Diem would never reform and acknowledged that the struggle against communism in Vietnam could not be won under Diem's rule. United States officials told South Vietnamese military leaders that the United States would not object to Diem's overthrow. With that encouragement, military leaders staged a coup in November 1963. They seized control of the government and, to Kennedy's dismay, assassinated Diem on November 2 as he tried to flee.

## Robert McNamara

**AMERICAN BIOGRAPHY** One of the American officials who gave up on Diem was Robert McNamara, Kennedy's Secretary of Defense. A Republican with a strong business background, McNamara became one of Kennedy's closest advisers on Vietnam. Later he would help shape the policies that drew the United States deeper into the war.

*Robert McNamara (b. 1916)*

Robert McNamara was born June 9, 1916, in San Francisco, California. He grew up across the bay in Oakland. McNamara attended the University of California at Berkeley and went on to earn a graduate degree at Harvard Business School in 1939. He used his degree to land a job at the Ford Motor Company. Through hard work and solid business decisions, McNamara moved quickly up the corporate ladder. He took over the presidency of Ford Motor in November 1960. This rising star caught the eye of President Kennedy, who offered him a position in his Cabinet just one month later.

As Secretary of Defense, McNamara applied his business knowledge, managing to cut costs while modernizing the armed forces. He turned the Pentagon's thinking away from reliance on the threat of nuclear bombs toward the development of a "flexible response" to military crises. He also began to focus his attention on how to handle the conflict in Vietnam.

Later, under Lyndon Johnson, McNamara would push for direct American involvement in the war. But in 1963 he still questioned whether a complete withdrawal was not the better alternative. Looking back on that period later, McNamara revealed his and Kennedy's feelings:

**AMERICAN VOICES** **"I believed that we had done all the training we could. Whether the South Vietnamese were qualified or not to turn back the North Vietnamese, I was certain that if they weren't, it wasn't for lack of our training. More training wouldn't strengthen them; therefore we should get out. The President agreed."**

—*Robert McNamara*

As you will read, the United States did not withdraw. It continued to back South Vietnam and the coup leaders who took over the government. ■

## *Johnson's War*

Three weeks after Diem's assassination, Kennedy himself fell to an assassin's bullet in Dallas, Texas. By then the new military government in South Vietnam was already in trouble. The ruling generals bickered among themselves and failed to direct the South Vietnamese army effectively.

**The Viet Cong** Meanwhile Communist guerrillas in the south, known as **Viet Cong,** gained control of more territory and earned the loyalty of an increasing number of South Vietnamese. Ho Chi Minh and the North Vietnamese aided the Viet Cong throughout the struggle.

Lyndon Johnson, the new United States President, was suspicious of Ho's Communist sympathies, as Kennedy had been. He believed strongly in the need for containment:

**"The Communists' desire to dominate the world is just like the lawyer's desire to be the ultimate judge on the Supreme Court. . . . You see, the Communists want to rule the world, and if we don't stand up to them, they will do it. And we'll be slaves. Now I'm not one of those folks seeing Communists under every bed. But I do know about the principles of power, and when one side is weak, the other steps in."**

—*Lyndon Johnson*

Just after he assumed office, Johnson met with Henry Cabot Lodge, United States ambassador to South Vietnam. Lodge told the new President that if he wanted to save Vietnam, he faced some tough choices. Johnson was determined to do whatever was necessary to win the war. "I am not going to lose Vietnam," he said. Referring to the Communist takeover of China in 1949, he went on: "I am not going to be the President who saw Southeast Asia go the way China went."

In his campaign for President in 1964, Johnson tried to keep the war from becoming an issue. "We are not about to send American boys nine or ten thousand miles away from home to do what Asian boys ought to be doing for themselves," he declared. He called Barry Goldwater,

Buddhist monks protested Ngo Dinh Diem's government by burning themselves to death on the streets of Saigon. ***Government*** *How does this picture symbolize the difficult problems Johnson inherited in Vietnam?*

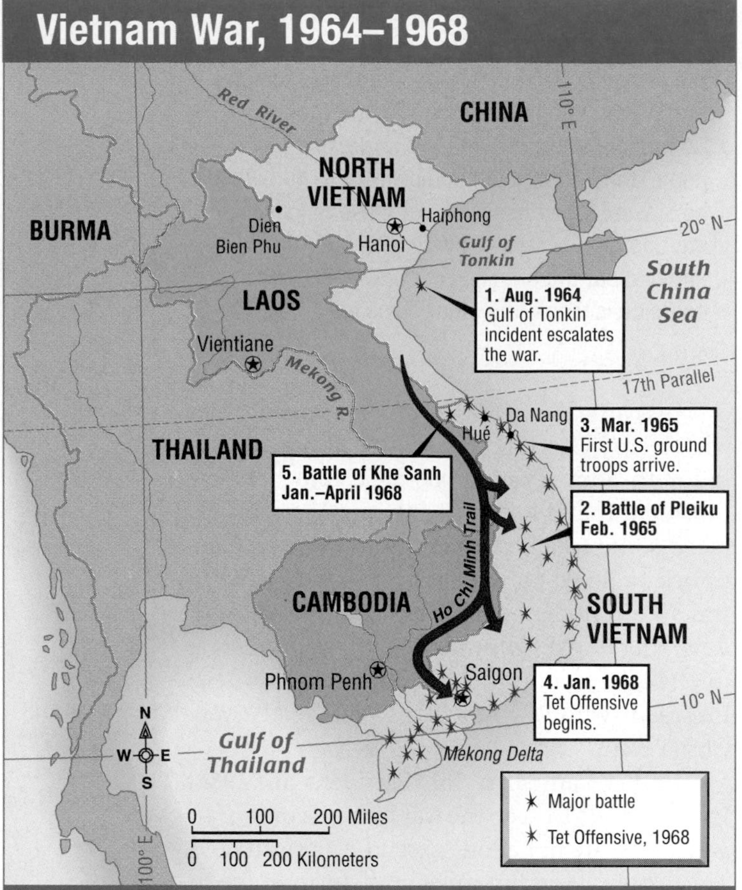

The Ho Chi Minh Trail, shown in the map above, was a supply route from North Vietnam through Laos and Cambodia into South Vietnam.

***Movement*** *How might the Ho Chi Minh Trail have contributed to the execution of the Tet Offensive?*

his Republican opponent in the election, an extremist who would lead the nation into nuclear war. Even when the Viet Cong attacked an airfield outside of Saigon, killing four Americans, Johnson declined to retaliate.

**Intensifying the War** In August 1964, during the presidential campaign, Johnson made a dramatic announcement. North Vietnamese torpedo boats, he said, had attacked United States destroyers in the international waters of the Gulf of Tonkin, 30 miles from North Vietnam. Those attacks would change the course of the war.

**Main Idea CONNECTIONS**

*What events led to an increase in American involvement in Vietnam in 1964?*

Details about the attacks were sketchy, and some people doubted that they had even taken place. In any case, Johnson used the Tonkin Gulf incident to deepen American involvement in Vietnam. Johnson asked Congress for and obtained a resolution giving him authority to "take all necessary measures to repel any armed attack against the forces of the United States and to prevent further aggression."

Congress passed this **Gulf of Tonkin Resolution** on August 7 by a vote of 414 to 0 in the House of Representatives and 88 to 2 in the Senate. Johnson had been waiting for some time for an opportunity to propose the resolution, which, he noted, "covered everything." The President now had nearly complete control over what the United States did in Vietnam, even without an official declaration of war from Congress.

After winning the election in 1964, Johnson started a gradual military **escalation,** or expansion, of the war, devoting ever more American money and personnel to the conflict. Enemy gains in South Vietnam led to this course of action.

Initially, United States soldiers had gone to Vietnam to advise the South Vietnamese. Now they took on the task of propping up the South Vietnamese government. The leader of that government in 1965 was military officer Nguyen Cao Ky. In 1967 Nguyen Van Thieu succeeded him as president. Ky and Thieu were more effective leaders than Diem had been, but they remained authoritarian. More important, they were unable to put together an army that could successfully defend the country.

By 1965 the Viet Cong were steadily expanding within South Vietnam. North Vietnamese troops and supplies poured into the south via the **Ho Chi Minh Trail,** a supply route that passed through Laos and Cambodia. The Communists appeared close to victory.

In February 1965 a Viet Cong attack at Pleiku in South Vietnam killed 8 Americans and wounded 126. President Johnson responded by authorizing the bombing of North Vietnam. Two weeks after the Pleiku attack, General William Westmoreland, the commander of United States forces in Vietnam, requested more soldiers. He asked Johnson for two battalions of marines to protect the American airfield at Da Nang.

Johnson heeded the request, beginning a rapid buildup of American combat troops. At the start of 1965 some 25,000 American soldiers were stationed in Vietnam. By the end of the year the number had risen to 184,000. The Americans brought with them advanced weaponry and new tactics and did achieve some successes. But they still failed to drive out the Viet Cong, who were masters at jungle warfare.

Month after month the fighting continued. United States planes bombed North Vietnam, and the flow of American soldiers into the south increased. Their number climbed to 385,000 by the end of 1966, to 485,000 by the end of 1967, and to 536,000 by the end of 1968. Despite the large United States presence in South Vietnam, the Communist forces only intensified their efforts.

**The Tet Offensive** Those efforts reached a climax in 1968, during Tet, the Vietnamese New Year. On January 30 the Viet Cong and North Vietnamese launched a major offensive. The **Tet Offensive,** shown in the map on the previous page, included surprise attacks on major cities and towns and American military bases throughout South Vietnam. In Saigon, the South Vietnamese capital, the Viet Cong boldly attacked the American embassy and the presidential palace. Fierce fighting continued in Saigon for several weeks. The siege of Khe Sanh, an American base near the border with North Vietnam, lasted until April.

Even though they were turned back with heavy losses, the Viet Cong had won a psychological victory. The Tet Offensive demonstrated that the Viet Cong could launch a massive attack on targets throughout South Vietnam. Furthermore, as images of the fighting flooded American television, many people at home began to express reservations about United States involvement in Vietnam. Many were discouraged, believing that once there the troops had not been allowed to win the war. In spite of the vocal "pro-peace" protesters, a majority of Americans supported a policy tougher than the one pursued by the administration. President Johnson, caught in the middle, saw his popularity plunge.

**FACT Finder** **The War in Vietnam Escalates**

| Year | Event |
|---|---|
| 1964 | Gulf of Tonkin Resolution passes. Gradual military escalation begins. |
| 1965 | President Johnson responds to attacks against American troops by authorizing the bombing of North Vietnam and by rapidly increasing the number of American combat troops in South Vietnam. |
| 1966–1967 | The number of American soldiers in South Vietnam continues to increase. |
| 1968 | The Viet Cong and North Vietnamese launch the Tet Offensive. |

**Interpreting Tables** The Gulf of Tonkin Resolution gave President Johnson increased authority over troops in Vietnam. ***Government What was the Tet Offensive?***

## SECTION 1 REVIEW

### Comprehension

1. *Key Terms* Define: (a) Geneva Conference; (b) Viet Cong; (c) Gulf of Tonkin Resolution; (d) escalation; (e) Ho Chi Minh Trail; (f) Tet Offensive.
2. *Summarizing the Main Idea* Why did the United States get more and more involved in the conflict in Vietnam?
3. *Organizing Information* Draw a line graph to show the changes in the number of American soldiers in Vietnam between 1960 and 1968. Write notes to describe events that influenced United States policy toward Vietnam, and connect them to points on the graph.

### Critical Thinking

4. *Analyzing Time Lines* Review the time line at the start of the section. Which event do you think affected Kennedy's viewpoint on Vietnam the most? Explain.
5. *Identifying Assumptions* What do you think Johnson hoped to gain by authorizing the bombing of targets in North Vietnam in 1965?

### Writing Activity

6. *Writing a Persuasive Essay* Imagine that you are Robert McNamara in 1963. Write an essay presenting President Kennedy with two options—withdraw from Vietnam or fully support Diem.

| 1966 | 1968 | 1969 | 1971 |
|---|---|---|---|
| *B-52 bomber first used in Vietnam* | *My Lai massacre* | *Americans first learn of My Lai massacre* | *Calley sentenced to life in prison* |

**1966** **1968** **1970** **1972**

# 2 The Brutality of the War

## SECTION PREVIEW

### Objectives

1 Describe the conditions under which American soldiers fought in Vietnam.
2 Identify the effects of the war on Vietnamese civilians.
3 Summarize the impact of the massacre at My Lai.
4 *Key Terms* Define: saturation bombing; napalm; My Lai massacre.

### Main Idea

The violence and brutality of the Vietnam War affected civilians as well as soldiers.

### Reading Strategy

*Reading for Evidence* Read the section that summarizes the effects of the war on American soldiers and Vietnamese civilians. As you read, list the different ways in which the soldiers and the civilians suffered.

*Images of brutality and bloodshed made American television viewers question U.S. involvement in Vietnam.*

When Americans first started arriving in Vietnam in large numbers, they encountered all the frustrations of guerrilla warfare. American forces had superior arms and supplies. The Communists, however, had advantages of their own. For one thing, the swamps and jungles of Vietnam offered them protection. Sanctuaries across the border in Cambodia and Laos were valuable too. Finally, the Communists could often count on the support of the local population. At times that support was gained through terrorist methods. But it was often genuine, especially in the early 1960s.

## Battlefield Conditions

Many American soldiers went to war enthusiastic about the job they were being asked to do. Some, like Ron Kovic of Long Island, worried about the Communist threat. Kovic was afraid that Communists "were infiltrating our schools, trying to take over our classes and control our minds." After high school, he joined the marines to do his part to defend his country. He proudly served a tour in Vietnam and signed up for a second tour. This second tour of duty would take a terrible toll on Kovic's body and mind.

He and other soldiers were finding the war confusing and disturbing. They were trying to defend the freedom of the South Vietnamese, but the people seemed indifferent to the Americans' effort. The dishonest and inept government in Saigon may have caused that indifference. "We are the unwilling working for the unqualified to do the unnecessary for the ungrateful," Kit Bowen of the First Infantry Division wrote to his father in Oregon.

Fighting conditions were also different from those they had seen in films. Carrying 60-pound packs, they had to walk through jungles of 10-foot-tall elephant grass and across flooded rice paddies. Much of the time they fought leeches, fever, and jungle rot—a tropical fungus that infected the skin.

American troops never knew what to expect next, and they never could be sure who was a friend and who was an enemy. The

Vietnamese woman selling soft drinks by the roadside might be a Viet Cong ally, counting government soldiers as they passed. A child peddling candy might be concealing a live grenade.

The Viet Cong lacked the sophisticated equipment of the United States troops, so they avoided head-on clashes. Instead they used guerilla warfare tactics, working in small groups to launch sneak attacks and practice sabotage. They often frustrated American search parties by hiding themselves in elaborate underground tunnels. Some of these were equipped with running water and electricity. The largest contained hospitals, stores, and weapons storage facilities.

The various booby traps of the guerrilla fighters posed constant hazards to the Americans. There were animal snares, camouflaged holes filled with razor-sharp punji stakes that were sometimes poisoned, carefully hidden land mines, and grenades triggered by concealed trip wires. GIs could go weeks without making contact with the enemy—in fact, most never did—but there was always the possibility of sudden danger.

In the face of the uncertain situation, a GI wrote home:

**AMERICAN VOICES** **"The VC [Viet Cong] are getting much stronger, so I think this war is going to get worse before it gets better. . . . I try and take great pride in my unit and the men I work with. A lot of the men have been in a lot of trouble and have no education or money. But I feel honored to have them call me a friend."**

*—Letter home from an American soldier*

Ron Kovic confronted his fears by making an aggressive effort to be a good soldier. But the horrors of war came to haunt him after he accidentally killed a United States corporal. Later he shot at shadowy figures in a village hut, only to learn that his unit had killed and wounded innocent children.

The final blow for Ron Kovic came when a sniper's bullet entered his spine. As his spinal column was severed and he lost the feeling in his legs, all he could think of was "the worthlessness of dying right here in this place at this moment for nothing." Kovic survived the bullet wound but was paralyzed from the chest down. The injury caused him to feel, in his words, "like a big clumsy puppet with all his strings cut."

## *Effects on Civilians*

**Main Idea CONNECTIONS**

***How were Vietnamese civilians affected by the war?***

The war was also devastating for Vietnamese civilians in both the north and the south. Because American soldiers were never sure who might be sympathetic to the Viet Cong, civilians suffered as much as soldiers. As the struggle intensified, the destruction worsened.

In April 1966 the Americans introduced the huge B-52 bomber into the war to smash roads and heavy bridges in North Vietnam. During air raids these planes could drop thousands of tons of explosives over large areas. This **saturation bombing** tore North Vietnam apart.

Many of the bombs used in these raids threw pieces of their thick metal casings in all directions when they exploded. These fragmentation bombs were not confined to the north alone. They were also used in the south, where they killed and maimed countless civilians.

United States forces also used chemical weapons against the Vietnamese. Pilots dropped an herbicide known as Agent Orange on dense jungle landscapes. By killing the leaves and thick undergrowth, the herbicide exposed Viet Cong hiding places. Agent Orange also killed crops, and later it was discovered to cause health problems in livestock and humans, including civilians and American soldiers.

In addition to killing and injuring many civilians, the war also forced many Vietnamese to flee their homes. ***Culture What impact did the war have on Vietnamese culture?***

VIEWING HISTORY

From the medic trying in vain to save a dying comrade (above), to the soldier finally giving in to anguished tears in a lonely barracks (right), the war left few untouched. ***Culture* How did the nature of the fighting add to the frustrations of American soldiers?**

Another destructive chemical used in Vietnam was called **napalm.** This jellylike substance, when dropped from planes as a "firebomb," burned uncontrollably. It stuck to people's bodies and seared off their flesh.

The war affected everyone in Vietnam. Le Thanh, a North Vietnamese, recalled the horrors he had witnessed as a child in the 1960s:

> **"Nobody could get away from the war. It didn't matter if you were in the countryside or the city. While I was living in the country I saw terrible things. . . . I saw children who had been killed, pagodas and churches that had been destroyed, monks and priests dead in the ruins, schoolboys who were killed when schools were bombed."**
>
> *—Le Thanh*

The situation was similar in the south. Near the village of My Thuy Phuong, the war suddenly intruded on the life of a peasant who later described the frightening incident:

> **"One day I was walking back home from the ricefield, carrying tools on my shoulder. Then behind me I heard a large, loud noise. A very bad noise. I looked back and saw an American helicopter following me, shooting down the path toward me. I was very scared, so [I] jumped into the water by the side. Just one moment later, the bullets went right by. So scary."**
>
> *—Vietnamese peasant*

## *The My Lai Massacre*

In March 1968 the brutality of the war came into sharp focus at My Lai, a small village in South Vietnam. In response to word that My Lai was sheltering 250 members of the Viet Cong, a United States infantry company moved in to clear out the village. Rather than enemy soldiers, the company found women, children, and old men. The American troops already had suffered heavy combat losses. They were worn down by the tensions, terrors, and frustrations of fighting a guerrilla war. Some lost control.

Lieutenant William L. Calley, Jr., was in charge. First he ordered, "Round everybody up." Then he gave the command for the prisoners to be killed. One soldier, Private Paul Meadlo, later described what happened to one group of Vietnamese:

> AMERICAN VOICES
>
> **"We huddled them up. We made them squat down. . . . I poured about four clips [about 68 shots] into the group. . . . Well, we kept right on firing. . . . I still dream about it. . . . Some nights, I can't even sleep. I just lay there thinking about it."**
>
> *—Private Paul Meadlo*

At least 175 and perhaps more than 400 Vietnamese died in the **My Lai massacre.** Even more would have perished without the heroic actions of a helicopter crew who stepped in to halt the slaughter. The pilot, Hugh Thompson, saw at least 10 villagers racing for a bunker, with a group of American soldiers in pursuit. From the air, he had already seen bodies piled in ditches and had witnessed the killing of a wounded woman by an American officer. So he knew what would happen if he did nothing.

At great risk to himself and his crew, Thompson landed the helicopter between the soldiers and the fleeing Vietnamese. He ordered his door gunner, 18-year-old Lawrence Colburn, to fire his machine gun at the American troops if they began shooting the villagers. Thompson got out, confronted the leader of the soldiers, and then arranged to evacuate the civilians. Thompson's crew chief, Glenn Andreotta, pulled a child from a ditch full of dead bodies.†

Despite Thompson's testimony about My Lai, his superiors covered up the incident. When the story finally came out, late in 1969, it shocked Americans at home. In 1971, for his role in the massacre, Lieutenant Calley began serving a sentence of life in prison with hard labor. Many Americans saw him as a scapegoat, however, and the public outcry was such that President Nixon reduced his life sentence to twenty years. He was released on good behavior three years later.

The publicity surrounding the My Lai massacre was so great that news accounts of atrocities in the city of Hué, also just coming to light, were completely overshadowed. During the Tet Offensive, the Communists had been uncommonly brutal, slaughtering anyone they labeled an enemy. This included harmless minor officials, teachers, and doctors. While the Communists had control of Hué, they ordered all civil servants, military personnel, and those who had worked for the Americans to report to special locations. Of those who obeyed, some 3,000 to 5,000 were killed. Their bodies were found in mass graves after American and South Vietnamese forces retook the city.

The helicopter was first widely used in warfare during the Vietnam War. ***Science and Technology*** ***Why did American troops with superior equipment fail to defeat the enemy?***

† The heroics of the helicopter crew did not surface until much later. Finally, in 1998 the United States honored all three men with the Soldier's Medal, the highest award for bravery unrelated to fighting an enemy.

## SECTION 2 REVIEW

### Comprehension

1. *Key Terms* Define: (a) saturation bombing; (b) napalm; (c) My Lai massacre.
2. *Summarizing the Main Idea* Why was the Vietnam War particularly brutal for American soldiers?
3. *Organizing Information* Create a chart to compare the effects of the war on American soldiers and Vietnamese civilians.

### Critical Thinking

4. *Analyzing Time Lines* Review the time line at the start of the section. What evidence do you see of a cause and an effect in the time-line events?
5. *Drawing Conclusions* Do you think that the United States made every effort to win the Vietnam War? Why or why not?

### Writing Activity

6. *Writing a Persuasive Essay* Write an essay either condemning or forgiving the actions of Lieutenant Calley at My Lai.

**1960** Students for a Democratic Society organized

**1964** Free speech movement begins

**1965** First teach-in

**1968** More than 200 demonstrations at U.S. colleges and universities

**1969** Weathermen clash with police in Chicago

**1971** Publication of Pentagon Papers

1960 | 1965 | 1970 | 1975

# 3 Student Protest

## SECTION PREVIEW

### Objectives

1. Describe student activism in the 1960s.
2. Identify actions some people took to resist the Vietnam War.
3. *Key Terms* Define: Pentagon Papers; New Left; teach-in; conscientious objector; deferment.

### Main Idea

Students in the 1960s demonstrated in support of free speech and other issues and protested against the Vietnam War.

### Reading Strategy

*Structured Overview* Write the main headings *Student Activism* and *Resistance to War* on a sheet of paper. As you read the section, write important details in the column under each heading.

*This 1969 poster advertised one of many antiwar demonstrations during the Vietnam War era.*

In June 1971 *The New York Times* began publishing articles based on a classified government study of United States involvement in the Vietnam War. The study came to be called the Pentagon Papers. The **Pentagon Papers** revealed that government officials had lied to Congress and the American people about the war. Presidents had made secret policy decisions, such as giving military aid to France and waging an undercover war against North Vietnam in the early 1960s.

Such revelations shocked the public and gave a boost to the growing antiwar movement. Popular support for the war began to drop. Still, many loyal and patriotic Americans defended their country's actions in Vietnam, and the issue created deep divisions within the United States.

## Student Activism

Students stood at the forefront of the antiwar movement. In the early 1960s members of the baby-boom generation started graduating from high school. Postwar prosperity gave many of these students opportunities unknown to previous generations. Instead of going directly into the working world after high school, these young men and women could afford to continue their education. College enrollments swelled with more students than ever before.

Change was in the air. It had been building for a while, even through the conformist years of the 1950s. The popular culture of that decade, including rock-and-roll music and rebellious youths on the movie screen, indicated that many young Americans were not satisfied with the values of their parents. The early 1960s saw a widening of this generation gap.

The civil rights movement, discussed in an earlier chapter, also became a steppingstone to other movements for change. Civil rights activists helped organize Students for a Democratic Society (SDS) in 1960. SDS's declaration of principles and goals, called the Port Huron Statement, appeared in 1962. Written largely by Tom Hayden, a student at the University of Michigan, the statement explained some of the feelings behind the antiwar movement:

KEY DOCUMENTS

"We are people of this generation, bred in at least modest comfort, housed now in universities, looking uncomfortably at the world we inherit. When we were kids the United States was the wealthiest and strongest country in the world. . . . As we grew, however, our comfort was penetrated by events too troubling to dismiss. . . . We would replace power rooted in possession, privilege, or circumstance by power and uniqueness rooted in love, reflectiveness, reason, and creativity. As a social system we seek the establishment of a democracy of individual participation."

—*Port Huron Statement*

SDS was a tiny organization at the start. Still, it had a major influence on the development of a new political movement that came to be called the **New Left.** Members of the New Left believed that problems such as poverty and racism called for radical changes.

**The Free Speech Movement** The first confrontation of the student revolution came at the University of California at Berkeley in September 1964. Students became angry when the university administration refused to allow them to distribute leaflets outside the main gate of the campus.

The students, who had fought for equal rights in the South, argued that their right to free speech was being challenged. They resisted the university's effort to restrict their political activity. When police came to arrest one of their leaders, students surrounded the police car and kept it from moving. The free speech movement was under way.

The university administration tried to find a compromise. But then the university governing board stepped in. The board had the final word over university policy. It decided to hold student leaders responsible for their actions and filed charges against some.

On December 2, 1964, thousands of irate students took over Sproul Hall and shut down the university administration. That night police moved in. They arrested more than 700 students in the hall. Other students, supported by some faculty members, went on strike. They stopped attending classes to show their support for the free speech demonstrators.

Berkeley remained the most radical campus, but the agitation there spread to other campuses across the United States. In the spring of 1965, activists at several schools launched protests against regulations they thought unfairly curbed their freedom. Students at Michigan State University and elsewhere challenged social restrictions, such as the hours when women and men could visit each others' dormitories. Students also sought greater involvement in college affairs. Others left their campuses to work in campaigns to improve conditions in the inner cities.

In October 1964, Berkeley student Mario Savio stood atop a police car to address a crowd of protesters demanding free speech. The building in the background is Sproul Hall. ***Culture*** ***How had the civil rights movement influenced the antiwar movement?***

**The Teach-in Movement** As American involvement in the Vietnam War grew, students were among the first to protest the war. Some opposed what they regarded as American imperialism. Others viewed the conflict as a civil war that should be resolved by the Vietnamese alone.

As escalation began (see the graphs on the next page), antiwar activists used new methods to protest the war. The first **teach-in** took place at the University of Michigan in March 1965. When a small

*What was a teach-in?*

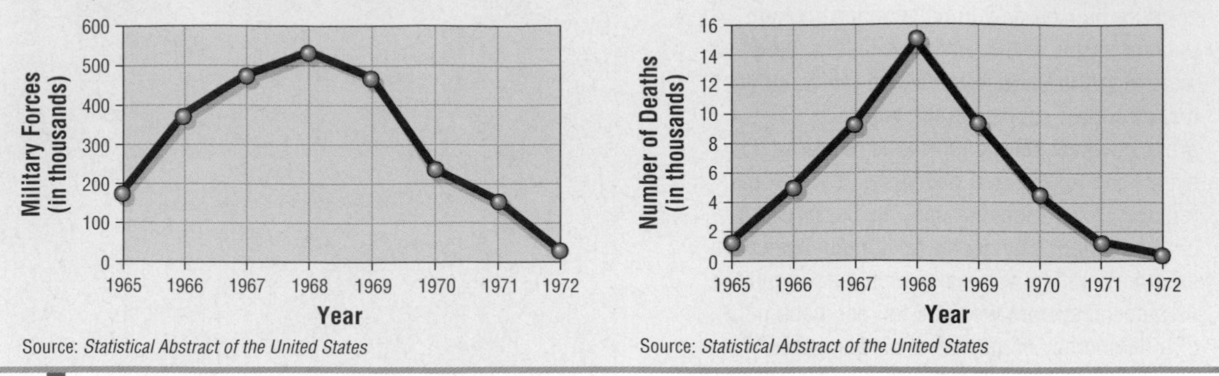


**Interpreting Graphs** United States involvement in Vietnam peaked in 1968. ***Foreign Relations*** ***How many United States soldiers were in Vietnam in 1968? How many United States soldiers died in battle in 1968?***

group of faculty members planned a strike to protest the war, the Michigan legislature threatened to fire them. Instead, an even larger group decided to make a public statement. Some 50 or 60 professors decided to teach a special night session in which issues concerning the war could be aired.

To their surprise, several thousand people showed up and made the evening a monumental success. Soon other teach-ins followed at colleges around the country. Supporters as well as opponents of the war appeared at the early teach-ins, but soon antiwar voices dominated the sessions.

## *Resistance to War*

A Selective Service Act allowing the government to draft men between the ages of 18 and 26 had been in place since 1951. Relatively few people refused to be drafted in the first half of the 1960s. Most who did were **conscientious objectors.** They opposed fighting in the war on moral or religious grounds.

In July 1965 President Johnson doubled the number of men who could be drafted into the armed forces. By the end of the year he had doubled the number again. These moves led to the rise of a draft-resistance movement that urged young men not to cooperate with their local draft board.

As more and more young men were called into service and sent to fight in Vietnam, Americans began to question the morality and fairness of the draft. College students could receive a **deferment,** or official postponement of their call to serve. Usually this meant they would not have to go to war. Those who could not afford college did not have this avenue open to them. In 1966 the Selective Service System announced that college students who ranked low academically could be drafted.

In 1967 resistance to the military draft began to sweep the country. Many young men tried to avoid the draft by claiming that they had physical disabilities. Others applied for conscientious-objector status. Still others left the country. By the end of the war more than 50,000 were believed to have gone to countries such as Canada.

Antiwar groups grew by leaps and bounds around the country. During demonstrations, marchers chanted "Hey, hey, LBJ. How many kids did you kill today?" In April 1967 some 200,000 opponents of the war marched in New York City. In October more than 50,000 protesters gathered in Washington, D.C., for a March on the Pentagon, home of the Defense Department.

In 1969 the National Chicano Moratorium Committee staged its own antiwar demonstrations. These protesters argued that Vietnam was a racial war, with black and brown Americans being used against their brothers and sisters in developing nations. In the first six months of 1968, more than 200 major demonstrations erupted at colleges and universities around the country.

Despite the widespread discontent, not all students agreed with the antiwar protesters. Some firmly supported American involvement in Vietnam. Others questioned the war but were troubled by the lawlessness and radicalism of many antiwar protests. These students did not receive the press coverage of their more outspoken classmates. But they did make their opinions known by writing letters to campus newspapers or by challenging the actions of antiwar groups in court. Many other Americans expressed their patriotism by putting flag decals on their car windows or attaching bumper stickers that read "My Country, Right or Wrong" and "Love It or Leave It."

The most dramatic confrontation of 1968 came in April at Columbia University in New York City. Students there linked the issues of civil rights and the war. An SDS chapter sought to get the university to cut its ties with a research institute that did work for the military. At the same time, an African American student organization tried to halt construction of a gymnasium that would encroach upon a nearby minority neighborhood.

As President Johnson dramatically stepped up the draft, antiwar sentiment stepped up, too. Antiwar protests, like this one in San Francisco in 1967, received much press coverage. Still, many Americans supported the war effort—some with bumper stickers like the one below. ***Diversity*** ***How else did students who supported the administration make their views known?***

**My Country Love it or Leave It**

Together these two groups took over the president's office. Finally the president of Columbia called the police, and hundreds of students were arrested. A student sympathy strike followed, and the university closed early that spring.

Sometimes the radical movement turned violent. Activists in one SDS faction called themselves the Weathermen, after a line in a Bob Dylan song—"You don't need a weatherman to know which way the wind blows." They were determined to bring about a revolution immediately.

In October 1969 the group converged on Chicago. Members dressed in hard hats, boots, and work gloves rampaged through the streets wielding pipes, clubs, rocks, and chains. They tangled with police (as they had planned), regrouped, and came back for still another confrontation. This kind of violence alarmed most Americans and turned some against the antiwar movement.

## SECTION 3 REVIEW

### Comprehension

1. *Key Terms* Define: (a) Pentagon Papers; (b) New Left; (c) teach-in; (d) conscientious objector; (e) deferment.
2. *Summarizing the Main Idea* What forms did student protest take in the 1960s?
3. *Organizing Information* Use a flowchart to show the sequence of important events related to student protests in the 1960s. You might start with the civil rights movement of the 1950s.

### Critical Thinking

4. *Analyzing Time Lines* Review the time line at the start of the section. Which event do you think had the strongest effect on American public opinion about the war? Explain.
5. *Determining Relevance* Do you think that the war protests of the 1960s could have taken place if there had never been a civil rights movement? Explain.

### Writing Activity

6. *Writing an Expository Essay* Write an essay about the forms of protest Americans used to express their views on the war in Vietnam.

# SKILLS FOR LIFE

**Critical Thinking**

Geography

Graphs and Charts

Historical Evidence

## Checking Consistency

Checking consistency means determining whether ideas that should agree, or follow logically one from the other, actually do. Government actions, for example, should always agree with the Constitution. Where no such overriding rules apply—in the creation of foreign policy, for instance—policy objectives are expected to be consistent with past decisions on similar issues.

Use the following steps to check for consistency in the examples at right.

**1.** ***Identify the principle or other factor to be used as the baseline for checking consistency.*** You should expect certain facts, ideas, or actions to agree, either with one another or with an overriding principle. Read the information in Items A and B, at right. (a) What rule or principle serves as the baseline for checking consistency in Item A? (b) In Item B, what did Johnson's description of the North Vietnamese in 1965 suggest about the goals of his policy in Vietnam at the time? (c) How can Johnson's statement serve as the baseline for checking his consistency in other statements about Vietnam?

**2.** ***Note the corresponding action or idea to be checked for consistency.*** (a) In Item A, what action did the Supreme Court take? (b) What probably happened as a result of this action? (c) In Item B, what did Johnson's description of the North Vietnamese (the "Communists") in 1966 suggest about the goals of his policy in Vietnam?

**3.** ***Check for consistency between the principle or baseline factor and the corresponding action or idea.*** In the examples below, compare the second action or idea against the baseline you have identified to see if the two ideas are consistent with or contradict each other. (a) In Item A, did the action taken by the Supreme Court agree or conflict with the First Amendment? Explain your answer. (b) In Item B, was Johnson's statement of his policy objective in 1966 consistent with the statement he had made in 1965? Explain your answer.

### TEST FOR SUCCESS

Compose a statement that Johnson might have made after the Tet Offensive. Label the statement either consistent or inconsistent with the statement he made in 1965. Explain your reasoning.

**A**

"Congress shall make no law . . . abridging the freedom of speech, or of the press. . . ."

—First Amendment, United States Constitution

In 1971 the United States Supreme Court denied the government's request to prohibit two newspapers from publishing the Pentagon Papers, a highly classified documentary history of United States involvement in Vietnam through May 1968.

**B**

"This war, like most wars, is filled with terrible irony. For what do the people of North Vietnam want? They want what their neighbors also desire: food for their hunger, health for their bodies, . . . an end to the bondage of material misery. . . . Neither independence nor human dignity will ever be won by arms alone. It also requires the works of peace."

—President Lyndon B. Johnson,
address at Johns Hopkins University (April 7, 1965)

"Aggression is on the march and the enslavement of free men is its goal. . . . If we allow the Communists to win in Vietnam, it will become easier and more appetizing for them to take over other countries in other parts of the world. . . . That is why it is vitally important to every American family that we stop the Communists in South Vietnam."

—President Lyndon B. Johnson,
Honolulu Conference (February 6, 1966)

| 1963 | 1965 | 1966 | 1969 |
|---|---|---|---|
| *Two Harvard researchers fired for LSD experiments* | *Miniskirt introduced* | *Masters and Johnson publish* Human Sexual Response | *Woodstock festival* |

1963 — 1965 — 1967 — 1969

# 4 The Counterculture

## SECTION PREVIEW

### Objectives

1. Identify the social changes promoted by members of the counterculture.
2. Describe the music world in the 1960s and how it both reflected and contributed to cultural changes.
3. *Key Terms* Define: counterculture; Woodstock festival.

### Main Idea

In the 1960s a youth culture arose that promoted freedom and individuality. Its new attitudes about personal relationships, drugs, and music shocked many Americans.

### Reading Strategy

*Reinforcing Key Ideas* As you read the section, note details that support the following sentence from this page: "In the 1960s many Americans began to look for alternatives to traditional patterns of living."

In the 1960s many Americans began to look for alternatives to traditional patterns of living. Young people, in particular, adopted values that ran counter to, or against, the mainstream culture. Drawing on the example of the Beat Generation of the 1950s, members of this **counterculture** rejected most of the conventional social customs. They experimented with new forms of dress, different attitudes toward sexual relationships, and the recreational use of drugs. Their rejection of accepted ways of life in favor of change and individual choice still affects society today.

## A Time of Change

People's appearances reflected the social changes that were taking place. Hippies—people who were "hip," or aware of the latest styles—wanted to look different. Some women wore their hair long and chose freer fashions, such as loose-fitting dresses. Others chose to wear tight miniskirts, which were introduced by British designer Mary Quant in 1965. Men often let their hair grow long and wore beards.

Many hippies adopted the dress of working people, which seemed somehow more "authentic" than the school clothes of middle-class youth. Both men and women wore blue jeans (often with bell bottoms), plain cotton shirts, and other simple garments that were intended to look natural.

**The Sexual Revolution** The new views of sexual behavior advanced by the counterculture were labeled "the sexual revolution." The young people who led this revolution demanded more freedom to make personal choices. Some argued that sex should be separated from its traditional ties to family life.

The sexual revolution in the counterculture led to more open discussion of sexual subjects. Newspapers, magazines, and books published articles that might not have been printed just a few years earlier. The 1962 book by Helen Gurley Brown, *Sex and the Single Girl,* became a bestseller. In 1966 William H. Masters and Virginia E. Johnson shocked

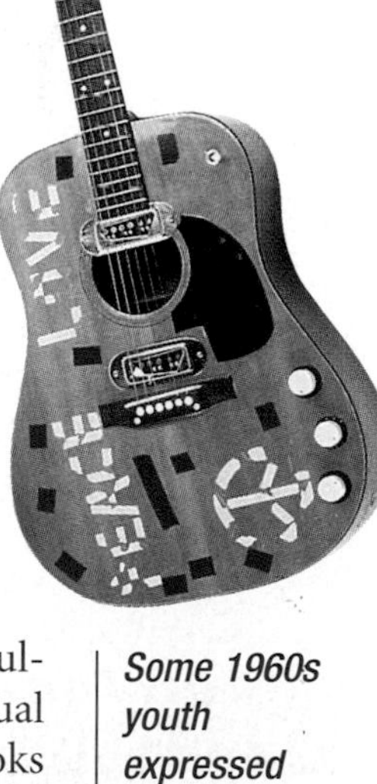

*Some 1960s youth expressed themselves by turning their possessions into works of art.*

This group of hippies lived together in the New Buffalo Commune. They turned out for the 1968 Fourth of July parade in El Rito, New Mexico, in their outrageously painted bus. ***Culture** In what other ways did people reject traditional social customs?*

many people when they published *Human Sexual Response,* a report on their scientific studies of sexuality.

Many men and women also experimented with new living patterns. Some hippies rejected traditional relationships and lived together in communal groups, where they often shared property and chores. More and more people simply lived together as couples, without getting married.

**The Drug Scene** Some members of the 1960s counterculture also turned to psychedelic drugs. These powerful chemicals cause the brain to behave abnormally. Users of psychedelic drugs experience hallucinations and other altered perceptions of reality. The beatniks had experimented with drugs a decade before, but they had been relatively few in number. Now the use of drugs, especially marijuana, became more widespread among the nation's youth.

**Main Idea CONNECTIONS**

*Why do you think the counterculture disturbed many Americans?*

One early proponent of psychedelic drug use was researcher Timothy Leary. Leary worked at Harvard University with Richard Alpert on the chemical compound lysergic acid diethylamide, commonly known as LSD. The two men were fired from their research posts in 1963 for using undergraduates in experiments with the drug. Leary then began to preach that drugs could help free the mind. He advised listeners, "Tune in, turn on, drop out."

Soldiers who had used drugs in Vietnam brought them home when their tours of duty were completed. Marijuana became common among middle-class college students. Todd Gitlin, a radical activist who became president of SDS, explained that "the point was to open up a new space, an inner space, so that we could space out, live for the sheer exultant point of living."

This view presented just one side of the drug scene. On the other side lay serious danger. The possibility of death from an overdose or from an accident while under the influence of drugs was very real. Three leading musicians—Janis Joplin, Jim Morrison, and Jimi Hendrix—died of complications from drug overdoses. They were not the only ones. Their deaths represented the tragic excesses to which some people were driven by their reliance on drugs as an escape.

## The Music World

Music both reflected and contributed to the cultural changes. The rock and roll of the 1950s and the folk music of the early 1960s gave way to a new kind of rock. The Beatles heavily influenced the music of this period, taking first their native England and then the United States by storm. Mick Jagger of the Rolling Stones was a dramatic and electrifying showman on stage. Janis Joplin was a hard-drinking singer whose powerful interpretations of classic blues songs catapulted her to superstardom.

**Woodstock** The diverse strands of the counterculture all came together at the Woodstock Music and Art Fair in upstate New York in August 1969. About 400,000 people gathered for several days in a large pasture in Bethel, New York, to listen to the major bands of the rock world. Despite brutal heat and rain, those who attended the **Woodstock festival** recalled the event with something of a sense of awe for the fellowship they experienced there. Police avoided confrontations with those attending by choosing not to enforce drug laws. The crowd remained under control. Tom Law, one participant at Woodstock, commented on the mood:

> **AMERICAN VOICES** **"The event was so much bigger than the music. It was a phenomenon. It was absolutely a phenomenon. And it was also the most peaceful, civilized gathering that was probably happening on the planet at the time."**
>
> —*Tom Law*

Other Americans, however, viewed both the festival and the mood it reflected with disgust. Even as some older people began growing their hair longer and wearing "hipper" clothing, they were alarmed at the changes they saw around them. These changes also disturbed many young people. In particular, people in the mainstream culture deplored the drugs, sex, and nudity they saw at the Woodstock festival and around the country. To them the counterculture represented a rejection of morals and honored values and seemed a childish reaction to the problems of the era.

The young people who attended the Woodstock Music and Art Fair in 1969 reflected the new fashions and social values of their times. ***Culture What were some of these values?***

**Altamont** The fears of those who criticized Woodstock came true at another rock festival that took place at the Altamont Speedway in California in December 1969. There, 300,000 people gathered for a concert by the Rolling Stones.

When promoters of the concert failed to provide adequate security, the Stones hired a band of Hell's Angels, an infamous and lawless motorcycle gang, to keep order. The cyclists ended up beating one man to death when he ventured onstage. The ugly violence at Altamont contradicted the values preached by the counterculture. It also signaled that the era of "peace and love" would not last forever.

Despite their celebration of simple lifestyles, most hippies were children of the comfortable middle class. American corporations marketed items such as blue jeans and stereo equipment to them, and they eagerly bought the products. When the counterculture fell apart, the hippies melted right back into the mainstream. By the 1980s many baby boomers who had protested the values of the 1950s and 1960s would hold executive positions in the same corporations they had once denounced.

## SECTION 4 REVIEW

### Comprehension

1. *Key Terms* Define: (a) counterculture; (b) Woodstock festival.
2. *Summarizing the Main Idea* What values did the counterculture reject in the 1960s and what did it embrace?
3. *Organizing Information* Create a web diagram to organize information related to the counterculture of the 1960s.

### Critical Thinking

4. *Analyzing Time Lines* Review the time line at the start of the section. Which event do you think reflected the sharpest break with the culture of the 1950s?
5. *Identifying Assumptions* What assumptions did members of the counterculture make about mainstream culture?

### Writing Activity

6. *Writing an Expository Essay* Write an essay describing the traditional values that members of the counterculture rejected.

| 1968 | 1969 | 1970 | 1973 | 1975 | 1982 |
|---|---|---|---|---|---|
| Johnson quits race for President | Nixon takes office | Kent State protest | Peace agreement signed | South Vietnam falls | Vietnam Memorial completed |

1965 1970 1975 1980 1985

# 5 The End of the War

## SECTION PREVIEW

### Objectives

1. Explain how opponents of the Vietnam War helped force Johnson's departure, and describe how they reacted to Nixon's policies.
2. Describe how the American troop withdrawal came about and what it meant for South Vietnam.
3. Identify elements that make up the legacy of the Vietnam War.
4. *Key Terms* Define: Paris peace talks; Vietnamization; Vietnam Veterans Memorial.

### Main Idea

The end of the Vietnam War involved slow-moving peace negotiations, the gradual withdrawal of American troops, and the fall of South Vietnam.

### Reading Strategy

*Predicting Content* Skim the section, reading headings and the first sentence of each paragraph. Then list the main headings on a sheet of paper. Under each heading, write a sentence or phrase predicting the content of that part of the section. When you have finished reading, compare your predictions with the actual content.

*The Vietnam Women's Memorial in Washington, D.C., honors the thousands of women who served in Vietnam.*

The Vietnam War created deep divisions in the Democratic party and in the country as a whole. These divisions forced Lyndon Johnson to leave the presidency at the end of his term and paved the way for the election of Republican Richard Nixon in 1968. Nixon pledged to withdraw the United States from the Southeast Asian struggle. He succeeded, but only after expanding the war outside Vietnam, which led to even more violent protest at home.

## Johnson's Departure

By 1968 the antiwar movement was in full swing. Political activists drew on all of their resources to mount the most extensive resistance campaign in American history. Marchers took to the streets, while artists, authors, and musicians contributed their talents to the antiwar crusade.

Years of protests and a growing list of American casualties had steadily increased public opposition to Johnson's handling of the war. By 1967 Robert McNamara, Johnson's Secretary of Defense, had lost faith in the war effort. Privately, he urged the President to turn more of the fighting over to the South Vietnamese and to stop the bombing of North Vietnam. Johnson, fearful of risking defeat on the battlefield, ignored the proposal. He continued to increase American troop levels and to authorize bombing raids on North Vietnam. Still, after the Tet Offensive, Johnson recognized that American public opinion had turned against him. He rarely left the White House near the end of his presidency for fear of being assaulted by angry crowds of protesters. He felt like "a jackrabbit in a hailstorm, hunkering up and taking it."

In early 1968 Johnson watched the campaign of antiwar candidate Eugene McCarthy gain momentum. On March 12 McCarthy almost beat the President in the New

Hampshire Democratic primary. Four days later another critic of the war, Robert Kennedy, joined the race for the Democratic nomination.

Johnson realized that he had lost his base of support. On March 31, 1968, he declared dramatically in a nationally televised speech that he would not run for another term as President:

> "I do not believe that I should devote an hour or a day of my time to any personal partisan causes or to any duties other than the awesome duties of this office—the presidency of your country. Accordingly, I shall not seek, and I will not accept, the nomination of my party for another term."
>
> —*Lyndon Johnson*

Earlier in the same speech, Johnson had ordered a pause in the relentless bombing of Vietnam to open the possibility of peace talks. In this way he hoped to end the war and so restore unity to the United States as he left public life. In April the North Vietnamese agreed to begin formal negotiations with the United States in Paris. A month later the **Paris peace talks** began.

## Public Opinion of U.S. Involvement in Vietnam

***"Do you approve or disapprove of the way President Johnson is handling the situation in Vietnam?"***

| | Approve | Disapprove | No opinion |
|---|---|---|---|
| December 1965 | 56% | 26% | 18% |
| May 1966 | 41% | 37% | 22% |
| April 1967 | 43% | 42% | 15% |
| July 1967 | 33% | 52% | 15% |
| December 1967 | 39% | 49% | 12% |
| February 1968* | 35% | 50% | 15% |

***"In view of the developments since we entered the fighting in Vietnam, do you think the United States made a mistake sending troops to fight in Vietnam?"***

| | Yes, made mistake | No, did not | No opinion |
|---|---|---|---|
| May 1966 | 36% | 49% | 15% |
| April 1967 | 37% | 50% | 13% |
| July 1967 | 41% | 48% | 11% |
| February 1968† | 49% | 41% | 10% |

* During Tet Offensive †After Tet Offensive
Source: *The Gallup Poll: Public Opinion 1935–1971*, by George H. Gallup

**Interpreting Tables** Public opinion of U.S. involvement in Vietnam changed over the course of the war. ***Culture*** ***What percentage of those polled in 1965 approved of Lyndon Johnson's handling of the war? What percentage approved in 1968?***

## Nixon's Policies

McCarthy's campaign for the presidency faltered, and on June 5 Robert Kennedy was assassinated. The Democrats eventually nominated Johnson's Vice President, Hubert Humphrey, at their party's convention in Chicago (see the next chapter). For the Republicans, Richard Nixon ran for the presidency with the claim that he had a secret plan to end the war in Vietnam. He never divulged the details, and critics doubted that a plan really existed, but his pledge still helped secure his election over Humphrey.

**Vietnamization** Once in the White House, Nixon dedicated himself to a policy of **Vietnamization.** This involved removing American forces and replacing them with South Vietnamese soldiers. Between 1968 and 1972 American troop strength dropped from 536,000 to 24,000, and opposition to the war among people in the United States declined. †

Even as he moved to bring American soldiers home, Nixon himself became caught up in the war. As much as he wanted to defuse antiwar sentiment at home, he was determined not to lose the war. Therefore, as he withdrew American troops, he resumed bombing raids, keeping his actions secret from his critics. The map later in this section shows the major targets of the bombing raids.

**Invading Cambodia** President Nixon also widened the war beyond the borders of Vietnam. Hoping to avoid more antiwar protests, Nixon ordered secret bombings in Cambodia. Later, in April 1970, Nixon publicly announced that United States and South

† In January 1973 Nixon announced the end of the military draft, which further defused antiwar protests.

## COMPARING PRIMARY SOURCES

### THE TRAGEDY OF KENT STATE

In May 1970 the National Guard opened fire on a crowd of antiwar protesters at Kent State University and killed four students.

| Opposed to National Guard's Actions | In Support of National Guard's Actions |
|---|---|
| "Nixon acts as if the kids had it coming. But shooting into a crowd of students, that is violence. They say it could happen again if the Guard is threatened. They consider stones threat enough to kill children. I think the violence comes from the government." —*Mother of Jeffrey Glenn Miller, a student killed at Kent State, quoted in* Life *magazine, May 15, 1970* | "He told me they didn't fire those shots to scare the students off. He told me they fired those shots because they knew the students were coming after them, coming for their guns. People are calling my husband a murderer; my husband is not a murderer. He was afraid." —*Wife of a member of the National Guard, quoted in* Newsweek *magazine, May 18, 1970* |

***ANALYZING VIEWPOINTS*** **How do these viewpoints reflect the issues that tore apart American society at that time?**

Vietnamese ground forces were moving into neighboring Cambodia. Their goal was to clear out Communist camps there, from which the enemy was mounting attacks on South Vietnam. The United States, he asserted, would not stand by like "a pitiful helpless giant" while the Viet Cong attacked from Cambodia:

**AMERICAN VOICES** **"We take this action not for the purpose of expanding the war into Cambodia but for the purpose of ending the war in Vietnam and winning the just peace we all desire. We have made and we will continue to make every possible effort to end this war through negotiation at the conference table rather than through more fighting on the battlefield."**

—*Richard Nixon*

**Main Idea CONNECTIONS**

*Why did the United States invade Cambodia?*

Nixon knew that invading Cambodia would not win the war, but he thought it would help at the bargaining table. He was willing to intensify the war in order to strengthen the American position at the peace talks. Nixon's actions, however, brought chaos and civil war in Cambodia and a fresh wave of protests at home.

**Kent State and Jackson State** Nixon's invasion of Cambodia in 1970 reignited the protest movement on college campuses in the United States. At Kent State University in Ohio, students reacted angrily to the President's action. On the weekend following his speech, they broke windows in the business district downtown. They also burned the army ROTC building on campus, which had become a hated symbol of the war.

In response, the governor of Ohio ordered the National Guard to Kent State. Tension mounted. When students threw rocks and empty tear-gas canisters at them, the guardsmen loaded their guns and donned gas masks. They knelt down and aimed their rifles at the students, as if warning them to stop. Then the guardsmen retreated to another position. At the top of a hill, they suddenly turned and began firing on the students below.

Seconds later, four students lay dead, with nine others wounded. Two of the dead had been demonstrators more than 250 feet away from the guardsmen. The other two were bystanders, almost 400 feet away.

Similar violence flared at Jackson State, a nearly all-black college in Mississippi. A confrontation between students and police left two students dead and eleven wounded.

These attacks horrified Americans. In a sign of the deep divisions in the nation, 100,000 construction workers marched in an angry demonstration in New York City in support of the President.

## *American Withdrawal*

The war dragged on, as did the Paris peace talks. In January 1972, while running for a second term as President, Nixon announced that North Vietnam had refused to accept a proposed settlement. At the end of March, the North Vietnamese began a major assault on South Vietnam. This led Nixon to order the most intensive bombing campaign of the war. The United States bombed Hanoi, the North Vietnamese capital, and mined North Vietnamese harbors.

**"Peace Is at Hand"** Just days before the 1972 election, National Security Adviser Henry Kissinger announced, "Peace is at hand." As it turned out, the settlement was not actually final.

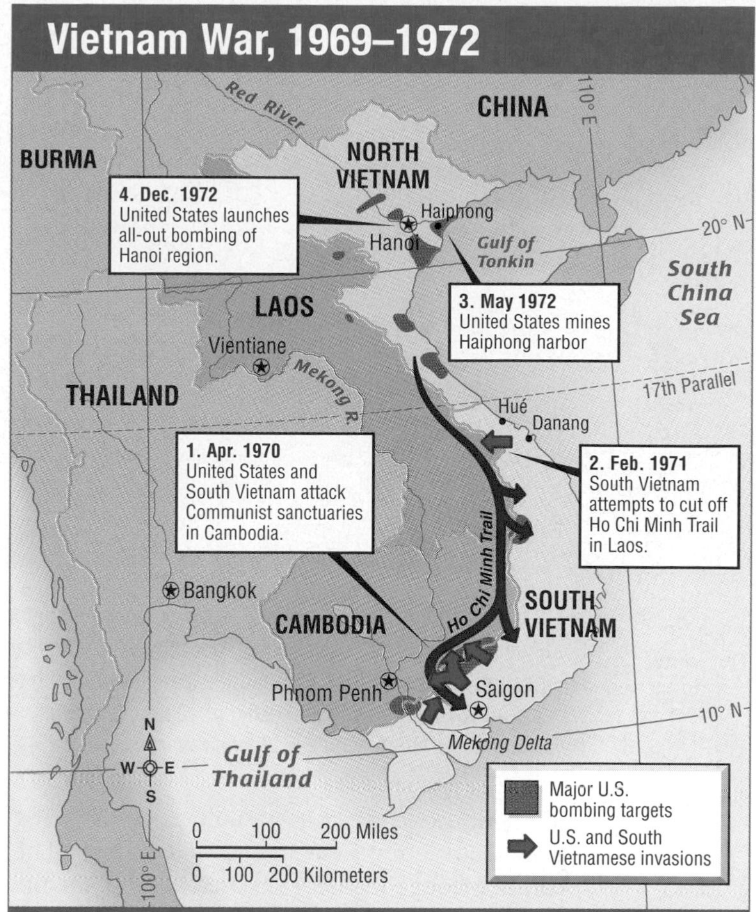


**MAP skills** Although Nixon began withdrawing troops from Vietnam in 1969, he stepped up bombing raids. ***Location*** *According to this map, in what areas were United States bombing raids concentrated during the later years of the war?*

But after Nixon's reelection in November and another round of B-52 bombings of North Vietnam in December, peace finally did arrive. In January 1973 the United States, South Vietnam, North Vietnam, and the Viet Cong signed a formal agreement in Paris. Among the provisions in the agreement were these:

(1) The United States would withdraw all its forces from South Vietnam within 60 days.

(2) All prisoners of war would be released.

(3) All parties to the agreement would end military activities in Laos and Cambodia.

(4) The 17th parallel would continue to divide North and South Vietnam until the country could be reunited.

**South Vietnam Falls** United States involvement in the war came to an end, but the fighting between North and South Vietnam continued for another two years. After the withdrawal of American forces, South Vietnamese soldiers steadily lost ground to their North Vietnamese enemies. In the spring of 1975, the North Vietnamese launched a campaign of strikes against strategic cities throughout South Vietnam, the final objective being the seat of government in Saigon.

South Vietnamese forces crumpled in the face of this campaign. On April 29, 1975, with Communist forces surrounding Saigon, the United States carried out a dramatic last-minute evacuation. American helicopters airlifted more than 1,000 Americans and nearly 6,000 Vietnamese from the city to aircraft carriers waiting offshore. On April 30 North Vietnam completed its conquest of South Vietnam, and the Saigon government officially surrendered. After decades of fighting, Vietnam was a single nation under a Communist government.

## *Legacy of the War*

The Vietnam War was the longest and least successful war in which the United States had ever participated. Its costs were enormous.

**Counting the Costs** The Vietnam War resulted in more than 58,000 Americans dead and 300,000 wounded. It cost at least $150 billion in direct expenses and produced a huge national debt and growing inflation.

The costs of the war were even higher for the Vietnamese. More bombs rained down on Vietnam than had fallen on all Axis powers during World War II. The number of dead and wounded Vietnamese soldiers ran into the millions, with countless civilian casualties. The landscape itself would long bear the scars of war.

*Prisoners of War (POWs) and soldiers missing in action (MIAs) were also part of the enormous costs of the Vietnam War.*

**Southeast Asia After the War** One of the reasons for American involvement in Vietnam was the belief in the domino theory. This was the assumption that the entire region would collapse if the Communists won in Vietnam. With the North Vietnamese victory, two dominoes did topple—Laos and Cambodia. The rest of the region, however, did not fall.

The suffering of the Cambodian people was one of the most tragic effects of the war in Vietnam. In April 1975, Cambodia fell to the Khmer Rouge, a force of Communists led by the fanatical Pol Pot. In five years of fighting, Cambodia had already suffered as many as a

In 1975 Nha Trang in South Vietnam was evacuated just before Communist troops took over. The man above was punched by an American official as he tried to board the last plane out, which was already overcrowded with fleeing refugees. ***Foreign Relations*** *Who finally won the Vietnam War?*

half million civilian casualties, mostly by American bombs. Worse was to come. The Khmer Rouge in effect declared war on anyone "tainted" with Western ways. They killed as many as 1.5 million Cambodians—a quarter of the population. Many were shot, while the rest died of starvation, disease, mistreatment in labor camps, or on forced marches.

Although not so extreme, Vietnam's new leaders also forced hundreds of thousands of South Vietnamese soldiers, civil servants, and other professionals into "re-education camps." Meanwhile, more than 1.5 million Vietnamese fled their country by boat, leaving behind all personal possessions in their determination to escape. In addition to these refugees, hundreds of thousands of Cambodians and Laotians also fled their homelands, many making their way to the United States.

**The United States After the War** In the United States the war splintered the foreign policy that had guided the nation during and after World War II. Americans had believed that they could defend the world from communism anywhere, at any time. American technology and money, they assumed, could always bring victory. Vietnam proved that assumption to be false. Many people called for a reassessment of America's global mission.

The impact of the war in the United States lingered on long after the last bomb had been dropped. Soldiers came home to a different reception from the ones their fathers and grandfathers had following World War II. There were no welcoming ticker-tape parades. Many veterans complained that Americans did not appreciate what they had gone through.

In 1979 a group of veterans began making plans for a **Vietnam Veterans Memorial.** They wanted to recognize the courage of American GIs during the Vietnam ordeal and to help heal the wounds the war had caused. The memorial was completed in 1982. In 1994 the United States announced an end to the long-standing American trade embargo against Vietnam. The next year the United States agreed to restore full diplomatic relations with its former enemy.

## SECTION 5 REVIEW

### Comprehension

1. *Key Terms* Define: (a) Paris peace talks; (b) Vietnamization; (c) Vietnam Veterans Memorial.
2. *Summarizing the Main Idea* Why did the end of the Vietnam War come so slowly?
3. *Organizing Information* Create a chart to show the events or other factors that led to an end to the war and the factors that kept the war going.

### Critical Thinking

4. *Analyzing Time Lines* Review the time line at the start of the section. How might the period 1968–1975 have been different if Johnson had been willing and able to end the war?
5. *Recognizing Cause and Effect* What did the complete withdrawal of American troops mean for South Vietnam?

### Writing Activity

6. *Writing an Expository Essay* Write an essay about the legacy of the Vietnam War.

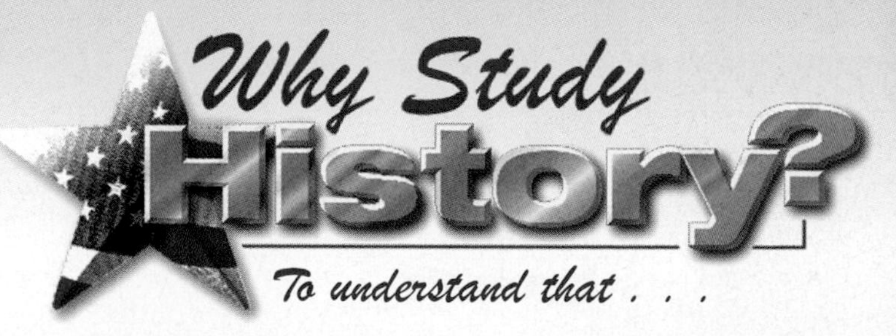


# Draft Registration Is Required Today

**Registration for the military draft, which provoked fierce opposition during the Vietnam War, is in effect today.**

*Young men burning draft cards to protest the Vietnam War*

One of the issues that divided the country during the Vietnam War was the military draft, or conscription. More than a million young American men were drafted into the army to fight in Southeast Asia. As the war dragged on and casualties increased, public support for the war declined. Increasing numbers of Americans began to question conscription.

## The Impact Today

Since the Civil War, the United States has used a draft in wartime to meet its military needs. Reacting to the start of World War II in Europe, President Franklin Roosevelt initiated the nation's first peacetime draft in 1940. About 10.1 million American men were drafted into the military between 1940 and 1946. After the war, the number of men drafted each year declined dramatically—except during the Korean War. Some 1.5 million men were drafted between 1950 and 1953 as a result of that conflict.

The manpower needs of the armed forces increased again with deepening American involvement in Vietnam. Between 1964 and 1973, about 1.8 million men were drafted into military service. College students, however, could receive draft deferments that exempted them from service as long as they remained in school. This meant that a high number of those drafted were young men too poor to afford college. Following complaints about the system, Congress eliminated the deferment in 1971.

In another effort to make the draft fairer, in 1969 the government instituted a lottery system. In a random drawing, all eligible men ages 18 and over were assigned a number according to their birth date. A person's number told him the likelihood that he would be called for service.

Despite these changes, opposition to the draft remained. Thousands even left the country to avoid the draft. In 1973 Congress ended conscription, and the United States converted to an all-volunteer military force. A law requiring 18-year-olds to register at local draft boards was suspended in 1975. It was resumed, however, in 1980 and remains in effect today. Male United States citizens ages 18 through 25 must register with the Selective Service System. In a national crisis, if the country needs more soldiers than an all-volunteer service can provide, the draft can be resumed.

*Army soldiers leave for Middle East, 1990*

## The Impact on You

List two arguments in support of maintaining the current all-volunteer system in the armed forces. Next to these, list two arguments in support of returning to a system of conscription. Then, below these two sets of arguments, write a paragraph explaining which position you favor and why.

## Personal Memorials

Visible in this photo are some of the names on the Vietnam Veterans Memorial.

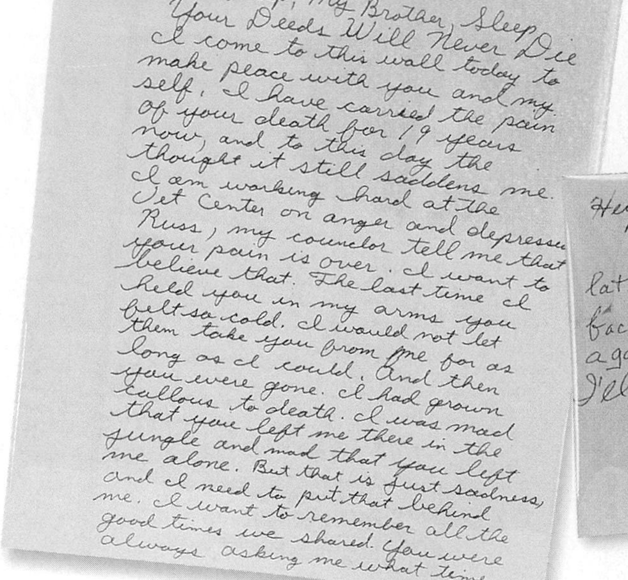

Your Deeds Will Never Die
I come to this wall today to
make peace with you and myself. I have carried the pain
of your death for 19 years
now, and to this day the
thought it still saddens me.
I am working hard at the
Vet Center on anger and depression.
Russ, my councelor tell me that
your pain is over. I want to
believe that. The last time I
held you in my arms you
felt so cold. I would not let
them take you from me for as
long as I could. And then
you were gone. I had grown
callous to death. I was mad
that you left me there in the
jungle and mad that you left
me alone. But that is just sadness,
and I need to put that behind
me. I want to remember all the
good times we shared. You were
always asking me what time

## Mementos

People leave objects, such as these stuffed animals, in memory of their loved ones.

## Boots and Helmet

The National Park Service collects items left at the wall, such as these boots and helmet that once belonged to a soldier.

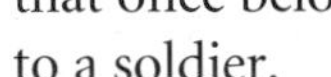

FROM EXHIBITIONS AND COLLECTIONS AT THE SMITHSONIAN INSTITUTION'S NATIONAL MUSEUM OF AMERICAN HISTORY

# THE VIETNAM VETERANS MEMORIAL

**The United States' involvement in the Vietnam War divided the country into two angry camps: those who supported it and those who opposed it. This division continued even after the American withdrawal from Vietnam in 1973. Returning veterans, instead of being honored for their service, were sometimes greeted with indifference or even hostility.**

**In 1982 the Vietnam Veterans Memorial was unveiled in Washington, D.C. Unlike most other monuments in the city, the wall is built on a small, human scale. Its two polished, black-granite walls hold the names of more than 58,000 Americans killed and missing in the war. *See* 1 .**

**With the dedication of the Vietnam Veterans Memorial, a healing of the war's bitter divisions seemed to begin. People began leaving personal tokens at the base of the monument to honor and remember the soldiers who fought in the war. These tokens ranged from stuffed animals, favorite magazines, beverages, and items of clothing to the everyday items of a soldier in Vietnam, such as helmets and combat boots. *See* 2 *and* 3 .**

**A few visitors have written notes to their loved ones and left those notes at the wall. Others have left dog tags and driver's licenses. Such items carry memories of the bond between soldier and mourner. *See* 4 *and* 5 .**

**This practice continues today. The National Park Service collects and preserves the artifacts. In 1992 the Smithsonian Institution put some of these items on display, where thousands of Americans view them each year.**

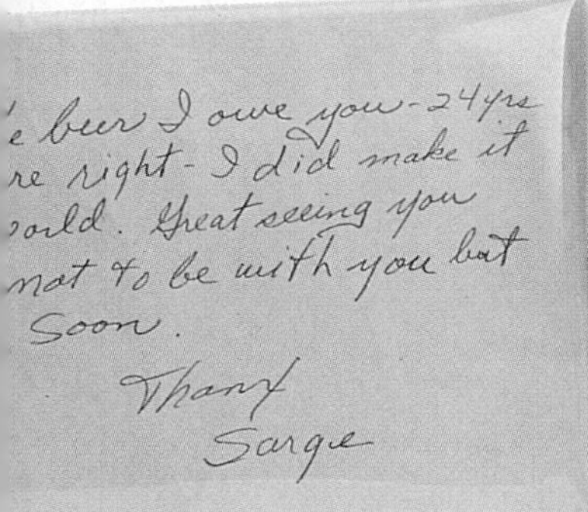
'e beer I owe you - 24 yrs
re right - I did make it
vorld. Great seeing you
not to be with you but
Soon.
Thanx
Sarge

4

## Letters

Family and friends have left letters for the soldiers whose names are on the wall.

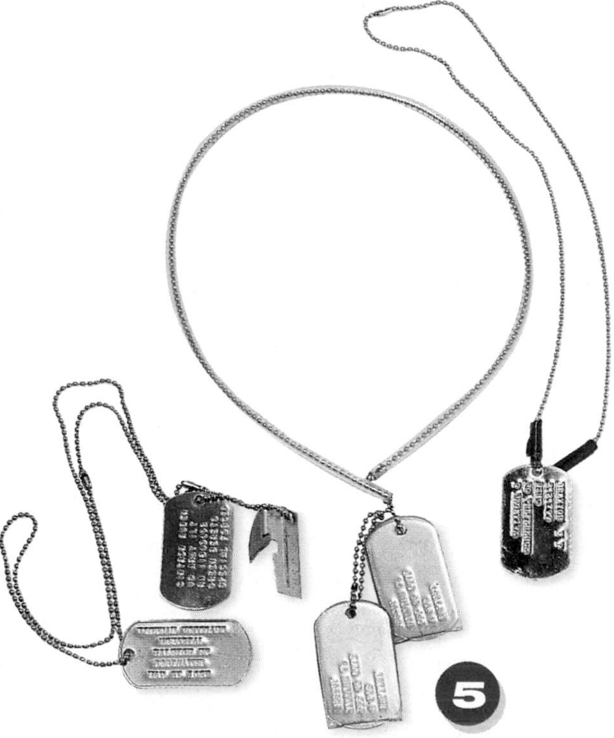

5

## Dog Tags

Listing information such as name, identification number, and blood type, "dog tags" were issued to each soldier. Many have been left at the wall.

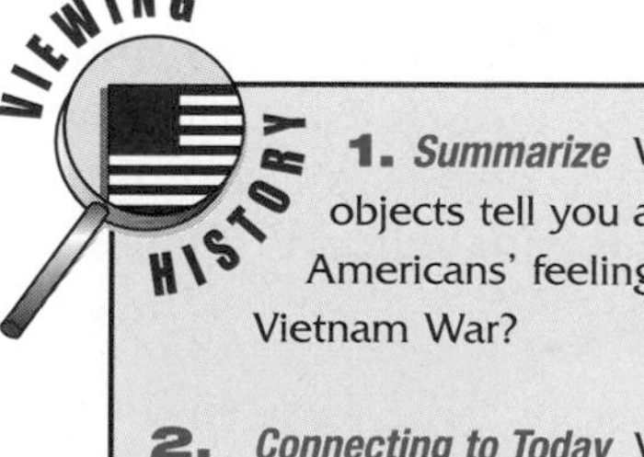


1. ***Summarize*** What do the objects tell you about Americans' feelings about the Vietnam War?

2. ***Connecting to Today*** What can the Vietnam Veterans Memorial and the objects that have been left there teach us about the war and the people whose lives it affected?

# Chapter 21 Review

## Chapter Summary

The major concepts of Chapter 21 are presented below. See also ***Guide to the Essentials of American History*** or ***Interactive Student Tutorial CD-ROM,*** which contains interactive review activities, time lines, helpful hints, and test practice.

### *Reviewing the Main Ideas*

Under Presidents Kennedy and Johnson, the country became deeply involved in stopping a Communist takeover in South Vietnam. As the war dragged on, many Americans began to question American participation in the war. At the same time a youthful counterculture arose, criticizing the traditional values of many Americans.

### *Section 1: Deepening American Involvement*

The United States entered the Vietnam War to defeat Communist forces threatening South Vietnam.

### *Section 2: The Brutality of the War*

The violence and brutality of the Vietnam War affected civilians as well as soldiers.

### *Section 3: Student Protest*

Students in the 1960s demonstrated in support of free speech and other issues and protested against the Vietnam War.

### *Section 4: The Counterculture*

In the 1960s a youth culture arose that promoted freedom and individuality. Its new attitudes about personal relationships, drugs, and music shocked many Americans.

### *Section 5: The End of the War*

The end of the Vietnam War involved slow-moving peace negotiations, the gradual withdrawal of American troops, and the fall of South Vietnam.

Registration for the draft, which provoked fierce opposition during the Vietnam War, is still in effect today.



## Key Terms

Use each of the terms below in a sentence that shows how it relates to the chapter.

1. counterculture
2. Viet Cong
3. deferment
4. Gulf of Tonkin Resolution
5. Vietnamization
6. conscientious objector
7. Pentagon Papers
8. escalation
9. Tet Offensive
10. teach-in
11. Woodstock
12. Ho Chi Minh Trail
13. My Lai massacre
14. napalm

## Comprehension

1. How did the Vietnam War escalate under President Johnson?
2. Why was the war so hard on American soldiers fighting in Vietnam?
3. What were some of the changes that student activists demanded during the 1960s?
4. What methods did activists use during the 1960s?
5. Why did many Americans view the counterculture with shock and dismay?
6. Why did Richard Nixon authorize the invasion of Cambodia in 1970?
7. What was the lasting impact of the war on Vietnam and on the United States?

## Using Graphic Organizers

On a separate sheet of paper, copy the web diagram below. Create additional circles to show (1) shifts in United States policy, from Kennedy to Nixon; (2) major events related to the war; and (3) main effects of the war on American soldiers,Vietnamese civilians, and American society.

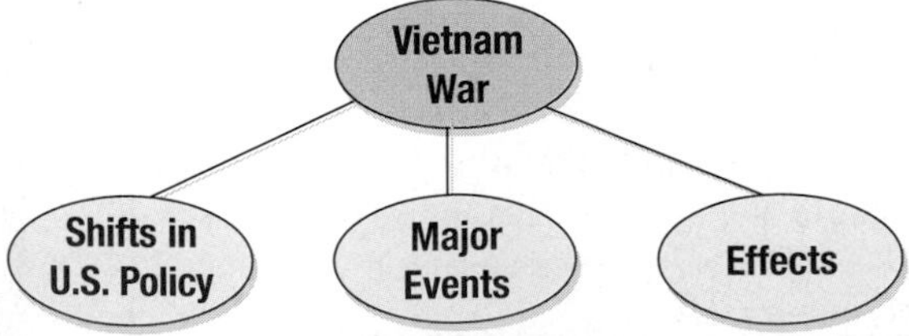

## Analyzing Political Cartoons ▶

1. Examine the images in the cartoon. Who are the two men?
2. What is the occasion shown in the cartoon?
3. (a) What is the significance of the documents held by the man on the right? (b) What does the gravestone refer to?
4. What point is the cartoonist trying to make?

## Critical Thinking

1. ***Applying the Chapter Skill*** President Nixon promised to end the war in Vietnam. Yet he authorized the heaviest bombing raids of the war and he expanded the war into Cambodia. Were these actions consistent with his promise? Explain.
2. ***Demonstrating Reasoned Judgment*** If you had been a student during the Vietnam War, do you think that your views of the conflict would have changed or remained the same throughout the course of the war? What factors might have influenced your views?
3. ***Expressing Problems Clearly*** Since the end of the Vietnam War, government officials have advised caution in global affairs so that the United States does not get involved in "another Vietnam." Explain what is meant by this warning.

### INTERNET ACTIVITY

***For your portfolio:***
**WRITE AN ARTICLE**

Access Prentice Hall's *America: Pathways to the Present* site at **www.Pathways.phschool.com** for the specific URLs to complete the activity. Additional resources and related Web sites are also available.

Use the links provided to read about the Kent State shootings on May 4, 1970. Write a newspaper article describing the incident. How did Americans react to the event? In what ways did the incident reflect the deep divisions in the nation?

### ANALYZING DOCUMENTS ▶ INTERPRETING DATA

Turn to the map titled "Vietnam War, 1969–1972" on page 637.

1. About how long was the Ho Chi Minh Trail? (a) 150 miles (b) 300 miles (c) 600 miles (d) 3,000 miles
2. What action would have helped prevent Soviet war supplies from reaching North Vietnam? (a) mining Haiphong harbor (b) attacking Communist bases in Cambodia (c) cutting off the Ho Chi Minh Trail (d) bombing Saigon
3. ***Writing*** Write an essay explaining how the neighboring countries of Laos and Cambodia became involved in the Vietnam War.

### Connecting to Today

Although we call it the Vietnam War, Congress never officially declared a war against North Vietnam. Write an essay about how American involvement in Vietnam might have changed if Congress had pursued its right to declare war.

American Heritage®

# My Brush with History

BY BRUCE KILLEBREW & JOAN W. MUSBACH

***INTRODUCTION*** The two passages below describe how two white Americans became aware of the system of racial segregation that existed in many parts of the country. In the first account, Bruce Killebrew recalls the integration of his third-grade class. In the second account, Joan W. Musbach remembers the day that she, as a high school student, came face to face with her own ignorance of segregation.

*In 1954 my father was stationed at the Pentagon* in Washington, D.C., and we lived on the now-defunct South Post of Fort Myer. My friends and I had a grand time romping through the nearby Civil War battlefields, taking turns being Yankee and Rebel. I couldn't decide whether to favor the Blue or the Gray. At the age of eight I'd really never thought about the issues that fueled the fighting.

Then, one day in the first week of September 1954, at the beginning of the year for our small military elementary school at Fort Myer, there were new faces in my class—and reporters from United Press and *Army Times* taking pictures. They were photographing the class while I led the Pledge of Allegiance for the first integrated class in the formerly Confederate state of Virginia. The two new students were black, and to me and the rest of my third-grade classmates they did not seem any different from the rest of us kids. But I was very proud to have been chosen to lead the Pledge of Allegiance on that day.

The event would help shape this nation's future, and my own. It brought home to me the idea that all men are created equal and have the right to equal opportunity. Much of my life as an individual and a social worker has been based on the premise I learned in that classroom in 1954.

—*Bruce Killebrew*

*Bruce Killebrew, Grade 3, Fort Myer*

***Bruce Killebrew appears in the far left of this photo.***

*On a crisp, cool, sunny Saturday in January,* a Midwestern café—a freestanding building with one counter, stools in front, grill behind—became the site of the most memorable experience of my high school years.

Segregation, announced in some places by signs like this, was practiced more quietly in other places.

It was 1960. I was a senior member of the debate team from John J. Ingels High School, in Atchison, Kansas. I was growing up within sixty miles of the origin of the 1954 Supreme Court case, *Brown* v. *Board of Education,* but, as of 1960, had never heard of Linda Brown or the case that bears her name. I was soon to discover that there was a great deal about which I was unaware.

We finished the Saturday-morning rounds and then went out for lunch before returning to the college to hear the semifinalists announced. We chose an appealing-looking cafeteria near the college. I was the only girl on the trip, and I was still just entering when Mr. Phipps and the boys turned around and came back out. I was busy talking and didn't ask why we had left. I assumed the cafeteria was too crowded. We got into Mr. Phipps's old car and drove a few blocks to a café. Business was sparse, and we spread out down the red-plastic-covered stools along the counter. John, my partner, was seated beside me. The waitress came down the counter distributing menus. John did not get one. We called this to her attention, and she quickly informed us that blacks were not served in there. I was shocked. I had never heard of such a thing. We all got up and went to the car, and Mr. Phipps went to a nearby hamburger stand and bought hamburgers and sodas for us all to eat in the car.

John wouldn't eat. He sat in the corner of the back seat, speechless. We didn't know what to say either. We just ate our hamburgers and went back to the college.

As I thought about the incident, I realized that John was the victim of our ignorance as well as of the prejudice of the management of the cafeteria and the café. He had probably never been exposed to such humiliation before, protected by parents or other adults who would have avoided such an incident. Strange as it may seem, a carful of high school students and their teacher were unaware of the segregation of public services just across the river from where they lived.

The look on John's face as we ate our hamburgers ensured that I would never forget that crisp January Saturday or the Kansas City café where I met Jim Crow.

*—Joan W. Musbach*

Source: *American Heritage* magazine, April 1991 and April 1994.

**ADDITIONAL READING**

**To learn more about the topics discussed in this selection, you might want to read the following books:**

- *The Children,* by David Halberstam (New York: Random House, 1998)
- *The Color Line: Legacy for the Twenty-first Century,* by John Hope Franklin (Columbia: University of Missouri Press, 1993)
- *Parting the Waters: America in the King Years, 1954–1963,* by Taylor Branch (New York: Simon & Schuster, 1989)
- *The Strange Career of Jim Crow,* by C. Vann Woodward (New York: Oxford University Press, 1974)

unit SIX

# Continuity and Change

## 1968–Present

*By 1968 many Americans were tired of the turmoil of the 1960s. The election of Richard Nixon as President that year marked the emergence of a Republican majority that lasted, with one brief exception, for more than twenty years. A recession following the election of George Bush in 1988, however, created growing dissatisfaction with Republican policies. When Democrat Bill Clinton defeated Bush in the 1992 presidential election and was reelected in 1996, Americans seemed ready to head in a new direction.*



### UNIT THEMES

**Government** The public lost confidence in the government as scandal forced President Nixon to resign from office.

**Economics** President Reagan embarked on major program of deregulation in order to spur business growth.

**Foreign Relations** In the mid- to late-1990s, the nation found itself trying to promote peace abroad while at the same time avoiding costly foreign entanglements.

**EVENTS IN THE UNITED STATES**

**1969** *SALT talks begin*

**1972** *Nixon travels to China and USSR*

**1973** *Trial of Watergate burglars begins*

**1974** *President Nixon resigns*

**1980** *Turning Point: The Election of 1980 (p. 701)*

**1981** *O'Connor first woman on Supreme Court*

Presidents: Nixon | Ford | Carter | Reagan

1968 — 1978

**EVENTS IN THE WORLD**

**1971** *China joins UN*

**1973** *OPEC oil embargo*

**1979** *Civil war begins in Nicaragua*

**1985** *Gorbachev leads USSR*

**VIEWING HISTORY** These recently sworn in citizens are symbolic of the cultural diversity that is one of the United States' greatest strengths. ***Culture*** ***What impact has recent immigration had on American society and politics?***

**1991**
*Persian Gulf War*

**1994**
*Senate ratifies NAFTA*

**1998**
*Clinton announces a federal budget surplus*

**2000**
*Clinton hosts Camp David Accords*

George H. Bush | Clinton | George W. Bush

**1988** — **1998**

**1988**
*Poland's Communist government falls*

**1991**
*Soviet Union breaks up*

**1995**
*Israeli leader Rabin assassinated*

**1998**
*U.S. embassies bombed in Kenya and Tanzania*

**1999**
*NATO goes to war over Kosovo*

CHAPTER

# 22 The Nixon Years

## 1969–1974

## CHAPTER FOCUS

This chapter examines the accomplished and ill-fated presidency of Richard M. Nixon. It looks at the bold policies for which he is remembered and the scandal that finally brought him down.

*The* **Why Study History?** *page at the end of this chapter explores the connection between Nixon's use of presidential power and the balance of power today.*

▲ **VIEWING HISTORY**
President Richard Nixon and his wife Pat tour the Great Wall of China in a historic visit to China in 1972. ***Foreign Relations*** ***How do presidential visits help diplomatic relations?***

| January | April | June | August | November |
|---|---|---|---|---|
| *Tet Offensive begins* | *Martin Luther King, Jr., assassinated* | *Robert F. Kennedy assassinated* | *Democratic National Convention* | *Richard M. Nixon elected President* |

**Jan. 1968** **June 1968** **Dec. 1968**

# 1 The Crises of 1968

## SECTION PREVIEW

### Objectives

1. Explain how the Tet Offensive increased antiwar sentiment.
2. Explain the impact of the assassinations of Martin Luther King, Jr., and Robert Kennedy.
3. Describe the impact of the 1968 Democratic convention on that year's presidential election.
4. *Key Terms* Define: Middle America; Poor People's Campaign.

### Main Idea

The year 1968 was a turbulent and painful time for the country that resulted in the election of Richard Nixon as President.

### Reading Strategy

*Finding Evidence* As you read the section, jot down facts to support the idea, stated on this page, that 1968 was "the most shattering year" of the 1960s.

In the troubled decade of the 1960s, perhaps the most shattering year was 1968. A series of tragic events hit with such force that, month by month, the nation seemed to be coming apart. Amid the turmoil, and partly because of it, the way was paved for the election of Richard Nixon.

Nixon's win marked the start of a Republican hold on the presidency that would last, with one interruption, for the next 20 years. This political shift reflected how distressing the 1960s had become for mainstream Americans, a group sometimes called **Middle America.** In an era of chaos and confrontation, Middle America turned to the Republican party for stability.

## Antiwar Sentiment Increases

The Vietnam War reached a crucial turning point in 1968. Beginning in January, as you have read, the Viet Cong launched the Tet Offensive. This massive surprise attack against South Vietnam ended in military defeat for the Viet Cong and their North Vietnamese allies. But it caused more and more Americans to question whether victory in the Vietnam War was possible.

The Johnson administration had been escalating the war for three years before the Tet Offensive. Many Americans wondered what had been achieved if the enemy could still mount such a blistering offensive. From a military perspective, Tet was a major defeat for the Viet Cong. But from a political perspective, it was a major defeat for the United States—and for Lyndon Johnson.

*LBJ's political career is crushed in this 1967 British cartoon, "The Time Machine."*

After Tet, polls showed for the first time that a majority of Americans opposed the war. Television news coverage of Tet increased the impact that the attack had on the public. Millions watched as news anchor Walter Cronkite, known for his objectivity, said in February, "It now seems more certain than ever that the bloody experience in Vietnam is to end in stalemate." President Johnson heard Cronkite's assessment of the war and reacted with dismay. Reportedly he said, "If I've lost Cronkite, I've lost Middle America."

## King Assassinated

For most Americans, the memory of President John F. Kennedy's assassination in 1963 was still vivid and haunting five years later. They looked to other leaders to carry on the spirit and idealism of the Kennedy years.

**Main Idea CONNECTIONS**

*How did the nation react to the murder of Martin Luther King, Jr.?*

One such leader was Martin Luther King, Jr. By the mid-1960s King had led the civil rights movement to several major political victories in battles ranging from integration to voting rights.

In 1968 King turned his attention to economic issues. Convinced that poverty bred violence, he broadened his approach to attack economic injustice. Calling his new crusade the **Poor People's Campaign,** King began planning a Poor People's March on Washington. Traveling around the United States to mobilize support, he went to Memphis, Tennessee, in early April. There he offered his assistance to striking garbage workers who were seeking better working conditions.

King spoke eloquently, referring to threats made against his life:

**AMERICAN VOICES** **"We've got some difficult days ahead. But it doesn't matter with me now, because I've been to the mountain top. And I don't mind. Like anybody, I would like to live a long life. . . . But I'm not concerned about that now. I just want to do God's will. And He's allowed me to go up to the mountain. And I've looked over. And I've seen the promised land."**

—*Martin Luther King, Jr.*
*April 3, 1968*

The next day, as King stood on the balcony of his motel, a bullet fired from a high-powered rifle tore into him. An hour later, King was dead.

King's assassination sparked violent reactions across the nation. In an outburst of rage and frustration, some African Americans rioted, setting fires and looting stores in 124 cities. The riots, and police responses to them, left 45 people dead. President Johnson ordered flags on federal buildings to be flown at half-mast to honor King, but it took more than 5,500 troops to quell the violence. For many Americans of all races, King's death eroded faith in the idea of nonviolent change.

**VIEWING HISTORY** Assassinations in 1968 shocked the nation. Above, Martin Luther King lies mortally wounded, while companions point frantically to the direction from which shots were fired. At right, busboy Juan Romero is the first to reach Robert Kennedy after he was shot in a hotel kitchen just after winning the California primary. ***Culture* *What effect did these murders have?***

## Robert Kennedy Assassinated

In March 1968 the battle for the Democratic presidential nomination intensified. Senator Eugene McCarthy, a vocal antiwar candidate, challenged President Johnson in the New Hampshire primary on March 12. McCarthy did well, losing by just 6 percentage points.

Senator Robert F. Kennedy, who had served his brother John as Attorney General, realized that Johnson was vulnerable. On March 16 Kennedy entered the campaign himself. His candidacy received a critical boost on March 31, when Johnson stunned the nation by announcing that he would not run for a second term as President.

In the years since his brother's death, Robert Kennedy had reached out to many Americans, including Chicanos in the California farm fields, Native Americans in the Southwest, African Americans in the Mississippi delta, and poor white families in New York tenements. Opposed to the Vietnam War, he condemned the killing of both Americans and Vietnamese. He criticized the Johnson administration for financing a war instead of funding the programs needed to help the poor and disadvantaged at home.

Kennedy spent the spring of 1968 battling McCarthy in the Democratic primary elections. On June 5 he won a key victory in California's primary. But just after midnight, after giving his victory speech in a Los Angeles hotel, Robert Kennedy was shot by an assassin. He died later that day.

Violence seemed to follow the Democratic party in the turbulent year 1968. At the Democratic National Convention, Chicago police and National Guardsmen used nightsticks, tear gas, and rifles against demonstrators and others caught up in the violence. ***Government* Why did the Democrats lose the 1968 presidential election?**

When the shooting was reported, several campaign workers who had watched the speech on TV were waiting for Kennedy in his hotel room. One of them, civil rights leader John Lewis, later said, "We all just fell to the floor and started crying. To me that was like the darkest, saddest moment." Looking back on Kennedy's death, Lewis said,

**AMERICAN VOICES** **"Something was taken from us. The type of leadership that we had in a sense invested in, that we had helped to make and to nourish, was taken from us."**

—*Civil rights leader John Lewis, 1987*

Kennedy's death ended many people's hopes for an inspirational leader who could heal the nation's wounds.

## *The 1968 Democratic Convention*

Delegates to the Democratic convention met in Chicago that summer to nominate candidates for President and Vice President. By the time the Democrats convened, their party was in shreds. Many of them backed McCarthy for President, but party regulars thought he was too far out of the mainstream. They supported Vice President Hubert Humphrey, longtime advocate of social justice and civil rights. Humphrey, however, was hurt by his defense of administration policies on Vietnam. In the face of growing antiwar protest, he hardly seemed the one to bring the party together.

Groups of radicals, peace activists, and hippies all vowed to descend on Chicago in August for the convention. The prospect of thousands of demonstrators in his city enraged Chicago mayor Richard J. Daley. He had the convention hall protected by barbed wire and chain-link fencing. He also ordered police to clear out protesters gathered in Lincoln Park, along the shore of Lake Michigan. As the police went in with tear gas and clubs, several violent confrontations took place.

The climax came when the convention delegates voted down a peace resolution and seemed ready to nominate Humphrey. As thousands of protesters gathered for a rally near the convention hotel, the police moved in, using their nightsticks to club anyone on the street, including bystanders, hotel guests, and reporters.

Historian Theodore H. White, chronicler of presidential elections, recorded the scene:

> **AMERICAN VOICES** "Slam! Like a fist jolting, like a piston exploding from its chamber, comes a hurtling column of police . . . into the intersection, and all things happen too fast: first the charge as the police wedge cleaves through the mob; then screams, whistles, confusion. . . . And as the scene clears, there are little knots in the open clearing—police clubbing youngsters, police dragging youngsters, police rushing them by the elbows, their heels dragging, to patrol wagons. . . ."
>
> —*Theodore H. White*

*George Wallace created trouble for the Democrats in 1968 by running as a third party candidate.*

Much of the violence took place in front of television cameras, while crowds chanted "The whole world is watching." As convention delegates voted, Senator Abraham Ribicoff of Connecticut denounced the "Gestapo tactics on the streets of Chicago," provoking an angry scene with Daley. Humphrey was nominated, but the party had been further torn apart.

## The Election of 1968

The Republicans had already held their convention, in early August. They had chosen Richard M. Nixon, who had narrowly lost to John Kennedy in 1960. In his campaign Nixon backed law and order and boasted of a secret plan to end the war in Vietnam.

Nixon was determined to stay "above the fray" and act presidential during the campaign. So he let his running mate, Governor Spiro Agnew of Maryland, make harsh accusations, such as calling Humphrey "squishy soft" on communism. With a well-run and well-financed campaign, Nixon quickly took the lead in public-opinion polls.

Adding to the Democrats' problems was a third-party candidate for President. Alabama governor George C. Wallace, a lifelong Democrat, had gained national fame for playing on racial tensions among southerners. In 1968, representing the American Independent party, he appealed to blue-collar voters in the North who resented campus radicals and antiwar activists. Wallace won support by attacking "left-wing theoreticians, briefcase-totin' bureaucrats, ivory-tower guideline writers, bearded anarchists, smart-aleck editorial writers, and pointy-headed professors."

Late in the campaign, Humphrey began to catch up to Nixon in the public-opinion polls. But even though President Johnson stopped the bombing of North Vietnam on October 31, it was too late. Many disillusioned Democrats stayed home on election day, voting for no one.

The election, held on November 5, was close. Nixon won 43.4 percent of the popular vote—less than one percentage point more than Humphrey's 42.7 percent. Nixon gained 302 electoral votes to 191 for Humphrey and 45 for Wallace. Although Democrats kept control of both houses of Congress, the Republicans had regained the White House.

## SECTION 1 REVIEW

### Comprehension

1. *Key Terms* Define: (a) Middle America; (b) Poor People's Campaign.
2. *Summarizing the Main Idea* Why did the Tet Offensive have such a strong impact on American politics?
3. *Organizing Information* Create a flowchart to show the sequence of events that led to the election of Richard Nixon as President.

### Critical Thinking

4. *Analyzing Time Lines* Review the time line at the start of the section. Which event do you think had the greatest impact on Americans? Explain your reasoning.
5. *Predicting Consequences* Choose one important event from 1968 and explain how history might have been different if the event had never happened.

### Writing Activity

6. *Writing an Expository Essay* Write an essay about the assassinations of Martin Luther King, Jr., and Robert F. Kennedy. In your essay explore what these killings said about American society at the time.

**1969** *Warren Burger becomes Chief Justice*

**1969** *America lands astronauts on the moon*

**1970** *Student protesters killed at Kent State U.*

**1971** *Supreme Court rules in favor of busing*

**1971** *Nixon imposes wage and price controls*

**1973** *OPEC oil embargo*

**1969** | **1971** | **1973**

# 2 The Nixon Administration

## SECTION PREVIEW

### Objectives

1. Describe how Nixon's personality might have affected his choice of staff members.
2. Describe how Nixon's domestic policy differed from that of his predecessors.
3. Explain how Nixon applied his "southern strategy" to the issue of civil rights and to his choice of Supreme Court justices.
4. *Key Terms* Define: deficit spending; Organization of Petroleum Exporting Countries (OPEC); embargo; silent majority.

### Main Idea

As President, Richard Nixon relied on several close advisers to help him move the country in a new direction.

### Reading Strategy

*Reinforcing Key Ideas* Create a two-column chart with the headings *Nixon's Personality* and *Nixon's Domestic Policies.* As you read the section, write details describing Nixon's personal traits and his policies in the proper column.

Richard Nixon's victory in 1968 was, for him, particularly sweet. His earlier bid for the presidency, in 1960, had failed. Two years later he had lost another election, for governor of California. Deeply unhappy, Nixon had vowed to retire from politics. Instead he came back from those bitter defeats to win the nation's highest office at a time when the country sorely needed strong leadership.

## Nixon in Person

Unlike most politicians, Richard Nixon was a reserved and remote man. Uncomfortable with people, he often seemed stiff and lacking in humor and charm. He overcame these drawbacks by using modern campaign techniques to get his message across.

Many Americans looked beyond these personal disadvantages. They respected Nixon for his experience and for his skillful handling of the vice presidency under Eisenhower. But many others neither trusted nor liked him.

Nixon grew up in a low-income family in Whittier, California. He never got over his sense of being an outsider. In 1963 he described how that feeling drove him to achieve:

> "What starts the process really are laughs and slights and snubs when you are a kid. Sometimes it's because you're poor or Irish or Jewish or Catholic or ugly or simply that you are skinny. But if you are reasonably intelligent and if your anger is deep enough and strong enough, you learn that you can change those attitudes by excellence, personal gut performance."
>
> —*Richard Nixon, 1963*

*Although he was a private man, Nixon loved the applause of a crowd.*

According to Patrick Buchanan, then a Nixon speech writer, there was "a mean side to his nature." He was willing to say or do any-

The Oval Office in the White House saw many meetings of Nixon and his inner circle of close advisers. Left to right in this photo are Kissinger, Ehrlichman, the President, and Haldeman. ***Government*** *What role did his advisers play in Nixon's presidency?*

thing to defeat his enemies. Those enemies included his political opponents, the government bureaucracy, the press corps, and leaders of the antiwar movement.

Nixon was fully prepared to confront these forces. He wrote, "I believe in the battle, whether it's the battle of the campaign or the battle of this office, which is a continuing battle. It's always there wherever you go."

**Main Idea CONNECTIONS**

*How did Nixon's personality affect his administration style?*

Nixon had few close friends, insulating himself from people and the press. He took support and security from his family: his wife, Pat, and their two daughters. He also established lasting associations with several activists in his political campaigns. Away from the White House, he secluded himself at his estates in Florida and California.

Nixon wanted the executive branch to dominate the other branches of government. When he took office, he gathered a close circle of trusted advisers around him to pursue that goal.

## Nixon's Staff

Cabinet members, who represent the major departments of government, have historically been a President's top advisers. They have tended to be independent-minded people. More than most other post–World War II Presidents, Nixon avoided his Cabinet and preferred to rely on his White House staff to develop broad policies. Staff members were team players. They gave him unswerving loyalty.

Two key appointees had direct access to the President. They shielded Nixon from the outside world and carried out his orders. One was H. R. Haldeman, an advertising executive who had campaigned tirelessly for Nixon. He became chief of staff. Haldeman once summarized how he served the President: "I get done what he wants done and I take the heat instead of him." The other key staffer was lawyer John Ehrlichman. Ehrlichman served as Nixon's personal lawyer and rose to the post of chief domestic adviser.

Haldeman and Ehrlichman framed issues and narrowed options for the President. They also stood between the President and anybody else who wanted to speak to him. Together they became known as the "Berlin Wall" for the way they protected Nixon's privacy.

A third trusted adviser was John Mitchell, a lawyer. Mitchell had worked with Nixon in New York and managed his presidential campaign. Nixon asked him to be Attorney General just after the 1968 election. Mitchell exerted great influence on the President, often speaking with him several times a day.

Another of Nixon's closest advisers did not fit the mold of Haldeman, Ehrlichman, and Mitchell. Henry Kissinger, a Harvard government professor, had no previous ties to Nixon. Still, he acquired tremendous power in the Nixon White House. Kissinger joined the administration as head of the National Security Council. In 1973 he became Nixon's Secretary of State. Kissinger played a major role in shaping foreign policy, both as an adviser to the President and in behind-the-scenes diplomacy.

## Domestic Policy

The Vietnam War and domestic policy had both been important in the 1968 political campaigns. On domestic issues, Nixon broke with many of the policies of his Democratic predecessors.

## OPEC Nations, c. 1970

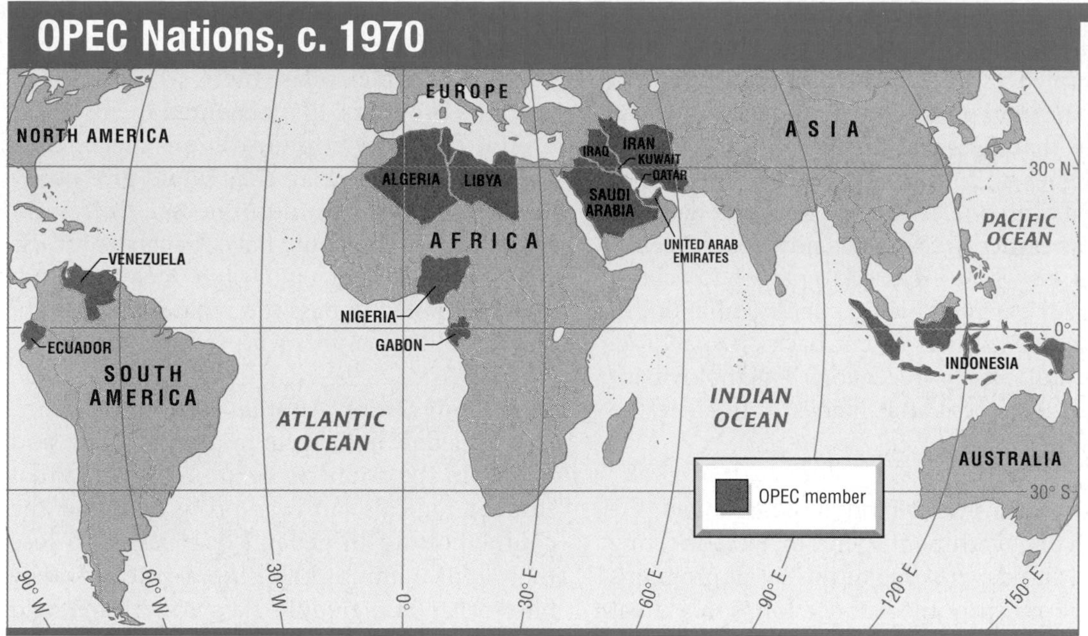

OPEC brought together the world's major oil producers. ***Regions*** ***In what region of the world are many of these nations concentrated?***

**Inflation** The economy was shaky when Nixon took office. Largely because of spending for the Vietnam War, inflation had doubled between 1965 and 1968. The budget had also gone out of balance, with government spending exceeding revenues. Meanwhile, unemployment continued to grow. Nixon's first priority was to halt inflation. He wanted to get federal spending under control, even if it led to further unemployment.

At the same time, Nixon was determined to avoid government control of wages and prices. He had seen such controls in action while working for the Office of Price Administration during World War II. "I will not take the nation down the road of wage and price controls, however politically expedient they may seem," he said in 1970.

During his first few years in office, however, controlling spending proved difficult. Unemployment and inflation both continued to rise. Although Republicans traditionally aimed for a balanced budget, Nixon began to consider **deficit spending.** By spending more money than the government received in revenues, he hoped to stimulate the economy.

This was the approach that Franklin Roosevelt had used during the Depression, following the advice of British economist John Maynard Keynes. "I am now a Keynesian in economics," Nixon announced in 1971, to the surprise of many people.

To slow the high rate of inflation, shown in the graph to the right, he imposed a 90-day freeze on wages, prices, and rents. Pressure from business and labor, however, led him to lift these controls, and inflation again soared.

**Oil Crisis** Unrest in the Middle East brought more disruptions to the troubled economy. Americans depended on cheap, imported oil for about a third of their energy needs. But in 1973 Israel and the Arab nations of Egypt and Syria went to war. The United States backed its ally Israel. In response, the Arab members of the **Organization of Petroleum Exporting Countries (OPEC)** imposed an **embargo,** or ban, on the shipping of oil to the United States.

## Rate of Inflation, 1968–1976

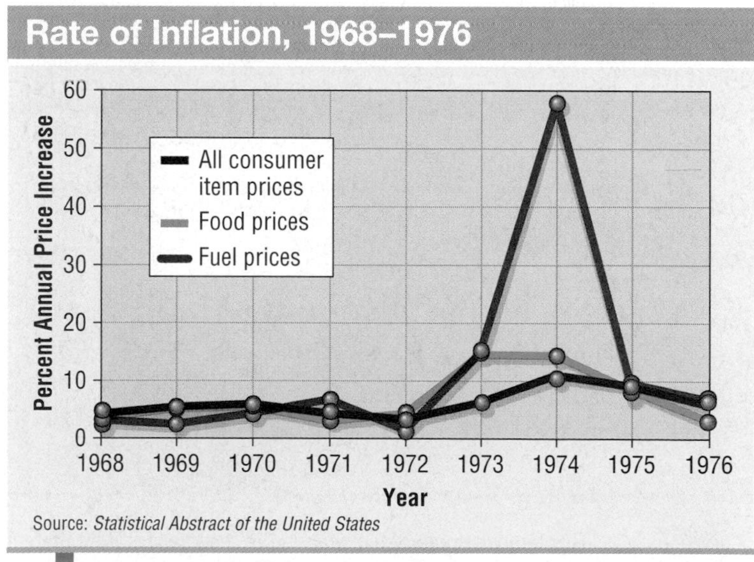


Source: *Statistical Abstract of the United States*

**Interpreting Graphs** Rising oil prices in the 1970s had a strong impact on all parts of the American economy. ***Economics*** ***When did fuel prices reach their peak?***

OPEC, a group of nations that cooperates to set oil prices and production levels, also quadrupled its prices. The cost of oil skyrocketed. The map on the previous page shows the nations that belonged to OPEC.

Higher oil prices added to inflation, which affected everyone. A loaf of bread that had cost 28 cents earlier in the 1970s now cost 89 cents. Americans who were used to paying 25 cents a gallon for gas now paid 65 cents. Inflation, in turn, led consumers to cut back on spending. The result was a recession. Unemployment reached 9 percent, the highest rate since the 1930s.

**Social Programs** Nixon hoped to halt the growth of government spending by redirecting or shutting down some of the social programs that had mushroomed under Johnson's Great Society. Critics claimed that these programs were wasteful, encouraged "welfare cheaters," and discouraged people from seeking work.

Nixon had exploited those complaints in his campaign, but he now faced a dilemma. On the one hand, he wanted to please conservative voters who demanded cutbacks. On the other hand, he hoped to appeal to traditionally Democratic blue-collar voters, who wanted to keep the programs that benefited them.

In 1969 the administration suggested a Family Assistance Plan that would give needy families a basic minimum income. In return, heads of families would have to register for job training and accept a job when one was found. The plan failed to pass the Senate but did gain Nixon political points with some voters.

**Law and Order** Another important campaign pledge had been to restore "law and order" in the country. Nixon recognized that student radicals, antiwar protesters, and the counterculture in general had begun to lose their appeal among the general public. Many blue-collar and middle-class Americans held those groups responsible for rising crime, growing drug use, and permissive attitudes toward sex. In a speech in 1969 Nixon referred to this large group of Americans as the **silent majority.**

To strengthen his position on law and order, Nixon aimed to discourage protest, especially against the war. In his "silent majority" speech he declared, "If a vocal minority, however fervent its cause, prevails over reason and the will of the majority, this nation has no future as a free society."

Tensions between antiwar activists and law-and-order supporters reached a peak in 1970. At a demonstration at Kent State University in Ohio, National Guardsmen opened fire on the crowd. Four student protesters were shot dead. Nixon implied that the students themselves had caused the tragedy:

AMERICAN VOICES

> **"The time has come for us to recognize that violence and terror have no place in a free society. Whatever the purported [supposed] cause of the perpetrators may be . . . no cause justifies violence."**
>
> —*Richard Nixon, speech at Kansas State University, 1970*

Other members of the administration backed up the President. Attorney General Mitchell stepped up the Justice Department's campaign against crime. Unhappy with press coverage of the White House, Vice President Spiro Agnew also accused television reporters of distorting administration actions.

This famous photo of the shooting of a student at Kent State University horrified the nation. ***Government*** *How did President Nixon regard such antiwar protests?*

## *The "Southern Strategy"*

Nixon believed that he had little to gain by supporting advances in civil rights. Few African Americans had voted for him in the 1960 race against John Kennedy, and in 1968 he had won just 12 percent of the black vote. Besides, he reasoned, any attempt to court the black electorate could threaten the white southern vote in a reelection bid.

Explaining his position, Nixon once observed that "there are those who want instant integration and those who want segregation forever. I believe that we need to have a middle course between those two extremes." In effect, this meant a slowdown in desegregation.

Nixon's aim was to find the proper "southern strategy" to win over white southern Democrats. Republican senator Strom Thurmond of South Carolina, who had left the Democratic party in 1948, became Nixon's strongest southern supporter. To keep him and his colleagues happy, Nixon sought to cut funding for the enforcement of fair housing laws. He also made it easier to comply with desegregation guidelines.

The Justice Department, headed by John Mitchell, tried to prevent the extension of the Voting Rights Act of 1965. This law had greatly increased the number of African Americans who could vote in the South. Congress went ahead with the extension, but Nixon had made his point to white southern voters.

Another controversial issue was the use of busing to end school segregation. In several cities, federal courts ordered school systems to bus students to other schools in order to end the pattern of all-black or all-white schools. Particularly in northern cities, such as Detroit and Boston, some white students and their parents met incoming black students with boycotts or violent protests.

In 1971 the Supreme Court issued guidelines for busing that went against Nixon's views. A federal judge in North Carolina had ruled that voluntary integration was not working. In *Swann* v. *Charlotte-Mecklenburg Board of Education,* the Court agreed, saying that busing was one possible option for ending school desegregation.

Nixon had long opposed busing. He now went on national television to say that he would ask Congress to halt it.† He also allowed the Department of Health, Education, and Welfare to restore federal funding to school districts that were still segregated. Nixon's refusal to enforce the Court ruling did not halt busing in the country but did limit it.

These demonstrators expressed their unhappiness with busing by burying a school bus. ***Government* How did Nixon's views on busing influence efforts to desegregate the schools?**

## *Nixon's Supreme Court*

During the election campaign, Nixon had criticized the Supreme Court as too liberal and soft on criminals. In his first term, four of the nine justices died, resigned, or retired. This gave him the extraordinary opportunity to name four new justices and thus reshape the Court. Nixon first named Warren Burger as Chief Justice, replacing Earl Warren. Burger, a moderate, was easily confirmed by the Senate in 1969.

Later nominations reflected Nixon's southern strategy and conservative views. The Senate rejected his first nominees from the South. Opponents charged that both men showed racial bias. Eventually Nixon successfully appointed Harry A. Blackmun (1970), Lewis F. Powell, Jr. (1972), and William H.

† One of Nixon's often-repeated lines was: "I think it is the job of the courts to interpret the law and not make the law."

Astronaut Buzz Aldrin takes a walk on the moon. ***Government*** *Why was the government so committed to the space program?*

Rehnquist (1972). All three were respected jurists who generally tilted the Court in a more conservative direction.

## *The First Moon Landing*

The Nixon years witnessed the fulfillment of President Kennedy's commitment in 1961 to achieve the goal, "before this decade is out, of landing a man on the moon." That man was *Apollo 11* astronaut Neil A. Armstrong.

On July 20, 1969, at 10:56 P.M. Eastern Daylight Time, Armstrong descended from the *Eagle* lunar landing craft and set foot on the moon's surface. As a TV camera aboard the *Eagle* captured the event, Armstrong radioed back the famous message: "That's one small step for man, one giant leap for mankind."

TV viewers around the world witnessed this triumph of the *Apollo* program, carried out by the National Aeronautics and Space Administration (NASA). The *Apollo 11* crew included Edwin E. "Buzz" Aldrin, Jr., who landed with Armstrong in the *Eagle,* and Michael Collins, who remained in the *Apollo 11* Command Module circling the moon.

Aldrin joined Armstrong in the two-hour moon walk, during which they collected rock and soil samples and set up scientific instruments to monitor conditions on the moon. They also photographed the landing area, a dusty plain in an area called the Sea of Tranquillity.

The *Eagle* and its crew stayed on the moon for 21 hours and 36 minutes before lifting off to rejoin Collins in the Command Module for the return trip. After a safe splashdown, the astronauts were quarantined for 18 days to ensure that they had not picked up any unknown lunar microbes. They emerged to a hero's welcome.

## SECTION 2 REVIEW

### Comprehension

1. *Key Terms* Define: (a) deficit spending; (b) Organization of Petroleum Exporting Countries (OPEC); (c) embargo; (d) silent majority.
2. *Summarizing the Main Idea* What was Nixon's "southern strategy," and how did it affect his domestic policies?
3. *Organizing Information* Create a web diagram to organize text information about the Nixon administration.

### Critical Thinking

4. *Analyzing Time Lines* Review the time line at the start of the section. Which event do you think may have had the greatest effect on the American people? Explain.
5. *Determining Relevance* Do you think that Nixon's use of his staff, rather than his Cabinet, as policy advisers reflected the President's personal traits? Explain.

### Writing Activity

6. *Writing a Persuasive Essay* Write an essay that might have appeared in 1970 either supporting or opposing the Nixon administration's position on antiwar protests.

| 1969 | 1971 | 1972 | 1972 | 1972 | 1973 |
|---|---|---|---|---|---|
| Strategic Arms Limitation Talks open | United States ends trade embargo with China | Nixon travels to China | Nixon visits Soviet Union | SALT I treaty signed | Kissinger appointed Secretary of State |

1969 — 1971 — 1973

# 3 Nixon's Foreign Policy

## SECTION PREVIEW

### Objectives

1. Analyze Henry Kissinger's role in relaxing tensions between the United States and the major Communist powers.
2. Outline Nixon's new approach toward the People's Republic of China.
3. Describe how the Nixon administration reached an agreement with the Soviet Union on limiting nuclear arms.
4. *Key Terms* Define: *realpolitik;* détente; proliferation; SALT I.

### Main Idea

President Nixon's foreign policy led to more positive relationships with China and with the Soviet Union.

### Reading Strategy

*Notetaking* As you read the section, take notes on the following topics: (a) Henry Kissinger and American foreign policy, (b) United States relations with China, and (c) United States relations with the Soviet Union.

As President, Richard Nixon's greatest achievements came in the field of foreign policy. "I've always thought this country could run itself domestically without a President," he observed. Nixon's creative approach to foreign affairs helped ease cold war tensions. Aided by the skillful diplomacy of Henry Kissinger, Nixon opened the way to establishing ties with China and crafted stronger relations with the Soviet Union.

## Henry Kissinger

AMERICAN BIOGRAPHY

While Nixon had a keen understanding of foreign policy, he still relied heavily on Henry Kissinger in charting his course. Kissinger quickly gained the President's confidence. By the time Nixon appointed him Secretary of State in 1973, he was a dominant figure in the administration.

Henry Kissinger (b.1923)

Kissinger came from a Jewish family that fled Nazi Germany in 1938, when he was 15, and settled in New York City. During the day, the young immigrant worked at a shaving brush company. At night he completed high school courses. Kissinger attended City College of New York and later transferred to Harvard. There he completed both undergraduate and graduate degrees.

Kissinger wrote his doctoral dissertation on Klemens von Metternich, an Austrian statesman and diplomat in the nineteenth century who helped maintain stability in Europe amid liberal change. Kissinger's studies in European history gave him an admiration for ***realpolitik,*** a German term for "practical politics." Nations that follow this policy make decisions based on maintaining their own strength rather than clinging to rigid moral principles. Kissinger would later apply this approach to dealing with China and the Soviet Union.

**Main Idea CONNECTIONS**

*How did Kissinger gain influence with Nixon?*

As a Harvard professor, Kissinger became a recognized expert on foreign relations. Nixon lured him away from Harvard in 1969 by offering him a job as his national security adviser.

Nixon liked to be flattered, and he liked people who could talk tough. Kissinger understood these things, and soon he became the man Nixon talked to most. "Henry, of course, was not a personal friend," Nixon later said, but the two spoke five or six times a day, sometimes in person, sometimes by phone, and often for hours at a time.

Both men were suspicious and secretive. They tended not to seek consensus, but to keep information to themselves. "They tried not to let anyone else have a full picture, even if it meant deceiving them," noted Lawrence Eagleburger, a State Department official.

Kissinger's actual influence in shaping American foreign policy was broader than his official role as Secretary of State. He knew how to frame questions in ways the President wanted. He could distill foreign policy issues into briefing papers that gave Nixon clear options for making decisions. In his memoirs, Kissinger wrote:

**"Nixon could be very decisive. Almost invariably during his Presidency, his decisions were courageous and strong and often taken in loneliness against all expert advice. But wherever possible Nixon made these decisions in solitude on the basis of memoranda or with a few very intimate aides."**

—*Henry Kissinger,*
The White House Years, *1979*

In addition to his intellectual skills, Kissinger understood the power of the press. He had a remarkable ability to use the media to shape public opinion. Journalists depended on him for stories, so they refrained from antagonizing him. "You know you are being played like a violin," a *Time* magazine reporter observed, "but it's still extremely seductive."

Kissinger's efforts in ending the Vietnam War and easing cold war tensions made him a celebrity. He shared the 1973 Nobel Peace Prize with North Vietnam's Le Duc Tho (who refused it); he appeared on 21 *Time* magazine covers; and in a 1973 Gallup Poll he led the list of the most-admired Americans. Kissinger's efforts in the Nixon administration left a lasting mark on American foreign policy.

President Nixon owed the success of much of his foreign policy to his Secretary of State, Henry Kissinger. ***Foreign Relations*** *Why did Nixon rely so heavily on Kissinger's advice?*

## *Relaxing Tensions*

Nixon's and Kissinger's greatest accomplishment was in bringing about **détente,** or a relaxation in tensions, between the United States and the two Communist giants. China and the Soviet Union were sworn enemies of the United States. Nixon's willingness to negotiate peacefully with them stunned many observers. In the 1950s Nixon had been one of the most bitter and active anti-Communists in government. He had made his reputation by demanding that the United States stand firm against the Communist threat.

As President, however, Nixon dealt imaginatively with both China and the Soviet Union. Nixon distrusted government bureaucracy, so he kept much of his diplomacy secret. Bypassing Congress, and often bypassing his own advisers, he and Kissinger reversed the direction of postwar American foreign policy.

Nixon drew on Kissinger's understanding that foreign affairs were more complex than a simple standoff between the United States and communism. Kissinger pointed out that the Communist world itself suffered from serious rifts, noting, "The deepest international conflict in the world today is not between us and the Soviet Union but between the Soviet Union and Communist China."

## *A New Approach to China*

The most surprising policy shift was toward China. In 1949 the Communist revolution had resulted in the establishment of the People's Republic of China. Americans saw all Communists in Asia as part of a united plot to dominate the world. As a result, the United States did not extend formal diplomatic recognition to the new Chinese government. In effect, the United States officially pretended that it did not exist.

Even when a Chinese-Soviet alliance crumbled, the United States clung to its rigid position. It insisted that the government of Jiang Jieshi, which was set up on the island of Taiwan when the Nationalists fled the Chinese mainland, was the rightful government of all China.

Quietly, Nixon began to prepare the way for a new policy of *realpolitik.* In his Inaugural Address in 1969, he referred indirectly to China when he declared, "We seek an open world . . . a world in which no people, great or small, will live in angry isolation." His first foreign policy report to Congress in 1970 began:

**AMERICAN VOICES** **"The Chinese are a great and vital people who should not remain isolated from the international community. . . . United States policy is not likely soon to have much impact on China's behavior, let alone its ideological outlook. But it is certainly in our interest, and in the interest of peace and stability in Asia and the world, that we take what steps we can toward improved practical relations with Peking [Beijing]."**

—*Richard Nixon,* report to Congress, *1970*

The administration undertook a series of moves designed to open a better relationship with China:

(1) In January and February 1970, American and Chinese ambassadors met in Warsaw, Poland.

(2) In October 1970, in a first for an American President, Nixon referred to China by its official title, the People's Republic of China.

(3) In March 1971, the United States government lifted restrictions on travel to China.

Chinese premier Zhou Enlai and President Richard Nixon congratulate each other on the new ties between their nations. ***Culture*** ***Why was it important for the press to capture such moments?***

(4) In April 1971, the American table-tennis team accepted a Chinese invitation to visit the mainland, beginning what was called "ping-pong diplomacy."

(5) In June 1971, the United States ended its 21-year embargo on trade with the People's Republic of China.

In July 1971, after extensive secret diplomacy by Kissinger, Nixon made the dramatic announcement that he planned to visit China the following year. He would be the first United States President ever to travel to that country.

Nixon understood that the People's Republic was an established government that would not simply disappear. Other nations had recognized the government, and it was time for the United States to do the same. Similarly, other countries wanted to give China's seat in the United Nations to the People's Republic. The United

*Mao Zedong*

President Nixon shakes hands with Egyptian President Anwar Sadat in front of Egypt's famous pyramids. Nixon's administration faced difficult diplomatic challenges in the Middle East, particularly during the 1973 Arab-Israeli war. ***Foreign Relations** What do you think was Nixon's greatest foreign policy success?*

States could no longer muster international opinion against this change.

*Intercontinental Ballistic Missile (ICBM)*

Nixon had other motives as well. He recognized that he could use Chinese friendship as a bargaining chip in his negotiations with the Soviet Union. Press coverage of the trip would give him a boost at home. Also, he believed that he could take this action without suffering political damage, because of his past reputation as a strong anti-Communist.

Nixon traveled to China in February 1972. He met with Mao Zedong, the Chinese leader who had spearheaded the revolution in 1949. He spoke with Premier Zhou Enlai about international problems and ways of dealing with them. He and his wife, Pat, toured the Great Wall and other Chinese sights, all in front of television cameras that sent the historic pictures home.

When he returned to the United States, Nixon waited in his plane until prime time so that his return would be seen by as many television viewers as possible. Formal relations were not yet restored—that would take a few more years—but the basis for diplomatic ties had been established.

## *Limiting Nuclear Arms*

Several months after his 1972 China trip, Nixon visited the Soviet Union. He received as warm a welcome in Moscow as he had in Beijing. In a series of cordial meetings between Nixon and Premier Leonid I. Brezhnev, the two nations reached several decisions. They agreed to work together to explore space, eased longstanding trade limits, and completed negotiations on a weapons pact.

Nixon viewed arms control as a vital part of his foreign policy program. Like many Americans, he was worried about the widespread **proliferation,** or growth, of nuclear weapons. The Limited Test Ban Treaty of 1963 had ended atmospheric testing of new bombs, but underground testing continued. The two superpowers were making bigger and better bombs all the time. Some people feared that the world might be destroyed unless these weapons were brought under control.

Nixon was determined to address the nuclear threat and to deal creatively with the Soviet Union at the same time. He had taken office intent on building more nuclear weapons to keep ahead of the Soviet Union. But he came to recognize that this kind of arms race made little sense. Each nation already had more than enough weapons to destroy its enemy many times over. The nuclear age demanded balance between the superpowers.

To address the issue, in 1969 the United States and the Soviet Union began Strategic Arms Limitation Talks. The talks produced a 1972 pact to limit offensive nuclear weapons, ready to be signed when Nixon went to Moscow.

The first Strategic Arms Limitation Treaty, known as **SALT I,** included a five-year agreement that held the number of intercontinental ballistic missiles (ICBMs) and submarine-launched ballistic missiles (SLBMs) at 1972 levels. Ballistic missiles ascend in a controlled manner, and descend in free-fall. The treaty also included an agreement restricting the development and deployment of antiballistic missile defense systems.

SALT I was a diplomatic triumph for the Nixon administration and an important step forward. But it did little to limit the number of warheads the two nations possessed or to stop them from improving nuclear weapons systems in other ways.

The cold war warmed slightly as Soviet premier Leonid Brezhnev (center, left) and President Nixon (center, right) met and SALT I was signed. ***Government How was SALT I both a success and a failure?***

The practical Kissinger called for respecting the limits imposed, but he also urged the American military to improve its defenses. "The way for us to use this freeze is for us to catch up," he said soon after the summit. "If we don't do this, we don't deserve to be in office." Still, SALT I showed that arms control agreements were possible, paving the way for more progress in the future.

About a year before the signing of SALT I, Nixon pointed out that the potential benefits of negotiating with the Soviet Union went beyond the issue of limiting nuclear arms:

**AMERICAN VOICES**

**"Perhaps for the first time, the evolving strategic balance allows a Soviet-American agreement which yields no unilateral [one-sided] advantages. The fact [that] we have begun to discuss strategic arms with the USSR is in itself important. Agreement in such a vital area could create a new commitment to stability, and influence attitudes toward other issues."**

*—Richard Nixon*

## SECTION 3 REVIEW

### Comprehension

1. *Key Terms* Define: (a) *realpolitik*; (b) détente; (c) proliferation; (d) SALT I.
2. *Summarizing the Main Idea* Why were Nixon's policies toward China and the Soviet Union so surprising?
3. *Organizing Information* Create a web diagram to organize information about Nixon's foreign policy.

### Critical Thinking

4. *Analyzing Time Lines* Review the time line at the start of the section. Do you think these events support the idea that in foreign relations change comes slowly? Explain.
5. *Demonstrating Reasoned Judgment* Considering its weaknesses, how important was the SALT I treaty? Why?

### Writing Activity

6. *Writing an Expository Essay* Write an essay that Henry Kissinger might have prepared to explain the importance of relaxing tensions between the United States and both China and the Soviet Union. Try to refer to *realpolitik* and détente in your essay.

**1969** Nixon White House wiretaps government employees

**1971** Pentagon Papers released

**1972** Watergate break-in; Nixon wins reelection

**1973** Trial of Watergate burglars; Senate Watergate hearings; "Saturday Night Massacre"

**1974** House committee recommends impeachment; Nixon resigns

1968 | 1970 | 1972 | 1974

# 4 The Watergate Scandal

## SECTION PREVIEW

### Objectives

1. Explain how the siege mentality at the White House led to illegal and unethical actions during Nixon's reelection campaign.
2. Describe the Watergate break-in and how the story of the Watergate scandal unfolded.
3. Describe the events that directly led to Nixon's resignation.
4. *Key Terms* Define: Watergate scandal; special prosecutor; impeachment.

### Main Idea

The break-in at the Watergate apartment complex started a scandal that led to President Nixon's resignation.

### Reading Strategy

*Taking Notes* As you read, take notes on the various events related to the Watergate scandal. Use the terms *Who, What, When, Where,* and *Why* to help you organize each piece of information.

Looking toward the 1972 election, Nixon was determined to win an overwhelming victory. With such a mandate he would be in a position to move his programs through Congress. Fiercely loyal aides concocted various schemes to help ensure that the President would win. Some of them committed crimes in the process. When Nixon tried to hide their illegal actions, he involved himself in a scandalous series of events that ended his presidency and shook the foundations of American government.

MR. PRESIDENT: RELEASE the TAPES!

A series of secret Oval Office recordings became the center of controversy.

## Siege Mentality

The President's suspicious and secretive nature caused the White House to operate as if it were in a state of siege, surrounded by political enemies. Nixon's staff responded to the President's attitude by trying to protect him at all costs from anything that might weaken his political position.

**The Enemies List** One result of this mind-set was what became known as the "enemies list." Special counsel Charles W. Colson helped develop a list of prominent people unsympathetic to the administration. It included politicians such as Senator Edward Kennedy, members of the media such as reporter Daniel Schorr, and a number of outspoken performers such as comedian Dick Gregory and actors Jane Fonda and Steve McQueen. Aides then considered how to harass these White House "enemies." One idea, for example, was to arrange income tax investigations of people on the list.

**Wiretaps** Despite his dedication to a domestic policy of law and order, Nixon was sometimes willing to take illegal actions. In 1969 someone in the National Security Council appeared to have leaked secret information to *The New York Times.* In response, Nixon ordered Henry Kissinger to install wiretaps, or listening devices, on the telephones of several of his own staff. He also ordered wiretaps on some news reporters' phones. These wiretaps, installed for national security reasons, were legal at the time. But they would lead to a flurry of illegal wiretapping, much of it done for political purposes.

At the same time, Nixon sought tighter coordination of intelligence activities. The FBI, under director J. Edgar Hoover, was already illegally monitoring radical activists by tapping their phones and opening mail. In mid-1970 Nixon's staff proposed a plan for wiretaps and other probes that was so far outside the law that even Hoover rejected it.

**The Plumbers** In the spring of 1971 Daniel Ellsberg, a former Defense Department official, handed *The New York Times* a huge, secret Pentagon study of the Vietnam War. In June 1971, as you have read, *The New York Times* began to publish this study, which became known as the Pentagon Papers. The documents showed that previous Presidents often had deceived Congress and the American people about the real situation in Vietnam and had deliberately escalated the conflict.

Nixon was upset that Ellsberg could get away with leaking secret government information. He was even more upset when leaks to the press continued. He and Kissinger were in the midst of secret discussions with China and the Soviet Union, and he did not want those delicate negotiations undermined.

Nixon approved a plan to organize a special White House unit to stop government leaks. The group, nicknamed the Plumbers, included E. Howard Hunt, a spy novelist and former CIA agent, and G. Gordon Liddy, a former FBI agent. In September 1971, with approval from White House chief domestic adviser John Ehrlichman, the undercover unit broke into the office of Ellsberg's psychiatrist. To punish Ellsberg for leaking the Pentagon Papers, they hoped to find and disclose damaging information about his private life.

## Nixon's Reelection Campaign

Determined to ensure Nixon's victory in 1972, the Committee to Reelect the President used other questionable tactics. Headed by former Attorney General John Mitchell, the Committee launched a special fund-raising campaign. It wanted to collect as much money as possible before a new law made it necessary to report such contributions. The money would fund both routine campaign activities and unethical stunts hidden from the public.

The Committee funded a variety of questionable actions. For example, in 1972 people on its payroll made up a letter attempting to discredit Edmund Muskie, a Democratic senator from Maine who was a leading presidential contender. Then they leaked the letter to a conservative New Hampshire newspaper.

Charging Muskie with making insulting remarks about French Canadians living in the state, the letter was timed to arrive two weeks before the New Hampshire primary. The letter also claimed that Muskie's wife was an alcoholic. The normally composed Muskie broke down in tears in front of TV cameras, which seriously damaged his candidacy.

Attempts such as this to sabotage Nixon's political opponents came to be known as "dirty tricks." They included sending hecklers to disrupt Democratic campaign meetings and assigning undercover "spies" to join the campaigns of major candidates.

Nixon's downfall began when burglars paid by the Committee to Reelect the President broke into Democratic party headquarters in Washington's Watergate apartment complex. ***Government*** ***What did Nixon do to become ensnared in the scandal?***

## The Watergate Break-In

Within the Committee to Reelect the President a group was formed to gather intelligence, or secret political information. It included "Plumbers" Liddy and Hunt. The group masterminded several outlandish plans.

One scheme called for wiretapping top Democrats to try to compromise delegates at their convention. Twice Mitchell

*Security guard Frank Willis discovered the Watergate break-in.*

refused to go along, not because the plan was illegal, but because it was too expensive.

Finally, in March 1972, he approved a different idea. Liddy would oversee the wiretapping of phones at Democratic National Committee headquarters in the Watergate apartment complex in Washington, D.C.

The first break-in to install illegal listening devices failed. A second attempt, begun late at night on June 16, 1972, ended with the arrest of the five men involved. One suspect was James McCord, a former CIA officer working as a security officer for the Committee to Reelect the President. The Watergate burglars carried money that could be traced to the Committee. Thus they tied the break-in directly to Nixon's reelection campaign.

**Main Idea CONNECTIONS**

*What was the purpose of the Watergate break-in?*

When the FBI traced the money carried by the Watergate burglars to the reelection committee, Nixon contacted the CIA. He authorized that organization to try to persuade the FBI to stop its investigation on the grounds that the matter involved "national security."

This action would come back to haunt the President. Although he had not been involved in planning the break-in, Nixon was now part of the illegal coverup. The break-in and the coverup are now known as the **Watergate scandal.**

In the months following the Watergate break-in, the incident barely reached the public's notice. Behind the scenes in the White House, some of the President's closest aides worked feverishly to keep the truth hidden.

In the summer of 1972, Haldeman, Ehrlichman, Mitchell, and others launched a scheme to bribe the Watergate defendants. They distributed hundreds of thousands of dollars in illegal "hush money" to buy their silence. Also, to shield the President, Mitchell and other top officials committed perjury by lying under oath in court.

Their efforts paid off in the November presidential election. Nixon trounced Democratic liberal Senator George McGovern of South Dakota by 520 to 17 electoral votes and a sizable majority of the popular vote. He had the mandate he wanted, though he did not get a Republican majority in either house of Congress.

*Washington Post* investigative reporters Bob Woodward (right) and Carl Bernstein (left) persisted in tracking down information to uncover the Watergate story. ***Culture*** ***How do you think their reporting affected the official investigation?***

## The Watergate Scandal Unfolds

Despite Nixon's victory in the election, the Watergate story refused to go away. Newspapers such as the *Washington Post* continued asking probing questions of administration officials. Nixon himself had proclaimed publicly that "no one in the White House staff, no one in this administration, presently employed, was involved in this very bizarre incident." Not everyone believed him.

**The Watergate Trial** The trial of the Watergate burglars began in January 1973, with Judge John J. Sirica presiding. All the defendants either pleaded guilty or were found guilty. Meanwhile the White House and the President himself were becoming more deeply involved. In March 1973, just before the judge handed down the sentences, Nixon personally approved the payment of "hush money" to defendant E. Howard Hunt.

At sentencing time Judge Sirica was not convinced that he had gotten to the bottom of the matter. Criticizing the prosecution, he said:

**AMERICAN VOICES** **"I have not been satisfied, and I am still not satisfied that all the pertinent facts that might be available—I say *might* be available—have been produced before an American jury. . . . I would hope that**

the Senate committee is granted the power by Congress . . . to try to get to the bottom of what happened in this case.❞

—*Judge John J. Sirica*

To prompt the burglars to talk, Sirica sentenced them to long prison terms, up to 40 years. But he suggested that their sentences could be reduced if they cooperated with the upcoming Senate hearings on Watergate.

**Woodward and Bernstein** Meanwhile, two *Washington Post* reporters were following a trail of leads. Bob Woodward and Carl Bernstein, both young and eager, sensed that the trail would lead to the White House.†

Even before the election, Woodward and Bernstein had learned about the secret funds at the Committee to Reelect the President. They had written about the political spying and sabotage. As they began to realize who was involved, they called John Mitchell and asked him to verify their story. He denied it angrily.

**The Senate Investigates** In February 1973 a Senate Select Committee on Presidential Campaign Activities had begun to investigate the Watergate affair. James McCord, one of the convicted Watergate burglars, responded to his lengthy prison sentence by testifying before the committee in secret session. He gave members a vague sense of what had gone on, and he suggested that Nixon staffers were involved. The stories by Woodward and Bernstein helped the probe. In turn, leaks from the Senate committee aided these and other reporters.

As rumors of White House involvement grew, Nixon tried to protect himself. In April 1973 he fired Haldeman and Ehrlichman, his two closest aides. On national television he proclaimed that he would take final responsibility for the mistakes of others, for "there can be no whitewash at the White House."

The investigation ground on. In May 1973 the Senate committee, chaired by Senator Sam Ervin of North Carolina, began televised public hearings on Watergate. Millions of Americans watched, fascinated, as the story unfolded like a mystery thriller. John Dean, the

†The reporters received key clues from a shadowy informant whose identity remains a secret today. The cloak-and-dagger story of the investigation became a popular book and movie, *All the President's Men.*

## Watergate Chronology

|  |  |
|---|---|
| June 1972 | Five men linked to Nixon's reelection campaign arrested for breaking into Democratic National Committee headquarters. |
| April 1973 | Nixon denies knowledge of the break-in. |
| May 1973 | Senate Select Committee on Presidential Campaign Activities begins hearings. |
| June 1973 | Former Nixon counsel John Dean tells the committee that Nixon authorized a coverup. |
| July 1973 | Committee discovers that Nixon had been secretly recording presidential conversations since 1971 and orders Nixon to release certain tapes. Nixon refuses. |
| Aug. 1973 | Special Prosecutor Archibald Cox sues Nixon for the tapes. |
| Oct. 1973 | Nixon offers summaries of the tapes, which Cox rejects. Nixon fires Cox, setting off a series of firings known as the "Saturday Night Massacre." The House takes steps to impeach Nixon. Nixon releases all but two of the requested tapes. |
| Nov. 1973 | An 18 1/2-minute gap is found on one of the tapes. |
| Jan. 1974 | Nixon claims "executive privilege." |
| April 1974 | Nixon is ordered to surrender more tapes and related documents. Nixon supplies 1,254 pages of edited transcripts. Special Prosecutor Leon Jaworski sues Nixon for the originals. |
| July 1974 | Supreme Court orders Nixon to surrender the tapes and documents. The House Judiciary Committee recommends impeachment. |
| Aug.1974 | Nixon releases transcripts that prove he learned of the break-in as early as June 23, 1972, and ordered the coverup. Nixon resigns August 9. |

**Interpreting Charts** As the investigation unfolded, it became increasingly clear that Nixon had something to hide. ***Government*** ***How was the investigation an example of the federal system of checks and balances?***

## COMPARING PRIMARY SOURCES

### SHOULD NIXON BE IMPEACHED?

In July 1974 the House Judiciary Committee debated the possible impeachment of President Richard Nixon.

| In Favor of Impeachment | Opposed to Impeachment |
|---|---|
| "My faith in the Constitution is whole, it is complete, it is total. I am not going to sit here and be an idle spectator to the diminution [lessening], the subversion [overthrow], the destruction of the Constitution. . . . The Framers confided in the Congress the power if need be to remove . . . a President swollen with power and grown tyrannical." *—Texas Representative Barbara Jordan, Democrat* | "As the trust is placed in Congress to safeguard the liberties of the people through the . . . powers to remove a President, so must Congress's vigilance be fierce in seeing that the trust is not abused. . . . Not only do I not believe that any crimes by the President have been proved beyond a reasonable doubt, but I do not think the proof even approaches the lesser standards of proof which some of my colleagues . . . suggested we apply." *—Michigan Representative Edward Hutchinson, Republican* |

***ANALYZING VIEWPOINTS*** **Compare the views of the two speakers toward impeachment of Nixon.**

President's personal legal counselor, sought to save himself by testifying that Nixon knew about the coverup. Other staffers described illegal activities at the White House.

The most dramatic moment came when one aide revealed the existence of a secret taping system in the President's office that recorded all meetings and telephone conversations. The system was set up to provide a historical record of Nixon's presidency. Now those audiotapes could show whether or not Nixon had actually been involved in the coverup.

**The "Saturday Night Massacre"** In an effort to prove his honesty, Nixon agreed in May 1973 to the appointment of a special Watergate prosecutor. A **special prosecutor** works for the Justice Department but conducts an independent investigation of alleged wrongdoing by government officials. Archibald Cox, a Harvard law professor, took the post and immediately asked for the tapes. Nixon refused to release them. When Cox persisted, Nixon ordered him fired during the weekend of October 20, 1973. This action triggered a series of resignations and firings that became known as the "Saturday Night Massacre."

**An Administration in Jeopardy** By this time, Nixon was in serious trouble. His public approval rating plummeted. After Cox's firing, *Time* magazine declared "The President Should Resign."

Cox's replacement as special prosecutor, Leon Jaworski of Texas, also asked for the tapes. Nixon then tried to show his innocence by releasing edited transcripts of some of his White House conversations. He carefully cut out the most damaging evidence. Still, many people were angry and disillusioned when they read even the edited comments of some of the conversations in the Oval Office.

Meanwhile, a subplot emerged in the troubled White House. Vice President Spiro Agnew stood accused of evading income taxes and taking bribes. Early in October 1973, just 10 days before the "Saturday Night Massacre," he resigned in disgrace. To succeed Agnew, Nixon named Gerald R. Ford, the House minority leader. For nearly two months, until the Senate confirmed Ford, the nation had a President in big trouble—and no Vice President.

**Impeachment Ahead?** Nixon had to do something. After the "Saturday Night Massacre," Congress had begun the process that could lead to **impeachment**—bringing charges of misconduct against a government official.

In July 1974 the House Judiciary Committee, which included 21 Democrats and 17 Republicans, began to hold hearings to determine if there were adequate grounds for impeachment. This debate, like the earlier hearings, appeared on national television. The country watched anxiously as even Republicans deserted the President. Representative M. Caldwell Butler of Virginia spoke for many of them when he said:

**AMERICAN VOICES** "For years we Republicans have campaigned against corruption and misconduct. . . . But Watergate is our shame. Those things have happened in our house and it is our responsibility to do what we can to clear it up. . . . It is a sad chapter in American history, but I cannot condone what I have heard; I cannot excuse it; and I cannot and will not stand for it."

*—Representative M. Caldwell Butler, 1974*

By sizable tallies, the House Judiciary Committee voted to impeach the President on charges of obstruction of justice, abuse of power, and refusal to obey a congressional order to turn over his tapes. To remove him from office, a majority of the full House of Representatives would have to vote for impeachment, and the Senate would then have to hold a trial. The outcome seemed obvious.

## *Nixon Resigns*

On August 5, after a brief delay, Nixon finally obeyed a Supreme Court ruling and released the tapes. They contained a disturbing gap of 18 1/2 minutes, during which the conversation had been mysteriously erased. Still, the tapes gave clear evidence of Nixon's involvement in the coverup.

Three days later Nixon appeared on television and painfully announced that he would leave the office of President the next day. On August 9, 1974, Nixon resigned, the first President ever to do so.

That same day, in a smooth constitutional transition, Vice President Gerald Ford was sworn in. "Our long national nightmare is over," he said. Many Americans wanted Nixon to face the charges against him in court. Ford, however, believed that a long, public trial might divide the country and draw the focus away from vital issues. A month after Nixon resigned, Ford granted him a presidential pardon.

The Watergate scandal still stands as a low point in American political history. It revealed how trusted government officials could abuse the power granted to them by the people. The scandal also proved the strength of the United States' constitutional system, especially its balance of powers. The judicial and legislative branches of government forced the members of the executive branch to answer for their criminal actions.

In this famous photograph, former President Richard Nixon offers the crowd his familiar salute as he leaves Washington, D.C., following his resignation. ***Government*** ***Why did President Ford pardon Nixon?***

### SECTION 4 REVIEW

**Comprehension**

1. *Key Terms* (a) Watergate scandal; (b) special prosecutor; (c) impeachment.
2. *Summarizing the Main Idea* Why was the Watergate break-in such an important event?
3. *Organizing Information* Create a cause-and-effect chart to organize information about the Watergate scandal.

**Critical Thinking**

4. *Analyzing Time Lines* Review the time line at the start of the section. Which events do you think are related to the siege mentality that gripped the Nixon White House? Explain.
5. *Formulating Questions* Imagine that you are a member of the House Judiciary Committee, preparing for impeachment hearings. What three questions would you want to ask President Nixon?

**Writing Activity**

6. *Writing a Persuasive Essay* Write an essay either in favor of or opposed to President Ford's pardon of Nixon.

# SKILLS FOR LIFE

**Historical Evidence**

Geography

Graphs and Charts

Critical Thinking

# Analyzing Presidential Records

Presidential papers record a President's time in office. They include letters, memoranda, notes on meetings, speeches, transcripts of press conferences, and more. They provide a valuable source of historical evidence.

In more recent times technology has added new forms of "papers" as historical evidence, such as audio- and videotapes. President Nixon's audiotapes, recorded in the Oval Office, loomed large in the Watergate affair. In fact, one of these tapes finally ended the affair. It was a recording of a conversation that took place just a few days after the Watergate break-in on June 16, 1972. Not released until August 5, 1974, it proved that Nixon knew of the cover-up all along.

**1.** ***Identify the source by asking who, when, where, and what.*** (a) Who are the speakers on the tape? (b) Who else is mentioned in it? (c) When did the conversation take place? (d) Where? (e) What is the major topic?

**2.** ***Identify the main points of information in the excerpts.*** (a) Why is Haldeman concerned about the FBI? (b) What recommendation does he put forward about using the CIA to end the investigation? (c) How does President Nixon respond to the recommendation?

**3.** ***Study the tape to find clues to the historical period.*** (a) What can you infer about the extent of the powers that Nixon believed he had over FBI and CIA operations? (b) What can you infer about Nixon's sense of priorities at the time the recording was made?

**TEST FOR SUCCESS**

What can you infer about the extent of Haldeman's influence on Nixon?

*June 23, 1972*
**Speakers**
President Nixon
H. R. Haldeman, Chief of Staff

**Haldeman** Now, on to the investigation, you know the Democratic break-in thing. We're back in the problem area because the FBI is not under control, because [acting FBI director L. Patrick] Gray doesn't exactly know how to control it and . . . their investigation is now leading into some productive areas—because they've been able to trace the money [that was found on the Watergate burglars]. . . . [John] Mitchell's recommendation [is] that the way to handle this now is for us to have [deputy CIA director Vernon] Walters call Pat Gray and just say, "Stay . . . out of this—this is ah, business here we don't want you to go any further on it." That's not an unusual development, and ah, that would take care of it.

**Nixon** What about Pat Gray—you mean Pat Gray doesn't want to?

**Haldeman** Pat does want to. He doesn't know how to, and he doesn't have any basis for doing it. Given [Walters's call], he will then have the basis.

**Nixon** Yeah.

**Haldeman** [Gray will] say, "We've got this signal from across the river [the CIA] to put a hold on this." And that will fit rather well because the FBI agents who are working the case, at this point, feel that's what it is.

**Nixon** They've traced the money? Who'd they trace it to?

*[Haldeman describes various people who contributed to the Committee to Reelect the President, and Nixon wonders if these people will say that the burglars, not the committee, asked for the money.]*

**Haldeman** Well, if they will. But then we're relying on more and more people all the time. That's the problem, and they'll stop if we could take this other route.

**Nixon** All right.

**Haldeman** And you seem to think the thing to do is get [the FBI] to stop?

**Nixon** Right, fine.

*—Excerpted from* The New York Times, *Tuesday, August 6, 1974*

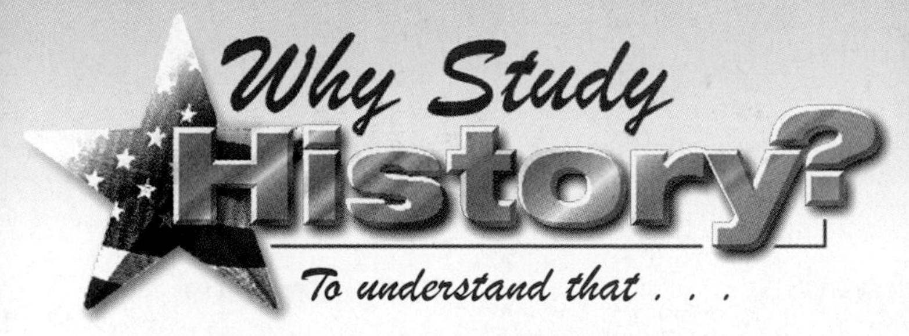


# Government Requires Checks and Balances

**The issue of presidential power, keenly reflected in the Watergate scandal, continues to shape American politics today.**

Senate Watergate hearings, 1973

The United States in 1968 seemed to be slipping into chaos. Protests against the Vietnam War multiplied after the Tet Offensive. The assassination of Martin Luther King, Jr., abruptly halted the Poor People's Campaign. Another assassin's bullet killed presidential candidate Robert F. Kennedy. Outside the Democratic Convention in Chicago, police wielded tear gas, nightsticks, and rifles against demonstrators as a horrified nation watched on television.

In November 1968, Richard Nixon won the presidency on the promise to restore law and order. Yet behind the scenes, President Nixon violated the standards that he publicly upheld. The Watergate scandal revealed the extent to which he abused his power as President.

## The Impact Today

Vast executive power was not what the Founding Fathers had in mind when they wrote the Constitution, with its system of checks and balances. The Constitution lists the powers of the executive, legislative, and judicial branches. But the language of the Constitution is sometimes general, and thus the extent of the three branches' powers is open to interpretation.

The balance of power between Congress and the President has shifted over time. In the cold war era, for example, presidential power expanded, especially in the area of military affairs. Though the Constitution gives Congress the power to declare war, Presidents deployed American military forces abroad on several occasions without a formal declaration of war.

In 1950, President Truman sent troops to South Korea. In 1965, President Johnson sent troops to Vietnam. In 1970, President Nixon launched an invasion of Cambodia. All these actions undermined Congress's war power. In response, in 1973 Congress passed the War Powers Act, which required congressional approval for sending troops overseas.

In recent years, the budget has become a battleground for disputes over presidential and congressional powers. In 1996, Congress passed the Line-Item Veto Act. It gave the President the power to veto specific items in the federal budget. (In the past, Presidents had to approve or veto the budget bill as a whole.) Yet two years later, the Supreme Court ruled the line-item veto unconstitutional.

## The Impact on You

Make a two-column table titled "Executive Versus Legislative Power." In the first column, list powers that you think the President should have. In the second column, list powers that should reside with Congress. Give a brief reason why each power on your table should belong to the President or to Congress.

President Clinton addresses Congress, 1997

# Chapter 22 Review

## Chapter Summary

The major concepts of Chapter 22 are presented below. See also ***Guide to the Essentials of American History*** or ***Interactive Student Tutorial CD-ROM,*** which contains interactive review activities, time lines, helpful hints, and test practice.

### *Reviewing the Main Ideas*

In 1968 a fateful series of events helped Richard Nixon win the presidential election. Relying on his close advisers to help develop domestic and foreign policy, Nixon tried to shift the country in a new direction. The Watergate scandal forced Nixon to resign in 1974.

### *Section 1: The Crises of 1968*

The year 1968 was a turbulent and painful time for the country that resulted in the election of Richard Nixon as President.

### *Section 2: The Nixon Administration*

As President, Richard Nixon relied on several close advisers to help him move the country in a new direction.

### *Section 3: Nixon's Foreign Policy*

President Nixon's foreign policy led to more positive relationships with China and the Soviet Union.

### *Section 4: The Watergate Scandal*

The break-in at the Watergate apartment complex started a scandal that led to President Nixon's resignation.

The issue of presidential power, reflected in the Watergate scandal, continues to shape American politics today.

## Key Terms

Use each of the terms below in a sentence that shows how it relates to the chapter.

1. SALT I
2. Poor People's Campaign
3. deficit spending
4. special prosecutor
5. *realpolitik*
6. Watergate scandal
7. détente
8. silent majority
9. proliferation
10. embargo
11. Organization of Petroleum Exporting Countries (OPEC)

## Comprehension

1. What effect did the Tet Offensive have on American public opinion in 1968? Why?
2. What factors hurt the Democrats' chances for victory in the presidential election of 1968?
3. Why were President Nixon's key staff members so important to him?
4. What was Nixon's "southern strategy"?
5. How did Henry Kissinger affect American foreign policy under President Nixon?
6. How did the Nixon administration change United States' policy toward China?
7. What measures did the Committee to Reelect the President take to win the 1972 election?
8. What illegal actions did Nixon take in attempting to cover up the Watergate break-in?

## Using Graphic Organizers

On a separate sheet of paper, copy the flowchart to organize the main ideas of the chapter. Fill in the blank boxes with important details.

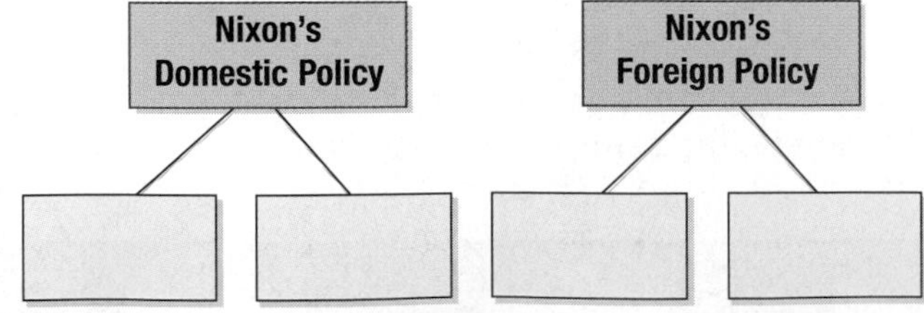

## Analyzing Political Cartoons ▶

1. This cartoon appeared during the Watergate scandal. (a) What is the building shown? (b) How has it been modified?
2. What does this modification represent?
3. What is the cartoon's message?

## Critical Thinking

1. ***Applying the Chapter Skill*** Compile a brief presidential record for one of the earlier American Presidents. The record may be a letter, speech, notes on a meeting, a memorandum, or the transcript of a press conference. It should focus on a critical issue or event. Other details might suggest the time period, the mood of the President, and the importance of the issue or event. Use your textbook as an aid.
2. ***Testing Conclusions*** Some observers have concluded that only a Republican veteran of the cold war like Richard Nixon could have reestablished relations with China. Do you agree, or do you believe that a Democratic President could have been equally successful? Explain.
3. ***Predicting Consequences*** What kind of President do you think Americans were looking for after Watergate and the Nixon resignation?

### INTERNET ACTIVITY

***For your portfolio:***
**PREPARING A SUMMARY**

Access Prentice Hall's *America: Pathways to the Present* site at **www.Pathways.phschool.com** for the specific URLs to complete the activity. Additional resources and related Web sites are also available.

Use the links provided to prepare a summary of the short- and long-term effects of the Watergate scandal. What impact did the scandal have on Nixon and his administration? What lasting impact did the scandal have on the presidency and the American public?

### ANALYZING DOCUMENTS ▶ INTERPRETING DATA

Turn to the line graph titled "Rate of Inflation, 1968–1976," in Section 2.

1. When did consumer prices reach their peak? (a) 1968 (b) 1971 (c) 1974 (d) 1976.
2. What is the best description of the rate of inflation through the period from 1968 to 1972? (a) stayed about the same (b) rose steadily (c) dropped steadily (d) rose and dropped wildly from year to year.
3. ***Writing*** Imagine that you are the manager of a grocery store in 1973. Customers have been complaining about rising food prices. Write a notice to your customers explaining why food prices go up when fuel prices rise. Think about the grocer's costs and how they might be affected by changes in fuel prices.

### Connecting to Today

***Essay Writing*** Today, in part because of the Watergate scandal, Congress and the press keep a watchful eye on top government officials. They eagerly probe any questionable activity, past or present, public or private. Is this level of watchfulness good for the country, or bad? Explain your answer in an essay.

# CHAPTER 23 The Post-Watergate Period

## 1974–1980

## CHAPTER FOCUS

*This chapter describes the years of the post-Watergate period when upheaval from the scandal continued to disrupt American society. Gerald Ford, the man who assumed the presidency after Nixon, tried to revive the confidence that had sustained the United States through past troubles. He was replaced after two years in office by a newcomer to national politics, Jimmy Carter, who promised the country honesty and morality.*

*The **Why Study History?** page at the end of this chapter explores the issue of trust in government, in the 1970s and today.*

▲ **VIEWING HISTORY** The fireworks shown here at Independence Hall in Philadelphia were part of the country's 200th birthday celebration. ***Culture*** ***How did the bicentennial celebration help revive a sense of optimism in the United States?***

| 1974 | 1974 | 1974 | 1975 | 1975 | 1976 |
|---|---|---|---|---|---|
| *Gerald Ford becomes President after Nixon resigns* | *Ford grants Nixon presidential pardon* | *Ford presents WIN economic program* | *U.S. Marines rescue Mayaguez crew* | *Helsinki Accords* | *United States celebrates bicentennial* |

**1974** **1975** **1976**

# 1 The Ford Administration

## SECTION PREVIEW

### Objectives

1. Describe how Gerald Ford became President and why he pardoned Richard Nixon.
2. Summarize the economic problems faced by the Ford administration.
3. Explain the foreign policy challenges that faced Ford.
4. Describe the importance of the nation's 200th birthday celebration.
5. *Key Terms* Define: stagflation; recession; War Powers Act; Helsinki Accords; bicentennial.

### Main Idea

After becoming President, Gerald Ford worked to reunite the country. He faced economic problems at home as well as foreign policy challenges abroad.

### Reading Strategy

*Outlining Information* Skim the section and use the headings and subheadings to create an outline for the section. As you read, fill in appropriate supporting details under each heading.

The new President, Gerald R. Ford, faced a difficult job. He had to help the United States emerge from its worst political scandal. At the same time, the economy was in trouble and the war in Vietnam had ended in defeat. At the start, Ford lost considerable support with a well-meant pardon for Richard Nixon. In the months that followed, he never recovered from the loss of support.

## Ford Becomes President

"Jerry" Ford was one of the most popular politicians in Washington when he was appointed Vice President in October 1973. (Vice President Spiro Agnew had resigned in disgrace for accepting bribes.) Ford had been in the House of Representatives since 1948, rising to become Minority Leader in 1965. He was an unassuming Republican from Michigan who believed in traditional American virtues like hard work and self-reliance. Ford had been a football star at the University of Michigan. He played on the national championship teams of 1932 and 1933, then with the College All-Stars. After earning a law degree and serving in the navy during World War II, he entered politics.

*Vice President Gerald Ford became President after Richard Nixon resigned in August 1974.*

Ford described himself as "conservative in fiscal affairs, moderate in domestic affairs, internationalist in foreign affairs." His stands on issues reflected those points of view. Over the years, he had opposed much government spending—federal aid to education, the antipoverty program, and spending for mass transit. He supported measures for law and order and defense spending.

Nixon chose Ford as a noncontroversial figure who might bolster his own support in Congress. When Ford was confirmed as Vice President, Congress and the public were interested mainly in his reputation for honesty, integrity, and stability. Some, however, questioned whether he was qualified to take over the presidency if that became necessary.

Betty Ford described her husband as "an accidental Vice President, and an accidental President, and in both jobs he replaced disgraced leaders." ***Culture*** ***What was the popular reaction to Ford's pardoning of Richard Nixon?***

Despite Ford's long experience in Congress, he had little experience as an administrator or in foreign affairs. Ford acknowledged his own limitations when he was sworn in, saying, "I am a Ford, not a Lincoln."

When Nixon resigned in August 1974, Ford became the first nonelected President. Other Vice Presidents who had moved into the White House had been elected to the vice presidency as part of the national ticket. To fill the vice-presidential vacancy, Ford named former New York governor Nelson Rockefeller. This created the unique situation of having both a President and a Vice President who had been appointed, not elected.

## The Nixon Pardon

Ford became President in the midst of what he called "our long national nightmare." The nation was disillusioned by Watergate. During the scandal, many Americans had wondered whether the Constitution would survive their leader's actions. Few people looked forward to the prospect of an impeachment trial. It would have been only the second in United States history, after that of Andrew Johnson in 1868. When Ford assumed the presidency, the nation needed a leader who could take it beyond the ugliness of Watergate.

In response to this public mood, President Ford declared that it was a time for "communication, conciliation, compromise and cooperation." Americans were on his side. *Time* magazine noted "a mood of good feeling and even exhilaration in Washington that the city had not experienced for many years."

All too quickly, Ford lost some popular support. On September 8, barely a month after Nixon had resigned, Ford pardoned the former President for "all offenses" he might have committed, avoiding further prosecution. On national television, Ford explained that he had looked to God and his own conscience in deciding "the right thing" to do about Nixon and "his loyal wife and family":

**AMERICAN VOICES** **"Theirs is an American tragedy in which we have all played a part. It could go on and on and on, or someone must write the end to it. I have concluded that only I can do that, and if I can I must. . . . My conscience tells me that only I, as President, have the constitutional power to firmly shut and seal this book. My conscience tells me that it is my duty not merely to proclaim domestic tranquillity but to use every means that I have to ensure it."**

*—President Ford*

Ford expected criticism of the pardon, but he underestimated the widespread negative reaction. Many of Nixon's loyalists were facing prison for their role in Watergate. The former President, however, walked away without a penalty. Although some people supported his action, Ford's generous gesture backfired. Some people suggested that a bargain had been made when Nixon resigned. Many also criticized the new President's judgment. Ford occasionally was booed when he made public speeches, just as Johnson and Nixon had been. To counter the reactions, he went before a House committee in October to explain his reasons. Still angry, the public voted a number of Republicans out of office in the 1974 congressional elections.

## "Stagflation," 1970–1979

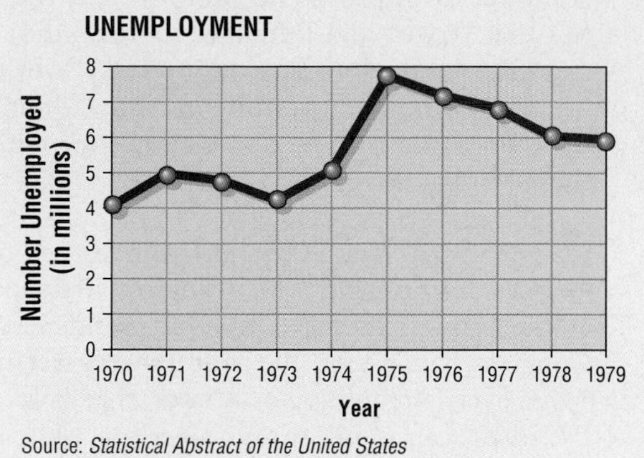


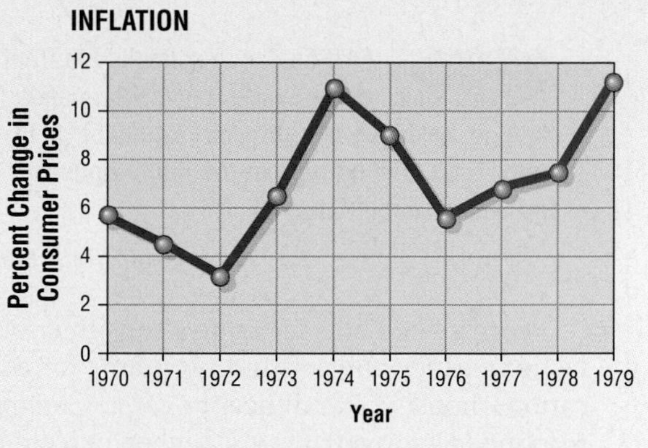


Source: *Statistical Abstract of the United States*

**Interpreting Graphs** Upon assuming office President Ford declared war on inflation, calling it "Public Enemy No. 1." Ford's administration, however, saw the worst economic slump in the United States since the Great Depression. ***Economics In what year were consumer prices highest in the 1970s? When did unemployment peak in this decade?***

## *Economic Problems*

The aftermath of Watergate was not the only difficult issue Ford faced. While focused on the scandal, the nation seemed to have stood still. Some conditions had grown worse. Now, facing a hostile Congress, the new administration found it hard to provide direction.

**The Economy Stalls** Months of preoccupation with Watergate had kept President Nixon from dealing with economic difficulties. By 1974 inflation was at about 11 percent, significantly higher than it had been in the past, while unemployment climbed to 5.6 percent. Home building, usually a sign of a healthy economy, slowed as interest rates rose. The fears of worried investors brought a drop in stock prices.

Usually, federal policymakers had to deal with either inflation—due to a rapidly growing economy—or unemployment, due to a slow economy. Most economists believed that each of those trends could balance out the other. For example, a moderate rise in inflation would help lower the rate of unemployment. Now, however, inflation and unemployment both rose, while the economy remained stalled and stagnant. Economists named this new situation **stagflation.**

By the time Ford assumed the presidency, the country was in a **recession,** a period of slow business activity. Not since Franklin Roosevelt took office during the Great Depression had a new President faced such harsh economic troubles.

Ford's approach (like Herbert Hoover's in the early 1930s) was to try to restore public confidence. Early in October 1974, he sent Congress an economic program called "WIN," or "Whip Inflation Now." The President asked Americans to wear red and white "WIN" buttons, to save instead of spending, conserve fuel, and plant vegetable gardens to counter high grocery store prices. The WIN campaign depended on people voluntarily changing their everyday actions, but had no real incentives. It soon faded away.

Eventually, Ford recognized the need for more direct action. The Federal Reserve tightened the money supply to control inflation, but that made the recession worse. There were widespread job layoffs. Unemployment soared to almost 8 percent in 1975. Congress then backed an anti-recession spending program. Despite his belief in less government spending, Ford backed an increase in unemployment benefits and a multibillion dollar tax cut. The economy recovered slightly, but inflation and unemployment remained high.

**Main Idea CONNECTIONS**

***What economic problems did the Ford administration face?***

**Conflicts with Congress** In spite of his long experience as a congressional leader, President Ford was often at odds with the Democratic-controlled Congress. He basically believed in limited government, while Congress wanted more government action in the economy.

Jerold F. terHorst, Ford's first press secretary, noted how Ford's own sense of decency came into conflict with his view of government:

**AMERICAN VOICES** **"If he saw a schoolkid in front of the White House who needed clothing, he'd give him the shirt off his back, literally. Then he'd go right in the White House and veto a school-lunch bill."**

— *Jerold F. terHorst*

Ford vetoed bills to create a consumer protection agency and to fund programs for education, housing, and health care. Congress responded by overriding a higher percentage of vetoes than it had since the presidency of Franklin Pierce in the 1850s.

## *Foreign Policy Actions*

In foreign policy Ford generally followed Nixon's approach, working for détente. He kept Henry Kissinger on as Secretary of State. In 1974 and 1975 Ford made a series of trips abroad. He met with European leaders and was the first American President to visit Japan. Ford also visited China in order to continue to improve the political and trade ties that Nixon had initiated. As revolutions in Africa and elsewhere around the world toppled colonial governments, the administration acted to develop relationships with the new regimes.

**War Powers Act** Ford bore the legacy of Nixon's relationship with Congress. Irritated at the growth of the "imperial presidency," Congress had passed the **War Powers Act** in 1973 over Nixon's veto. Under this law, a President can send troops overseas only if there is a declaration of war, a specific law is passed, or if there is a national emergency. There are limits on his emergency powers:

(1) The President can send troops but must notify Congress within 48 hours.

(2) Troops may not stay overseas more than 60 days without congressional approval.

(3) Congress can demand that the President bring troops home by passing a concurrent resolution.

**Southeast Asia** The involvement of the United States in Vietnam was officially over. In the spring of 1975, however, North Vietnam began a new offensive against the South. Ford asked for military aid for South Vietnam, but Congress used the War Powers Act to say no. Most Americans also had no wish to become involved in Vietnam again. By late April, the South Vietnamese capital, Saigon, was about to fall. Ford agreed to an American airlift that helped evacuate thousands of people, both Americans and Vietnamese.

Southeast Asia remained a foreign policy problem. In May 1975, soldiers from Communist Cambodia (which had fallen to the Khmer Rouge) captured the *Mayaguez,* an American merchant ship cruising in Cambodian waters. When protests went unanswered, Ford sent the marines to recapture the ship. Although the rescue succeeded, 41 Americans were killed. Later investigations showed that the Cambodian government apparently was preparing to return both ship and crew. For the administration, however, the incident was a chance to counteract the impression of American weakness in Southeast Asia.

**Europe and the Soviet Union** On another foreign policy front, President Ford signed the

Continuing Nixon's policy of détente, President Ford (right), shown with Soviet General Secretary Leonid Brezhnev (left), signed the Helsinki Accords in Finland in 1975. ***Government*** ***What were the Helsinki Accords?***

**Helsinki Accords,** a series of agreements on European security made at a 1975 summit meeting in Finland. The United States, Canada, the Soviet Union, and about 30 European countries pledged to cooperate economically, respect existing national boundaries, and promote human rights. Ford also continued Strategic Arms Limitation Talks (SALT) with the Soviet Union, holding out hope for further limits on nuclear weapons.

A parade of majestic tall ships during the nation's bicentennial celebration reminded the country of its long and glorious past. ***History*** ***What image do these tall ships portray of the nation's past?***

## *The Nation's Birthday*

Looking for a way to forget Watergate and the recession, Americans held a nationwide birthday party. July 4, 1976, marked the **bicentennial,** or the 200th anniversary, of the Declaration of Independence. Throughout the summer, people in small towns and great cities across the country celebrated with parades, concerts, air shows, political speeches, and fireworks.

The climax of the national party was the Fourth of July itself. In New York City, more than 200 sailing ships, including majestic "tall ships," sailed into the harbor while millions watched from the shore. Other cities competed to have the most spectacular fireworks display or the longest parade. Many observers saw the bicentennial mood as an optimistic revival after years of gloom.

## SECTION 1 REVIEW

### Comprehension

1. *Key Terms* Define: (a) stagflation; (b) recession; (c) War Powers Act; (d) Helsinki Accords; (e) bicentennial.
2. *Summarizing the Main Idea* What were the major issues facing Gerald Ford when he became President?
3. *Organizing Information* Create a web with *U.S. Economy* at the center, showing the different problems and pressures that affected the economy during the 1970s.

### Critical Thinking

4. *Analyzing Time Lines* Review the time line at the start of the section. Write a sentence that explains the broader effect of each event.
5. *Predicting Consequences* Should Gerald Ford have pardoned Richard Nixon? What might have happened if he had not done so?

### Writing Activity

6. *Writing an Expository Essay* Imagine that you are the editorial writer for a local newspaper in 1976. Write the lead editorial for the bicentennial edition of the paper, explaining the historical background of this event and why it is still important.

February 1976 Jimmy Carter wins New Hampshire primary

August 1976 Gerald Ford wins Republican nomination

November 1976 Carter wins presidential election

January 1977 Jimmy Carter is sworn in as President

1976 — 1977

# 2 The Carter Transition

## SECTION PREVIEW

### Objectives

1 Explain the background and outcome of the 1976 presidential election.
2 Describe Barbara Jordan's political career.
3 Summarize the changes that Carter brought to the office of the presidency.
4 *Key Terms* Define: incumbent.

### Main Idea

Partly in reaction to Watergate, voters in 1976 elected a little-known Democrat, Jimmy Carter of Georgia, who stressed trust and honesty in his campaign for the presidency.

### Reading Strategy

*Outlining Information* Write *Jimmy Carter* in the center of a web diagram. As you read the section, note major details about Carter in surrounding circles.

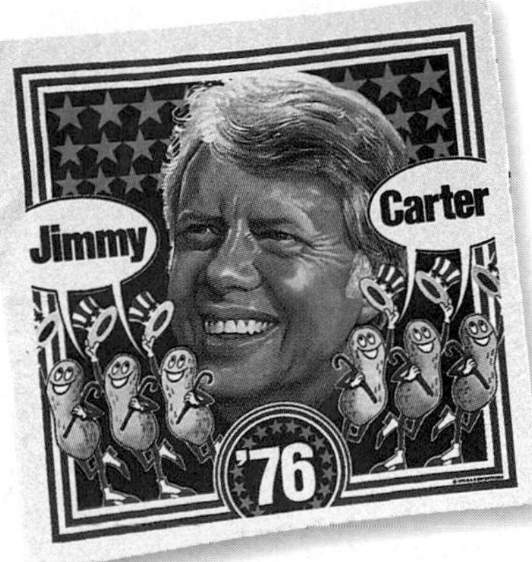


*One writer described Jimmy Carter's famous smile as "the biggest grin of any President since TR."*

The 1976 party conventions brought surprises for both political parties. Even though Ford was the **incumbent**—the current office holder—he faced strong opposition from conservatives inside his own Republican party. At the beginning of the campaign, few Americans even recognized the name of Jimmy Carter, a former governor of Georgia. "Jimmy who?" they asked. By the time of the convention, though, James Earl Carter, Jr., easily won the Democratic nomination.

## The Election of 1976

Gerald Ford had initially said that he would not seek election to the office he had inherited, but by 1976 he had changed his mind. A number of qualities, however, continued to hurt his chances. While most people liked him, they said that Ford did not appear "presidential," and he never fully won the people's confidence. The press joked about his supposed clumsiness. Ford faced a strong challenge in the primaries from Ronald Reagan, an affable former actor and governor of California, who was backed by conservative Republicans. At the convention in August, Ford won the nomination by a close vote. He chose Kansas senator Robert Dole as his vice-presidential running mate.

**Carter's Campaign** The Democratic candidate, Jimmy Carter, was a relative newcomer to politics. Nationally, he began as a virtual unknown with a broad smile and soft southern accent. After taking the New Hampshire primary in February, he kept up a skillful campaign and appealed to a wide audience. A white southerner, Carter had the support of civil rights leaders because of his stand against racial discrimination in Georgia. His running mate was Walter Mondale, a senator from Minnesota.

Carter's campaign played on the distrust of politicians that followed Watergate. He stressed that he was not a lawyer and not part of the Washington establishment. He said he would bring a new perspective to the nation's capital. Carter emphasized the themes of honesty and straightforwardness.

Carter's appeal succeeded. The basic issue in 1976 was trust, and he used it well. His status as an outsider was another advantage. Patrick Caddell, a public opinion pollster, noted that people "had no reason to distrust him [Carter] and he didn't give them one." In addition, the state of the economy hurt Ford's chances.

**Election Results** Carter took an early lead in the campaign. He then nearly lost it as voters wondered whether he could be a national leader. Ford hurt his own cause with a number of embarrassing mistakes. During a television debate, for instance, he declared that the Soviets did not dominate Eastern Europe.

In the end, Carter gained the support of most factions of the old Democratic coalition. He was successful with blue-collar, African American, and some Catholic voters. Also, as the map at right shows, he won back most of the South. Though Democrats in races for Congress and local contests generally swept the election, Carter had only a narrow margin of the popular vote. The electoral vote, 297 to 240, was also close.

## Presidential Election of 1976

| Candidate/Party | Electoral Vote | Popular Vote | % Electoral Vote | % Popular Vote |
|---|---|---|---|---|
| Jimmy Carter (Democrat) | 297 | 40,827,394 | 55.3 | 49.9 |
| Gerald R. Ford (Republican) | 240 | 39,145,977 | 44.7 | 47.9 |
| Minor parties | | 1,577,333 | | 2.2 |

Notice the regional voting pattern shown in this map. ***Regions*** ***What do you know about each candidate's background that might help to explain it?***

# *Barbara Jordan*

**AMERICAN BIOGRAPHY** Jimmy Carter's nomination was not the only exciting event of the 1976 Democratic National Convention in New York City. Another highlight was the stirring keynote speech by Representative Barbara Jordan of Texas. Jordan was both the first woman and the first African American to address a national convention. In a rich, deep speaking voice, she pointed out that there was "something special about tonight":

**AMERICAN VOICES** **"A lot of years have passed since 1832 [the first Democratic convention] and during that time it would have been most unusual for any national political party to ask that Barbara Jordan deliver a keynote address, but tonight here I am. And I feel notwithstanding the past that my presence here is one additional bit of evidence that the American Dream need not forever be deferred."**

—*Barbara Jordan*

Barbara Jordan's political career included many "firsts." Born in Houston in 1936, she grew up in a segregated southern society. She graduated from Texas Southern University, where she led the debating team, then earned a law degree from Boston University in 1959. She considered staying in the North but returned to Houston to practice law. She was elected to the Texas state legislature in 1966—the first African American in the state senate since Reconstruction. People

*Barbara Jordan (1936–1996)*

Abandoning the traditional limousine ride, President Jimmy Carter takes an inaugural stroll with his wife, Rosalynn, and daughter, Amy. ***Government*** ***How did Carter hope to be a different kind of President?***

soon recognized Jordan as an outstanding leader and an inspiring speaker. In June 1972, fellow members of the state legislature named her "Governor for a Day," a traditional honor for outstanding state legislators.

Winning election to the House of Representatives that fall, Jordan was again "first"—the first woman and the first African American from Texas. As a member of the House Judiciary Committee, Jordan took part in the Watergate hearings in July 1974. Her strong opinions were based on her belief that Nixon's actions threatened the Constitution.

Jordan was reelected to the House for two more terms, in 1974 and 1976. Retiring from politics in 1978, she taught political ethics at the Lyndon B. Johnson School of Public Affairs (University of Texas). Jordan was again the keynote speaker at the Democratic convention in 1992. She died in 1996. ■

## Carter's Presidency

Jimmy Carter, a southerner with no national political experience, was different from his recent predecessors in the White House. His family had lived for generations in the rural South. A 1946 graduate of the United States Naval Academy, Carter served as an engineering officer on nuclear submarines. When his father died, he took over management of the family's prosperous peanut farm and warehouse. He did not enter politics until 1962, and was elected governor of Georgia in 1970.

**Main Idea CONNECTIONS**

*How did Carter's background shape his approach to the presidency?*

Carter was a born-again Baptist who noted that his life had been "shaped in the church." His deeply felt religious faith was central to his view of the world. His faith, he believed, would keep him from taking on "the same frame of mind that Nixon or Johnson did—lying, cheating, and distorting the truth."

While holding his own strong religious beliefs, Carter respected those of others. In campaigning he emphasized his belief in the "absolute and total separation of church and state." In Georgia, for instance, he had opposed prayer in the public schools.

**Approach to the Presidency** In the first months of Carter's presidency, he appeared to be a strong supporter of social programs and political activism. When he accepted his party's nomination, he demanded "an end to discrimination because of race or sex." He also challenged the established "political and economic elite" and suggested new welfare and health care programs.

The new President appointed significantly more women and minorities to his staff than previous administrations had done. Of about 1,200 full-time appointees, 12 percent were women, 12 percent were African American, and another 4 percent were Hispanic. In nominating federal judges, he chose four times as many women as had all previous Presidents combined.

In other areas, especially the economy, Carter moved away from Democratic stands. He supported spending cuts, which were meant to reduce inflation but which hit social programs. As a result, support from his own party began to dwindle. Since he had won by only a narrow margin, other Democrats felt they owed him less than if he had had a sweeping victory. The press, too, became more critical as the Carter presidency seemed to lose its momentum.

**Staff Problems** The "Washington outsider" role turned out to have disadvantages. The White House staff and other close advisers were also southerners, mostly Georgians. They had little sense of how crucial it was for the President to work with Congress. Carter himself was uneasy with Congress's demands and found it difficult to get legislation passed. He had no experience or former colleagues in Congress. He lacked Lyndon Johnson's ability to win over reluctant politicians.

Carter also suffered from hints of scandal in an administration that took pride in being pure. Banker Bert Lance, the director of the Office of Management and Budget, was an old friend from Georgia. When Lance was accused of having allowed large bank overdrafts and other irregularities in his bank, Carter at first strongly defended him. Finally Carter had to conclude that Lance must resign.

Carter's brother Billy posed another problem. He was an irreverent character who relished the attention he received as part of the presidential family. His careless comments were embarrassing. When he accepted $200,000 in "loans" from friends in Libya, it looked as if family business was entwined with foreign affairs.

**Personal Style** At first, people responded warmly to Carter's "down home" approach.

The Carters brought a folksy style to the presidency. In spite of the President's low-key image, he was known among friends as a "super-achiever." One friend called Carter "the most disciplined person I've ever seen." ***Government*** ***Why do you think Carter's style appealed to many people?***

They loved it when he and his wife, Rosalynn, dismissed their limousine after the inauguration and strolled down Pennsylvania Avenue with their young daughter. He spoke to the nation on television wearing a cardigan sweater instead of a business suit. He cut out many of the ceremonial details of White House life, such as trumpets to announce his entrance at official receptions. Some critics, however, began to complain about a lack of dignity and ceremony.

Carter finally moderated his low-key approach. After a while, he let the band play "Hail to the Chief" on "special occasions," noting, "I found it to be impressive and enjoyed it."

## SECTION 2 REVIEW

### Comprehension

1. *Key Terms* Define: incumbent.
2. *Summarizing the Main Idea* What were the major issues that won the presidency for Jimmy Carter?
3. *Organizing Information* Create a two-column chart to compare the two candidates in the 1976 election.

### Critical Thinking

4. *Analyzing Time Lines* Review the time line at the start of the section. Write a sentence or phrase that explains the significance of each event.
5. *Identifying Central Issues* What was special about having Barbara Jordan as the keynote speaker at the 1976 Democratic convention?

### Writing Activity

6. *Writing a Persuasive Essay* Imagine that you are the chairperson of a political rally for either Jerry Ford or Jimmy Carter during the 1976 campaign. Write the speech in which you will introduce your candidate, stressing ideas and issues that will make the audience welcome and support him.

**1977** *Carter signs Panama Canal treaties*

**1978** *Egypt and Israel work toward peace in the Camp David Accords*

**1979** *U.S. establishes diplomatic relations with People's Republic of China*

**1979** *Carter and Brezhnev sign SALT II agreement*

**1979** *Iranian revolutionaries take Americans hostage*

**1981** *Iranian hostages return home*

**1977** **1979** **1981**

# 3 Carter's Foreign Policy

## SECTION PREVIEW

### Objectives

1. Explain Carter's support for human rights and his accomplishments in the Middle East.
2. Discuss the new policy directions Carter took in foreign affairs and the complex relationship between the United States and the Soviet Union.
3. Describe how the Iran hostage crisis began and ended.
4. *Key Terms* Define: shuttle diplomacy; Camp David Accords; dissident.

### Main Idea

Carter's religious beliefs and principles led him to emphasize peacemaking and human rights in foreign affairs. This approach brought some notable results but caused disagreements with the Soviet Union and a crisis with Iran.

### Reading Strategy

*Formulating Questions* Reread the main idea above. Then rewrite it as a question. As you read the section, look for answers to your question.

Although Jimmy Carter had little diplomatic experience when he took office, his personal high standards greatly influenced decisions he made about foreign affairs. During the campaign he had declared, "Peace is the unceasing effort to preserve human rights . . . a combined demonstration of strength and goodwill." The emphasis he placed on human rights brought notable achievements, but complicated the relationship of the United States with some nations.

## Human Rights Diplomacy

Support for human rights was the cornerstone of Carter's foreign policy. In his inaugural speech, he declared, "Our commitment to human rights must be absolute. . . . We can never be indifferent to the fate of freedom elsewhere."

Later Carter wrote, "Our country has been strongest and most effective when morality and a commitment to freedom and democracy have been most clearly emphasized in our foreign policy." Since the Truman era the country had not kept to that standard, he went on:

**AMERICAN VOICES** "Instead of promoting freedom and democratic principles, our government seemed to believe that in any struggle with evil, we could not compete effectively unless we played by the same rules or lack of rules as the evildoers. . . . When I announced my candidacy in December 1974, I expressed a dream: 'That this country set a standard within the community of nations of courage, compassion, integrity, and dedication to basic human rights and freedoms.'"

—*Jimmy Carter*

## A Step Toward Middle East Peace

Carter's commitment to finding ethical solutions to complicated problems was most visible in the Middle East. In that unstable region, conflicts between Israel and the Arab nations had existed for nearly 30 years, most recently in 1967 and 1973. After the last Arab-Israeli war, Henry Kissinger had undertaken **shuttle diplomacy,** traveling back and forth between nations in an attempt to arrange peace. Differences still remained.

At first, Carter hoped to call an international conference on the Middle East. Then Egypt's president Anwar el-Sadat made a historic visit to Israel to begin negotiations with Prime Minister Menachem Begin. The two men had such different personalities, however, that they had trouble compromising. Carter intervened, sending Secretary of State Cyrus Vance to invite them to Camp David, the rustic presidential retreat in the Maryland hills. In such a setting, he hoped that he could smooth their differences and move the peace process forward.

Carter knew it was a bold step. In his diary entry for July 31, 1978, he wrote, "We understand the political pitfalls involved, but the situation is getting into an extreme state." He and the two Middle Eastern leaders maintained tight secrecy about the coming conference.

At Camp David in September 1978, Carter assumed the role of peacemaker. He practiced highly effective personal diplomacy to bridge the gap between Sadat and Begin. They finally agreed on a framework for peace that became known as the **Camp David Accords.** Under the resulting peace treaty, Israel would withdraw from the Sinai peninsula, which it had occupied in 1967. Egypt, in return, became the first Arab country to recognize Israel's existence as a nation.

The Camp David Accords, of course, did not solve all the problems of the Middle East. Among the remaining problems was the question of what to do about the Palestinians. Many had fled their homes when Arab nations declared war on Israel immediately after that country was established in 1948. Still, as Secretary of State Vance noted:

AMERICAN VOICES **"The Camp David Accords rank as one of the most important achievements of the Carter administration. First, they opened the way to peace between Egypt and Israel, which transformed the entire political, military, and strategic character of the Middle East dispute. Genuine peace between Egypt and Israel meant there would be no major Arab-Israeli war, whatever the positions of [other Arab groups]."**

—*Cyrus Vance*

Moreover, Vance pointed out, the agreement also let negotiators focus on the Palestinian question. It established a process for future talks.

A jubilant President Carter congratulates Egypt's President Sadat (left) and Israel's Prime Minister Begin (right) on the signing of the Camp David Accords. ***Foreign Relations*** *What were the major achievements of the accords?*

## *New Policy Directions*

Carter's foreign policy team took new steps in other parts of the world as well. Often these reflected the President's own philosophy. In Latin America, for example, the United States had for years backed military dictators against Communist or leftist rebels. Now the United States stopped helping regimes that seriously abused human rights, such as those in Nicaragua and Chile.

**Main Idea CONNECTIONS**

*How did Carter's principles influence his policies regarding Latin America?*

**The Panama Canal** Another diplomatic milestone was Carter's successful fight to have the Senate ratify treaties that would return the Panama Canal to Panama. In the early 1900s, President Theodore Roosevelt was proud of the way he had gained control of land for the canal. Now, however, many Latin Americans resented the continuing United States presence. For Carter, the treaties were a way to show that the United States could deal fairly with smaller nations.

The canal treaties, signed in 1977, caused bitter debate in Congress. In 1978 the Senate

President Carter and Soviet president Leonid Brezhnev sign SALT II in Vienna, Austria. Carter believed that the arms limitation agreement would "make the world a safer place for both sides." ***Foreign Relations*** ***Why did relations with the Soviets worsen, despite SALT II?***

*What were the main provisions of the Panama Canal treaties?*

approved them by a margin of one vote. One treaty was an agreement to return the canal to Panama by the year 2000. The other gave the United States the right to take military action to keep it open. The pacts protected American interests while improving relations with Latin America.

**Recognition of China** Building on Nixon's initiative in Asia, Carter took the next step. He established diplomatic relations with the People's Republic of China as of January 1979. The Chinese wanted American technology and expertise in modernizing their country. The United States hoped that closer ties with China would provide an advantage in dealing with the Soviet Union. Businesses in the United States also were eager to open the Chinese market of nearly a billion people.

**Africa** Great changes were taking place in Africa, where independent nations that had once been European colonies were struggling to create prosperity. Carter had named civil rights leader Andrew Young as the U.S. ambassador to the United Nations. Young played a large role in policies toward Africa.

Carter called for rule by the black majority in South Africa and in Rhodesia. He also declared that Cuba and the Soviet Union should stop interfering in African nations. When Carter visited Nigeria and Liberia in March 1978, the popularity of this approach was evident as thousands cheered him in the streets.

## *Soviet-American Relations*

Several issues complicated the relationship between the United States and the Soviet Union. Détente—a relaxation of the tensions between the superpowers—was at a high point when Carter took office. In his first year, he declared optimistically that the United States and Soviet Union would forge even closer ties.

Then Carter's stand on human rights alienated Soviet leaders, undermining efforts to work together. The Soviets were annoyed when the President spoke in support of Soviet **dissidents**—writers and other activists who criticized the actions of their government.

**SALT II** The discord directly affected further agreements on arms control. Negotiations were already under way for a second round of Strategic Arms Limitation Talks (SALT II). Misjudging the Soviets, Carter offered new weapons reduction proposals that went further than earlier agreements. The Soviets were already suspicious of Carter and balked at the proposals.

Nevertheless, in June 1979, Carter and Soviet leader Leonid Brezhnev signed a new treaty in Vienna. More complicated than SALT I, it limited the number of nuclear warheads and missiles each power retained. SALT II still needed Senate approval. Its backers said it would slow the arms race. Opponents claimed it would weaken American defenses.

**Afghanistan** Late in 1979, before the Senate could ratify SALT II, the Soviet Union invaded Afghanistan, a country on its southern border. It sent troops to end agitation against the Soviet-supported government there.

Carter quickly called Brezhnev on the "hot line," the open telephone line between

Washington and Moscow, and told him that the invasion was "a clear threat to the peace." He also added, "Unless you draw back from your present course of action, this will inevitably jeopardize the course of United States–Soviet relations throughout the world." A United Nations resolution also called for Soviet withdrawal.

Carter halted grain shipments and took other steps to show disapproval of Soviet aggression. Realizing that SALT II surely would be turned down, he did not send it to the Senate. He also imposed a boycott on the 1980 summer Olympic Games to be held in Moscow. Eventually, some 60 other nations joined the Olympic boycott.† Détente was effectively dead.

## *The Iran Hostage Crisis*

Iran, Afghanistan's neighbor to the west, was the scene of the worst foreign policy crisis of the Carter administration. For years the United States had supported the rule of Muhammed Reza Shah Pahlevi, who had taken many steps to modernize Iran. Americans overlooked the corruption and harsh repression of the shah's government because he was a reliable supplier of oil and a pro-Western force. Carter himself praised the shah on a visit to Tehran, Iran's capital, in late 1977.

In January 1979, revolution broke out in Iran. It was led by Muslim fundamentalists, who wanted to bring back traditional ways, and by liberal critics of the shah, who wanted more political and economic reforms. As the revolution spread, the shah fled the country. He was replaced by an elderly Islamic leader, the Ayatollah Ruholla Khomeini, who had been in exile.†† Khomeini and his followers were aggressively anti-Western, determined to make Iran a strict Islamic state.

In October, in what was intended as a humanitarian gesture, Carter let the exiled shah enter the United States for medical treatment. Many Iranians were outraged. On November 4, 1979, angry followers of Khomeini seized the American embassy in Tehran. They took 66 Americans hostage, mostly embassy workers. More than 50 men and women were held for over a year. The situation caused bitter animosity between the United States and Iran.

**The Hostages' Ordeal** For 444 days, revolutionaries kept the hostages prisoner in different locations. The prisoners were blindfolded and moved from place to place. Some were tied up and beaten. Others spent time in solitary confinement and faced mock executions intended to keep them constantly afraid.

Kathryn Koob, a cultural exchange official, described part of her experiences:

**AMERICAN VOICES** **"And the sounds outside the embassy were nerve-wracking. . . . There seemed to be a continuous crowd of people shouting anti-American slogans, listening to the exhortations [cries] of the students and mullahs [clergymen] who were always on hand. In addition to the crowd noises, there were three or four loudspeakers blaring newscasts. . . . As I sat confined in my chair I thought, I can't take this, I just can't take this."**

—*Kathryn Koob*

Meanwhile, the American public became increasingly frustrated and impatient for the hostages' release. Nightly newscasts made the crisis a national issue.

In spite of the sentiments of anti-American Iranians, personnel from the United States embassy in Tehran, Iran, were freed after being held hostage for more than a year. ***Foreign Relations*** ***How did Carter try to resolve the hostage crisis?***

† In retaliation, the Soviet Union and several other Communist nations boycotted the 1984 Olympic games hosted by the United States in Los Angeles, California.

†† *Ayatollah* is a title given to a Shiite Muslim religious leader.

VIEWING HISTORY Jubilant Americans returned home after being held hostage by Iranians. ***Foreign Relations*** *How did Carter's handling of the hostage crisis affect his career?*

**The End of the Crisis** People expected the President to secure the hostages' freedom. He tried many approaches. He broke diplomatic relations with Iran and froze all Iranian assets in the United States. Khomeini held out, insisting that the shah be sent back for trial. Under pressure, in April 1980, Carter authorized a risky commando rescue mission. It ended in disaster when several helicopters broke down in the desert sands and eight American soldiers were killed. The government was humiliated, and Carter's popularity dropped further. Even after the shah died in July, the standoff continued. The unending crisis damaged Carter's chances for reelection.

Carter himself was torn apart by the crisis. At one point, just weeks after the Americans had been taken prisoner, he confided his feelings to Hamilton Jordan, one of his closest aides:

> **AMERICAN VOICES** **"You know, I've been worried all week about the hostages as a problem for the country and as a political problem for me. But it wasn't until I saw the grief and hope on the faces of their wives and mothers and fathers that I felt the personal responsibility for their lives. It's an awesome burden."**
>
> —*President Carter*

After months of secret talks, the Iranians agreed to release the 52 remaining hostages in early 1981. Not until the day Carter left office, however, were they allowed to come home. The new President, Ronald Reagan, sent Carter to greet the freed hostages as they arrived at a United States military base in West Germany.

## SECTION 3 REVIEW

### Comprehension

1. *Key Terms* Define: (a) shuttle diplomacy; (b) Camp David Accords; (c) dissident.
2. *Summarizing the Main Idea* What ideals guided foreign policy during the Carter administration?
3. *Organizing Information* Create a flowchart tracing the progress of Soviet-American diplomatic relations during the Carter administration.

### Critical Thinking

4. *Analyzing Time Lines* Review the time line at the start of the section. Write a sentence that explains the broader effect of each event.
5. *Making Comparisons* Give examples of the positive and negative results of Carter's approach to foreign policy.

### Writing Activity

6. *Writing a Persuasive Essay* How much should human rights influence foreign policy? Write an editorial setting out your ideas on when it is and is not appropriate to ignore human rights concerns in dealing with other nations.

# SKILLS FOR LIFE

**Critical Thinking**

Geography

Graphs and Charts

Historical Evidence

## Recognizing Ideologies

An ideology is a set of beliefs that guide a person, a group, or a culture. If you can recognize ideologies, you can better understand why certain actions are taken or statements are made. Use the following steps to help you recognize the ideologies behind two opposing statements in the debate over the Panama Canal treaties.

**1.** ***Identify the main topic of the statements and the people who made them.*** (a) What is the subject in these statements? (b) Who made each statement? (c) In which branch of government does each speaker serve? (d) To what party does each belong?

**2.** ***Locate the major points that each speaker makes.*** (a) What reasons does Speaker A give for rejecting the proposed change? (b) What reasons does Speaker B give for accepting it?

**3.** ***Identify the beliefs that underlie the reasons given.*** (a) What does Speaker A believe about the rights of property with regard to the Panama Canal? (b) What attribute of the national character does he believe should guide American foreign policy? (c) What does Speaker B believe about the role of fairness with regard to the canal? (d) What attributes of national character does he think should guide American foreign policy?

### TEST FOR SUCCESS

Choose a current issue before Congress and find speeches or articles expressing different points of view about it. Identify (a) the background of each person in the debate and (b) the beliefs that underlie his or her opinion.

**A**

The case for rejecting the proposed treat[ies] . . . begins with one crucial point: The Panama Canal is United States property, and the Canal Zone is United States territory. According to the terms of the 1903 treaty with Panama, we acquired sovereign rights over the Canal Zone "in perpetuity" [forever]. The Supreme Court upheld our exercise of sovereignty in 1907. . . . Moreover, the maps of the world show the Canal Zone as part of the United States.

Thus, it is clear that the burden of proof rests on those who favor the treaties; those who oppose them are merely standing up for American rights. Proponents must show that it is in the national interest to dispose of American property which, in addition to its strategic and economic value, represents a cumulative investment of roughly $7 billion.

. . . Would we give up Alaska to the Russians if they were suddenly to demand it? Such weakness is entirely contrary to our national character and heritage.

*—Strom Thurmond, Republican (South Carolina), "Why the U.S. Should Keep the Panama Canal,"* The Christian Science Monitor, *September 13, 1977*

**B**

The most important reason, the only reason, to ratify the treaties is that they are in the highest national interest of the United States and will strengthen our position in the world. Our security interest will be stronger; our trade opportunities will be improved. We will demonstrate that as a large and powerful country we are able to deal fairly and honorably with a proud but smaller sovereign nation.

. . . We Americans want a more humane and stable world. We believe in goodwill and fairness as well as strength. This agreement with Panama is something we want because we know it is right.

. . . If Theodore Roosevelt were to endorse the treaties, as I'm quite sure he would, it would be mainly because he could see the decision as one by which we are demonstrating the kind of great power we wish to be. . . . In this historic decision, he would join us in our pride for being a great and generous people with a national strength and wisdom to do what is right for us and what is fair to others.

*—President Jimmy Carter, televised speech, February 1, 1978*

**1977** *Carter grants amnesty to Vietnam War draft evaders*

**1977** *Carter presents energy conservation program*

**1977** *Department of Energy created*

**1978** *Supreme Court decides Bakke case*

**1978** *Airline deregulation begins*

**1979** *Nuclear accident at Three Mile Island, Pennsylvania*

**1977** | **1978** | **1979**

# 4 Carter's Domestic Issues

## SECTION PREVIEW

### Objectives

1. Describe the economic instability facing the Carter administration.
2. List the elements of Carter's energy policy.
3. Summarize other domestic issues that weakened Carter's presidency and the outcome of the 1980 presidential election.
4. *Key Terms* Define: deregulation; amnesty; affirmative action.

### Main Idea

Facing problems with the economy, Carter had trouble getting legislation through Congress and winning strong public support for his energy program and other policies.

### Reading Strategy

*Reading for Evidence* As you read the section, look for evidence to support the statement below that President Carter "had little success in programs at home."

*Oil shortages caused American drivers to face long lines at the gas pumps—when gas was available.*

Jimmy Carter had little success in programs at home. He could not find a way to work effectively with Congress, which blocked his plans in many areas, especially energy and the economy. Looking back, he wrote, "I quickly learned that it is a lot easier to hold a meeting, reach a tentative agreement, or make a speech than to get a controversial program through Congress."

That was not the only problem. As *The New York Times* columnist Tom Wicker observed, Carter "never established a politically coherent administration." His strategies were not clearly defined. Public support faded as his programs floundered.

## More Economic Instability

Carter inherited an unstable economy. Like his predecessors, he had trouble controlling inflation without hurting growth. Inflation had also been a problem for Ford, but had seemed under control after the recession in 1974–1976. Carter tried to prevent another recession by stimulating growth with government deficit spending. As deficits grew, the Federal Reserve Board increased the money supply, but inflation then rose to about 10 percent.

**Spending Cuts** In an attempt to stop inflation, slow the economy, and reduce the deficit, Carter cut spending. The cuts fell mostly on social programs, which angered liberal Democrats. At the same time, the slowdown in the economy increased unemployment and the number of business failures. Things got worse in 1980, when the new federal budget called for continued high spending. In reaction, bond prices fell and interest rates soared. Borrowers were angry at having to pay high interest rates—sometimes over 20 percent—for mortgages and other loans.

People lost confidence in Carter and his economic advisers. The administration's back-and-forth efforts—trying first one approach, then another—gave the impression that it had no idea what was happening or how to fix it.

**Deregulation** Another economic move was toward **deregulation**—the reduction or

## Comparison of Energy Sources

| Source | Advantages | Disadvantages |
|---|---|---|
| Oil | • Currently widely available to consumers.<br>• Relatively affordable. | • Nonrenewable resource.<br>• Supplies are concentrated in relatively few regions.<br>• Oil exploration, production, and transportation risk oil spills and other environmental damage.<br>• Significant source of air pollution. |
| Natural Gas | • Low emission levels of air pollutants, carbon monoxide, and solid wastes such as sludge and ash. | • Nonrenewable resource.<br>• Majority of gas reserves located in just a few countries.<br>• Difficult to transport. |
| Coal | • Most abundant nonrenewable energy source.<br>• Least expensive of the fossil fuels. | • Nonrenewable resource.<br>• Major source of air pollution.<br>• Contributes to chronic and acute respiratory conditions.<br>• Strip mining causes extensive erosion. |
| Nuclear Energy | • Uses uranium, a naturally occurring element. One ton of uranium can be used to produce more than 10,000 times the amount of electricity of a ton of oil. | • Produces hazardous radioactive waste that is difficult to dispose of safely.<br>• Mechanical or human error could have serious or fatal results for workers and the general population. |
| Solar Energy | • Unlimited resource.<br>• Produces no pollutants. | • Present equipment too expensive to put into general usage. |
| Wind Energy | • Unlimited resource.<br>• Produces no pollutants.<br>• Considered most environmentally safe energy source. | • Location has direct bearing on the productivity of the plant.<br>• Wind doesn't always blow at adequate speeds. |
| Hydroelectric Power | • Renewable resource.<br>• Produces no pollutants. | • Hydroelectric dams alter the environment.<br>• Large dams can occasionally flood acres of productive land or wilderness area. |

***Interpreting Tables*** Oil shortages caused by United States dependence on foreign oil fueled the search for alternative forms of energy. ***Geography*** ***Which alternative source seems to have the most advantages? The fewest?***

removal of government controls in several industries. In the late 1800s and early 1900s, agencies such as the Interstate Commerce Commission had been established to regulate rates and business practices. Over the years, regulations had multiplied. Carter now argued that they hurt competition and increased consumer costs.

To encourage greater energy production, Carter proposed removing controls on prices for oil and natural gas. He also took steps to deregulate railroads, trucking, and airlines. While consumer groups and many liberal Democrats opposed deregulation, it continued during the next two administrations, both Republican.

## A Program to Save Energy

Carter made energy conservation a major goal, but he had trouble winning support from Congress and the public. Despite earlier embargoes and shortages, Americans still depended heavily on imported oil. In the late 1970s, more than 40 percent of the oil used in the United States came from other countries. Some thought the country should be more energy self-sufficient. Others urged cutting down overall energy use, warning that oil reserves were limited.

**Main Idea CONNECTIONS**

*How did oil price increases and shortages affect Carter's popularity?*

## Nuclear Power Plant

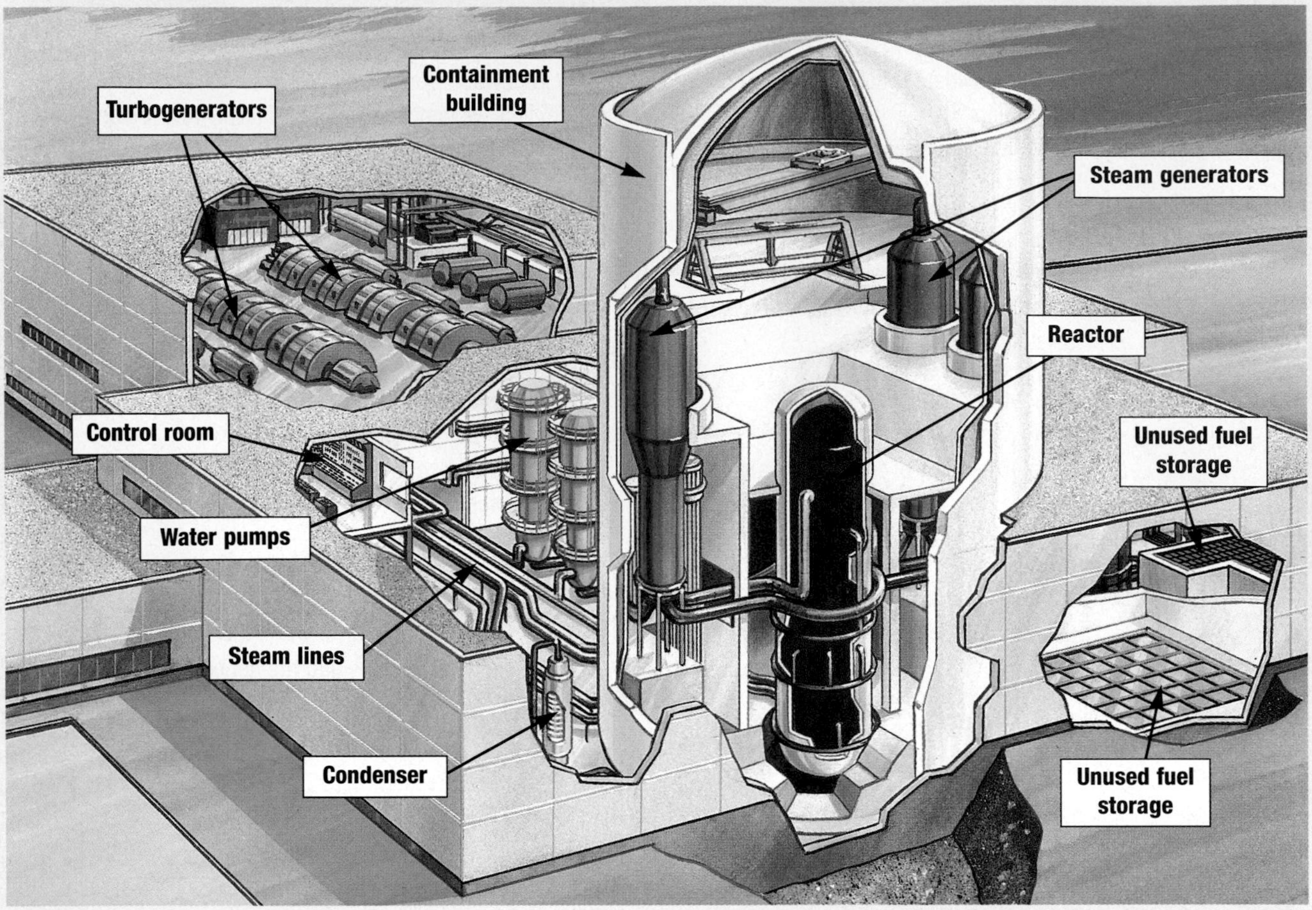

**Inside the reactor, uranium or plutonium atoms are split in half, releasing energy in the form of heat and radiation. The heat is used to heat water and generate steam. Steam pipes carry the steam to the plant's turbogenerators, which produce electricity.** ***Science and Technology*** ***What are the drawbacks of nuclear energy production?***

OPEC, the Organization of Petroleum Exporting Countries, had been raising oil prices steadily since 1973. People grumbled about rising prices, shortages, and long lines at the gas station. Although the President was not responsible for oil prices or shortages, he often was the focus of people's complaints.

In April 1977, Carter presented his comprehensive energy program to Congress and the public. He asked people to save fuel by driving less and by using less fuel to heat or cool their homes and offices. He also created a new Cabinet department, the Department of Energy. It would coordinate various federal programs promoting conservation and looking for new energy sources. Carter took energy problems seriously, calling the need for conservation the "moral equivalent of war." Critics, however, created the acronym MEOW (from the first letter of each word) to make fun of it.

Representatives from states that produced oil and gas fiercely opposed the energy proposals. Many proposals were stalled in Congress for months. In 1978, though, the National Energy Act finally passed. It included these provisions:

(1) taxes on inefficient "gas-guzzling" cars

(2) conversion of new utilities to fuels other than oil or natural gas

(3) deregulation of prices for domestic oil and natural gas

(4) tax credits or loans to homeowners for using solar energy and improving insulation

(5) research funds for alternative energy sources such as solar energy and synthetic fuels.

**Three Mile Island** Nuclear power seemed to be one exciting alternative energy source. Serious questions persisted about its costs and safety, however. Since the 1960s, grassroots activists and some scientists had been criticizing the nuclear power industry. In March 1979, people's doubts seemed to be confirmed by an accident at the nuclear power plant at Three Mile Island, near Harrisburg, Pennsylvania.

A small leak through a faulty seal in the cooling system stopped the pumps that circulated the coolant. Temperatures in the reactor core rose, but plant operators misread the symptoms and shut down an emergency cooling system. A partial meltdown of the core occurred, releasing some radiation. People near the plant were terrified by the idea of a radioactive leak, and 140,000 people fled their homes. The story made headlines around the world.

**The Future of Nuclear Power** Carter named a commission to investigate the accident at Three Mile Island. Its report identified operator errors that had made the initial problem worse. In his response to the report, Carter noted "very serious shortcomings in the way that both the government and the utility industry regulate and manage nuclear power." He proposed reorganizing the Nuclear Regulatory Commission, the agency in charge of nuclear power. He also called on utility companies to improve standards.

In spite of Carter's efforts, the nuclear industry fell on hard times. People were angry at cost overruns in building new plants, which often increased their electric bills. Protesters blocked building sites. Orders for new plants were canceled, and some construction was halted.

## Other Domestic Issues

Carter's concern for moral and humanitarian values influenced his approach to domestic questions as well as foreign policy. Some of his actions were controversial. Soon after taking office, he carried out his promise to grant **amnesty**—a general pardon—to those who had evaded the draft during the Vietnam War. Because that war still divided Americans, reactions were mixed.

**Civil Rights** As governor of Georgia, Carter had had a good civil rights record. During the 1976 campaign, he won African American support with what columnist David Broder called "an eloquence, a simplicity, a directness that moved listeners of both races."

Carter tried to move beyond the civil rights battles of the 1950s and 1960s. As a white southerner himself, he understood the South's need to overcome the negative images of the past decades:

**AMERICAN VOICES** "The most important [message] was that we in the South were ready for reconciliation, to be accepted as equals, to rejoin the mainstream of American political life. This yearning for what might be called political redemption was a significant factor in my successful campaign."

—*Jimmy Carter*

Many of Carter's staff appointments, such as the United Nations ambassadorship for Andrew Young, won the approval of black Americans. On the other hand, his weak support of social programs disappointed many African Americans.

**Affirmative Action** In 1978 the Supreme Court ruled on a civil rights case that had important implications for **affirmative action** policies. Such policies give special consideration to women and members of minorities to make up for past discrimination against them. Allan Bakke, who was white, applied to the medical school at the University of California

## COMPARING PRIMARY SOURCES

### ON NUCLEAR ENERGY

The need to reduce the dependence on foreign oil prompted viewpoints strongly for and against nuclear power.

**In Favor of Nuclear Energy**

"When you debate the issue of nuclear energy, you are actually debating the issue of growth. Growth will be the key issue for the remainder of this century, and it is the resolution of that issue which will determine the lifestyles of most Americans for generations to come. . . . Economic growth has been inextricably linked to the growth of the supply of energy throughout history."

—*Senator James A. McClure (Idaho), address before the National Conference on Energy Advocacy, February 2, 1979*

**Opposed to Nuclear Energy**

"If this country . . . continues to rely more and more on nuclear power a meltdown disaster is almost predictable. . . . For years now, the utilities and nuclear power industry have refused to listen to scientific logic and reasoning concerning the dangers of this technology. . . . Perhaps it is time for emotion and for passion and for commitment to stir our souls and our hearts and our minds once again into action."

—*Dr. Helen Caldicott, in* Nuclear Madness, What You Can Do! *1980*

***ANALYZING VIEWPOINTS*** **What are the main concerns of each of these speakers?**

wrote six separate opinions. While the Court ordered Bakke's admission to the California medical school, it also upheld the school's right to consider race as one factor in admission decisions. It did not, however, allow actual quotas. The Court decision supported the concept of affirmative action, but the case signaled the start of a backlash against the policy.

VIEWING HISTORY

Allan Bakke (above center) sued to gain a spot at the University of California. His case caused some people to march in support of affirmative action. ***Culture*** ***What was the outcome of the trial?***

## The 1980 Election

Despite Carter's notable foreign policy achievements and his commitment to serious goals, his administration lost many people's confidence. Rising inflation in early 1980 dropped his approval rating to 21 percent in public opinion polls. Unemployment was still over 7 percent. At times Carter himself seemed to have lost confidence. In two speeches in July, he spoke of a national "crisis of confidence" and a "national malaise."

In the Democratic primaries leading up to the 1980 elections, Massachusetts Senator Edward M. Kennedy won a large number of delegate votes. Kennedy withdrew, however, just as the Democratic National Convention began, and Carter was nominated again. Nonetheless, many people were ready for the optimism and hopeful rhetoric of the Republican candidate, Ronald Reagan.

(Davis) in 1973 and 1974. After being turned down twice, he sued the school for "reverse discrimination." Bakke charged that the policy of reserving 16 of 100 class spaces for minority group applicants violated both the Civil Rights Act of 1964 and the Constitution.

In a complex ruling in *Regents of the University of California* v. *Bakke,* the justices

## SECTION 4 REVIEW

### Comprehension

1. *Key Terms* Define: (a) deregulation; (b) amnesty; (c) affirmative action.
2. *Summarizing the Main Idea* Why was it difficult for Carter to win public and congressional support for his energy program?
3. *Organizing Information* Create a flow map to show the causes and effects of the Carter administration's economic decisions.

### Critical Thinking

4. *Analyzing Time Lines* Review the time line at the start of the section. Write a paragraph explaining how each event relates to Carter policies.
5. *Demonstrating Reasoned Judgment* Many politicians since 1980 have continued Carter's policy of deregulation. In what ways do you think this policy has helped or hurt consumers?

### Writing Activity

6. *Writing a Persuasive Essay* President Carter had trouble getting Americans to support his efforts to conserve energy. Write a letter to the editor in which you support or oppose such efforts.

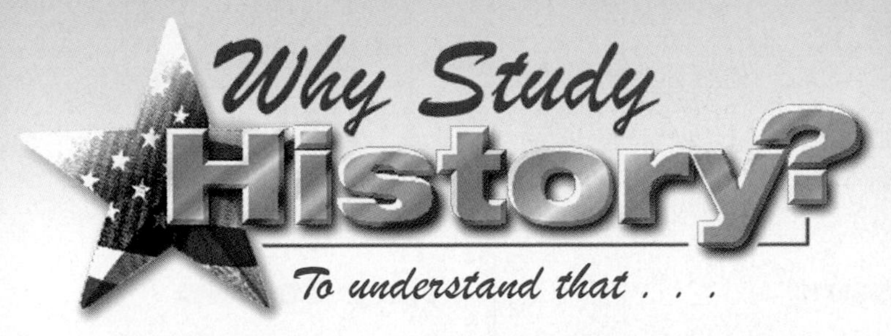


# Americans Are Skeptical About Government

**Since the early 1970s, distrust of government has become widespread, and Americans have become more cynical about their leaders.**

*Vietnam protest march, 1969*

Whom do you trust to make big decisions that affect your life? What about decisions that affect the entire nation? Whom can you trust to make such decisions wisely?

During and after World War II, most Americans trusted the nation's leaders in Washington to solve enormous problems. However, public trust in government plummeted after the Vietnam War and the Watergate scandal. Presidents Ford and Carter tried but largely failed to restore public trust. Today, many Americans do not trust the federal government to solve problems. They believe that the government itself is the problem.

## The Impact Today

In 1964, a national poll showed that 76 percent of Americans trusted Washington to do what is right "always" or "most of the time." By 1997, however, only 22 percent of Americans expressed confidence in the federal government. (State and local governments fared somewhat better in the 1997 poll.) Some Americans resent the cost and size of government or its interference in their lives. Others see a lack of political leadership as the greatest problem.

Despite these bleak statistics, most Americans still believe that government has important responsibilities in areas such as foreign relations, civil rights, environmental protection, health, and safety. Public mistrust of government could make it difficult for government to perform these tasks.

Such mistrust might even threaten the nation's democratic institutions. A cynical public is less likely to vote and participate in other ways in the political process. (Indeed, during the 1950s and 1960s more than 60 percent of Americans usually voted in presidential elections. That percentage has since dropped, falling below 50 percent in 1996.) Mistrustful citizens are also less willing to support their government by paying taxes, obeying laws, and entering public service.

How can government improve its performance to restore Americans' trust? Some suggest that the government draw on the talents of business leaders to improve management of the public sector. Others say cynicism will persist as long as public officials serve their own interests rather than the nation's good.

## The Impact on You

Take a poll of your classmates to find out what they trust about the federal government and what they mistrust about it. Compile the answers into a list. Then use the list to make a bar graph of the top five answers.

DON'T VOTE, IT ONLY ENCOURAGES THEM

*Bumper sticker with a modern message*

# Chapter 23 Review

## Chapter Summary

The major concepts of Chapter 23 are presented below. See also ***Guide to the Essentials of American History*** or ***Interactive Student Tutorial CD-ROM,*** which contains interactive review activities, time lines, helpful hints, and test practice.

### *Reviewing the Main Ideas*

Gerald Ford, who took over as President after Nixon's resignation, also inherited a troubled economy and foreign policy challenges. After two years, he lost the presidency to a little-known Democrat, Jimmy Carter, who campaigned on issues of trust and morality. Along with the aftereffects of Watergate, controlling inflation and unemployment remained problematic for political leaders throughout the 1970s.

### *Section 1: The Ford Administration*

After becoming President, Gerald Ford worked to reunite the country. He faced economic problems at home as well as foreign policy challenges abroad.

### *Section 2: The Carter Transition*

Partly in reaction to Watergate, voters in 1976 elected a little-known Democrat, Jimmy Carter of Georgia, who stressed trust and honesty in his campaign for the presidency.

### *Section 3: Carter's Foreign Policy*

Carter's religious beliefs and principles led him to emphasize peacemaking and human rights in foreign affairs. This approach brought some notable results but caused disagreements with the Soviet Union and a crisis with Iran.

### *Section 4: Carter's Domestic Issues*

Facing problems with the economy, Carter had trouble getting legislation through Congress and winning strong public support for his energy program and other policies.

Since the early 1970s, distrust of government has become widespread, and Americans have become much more cynical about their leaders.

## Key Terms

Use each of the terms below in a sentence that shows how it relates to the chapter.

1. stagflation
2. recession
3. War Powers Act
4. Helsinki Accords
5. bicentennial
6. incumbent
7. Camp David Accords
8. deregulation
9. amnesty
10. affirmative action

## Comprehension

1. What problems did the economy face during the Ford administration? What programs did Ford propose to solve them?
2. What were Ford's reasons for giving a pardon to former President Nixon? What was the public reaction?
3. What authority does Congress gain from the War Powers Act?
4. What were the main issues of the 1976 election? What gave Carter an advantage?
5. How did Carter's lack of Washington experience hurt his administration?
6. What brought about the Iran hostage crisis?
7. What factors made relations with the Soviet Union worse in the late 1970s?

## Using Graphic Organizers

On a separate sheet of paper, copy the tree map to organize the main ideas of the chapter. Each section of the tree map should focus on developments in one political issue in the Ford and Carter administrations: economic policy, foreign policy, civil rights, energy. Supply in your own words the main ideas and supporting details for each section.

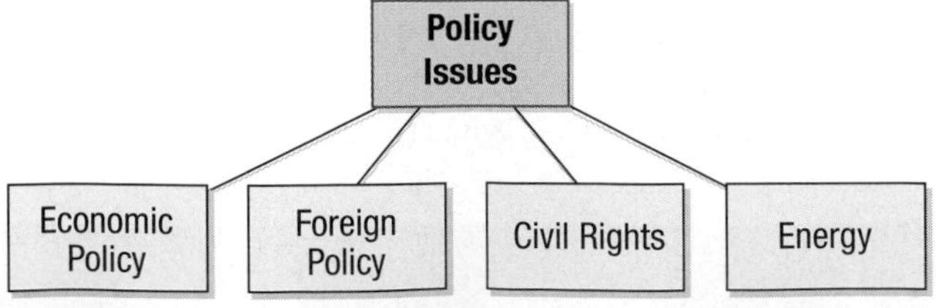

## Analyzing Political Cartoons ▶

1. Examine the images in the cartoon. What is the significance of the two people being seated at the back of the bus?
2. Who is the man on the left?
3. Explain the woman's comment. What is her perspective?
4. What point might the cartoonist be trying to make?

## Critical Thinking

1. *Applying the Chapter Skill* Trying to make peace in the Middle East was a risky move politically. Identify the beliefs that led President Carter to step in as peacemaker between Israel and Egypt.
2. *Checking Consistency* Although people complained about fuel shortages during the 1970s, many did not support Carter's energy program or try to conserve oil and gas. How do you explain this inconsistent behavior?
3. *Drawing Conclusions* Which do you think played a larger role in Congress's refusal to send military aid to South Vietnam in 1975—the War Powers Act or public opinion about involvement in Vietnam?
4. *Identifying Central Issues* In the 1976 election, trust was one of the most important issues. What do you think are the most important issues for voters today when electing a President?

### INTERNET ACTIVITY

***For your portfolio:***
**ORGANIZE A DEBATE**

Access Prentice Hall's *America: Pathways to the Present* site at **www.Pathways.phschool.com** for the specific URLs to complete the activity. Additional resources and related Web sites are also available.

Follow the links to find information that supports a pro- or anti-nuclear position. Then organize a debate on the future of nuclear power as an energy source, considering its benefits and drawbacks.

### ANALYZING DOCUMENTS ▶ INTERPRETING DATA

Turn to the 1976 election map on page 681.

1. Ford won the votes of all the states in the (a) Midwest. (b) West and Southwest. (c) South. (d) Northeast.
2. Why would Carter's winning margin of electoral votes be greater than his margin of the popular vote? (a) He won more states than Ford. (b) He won states with more electoral votes. (c) He won states with smaller populations. (d) He lost only states in the West.
3. *Writing* Using this map and the rest of the chapter, write two paragraphs that explain why each candidate appealed to different groups of voters and different regions of the country.

## Connecting to Today

*Essay Writing* Reread the account of the 1979–1981 Iranian hostage crisis. Then research newspapers and news magazines and write an essay explaining how that event has affected U.S.-Iran relations since that time.

CHAPTER

# 24 The Conservative Revolution

## 1980–1992

**VIEWING HISTORY**
Ronald Reagan's genial personality helped make him a popular President. His wife, Nancy, strongly influenced his decision making. *Government* ***Why do you think Americans chose a conservative President in 1980?***

## CHAPTER FOCUS

*This chapter examines the rise of conservatives to power in the 1980s, beginning with the election of President Ronald Reagan. It looks at the shift in values and policies that occurred in government during the Reagan and Bush presidencies and details the key events of their combined 12 years in office.*

*The **Why Study History?** page at the end of this chapter explores the connection between Reagan's efforts to reduce the size and scope of the federal government and such efforts today.*

**1964**
*In setback for conservatives, Johnson crushes Goldwater in presidential race*

**1965**
*Great Society program expands government's role*

**1968**
*Nixon elected President, restoring Republican power*

**1973**
*Roe v. Wade legalizes abortion, mobilizes conservatives*

**1980**
*Conservatives triumph as Reagan elected President*

**1960** **1965** **1970** **1975** **1980**

# 1 Roots of the New Conservatism

## SECTION PREVIEW

### Objectives

1. Outline the major events in Ronald Reagan's political career.
2. Trace the rise of modern political conservatism.
3. Evaluate the significance of the election of 1980.
4. *Key Terms* Define: New Right; televangelism.

### Main Idea

After decades of government growth and social and cultural change, a conservative backlash grew during the 1970s. In 1980 it brought Ronald Reagan to power.

### Reading Strategy

*Arranging Events in Order* As you read, make a list of dates that mark major events in the development of the conservative movement from the 1930s to 1980.

The inauguration of Ronald Reagan in early 1981 marked a major shift in American politics. The new President voiced the growing frustrations of voters around the country who believed that government had grown too large and had lost touch with the needs of the people. Reagan's own political journey reflected the growing conservatism of millions of Americans.

## Reagan's Political Career

Reagan was originally a Democrat and voted for Franklin D. Roosevelt, architect of the New Deal, in 1932. When Reagan began his career as a movie actor in Hollywood, he became actively involved in the political affairs of the actors' union.

After World War II, Reagan found himself less comfortable with the Democratic party and joined the Republican party. In the 1950s he served as a spokesman for General Electric, making speeches praising capitalism and attacking government regulation. He also spoke out strongly against Communists in the United States. Ronald Reagan was now clearly in the conservative camp.

Reagan gained national attention in 1966, when he was elected governor of California. Likeable, photogenic, genial—and committed to conservative values—he gained support for cutbacks in social programs in his state. He also called for the same approach in the federal government.

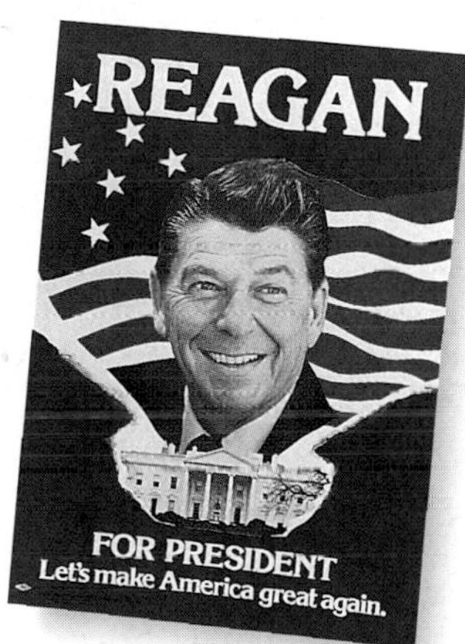


*With this 1980 campaign poster, Ronald Reagan appealed to voters' patriotism.*

## The Rise of Conservatism

Americans have debated the proper size and scope of government since the nation's founding. That debate greatly intensified with Franklin Roosevelt's New Deal, which greatly enlarged the federal government.

**New Deal Opponents** New Deal agencies, which furnished banking regulation, assistance to farmers, aid for the unemployed, and a great deal more, changed the role of the President and the federal government. Critics argued that in a capitalist country, government should not undertake these tasks. They said

*Pro-choice and anti-abortion activists gathered at this rally.*

the nation could not afford the high federal spending that resulted.

Some of these critics joined together in the American Liberty League. Established in 1934, this organization included both industrialists and disgruntled politicians. The Liberty League sought to teach respect for the rights of individuals and property and to underscore the importance of individual enterprise. All of these values, members claimed, were being undermined by FDR's large government programs.

In 1937 an attempt by Roosevelt to "pack" the Supreme Court by adding new justices caused a backlash. Opponents formed a bipartisan coalition that opposed any further New Deal legislation.

**From Eisenhower to Goldwater** The election of Dwight D. Eisenhower as President in 1952 began eight years of Republican rule. Ike called his approach to government "modern Republicanism." He accepted the basic outlines of the New Deal. He never attempted to dismantle the federal bureaucracy. There was even occasional bureaucratic expansion, as in the 1953 creation of a new Department of Health, Education, and Welfare, headed by Oveta Culp Hobby.

**Main Idea CONNECTIONS**

*What was Eisenhower's approach to government?*

In 1964 the Republican candidate for President, Senator Barry Goldwater of Arizona, ran on a staunchly conservative platform. Facing Democrat Lyndon B. Johnson, Goldwater opposed government activism, including civil rights laws and antipoverty programs. He also demanded a military buildup against an expected Soviet attack.

Johnson portrayed Goldwater as a dangerous extremist and crushed him in the 1964 election. Some analysts concluded that Goldwater's conservatism would never gain wide support.

**The Great Society** Conservatives found themselves silenced for a time following Goldwater's decisive defeat in 1964. The Democratic landslide in the election gave liberals the political upper hand in the mid-1960s. Congress cooperated as President Johnson pushed ahead with his Great Society program, an extension of the New Deal, starting in 1965.

"Is a new world coming?" Johnson asked. "We welcome it, and we will bend it to the hopes of man."

The Great Society promised something for everyone. The Office of Economic Opportunity helped the poor and gave them a voice in handling their own affairs. Medicare ensured medical care for the elderly, while Medicaid gave similar aid to the poor. The Great Society included the most far-reaching school support program in American history. In 1965 a new Department of Housing and Urban Development gave Cabinet-level visibility to the effort to revive the nation's cities.

**Nixon and the Welfare State** In 1968 Richard Nixon won the presidency, bringing Republicans back into power. Nixon wanted to trim social welfare programs, which he claimed encouraged people not to work, and to bring the budget under control.

Yet in fact, the federal government continued to grow during Nixon's presidency. The Occupational Safety and Health Act (OSHA) of 1970 provided for employee rights in the workplace and demanded that safety standards be maintained, with federal enforcement regulation. Also in 1970 the Environmental Protection Agency (EPA) was created to oversee federal antipollution laws. Opponents of government growth bridled at these efforts.

**Social Issues** Many conservatives were deeply troubled by rapid cultural changes of the time. Rock music was becoming increasingly shocking, its lyrics more openly sexual and drug-oriented. Illegal drugs became widespread on college campuses.

The sexual revolution was another source of conservative concern. The use of the new birth control pill encouraged promiscuity, critics said. Also, after the 1973 Supreme Court ruling in *Roe* v. *Wade* legalized abortion, antiabortion forces launched a campaign to overturn that ruling. The movement for gay and lesbian rights further angered many conservative Americans.

The women's movement caused still another rift. As women worked for equal rights and began to gain new opportunities, some conservatives reacted vigorously. A woman's place was at home, they argued. Phyllis Schlafly, who campaigned against ratification of the Equal Rights Amendment, echoed the desire to retain women's traditional roles.

Another controversy involved affirmative action. This is a policy whereby employers try to make up for past discrimination by giving special consideration to the hiring of women and minority applicants. When the government and private companies adopted affirmative action, some critics called the policy "reverse discrimination." This issue attracted some Democratic blue-collar workers to the Republican ranks, where they would help elect Ronald Reagan to the presidency.

## *Turning Point: The Election of 1980*

In 1976, Ronald Reagan had challenged President Gerald Ford for the Republican nomination. He lost by a narrow margin. In 1980 Reagan again sought the nomination. Republican moderates claimed that he, like Goldwater in 1964, was too conservative to defeat the Democratic President, Jimmy Carter. Yet in fact, social changes were under way that would prove this prediction wrong.

**The New Right Coalition** By 1980, conservative groups had formed a powerful political

## TURNING POINT: *Election of 1980*

**Ronald Reagan's election as President in 1980 reflected a growing public demand for smaller, less expensive government.**

**1980**
*Ronald Reagan, promising to reduce the size and cost of government, is elected President.*

**1981**
*Congress approves cuts in taxes and domestic spending.*

**1988**
*George Bush wins the presidency on a pledge of "no new taxes."*

**1990**

**1994**
*Congress defeats President Clinton's plan for comprehensive health care.*

**1996**
*President Clinton declares that "the era of big government is over."*

**1998**
*The federal budget deficit is eliminated.*

**2000**

Jerry Falwell and other televangelists helped change the way political candidates portrayed themselves and their opponents in the media. ***Culture*** *What were some of the issues addressed by the New Right?*

coalition known as the **New Right.** A key concern of many conservatives in the New Right was the size of government and its role in the economy. They proposed cutting government-funded social programs.

Other groups in the New Right wanted to restore what they considered Christian values to society. Members of the Moral Majority, led by the Reverend Jerry Falwell of Virginia, wanted to follow the dictates of the Bible and revive the traditional values they believed had strengthened the country in the past.

Falwell and other evangelists used the power of television to reach millions of people. In a format that became known as **televangelism,** they appealed to viewers to contribute money to their campaign. They delivered fervent sermons on specific political issues and used the money they raised to back conservative politicians.

**A Reagan Landslide** The growing strength of conservatives in the Republican party gave Ronald Reagan the GOP presidential nomination in 1980. During the campaign, Reagan seized on growing discontent. His attacks on incumbent Jimmy Carter's handling of the economy were particularly effective. Criticizing Carter's economic record, he poked fun at the President's use of technical language:

AMERICAN VOICES **"I'm talking in human terms and he is hiding behind a dictionary. If he wants a definition, I'll give him one. A recession is when your neighbor loses his job. A depression is when you lose yours. A recovery is when Jimmy Carter loses his."**

*—Ronald Reagan, 1980*

The continuing hostage crisis in Iran, as well as other issues, hurt Carter, and Reagan won in a landslide. He gained 51 percent of the popular vote to Carter's 41 percent. (Illinois Representative John Anderson ran as a third-party candidate.) Carried along by Reagan's popularity, the Republicans gained control of the Senate for the first time in 25 years.

Conservatism now controlled the nation's agenda. The effects of this power shift are shown in the Turning Point on the previous page.

## SECTION 1 REVIEW

### Comprehension

1. *Key Terms* Define: (a) New Right; (b) televangelism.
2. *Summarizing the Main Idea* What types of social changes in the 1960s and 1970s led to a conservative backlash in 1980?
3. *Organizing Information* Create a table listing all the Presidents mentioned in this section and summarizing their approaches to government.

### Critical Thinking

4. *Analyzing Time Lines* Refer to the time line at the start of the section. (a) Identify entries that show a shift in political power. (b) Why do you think power tends to swing between liberalism and conservatism?
5. *Recognizing Cause and Effect* How did Reagan use modern technology and new political techniques to increase his popularity?

### Writing Activity

6. *Writing an Expository Essay* Many political analysts at first disregarded candidate Reagan as too conservative to win widespread support. Write an essay explaining how he was able not just to win the election, but to win in a landslide.

| 1981 | 1981 | 1982 | 1983 | 1983 | 1983 |
|---|---|---|---|---|---|
| 5 percent tax cut; severe recession begins | Reagan wounded in assassination attempt | 10 percent tax cut | Strategic Defense Initiative announced | Inflation and unemployment drop below 10 percent | Bombing in Lebanon kills 241 marines; American victory in Grenada |

1981 — 1982 — 1983

# 2 The Reagan Revolution

**SECTION PREVIEW**

### Objectives

1. Describe how Reagan sought to change the economy and the government.
2. List the major initiatives and key foreign policy crises during Reagan's first term.
3. Describe the economic recession of the early 1980s.
4. *Key Terms* Define: supply-side economics; New Federalism; Strategic Defense Initiative (SDI).

### Main Idea

Ronald Reagan aimed to boost the nation's pride and prosperity by cutting taxes, shrinking the federal government, and increasing defense spending.

### Reading Strategy

*Outlining Information* On a separate sheet of paper, copy down the headings and subheadings in this section. As you read, add at least two key facts under each subheading to create an outline of the section.

During the 1980 campaign, Ronald Reagan stressed three broad policies that he would pursue if elected President: slashing taxes, eliminating unnecessary government programs, and bolstering the defense capability of the United States. In his first term, he moved aggressively to implement those policies.

## Changing the Economy

President Reagan brought to Washington a plan for economic change that conservatives had long sought to put into action. In simple terms, he wanted to put more money back into people's paychecks instead of into tax coffers.

**Supply-Side Economics** Reagan's main goal was to spur business growth. His economic program, dubbed "Reaganomics," rested on the theory of supply-side economics. This theory reversed earlier policies based on the ideas of English economist John Maynard Keynes.

In the 1920s and 1930s, Keynes had argued that the government could best improve the economy by increasing consumers' demand for goods. This meant giving people more money—either directly, through government aid, or indirectly, by creating jobs. Once people had more money to spend, Keynes argued, they would purchase more goods and services, which would cause the economy to grow.

Keynesian theory had helped explain the Great Depression and the recovery that took place as the United States began a massive military spending program during World War II. In the postwar years, most economists accepted Keynesian arguments.

In contrast to Keynesian theory, **supply-side economics** focused not on the demand for goods but on the supply of goods. It predicted that cutting taxes would put more money into the hands of businesses and investors—those who supplied the goods for consumers to buy.

The theory assumed that businesses would then hire more people and produce more goods and services, making the economy grow faster. The real key, therefore, was encouraging business leaders to invest. Their individual actions would create and promote greater national economic abundance. Prosperity would eventually "trickle down" from the top to those at the lower levels of the economy.

George Bush, a rival candidate for the Republican presidential nomination, called Reagan's economic plan "voodoo economics." Only later, when he became Reagan's running mate, did Bush change his stand.

**Cutting Taxes** Reagan's first priority was a tax cut. In October 1981, a 5 percent cut went into effect, followed by 10 percent cuts in 1982 and 1983. In 1986, during Reagan's second term, Congress passed the most sweeping tax reform in history. The law closed loopholes that had allowed some people to avoid paying their fair share of taxes. It simplified the tax system by reducing the number of income brackets that determined how much tax a person paid. While all taxpayers benefited from these measures, the wealthy Americans benefited most. The tax rate on the highest incomes dropped from 50 percent to 28 percent.

**Main Idea CONNECTIONS**

*What was the effect of Reagan's tax cuts?*

## *Changing the Government*

As you read in the previous section, for generations conservatives had criticized government growth. Now, however, they had a Chief Executive committed to limiting both the size and the role of the federal government.

**Cutting Regulations** Reagan embarked on a major program of deregulation. Like President Carter before him, Reagan wanted to eliminate government regulations that he said stifled free market competition.

By the time of Reagan's presidency, regulation had been expanding for nearly a century. The Interstate Commerce Commission, established in 1887, was the first step. Government regulations grew during the Progressive era of the early 1900s and in the New Deal years of the 1930s. Regulation was intended to protect companies from unfair competition, workers from unsafe working conditions, and consumers from ineffective or unsafe products.

Reagan continued and expanded the deregulation of the energy, transportation, and banking industries begun under the Carter administration. He cut the number and size of regulatory agencies like the Environmental Protection Agency, which had its budget, and therefore its functions, reduced. Reagan argued that regulations made life difficult for producers, which meant fewer jobs for workers and higher prices for consumers. The more

In 1981, the Professional Air Traffic Controllers Association (PATCO) went on strike. Citing that federal employees were prohibited from striking, Reagan fired 11,500 strikers and banned them from their careers. ***Government*** ***Why do you think Reagan felt there was the need for decisive action?***

that businesses spent to comply with government rules, he charged, the less they could spend on new factories and equipment.

**Slowing Federal Growth** Reagan also attempted to cut the size of the federal government. The President believed that any American could succeed through individual effort. This belief ran counter to the argument on which welfare was based: that government should help people who could not help themselves. Reagan charged that the government had become too intrusive in people's lives:

> **AMERICAN VOICES** **"It is . . . my intention . . . to make [government] work—work with us, not over us; to stand by our side, not ride on our back. Government can and must provide opportunity, not smother it; foster productivity, not stifle it."**
>
> —*President Ronald Reagan, First Inaugural Address, 1981*

Drawing support from opponents of the programs created by Lyndon Johnson's Great Society, Reagan attacked these programs head-on. The administration eliminated public service jobs that were part of an employment training program. It reduced unemployment compensation. It lowered welfare benefits and reduced allocations for food stamps. It raised fees for Medicare patients. Despite cuts to specific programs, total federal spending on social welfare rose between 1980 and 1982.

While he cut back the role of the federal government, Reagan sought to give more responsibility to state and local governments. Borrowing a term from the Nixon administration, he called his plan the **New Federalism.** Under this plan, the federal government would no longer tell states exactly how federal aid had to be used. Rather it would let states create and pay for programs as they saw fit.

The New Federalism program never worked as planned. A recession early in Reagan's presidency left a number of cities and states nearly bankrupt. They now had responsibility but not enough money for programs formerly funded by the federal government.

## *Reagan's Foreign Policy*

While taking decisive measures to change the direction of domestic policy, Reagan was equally determined to defend American interests in the cold war. He believed in a tough approach toward the Soviet Union, which he called an "evil empire." He favored large defense budgets to strengthen both conventional military forces and the nuclear arsenal.

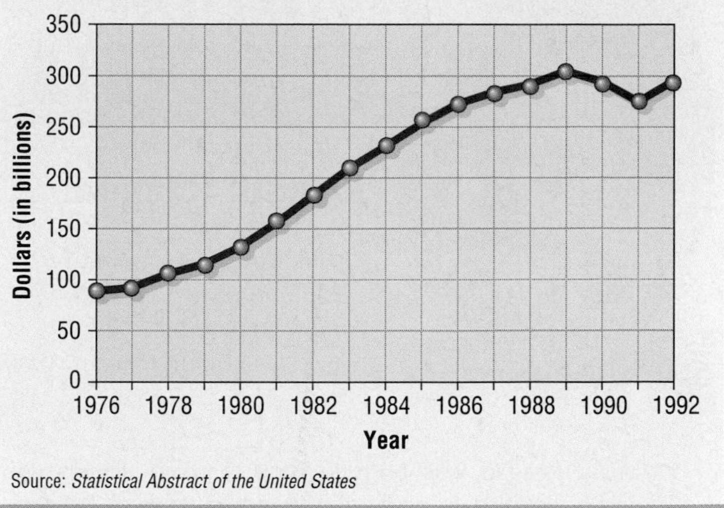


**Interpreting Graphs** Notice the change in defense spending in the early 1980s. ***Economics*** ***By how much did the defense budget increase during President Reagan's two terms in office?***

**Military Buildup** The costs of the buildup were enormous. Over a five-year period, the United States spent an unprecedented $1.1 trillion on defense. By 1985, the nation was spending half a million dollars every minute on defense. These expenditures contributed to the growing budget deficits.

Much of this money went into new weapons. The United States continued to develop new missiles, such as the intercontinental MX, as well as new bombers and submarines that could carry nuclear weapons. Reagan also explored ways to protect Americans against nuclear attack. In 1983 Reagan announced the **Strategic Defense Initiative (SDI),** popularly known as "Star Wars," after the 1977 film. SDI proposed the creation of a massive satellite shield in space to intercept and destroy incoming Soviet missiles.

***President Reagan (left) reviews an honor guard at a Pentagon ceremony in 1987.***

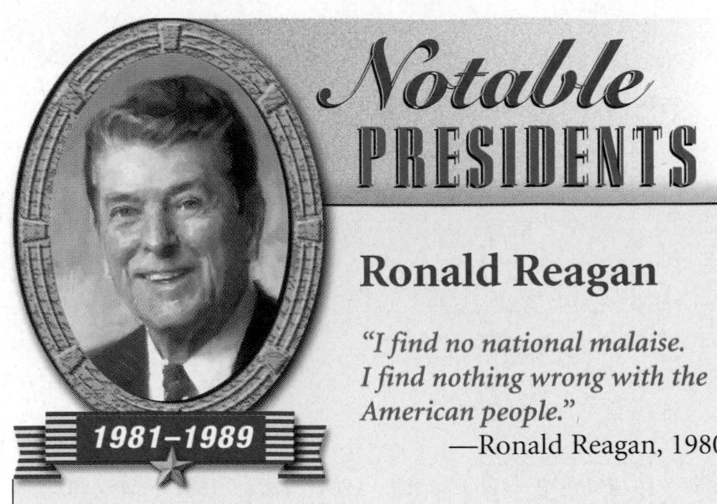


## Ronald Reagan

*"I find no national malaise. I find nothing wrong with the American people."*
—Ronald Reagan, 1980

Ronald Reagan was born in rural Tampico, Illinois, in 1911. The first in his family to go to college, Reagan became a radio sportscaster after graduating. The Iowa radio station could not afford to send him to Chicago to broadcast the Chicago Cubs baseball games, so Reagan used the wire service's running accounts and dramatized the rest. His ability to spin dramatic stories from a few dry facts helped him become known in later years as the "Great Communicator." During a business trip to California in 1937, Reagan took a screen test at the Warner Brothers studio. He spent the next ten years building a film career.

In 1947, Reagan became president of the film actors' union, the Screen Actors' Guild. He used his position to fight communism. In the mid- and late 1950s, he became the spokesman for General Electric. He spoke against communism and the "containment" policy. During the 1964 presidential campaign he gave a nationally televised speech, which outlined major conservative views. The speech made Reagan a national political figure.

In 1966 Reagan was elected governor of California. Likable and articulate, Reagan was a natural politician who appealed to any audience. In the presidential election of 1980, he asked the voters, "Are you better off today than you were four years ago?" The answer was apparent in his landslide victory over President Carter.

In 1984, Reagan was reelected, becoming the third Republican President to win reelection since the Depression. His aggressive defense policy helped bring about the end of the cold war and reshaped postwar politics.

Americans remember Reagan for his presidential style—unassuming, personable, candid, and optimistic. A later President, Bill Clinton, summed it up: " [Reagan's] unwavering hopefulness reminded us that optimism is one of our most fundamental virtues."

### Connecting to Today

Ronald Reagan reminded Americans how important the role of the President is in helping overcome national self-doubt.

***How has the United States' self-confidence changed since 1980? Explain.***

**Trouble Spots Abroad** Relations with the Soviet Union remained frosty during Reagan's first term. The Soviets criticized the American defense buildup. They also complained when the United States stationed new intermediate-range nuclear missiles in Western Europe.

The United States was active in the Middle East as well. The country of Lebanon had become a battleground for a variety of armed political groups. In 1982, Reagan sent several thousand marines to Beirut, the Lebanese capital, as part of a peacekeeping force. In October 1983 a terrorist truck loaded with explosives crashed through the gates of a marine barracks, killing 241 Americans.

The attack horrified the nation. Many Americans demanded an immediate withdrawal from Lebanon, and by the following February, all the troops had left.

In Latin America, Reagan feared that Communist forces would gain power and threaten American interests. In El Salvador, the United States supported a repressive military regime in resisting guerrillas, some of whom were Marxists. Reagan increased military aid to El Salvador to the level of about $1 million a day. In Nicaragua, as you will read in the next section, the United States helped guerrillas who were fighting to overthrow that nation's leftist government.

Reagan claimed a victory on the tiny Caribbean island of Grenada. He ordered United States military forces to Grenada in October 1983, after a military coup installed a government sympathetic to Communist Cuba. The official aim of the invasion was to safeguard several hundred American medical students on the island. However, United States forces also overthrew the Grenadian government and remained in Grenada to oversee free elections.

## Recession and Recovery

During Reagan's first two years in office, the United States experienced the worst recession since the Great Depression. High interest rates discouraged Americans from borrowing to purchase goods or invest in new equipment. Foreign competition cost thousands of American jobs. By 1982 several hundred businesses were going bankrupt each week.

The 1981–1982 recession did, however, pave the way for an economic recovery. The high interest rates cooled down inflation, and as Reagan's tax cuts took effect, consumer spending began to rise. By 1983, both inflation and unemployment had already dropped below 10 percent. Business leaders gained new confidence, and increased their investments. The stock market pushed upward. Republicans claimed that the recovery demonstrated the wisdom of supply-side economics.

Yet an important prediction of the supply-side theorists had not come true. Cuts in tax rates were supposed to generate so much economic growth that the government's tax revenues would actually increase. As a result, the federal deficit, or the amount by which the government's spending exceeds its income in a given year, was supposed to decrease.

During the 1980 campaign, Reagan had vowed to balance the federal budget if elected. But, the combination of the Reagan tax cuts and defense spending pushed the deficit up, not down. The deficit ballooned from nearly $80 billion in 1980 to a peak of $221 billion in 1986.

While the rising deficits did help the government cut back on domestic spending, they drove the nation as a whole deeper into debt. The national debt, the total amount of money owed by the government, rose from $909 billion in 1980 to $3.2 trillion in 1990. Future generations would have to bear the burden of interest payments on this monumental debt.

Yet in spite of these problems, most Americans supported Reagan. They shared his values and principles.

In 1981, Reagan was wounded in an assassination attempt. The courage and humor with which he faced the situation ("Please tell me you're all Republicans," he quipped to the doctors treating him) only reinforced Americans' respect for their President.

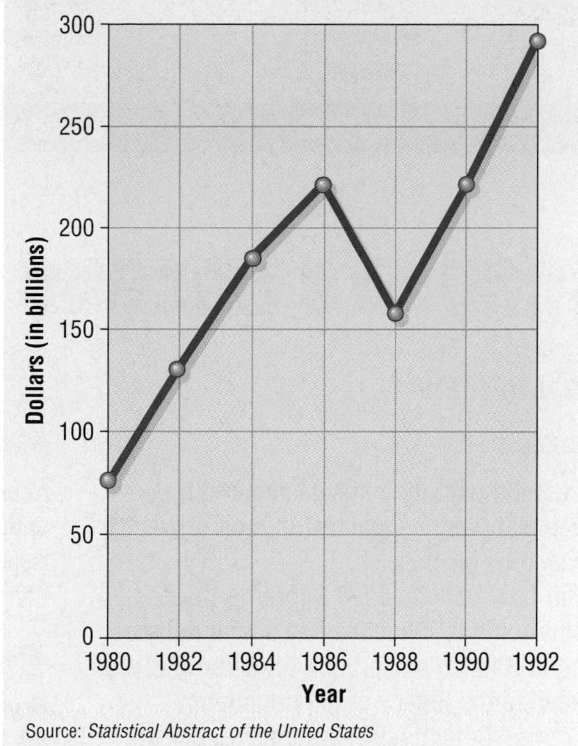


**Interpreting Graphs** Examine the graph above showing the federal deficit from 1980 to 1992. ***Economics*** ***What happened to the federal deficit during Reagan's years in office? How did Reagan's policies contribute to that trend?***

## SECTION 2 REVIEW

### Comprehension

1. *Key Terms* Define: (a) supply-side economics; (b) New Federalism; (c) Strategic Defense Initiative (SDI).
2. *Summarizing the Main Idea* What major shifts in philosophy and policies did Reagan bring to the government?
3. *Organizing Information* Create a three-column table entitled *Changes Under Reagan.* The columns should have the headings *Economy, Government,* and *Foreign Policy.* Fill in at least three entries under each column.

### Critical Thinking

4. *Analyzing Time Lines* Refer to the time line at the start of the section. Why was 1983 an active year for foreign policy in Reagan's first term?
5. *Drawing Conclusions* What consequences could result from cutting regulations enforced by the federal government?

### Writing Activity

6. *Writing a Persuasive Essay* Take a stand for or against the theory of supply-side economics. Use specific details and examples to argue your position.

| 1981 | 1982 | 1984 | 1985 | 1986 | 1987 |
|---|---|---|---|---|---|
| *O'Connor becomes first woman on Supreme Court* | *Equal Rights Amendment defeated* | *Reagan wins reelection* | *Gorbachev takes power in Soviet Union* | *Iran-contra affair revealed* | *Reagan, Gorbachev sign INF Treaty* |

1980 · 1982 · 1984 · 1986 · 1988

# 3 Reagan's Second Term

**SECTION PREVIEW**

### Objectives

1. Contrast the patriotic renewal inspired by Reagan with the unequal distribution of wealth increased by his policies.
2. Explain how Reagan used Supreme Court appointments to influence key social debates.
3. Describe Reagan's approach to governing, and summarize the legacy of his presidency.
4. *Key Terms* Define: AIDS; Sandinista; contra; Iran-contra affair; INF Treaty; entitlement.

### Main Idea

After a decisive reelection victory in 1984, Reagan continued his conservative policies on economic and social issues. In domestic and foreign affairs, the administration had key successes but also serious missteps.

### Reading Strategy

*Organizing Information* As you read the section, list the key events and crises described. For each event, summarize the significance or outcome.

Campaigning for reelection in 1984, Ronald Reagan asked voters if they were better off than they had been four years before. As they roared their approval, he told them, "You ain't seen nothing yet." His campaign advertisements, such as one depicting "Morning in America," heralded a new day of optimism.

Reagan faced Democrat Walter Mondale, former Vice President under Carter. Mondale's running mate was New York Representative Geraldine Ferraro, the first woman ever on a major party's presidential ticket.

*Ronald Reagan's charisma appealed to many voters.*

The relative strength of the economy and Reagan's popularity gave the President a landslide victory over Mondale. Reagan took 59 percent of the popular vote and all the electoral votes except those of the District of Columbia and Mondale's home state of Minnesota. It was the second largest electoral-vote margin in history.

## Patriotic Renewal

Reagan wanted to re-create the sense of community he had known in his youth and to help revive the virtues that had made America strong. The nation had endured turbulence in the years following the Vietnam War. The 1980s offered several occasions to celebrate patriotic renewal.

**1984 Olympic Games** The 1984 Olympic Games were held in Los Angeles, the first time the Summer Games had come to the United States in half a century. The ceremonies, televised worldwide to hundreds of millions of viewers, were festive, patriotic affairs.

Some Communist countries, including the Soviet Union and East Germany, boycotted the games. The move was in retaliation to an American-led boycott of the 1980 Moscow games to protest the Soviet invasion of Afghanistan in 1979. As a result of the boycott, the United States won an unusually high number of medals.

**Statue of Liberty Centennial** Two years later, in 1986, the nation celebrated the centennial of the Statue of Liberty in New York harbor. This monument, the first structure many immigrants had seen as they entered the United

States, was a symbol of freedom around the world. But the copper lady in flowing robes had deteriorated over the course of 100 years. Now, after a massive campaign to refurbish the statue, the nation held a spectacular centennial celebration.

**Bicentennial of the Constitution** The following year the United States celebrated the 200th anniversary of the Constitution, drafted in 1787. Government and private groups sponsored lectures, workshops, and meetings focusing on the features of the Constitution that made the nation strong. This observance helped renew public appreciation of such enduring ideas as balanced government and separation of powers.

## Unequal Wealth

The truly wealthy, more than anyone else, flourished under Reagan. The net worth of *Forbes* magazine's 400 richest Americans nearly tripled in the Reagan years. Political analyst Kevin Phillips described this new class of "upper America":

AMERICAN VOICES

> **"The truth is that the critical concentration of wealth in the United States was developing at higher levels—decamillionaires, centimillionaires, half-billionaires and billionaires. Garden variety millionaires had become so common that there were about 1.5 million of them by 1989."**
>
> —*Political analyst Kevin Phillips,* New York Times Magazine, *June 24, 1990*

By the late 1980s, wealth was more unevenly distributed than at any time since the end of World War II. Many families increased their total income by having both husband and wife work outside the home. Individual wages, however, declined. For the poorest one fifth of the population, total family income dropped.

## Continuing Social Debates

In the years leading to Reagan's election, conservatives gained public support with their stands on social issues as well as economic ones. In the 1980s, conservative policies on social issues made these "hot" issues even hotter.

**Civil Rights** The federal commitment to extend voting rights had given the vote to millions of African Americans who had been denied it for decades. These new voters elected an increasing number of African American candidates to local, state, and national offices.

Resistance to civil rights initiatives was growing, however, as critics complained that many of these policies trampled on the rights of state and local governments. Reagan tried to prevent the extension of the Voting Rights Act of 1965, backing off only after intense criticism. He appointed federal judges who were less sympathetic to civil rights goals. The administration also worked to end some affirmative action programs.

**The Women's Movement** As women gained access to jobs and other opportunities previously denied to them, the women's movement met with a backlash. One sign of this backlash was the defeat in 1982 of the proposed Equal Rights Amendment, which failed to gain the approval of enough state legislatures to be ratified.

Anti-abortion groups took aim at the right to abortion granted in the 1973 *Roe* v. *Wade*

### COMPARING PRIMARY SOURCES

### THE LEGACY OF THE CIVIL RIGHTS MOVEMENT

Decades after the civil rights movement, Americans disagreed on how much progress had been made.

**Substantial Progress**

"Before the civil rights movement, there was a very wide separation between blacks and whites. I don't think the separation is as great today. There has been more speaking out. Blacks now let themselves open up and say how they feel in no uncertain terms. I think there are friendships between blacks and whites that didn't exist before. In spite of everything, I think the racial situation is healthier than it was before. Blacks are no longer invisible."

—*Eileen Barth, retired social worker, quoted in Studs Terkel's* Race, *1992*

**Little or No Progress**

"The country is more segregated today than it was when [Martin Luther] King and [Robert] Kennedy were alive. What Dr. King and Bobby were fighting was segregation and discrimination imposed by law, by the state. . . . All of that has changed. . . . But in the North, everybody knows what's happened in the cities. At universities, there's much more black withdrawal into separate communities. I grew up thinking we were going to have an integrated society, not just an end to official racism."

—New York Times *columnist Anthony Lewis, April 1993*

*ANALYZING VIEWPOINTS* **Compare the main arguments in the two quotations above.**

Supreme Court decision. Opponents lobbied to halt federal funding of abortions for the poor.

**Sexual Orientation** The campaign for homosexual rights caused similar polarization. Contributing to the backlash was the discovery in 1981 of acquired immuno-deficiency syndrome, known simply as **AIDS.** At first, most of its victims were intravenous drug users and homosexual men. Some Americans therefore viewed AIDS as a curse that punished certain people for their habits and lifestyles. Even as AIDS spread into the larger community, the resistance to gay rights grew more vocal.

## *Conservatives on the Supreme Court*

Many of these social issues wound up in the courts. Reagan used his years in office to appoint conservative federal judges. In 1981 he selected Arizona judge Sandra Day O'Connor as the nation's first woman Supreme Court justice. In 1986 Reagan chose another conservative, Antonin Scalia, for the Supreme Court.

While O'Connor and Scalia won Senate confirmation, Reagan's next Supreme Court appointment, conservative judge and former law professor Robert Bork, did not. Liberal groups joined together in 1987 to convince the Senate to reject Bork's nomination. The nominee whom the Senate finally approved, Anthony Kennedy, was known as a moderate conservative. He joined the Court in 1988.

## *Sandra Day O'Connor*

AMERICAN BIOGRAPHY

Among the conservatives on the Court, Sandra Day O'Connor emerged as someone who went her own way and often helped to reconcile differences. These were skills that she *had* to learn—a long time ago.

Born in El Paso, Texas, in 1930, Sandra Day grew up on her parents' ranch in Arizona. Graduating early from Austin (Texas) High School, at age 16 she entered Stanford University in California, where she earned an economics degree and high honors in 1950. Two years later she graduated third in her class at Stanford Law School and made the prestigious Law Review.

*Sandra Day O'Connor (b.1930)*

These credentials should have landed the young lawyer an excellent job. However, as she later recalled, "When I graduated from law school in 1952, there were still only a handful of women lawyers in the United States. None of the larger law firms had ever hired a woman attorney. I was unable to get a job on graduation as a lawyer in a law firm, although I did get a job as an attorney in a county government office."

Day married Stanford classmate John Jay O'Connor III in 1952. They eventually settled in Arizona, where Sandra Day O'Connor opened her own law firm, serving as a court-appointed attorney for impoverished clients. She discontinued her practice with the birth of the first of her three children in 1957 and began working for the Republican party in Arizona.

In 1965 she returned to full-time work, serving in a variety of roles: assistant attorney general, state senator (and the first woman majority leader), and superior court judge. In 1979, Arizona governor Bruce Babbitt appointed O'Connor to the state appeals court. Just 18 months later, in 1981, President Reagan nominated her to become the first woman justice of the United States Supreme Court. She was sworn in on September 26, 1981.

In her years on the Court, which included a battle with cancer, O'Connor gained the respect of both conservatives and liberals. Her opinions in several landmark cases showed a tendency to look for practical solutions instead of ruling along strictly ideological lines. She broke ranks with her fellow conservatives to support the Equal Rights Amendment and took a leadership role on women's issues. ■

## *Reagan's Hands-off Style*

Ronald Reagan favored less government regulation of the economy. A decade later, neither party—the Republicans or the Democrats—would argue with that. Reagan also followed a hands-off style in running the government. He delegated authority to those who worked for him rather than be involved in every decision. Several times this approach led to notable problems.

**The S & L Scandal** "Thrift institutions" or savings and loan banks, often called S&Ls, made home mortgage loans to individuals. The Reagan administration, with the help of Democrats in Congress, pressed for the deregulation of S&Ls to permit them to make riskier but more profitable investments.

Officials at some deregulated S&Ls took advantage of the new laws to make huge fortunes for themselves. Many made risky investments in an overheated real estate market. When the market cooled down in the late 1980s, many S&Ls collapsed, taking with them about $2.6 billion in depositors' savings.

Because bank accounts are insured by the federal government, taxpayers had to make up the billions of dollars lost when hundreds of S&Ls failed. A number of banking officials were prosecuted for their role in the scandal and their efforts to cover it up.

**The Iran-contra Affair** In Nicaragua, the Reagan administration sought to undermine the Marxist government that had seized power in 1979. The ruling group, the **Sandinistas,** was named after a Nicaraguan freedom fighter from the 1920s. Reagan feared that the Sandinistas' revolution would spread Marxist upheaval to other Latin American countries.

Working through the Central Intelligence Agency, the United States trained and armed Nicaraguan guerrillas known as **contras** (Spanish for "counterrevolutionaries"). This policy, however, violated American neutrality laws.

Congress discovered these secret missions and in 1984 cut off military aid to the contras. Some members of the Reagan administration still believed that aid to the contras was justified. These officials took the profits from secret arms sales to Iran and then sent those profits to the contras. (The arms sales were meant to encourage the release of American hostages held in Lebanon by pro-Iranian terrorists.)

When the secret actions became public in the fall of 1986, Oliver North, the marine colonel who had made the arrangements, took the blame. The **Iran-contra affair,** as this scandal came to be called, caused the most serious criticism that the Reagan administration ever faced. The President himself claimed no knowledge of North's operations.

Relations between the United States and the Soviet Union warmed during Reagan's second term. Here, Reagan and Soviet leader Mikhail Gorbachev meet outside St. Basil's Cathedral in Moscow. ***Foreign Relations*** ***Why do you think glasnost and perestroika helped smooth relations between the two countries?***

## *The Reagan Legacy*

The Iran-contra affair did not damage Ronald Reagan's personal approval ratings. When he left office in 1989, polls showed that over 60 percent of the American people gave him high marks for his overall performance.

**Foreign Policy Success** One reason for the President's continued popularity was the improvement in relations between the United States and the Soviet Union during Reagan's second term. Despite his fierce anti-Communist stance, Reagan developed a close relationship with Mikhail Gorbachev, who became the Soviet leader in 1985.

To reform the ailing Soviet system, Gorbachev proposed a program of *glasnost,* a Russian word meaning "political openness." He also initiated *perestroika,* or "restructuring," an economic policy to allow limited free enterprise.

**Main Idea CONNECTIONS**

***What changes did Gorbachev bring to the Soviet Union?***

These moves paved the way toward better relations between the United States and the Soviet Union. Reagan and Gorbachev signed the Intermediate-Range Nuclear Forces (INF) Treaty in 1987. The **INF Treaty** provided for

## FACT Finder: Arms Control Agreements, 1979–1993

| Date | Legislation | Purpose |
|---|---|---|
| 1979 | SALT II (Strategic Arms Limitation Treaty) | • Reinforcement of SALT I Treaty between the United States and the USSR. Required reduction of strategic offensive weapons systems, specifically nuclear arms. Set limits on the types and numbers of weapons each side could acquire. |
| 1987 | INF (Intermediate-Range Nuclear Forces) Treaty | • Treaty between the United States and the USSR that required each party to destroy ground-launched and ballistic cruise missiles and their launchers within three years. |
| 1993 | START II (Strategic Arms Reduction Treaty) | • Treaty between the United States and former Soviet republics. The treaty parties reserved the right to conduct annual inspections at former INF missile sites to ensure that no missiles are being manufactured. |

**Interpreting Tables** Soviet leader Mikhail Gorbachev's policy of glasnost helped slow the arms race between the United States and the USSR. ***Foreign Relations*** ***Why do you think arms control agreements were still necessary in the post-Soviet era?***

the destruction of 2,500 Soviet and American missiles in Europe.

**Domestic Policy Initiatives** Another reason for Reagan's popularity was his stated commitment to reducing government. Actually Reagan's policies did not succeed in dramatically reducing Washington bloat. Payments for **entitlements**—programs like Social Security, Medicare, and Medicaid, which guarantee payments to a particular group of recipients—grew faster than policymakers expected. Social Security expenditures, for example, skyrocketed as the nation's elderly population continued to rise. Reagan failed to restrain the growth of these programs.

Economic turmoil erupted near the end of Reagan's presidency. Investor fears about the huge budget deficits and rising national debt prompted a stock market crash in 1987. Following six weeks of falling prices, the market suffered a huge 22.6 percent drop on October 19. The speculative bubble of the 1980s had burst.

While the stock market did recover, Reagan's successor, George Bush, inherited many economic problems. By the end of the decade the nation found itself in the midst of another recession.

For most Americans, Ronald Reagan's two-term presidency was marked by his vigorous emphasis on national pride and the force of his own optimistic personality. Reagan's presidency made many Americans feel confident for the first time since the Kennedy years.

## SECTION 3 REVIEW

### Comprehension

1. *Key Terms* Define: (a) AIDS; (b) Sandinista; (c) contra; (d) Iran-contra affair; (e) INF Treaty; (f) entitlement.
2. *Summarizing the Main Idea* List some successes and failures of Reagan's second term.
3. *Organizing Information* Make a web diagram called *Results of Reagan's Style of Governing.* Fill in entries that show the effects of Reagan's administrative approach.

### Critical Thinking

4. *Analyzing Time Lines* Refer to the time line at the start of the section. Identify three events seen as successes for the Reagan administration, and explain why.
5. *Analyzing Cause and Effect* Despite some failures and scandals, Reagan was a highly popular President. Analyze Reagan's legacy and the effect of his patriotism on public opinion.

### Writing Activity

6. *Writing an Expository Essay* In an essay, explain how the influence of conservatives was felt during the Reagan years, both in social issues and in changes in the Supreme Court.

# SKILLS FOR LIFE

**Critical Thinking**

Geography

Graphs and Charts

Historical Evidence

## Demonstrating Reasoned Judgment

Making connections between ideas is the basis for reasoned judgment. This critical thinking skill enables you to analyze the merits of a statement or opinion and thus to reach your own conclusions about its validity.

The passage below is an analysis of the effects of Reagan's economic policies. In order to decide whether you agree with the analysis, you must first evaluate the reasoning process the writer used to make his judgments.

Read the passage. Then use the following steps to analyze the response and to test the reasonableness of both the writer's judgment and your own. Keep in mind that you do not have to agree with the viewpoint expressed in order to find that the reasoning is valid.

**1.** ***Examine the source and nature of the evidence by asking* who, when, where, *and* what.** (a) Who is the writer? (b) Is he qualified to speak on the subject? (c) Might he have any biases that affected his view of Reagan's economic policies or Republican policies in general?

**2.** ***Identify the major points in the argument.*** (a) What is the writer's main point? (b) What other points does he make?

**3.** ***Evaluate the evidence offered and the speaker's reasoning.*** (a) How does the writer support his points? (b) How convincing do you find his arguments? Explain. (c) What grade—from A down to F (failing)—would you give the speaker on how well he demonstrates reasoned judgment? Why did you choose that grade?

### TEST FOR SUCCESS

Turn to Section 3 and reread the Comparing Primary Sources quotation by Anthony Lewis. Does the quotation show reasoned judgment? Why or why not?

**"Of the many self-inflicted wounds suffered by America in the last thirty years, none was as deep, corrosive, and enduring as the series of huge, chronic federal budget deficits created by the policies of Ronald Reagan in his eight years in office. During that period, the average budget deficit was $211 billion, with the result that the federal debt (which had been less than $1 trillion over the entire course of the nation's history until then, including two world wars) nearly tripled to a total of $2.7 trillion, while the size of the nation's economy increased barely by half.**

**Bush went Reagan one better: in his four years, the deficit averaged $355 billion, adding another $1.4 trillion to the debt, for a total of more than $4 trillion. . . .**

**Over the sixteen-year period covering Johnson, Nixon, Ford, and Carter, the federal debt had risen only an average of $35 billion a year, for a total of $579 billion. Thus, in any three years of the Reagan-Bush twelve, the budget deficit expanded more than it had in the sixteen years of the four prior administrations.**

**Reagan presided over an economy in which investment and savings stagnated and real wages declined, transforming America from the world's number one creditor nation to the number one debtor. Incredibly, America's foreign debt began to exceed that of Mexico or Brazil. . . . If Reagan was right to suggest in [his] 1980 [campaign for President] that Americans were "worse off" than they were in 1976, at the beginning of the Carter years, Bill Clinton could rightly argue during the 1992 presidential campaign that they had made no gains in the entire decade of the 1980s."**

*—Hobart Rowen, economics columnist of* The Washington Post, *in his 1994 book* Self-Inflicted Wounds: From LBJ's Guns and Butter to Reagan's Voodoo Economics

| 1988 | 1988 | 1989 | 1990 | 1991 | 1991 | 1991 |
|---|---|---|---|---|---|---|
| Bush elected President | Poland's Communist government falls | Berlin Wall opened | Germany reunified | Persian Gulf War | Bush and Gorbachev sign arms treaty; Soviet Union breaks up | Economic recession hits |

1988 1989 1990 1991

# 4 The Bush Presidency

## SECTION PREVIEW

### Objectives

1. Evaluate the outcome of the 1988 presidential election.
2. Analyze President Bush's foreign policy successes, including the end of the cold war and victory in the Persian Gulf War.
3. Describe the effect of domestic issues on Bush's popularity.
4. *Key Terms* Define: Strategic Arms Reduction Treaty (START); Persian Gulf War; downsizing.

### Main Idea

George Bush achieved notable foreign policy successes, including a popular victory in the Gulf War. However, his record on domestic issues, the economy in particular, eroded his public support.

### Reading Strategy

*Analyzing Cause and Effect* As you read, identify as many cause-and-effect relationships as you can. List them in a chart.

*George Bush remained in Reagan's shadow throughout his presidency.*

It is not easy to follow a legendary President. George Bush had the same problem as William Howard Taft, who succeeded Theodore Roosevelt in 1909. So did Harry S. Truman, who inherited the presidency upon the death of Franklin D. Roosevelt in 1945. Ronald Reagan remained enormously popular as he left office in 1989, and Bush sought to continue the revolution his predecessor had begun. But he lacked Reagan's charismatic appeal and found that it was not always easy to measure up.

## The 1988 Election

Son of a well-to-do Connecticut senator, Bush served in World War II as a bomber pilot in the Pacific and was awarded the Distinguished Flying Cross. After the war he had a profitable career in the Texas oil industry.

In 1966 he entered a long and brilliant political career, serving in many roles: congressman from Texas; ambassador to the United Nations under Nixon; chairman of the Republican National Committee; American envoy to China under President Ford; and head of the Central Intelligence Agency (CIA) until 1977. He was well connected, with a reputation as a moderate and loyal Republican.

Despite these impressive credentials, Bush lacked the support of conservatives in the Republican party. Some Republicans, whose hero was Ronald Reagan, questioned Bush's commitment to their cause. They were concerned about his apparent early sympathy for abortion rights. They never truly forgave him for calling Reagan's economic plans "voodoo economics" in 1980. Bush's loyal service as Reagan's Vice President for eight years failed to ease their fears.

Bush began the 1988 campaign far behind his Democratic opponent, Governor Michael Dukakis of Massachusetts. Dukakis had revived his state after years of economic distress and promised to do the same thing nationally.

Bush took the offensive in what became a nasty contest. One part of his campaign was a pledge that there would be "no new taxes."

Reagan's popular tax cuts had contributed to the huge budget deficit and national debt. Reagan's successor would be under great pressure to raise taxes in order to reduce the deficit. Yet Bush publicly committed himself to holding the line on taxes.

Bush also attacked Dukakis as soft on crime. He launched attack ads that apparently alienated many voters. Americans complained that neither candidate addressed the major issues facing the country. Nearly half of all eligible voters stayed home in frustration.

Bush won a solid 54 percent of the popular vote and carried 40 states in a 426-111 electoral vote win. But he failed to gain the mandate Reagan had enjoyed, as Democrats now controlled both houses of Congress.

## *The Cold War Ends*

Bush's major triumphs came in foreign policy. Even more than Reagan, Bush benefited from the historic changes in the Communist world unleashed by Mikhail Gorbachev.

The Soviet leader started a chain reaction that would eventually bring down Europe's "Iron Curtain" and dissolve the Soviet Union. It began with Gorbachev's public statements encouraging Eastern European leaders to adopt perestroika and glasnost. The suggestion was unthinkable in a region where police states efficiently smothered all opposition. Yet it was enough to give hope and inspiration to anti-Communist movements throughout Eastern Europe that had worked for decades, at great risk, to keep a democratic spirit alive.

*What events led to the fall of the USSR?*

**Poland** In Poland the stage was set for the downfall of Soviet communism. The story had begun in 1970, when severe food shortages provoked riots in the city of Gdansk. A witness to those riots was a young electrician named Lech Walesa, who worked in the huge Lenin Shipyard at Gdansk. Walesa became involved in anti-Communist organizing and lost his job after helping to lead a protest in 1976.

When shipyard workers at Gdansk launched a strike in 1980, Walesa climbed over the fence of the facility and joined them, becoming

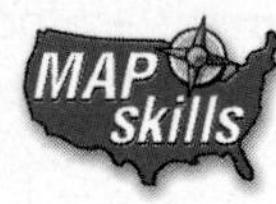


In the late 1980s the Eastern bloc shattered into a jigsaw puzzle of diverse republics (above). Above right, a giant statue of Vladimir Lenin, founder of the Russian Communist party, is removed from Moscow in pieces. ***Place*** ***What kinds of problems do you think might follow the breakup of such a large nation as the Soviet Union?***

VIEWING HISTORY

Berliners celebrated the fall of the Berlin Wall with joyous, all-night celebrations. ***Foreign Relations*** *What set off the end of the cold war?*

head of a movement that grew with great speed. After two tense weeks, the government gave in to workers' demands for the right to form a free and independent trade union.

Union activity spread throughout Poland, forming an alliance called Solidarity. The Communist government launched a crackdown in 1981, banning Solidarity and jailing its leaders, including Walesa.† But support for Solidarity remained alive.

In 1988, further economic collapse in Poland sparked a new round of protests and strikes that brought down the government. The next year, Poland held its first free elections in half a century. It chose as its president the electrician from Gdansk, Lech Walesa.

† The Western world watched in admiration as events unfolded in the Gdansk shipyard. In 1983, Walesa, a plain-speaking man with minimal education, won the Nobel Peace Prize for his acts of courage.

**The Wall Falls** Throughout Eastern Europe, anti-Communist revolts broke out. Each had its own stories of courage and its own heroes. In Czechoslovakia, a poet and playwright once persecuted by the Communists, Vaclav Havel, was elected president. Eventually, new regimes took charge in Bulgaria, Hungary, Romania, and Albania as well. But the most dramatic events of 1989 took place in East Germany.

In East German cities, nonviolent protests pressured the country's dictator, Erich Honecker, to institute reforms and open border crossings. On November 9, the government announced that East Germans could travel freely to West Germany.

East Germans flooded around and over the hated Berlin Wall. Germans scaled it from both sides and stood atop the structure, cheering and chanting and waving signs. They came with sledgehammers and smashed it with glee. The wall, the most potent symbol of the cold war, had been breached. Within a month the Communist party was in collapse. A year later East and West Germany reunified.

**The Soviet Union** By the end of 1991 the Soviet Union no longer existed. It had been replaced by a loose alliance of former Soviet republics called the Commonwealth of Independent States. Russia's new president, Boris Yeltsin, emerged as the dominant leader in this fragmented land.

As the Soviet Union disintegrated, Bush continued arms-control talks with Gorbachev and later with Yeltsin. The Soviets and Americans signed a number of pacts that signaled the end of the cold war. Agreements in 1989 and 1990 limited the buildup of nuclear and chemical weapons. The first **Strategic Arms Reduction Treaty,** known as START I, called for dramatic reductions in the two nations' supplies of long-range nuclear weapons. It was signed in 1991.

"The cold war is now behind us," Gorbachev declared. "Let us not wrangle over who won it." But clearly the United States was now the world's lone superpower.

## *The Persian Gulf War*

In August 1990 the Arab nation of Iraq, headed by a brutal dictator, Saddam Hussein, launched a sudden invasion of neighboring Kuwait. Saddam justified the assault by citing centuries-old territorial claims. But in fact he had his sights on Kuwait's substantial oil wealth. The conquest promised to yield new riches and stir up patriotic support for Saddam's impoverished regime.

Of concern to the Bush administration was the flow of Kuwaiti oil to the West. Bush viewed the protection of those oil reserves as an issue of national security. The administration was also concerned for the security of Saudi Arabia, a key Arab ally in the region. Bush responded strongly:

**AMERICAN VOICES** **"There is much in the modern world that is subject to doubts or questions—washed in shades of gray. But not the brutal aggression of Saddam Hussein against a peaceful, sovereign nation and its people. It's black and white. The facts are clear. The choice is unambiguous—right versus wrong."**

*—President George Bush, 1990*

U.S. army helicopters hover over the Kuwaiti desert, as oilfields bombed by Iraq blaze in the background (above). American soldiers (right) fought a brief, victorious war, aided by the open terrain, which provided no cover for Saddam's armies. ***Foreign Relations*** *Why did the Bush administration decide to intervene militarily in this regional conflict?*

Americans at first seemed reluctant to get involved in a territorial matter between Arab nations. As the weeks passed, however, reports of rampaging Iraqi soldiers and atrocities against Kuwaiti civilians drew increasing concern.

Months of diplomatic efforts failed to persuade Saddam to withdraw. Finally, the United States, working through the United Nations, mobilized an alliance of 28 nations to launch the **Persian Gulf War.** It was a limited military operation to drive Iraqi forces out of Kuwait.

To organize military operations, President Bush turned to General Colin Powell. Powell had risen quickly through the ranks of the military. In 1979, at age 42, he had become the Army's youngest brigadier general. He was the first African American to serve as national security adviser. In 1989, he had been named the nation's top military officer, Chairman of the Joint Chiefs of Staff, the youngest ever.†

Powell's battle plan was simple. He would use airpower to destroy Iraq's ability to wage war and then smash the Iraqi forces occupying Kuwait. UN forces, directed by General Powell and led by General Norman Schwarzkopf, did just that. A series of massive air strikes, known as "Operation Desert Storm," was launched on January 16–17, 1991. In a war that lasted just 42 days, UN forces liberated Kuwait. The allies lost fewer than 300 soldiers, while tens of thousands of Iraqi troops died.

† After the war, both Republicans and Democrats wooed Powell as a possible candidate for Vice-President in the 1992 election. Powell declined, but did not rule out a future political career.

Bush opted not to extend the war by sending troops into Iraq to oust Saddam, expecting Saddam's opponents to soon overthrow the weakened regime. Yet Saddam proved stronger and his opposition weaker than Bush's advisers thought. Saddam remained in power in Iraq.

## Domestic Issues

Bush's leadership during the Persian Gulf War drove his approval rate up to an astounding 91 percent. Yet while his handling of foreign policy generally won him praise, Americans began to believe that Bush did not have a clear plan for handling domestic problems. In the end, this perception helped usher him out of office.

Bush angered many moderates and liberals with his nomination of Clarence Thomas, a conservative black judge, to the Supreme Court in 1991. Thomas faced grilling about his views on civil rights and about charges of past sexual harassment. Thomas won confirmation after stormy televised Senate hearings that ignited public debate on the issue of sexual harassment.

Bush's real undoing was a recession, with roots in the Reagan years, that began in the early 1990s. Unemployment climbed again. Companies laid off workers to cut costs in a process called **downsizing.** By 1991 the jobless rate reached 7 percent, the highest level in nearly five years.

Bush countered by slowing spending for social programs. Finally, he agreed to a deficit reduction plan that included new taxes. The tax hike broke Bush's 1988 campaign promise and generated public fury.

## SECTION 4 REVIEW

### Comprehension

1. *Key Terms* Define: (a) Strategic Arms Reduction Treaty (START); (b) Persian Gulf War; (c) downsizing.
2. *Summarizing the Main Idea* What were the major successes and failures of the Bush administration?
3. *Organizing Information* Create a cause-and-effect chart on the end of the cold war. Include information about the Soviet Union and Eastern Europe.

### Critical Thinking

4. *Analyzing Time Lines* Refer to the time line at the start of the section. Choose a year that you think had historic significance, and explain your choice.
5. *Making Comparisons* Compare public opinion in the 1988 presidential election with public opinion of Bush near the end of his term.

### Writing Activity

6. *Writing a Persuasive Essay* Is it fair to characterize Bush's successes and failures as largely the result of Reagan-era policies? Write an essay to support your views.

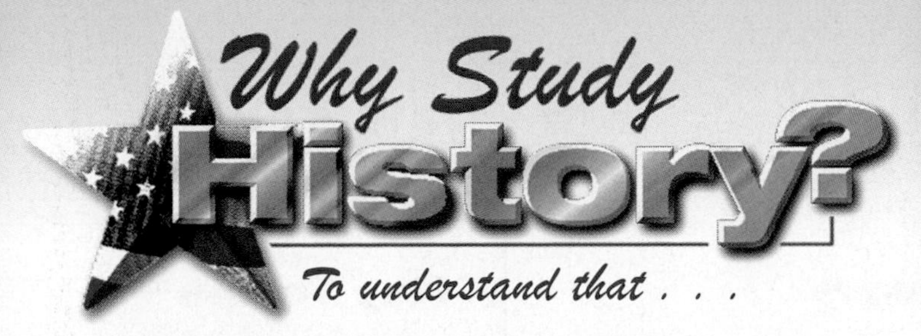


# Government Efficiency Can Be Improved

**President Reagan's vision of a government that is less expensive and more efficient appeals to many Americans today.**

*Anti-tax demonstration*

What's the scariest day of the year? Most adults would say it's April 15, when tax returns are due at the Internal Revenue Service. The happiest? Some might choose "Tax Freedom Day," the day by which the average taxpayer has earned enough money to pay his or her taxes for the year. In 1998, for example, May 10 was Tax Freedom Day. That means that the average taxpayer's total taxes for 1998 amounted to his or her total income from January 1 to May 10.

Many taxpayers complain that their taxes are high because the federal government is wasting money. Republicans controlled the presidency through the 1980s by appealing to public complaints about bloated and ineffective federal programs.

## The Impact Today

In his First Inaugural Address, President Reagan promised to make government "work with us, not over us; to stand by our side, not ride on our back." Reagan's speech reflected his views about the federal government: It was too big, too costly, and too involved in regulation.

During his presidency, Reagan made cuts in a number of federal programs and reduced federal regulations. Yet total federal spending actually increased during Reagan's two terms because of growth in defense spending and in programs such as Social Security and Medicare.

Many Americans still want to "reinvent" government, making it more efficient. In 1993 President Clinton named Vice President Al Gore as head of the National Performance Review (NPR). The NPR sought to create a government that "works better, costs less, and gets results Americans care about."

The NPR, later renamed the National Partnership for Reinventing Government, made impressive gains. It recommended about $177 billion in savings over a five-year period and helped cut the federal civilian work force by 348,000. Federal agencies eliminated unnecessary regulations, adopted innovative practices, and raised customer service standards. President Clinton even ordered all federal agencies to use "plain language" rather than bureaucratic jargon when communicating with the public.

Still, many people still see the federal government as too costly. Others view the government more favorably and support programs to protect the environment, help the poor, and improve education.

*Clinton and Gore present report on reforming government, 1993*

## The Impact on You

"The federal government is too large, too costly, and inefficient." Write a letter to the editor either agreeing or disagreeing with this statement.

# Chapter 24 Review

## Chapter Summary

The major concepts of Chapter 24 are presented below. See also ***Guide to the Essentials of American History*** or ***Interactive Student Tutorial CD-ROM,*** which contains interactive review activities, time lines, helpful hints, and test practice.

### *Reviewing the Main Ideas*

This chapter examines the rise of conservatives to power in the 1980s, beginning with the election of President Ronald Reagan. It looks at the shift in values and policies that occurred in government during the Reagan and Bush presidencies and details the key events of their combined 12 years in office.

### *Section 1: Roots of the New Conservatism*

After decades of government growth and social and cultural change, a conservative backlash grew during the 1970s. In 1980 it brought Ronald Reagan to power.

### *Section 2: The Reagan Revolution*

Ronald Reagan aimed to boost the nation's pride and prosperity by cutting taxes, shrinking the federal government, and increasing defense spending.

### *Section 3: Reagan's Second Term*

After a decisive reelection victory in 1984, Reagan continued his conservative policies on economic and social issues. In domestic and foreign affairs, the administration had key successes but also serious missteps.

### *Section 4: The Bush Presidency*

George Bush achieved notable foreign policy successes, including a popular victory in the Gulf War. However, his record on domestic issues, the economy in particular, eroded his public support.

Reagan's vision of a less expensive, more efficient government appeals to many Americans today.

## Key Terms

Use each of the terms below in a sentence that shows how it relates to the chapter.

1. downsizing
2. entitlement
3. AIDS
4. supply-side economics
5. televangelism
6. Sandinistas
7. START
8. Iran-contra affair

## Comprehension

1. What were some of the goals of the New Right?
2. Why did the United States go to war with Iraq?
3. What arms-control treaties were signed during the Reagan and Bush administrations?
4. Why did the United States government support the contras in Nicaragua?
5. Name one positive effect and one negative effect of Reagan's economic policies.
6. Who is Sandra Day O'Connor, and what were her major accomplishments?
7. What was the impact of Gorbachev's call for perestroika and glasnost?
8. What role did Supreme Court appointments have in Reagan's conservative strategy?

## Using Graphic Organizers

On a separate sheet of paper, copy the chart below. In each box fill in key facts from the chapter.

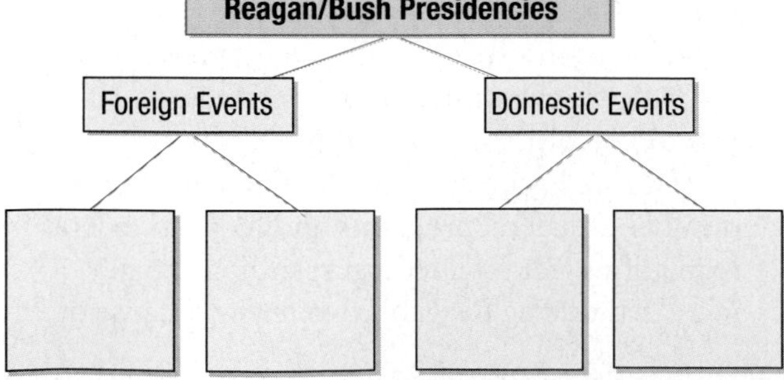

## Analyzing Political Cartoons ▶

1. Analyze the images in the cartoon. (a) Who is the man? (b) What does the ship symbolize? (c) How do you know?
2. (a) Where is the ship headed? (b) What is the man's attitude about the ship's course?
3. Summarize the cartoonist's message.

## Critical Thinking

1. *Applying the Chapter Skill* Reread the American Voices quotation of President Bush in Section 4. Do you think this is an example of reasoned judgment? Why or why not?
2. *Recognizing Ideologies* (a) How did conservative beliefs affect Reagan's policies? (b) How did they affect Bush's policies?
3. *Analyzing Cause and Effect* How did the policies of the Reagan administration influence the outcome of the Bush presidency?
4. *Drawing Conclusions* During his first term, Reagan called the Soviet Union "the evil empire." In his second term, he developed a working relationship with Gorbachev. What do you think accounts for this change in strategy?

### INTERNET ACTIVITY

***For your portfolio:***
**CREATE A TIMELINE**

Access Prentice Hall's *America: Pathways to the Present* site at **www.Pathways.phschool.com** for the specific URL to complete the activity. Additional resources and related Web sites are also available.

Use the links provided to read about the START treaties. Create a time line of important events relating to the treaties. Provide a caption to your time line. What is the importance of START?

## ANALYZING DOCUMENTS ▶ INTERPRETING DATA

Turn to the Federal Budget Deficit graph in Section 2.

1. During the Reagan years, what happened to the overall course of the budget deficit? (a) It rose steadily. (b) It fell. (c) It increased by about $210 billion. (d) It increased, then fell back to its original level.
2. What was the major cause of deficit increases during the period shown in the graph? (a) the cost of the Persian Gulf War (b) the Strategic Defense Initiative (c) increased defense spending and tax cuts under Reagan (d) Bush's pledge not to raise taxes.
3. *Writing* Do you think the government should be allowed to spend more money in any given year than it earns in revenues from taxes and other sources? Why or why not?

## Connecting to Today

*Essay Writing* Is the conservative revolution alive and well today? Write an essay to explain your answer. Include examples of issues from the Reagan/Bush era that have either continued to be debated today or have faded in significance.

CHAPTER

# 25 Entering a New Era

## 1992-Present

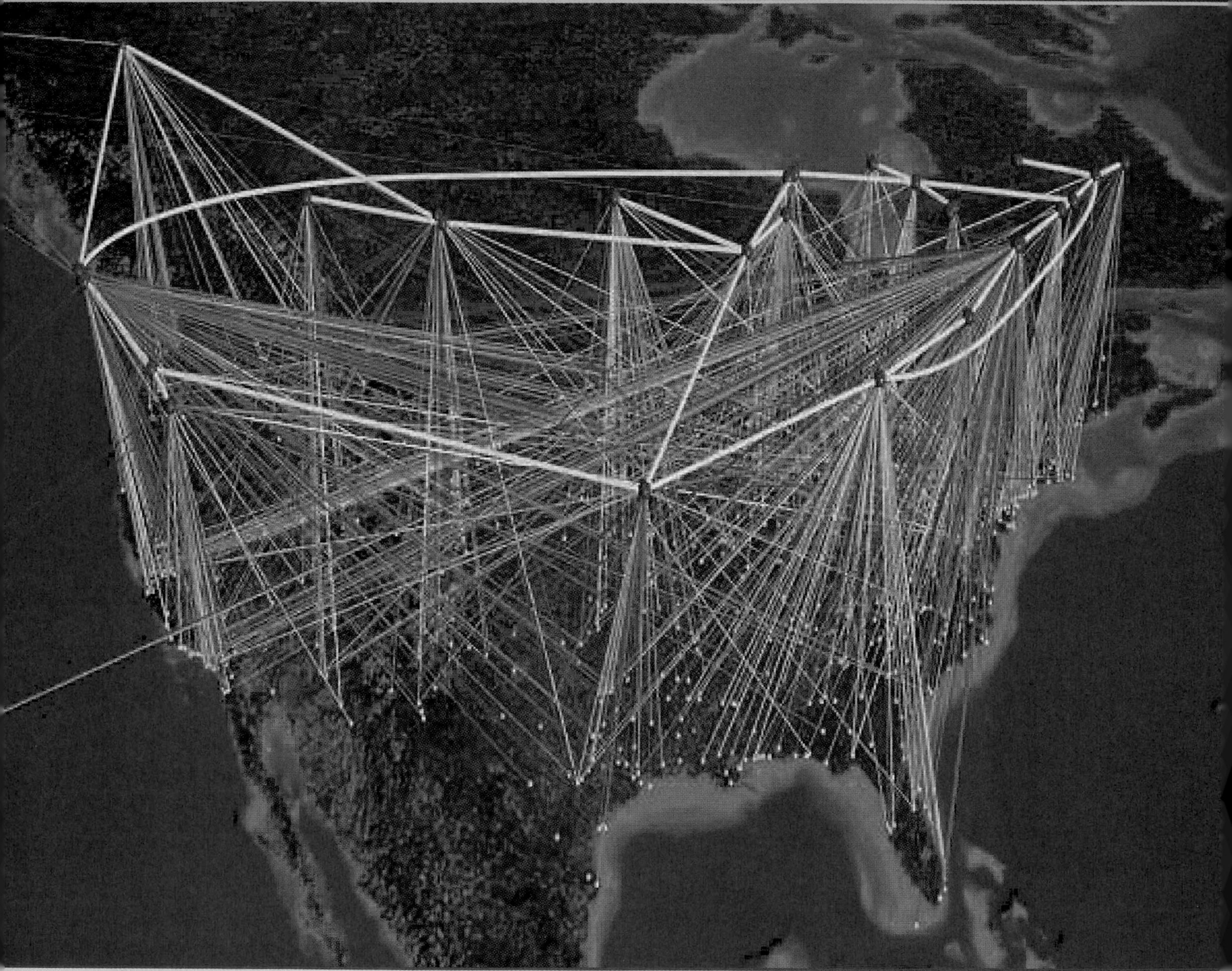

### CHAPTER FOCUS

*In 1993 Democrat Bill Clinton ended twelve years of Republican control of the White House when he became the forty-second President. In 1996, he won a second term. In this chapter you will read about the challenges that Clinton and the American people faced in the post–cold war era abroad and in a changing cultural climate at home.*

*The **Why Study History?** page at the end of this chapter explores the connection between the computer revolution and the public's access to information on the Internet.*

▲ **VIEWING HISTORY** The map above shows the National Science Foundation's Internet network. *Culture* ***How are telecommunication advances changing the ways Americans live, learn, work, and play?***

| 1992 | 1994 | 1995 | 1996 | 1998 | 1999 |
|---|---|---|---|---|---|
| Bill Clinton elected President | Republicans promote Contract with America | Republicans take control of House and Senate | Clinton reelected President | Clinton announces a federal budget surplus | Bill Clinton impeached |

1992 1994 1996 1998 2000

# 1 Politics in the 1990s

## SECTION PREVIEW

### Objectives

1. Describe Clinton's path to the presidency.
2. List the reforms that Clinton tried to accomplish during his first term.
3. Describe the goals of the Republicans' Contract with America.
4. Summarize the challenges Clinton faced during his second term.
5. *Key Terms* Define: Contract with America; Whitewater affair.

### Main Idea

American voters, concerned with a sluggish economy, elected Bill Clinton to the presidency in 1992. Despite showing strong support for Republicans in the 1994 midterm elections, voters reelected Clinton in 1996. His second term, although filled with scandal, was marked by a strong, rapidly growing economy.

### Reading Strategy

*Organizing Information* As you read the section, create a graphic organizer to record the proposed reforms that did and did not take effect during Clinton's two terms as President.

An earnest young man named Bill Clinton reached out and firmly grasped President John F. Kennedy's hand. At just 17, this high school student from a small town in Arkansas was actually shaking hands with the President! Clinton was in Washington as a member of Boys Nation, a program that teaches young people about government. Later, the experience contributed to Clinton's decision to pursue a career in politics. In 1993, some three decades after this meeting, Clinton was back in the White House. This time he stayed, for he was now the forty-second President of the United States.

## Clinton's Path to the Presidency

Bill Clinton's political career got off to a fast start. In 1976, just three years after earning his law degree at Yale, he was elected Attorney General of Arkansas. Two years later, at age 32, Clinton won election as the state's governor. Though he was defeated in his reelection bid in 1980, Clinton made a remarkable comeback. He was returned to office in the 1982 election and remained governor of Arkansas through the 1980s.

*After meeting President Kennedy at age 17, Bill Clinton decided to pursue a career in politics.*

One of Clinton's closest advisers was his wife, Hillary Rodham Clinton, whom he had met at law school. Mrs. Clinton became a leader in efforts to reform education in Arkansas during the 1980s. She was praised by many for her intelligence and energy. Others criticized her active role in government, arguing that a governor's wife should confine herself to ceremonial duties.

**The 1992 Campaign** The 1992 presidential campaign was a three-way race. Not since 1912, when President Taft faced both Woodrow Wilson and former President Theodore

Roosevelt, did a third candidate play such a major role in a presidential election.

On the Republican side, President George Bush sought a second term. Discouraged by Bush's high approval ratings, several prominent Democrats chose not to seek their party's nomination. This created an opening for the likable and eloquent Bill Clinton, who decided to run for the presidency.

Some critics charged that Clinton would say whatever was necessary—regardless of the truth—to get what he wanted. When a woman claimed to have been Clinton's mistress, and produced evidence that seemed to support her story, the candidate denied her charges. In addition, Clinton's statements about how and why he had avoided the draft during the Vietnam War seemed evasive to some. Clinton supporters praised his refusal to quit and called him the "comeback kid."

The third candidate was H. Ross Perot, a billionaire Texas businessman. He entered the race out of frustration over the government's policies on the federal budget and the economy. As an independent, however, Perot had no party base. So he organized a large network of volunteers who collected enough signatures on petitions to get his name on the ballot in each of the 50 states.

**Campaign Issues** The Republicans tried to focus the election on what they perceived to be a decline in family values. In addition, President Bush had won wide praise for his role in ending the cold war and winning the Gulf War. However, the recession of the early 1990s continued, and economic issues dominated the campaign.

Clinton promised to use government measures to end the recession and deal with the nation's other nagging economic problems. He also pledged to address the federal budget deficit and the problems in the health care system. Like his hero, President Kennedy, Clinton believed that government was necessary "to make America work again." At the same time, he called himself a "New Democrat," meaning he would look for new ways to make government more efficient and responsive. Clinton's message appealed to Americans who were frustrated at the seemingly endless bickering and deadlock between Democrats and Republicans in Congress. These voters were eager for action and change.

Like Clinton, Perot also focused on the economy. As a successful businessman, he argued, he had the necessary skills to cut costs, balance the budget, and restore prosperity. Perot ran as a Washington "outsider." He noted that he had no ties to special interest groups, and he pledged that he would consider the needs of the country as a whole.

**Clinton Wins the Election** Television played an important role in the campaign. In addition to the usual political ads and debates, all three candidates appeared on talk shows and interview programs in an effort to shape public opinion.

On election day, Clinton received 43 percent of the votes, while Bush polled nearly 38 percent. Perot's strong showing of about 19 percent meant that Clinton became President with less than a majority of the popular vote. Republicans claimed that Perot had prevented Bush's reelection by attracting support from conservative voters that otherwise would have chosen Bush. In the electoral college

Even before he ran for President of the United States, Bill Clinton had a reputation as a brilliant campaigner. Here he greets a crowd of supporters during his successful 1992 presidential campaign. ***Culture*** ***How does this photo illustrate some of the challenges of campaigning for President?***

Clinton won 370 votes versus 168 for Bush. Perot won no electoral votes.

## *Clinton's First Term*

Bill Clinton began his first term as President in January 1993. He recognized that the voters wanted a change from the politics of the past:

> AMERICAN VOICES **"Thomas Jefferson believed that to preserve the very foundations of the nation we would need dramatic change from time to time. Well, my fellow Americans, this is our time. Let us embrace it. . . . Today we pledge an end to the era of deadlock and drift, and a new season of American renewal has begun."**
>
> — *Bill Clinton, First Inaugural Address*

Clinton was buoyed by the fact that Democratic majorities existed in both the House and the Senate. For the first time in more than a decade, the executive and legislative branches would be in the hands of the same political party. The new President looked forward to working with Congress to fulfill the pledges he had made during the campaign. However, these promises proved difficult to accomplish.

**Economic Reform** In dealing with the economy, Clinton tried to follow a middle course. He wanted to end the lingering recession by raising spending or cutting taxes. At the same time, he needed to reduce the budget deficit, which meant cutting spending or raising taxes. Stimulating the economy and reducing the deficit involved contradictory actions. It was like a driver putting one foot on the gas pedal and the other on the brake, some said. Following this course proved more challenging than Clinton had realized.

Over and over, the President talked of the need to "grow the economy" with new government programs to create jobs and to provide job training. However, even with Democratic majorities in Congress, he could not muster the necessary support. Legislators sensed a conservative mood in the country and refused to pass his package.

Congress did approve Clinton's first budget, but just barely. The House passed the measure by only two votes, while in the Senate, Vice President Al Gore of Tennessee had to break a 50-50 tie. To reduce the deficit, the budget included both spending cuts and tax increases. Neither action was well received by the public. The tax increases fell most heavily on the wealthiest Americans, but still irritated people with lower incomes.

**The Battle over Health Care** An estimated 37 million Americans had no health insurance in 1993. For years, this number had been rising, as were the costs of health care. Many Americans were finding it increasingly difficult to afford medical care. Soon after taking office, Clinton appointed his wife Hillary to head a task force to analyze health care and propose reforms.

"This health care system of ours is badly broken, and it is time to fix it," Clinton declared

## COMPARING PRIMARY SOURCES

### REGULATING HEALTH MAINTENANCE ORGANIZATIONS (HMOS)

During the 1990s, many people debated whether stricter regulations should be placed on HMOs to ensure that patients were not being denied treatments in order to cut costs.

#### Opposed to Stricter HMO Regulations

"Proponents of [greater regulation of HMOs] say their intention is only to improve a managed care system that's put too much emphasis on finances and not enough emphasis on patient care. . . . However, . . . HMOs have brought revolutionary changes to a health care system that had the exact opposite problem only a few decades ago—too little attention to finances and too much wasteful spending in order to pay for new buildings, equipment, and other dubious expenditures that led to double-digit cost increases."

—*Editorial,* Boston Business Journal, *April 10–16, 1998*

#### In Favor of Stricter HMO Regulations

"Market discipline [of HMO's] must include legal constraints that enforce remedies for broken contracts and civil injuries. Without the sanction of having to compensate the victims of their wrongdoing, HMOs will continue to cut their expenditures by withholding deserved treatment and paying their managers bonuses for actions that drive down the quality of care. Horror stories. . . will continue, and managed care will never achieve its fundamental purpose—to reduce cost without impairing the quality of care."

—*Editorial by Ronald F. Hoffman and Mark O. Heipler,* The Washington Post, *April 4, 1998*

***ANALYZING VIEWPOINTS*** **What concerns do these two editorials raise regarding the regulation of HMOs?**

In an outdoor press conference, Newt Gingrich outlines the accomplishments of the Republican's Contract with America. ***Government*** ***How did the Contract change the debate on cutting government spending?***

to a national TV audience in September 1993. "We must make this our most urgent priority." The proposal he presented to Congress called for creation of a government-supervised health insurance program that would guarantee affordable coverage to every American.

Although the public at first seemed to favor Clinton's plan, it was vigorously opposed by a number of insurance, professional, and small-business groups. Congressional Republicans charged the program would be expensive to taxpayers, and they attacked it as an example of big government.

The debate continued for about a year. During this time, lobbyists representing groups opposed to the President's plan lined up congressional support against it. In the end Clinton's plan for health care reform failed to gain the necessary support in Congress.

## *The Republicans' Contract with America*

**Main Idea CONNECTIONS**

*What factors led to a sweeping Republican victory in the 1994 midterm elections?*

The failure of his health care plan signaled trouble for the President. During the 1994 midterm elections, Georgia representative Newt Gingrich called on Republican candidates to endorse what he called a **Contract with America.** This was a pledge, in writing, to scale back the role of the federal government, eliminate bothersome regulations, cut taxes, and balance the budget.

Many voters, feeling that the Democratic-controlled Congress had lost touch with their concerns, responded enthusiastically. In November 1994, voters elected Republicans in large numbers, giving them a majority in both houses of Congress for the first time in more than four decades.

**Congress Versus the President** The first-term Republicans quickly became a potent force in the House. For leadership they looked to Newt Gingrich, who was elected Speaker of the House. There was talk of a new era in American politics in which Congress, not the President, set the nation's course.

The Republicans in Congress moved quickly to keep the pledges they had made during the campaign. They demanded that the budget be balanced in seven years and proposed cuts in virtually all social services. Recalling the achievements of the "hundred days" of the New Deal in 1933, Gingrich demanded action on these items within the session's first hundred days. In most cases, approval was given.

Many of the bills approved by the House never became law, however. Some were rejected by the Senate, while others were vetoed by Clinton. Even so, Gingrich claimed that he had "changed the whole debate in American politics." That is, Americans were no longer debating whether to cut government and balance the budget, but rather *how* to do so.

**The Budget and Welfare Reform** The budget remained a point of contention. At the end of 1995, Clinton and Gingrich clashed over the size of budget cuts and the timetable for balancing the budget. When they were unable to compromise, government offices and operations temporarily shut down, disrupting services to millions of Americans. Not until the spring of 1996 did Congress and the President come to a permanent agreement on the budget.

The battle over the budget marked the start of yet another Clinton comeback. Many Americans blamed congressional Republicans for the government shutdown and began to regard them as uncompromising and extreme. By labeling proposed Republican cuts as mean-spirited and presenting himself as one who could make needed reforms, Clinton raised his approval rating in national polls.

In August 1996 Congress and Clinton did agree on a sweeping reform of the nation's welfare system. Affected were 12.8 million people receiving Aid to Families with Dependent Children (AFDC) and 25.6 million people receiving food stamps. The new law eliminated federal guarantees of cash assistance and gave states authority to run their own welfare programs with block grants of federal money. It also established a lifetime limit of five years of aid per family and required most adults to work within two years of receiving aid. The historic policy change reversed six decades of social welfare legislation dating back to the New Deal in the 1930s.

## *Clinton's Second Term*

When the Republicans took control of Congress in 1995, Clinton's chances for reelection had seemed slim. The Republican message seemed to have great appeal to voters. In the months that followed, Clinton worked hard to counter that message and to show that he was not a "tax-and-spend liberal."

**The 1996 Campaign** The Republican candidate in 1996 was Bob Dole, Senate Majority Leader and a respected member of Congress for 35 years. Ross Perot again entered the race, this time as the nominee of the newly created Reform Party.

As the election approached, Clinton successfully maneuvered several popular bills through Congress, including a higher minimum wage. In addition the economy, which had been an important factor in the 1992 campaign, was now strong. Thus it again worked in Clinton's favor.

On election day, voters returned Clinton to office with 49 percent of the popular vote. Dole received 41 percent while Perot dropped off to 8 percent. In the electoral college, Clinton gathered 379 votes to 159 for Dole.

**Scandal and the Second Term** Charges of scandal in Clinton's first term, which Bob Dole emphasized in the 1996 election, continued into his new administration.

In what came to be known as the **Whitewater affair,** Clinton was accused of having participated in fraudulent loans and land deals in Arkansas and of having used his influence as governor to block investigation of his business partners. Attorney General Janet Reno appointed a special prosecutor to look into these charges. As a result, some of Clinton's friends and former associates were convicted of various crimes and jailed. Yet no evidence was found to link the President to any wrongdoing.

Another charge was made by Republicans, shortly after Clinton's reelection, that he had accepted illegal campaign donations in return for political favors. A Senate committee found violations of campaign finance laws by members of both political parties, but Clinton was not directly implicated.

**Clinton Impeached** Clinton's sixth year in office, 1998, began with better news: the historic announcement that the government had achieved its first budget surplus since 1962. The moment was short-lived, however. Later that month a scandal erupted that engulfed the President and the Congress and led to only the second impeachment in the nation's history.

The crisis arose when the special prosecutor, Kenneth Star, began to investigate the relationship between Clinton and a young White House intern. Under oath in a separate sexual harassment lawsuit, Clinton denied having had sexual relations with the intern. He repeated this denial again to a grand jury convened by Starr in August. Finally, Clinton did admit to having had an "inappropriate relationship" and to having "misled" his family and the country.

In September, Starr sent a report listing numerous grounds for impeachment to the

Wall Street traders celebrate in 1999 as the Dow Jones reaches its highest levels ever (inset). The rising stocks reflected the explosion of the U.S. economy in the late 1990s. ***Government*** *How might the economic boom have influenced the public's attitude toward the Clinton scandals?*

George W. Bush, shown here with his wife Laura, emerged as the victor in one of the closest presidential elections in United States history in 2000.

House of Representatives. This led to a bitterly partisan debate in the House and throughout the country.

Polls showed that while most did not approve of Clinton's actions, a majority of Americans believed that he was doing a good job as President and should not be impeached. However, on December 19, 1998, the full House voted to impeach Clinton on charges of perjury and obstruction of justice. Most Republicans voted yes, and most Democrats voted no.

The Senate trial that followed opened on January 7, 1999. Many senators believed that Clinton had committed offenses, but debate centered around whether these offenses qualified as "high crimes and misdemeanors," the constitutional requirement for conviction of a President.

On February 12, 1999, the trial ended as most people expected, with the Senate voting to acquit Clinton on both charges. The episode, while raising serious constitutional issues, also fueled more partisan debate throughout the country.

Support for Clinton throughout the process may have been bolstered by an unprecedented economic boom. The Clinton presidency marked the longest period of economic expansion in American history. As the economy continued to grow, the nation maintained low levels of unemployment and inflation.

**The 2000 Election** The mixture of a strong economy and a scandal-ridden presidency would make for an interesting presidential election in 2000. Partisan debate and battles began anew throughout the campaign process. For months leading up to the election, national polls showed that the Republican candidate, Texas governor George W. Bush, was virtually tied with the Democratic nominee, Vice President Al Gore.

On election night the votes in several states were too close to call and neither candidate captured the 270 electoral votes needed to win the presidency. One undecided state, Florida, would give either candidate the electoral votes needed to win. A recount of the votes there was then ordered by law. Florida became a battleground for the presidency as lawyers, politicians, and the media swarmed there to monitor the recount.

Democrats and Republicans argued bitterly over how the recount process should proceed. Charges were made on both sides that the recounts were not fair or accurate. For 36 days, the nation waited and watched as a variety of court battles ensued between the two parties.

Eventually, matters reached the U.S. Supreme Court in *Bush* v. *Gore.* The nine justices were sharply divided about how to remedy the election crisis. By a majority of five to four, they issued a ruling that discontinued all recounts in Florida. This decision overturned a Florida Supreme Court decision to allow recounts to proceed, and effectively secured the presidency for George W. Bush. Although Gore won the national popular vote, Bush won 271 electoral votes to Gore's 266. President-elect Bush promised to bridge partisan gaps and find a common ground for renewed progress.

## SECTION 1 REVIEW

### Comprehension

1. *Key Terms* Define: (a) Contract with America; (b) Whitewater affair.
2. *Summarizing the Main Idea* Describe the election outcomes in 1992, 1996, and 2000.
3. *Organizing Information* Create a graphic organizer that summarizes the results of the elections of 1992, 1996, and 2000.

### Critical Thinking

4. *Analyzing Time Lines* Review the time line at the start of the section. What factors led to Clinton's election in 1992? What challenges did Clinton face after his reelection in 1996?
5. *Recognizing Ideologies* Describe the impact of the Contract with America.

### Writing Activity

6. *Writing a Persuasive Essay* Write an essay urging Congress to either accept or reject Clinton's proposal for health care reform.

SKILLS FOR LIFE

Critical Thinking

Geography

Graphs and Charts

Historical Evidence

# Predicting Consequences

Many social scientists, especially those who work for the government, try to look into the future. They study what has happened in the past, and on the basis of that, they try to predict what might happen next.

Every ten years the government takes a census of the national population. Social scientists study the data from the census to see what they can predict from it. For example, what has the rate of population growth been over the past decades? What does this suggest about the rate of population growth in the next few years? Which groups are likely to grow faster and which slower?

The table at right focuses on census information on the changing number of families in three ethnic groups in the United States and family income in those groups over a fifteen-year period. Use the following steps to analyze the information in the table. Draw on your understanding of history to predict possible trends for the twenty-first century.

**1.** *Identify the kinds of information in the table.* (a) What does this table tell you about the number of families in various ethnic groups in the United States? (b) By what percentage did the number of Latino families increase between 1990 and 1995? (c) The median income for a given group represents the center of the income distribution—in each group, exactly half of the families earn more and half earn less than the median income. What does it mean if one group has a lower median income than another group?

**2.** *Analyze the rate of change.* (a) Which group of families is growing at the fastest rate? (b) Which group's median income has grown at the fastest rate? (c) Which group seems the most economically vulnerable—that is, which has the least stable median income?

**3.** *Use your knowledge of history to predict the consequences that your findings might have in the future.* The Immigration Act of 1965 allowed more people from places other than Europe to immigrate to the United States. The Immigration Act of 1990 further increased immigration quotas by 40 percent. (a) How might the table illustrate the consequences of the 1965 law? (b) What consequences might the 1990 law have by the year 2005? (c) If an economic recession began in the first years of the twenty-first century, which group's median income would you expect to drop the most? (d) What changes in the trends shown on the table would have to take place in order to alter your predictions?

**TEST FOR SUCCESS**

Given the data on percent changes in median income, do you think the median income of Latino families will be higher or lower than the median income of African American families in the near future?

**Change in Number of Families and Median Income,* by Selected Ethnic Groups, 1980—1995**

| | Year | Number of Families (in thousands) | Percent Change (from preceding figure) | Median Income (dollars) | Percent Change (from preceding figure) |
|---|---|---|---|---|---|
| White Families | 1980 | 52,710 | — | 40,561 | — |
| | 1990 | 56,803 | +7.8 | 43,044 | +6.1 |
| | 1995 | 58,872 | +3.6 | 42,646 | –1.0 |
| African American Families | 1980 | 6,317 | — | 23,469 | — |
| | 1990 | 7,471 | +18.3 | 24,980 | +6.4 |
| | 1995 | 8,055 | +7.8 | 25,970 | +4.0 |
| Latino Families | 1980 | 3,235 | — | 27,251 | — |
| | 1990 | 4,981 | +54.0 | 27,321 | +0.3 |
| | 1995 | 6,287 | +26.2 | 24,570 | –10.0 |

* In 1995 dollars

Source: *Statistical Abstract of the United States*

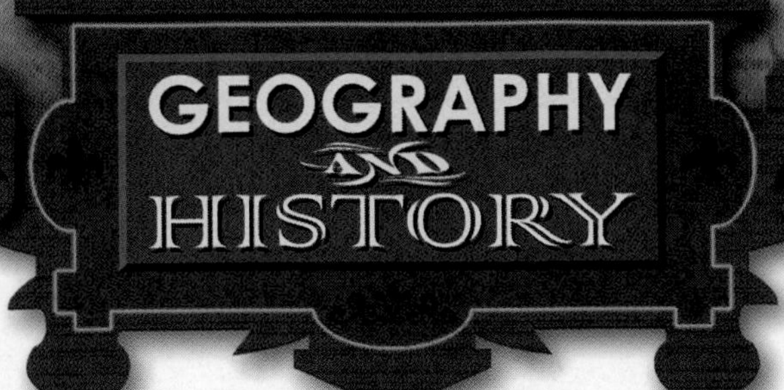


# The Rise of the Sunbelt

Atlanta, Georgia

***The geographic theme of movement explores ways in which people, goods, and ideas travel from one place to another. By 1990, large numbers of people had flocked to one region of the United States—the Sunbelt. What caused this? How did it affect politics and the economy?***

In the years after World War II, the southern states—mainly agricultural, often poor—suddenly exploded into growth and prosperity. Writers in the 1970s used the term "Sunbelt" to describe this change. Generally, the Sunbelt included the warm-weather states south of the 37th parallel, from North Carolina to Arizona. Neighboring states such as California and Colorado are often included as well.

## Moving for New Jobs

The key reason for Sunbelt growth was jobs, both new and transplanted. New manufacturing industries were started in the South or moved there from other areas. Sunbelt cities such as Houston, Dallas, and Atlanta grew quickly, with more room to spread out than crowded metropolitan areas in the North. People flocked to the area, leaving behind hard times and cold weather. They turned their backs on the decaying industries and cities in northern states, which soon acquired unflattering nicknames, like "Frost Belt" and "Rust Belt."

Other factors attracted businesses to the Sunbelt. Hydroelectric power was inexpensive and widely available. Warmer weather reduced the expense of heating fuels. And lower taxes and costs of living attracted both workers and industry. As the Sunbelt economy grew, so did defense industries and aerospace and electronics companies.

While manufacturing jobs increased, other types of businesses grew. Newcomers built homes and offices, bringing a boom in construction and building supplies. Service businesses opened, from realtors to supermarkets to video rentals. Southern cities won franchises for expansion teams of professional sports, even for that most wintry sport, ice hockey.

**In addition to jobs, good weather and mild winters drew retired people and families. For younger families, quality of life was a big attraction.**

## Quality of Life

In addition to jobs, good weather and mild winters drew retired people and families. For younger families, quality of life was a big attraction. This meant a slower-paced way of life, clean air, a friendlier and safer atmosphere, and more outdoor recreation.

For the first time in decades, many new southerners were African American. Earlier in the century, many had left the South to escape racial prejudice and find jobs in industry. Now, many returned, deciding that racial attitudes and quality of life were better in the South than in many northern cities.

## 1990 Reapportionment

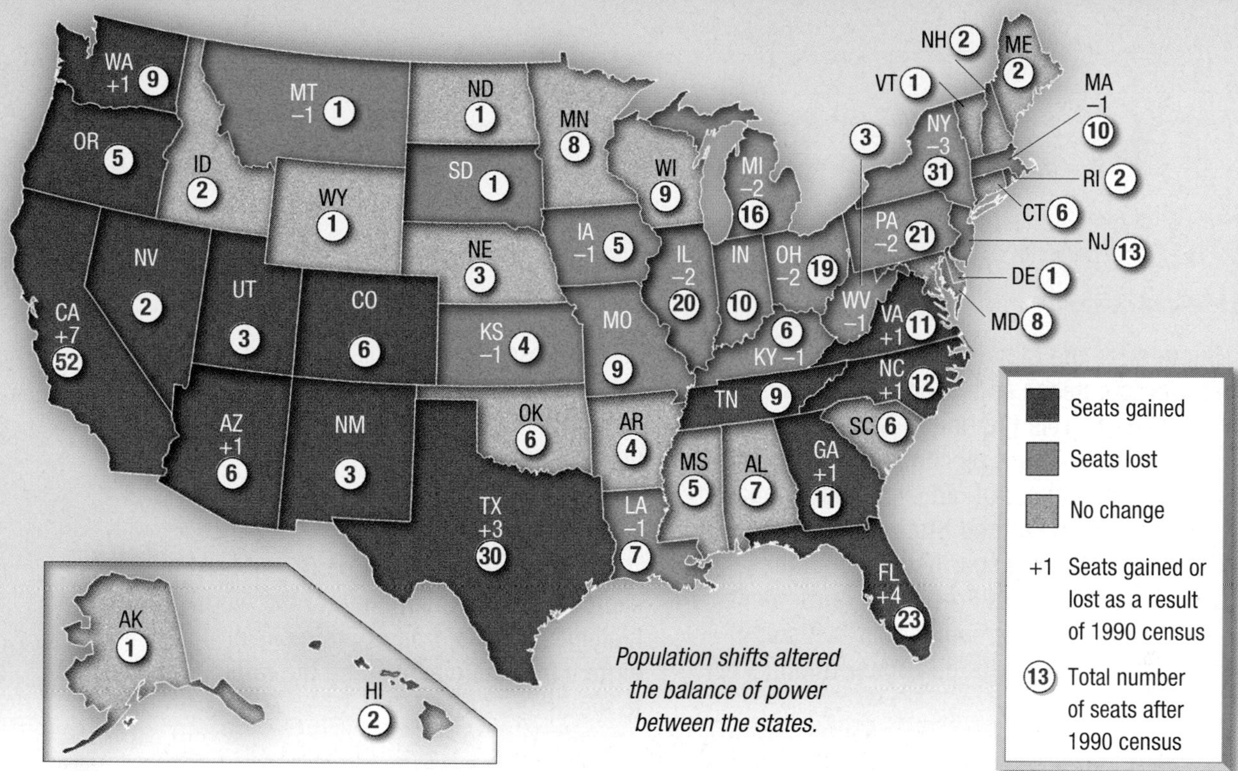


Population shifts altered the balance of power between the states.

### New Political Influence

The shift of people to the Sunbelt has brought a dramatic shift in national political power. Every ten years, after the census, the 435 seats in the U.S. House of Representatives are reapportioned among the states on the basis of population changes. As the map shows, after the 1990 census, many southern and western states added congressional seats, while the Northeast lost representatives. These shifts have given the South and West greater influence on both politics and social issues.

The Sunbelt's voting strength is reflected in presidential politics. Since the mid-1960s, most Presidents have been from Sunbelt states. In 1996, for the first time, southern Republicans led both houses of Congress: Speaker of the House Newt Gingrich of Georgia and Senate Majority Leader Trent Lott of Mississippi.

Southern voting patterns have also changed. Once a stronghold for Democrats, the South has become more strongly Republican and conservative.

Sunbelt population growth is expected to continue. Of the 20 cities expected to grow the most between 1995 and 2005, 15 are in Sunbelt states, and 11 are in just three states: Texas, Florida, and California.

Eighteen of the 20 cities with the fastest projected job growth for the same period are also in the South and West. Whether the rest of the country can keep up with the growth of the Sunbelt remains to be seen.

1. What were some factors that attracted people and businesses to the Sunbelt?
2. What political changes took place as a result of the growth of the Sunbelt?

#### Themes in Geography

3. *Movement* What could northern states and communities do to keep businesses and people from moving to the Sunbelt?

| 1993 Peace agreement between Israel and Palestinians | 1994 United States–led intervention in Haiti | 1994 Senate ratifies NAFTA | 1995 Bosnian peace agreement | 1996 Boris Yeltsin reelected Russian president | 1998 Northern Ireland peace accord | 1999 NATO goes to war over Kosovo |
|---|---|---|---|---|---|---|

1992 | 1994 | 1996 | 1998 | 2000

# 2 The United States in a New World

## SECTION PREVIEW

### Objectives

1. Summarize the Clinton administration's efforts to promote peace and freedom abroad.
2. Describe the role the United States played in helping nations torn by conflict in the 1990s.
3. Analyze the impact of an expanding global economy on the United States.
4. *Key Terms* Define: apartheid; economic sanction; North American Free Trade Agreement (NAFTA); General Agreement on Tariffs and Trade (GATT); World Trade Organization (WTO).

### Main Idea

The collapse of communism and an increase in ethnic tensions in various parts of the world caused Americans to examine their nation's political and economic role in the post–cold war era.

### Reading Strategy

*Organizing Information* Before you read the section, sketch a rough outline map of the world. As you read, highlight areas of United States involvement and write a brief note explaining the region's connection to the United States.

*F. W. de Klerk and Nelson Mandela shared the 1993 Nobel Peace Prize for their work in ending apartheid.*

Witnessing the collapse of communism in the Soviet Union and Eastern Europe, President Bush had spoken hopefully of the dawn of a "New World Order." By this, he meant a more stable and peaceful world, in which "the strong respect the rights of the weak." However, President Clinton found that in some ways the world was becoming less stable. While some nations had thrown off repressive governments and become more open and democratic, others were being torn apart by racial, cultural, or religious tensions. A few observers joked grimly of a "New World Disorder." Meanwhile, economic ties between nations continued to expand.

## The Search for Peace and Freedom

In the 1980s, communism in the Soviet Union, racial oppression in South Africa, and conflict in the Middle East had seemed like permanent world problems. For decades they had been considerations in shaping American foreign policy. By the late 1990s, however, historic events had changed conditions in these and other regions.

**Russia and Eastern Europe** As the old Soviet empire crumbled, the United States tried to promote the move toward Western-style democracy in many of the former Soviet republics. It applauded the election of Boris Yeltsin as president of Russia.

To help that nation create a free market economy, the United States offered a $2.5 billion aid package. Yet even that was not enough. Goods remained in short supply, and the Russian economy remained unstable. In the fall of 1993 the Russian parliament resisted reforms that Yeltsin argued were necessary. In response, he dissolved the parliament and tightened censorship in a bid to silence his political opponents.

Russian reformers, angry at these curbs on freedom, soon grew angrier. In 1994, Yeltsin ordered troops into Chechnya, a self-governing republic that sought independence from Russia. After 21 months of fierce fighting, a cease-fire was finally reached, and the Russian troops were withdrawn. Although Yeltsin postponed the crisis, the bloody conflict had already taken thousands of lives. It cost Yeltsin much of his public support.

In 1999, this same conflict would be the source of great public support for newly appointed Russian Prime Minister Vladimir Putin. A series of Chechnyan terrorist attacks in Russia late in the year prompted Putin to assault the republic with air raids and a full-scale ground invasion. This act made Putin a popular figure in Russia. Political parties aligned with Putin won great support in the December parliamentary elections. Many people saw this as a mandate for Putin and at the end of the year, Yeltsin resigned his post, making Putin the acting president of Russia.

Great political change also continued to occur in other parts of Eastern Europe. In the early 1990s Poland, led by Solidarity hero Lech Walesa, had undertaken bold economic reforms to create a free market. Economic progress was initially slow and many people were quick to worry. In 1995, Polish voters elected Aleksander Kwasniewski as president. Despite his communist background, Kwasniewski continued the push for a free market economy and eventually the economy began to rebound.

In a clear sign that there was no returning to the past, in 1999, Poland, Hungary, and the Czech Republic all became members of NATO. The NATO allies also held out hope of membership to other former Communist nations in the region if they continued to make progress toward democracy.

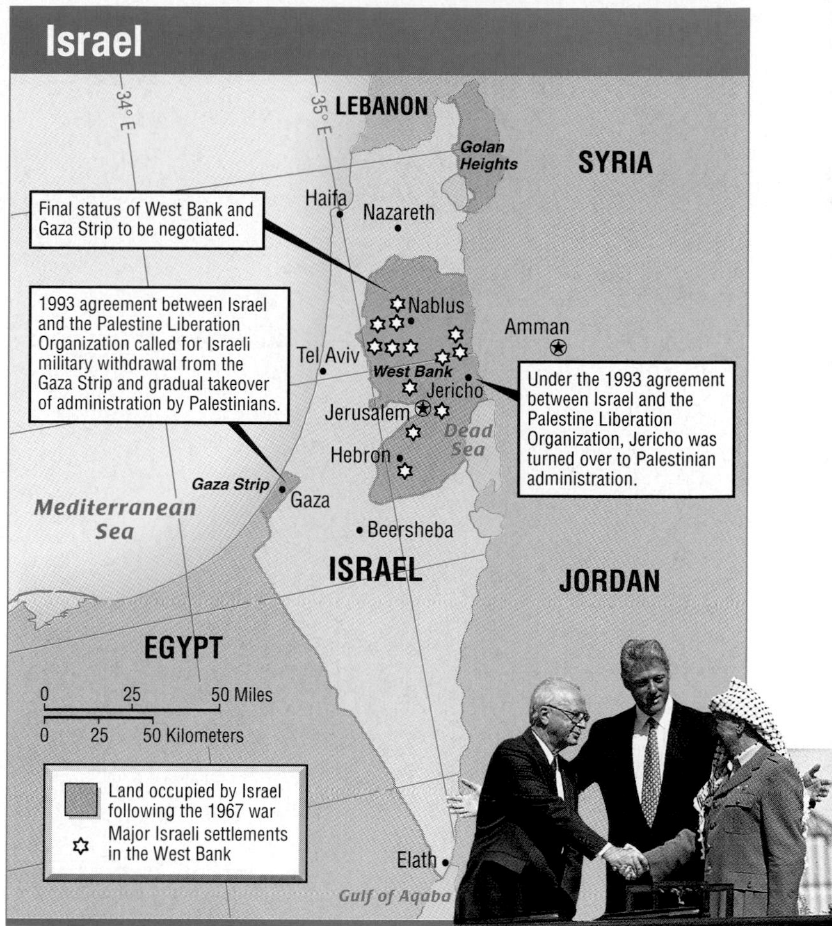


**MAP skills** The map above shows the effects of the peace accord between Israel's Yitzhak Rabin (left) and the PLO's Yasir Arafat (right), presided over by President Clinton (center) in 1993. ***Regions*** ***How did the accord affect the West Bank and the Gaza strip?***

**South Africa** The United States and nations around the world hailed South Africa's effort to overturn **apartheid,** the systematic separation of people of different racial backgrounds. South Africa's white minority, which made up only about 15 percent of the population, had long denied equal rights to the black majority. The United States and other nations had used **economic sanctions,** or trade restrictions and other economic measures intended to punish another nation, to encourage reform. Finally, in 1990, Prime Minister F. W. de Klerk released anti-apartheid leader Nelson Mandela from jail. Mandela had been held prisoner for 27 years.

Former rivals de Klerk and Mandela worked together to end apartheid. In 1994, South Africa held its first elections in which blacks as well as whites voted. These elections produced a new government, led by a new president, Nelson Mandela, and his anti-apartheid organization, the African National Congress (ANC). Although the world watched in fear that a civil war might erupt, South Africa made a peaceful transition to black majority rule. From 1996 to 1998, a government-appointed Truth and Reconciliation Commission investigated the atrocities of the apartheid era. Its final report, published in 1998, won international praise as it addressed wrongdoings on both sides and continued the nation's move toward peace.

**The Middle East** In September 1993, Palestine Liberation Organization (PLO) leader Yasir Arafat and Israel's prime minister Yitzhak Rabin signed the historic peace

**MAP skills** This map shows the regions of Bosnia-Herzegovina controlled by various groups. ***Regions*** ***How does it demonstrate the problems in many former Communist nations after their governments collapsed in the late 1980s and early 1990s?***

agreement in Washington, D.C. It was a difficult step for both sides. However, as Rabin noted, "Peace is not made with friends. Peace is made with enemies."

The pact provided for Palestinian self-rule in the Gaza Strip (between Israel and the Sinai Peninsula) and in the town of Jericho on the West Bank of the Jordan River. The agreement also set the stage for negotiations on the status of the rest of the West Bank. Israel had seized these areas in the Six-Day War of 1967. At the same time, the PLO recognized Israel's right to exist.

The Middle Eastern peace process had other successes. In 1994, Israel and Jordan signed a treaty ending the state of war that had existed between them. Israel and Syria began talks as well. Extremists on both sides, meanwhile, tried to destroy prospects for peace through terrorist attacks. In 1995 a Jewish extremist assassinated Rabin.

Benjamin Netanyahu became the next prime minister and was more reluctant than Rabin to grant concessions to the Palestinians. The peace process faltered under his leadership, but in 1999, moderate leader Ehud Barak, touted as a soldier for peace, was elected prime minister of Israel by a landslide. Under Barak, the 1998 Wye River Accords between Israel and Palestine were implemented, in which both sides made concessions to further the peace process. The 2000 Camp David Summit between Barak and Arafat sought to build on the peacemaking efforts of the Wye River Accords.

**Haiti** Several other nations likewise took steps toward stability. In Haiti, military leaders had overthrown that country's first freely elected president, Jean-Bertrand Aristide, in 1991. Three years later, a United States–led military intervention forced Haiti's military to give up power. U.S. troops stayed in Haiti for many months, helping to restore democracy.

**Northern Ireland** In Northern Ireland, the United States encouraged renewed efforts in the 1990s to end decades of violence between Protestants and Catholics. In 1996, Clinton asked former U.S. senator George Mitchell to lead talks that included representatives of the warring factions and the British and Irish governments.

After 22 months of tense negotiations, Mitchell's efforts paid off. In 1998, all parties signed the Good Friday Accords, agreeing to major reforms in the government of the British province. The agreement was approved by a vast majority of voters in both Northern Ireland and Ireland. It stopped short of providing for unification of the two Irelands, which Catholics had desired. However, it offered the best hope yet for ending the shootings and bombings that in 30 years had taken over 3,000 lives.

## *Nations Torn by Conflict*

For the United States, promoting peace and the spread of democracy were satisfying foreign policy challenges. Far less satisfying was the task of trying to stop the terrifying violence that erupted within several disintegrating countries. President Clinton had to balance Americans' desire to help other nations against Americans' fear of costly commitments. This fear was magnified by memories of the Vietnam War.

**The Balkan Nations** The nation of Yugoslavia had long been burdened with deep-rooted ethnic and religious tensions. Under communism, following World War II, these tensions remained below the surface. With the end of the cold war, however, these underlying problems erupted, resulting in a decade of violent conflict.

Some of the Yugoslav republics wanted to separate and become independent nations. Serbia, and its leader, Slobodan Milosevic, wanted to preserve a unified Yugoslavia, dominated by Serbia. When the Muslim and Croatian majority in Bosnia declared its independence in 1991, Bosnian Serbs, backed by Milosevic and Serbia, attacked. They began a siege of Sarajevo, Bosnia's major city, and carried on a ferocious "ethnic cleansing" campaign to remove non-Serbs from the republic. Millions were forced to flee their homes and 300,000 people were killed in the worst atrocities seen in Europe since World War II.

When Clinton campaigned for President in 1992, he promised strong action in Bosnia. Once in office, however, he hesitated when America's European allies resisted the use of force. Finally, in mid-1995, an American-led NATO bombing campaign pushed the Bosnian Serbs into peace talks. These talks, held in Dayton, Ohio, produced a cease-fire and the commitment of foreign peacekeeping troops, thousands of whom were U.S. troops.

Steps toward peace had been made, but none of the underlying problems had gone away. New troubles began in Kosovo, another part of the former Yugoslavia. As a part of Serbia, Kosovo was subject to Serbian rule. Much like Bosnia, however, Kosovo's majority population was not Serbian. Most people living there were ethnic Albanians and they had demanded more self-rule. This led to another brutal round of violence, this time between the Serbs and the Kosovars.

Thousands of ethnic Albanian refugees fled Kosovo as the fighting became more widespread throughout 1998. By July, the Kosovo Liberation Army (KLA) occupied 40 percent of Kosovo before being defeated by the Serbs. Following this victory, the Serbians took control and began a violent campaign closely resembling their actions in Bosnia.

In early 1999, the U.S. and NATO threatened airstrikes if both sides would not commit to a Kosovo peace conference. While Kosovo Albanians signed a peace deal authorizing the stationing of a NATO peacekeeping force there, the Serbs refused. After the failure of Serbs to commit to NATO peacekeeping efforts, NATO launched a series of airstrikes which forced them to reconsider. Eventually, Milosevic agreed to the international peacekeeping force in Kosovo and the Albanian refugees were able to return home.

**Main Idea CONNECTIONS**

*What role did the United States play in ending the conflicts in Bosnia and Kosovo?*

**Somalia** In the early 1990s the East African nation of Somalia had suffered from a devastating famine, made worse by a civil war. In 1992 President Bush sent American troops to assist a United Nations relief effort. The food crisis eased, but Somalia's government remained unable to control the armed groups that ruled the countryside. The following year, after several United States soldiers were killed in a battle with Somali rebels, Clinton recalled the troops without order having been restored. By 1998, the end of the long civil war seemed to be in sight after leaders of the rival factions signed a peace agreement. It remained to be seen whether a functioning government could be formed.

The war in Kosovo tore apart cities and towns throughout the region. Here, U.S. soldiers patrol through the village of Cuernica as part of a NATO peacekeeping operation. NATO played an integral role in rebuilding the infrastructure in villages such as these. ***Foreign Relations*** ***Why did the U.S. support sending troops into Kosovo?***

Secretary of State Madeleine Albright, seen here during a trip to China, worked hard to establish a new leadership role for the United States in the post–cold war era. ***Government*** ***What issues faced the Secretary of State during the Clinton administration?***

**Rwanda and Zaire** In 1994 the death of Rwanda's president in a suspicious plane crash wrecked an uneasy peace that had existed between the nation's two main ethnic groups, the Hutus and Tutsis. The Hutus, blaming the Tutsis for the crash, embarked on a massive genocidal campaign, slaughtering hundreds of thousands of Tutsis. Later that year, Tutsi rebels countered and overthrew the Hutu government prompting an estimated one million Hutus to flee the country.

Many of the Hutus fled to neighboring Zaire, one of Africa's largest nations. Zaire was then under the leadership of longtime dictator and U.S. ally Mobutu Sese Seko, whose power had recently been weakened. From Zaire, the Hutu refugees staged raids on the Tutsi-dominated Rwandan government. The ethnic Tutsis in Zaire responded by rebelling against Zaire's government.

In 1997, supported by Rwanda and other nearby countries, the rebels forced Sese Seko to resign. Rebel leader Laurence Kabila became president and renamed Zaire to the Democratic Republic of Congo. Since then, Kabila has failed to initiate basic reforms and has turned against the Tutsi and Rwandan influences that once supported him. A new rebellion formed, followed by a violent civil war, which by 2000 claimed an estimated 1.7 million lives.

**India, Pakistan, and China** At the same time that tensions were easing in Northern Ireland, Asia suddenly became less stable. In 1998, India exploded nuclear weapons for the first time in a series of underground tests. India's neighbor and rival, Pakistan, quickly responded with its first nuclear tests. A border dispute between the two nations had already embroiled them in three wars in the past half-century. The United States feared that their long-standing territorial and religious tensions would touch off nuclear war in the region.

Much of the world, including nearby China, viewed the developments in India and Pakistan with alarm. China's economic growth, combined with its size, made it an increasingly important power in the 1990s. As a result, the United States began working more closely with China on various issues, including trade and regional security.

## *Trade and the Global Economy*

Despite dramatic events within countries, the most important world development of the mid- and late-1990s may have been one that took place between countries. That development was the continuing growth of global trade. The United States was active in promoting closer economic ties with other countries.

**The European Union** In 1957 six European nations set up the Common Market to coordinate economic and trade policies. Over time, new nations joined the Common Market. In 1986, member nations agreed to dismantle all tariffs on one another's exports, thereby creating a single market.

In 1993, the Common Market nations formed the European Union (EU) to provide political and monetary coordination as well. The EU, now with more than a dozen members, has a parliament and a council in which all member nations are represented. In the late 1990s member nations agreed to gradually replace their individual monetary systems with a single new currency called the eurodollar, or euro, by 2001.

The EU's goal is to create an economic unit that rivals the size and strength of the American economy. The United States has generally supported Europe's progress toward economic cooperation. As a Clinton administration official stated, "Close partnership between the United States and the European Union is essential to our common agenda of democratic renewal." The EU is today the largest trading partner of the United States.

**NAFTA** Meanwhile, the United States also sought to encourage greater economic cooperation in its own backyard. **The North American Free Trade Agreement (NAFTA)** called for removal of trade restrictions among the United States, Canada, and Mexico. The resulting free trade zone created a single market similar to the market of the European Union.

The NAFTA measure aroused tremendous controversy in the United States. NAFTA opponents worried that American factories would relocate to Mexico, where wages were lower and government regulations, such as environmental controls, were less strict. Supporters of NAFTA claimed that it would instead create more American jobs by increasing exports to Mexico and Canada. In 1994 the United States Senate ratified NAFTA, but only after a bruising battle. Three years later, the government's first study of NAFTA revealed it to be only a limited success. The report cited a "modest" increase in United States exports to Mexico and estimated that perhaps 90,000 to 160,000 new, NAFTA-related jobs had been created. However, some 128,300 American jobs had disappeared. Even with these mixed results, Clinton and others continued their efforts to expand the NAFTA agreement to include other countries in the Western Hemisphere.

**International Agreements** Clinton's support for NAFTA reflected his foreign policy goal of expanding United States trade throughout the world. As part of this effort, the United States joined many other countries in adopting a revised version of the **General Agreement on Tariffs and Trade (GATT)** in 1994.† The goal of GATT, originally established in 1948, was to reduce tariffs and expand world trade. In 1995 the **World Trade Organization (WTO)** was established to ensure compliance with GATT, to negotiate new trade agreements, and to resolve trade disputes.

† The GATT agreement was revised between 1986 and 1994 at a conference known as the Uruguay Round.

## ECONOMICS CONCEPTS

***tariffs:* *taxes on foreign goods imported into a country***

- ▼ **The Historical Context:** In the 1980s and 1990s, a number of governments worked together to reduce tariffs in the hope that expanded trade would stimulate economic growth. These efforts produced regional trade agreements, such as NAFTA, and the formation of the World Trade Organization to resolve trade disputes.
- ▼ **The Concept Today:** Tariffs remain a controversial issue in the United States. Some Americans worry that as American tariffs are lowered, jobs will shift from the United States to less-developed nations. Other Americans, in contrast, argue that lower tariffs worldwide will boost American exports and create new jobs.

## SECTION 2 REVIEW

### Comprehension

1. *Key Terms* Define: (a) apartheid; (b) economic sanction; (c) North American Free Trade Agreement (NAFTA); (d) General Agreement on Tariffs and Trade (GATT); (e) World Trade Organization (WTO).
2. *Summarizing the Main Idea* What questions did Americans raise about their nation's political and economic role in the post–cold war era?
3. *Organizing Information* Create a chart summarizing the United States' role in conflicts in the following places: Bosnia, Kosovo, Somalia, and Rwanda.

### Critical Thinking

4. *Analyzing Time Lines* Review the time line at the start of the section. Select one event on the time line and tell how it reflects the Clinton administration's efforts to promote peace and freedom abroad.
5. *Identifying Central Issues* Why have efforts to reduce tariffs and expand free trade been controversial in the United States?

### Writing Activity

6. *Writing a Persuasive Essay* Write an essay to your senator either in support of or against the expansion of NAFTA to other countries in the Western Hemisphere.

1

### Communications Satellite

Telstar was the world's first communications satellite. On the day it was launched, July 10, 1962, it transmitted the first live television pictures from the United States to Europe.

4

### Bar Codes

*Mad Magazine* makes fun of bar codes—lines of varying thickness carrying information that can be read by laser light.

2

### Fiber-Optic Cable

Hair-thin glass fibers can carry sound and data long distances using coded light pulses.

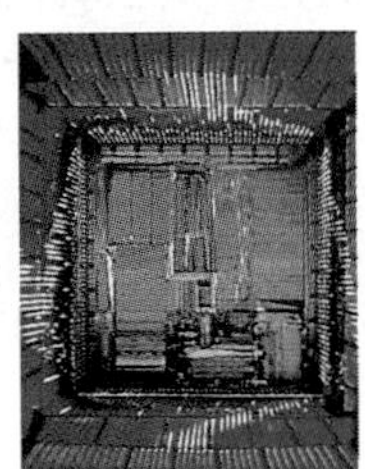

5

### Silicon Chip

The miracle of the information age is this chip of impure silicon—a microprocessor. Computers with silicon chips are more complex, faster, and can handle many times more information than the original room-sized computers that used vacuum tubes and transistors.

### Laser Head

Theodore Maiman developed this early laser in 1960. Laser light can carry more information than radio waves.

3

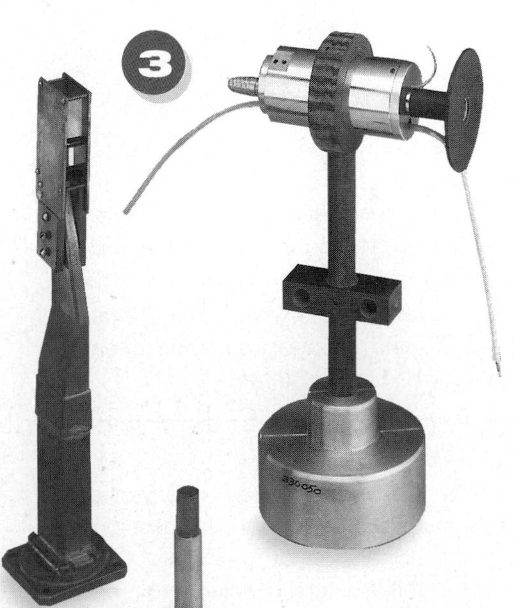

6

### Hand-Held Computer

The ability of a single silicon chip to store and process great amounts of information has shrunk the size of the computer. A person can carry this computer anywhere and operate it at any time with a small stylus.

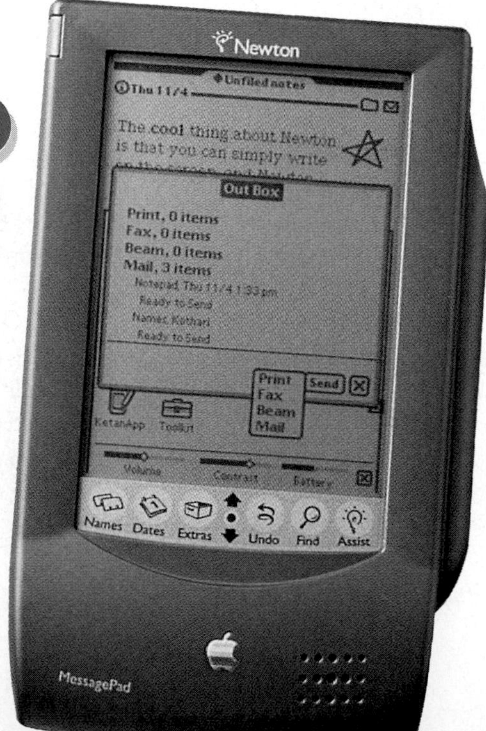

**Early Computer**

The very first computers had no keyboards with which to enter information, no screens to view what was entered, and no storage devices. The Osborne, shown here, was a personal computer that offered all these improvements.

7

**Watergate Bugs**

The burglars who broke into the Democratic National Committee headquarters at the Watergate apartment complex in Washington, D.C., carried these "bugs."

8

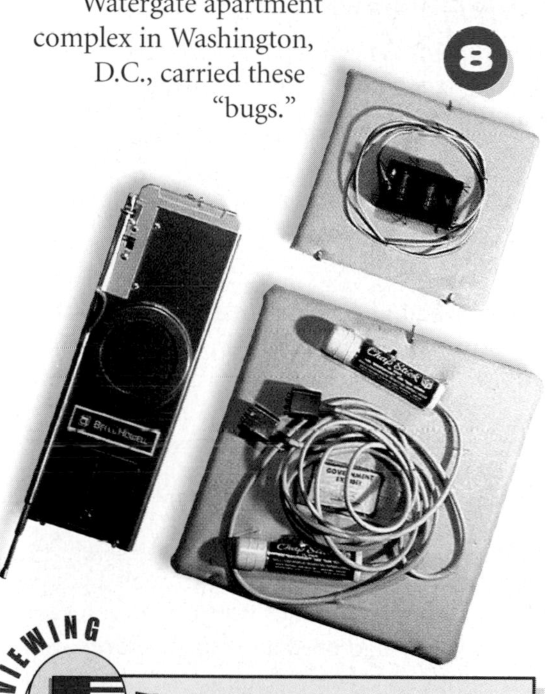

**VIEWING HISTORY**

1. ***Summarize*** What do the objects tell you about technological changes over the years?

2. ***Connecting to Today*** Think about how new technology affects our daily lives. Report the following to your class: (a) several ways in which computers have changed everyday activities; (b) what changes might take place as a result of technological advances in the next five to ten years.

American ARTIFACTS

FROM EXHIBITIONS AND COLLECTIONS AT THE SMITHSONIAN INSTITUTION'S NATIONAL MUSEUM OF AMERICAN HISTORY

# THE INFORMATION AGE

You may not believe this, but there was a time before computers, before hand-held video games and CD-ROMs. The fact is that people have always needed ways to store and keep track of information. Do you know how people did this in the days before computers? You're probably holding the answer right in your hands—a book.

Technology has come a long way in a short period of time. In fact, the present era is called the Information Age because so many changes are happening so rapidly. Starting in the last century, people began to develop new forms of communication—the telegraph, the telephone, and the radio. In the last few decades, the invention of many more ways to store, retrieve, and transmit information has created an information explosion.

Developed in 1962, the first communications satellite transmitted television pictures across the globe. Today, fiber-optics technology is improving telephone and Internet service. Cables made of these optical fibers are lighter, cost less to use, and can carry more information than can metal cables. *See* 1 *and* 2.

Laser light is used to decode information stored on CD-ROM and compact audio disks. Lasers have also made shopping easier. Using lasers that "read" the bar codes printed on consumer goods, store cashiers can add up a consumer's purchases far more efficiently. *See* 3 *and* 4.

The centerpiece of the Information Age, of course, is the computer. Originally the size of a room, computers have shrunk in size as they grow in their ability to store information. *See* 5, 6, *and* 7.

Many people worry that such huge technological strides have not come without a price. The ability to listen in on private conversations and invade privacy is seen by some as just one unwelcome by-product of the Information Age. Still, most people feel the benefits far outweigh the costs. We can only guess how far technology will take us. After all, who ever would have believed that some day you could talk on the phone while walking your dog? *See* 8.

| 1986 | 1990 | 1992 | 1996 | 2000 |
|---|---|---|---|---|
| *Immigration Reform and Control Act* | *Immigration Act increases quotas* | *Carol Moseley Braun elected to Senate* | *California passes Proposition 209* | *Federal judge orders breakup of Microsoft* |

1985 | 1990 | 1995 | 2000

# 3 Twenty-First Century Americans

## SECTION PREVIEW

### Objectives

1. Describe the changing makeup of the nation's diverse population.
2. List the differences of opinion that emerged as Americans struggled to make diversity work.
3. Summarize the economic and political impact of the nation's aging population.
4. Analyze the impact of the computer revolution on the future of the United States.
5. *Key Terms* Define: multiculturalism, Internet.

### Main Idea

In the 1990s, the United States sought new ways to create unity out of its ethnic and cultural diversity and to deal with the consequences of an "aging" population and a technological revolution.

### Reading Strategy

*Organizing Information* As you read the section, create a graphic organizer summarizing the many changes facing the United States.

*This California road sign warns drivers to be on the lookout for undocumented aliens who might have crossed the border from Mexico.*

The Latin motto of the United States, found on American coins, is *"E pluribus unum"* meaning in English, "From many, one." This brief phrase reflects the patterns of the nation's past and the possibilities for its future. The United States was created when 13 separate colonies agreed to form a single union. Since then, people from an astonishing variety of lands have come to the United States and have enriched the culture of the nation. That process continued in the 1990s, and new priorities emerged as the nation matured. Creating unity out of diversity remains one of the nation's biggest challenges and a key to its future prosperity.

## A Nation of Diversity

In the 1990s, as a result of another wave of immigration, the United States became more diverse than ever before. Throughout American history, each wave of immigration has been characterized by people from a different part of the world. Most immigrants in the 1600s came from England. Great numbers of German and Irish immigrants arrived in the mid-1800s. In the late 1800s and early 1900s most immigrants were from southern and eastern Europe. By the late 1900s, close to 90 percent of all legal immigrants came from Asia and Latin America. As points of origin shifted away from Europe, Los Angeles became the major port of entry, just as New York City had been a century before.

In 1996 an all-time high of 28 percent of the nation's people were African American, Hispanic, Asian American, or Native American. This expanding diversity meant that the United States was becoming, in the words of writer Ben J. Wattenberg, "the first universal nation."

**Changing Immigration Policies** American immigration policy contributed to the nation's growing diversity. Laws passed in the 1920s had strictly limited immigration and had given preference to immigrants from northern and western Europe. The Immigration Act of 1965 eliminated the bias that favored European immigrants. In 1986 the Immigration Reform and Control Act sought to curb illegal immigration, in part by forbidding employers to hire illegal aliens. At the same time, however, it permitted illegals who had lived in the United States since 1982 to register to become citizens. The Immigration Act of 1990 increased immigration quotas by 40 percent. It also erased restrictions that had denied entrance to many people in the past.

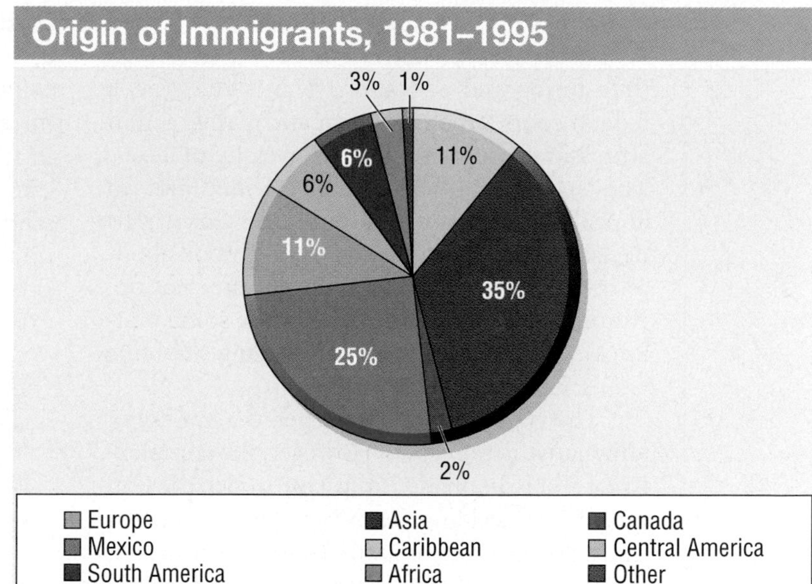


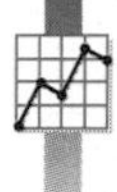

**Interpreting Graphs** Immigration continues to keep the American population diverse. ***Diversity* *Which group comprised the largest percentage of immigrants to the United States between 1981 and 1995? How would you expect these statistics to affect the overall ethnic composition of the United States over several decades?***

**Changing Population Patterns** Changes in immigration caused changes in the nation's demographics, or population characteristics and patterns. While earlier immigrants had settled mainly on the East Coast, many of the new arrivals chose the Sun Belt. (The Sun Belt stretches from Florida to California.) Like their predecessors, most immigrants of the late 1900s settled in urban areas.

In 1990 minorities made up at least half the population in 15 of the nation's 28 largest cities. African Americans predominated in Detroit, Chicago, New Orleans, and Washington, D.C. Latinos were most heavily concentrated in Phoenix, El Paso, and San Antonio. Large numbers of Asian Americans settled in San Francisco. Los Angeles experienced the most dramatic variety of all. Korean, Vietnamese, Cambodian, Samoan, and Taiwanese newcomers joined established groups of Mexican Americans, African Americans, and European Americans. Like the many nationalities that had crowded into New York City a century earlier, these groups competed for jobs and housing. Similar competition occurred in other cities with large immigrant populations.

**Minorities in Politics** As minority groups grew in size, they also gained a new voice in the nation's political system. In 1992 Carol Moseley Braun, an Illinois Democrat, became the first African American woman to win election to the United States Senate. Also in 1992 Ben Nighthorse Campbell, a Republican from Colorado, became the first Native American to win election to the United States Senate. The 1994 midterm election sent 38 African Americans and 18 Latinos to the House. As Representative Nydia Velázquez of New York State observed, "Many of the new members were elected on [the promise of] changing 'business as usual.'" Minority political participation continued to grow as the century drew to a close. The House that took office at the start of Clinton's second term boasted 39 African Americans, 21 Latinos, and 5 Asian Americans.

## *Making Diversity Work*

As American society became more diverse, government, private organizations, and individual citizens all undertook efforts to make diversity work. Some of these efforts aroused controversy.

**Affirmative Action** One of the most heated debates concerned affirmative action. President Johnson had introduced affirmative action policies under the Civil Rights Act of 1964 and an executive order in 1965. Its purpose was to improve employment and educational opportunities by giving preferences to African Americans and later to other minorities and women. Supporters of affirmative action argued that it succeeded in giving increased opportunities to tens of thousands of women and minorities. Opponents claimed that giving preferential treatment to some groups was unfair to everyone else. Americans should not "trample individual rights" in this way, argued California governor Pete Wilson.

In 1996, California voters passed Proposition 209, ending affirmative action in state hiring and education. That same year, a federal court struck down an affirmative action admissions program at the University of Texas. The state's attorney general decided not to appeal the ruling to the Supreme Court. His decision reflected a growing public mood about affirmative action throughout the nation. Among the critics of the policy were some well-known African Americans, including Supreme Court Justice Clarence Thomas.

The courts in the 1990s heard a variety of affirmative action cases. However, the complexity of the issue made it difficult to decide. Can race be the deciding factor in a decision such as hiring, or just one of many factors? Is it proper for an organization to set numerical targets for selecting minorities or women? Should a less-qualified applicant ever be selected over a more-qualified one, simply because he or she belonged to a group discriminated against in the past? While both supporters and opponents of affirmative action agreed on the *idea* of fairness, fairness was not always easy to define.

## Changing Ethnic Composition

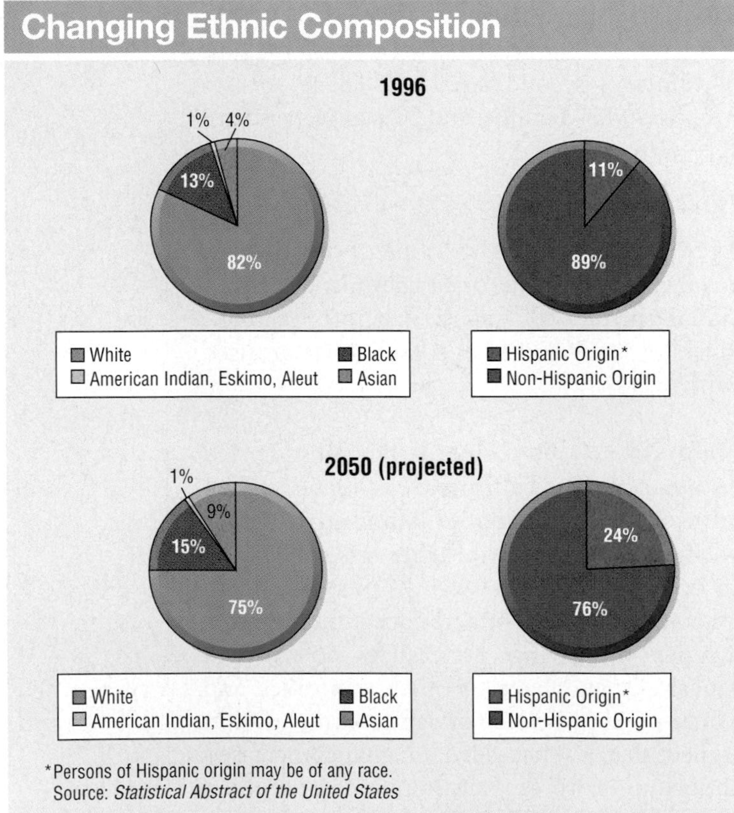


*Persons of Hispanic origin may be of any race.
Source: *Statistical Abstract of the United States*

**Interpreting Graphs** These graphs show recent and projected ethnic makeup of the United States. ***Diversity** According to the graphs, which group in the United States will experience the most dramatic rate of growth between 1996 and 2050?*

**Multiculturalism** Another effort to make diversity work was **multiculturalism.** Multiculturalism was a movement that called for greater attention to non-European cultures in such areas as education. For example, advocates of multicultural education argued that school textbooks should include information on the contributions of people from all groups. Professor of education Jaime S. Wurzel explained the thinking behind this belief:

**AMERICAN VOICES** **"The multicultural person questions the arbitrary nature of his or her own culture and accepts the proposition that others who are culturally different can enrich their experience."**

—*Jaime S. Wurzel*

Others disapproved of this approach. History professor Arthur M. Schlesinger, Jr., referred to multiculturalism as "ethnic cheerleading." He criticized the use of history to make people feel good about themselves rather than to discover the truth about the past. Other critics worried that extreme versions of multiculturalism could damage the unity of society. They argued that the approach emphasized differences between groups rather than the shared values and experiences of all Americans.

**The Future of Immigration** In addition to debates over diversity, concerns about the economy in the 1990s caused some people to question government immigration policies. Some citizens proposed lowering the number of immigrants admitted each year. Other proposals included requiring schools to teach children only in English and limiting the rights of illegal immigrants.

In 1994, for example, California voters approved Proposition 187. This law required teachers and clinic doctors to deny assistance to illegal aliens and to report them to police. Supporters of the measure argued that states that were home to a large number of immigrants, like California, were unfairly burdened by heavy social welfare costs. The welfare reform passed by Congress in 1996 recognized this argument. It cut off food stamps for nearly all needy immigrants. In 1997 Congress reconsidered this drastic action and restored benefits to most immigrants who were legal residents of the United States. Also in 1997 a federal judge overturned Proposition 187 ruling it unconstitutional. It seemed likely that the public debate over immigration would continue.

## America's Aging Population

As the United States approached the turn of the century, its population was older than ever before. Elderly people made up the fastest-growing age group in the country. The number of people age 65 and over increased nearly elevenfold between 1900 and 1995. At the same time the nation's total population only tripled. Advances in medical care increased average life expectancy for newborns from 47 to 76 years. Between 1980 and 1995 alone, the number of people age 75 and over grew by 48 percent. An "aging revolution" was clearly under way.

The "graying of America" had important political and economic effects. Many older Americans pushed successfully for legislation that prohibited forced retirement at a given age. In addition, because older Americans were growing in number and living longer, entitlement payments increased greatly.

The Social Security system, for example, faced difficulties because the number of retirees receiving benefits was rising faster than the number of workers. In 1983, Congress tried to deal with the problem by raising taxes for workers and setting a later age for retirement benefits to begin. However, experts warned that more radical steps would have to be taken before the huge baby boom generation began retiring in the twenty-first century.

In the mid-1990s polls showed that many young Americans doubted that the Social Security system would exist when they reached retirement age. Some of them also indicated that they resented paying high taxes to provide benefits for people who were already retired. Some observers suggested that inter-generational conflict could become another tension in American society. Clearly, a solution to the Social Security problem needs to be found.

There was similar pressure on the medical care system. Medicare, established during the Great Society of the 1960s, provided many of the medical expenses of older Americans. As the number of recipients and health care costs rose, however, Medicare payouts exploded from $7.5 billion in 1970 to over $200 billion in the 1990s. As with Social Security, Congress agreed that long-term changes were needed. Clinton appointed a panel of Republicans and Democrats to study the future of Medicare.

## The Computer Revolution

The pace of change today is increasing, and the computer is perhaps the best symbol of this change. Between 1983 and 1995, the percentage of American households with a computer jumped from 7 percent to 37 percent. Computers navigate spacecraft, route telephone calls, and assist in all kinds of scientific research. The **Internet,** a computer network that links millions of people around the world, is revolutionizing American education and business.

How will these changes affect employment? While computers have replaced some human workers, the growth of "high tech" industries has created thousands of new jobs. These jobs demand a high level of education and skills. One feature of the emerging economy is the lack of stable, well-paying jobs for unskilled workers. Education, therefore, has become more important than ever before.

**Main Idea CONNECTIONS**

*How will the computer revolution affect employment opportunities?*

The computer's ability to store, manipulate, and transfer information with astonishing speed will continue to transform the American economy and society in the new century. ***Culture* *Describe some of the ways in which the computer and the Internet have influenced American culture in recent years.***

## Bill Gates

**AMERICAN BIOGRAPHY** In 1975, Bill Gates envisioned the future of computers and set to work turning that vision into reality. That year, at the age of 19, Gates dropped out of Harvard University to join his high school friend Paul Allen in establishing a new company. During high school Bill had used his computer knowledge to help create a company that sold traffic data to local governments. In 1975 the two friends first read about a kit computer in *Popular Electronics* magazine. "Paul and I didn't know exactly how it would be used, but we were sure it would change us and the world of computing."

*Bill Gates (b.1955)*

At first, people couldn't make the kit computer do much. Gates and Allen changed that by writing software, or the coded instructions for performing specific tasks, to run on the computer. Their efforts transformed it from a device with limited uses into a general-purpose computer similar (though much less powerful) to those we use today.

The company that the two friends started for marketing their software, later named Microsoft, grew to become a giant in the computer industry. Located in Seattle, Washington, where Gates was born, its success made Gates a billionaire by the age of 31. By 1998 Microsoft had become the world's second most valuable company, worth some $200 billion. Gates had become the richest person on Earth, with a personal fortune of about $45 billion.

Microsoft's size and success resulted in problems for Gates. In 1998 the Justice Department sued the company for violating the Sherman Antitrust Act of 1890. The government accused Microsoft of using its power to gain a monopoly over software needed to browse the Internet. In 2000 a federal judge agreed and ordered that Microsoft be split into two smaller companies. Microsoft then began an appeals process in an effort to reverse this decision. Despite these setbacks, Gates remained steadfast in his vision of the future. ■

## Facing the Future

In the future lie our hopes and dreams, as well as the struggles that bind us together as a nation. The next seven chapters focus on issues of our common future. By tackling these issues, we will make our own future together.

Near the end of his life, Thomas Jefferson wrote, "If a nation expects to be ignorant and free . . . it expects what never was and never will be." True as this statement was nearly 200 years ago, it is all the more true as we enter a century whose advances we can scarcely imagine.

### SECTION 3 REVIEW

#### Comprehension

1. *Key Terms* Define: (a) multiculturalism; (b) Internet.
2. *Summarizing the Main Idea* Describe some of the major changes facing the United States at the end of the twentieth century.
3. *Organizing Information* Create a cause-effect graphic organizer showing the effects of the aging of the country's population.

#### Critical Thinking

4. *Analyzing Time Lines* Review the time line at the start of the section. How is the diverse nature of the nation's population reflected in the events shown?
5. *Drawing Inferences* How are economic issues related to questions about the country's immigration policies?

#### Writing Activity

6. *Writing an Expository Essay* Write an essay describing different points of view on affirmative action or multiculturalism.

# Why Study History?

To understand that . . .

## You Need to Stay Informed

**As the world's supply of information explodes, learning how to obtain the information you need is becoming more important than ever.**

*Traditional source of information, the newspaper*

Katherine Chiao reads a daily newspaper and a weekly news magazine. She listens to news programs on the radio and watches documentaries on television. In addition, Chiao regularly uses the Internet, checking her favorite Web sites to find information on current topics of special interest. In short, she has learned to take advantage of the many sources of information that are available today.

### The Impact Today

The 1990s represented the beginning of a new era in the United States. The end of the decades-long cold war prompted Americans to focus on domestic issues and challenges. At the same time, advances in communication technology produced a flood of information directed every day at average Americans.

Traditional forms of media, such as television, radio, and newspapers, remain the primary sources of news and information for most Americans. In the 1990s some 190 million Americans watched television regularly, while roughly 85 million listened to the radio and about 83 million read newspapers.

The Internet, however, has the potential to surpass all of these traditional forms in importance. Tens of millions of Americans are now connected to the Internet, which provides access to thousands of online magazines and newspapers. The Internet also has millions of articles, documents, and pictures from governments, businesses, and individuals.

With so much information becoming available, our challenge today lies not in obtaining information but in sorting through it to find what is both useful and reliable. Anyone can post materials on the Internet, and thus the quality of information there varies enormously. Many materials come from respected sources, such as universities and government agencies. Other materials are placed on the Internet by groups or individuals who have little expertise but want to express a certain point of view. Some materials are designed to deceive or to spread hatred. Internet users must therefore become intelligent "information consumers," distinguishing between reliable and unreliable sites.

### The Impact on You

Watch the TV news coverage of an important event. Read about the same event in newspapers and magazines. Listen to radio accounts of the event. Search for documents about the event on the Internet, and read those as well. Discuss in class how the presentation of the event is similar or different in the various media. Then create a media report card that shows which medium you think is best for obtaining reliable information.

*A dizzying array of information available on the Internet*

# Chapter 25 Review

## Chapter Summary

The major concepts of Chapter 25 are presented below. See also ***Guide to the Essentials of American History*** or ***Interactive Student Tutorial CD-ROM,*** which contains interactive review activities, time lines, helpful hints, and test practice.

CD-ROM REVIEW

### *Reviewing the Main Ideas*

Despite opposition from Congress and charges of political and personal scandal, Clinton remained a popular President. Throughout the 1990s, the country struggled to find its way through uncharted waters in post–cold war international relations. The country also worked to maintain a strong sense of unity and economic well-being in the face of demographic and technological changes.

### *Section 1: Politics in the 1990s*

American voters, concerned with a sluggish economy, elected Bill Clinton to the presidency in 1992. Despite showing strong support for Republicans in the 1994 midterm elections, voters reelected Clinton in 1996. His second term, although filled with scandal, was marked by a strong, rapidly growing economy.

### *Section 2: The United States in a New World*

The collapse of communism and an increase in ethnic tensions in various parts of the world caused Americans to examine their nation's political and economic role in the post–cold war era.

### *Section 3: Twenty-First Century Americans*

In the 1990s, the United States sought new ways to create unity out of its ethnic and cultural diversity and to deal with the consequences of an "aging" population and a technological revolution.

As the world's supply of information explodes, learning how to obtain the information you need is becoming more important than ever. Internet users must become intelligent "information consumers," distinguishing between reliable and unreliable sites.

## Key Terms

For each of the terms below, write a sentence explaining how it relates to the chapter.

1. Contract with America
2. Whitewater affair
3. apartheid
4. economic sanctions
5. NAFTA
6. GATT
7. World Trade Organization
8. multiculturalism
9. Internet

## Comprehension

1. Why did Clinton's health care plan fail to win passage in Congress?
2. After 1994, why did Republicans believe that they had a mandate to reduce the size of the federal government?
3. What role did the United States play in producing cease-fires in Bosnia and Kosovo?
4. Give reasons why some people supported NAFTA and others opposed it.
5. Which two regions of the world sent the most immigrants to the United States during the 1990s?
6. How did federal policy add to the diversity of the United States?

## Using Graphic Organizers

On a separate sheet of paper, draw a web diagram similar to the one below. In each circle summarize an international event that occurred during the Clinton administration.

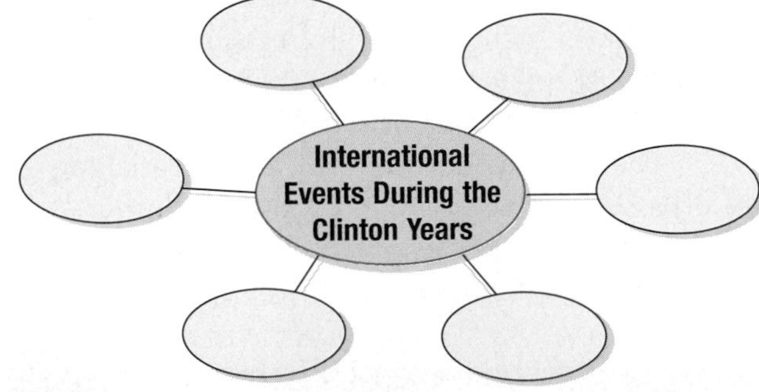

## Analyzing Political Cartoons ▶

1. Read the title of the cartoon. What do you normally associate with vacations?
2. Examine the scene. (a) What do you traditionally associate with a trip to the beach? (b) How is this scene different?
3. What comment is the cartoonist making about 1990s lifestyle?

## Critical Thinking

1. *Applying the Chapter Skill* Describe the consequences of the nation's aging population.
2. *Demonstrating Reasoned Judgment* The United States intervened in some world conflicts during the 1990s. What do you think should be the role of the United States in future conflicts throughout the world?
3. *Identifying Assumptions* What reasons do people who oppose affirmative action cite in support of their position?
4. *Drawing Inferences* President Clinton gave his speech regarding the need for health care reform to a national TV audience in 1993 as a way of rallying public support for reform. What benefits and drawbacks does television offer to Presidents?

### INTERNET ACTIVITY

***For your portfolio:***
**PREPARE A REPORT**

Access Prentice Hall's *America: Pathways to the Present* site at **www.Pathways.phschool.com** for the specific URLs to complete the activity. Additional resources and related Web sites are also available.

Use information and trade data from the links provided to prepare a report on the purpose and goals of the European Union. Include a graph or chart in your report using data on trade.

### ANALYZING DOCUMENTS ▶ INTERPRETING DATA

Turn to the ethnic composition graphs on page 742.

1. Which of the following groups made up 13 percent of the United States population in 1996?
(a) White (b) Black
(c) American Indian, Eskimo, and Aleut (d) Asian.
2. Which of the following groups will more than double its percentage of the United States population by 2050? (a) White (b) Black (c) Asian (d) Hispanic Origin.
3. *Write* What will happen to the white population as a percent of the total population?

## Connecting to Today

*Making Inferences*
Reread the statement by Thomas Jefferson on page 744. Describe in your own words how education and freedom are related. Why will education be so important to workers of the twenty-first century?

# American Heritage®

## My Brush with History

BY CRAIG B. GREENFIELD

***INTRODUCTION*** The cold war decades were a boom time for the American defense industry. The billions spent each year to develop and produce modern weapons not only helped protect the nation, but boosted its economy. In the passage below, Craig B. Greenfield, whose father worked for a defense contractor, describes a visit to see his father's handiwork in action.

*It was 1974.* As your average twelve-year-old, my world was one of mischievous after-school activities, mixed with the usual sandlot sports, awkward encounters with girls, and homework. With the exception of the trendy peace-sign belt buckle and fingers-gesturing peace-sign T-shirt that I owned, I had only a faint familiarity with the politics of peace and war in faraway Vietnam. In fact, my only real exposure to those events came from those television voices that came between "Gilligan's Island" and "Adam 12," who spoke of the specter of nuclear holocaust that losing to communism in Asia might invite. All that changed one winter with a brief but profound encounter with the inner workings and realities of the Cold War.

My family had taken a vacation that December. With my father employed as an electrical engineer by the Sperry Corporation, a leading Long Island defense contractor, and my mother keeping busy with her family at home, we set out for Fort Lauderdale to combine some sunshine with the duty of visiting all our recently retired relatives. A much-anticipated highlight of this trip for me was to be a visit to the newly opened Disney World. But compared with the show I was to see, that children's mecca turned out to be just a roadside attraction.

We were relaxing in the cool comfort of my uncle's condominium when my father proudly announced that he had arranged for a side trip to Cape Canaveral for what he called, in the acronymistic vernacular of the defense industry, a DASO, or "daytime at sea operation," wherein a Poseidon missile would be launched from an actual submarine. Although I viewed this development as one more dreaded lengthy car ride full of slap fighting with my brother, to my father, who had worked hard on developing submarine navigation systems, it was a rare and valuable chance to see his engi-

Poseidon Missile Test

***A Poseidon missile submarine (left) launches one of its missiles (right).***

neering achievement at work—a demonstration otherwise possible only in an apocalyptic armed launch situation.

With a quick good-bye we set off on our three-hour journey to Port Canaveral, neighboring the cape, where so many televised space shots originated, my father's excitement manifesting itself in driving at a clip that ultimately got him ticketed.

We arrived at Cape Canaveral and were processed in true Cold War fashion: security clearance, identification cards, and a short, sharp admonishment to stay only in certain areas of the host Navy ship during our day at sea. Then we proceeded up the gangplank and onto the huge auxiliary ship *Compass Island* (EAG 153), which had seen action over the years as a part of the U.S. Military Sealift Command.

I spent the hours-long voyage out to sea exploring the ship and listening to a succession of lectures about this and that capability, guidance system, and the like on both the *Compass Island* and the day's feature attraction, the five-hundred-foot long Poseidon submarine USS *Lafayette* (SSBN 616), which rode regally beside us until it majestically submerged into the sparkling Atlantic water, trailed only by its perfect wake and the indiscreet presence of an antenna-laden Soviet "fishing trawler."

At dusk, with the Florida sun low on the horizon, everyone aboard became aware of the countdown that had actually been going on all day. With fifteen seconds left and our formidable companion well hidden under the sea, the boat buzzed with anticipation and excitement.

At about five seconds to launch, our immense host ship began to rock to and fro, despite the relative tranquillity of the Atlantic shortly before. At four seconds to launch the boat was heaving so violently that all of us had to brace ourselves. At three seconds to launch the rumbling became so loud that I imagined myself being in the center of a thunderclap. At two seconds to launch, with the blocks-long ship in its turbulent pitch and roll and the noise of eruption becoming ever louder, the inside missile hatch of the submarine blew open explosively far below. Finally, rising on a column of fire, the thirty-four-foot body of the C-3 Poseidon missile emerged from the boiling sea and, with a zig right and a zag left, rocketed skyward and headed toward its destination in the Indian Ocean, nearly three thousand miles away. As I gazed awestruck, my jaw opened wide, that image implanted itself indelibly in my memory.

Today, more than twenty years later, with the disintegration of soviet communism receding into history, what occurred on that winter day at sea seems almost to have been staged for a movie rather than the profound and scary reality that it was.

However, that vivid childhood memory allows me as an adult to appreciate fully the magnitude of the resources involved in that endeavor called the Cold War. Having personally lived with the practical realities of the Cold War —and having been fed, clothed, and educated with the money that the employment of thousands like my father in the defense industry brought—I greet these new historical developments with both a sense of hope for a peaceful future and a sense of what brought them about.

Source: *American Heritage* magazine, July 1995.

## ADDITIONAL READING

**To learn more about the topics discussed in this selection, you might want to read the following books:**

- *The Cold War: A History,* by Martin Walker (New York: Henry Holt, 1994)
- *Grand Expectations: The United States, 1945–1974,* by James T. Patterson (New York: Oxford University Press, 1996)
- *The Nuclear Question: The United States and Nuclear Weapons, 1946–1976,* by Michael Mandelbaum (Cambridge: Cambridge University Press, 1979)
- *The Wizards of Armageddon,* by Fred Kaplan (New York: Simon & Schuster, 1983)

unit SEVEN

# Pathways to the Future

## Themes for the Twenty-first Century

**Chapter 26**

### Immigration and the Golden Door

In the 1990s, immigrants had a profound impact on the nation. Both the sheer numbers of immigrants and their cultural diversity are reshaping American society.

**Chapter 27**

### Gun Control and Crime

In recent years, America has experienced a wave of violent crime, with a significant percentage of these crimes involving the use of guns. The Second Amendment to the Constitution protects the right to "keep and bear arms." But does it refer only to states' needs for security, or does it include individuals' needs as well?

**Chapter 28**

### The Minimum Wage

In the 1990s the gap between the rich and the poor continued to widen. To narrow this gap, President Clinton proposed an increase in the minimum wage. While economists and politicians debated the effect of such a raise on the economy, others questioned whether the federal government should be setting a minimum wage at all.

**Chapter 29**

### Rethinking Entitlements

In the 1990s increasing numbers of people receiving assistance in the form of cash benefits, food stamps, and medical care put a strain on the federal budget. Balancing the needs of the poor and the elderly against the needs of the budget is a challenge facing all Americans.

**Chapter 30**

### The Debate Over Trade

With the end of the cold war and the rise of democratic institutions in the Western Hemisphere, trade has become a major concern of the United States and its neighbors. The North American Free Trade Agreement (NAFTA) is the lightning rod for the debate over what the model should be for relations among the countries of the Americas.

**Chapter 31**

### Foreign Policy After the Cold War

What is the proper role of the United States in the world today? Should it continue its role of world leadership? Should it seek to be a peacekeeper or a humanitarian relief agency? These and other questions on the nation's role in world affairs will be debated into the next century.

**Chapter 32**

### Technology and You in the Next Century

Technology has always had a profound effect on American society. Today it is the computer industry that is changing the way Americans live and work. What is the role of schools in preparing students to use and understand this technology, which will dominate the next century?

*Ticker tape parade, New York City*

# CHAPTER 26 Immigration and the Golden Door

Ellis Island postcards

## INTRODUCING THE THEME

**A poem inscribed at the base of the Statue of Liberty begins: "Give me your tired, your poor, Your huddled masses yearning to breathe free. . . ." Emma Lazarus wrote these lines in 1883, during a new wave of immigration to the United States. More than a hundred years later, immigration is again on the rise. Both the sheer numbers of immigrants and their cultural diversity are profoundly reshaping American society—everything from foods and phone books to schools and politics.**

## DEBATE

**Should we continue to welcome people from other lands, or do we need to restrict immigration?**

## KEY TERMS

undocumented immigrant, political asylum, green card, nativist, bilingual education

## VIEWING THE PRESENT

Ovidiu Colea spent five years in a Romanian labor camp as punishment for trying to escape to the United States. He finally emigrated in 1978 and settled in New York. In 1985 he won the only contract to make replicas of the Statue of Liberty for the centennial celebration the next year. With the help of about two dozen other immigrants in his factory in Blissville, Queens, Colea and his business became very successful, manufacturing the very symbol of the American dream.

Not all immigrant stories end so happily. For example, in El Monte, California, 72 immigrants from Thailand lived and worked locked inside an apartment complex surrounded by razor wire. They sewed garments for up to 115 hours a week in cramped sweatshops. From their meager wages, their employer deducted the nearly $5,000 cost of transportation to the United States. "Living in there was like death, never able to see the world outside," said one woman. Eventually a worker escaped and notified authorities, who freed the others.

### *Rising Immigration*

Between the extremes of these two experiences lie the stories of millions of newcomers to the United States in recent years. In the 1980s immigration skyrocketed. During that decade, the number of newcomers soared to about 7.3 million, more than one and a half times what it had been in the previous decade. This surge continued into the 1990s. In 1991, the number of official immigrants entering the United States totaled 1,827,200

*Ovidiu Colea with a replica of the Statue of Liberty*

people. The figures dropped in succeeding years, with 660,447 arriving in 1998—the lowest numbers since 1988.

To appreciate the full impact of recent immigration, however, one must add to these figures the number of **undocumented immigrants.** (These are immigrants who have entered the United States illegally.) The Immigration and Naturalization Service estimated that in 1996 some 5 million people were living in this country illegally.

You only need go as far as your local grocery store to see that immigration affects American culture. ***Economics*** *Which of the foods in this photograph can you find in your local grocery store? Do those foods reflect the background of the people who live in your area? How do they reflect the diversity of America as a whole?*

## *Reasons for Immigration*

Immigrants can legally enter the United States for the following reasons:

1. They have relatives who are American citizens.
2. They possess needed job skills.
3. They are refugees from war or are seeking **political asylum** to escape persecution.

The principal reason immigrants come to the United States is family ties. In 1998, about 72 percent of legal immigrants were family members of American citizens. Another 12 percent were granted entry because they had specialized work skills. About 8 percent were refugees and asylum seekers. The rest fell into special categories of the immigration law.

## *Sources of Immigration*

The largest group of immigrants in 1998—about 38 percent—came from North America and the Caribbean, with Mexico in the lead. Approximately one third of all immigrants in that year came from Asia, with the largest contingent from China. About 14 percent came from Europe, 7 percent from South America, and 6 percent from Africa. All in all, more people are coming to the United States from more countries than ever before.

## *Finding Homes*

Once they arrive, newcomers face seemingly endless challenges, the first of which is finding a place to live. Immigrants move to every state of the Union, with the greatest concentrations in California, New York, Florida, and Texas. Most settle in cities with ethnic neighborhoods where they can find familiar food, language, and customs, as well as a network of people to help them learn the American way of life.

Nur Emirgil, a Turkish immigrant to Queens, New York, describes how her neighborhood works: "Somebody calls or knocks on the door and asks, 'Can this person stay on your couch for a few days?' 'Do you know any job they can get, someplace that doesn't care about **green cards** [work permits for foreigners]?' 'Can you go with them to the doctor to translate?'"

## *Adjusting to America*

For immigrants, striking a balance between preserving old ways and learning new ones can be difficult. Many immigrants discover they have to give up their old line of work and take the lowest-paying unskilled jobs just to be employed at all. While they want their children to learn English, they also want them to maintain their heritage.

Just as immigrants have changed to adjust to America, this nation has changed to adjust to them. New products and services have appeared to appeal to the nearly 10 percent of Americans who are foreign-born. Television and radio now broadcast in several dozen languages. Yellow pages have been published for different ethnic groups. Foods imported from places as different as Southeast Asia and Mexico line the shelves of grocery stores in small towns like Garden City, Kansas.

## *Caring for Immigrants*

The arrival of so many immigrants of such diverse origins has placed a strain on the United States. Areas with large foreign-born populations must provide ballots in one or more languages besides English. Big-city school systems like those in Chicago and Los Angeles must devise ways to teach classes representing dozens of different languages. Public hospitals must treat poor immigrants who cannot afford to pay for health care. All of these services cost money at a time when federal, state, and local governments have less to spend.

## REVIEWING THE PAST

We are, as President Kennedy put it, a "nation of immigrants." With the exception of Africans, who were brought to the Americas against their will, all other immigrants have come here in search of a better life. They see America as a land of opportunity. But opportunity has always involved risk, loss, and change.

Coming to the United States has meant wrenching changes for immigrants, who had to leave their homelands behind and adapt to new circumstances. It has also meant the growth of a unique American culture. Some call it a melting pot. Others describe it as a salad bowl or a mosaic. But whatever the metaphor, American society is indeed the product of many people from many nations.

## *Early Diversity*

Archaeologists estimate that perhaps as long as 40,000 years ago, people began migrating to the Americas across a land bridge from Asia. Their descendants, today's Native Americans, disagree. They claim instead that their people have lived in the Americas since Earth's creation. In either case, Native Americans had formed about 500 nations by the time Europeans began colonization in the sixteenth and seventeenth centuries.

The European countries that colonized North America had a variety of goals and thus a variety of immigration patterns. The Spanish set up colonies to extract wealth from the land and to convert Native Americans to Christianity, but not primarily to relocate Spaniards. The French, similarly, did not emphasize settlement. They too wanted the riches of the land, and in the 1600s and 1700s that meant trapping and trading with Native Americans for furs.

The English and Dutch, on the other hand, did want to settle North America. The Dutch settlement of New Amsterdam advertised to recruit people. The Dutch were so successful in drawing people from many places that as early as 1644, 18 languages were spoken in New Amsterdam. William Penn also advertised throughout Europe for people to come to Pennsylvania. In 1750, in fact, more than half the people of the English colonies were non-English. Almost 20 percent were African, and the rest were Scotch-Irish, German, Irish, Scottish, Welsh, Dutch, French, and Swedish.

This Russian family came to the United States in the early 1900s. In those years, thousands of new arrivals passed through the Ellis Island immigration center each day. ***Government** How did Americans respond to this wave of immigration?*

## *Immigration and Backlash*

In his 1782 *Letters from an American Farmer,* J. Hector St. John de Crèvecoeur wrote, "I could point out to you a family whose grandfather was an Englishman, whose wife was Dutch, whose son married a French woman, and whose present four sons have now four wives of different nations." As the new nation, founded on principles of equality, grew, so did its immigration from many nations. Until 1846 those nations were mostly in western and northern Europe, and almost all their emigrants were Protestant. In America there were jobs and land enough for all.

Starting in 1846 the immigrant population changed rapidly as the potato famine in Ireland sent hundreds of thousands of Irish Catholics to America. Most settled in northeastern cities, taking jobs in factories or on canals or railroads. Joining them were hundreds of thousands of German immigrants fleeing political oppression. This new wave of immigrants settled largely in the cities of the Northeast or bought farmland in the Midwest.

The Irish and many of the Germans were Catholic. Some native-born Americans, fearing control by the Pope and loss of jobs to newcomers, were hostile toward the foreign-born. Many of these **nativists** formed the Know-Nothing party, which became an important political force in 1854. The Know-Nothings wanted to keep Catholics and foreigners out of public office and to require 21-years of residence before an immigrant could qualify for citizenship.

Although the Know-Nothing party fell apart, nativist feelings grew as Chinese immigrants arrived in the mid-1800s. Fearing competition for jobs, nativists succeeded in passing the Chinese Exclusion Act of 1882. This federal law cut off all immigration from China. Anti-Asian sentiment also curtailed Japanese immigration with the Gentlemen's Agreement of 1907.

THE ONLY WAY TO HANDLE IT.

This cartoon refers to a 1921 law that restricted immigration from European countries. That law set quotas based on national origin. Immigration from a particular country could not exceed 3 percent of the number of people of the same nationality living in the United States in 1910. ***Culture*** ***How does the cartoon portray immigrants?***

## *The New Immigration*

Beginning in the 1880s, immigration to the United States increased rapidly. Between 1870 and the end of the 1880s, immigration doubled. This new wave of immigrants was different from the ones before. Instead of coming from western and northern Europe, as earlier, they came from southern and eastern Europe. Instead of being mainly Protestant, they were Catholic and Jewish. Instead of spreading out over the farmlands of the Midwest and Great Plains, they settled in cities, where they found work in factories and mills.

## Origins of Immigrants to the U.S., 1981–1995

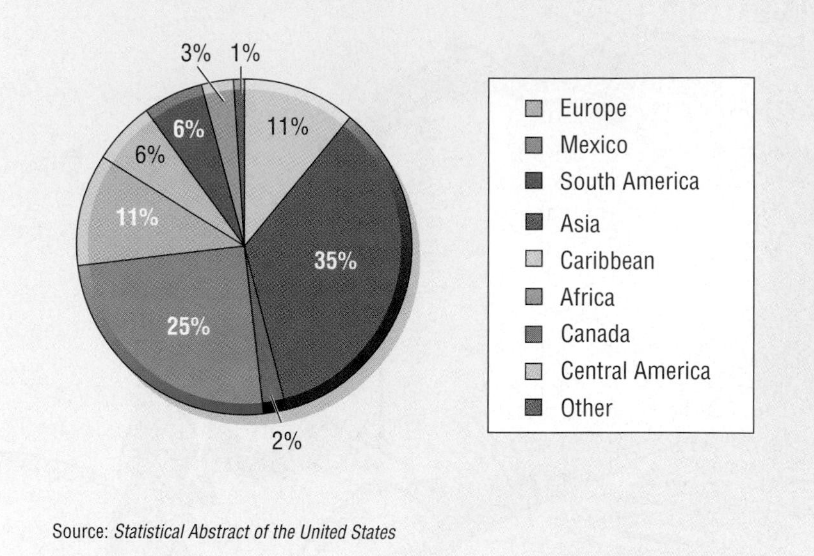


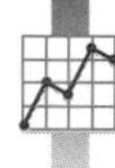

**Interpreting Graphs** As the 1990s drew to a close, immigration was helping to create an increasingly diverse American population. ***Diversity* From which region did most immigrants originate during the 1980s and early 1990s?**

Even as these newcomers were becoming part of the country's mainstream, opposition to immigrants continued to flourish. During World War I, government propaganda fanned nativist sentiment.

### *Immigration Laws*

After the war, America went through a period of intense fear of foreigners. Believing political radicals were spreading communism and revolution, the Justice Department jailed or deported hundreds of innocent people between 1919 and 1921. Wanting no part of European politics, American foreign policy became isolationist.

In this spirit, Congress passed the Immigration Law of 1921, which limited immigration to 350,000 people per year and set up quotas for nationalities. The Immigration Law of 1924 went even further. It capped immigration at 164,000, banned all Asians, and limited the number of immigrants from each country to 2 percent of the number of people of the same nationality living in the United States in 1890. This last provision aimed to halt immigration from southern and eastern Europe.

With these laws in place, immigration slowed to a trickle. During the next 30 years, only about 100,000 people came to the United States each year. Then, in 1965, Congress passed a new law lifting all immigration quotas, thus opening the Golden Door to more non-Europeans. As a result, the number of immigrants has greatly increased, and their countries of origin have changed. Between 1930 and 1960, about 80 percent of all immigrants came from Europe or Canada. Since 1960, about 80 percent have come from Asia, Latin America, and the Caribbean.

As the number of legal immigrants has grown, so has the number of illegal, or undocumented, immigrants. To combat this problem, Congress passed the Immigration Reform and Control Act of 1986. This law punished employers who knowingly hired illegals. It also granted amnesty to illegals who had lived in the United States since 1982, to enable them to register to become citizens. The Immigration Act of 1990 raised immigration totals and removed certain restrictions on people who had been denied entry in the past.

The impact of these laws is reflected in the changing composition of American society. At nearly 10 percent of the total population, America's foreign-born population is at its highest level since 1940. This greater diversity has, in turn,

***Some Americans today believe that immigration to the United States should be restricted or even stopped completely.***

sparked intense debate about the future of American immigration policy.

## DEBATING THE FUTURE

Massive immigration will destroy America, says author Lawrence Auster. "As whites lose their numerical, political, and cultural dominance, American civilization with all its constituent virtues will also come to an end." Not so, counters Julian L. Simon, a professor at the University of Maryland. He believes that "Talented young immigrants help us achieve every one of our national goals. They make us richer and not poorer, stronger and not weaker." Arguments such as these are representative of much of the national debate about immigration policy.

### *Arguments Against Immigration*

Opponents of current policy argue that high levels of immigration hurt the American economy. Because immigrants are willing to work for low wages, many fear they will take jobs away from native-born Americans. "How can we keep bringing people into this country when our own people don't have jobs?" asks Clark Yates, an auto mechanic in Chicago, Illinois.

Illegal immigrants, in particular, will work for less than minimum wage, which drives down other workers' pay. "Undocumented immigrants tend to compete unfairly for low-skilled jobs, and they can sometimes bring down the level of wages and working conditions," according to Charles Wheeler, executive director of the National Immigration Law Center.

There are political arguments against immigration as well. The federal government sets immigration policy, but it does not pay for all the services immigrants require. By and large, state and local governments must cover the costs of welfare, health care, and education for immigrants and for their children, who are citizens if born in the United States.

Many Californians oppose immigration because their state receives the largest number of immigrants, both legal and illegal. The costs for the state are enormous. Said a California state assembly aide in 1993:

**AMERICAN VOICES** **"The state is broke. We've had a multibillion-dollar deficit three years in a row, and yet we continue to pay medical benefits for these illegal immigrants. We take better care of them than of our own people."**

*—California State assembly aide*

In 1994 Governor Pete Wilson asked the President to declare an emergency in California and repay the state the $2.4 billion it spends each year on undocumented immigrants. Also that year, by a margin of 59 to 41 percent, California voters approved Proposition 187, which denied public services to illegal immigrants.

Finally, immigration opponents see the new immigrant groups as fragmenting American society, dividing it into ethnic enclaves rather than adapting to American culture. Language has become a rallying point, with campaigns for "English only" as the official language. In 1975, Congress amended the voting rights act to require bilingual ballots. English-only advocates point out that naturalized citizens are supposed to know the language and claim that many have cheated to pass the naturalization exam. John Silber, former chairman of the Massachusetts State Board of Education, argues:

**AMERICAN VOICES** **"Citizens who are not proficient in English cannot, in most cases, follow a political campaign, talk with candidates, or petition their representatives. They are citizens in name only and are unable to exercise their rights. Providing them with bilingual ballots does not enable them to exercise those rights in any meaningful way."**

*—John Silber*

SPECIAL ISSUE TIME

Take a good look at this woman. She was created by a computer from a mix of several races. What you see is a remarkable preview of...

THE NEW FACE OF AMERICA

How Immigrants Are Shaping the World's First Multicultural Society

*Time* magazine created this computer-generated portrait by combining the characteristics of all the races present in the United States in 1993. ***Culture*** *What are some arguments in favor of immigration?*

**Bilingual education** is another source of frustration for those who want to limit immigration. In bilingual programs, students are taught in their native language as well as English while their English-language skills improve. Opponents of bilingual education argue that these programs only perpetuate separateness rather than promote assimilation into the American mainstream. Without a common language, they believe, our common culture is in danger.

Opponents received a boost from voters in California. In 1998 Californians approved Proposition 227, which severely limits bilingual education in that state. The law gives all children with limited English skills just one year to learn English before joining regular classes. Proposition 227 ended 30 years of full-scale bilingual instruction in the nation's largest school system.

## *Arguments for Immigration*

Immigrants help, not hurt, the economy, claim immigration supporters. They come highly motivated to work, with strong family units that promote discipline and high standards.

Immigrants contribute to the economy as consumers, small-business owners, and taxpayers. They also take jobs few native-born Americans want. As Chicago carpenter Eddy Jerena explains:

AMERICAN VOICES **"My brother . . . has a business, and the Mexicans work hard for him 12 hours a day and they don't complain. You get these American-born guys, they don't work like that. This country was built by immigrants. The Mexicans deserve to be here."**

—*Eddy Jerena*

Immigration supporters point out that most immigrants do not receive public assistance. Most legal immigrants have to wait five years to be eligible for welfare. Illegal immigrants are not eligible for any social services except emergency Medicaid and vital programs related to child welfare. A study in 1997 showed that 4.9 percent of immigrants receive help, in contrast to 3.3 percent of the native-born population. But many of those immigrants are refugees or the elderly, who do not qualify for Social Security as older Americans do.

Finally, supporters say immigration is an investment that will pay off in a trained work force and future taxpayers. To those who would deny education to the children of illegal immigrants, Indianapolis Superintendent of Schools Esperanza Zendejas replies:

**"These kids are going to be here for a long time. So the question is whether we want to educate these kids now or pay for increased social welfare costs later down the line. I think it's an easy choice."**

—*Esperanza Zendejas*

***The Statue of Liberty was what many immigrants first saw when they arrived in the United States. For some, trunks like the one below carried all the possessions they were able to bring from home.***

## *The Debate Continues*

Although both supporters and opponents of immigration believe it is necessary to exert greater control over illegal immigrants, they disagree over how to do it. They also disagree over the level of legal immigration and whether legal immigrants should be eligible for social services. Voters will need to weigh the Statue of Liberty's promise against their perception of America's ability to keep that promise.

# Chapter 26 Review

## Key Terms

1. undocumented immigrant
2. political asylum
3. green card
4. nativist
5. bilingual education

## Creating a Time Line

6. To set the events of this chapter in context, construct a time line that includes eight to ten significant milestones in the modern history (since colonial times) of immigration to the United States. Include both events and legislation. You can refer to previous chapters of this textbook for information.

## Portfolio Activity

7. Think about your own attitude toward immigration and the services to which immigrants are entitled. Then consider how you can best express this opinion: for instance, a newspaper editorial, a pictorial essay, a series of interviews, a poem, a cartoon or drawing, a poster. When you have chosen a presentation that is acceptable to your teacher, put it in an appropriate format.

### INTERNET ACTIVITY

***For your portfolio:***
**PREPARE A SUMMARY**

8. Access Prentice Hall's *America: Pathways to the Present* site at **www.Pathways.phschool.com** for the specific URL to complete the activity. Additional resources and related Web sites are also available.

   Use the link provided and choose a bill related to immigration that is currently pending in Congress. Summarize the bill and explain two arguments for and against passing it.

## Using Graphic Organizers

9. Review the arguments in the Debating the Future section of the chapter. Then fill in the blanks in the graphic organizer below that show political movements and legislation affecting immigration between the mid-1800s and the 1990s. Large boxes show the major developments or laws. Specific details or effects appear in the smaller boxes. You can copy the organizer on another sheet of paper.

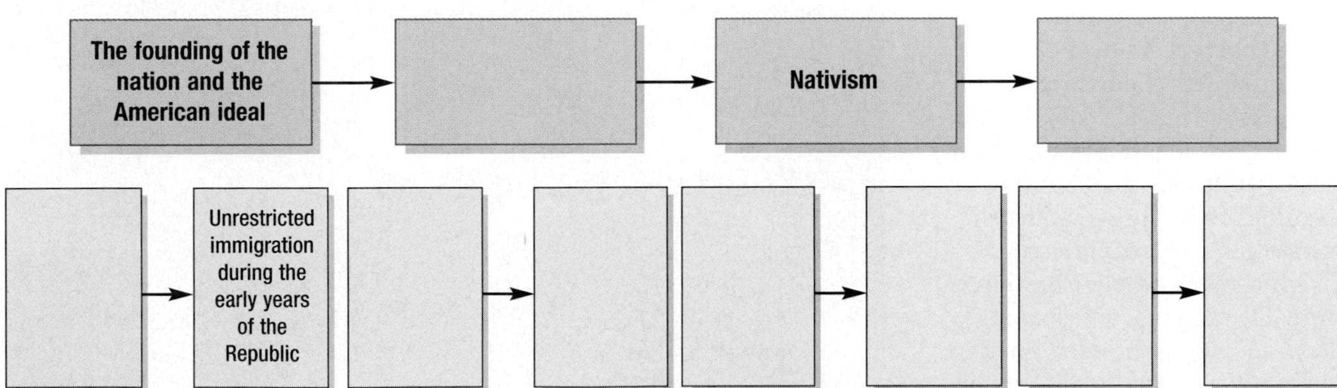

CHAPTER 27

# Gun Control and Crime

Colonial woodcut

## INTRODUCING THE THEME

**Violent crime and the criminal use of guns have become part of life in the United States. At the same time, more private citizens are arming themselves in self-defense. Since the earliest days of this nation, Americans have debated the right to private ownership of guns. At the heart of this debate is the Second Amendment to the Constitution, which protects the right to "keep and bear arms." The meaning of this amendment is highly controversial and the subject of lawsuits. Some advocate an interpretation that guarantees all Americans the right to bear arms without restrictions from any government. Other experts believe that the amendment is important for its guarantee of the right of the states to maintain a militia.**

**Given the widespread public concern over violent crime, is stiffer gun control an effective way to restore tranquillity?**

### KEY TERMS

homicide, militia,
Second Amendment,
National Rifle Association (NRA)

## VIEWING THE PRESENT

Under a Chicago railroad bridge the police found "Yummy" in a mud puddle. His face was torn apart by bullets fired through the back of his head. Eleven-year-old Robert "Yummy" Sandifer had been gunned down by members of his own gang. He was supposed to shoot members of a rival gang, but killed an unrelated 14-year-old girl instead. When police went after him, Yummy became too big a risk and fell victim to gang violence himself.

In Collingswood, New Jersey, Amy Fleming practices loading her handgun in the dark. She can do it in five seconds flat. Amy lives with her son, Justy, her dog, and her fear of her ex-husband, Ed. A drug user who has been convicted of two violent assaults and theft of a firearm, Ed has repeatedly

*Some people, like this woman, find that owning a handgun makes them feel more secure.*

threatened to kill Amy. No help is available from the police, who can only recommend that she run away and hide. Since Ed has no trouble finding out where she lives, Amy believes that her gun is the only protection she has.

### *Public Fears About Crime*

How typical are these two stories? While they don't give the full picture, they do put human faces on some startling statistics. Every two minutes someone is shot in this country. The Federal Bureau of Investigation reports that Americans are much more likely to be the victim of a violent crime than to be hurt in a traffic accident. Violent crime includes murder, rape, robbery, and aggravated assault. Crime rates increased in the 1980s and through the recession years of the mid-1990s.

Crime has declined significantly in recent years, however. In fact, violent crime decreased about 19 percent from 1994 to 1999, reaching the lowest levels of violent crime ever recorded in this country. Despite this decline, public concern about crime remains high. Crime consistently placed one or two among the nation's leading concerns in Gallup polls conducted since 1959. People continue to think of crime as a more serious problem than other concerns like unemployment or taxes. Why?

**Murder Weapons, 1995**

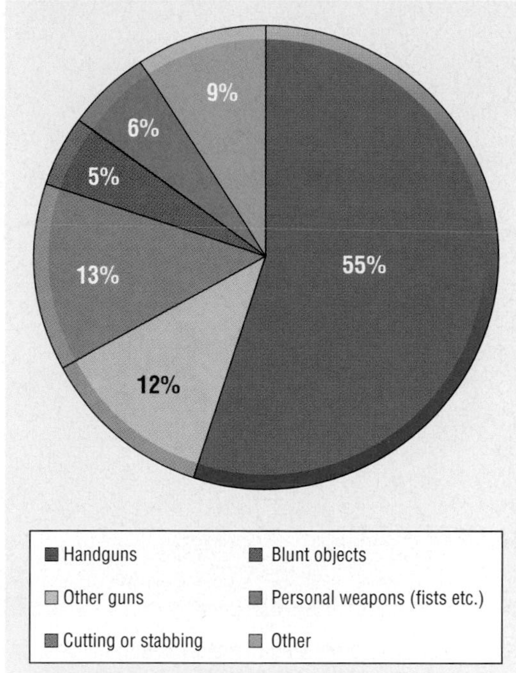


Source: *Statistical Abstract of the United States*

**Interpreting Graphs** In 1995, 20,220 murders were committed. Handguns were used in more than half of these killings. ***Culture How do you think the statistics presented in this graph influence the debate on handgun control?***

### *Crime Trends*

Criminologists (social scientists who study crime) cannot say for certain what makes crime rates increase or decrease. Still, they can identify historical trends. During the 1940s and 1950s the United States enjoyed relatively low crime rates. Things began to change in the mid-1960s, as a look at the rate of **homicide,** or murder, reveals. In 1965 the murder rate was about 5 per 100,000 people. By 1974 it had doubled. After falling in the mid-1970s, the murder rate rose to 10 per 100,000 people in 1980. Then it dropped again until the late 1980s. According to the FBI, the murder rate in 1998 was about 6 per 100,000 people.

There are no clear-cut explanations of these ups and downs. Still, Professor Lawrence M. Friedman of Stanford University suggests that crime rates may be connected with larger social, economic, and cultural trends. For example, the rise in murder rates in the late 1960s took place during a period of great social and political turmoil. The increase in murder rates in the late 1980s coincided with high inner-city unemployment and poverty and the get-rich-quick appeal of the crack cocaine trade.

***Western frontier myths turned the sheriff's badge into a symbol of frontier justice in the popular imagination.***

### *A Cause of Crime*

There is a direct link between drugs and violent crime. Reasons for the relationship between drug trafficking and violence include the following: competition for drug markets and customers, disputes among individuals involved in the illegal drug market, and the tendency toward violence of those who participate in drug trafficking.

The number of drug-related homicides, however, has been decreasing in recent years. In 1991, 6.2 percent of all homicides were drug-related, whereas in 1998, this figure dropped to 4.8 percent. Despite this decrease, drug-related homicides remain the fourth most documented type of murder.

There were as many guns as colonists in early Jamestown. In the new setting, people needed guns to hunt and to protect themselves.

The colonists also had English tradition to support their ownership of weapons. That tradition gave them the right to defend themselves and their homes and the duty to have weapons to protect the public peace. Dating back to the Middle Ages, the English chose to arm themselves for defense rather than have an army under the direction of a monarch. They recognized that the monarch could become a tyrant and use the army against them.

During the American Revolution, volunteers organized themselves into militias, or small defense forces, known as minutemen. They got their name because they were ready to respond in a minute's notice to fight British troops. ***Government*** ***Why did American colonists believe in their right to own guns?***

## *Guns and Crime: A Deadly Combination*

Crime, especially murder, is reported widely in newspapers, magazines, and on television and radio. Major television networks tripled the time allotted to their news coverage of murder stories in 1993. These broadcasts draw attention to the fact that crime increasingly involves young people. Between 1987 and 1996 the rate of juvenile arrests for violent crime rose 60 percent. During the same period the rate of violent crime for all ages dropped by 5 percent.

An overwhelming proportion of violent crimes, whether juvenile or adult, are committed with a gun. In 1998 about 69 percent of all homicides involved firearms, and four out of five of these were handguns. Many Americans wonder if stiffer gun control is an effective way to reduce crime.

## REVIEWING THE PAST

Foreign visitors are often surprised by the number of guns—some 230 million—owned by civilians in the United States. In many other countries, guns are banned or tightly controlled. For example, Britain strictly limits gun ownership, and it completely banned handguns in 1997. Since the assassinations of President Kennedy, Martin Luther King, Jr., and Robert F. Kennedy, there have been a number of attempts to pass gun-control laws in the United States. Each bill has met with heated debate because of the history of gun ownership in this country.

## *The English Tradition*

Guns have been part of the American way of life since the first Europeans came to North America.

Over time, tensions increased as the English kings sought more power. After the Glorious Revolution of 1688 overthrew James II, Parliament placed limits on the monarchy through the Bill of Rights. For one thing, it established the right to keep arms for the common defense. Thus English people, both before and after the Glorious Revolution, brought to the American colonies their strongly held belief in their rights to own guns and to protect themselves from absolute government power.

## *Colonists Fight for Their Rights*

When American colonists believed that the British were trying to limit their rights, they fought back. The colonists had enjoyed a fair amount of self-government until Britain began to tighten its control after the French and Indian War. The British wanted to maintain their vast new North American empire, so they kept a standing army in the colonies. They expected the colonists to help pay for it.

Resistance to the British grew after passage of the Stamp Act. **Militias** began to form in 1774 and 1775. Militias are bands of citizens armed to defend themselves. One such group, known as minutemen, fought the British to protect supplies of ammunition at Lexington and Concord in Massachusetts. This "shot heard round the world" touched off the American Revolution.

## The Second Amendment

After the American Revolution, the new nation had to form a stable, unified government. The result was the Constitution. That document, however, met with stiff resistance from those who feared it would not protect individuals' and states' rights. In order to get the Constitution ratified, its sponsors agreed to add a Bill of Rights. These are the first 10 amendments of the present-day Constitution.

Americans had fought the British to preserve their rights to self-defense and self-taxation. They had been able to resist the British because they had had their own militias. Following the war, Americans were not about to give up that protection. After all, who knew how the new government would turn out?

During the debate on ratifying the Constitution, many delegates demanded that the right to bear arms be included in a Bill of Rights. As a result, James Madison drafted the **Second Amendment.** In its final form it states, "A well-regulated militia being necessary to the security of a free state, the right of the people to keep and bear arms shall not be infringed."

## An American Symbol

Thus guns were present at the creation of this country and became part of the law of the land. Firearms have also become the stuff of American legend. Think of the early pioneer, the mountain man, and the cowhand. These are strong, independent, free, and rugged individuals, symbols of an American ideal. Take away their guns, and what happens to those symbols?

Today the United States is far more urban than rural, and gun violence is alarmingly high. These are facts. So, should the right to have a gun continue to be part of the American way of life? Americans have wrestled with that question and have put some restrictions on the books.

Thousands of laws regulate firearms in the United States. Most of these are state and local laws that license gun dealers, provide permits for gun buyers, and, in some places, ban certain types of guns. On the federal level, the 1968 Gun Control Act (GCA) prohibits criminals, minors, the mentally ill, and illegal aliens from owning guns.

A 1993 amendment to the GCA known as the Brady Law required a five-day waiting period, as well as a police background check, before someone could purchase a gun. (This law was named for James Brady, who was paralyzed by a gunshot aimed at President Reagan.) In 1997 the Supreme Court struck down the requirement that police do a background check. Still, in 1998 every state was conducting voluntary background checks on gun purchasers.

Yet another federal law, the Assault Weapons Act of 1994, bans certain types of semiautomatic firearms. In 1998 President Clinton, through an executive order, also banned the importation

Frederic Remington's 1902 painting, *The Cowboy,* illustrates the popular notion of Americans' rugged individualism. ***Culture* What American ideals did the cowboy represent?**

of semiautomatic assault-style weapons that have been modified for sporting purposes. With so many regulations on firearms, what more is necessary?

## DEBATING THE FUTURE

Natisha Campbell, whose friend Hank Lloyd was shot and killed in Washington, D.C., asks, "Why should you be able to have a gun laying under your pillow so that a baby can pick it up and shoot themselves?" "I say all guns are good guns," counters Joe Foss, former president of the **National Rifle Association (NRA),** the leading organization working against gun control. "There are no bad guns. I say the whole nation should be an armed nation. Period."

### *Against Gun Control*

The National Rifle Association's members cite the Second Amendment phrase, "the right of the people to keep and bear arms shall not be infringed," as the basis for their belief that individuals have the right to own guns. Gun prohibition, besides being unconstitutional, would endanger society, says the NRA. Members believe that people must have guns to protect themselves against criminals. They point out that most gun owners are law-abiding citizens.

Says Mary Sue Faulkner of the NRA, "We know criminals fear armed citizens more than they do the police." Statistics support this statement: handguns are used more often in repelling crimes than in committing them. As one Florida rifle association member put it, "If I want to mug someone, I'll avoid a person who may have a handgun."

NRA members say that gun control is not the answer to the crime problem. "Gun control is a cop-out," said NRA lobbyist James Jay Baker, "an easy solution to a complex problem. And it doesn't work." People bent on committing crime will find a way, says the NRA. So will people intent on getting a gun. "There is absolutely no way the legislation is going to stop the bad guys from getting guns," says a veteran Maryland police officer.

A 1991 Justice Department study showed that only 27 percent of state-prison inmates had bought their guns legally. The others got them from family or friends, stole them, or purchased them on the black market. Commented one gun-shop customer, "It's easier to get a firearm delivered in the Washington area than it is to get a pizza."

Some Americans believe that the right to keep and bear arms, without federal or state regulations, is part of their constitutional rights as stated in the Second Amendment. ***Culture What arguments does the NRA make opposing gun control?***

Many members of the NRA believe that any attempt to regulate firearms will lead to total gun prohibition. Before the 1994 federal laws were passed, former NRA president Jim Reinke said:

**AMERICAN VOICES** **"If we give in on the gun waiting period and assault rifles, we'd lose half our membership, and six months later the anti-gunners will want our long guns."**

—*Jim Reinke*

If gun control is not the answer to violent crime, what is? The NRA's J. Warren Cassidy, an executive vice president, responded to that question in 1990 this way:

**AMERICAN VOICES** **"Tough laws designed to incarcerate violent offenders offer something gun control cannot: swift, sure justice meted out with no accompanying erosion of individual liberty."**

—*J. Warren Cassidy*

### *For Gun Control*

Supporters of gun control focus on the first phrase of the Second Amendment, "A well-regulated militia being necessary to the security of a free state." They emphasize that the purpose of the amendment is to provide protection for the entire community.

Restricting criminals' access to guns is absolutely essential to reduce violent crime, argues Dewey Stokes, national president of the Fraternal Order of Police. "The police are definitely outgunned in this country." Criminals are carrying more dangerous weapons and are more willing to use them. Al Baker of the Houston Police Department says:

**AMERICAN VOICES** **"Just about everybody committing a crime has a gun. Not cheap Saturday-night specials, but guns they can count on. And they're willing to shoot it out rather than go to jail."**

—*Al Baker*

Gun-control advocates point out that in 1939 the Supreme Court upheld a law against short-barreled shotguns because their use could not "contribute to the common defense." In 1983, the Court refused to hear a case challenging the first ban on handguns in the nation.

Far from making society safer, gun-control advocates say, guns kept for defense against criminals make life more dangerous. A 1993 study appearing in *The New England Journal of Medicine* supported that claim. It showed that the risk of homicide in the home is three times greater in households with guns.

Children are often the victims of firearms both inside and outside the home. In 1997, according to the National Center for Health Statistics, 12 children were killed with guns every day in the United States.

Some of these incidents have shocked the nation. In 1998 five were killed by a student in a Jonesboro, Arkansas high school. One year later, two students armed with semi-automatic guns and bombs killed twelve classmates, a teacher, and later themselves at Columbine High School in Littleton, Colorado.

### *The Debate Continues*

A Gallup survey in 1999 showed that 89 percent of Americans favor requiring a five-day waiting period on the purchase of guns. Another Gallup survey found that 68 percent support a ban on semi-automatic assault weapons. Yet according to another poll also conducted by Gallup in that same year, 62 percent of Americans oppose a ban on the possession of handguns. Given these mixed feelings, Americans will need to look more closely and considerately at both sides of the gun-control issue to develop effective public policy in combatting crime.

*James Brady, White House press secretary during President Reagan's first term, was paralyzed by a gunshot wound during an assassination attempt on President Reagan in 1981. Brady and his wife, Sarah, became strong advocates of gun control. Their efforts brought about the 1994 passage of the Brady law.*

# Chapter 27 Review

## Key Terms

1. homicide
2. militia
3. Second Amendment
4. National Rifle Association (NRA)

## Creating a Time Line

5. To place the issue of gun control in context, construct a time line that traces the English and American traditions toward gun ownership from the Middle Ages to the inclusion of the Second Amendment in the Constitution (from the Reviewing the Past section). Use your textbook as a reference.

## Portfolio Activity

6. Think about your own opinions about crime and the role of gun control in reducing violent crime. Express the opinions in your own way. Consider the following: a poster or drawing, a letter to the editor, a poem or personal essay, a photo essay. When you have chosen a presentation that is acceptable to your teacher, put it in an appropriate format.

### INTERNET ACTIVITY

*For your portfolio:*
**WRITE AN ESSAY**

7. Access Prentice Hall's *America: Pathways to the Present* site at **www.Pathways.phschool.com** for the specific URL to complete the activity. Additional resources and related Web sites are also available.

   Review the constitutions of two nations other than the United States for information on firearms. Write an essay comparing their stance on fireams to the one presented in the Second Amendment to the United States Constitution. Which nation do you think handles the issue the best?

## Using Graphic Organizers

8. Review the arguments in the Debating the Future section of the chapter. Then fill in the blank webs in the graphic organizer below, which compares and contrasts views on gun control. You can copy the web on a separate sheet of paper.

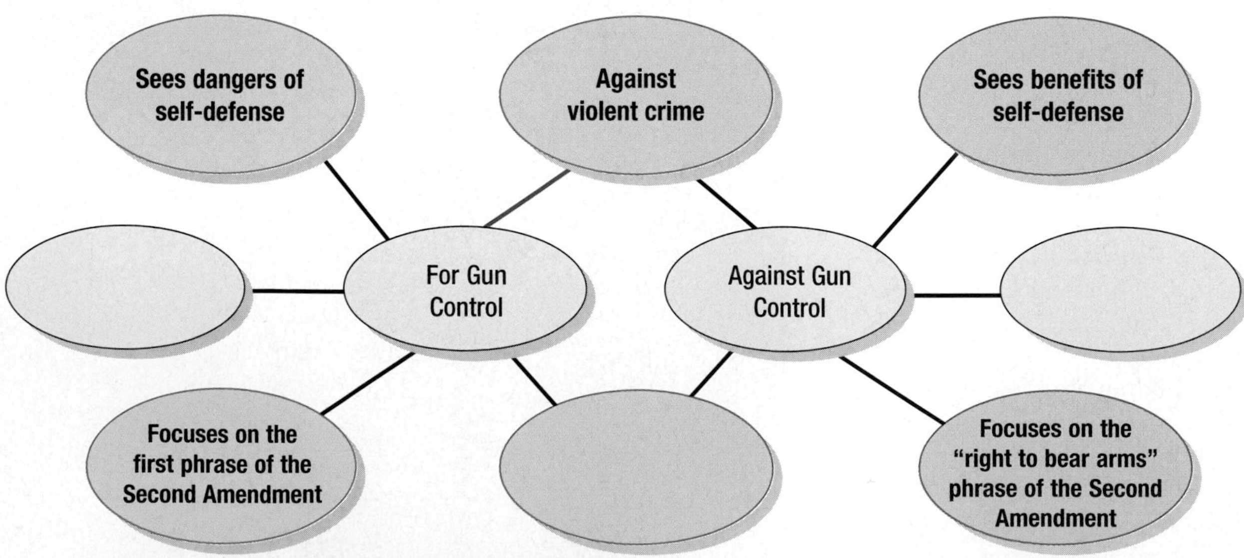

CHAPTER

# 28 The Minimum Wage

## INTRODUCING THE THEME

**For the last century, Americans have debated the role of the federal government in the economy. Should government have any control over industries in a free enterprise system? Americans continue to argue about agencies and laws regulating business, monitoring product safety, and assuring a safe workplace. A related issue is the government-mandated minimum wage. Most Americans agree that the government has the right to set a minimum wage. They disagree, however, over what that wage should be and how often it should change to reflect increases in the cost of living.**

## DEBATE

**What is the proper role of the federal government in protecting workers' incomes?**

### KEY TERMS

progressive,
New Deal,
work ethic

## VIEWING THE PRESENT

Jacqueline Barnes wants to be a doctor. To pay her way through medical school, she works eight-hour shifts at a sandwich shop in Washington, D.C., between semesters. The minimum-wage raise of 1996 promised to increase her earnings by 15 cents an hour. Does she turn her nose up at such a small raise? Not at all. "Fifteen cents might not sound like much, but you know what? Even after taxes that's enough to buy me at least one extra textbook at college."

Barnes works for a large chain of sandwich shops, but across town Karen Audia Shannon runs her own restaurant. She worries that an increase in the minimum wage will have a ripple effect, forcing her to increase wages to her lowest-paid employees, even though they earn slightly

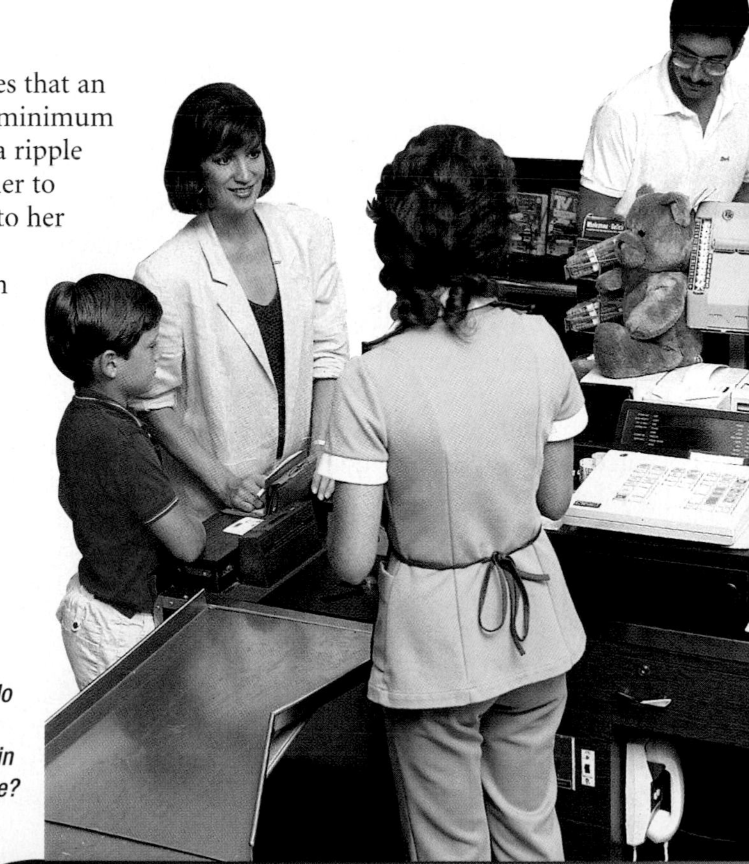

The majority of minimum-wage workers are adults. *Economics* *Why do some Americans oppose increases in the minimum wage?*

Workers toil away in this Progressive Era factory. During the Progressive Era, reformers tried to make factories less dangerous and improve overall working conditions. ***Government*** ***What role did progressive reformers believe government should play in protecting workers?***

more than the minimum now. Said Shannon, "It would put my business in serious jeopardy, so much so that I almost feel I'd be forced to close. I would be put in a position where operating as a profitable restaurant would no longer be a possibility." If the restaurant closed, she and her 26 employees would be out of a job.

## *Minimum-Wage Workers*

In 1997 the minimum wage rose to $5.15 per hour for most jobs. Of the 130 million workers in the United States, some 2 million earn the minimum wage. Another 4 million, whose jobs are not covered by the law, earn less than the minimum wage. Who are these workers? What kinds of jobs do they have? Where do they live?

When you think of someone making minimum wage, you probably picture a teenager flipping hamburgers at a fast-food restaurant. As with many stereotypes, this picture is partly accurate. But the reality of minimum-wage work is much more complex.

1. A quarter of the people who are paid the minimum wage or less are food-service workers.
2. Only a small percentage of these are teenagers. The majority of workers earning up to minimum wage—about 70 percent—are adults.
3. The majority are also women—about 60 percent.
4. Just under half of the workers paid minimum wage or less work full time, and another third work 20 to 34 hours per week.
5. About 12 percent are the sole breadwinners in families with children.

Jobs paying the minimum wage include retail sales in shops and malls, restaurant work, gardening, farm work, motel cleaning, dry cleaning, child care, and garment work. These jobs can be found all over the country. Some, however, are more concentrated in particular areas. They include farm work in California; garment work in the Northeast, San Francisco, and Los Angeles; and textile jobs in the Southeast. Overall, the South has the highest concentration of minimum-wage workers.

## REVIEWING THE PAST

The idea of government legislation to protect workers began with a group of political and social reformers in the late 1800s and early 1900s. These **progressives,** largely well-educated middle-class people, were appalled by the effects of rapid industrial growth. They saw corrupt politicians lining their own pockets and captains of industry amassing great wealth.

Meanwhile, workers labored long hours in unsafe conditions for low wages. To improve society, various progressive groups sought to end corruption in government. They tried to limit the abuses of power by giant corporations. They also worked to improve the living and working conditions of the poor, starting at the state level.

### *State Regulations*

Instead of counting on public opinion or private charity to bring about social reform, the progressives looked to government to solve problems. They believed government had to increase its responsibility for the well-being of its citizens.

To protect workers, progressives pushed for state laws regulating workplace conditions, maximum hours, and minimum wages. They met with stiff resistance, however. At that time, such laws were considered restrictions on personal liberties. In 1905, for example, the Supreme Court overturned a New York law setting a maximum 10-hour workday for bakers. Wrote Supreme Court Justice Rufus W. Peckham, "[Statutes] limiting the hours in which grown and intelligent men may labor to earn their living, are mere meddlesome interferences with the rights of the individual."

It took a terrible tragedy to awaken public demand for more legislation to protect workers. On March 25, 1911, fire swept through the Triangle Shirtwaist Factory in New York City. As a result of locked doors and an inadequate fire escape system, many young women workers were trapped inside. More than 140 were killed. Some plunged to their deaths from the eighth, ninth, and tenth floors. As a result, the New York State legislature formed the Factory Inspection Commission.

The Commission recommended legislation on factory safety, workers' accident insurance, protection for women and children in industry, and minimum wages. The commission's work led to the adoption of a new Industrial Code in New York. This code became a model for legislation in other states.

## *First Minimum-Wage Law*

Progressives like Frances Perkins, who had worked to set up the Factory Inspection Commission, believed that the minimum wage was essential. In 1912 Massachusetts became the first state to pass a minimum-wage law. That year Theodore Roosevelt made the minimum wage a part of his Progressive party platform. In 1913 eight additional states passed minimum-wage laws.

When the United States entered World War I, the federal government took on a larger role. To ensure defense production, it regulated wages, hours, and working conditions through the War Labor Policies Board. After the war, however, the military need for regulation ended, and public interest in workers' conditions dropped off.

## *Depression and New Deal*

When the glamour of the Roaring Twenties gave way to the grim realities of the Great Depression, interest in protecting workers revived. As more and more people lost their jobs, those still employed often saw their wages drop. Between 1928 and 1932, for example, the average weekly earnings for factory workers dropped from $27.80 to $17.05.

When he took office in 1933, President Franklin D. Roosevelt made good on his campaign promise of a **New Deal** for Americans. He offered programs to provide relief, create jobs, and stimulate the economy. He also appointed Frances Perkins to be Secretary of Labor, the first woman to hold a Cabinet post. Perkins, who had fought tirelessly for worker protection in New York, continued her crusade in Washington.

The New Deal's first attempt to set minimum wages and shorter hours was part of the National Industrial Recovery Act of 1933. When the Supreme Court declared that law unconstitutional, workers renewed their demands for protection. With Perkins's help, FDR sent the Fair Labor Standards bill to Congress in 1937. He said, "A self-supporting and self-respecting democracy can plead no justification for the existence of child labor, no economic reason for chiseling workers' wages or stretching workers' hours."

The fire at the Triangle Shirtwaist Factory in New York City in 1911 brought national attention to the issue of workplace safety and workers' rights. ***Government*** *What impact did the fire have on government legislation?*

Many of the labor laws to which we have become accustomed were either enacted or proposed during FDR's New Deal. ***Government*** ***How many familiar workplace laws and guarantees can you identify in this painting?***

## *Recent Developments*

Since 1938 the minimum wage has become part of American working life. Following the New Deal came Harry Truman's Fair Deal, during which Congress raised the minimum wage to 75 cents an hour. Six years later it rose to $1 an hour, and another six years took it to $1.25. It has inched upward since then until it reached $4.25 in 1991.

Congress considered raising the minimum wage in the election year of 1996. Although many members opposed it, the bill finally passed, and President Clinton signed it. As the new law provided, the rate went to $5.15 on September 1, 1997. Three years later Clinton asked Congress to raise the minimum wage further—to $6.15. Other Democrats called for an even greater hike. Any attempt to raise the minimum wage again is sure to provoke heated debate.

*The Works Progress Administration (WPA) was a New Deal agency set up in 1935. It lasted for eight years and provided work for more than eight million Americans.*

Congress passed the Fair Labor Standards Act the next year. It banned child labor and set the minimum wage at 25 cents per hour, increasing to 40 cents per hour over seven years. The maximum work week was set at 44 hours, to drop to 40 hours in the next three years. When the law took effect in 1938, it immediately helped about 300,000 workers earning less than 25 cents an hour and 1,384,000 others working more than 44 hours a week. The next year, when the minimum wage went up to 30 cents and maximum hours went down to 42, some 3 million more workers benefited.

### DEBATING THE FUTURE

Jill Mattioli could no longer afford an apartment in Telluride, Colorado. She had to move to the outskirts of town. "If I wait [tables] and serve these people," she says, "I should be able to live here and have a decent standard of living." But to do so would involve raising the minimum wage. That is something Atlanta radio talk show host Sean Hannity opposes. "How much more can you pay someone who flips burgers for a living? Are you willing to pay more for a hamburger?" he argues.

A national poll taken by the *Los Angeles Times* in 1999 showed that more than three fourths of Americans favored increasing the minimum wage. Moreover, more than half of the people surveyed in every Gallup poll taken on this topic since 1945 have supported a higher minimum wage. Yet despite public opinion and congressional action, debate continues to swirl around the minimum-wage issue.

## In Favor of Raising the Minimum Wage

In 1997 the average chief executive officer (CEO) of a corporation earned 326 times as much as the average factory worker. Proponents of increasing the minimum wage point to the vast gap between the rich and poor in America to argue their case. "It's a moral issue," says Representative John Lewis of Georgia. "Raising the minimum wage is the right thing to do."

It is the right thing to do, argue those in favor, because in 1998 a minimum-wage earner working full time earned $10,700. If that worker had three dependents, his or her earnings fell far below the federal poverty line of $16,450. Said Philadelphian John Trendler of the $4.25 minimum wage:

**AMERICAN VOICES** **"I don't know of anyone trying to support a family who can get by on that."**

—*John Trendler*

For most minimum-wage earners with families, getting by at that level has required government assistance. This means food stamps and even welfare.

Inflation is one reason often cited for continuing increases in the minimum wage. As prices rise, people with fixed incomes find it harder and harder to support a family. Reduced buying power means minimum-wage earners must skimp on everything.

That skimping, in turn, has far-reaching consequences for society as a whole. For example, an uninsured driver who gets into an accident forces someone else to pay and pushes up everyone else's premiums. Pregnant women who do not get adequate medical care are more at risk for having babies with birth defects. Caring for these children drives up everyone's medical costs.

## Opposed to Raising the Minimum Wage

Restaurant owner Robert Bobbitt, Sr., of Canton, Ohio, argues that wages are not a matter of "employer whim." Mr. Bobbitt worked a second job at night to get enough training to qualify for ownership of a McDonald's franchise. Now he owns four of the restaurants. He opposes a wage increase. "Before, I would have thought of the minimum wage as a social issue. Then you start working for yourself, and all the risk and responsibilities are on you. Raising the minimum wage will

Those who support a rise in the minimum wage say that most families cannot support themselves on a low minimum wage. Families who cannot support themselves increase the burden on public assistance programs. ***Economics*** ***What are the main arguments of those who favor raising the minimum wage?***

Robert Bobbitt, Sr., of Canton, Ohio, is a restaurant owner. He, like many small-business owners, fears that a rise in the minimum wage cannot be absorbed by a small business like his. He thinks the rise will result in worker layoffs. ***Economics*** ***How do higher wages affect consumers?***

take money out of the entrepreneur's pocket," Bobbitt claims. In other words, the level of wages can make or break a small business.

Opponents of an increase say holding the minimum wage steady is also important to consumers. Typically, a producer of goods or services passes along any increase in costs to customers. "Businesses simply don't absorb increased wage costs," according to presidential adviser Rob Shapiro. "They pass them on in the form of higher prices, which are regressive [hardest on the poor] because they're borne equally by all." Higher prices hurt those least able to pay. They can also trigger inflation.

Consumers aren't the only ones who will suffer from raising the minimum wage, opponents say. Workers on the lowest rungs of the economic ladder will be hurt, too. When employers must raise the minimum wage, they often have to cut employee hours or drop employees from the payroll. Like Robert Bobbitt of Ohio, Maryland restaurant owner Chris Gallant says,

**AMERICAN VOICES** **"These people need their jobs. Congress would only be hurting us, and our employees, if they raised the minimum wage."**

—*Chris Gallant*

So, what is the value of the minimum wage? The laws of supply and demand in the marketplace, not the government, should determine wages, according to these opponents of the minimum wage.

## *The Debate Continues*

The majority of Americans favor increasing the minimum wage. Yet the debate among politicians over the minimum wage is intense because it pits two deeply held American values against each other. Americans hold fast to their belief in the **work ethic**—the idea that hard work will produce a decent life. The American dream, after all, is based on the notion that anyone who tries hard enough can achieve a comfortable standard of living. The minimum wage, therefore, should meet that standard.

On the other hand, Americans also believe in free enterprise. Government regulation that restricts free enterprise interferes with the workings of the marketplace and will ultimately hurt the economy. The challenge to Americans, then, is to find a way to reconcile these two beliefs in an era when government regulation is mistrusted but poverty is increasing.

# Chapter 28 Review

## Key Terms

1. progressive
2. New Deal
3. work ethic

## Creating a Time Line

4. To set the issues of this chapter in context, construct a time line that includes major events and legislation in twentieth-century United States history related to worker protection and the minimum wage. Begin with the Triangle Shirtwaist Factory fire. You may use your textbook as a reference.

## Portfolio Activity

5. Review the issues of the debate about the minimum wage in the Debating the Future section of the chapter. How do they affect you personally and the country as a whole? Choose a way to express your opinion. Draw a cartoon, write a letter to a member of Congress, or construct a poster. When you have chosen a presentation that is acceptable to your teacher, put it in the appropriate format.

### INTERNET ACTIVITY

***For your portfolio:***
**CREATE A GRAPH**

6. Access Prentice Hall's *America: Pathways to the Present* site at **www.Pathways.phschool.com** for the specific URL to complete the activity. Additional resources and related Web sites are also available.

   Use the data provided to graph the change in wages between 1973 and 1997 for workers of various education levels. Describe the trend in wages for each category of education level. Have wages increased or decreased during this time period? Which group of workers has fared the best? The worst?

## Using Graphic Organizers

7. Review the arguments in the Debating the Future section of the chapter. Fill in the blank circles in the web diagram below, which shows the connections among employers, wage earners, and the government.

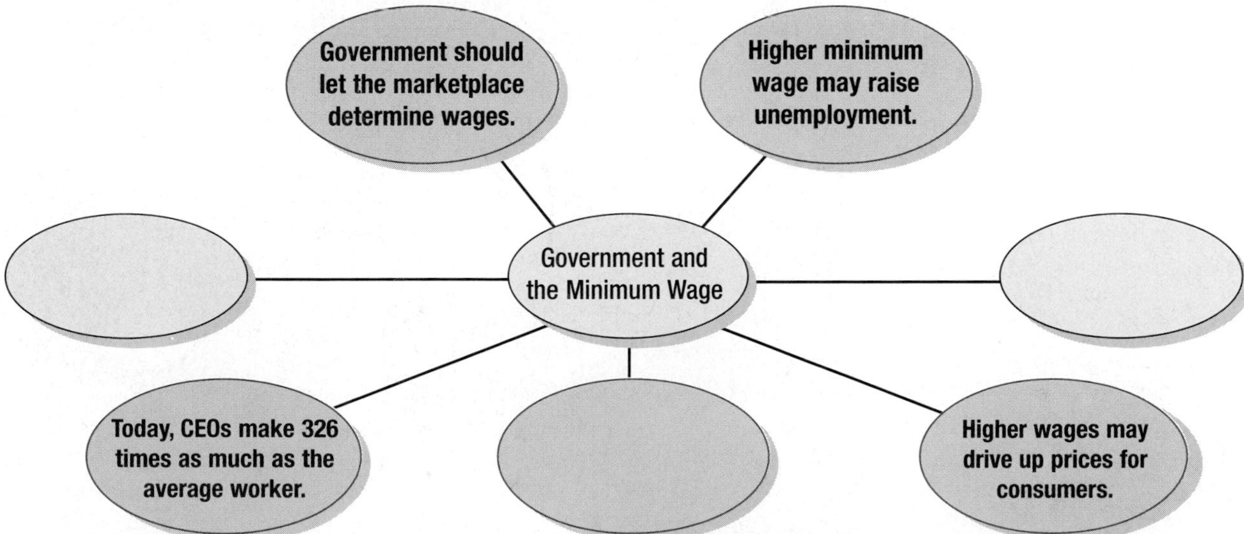

CHAPTER 29

# Rethinking Entitlements

## INTRODUCING THE THEME

**Millions of people in the United States receive some form of government assistance, such as food stamps, health insurance, or medical care. While federal social welfare programs have existed since the 1930s, the rising cost of such programs has raised controversy in recent years. Critics of social welfare programs argue that they encourage dependency and unfairly burden taxpayers. Defenders of social welfare programs counter that such programs are needed to protect vulnerable groups, such as the elderly and children.**

*Social Security card*

## DEBATE

**How do we balance the needs of the poor and the elderly against the needs of the budget, both for the present and for the future?**

## KEY TERMS

Medicare, entitlement, AFDC, federal deficit, national debt, food stamp, block grant

## VIEWING THE PRESENT

When she was in the tenth grade in Milwaukee, Wisconsin, Keyola Lackey dropped out of school because she was pregnant. A year after her first baby was born, she had another child. Without a husband and without job skills, Lackey got by on welfare, or public assistance. She fit the welfare stereotype almost exactly: an unwed teenage

A welfare reform law passed in 1996 brought about sweeping changes in social welfare programs. ***Economics*** *What was one of the major goals of the law?*

The United States' elderly population is the fastest-growing segment of American society. Almost all Americans aged sixty-five and over are insured by Medicare. ***Economics What challenges does the Medicare system face?***

mother with several children and no way to support them.

When 75-year-old J. S. Russell learned that he needed heart surgery, his family worried a lot about how to pay for it. The costs of a pacemaker, the operation itself, and a week of care at Stanford University Hospital seemed enormous. As it turned out, the family had to pay much less than they feared. **Medicare,** a federal health-insurance program for elderly and disabled Americans, paid for almost everything except Russell's medications.

## What Are Entitlements?

Welfare and Medicare are two examples of federal programs called entitlements. **Entitlements** are social welfare programs that people are "entitled to" by being at a certain income level or age. The federal government guarantees assistance for all those who qualify. As the number of people who qualify increases, so do the costs. As a result, managing costs has become a major concern.

In the 1990s politicians were quick to attack the idea of welfare but reluctant to question the need for Medicare. A 1995 *Time*/CNN poll reflected this split. Some 65 percent of those surveyed favored cutting welfare benefits, while 81 percent opposed cuts in Medicare. Yet despite these differences in public opinion, most Americans agreed that both programs needed to be reformed. There was little agreement, however, on how to do so.

## Welfare

Welfare is a broad term that covers many forms of public assistance. Yet when most people hear the word "welfare," they think of Aid to Families with Dependent Children **(AFDC).** Before major reform of the welfare system in 1996, AFDC was the largest and best-known program of public assistance. Federal outlays to AFDC families made up roughly 4 percent of the national budget. Medicaid, which provides health care services to more than 36 million Americans receiving public assistance, accounted for about 6 percent of the budget in 1996.

The federal government set the guidelines for who could receive AFDC and Medicaid and how money would be distributed. Slightly more than half of the costs of AFDC were paid for by the federal government. The rest was paid by the states. The federal government also paid at least half of each state's Medicaid expenses.

In 1996, roughly 12.8 million people received AFDC, about two thirds of them children. Approximately one in seven American children was on AFDC, and of these AFDC children, nearly 60 percent were African American or Hispanic.

Some people have been able to stop receiving welfare aid after a short time. Many others, however, have remained on the welfare system for extended periods. According to Ladonna Pavetti of the Urban Institute, about 63 percent of those receiving welfare in the past eventually spent nine years or more on public assistance. Critics of welfare point to such figures as proof that people have abused the system or at least have become dependent on it.

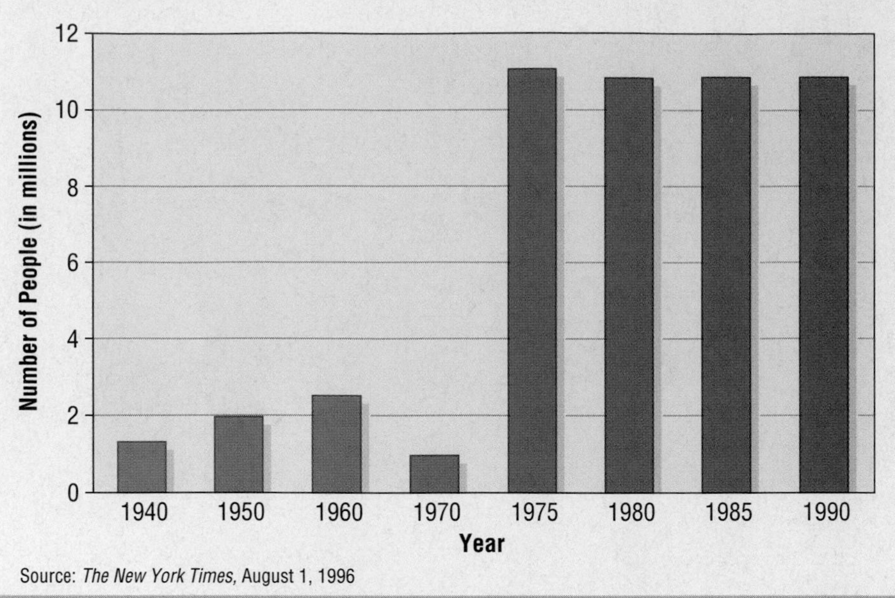


**Interpreting Graphs** The number of people receiving AFDC grew rapidly after 1970. ***Culture*** ***What connection is there between these figures and the public's view of social welfare?***

## *Medicare*

Medicare provides health insurance for Americans over 65 and for people with disabilities—over 40 million people in 2001. Medicare pays for both hospital care and doctors' visits, but it does so in different ways. Money for Part A of Medicare, which covers hospital expenses, comes from a payroll tax paid for by workers and employers. About one fourth of the money for Part B, which covers doctors' visits, comes from premiums paid by Medicare recipients themselves. The other three fourths comes from congressional outlays. In 2001, government Medicare payments accounted for 12 percent of the federal budget.

Medicare faces several problems, but the biggest is financial. The hospital insurance fund, which had a surplus in the mid-1990s, is expected to run out of money by 2008 because of soaring costs. The main reason for the rising costs of medical care is the expense of new technology.

The number of people eligible for Medicare is growing steadily. By 2010, when baby boomers start to retire, the number of Americans over 65 will be about 40 million. Adding to the problem is the fact that the fastest-growing population group is also the group needing the most medical care. This is the group over age 85.

Unlike welfare, the main requirement for receiving Medicare is not income but age. In 1995, there were four people paying Medicare taxes for every Medicare recipient. By the middle of the next century there will only be two people paying taxes for every recipient.

## *Rethinking Entitlements*

Every year from 1970 to 1996 the United States spent more money than it took in through taxes. This meant that in each of those years there was a **federal deficit.** Each year's deficit adds to the **national debt**—all the money that the federal government owes. By mid-1998 the national debt had reached around $5.5 trillion.

Like anyone who borrows money, the federal government must pay interest on this debt. For the fiscal year ending in September 1997, that interest totaled more than $244 billion. This amount represented about 14 percent of the entire federal budget.

Reducing the national debt would lower the government's annual interest payments. To do this, Congress either has to cut federal spending in another area or raise more money from the taxpayers. Because no one wants a tax increase, the government looks to make budget cuts. Entitlements have become a logical target for those cuts.

Tensions over budget cuts eased somewhat in 1998 when the U.S. recorded a budget surplus—the first one since 1969. The government's interest payments towards the national debt decreased to 11 percent of the federal budget in 2001. As a result, the budget gains flexibility and there is less pressure to slash spending in other areas.

## REVIEWING THE PAST

To most people the "American Dream" is the belief that through hard work and determination, anyone can become successful in America. For most of this nation's history, people did not believe it was the government's responsibility to help the poor or the needy.

By the end of the nineteenth century, however, many people seemed to find it much more difficult to make it on their own. The Industrial Revolution had drawn people from the farm to the city. As working and living conditions in the growing cities became harsh, progressives worked for government regulation of some aspects of private industry. Passage of these laws signaled a shift in public opinion. It paved the way for greater government involvement in solving social problems.

### *FDR's New Deal*

The economic crisis of the Great Depression motivated President Franklin D. Roosevelt (FDR) to set up a number of social welfare programs in the United States. Under his New Deal, work-relief projects like the Works Progress Administration provided billions of dollars for jobs for the poor. Such programs kept many families from starving.

Social Security was another New Deal program. The Social Security Act provided retirement pensions for workers over 65 and unemployment benefits for those who lost their jobs. Social Security was funded by deductions from workers' paychecks as well as by contributions from employers.

Added to the original Social Security Act was a section to provide Aid to Dependent Children (ADC)—direct payments to children whose fathers had died or deserted the family. Money for ADC was to come from both the federal government and the states, with the federal government handling a larger share. ADC became Aid to Families with Dependent Children (AFDC) in 1950. In that year, Congress broadened its coverage to include mothers in its benefits.

During the prosperous 1950s, most Americans thought little about the poor. Unknown to them, pockets of poverty existed in the midst of national prosperity—in Appalachia, in the Deep South, and in the big cities of the Northeast and Midwest. Michael Harrington brought these problems to light in his 1962 book, *The Other America.*

In response, President John Kennedy asked Congress for laws to eliminate poverty. One direct result was the food stamp program to help feed the poor. Under this

This photograph of a family during the Depression was taken by Dorothea Lange in 1936. The Social Security Act of 1935 provided direct payments to children whose fathers had died or deserted the family. ***Government How did the role of government change during the New Deal?***

program, people receive **food stamps,** which are printed slips of paper that can be used like money to purchase groceries.

## *Johnson's Great Society*

After Kennedy's assassination, President Lyndon Johnson enlarged Kennedy's ideas into his own vision of "The Great Society." To create it, he declared "an unconditional war on poverty in America." In 1964 and 1965 Congress passed laws that raised AFDC payments and broadened eligibility, increased Social Security benefits, set up Medicare and Medicaid, and established job training and education programs like Head Start. Johnson, who had begun his political career as a strong New Dealer, believed that the federal government could and should solve the problems of poverty in America.

During the Johnson administration, federal welfare spending increased each year. It continued to grow during the Nixon, Ford, and Carter administrations as well. One reason for the increase was the growing number of people on welfare. Yet spending more money on more people did not create a Great Society. It did, however, generate a major backlash against federal anti-poverty programs.

*The food stamp program in the United States came about in part because of the publication of* The Other America, *by Michael Harrington. Shown here is the original cover of the 1962 book.*



## *Reagan's Revolution*

Ronald Reagan was elected President in 1980, declaring that "government is not the solution to our problem. Government is the problem." Reagan wanted to reduce the size of government in most areas. Social welfare programs were a prime target. Welfare payments robbed people of their dignity and of their drive to work, Reagan believed. Promising to maintain a "safety net" for the neediest, he made dramatic cuts in social welfare budgets. For example, during the Reagan years, funding for food stamps dropped 18.8 percent and funding for AFDC decreased 17.7 percent. About 600,000 people found themselves excluded from Medicaid.

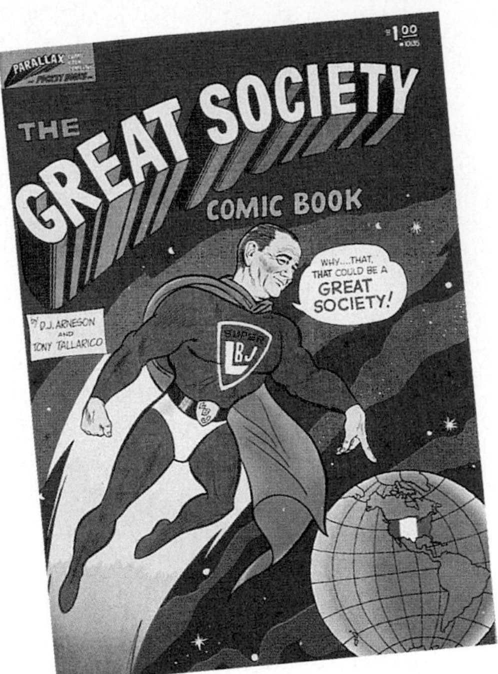


**VIEWING HISTORY** This comic book cover shows the energy with which President Johnson rallied Congress and the country behind his ambitious social programs. ***Government*** ***What programs were established during Johnson's Great Society program?***

## *After Reagan*

George Bush, elected President in 1988, carried on Reagan's legacy and continued to cut spending for social programs. Although Bush was defeated in 1992, the conservative desire to spend less on social programs gained momentum. Democrat Bill Clinton promised to "end welfare as we have known it" in his campaign for the presidency in 1992. When conservative Republicans won control of Congress in 1994, their "Contract with America" called for basic welfare reform.

## *1996 Welfare Reform*

In 1996 President Clinton signed the Personal Responsibility and Work Opportunity Reconciliation

Act. This welfare reform law made sweeping changes in the welfare system. It eliminated AFDC. No longer will needy people receive cash assistance for an indefinite period of time.

Instead, the federal government makes funds available to the states in the form of **block grants.** By distributing these lump sums of money, which are intended to stay about the same from year to year, the federal government may be better able to control its budget.

The block grants carry some restrictions. To continue to receive the grants, states must devise programs to remove people from the welfare rolls. By the year 2002 at least 50 percent of a state's welfare recipients must have a job.

Even without welfare reform, the number of people receiving assistance began to drop in the mid-1990s. In 1994 the welfare rolls reached their highest level, and then they started declining. By 2000 they had fallen by nearly 59 percent. Part of the reason for the decline was the booming economy during this period, which tamed inflation, increased employment, and also helped produce a balanced budget. Another reason was the establishment of reform programs, at both the state and the federal level. Still another reason, some suggest, was that the old-fashioned work ethic had been restored.

Since passage of the federal welfare reform law, welfare cases did shrink at a faster pace. This suggests that the law is working. But President Clinton did not like all the provisions in the law. He promised to revise some of those provisions to make them less severe, especially on children. His voice joined those of others in the debate about the future of welfare.

## DEBATING THE FUTURE

Clinton signed the welfare reform law in part because most people agreed that the welfare system needed to be overhauled. As Andrew Cuomo, Clinton's Assistant Secretary of Housing and Urban Development, said, "Nobody likes welfare. Nobody thinks it works."

There is similar agreement on the need to revamp Medicare. According to Frank Luntz, a Republican pollster:

**AMERICAN VOICES** "When the public realizes and personalizes the financial situation of Medicare, they end up backing significant reform."

—*Frank Luntz*

Yet that is about as far as agreement goes. When it comes to actually cutting welfare and Medicare, the debate centers on one question: "How deep?"

### *In Favor of Deep Cuts*

Welfare is by no means the largest item in the federal budget, but it provokes some of the sharpest attacks. Many people see welfare as a threat to the American belief in individual effort. They believe welfare recipients would rather take a handout than work. They see people getting something for nothing while the rest of America works hard and pays high taxes.

*Medicare funding has been a hot issue in the entitlements debate.*

Tom DeLay, Republican whip in the House of Representatives, summed up this argument:

**AMERICAN VOICES** "**The current welfare system undermines incentives to work, encourages expansion of the underclass, breaks up families, and promotes welfare as a way of life.**"

—*Tom DeLay*

DeLay and others have argued that sharply limiting the time people can receive assistance will get them out into the work force. The 1996 welfare reform law gives new welfare recipients two years to find work.

Some states already have programs in place to train welfare recipients. Wisconsin's Learnfare requires young people to stay in school or lose their benefits. Teenage mother Keyola Lackey supports Learnfare because it made her return to school to prepare for a job. "The people who criticize it want the money free and do nothing for it. But nothing comes free," she says.

Welfare critics have also suggested that Congress allocate a fixed amount of money for welfare each year. To promote efficiency, reformers of welfare believe that the states, not the federal government, should administer welfare programs. The 1996 welfare reform bill, with its block grants, accomplished both of these goals.

Those who want to make stiff cuts in Medicare believe that it, too, must be more efficient and less generous. They point out that Medicare covers everyone, even those who could afford to pay for their own health care. Clyle Dwyer, retired truck driver in Fargo, North Dakota, believes that Medicare is too generous. "I know guys who have stuff done that they shouldn't because Medicare will pay for it."

To rein in the growth of Medicare, former Speaker of the House Newt Gingrich and others advocated several cost-cutting measures.

1. Raise Part B premiums (which help cover doctors' visits) for people with higher incomes.
2. Promote the establishment of medical savings accounts, in which older Americans could deposit funds for use when they needed them.
3. Turn health care for older Americans over to private insurers such as health maintenance organizations (HMOs).

Gingrich believed that the private sector can do a better job than the government, especially at cutting costs. He predicted that the Health Care Financing Administration, which handles Medicare, "will wither on the vine because we think people are voluntarily going to leave it."

As this political cartoon shows, the federal government is making the states take more responsibility for public-assistance programs. ***Government*** ***How does the cartoonist portray the ability of state governments to handle this responsibility?***

## *In Favor of Moderate Cuts*

In the early 1990s the welfare population skyrocketed. Increasing poverty accounted for this growth far more than individual laziness. So said those who favor moderate welfare cuts. Rebecca Blank, a leading poverty economist, explained that the increase did not come about because of generous benefits or because single mothers were working less. In fact, she said, they were working more. The reason, according to Blank, was that inflation had decreased the value of food stamps and AFDC 26 percent between 1972 and 1992.

Those who favor moderate cuts also point out that most people who receive benefits want to work but cannot find jobs that pay a decent wage. Many of them lack job skills. According to Christopher Jencks, a professor at Northwestern University:

**AMERICAN VOICES** "For a very large proportion of single mothers, it's impossible to find a job that pays as well as being on welfare."

—*Christopher Jencks*

Removing these women from the welfare rolls will send them into minimum-wage jobs, observers point out. There they will earn less. They will also lose Medicaid coverage for themselves and their children.

Deep welfare cuts would harm children the most, say the moderates, and block grants will remove the federal guarantee of protection for all. Since each state can administer its money as it chooses, there may be areas where people completely lose their safety net. Reverend Sam Myskens of Wichita, Kansas, gives this illustration: "If the wheat crop is bad one year or Boeing lays off 5,000 people, there will be more hungry children but no more money available to feed them."

Moreover, cutting back welfare will not result in great savings, say the moderates. A better long-term solution would include child care services and job training or retraining. While these programs would cost money, they would be investments in a better-educated work force and healthier children in the future.

Some specialists who want moderate cuts in Medicare claim that privatizing this program will not produce the desired savings. They cite studies showing that private insurers are no more cost-effective than Medicare.

Furthermore, they say, shifting additional responsibilities for financing Medicare Part B to older Americans does nothing to stop the pressures that are driving health care inflation. Among those pressures is the soaring cost of new medical technology. In addition, this scheme does not rescue Part A, the hospital insurance fund.

## *The Debate Continues*

The need to reduce the national debt is very real. Entitlements are one area of spending that can be cut to help keep the federal budget balanced. Like a household budget, the federal budget is more than a list of numbers. It is also a statement of priorities. The statement would have to consider what is most important to the household at the present time and how it will affect the household in the future. How America's leaders ultimately rethink and revise entitlements will reflect the nation's priorities for the future.

In 1994 Republicans in Congress under the leadership of Speaker of the House Newt Gingrich (above), proposed a "Contract with America" to reduce the role of federal government. ***Government*** ***How did Speaker Gingrich believe health care should be handled?***

# Chapter 29 Review

## Key Terms

1. entitlement
2. AFDC
3. Medicare
4. federal deficit
5. national debt
6. food stamp
7. block grant

## Creating a Time Line

8. To set a background for the entitlement debate, construct a time line that includes six to ten significant milestones related to social welfare programs. Include events and legislation from the New Deal to the present.

## Portfolio Activity

9. Think about the history of social welfare programs in the United States. What events or legislation do you think were the most important in creating the system of entitlements that exists today? Choose one or two of these landmarks and describe them in your own way. You may make a poster, an album of magazine or newspaper photographs, or choose another format acceptable to your teacher.

**INTERNET ACTIVITY**

***For your portfolio:***
**PREPARE A REPORT**

10. Access Prentice Hall's *America: Pathways to the Present* site at **www.Pathways.phschool.com** for the specific URL to complete the activity. Additional resources and related Web sites are also available.

Use the links provided to research debate on Social Security. Write a report on the current debate. What are seen as the problems with Social Security? What are the proposed solutions?

## Using Graphic Organizers

11. Review the arguments in the Debating the Future section of the chapter. Study the web diagram below, and then create a new web that shows arguments for making *deep* cuts in entitlements. (Include information from elsewhere in the chapter as needed.)

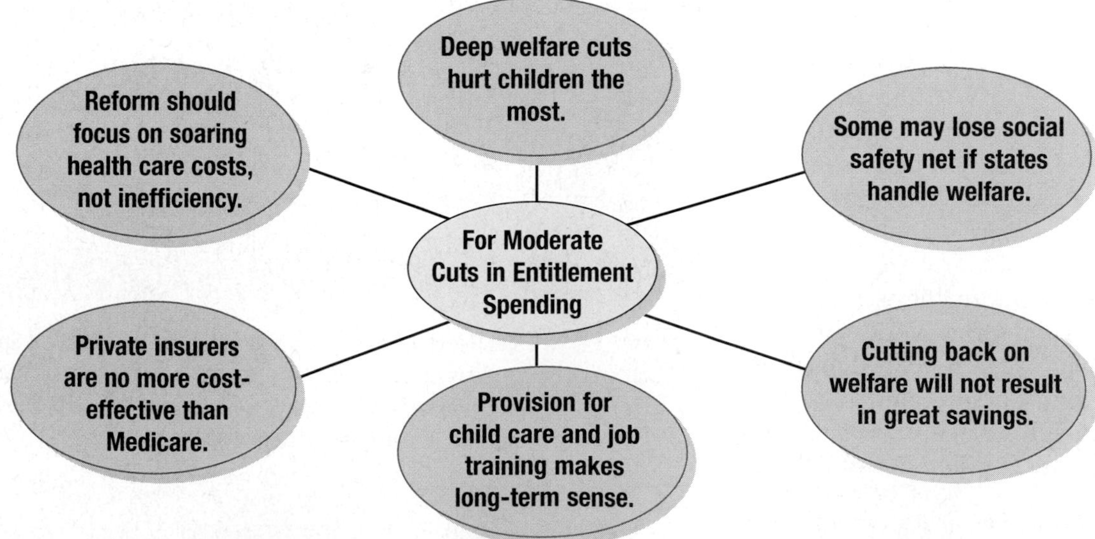

# The Debate over Trade

CHAPTER 30

## INTRODUCING THE THEME

**When the North American Free Trade Agreement (NAFTA) took effect on January 1, 1994, the economy of the United States became more closely linked with the economies of Canada and Mexico. Since then, NAFTA has been a lightning rod for debate over free trade. While supporters of NAFTA argue that free trade will increase jobs and exports in the United States, opponents believe that it will result in a loss of American jobs. NAFTA may become the model for a trade agreement proposed for 2005 that would include all of North and South America.**

**How well has NAFTA worked? How good a model is it for our dealings with the other countries of the Americas?**

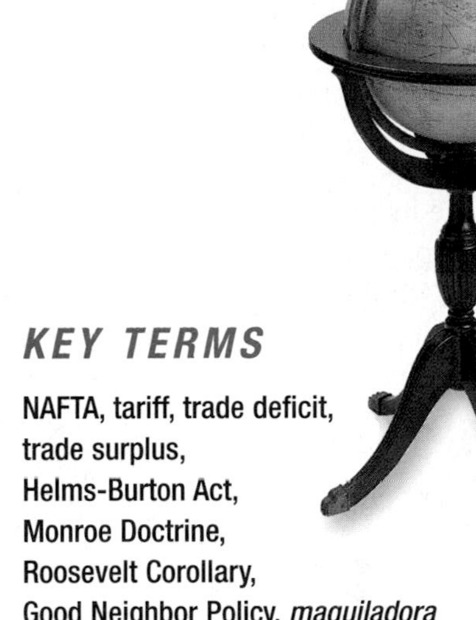

### KEY TERMS

NAFTA, tariff, trade deficit, trade surplus, Helms-Burton Act, Monroe Doctrine, Roosevelt Corollary, Good Neighbor Policy, *maquiladora*

## VIEWING THE PRESENT

Nelson Silva used to operate a forklift at a TV-assembly plant in Elmwood Park, New Jersey. When the factory shut down and moved to Tijuana, Mexico, in 1995, he lost his job. "I'm bitter that we lost these people, lost these jobs, not just at JVC but all over America," he says. "We invented the television in the

VIEWING HISTORY Some American companies have their products assembled in Mexican factories, such as the one at right. ***Economics*** *How has this phenomenon been both good and bad for American workers?*

United States, and they're going to take it completely out of the country."

Key Tronic Corporation used to manufacture computer keyboards in Spokane, Washington. It too moved to Mexico. Although Key Tronic had to lay off workers, chief financial officer Ronald F. Klawitter points out that the move turned out to be good for Spokane. Lower labor costs for his company meant lower prices for the keyboards. Lower prices, in turn, meant more sales, which increased the demand for keyboard components made in Spokane. A greater number of people in Washington ended up with jobs making parts that are then assembled in Mexico.

VIEWING HISTORY Ross Perot was the Independent candidate for president in 1992 and 1996. ***Economics*** *Why did he oppose the North American Free Trade Agreement?*

## *What Is NAFTA?*

Both of these factories relocated as a result of **NAFTA,** the North American Free Trade Agreement, which took effect on January 1, 1994. Their stories illustrate two sides of the argument over NAFTA.

The main purpose of NAFTA is to stimulate economic growth in the United States, Canada, and Mexico. To this end NAFTA removed **tariffs,** or import taxes, and other barriers to trade. In this way it created a continent-wide free-trade zone. Without tariffs, companies can sell their goods more cheaply to a larger market. Since lower prices will bring higher sales, companies like JVC and Key Tronic moved some of their plants to Mexico, where labor costs less. They no longer have to pay tariffs if they want to sell such foreign-made goods in the United States.

Before 1994, when NAFTA took effect, opponents argued that it would mean an enormous loss of American jobs to Mexico. In 1992, H. Ross Perot described the potential disaster as a "giant sucking sound" that would be heard as American jobs drained south of the border. Supporters of NAFTA like Presidents Bush and Clinton countered that the increased demand for American goods to Canada and Mexico would create more higher-skilled, higher-paying jobs in the United States, as well as more investment opportunities.

**FACT Finder** **The North American Free Trade Agreement (NAFTA), 1994**

| The Agreement | The Result | The Controversies |
|---|---|---|
| The United States, Canada, and Mexico will remove tariffs and most other mutual trade restrictions over the next 15 years. | The resulting free-trade zone formed a single market similar to, but much larger than, the European Community. | Despite NAFTA's "side agreements" and other provisions, concern remains over its potential effects on the environment and the United States job market. |

**Interpreting Tables** This table provides an overview of the NAFTA agreement and its consequences. ***Economics*** *What controversies were created by NAFTA?*

## *NAFTA and Canada*

Trade between the United States and Canada has been strong for many years. President Kennedy summed up this relationship: "Geography made us neighbors. History made us friends. And economics made us partners."

Even before NAFTA, Canada and the United States were each other's largest trading partner. In 1988, the two countries agreed to the Free Trade Agreement. This pact, signed 6 years before NAFTA,

Opponents of NAFTA argued that many of the new jobs created in Mexico would pay low wages. They also argued that Mexican workers would take work that otherwise would be performed by Americans. ***Economics* How was trade between Mexico and the United States affected by NAFTA?**

was designed to eliminate tariffs over a 10-year period.

Since NAFTA took effect, both countries have greatly increased exports to each other. The United States, however, buys more than it sells to Canada, thus producing a **trade deficit** in the United States.

## *NAFTA and Mexico*

The effect of trade with Mexico since NAFTA is more complicated. On the one hand, fewer jobs disappeared than had been predicted. Instead of the 6 million jobs that Perot claimed would be lost, the Labor Department reported in 1997 that 128,300 job losses were NAFTA-related.

On the other hand, not as many new jobs were created as had been anticipated. Supporters of NAFTA had predicted that it would bring about 200,000 new jobs in its first year. That did not happen. While the number of people employed in the United States has risen steadily since NAFTA, it is impossible to say how many of the new jobs are directly a result of the free-trade agreement.

## *Mexican Debt Crisis*

Overall, the two-way trade between the United States and Mexico rose nearly 93 percent between 1993 and 1997. But the balance of trade was not always in favor of the United States. During NAFTA's first year, 1994, exports from the United States to Mexico rose from $41.6 billion to $50.8 billion and also produced a **trade surplus.** This meant that the United States sold more to Mexico than it bought from Mexico. During 1995, however, United States exports dropped to $46.3 billion, but imports soared, leaving a trade deficit.

This shift in balance of payments resulted from a drop in the value of the Mexican peso in December 1994. With that drop, a severe recession hit Mexico. Foreign investors became nervous. It did not help that an uprising for land reform and a scandal involving Mexico's president happened at the same time.

## *Loan to Mexico*

To promote stability, in 1995 the United States granted Mexico a loan of $12.5 billion. With this help, Mexico was able to start to recover from its recession.

Much to the surprise of the loan's critics, by January 1997

Mexico had paid back the entire loan, three years ahead of schedule. Mexico also began making political reforms in 1996. Even so, the Mexican recession left many Americans wondering whether it was wise to be so closely tied economically to an unstable neighbor.

John M. Hay, future Secretary of State, wrote his friend Teddy Roosevelt that the 1898 Spanish-American War was "a splendid little war." It marked the beginning of United States involvement in Latin America for the next century. Shown here are the African American soldiers of the Tenth United States Cavalry who fought in Cuba. ***Foreign Policy*** *How has trade influenced foreign policy?*

## *Balancing Economics and Politics*

With the signing of NAFTA, the United States established a special economic relationship with its immediate neighbors. But what impact does the agreement have on political relations? What happens, for example, if Mexico or Canada wants to trade with a country to which the United States has restricted its trade?

In 1996 Congress passed the **Helms-Burton Act.** That act penalizes foreign companies that do business with Cuba. Canada and Mexico, as well as other nations of Latin America, loudly objected to it. They claimed that it violated NAFTA and international law. They saw the Helms-Burton Act as an abuse of United States power and the latest example of Uncle Sam's muscle-flexing in the Western Hemisphere.

This 1901 political cartoon suggests how the United States applied the Monroe Doctrine.

### REVIEWING THE PAST

The history of relations between the United States and Latin America shows how hard it is to separate economics and politics. In 1995 Deputy Secretary of State Strobe Talbott stated the government's two main goals in the Americas. He said, ". . . one is to support the growth of democratic institutions; the other is to advance prosperity through open markets and free trade." These objectives, democracy and trade, have shaped American foreign policy in the Western Hemisphere from the nation's earliest days. However, the ways the United States has chosen to pursue these goals have often made its neighbors wary of American power.

## *The Monroe Doctrine*

In the early 1820s, independence movements rocked Spain's and Portugal's American colonies.

Several European monarchies seemed poised to help these countries regain their former colonies. To head them off, the United States issued the **Monroe Doctrine.** Remembering its own recent colonial status, the United States warned, "The American continents, by the free and independent condition which they have assumed and maintain, are henceforth not to be considered as subject for future colonization by any European powers."

Behind this hands-off message was the desire to promote trade. One enterprising American, Minor C. Keith, built banana plantations and a railroad in Costa Rica in the late 1800s. Keith and his partners made their business, the United Fruit Company, the largest employer in Central America. With its vast economic power, United Fruit also had enormous political influence. In the independent republics of Costa Rica, Guatemala, and Honduras, the company's power was especially strong. For this reason, some people called these nations "banana republics."

In most of the new Central American nations, a small number of families controlled the wealth, leaving the rest of the population in poverty. This ruling class generally backed military dictatorships that would defend their wealth and privilege. Dictators often replaced each other in rapid succession. Yet political stability was essential to maintain the profitability of American investments in the region.

## *Gunboats and Dollars*

Extending the Monroe Doctrine, President Theodore Roosevelt announced in 1904 that the United States would exercise "international police power" to promote stability in Latin America. He called this policy the **Roosevelt Corollary.** It aimed to prevent European interference in the weak and unstable governments of the region. In practice, it meant that the United States sent troops to the Dominican Republic, Cuba, Nicaragua, and Haiti to keep the peace and protect American property.

In contrast to this style of "gunboat diplomacy," Roosevelt's successor, William Howard Taft, favored "dollar diplomacy." This term meant building regional stability through American investments in Latin America. Mexico, for example, attracted American investors. In time, Americans owned a large share of that nation's oil, railroads, mines, and rubber plantations. Yet dollar diplomacy just masked gunboat diplomacy. The United States continued to wield military power in Latin America to protect its interests, and many Latin Americans resented it bitterly.

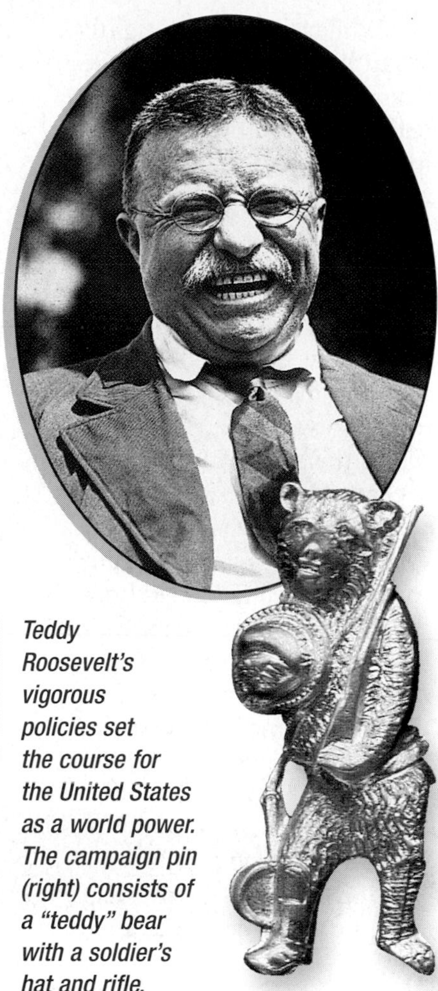

*Teddy Roosevelt's vigorous policies set the course for the United States as a world power. The campaign pin (right) consists of a "teddy" bear with a soldier's hat and rifle.*

## *Good Neighbors*

After World War I the United States no longer needed to warn European nations away, and during the Depression it could no longer afford military occupation in Latin America. Instead of direct intervention, President Franklin D. Roosevelt promoted the **Good Neighbor Policy.** Stability would come from a higher standard of living, Roosevelt believed, and so his policy was to encourage trade by lowering tariffs. The United States also loaned money to Latin American governments to build public works such as bridges, roads, schools, hospitals, and water systems.

Latin America sorely needed economic development. A number of corrupt dictators still controlled countries in which the majority of people lived in poverty.

## *After World War II*

Protecting American interests after World War II meant opposing communism. Americans worried that the masses of poor people in Latin America might be attracted to communism's philosophy.

In 1959 Fidel Castro took control of Cuba. Within two years he had nationalized American property in Cuba and allied his country with the Soviet Union. Americans feared that Castro would export communism to the rest of Latin America. To gain support in blocking the spread of communism, the United States backed a number of governments headed by military strongmen.

While these leaders tightly controlled their countries, they mismanaged the finances. Many had borrowed huge sums from foreign banks. By the early 1980s the loans could not be paid off, and Latin America plunged into a debt crisis. To get out of it, governments had to agree to plans that led to the restructuring of their economies. In time, better economic management brought new foreign investment.

In the course of these economic changes, governments were changing, too. Democracy was spreading throughout Latin America, given an added boost by the collapse of the Soviet Union. By 1995, all of the governments of the Western Hemisphere except Cuba had democratic institutions. As economies improved, political stability grew. So too did the potential for increased trade among the nations of the region.

## DEBATING THE FUTURE

Opponents of NAFTA argue that the agreement is not fair to the United States. Politician Pat Buchanan believes the American people were misled by NAFTA supporters because none of the promises made about it have been kept. He says, "NAFTA should be canceled. A contract negotiated in deceit is no contract at all." President Clinton, on the other hand, says "NAFTA . . . is working superbly." What does our experience with NAFTA teach us about free trade and international relations?

### *In Favor of NAFTA*

"The premise of NAFTA is that trade is not a zero-sum game," says former Secretary of Labor Robert B. Reich. In other words, both players win. Benefits for the United States include a net increase in jobs and a 57 percent growth in exports to Mexico and Canada in NAFTA's first four years. Both Canada and Mexico have enjoyed an increase in exports, too. NAFTA has also created jobs in those countries, particularly in the ***maquiladoras,*** Mexican border factories that assemble parts imported from the United States.

Some might say that these short-term gains are small. But those who support free trade also claim that NAFTA will build long-term confidence in the economy. As Professor Edward Leamers of Yale and UCLA explains:

After the missile crisis in Cuba in 1962, the United States was determined to stop the spread of communism in Latin America. By 1995, all of the governments of the Western Hemisphere except Cuba had democratic institutions. ***Economics*** *Today the region's political leaders are working to create a Free Trade Area of the Americas (FTAA). How is political stability related to a country's economy?*

## Latin America, 1965

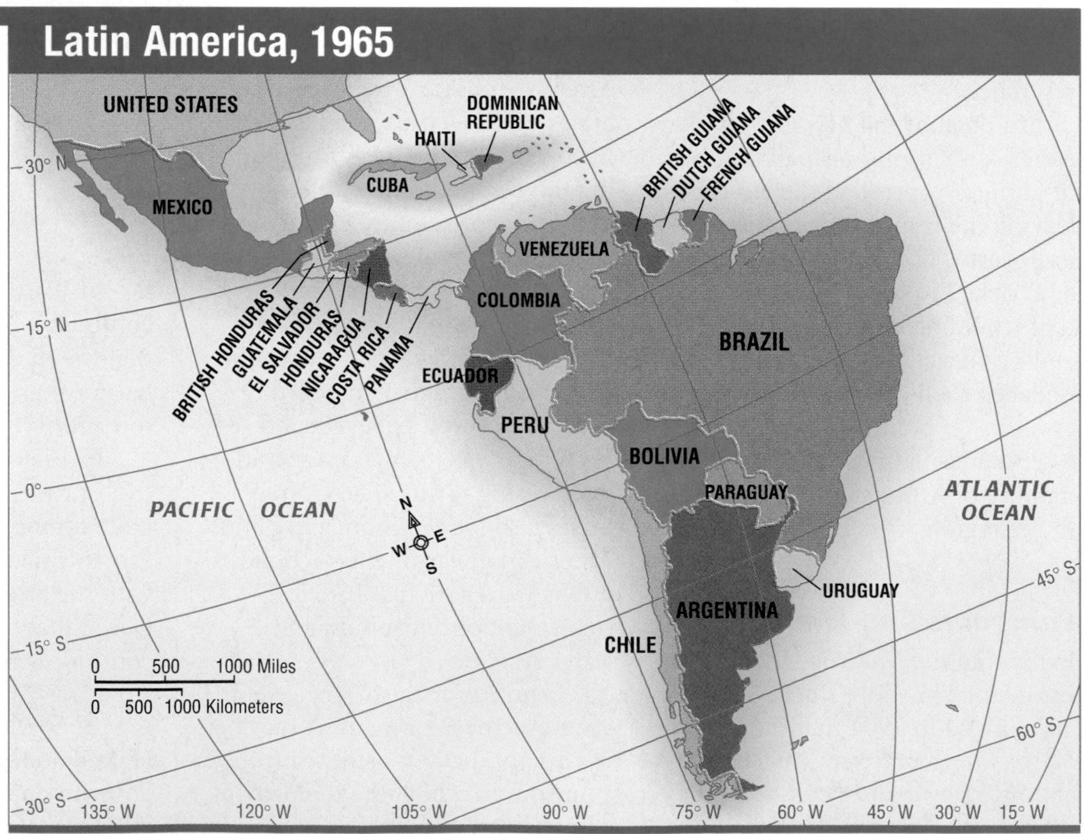

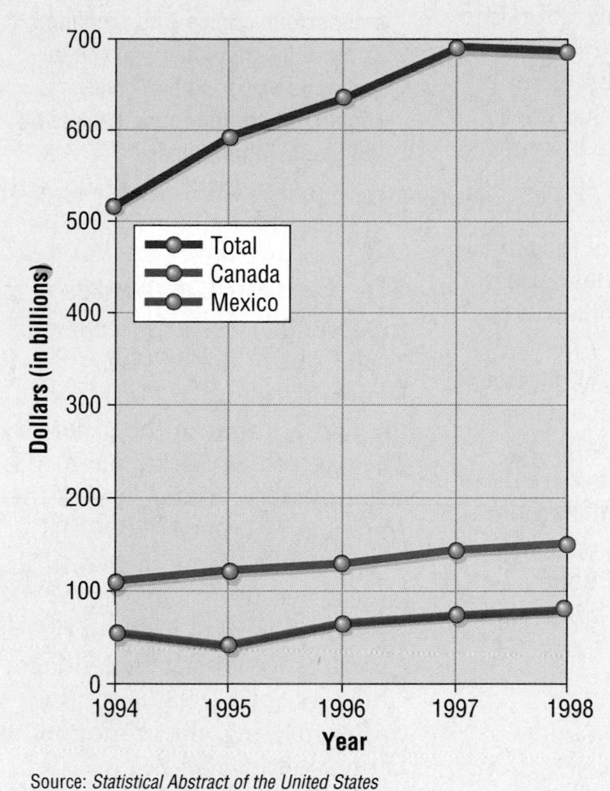


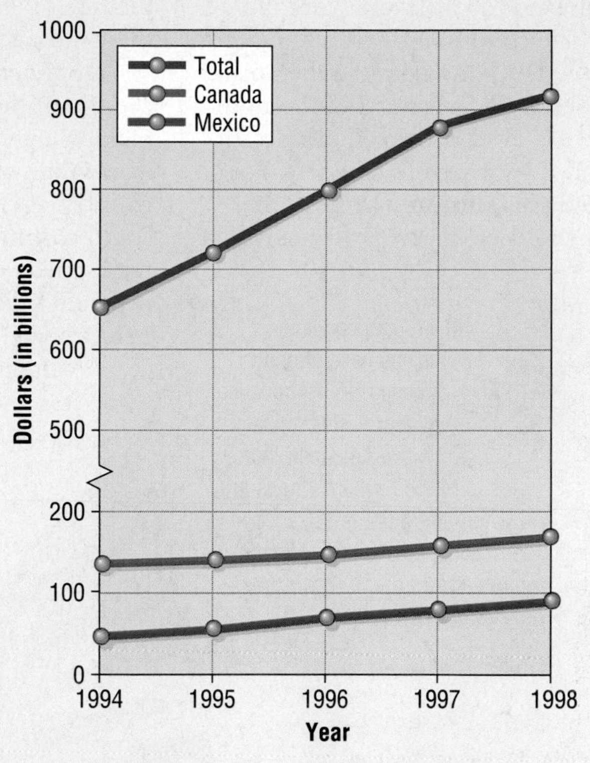


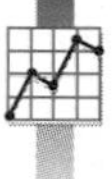

**Interpreting Graphs** Although the value of United States exports to Mexico and Canada increased between 1994 and 1998, so too did the value of its imports from these countries. ***Economics*** ***Compare the value of United States imports from Canada for each year on the graph. Which country experienced a trade deficit with the other?***

AMERICAN VOICES **"NAFTA guarantees that tariffs won't suddenly be raised. It is a major risk reduction document for investors. If your time clock is year by year, then NAFTA was definitely oversold. If your clock runs decade by decade, this is a more important event."**

—*Edward Leamers*

Advocates of free trade believe that it will improve the Mexican economy over time. This, they say, is the best way to build political stability in Mexico. A more stable and economically successful Mexico will also mean fewer illegal immigrants to the United States in the years ahead.

Based on NAFTA, supporters believe that free trade is the wave of the future. Free trade "is simply going to happen, and no President or Congress can stand in the way of it or they will be eaten alive," predicts former Congressman Bill Frenzel. A free-trade agreement is essential, says G. Philip Hughes, former ambassador to Barbados, because "we simply cannot afford to be left behind."

## *Against NAFTA*

NAFTA has been a bad deal, say opponents of free trade. It has not increased trade to the levels that were promised. It has mostly benefited large multinational corporations and has hurt workers. Public Citizen, a lobbying group, says:

AMERICAN VOICES **"NAFTA is causing the loss of existing jobs, while the new jobs that were promised aren't being created."**

—*Public Citizen*

To make matters worse, NAFTA is pushing down wages for some existing jobs. For these reasons, labor unions have vigorously opposed NAFTA.

NAFTA has not been uniformly good for Mexico either, opponents say. Mexican workers are still paid too little and work in unsafe conditions. Factory and job growth is strong only in the north. Investment in the rest of the country has dried up. Small businesses find it very hard to compete. For example, Mexican farmers suffer when American crops like corn undersell theirs. With these economic woes, NAFTA has not made good on its promise to stem the tide of illegal immigration into the United States.

Opponents like Ross Perot claim that the United States is making a great mistake by tying its economy to that of an unstable country. A crisis in that country could cost thousands of jobs in the United States. It could also wipe out billions of dollars in investments.

Other critics say that free trade is not unavoidable. Nor should it be the driving force in government policy. Lori Wallach of Public Citizen says:

**"The notion that free trade is inevitable is just not right; trade is a conscious choice. The problem is, recently, trade has become an end in itself. . . . Public policy should not be determined solely by the global marketplace."**

*—Lori Wallach*

VIEWING HISTORY Most American labor unions have strongly opposed NAFTA because they fear that companies will move American factories to Mexico, where wages are lower and where there are fewer environmental restrictions. ***Economics*** ***What do these demonstrators mean when they say "Fighting for Good Jobs"?***

## *The Debate Continues*

In December 1994 the leaders of 34 nations in the Western Hemisphere met in Florida for the first Summit of the Americas. They agreed to work for the creation of a Free Trade Area of the Americas (FTAA) by 2005. This area would become the world's largest free-trade zone.

The second Summit of the Americas took place in Santiago, Chile, in April 1998. Since the earlier meeting, the economies of Latin America had begun to boom. The United States wants access to those fast-growing markets before European or other nations step in.

The main stumbling block for the United States involves labor and environmental issues. As with NAFTA, opponents fear that FTAA will lower wage rates. They also fear that businesses outside the United States will not meet American environmental standards. Democrats in Congress, especially, insist that these issues be addressed in any agreement.

Clearly, economic isolationism is no longer possible in the age of multinational corporations. But just what form the new trade pact will take remains to be seen. Congress must ratify it, and they will look closely at the effects of NAFTA before agreeing to FTAA. The debate is sure to be lively.

# Chapter 30 Review

## Key Terms

1. NAFTA
2. tariff
3. trade deficit
4. trade surplus
5. Helms-Burton Act
6. Monroe Doctrine
7. Roosevelt Corollary
8. Good Neighbor Policy
9. *maquiladora*

## Creating a Time Line

10. To see the pattern of United States relations with Latin America, construct a time line tracing major events and developments from the Monroe Doctrine to NAFTA. Include at least six items and be sure you can explain the significance of each event on the time line.

## Portfolio Activity

11. Decide whether you agree with those who favor NAFTA or those who oppose it, and why. Then choose a way to express your opinion, such as an editorial, a cartoon, a photo essay, a letter to the President or your representatives in Congress, or another format that is acceptable to your teacher.

### INTERNET ACTIVITY

***For your portfolio:***

**ORGANIZE A DEBATE**

12. Access Prentice Hall's *America: Pathways to the Present* site at **www.Pathways.phschool.com** for the specific URL to complete the activity. Additional resources and related Web sites are also available.

Organize two debate teams. Furnish one with the Global Trade Watch anti-NAFTA report and the other with the Executive Summary from the U.S. Trade Representative site. Have teams use the data provided to debate the success of NAFTA.

## Using Graphic Organizers

13. Review the arguments in the Debating the Future section of the chapter. Then fill in the blank portion in the graphic organizer below, which shows the different major stages in the policies of the United States toward its neighbors. You should provide at least three supporting details. Copy the organizer on another sheet of paper.

**U.S. Foreign Policy in the Western Hemisphere**

**Monroe Doctrine**
- Anti-colonialism
- Pro-democracy
- Trade encouraged

**Dollar Diplomacy**
- Regional stability promoted
- United States corporate investment
- Military enforcement of stability

**Good Neighbor Policy**

**NAFTA**

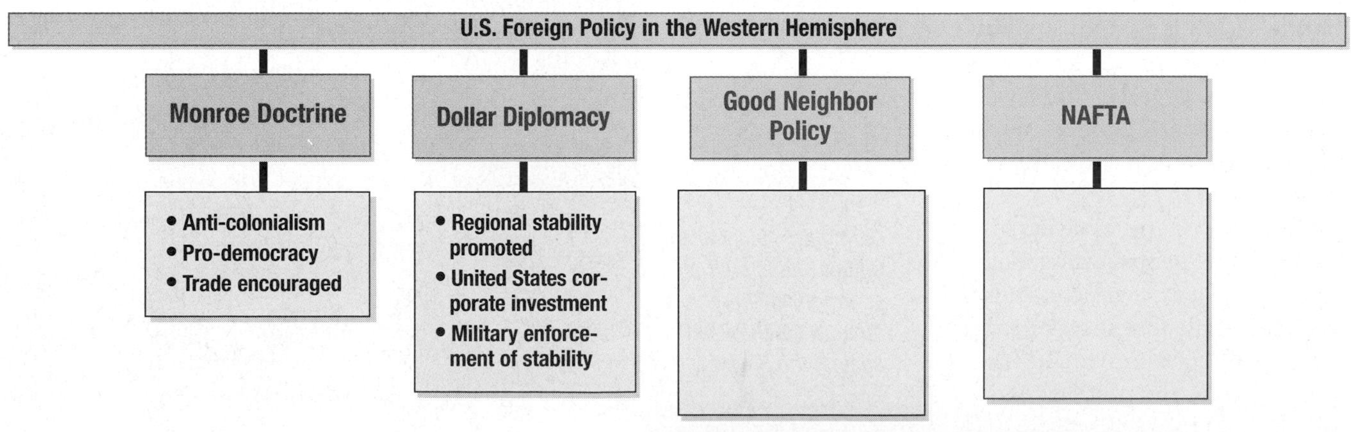

CHAPTER 31

# Foreign Policy After the Cold War

## INTRODUCING THE THEME

**From Theodore Roosevelt's "big stick diplomacy" to Ronald Reagan's talk of the Soviet Union as an "evil empire," the question has remained the same: What role should the United States play in the world? Since the end of the cold war, America's role as a world leader has continued to be a source of debate. While some argue that the United States should end the foreign alliances forged during the cold war, others argue that the United States must always maintain a leadership position in world affairs.**

**What should be the American role in world affairs now that the cold war is over?**

### KEY TERMS

cold war,
Truman Doctrine,
NATO, Warsaw Pact

## VIEWING THE PRESENT

In Woodside, California, Stephen Shapiro slices vegetables for a Malaysian gourmet dinner he's preparing. Shapiro was formerly an equipment operator in the Missile and Space Division of Lockheed Corporation, one of the nation's leading weapons manufacturers. Shapiro was laid off after Lockheed began receiving fewer and fewer government contracts. Now he works as a cook in an artists' colony.

Some 3,000 miles away, in Valley Forge, Pennsylvania, Sally Kain looks out her office window at a crab apple tree she planted in a company ceremony in 1971. Employed for the past 28 years by Martin Marietta Corporation, another major weapons producer, Kain is losing her job as well. Her layoff is one part of a company-wide reorganization announced after Lockheed and Martin Marietta merged in 1995, creating a new company called Lockheed Martin.

*During the cold war the United States built an enormous military force to defend itself against the Soviet Union.*

### *The Defense Boom Busts*

Shapiro and Kain are two unlikely victims of the end of a decades-long conflict between the United

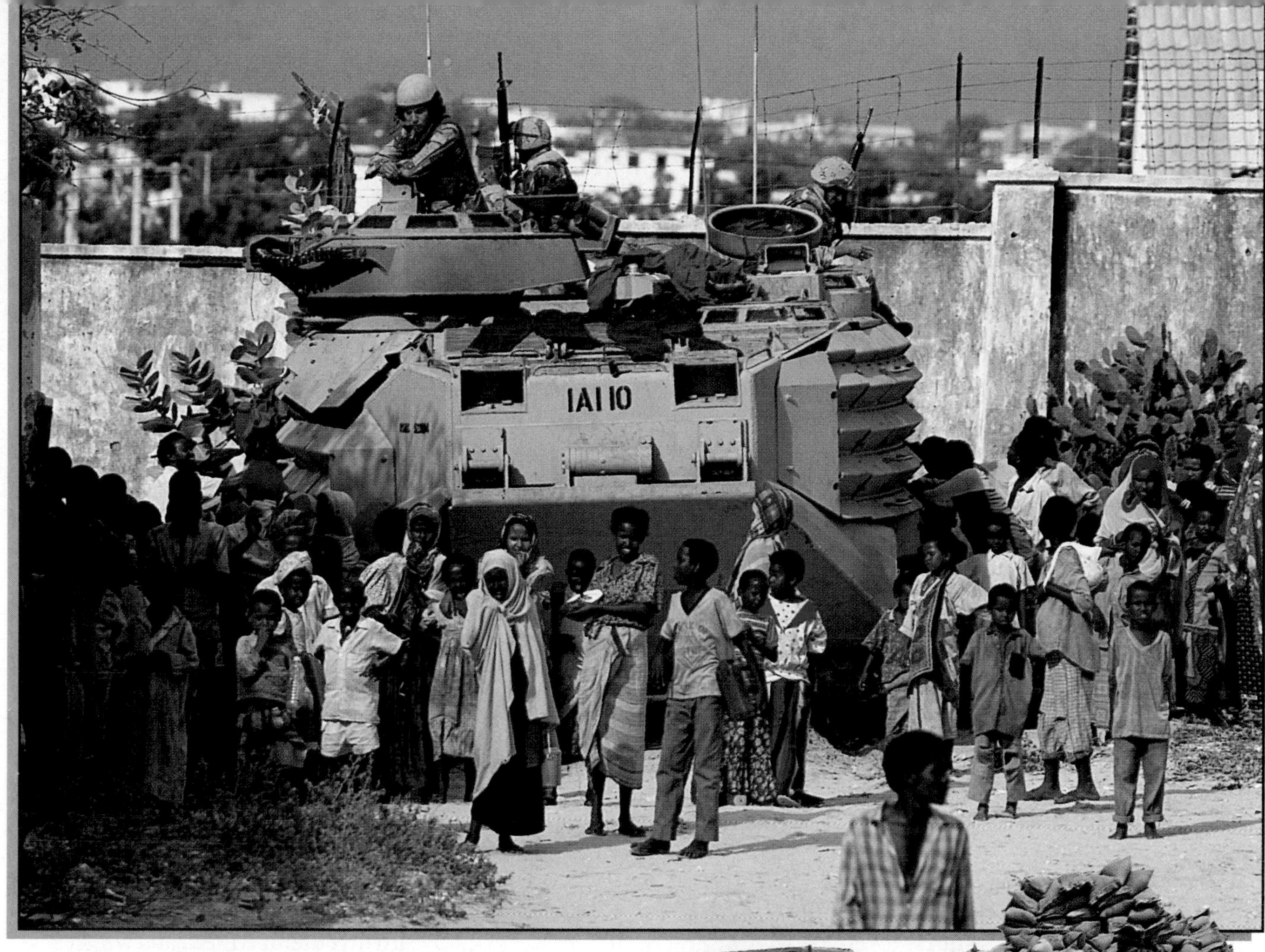


VIEWING HISTORY One of the roles the United States played during the 1990s was that of peacekeeper. United States troops were sent to Somalia in 1993 to distribute truckloads of food and other vital supplies in the famine stricken East African nation. ***Economics*** ***What role did the cold war play in the defense industry?***

States and the Soviet Union. The two superpowers never actually fought each other on the battlefield. This was a **cold war,** marked by the buildup of arms and armies for use, if necessary, in "hot" combat. The United States spent billions each year on defense—as much as $300 billion a year by the late 1980s. Companies that made weapons thrived.

As cold war tensions began to ease, defense spending fell. Defense contractors reacted in three ways. First, they laid off workers. Employment in airplane manufacturing, for example, fell from around 905,000 to around 585,000 between 1989 and 1994. Lockheed cut more than 10,000 jobs in its San Francisco–area plants alone.

Second, defense contractors negotiated mergers and takeovers with their competitors. Stronger companies swallowed weaker ones, and troubled companies sought stability by growing larger. Combining companies made more job cuts necessary to eliminate duplication of services. The merger of Lockheed and Martin Marietta resulted in the closing of 12 plants and the layoffs of 12,000 workers, some 7 percent of the companies' combined work force.

The defense contractors' third response to the budget cuts was to move into non-defense areas of production. They believed that companies less dependent on the size of the government's military budget would be more stable over the long run. Lockheed's Missiles and Space Division (Stephen Shapiro's former employer) worked on the Hubble space telescope. It also signed a large contract with Motorola to build a string of communications satellites. Still, more than half of Lockheed Martin's sales come from defense contracts, which have declined significantly since their peak in the late 1980s.

### Future Security

The health of the defense industry changes with the size of the military budget. In the same way, the size of the military budget changes with the extent of threats to American security. Cuts in the military budget have taken place because the collapse of the Soviet Union eliminated the most dangerous rival of the United States and ended the cold war.

Now the world, like the American defense industry, is in a state of transition. Will the next century be more dangerous, less dangerous, or simply dangerous in a different way from the cold war era? How will the United States deal with this new world? These questions lie at the heart of the present debate over the future of American foreign policy.

## REVIEWING THE PAST

George Washington advised in his Farewell Address in 1796, "The great rule of conduct for us in regard to foreign nations is, in extending our commercial relations, to have with them as little political connection as possible." In other words, while trade with other nations would benefit Americans, entanglements in foreign conflicts could only threaten American democracy.

Most American leaders of the 1800s followed Washington's advice. Events during the first half of the twentieth century, however, changed that policy. The United States felt compelled to enter into foreign wars, permanent alliances, and involvement around the globe.

### World War I

Millions of Americans had ties to the nations involved in World War I. Yet when the war started in 1914, most Americans wanted to stay out of it, just as they had stayed out of earlier European conflicts.

*About 2 million American soldiers served "Over There" in World War I. The use of poisonous gases as weapons forced soldiers to wear masks such as this.*

For three years the United States remained neutral. Still, the government and a majority of the people sympathized more with Britain and France than with Germany. German submarine attacks on American ships inflamed American anger at Germany. In 1917 those attacks drew the United States into the war on the side of Britain and France.

American soldiers helped turn back the last great German offensive in 1918. By November 1918, Germany was ready to sign an armistice.

Having played a key role in the war, the United States was in a position to help shape Europe's future. President Woodrow Wilson looked forward to a strong American presence in the League of Nations, the newly created international peacekeeping body. Still, the war had not converted Americans to the cause of global involvement. Americans worried that the League might dictate American foreign policy and even drag the United States into future European wars.

In 1919 the United States Senate rejected American participation in the League of Nations. For the next two decades the United States returned to its eighteenth-century approach to foreign policy. It would seek trading partners around the world while avoiding political entanglements.

### World War II

The American people opposed involvement in World War II at first, just as they had in World War I. The United States had entered World War I with the goal of creating lasting peace in Europe. Many Americans saw the outbreak of World War II in 1939 as proof that no good could come of American participation in European wars. Nor did Americans favor war against Japan, despite Japanese aggression in East Asia.

Congress reflected the people's desire to keep out of the war. In August 1941, for example, a proposal to extend the service of Army draftees passed the House of Representatives by only one vote.

That attitude changed in a single day. On December 7, 1941, Japanese war planes attacked the American naval base at Pearl Harbor, Hawaii. Shocked and angered, Americans of all backgrounds rallied in defense of their nation and the Congress declared war. Three days later the other Axis powers—Germany and Italy—declared war on the United States.

The Japanese attack on Pearl Harbor pushed American sentiment in favor of entering World War II (below). Photographer Joe Rosenthal's study of victorious marines hoisting the American flag on the Pacific island of Iwo Jima (above) is one of the most famous photographs of the war. ***Geography** How did involvement in World War II help make the United States a global power?*

To a far greater degree than World War I, World War II was a global war. Involvement in that war helped make the United States a truly global power. American troops, alongside Allied troops from Britain and Russia, fought battles from the Philippines to Morocco to France. American ships confronted German U-boats in the North Atlantic and Japanese aircraft carriers in the South Pacific. American bombers and supply planes crossed tens of thousands of miles of land and sea.

The war ended with an Allied victory in 1945. The United States now had the power to shape events nearly everywhere on the globe. It had done more than any other nation to defeat the Axis powers, and its economy was bigger than that of all other nations combined. Finally, only the United States possessed the awesome destructive power of the atomic bomb.

All these factors meant that the United States would not return to a policy of isolationism, as it had after World War I. Like Wilson, President Franklin Roosevelt set out to create an international peacekeeping body, to be called the United Nations. He wanted the United States to be a strong member, and this time most Americans agreed.

## *The Cold War*

Between 1945 and 1950 the United States and Soviet Union changed from wartime allies to bitter rivals. As a result, a new American foreign policy took shape. The Communist government of the Soviet Union was aimed at world conquest, American leaders said, and only the United States had the strength to lead the free world against it. From roughly 1947 to 1991, the cold war was the centerpiece of American foreign policy.

In 1947 President Harry Truman announced a bold new foreign policy. Known as the **Truman Doctrine,** this policy committed the United States to defend "free peoples who are resisting attempted subjugation by armed minorities or by outside pressures." The United States, in other words, would intervene wherever communism threatened to expand.

Under this commitment, the United States helped create **NATO** (the North Atlantic Treaty Organization), and promised to defend Western Europe against attack. The United States also signed agreements with other allies, such as Japan, and made large commitments to small and distant countries that faced a Communist threat.

### *Wars in Korea and Vietnam*

Twice in Asia, the United States joined wars within divided nations to stop the spread of communism. In Korea, American forces rushed to defend South Korea after an invasion by Communist North Korea in 1950. Three years of bloody fighting brought stalemate on the battlefield and frustration within the United States. Still, American intervention had saved South Korea.

The United States would not manage to save South Vietnam. Despite American military involvement from 1961 to 1973, Communist North Vietnam overran South Vietnam and reunified the country in 1975.

The Vietnam War cost the United States some 58,000 lives and more than $150 billion. It also convinced most Americans that the United States should reduce its foreign commitments. The United States, more and more Americans argued, could not afford to be what some called "the world's policeman."

### *The Collapse of Communism*

Whether and when to intervene in foreign countries remained controversial issues throughout the 1970s and 1980s. Americans still feared Communist expansion. But they did not think that they alone could, or should, fight it.

American defense spending declined after the Vietnam War, but then rose sharply in the 1980s under President Ronald Reagan. Reagan won election in 1980 on a promise of a stronger anti-Soviet policy. Americans supported the defense increases but remained wary of military intervention abroad.

During the late 1980s Americans began to question their commitment to the cold war, with its huge defense budgets. At the same time the list of America's cold war enemies began to shrink. One by one the nations of Eastern Europe, fed up with the brutalities and inefficiencies of communism, rejected their Communist leaders.

The Soviet Union tried to hold itself together in the face of this rejection of communism. Mikhail Gorbachev, who became leader of the Soviet Union in 1985, tried to improve the Soviet system. But his reforms only quickened the pace of communism's decline. On December 31, 1991, the Soviet Union officially ceased to exist. The cold war was over.

*The Vietnam Women's Memorial in Washington, D.C.*

#### DEBATING THE FUTURE

E-mail messages raised the spirits of American troops stationed in Bosnia in 1996. A student in the 6th grade in Melbourne, Florida, wrote, "I would like to thank you for putting your life on the line for our country." From Jackson, Mississippi, came this message: "Being a Vietnam vet, I know how hard it is being away from family and friends." Another American wrote, "It seems that having U.S. troops abroad has become a traditional part of the holiday season. Please know that we miss you guys and are proud of the commitment that you have made to serve your country. . . . Hurry Home!"

While these letters used the new technology of the Internet, they contained a message that is as old as American commitments abroad. Americans are proud of their country's global role. Yet they also hope that Americans serving overseas will soon be able to return home.

As you have read, during the cold war the United States promised to protect other countries in case of attack. To meet these many foreign commitments, the United States spent hundreds of billions of dollars each year on defense. As the nation approaches the next century, it must confront two basic foreign-policy questions:

1. Now that the Soviet Union has collapsed, what are the benefits to the United States of maintaining its foreign commitments?
2. Now that the national debt has skyrocketed and other nations have become stiff trading competitors, can the United States afford the high cost of its foreign commitments?

### *Benefits of Foreign Commitments*

Some foreign-policy analysts argue that the United States should cancel cold war–era alliances such as NATO and defense treaties with other nations, including Japan and South Korea. "It is time to recognize that with the disintegration of the Soviet Union, the mission of America's cold war alliances has been accomplished," writes Ted Galen Carpenter, a foreign-policy analyst at a research organization called the Cato Institute.

NATO, for example, was created to defend Western Europe against attack by the Soviet Union and the Eastern European countries under its influence. The danger increased when those Communist countries became allies under the **Warsaw Pact** in 1955.

VIEWING HISTORY Soviet and American leaders Khrushchev and Eisenhower balanced on a 1959 *Newsweek* cover. ***Government*** *How did cold war tensions influence American foreign policy?*

Carpenter and others point out that the nations that once made up the Warsaw Pact are now joining NATO rather than attacking it. Recently, three former Soviet allies: Poland, the Czech Republic, and Hungary accepted membership into the organization. Also, for the first time, Russian ground combat troops joined a NATO peacekeeping exercise. Russia, NATO's long-time foe joined the Partnership for Peace, a NATO program designed to ensure security throughout Europe. There is no reason, critics like Carpenter argue, to defend Western Europe against an enemy that no longer exists. Thus, the NATO alliance is unnecessary.

Many analysts disagree with this assessment. Some believe that NATO's role should change from that of a strictly military organization to one that can help solve global crises. Others prefer to keep the alliance focused on military defense.

Former President Richard Nixon favored keeping NATO a military alliance. In his book *Seize the Moment: America's Challenge in a One-Superpower World,* he also warned of any withdrawal from our global responsibilities:

**AMERICAN VOICES** **"For many on the American left and right, the knee-jerk response to the decline of the Soviet Union . . . is to withdraw into a new isolationism. But in fact American world leadership will be indispensable in the coming decades. . . . The real world revolves not around wishful thinking about 'peace breaking out all over' but around the enduring realities of geopolitics. . . . In a world of competing states, clashing interests and national conflicts are inevitable."**

—*Richard Nixon*

Put most simply, Nixon's point is that nations will always need friends because they will always have enemies. Although the collapse of the Soviet Union removed the chief rival of the United States, Nixon argued, other rivals will surely emerge. The United States will need the help of allies against those new rivals. As Caspar Weinberger, who was Secretary of Defense under President Reagan, wrote:

**AMERICAN VOICES** **"Clearly, no nation is strong enough alone to keep its own freedom. Every nation requires alliances, friendships or associations of one kind or another with other countries who share its goals and ideals."**

—*Caspar Weinberger*

One of the most prominent symbols of the cold war was the barbed wire and concrete of the Berlin Wall. Shown here is the celebration of the wall's destruction in 1989. ***Government*** *How has the end of the cold war influenced American foreign policy?*

## *Cost of Foreign Commitments*

"Today there is not, as some argue, a single superpower, the United States," columnist William Pfaff wrote in the quarterly *Foreign Affairs.* "There are none." Pfaff and others claim that the United States, with a national debt of more than $5 trillion, is not wealthy enough to try to control world events.

The Cato Institute's Ted Galen Carpenter agrees. He writes, "We cannot afford to maintain alliances for the sake of having alliances." Carpenter continues:

**AMERICAN VOICES** **"The NATO commitment alone cost American taxpayers more than $120 billion a year during the latter stages of the cold war. . . . Washington's obligation to defend Japan, South Korea, and other East Asian allies costs another $40 billion. . . .The United States currently spends nearly seven times as much on the military as does any other member of the [major] industrial powers. Indeed, it spends some 60 percent more than all of the other [major industrial] countries combined."**

—*Ted Galen Carpenter*

A nation that faces serious domestic problems cannot afford this burden, Carpenter concluded. High American defense spending does not only take money away from domestic programs like education, Carpenter and others argue. It also enables trading competitors of the United States, such as Germany and Japan, to spend less on defense, because those countries can rely on American military protection.

A number of other analysts believe that the United States can indeed afford the cost of remaining a superpower. Caspar Weinberger, for example, writes that "the United States could obviously afford larger defense budgets, provided that sacrifices were made elsewhere." Former President Nixon argued that in the long run, reducing foreign commitments would cost the United States even more money than maintaining them:

**AMERICAN VOICES** **"The security of our home in this . . . interdependent world is affected by changes everywhere. Walking away from global challenges will carry a dangerous price. History may once again produce nations aspiring to regional or global dominance. . . . With imports and exports comprising over 20 percent of our economy, our prosperity depends on international stability."**

—*Richard Nixon*

## *The Debate Continues*

The questions outlined here have no simple or permanent answers. The United States' need for foreign commitments is influenced by events around the world. These can create or remove threats to American security almost overnight. The ability of the United States to afford foreign commitments depends on the continually changing health of the American economy. Each generation of Americans, therefore, must decide for itself the role its nation will play in the world.

# Chapter 31 Review

## Key Terms

1. cold war
2. Truman Doctrine
3. NATO
4. Warsaw Pact

## Creating a Time Line

5. To see this chapter in context, construct a time line showing 6 to 12 major events of the twentieth century that had an important impact on American foreign policy.

## Portfolio Activity

6. Decide which point of view on foreign policy you generally agree with. Then choose a way to express it: a magazine or newspaper article, a poster or cartoon, a letter to your representatives in Congress, an editorial, or some other format acceptable to your teacher.

**INTERNET ACTIVITY**

*For your portfolio:*
**PREPARE A SUMMARY**

7. Access Prentice Hall's *America: Pathways to the Present* site at **www.Pathways.phschool.com** for the specific URL to complete the activity. Additional resources and related Web sites are also available.

Use the State Department links to read about "Hot Topics" in U.S. foreign policy. Select a topic and summarize current policy. What is the issue? Why is the United States concerned? What is the government's official stance on the issue?

## Using Graphic Organizers

8. Review the arguments in the Debating the Future section of the chapter. Then fill in the blank webs in the graphic organizer below. This web diagram shows the connection between various issues and arguments that have affected United States foreign policy in the years after the cold war. Copy the diagram on a separate sheet of paper.

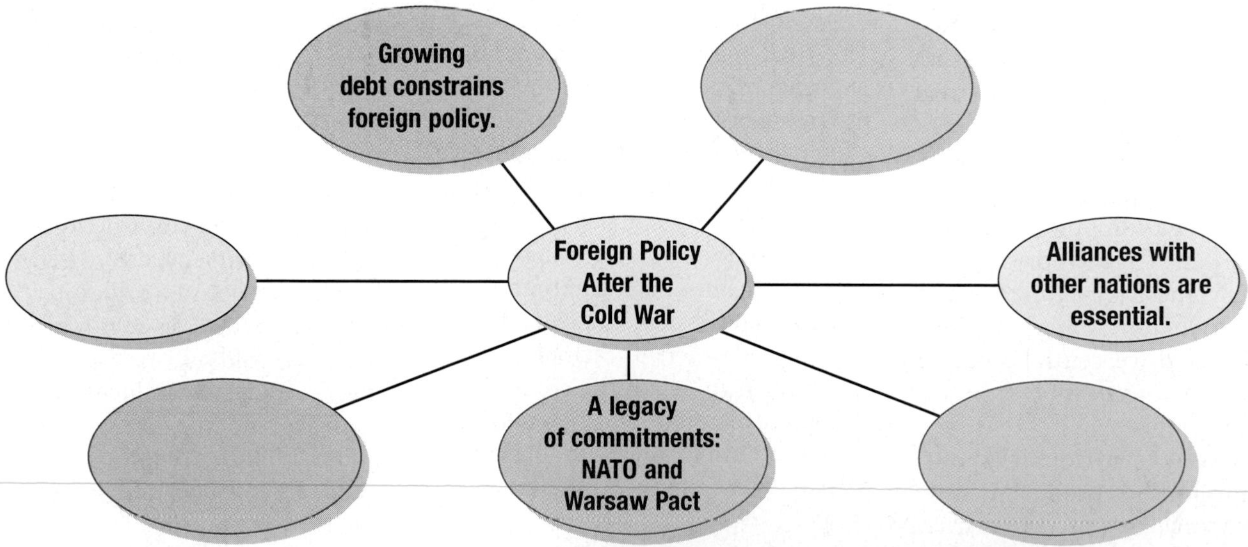

# CHAPTER 32 Technology and You in the Next Century

## INTRODUCING THE THEME

**Technological advances have changed the face of America many times. The cotton gin made possible the rise of King Cotton. Following the Bessemer steelmaking process came the expansion of the railroads and the rise of modern industry. The automobile revolutionized not only how people traveled, but also where they lived and how they spent their time. The computer, however, may prove to be the most impressive technological advance of them all.**

## DEBATE

**How can schools best prepare students to use and take advantage of the technology of the next century?**

## KEY TERMS

e-mail, globalization, modem, telecommunications, software, productivity, automation, World Wide Web

## VIEWING THE PRESENT

"Buy American," the principal told the school librarian, so she ordered a computer from a California company. Yet when she opened the boxes, she was surprised. She found a monitor made in Japan, a mouse made in China, a keyboard manufactured in Mexico from American parts, and a computer assembled in Taiwan. The memory chips were from Malaysia, the floppy disk drive from Korea, and the hard disk drive, central processing unit, and power supply from the United States.

It took many countries to create this finished product. It also took many computers to deliver it. To order this computer, the librarian sent a fax to a dealer. The dealer's computerized inventory system noted the sale and kept track of how many more computers to buy.

Each month the dealer places orders by electronic mail, or **e-mail,** with the computer's California manufacturer. From the company's computerized order department, the information goes electronically to the billing department, the shipping department, and also the manufacturing department. There, computers automatically tally the demand and send orders to each of the suppliers in Asia. With computers talking to computers, this information can travel within the company and halfway around the globe in seconds.

### *The Global Economy*

How typical is this computer use for the average American product? It is more typical than you might think. It illustrates an economic trend called **globalization.** This refers to a system of producing and selling goods that involves many countries. It also highlights the increasing importance of computer networks.

Reflecting this trend, administrators at Boeing, an American aerospace company, advertised, "It takes the entire world to pay our bills. . . . 70% of all our airplanes are sold outside the U.S." Foreign trade, which includes the exporting and importing of all kinds of goods, occupies a larger and larger position in the American economy.

As the computer example shows, the Asian countries of the Pacific Rim have become important trading partners of the United States. The computer also illustrates another side of globalization: the blurring of national boundaries in making products. Says Jeffrey Garten, dean of the Yale School of Management, "An increasing number of the goods we make are composed of both foreign and American components, and multinational companies, with plants all over the world, are responsible for an increased portion of international trade."

American companies not only buy foreign parts but also own factories in other countries. For example, Ford makes cars on every continent except Antarctica. Likewise, foreign companies like Honda build their cars in the United States. In some places, such as the NUMMI plant in Fremont, California, foreign and domestic companies team up to manufacture cars.

Computers have made many tasks easier. Students often use computers in classrooms and libraries for research projects. They also use computers at home for both school projects and for their own entertainment. ***Culture How are e-mail and the Internet likely to influence American culture?***

## *Shift to Service Jobs*

Why are American companies buying foreign parts and building factories overseas? One reason is lower labor costs. Since the 1970s foreign countries such as Japan and Korea have been able to sell their products in the United States at lower prices than American products. To be competitive, American companies have had to reduce their costs, the largest of which is labor. So they have looked around the world for places with cheaper labor. As a result, more and more traditional manufacturing jobs have left the United States for other countries.

Meanwhile, service industries have grown strong in the American economy. Gaining importance within the service sector are jobs that involve managing information. Think of what happened when the librarian ordered the computer. Workers in California handled the flow of information that generated the bill, directed shipping, regulated the supply of parts, and determined levels of production. Most of the manufacturing was done abroad. Still, it was American engineers, highly skilled and well paid, who had designed these complex computer systems.

As the economies of the world grow more interconnected, countries are starting to specialize in what they do well. Countries with low labor costs are specializing in manufacturing, while the United States is specializing in managing information. For example, large American corporations with plants around the world still centralize their accounting in the United States.

## *Computer Networks*

What makes these two trends possible is the widespread use of computer networks. A network enables one computer to send information to another through a central computer called a server. Although a single computer can store massive amounts of data, it is much more valuable when it can share data with other computers. Some businesses and schools have local area networks that link their computers. As a result, they can exchange data and e-mail.

Picture a network linking computers around the world. This is the Internet. The Internet is a global network that connects computers by sending electronic information from one to another. Most of this information travels over telephone wires, but it also can follow television cables or even travel as radio waves. Each computer needs a device called a **modem** to transmit its data.

The Internet makes it possible to use a computer to conduct research all over the world. It also makes it possible for anyone to send and receive information instantly.

Using this global computer network is a prime example of **telecommunications,** which is the sending of information over long distances. Says one California executive, "A modern company operating globally can't do anything without telecommunications."

For example, his company uses workers on opposite sides of the globe to prepare a new computer product. The company has computer programmers in India writing **software**—instructions telling the computer what to do. At the end of the day, the programmers can send their work via the Internet to California to be tested. While the programmers are sleeping, technicians half a world away test the program and send it back over the Internet, in time for the next workday in India.

## Computers and Education

In this increasingly high-tech world, schools face the question of how best to prepare students for the next century. How much should they use computers to teach? How much should they teach students about using computers? Or should schools concentrate on traditional writing, computation, and thinking skills? Computers are, after all, only as smart as the people using them.

Some people argue that computers are the answer to preparing America's students for the future. But are they really?

## REVIEWING THE PAST

The computer has brought American society to the turning point of a new age. Yet it is only the latest in a series of inventions that have changed the way Americans live, work, and learn. The automobile, electric power, and the telephone are probably the only other technologies that have had such a profound effect on American life.

Before the Industrial Revolution, the United States was a land of farmers and independent artisans. In today's terms, they would be considered "small-business people," owning their own tools and working for themselves. An artisan like Paul Revere would make his products in his own workshop, fashioning each piece of silver by hand from start to finish. Learning these skills took many years.

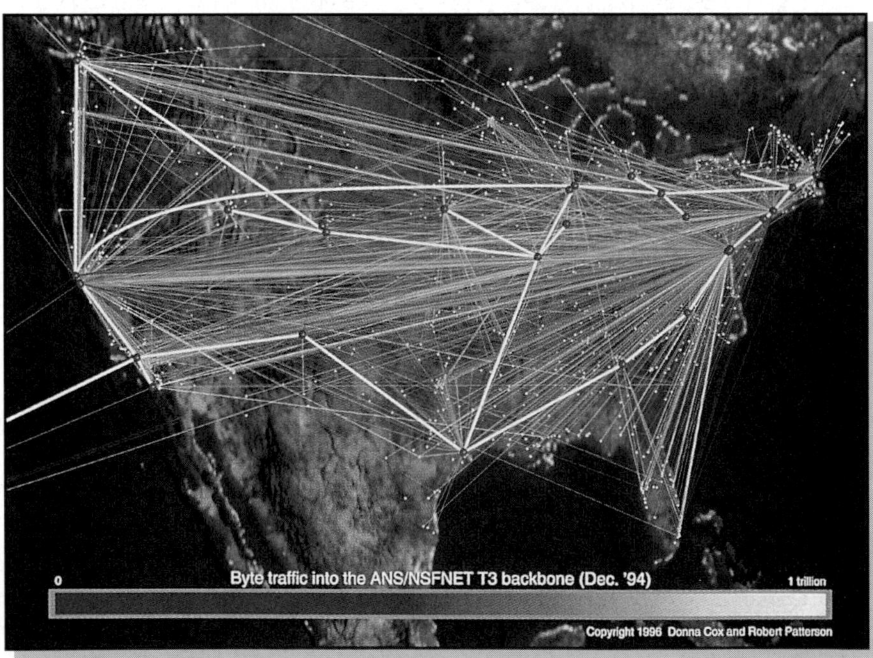

Not only do computers have the power to do many complex operations at lightning speed, they can also share the information with other computers almost instantly. This telecommunications network map of the United States illustrates the idea. ***Economics*** *How have telecommunications helped bring about a global economy?*

## The Production Revolution

Making goods by machine began in the United States in 1793 when Samuel Slater built the first successful mill to spin cotton. Soon, New England had a number of factories to spin and weave cotton, each built beside a river.

Water powered the machines, and workers kept them running smoothly. Many of these workers were young women who had left small family farms to move near the factories. Unlike their mothers, who had to know all the steps of carding, spinning, and weaving wool to make cloth, these workers had to learn only one job: how to run their machine.

Manufacturing grew rapidly in the early 1800s, especially in the Northeast. In addition to textiles, factories turned out guns, shoes, and other goods. However, most American goods in this era were still made by skilled craftsworkers.

Not until the Civil War did industry really take off. After the war, cities grew rapidly as new factories attracted workers, both native-born and immigrant. In the 1870s and 1880s factories replaced workshops in the production of goods.

## exploring TECHNOLOGY *A Textile Mill*

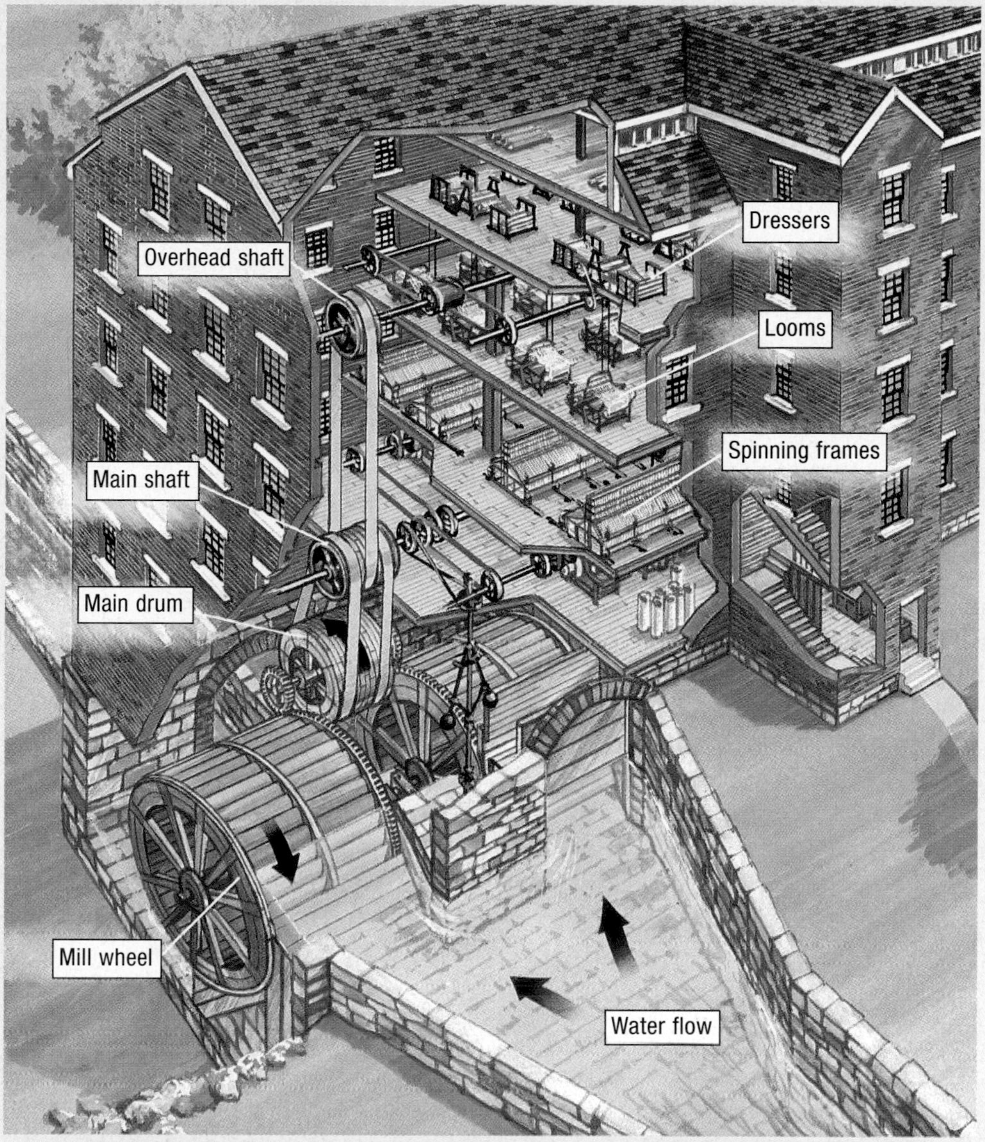

**In the early 1800s, the textile mills of the Northeast had plenty of rivers and streams suitable for mill sites, busy ports for shipping, and an abundance of people in search of work. *Science and Technology* *How did the advent of factories change the nature of work?***

In this industrial transformation, workers no longer made all parts of a product. Instead, they performed only one step in the production process. Craftsworkers' skills learned through long years of apprenticeship were no longer needed. Industrial workers typically had to know only one task, and they learned it on the job.

Through his use of the assembly line, automobile maker Henry Ford ushered in the age of mass production. Now workers stood beside a moving conveyor belt to assemble a product. Each worker added one part, performing the same step over and over at a steady pace. This innovation greatly increased **productivity,** the amount of goods or services each worker produces in a given period of time.

Productivity grew even faster following World War II, with the coming of automation. **Automation** is the use of sophisticated machines in place of human labor. Automation is used in farming, mining, and manufacturing. In some cases a single worker, at the controls of such a machine, could now produce as many goods or services as 100 people had in the past.

Automation reduced the number of workers needed in manufacturing. More and more Americans turned to sales and service for employment. The service sector included not only jobs like auto repair and dry cleaning but also office work. These jobs involved reading, writing, and calculating, which are skills learned in school rather than on the job. Tools that increased productivity among office workers included the typewriter and the telephone. But these improvements pale beside the achievements of the computer.

## *The Information Age*

The workplace of the 1990s changed profoundly because of the computer. The American inspiration for it came not from a car factory or law office, but from the United States census. Herman Hollerith, an 1890 census agent, devised a time-saving machine that used punch cards to tabulate data.

By 1946, scientists had developed the Electronic Numerical Integrator and Computer, or ENIAC for short. ENIAC could do 5,000 addition problems per second. But its tremendous size and weight made it impractical for most uses.

Since ENIAC, transistors have replaced vacuum tubes, and computers have become much smaller, faster, and more sophisticated. In the 1960s and 1970s most computers in universities, businesses, and government offices were still just large calculating machines. Only a handful of people in any organization knew how to operate them. Some offices had a central computer, with connections to terminals beside a few workers' desks. But computer skills were limited to specially trained employees.

During the 1980s several breakthroughs in computer technology revolutionized the workplace. The first was the personal computer. After it appeared, early in the decade, millions of workers had a computer on their desk. Once they learned how to use it to write, calculate, and sort data, workers found that their productivity increased.

Another time-saver of the 1980s was the fax (facsimile) machine. The fax machine used computer technology to scan a page, turn its contents into electronic signals, and transmit them over telephone lines. Another fax machine received and decoded the electronic signals. An even faster way to send information was through computer networks, which were operating in many businesses by the end of the decade.

The Internet became the world's hottest telecommunications tool in the 1990s. Begun in the 1960s as a government project to link university science departments, the Internet grew to include millions of business, governmental, educational, and individual computers.

To help users find what they're looking for, the Internet has a system called the **World Wide Web.** Using software called a Web browser, users can retrieve electronic files to get information and use links to jump to related files.

Access to the Internet has spread to schools, businesses, libraries, homes, and even some cafés, where "Net-surfing" has replaced video games as a way to attract customers. With a global audience of millions, businesses scrambled to find ways to use the Internet.

# Advances in Technology, 1775–Present

**1793**
*Eli Whitney invents the cotton gin.*

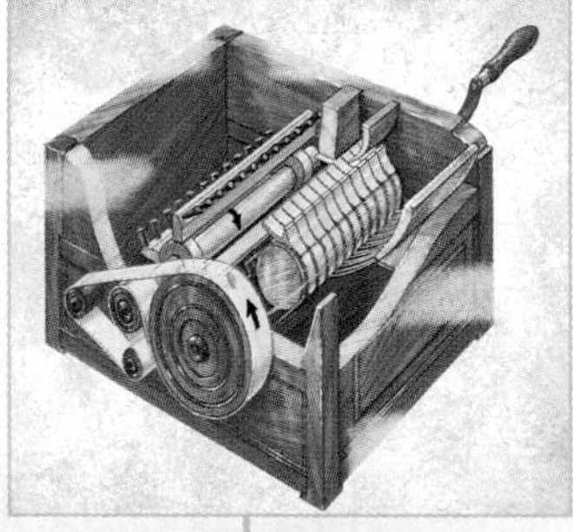

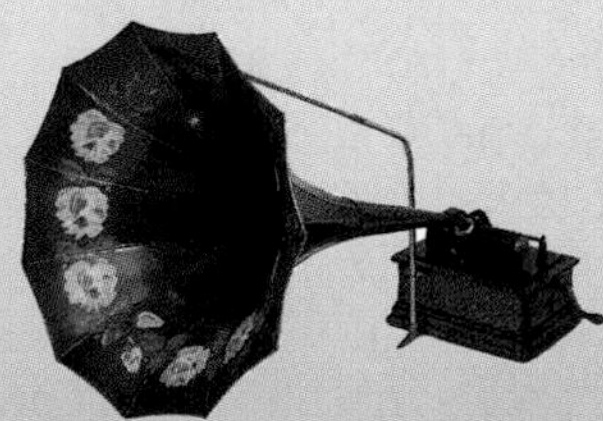

**1775**
*James Watt perfects his invention of the steam engine.*

**1793**
*Samuel Slater builds first successful mill to spin cotton.*

**1876**
*Alexander Graham Bell invents the telephone.*

**1877**
*Thomas Edison invents the phonograph.*

**Industrial Revolution**

**Electric Age**

## DEBATING THE FUTURE

A high school junior in a tiny town in Alaska is writing a term paper on the migration of gray whales. The nearest public library is more than a hundred miles away, but she is able to do research at school. Using a computer and modem, she browses the World Wide Web and within a few hours finds the most up-to-date information. Her teacher is very pleased with her paper, because her research far exceeded what the library has to offer.

At a high school in California, two seniors create a multimedia presentation on the stegosaurus for a geology assignment. They scan pictures into the computer, color them, and add sound clips downloaded from the Internet. While their presentation amuses their classmates, the teacher is not impressed. He says it's too little information dressed up in a flashy package.

How much do computers really add to a student's educational experience? Stories such as these fuel the debate over what place computer technology should have in school.

### High-Tech Is the Answer

One of the most important jobs of the schools is to prepare students for work. Computer skills have become absolutely essential in the workplace, say advocates of educational technology. To support this position, they point to "What Work Requires of Schools," a 1991 report from the Department of Labor. The report states that understanding and applying technology and using computers to process information are essential requirements for workers.

**1974**
*The first fax machine transmits one page in six minutes.*

**1983**
*The Federal Communications Commission issues a license for the first cellular phone system.*

**1984**
*Philips and Sony develop the compact disc read-only memory (CD-ROM)*

**1896**
*Henry Ford builds his first car.*

**1969**
*American astronauts complete the first moon walk.*

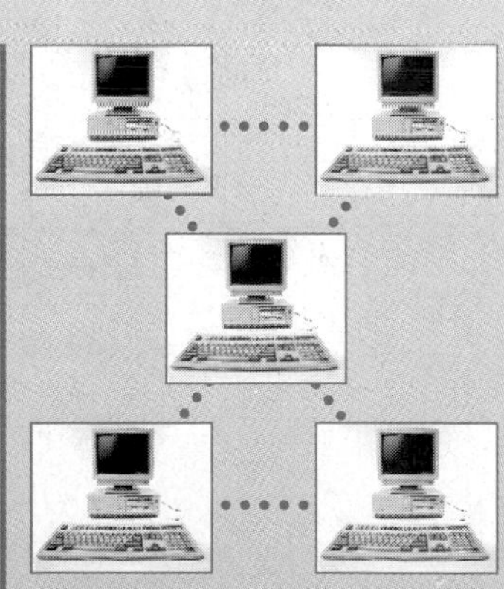

**1992**
*The World Wide Web is released by the European Laboratory for Particle Physics.*

**Electronic Age** | **Information Age**

Colleges have already recognized the importance of computer skills. Some even require freshmen to bring their own computer to school with them.

Like today's mechanic who analyzes a car's problems electronically instead of poking around under the hood, more and more jobs of the future will rely on computers. In fact, the three fastest-growing occupations are in computer-related fields, according to the Labor Department. Labor economist Audrey Freedman says:

> **AMERICAN VOICES** "The jobs that are being created are computer-using jobs. They're service, white-collar types of work."
>
> —*Audrey Freeman*

Moreover, computer users earn more money than workers without computers in similar jobs—about 15 percent more in 1995. To prevent widening the gap between the rich and poor in this country, high-tech boosters argue, all students must learn how to use computers.

The ability to adapt to change is a key characteristic of the successful worker of the future. Computer skills provide that adaptability, supporters claim. They cite examples like Lizanne Gottung, a manager in a Connecticut factory. She says, "When we hire now, we're thinking about how easily a person can be trained to do different jobs." Mike Thomas, one of her employees, knows how adaptable workers need to be. "I'm an old dog who's adjusted to three product changes in the last year," he reports. He monitors computers that control production. Without his computer skills, he would have been out of a job.

Using computers and the Internet in schools not only prepares students for the future, advocates say, but also improves the quality of education. Computer-assisted learning gives students a chance to advance at their own pace. It gives them immediate feedback and the opportunity to repeat a lesson as many times as necessary. Computer programs such as word processing, spreadsheets, and databases let students write, calculate, and do research more efficiently than ever before. In addition, computers enable disabled students to complete many educational tasks that they could not perform in the past.

Computers with access to the Internet can connect students to a huge global pool of information. Says Jim Dunnigan, a high school teacher in Seattle, Washington:

In 1946, the University of Pennsylvania's Electronic Numerical Integrator and Computer (ENIAC) took up a huge room, weighed 30 tons, and had 17,000 vacuum tubes. ***Science and Technology*** ***How has computer technology changed since 1946?***

## An Introduction to the Internet

| | |
|---|---|
| ***What is the Internet?*** | The Internet is a global network of computers that are linked together. It was set up as a government project to connect university science departments in the 1960s. Today individuals, businesses, schools, and many other groups use the Internet. |
| ***What is the World Wide Web?*** | The World Wide Web (WWW) is a group of electronic documents (called Web pages) and links that lead from one document to another. Documents on the Web can contain text, pictures, audio clips, and video clips. |
| ***Who uses the Web?*** | Millions of people use the Web every day. Hundreds of thousands of companies and individuals have Web sites, called home pages. |
| ***How do you get on the Web?*** | To get on the Web, you need a computer, a modem, and a computer application called a browser. The modem provides the link between your computer and the other computers on the Web. The browser helps you find and read Web pages. |
| ***What does the future hold?*** | Today people can do everything from grocery shopping to medical research on the Internet. Over time it will have even more uses. Almost any use you can think of for the Internet may someday become a reality. You could even be the one to make your idea come true. |

**Interpreting Tables** Although the Internet is a product of fairly recent technology, use of the Internet skyrocketed during the 1990s. ***Science and Technology*** ***What do you think will be the long-term significance of the Internet?***

**"We have students in my school district who know no bounds to the classroom walls. They use electronic mail to talk with archaeologists in South America; they publish Civil War history research projects on the Internet; and they maintain e-mail correspondence with other students in the Czech Republic."**

—*Jim Dunnigan*

Learning how to use computers and the Internet has enriched these students' education in ways that no one could have predicted. Students will be well prepared when they enter the increasingly global and increasingly computerized workplace. They will know how to find information and communicate internationally.

### *Good Teaching Is the Answer*

Good teaching is far more important than electronic gadgets, say critics of computers in education. Clifford Stoll, an astrophysicist and one of the best-known critics of educational technology, describes the most important thing in a classroom:

AMERICAN VOICES **"A good teacher interacting with motivated students. Anything else that separates them—filmstrips, instructional videos, multimedia displays, e-mail, TV sets, interactive computers—is of questionable educational value."**

—*Clifford Stoll*

Stoll and others would have school districts spend their limited funds on more teachers rather than on computers.

Computer-assisted instruction sugarcoats the learning process, opponents argue. Learning takes hard work, concentration, and self-discipline. This calls for far more sustained effort than zapping an alien on a computer screen to get a correct answer. Critics argue that computer-assisted instruction promotes short attention spans among students rather than dedicated study and critical thinking skills.

Moreover, computer simulations are no substitute for real life. Students need to know how to conduct experiments and perform calculations in the real world, not just on the computer.

Those who favor a more traditional approach to education claim that students need basic skills more than computer skills. By focusing on technology, they say, computer lovers have missed the main point of the "What Work Requires of

Schools" report. The Labor Department report pays far more attention to other requirements, which call for fundamental academic skills, thinking skills, and personal qualities.

Critics of educational technology believe that emphasizing computer skills is not the best way to prepare students for the workplace. Even more than computer literacy, jobs of the future will require educated workers who can reason well, express themselves clearly, and work well with others.

Indeed, computer skills are easy to acquire and can be learned outside of school. Critics point out that computers can be found in many public libraries and in more than 40 percent of American households. Free time, they say, is better than school time for developing computer expertise. Moreover, school assignments that require high-tech delivery distract students from the subject matter that they should be studying. Students end up spending more time using the software than they spend researching and thinking.

Turning students loose on the Internet to do research makes a lot of data available to them but gives them no organization or context for it, say opponents. It is also easy for students to download a file from the Internet and then cut and paste parts of it into their own work. Missing is any critical thought about the value of the source or any understanding of the true purpose of doing research.

### *The Debate Continues*

Computers have become an essential part of American society, but their place in schools is still being determined. Some school systems are resisting the computer revolution. Many others are trying to deal with it in a way that makes sound educational sense for their students.

A big challenge for schools will be to find the right balance between traditional teaching and new technology. This may mean limiting the role of the computer to tasks for which it is most useful. Alternately, it may mean adapting the computer to reinforce traditional skills. An even bigger challenge will be to find enough money to fund the new technology and all the changes that come with it.

Technology alone cannot solve the problems of education. The answer lies instead in studying the issues, communicating points of view, and working together to find solutions. As computers continue to play a larger role in daily life, we must ensure that everyone will be able to understand and use them. In this way the new technology can most effectively help people learn, communicate, and work together.

VIEWING HISTORY Using computers is a requirement in many colleges today. Computers are even more common in the workplace. ***Diversity*** *Why is equal access to computers for all students important?*

# Chapter 32 Review

## Key Terms

1. e-mail
2. globalization
3. modem
4. telecommunications
5. software
6. productivity
7. automation
8. World Wide Web

## Creating a Time Line

9. Using information in the Reviewing the Past section, construct a time line that shows the progress and changes in American technology. Include six to eight major developments, and be ready to explain why each step was important.

## Portfolio Activity

10. From your experience and from the information in this chapter, decide what you think about how useful computers are and could be in schools. Then choose a way to express your point of view: a selection of magazine or newspaper articles, a poster or cartoon, a letter to the editor, or another format acceptable to your teacher. If possible, use a computer to prepare or present your project.

### INTERNET ACTIVITY

*For your portfolio:*
**WRITE AN ARTICLE**

11. Access Prentice Hall's *America: Pathways to the Present* site at **www.Pathways.phschool.com** for the specific URL to complete the activity. Additional resources and related Web sites are also available.

    Read about evaluating the quality of Internet resources. Write an article explaining how Internet resources differ from printed resources. Outline the necessity and methods of evaluating Web sites.

## Using Graphic Organizers

12. The multiflow chart below gives an example of the ways that information travels today. On a separate sheet of paper, construct a similar chart to show how you might gather information from different sources to present a paper on why and how schools use computers.

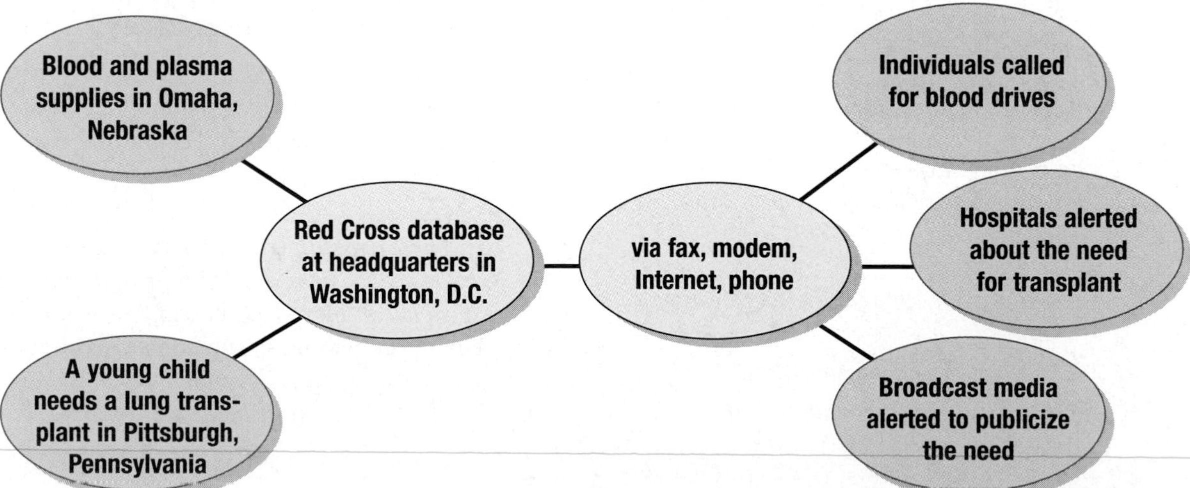

# Why Study History?

## A Nation Looks Ahead

Your textbook began with a question: Why Study History? As you studied each chapter, you learned that there are many answers to this question. Most can be summed up in a simple statement: The people and events of the past have created the world in which we live today. You can understand your world only by understanding the people whose vision of the future shaped our society. To do this you must study history and engage in an active, imaginative journey into the past. Although the people you encounter on this journey may have spoken, thought, and dressed differently from you, they, like you, were motivated by universal concerns and a wish for a better future.

Today, Americans look forward to a new century with a sense of hope. We have tremendous resources to use as we help shape tomorrow's world. Among these resources are our system of government, our vision of the future, and, of course, our history.

Foremost of America's strengths is the nation's unique system of government, which allows Americans to face the future with confidence. Our representative democracy strikes a balance between the rights of the people and the responsibilities that are assigned to the government. The tone of our various national debates might sometimes be shrill, but the discussion itself is a testament to the power of democracy as a means of settling disputes.

Americans have always tried their best to work together. Although at times separated by race, religion, and culture, all have played a part in building a strong nation. Now, as we face the challenges of the future we look, as always, to the lessons of the past.

On January 6, 1941, President Franklin D. Roosevelt delivered a famous speech before both houses of Congress. In that speech President Roosevelt outlined what he hoped would be goals for all Americans:

*There is nothing mysterious about the foundations of a healthy and strong democracy. The basic things expected by our people of their political and economic systems are simple. They are:*

- *Equality of opportunity for youth and for others.*
- *Jobs for those who can work.*
- *Security for those who need it.*
- *The ending of special privilege for a few.*
- *The preservation of civil liberties for all.*
- *The enjoyment of the fruits of scientific progress in a wider and constantly rising standard of living.*

*These are simple and basic things that must never be lost sight of in the turmoil and unbelievable complexity of the modern world. The inner and abiding strength of our economic and political systems is dependent upon the degree to which they fulfill these expectations. . . .*

Americans have built a nation that is unique. It is unique in its diversity, its exciting opportunities, and the ability of its citizens to meet new challenges.

*In the future days, which we seek to make secure, we look forward to a world founded upon four essential human freedoms.*

*THE FIRST IS FREEDOM OF SPEECH and expression everywhere in the world.*

*THE SECOND IS THE FREEDOM OF EVERY PERSON TO WORSHIP GOD in his own way everywhere in the world.*

*THE THIRD IS FREEDOM FROM WANT which, translated into world terms, means economic understandings which will secure to every nation a healthy peacetime life for its inhabitants everywhere in the world.*

*THE FOURTH IS FREEDOM FROM FEAR which, translated into world terms, means a worldwide reduction of armaments to such a point and in such a thorough fashion that no nation will be in a position to commit an act of physical aggression against any neighbor—anywhere in the world. . . . Since the beginning of our American history we have engaged in change—in perpetual peaceful revolution—a revolution which goes on steadily, quietly adjusting itself to changing conditions. . . .*

*Freedom means the supremacy of human rights everywhere. Our support goes to those who struggle to gain those rights or keep them. Our strength is in our unity of purpose.*

*—Franklin Delano Roosevelt*

SEAL OF THE PRESIDENT OF THE UNITED STATES
E PLURIBUS UNUM
NEW-YORK

# Reference Section

History is a collection of stories of the past. Literature also offers dramatic stories in every sphere of human activity. The study of literature makes history come alive and deepens our understanding of that past.

The following pages contain literature selections for every unit of your textbook. The selections range from fiction to autobiography to letters to song lyrics, and their authors are similarly diverse. All of the selections, however, can add to our understanding of American history and the American people.

# April Morning

BY HOWARD FAST

***INTRODUCTION*** The fighting at Lexington and Concord, Massachusetts, on April 19, 1775, marked the beginning of the American Revolution. In the following excerpt from his historical novel *April Morning*, Howard Fast captures the sights and sounds of the skirmish at Lexington Green.

***VOCABULARY*** Before you read the selection, find the meaning of these words in a dictionary: *dissipate, jubilation.*

When the British saw us, they were on the road past Buckman's [Tavern]. First, there were three officers on horseback. Then two flagbearers, one carrying the regimental flag and the other bearing the British colors. Then a corps of eight drums. Then rank after rank of the redcoats, stretching back on the road and into the curtain of mist, and emerging from the mist constantly, so that they appeared to be an endless force and an endless number. It was dreamlike and not very believable, and it caused me to turn and look at the houses around the common, to see whether all the rest of what we were, our mothers and sisters and brothers and grandparents, were watching the same thing we watched. My impression was that the houses had appeared by magic, for I could only remember looking around in the darkness and seeing nothing where now all the houses stood—and the houses were dead and silent, every shutter closed and bolted, every door and storm door closed and barred. Never before had I seen the houses like that, not in the worst cold or the worst storms.

And the redcoats did not quicken their pace or slow it, but marched up the road with the same even pace, up to the edge of the common; and when they were there, one of the officers held up his arm—and the drums stopped and the soldiers stopped, the line of soldiers stretching all the way down the road and into the dissipating mist. They were about one hundred and fifty paces from us.

The three officers sat on their horses, studying us. The morning air was cold and clean and sharp, and I could see their faces and the faces of the redcoat soldiers behind them, the black bands of their knapsacks, the glitter of their buckles. Their coats were red as fire, but their light trousers were stained and dirty from the march.

Then, one of the officers sang out to them, "Fix bayonets!" and all down the line, the bayonets sparkled in the morning sun, and we heard the ring of metal against metal as they were clamped onto the guns. . . .

***British uniform jacket like those worn at Lexington***

Then another British officer—I discovered afterward that he was Major Pitcairn—called out orders: "Columns right!" and then, "By the left flank," and, "Drums to the rear!" The drummers stood still and beat their drums, and the redcoats marched past them smartly, wheeling and parading across the common, while the three mounted officers spurred over the grass at a sharp canter, straight across our front and then back, reining in their prancing horses to face us. Meanwhile, the redcoats marched onto the common, the first company wheeling to face us when it was past our front of thirty-three men, the second company repeating the exercise, until they made a wall of red coats across the common, with no more than thirty or forty paces separating us. Even so close, they were unreal; only their guns were real, and their glittering bayonets too—and suddenly, I realized, and I believed that everyone else around me realized, that this was not to be an exercise or a parade or an argument, but something undreamed of and unimagined.

I think the Reverend was beginning to speak when Major Pitcairn drove down on him so that he had to leap aside. My father clutched the Reverend's arm to keep him from falling, and wheeling his horse, Major Pitcairn checked the beast so that it pawed at the air and neighed shrilly. The Reverend was speaking again, but no one heard his words or remembered them. The redcoats were grinning; small, pinched faces under the white wigs—they grinned at us. Leaning over his horse, Major Pitcairn screamed at us:

"Lay down your arms . . . Disperse, do you hear me! Disperse, you lousy peasant scum! Clear the way, do you hear me! Get off the King's green!"

At least, those were the words that I seem to remember. Others remembered differently; but the way he screamed, in his strange London accent, with all the motion and excitement, with his horse rearing and kicking at the Reverend and Father, with the drums beating again and the fixed bayonets glittering in the sunshine, it's a wonder that any of his words remained with us.

Yet for all that, this was a point where everything appeared to happen slowly. Abel Loring clutched my arm and said dryly, "Adam, Adam, Adam." He let go of his gun and it fell to the ground. "Pick it up," I said to him, watching Father, who pulled the Reverend into the protection of his body. Jonas Parker turned to us and cried at us:

"Steady! Steady! Now just hold steady!"

We still stood in our two lines, our guns butt end on the ground or held loosely in our hands. Major Pitcairn spurred his horse and raced between the lines. Somewhere, away from us, a shot sounded. A redcoat soldier raised his musket, leveled it at Father, and fired. My father clutched at his breast, then crumpled to the ground like an empty sack and lay with his face in the grass. I screamed. I was two [persons]. One part of me was screaming; another part of me looked at Father and grasped my gun in aching hands. Then the whole British front burst into a roar of sound and flame and smoke, and our whole world crashed at us, and broke into little pieces that fell around our ears, and came to an end; and the roaring, screaming noise was like the jubilation of the damned.

I ran. I was filled with fear, saturated with it, sick with it. Everyone else was running. The boys were running and the men were running. Our two lines were gone, and now it was only men and boys running in every direction that was away from the British, across the common and away from the British.

**Use the passage on these pages to answer the following questions.**

**1.** How did the British force at Lexington compare with the colonists' force?

**A** The two forces were roughly equal.
**B** The colonists' force was much larger.
**C** The British force was much larger.
**D** The mist made it impossible to compare the two forces.

**2.** What did the narrator mean by the use of such words as "dreamlike" and "unreal" to describe the events of that morning?

**A** He had not witnessed the events and was only imagining how they must have looked.
**B** He had arrived on the scene too late to understand what was happening.
**C** He was too young to understand what was happening.
**D** He had difficulty believing what was happening.

**3.** ***Critical Thinking: Drawing Conclusions*** Based on this account, what do you think caused the fighting at Lexington? Explain your answer.

# Benjamin Franklin Campaigns for the Constitution

***INTRODUCTION*** "It is much easier to pull down a government . . . than to build up, at such a season as the present," wrote John Adams early in 1787. Yet on September 17, 1787, the completed Constitution of the United States was put before the delegates for their signatures. It was fitting that Benjamin Franklin, who for so long had been part of the revolutionary changes sweeping the nation, should rise at that point and give the delegates the benefits of his wisdom.

***VOCABULARY*** Before you read the selection, find the meaning of these words in a dictionary: *sect, infallible, despotism, constituent, partisan, salutary, manifest, vicissitude.*

**Monday, September 17, 1787: In Convention:**

The engrossed [that is, formally written] Constitution being read, Doctor Franklin rose with a speech in his hand, which he had reduced to writing for his own conveniency, and which Mr. Wilson read in the words following.

Mr. President

I confess that there are several parts of this constitution which I do not at present approve, but I am not sure I shall never approve them: For having lived long, I have experienced many instances of being obliged by better information, or fuller consideration, to change opinions even on important subjects, which I once thought right, but found to be otherwise. It is therefore that the older I grow, the more apt I am to doubt my own judgment, and to pay more respect to the judgment of others. Most men indeed as well as most sects in Religion, think themselves in possession of all truth, and that wherever others differ from them it is so far error. Steele, a Protestant, in a Dedication tells the Pope that the only difference between our Churches in their opinions of the certainty of their doctrines is, the Church of Rome is infallible and the Church of England is never in the wrong. But though many private persons think almost as highly of their own infallibility as of that of their sect, few express it so naturally as a certain French lady, who in a dispute with her sister, said "I don't know how it happens, Sister but I meet with no body but myself, that's always in the right—*Il n'y a que moi qui a toujours raison.*"

Benjamin Franklin

In these sentiments, Sir, I agree to this Constitution with all its faults, if they are such; because I think a general Government necessary for us, and there is no form of Government but what may be a blessing to the people if well administered, and believe farther that this is likely to be well administered for a course of years, and can only end in Despotism, as other forms have done before it, when the people shall became so corrupted as to need despotic Government, being incapable of any other. I doubt too whether any other Convention we can obtain, may be able to make a better Constitution. For when you assemble a number of men to have the advantage of their joint wisdom, you inevitably assemble with those men, all their prejudices, their passions, their errors of opinion, their local interests, and their selfish views. From such an assembly can a perfect production be expected? It therefore astonishes me, Sir, to find this system approaching so near to perfection as it does; and I think it will astonish our enemies, who are waiting with confidence to hear that our councils are confounded like those of the Builders of Babel; and that our States are on the point of separation, only to meet hereafter for the purpose of cutting one another's throats. Thus I consent, Sir, to this Constitution because I expect no better, and because I am not sure, that it is not the best. The opinions I have had of its errors, I sacrifice to the public good. I have never whispered a syllable of them abroad. Within these walls they were born, and here they shall die. If every one of us in returning to our Constituents were to report the objections he has had to it, and endeavor to gain partisans in support of them, we might prevent its being generally received, and thereby lose all the salutary effects & great advantages resulting naturally in our favor among foreign Nations as well as among ourselves, from our real or apparent unanimity. Much of the strength & efficiency of any Government in procuring and securing happiness to the people, depends, on opinion, on the general opinion of the goodness of the Government, as well as of the wisdom and integrity of its Governors. I hope therefore that for our own sakes as a part of the people, and for the sake of posterity, we shall act heartily and unanimously in recommending this Constitution (if approved by Congress & confirmed by the Conventions) wherever our influence may extend, and turn our future thoughts & endeavors to the means of having it well administered.

**Philadelphia's Independence Hall, site of the Constitutional Convention**

On the whole, Sir, I can not help expressing a wish that every member of the Convention who may still have objections to it, would with me, on this occasion doubt a little of his own infallibility, and to make manifest our unanimity, put his name to this instrument. . . .

Whilst the last members were signing it Doctor Franklin looking towards the President's Chair, at the back of which a rising sun happened to be painted, observed to a few members near him, that Painters had found it difficult to distinguish in their art a rising from a setting sun. I have, said he, . . . often in the course of the Session, and the vicisitudes [vicissitudes] of my hopes and fears as to its issue, looked at that behind the President without being able to tell whether it was rising or setting: But now at length I have the happiness to know that it is a rising and not a setting Sun.

The Constitution being signed by all the members except Mr. [Edmund] Randolph [of Virginia], Mr. Mason, and Mr. Gerry who declined giving it the sanction of their names, the Convention dissolved itself by an Adjournment *sine die*—

## ANALYZING LITERATURE

**Use the passage on these pages to answer the following questions.**

**1.** Franklin believed that the Constitution should be approved because he
- **A** thought no other convention could create a better one.
- **B** agreed with all of its provisions.
- **C** had complete confidence in his own judgment.
- **D** had written the first draft.

**2.** Franklin's request that the delegates "doubt a little of [their] own infallibility" meant that he wanted them to
- **A** trust their best judgment.
- **B** recognize the errors in the Constitution.
- **C** understand his objections to the Constitution.
- **D** set aside their objections to the Constitution.

**3.** ***Critical Thinking: Determining Relevance*** How did Franklin's age and experience affect his thinking regarding whether or not to support the Constitution?

# *Incidents in the Life of a Slave Girl*

BY HARRIET ANN JACOBS

***INTRODUCTION*** Harriet Ann Jacobs was born into slavery in Edenton, North Carolina, in 1813. Her long and remarkable road to freedom began in 1835, when she and her two young children went into hiding in her hometown. In 1842, Jacobs escaped to New York with her son and daughter. There she made a home for her children and was eventually bought by the Colonization Society and freed in 1852. Shortly afterward she wrote her autobiography, which provides a personal account of what it was like to be enslaved in the 1800s.

***VOCABULARY*** Before you read the selection, find the meaning of these words in a dictionary: *toilsome, bequeath, chattel, defraud.*

I was born a slave; but I never knew it till six years of happy childhood had passed away. My father was a carpenter, and considered so intelligent and skillful in his trade, that, when buildings out of the common line were to be erected, he was sent for from long distances, to be head workman. On condition of paying his mistress two hundred dollars a year, and supporting himself, he was allowed to work at his trade, and manage his own affairs. His strongest wish was to purchase his children; but, though he several times offered his hard earnings for that purpose, he never succeeded.

I was so fondly shielded that I never dreamed I was a piece of merchandise, trusted to them for safe keeping, and liable to be demanded of them at any moment. . . .

Such were the unusually fortunate circumstances of my early childhood.

When I was six years old, my mother died; and then, for the first time, I learned, by the talk around me, that I was a slave. My mother's mistress was the daughter of my grandmother's mistress. She was the foster sister of my mother; they were both nourished at my grandmother's breast. In fact, my mother had been weaned at three months old, that the babe of the mistress might obtain sufficient food. They played together as children; and, when they became women, my mother was a most faithful servant to her white foster sister. On her death-bed her mistress promised that her children should never suffer for any thing; and during her lifetime she kept her word. They all spoke kindly of my dead mother, who had been a slave merely in name, but in nature was noble and womanly. I grieved for her, and my young mind was troubled with the thought who would now take of me and my little brother. I was told that my home was now to be with her mistress; and I found it a happy one. No toilsome or disagreeable duties were imposed upon me. My mistress was so kind to me that I was always glad to do her bidding, and proud to labor for her as much as my young years would permit. . . .

***Antislavery logo linking the women's rights and abolitionist movements***

When I was nearly twelve years old, my kind mistress sickened and died. As I saw the cheek grow paler, and the eye more glassy, how earnestly I prayed in my heart that she might live! I loved her; for she had been almost like a mother to me. My prayers were not answered. She died, and they buried her in the little churchyard, where, day after day, my tears fell upon her grave.

I was sent to spend a week with my grandmother. I was now old enough to begin to think of the future; and again and again I asked myself what they would do with me. I felt sure I should never find another mistress so kind as the one who was gone. She had promised my dying mother that her children would never suffer for any thing; and when I remembered that, and recalled her many proofs of attachment to me, I could not help having some hopes that she had left me free. . . .

After a brief period of suspense . . . we learned that she had bequeathed me to her sister's daughter, a child of five years old. So vanished our hopes. My mistress had taught me the precepts of God's Word: "Thou shalt love thy neighbor as thyself." "Whatsoever ye would that men should do unto you, do ye even so unto them." But I was her slave, and I suppose she did not recognize me as her neighbor. I would give much to blot out from my memory that one great wrong. As a child, I loved my mistress; and, looking back on the happy days I spent with her, I try to think with less bitterness of this act of injustice. While I was with her, she taught me to read and spell; and for this privilege, which so rarely falls to the lot of a slave, I bless her memory. . . .

My grandmother's mistress had always promised her that, at her death, she should be free; and it was said that in her will she made good the promise. But when the estate was settled, Dr. Flint told the faithful old servant that, under existing circumstances, it was necessary she should be sold.

On the appointed day, the customary advertisement was posted up, proclaiming that there would be a "public sale of negroes, horses, &c." Dr. Flint called to tell my grandmother that he was unwilling to wound her feelings by putting her up at auction, and that he would prefer to dispose of her at private sale. My grandmother saw through his hypocrisy; she understood very well that he was ashamed of the job. She was a very spirited woman, and if he was base enough to sell her, when her mistress intended she should be free, she was determined the public should know it. She had for a long time supplied many families with crackers and preserves; consequently, "Aunt Marthy," as she was called, was generally known, and everybody who knew her respected her intelligence and good character. Her long and faithful service in the family was also well known, and the intention of her mistress to leave her free. When the day of sale came, she took her place among the chattels, and at the first call she sprang upon the auction-block. Many voices called out, "Shame! Shame! Who is going to sell you, Aunt Marthy? Don't stand there! That is no place for you." Without saying a word, she quietly awaited her fate. No one bid for her. At last, a feeble voice said, "Fifty dollars." It came from a maiden lady, seventy years old, the sister of my grandmother's deceased mistress. She had lived forty years under the same roof with my grandmother; she knew how faithfully she had served her owners, and how cruelly she had been defrauded of her rights; and she resolved to protect her.

## ANALYZING LITERATURE

**Use the passage on these pages to answer the following questions.**

**1.** How did Jacobs learn that she was born a slave?

**A** Her mother told her before she died.
**B** Her father told her when he purchased her freedom.
**C** Others mentioned it after her mother died.
**D** She was sold at a public auction.

**2.** Why did people not make bids for Jacobs's grandmother when she was put up for sale at an auction?

**A** Dr. Flint told people that he preferred not to sell her.
**B** People disapproved of the selling of human beings.
**C** People thought she was too old to be a useful worker.
**D** People knew that her mistress had wanted her to be freed upon the mistress's death.

**3.** ***Critical Thinking: Identifying Central Issues*** How does the passage show how little control slaves had over their lives?

# Classics from the Civil War

***INTRODUCTION*** Two of the best-known writings of the Civil War are presented below. After a tour of Union army camps in 1861, writer and reformer Julia Ward Howe wrote "The Battle Hymn of the Republic," to be sung to the tune of "John Brown's Body." Published in 1862, the song became a favorite of Union soldiers. President Lincoln's address at the November 19, 1863, dedication ceremony at the Gettsysburg cemetery was so short that a photographer who meant to take a picture of Lincoln did not have time to focus his camera. Yet Lincoln's message on the ideals of the war, and the nation, has been called the greatest address in the nation's history.

***VOCABULARY*** Before you read the selections, find the meaning of these words in a dictionary: *contemners, consecrate, hallow.*

## "The Battle Hymn of the Republic"

**JULIA WARD HOWE**

Mine eyes have seen the glory of the coming of the Lord:
He is trampling out the vintage where the grapes of wrath are stored;
He hath loosed the fateful lightning of His terrible swift sword:
His truth is marching on.

I have seen Him in the watch-fires of a hundred circling camps,
They have builded Him an altar in the evening dews and damps;
I can read His righteous sentence by the dim and flaring lamps:
His day is marching on.

I have read a fiery gospel writ in burnished rows of steel:
"As ye deal with my contemners, so with you my grace shall deal;
Let the Hero, born of woman, crush the serpent with his heel,
Since God is marching on."

He has sounded forth the trumpet that shall never call retreat;
He is sifting out the hearts of men before His judgment-seat:
Oh, be swift, my soul, to answer Him! be jubilant, my feet!
Our God is marching on.

In the beauty of the lilies Christ was born across the sea,
With a glory in his bosom that transfigures you and me:
As he died to make men holy, let us die to make men free,
While God is marching on.

# The Gettysburg Address

**ABRAHAM LINCOLN**

Fourscore and seven years ago our fathers brought forth on this continent, a new nation, conceived in Liberty, and dedicated to the proposition that all men are created equal.

Now we are engaged in a great civil war, testing whether that nation, or any nation so conceived, and so dedicated, can long endure. We are met on a great battlefield of that war. We have come to dedicate a portion of that field, as a final resting place for those who here gave their lives, that that nation might live. It is altogether fitting and proper that we should do this.

But, in a larger sense, we can not dedicate—we can not consecrate—we can not hallow—this ground. The brave men, living and dead, who struggled here, have consecrated it far above our poor power to add or detract. The world will little note, nor long remember what we say here, but it can never forget what they did here. It is for us the living, rather, to be dedicated here to the unfinished work which they who fought here have thus far so nobly advanccd. It is rather for us to be dedicated to the great task remaining before us—that from these honored dead we take increased devotion to that cause for which they gave the last full measure of devotion—that we here highly resolve that these dead shall not have died in vain—that this nation, under God, shall have a new birth of frccdom—and that government of the people, by the people, for the people, shall not perish from the earth.

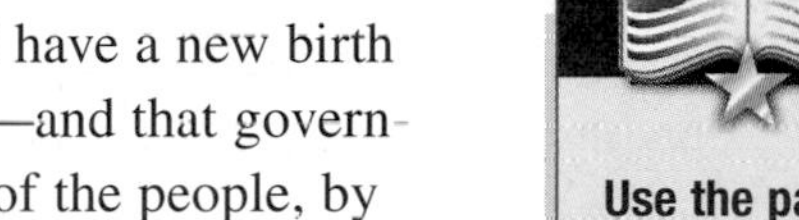

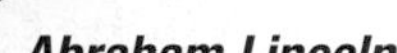

***Abraham Lincoln***



## ANALYZING LITERATURE

**Use the passages on these pages to answer the following questions.**

**1.** In "The Battle Hymn of the Republic," the line "As he died to make men holy, let us die to make men free" compares the death of Jesus Christ to the death of

**A** Abraham Lincoln.
**B** Union soldiers.
**C** freedom.
**D** slavery.

**2.** In the Gettysburg Address, why, according to Lincoln, could the assembled crowd not consecrate the cemetery ground?

**A** History would not remember their words.
**B** They had not personally fought for freedom.
**C** The final victory had not yet been won.
**D** Those who fought there had already consecrated it.

**3.** ***Critical Thinking: Determining Relevance*** What are some of the ideals expressed in the Gettysburg Address that we still find relevant today?

# Hungry Hearts

BY ANZIA YEZIERSKA

***INTRODUCTION*** Like many other immigrants who flooded into the nation's cities during the late 1800s, Anzia Yezierska and her family came to New York to escape ethnic persecution in their homeland. In her autobiography, *Hungry Hearts*, Yezierska describes what it was like to leave her Russian village and begin a new life in the United States.

***VOCABULARY*** Before you read the selection, find the meaning of these words in a dictionary: *Cossack, dilapidated, maw, galling.*

Steerage—dirty bundles—foul odors—seasick humanity—but I saw and heard nothing of the foulness and ugliness around me. I floated in showers of sunshine. Vision upon vision of the new world opened before me. From everyone's lips flowed the golden legend of the golden country:

"In America you can say what you feel—you can join your friends in the open streets without fear of Cossack."

"In America is a home for everyone. The land is your land. Not like in Russia where you feel yourself a stranger in the village where you were born and lived—the village in which your father and grandfather lie buried." . . .

"Everybody can do what he wants with his life in America."

"There are no high or low in America. Even the President holds hands with Gedalyeh Mindel."

"Plenty for all. Learning flows free like milk and honey."

"Learning flows free."

The words painted pictures in my mind. I saw before me free schools, free colleges, free libraries, where I could learn and learn and keep on learning. . . .

"Land! Land!" came the joyous shout.

"America! We're in America!" cried my mother, almost smothering us in her rapture.

All crowded and pushed on deck. They strained and stretched to get the first glimpse of the "golden country," lifting their children on their shoulders that they might see beyond them.

Men fell on their knees to pray. Women hugged their babies and wept. Children danced. Strangers embraced and kissed like old friends. Old men and women had in their eyes a look of young people in love.

Age-old visions sang themselves in me—songs of freedom of an oppressed people.

America! America! . . .

Between buildings that loomed like mountains, we struggled with our bundles, spreading around us the smell of the steerage. Up Broadway, under the bridge, and through the swarming streets of the ghetto, we followed Gedalyeh Mindel.

I looked about the narrow streets of squeezed-in stores and houses, ragged clothes, dirty bedding oozing out of the windows, ash cans and garbage cans cluttering the sidewalk. A vague sadness pressed down my heart—the first doubt of America.

"Where are the green fields and open spaces in America?" cried my heart. "Where is the golden country of my dreams?"

A loneliness for the fragrant silence of the woods that lay beyond our mud hut welled up in my heart, a longing for the soft, responsive earth of our village streets. All about me was the hardness of brick and stone, the stinking smells of crowded poverty.

"Here's your house with separate rooms like in a palace." Gedalyeh Mindel flung open the door of a dingy, airless flat.

"Oi weh!" my mother cried in dismay. "Where's the sunshine in America?"

She went to the window and looked out at the blank wall of the next house. "Gottuniu! Like in a grave so dark."

"It ain't so dark, it's only a little shady." Gedalyeh Mindel lighted the gas. "Look only." He pointed with pride to the dim gaslight. "No candles, no kerosene lamps in America, you turn on a screw and put to it a match and you got it light like with sunshine."

Again the shadow fell over me, again the doubt of America!

In America were rooms without sunlight, rooms to sleep in, to eat in, to cook in, but without sunshine. And Gedalyeh Mindel was happy. Could I be satisfied with just a place to sleep and eat in, and a door to shut people out—to take the place of sunlight? Or would I always need the sunlight to be happy?

And where was there a place in America for me to play? I looked out into the alley below and saw pale-faced children scrambling in the gutter. "Where is America?" cried my heart. . . .

"Heart of mine!" my mother's voice moaned above me. "Father is already gone an hour. You know how they'll squeeze from you a nickel for every minute you're late. Quick only!"

I seized my bread and herring and tumbled down the stairs and out into the street. I ate running, blindly pressing through the hurrying throngs of workers—my haste and fear choking each mouthful.

I felt a strangling in my throat as I neared the sweatshop prison [factory where she worked]; all my nerves screwed together into iron hardness to endure the day's torture.

For an instant I hesitated as I faced the grated window of the old dilapidated building—dirt and decay cried out from every crumbling brick.

In the maw of the shop, raging around me the roar and the clatter, the clatter and the roar, the merciless grind of the pounding machines. Half maddened, half deadened, I struggled to think, to feel, to remember—what am I—who am I—why was I here?

I struggled in vain—bewildered and lost in a whirlpool of noise.

"America—America—where was America?"

It cried in my heart.

The factory whistle—the slowing-down of the machines—the shout of release hailing the noon hour.

I woke as from a tense nightmare—a weary waking to pain.

In the dark chaos of my brain reason began to dawn. In my stifled heart feelings began to pulse. The wound of my wasted life began to throb and ache. My childhood choked with drudgery—must my youth too die—unlived?

The odor of herring and garlic—the ravenous munching of food—laughing and loud, vulgar jokes. Was it only I who was so wretched? I looked at those around me. Were they happy or only insensible to their slavery? How could they laugh and joke? Why were they not torn with rebellion against this galling grind—the crushing, deadening movements of the body, where only hands live and hearts and brains must die?

A touch on my shoulder. I looked up. It was Yetta Solomon from the machine next to mine.

"Here's your tea."

I stared at her, half hearing.

"Ain't you going to eat nothing?"

"Oi weh! Yetta! I can't stand it!" The cry broke from me. "I didn't come to America to turn into a machine. I came to America to make from myself a person. Does America want only my hands—only the strength of my body—not my heart—not my feelings—my thoughts?"

## ANALYZING LITERATURE

**Use the passage on these pages to answer the following questions.**

**1.** Which statement best describes Anzia Yezierska's image of the United States before she arrived?

**A** It was her homeland.
**B** It was a land of freedom for all.
**C** It was a crowded and dark country.
**D** It was not a place of safety.

**2.** What was her biggest disappointment about the United States?

**A** It reminded her too much of her former home.
**B** It had too much open space.
**C** It had no jobs.
**D** It seemed to want her only as a laborer, not a complete person.

**3.** ***Critical Thinking: Predicting Consequences*** In what different ways might immigrants have reacted to disappointments in the United States?

# Songs of World War I

***INTRODUCTION*** Popular songs about World War I played an important role in boosting the morale of both American soldiers abroad and civilians at home. As one soldier said, "Music keeps us from getting blue. We all have a country, a home and a girl, and music talks about these things without making you say anything." George M. Cohan was perhaps one of the most famous songwriters of the time. His song "Over There" expressed the patriotic spirit of citizens on the home front. It was also a favorite marching song of the men in the American Expeditionary Force. Songs like Geoffrey O'Hara's "K-K-K-Katy," helped civilians and soldiers alike to rally their spirits and gave them hope for the future.

***VOCABULARY*** Before you read the selections, find the meaning of these words in a dictionary: *hoist, gawk, foe.*

## "Over There"

### GEORGE M. COHAN

Johnnie get your gun, get your gun, get your gun,
Take it on the run, on the run, on the run;
Hear them calling you and me;
Every son of liberty.
Hurry right away, no delay, go today,
Make your daddy glad, to have had such a lad,
Tell your sweetheart not to pine,
To be proud her boy's in line.

*Chorus:*
Over there, over there,
Send the word, send the word over there,
That the Yanks are coming, the Yanks are coming,
The drums rum-tumming everywhere.
So prepare, say a prayer,
Send the word, send the word to beware,
We'll be over, we're coming over,
And we won't come back till it's over over there.

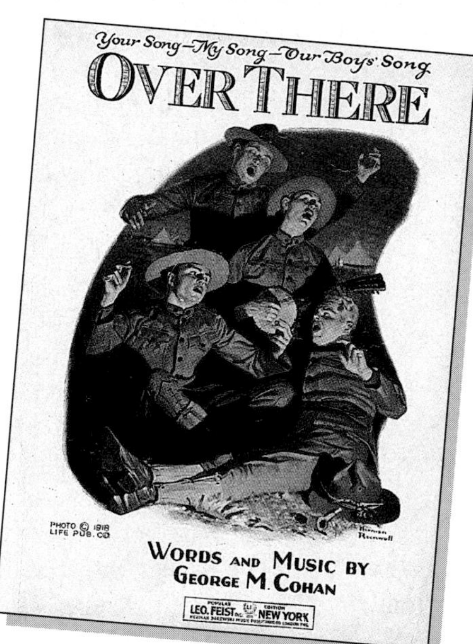


***Original cover of sheet music for "Over There"***

Johnnie get your gun, get your gun, get your gun,
Johnnie show the Hun [a derogatory term for Germans], you're a son-of-a-gun,
Hoist the flag and let her fly,
Like true heroes do or die.
Pack your little kit, show your grit, do your bit,
Soldiers to the ranks from the towns and the tanks,
Make your mother proud of you,
And to liberty be true.

# "K-K-K-Katy"

## GEOFFREY O'HARA

Jimmy was a soldier brave and bold,
Katy was a maid with hair of gold,
Like an act of fate,
Kate was standing at the gate,
Watching all the boys on dress parade.
Jimmy with the girls was just a gawk,
Stuttered every time he tried to talk,
Still that night at eight
He was there at Katy's gate,
Stuttering to her this lovesick cry:
"K-K-K-Katy, beautiful Katy,
You're the only g-g-g-girl that I adore;
When the m-moon shines over the cowshed,
I'll be waiting at the k-k-k-kitchen door."
No one ever looked so nice and neat,
No one could be just as cute and sweet.
That's what Jimmy thought,
When the wedding ring was bought;
Now he's off to France, the foe to meet.
Jimmy thought he'd like to take a chance,
See if he could make the Kaiser dance,
Stepping to a tune,
All about a silvery moon —
This is what they hear in far-off France:
"K-K-K-Katy, beautiful Katy,
You're the only g-g-g-girl that I adore;
When the m-moon shines over the cowshed,
I'll be waiting at the k-k-k-kitchen door."

***World War I patriotic poster***

## ANALYZING LITERATURE

**Use the passages on these pages to answer the following questions.**

**1.** In "Over There," the line "And we won't come back till it's over over there" means that the United States is committed to
- **A** winning the war.
- **B** staying out of the war.
- **C** redrawing European boundaries.
- **D** defending the United States from invasion.

**2.** In "K-K-K-Katy," what is meant by the lines "Jimmy thought he'd like to take a chance, /See if he could make the Kaiser dance"?
- **A** Jimmy was in love with a girl named Kaiser.
- **B** Jimmy thought there was a chance he could avoid overseas service.
- **C** Jimmy had been drafted to fight against Germany's kaiser, or leader.
- **D** Jimmy wanted to enlist to fight against Germany's kaiser, or leader.

**3.** ***Critical Thinking: Recognizing Cause and Effect*** How do you think these songs affected American soldiers serving in Europe?

# Growing Up

BY RUSSELL BAKER

***INTRODUCTION*** Single parents rarely have an easy life, and during the Depression their families' very survival was threatened. Because they were the sole caregivers for their children, they could not travel to look for work. Many had no choice but to accept aid from the government. In the following excerpt from his 1982 autobiography, *Growing Up*, Russell Baker, a *New York Times* columnist, remembers those difficult days and one trying day in particular.

***VOCABULARY*** Before you read the selection, find the meaning of these words in a dictionary: *dilapidation, appetizing, edible, incriminating, ostentatious.*

The paper route earned me three dollars a week, sometimes four, and my mother, in addition to her commissions on magazine sales, also had her monthly check coming from Uncle Willie, but we'd been in Baltimore a year before I knew how desperate things were for her. One Saturday morning she told me she'd need Doris and me to go with her to pick up some food. I had a small wagon she'd bought me to make it easier to move the Sunday papers, and she said I'd better bring it along. The three of us set off eastward, passing the grocery stores we usually shopped at, and kept walking until we came to Fremont Avenue, a grim street of dilapidation and poverty in the heart of East Baltimore.

"This is where we go," she said when we reached the corner of Fremont and Fayette Street. It looked like a grocery, with big plate-glass windows and people lugging out cardboard cartons and bulging bags, but it wasn't. I knew very well what it was.

"Are we going on relief?" I asked her.

"Don't ask questions about things you don't know anything about," she said. "Bring that wagon inside."

I did, and watched with a mixture of shame and greed while men filled it with food. None of it was food I liked. There were huge cans of grapefruit juice, big paper sacks of cornmeal, cellophane bags of rice and prunes. It was hard to believe all this was ours for no money at all, even though none of it was very appetizing. My wonder at this free bounty quickly changed to embarrassment as we headed home with it. Being on relief was a shameful thing. People who accepted the government's handouts were scorned by everyone I knew as idle no-accounts without enough self-respect to pay their own way in the world. I'd often heard my mother say the same thing of families in the neighborhood suspected of being on relief. These, I'd been taught to believe, were people beyond hope. Now we were as low as they were.

Pulling the wagon back toward Lombard Street, with Doris following behind to keep the edible proof of our disgrace from falling off, I knew my mother was far worse off than I'd suspected. She'd never have accepted such shame otherwise. I studied her as she walked along beside me, head high as always, not a bit bowed in disgrace, moving at her usual quick, hurry-up pace. If she'd given up on life, she didn't show it, but on the other hand she was unhappy about something. I dared to mention the dreaded words only once on that trip home.

***Taken at a relief center in Kentucky, this photograph offers an ironic comment on the Great Depression.***

"Are we on relief now, Mom?"

"Let me worry about that," she said.

What worried me most as we neared home was the possibility we'd be seen with the incriminating food by somebody we knew. There was no mistaking government-surplus food. The grapefruit-juice cans, the prunes and rice, the cornmeal—all were ostentatiously unlabeled, thus advertising themselves as "government handouts." Everybody in the neighborhood could read them easily enough, and our humiliation would be gossiped through every parlor by sundown. I had an inspiration.

"It's hot pulling this wagon," I said. "I'm going to take my sweater off."

It wasn't hot, it was on the cool side, but after removing the sweater I laid it across the groceries in the wagon. It wasn't a very effective cover, but my mother was suddenly affected by the heat too.

"It is warm, isn't it, Buddy?" she said. Removing her topcoat, she draped it over the groceries, providing total concealment.

"You want to take your coat off, Doris?" asked my mother.

"I'm not hot, I'm chilly," Doris said.

It didn't matter. My mother's coat was enough to get us home without being exposed as three of life's failures.

## ANALYZING LITERATURE

**Use the passage on these pages to answer the following questions.**

**1.** What conclusion did Baker draw from his mother's decision to accept government relief?

**A** His mother had given up on life.
**B** His mother no longer cared what others thought of her.
**C** His mother wanted him to quit his paper route.
**D** His mother was desperately poor.

**2.** Baker placed his sweater in the wagon because he was

**A** hot.
**B** ashamed of the government-surplus food.
**C** ashamed of his mother.
**D** ashamed of the wagon.

**3.** ***Critical Thinking: Distinguishing False from Accurate Images*** How might this experience have changed Baker's image of those who accepted government help?

# Night

BY ELIE WIESEL

***INTRODUCTION*** Elie Wiesel, a Hungarian Jew, lost his parents and a sister in the Holocaust. Released from the Buchenwald concentration camp in 1945, he waited ten years before writing of his experiences. *Night,* the book he eventually wrote, is one of the most powerful memoirs written by survivors of the Nazi camps. The excerpt below recalls Wiesel's first night in the camp.

***VOCABULARY*** Before you read the selection, find the meaning of these words in a dictionary: *nocturnal, antechamber, bestial, truncheon, crematory, lucidity, redemption, Talmud.*

Never shall I forget that night, the first night in camp, which has turned my life into one long night, seven times cursed and seven times sealed. Never shall I forget that smoke. Never shall I forget the little faces of the children, whose bodies I saw turned into wreaths of smoke beneath a silent blue sky.

Never shall I forget those flames which consumed my faith forever.

Never shall I forget that nocturnal silence which deprived me, for all eternity, of the desire to live. Never shall I forget those moments which murdered my God and my soul and turned my dreams to dust. Never shall I forget these things, even if I am condemned to live as long as God Himself. Never.

The barracks we had been made to go into was very long. In the roof were some blue-tinged skylights. The antechamber of Hell must look like this. So many crazed men, so many cries, so much bestial brutality!

There were dozens of prisoners to receive us, truncheons in their hands, striking out anywhere, at anyone, without reason. Orders:

"Strip! Fast! *Los*! Keep only your belts and shoes in your hands. . . ."

We had to throw our clothes at one end of the barracks. There was already a great heap there. New suits and old, torn coats, rags. For us, this was the true equality: nakedness. Shivering with the cold.

Some SS officers moved about in the room, looking for strong men. If they were so keen on strength, perhaps one should try and pass oneself off as sturdy? My father thought the reverse. It was better not to draw attention to oneself. Our fate would then be the same as the others. (Later, we were to learn that he was right. Those who were selected that day were enlisted in the Sonder-Kommando, the unit which worked in the crematories. Bela Katz—son of a big tradesman from our town—had arrived at Birkenau with the first transport, a week before us. When he heard of our arrival, he managed to get word to us that, having been chosen for his strength, he had himself put his father's body into the crematory oven.)

Blows continued to rain down.

"To the barber!"

***Survivors of a Nazi concentration camp***

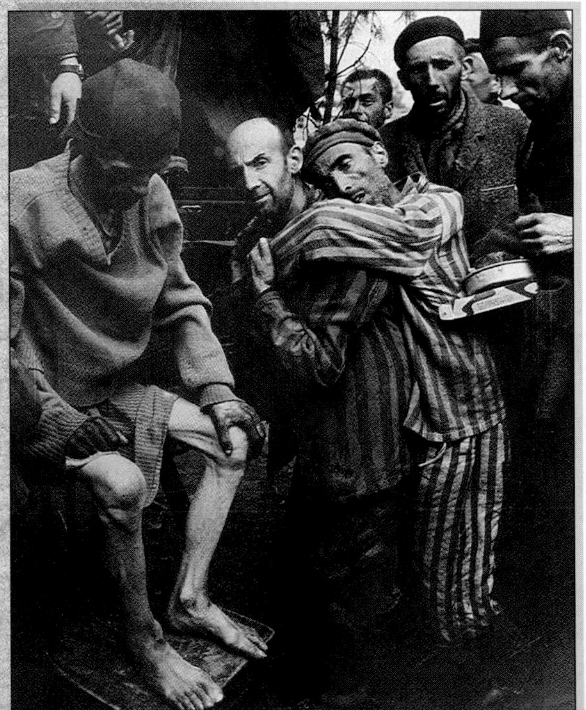

Belt and shoes in hand, I let myself be dragged off to the barbers. They took our hair off with clippers, and shaved off all the hair on our bodies. The same thought buzzed all the time in my head—not to be separated from my father.

Freed from the hands of the barbers, we began to wander in the crowd, meeting friends and acquaintances. These meetings filled us with joy—yes, joy—"Thank God! You're still alive!"

But others were crying. They used all their remaining strength in weeping. Why had they let themselves be brought here? Why couldn't they have died in their beds? Sobs choked their voices.

Suddenly, someone threw his arms round my neck in an embrace: Yechiel, brother of the rabbi of Sighet. He was sobbing bitterly. I thought he was weeping with joy at still being alive.

"Don't cry, Yechiel," I said. "Don't waste your tears. . . ."

"Not cry? We're on the threshold of death. . . . Soon we shall have crossed over. . . . Don't you understand? How could I not cry?"

Through the blue-tinged skylights I could see the darkness gradually fading. I had ceased to feel fear. And then I was overcome by an inhuman weariness.

Those absent no longer touched even the surface of our memories. We still spoke of them—"Who knows what may have become of them?"—but we had little concern for their fate. We were incapable of thinking of anything at all. Our senses were blunted; everything was blurred as in a fog. It was no longer possible to grasp anything. The instincts of self-preservation, of self-defense, of pride, had all deserted us. In one ultimate moment of lucidity it seemed to me that we were damned souls wandering in the half-world, souls condemned to wander through space till the generations of man came to an end, seeking their redemption, seeking oblivion—without hope of finding it.

Toward five o'clock in the morning, we were driven out of the barracks. The Kapos beat us once more, but I had ceased to feel any pain from their blows. An icy wind enveloped us. We were naked, our shoes and belts in our hands. The command: "Run!" And we ran. After a few minutes of racing, a new barracks.

A barrel of petrol at the entrance. Disinfection. Everyone was soaked in it. Then a hot shower. At high speed. As we came out from the water, we were driven outside. More running. Another barracks, the store. Very long tables. Mountains of prison clothes. On we ran. As we passed, trousers, tunic, shirt, and socks were thrown to us.

Within a few seconds, we had ceased to be men. If the situation had not been tragic, we should have roared with laughter. Such outfits! Meir Katz, a giant, had a child's trousers, and Stern, a thin little chap, a tunic which completely swamped him. We immediately began the necessary exchanges.

I glanced at my father. How he had changed! His eyes had grown dim. I would have liked to speak to him, but I did not know what to say.

The night was gone. The morning star was shining in the sky. I too had become a completely different person. The student of the Talmud, the child that I was, had been consumed in the flames. There remained only a shape that looked like me. A dark flame had entered into my soul and devoured it.

So much had happened within such a few hours that I had lost all sense of time. When had we left our houses? And the ghetto? And the train? Was it only a week? One night—one single night?

How long had we been standing like this in the icy wind? An hour? Simply an hour? Sixty minutes?

Surely it was a dream.

## ANALYZING LITERATURE

**Use the passage on these pages to answer the following questions.**

**1.** Prisoners who appeared stronger than others were
**A** killed immediately.
**B** given special privileges.
**C** assigned to work in crematories.
**D** beaten more severely.

**2.** The reference to fog on the first night describes the
**A** mental confusion of the prisoners.
**B** mental confusion of the guards.
**C** atmosphere surrounding the camp.
**D** atmosphere within the crowded barracks.

**3.** ***Critical Thinking: Drawing Conclusions*** Explain what Wiesel meant by the sentence, "Surely it was a dream."

LITERATURE

# "Letter from the Birmingham Jail"

BY MARTIN LUTHER KING, JR.

***INTRODUCTION*** In 1963 the Reverend Martin Luther King, Jr., and the Southern Christian Leadership Conference staged a mass protest in Birmingham, Alabama. King was arrested for his participation in the protest, and from his jail cell he wrote a letter, which is excerpted below. The letter was his answer to eight Birmingham clergymen who had condemned the civil rights demonstration and criticized King as an "outside agitator" coming to stir up trouble in Birmingham.

***VOCABULARY*** Before you read the selection, find the meaning of these words in a dictionary: *deplore, unduly, ominous, complacency, manifest.*

**My Dear Fellow Clergymen:**

You deplore the demonstrations taking place in Birmingham. But your statement, I am sorry to say, fails to express a similar concern for the conditions that brought about the demonstrations. . . .

We know through painful experience that freedom is never voluntarily given by the oppressor; it must be demanded by the oppressed. Frankly, I have yet to engage in a direct-action campaign that was "well timed" in the view of those who have not suffered unduly from the disease of segregation. For years now I have heard the word "Wait!" It rings in the ear of every Negro with piercing familiarity. This "Wait!" has almost always meant "Never." We must come to see, with one of our distinguished jurists, that "justice too long delayed is justice denied." . . .

Perhaps it is easy for those who have never felt the stinging darts of segregation to say, "Wait." But when you have seen vicious mobs lynch your mothers and fathers at will and drown your sisters and brothers at whim; when you have seen hate-filled policemen curse, kick, and even kill your black brothers and sisters; when you see the vast majority of your twenty million Negro brothers smothering in an airtight cage of poverty in the midst of an affluent society; when you suddenly find your tongue twisted and your speech stammering as you seek to explain to your six-year-old daughter why she can't go to the public amusement park that has just been advertised on television, and see tears welling up in her eyes when she is told that Funtown is closed to colored children, and see ominous clouds of inferiority beginning to form in her little mental sky, and see her beginning to distort her personality by developing an unconscious bitterness toward white people. . . then you will understand why we find it difficult to wait. . . .

You speak of our activity in Birmingham as extreme. At first I was rather disappointed that fellow clergymen would see my nonviolent efforts as those of an extremist. I began thinking about the fact that I stand in the middle of two opposing forces in the Negro community. One is a force of complacency, made up in part of Negroes who, as a result of long years of oppression, are so drained of self-respect and a sense of "somebodiness" that they have adjusted to segregation; and in part of a few middle-class Negroes who, because of a degree of academic and economic security and because in some ways they profit by segregation, have become insensitive to the problems of the masses. The other force is one of bitterness and hatred, and it comes perilously close to advocating violence. It is expressed in the various black nationalist groups that are springing up across the nation, the largest and best-known being Elijah Muhammad's Muslim movement. . . .

I have tried to stand between these two forces, saying that we need emulate neither the "do-nothingism" of the complacent nor the hatred and despair of the black nationalist. For there is the more excellent way of love and nonviolent protest. I am grateful to God that, through the influence of the Negro church, the way of nonviolence became an integral part of our struggle. . . .

Oppressed people cannot remain oppressed forever. The yearning for freedom eventually manifests itself, and that is what has happened to the American Negro. Something within has reminded him of his birthright of freedom, and something without has reminded him that it can be gained.

*As his son looks on, Martin Luther King, Jr., removes a cross that had been burned in front of his home in Atlanta, Georgia, in 1960.*

LITERATURE

## ANALYZING LITERATURE

**Use the passage on these pages to answer the following questions.**

**1.** Why, according to King, could African Americans not expect whites to grant them freedom?

**A** Those in power never give up power without a struggle.
**B** African Americans did not yet deserve full freedom.
**C** African Americans were too divided on the issue of segregation.
**D** "Do-nothingism" was too common among African Americans.

**2.** Between which two groups did King see himself as standing?

**A** blacks and whites
**B** black clergymen and white clergymen
**C** blacks who favored him and blacks who favored his enemies
**D** blacks who accepted segregation and blacks who advocated hatred

**3.** ***Critical Thinking: Expressing Problems Clearly*** Restate in your own words the message that "justice too long delayed is justice denied."

# "Straw into Gold: The Metamorphosis of the Everyday"

BY SANDRA CISNEROS

***INTRODUCTION*** Recent years have witnessed an explosive growth in the diversity of American literature. Works by women, African Americans, Hispanic Americans, and Asian Americans have been both critical and sales successes, and these works reflect themes as diverse as their authors. One member of the new generation of writers is Sandra Cisneros, who was born in Chicago in 1954. The following selection is taken from her essay "Straw into Gold: The Metamorphosis of the Everyday."

***VOCABULARY*** Before you read the selection, find the meaning of these words in a dictionary: *threshold, taboo, vagabonding, sappy.*

I've managed to do a lot of things in my life I didn't think I was capable of and which many others didn't think me capable of either. Especially because I am a woman, a Latina, an only daughter in a family of six men. My family would've liked to have seen me married long ago. In our culture, men and women don't leave their father's house except by way of marriage. I crossed my father's threshold with nothing carrying me but my own two feet. A woman whom no one came for and no one chased away.

Sandra Cisneros

To make matters worse, I had left before any of my six brothers had ventured away from home. I had broken a terrible taboo. Somehow, looking back at photos of myself as a child, I wonder if I was aware of having begun already my own quiet war.

I like to think that somehow my family, my Mexicanness, my poverty all had something to do with shaping me into a writer. I like to think my parents were preparing me all along for my life as an artist even though they didn't know it. From my father I inherited a love of wandering. He was born in Mexico City but as a young man he traveled into the U.S. vagabonding. He eventually was drafted and thus became a citizen. Some of the stories he has told about his first months in the U.S. with little or no English surface in my stories in *The House on Mango Street* as well as others I have in mind to write in the future. From him I inherited a sappy heart. (He still cries when he watches the Mexican soaps [soap operas]—especially if they deal with children who have foresaken their parents.)

My mother was born like me—in Chicago, but of Mexican descent. It would be her tough, streetwise voice that would haunt all my stories and poems. An amazing woman who loves to draw and read books and can sing an opera. A smart cookie. . . .

What would my teachers say if they knew I was a writer? Who would've guessed it? I wasn't a very bright student. I didn't much like school because we moved so much and I was always new and funny-looking. In my fifth-grade report card, I have nothing but an avalanche of C's and D's, but I don't remember being that stupid. I was good at art and I read plenty of library books and Kiki [her brother] laughed at all my jokes. At home I was fine, but at school I never opened my mouth except when the teacher called on me, the first time I'd speak all day.

When I think how I see myself, it would have to be at age eleven. I know I'm thirty-two on the outside, but inside I'm eleven. I'm the girl in the picture with skinny arms and a crumpled shirt and crooked hair. I didn't like school because all they saw was the outside me. School was lots of rules and sitting with your hands folded and being afraid all the time. I liked looking out the window and thinking. I liked staring at the girl across the way writing her name over and over again in red ink. I wondered why the boy with the dirty collar in front of me didn't have a mama who took better care of him.

I think my mama and papa did the best they could to keep us warm and clean and never hungry. We had birthday and graduation parties and things like that, but there was another hunger that had to be fed. There was a hunger I didn't even have a name for. Was this when I began writing?

In 1966 we moved into a house, a real one, our first real home. This meant we didn't have to change schools and be the new kids on the block every couple of years. We could make friends and not be afraid we'd have to say goodbye to them and start all over. My brothers and the flock of boys they brought home would become important characters eventually for my stories—Louie and his cousins, Meme Ortiz and his dog with two names, one in English and one in Spanish.

My mother flourished in her own home. She took books out of the library and taught herself to garden, producing flowers so envied we had to put a lock on the gate to keep out the midnight flower thieves. My mother is still gardening to this day.

This was the period in my life, that slippery age when you are both child and woman and neither, I was to record in *The House on Mango Street.* I was still shy. I was a girl who couldn't come out of her shell.

How was I to know I would be recording and documenting the women who sat their sadness on an elbow and stared out a window? It would be the streets of Chicago I would later record, but from a child's eyes.

I've done all kinds of things I didn't think I could do since then. I've gone to a prestigious university, studied with famous writers, and taken away an MFA [Master of Fine Arts] degree. I've taught poetry in the schools in Illinois and Texas. I've gotten an NEA [National Endowment for the Arts] grant and run away with it as far as my courage would take me. I've seen the bleached and bitter mountains of the Peloponnesus. I've lived on a Greek island. I've been to Venice twice. In Rapallo, I met Ilona once and forever and took her sad heart with me across the south of France and into Spain. . . .

I've moved since Europe to the strange and wonderful country of Texas, land of polaroid-blue skies and big bugs. I met a mayor with my last name. I met famous Chicana/o artists and writers and politicos [politicians].

Texas is another chapter in my life. It brought with it the Dobie-Paisano Fellowship, a six-month residency on a 265-acre ranch. But most important Texas brought Mexico back to me.

Sitting at my favorite people-watching spot, the snaky Woolworth's counter across from the Alamo, I can't think of anything else I'd rather be than a writer. I've traveled and lectured from Cape Cod to San Francisco, to Spain, Yugoslavia, Greece, Mexico, France, Italy, and finally today to Seguin, Texas. Along the way there is straw for the taking. With a little imagination, it can be spun into gold.

## ANALYZING LITERATURE

**Use the passage on these pages to answer the following questions.**

**1.** How does Cisneros think her family and background affected her as a writer?

**A** They shaped the kind of writer she became.
**B** She became a writer in order to escape them.
**C** They prevented her from becoming a serious writer.
**D** They played no role in her career as a writer.

**2.** Cisneros's teachers would be surprised at her choice of occupation because she

**A** always hated writing.
**B** was not curious about the world around her.
**C** got poor grades and participated little in class.
**D** was constantly changing schools.

**3.** ***Critical Thinking: Formulating Questions*** In this excerpt, Cisneros refers to accomplishing things she did not expect to accomplish. If you were interviewing Cisneros for a newspaper story on this topic, what questions might you ask her?

UNIT 7 LITERATURE

# My American Journey

BY COLIN POWELL

*INTRODUCTION* The son of Jamaican immigrants, Colin Powell began his army career after college and served two tours of duty in Vietnam. In 1987 President Reagan appointed him national security adviser. Two years later Powell became Chairman of the Joint Chiefs of Staff. As Chairman he played a major role in planning and executing American strategy during the Persian Gulf War of 1991. Powell retired from the military in 1993 and became a prominent public speaker on issues related to public service.

*VOCABULARY* Before you read the selection, find the meaning of these words in a dictionary: *hyphenated, malcontent, fractious, resilience, hybrid.*

As I travel around the country, I invite questions from my audiences, which range from trade associations to motivational seminars, from prison inmates to the youngsters at my pride and joy, the Colin L. Powell Elementary School in Woodlands, Texas. What people ask gives me a good idea of what is on America's mind. . . .

American voters [are] looking, in my judgment . . . for a different spirit in the land, something better. How do we find our way again? How do we reestablish moral standards? How do we end the ethnic fragmentation that is making us an increasingly hyphenated people? How do we restore a sense of family to our national life? On the speech circuit, I tell a story that goes to the heart of America's longing. The ABC correspondent Sam Donaldson was interviewing a young African-American soldier in a tank platoon on the eve of battle in Desert Storm. Donaldson asked, "How do you think the battle will go? Are you afraid?"

Colin Powell

"We'll do okay. We're well trained. And I'm not afraid," the GI answered, gesturing toward his buddies around him. "I'm not afraid because I'm with my family."

The other soldiers shouted, "Tell him again. He didn't hear you."

The soldier repeated, "This is my family and we'll take care of each other."

That story never fails to touch me or the audience. It is a metaphor for what we have to do as a nation. We have to start thinking of America as a family. We have to stop screeching at each other, stop hurting each other, and instead start caring for, sacrificing for, and sharing with each other. We have to stop constantly criticizing, which is the way of the malcontent, and instead get

LITERATURE

***According to Colin Powell, American voters are looking for "a different spirit in the land, something better."***

LITERATURE

back to the can-do attitude that made America. We have to keep trying, and risk failing, in order to solve this country's problems. We cannot move forward if cynics and critics swoop down and pick apart anything that goes wrong to a point where we lose sight of what is right, decent, and uniquely good about America. . . .

We are a fractious nation, always searching, always dissatisfied, yet always hopeful. We have an infinite capacity to rejuvenate ourselves. We are self-correcting. And we are capable of caring about each other. . . .

We will prevail over our present trials. We will come through because our founders bequeathed us a political system of genius, a system flexible enough for all ages and inspiring noble aspirations for all time. We will continue to flourish because our diverse American society has the strength, hardiness, and resilience of the hybrid plant we are. . . . Jefferson once wrote, "There is a debt of service due from every man to his country, proportioned to the bounties which nature and fortune have measured to him." . . . My responsibility, our responsibility as lucky Americans, is to try to give back to this country as much as it has given to us, as we continue our American journey together.

## ANALYZING LITERATURE

**Use the passage on these pages to answer the following questions.**

**1.** What lesson did Powell learn from the conversation between Sam Donaldson and the black soldier?

**A** Americans have too little faith in the news media.
**B** Americans need to ask each other fewer questions.
**C** Americans need to trust each other more.
**D** Americans need to work together more.

**2.** The quotation from Jefferson, cited by Powell, means that

**A** people who have more advantages owe more to their nation.
**B** all Americans owe their nation the same degree of service.
**C** Americans owe their success entirely to their nation.
**D** fortune, or luck, is more important than natural gifts.

**3.** ***Critical Thinking: Drawing Conclusions*** Two of the nation's strengths that Powell cited were its political system and its diverse society. Explain how each of these is a source of strength for the United States.

# A Correlation to Prentice Hall Literature
## *The American Experience*

| AMERICA: PATHWAYS TO THE PRESENT | THE AMERICAN EXPERIENCE | | |
|---|---|---|---|
| ***Chapter*** | ***Author*** | ***Title and Page Number*** | ***Genre*** |
| **Unit 1: Building a Powerful Nation** | | | |
| **1 American History to the Civil War Beginnings–1861** | Michael J. Caduto and Joseph Bruchac | "The Earth on Turtle's Back" page 22 | myth |
| | Alvar Núñez Cabeza de Vaca | "A Journey Through Texas" page 34 | nonfiction |
| | Olaudah Equiano | from *The Interesting Narrative of the Life of Olaudah Equiano* page 44 | nonfiction |
| | Benjamin Franklin | from *The Autobiography* page 131 | nonfiction |
| | Abigail Adams | "Letter to Her Daughter From the New White House" page 194 | letter |
| | Benjamin Franklin | "Speech in the Convention" page 172 | speech |
| | Washington Irving | "The Devil and Tom Walker" page 236 | short story |
| | Ralph Waldo Emerson | from *Self-Reliance* page 366 | nonfiction |
| | Henry David Thoreau | from *Civil Disobedience* page 380 | nonfiction |
| | Chief Joseph | "I Will Fight No More Forever" page 551 | speech |
| | Frederick Douglass | from *My Bondage and My Freedom* page 458 | nonfiction |
| **2 The Civil War 1861–1865** | Ambrose Bierce | "An Occurrence at Owl Creek Bridge" page 468 | short story |
| **3 Reconstruction 1863–1877** | Sojourner Truth | "An Account of an Experience With Discrimination" page 503 | nonfiction |
| **4 The Expansion of American Industry 1865–1900** | Edwin Arlington Robinson | "Richard Cory" page 607 | poem |
| **5 Looking to the West 1861–1865** | Bret Harte | "The Outcasts of Poker Flat" page 534 | short story |
| **6 Politics, Immigration, and Urban Life 1870–1915** | Bernard Malamud | "The First Seven Years" page 892 | short story |
| **7 Daily Life in the Gilded Age 1870–1915** | Kate Chopin | "The Story of an Hour" page 592 | short story |

| AMERICA: PATHWAYS TO THE PRESENT | THE AMERICAN EXPERIENCE | | |
|---|---|---|---|
| **Chapter** | **Author** | **Title and Page Number** | **Genre** |
| **Unit 2: The United States on the Brink of Change, 1890–1920** | | | |
| 8 Becoming a World Power 1890–1913 | William Carlos Williams | "This Is Just to Say" page 663 | poem |
| 9 The Era of Progressive Reform 1890–1920 | Carl Sandburg | "Chicago" page 770 | poem |
| 10 The World War I Era 1914–1920 | Ernest Hemingway | "In Another Country" page 731 | short story |
| **Unit 3: Boom Times to Hard Times, 1919–1938** | | | |
| 11 The Twenties 1920–1929 | Zora Neale Hurston | from *Dust Tracks on a Road* page 830 | nonfiction |
| 12 Crash and Depression 1929–1933 | F. Scott Fitzgerald | "Winter Dreams" page 670 | short story |
| 13 The New Deal 1933–1938 | E.B. White | from *Here Is New York* page 822 | nonfiction |
| **Unit 4: Hot and Cold War, 1939–1960** | | | |
| 14 World War II 1939–1945 | Randall Jarrell | "The Death of the Ball Turret Gunner" page 1045 | poem |
| 15 World War II at Home 1941–1945 | Ezra Pound | "In a Station of the Metro" page 661 | poem |
| 16 The Cold War 1945–1960 | John Hersey | "Hiroshima" (page 1036) | nonfiction |
| 17 The Postwar Years at Home 1945–1960 | W.H. Auden | "The Unknown Citizen" page 696 | poem |
| **Unit 5: The Upheaval of the Sixties, 1960–1975** | | | |
| 18 The Kennedy and Johnson Years 1961–1969 | Robert Hayden | "Frederick Douglass" page 1053 | poem |
| 19 The Civil Rights Movement 1954–1968 | Colleen McElroy | "For My Children" page 1060 | poem |
| 20 Other Social Movements 1960–1975 | James Baldwin | "The Rockpile" page 1026 | short story |
| 21 The Vietnam War and American Society 1960–1975 | Yusef Komunyakaa | "Camouflaging the Chimera" page 1080 | poem |
| | Tim O'Brien | "Ambush" page 1082 | short story |
| **Unit 6: Continuity and Change, 1968–Present** | | | |
| 22 The Nixon Years 1969–1974 | Theodore Roethke | "The Adamant" page 919 | poem |
| 23 The Post-Watergate Period 1974–1980 | Anne Tyler | "Average Waves in Unprotected Waters" page 926 | short story |
| 24 The Conservative Revolution 1980–1992 | Ian Frazier | "Coyote v. Acme" page 998 | nonfiction |
| 25 Entering a New Era 1992–Present | Sandra Cisneros | "Straw Into Gold: The Metamorphosis of the Everyday" page 1006 | nonfiction |
| **Unit 7: Pathways to the Future: Themes for the Twenty-First Century** | | | |
| Chapters 26–32 | Amy Tan | "Mother Tongue" page 1012 | nonfiction |

# Illustrated Data Bank

The following maps, tables, and graphs that make up this Illustrated Data Bank are designed as reference materials to help you in your study of United States history:

- United States Population Density, 1790
- United States Ethnic Groups, 1790
- Enslaved Population of the United States, 1790
- United States Population Density, 1890
- United States Foreign-Born Population, 1890
- United States Territorial Growth
- United States Birth Rate, 1910–2000
- United States Gross Domestic Product, 1960–1996
- United States Median Age, 1840–2040
- United States Population by Race, 1995
- United States Latino Population, 1990
- United States Population Density, 1995
- Political Map of the United States
- Physical Map of the United States
- Natural Resources of the United States
- Political Map of the World
- Profile of the Fifty States
- Presidents of the United States

## United States Population Density, 1790

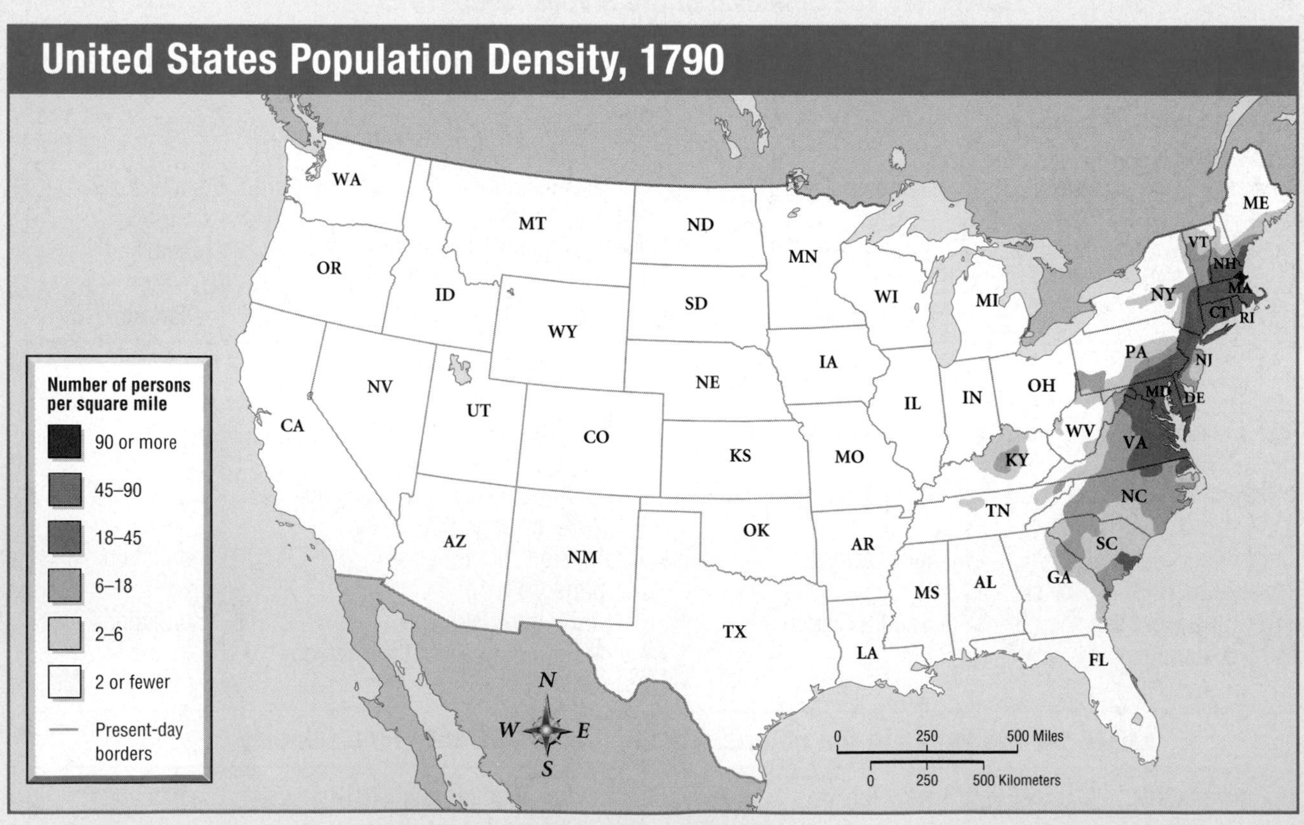

## United States Ethnic Groups, 1790

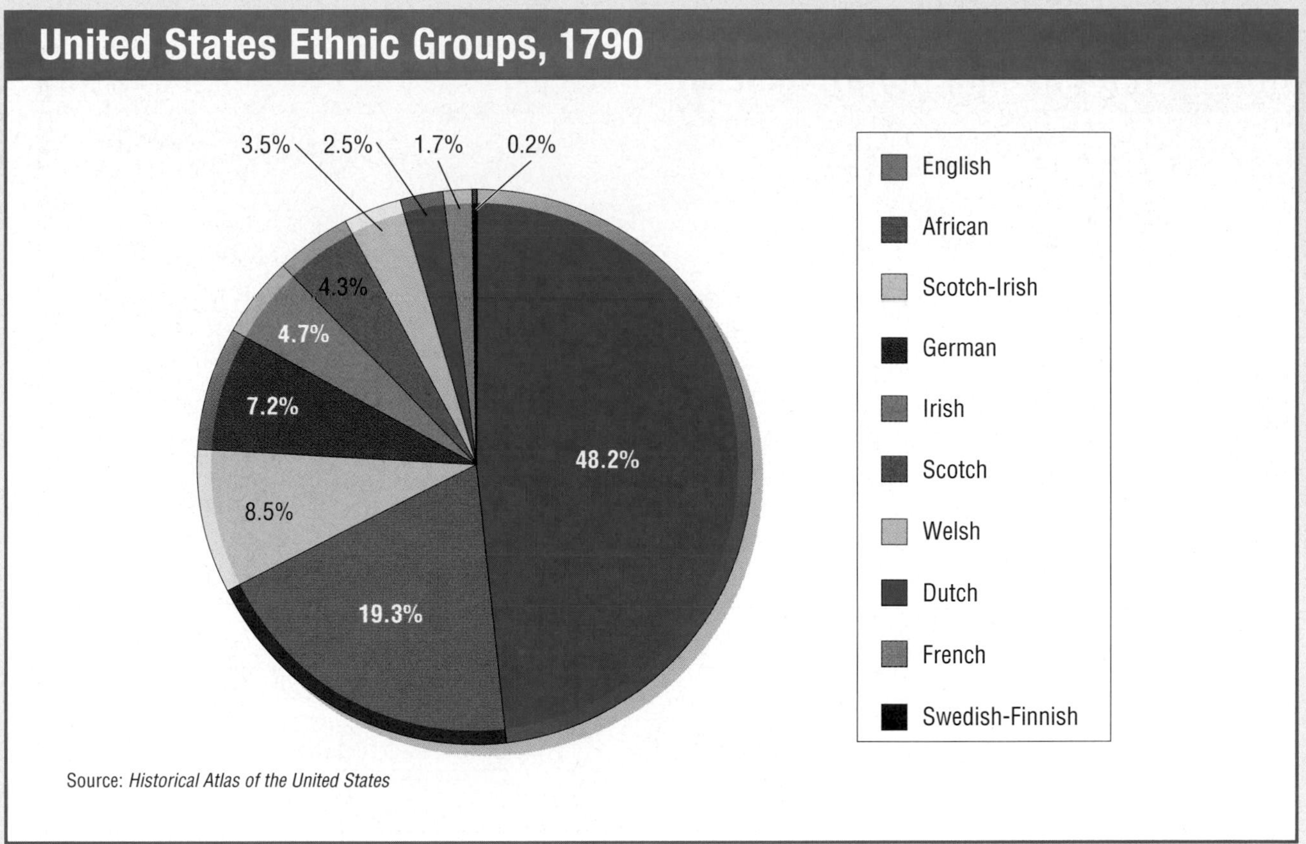


Source: *Historical Atlas of the United States*

## Enslaved Population of the United States, 1790

| *State* | *Total Population* | *Enslaved Population* | *Percent Enslaved* |
|---|---|---|---|
| Connecticut | 237,946 | 2,648 | 1.11 |
| Delaware | 59,096 | 8,837 | 14.95 |
| Georgia | 82,548 | 29,624 | 35.89 |
| Maryland | 319,728 | 103,036 | 32.33 |
| Massachusetts | 475,307 | 0 | 0.00 |
| New Hampshire | 141,885 | 157 | 0.11 |
| New Jersey | 184,139 | 11,423 | 6.20 |
| New York | 340,120 | 21,193 | 6.23 |
| North Carolina | 393,751 | 100,783 | 25.60 |
| Pennsylvania | 434,373 | 3,707 | 0.85 |
| Rhode Island | 68,825 | 958 | 1.39 |
| South Carolina | 249,073 | 107,094 | 43.00 |
| Virginia | 747,600 | 292,627 | 39.14 |

Source: *Historical Statistics of the United States, Colonial Times to 1970*

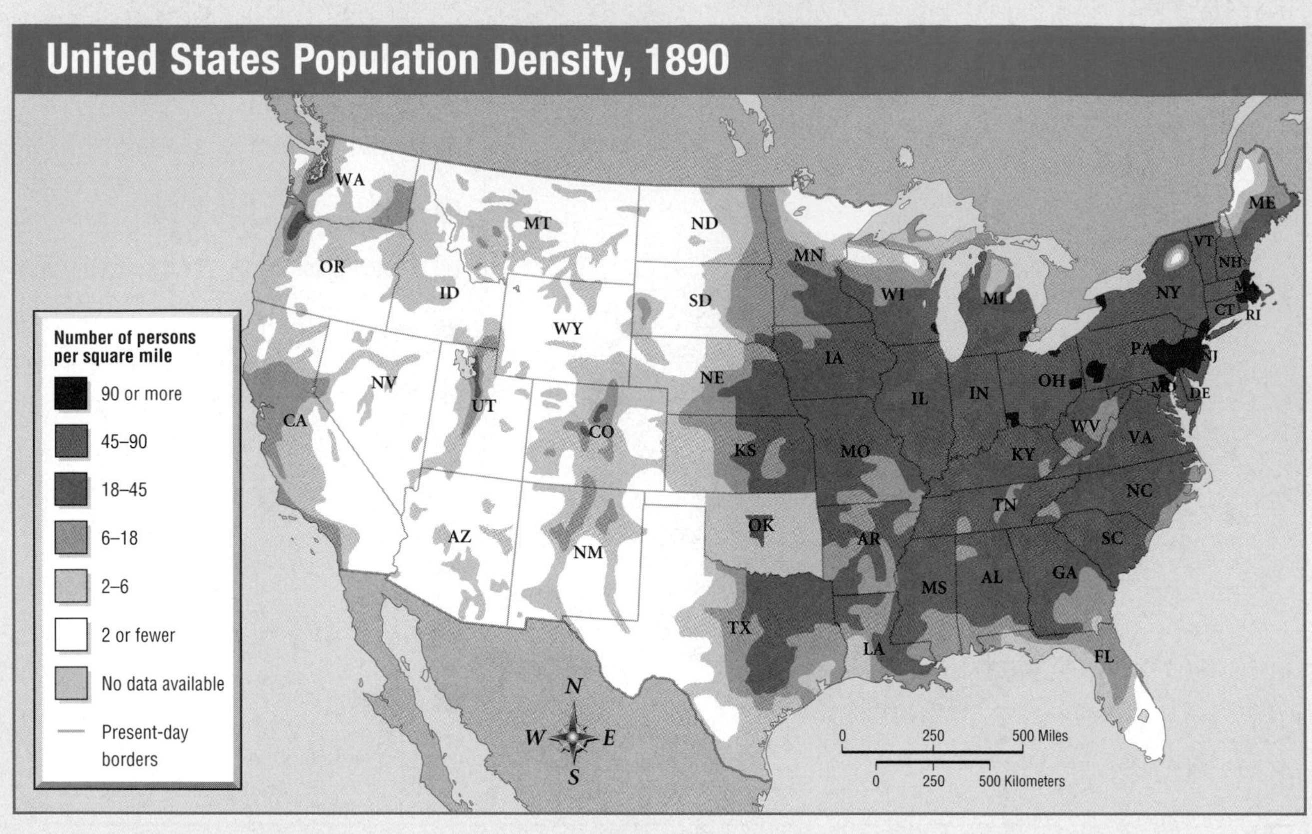
United States Population Density, 1890
Number of persons per square mile
90 or more
45–90
18–45
6–18
2–6
2 or fewer
No data available
Present-day borders
WA
OR
CA
ID
NV
MT
WY
UT
AZ
CO
NM
ND
SD
NE
KS
OK
TX
MN
IA
MO
AR
LA
WI
IL
MS
MI
IN
KY
TN
AL
OH
WV
VA
NC
SC
GA
FL
PA
NY
VT
NH
ME
MA
CT
RI
NJ
DE
MD
N
W
E
S
0
250
500 Miles
0
250
500 Kilometers

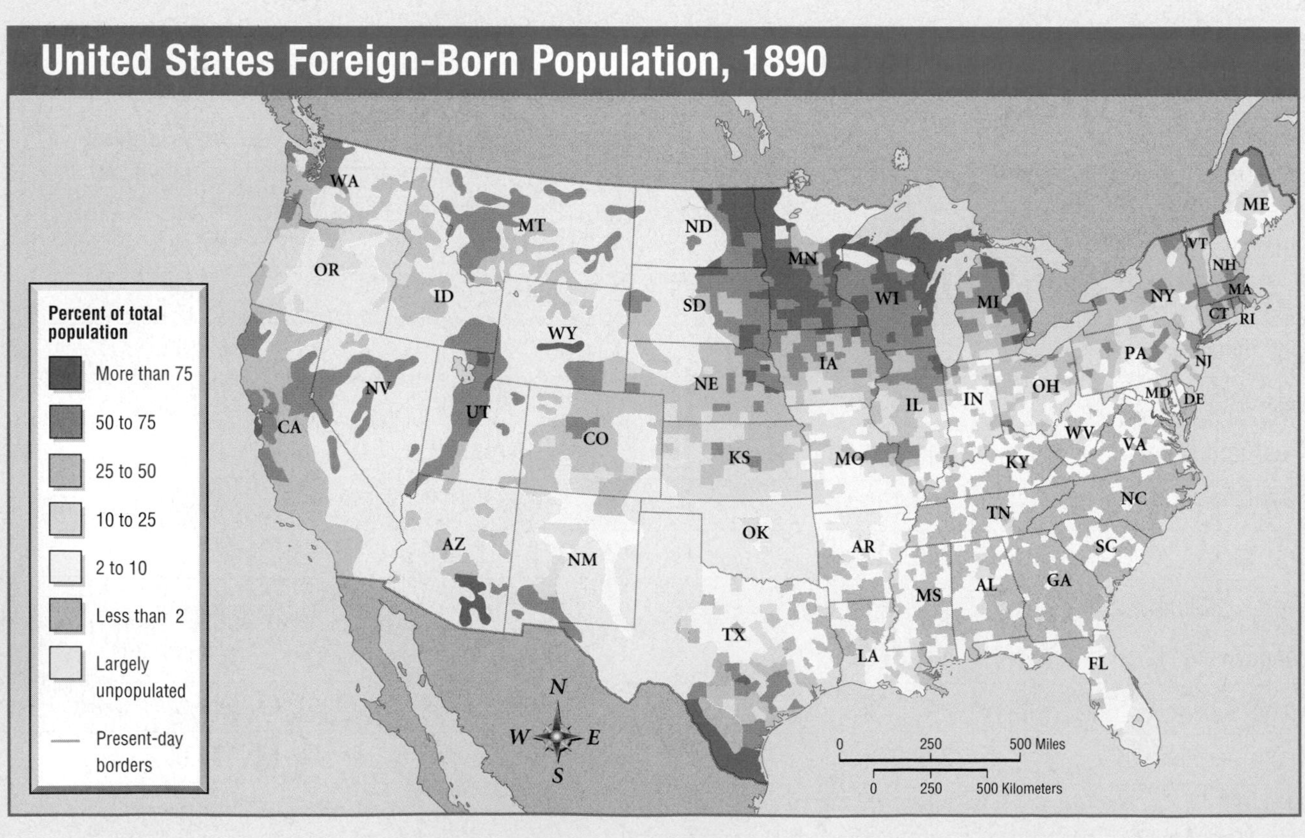
United States Foreign-Born Population, 1890
Percent of total population
More than 75
50 to 75
25 to 50
10 to 25
2 to 10
Less than 2
Largely unpopulated
Present-day borders
WA
OR
CA
ID
NV
MT
WY
UT
AZ
CO
NM
ND
SD
NE
KS
OK
TX
MN
IA
MO
AR
LA
WI
IL
MS
MI
IN
KY
TN
AL
OH
WV
VA
NC
SC
GA
FL
PA
NY
VT
NH
ME
MA
CT
RI
NJ
DE
MD
N
W
E
S
0
250
500 Miles
0
250
500 Kilometers

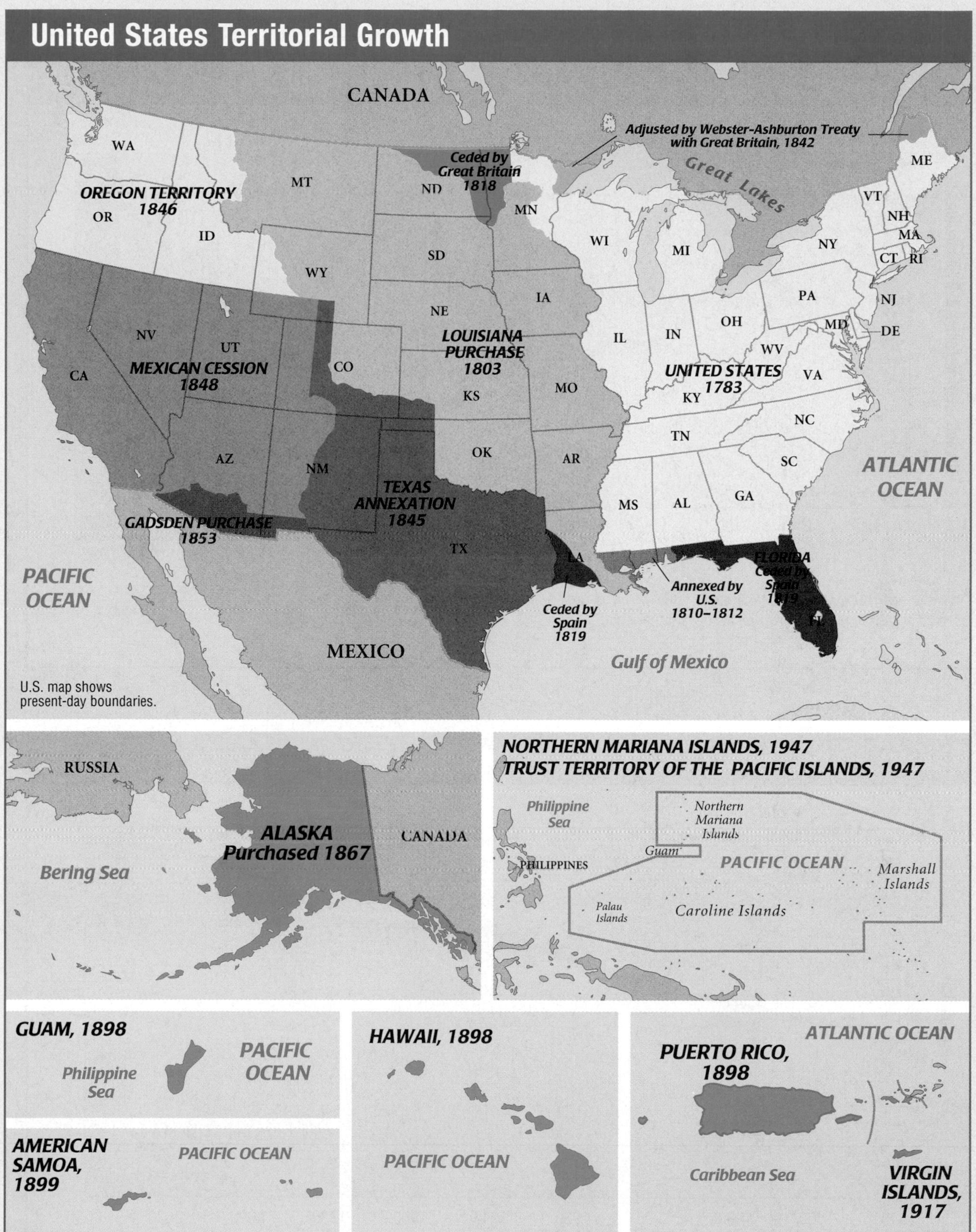


ILLUSTRATED DATA BANK

## United States Birth Rate, 1910–2000

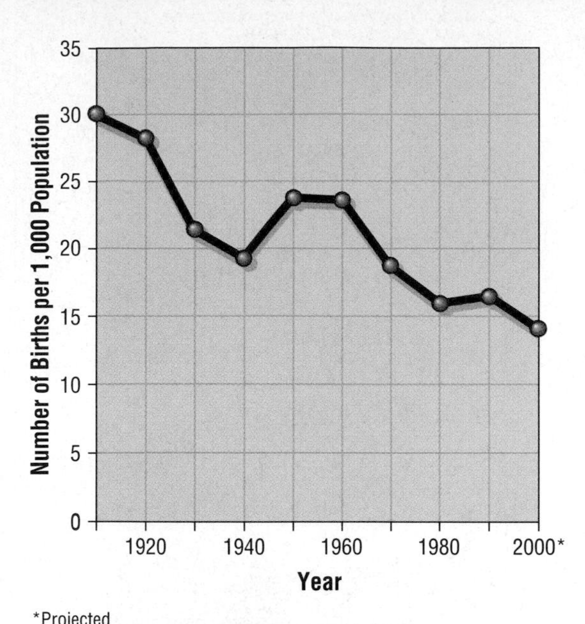


*Projected
Sources: *Historical Statistics of the United States, Colonial Times to 1970; Statistical Abstract of the United States; The Universal Almanac*

## United States Gross Domestic Product, 1960–1999

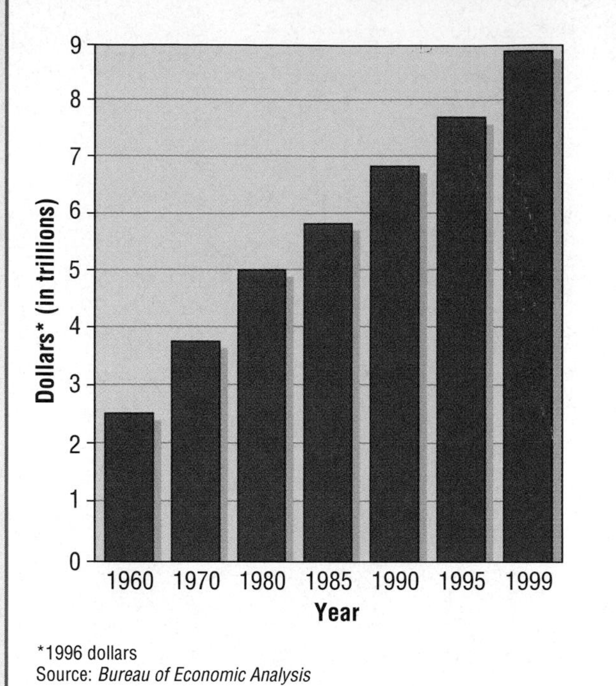


*1996 dollars
Source: *Bureau of Economic Analysis*

## United States Median Age, 1840–2040

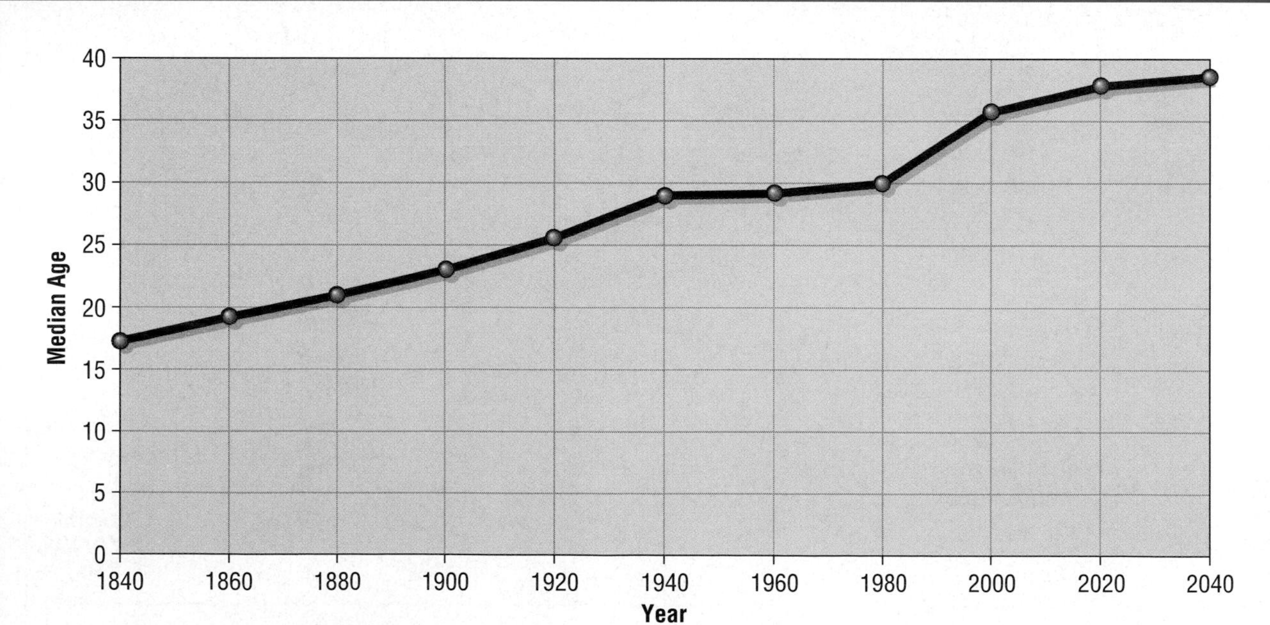


Sources: *Current Population Reports; Historical Statistics of the United States, Colonial Times to 1970; The Universal Almanac; World Almanac*

## United States Population by Race, 1995

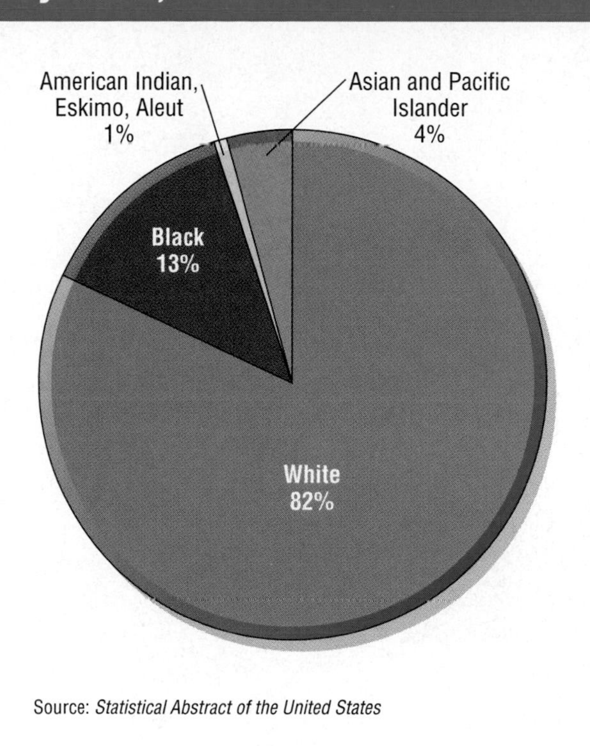


Source: *Statistical Abstract of the United States*

## United States Latino Population, 1990

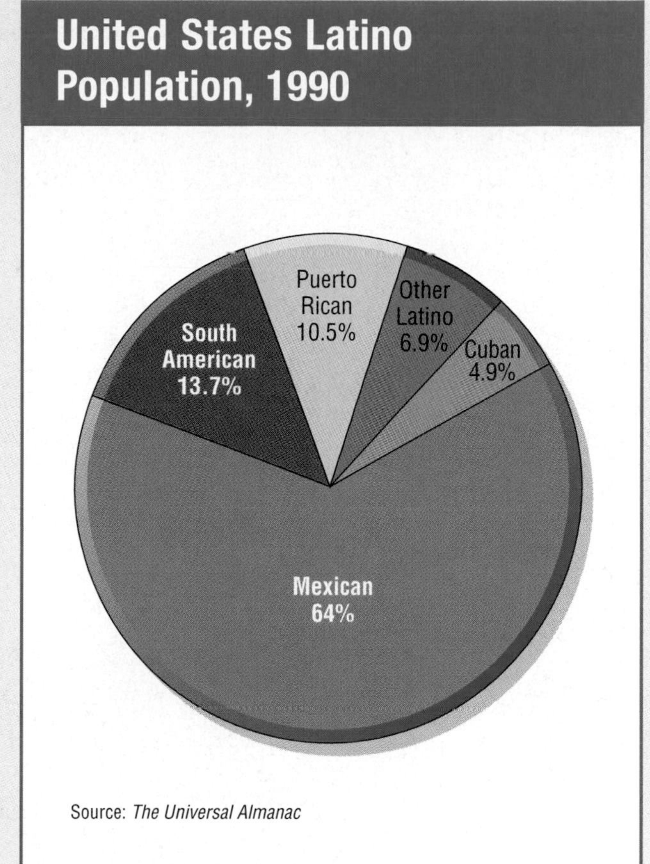


Source: *The Universal Almanac*

## United States Population Density, 1995

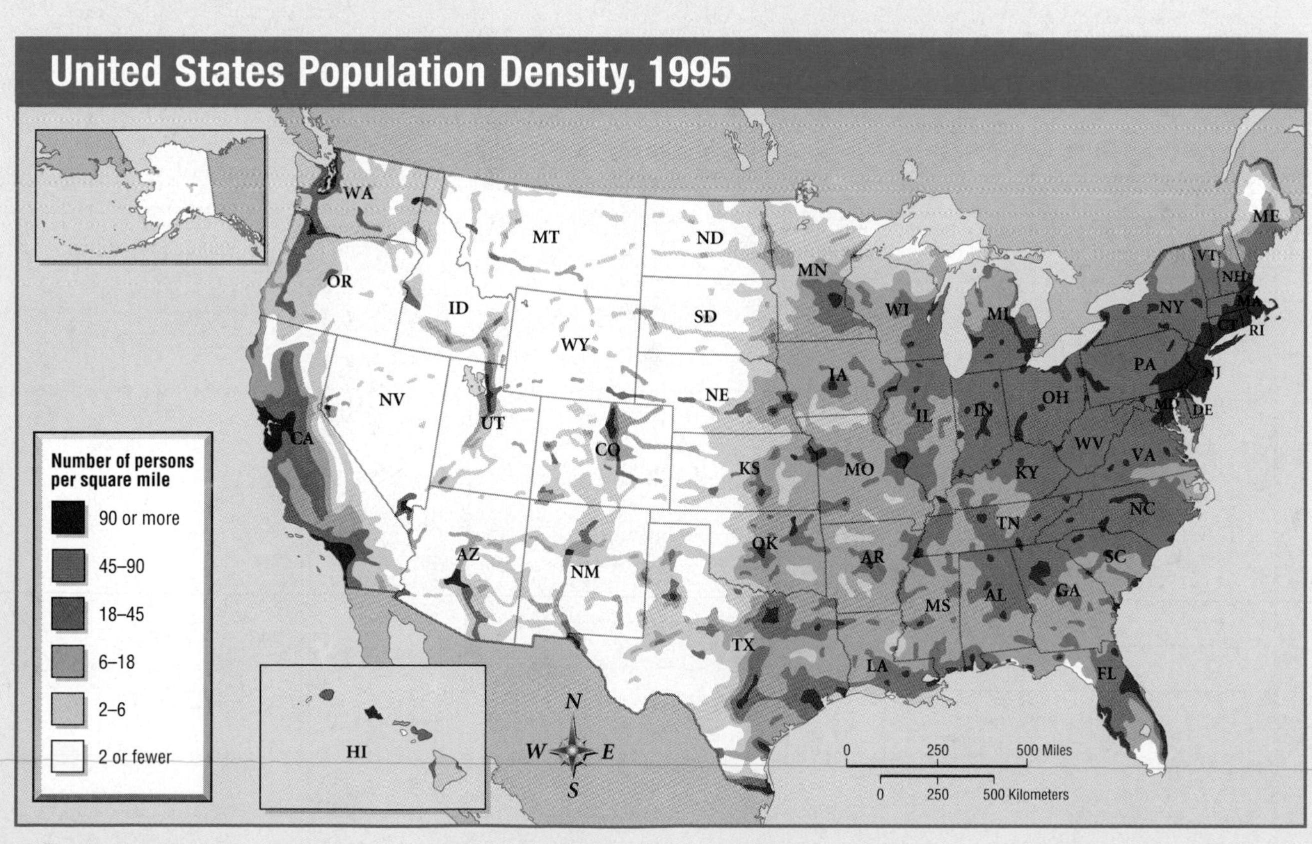

# Political Map of the United States

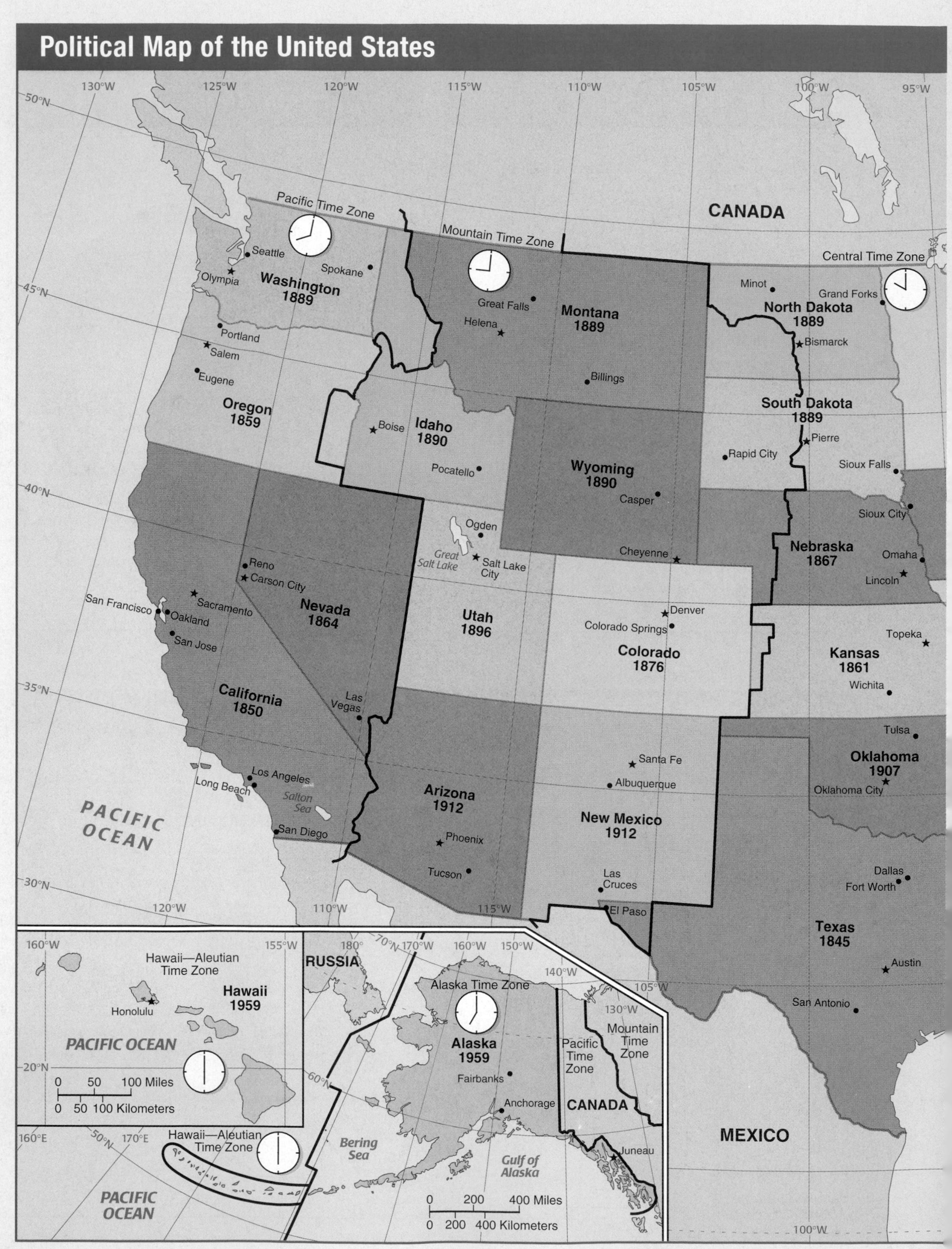

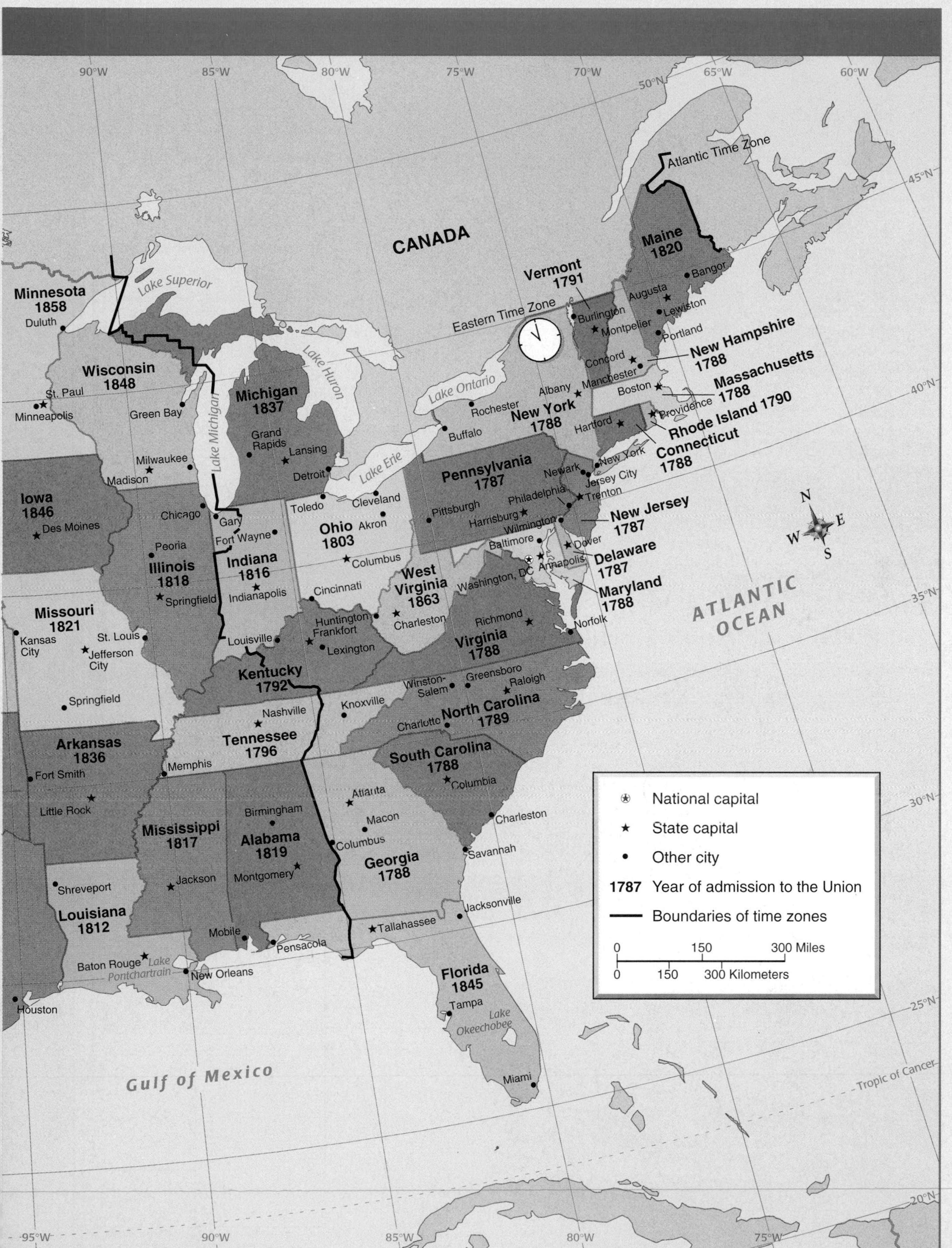

CANADA
Atlantic Time Zone
Eastern Time Zone
Lake Superior
Lake Michigan
Lake Huron
Lake Ontario
Lake Erie
Minnesota
1858
Duluth
St. Paul
Minneapolis
Wisconsin
1848
Green Bay
Milwaukee
Madison
Michigan
1837
Grand Rapids
Lansing
Detroit
Iowa
1846
Des Moines
Illinois
1818
Chicago
Peoria
Springfield
Indiana
1816
Gary
Fort Wayne
Indianapolis
Ohio
1803
Toledo
Cleveland
Akron
Columbus
Cincinnati
Missouri
1821
Kansas City
St. Louis
Jefferson City
Springfield
Kentucky
1792
Louisville
Frankfort
Lexington
West Virginia
1863
Huntington
Charleston
Pennsylvania
1787
Pittsburgh
Harrisburg
Philadelphia
New York
1788
Buffalo
Rochester
Albany
New York
Vermont
1791
Burlington
Montpelier
Maine
1820
Augusta
Bangor
Lewiston
Portland
New Hampshire
1788
Concord
Manchester
Massachusetts
1788
Boston
Rhode Island 1790
Providence
Connecticut
1788
Hartford
New Jersey
1787
Newark
Jersey City
Trenton
Delaware
1787
Wilmington
Dover
Maryland
1788
Baltimore
Annapolis
Washington, DC
Virginia
1788
Richmond
Norfolk
North Carolina
1789
Winston-Salem
Greensboro
Raleigh
Charlotte
Tennessee
1796
Nashville
Knoxville
Memphis
South Carolina
1788
Columbia
Charleston
Georgia
1788
Atlanta
Macon
Columbus
Savannah
Arkansas
1836
Fort Smith
Little Rock
Mississippi
1817
Jackson
Alabama
1819
Birmingham
Montgomery
Mobile
Louisiana
1812
Shreveport
Baton Rouge
Lake Pontchartrain
New Orleans
Houston
Florida
1845
Pensacola
Tallahassee
Jacksonville
Tampa
Lake Okeechobee
Miami
ATLANTIC OCEAN
Gulf of Mexico
Tropic of Cancer
N
E
S
W
90°W
85°W
80°W
75°W
70°W
65°W
60°W
50°N
45°N
40°N
35°N
30°N
25°N
20°N
95°W
90°W
85°W
80°W
75°W
National capital
State capital
Other city
1787 Year of admission to the Union
Boundaries of time zones
0
150
300 Miles
0
150
300 Kilometers

# Physical Map of the United States

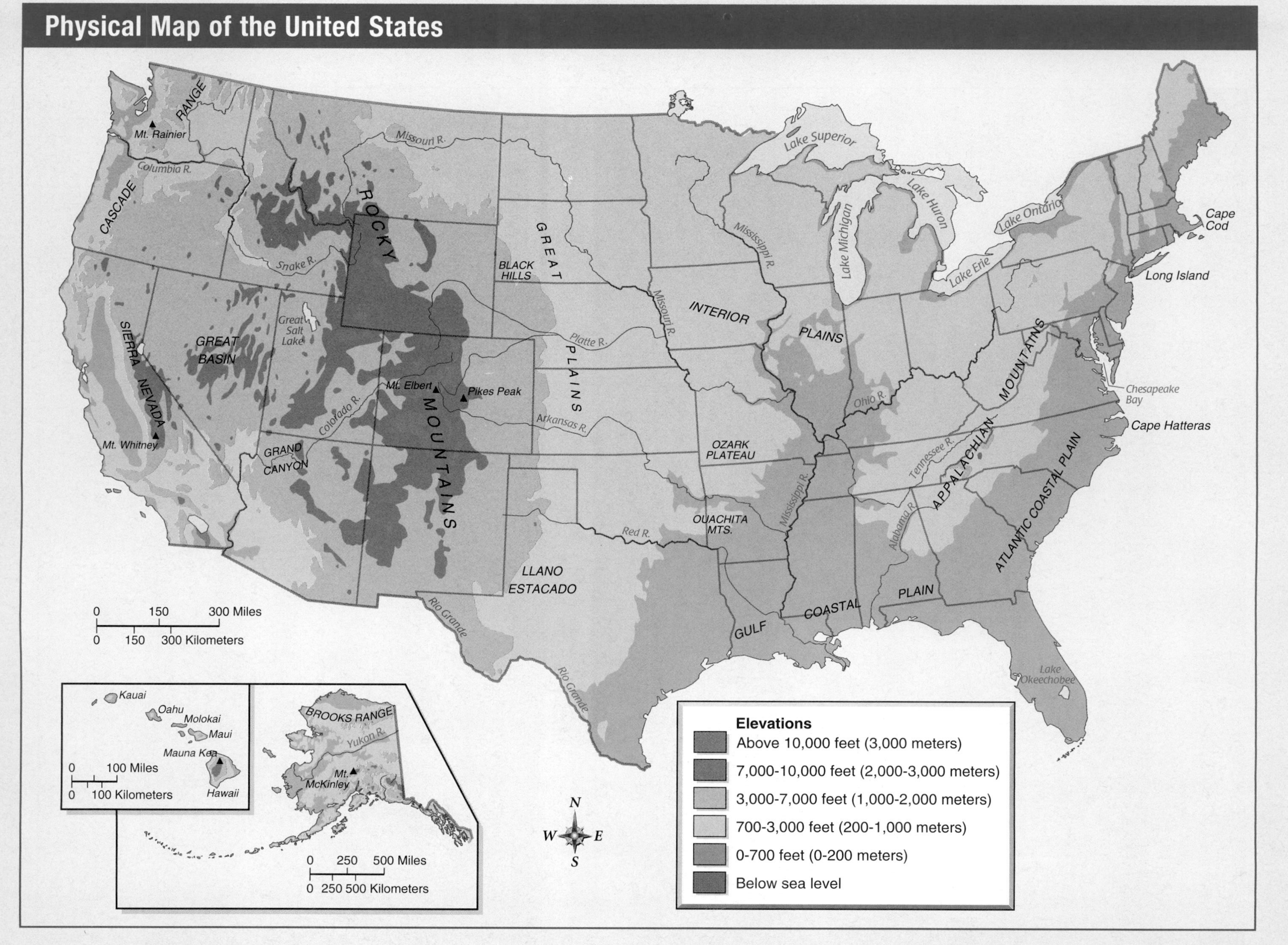

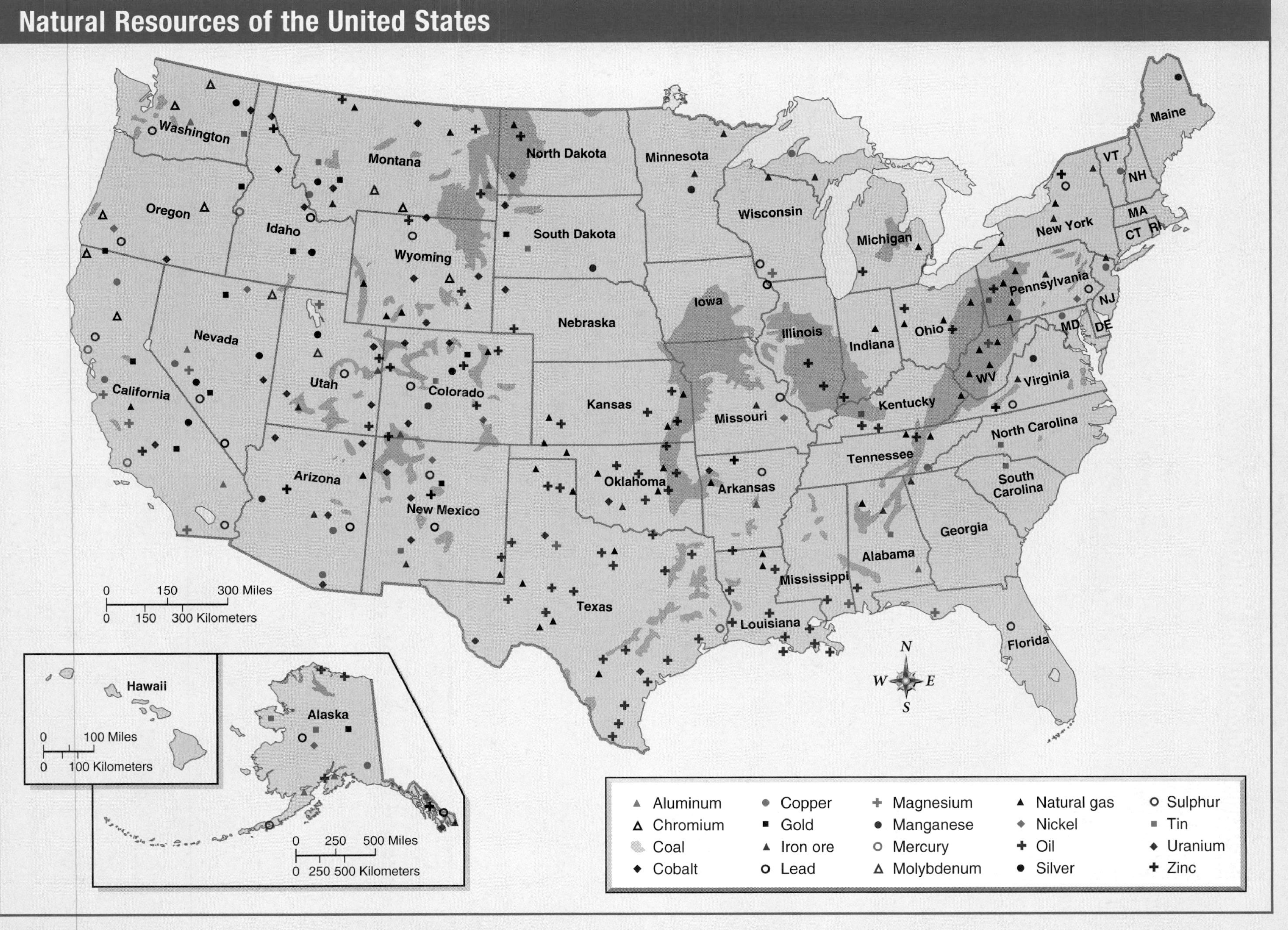

Natural Resources of the United States
Washington
Oregon
California
Nevada
Idaho
Montana
Wyoming
Utah
Arizona
Colorado
New Mexico
North Dakota
South Dakota
Nebraska
Kansas
Oklahoma
Texas
Minnesota
Iowa
Missouri
Arkansas
Louisiana
Wisconsin
Illinois
Michigan
Indiana
Ohio
Kentucky
Tennessee
Mississippi
Alabama
Georgia
Florida
South Carolina
North Carolina
Virginia
WV
Pennsylvania
New York
MD
DE
NJ
CT
RI
MA
VT
NH
Maine
Hawaii
Alaska
0 150 300 Miles
0 150 300 Kilometers
0 100 Miles
0 100 Kilometers
0 250 500 Miles
0 250 500 Kilometers
N
S
E
W
Aluminum
Chromium
Coal
Cobalt
Copper
Gold
Iron ore
Lead
Magnesium
Manganese
Mercury
Molybdenum
Natural gas
Nickel
Oil
Silver
Sulphur
Tin
Uranium
Zinc

# Political Map of the World

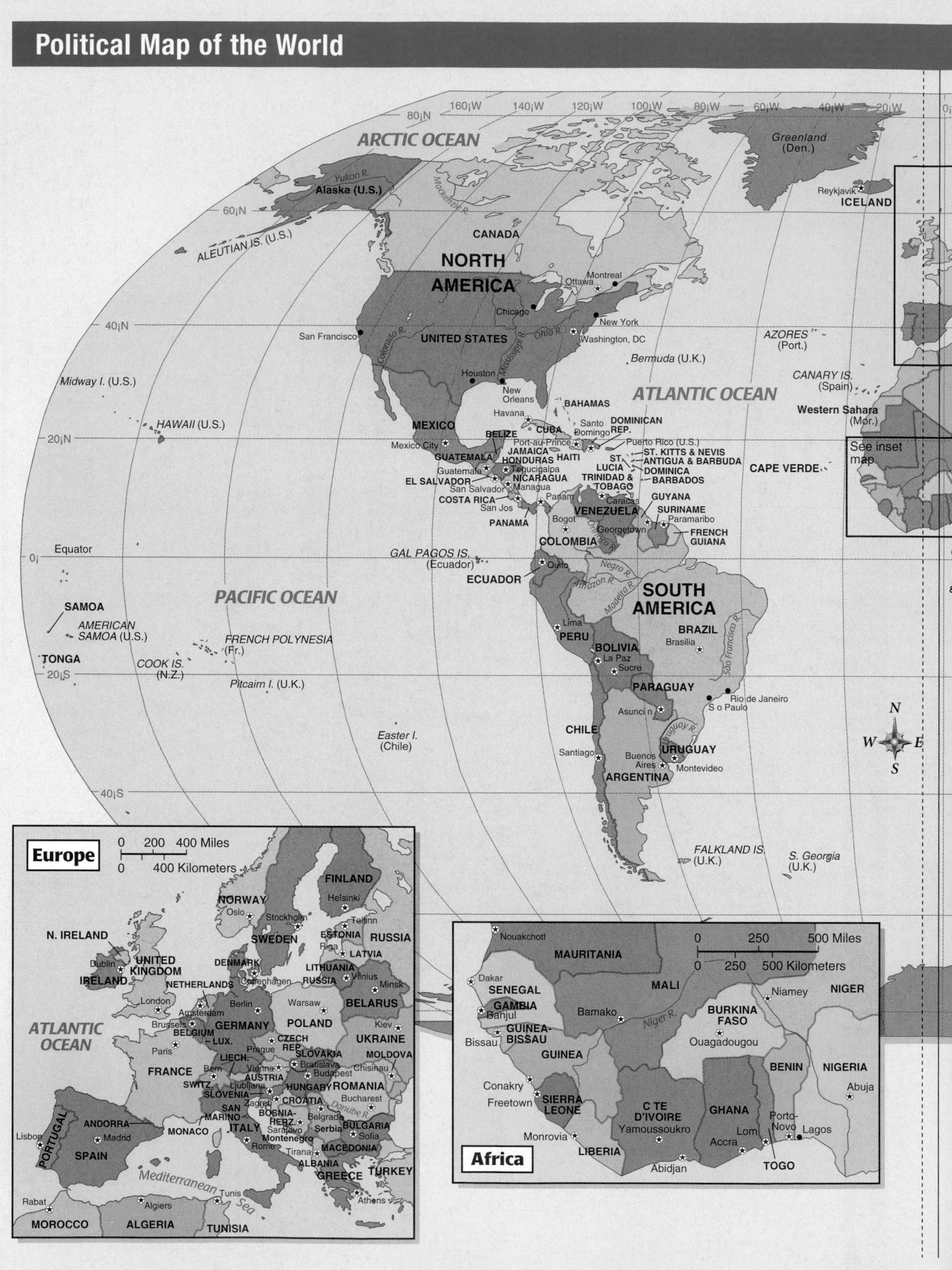

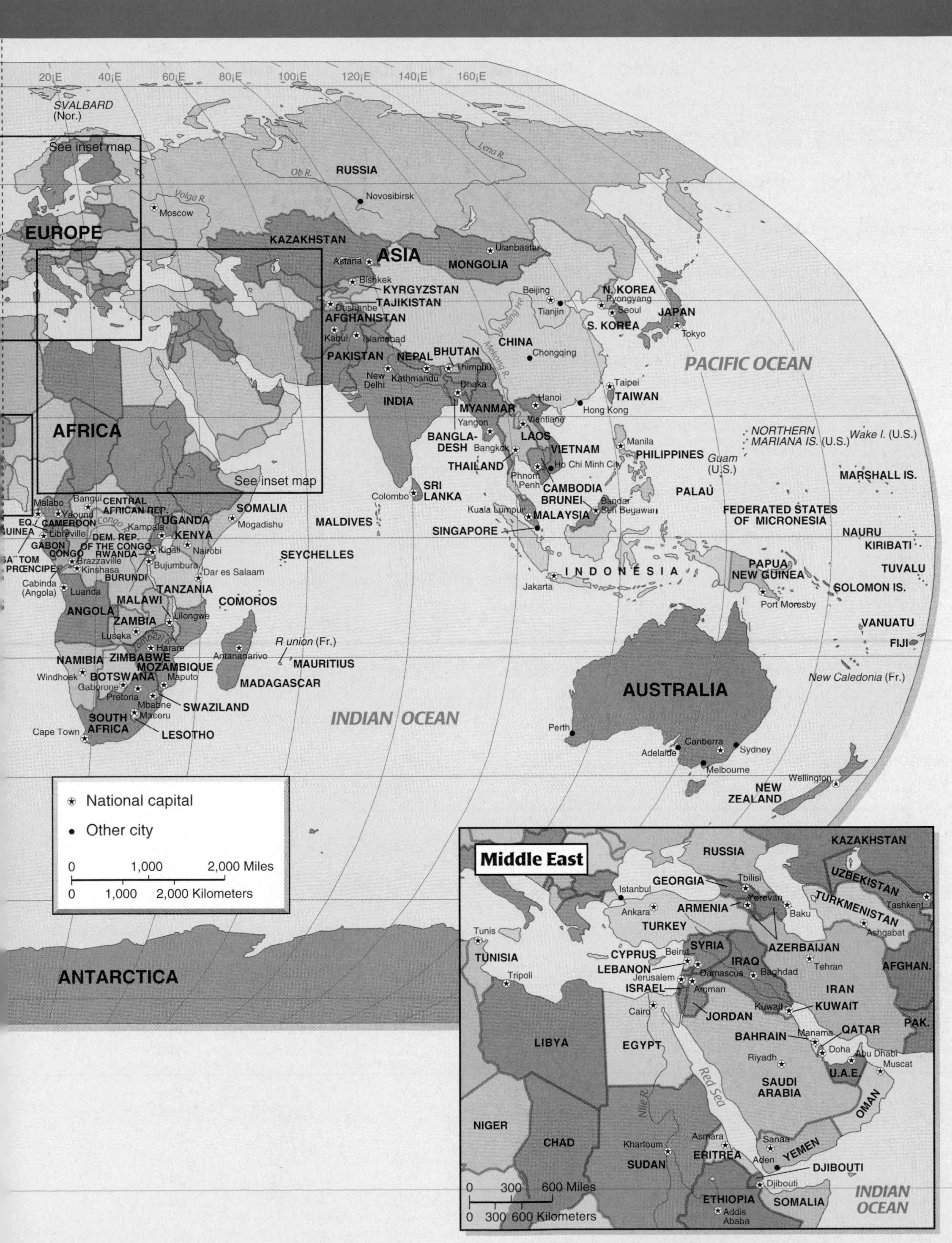
20¡E
40¡E
60¡E
80¡E
100¡E
120¡E
140¡E
160¡E
SVALBARD (Nor.)
See inset map
RUSSIA
Ob R.
Lena R.
Volga R.
Novosibirsk
Moscow
EUROPE
KAZAKHSTAN
Astana
ASIA
Ulanbaatar
MONGOLIA
Bishkek
KYRGYZSTAN
Dushanbe
TAJIKISTAN
AFGHANISTAN
Kabul
Islamabad
PAKISTAN
NEPAL
BHUTAN
Thimphu
New Delhi
Kathmandu
Dhaka
INDIA
Beijing
Tianjin
Huang He
N. KOREA
Pyongyang
Seoul
S. KOREA
JAPAN
Tokyo
CHINA
Chongqing
Mekong R.
PACIFIC OCEAN
Taipei
TAIWAN
Hanoi
Hong Kong
MYANMAR
Yangon
Vientiane
LAOS
BANGLA-DESH
Bangkok
THAILAND
VIETNAM
Manila
PHILIPPINES
Ho Chi Minh City
Phnom Penh
CAMBODIA
BRUNEI
Bandar Seri Begawan
Kuala Lumpur
MALAYSIA
SINGAPORE
NORTHERN MARIANA IS. (U.S.)
Wake I. (U.S.)
Guam (U.S.)
MARSHALL IS.
PALAU
FEDERATED STATES OF MICRONESIA
NAURU
KIRIBATI
PAPUA NEW GUINEA
TUVALU
SOLOMON IS.
Port Moresby
I N D O N E S I A
Jakarta
VANUATU
FIJI
New Caledonia (Fr.)
AFRICA
See inset map
Malabo
Bangui
CENTRAL AFRICAN REP.
Yaoundé
CAMEROON
EQ. GUINEA
Libreville
GABON
SAO TOME PRINCIPE
Congo R.
DEM. REP. OF THE CONGO
CONGO
Brazzaville
Kinshasa
RWANDA
Kigali
BURUNDI
Bujumbura
UGANDA
Kampala
KENYA
Nairobi
SOMALIA
Mogadishu
MALDIVES
SRI LANKA
Colombo
SEYCHELLES
Dar es Salaam
TANZANIA
Cabinda (Angola)
Luanda
ANGOLA
MALAWI
Lilongwe
ZAMBIA
Lusaka
COMOROS
Zambezi R.
Harare
ZIMBABWE
NAMIBIA
Windhoek
BOTSWANA
Gaborone
Pretoria
MOZAMBIQUE
Maputo
Mbabane
SWAZILAND
Maseru
SOUTH AFRICA
LESOTHO
Cape Town
Antananarivo
MADAGASCAR
Réunion (Fr.)
MAURITIUS
INDIAN OCEAN
AUSTRALIA
Perth
Adelaide
Canberra
Sydney
Melbourne
Wellington
NEW ZEALAND
National capital
Other city
0 1,000 2,000 Miles
0 1,000 2,000 Kilometers
ANTARCTICA
Middle East
RUSSIA
KAZAKHSTAN
UZBEKISTAN
Tashkent
TURKMENISTAN
Ashgabat
GEORGIA
Tbilisi
Istanbul
Ankara
ARMENIA
Yerevan
Baku
TURKEY
AZERBAIJAN
Tunis
TUNISIA
Tripoli
SYRIA
CYPRUS
Beirut
LEBANON
Damascus
IRAQ
Baghdad
Tehran
IRAN
AFGHAN.
Jerusalem
ISRAEL
Amman
JORDAN
Cairo
Kuwait
KUWAIT
PAK.
LIBYA
EGYPT
BAHRAIN
Manama
QATAR
Doha
Abu Dhabi
Muscat
Riyadh
U.A.E.
SAUDI ARABIA
Red Sea
Nile R.
OMAN
NIGER
CHAD
Khartoum
SUDAN
Asmara
ERITREA
Sanaa
YEMEN
Aden
DJIBOUTI
Djibouti
ETHIOPIA
Addis Ababa
SOMALIA
INDIAN OCEAN
0 300 600 Miles
0 300 600 Kilometers

## Profile of the Fifty States

| State | Capital | Entered Union | Population (1998) | Population Rank | Land Area (Square Miles) | Land Area Rank |
|---|---|---|---|---|---|---|
| Alabama | Montgomery | 1819 | 4,352,000 | 23rd | 51,705 | 29th |
| Alaska | Juneau | 1959 | 614,000 | 48th | 591,004 | 1st |
| Arizona | Phoenix | 1912 | 4,669,000 | 21st | 114,000 | 6th |
| Arkansas | Little Rock | 1836 | 2,538,000 | 33rd | 53,187 | 27th |
| California | Sacramento | 1850 | 32,667,000 | 1st | 158,706 | 3rd |
| Colorado | Denver | 1876 | 3,971,000 | 24th | 104,091 | 8th |
| Connecticut | Hartford | 1788 | 3,274,000 | 29th | 5,018 | 48th |
| Delaware | Dover | 1787 | 744,000 | 45th | 2,044 | 49th |
| Florida | Tallahassee | 1845 | 14,916,000 | 4th | 58,664 | 22nd |
| Georgia | Atlanta | 1788 | 7,642,000 | 10th | 58,910 | 21st |
| Hawaii | Honolulu | 1959 | 1,193,000 | 41st | 6,470 | 47th |
| Idaho | Boise | 1890 | 1,229,000 | 40th | 83,564 | 13th |
| Illinois | Springfield | 1818 | 12,045,000 | 5th | 56,345 | 24th |
| Indiana | Indianapolis | 1816 | 5,899,000 | 14th | 36,185 | 38th |
| Iowa | Des Moines | 1846 | 2,862,000 | 30th | 56,275 | 25th |
| Kansas | Topeka | 1861 | 2,629,000 | 32nd | 82,277 | 14th |
| Kentucky | Frankfort | 1792 | 3,936,000 | 25th | 40,409 | 37th |
| Louisiana | Baton Rouge | 1812 | 4,369,000 | 22nd | 47,751 | 31st |
| Maine | Augusta | 1820 | 1,244,000 | 39th | 33,265 | 39th |
| Maryland | Annapolis | 1788 | 5,135,000 | 19th | 10,460 | 42nd |
| Massachusetts | Boston | 1788 | 6,147,000 | 13th | 8,284 | 45th |
| Michigan | Lansing | 1837 | 9,817,000 | 8th | 58,527 | 23rd |
| Minnesota | St. Paul | 1858 | 4,725,000 | 20th | 84,402 | 12th |
| Mississippi | Jackson | 1817 | 2,752,000 | 31st | 47,689 | 32nd |
| Missouri | Jefferson City | 1821 | 5,439,000 | 16th | 69,697 | 19th |
| Montana | Helena | 1889 | 880,000 | 44th | 147,046 | 4th |
| Nebraska | Lincoln | 1867 | 1,663,000 | 38th | 77,355 | 15th |
| Nevada | Carson City | 1864 | 1,747,000 | 36th | 110,561 | 7th |
| New Hampshire | Concord | 1788 | 1,185,000 | 42nd | 9,279 | 44th |
| New Jersey | Trenton | 1787 | 8,115,000 | 9th | 7,787 | 46th |
| New Mexico | Santa Fe | 1912 | 1,737,000 | 37th | 121,593 | 5th |
| New York | Albany | 1788 | 18,175,000 | 3rd | 49,108 | 30th |
| North Carolina | Raleigh | 1789 | 7,546,000 | 11th | 52,669 | 28th |
| North Dakota | Bismarck | 1889 | 638,000 | 47th | 70,703 | 17th |
| Ohio | Columbus | 1803 | 11,209,000 | 7th | 41,330 | 35th |
| Oklahoma | Oklahoma City | 1907 | 3,347,000 | 27th | 69,956 | 18th |
| Oregon | Salem | 1859 | 3,282,000 | 28th | 97,073 | 10th |
| Pennsylvania | Harrisburg | 1787 | 12,001,000 | 6th | 45,308 | 33rd |
| Rhode Island | Providence | 1790 | 988,000 | 43rd | 1,212 | 50th |
| South Carolina | Columbia | 1788 | 3,836,000 | 26th | 31,113 | 40th |
| South Dakota | Pierre | 1889 | 738,000 | 46th | 77,116 | 16th |
| Tennessee | Nashville | 1796 | 5,431,000 | 17th | 42,144 | 34th |
| Texas | Austin | 1845 | 19,760,000 | 2nd | 266,807 | 2nd |
| Utah | Salt Lake City | 1896 | 2,100,000 | 34th | 84,899 | 11th |
| Vermont | Montpelier | 1791 | 591,000 | 49th | 9,614 | 43rd |
| Virginia | Richmond | 1788 | 6,791,000 | 12th | 40,767 | 36th |
| Washington | Olympia | 1889 | 5,689,000 | 15th | 68,138 | 20th |
| West Virginia | Charleston | 1863 | 1,811,000 | 35th | 24,231 | 41st |
| Wisconsin | Madison | 1848 | 5,224,000 | 18th | 56,153 | 26th |
| Wyoming | Cheyenne | 1890 | 481,000 | 50th | 97,809 | 9th |

Source: *World Almanac, Statistical Abstract of the United States*

# Presidents of the United States

**George Washington**
***(1732–1799)***

*Years in office:* 1789–1797
No political party
*Elected from:* Virginia
*Vice Pres.:* John Adams

**John Adams**
***(1735–1826)***

*Years in office:* 1797–1801
Federalist
*Elected from:* Massachusetts
*Vice Pres.:* Thomas Jefferson

**Thomas Jefferson**
***(1743–1826)***

*Years in office:* 1801–1809
Democratic Republican
*Elected from:* Virginia
*Vice Pres.:* Aaron Burr, George Clinton

**James Madison**
***(1751–1836)***

*Years in office:* 1809–1817
Democratic Republican
*Elected from:* Virginia
*Vice Pres.:* George Clinton, Elbridge Gerry

**James Monroe**
***(1758–1831)***

*Years in office:* 1817–1825
National Republican
*Elected from:* Virginia
*Vice Pres.:* Daniel Tompkins

**John Quincy Adams**
***(1767–1848)***

*Years in office:* 1825–1829
National Republican
*Elected from:* Massachusetts
*Vice Pres.:* John Calhoun

**Andrew Jackson**
***(1767–1845)***

*Years in office:* 1829–1837
Democrat
*Elected from:* Tennessee
*Vice Pres.:* John Calhoun, Martin Van Buren

**Martin Van Buren**
***(1782–1862)***

*Years in office:* 1837–1841
Democrat
*Elected from:* New York
*Vice Pres.:* Richard Johnson

**William Henry Harrison***
***(1773–1841)***

*Years in office:* 1841
Whig
*Elected from:* Ohio
*Vice Pres.:* John Tyler

**John Tyler**
***(1790–1862)***

*Years in office:* 1841–1845
Whig
*Elected from:* Virginia
*Vice Pres.:* none

**James K. Polk**
***(1795–1849)***

*Years in office:* 1845–1849
Democrat
*Elected from:* Tennessee
*Vice Pres.:* George Dallas

**Zachary Taylor***
***(1784–1850)***

*Years in office:* 1849–1850
Whig
*Elected from:* Louisiana
*Vice Pres.:* Millard FIllmore

**Millard Fillmore**
***(1800–1874)***

*Years in office:* 1850–1853
Whig
*Elected from:* New York
*Vice Pres.:* none

**Franklin Pierce**
***(1804–1869)***

*Years in office:* 1853–1857
Democrat
*Elected from:* New Hampshire
*Vice Pres.:* William King

**James Buchanan**
***(1791–1868)***

*Years in office:* 1857–1861
Democrat
*Elected from:* Pennsylvania
*Vice Pres.:* John Breckinridge

**Abraham Lincoln****
***(1809–1865)***

*Years in office:* 1861–1865
Republican
*Elected from:* Illinois
*Vice Pres.:* Hannibal Hamlin, Andrew Johnson

**Andrew Johnson**
***(1808–1875)***

*Years in office:* 1865–1869
Republican
*Elected from:* Tennessee
*Vice Pres.:* none

**Ulysses S. Grant**
***(1822–1885)***

*Years in office:* 1869–1877
Republican
*Elected from:* Illinois
*Vice Pres.:* Schuyler Colfax, Henry Wilson

19

**Rutherford B. Hayes**
***(1822–1893)***

*Years in office:* 1877–1881
Republican
*Elected from:* Ohio
*Vice Pres.:* William Wheeler

20

**James A. Garfield****
***(1831–1881)***

*Years in office:* 1881
Republican
*Elected from:* Ohio
*Vice Pres.:* Chester A. Arthur

21

**Chester A. Arthur**
***(1830–1886)***

*Years in office:* 1881–1885
Republican
*Elected from:* New York
*Vice Pres.:* none

22

**Grover Cleveland**
***(1837–1908)***

*Years in office:* 1885–1889
Democrat
*Elected from:* New York
*Vice Pres.:* Thomas Hendricks

23

**Benjamin Harrison**
***(1833–1901)***

*Years in office:* 1889–1893
Republican
*Elected from:* Indiana
*Vice Pres.:* Levi Morton

24

**Grover Cleveland**
***(1837–1908)***

*Years in office:* 1893–1897
Democrat
*Elected from:* New York
*Vice Pres.:* Adlai Stevenson

25

**William McKinley****
***(1843–1901)***

*Years in office:* 1897–1901
Republican
*Elected from:* Ohio
*Vice Pres.:* Garret Hobart, Theodore Roosevelt

26

**Theodore Roosevelt**
***(1858–1919)***

*Years in office:* 1901–1909
Republican
*Elected from:* New York
*Vice Pres.:* Charles Fairbanks

27

**William Howard Taft**
***(1857–1930)***

*Years in office:* 1909–1913
Republican
*Elected from:* Ohio
*Vice Pres.:* James Sherman

28

**Woodrow Wilson**
***(1856–1924)***

*Years in office:* 1913–1921
Democrat
*Elected from:* New Jersey
*Vice Pres.:* Thomas Marshall

29

**Warren G. Harding***
***(1865–1923)***

*Years in office:* 1921–1923
Republican
*Elected from:* Ohio
*Vice Pres.:* Calvin Coolidge

30

**Calvin Coolidge**
***(1872–1933)***

*Years in office:* 1923–1929
Republican
*Elected from:* Massachusetts
*Vice Pres.:* Charles Dawes

31

**Herbert C. Hoover**
***(1874–1964)***

*Years in office:* 1929–1933
Republican
*Elected from:* New York
*Vice Pres.:* Charles Curtis

32

**Franklin D. Roosevelt***
***(1882–1945)***

*Years in office:* 1933–1945
Democrat
*Elected from:* New York
*Vice Pres.:* John Garner,
Henry Wallace,
Harry S. Truman

33

**Harry S. Truman**
***(1884–1972)***

*Years in office:* 1945–1953
Democrat
*Elected from:* Missouri
*Vice Pres.:* Alben Barkley

34

**Dwight D. Eisenhower**
***(1890–1969)***

*Years in office:* 1953–1961
Republican
*Elected from:* New York
*Vice Pres.:* Richard M. Nixon

35

**John F. Kennedy****
***(1917–1963)***

*Years in office:* 1961–1963
Democrat
*Elected from:* Massachusetts
*Vice Pres.:*
Lyndon B. Johnson

36

**Lyndon B. Johnson**
***(1908–1973)***

*Years in office:* 1963–1969
Democrat
*Elected from:* Texas
*Vice Pres.:* Hubert Humphrey

37

**Richard M. Nixon*****
***(1913–1994)***

*Years in office:* 1969–1974
Republican
*Elected from:* New York
*Vice Pres.:* Spiro Agnew,
Gerald R. Ford

38

**Gerald R. Ford**
***(1913– )***

*Years in office:* 1974–1977
Republican
*Elected from:* Michigan
*Vice Pres.:*
Nelson Rockefeller

39

**Jimmy Carter**
***(1924– )***

*Years in office:* 1977–1981
Democrat
*Elected from:* Georgia
*Vice Pres.:* Walter F. Mondale

40

**Ronald W. Reagan**
***(1911– )***

*Years in office:* 1981–1989
Republican
*Elected from:* California
*Vice Pres.:* George H.W. Bush

41

**George H.W. Bush**
***(1924– )***

*Years in office:* 1989–1993
Republican
*Elected from:* Texas
*Vice Pres.:* J. Danforth Quayle

42

**William J. Clinton**
***(1946– )***

*Years in office:* 1993–2001
Democrat
*Elected from:* Arkansas
*Vice Pres.:* Albert Gore, Jr.

43

**George W. Bush**
***(1946– )***

*Years in office:* 2001–
Republican
*Elected from:* Texas
*Vice Pres.:* Richard Cheney

* **Died in office**
** **Assassinated**
*** **Resigned**

# Supreme Court Cases

*These pages provide summaries of key Supreme Court rulings over the course of the nation's history. For additional material and links to Supreme Court cases, see* America: Pathways to the Present *companion Web site at* http://www.Pathways.phschool.com

### *Baker* v. *Carr,* 1962

(14th Amendment) Rapid population growth in Nashville and reluctance of the rural-dominated Tennessee legislature to redraw state legislature districts led Mayor Baker of Nashville to ask for federal court help. The federal district court refused to enter the "political thicket" of redistricting, and the case was appealed. The Court directed a trial to be held in a Tennessee federal court. The case led to the 1964 Westberry decision, which created the "one man, one vote" equal representation concept.

### *Bob Jones University* v. *United States,* 1983

(14th and 1st amendments) Bob Jones University, a private school, denied admission to applicants in an interracial marriage or who "espouse" interracial marriage or dating. The Internal Revenue Service then denied tax-exempt status to the school because of racial discrimination. The university appealed, claiming that its policy was based on the Bible. The Court upheld the IRS ruling, stating that "Government has a fundamental overriding interest" in ending race discrimination in education.

### *Brown* v. *Board of Education of Topeka,* 1954

(14th Amendment) Probably no 20th-century Supreme Court decision so deeply stirred and changed life in the United States as *Brown.* A 10-year-old girl from Topeka, Kansas, was not permitted to attend her neighborhood school because she was an African American. The Court found that segregation itself was a violation of the Equal Protection Clause, commenting that "in the field of public education the doctrine of 'separate but equal' has no place. . . . Segregation is a denial of the equal protection of the laws." The decision overturned *Plessy,* 1896.

### *The Civil Rights Cases,* 1883

(14th Amendment) The Civil Rights Acts of 1875 included punishments for businesses that practiced discrimination. The Court ruled on a number of cases involving the Acts in 1883, finding that the Constitution, "while prohibiting discrimination by governments, made no provisions . . . for acts of racial discrimination by private individuals." The decision limited the impact of the Equal Protection Clause, giving tacit approval for segregation in the private sector.

### *Cruzan* v. *Director, Missouri Dept. of Health,* 1990

(9th Amendment, right to die) A Missouri woman was in a coma from an automobile accident in 1983. Her family, facing astronomical medical bills and deciding that "her life had ended in 1987," directed the health care providers to end intravenous feeding. The State of Missouri opposed the family's decision, and the family went to court. The Court ruled that states could require "clear and convincing" evidence that Cruzan would have wanted to die. However, the Court did not require other states to meet the Missouri standard. At a subsequent hearing, "clear and convincing evidence" was presented. The intravenous feeding was ended, and Cruzan died on December 26, 1990.

### *Dennis* v. *United States,* 1951

(1st Amendment) The Smith Act of 1940 made it a crime for any person to work for the violent overthrow of the United States in peacetime or war. Eleven Communist party leaders, including Dennis, had been convicted of violating the Smith Act, and they appealed. The Court upheld the Act. Much modified by later decisions, the Dennis case focused on anti-government speech as an area of controversy.

### *Dred Scott* v. *Sandford,* 1857

(6th Amendment) This decision upheld property rights over human rights by saying that Dred Scott, a slave, could not become a free man just because he had traveled in "free soil" states with his master. A badly divided nation was further fragmented by the decision. "Free soil" federal laws and the Missouri Compromise line of 1820 were held unconstitutional because they deprived a slave owner of the right to his "property" without just compensation. This narrow reading of the Constitution, a landmark case of the Court, was most clearly stated by Chief Justice Roger B. Taney, a states' rights advocate.

### *Engel* v. *Vitale,* 1962

(1st Amendment) The state Board of Regents of New York required the recitation of a 22-word nonsectarian prayer at the beginning of each school day. A group of parents filed suit against the required prayer, claiming it violated their First Amendment rights. The Court ruled New York's action unconstitutional, observing, "There can be no doubt that . . . religious beliefs [are] embodied in the Regents' prayer."

### *Escobedo* v. *Illinois,* 1964

(6th Amendment) A person known to Chicago-area police confessed to a murder but had not been provided with a lawyer while under interrogation. The Court's decision in the case extended the "exclusionary rule" to illegal confessions in state court proceedings. Carefully defining an "Escobedo Rule," the Court said, "where . . . the investigation is no longer a general inquiry . . . but has begun to focus on a particular suspect . . . (and where) the suspect has been taken into custody . . . the suspect has requested . . . his lawyer, and the police have not . . . warned him of his right to remain silent, the accused has been denied . . . counsel in violation of the Sixth Amendment."

### *Everson* v. *Board of Education,* 1947

(1st Amendment) In a case known as "the New Jersey School Bus Case," the Court considered New Jersey's use of public funds to operate school buses that carried some students to parochial schools. The Court permitted New Jersey to continue the payments, saying that the aid to children was not governmental support for religion. The decision, however, strongly stated that the wall separating church and state must be kept "high and impregnable." This was a clear incorporation of 1st Amendment limits of states.

### *Ex Parte Milligan,* 1866

(Article II) An Indiana man was arrested, treated as a prisoner of war, and imprisoned by a military court during the Civil War under presidential order. He claimed that his right to a fair trial was interfered with and that military courts had no authority outside of "conquered territory." The Court ordered him to be released on the grounds that the Constitution "is a law for rulers and people, equally in war and peace" and covers all people "at all times, and under all circumstances." The Court held that presidential powers in time of war did not extend to creating another court system run by the military.

### *Furman* v. *Georgia,* 1972

(8th Amendment) Three death penalty cases, including *Furman,* raised the issue of racial imbalances in the use of death sentences by state courts. Furman had been sentenced to death in Georgia. Overturning state death penalty laws, the Court noted an "apparent arbitrariness of the use of the sentence." Many states rewrote their death penalty statutes, and these were generally upheld in *Gregg,* 1976.

### *Gibbons* v. *Ogden,* 1824

(Article I, Section 8) This case examined the power of Congress to regulate interstate commerce. Ogden's exclusive New York ferry license gave him the right to operate steamboats to and from New York. Ogden claimed that Gibbons's federal license did not give him landing rights in New York City. Federal and state regulation of commerce conflicted. The Court strengthened the power of the United States to regulate interstate business. Federal controls on television, pipelines, and banking are based on *Gibbons.*

### *Gideon* v. *Wainwright,* 1963

(14th Amendment) Gideon was charged with breaking into a poolroom. He could not afford a lawyer, and Florida refused to provide counsel for trials not involving the death penalty. Gideon defended himself poorly and was sentenced to five years in prison. The Court called for a new trial, arguing that the due-process clause of the 14th Amendment applied to the 6th Amendment's guarantee of counsel for all poor persons facing a felony charge. Gideon later was found not guilty with the help of a court-appointed attorney.

### *Gitlow* v. *New York,* 1925

(1st and 14th amendments) For the first time, the Court considered whether the 1st and 14th amendments had influence on state laws. The case, involving "criminal anarchy" under New York law, was the first consideration of what came to be known as the "incorporation" doctrine, under which, it was argued, the provisions of the 1st Amendment were "incorporated" by the 14th Amendment. Although New York law was not overruled in the case, the decision clearly indicated that the Court could make such a ruling. Another important incorporation case is *Powell,* 1932.

## *Gregg* v. *Georgia*, 1976

(8th Amendment) In the 1970s activists tried to get the death penalty reinstated. Several test cases failed when the Court found the sentence had been motivated by racism, issued arbitrarily, or without due process. The case of Gregg, convicted of murdering two men, was considered to be free from such problems. Finding that his conviction and death sentence were fair and consistent with state law, the Court ruled that Georgia's death penalty did not violate the "cruel and unusual punishment" clause of the 8th Amendment. For the first time, the Court clearly affirmed that "punishment of death does not invariably violate the Constitution."

## *Griswold* v. *Connecticut*, 1965

(14th Amendment) A Connecticut law forbade the use of "any drug, medicinal article, or instrument for the purpose of preventing conception." Griswold, director of Planned Parenthood in New Haven, was arrested for counseling married couples. After conviction, he appealed. The Court overturned the Connecticut law, saying that "various guarantees (of the Constitution) create zones of privacy" and asking, " would we allow the police to search the sacred precincts of marital bedrooms . . . ?" The decision is significant for examining the concept of "unenumerated rights" in the 9th Amendment, later central to *Roe*, 1973.

## *Heart of Atlanta Motel, Inc.* v. *United States*, 1964

(Article I, Section 8) The Civil Rights Act of 1964 outlawed race discrimination in "public accommodations," including motels that refused rooms to blacks. Although local desegregation appeared to fall outside federal authority, the government argued that it was regulating interstate commerce. The Court agreed, declaring, "The power of Congress to promote interstate commerce also includes the power to regulate the local incidents thereof, including local activities . . . which have a substantial and harmful effect upon that commerce." Racial segregation of private facilities engaged in interstate commerce was found unconstitutional.

## *In Re Gault*, 1966

(14th Amendment) Before *Gault*, proceedings against juveniles were generally handled as "family law," not "criminal law," and offenders received few due-process rights. Gault was sentenced to six years in state juvenile detention for an alleged obscene phone call. He was not provided counsel and not permitted to confront or cross-examine the key witness. The Court overturned the juvenile proceedings and required that states provide juveniles "some of the due process guarantees of adults," including a right to a phone call, to counsel, to cross-examine, to confront their accuser, and to be advised of their right to silence.

## *Katz* v. *United States*, 1967

(4th Amendment) Arrested for illegal gambling after using a public phone to transmit information about betting, Katz claimed that the wiretapping of the phone, done without a warrant, was a violation of his 4th Amendment rights. The Court expanded the protections of the 4th Amendment, observing that people, not just property, are protected against illegal searches. Whatever a citizen "seeks to preserve as private, even in an area accessible to the public, may be constitutionally protected."

## *Korematsu* v. *United States*, 1944

(5th Amendment) Two months after Japan attacked Pearl Harbor, President Roosevelt ordered the internment of more than 110,000 Japanese Americans living on the West Coast. Although many Japanese Americans were United States citizens, they had to abandon their property and live in primitive camps far from the coast. Korematsu refused to report to an assembly center and was arrested. The Court rejected his appeal, noting that "pressing public necessity [World War II] may sometimes justify the existence of restrictions which curtail the civil rights of a single racial group" but added that "racial antagonism" never can justify such restrictions. The *Korematsu* decision has been widely criticized, particularly since few Americans of German or Italian descent were interned.

## *Lemon* v. *Kurzman*, 1971

(1st Amendment, Establishment Clause) In overturning state laws regarding aid to church-supported schools in this and a similar Rhode Island case, the Court created the Lemon test limiting "excessive government entanglement with religion." The Court noted that any state law about aid to religion must meet three criteria: (1) purpose of the aid must be clearly secular, not religious; (2) its primary effect must neither advance nor inhibit religion; and (3) it must avoid "excessive entanglement of government with religion."

## *Mapp* v. *Ohio*, 1961

(4th and 14th amendments) Before *Mapp*, the admission of evidence gained by illegal searches was permitted by some state constitutions. Cleveland police raided Mapp's home without a warrant and found obscene materials. She appealed her conviction, saying that the 4th and 14th amendments protected her against improper police behavior. The Court agreed, extending "exclusionary rule" protections to citizens in state courts. The Court said that the prohibition against unreasonable searches would be "meaningless" unless evidence gained in such searches was excluded. The case developed the concept of "incorporation" begun in *Gitlow*, 1925.

## *Marbury* v. *Madison*, 1803

(Article III) Chief Justice Marshall established "judicial review" as a power of the Supreme Court. After defeat in the 1800 election, President Adams appointed many Federalists to the federal courts, but the commissions were not delivered. New Secretary of State James Madison refused to deliver them. Marbury sued in the Supreme Court. The Court declared a portion of the Judiciary Act of 1789 unconstitutional, thereby declaring the Court's power to find acts of Congress unconstitutional.

### ***Massachusetts* v. *Sheppard*, 1984**

(4th Amendment) A search in Massachusetts was based on a warrant issued on an improper form. Sheppard argued that the search was illegal and the evidence was inadmissible under *Mapp*, 1961. Massachusetts argued that the police acted in "good faith," believing that the warrant was correct. The Court agreed with Massachusetts, noting that the exclusionary rule should not be applied when the officer conducting the search had acted with the reasonable belief that he was following proper procedures.

### ***McCulloch* v. *Maryland*, 1819**

(Article I, Section 8) Called the "Bank of the United States" case. A Maryland law required federally chartered banks to use only a special paper to print money, which amounted to a tax. McCulloch, the cashier of the Baltimore branch of the bank, refused to use the paper, claiming that states could not tax the federal government. The Court declared the Maryland law unconstitutional, commenting ". . . the power to tax implies the power to destroy."

### ***Miller* v. *California*, 1973**

(1st Amendment) In *Miller*, the Court upheld a stringent application of California obscenity law by Newport Beach, California, and attempted to define what is obscene. The "Miller Rule" included three criteria: (1) That the average person would, applying contemporary community standards, find that the work appealed to the prurient interest; (2) that the work depicts or describes, in an offensive way, sexual conduct defined by state law; and (3) that "the work, taken as a whole, lacks serious literary, artistic, political or scientific value. . . ."

### ***Miranda* v. *Arizona*, 1966**

(5th, 6th, and 14th amendments) Arrested for kidnapping and sexual assault, Miranda signed a confession including a statement that he had "full knowledge" of his legal rights. After conviction, he appealed, claiming that without counsel and without warnings, the confession was illegally obtained. The Court agreed with Miranda that "he must be warned prior to any questioning that he has the right to remain silent, that anything he says can be used against him in a court of law, that he has a right to . . . an attorney and that if he cannot afford an attorney one will be appointed for him. . . ." Although later modified, *Miranda* firmly upheld citizens' rights to fair trial in state courts.

### ***Mueller* v. *Allen*, 1983**

(1st and 14th amendments) Minnesota law allowed taxpayers to deduct the costs of tuition, textbooks, and transportation for children in elementary and secondary schools. Several taxpayers sued to prevent parents with children in religious schools from claiming this deduction, arguing that this would constitute state sponsorship of religion. The Court disagreed, ruling that the deduction was not intended to promote religion and was available to all parents with school-age children. The Court argued that a law must have the advancement of religion as its primary purpose to be found unconstitutional.

### ***New York Times* v. *United States*, 1971**

(1st Amendment) In June 1971 *The New York Times* published the first in a series of secret government documents known as the "Pentagon Papers," which detailed how the United States became involved in the Vietnam War. The Justice Department obtained a court order forbidding the newspaper from printing more documents. *The New York Times* and other newspapers challenged the order. The Court cited the 1st Amendment guarantee of a free press and refused to uphold the ban, noting that the government must prove that publication would harm the nation's security. The decision limited "prior restraint" of the press.

### ***Nix* v. *Williams*, 1984**

(4th Amendment, illegal evidence) A man was convicted of murdering a 10-year-old girl after he led officers to the body. He had been arrested, but not advised of his rights, in a distant city, and in transit, he had conversed with a police officer. Williams agreed that the child should have a proper burial and directed the officer to the body. Later, on appeal, Williams's attorneys argued that the body should not be admitted as evidence because the questioning was illegal. The Court disagreed, observing that search parties were within two and one-half miles of the body. "Evidence otherwise excluded may be admissible when it would have been discovered anyway." The decision was one of several "exceptions to the exclusionary rule" handed down by the Court in the 1980s.

### ***Plessy* v. *Ferguson*, 1896**

(14th Amendment, Equal Protection Clause) A Louisiana law required separate seating for white passengers and black passengers on public railroads. Plessy argued that the policy violated his right to "equal protection of the laws." The Court disagreed, saying that segregation was permissible if facilities were equal. It ruled that the 14th Amendment was "not intended to give Negroes social equality but only political and civil equality. . . ." The Louisiana law was seen as a "reasonable exercise of (state) police power. . . ." This "separate but equal" ruling allowed the segregation of public facilities throughout the South until *Plessy* was overturned by the *Brown* v. *Board of Education* case of 1954.

### *Powell* v. *Alabama,* 1932

(6th Amendment, right to counsel) The case involved the "Scottsboro Boys," seven black men accused of rape. The men were quickly prosecuted without counsel and sentenced to death. The Court overturned the decision, stating that poor people facing the death penalty in state courts must be provided counsel, saying that "there are certain principles of Justice which . . . no [state] may disregard." The case was a step toward incorporating the Bill of Rights into state constitutions.

### *Regents of the University of California* v. *Bakke,* 1978

(14th Amendment) Under an affirmative action program, the medical school of the University of California at Davis reserved 16 of 100 slots in each class for "disadvantaged citizens." When Bakke, who is white, was not accepted by the school, he claimed racial discrimination in violation of the 14th Amendment. The Court ruled narrowly, requiring Bakke's admission but not overturning affirmative action, preferring to review such questions on a case-by-case basis.

### *Roe* v. *Wade,* 1973

(9th Amendment) A Texas woman challenged a state law forbidding the artificial termination of a pregnancy, saying that she "had a fundamental right to privacy." The Court upheld a woman's right to choose, noting that the state's "important and legitimate interest in protecting the potentiality of human life" became "compelling" at the end of the first trimester, but that before then "the attending physician, in consultation with his patient, is free to determine, without regulation by the state, that . . . the patient's pregnancy should be terminated." The decision struck down state regulation of abortion in the first three months of pregnancy and was modified by *Webster,* 1989.

### *Rostker* v. *Goldberg,* 1981

(5th Amendment) In 1980, President Carter reinstated draft registration. For the first time both sexes were ordered to register. When Congress refused to fund the registration of women, several men sued, arguing that a selective draft violated their due process rights. The Court disagreed, noting that "the purpose of registration was to prepare for draft of combat troops" and that "Congress and the Executive have decided that women should not serve in combat."

### *Roth* v. *United States,* 1957

(1st Amendment) A New York man named Roth operated a business that used the mail to invite people to buy materials considered obscene by postal inspectors. The Court, in its first consideration of censorship of obscenity, created the "prevailing community standards" rule, which required a consideration of the work as a whole. In its decision, the Court defined as obscene that which offended "the average person, applying contemporary community standards."

### *Schenck* v. *United States,* 1919

(1st Amendment) Schenck, a member of an antiwar group, had urged men who were drafted into military service in World War I to resist and to avoid induction. He was charged with violating the Espionage Act of 1917, which outlawed active opposition to the war. The Court limited free speech in time of war, stating that Schenck's words presented a "clear and present danger. . . ." Although later decisions modified the decision, the Schenck case created a precedent that 1st Amendment rights were not absolute.

### *School District of Abington Township, Pennsylvania* v. *Schempp,* 1963

(1st Amendment) Some Pennsylvania parents challenged a state law that required Bible readings each day at school. The Court agreed with the parents, saying that the Establishment Clause and Free Exercise Clause forbade states from engaging in religious activity. The Court ruled that if the purpose and effect of a law "is the advancement or inhibition of religion," it "exceeds the scope of legislative power."

### *Sheppard* v. *Maxwell,* 1966

(14th Amendment) Sam Sheppard was convicted of murdering his wife in a trial sensationalized by the national media. Sheppard appealed, claiming that the pretrial publicity had made it impossible to get a fair trial. Rejecting arguments about freedom of the press, the Court overturned the conviction and ordered a new trial. Because of *Sheppard,* judges have issued "gag" orders limiting pretrial publicity.

### *South Dakota* v. *Dole,* 1986

In 1984, Congress voted to withhold five percent of federal highway funds from any state which did not set a minimum drinking age at 21. South Dakota, which would lose money under the new law, challenged the government's right to coerce states to adopt specific policies through funding cuts. The Court ruled that highway funding was not an entitlement, and the national government could impose reasonable conditions upon the states in the interest of the "general welfare." All states that wished to continue to receive full federal highway aid were required to raise the legal age to purchase and consume alcohol to 21 years. In later years, the threat of spending cuts became a powerful tool of federal policy.

### *Tennessee Valley Authority* v. *Hiram G. Hill, Jr., et al.,* 1978

The Tellico Dam was nearly completed—and $100 million had been spent on it—when local residents succeeded in halting construction to save a tiny, nearly extinct fish called the snail darter. The fish's only habitat would have been flooded by the dam. The Court found the injunction against the TVA's completion of the nearly finished dam to be proper to prevent violation of the Endangered Species Act. Congress had declared the value of endangered species "incalculable." The Court refused to overrule Congress's judgment. The ruling affirmed the Environmental Protection Agency's power to protect the environment.

### *Texas* v. *Johnson,* 1989

(1st Amendment) To protest national policies, Johnson doused a United States flag with kerosene and burned it outside the 1984 Republican National Convention in Dallas. He was arrested and convicted under a Texas law prohibiting the desecration of the Texas and United States flags. The Court ruled that the Texas law placed an unconstitutional limit on "freedom of expression," noting that ". . . nothing in our precedents suggests that a state may foster its own view of the flag by prohibiting expressive conduct relating to it."

### *Thompson* v. *Oklahoma,* 1988

(8th Amendment, capital punishment) A 15 year old from Oklahoma was convicted of murder and was sentenced to death at age 16. The Court overturned the death sentence, holding that "[t]he Eighth and Fourteenth Amendments prohibit the execution of a person who was under 16 years of age at the time of his or her offense." A death penalty was deemed cruel and unusual punishment for someone so young.

### *United States* v. *Nixon,* 1974

President Nixon was widely suspected of participating in the coverup of the Watergate break-in. After journalists discovered that he had recorded all of his conversations in the White House, Congress demanded that Nixon hand over the tapes. The President cited executive privilege, arguing that his office placed him above the law. The Court overruled Nixon and ordered him to surrender the tapes. Limiting executive privilege, it ruled that the President's "generalized interest in confidentiality" was subordinate to "the fundamental demands of due process of law in the fair administration of criminal justice." The tapes implicated Nixon in the coverup and led to his resignation.

### *Walz* v. *Tax Commission of the City of New York,* 1970

(1st Amendment, Establishment Clause) State and local governments routinely exempt church property from taxes. Walz claimed that such exemptions were a "support of religion." The Court disagreed, noting that such exemptions constituted a "benevolent neutrality" between government and churches, not a support of religion. Governments must avoid taxing churches, because taxation would give government a "control" over religion prohibited by the "wall of separation of church and state" noted in *Everson,* 1947.

### *Webster* v. *Reproductive Health Services,* 1989

(9th Amendment) A 1986 Missouri law stated that (1) life begins at conception; (2) unborn children have rights; (3) public funds could not be used for abortions not necessary to save the life of the mother; and (4) public funds could not be used for abortion counseling. Health care providers in Missouri filed suit, challenging the law, claiming it was in conflict with *Roe,* 1973, and intruded into "privacy questions." A 5-4 Court upheld the Missouri law, stating that the people of Missouri, through their legislature, could put limits on the use of public funds. The *Webster* decision narrowed the *Roe* decision.

### *Weeks* v. *United States,* 1914

(4th Amendment) A search without proper warrant was conducted in San Francisco, and the evidence collected was used by a postal inspector to prosecute Weeks. Weeks claimed that the evidence was gained by an illegal search, and thus was inadmissible. The Court agreed, applying for the first time an "exclusionary rule" for illegally gained evidence in federal courts. The decision stated ". . . if letters and private documents can thus be seized and used as evidence . . . his right to be secure against such searches . . . is of no value, and . . . might as well be stricken from the Constitution." See also *Mapp* v. *Ohio,* 1961; *Massachusetts* v. *Sheppard,* 1984; and *Nix* v. *Williams,* 1984.

### *West Virginia Board of Education* v. *Barnette,* 1943

The beliefs of Jehovah's Witnesses forbid them to salute the United States flag. In the patriotic climate of World War II, thousands of children who refused to salute were expelled from public schools. The Court ruled that a compulsory flag salute violated the 1st Amendment's exercise of the religion clause and was therefore unconstitutional. "No official, high or petty, can prescribe what shall be orthodox in politics, nationalism, religion, or other matters of opinion."

### *Westside Community Schools* v. *Mergens,* 1990

(1st Amendment, Establishment Clause) A request by Mergens to form a student Christian religious group at school was denied by an Omaha high school principal. Mergens took legal action, claiming that a 1984 federal law required "equal access" for student religious groups. The Court ordered the school to permit the formation of the club, stating, "a high school does not have to permit any extracurricular activities, but when it does, the school is bound by the Act of 1984. Allowing students to meet on campus and discuss religion is constitutional because it does not amount to a 'State sponsorship of a religion.' "

# Glossary

*This Glossary defines all key terms listed in section previews. The page number at the end of each entry indicates the text page on which the term appears in boldface. Other related terms are also included without page numbers. Key people are defined in the Biographical Dictionary.*

### Pronunciation Key

Pronunciations are provided for some of the entries in this Glossary. A syllable printed in SMALL CAPITAL LETTERS receives the greatest stress. The pronunciation key below lists the letters that will help you pronounce the word.

| Symbol | Example | Respelling |
|---|---|---|
| a | hat | (hat) |
| ay | late | (layt) |
| ah | hot | (haht) |
| ai | air | (air) |
| aw | law | (law) |
| eh | met | (meht) |
| ee | eat | (eet) |
| er | learn | (lern) |
| ih | fit | (fiht) |
| ī | mile | (mīl) |
| ir | ear | (ir) |
| oh | no | (noh) |
| oi | boy | (boi) |
| oo | rule | (rool) |
| or | door | (dor) |
| ow | out | (owt) |
| u | book | (buk) |
| uh | fun | (fuhn) |
| yoo | few | (fyoo) |
| ch | reach | (reech) |
| g | go | (goh) |
| j | gently | (JENT lee) |
| k | cup | (kuhp) |
| ks | mix | (mihks) |
| kw | quick | (kwihk) |
| ng | bring | (brihng) |
| s | cent | (sehnt) |
| sh | she | (shee) |
| th | three | (three) |
| y | onion | (UHN yuhn) |
| z | always | (AWL ways) |
| zh | treasure | (TREH zher) |

## A

**abolitionist movement** Movement to end slavery

**abstinence** Refrain from some activity, such as drinking alcoholic beverages

**Adams-Onís Treaty** 1819 treaty between the United States and Spain in which Spain ceded Florida to the United States

**administration** Term of office; also the members and agencies of the executive branch as a whole (p. 42)

**AFDC** Aid to Families with Dependent Children, a public-assistance program commonly referred to as welfare (p. 775)

**affirmative action** Policy which gives special consideration to women and members of minorities to make up for past discrimination (p. 693)

**agenda** List of items to accomplish

**AIDS** Acquired immuno-deficiency syndrome, a virus that killed many people starting in the early 1980s (p. 710)

**Albany Movement** Organization of African Americans formed in Georgia to promote civil rights (p. 572)

**Albany Plan of Union** Proposal by Benjamin Franklin in 1754 for the creation of a grand council made up of representatives from Britain's American colonies

**alien** A noncitizen (p. 215)

**Alien and Sedition Acts** Laws passed by Congress in 1798 that enabled the government to imprison or deport aliens and to prosecute critics of the government

**Alliance for Progress** President Kennedy's proposal for cooperation among nations of the Western Hemisphere to meet the basic needs of their people (p. 556)

**Allies** In World War I, Russia, France, Great Britain, and later the United States; in World War II, the alliance of Great Britain, the United States, the Soviet Union, and other nations (pp. 310, 432)

**almanac** Book containing information such as calendars and weather predictions

**amend** Revise (p. 37)

**American Expeditionary Force (AEF)** Name given to American troops in Europe in World War I (p. 317)

**American Indian Movement (AIM)** Organization formed in 1968 to help Native Americans (p. 602)

**American Liberty League** Organization opposed to the New Deal (p. 412)

**amnesty** General pardon for certain crimes (p. 693)
**anarchist** Radical who violently opposes all government (p. 171)
**annex** Join or attach (pp. 78, 260)
**Antifederalist** An opponent of the Constitution during the debate over ratification; opposed the concept of a strong central government (p. 41)
**anti-Semitism** Hostility or discrimination toward Jews (p. 451)
**apartheid** (uh PAHRT hīt) South Africa's systematic separation of the white and black races (p. 733)
**appeasement** Policy of giving in to someone's demands in order to preserve the peace (p. 431)
**apportionment** Distribution of seats in a legislative body (p. 549)
**apprentice** Person placed under a legal contract to work for another person in exchange for learning a trade
**arbitration** Settlement of a dispute by a person chosen to listen to both sides and come to a decision (p. 263)
**armistice** Cease-fire or truce (p. 320)
**arms race** A contest between nations in which both expand their arms stockpiles in an effort to gain superiority (p. 505)
**arsenal** Place where weapons are made or stored
**Articles of Confederation** Plan of government under which the United States operated from 1781 until its replacement by the Constitution of the United States (p. 37)
**assembly line** Manufacturing process in which each worker does one specialized task in the construction of the final product (p. 349)
**assimilation** Process by which people of one culture merge into and become part of another culture (p. 232)
**Atlantic Charter** Agreement signed by Roosevelt and Churchill in 1941 outlining the two nations' war aims (p. 436)
**autocrat** Ruler with unlimited power (p. 311)
**automation** The use of sophisticated machines in place of human labor (p. 803)
**autonomy** Self-government with respect to local matters (p. 602)
**Axis Powers** In World War II, the alliance of Germany, Italy, and Japan (p. 430)

# B

**baby boom** Dramatic increase in birthrate during and after World War II (p. 514)
**Bacon's Rebellion** Revolt in 1676 by Virginia colonists against the royal governor
**balance of trade** Difference in value between imports and exports (p. 23)
**banana republic** Term used to describe a Central American nation dominated by United States business interests (p. 261)
**bank note** Piece of paper that a bank issues to its customers and that can be exchanged for gold or silver coin
**barrio** Spanish-speaking neighborhood (p. 355)
**barter** To trade goods or services without money
**Bataan Death March** Brutal march of American and Filipino prisoners by Japanese soldiers in 1942 (p. 445)
**Battle of the Alamo** Capture by Mexican troops of a Texas-held mission in San Antonio in 1836
**Battle of Antietam** Civil War battle in 1862 in Maryland (p. 94)
**Battle of the Bulge** World War II battle in which German forces launched a final counterattack in the west (p. 442)
**Battle of Bunker Hill** Revolutionary War battle in 1775 north of Boston
**Battle of Chancellorsville** Civil War battle in 1863 in Virginia, won by the Confederacy (p. 107)
**Battle of Cold Harbor** Civil War battle in 1864 in Virginia (p. 114)
**Battle of the Coral Sea** World War II battle in 1942 between American and Japanese aircraft (p. 445)
**Battle of Fredericksburg** Civil War battle in 1862 in Virginia, won by the Confederacy (p. 106)
**Battle of Gettysburg** Civil War battle in 1863 in Pennsylvania, won by the Union and a turning point in the war (p. 108)
**Battle of Guadalcanal** (gwahd uhl cuh NAL) World War II battle in 1942–1943 between the United States and Japan (p. 446)
**Battle of Iwo Jima** World War II battle in 1945 between the United States and Japan (p. 447)
**Battle of Little Bighorn** Sioux victory in 1876 over army troops under George Custer (p. 182)
**Battle of Midway** World War II battle in 1942 between the United States and Japan, a turning point in the war in the Pacific (p. 445)
**Battle of New Orleans** Battle in 1815 between American and British troops for control of New Orleans, ending in an American victory
**Battle of Okinawa** World War II battle in 1945 between the United States and Japan (p. 447)
**Battle of Saratoga** Revolutionary War battle in 1777 in New York, a turning point in the war
**Battle of Shiloh** Civil War battle in 1862 in Tennessee (p. 91)
**Battle of Spotsylvania** Civil War battle in 1864 in Virginia (p. 114)
**Battle of Stalingrad** World War II battle in the Soviet Union that marked a turning point in the war in the east (p. 440)
**Battle of Tippecanoe** Battle in the Indiana Territory in 1811 between American and Native American forces that led to the defeat of the Native Americans

**counterculture** Group of young Americans in the 1960s who rejected conventional customs (p. 631)
**Crusades** Series of military campaigns by European Christians from 1096 to 1291 to win the Holy Land from the Muslims
**Cuban Missile Crisis** 1962 crisis that arose between the United States and the Soviet Union over a Soviet attempt to deploy nuclear missiles in Cuba (p. 554)
**Cumberland Road** A federally built road that began in Cumberland, Maryland, in 1811 and was extended westward to Ohio and beyond

# D

***Dartmouth College* v. *Woodward*** 1819 case in which the Supreme Court ruled that states could not interfere with contracts
**Dawes Act** 1887 law that divided Native American land into private family plots (p. 182)
**daylight saving time** Turning clocks ahead one hour for the summer (p. 323)
**D-Day** Code name for the Allied invasion of France on June 6, 1944 (p. 442)
**death camp** In World War II, a German camp created solely for mass murder (p. 453)
**Declaration of Independence** 1776 statement, issued by the Second Continental Congress, explaining why the colonies wanted independence from Britain (p. 30)
**de facto segregation** Segregation based not on law but on poverty and ghetto conditions (p. 583)
**deferment** Official postponement of a person's call to serve in the armed forces (p. 628)
**deficit spending** Government spending of borrowed money (p. 463)
**deflation** Drop in the prices of goods (p. 191)
**de jure segregation** Segregation based on law (p. 583)
**demagogue** (DEHM uh gawg) A leader who manipulates people through such means as half-truths and scare tactics (p. 412)
**demographics** Statistics that describe a population, such as data on race or income (p. 354)
**department store** Store that carries a variety of goods and sells in large quantities (p. 248)
**depression** A severe economic downturn marked by a decrease in business activity, widespread unemployment, and falling prices and wages (p. 73)
**deregulation** Reduction or removal of government controls (p. 690)
**détente** A relaxation in political tensions between nations (p. 660)
**direct primary** Election in which voters cast ballots to select nominees for upcoming elections (p. 292)
**disarmament** Program in which nations voluntarily give up their weapons (p. 344)
**discrimination** Unequal treatment of a group of people because of their nationality, race, sex, or religion
**dissident** Person who criticizes the actions of his or her government (p. 686)
**diversity** Variety (p. 24)
**division of labor** Way of producing in which different tasks are performed by different persons (p. 165)
**dollar diplomacy** President Taft's policy of encouraging American investment abroad (p. 275)
**domestic affairs** Issues relating to a country's internal affairs
**domino theory** Belief that if one country fell to communism, neighboring countries would likewise fall (p. 503)
**"Double V" campaign** An effort, launched by an African American newspaper, for victory against the Axis powers and victory in winning racial equality at home (p. 477)
**Dow Jones Industrial Average** Measure of average stock prices of major industries (p. 379)
**downsizing** Practice by companies of laying off workers in order to cut costs (p. 718)
**draft** Program of required military service (p. 95)
**dry farming** Techniques used to raise crops in areas that receive little rain (p. 184)
**Dust Bowl** A region in the Great Plains that had a period of drought and dust storms during the 1930s (p. 384)
**duty** A tax on imports

# E

**economic sanctions** Trade restrictions and other economic measures intended to punish another nation (p. 733)
**economies of scale** Phenomenon that as production increases, the cost of each item produced is often lower (p. 161)
**Electoral College** Group of electors, chosen by the voters, who vote for President (p. 40)
**e-mail** Electronic mail transmitted via computer networks (p. 800)
**emancipation** Freeing of enslaved people
**Emancipation Proclamation** Presidential decree, effective January 1, 1863, that freed slaves in Confederate-held territory (p. 99)
**embargo** Restriction on trade (pp. 72, 655)
**emigrate** To move out of one country or region to settle in another
**Enlightenment** 18th-century movement that emphasized science and reason as key to improving society
**entitlement** Government program that guarantees payments to a particular group, such as the elderly (pp. 712, 775)
**Environmental Protection Agency (EPA)** Government organization formed in 1970 to deal with issues such as air and water pollution (p. 608)
**Equal Rights Amendment (ERA)** Proposed constitu-

tional amendment, never ratified, to prohibit discrimination on account of sex (p. 593)

**Erie Canal** Canal in New York State, completed in 1825, that linked the Hudson River with Lake Erie

**escalation** Expansion by stages, as from a limited or local conflict into a general, especially nuclear, war (p. 620)

**evangelical** (ee van JEHL ih cuhl) Focusing on emotionally powerful preaching, rather than formal ceremonies, and on the teachings of the Bible

**executive branch** Branch of government that enforces the laws

**Exoduster** An African American who migrated to the West following the Civil War (p. 179)

# F

**faction** Group organized around a common interest and concerned only with furthering that interest

**fascism** Political philosophy that places the importance of the nation over that of the individual (p. 429)

**federal** Of or formed by a compact of a union of states that agree to divide power with a central government

**Federal Reserve system** Nation's central banking system, established in 1913 (p. 299)

**Federalist** Supporter of the Constitution during the debate over its ratification; favored a strong central government (p. 41)

**federal deficit** The sum of money lost when federal government expenditures exceed revenues (p. 776)

**feminism** Theory favoring the political, economic, and social equality of men and women (p. 589)

**feudalism** Political and economic system in medieval Europe, in which lesser lords received lands from powerful nobles in exchange for service

**Fifteenth Amendment** Constitutional amendment, ratified in 1870, that guaranteed African Americans voting rights (p. 135)

**filibuster** Tactic in which senators take the floor, begin talking, and refuse to stop talking to permit a vote on a measure (p. 316)

**First Battle of Bull Run** First battle of the Civil War, won by the Confederates in July 1861 (p. 88)

**First Continental Congress** Assembly of representatives from the colonies that first met in Philadelphia in September 1774 (p. 29)

**flapper** Term coined during the 1920s to describe a young woman with a fondness for dancing and brash actions (p. 353)

**food stamp** Federal coupon given to qualifying low-income persons for use in purchasing food (p. 778)

**Fort Sumter** Federal fort in the harbor of Charleston, South Carolina; the Confederate attack on the fort marked the start of the Civil War

**Fourteen Points** President Wilson's proposal in 1918 for a postwar European peace (p. 328)

**Fourteenth Amendment** Constitutional amendment, ratified in 1868, that guaranteed citizens equal protection of the laws (p. 132)

**franchise** Right to open a restaurant using a parent company's brand name and system (p. 512)

**Freedom Rides** Civil rights protest in which a racially mixed group of protesters challenged racially segregated bus terminals (p. 571)

**free enterprise system** Economic system in which companies compete for profits

**free soiler** Person dedicated to preventing the expansion of slavery into the western territories

**French and Indian War** War from 1754 to 1763 between France, with allied Indian nations, and Britain and its colonists, for control of eastern North America (p. 27)

**Fugitive Slave Act** Part of the Compromise of 1850, a law ordering all citizens of the United States to assist in the return of slaves

**fundamentalism** Set of religious beliefs including traditional Christian ideas about Jesus Christ, the belief that the Bible was inspired by God and does not contain contradictions or errors, and the belief that the Bible is literally true (p. 368)

# G

**Gadsden Purchase** 1853 purchase by the United States of southwestern lands from Mexico

**gag rule** Rule passed by the House in 1836 prohibiting antislavery petitions from being read or acted upon

**General Agreement on Tariffs and Trade (GATT)** International agreement on reducing tariffs and expanding world trade (p. 737)

**Geneva Conference** An international conference in 1954 in which Vietnam was divided into two nations (p. 617)

**genocide** Deliberate murder of an entire people (p. 321)

**Gentleman's Agreement** 1907 agreement between the United States and Japan that restricted Japanese immigration (p. 215)

**gentry** In colonial America, men and women wealthy enough to hire others to work for them

**Gettysburg Address** A famous speech by President Lincoln on the meaning of the Civil War, given in November 1863 at the dedication of a national cemetery on the site of the Battle of Gettysburg (p. 112)

**ghetto** Area in which one ethnic or racial group dominates (p. 219)

**ghost town** Town that has been abandoned due to lack of economic activity

**GI** Term used for American soldiers in World War II, derived from "Government Issue" (p. 436)

***Gibbons* v. *Ogden*** 1824 case in which the Supreme Court ruled that states could not regulate commerce on interstate waterways

**GI Bill** Law passed in 1944 that helped returning veterans buy homes and pay for college (p. 514)

**Gilded Age** Term used to describe the period from 1877 to 1900 (p. 205)

**globalization** Trend toward word-wide organization, such as in the manufacture and sale of goods (p. 800)

**Good Neighbor Policy** President Franklin D. Roosevelt's policy to promote good relations with Latin American nations (p.787)

**graft** Use of one's job to gain profit (p. 221)

**grandfather clause** Passage that exempts a group of people from obeying a law if they met certain conditions before the law was passed (p. 242)

**Grange, the** Organization formed to help farmers cooperate economically and politically; also known as the Patrons of Husbandry (p. 192)

**Great Awakening** Religious revival in the American colonies during the 1730s and 1740s

**Great Compromise** Compromise at the Constitutional Convention calling for a two-house legislature, with one house elected on the basis of population and the other representing each state equally

**Great Crash** Collapse of the American stock market in 1929 (p. 380)

**Great Depression** Severe economic decline that lasted from 1929 until about 1939 (p. 380)

**Great Migration** Migration of English settlers to the Massachusetts Bay Colony beginning in the 1630s

**Great Plains** Vast grassland that lies between the Mississippi River and the Rocky Mountains

**Great Society** President Lyndon Johnson's proposals to aid public education, provide medical care for the elderly, and eliminate poverty (p. 547)

**Great White Fleet** A force of United States Navy ships that undertook a world cruise in 1907 (p. 280)

**greenbacks** Name given the national paper currency created in 1862 (p. 97)

**green card** Permit granting an alien permission to reside and work in the United States (p. 1009)

**Gross National Product** Total annual value of goods and services that a country produces (p. 380)

**guerrilla** (guh RIHL uh) A soldier who uses hit-and-run tactics (p. 117)

**Gulf of Tonkin Resolution** 1964 congressional resolution authorizing President Johnson to take military action in Vietnam (p. 620)

# H

**Harlem Renaissance** African American literary awakening of the 1920s, centered in Harlem (p. 363)

**Hawley-Smoot Tariff** An especially high import tariff passed by Congress in 1930 (p. 394)

**Haymarket Riot** 1886 labor-related violence in Chicago (p. 171)

**Helms-Burton Act** 1996 act that penalizes foreign companies that do business with Cuba (p. 786)

**Helsinki Accords** Series of agreements on European security made in 1975 (p. 679)

**hidalgo** (hih DAL goh) A Spanish noble

**Ho Chi Minh Trail** Supply route that carried troops and supplies from North Vietnam to South Vietnam (p. 620)

**holding company** Corporation that holds the stocks and bonds of numerous companies (p. 293)

**Holocaust** Nazi Germany's attempt to murder all European Jews (p. 451)

**Hollywood Ten** Group of people in the film industry who were jailed for refusing to answer congressional questions regarding Communist influence in Hollywood (p. 498)

**home rule** System by which cities exercise a limited amount of self-rule (p. 286)

**Homestead Act** 1862 law that offered 160 acres of western land to settlers (p. 177)

**Homestead Strike** 1892 strike in Pennsylvania against Carnegie Steel (p. 171)

**homicide** The killing of one human being by another (p. 761)

**Hooverville** Makeshift shelter of the homeless during the early years of the Great Depression (p. 383)

**House of Burgesses** Virginia legislature formed in 1619 (p. 22)

**horizontal consolidation** Process of bringing together many firms that are in the same business to form one large company (p. 161)

**HUAC** House Un-American Activities Committee; congressional committee that investigated Communist influence in the United States in the 1940s and 1950s (p. 497)

**hundred days** Period at the start of Franklin Roosevelt's presidency in 1933, when many New Deal programs were passed by Congress (p. 404)

# I

**ICBM** An intercontinental ballistic missile (p. 506)

**immigrant** Person who enters a new country to settle

**Immigration Act of 1965** Law that ended quotas for individual countries and replaced them with more flexible limits (p. 548)

**impeach** Charge a public official with wrongdoing in office (pp. 134, 668)

**imperialism** Policy by a stronger nation to create an empire by dominating weaker nations economically, politically, culturally, or militarily (p. 259)

**impressment** Policy of forcing people into military or public service

**inauguration** Official swearing-in ceremony (p. 42)
**incumbent** Person already in office (p. 680)
**indentured servant** Person who agrees to work for another person for a specified time in return for transportation, food, and shelter
**Indian Removal Act** 1830 law calling for the forced movement of Native Americans to west of the Mississippi River (pp. 75, 77)
**indigo** Type of plant used in making a blue dye for cloth
**industrialization** Growth of industry
**Industrial Revolution** Effort, beginning in Britain in the late 1700s, to increase production by using machines powered by sources other than humans or animals
**infant mortality rate** Rate at which babies less than one year old die in a population
**inflation** A steady increase in prices over time, reducing the ability to buy (p. 29)
**infrastructure** The public property and services that a society uses (p. 140)
**initiative** Process by which citizens propose new laws by gathering signatures on a petition (p. 292)
**injunction** Court order prohibiting some action (p. 286)
**installment plan** A system that lets customers make partial payments (installments) at set intervals over a period of time (p. 347)
**integration** Process of bringing together of different races (p. 531)
**interchangeable parts** A system of manufacturing in which all parts are made to an exact standard for easy mass-assembly
**interest** An extra sum of money that borrowers have to repay creditors in return for the loan
**Intermediate-Range Nuclear Forces (INF) Treaty** 1987 treaty between the United States and the Soviet Union calling for the destruction of 2,500 missiles in Europe (p. 711)
**Internet** The network that links computers around the world (p. 743)
**internment camp** A camp to which Japanese Americans were forcibly sent during World War II (p. 479)
**interracial** Between, among, or involving people of different races (p. 564)
**Interstate Commerce Act** 1887 law that regulated railroads and other interstate businesses (p. 193)
**Iran-contra affair** Scandal in the Reagan administration involving the use of money from secret Iranian arms sales to support the Nicaraguan contras (p. 711)
**Irish Potato Famine** Famine in Ireland in the 1840s that led to a surge in immigration to the United States
**iron curtain** Winston Churchill's term for the extension of Communist control over Eastern Europe (p. 489)
**isolationism** Policy of avoiding political or economic alliances with foreign countries (p. 344)
**isthmus** A narrow strip of land that joins two larger land areas
**itinerant** (Ī TIHN uhr uhnt) Traveling from place to place or on a circuit

# J

**Japanese American Citizens League (JACL)** Organization of Japanese Americans working to promote the rights of Asian Americans (p. 599)
**Jay's Treaty** Treaty signed in 1794 between the United States and Britain in which Britain agreed to withdraw from forts in the Northwest Territory and which sought to improve trade relations
**Jazz Age** Term used to describe the 1920s (p. 360)
**Jim Crow** System of laws that segregated public services by race, beginning in the 1890s (p. 243)
**jingoism** A feeling of intense national pride and a desire for an aggressive foreign policy (p. 265)
**joint-stock company** Company funded and run by a group of investors who share the company's profits and losses
**judicial branch** Branch of government that interprets and applies the laws
**judicial review** Power of federal courts to decide whether laws are constitutional (p. 69)

# K

***kamikaze*** (kah mih KAH zee) In World War II, a Japanese suicide plane (p. 447)
**Kansas-Nebraska Act** 1854 law that called on citizens in each territory to decide the issue of slavery there (p. 81)
**Kellogg-Briand Pact** Agreement signed in 1928 in which nations agreed not to use war in their dealings with one another (p. 346)
**King Philip's War** War, beginning in 1675, between English colonists and Native Americans
**kinship** Family relationships
**Korean War** Conflict over the future of the Korean peninsula, fought between 1950 and 1953 and ending in a stalemate (p. 500)
***Kristallnacht*** The name given to the night of violence on November 9, 1938, when Nazi storm troopers attacked Jews in Germany and Austria (p. 452)

# L

**labor union** Organization of workers formed to protect the interest of its members
**laissez-faire** (LES ay FAYR) A government policy of not interfering in private business (p. 205)

**land speculator** Person who buys up large areas of land in the hope of later selling it for a profit (p. 177)

**Latino** Person whose family origins are in Spanish-speaking Latin America (p. 596)

**League of Nations** International organization, formed after World War I, that aimed to promote security and peace for all members (p. 329)

**legislative branch** Branch of government that makes the laws

**legislature** A lawmaking assembly

**Lend-Lease Act** 1941 law that authorized the President to provide aid to any nation whose defense he believed was vital to American security (p. 434)

**Lewis and Clark expedition** Journey by Meriwether Lewis and William Clark through the Louisiana Territory during 1804–1806 (p. 71)

**Liberty Bond** Special war bonds sold to support the Allied cause during World War I (p. 322)

**Liberty ship** A large, sturdy merchant ship built during World War II (p. 461)

**Limited Test Ban Treaty** Treaty, signed in 1963, in which the United States and the Soviet Union agreed not to test nuclear weapons above the ground

**lineage** Kinship groups that trace their origin to a common ancestor

**literacy** Ability to read and write (p. 231)

**long drive** Moving of cattle from distant ranges to busy railroad centers that shipped the cattle to market (p. 186)

**loose construction** Belief that the government can do anything that the Constitution does not say it cannot

**Lost Generation** Group of writers of the 1920s who shared the belief that they were lost in a greedy, materialistic world that lacked moral values (p. 361)

**Louisiana Purchase** Purchase by the United States of the Louisiana Territory from France in 1803 (p. 70)

**Lower South** States of Texas, Louisiana, Mississippi, Alabama, Florida, Georgia, and South Carolina

**Loyalist** Person who remained loyal to Great Britain during the Revolution

**lynching** Illegal seizure and execution of a person by a mob (p. 243)

# M

**Magna Carta** A "great charter" signed in 1215 that granted certain rights to English nobles (p. 22)

**mail-order catalog** Catalog advertising a wide range of goods that can be purchased by mail (p. 248)

**mandate** A set of wishes expressed to a candidate by the voters (p. 542)

**Manhattan Project** Secret American program during World War II to develop an atomic bomb (p. 448)

**manifest destiny** Argument that the United States was destined to expand across North America (p. 77)

**manufacturing** Making of goods by machinery

***maquiladora*** Mexican factory located along the United States–Mexico border that assembles products for U.S. companies (p. 788)

***Marbury* v. *Madison*** 1803 Supreme Court case that established the principle of judicial review

**March on Washington** 1963 civil rights demonstration in Washington, D.C. (p. 576)

**Market Revolution** Shift from a home-based economy to one based on money and the buying and selling of goods

**Marshall Plan** Program of American economic assistance to Western Europe, announced in 1947 (p. 492)

**martial law** Emergency rule by military authorities (p. 98)

**Massacre at Wounded Knee** 1890 shooting by army troops of a group of unarmed Sioux (p. 182)

**mass media** Print and broadcast methods of communicating information to large numbers of people (p. 358)

**mass production** Manufacture of goods in great amounts (p. 155)

**Mayflower Compact** Agreement in which settlers of Plymouth Colony agreed to obey their government's laws

**McCarran-Walter Act** 1952 immigration law that discriminated against potential immigrants from Asia and Southern and Central Europe (p. 498)

***McCulloch* v. *Maryland*** 1819 case in which the Supreme Court ruled that Congress has the authority to take actions necessary to fulfill its constitutional duties

**median age** Age that divides a population in half, with half the population above that age and half below it

**Medicaid** Federal program that provides medical benefits to poor Americans (p. 548)

**Medicare** Federal program that provides medical benefits for older Americans (pp. 548, 775)

**mercantilism** Economic theory that argued that a country should try to get and keep as much bullion, or gold and silver, as possible, by exporting more goods than it imported (p. 23)

**mestizo** (mehs TEE zoh) A person of mixed Spanish and Native American heritage

**Mexican War** Conflict between the United States and Mexico from 1846 to 1848, ending with a United States victory (p. 78)

**Middle Ages** Era in European history from about A.D. 500 to 1300

**Middle America** Term sometimes used to describe mainstream Americans (p. 649)

**middle class** A new class of merchants, traders, and

artisans that arose in Europe in the late Middle Ages; in modern times, the social class between the very wealthy and the lower working class

**Middle Colonies** English colonies of New York, New Jersey, Pennsylvania, and Delaware

**Middle Passage** Part of the triangular trade in which Africans were forcibly taken from Africa to slavery in the Americas (p. 24)

**migrant farm worker** Worker who moves from farm to farm planting and harvesting various crops (p. 597)

**militarism** Policy of aggressively building up a nation's armed forces in preparation for war (p. 309)

**militia** Armed citizens who serve as soldiers during an emergency (p. 763)

**Miranda Rule** Rule that police must inform persons accused of a crime of their legal rights (p. 549)

**missions** Headquarters from which people from another country seek to spread their religion

**Missouri Compromise** 1820 agreement calling for the admission of Missouri as a slave state and Maine as a free state, and outlawing slavery in future states to be created north of 36° 30' N latitude (p. 74)

**mobile society** A society in which people are constantly moving about

**mobilization** The readying of troops for war (p. 310)

**modem** A device that converts data into signals that can be transmitted by telephone (p. 801)

**modern republicanism** President Eisenhower's approach to government, described as "conservative when it comes to money, liberal when it comes to human beings" (p. 527)

**monarch** Ruler of a kingdom

**monetary policy** Federal government plan for the makeup and quantity of the nation's money supply (p. 191)

**monopoly** Complete control of a product or service (p. 160)

**Monroe Doctrine** Declaration by President Monroe in 1823 that the United States would oppose efforts by any outside power to control a nation in the Western Hemisphere (pp. 73, 787)

**Montgomery bus boycott** Protest in 1955–1956 by African Americans against racial segregation in the bus system of Montgomery, Alabama (p. 531)

**Morrill Land-Grant Act** 1862 law in which the federal government distributed millions of acres of western lands to state governments in order to fund state agricultural colleges (p. 177)

**mountain man** An American fur trader who explored the Rocky Mountains and regions farther west in the early 1800s

**muckraker** Journalist who uncovers wrongdoing on the part of politicians or corporations (p. 287)

**multiculturalism** Movement calling for greater attention to non-European cultures in such areas as education (p. 742)

**municipal** Relating to a city, as in municipal government (p. 286)

***Munn* v. *Illinois*** 1877 Supreme Court decision that allowed states to regulate certain businesses within their borders (p. 208)

**mutiny** Revolt against superior authority

**My Lai massacre** Killing of several hundred Vietnamese by American soldiers in 1968 (p. 624)

# N

**napalm** (NAY pahm) Highly flammable chemical used in firebombing attacks; dropped from U. S. planes during Vietnam War to burn away vegetation and expose Viet Cong hideouts (p. 624)

**National American Woman Suffrage Association (NAWSA)** Organization formed in 1890 to push for women's voting rights (p. 302)

**National Association for the Advancement of Colored People (NAACP)** Organization formed in 1909 to advance the cause of African Americans (p. 244)

**national debt** The total amount of money owed by the national government (pp. 416, 776)

**National Defense Education Act** 1958 bill to improve science and mathematics instruction in schools (p. 528)

**nationalism** Devotion to one's nation (p. 259)

**nationalization** Conversion to government ownership (p. 413)

**National Organization for Women (NOW)** Organization formed in 1966 to promote full participation of women in American society (p. 591)

**National Rifle Association (NRA)** Leading organization working against gun control (p. 764)

**Nation of Islam** Organization, also called the Black Muslims, dedicated to black separation and self-help (p. 581)

**nativism** Movement to ensure that native-born Americans received better treatment than immigrants (p. 223)

**nativist** Supporter of the policy of favoring native-born citizens over immigrants (p. 755)

**naturalize** To apply for and be granted American citizenship

**natural rights** Rights which belong to people simply because they are human

**neutral** Not taking sides in a conflict or dispute

**New Deal** President Franklin Roosevelt's program of relief, recovery, and reform programs to combat the Great Depression (pp. 403, 769)

**New England Colonies** English colonies which became the states of Connecticut, Rhode Island, Massachusetts, Vermont, New Hampshire, and Maine

**New Federalism** President Reagan's plan to give states

more control over the use of federal aid (p. 705)

**New Freedom** Woodrow Wilson's 1912 campaign platform calling for antitrust action without threatening free competition (p. 298)

**New Frontier** President Kennedy's proposals to improve the economy, help the poor, and advance the space program (p. 542)

**New Left** New political movement of the late 1960s that called for radical changes to fight poverty and racism (p. 627)

**New Nationalism** Theodore Roosevelt's program of greater federal regulation of business and workplaces, income and inheritance taxes, and electoral reforms (p. 297)

**New Right** A coalition of conservative groups that emerged by 1980 (p. 702)

**Niagara Movement** Organization, founded in 1905 by W.E.B. Du Bois and other black leaders, that called for full civil liberties for African Americans, an end to racial discrimination, and recognition of human brotherhood (p. 235)

**Nisei** (nee SAY) A Japanese American whose parents were born in Japan (p. 479)

**nomad** Person who continually migrates instead of living permanently in one place

**nonviolent protest** Form of protest in which protesters do not resist or fight back when attacked (p. 565)

**North American Free Trade Agreement (NAFTA)** Agreement calling for removal of trade restrictions among the United States, Canada, and Mexico (pp. 737, 784)

**North Atlantic Treaty Organization (NATO)** Alliance between the United States, Canada, and Western European nations, formed in 1949 (p. 495)

**Nuclear Regulatory Commission** Government organization formed in 1974 to oversee the civilian uses of nuclear materials (pp. 607, 796)

**nullification** A state's refusal to recognize a federal law

# O

**obsolete** Outdated

**Office of War Information** Federal agency created in 1942 to enlist public support for the war effort during World War II (p. 466)

**Office of War Mobilization** Federal agency formed in 1943 to coordinate issues related to war production during World War II (p. 460)

**Olive Branch Petition** Plea by the American colonists to King George III in 1775 that he halt the fighting

**Open Door Policy** American approach to China around 1900, favoring open trade relations between China and other nations (p. 269)

**oral history** Traditions passed from generation to generation by word of mouth

**Oregon Trail** Trail linking Independence, Missouri, and Oregon, used by pioneers during the 1840s

**Organization of Petroleum Exporting Countries (OPEC)** Group of nations that worked together to regulate the price and supply of oil (p. 655)

# P

**pardon** An official forgiveness of a crime (p. 127)

**Paris peace talks** Negotiations between the United States and North Vietnam, beginning in 1968 (p. 635)

**patent** A license to make, use, or sell an invention (p. 152)

**patronage** Practice of hiring political supporters for government jobs

**Peace Corps** Federal program established to send volunteers to help developing nations around the world (p. 557)

**Pendleton Civil Service Act** 1883 law that created a Civil Service Commission and stated that federal employees could not be required to contribute to campaign funds and could not be fired for political reasons (p. 207)

**Pentagon Papers** Government study of United States involvement in the Vietnam War, made public in 1971 (p. 626)

**Pequot War** War between English settlers and Pequot Indians in 1637

**per capita income** Average income per person (p. 511)

**persecute** To oppress someone because of his or her beliefs

**Persian Gulf War** 1991 war in which United Nations forces expelled an Iraqi occupation army from Kuwait (p. 718)

**philanthropist** Person who gives donations to worthy causes (p. 233)

**Pickett's Charge** Unsuccessful charge by Confederate infantry during the Battle of Gettysburg (p. 109)

**piecework** System in which workers are paid not by the hour but by what they produce (p. 164)

**Pilgrim** One of the group of English Separatists who established Plymouth Colony in 1620

**Pinckney Treaty** Treaty between the United States and Spain in 1795 that set the southern boundary of the United States

**placer mining** A method of mining used by individual prospectors (p. 185)

**plantation** Large farm on which crops are raised mainly for sale

***Plessy* v. *Ferguson*** 1896 case in which the Supreme Court ruled that racial segregation was legal as long as the separate facilities were equal for both races (p. 243)

**political asylum** Protection given by one country to refugees from another (p. 753)

**political machine** Unofficial organization designed to keep a particular party or group in power and usually headed by a single, powerful boss (p. 220)

**political party** Group of people who seek to win elections and hold public office in order to control government policy and programs

**poll tax** Special fee that must be paid before a person can vote (p. 242)

**Pontiac's Rebellion** Rebellion by Native Americans in the Great Lakes region against the British in 1763

**Poor People's Campaign** Crusade against economic injustice organized in 1968 by Martin Luther King, Jr. (p. 650)

**popular sovereignty** Policy of letting the people in a territory decide whether slavery would be allowed there

**population density** The average number of people living within a given area

**Populist** Supporter of the Populist party, formed in 1891 to advocate a larger money supply and other economic reforms (p. 193)

**precedent** (PREHS ih dehnt) Something done or said that becomes an example, rule, or tradition to be followed

**prejudice** An unreasonable, usually unfavorable opinion of another group

**presidio** (prih SEE dee oh) Fort built in Southwest by Spanish

**price controls** System of pricing determined by the government (p. 323)

**prime minister** Top official in a parliamentary government

**privateer** Privately owned ship hired by a government to attack enemy ships

**Proclamation of 1763** Order by the British king that closed the region west of the Appalachian Mountains to all settlement by colonists

**productivity** Amount that a worker produces in a given period of time (p. 152)

**profiteering** Selling scarce items at unreasonably high prices

**progressive** Political and social reformer of the late 1800s and early 1900s (p. 768)

**Progressive Era** Period from about 1890 to 1920, during which a variety of reforms were enacted at the local, state, and federal levels (p. 287)

**progressive income tax** Tax in which the percentage of taxes owed increases with income (p. 193)

**prohibition** A legal ban on the manufacture and sale of alcoholic beverages (p. 224)

**proliferation** Rapid growth in number, spread (p. 662)

**proprietary colony** Colony granted by a king or queen to an individual or group who have full governing rights

**public works program** Government-funded project to build public facilities (p. 405)

**Pueblo Revolt of 1680** Revolt by the Pueblo people in New Mexico against Spain

**Pullman Strike** 1894 railway workers' strike that spread nation-wide (p. 172)

**Puritan** Person who favored the purification of England's Anglican Church

# Q

**Quaker** Member of a Protestant group that emphasizes equality

**quarantine** A time of isolation to prevent the spread of a disease (p. 212)

**quota** A numerical limit (p. 345)

# R

**racism** Belief that differences in character or intelligence are due to one's race and that asserts the superiority of one race over another or others (p. 278)

**ragtime** Style of music consisting of melodies with shifting accents over a steady beat (p. 239)

**ratify** Approve or sanction

**rationing** Distributing goods to consumers in a fixed amount (p. 323)

***realpolitik*** (ray AHL poh lih teek) German for "practical politics," or a foreign policy based on interests rather than moral principles (p. 659)

**recall** Process by which voters remove a public official from office before the next election (p. 292)

**recession** Period of slow business activity (p. 677)

**recognition** Official acceptance (p. 96)

**Reconstruction** Federal government's effort between 1865 and 1877 to repair the damage to the South caused by the Civil War and to restore southern states to the Union (p. 125)

**red scare** A period of intense fear of communism and other extreme ideas (p. 342)

**referendum** Process by which citizens vote on a law passed by their legislature (p. 292)

**Reformation** Revolt against the Catholic Church that began in 1517

**religious tolerance** Idea that people of different religions should live in peace together

**Renaissance** Era of European history extending from the 1300s to the 1500s

**reparations** Payment from an enemy for economic injury suffered during a war (p. 330)

**republic** A government run by the people through their elected representatives (p. 42)

**republican virtues** Virtues the American people would need to govern themselves, such as sacrificing individual needs for the good of the community, self-reliance, industry, frugality, and harmony

**reservation** Area that the federal government set aside for Native Americans who had lost their homelands (p. 180)

**restrictive covenant** Agreement among homeowners

not to sell real estate to certain groups of people, such as African Americans or Jews (p. 219)

**revenue** Income of a government (p. 416)

**revival** A gathering where people are "revived," or brought back to a religious life

**Revolutionary War** American colonists' war of independence from Britain, fought from 1775 to 1783 (p. 30)

**rock and roll** Type of music that grew out of rhythm and blues and that became popular in the 1950s (p. 521)

***Roe* v. *Wade*** 1973 Supreme Court decision that legalized abortion (p. 593)

**Roosevelt Corollary** President Theodore Roosevelt's 1904 extension of the Monroe Doctrine in which he asserted the right of the United States to intervene in Latin American nations (pp. 273, 787)

**Rosie the Riveter** Term used to symbolize the many women who worked in defense industries during World War II (p. 470)

**royal colony** Colony with a governor appointed by the king

**rural** Pertaining to the countryside rather than cities

**rural free delivery** Free delivery of packages to rural areas, begun in 1896 (p. 248)

**Russian Revolution** Collapse of the czar's government in Russia in 1917, leading ultimately to the Bolshevik takeover (p. 316)

# S

**sachem** A Native American leader

**Salem witch trials** The prosecution and execution of twenty women and men for witchcraft in Massachusetts in 1692

**SALT I** Strategic Arms Limitation Treaty, a 1972 agreement between the United States and the Soviet Union on limiting nuclear weapons (p. 662)

**salutary neglect** Great Britain's policy in the early 1700s of not interfering in the American colonies' politics and economy as long as such neglect served British economic interests

**Sandinista** Member of the group of Nicaraguans who took control of the government in 1979 (p. 711)

**Santa Fe Trail** Trail linking Independence, Missouri, and Santa Fe, New Mexico in the mid-1800s

**satellite nation** A country dominated politically and economically by another nation, especially by the Soviet Union during the cold war (p. 487)

**saturation bombing** The dropping of a large concentration of bombs over a certain area (p. 623)

**savanna** Region near the equator with tropical grasslands and scattered trees

**scab** Worker called in by an employer to replace striking laborers (p. 170)

**scalawag** An insulting nickname for a white southern Republican following the Civil War (p. 136)

**scarce** In short supply

**Scopes trial** 1925 trial in Tennessee on the issue of teaching evolution in public schools (p. 368)

***Scott* v. *Sandford*** 1857 Supreme Court decision that declared slaves not to be citizens and ruled the Missouri Compromise as unconstitutional

**secede** To withdraw formally from membership in a group or organization (p. 82)

**secessionist** Person who wanted the South to secede

**Second Amendment** Amendment to the United States Constitution giving states the right to armed militias (p. 763)

**Second Continental Congress** Assembly of representatives from the colonies that first met in Philadelphia in May 1775 (p. 30)

**Second Great Awakening** Religious movement of the early 1800s

**Second New Deal** Period of legislative activity launched by President Franklin Roosevelt in 1935 (p. 408)

**section** A geographic region

**secularize** To put under the control of the government rather than the church

**sedition** Speech or actions that encourage rebellion (p. 324)

**segregation** Forced separation (p. 214)

**Selective Service Act** 1917 law authorizing a draft of young men for military service (p. 317)

**self-determination** Power to make decisions about one's own future (p. 328)

**self-sufficient** Having the necessary resources to get along without help

**Seneca Falls Convention** The first women's rights convention in United States history, held in 1848

**seniority** Status derived from length of service (p. 472)

**separation of powers** The Constitutional allotting of powers within the federal government among the legislative, executive, and judicial branches

**settlement house** Community center organized to provide various services to the urban poor (p. 225)

**sharecropping** System of farming in which a farmer farms some portion of a planter's land and receives a share of the crop at harvest time as payment (p. 138)

**Shays' Rebellion** An uprising against taxes in Massachusetts in 1786 and 1787

**shell** Device that explodes in the air or when it hits a solid target (p. 90)

**Sherman Antitrust Act** Law passed in 1890 that outlawed any combination of companies that restrained trade or commerce (p. 161)

**shuttle diplomacy** Repeated trips by a mediator between disputing nations in order to reach an agreement (p. 684)

**siege** Tactic in which an enemy is surrounded and starved in order to make it surrender (p. 110)

**silent majority** Term used by President Nixon to describe Americans who disapproved of the counterculture (p. 656)
**sit-down strike** Labor protest in which workers stop work but refuse to leave the workplace (p. 417)
**sit-in** Form of protest in which protesters seat themselves and refuse to move (p. 570)
**social Darwinism** Theory, derived from Darwin's theory of natural selection, that society should do as little as possible to interfere with people's pursuit of success (p. 160)
**social gospel movement** Reform movement that developed within religious institutions and that sought to apply the gospel of Jesus directly to society (p. 225)
**socialism** An economic and political philosophy that favors public (or social) control of property and income (p. 167)
**Social Security system** Publicly run system that provides regular payments to people who cannot support themselves (p. 409)
**social welfare program** Program designed to ensure a basic standard of living for all citizens (p. 288)
**software** Program for a computer (p. 802)
**solid South** Term used to describe the domination of post–Civil War southern politics by the Democratic party (p. 142)
**sooner** Person who marked his or her claims in Indian Territory before it was legally opened to settlement (p. 183)
**Southern Christian Leadership Conference (SCLC)** Civil rights organization formed in 1957 by Dr. Martin Luther King, Jr., and other leaders (p. 565)
**Southern Colonies** The English colonies of Virginia, Maryland, the Carolinas, and Georgia
**speakeasy** During Prohibition, a place where alcoholic drinks were served illegally (p. 366)
**special prosecutor** An attorney appointed by the Justice Department to investigate wrongdoing by government officials (p. 668)
**specie** (SPEE shee) Gold or silver coin
**speculation** Making high-risk investments in hopes of getting a high gain (p. 377)
**sphere of influence** Area of economic and political control exerted by one nation over another nation or other nations (p. 269)
**spiritual** A folk hymn
**spoils** Rewards gained through military victory (p. 329)
**spoils system** System or practice of giving appointed offices as rewards from the successful party in an election; name for the patronage system under President Jackson
***Sputnik*** First artificial satellite to orbit Earth, launched by the Soviet Union in 1957 (p. 506)
**stagflation** Combination of high inflation and high unemployment, with no economic growth (p. 677)
**stalemate** Situation in which neither side in a conflict is able to gain the advantage (p. 310)
**Stamp Act** 1765 law passed by the British Parliament which taxed newspapers, legal documents, and other printed materials in the colonies (p. 28)
**staple crop** A crop that is in constant demand, such as cotton, wheat, or rice
**states' rights** Theory that holds that the Constitution divided power between the states and the federal government and that a strict interpretation of that division must be respected.
**steerage** Large open area beneath the ship's deck, in which many poorer immigrants traveled (p. 211)
**stereotype** A fixed conception held by a number of people (p. 200)
**Stono Rebellion** 1739 slave revolt in South Carolina
**Strategic Arms Reduction Treaty** Agreement, known as START, signed in 1991, that called for dramatic reductions in Soviet and American nuclear weapons (p. 717)
**Strategic Defense Initiative (SDI)** President Reagan's proposed defense system against Soviet missile attack, popularly known as "Star Wars" (p. 705)
**strict construction** Belief that the government should not do anything that the Constitution does not specifically say it can do
**strike** A work stoppage intended to force an employer to meet certain demands, as for higher wages. (p. 239)
**Student Nonviolent Coordinating Committee (SNCC)** Student civil rights organization founded in 1960 (p. 567)
**subsidy** Payment made by the government to encourage the development of certain key industries (p. 206)
**suburb** Residential community surrounding a city (p. 218)
**suffrage** The right to vote
**supply-side economics** Theory that tax reductions will increase investment and thereby encourage business growth (p. 703)
**Sussex pledge** Pledge by the German government in 1916 that its submarines would warn ships before attacking (p. 315)
**synagogue** Jewish house of worship

# T

**Taft-Hartley Act** 1947 law that allowed the President to order striking workers in some industries back to work (p. 524)
**tariff** Tax on foreign goods imported into a country (pp. 68, 784)
**Tariff of 1828** A high tariff on manufactured goods; called the "Tariff of Abominations" by southerners
**teach-in** Special session of lecture and discussion on a controversial topic (p. 627)

**Teapot Dome scandal** Scandal of the Harding administration involving the granting of oil drilling rights on government land in return for money (p. 345)
**telecommunications** Communication over long distances by electronic means (p. 802)
**televangelism** Use by religious organizations of television, especially for fund-raising (p. 702)
**temperance movement** An organized campaign to eliminate alcohol consumption (p. 224)
**tenant farming** System of farming in which a farmer rented land to farm from a planter (p. 138)
**tenement** Crowded apartment building with poor standards of sanitation, safety, and comfort (p. 218)
**Tennessee Valley Authority (TVA)** A federal project to provide electric power, flood control, and recreational opportunities to the Tennessee River valley (p. 406)
**Tet Offensive** 1968 attack by Viet Cong and North Vietnamese forces throughout South Vietnam (p. 621)
**Texas War for Independence** Successful revolt by Texans against Mexican rule in 1835–1836 (p. 78)
**Thirteenth Amendment** Constitutional amendment, ratified in 1865, that abolished slavery (p. 116)
**38th parallel** Latitude line that divided North and South Korea (p. 500)
**Three-Fifths Compromise** Compromise at the Constitutional Convention calling for three fifths of a state's slave population to be counted for purposes of representation
**totalitarian** Describing a form of government that controls every aspect of its citizens' lives (p. 429)
**trade deficit** The sum of money lost when a nation spends more on imports than it earns with exports (p. 785)
**trade surplus** The sum of money gained when a nation earns more with exports than it spends on imports (p. 785)
**Trail of Tears** The forced movement of Cherokees in 1838–1839 to land west of the Mississippi River (p. 75)
**trans-Appalachia** Area west of the Appalachian Mountains
**transcendentalism** Philosophical movement of the mid-1800s that emphasized spiritual discovery and insight rather than reason
**transcontinental railroad** Railway extending from coast to coast (p. 152)
**transistor** Tiny circuit device that amplifies, controls, and generates electrical signals (p. 512)
**Treaty of Ghent** Agreement, signed in 1814, that ended the War of 1812
**Treaty of Greenville** Treaty signed in 1795 by the United States and several Native American peoples in which the Native Americans gave up control of most of Ohio
**Treaty of Guadalupe Hidalgo** Treaty signed in 1848 by the United States and Mexico, ending the Mexican War
**Treaty of Paris (1763)** Treaty that ended the French and Indian War and in which France gave up its land claims in North America to Britain
**Treaty of Paris (1783)** Treaty that ended the Revolutionary War and in which Britain acknowledged American independence (p. 31)
**Treaty of Tordesillas** Treaty signed in 1494 in which Portugal and Spain divided the non-Christian world
**Triangular Trade** Trade between the Americas, Europe, and Africa (p. 24)
**Truman Doctrine** 1947 declaration by President Truman that the United States would support nations that were being threatened by communism (pp. 490, 795)
**trust** A group of separate companies that are placed under the control of a single managing board (p. 161)
**trustee** Someone entrusted to look after a business
**Turner's Rebellion** Unsuccessful slave revolt led by Nat Turner in 1831
**Turner thesis** Argument, made by Frederick Jackson Turner in 1893, that the frontier had shaped American life (p. 198)
**turnpike** A road that requires users to pay a toll
**Twenty-first Amendment** Constitutional amendment, ratified in 1933, that ended Prohibition (p. 391)

# U

**U-boat** A German submarine (p. 314)
**Underground Railroad** Network of escape routes for slaves fleeing north to freedom
**undocumented immigrant** Immigrant who has entered the United States illegally (p. 753)
**Union** The United States as a national unit; or, during the Civil War, the North
**United Farm Workers (UFW)** Union organized by Cesar Chavez to organize Mexican field hands in the West (p. 598)
**Upper South** The states of Virginia, North Carolina, Tennessee, and Arkansas; designation used in the Civil War
**urban** Relating to a city
**utopian community** A small society dedicated to perfection in social and political conditions
**U-2 incident** The shooting down of an American spy plane over the Soviet Union in 1960 (p. 506)

# V

**vaudeville** Variety show that featured acts such as comic sketches and song-and-dance routines, popular in the late 1800s and early 1900s (p. 236)
**Versailles Treaty** 1919 treaty that ended World War I (p. 330)

**vertical consolidation** Process of gaining control of the many different businesses that make up all phases of a product's development (p. 161)
**veto** To prevent from becoming law (p. 41)
**vice** Immoral or corrupt behavior (p. 224)
**victory garden** A home garden created to boost food production during World War II (p. 466)
**Viet Cong** A force of Communist guerrillas in South Vietnam who, with North Vietnamese support, fought against the South Vietnamese government in the Vietnam War (p. 619)
**Vietnamization** President Nixon's policy of replacing American military forces with those of South Vietnam (p. 635)
**Vietnam Veterans Memorial** Monument in Washington, D.C., built to honor those killed in the Vietnam War (p. 638)
**vigilante** Citizen who takes the law into his or her own hands (p. 324)
**Virginia and Kentucky Resolutions** Resolutions passed in 1798 that attacked the Alien and Sedition Acts as unconstitutional
**Volunteers in Service to America (VISTA)** Federal program organized to send volunteers to help people in poor communities (p. 547)
**Voting Rights Act of 1965** Law aimed at reducing barriers to African American voting, in part by increasing federal authority to register voters (p. 579)

# W

**Wagner Act** Law passed in 1935 that aided unions by legalizing collective bargaining and establishing the National Labor Relations Board (p. 409)
**Wannsee Conference** 1942 conference in Germany concerning the plan to murder European Jews (p. 453)
**war bond** Government savings bond that is sold to raise money for a war (p. 463)
**War of 1812** War between the United States and Great Britain (p. 72)
**war of attrition** A war in which one side inflicts continuous losses on the enemy in order to wear down its strength (p. 89)
**War Powers Act** 1973 law limiting the President's power to deploy troops abroad (p. 678)
**War Refugee Board** Federal agency created in 1944 to try to help people threatened with murder by the Nazis (p. 454)
**Warren Commission** Commission, headed by Chief Justice Earl Warren, that investigated the assassination of President Kennedy (p. 544)
**Warsaw Pact** Military alliance between the Soviet Union and nations of Eastern Europe, formed in 1955 (pp. 495, 797)
**Watergate scandal** Scandal involving illegal activities that led ultimately to the resignation of President Nixon in 1974 (p. 666)
**welfare capitalism** An approach to labor relations in which companies met some of their workers' needs without prompting by unions (p. 376)
**Whiskey Rebellion** Unrest in 1794 caused by opposition to a tax on whiskey
**Whitewater affair** Charges that President Clinton had engaged in improper business transactions before becoming President (p. 727)
**wildcat strike** A strike organized by workers rather than union leaders (p. 462)
**Wilderness Road** Road built in the 1770s that became the main route across the Appalachian Mountains
**Woodstock festival** 1969 music festival in upstate New York (p. 632)
**work ethic** System of values stressing the importance of hard work in building success and a strong character (p. 772)
**World Trade Organization (WTO)** International organization formed in 1995 to encourage the expansion of world trade (p. 737)
**World Wide Web** Organization of global computer networks by which users can access information (p. 805)
**writ of *habeas corpus*** A legal protection requiring that a court determine if a person is lawfully imprisoned (p. 98)

# X

**XYZ Affair** Controversy in 1798 over French demands for bribes from American negotiators

# Y

**Yalta Conference** 1945 meeting between Churchill, Stalin, and Roosevelt in which the leaders discussed plans for the postwar world (p. 443)
**yellow journalism** Type of newspaper coverage that emphasized sensational stories of crime and scandal (p. 238)

# Z

**Zimmermann note** 1917 note by a German diplomat proposing an alliance with Mexico (p. 316)

# Spanish Glossary

## A

**abolitionist movement (movimiento abolicionista)** el movimiento para terminar con la esclavitud

**abstinence (abstinencia)** evitar alguna actividad, como beber bebidas alcohólicas

**Adams-Onís Treaty (Tratado Adams-Onís)** un tratado de 1819 entre Estados Unidos y España por el cual España cedió la Florida a los Estados Unidos

**administration (administración)** duración del cargo; también, los miembros y agencias del poder ejecutivo en su totalidad (p. 42)

**AFDC** Ayuda a Familias con Menores a Cargo, un programa de asistencia pública, popularmente conocido como welfare (p. 775)

**affirmative action (acción afirmativa)** la política que da consideración especial a las mujeres y miembros de las minorías como compensación a la discriminación sufrida en el pasado (p. 693)

**agenda (agenda)** una lista de artículos que se quieren conseguir

**AIDS (SIDA)** síndrome de inmunodeficiencia adquirida, un virus que ha matado a mucha gente desde la década de 1980 (p. 710)

**Albany Movement (Movimiento de Albany)** una organización de afroamericanos formada en Georgia para promover los derechos civiles (p. 572)

**Albany Plan of Union (Plan de Unión de Albany)** una propuesta que Benjamin Franklin hizo en 1754 para la creación de un gran consejo formado por representantes de las colonias británicas en Norteamérica

**alien (extranjero)** una persona que no es ciudadano (p. 215)

**Alien and Sedition Acts (Leyes de Extranjería y Sedición)** leyes aprobadas por el Congreso en 1798 que permitían que el gobierno encarcelara o deportara a los extranjeros y procesara a sus críticos

**Alliance for Progress (Alianza para Progreso)** Propuesta para la cooperación entre las naciones del Hemisferio Occidental para satisfacer las necesidades básicas de sus pueblos (p. 556)

**Allies (aliados)** en la primera guerra mundial, Rusia, Francia, Gran Bretaña y, más tarde, los Estados Unidos; en la segunda guerra mundial, la alianza entre Gran Bretaña, los Estados Unidos, la Unión Soviética y otras naciones (pp. 310, 432)

**almanac (almanaque)** un libro que contiene información, como calendarios y predicciones meteorológicas

**amend (enmendar)** revisar (p. 37)

**American Expeditionary Force (AEF) (Fuerza Expedicionaria Norteamericana)** nombre que recibían las tropas norteamericana en Europa durante la primera guerra mundial (p. 317)

**American Indian Movement (AIM) (Movimiento Indio Norteamericano)** una organización formada en 1968 para ayudar a los nativos norteamericanos (p. 602)

**American Liberty League (Liga Norteamericana de la Libertad)** una organización que se oponía al Nuevo Trato

**amnesty (amnistía)** perdón general de ciertos crímenes (p. 693)

**anarchist (anarquista)** un radical que se opone violentamente a cualquier forma de gobierno (p. 171)

**annex (anexar)** juntar o unir (pp. 78, 260)

**Antifederalist (antifederalista)** opositor a la Constitución durante el debate para su ratificación (p. 41)

**anti-Semitism (antisemitismo)** hostilidad o discriminación contra los judíos (p. 451)

**apartheid (apartheid; segregación racial)** en Suráfrica, separación sistemática de las razas blanca y negra (p. 733)

**appeasement (apaciguamiento)** política de ceder a las exigencias de alguien para preservar la paz (p. 431)

**apportionment (reparto)** distribución de los escaños en un cuerpo legislativo (p. 549)

**apprentice (aprendiz)** una persona que está obligada por contrato a trabajar para otra a cambio del aprendizaje de un oficio

**arbitration (arbitración)** la solución de una disputa por una persona elegida para escuchar a ambas partes y llegar a una decisión (p. 263)

**armistice (armisticio)** alto el fuego o tregua (p. 320)

**arms race (carrera armamentista)** una competición entre dos naciones en la que ambas aumentan sus reservas de armas en un intento por conseguir la superioridad (p. 505)

**arsenal (arsenal)** un lugar en el que se hacen o almacenan armas

**Articles of Confederation (Artículos de la Confederación)** el plan de gobierno que siguió los Estados Unidos desde 1781 hasta su sustitución por la Constitución de los Estados Unidos (p. 37)

**assembly line (cadena de montaje)** un proceso de manufacturación en el que cada trabajador realiza un trabajo especializado para la construcción del producto final (p. 349)

**assimilation (asimilación)** el proceso por el que personas de una cultura se combinan y convierten en parte de otra cultura (p.232)

**Atlantic Charter (Acuerdo Atlántico)** un acuerdo firmado por Roosevelt y Churchill en 1941 que perfilaba el objeto de los propósitos de guerra de las dos naciones (p. 436)

**autocrat (autócrata)** un gobernante con poder ilimitado (p. 311)

**automation (automatización)** el uso de máquinas sofisticadas en lugar de trabajadores (p. 803)

**autonomy (autonomía)** autogobierno en los asuntos locales (p. 602)

**Axis Powers (poderes del Eje)** en la segunda guerra mundial, la alianza entre Alemania, Italia y Japón (p. 430)

# B

**baby boom (incremento de la natalidad)** el dramático aumento del número de nacimientos durante y después de la segunda guerra mundial (p. 514)

**Bacon's Rebellion (la rebelión de Bacon)** revuelta de los colonos de Virginia contra el gobernador real

**balance of trade (déficit comercial)** la diferencia entre el valor de las importaciones y las exportaciones

**banana republic (república bananera)** un término que describe a una nación centroamericana dominada por los intereses económicos de los Estados Unidos (p. 261)

**bank note (nota bancaria)** un papel que un banco emite para sus clientes y que puede cambiarse por monedas de oro o plata

**barrio (barrio)** un vecindario en el que se habla español (p. 355)

**barter (cambiar)** cambio o trueque de bienes sin intervención de dinero

**Bataan Death March (Marcha de la Muerte de Batán)** la marcha brutal a la que fueron obligados los prisioneros norteamericanos y filipinos por los soldados japoneses en 1942 (p. 445)

**Battle of the Alamo (batalla del Álamo)** en 1836, la captura por las tropas mexicanas de una misión en San Antonio en poder de los texanos

**Battle of Antietam (batalla de Antietam)** una batalla de la guerra Civil en 1862, en Maryland (p. 94)

**Battle of the Bulge (batalla de las Ardenas)** la batalla de la segunda guerra mundial en la que las fuerzas alemanas lanzaron un contraataque final en el frente occidental (p. 442)

**Battle of Bunker Hill (batalla de Bunker Hill)** una batalla de la guerra de la Independencia que se libró en 1775 al norte de Boston

**Battle of Chancellorsville (batalla de Chancellorsville)** una batalla de la guerra Civil que ganaron los confederados en Virginia en 1863 (p. 107)

**Battle of Cold Harbor (batalla de Cold Harbor)** una batalla de la guerra Civil en Virginia (p. 114)

**Battle of the Coral Sea (batalla del Mar de Coral)** la batalla aérea que aviones norteamericanos y japoneses libraron en la segunda guerra mundial en 1942 (p. 445)

**Battle of Fredericksburg (batalla de Fredericksburg)** una batalla de la guerra Civil que ganó la Confederación en Virginia en 1861 (p. 106)

**Battle of Gettysburg (batalla de Gettysburg)** una batalla de la guerra Civil que ganó la Unión en 1863 en Pennsylvania, y que fue un momento crucial en la guerra (p. 108)

**Battle of Guadalcanal (batalla de Guadalcanal)** la batalla de la segunda guerra mundial en 1942–1943 entre Estados Unidos y Japón (p. 446)

**Battle of Iwo Jima (batalla de Iwo Jima)** la batalla de la segunda guerra mundial en 1945 entre los Estados Unidos y Japón (p. 447)

**Battle of Little Bighorn (batalla de Little Bighorn)** victoria de los siux en 1876 sobre las tropas del ejército bajo el mando de George Custer (p. 182)

**Battle of Midway (batalla de Midway)** la batalla de la segunda guerra mundial en 1942 entre los Estados Unidos y Japón, un momento crucial en la guerra del Pacífico (p. 445)

**Battle of New Orleans (batalla de Nueva Orleans )** la batalla por el control de Nueva Orleans en 1815 entre tropas norteamericanas y británicas, con victoria para los norteamericanos

**Battle of Okinawa (batalla de Okinawa)** la batalla de la segunda guerra mundial en 1945 entre los Estados Unidos y Japón (p. 447)

**Battle of Saratoga (batalla de Saratoga)** una batalla de la guerra de la Independencia en 1777 en Nueva York, un momento crucial en la guerra

**Battle of Shiloh (batalla de Shiloh)** una batalla de la guerra Civil en 1862 en Tennessee (p. 91)

**Battle of Spotsylvania (batalla de Spotsylvania)** una batalla de la guerra Civil en 1864 en Virginia (p. 114)

**Battle of Stalingrad (batalla de Estalingrado)** la batalla de la segunda guerra mundial en la Unión Soviética que marcó un momento crucial en la guerra en el este (p. 440)

**Battle of Tippecanoe (batalla de Tippecanoe)** la batalla en el territorio de Indiana en 1811 entre fuerzas norteamericanas e indias con derrota de los indígenas norteamericanos

**Battle of Trenton (batalla de Trenton)** una batalla de la guerra de la Independencia en 1776 en Nueva Jersey

**Battle of the Wilderness (batalla de Wilderness)** una batalla de la guerra Civil en 1864 en Virginia, ganada por la Confederación (p. 113)

**Battle of Yorktown (batalla de Yorktown)** una batalla de la guerra de la Independencia en 1781 en Virginia, una victoria norteamericana decisiva (p. 31)

**Battles of Lexington and Concord (batallas de Lexington y Concord)** las primeras batallas de la Guerra de la Independencia, el 19 de abril de 1775 (p. 30)

**Bay of Pigs invasion (invasión de Bahía Cochinos)** la fallida invasión de Cuba en 1961 por un grupo de fuerzas anticastristas (p. 552)

**beatnik (beatnik)** en la década de 1950, una persona que criticaba la sociedad norteamericana por ser apática y conformista (p. 521)

**Berlin airlift (puente aéreo de Berlín)** los suministros que los aviones norteamericanos y británicos lanzaron sobre Berlín Occidental durante el bloqueo soviético de 1948–1949 (p. 494)

**Berlin Wall (Muro de Berlín)** una barrera construida en 1961 por el gobierno de Alemania del Este para impedir que la gente escapara a Berlín Occidental (p. 553)

**Bessemer process (proceso Bessemer)** un nuevo proceso, patentado en 1856, para mejorar la fabricación del acero (p. 155)

**bicentennial (bicentenario)** ducentésimo aniversario (p. 679)

**bilingual education (educación bilingüe)** enseñar a los estudiantes en su lengua materna así como en inglés (p. 758)

**Bill of Rights (Declaración de Derechos)** las primeras diez enmiendas a la Constitución (p. 42)

**black codes (códigos negros)** las leyes que restringían los derechos de los libertos (p. 131)

**blacklist (lista negra)** una lista que circulaba entre los patronos y que contenía los nombres de personas que no debían ser contratadas (p. 498)

**black nationalism (nacionalismo negro)** la creencia en una identidad separada y la unidad racial en la comunidad afroamericana (p. 581)

**black power (poder negro)** movimiento afroamericano que busca la unidad y la autosuficiencia (p. 582)

**Black Tuesday (Martes Negro)** el 29 de octubre de 1929, día en que empezó el Gran Crack de la bolsa (p. 380)

**Bland-Allison Act (Acta Bland-Allison)** una ley de 1878 que disponía que el gobierno federal comprara y acuñara más plata (p. 191)

***blitzkrieg* (guerra relámpago)** un tipo de conflico bélico que enfatiza el movimiento rápido y mecanizado (p. 431)

**blockade (bloqueo)** aislar un lugar del contacto exterior

**block grant (subvención en bloque)** fondos federales entregados a los estados en un pago único (p. 779)

**blue law (ley azul)** una ley que prohibe ciertas actividades privadas, como tomar bebidas alcohólicas los domingos (p. 206)

**Bonanza farm (granja bonanza)** una granja controlada por una compañía grande y dirigida por profesionales (p. 185)

**Bonus Army (ejército Bonus)** un grupo de veteranos de la primera guerra mundial y sus familias, que en 1932 protestaron en Washington, D.C., por sus pensiones (p. 395)

**boomer (boomer)** uno de los colonos que se apresuraron en llegar al territorio indio después de que éste fuera abierto para su colonización en 1889 (p. 183)

**boom town (ciudad de rápido desarrollo)** una ciudad que ha experimentado un crecimiento rápido

**bootlegger (contrabandista de alcohol)** durante la prohibición, un suministrador de alcohol ilegal (p. 360)

**Border States (estados fronterizos)** los estados entre el Norte y el Sur: Delaware, Maryland, Kentucky y Misuri

**Boston Massacre (la masacre de Boston)** un incidente ocurrido el 5 de marzo de 1770 en el que los soldados británicos mataron a cinco colonos

**boycott (boicó)** la negativa a comprar cierto producto o a usar cierto servicio

**brinkmanship (diplomacia arriesgada)** la política de arriesgarse a ir a la guerra para proteger intereses nacionales (p. 505)

***Brown* v. *Board of Education* (*Brown* contra *la Junta de Educación*)** un caso por el que en 1954 el Tribunal Supremo declaró ilegal al segregación racial en las escuelas públicas (p. 530)

**buffalo soldier (soldado "búfalo")** nombre que los indios norteamericanos daban a los soldados negros del ejército de los Estados Unidos que sirvieron en el Oeste hacia finales de los 1800 y principios de los 1900 (p. 198)

**bureaucracy (burocracia)** los departamentos que componen una organización grande, como un gobierno

**business cycle (ciclo económico)** el crecimiento y la contracción periódicos de la economía de una nación (pp. 162, 380)

**buying on margin (comprar por una fracción)** la práctica por la que inversores compran acciones por sólo una fracción de su precio, tomando prestado el resto (p. 377)

# C

**Cabinet (gabinete)** los líderes de los departamentos ejecutivos del gobierno federal (p. 42)

**California gold rush (carrera del oro de California)** emigración masiva a California en 1848 inmediatamente después del descubrimiento de oro (p. 78)

**Camp David Accords (acuerdos de Camp David)** en 1978, acuerdo entre Israel y Egipto que hizo posible el tratado de paz entre las dos naciones (p. 685)

**canister (obús de metralla)** un tipo especial de obús lleno de balas (p. 90)

**capital (capital)** riqueza que puede invertirse para producir bienes y hacer dinero (p. 73)

**carpetbagger (carpetbagger)** apodo insultante que recibían los republicanos del Norte que se mudaron al Sur después de la guerra Civil (p. 136)

**carpet bombing (manto de bombas)** un método de bombardeo aéreo por el que se suelta un gran número de bombas en una área extensa (p. 441)

**cartel (cártel)** una asociación informal de negocios que producen el mismo producto

**cash crop (cultivo para la venta)** una cosecha que se cultiva para ser vendida

**casualty (baja)** una persona muerta o herida (p. 88)

**cede (ceder)** rendirse oficialmente o informalmente

**centralized (centralizado)** concentrado en un lugar

**Central Powers (poderes centrales)** en la primera guerra mundial, Alemania y Austro-Hungría (p. 310)

**charter (acuerdo)** un certificado o permiso que da un gobierno

**checks and balances (sistema de revisión)** el sistema en el que cada una de las ramas del gobierno federal puede comprobar las acciones de las otras ramas (p. 41)

**Chinese Exclusion Act (Acta de Exclusión de los Chinos)** una ley aprobada en 1882 que prohibía la entrada en el país a los trabajadores chinos (p. 214)

**civil disobedience (desobediencia civil)** negativa no violenta a obedecer la ley en un esfuerzo por cambiarla (p. 301)

**civil rights (derechos civiles)** las libertades personales de los ciudadanos garantizadas por la ley (p. 133)

**Civil Rights Act of 1964 (Ley de Derechos Civiles de 1964)** una ley que declaraba ilegal la discriminación en varias áreas, incluidos el voto, las escuelas y el lugar de trabajo (p. 577)

**civil service (servicio civil)** el sistema de trabajadores gubernamentales no elegidos por votación (p. 207)

**Civil War (guerra Civil)** la guerra entre la Unión y la Confederación, desde 1861 a 1865 (p. 87)

**clan (clan)** grupos de familias en los que todos los miembros descienden de un antepasado común

**Clayton Antitrust Act (Acta Antimonopolio Clayton)** una ley aprobada en 1914 para fortalecer la política federal antimonopolio, en la que se detallan las actividades comerciales que estaban prohibidas (p. 298)

**Clean Air Act (Ley del Aire Limpio)** una ley aprobada en 1970 que pretendía controlar la polución causada por las emisiones industriales y automovilísticas (p. 608)

**Clean Water Act (Ley del Agua Limpia)** una ley aprobada en 1972 que pretendía controlar la polución causada por la descarga de aguas residuales industriales y municipales (p. 609)

**cloture (limitación)** en el Senado, una votación que cuenta con las tres quintas partes de los votos y que permite terminar el debate de un asunto (p. 577)

**coalition (coalición)** una alianza de grupos con objetivos similares (p. 417)

**cold war (guerra fría)** la competencia que hubo entre los Estados Unidos y la Unión Soviética a partir de la década de 1940 hasta el colapso de la Unión Soviética (pp. 489, 793)

**collective bargaining (negociación colectiva)** un proceso en el que los empleados negocian en grupo con los propietarios (p. 169)

**collective security (seguridad colectiva)** una política por la que las naciones establecen un acuerdo para protegerse una a otra en caso de ataque (p. 495)

**colony (colonia)** un área establecida por inmigrantes que continúan siendo gobernados por el país del que provienen (p. 20)

**Columbian Exchange (Intercambio colombino)** el comercio trasatlántico de productos agrícolas, tecnología y cultura que se produjo entre las Américas y Europa, África y Asia, y que comenzó en 1492 con el primer viaje de Colón a las Américas (p. 20)

***Common Sense* (*Sentido común*)** un panfleto escrito por Thomas Paine y publicado en enero de 1776, en el que se pedía la independencia norteamericana de Gran Bretaña

**communism (comunismo)** la ideología oficial de la Unión Soviética, caracterizada allí porque el gobierno poseía la total propiedad de la tierra y los bienes, control del gobierno por un solo partido, falta de derechos individuales y la llamada a la revolución en todo el mundo (p. 342)

**Compromise of 1850 (Compromiso de 1850)** un acuerdo designado para facilitar las tensiones producidas por la expansión de la esclavitud en los territorios del oeste

**Compromise of 1877 (Compromiso de 1877)** un acuerdo por el que los demócratas estaban de acuerdo en dar la victoria a Rutherford B. Hayes en la elección presidencial de 1876 y Hayes, a cambio, estaba de acuerdo en sacar de los estados del Sur las tropas federales que quedaban (p. 143)

**compulsory (obligatorio)** compulsivo (p. 279)

**concentration camp (campo de concentración)** un lugar en el que se confina a prisioneros de guerra y a otros prisioneros, usualmente en condiciones crueles (p. 452)

**concession (concesión)** cesión de una parcela de tierra a cambio de la promesa de usar la tierra para un propósito específico (p. 271)

**Confederate States of America (Estados Confederados de Norteamérica)** la asociación de siete estados secesionistas del sur, formada en 1861

**conglomerate (conglomerado)** una corporación grande que es propietaria de muchas compañías pequeñas que producen variedad de bienes y servicios (p. 511)

**congregation (congregación)** los miembros de una iglesia; una reunión religiosa

**Congress of Racial Equality (CORE) (Congreso para la Igualdad Racial)** una organización fundada en 1942 para promover la igualdad por medios pacíficos (p. 564)

**Congressional Union (CU) (Unión Congresional)** una organización radical liderada por que hizo campaña a favor de una enmienda contitucional para garantizar el sufragio de la mujer (p. 303)

**conquistador (conquistador)** conquistador español

**conscientious objector (objetor de conciencia)** alguien que se opone a la guerra por razones morales o religiosas (p. 628)

**conservationist (conservacionista)** una persona preocupada por el cuidado y protección de los recursos naturales (p. 296)

**constitution (constitución)** un plan de gobierno que describe las distintas partes del gobierno y sus deberes y poderes

**consumer economy (economía de consumo)** una economía que se basa en que los individuos compren muchas cosas (p. 347)

**containment (contención)** política norteamericana que se resiste a la expansión del comunismo en el mundo (p. 489)

**contra (Contra)** en español, "contrarrevolucionario" (p. 711)

**contraband (contrabando)** objetos confiscados al enemigo durante la guerra (p. 100)

**Contract with America (Contrato con Norteamérica)** una promesa hecha por los candidatos republicanos en la campaña para la elección presidencial de 1994 en la que se comprometían a reducir el aparato de gobierno, eliminar algunas leyes, reducir los impuestos y equilibrar el presupuesto (p. 726)

**convoy (convoy)** un grupo de barcos armados y desarmados desplegados para proteger de los ataques a los barcos mercantes (p. 318)

**Copperhead (Copperhead)** durante la guerra Civil, un demócrata del Norte en contra de la guerra (p. 98)

**cotton gin (desmotadora de algodón)** una máquina para separar las semillas de las fibras de algodón en rama

**counterculture (contracultura)** en la década de 1960, un grupo de jóvenes norteamericanos que rechazaban las costumbres tradicionales (p. 631)

**Crusades (Cruzadas)** de 1096 a 1291, una serie de campañas militares de los cristianos europeos para arrebatarles la Tierra Sagrada a los musulmanes

**Cuban Missile Crisis (crisis cubana de los misiles)** la crisis que en 1962 se produjo entre los Estados Unidos y la Unión Soviética por el intento de los soviéticos de instalar misiles nucleares en Cuba (p. 554)

**Cumberland Road (camino Cumberland)** una carretera federal que se comenzó en Cumberland, Maryland, en 1811, y se extendió hacia el oeste hasta Ohio y más allá

# D

***Dartmouth College* v. *Woodward* (*Dartmouth College* contra *Woodward*)** un caso en 1819 en el que el Tribunal Supremo falló que los estados no podían interferir en los contratos

**Dawes Act (Acta Dawes)** una ley de 1887 que dividió los territorios de los indígenas norteamericanos en parcelas familiares privadas (p. 182)

**daylight saving time (cambio horario diurno)** adelantar los relojes una hora en el verano (p. 323)

**D-Day (día D)** el nombre codificado para la invasión aliada de Francia, el 6 de junio de 1944 (p. 442)

**death camp (campo de exterminio)** en la segunda guerra mundial, un campo alemán creado con el único propósito de asesinar en masa (p. 453)

**Declaration of Independence (Declaración de Independencia)** la declaración, proclamada por el Segundo Congreso Continental en 1776, que explicaba por qué las colonias buscaban independizarse de Gran Bretaña (p. 30)

**de facto segregation (segregación de facto)** la segregación basada no en la ley sino en la pobreza y las condiciones de los guetos (p. 583)

**deferment (aplazamiento)** la prórroga oficial de la llamada de una persona al servicio militar en el ejército (p. 628)

**deficit spending (gasto deficitario)** cuando el gobierno gasta dinero prestado (p. 463)

**deflation (deflación)** una caída del precio de los bienes de consumo (p. 191)

**de jure segregation (segregación de iure)** segregación según la ley (p. 583)

**demagogue (demagogo)** un líder que manipula a la gente por medio de verdades a medias y tácticas alarmantes (p. 412)

**demographics (demografía)** las estadísticas que describen a la población, como información sobre la raza o los ingresos económicos (p. 354)

**denomination (denominación)** un subgrupo religioso

**department store (grandes almacenes)** un almacén que tiene gran variedad de productos y vende en grandes cantidades (p. 248)

**depression (depresión)** una recesión económica severa (p. 73)

**deregulation (desregulación)** la reducción o supresión de los controles gubernamentales (p. 690)

***détente* (*détente*)** una relajación de la tensión entre naciones (p. 660)

**direct primary (primaria directa)** una elección en la que los votantes depositan sus votos para elegir a los candidatos de las futuras elecciones (p. 292)

**disarmament (desarmamento)** un programa en el que las naciones entregan sus armas voluntariamente (p. 344)
**discrimination (discriminación)** el trato desigual a un grupo de personas por su nacionalidad, raza, género o religión
**dissent (disentir)** diferencia de opinión o creencia
**dissident (disidente)** una persona que critica las acciones de su gobierno (p. 686)
**diversity (diversidad)** variedad (p. 24)
**division of labor (división del trabajo)** una forma de producción en la que diferentes personas realizan distintas tareas (p. 165)
**dollar diplomacy (diplomacia del dólar)** la política del Presidente Taft que fomentaba la inversión norteamericana en el extranjero (p. 275)
**domestic affairs (asuntos domésticos)** temas referentes a los asuntos internos del país
**domino theory (teoría dominó)** la creencia de que si un país se hace comunista, los países vecinos seguramente también se harán (p. 503)
**"Double V" campaign (campaña "Doble V")** un esfuerzo impulsado por un periódico afroamericano en favor de la victoria contra los poderes del Eje y la victoria en favor de la igualdad racial en el país (p. 477)
**Dow Jones Industrial Average (Promedio Industrial Dow Jones)** una medida promedio de los precios de las acciones de las principales industrias (p. 379)
**downsizing (reducción de personal)** la práctica empresarial de despedir a trabajadores para reducir los costos (p. 718)
**draft (llamada a filas)** un programa de servicio militar obligatorio (p. 95)
**dry farming (cultivo en seco)** las técnicas usadas para cultivar en áreas que reciben poca agua (p. 184)
**Dust Bowl (Dust Bowl)** una región de las grandes llanuras en la que hubo un periodo de sequía y tormentas de polvo durante la década de 1930 (p. 384)
**duty (impuesto)** una tasa

# E

**economic sanctions (sanciones económicas)** restricciones en el comercio y otras medidas económicas con el propósito de castigar a otra nación (p. 733)
**economies of scale (economías a escala)** el fenómeno por el cual conforme la producción aumenta, el costo de cada objeto producido es frecuentemente menor (p. 161)
**Electoral College (colegio electoral)** el grupo de electores, elegidos por los votantes, que eligen al Presidente (p. 40)
**e-mail** correo electrónico transmitido por las redes informáticas (p. 800)
**emancipation (emancipación)** liberación de esclavos
**Emancipation Proclamation (Proclamación de Emancipación)** el decreto presidencial, efectivo a partir del 1 de enero de 1863, que liberó a los esclavos en territorio confederado (p. 99)
**embargo (embargo)** una restricción del comercio (p. 655)
**emigrate (emigrar)** salir del propio país o región para establecerse en otro
**Enlightenment (Ilustración)** un movimiento del S. XVIII que enfatizaba la ciencia y la razón como claves para mejorar la sociedad
**entitlement (tener derecho)** un programa del gobierno que garantiza pagos a un grupo en particular, como a los ancianos (pp. 712, 775)
**Environmental Protection Agency (EPA) (Agencia para la Protección del Medio Ambiente)** una organización gubernamental formada en 1970 para tratar asuntos como la polución del aire y del agua (p. 608)
**Equal Rights Amendment (ERA) (Enmienda para la Igualdad de Derechos)** una propuesta de enmienda constitucional, nunca ratificada, que propone la igualdad de derechos para ambos sexos (p. 593)
**Erie Canal (Canal de Erie)** un canal en el estado de Nueva York, acabado en 1825, que unía el río Hudson con el lago Erie
**escalation (escalada)** expansión (p. 620)
**evangelical (evangélico)** que consiste en sermones emocionalmente poderosos y en las enseñanzas de la Biblia, en lugar de en ceremonias formales
**executive branch (poder ejecutivo)** la rama del gobierno que hace cumplir las leyes
**Exoduster (Exoduster)** uno de un grupo de afroamericanos que emigró al Oeste a continuación de la guerra Civil (p. 179)

# F

**faction (facción)** un grupo organizado en torno a un interés común y preocupado únicamente por el progreso de dicho interés
**fascism (fascismo)** una filosofía política que sitúa la importancia de la nación por encima de la del individuo (p. 429)
**federal (federal)** un tipo de gobierno en el que el poder está dividido entre el gobierno central y gobiernos más pequeños
**Federal Reserve System (Sistema Federal de Reserva)** el sistema bancario central de la nación, establecido en 1913 (p. 299)
**Federalist (federalista)** partidario de la Constitución durante el debate sobre su ratificación; a favor de un gobierno central fuerte (p. 41)
**federal deficit (déficit federal)** la suma de dinero que se pierde cuando los gastos del gobierno federal superan a los ingresos (p. 1032)
**feminism (feminismo)** una teoría que favorece la igual-

dad política, económica y social de hombres y mujeres (p. 589)

**feudalism (feudalismo)** un sistema político y económico de la Europa medieval en el que los señores menos importantes recibían tierras de nobles poderosos a cambio de servicios

**Fifteenth Amendment (Decimoquinta Enmienda)** la enmienda constitucional, ratificada en 1870, que garantizaba el derecho al voto de los afroamericanos (p. 135)

**filibuster (filibusterismo)** una táctica en la que los senadores piden la palabra, empiezan a hablar, y se niegan a dejar de hablar impidiendo así la votación sobre una medida (p. 316)

**First Battle of Bull Run (primera batalla de Bull Run)** la primera batalla de la guerra Civil, que ganaron los confederados en julio de 1861 (p. 88)

**First Continental Congress (Primer Congreso Continental)** una asamblea de representantes de las colonias que se reunió por primera vez en Filadelfia en septiembre de 1774 (p. 29)

**flapper (descocada)** un término acuñado durante la década de 1920 que describía a una mujer joven de silueta erguida y delgada y gusto por el baile y las acciones atrevidas (p. 353)

**food stamp (estampilla de comida)** cupón federal para comprar alimentos que reciben las personas de bajos ingresos que tienen derecho a recibir asistencia (p. 778)

**Fort Sumter (Fuerte Sumter)** un fuerte federal en la bahía de Charleston, Carolina del Sur; el ataque confederado al fuerte supuso el inicio de la guerra Civil

**Fourteen Points (los Catorce Puntos)** la propuesta del Presidente Wilson en 1918 para la paz europea de posguerra (p. 328)

**Fourteenth Amendment (Decimocuarta Enmienda)** la enmienda constitucional, ratificada en 1868, que garantizaba a todos los ciudadanos la misma protección de la ley (p. 132)

**franchise (franquicia)** el derecho a abrir un restaurante usando el nombre de marca y el sistema de una compañía principal (p. 512)

**Freedom Ride (Marcha de la Libertad)** una protesta a favor de los derechos civiles en la que un grupo racial mixto de manifestantes desafiaron a las estaciones de autobús que practicaban la segregación (p. 571)

**free enterprise system (sistema de libre empresa)** un sistema económico en el que las compañías compiten para conseguir beneficios

**free soiler (antiesclavista)** una persona dedicada a prevenir la expansión de la esclavitud hacia los territorios del oeste

**French and Indian War (Guerra Franco-india)** la guerra que, de 1754 a 1763, mantuvieron Francia, con naciones indias aliadas, y Gran Bretaña y sus colonos, por el control del este de Norteamérica (p. 27)

**Fugitive Slave Act (Acta de Esclavos Fugitivos)** parte del Compromiso de 1850, era una ley que ordenaba que todos los ciudadanos de los Estados Unidos ayudaran a la devolución de los esclavos fugitivos

**fundamentalism (fundamentalismo)** una serie de creencias religiosas que incluyen ideas cristianas tradicionales sobre Jesucristo, la creencia en que la Biblia fue inspirada por Dios y no contiene contradicciones o errores, y la creencia en que la Biblia es literalmente cierta (p. 368)

# G

**Gadsden Purchase (Compra Gadsden)** la compra de las tierras del suroeste que en 1853 hizo los Estados Unidos a México

**gag rule (regla de la mordaza)** una regla aprobada por el Congreso que prohibía que se oyeran o se emprendieran acciones en favor de las peticiones antiesclavistas

**General Agreement on Tariffs and Trade (GATT) (Acuerdo General sobre Aranceles Aduaneros y Comercio)** un acuerdo internacional para la reducción de tarifas y la expansión del comercio mundial (p. 737)

**Geneva Conference (Conferencia de Ginebra)** una conferencia internacional en 1954 en la que Vietnam fue dividido en dos naciones (p. 617)

**genocide (genocidio)** el asesinato deliberado de todo un pueblo (p. 321)

**Gentleman's Agreement (Acuerdo entre Caballeros)** un acuerdo en 1907 entre los Estados Unidos y Japón que restringía la inmigración japonesa (p. 215)

**Gettysburg Address (Discurso de Gettysburgh)** famosa alocución del Presidente Lincoln en noviembre de 1863 sobre el significado de la guerra Civil, con motivo de la dedicación de un cementerio nacional en el sitio de la batalla de Gettysburg (p. 112)

**ghetto (gueto)** una área en la que domina un grupo étnico o racial (p. 219)

**ghost town (ciudad fantasma)** una ciudad que ha sido abandonada por falta de actividad económica

**GI (Government Issued) (Aprobado por el Gobierno)** él término que designaba a los soldados norteamericanos en la primera guerra mundial, derivado de "Government Issued" (p. 436)

***Gibbons* v. *Ogden* (*Gibbons* contra *Ogden*)** un caso de 1824 en el que el Tribunal Supremo falló que los estados no podían regular el comercio en los cauces de agua interestatales

**GI Bill (Ley del GI)** una ley aprobada en 1944 para ayudar a los soldados veteranos a comprar casas y pagar estudios universitarios a su retorno (p. 514)

**Gilded Age (edad de oro)** término que describe el periodo comprendido entre 1877 y 1900 (p. 205)

**globalization (globalización)** tendencia a la organización mundial, como en la manufactura y venta de bienes (p. 800)
**Good Neighbor Policy (Política de buena vecindad)** la política del Presidente Franklin D. Roosevelt para promover buenas relaciones con naciones latinoamericanas (p. 787)
**graft (cohecho)** el uso del propio puesto para enriquecerse (p. 221)
**grandfather clause (cláusula del abuelo)** pasaje que exime a un grupo de gente de obedecer una ley si dicho grupo reúne ciertas condiciones antes de que se apruebe la ley (p. 242)
**Grange (Grange)** también conocida como Patrons of Husbandry (Protectores de la Economía Doméstica), una organización formada para fomentar la cooperación económica y política entre los agricultores (p. 192)
**Great Awakening (Gran Despertar)** un renacimiento religioso en las colonias norteamericanas durante las décadas de 1730 y 1740
**Great Compromise (Gran Compromiso)** el compromiso adoptado en la Convención Constitucional que pedía una legislatura con dos cámaras, una de ellas elegida por la población y la otra justamente representativa de cada estado
**Great Crash (Gran Crack)** el colapso de la bolsa norteamericana en 1929 (p. 380)
**Great Depression (Gran Depresión)** el severo deterioro económico que duró desde 1929 hasta aproximadamente 1939 (p. 380)
**Great Migration (Gran Migración)** la emigración de colonos ingleses a la colonia de la bahía de Massachusetts que comenzó en la década de 1630
**Great Society (Gran Sociedad)** propuestas del Presidente Johnson para mejorar la educación pública, proveer cuidado médico a los ancianos y eliminar la pobreza (p. 547)
**Great White Fleet (Gran Flota Blanca)** una fuerza de barcos de la Marina de los Estados Unidos que emprendió un crucero mundial en 1907 (p. 280)
**greenbacks (greenbacks)** el nombre que recibe la moneda nacional en papel, creada en 1862 (p. 97)
**green card (tarjeta verde)** permiso de residencia y trabajo que se otorga a los extranjeros en los Estados Unidos (p. 753)
**Gross National Product (producto nacional bruto)** el valor total de los bienes y servicios que produce un país en un año (p. 380)
**guerrilla (guerrillero)** un soldado que usas tácticas de ataque y huida (p. 117)
**Gulf of Tonkin Resolution (Resolución del Golfo de Tonkin)** resolución del Congreso que en 1964 autorizó al Presidente Johnson a emprender acción militar en Vietnam (p. 620)

# H

**Harlem Renaissance (Renacimiento de Harlem)** el despertar literario afroamericano en la década 1920, centrado en Harlem, ciudad de Nueva York (p. 363)
**haven (asilo)** un lugar seguro
**Hawley-Smoot tariff (tarifa Hawley-Smoot)** una tarifa de importación especilmente elevada, aprobada por el Congreso en 1930 (p. 394)
**Haymarket Riot (Revuelta de Haymarket)** la violencia sindical en Chicago, en 1886 (p. 171)
**Helms-Burton Act (Ley Helms-Burton)** una ley de 1996 que penaliza a las compañías extranjeras que tienen negocios con Cuba (p. 786)
**Helsinki Accords (Acuerdos de Helsinki)** una serie de acuerdos sobre seguridad europea, firmados en 1975 (p. 679)
**Ho Chi Minh Trail (Pista Ho Chi Minh)** la ruta de suministros que llevaba tropas y materiales desde Vietnam del Norte a Vietnam del Sur (p. 620)
**holding company (compañía de valores)** una corporación que tiene acciones y contratos en numerosas compañías (p. 293)
**Holocaust (Holocausto)** El intento de la alemania nazi de asesinar a todos los judíos europeos (p. 451)
**Hollywood Ten (los Diez de Hollywood)** un grupo de personas de la industria cinematográfica que fueron encarceladas por negarse a responder preguntas del Congreso sobre la influencia comunista en Hollywood (p. 498)
**home rule (autonomía)** un sistema en el que las ciudades ejercen una cantidad limitada de autogobierno (p. 286)
**Homestead Act (Acta de Protección a las Tierras de Colonización)** una ley de 1862 que les ofrecía a los colonos 160 acres de tierra en el Oeste (p. 177)
**Homestead Strike (huelga Homestead)** la huelga contra los aceros Carnegie que hubo en Pennsylvania en 1892 (p. 171)
**homicide (homicidio)** el asesinato de un ser humano por otro (p. 761)
**Hooverville (Hooverville)** un refugio para personas sin hogar durante los primeros años de la La Gran Depresión (p. 383)
**House of Burgesses (House of Burgesses)** la legislatura formada en Virginia en 1619 (p. 22)
**House Un-American Activities Committee (HUAC) (Comité de Investigación de Actividades Antinorteamericanas del Congreso)** un comité del Congreso que investigó la influencia comunista en los Estados Unidos en las décadas de 1940 y 1950 (p. 497)
**horizontal consolidation (consolidación horizontal)** proceso de consolidación de muchas compañías que trabajan en el mismo ramo para formar una única gran compañía (p. 161)

**hundred days (cien días)** en 1933, el periodo al comienzo de la presidencia de Franklin Roosevelt, durante el cual el Congreso aprobó muchos programas del Nuevo Trato (p. 404)

# I

**ICBM** un misil balístico intercontinental (p. 506)
**immigrant (inmigrante)** una persona que entra en un país nuevo para establecerse
**Immigration Act of 1965 (Ley de Inmigración de 1965)** una ley que terminó con las cuotas para países específicos y las reemplazó con restricciones más flexibles (p. 548)
**impeach (inculpar)** acusar a un funcionario público de corrupción en el cargo (pp. 134, 668)
**imperialism (imperialismo)** política de una nación más fuerte de crear un imperio basado en la dominación económica, política, cultural o militar de naciones más débiles (p. 259)
**impressment (leva, enganche)** política de forzar a las personas a hacer el servicio militar o civil
**inauguration (inauguración)** una ceremonia oficial de juramento (p. 42)
**incumbent (titular)** una persona que tiene el cargo oficialmente (p. 680)
**indentured servant (aprendiz bajo contrato)** una persona que está de acuerdo en trabajar para otra persona por un plazo de tiempo específico a cambio de transporte, alimento y cobijo
**Indian Removal Act (Acta de Traslado de los Indios)** una ley de 1830 que obligaba el traslado forzado de los indígenas norteamericanos al oeste del río Misisipí (pp. 75, 77)
**indigo (índigo)** una clase de planta usada para hacer un tinte azul para tela
**industrialization (industrialización)** el crecimiento de la industria
**Industrial Revolution (Revolución Industrial)** el esfuerzo que comenzó en Gran Bretaña a finales de los 1700 por aumentar la producción por medio de máquinas impulsadas por fuentes distintas de la fuerza humana o animal
**infant mortality rate (tasa de mortalidad infantil)** el porcentaje de niños menores de un año que mueren en una población
**inflation (inflación)** un aumento continuado del precio en un periodo de tiempo dado, que reduce la capacidad de compra
**infrastructure (infraestructura)** los servicios de propiedad pública que usa una sociedad (p. 140)
**INF Treaty (Tratado INF)** un tratado entre los Estados Unidos y la Unión Soviética firmado en 1987 que establece la destrucción de los misiles en Europa (p. 711)
**initiative (iniciativa)** un proceso por el que los ciudadanos proponen nuevas leyes por medio de la recogida de firmas en una petición (p. 292)
**injunction (orden judicial)** orden de un juzgado que prohibe alguna acción (p. 286)
**installment plan (pago a plazos)** un sistema que permite a los clientes hacer pagos parciales (plazos) a intervalos establecidos sobre un periodo de tiempo (p. 347)
**integration (integración)** el acercamiento de razas distintas (p. 531)
**interchangeable parts (repuestos)** un sistema de fabricación en el que se hacen todas las partes según un estándar exacto
**interest (interés)** una suma adicional de dinero que los que reciben dinero prestado deberán pagar al acreedor por el préstamo
**Internet** la red electrónica que une a los computadores por todo el mundo (p. 743)
**internment camp (campo de internamiento)** uno de los campos a los que se obligó a ir a los norteamericanos de origen japonés durante la segunda guerra mundial (p. 479)
**interracial (interracial)** que se realiza, contiene, o en el que participan gentes de razas diferentes (p. 564)
**Interstate Commerce Act (Ley para el Comercio Interestatal)** una ley de 1887 que regulaba los ferrocarriles y otros negocios interestatales (p. 193)
**Iran-Contra affair (asunto Irán-Contra)** el escándalo en la administración Reagan producido por la desviación de fondos hacia los contras nicaragüenses del producto de las ventas secretas de armas a los iraníes (p. 711)
**Irish Potato Famine (Hambruna de la Patata en Irlanda)** una epidemia de hambre en Irlanda en la década de 1840 que causó el aumento de la inmigración a los Estados Unidos
**iron curtain (Telón de Acero)** término con el que Winston Churchill describió la extensión del control comunista por Europa Oriental (p. 489)
**isolationism (isolacionismo)** la política de evitar alianzas políticas o económicas con países extranjeros (p. 344)
**isthmus (istmo)** una estrecha franja de tierra que une dos áreas de tierra más grandes
**itinerant (itinerante)** que de un lugar a otro, o por un circuito

# J

**Japanese American Citizens League (JACL) (Liga de Ciudadanos Japonés-norteamericanos)** una organización de japonés-norteamericanos formada para promover los derechos de los asiático-americanos (p. 599)
**Jay's Treaty (Tratado de Jay)** un tratado firmado en 1794 entre los Estados Unidos y Gran Bretaña por el

que Gran Bretaña estaba de acuerdo en salir de los fuertes en los territorios del noroeste y ambos países en mejorar las relaciones comerciales

**Jazz Age (Era del Jazz)** un término usado para describir la década de 1920 (p. 360)

**Jim Crow (Leyes Jim Crow)** sistema de leyes que aplicaba la segregación en los servicios públicos a principios de la década de 1890 (p. 243)

**jingoism (jingoísmo)** un sentimiento intenso de orgullo nacional y deseo de una política exterior agresiva (p. 265)

**joint-stock company (sociedad anónima)** una compañía fundada y dirigida por un grupo de inversores que comparten las ganancias y pérdidas de la compañía

**judicial branch (poder judicial)** la rama del gobierno que interpreta y aplica las leyes

**judicial review (revisión judicial)** el poder de los tribunales federales para decidir qué leyes son constitucionales (p. 69)

# K

***kamikaze* (kamikaze)** en la segunda guerra mundial, un avión suicida japonés (p. 447)

**Kansas-Nebraska Act (Decreto de Kansas-Nebraska)** una ley de 1854 que pedía que los ciudadanos de cada territorio decidieran sobre el tema de la esclavitud en ellos (p. 81)

**Kellogg-Briand Pact (Pacto Kellogg-Briand)** un acuerdo firmado en 1928 por el que las naciones firmantes se ponían de acuerdo en no recurrir a la guerra para resolver sus diferencias (p. 346)

**King Philip's War (guerra del rey Felipe)** la guerra que empezó en 1675 entre los colonos ingleses y los indígenas norteamericanos

**kinship (parentesco)** las relaciones familiares

**Korean War (guerra de Corea)** el conflicto sobre el futuro de la península de Corea, que transcurrió entre 1950 y 1953 y acabó en punto muerto (p. 500)

***Kristallnacht* (Noche de los cristales)** nombre que recibe la noche de violencia, el 9 de noviembre de 1938, en contra de los judíos en Alemania y Austria, en 1938 (p. 452)

# L

**labor union (sindicato)** una organización de trabajadores formada para proteger los intereses de sus miembros

**laissez-faire (liberalismo)** la política gubernamental de no interferencia en los negocios privados (p. 205)

**land speculator (especulador del suelo)** una persona que compra grandes terrenos con la esperanza de venderlos después y obtener provecho (p. 177)

**Latino (latino)** una persona con orígenes familiares en la Latinoamérica hispanohablante (p. 596)

**League of Nations (Liga de las Naciones)** una organización internacional, formada después de la primera guerra mundial, que pretendía promover la seguridad y la paz para todos sus miembros (p. 329)

**legislative branch (poder legislativo)** la rama del gobierno que hace las leyes

**legislature (legislatura)** una asamblea legislativa

**Lend-Lease Act (Ley de Préstamo-Alquiler)** una ley de 1941 que autorizaba al Presidente a prestar ayuda a cualquier nación cuya defensa fuera, en su opinión, vital para la seguridad de los Estados Unidos (p. 434)

**Lewis and Clark expedition (expedición de Lewis y Clark)** el viaje de Meriwether Lewis y William Clark a través del territorio de Luisiana durante 1804–1806 (p. 71)

**Liberty Bond (bonos de la libertad)** unos bonos de guerra especiales que se vendían para apoyar la causa de los Aliados durante la primera guerra mundial (p. 322)

**Liberty ship (barco de la libertad)** un barco mercante grande y robusto construido durante la segunda guerra mundial (p. 461)

**Limited Test Ban Treaty (Tratado para la Limitación de Pruebas Nucleares)** en el tratado, firmado en 1963, los Estados Unidos y la Unión Soviética acordaron no probar armas nucleares por encima de la superficie terrestre

**literacy (alfabetismo)** la capacidad de leer y escribir (p. 231)

**long drive (gran travesía)** la conducción de ganado desde las lejanas montañas a los bulliciosos centros ferroviarios que transportaban el ganado al mercado (p. 186)

**loose construction (vaga interpretación)** la creencia en que el gobierno puede hacer cualquier cosa que la Constitución no dice que no puede hacer

**Lost Generation (generación perdida)** un grupo de escritores de la década de 1920 que compartían la creencia de que estaban perdidos en un mundo codicioso y materialista que carecía de valores morales (p. 361)

**Louisiana Purchase (adquisición de Luisiana)** la compra por los Estados Unidos a Francia del territorio de Luisiana, en 1803 (p. 70)

**Lower South (Bajo Sur)** Los estados de Texas, Luisiana, Misisipí, Alabama, Florida, Georgia y Carolina del Sur

**lynching (linchamiento)** el secuestro y ejecución ilegal de una persona por una multitud (p. 243)

# M

**Magna Carta (carta grande)** una "carta grande" firmada en 1215 que cedo ciertas derechas a los nobles ingleses (p. 22)

**mail-order catalog (catálogo de pedidos por correo)** un catálogo que anuncia una gran variedad de objetos que se pueden comprar por correo (p. 248)

**mandate (mandato)** una serie de deseos que los votantes piden a un candidato (p. 542)

**Manhattan Project (Proyecto Manhattan)** en la segunda guerra mundial, el programa secreto norteamericano para fabricar una bomba atómica (p. 448)

**manifest destiny (destino manifiesto)** el razonamiento que defendía que los Estados Unidos estaba destinado a expandirse por Norteamérica (p. 77)

**manufacturing (manufactura)** la fabricación de bienes por medio de máquinas

***maquiladora* (*maquiladora*)** factoría mexicana instalada en las cercanías de la frontera entre los Estados Unidos y México, que produce y monta productos para compañías estadounidenses (p. 788)

**March on Washington (marcha sobre Washington)** la manifestación en favor de los derechos civiles, en 1963, en Washington, D.C. (p. 576)

***Marbury* v. *Madison* (*Marbury* contra *Madison*)** en 1803, un caso en el que el Tribunal Supremo estableció el principio de revisión judicial

**Market Revolution (revolución de mercado)** el cambio de la economía doméstica a la economía basada en el dinero y en la compra y venta de bienes

**Marshall Plan (Plan Marshall)** el programa de ayuda económica norteamericana a Europa Occidental, anunciado en 1947 (p. 492)

**martial law (ley marcial)** gobierno de emergencia de las autoridades militares (p. 98)

**Massacre at Wounded Knee (masacre de Wounded Knee)** el asesinato a tiros por tropas del ejército de un grupo de siux desarmados, en 1890 (p. 182)

**mass media (medios de comunicación)** métodos para la comunicación de información a gran número de personas por medio de letra impresa o transmisión (p. 358)

**mass production (producción en masa)** producción de bienes en gran cantidad (p. 155)

**Mayflower Compact (pacto del Mayflower)** el acuerdo por el que los colonos de la colonia Plymouth se comprometían a obedecer las leyes de su gobierno

**McCarran-Walter Act (Decreto McCarran-Walter)** una ley de inmigración de 1952 que discriminaba en contra de potenciales inmigrantes de Asia y Europa Meridional y Central (p. 498)

***McCulloch* v. *Maryland* (*McCulloch* contra *Maryland*)** en 1819, un caso en el que el Tribunal Supremo falló que el Congreso tiene la autoridad para llevar a cabo las acciones necesarias para cumplir sus deberes constitucionales

**median age (edad mediana)** la edad que divide a la población en dos mitades: una mitad por encima de esa edad y la otra por debajo

**Medicaid** un programa federal que provee ayuda médica para los norteamericanos pobres (p. 548)

**Medicare** un programa federal que provee ayuda médica para los ancianos norteamericanos (pp. 548, 775)

**mercantilism (mercantilismo)** una teoría económica que razonaba que un país debía tratar de acumular tantos lingotes de oro y plata como le fuera posible, exportando más bienes de los que importa (p. 23)

**mercenary (mercenario)** un soldado extranjero que lucha por dinero

**mestizo (mestizo)** una persona de herencia mixta hispana e indígena americana

**Mexican War (guerra Mexicana)** el conflicto entre los Estados Unidos y México, de 1846 a 1848, que acabó con la victoria de Estados Unidos (p. 78)

**Middle Ages (Edad Media)** era de la historia europea que comprende desde el año 500 d. de C. hasta el año 1300

**Middle America (Norteamérica moderada)** un término usado a veces para describir la tendencia principal entre los norteamericanos (p. 649)

**middle class (clase media)** una nueva clase de comerciantes, negociantes y artesanos que surgió en Europa al final de la Edad Media; en los tiempos modernos, la clase social entre los muy ricos y la clase trabajadora menos pudiente

**Middle Colonies (colonias centrales)** las colonias inglesas de Nueva York, Nueva Jersey, Pennsylvania y Delaware

**Middle Passage (paso medio)** la parte del comercio triangular en la que los africanos eran sacados a la fuerza de África para ser llevados como esclavos a las Américas (p. 24)

**migrant farm worker (trabajador agrícola migratorio)** un trabajador que va de granja en granja sembrando y cosechando cosechas distintas (p. 597)

**militarism (militarismo)** la política de aumento de las fuerzas armadas de una nación, como preparación previa a la guerra (p. 309)

**militia (milicia)** ciudadanos armados que sirven de soldados durante una emergencia (p. 763)

**Miranda rule (Ley de Miranda)** obligación que tiene la policía de informar de sus derechos legales a los acusados de cometer un crimen (p. 549)

**mission (misión)** la sede desde la cual personas de otro país pretenden la difusión de su religión

**Missouri Compromise (Compromiso de Misuri)** un acuerdo al que se llegó en 1820 que pedía la admisión de Misuri como estado esclavista y de Maine como estado libre, declarando ilegal la esclavitud en los futuros estados que se crearan al norte de los 36° 30' N de latitud (p. 74)

**mobile society (sociedad móvil)** una sociedad en la que las personas están constantemente yendo de lado a lado

**mobilization (mobilización)** la preparación de tropas para la guerra (p. 310)

**modem (módem)** un dispositivo que convierte datos

en señales que pueden transmitirse por teléfono (p. 801)

**modern republicanism (republicanismo moderno)** propuesta de gobierno del Presidente Eisenhower, descrito como "conservador en lo referente al dinero, liberal en lo referente a los seres humanos" (p. 527)

**monarch (monarca)** alguien que gobierna un reino, como un rey o una reina

**monetary policy (política monetaria)** el plan del gobierno federal para la fabricación y reserva del suministro de dinero de la nación (p. 191)

**monopoly (monopolio)** control completo de un producto o servicio (p. 160)

**Monroe Doctrine (Doctrina Monroe)** la declaración que hizo el Presidente Monroe en 1823 en la que decía que Estados Unidos se opondría a los esfuerzos de cualquier potencia extranjera que quisiera controlar a otra nación en el Hemisferio Occidental (pp. 73, 787)

**Montgomery bus boycott (boicó a los autobuses de Montgomery)** la protesta que en 1955–1956 hicieron los afroamericanos contra la segregación racial en el sistema de autobuses de Montgomery, Alabama (p. 531)

**Morrill Land-Grant Act (Acta Morrill de Concesión de Tierra)** una ley 1862 por la que el gobierno federal distribuyó millones de acres de tierras en el oeste entre los gobiernos de los estados para fundar colegios agrícolas estatales (p. 177)

**mountain man (hombre montañés)** uno de los comerciantes de pieles norteamericanos que exploraron las Montañas Rocosas y otras regiones más al oeste en los 1800

**muckraker (reportero investigador)** un periodista que investiga fechorías cometidas por políticos o corporaciones (p. 287)

**multiculturalism (multiculturalismo)** movimiento que pide más atención a las culturas no europeas en distintas áreas, como la educación (p. 742)

**municipal (municipal)** relativo a la ciudad, como el gobierno municipal (p. 286)

***Munn* v. *Illinois* (*Munn* contra *Illinois*)** una decisión del Tribunal Supremo en 1877 que permitía que los estados regularan ciertos negocios dentro de sus fronteras (p. 208)

**mutiny (motín)** revuelta contra la autoridad superior

**My Lai massacre (masacre de My Lai)** la matanza de varios cientos de vietnamitas por soldados norteamericanos en 1968 (p. 624)

# N

**napalm** una sustancia química muy inflamable usada en ataques con bombas incendiarias (p. 624)

**National American Woman Suffrage Association (Asociación Nacional Norteamericana para el Sufragio Femenino)** una organización formada en 1890 para impulsar el derecho de la mujer al voto (p. 302)

**National Association for the Advancement of Colored People (Asociación Nacional para el Progreso de las Personas de Color)** una organización formada en 1909 para el progreso de la causa de los afroamericanos (p. 244)

**national debt (deuda nacional)** la cantidad total de dinero que debe el gobierno nacional (pp. 416, 776)

**National Defense Education Act (Ley Nacional para la Defensa de la Educación)** una ley de 1958 para mejorar la enseñanza de ciencias y matemáticas en las escuelas (p. 528)

**National Rifle Association (NRA) (Asociación Nacional del Rifle)** organización destacada que está en contra del control de armas (p. 764)

**nationalism (nacionalismo)** devoción hacia la propia nación (p. 259)

**nationalization (nacionalización)** conversión en propiedad del gobierno (p. 413)

**National Organization for Women (NOW) (Organización Nacional de Mujeres)** una organización formada en 1966 para promover la participación total de las mujeres en la sociedad norteamericana (p. 591)

**Nation of Islam (Nación del Islam)** una organización, llamada también Musulmanes Negros, dedicada a la separación de las personas de raza negra y a la ayuda a sí mismos (p. 581)

**nativism (indigenismo)** un movimiento que promueve un mejor trato para los norteamericanos nacidos en el país que para los inmigrantes (p. 223)

**nativist (natalista)** que apoya la política de favorecer a los ciudadanos nacidos en el país y desfavorecer a los inmigrantes (p. 755)

**naturalize (naturalizar)** solicitud y concesión de la ciudadanía norteamericana

**natural rights (derechos naturales)** derechos que tiene la gente simplemente por ser humanos

**neutral (neutral)** que no toma partido en un conflicto o disputa

**New Deal (Nuevo Trato)** los programas de ayuda, recuperación y reforma del Presidente Franklin Roosevelt para combatir la Gran Depresión (pp. 403, 769)

**New England Colonies (colonias de Nueva Inglaterra)** las colonias inglesas que se convirtieron en los estados de Connecticut, Rhode Island, Massachusetts, Vermont, Nueva Hampshire y Maine

**New Federalism (Nuevo Federalismo)** el plan del Presidente Reagan para dar a los estados más control sobre el uso de la ayuda federal (p. 705)

**New Freedom (Nueva Libertad)** la plataforma de la campaña de Woodrow Wilson en 1912, en la que se pedía acción antimonopolio sin amenazar la libre competencia (p. 298)

**New Frontier (Nueva Frontera)** las propuestas del

Presidente Kennedy para mejorar la economía, ayudar a los pobres y acelerar el programa espacial (p. 542)

**New Left (Nueva Izquierda)** un movimiento político nuevo de finales de la década de 1960 que pedía cambios radicales para luchar contra la pobreza y el racismo (p. 627)

**New Nationalism (Nuevo Nacionalismo)** el programa de Theodore Roosevelt para aumentar la regulación federal de los negocios y lugares de trabajo, los impuestos sobre la renta y las herencias y reformas electorales (p. 297)

**New Right (nueva derecha)** una coalición de grupos conservadores que surgió hacia 1980 (p. 702)

**Niagara Movement (Movimiento Niágara)** una organización fundada en 1905 por W.E.B. Du Bois y otros líderes negros que pedía libertades civiles totales para los afroamericanos, el fin de la discriminación racial y el reconocimiento de la hermandad de los seres humanos (p. 235)

**Nisei (nisei)** un japonés-americano cuyos padres nacieron en Japón (p. 429)

**nomadic (nómada)** que cambia de lugar regularmente en busca de alimento

**nomad (nómada)** una persona que emigra constantemente, en lugar de vivir permanentemente en un lugar

**nonviolent protest (protesta no-violenta)** una forma de protesta en la que los protestantes no se resisten o devuelven los golpes al ser atacados (p. 565)

**North American Free Trade Agreement (NAFTA) (Zona de Libre Comercio del Atlántico Norte)** un acuerdo por el que se suprimen las restricciones al comercio entre Estados Unidos, Canadá y México (pp. 737, 784)

**North Atlantic Treaty Organization (NATO) (Organización del Tratado del Atlántico Norte) (OTAN)** la alianza entre Estados Unidos, Canadá y naciones de Europa Occidental, formada en 1949 (pp. 495, 796)

**Nuclear Regulatory Commission (Comisión para la Regulación Nuclear)** una organización gubernamental formada en 1974 para supervisar los usos civiles de materiales nucleares (p. 607)

**nullification (anulación)** negativa de un estado a reconocer una ley federal

# O

**obsolete (obsoleto)** anticuado

**Office of War Information (Oficina de Información para la Guerra)** una agencia federal creada en 1942 para conseguir apoyo público para el esfuerzo de guerra de la segunda guerra mundial (p. 466)

**Office of War Mobilization (Oficina de Mobilización para la Guerra)** una agencia federal creada en 1943 para coordinar asuntos relacionados con la producción de guerra durante la segunda guerra mundial (p. 460)

**Olive Branch Petition (Petición de la Rama de Olivo)** una petición que los colonos norteamericanos hicieron al rey Jorge III en 1775 para que él parara la lucha

**Open Door Policy (política de puertas abiertas)** la estrategia norteamericana con China hacia el 1900, que favorecía relaciones comerciales abiertas entre China y otras naciones (p. 269)

**oral history (historia oral)** tradiciones transmitidas por la palabra de generación en generación

**Oregon Trail (Pista Oregón)** una ruta que unía Independence, Misuri, y Oregón, usada por muchos pioneros durante la década de 1840

**Organization of Petroleum Exporting Countries (OPEC) (Organización de Países Exportadores de Petróleo) (OPEP)** un grupo de naciones que colaboraban para regular el precio y suministro de petróleo (p. 655)

# P

**pardon (perdón)** absolución oficial de un crimen (p. 127)

**Paris peace talks (conferencias de París para la paz)** las negociaciones entre los Estados Unidos y Vietnam del Norte, que comenzaron en 1968 (p. 635)

**pass (paso)** un lugar a poca altura en una cadena montañosa que permite el paso de viajeros al otro lado

**patent (patente)** una licencia para fabricar, usar o vender un invento (p. 152)

**patronage (patrocinio)** la práctica de contratar a partidarios políticos para puestos de trabajo en el gobierno

**Peace Corps (Cuerpo de Paz)** un programa federal establecido para mandar voluntarios para ayudar a las naciones en desarrollo en todo el mundo (p. 557)

**Pendleton Civil Service Act (Acta Pendleton de Servicio Civil)** una ley de 1883 que creó una Comisión para el Servicio Civil y declaró que a los empleados federales no se les podía exigir que contribuyeran a los fondos para las campañas electorales y no podían ser despedidos por razones políticas (p. 207)

**Pentagon Papers (Papeles del Pentágono)** un estudio del gobierno sobre la participación de los Estados Unidos en la guerra de Vietnam, hecho público en 1971 (p. 626)

**Pequot War (guerra Pequot)** la guerra entre los colonos ingleses y los indios pequot en 1637

**per capita income (renta per cápita)** promedio de los ingresos por persona (p. 511)

**persecute (perseguir)** oprimir a alguien a causa de sus creencias

**Persian Gulf War (guerra del Golfo Pérsico)** la guerra en la que fuerzas de las Naciones Unidas expulsaron de Kuwait al ejército invasor iraquí en 1991 (p. 718)

**philanthropist (filántropo)** persona que hace donaciones a causas que lo merecen (p. 233)

**Pickett's Charge (Carga de Pickett)** la desafortunada carga de la infantería confederada durante la batalla de Gettysburg (p. 109)

**piecework (trabajo a destajo)** un sistema en el que a los trabajadores no se les paga por horas sino por lo que producen (p. 164)

**Pilgrim (peregrino)** un miembro del grupo de separatistas ingleses que establecieron la colonia de Plymouth en 1620

**Pinckney Treaty (Tratado Pinckney)** un tratado entre los Estados Unidos y España en 1795 que estableció los límites de los Estados Unidos por el sur

**placer mining (minería de lavadero)** un método minero usado por buscadores particulares (p. 185)

**plantation (plantación)** una gran instalación agrícola en la que las cosechas se cultivan principalmente para la venta

***Plessy* v. *Ferguson* (*Plessy* contra *Ferguson*)** un caso de 1896 en el que el Tribunal Supremo falló que la segregación racial era legal siempre que las instalaciones separadas fueran iguales para ambas razas (p. 243)

**political asylum (asilo político)** protección que un país da a los refugiados de otro país (p. 753)

**political machine (maquinaria política)** una organización no oficial diseñada para mantener en el poder a un partido o grupo en particular, dirigida normalmente por un único y poderoso jefe (p. 220)

**political party (partido político)** un grupo de personas que tratan de ganar las elecciones y los cargos públicos para controlar la política y los programas del gobierno

**poll tax (impuesto por persona)** una tarifa especial que se debe pagar antes de que una persona pueda votar (p. 242)

**Pontiac's Rebellion (rebelión de Pontiac)** una rebelión de los indígenas norteamericanos contra los británicos en la región de los Grandes Lagos, en 1763

**Poor People's Campaign (Campaña de los Pobres)** una cruzada contra la injusticia económica organizada en 1968 por Martin Luther King, Jr. (p. 650)

**popular sovereignty (soberanía popular)** dejar que la gente de un territorio decida si se va a permitir la esclavitud en él

**population density (densidad de población)** el número de personas promedio que viven en un espacio dado

**Populist (populista)** un seguidor del partido populista, formado en 1891, que apoyaba la creación de una provisión mayor de dinero y otras reformas económicas (p. 193)

**precedent (precedente)** algo que se ha hecho o dicho que se convierte en un ejemplo, regla o tradición a seguir

**prejudice (prejuicio)** una opinión irracional, generalmente desfavorable, sobre otro grupo

**presidio (presidio)** fuerte construido en el Suroeste por los españoles

**price controls (control de precios)** un sistema de precios determinados por el gobierno (p. 323)

**prime minister (primer ministro)** el funcionario más alto de un gobierno parlamentario

**privateer (corsario)** un barco propiedad de un particular que es contratado por un gobierno para atacar a barcos enemigos

**Proclamation of 1763 (Proclamación de 1763)** una orden del rey británico que cerró la región al oeste de los Apalaches y prohibió el asentamiento de colonos

**productivity (productividad)** la cantidad que produce un trabajador en un periodo de tiempo (pp. 152, 803)

**profiteering (acaparamiento)** venta de bienes escasos a precios irracionalmente altos

**progressive (progresista)** reformista político y social de finales de los 1800 y principios de los 1900 (p. 768)

**Progressive Era (Era Progresista)** el periodo entre 1890 y 1920 durante el cual se realizaron una serie de reformas a nivel local, estatal y federal (p. 287)

**progressive income tax (impuesto progresivo sobre la renta)** un impuesto en el que el porcentaje de tasas que se deben aumenta con la renta percibida (p. 193)

**prohibition (prohibición)** prohibición legal de manufacturación y venta de bebidas alcohólicas (p. 224)

**proliferation (proliferación)** aumento rápido del número, esparcimiento (p. 662)

**proprietary colony (colonia propiedad)** concesión de una colonia con plenos derechos de gobierno que el rey o reina hace a un individuo o grupo

**public works program (programa de obras públicas)** un programa financiado por el gobierno para construir obras públicas (p. 405)

**Pueblo Revolt of 1680 (revuelta de los Pueblo de 1680)** una revuelta de los indios pueblo de Nuevo México contra España

**Pullman Strike (huelga Pullman)** la huelga de trabajadores del ferrocarril que se extendió por toda la nación (p. 172)

**Puritan (puritano)** una persona a favor de la purificación de la Iglesia Anglicana de Inglaterra

## Q

**Quaker (cuáquero)** un miembro de un grupo protestante que pone énfasis en la igualdad

**quarantine (cuarentena)** un periodo de aislamiento para prevenir la extensión de una enfermedad (p. 212)

**quorum (quórum)** el numero minimo de miembros necesarios para votar

**quota (cuota)** un número límite (p. 345)

# R

**racism (racismo)** la creencia que sostiene que las diferencias en carácter o inteligencia se deben a la raza de la persona (p. 278)

**ragtime (ragtime)** un estilo de música que consiste en melodías con acentos sincopados sobre un pulso constante (p. 239)

**ratify (ratificar)** aprobar o sancionar

**rationing (racionar)** distribuir cantidades fijas de bienes entre los consumidores (p. 323)

***realpolitik* (realpolitik)** en alemán, "política práctica," o política exterior basada en el interés en lugar de en principios morales (p. 659)

**recall (retirar)** un proceso por el que los votantes destituyen a un funcionario público de su puesto antes de la próxima elección (p. 292)

**recession (recesión)** un periodo de poca actividad económica (p. 677)

**recognition (reconocimiento)** aceptación oficial (p. 96)

**Reconstruction (reconstrucción)** el esfuerzo del gobierno federal entre 1865 y 1877 por reparar los daños causados al Sur y devolver los estados sureños a la Unión (p. 125)

**red scare (miedo a los rojos)** miedo al comunismo y a otras ideas extremas (p. 342)

**referendum (referéndum)** un proceso por el que los ciudadanos votan una ley aprobada por su legislatura (p. 292)

**Reformation (Reforma)** una revuelta contra la Iglesia Católica, que comenzó en 1517

**religious tolerance (tolerancia religiosa)** la idea que mantiene que personas de religiones distintas deberían vivir juntas en paz

**Renaissance (Renacimiento)** una era de la historia europea, desde el año 1300 al 1500

**reparations (compensación)** pago que un enemigo debe hacer por daños económicos sufridos durante una guerra (p. 330)

**republic (república)** gobierno del pueblo por medio de sus representantes electos (p. 42)

**republican virtues (virtudes republicanas)** las virudes que el pueblo norteamericano necesitaría para gobernarse a sí mismo, como sacrificar las necesidades individuales por el bien de la comunidad, autoconfianza, industria, frugalidad y armonía

**reservation (reserva)** una área que el gobierno federal reservó para los indígenas norteamericanos que habían perdido su tierra natal (p. 180)

**restrictive covenant (pacto restrictivo)** un acuerdo entre propietarios de viviendas para no vender propiedades inmobiliarias a ciertos grupos de personas, como a los afroamericanos o a los judíos (p. 219)

**revenue (ingresos)** renta (p. 416)

**revival (renacer)** una reunión en la que las personas "renacen," o son devueltas a una vida religiosa

**Revolutionary War (guerra de Independencia)** la guerra de los colonos norteamericanos por conseguir la independencia de Gran Bretaña, que duró de 1775 a 1783 (p. 30)

**rock and roll** un tipo de música que surge del rhythm and blues y que se hizo popular en la década de 1950 (p. 521)

***Roe* v. *Wade* (*Roe* contra *Wade*)** en 1973, la decisión del Tribunal Supremo que legalizó el aborto (p. 593)

**Roosevelt Corollary (Corolario de Roosevelt)** la ampliación que el Presidente Theodore Roosevelt hizo en 1904 de la Doctrina Monroe, en la que Roosevelt afirmaba el derecho de los Estados Unidos a intervenir en naciones latinoamericanas (pp. 273, 787)

**Rosie the Riveter (Rosie "la remachadora")** un término que simboliza a las muchas mujeres que trabajaron en la industria de defensa durante la segunda guerra mundial (p. 470)

**royal colony (colonia real)** una colonia con un gobernador nombrado por el rey

**rural (rural)** ambiente de campo, en vez de ambiente de ciudad

**rural free delivery (reparto rural gratuito)** la entrega gratuita de paquetes en las áreas rurales, que comenzó en 1896 (p. 248)

**Russian Revolution (revolución Rusa)** el colapso del gobierno del zar en Rusia en 1917, que finalmente llevó a la toma del poder por los bolcheviques (p. 316)

# S

**sachem (cacique)** un líder indígena norteamericano

**Salem witch trials (juicios por brujería de Salem)** el procesamiento y ejecución de veinte mujeres y hombres acusados de brujería en Massachusetts, en 1692

**SALT I (Strategic Arms Limitation Treaty) (tratado para la limitación de armas estratégicas)** un acuerdo firmado en 1972 por los Estados Unidos y la Unión Soviética sobre la limitación de armas nucleares (p. 662)

**salutary neglect (negligencia saludable)** la política británica a principios de los 1700 consistente en no interferir en la política y la economía de las colonias norteamericanas, siempre que dicha negligencia sirviera a los intereses económicos británicos

**Sandinista (sandinista)** un miembro del grupo de nicaragüenses que se hicieron con el gobierno en 1979 (p. 711)

**Santa Fe Trail (Pista de Santa Fe)** un camino que unía Independence, Misuri, con Santa Fe, Nuevo México, a mediados del siglo XIX

**satellite nation (nación satélite)** un país dominado política y económicamente por otro país, especialmente por la Unión Soviética durante la guerra fría (p. 487)

**saturation bombing (bombardeo de saturación)** arrojar grandes concentraciones de bombas sobre cierta área (p. 623)

**savanna (sabana)** una región cerca del ecuador con praderas tropicales y árboles dispersos

**scab (esquirol)** un trabajador contratado por un patrón para reemplazar a obreros en huelga (p. 170)

**scalawag (republicano del Sur)** un apodo insultante para un republicano blanco del Sur después de la guerra Civil (p. 136)

**scarce (escaso)** que hay poco

**Scopes trial (juicio Scopes)** un juicio en Tennessee en 1925 sobre la enseñanza de la teoría de la evolución en las escuelas públicas (p. 368)

***Scott* v. *Sandford* (*Scott* contra *Sandford*)** una decisión del Tribunal Supremo en 1857 que declaró que los esclavos no eran ciudadanos y reguló el Compromiso de Misuri era inconstitucional

**secede (secesión)** renunciar formalmente a ser miembro de un grupo u organización (p. 82)

**secessionist (secesionista)** una persona que quería que el Sur se separara

**Second Amendment (Segunda Enmienda)** enmienda a la Constitución de los Estados Unidos que concede a los estados el derecho a formar milicia armada (p. 763)

**Second Continental Congress (Segundo Congreso Continental)** una asamblea de representantes de las colonias que se reunió por primera vez en Filadelfia en mayo de 1775 (p. 30)

**Second Great Awakening (Segundo Gran Despertar)** un movimiento religioso de principios del S. XIX

**Second New Deal (Segundo Nuevo Trato)** un periodo de actividad legislativa emprendido por el Presidente Franklin Roosevelt en 1935 (p. 408)

**section (sección)** una región geográfica

**secularize (secularizar)** poner bajo el control del gobierno en vez del de la iglesia

**sedition (sedición)** palabras o acciones que fomentan la rebelión (p. 324)

**segregation (segregación)** separación por la fuerza (p. 214)

**Selective Service Act (Ley de Servicio Selectivo)** una ley de 1917 que autorizaba la leva de hombres jóvenes para el servicio militar (p. 317)

**self-determination (autodeterminación)** el poder de tomar decisiones sobre el propio futuro (p. 328)

**self-sufficient (autosuficiente)** capaz de hacer todo lo necesario para mantenerse a sí mismo

**Seneca Falls Convention (Convención de Seneca Falls)** la primera convención sobre los derechos de la mujer en la historia de los Estados Unidos, celebrada en 1848

**seniority (antigüedad)** estado derivado de la duración del servicio (p. 472)

**separation of powers (separación de poderes)** la separación de poderes en el gobierno federal entre el poder legislativo, executivo y judicial

**settlement house (centro de residencia)** un centro comunitario organizado para proveer varios servicios a los pobres de la ciudad (p. 225)

**sharecropping (aparcería)** un sistema de cultivo en el que un agricultor cultivaba una porción de tierra de otro propietario y recibía como pago parte de la cosecha en el momento de la recolección (p. 138)

**Shays' Rebellion (Rebelión de Shay)** una revuelta contra los impuestos en Massachusetts en 1786 y 1787

**shell (granada)** un artefacto que explota en el aire o cuando choca contra un objetivo sólido (p. 90)

**Sherman Antitrust Act (Acta Antimonopolios Sherman)** una ley aprobada en 1890 que prohibía cualquier combinación de compañías que limitaran el comercio (p. 161)

**shuttle diplomacy (diplomacia itinerante)** viajes repetidos de un mediador entre naciones en disputa con la intención de llegar a un acuerdo (p. 684)

**siege (asedio)** una táctica en la que se rodea al enemigo y se le hace pasar hambre para que se rinda (p. 110)

**silent majority (mayoría silenciosa)** un término usado por el Presidente Nixon para describir a los norteamericanos que no estaban de acuerdo con la contracultura (p. 656)

**sit-down strike (huelga de brazos caídos)** una protesta laboral en la que los trabajadores dejan de trabajar pero se niegan a abandonar el lugar de trabajo (p. 417)

**sit-in (sentada)** forma de protesta en la que los protestantes se sientan y se niegan a moverse; los defensores de los derechos civiles las usaron a veces para protestar pacíficamente (p. 570)

**social Darwinism (darwinismo social)** una teoría, derivada de la teoría sobre la selección natural de Darwin, según la cual la sociedad debe interferir lo menos posible en la búsqueda de la felicidad de sus individuos (p. 160)

**social gospel movement (movimiento del evangelio social)** un movimiento de reforma social que se desarrolló en instituciones religiosas y que buscaba la aplicación directa de la palabra de Jesús en la sociedad (p. 225)

**socialism (socialismo)** una filosofía económica y política que favorece el control público (o social) de la propiedad y los ingresos (p. 167)

**Social Security system (sistema de Seguridad Social)** un sistema público que proporciona pagos regulares a personas que no pueden mantenerse a sí mismas (p. 409)

**social welfare program (programa de bienestar social)**

un programa diseñado para asegurar un estándar de vida básico para todos los ciudadanos (p. 288)

**software (software)** programa para una computadora (p. 802)

**solid South (Sólido Sur)** un término que describe la dominación ejercida por el partido demócrata en el Sur desde la guerra Civil (p. 142)

**sooner (primer colono)** una persona que señalaba su propiedad en territorio indio antes de que éste se abriera legalmente a la colonización (p. 183)

**Southern Christian Leadership Conference (SCLC) (Conferencia de Liderazgo Cristiano del Sur)** una organización en favor de los derechos civiles formada en 1957 por el Dr. Martin Luther King, Jr., y otros líderes (p. 565)

**Southern Colonies (colonias del sur)** las colonias inglesas de Virginia, Maryland, las Carolinas y Georgia

**speakeasy (bar clandestino)** durante la Prohibición, un bar donde se servían ilegalmente bebidas alcohólicas (p. 366)

**special prosecutor (fiscal especial)** un investigador nombrado por el Departamento de Justicia para investigar irregularidades cometidas por funcionarios del gobierno (p. 668)

**specie (metálico)** moneda de oro o plata

**speculation (especulación)** inversiones de alto riesgo con la esperanza de obtener mucha ganancia (p. 377)

**sphere of influence (esfera de influencia)** área de control económico y político que ejerce una nación sobre otra u otras naciones (p. 269)

**spiritual (espiritual)** un himno popular

**spoils (botín)** recompensa (p. 329)

**spoils system (sistema de sinecuras)** sistema o práctica por el que el partido ganador en una elección concede cargos oficiales como recompensa; el nombre del sistema de padrinazgo bajo la presidencia de Jackson

***Sputnik*** el primer satélite artificial en orbitar la Tierra, lanzado por la Unión Soviética en 1957 (p. 506)

**stagflation (estanflación)** una combinación de alta inflación y alto desempleo, sin crecimiento económico (p. 677)

**stalemate (punto muerto)** una situación en la que ninguna de las partes en conflicto es capaz de conseguir ventaja (p. 310)

**Stamp Act (Ley del Impuesto de los Sellos)** una ley aprobada por el Parlamento británico en 1765 que exigía un impuesto sobre los periódicos, documentos legales y otros materiales impresos en las colonias (p. 28)

**staple crop (cultivo básico)** una cosecha que está en constante demanda, como el algodón, el trigo o el arroz

**states' rights (derechos de los estados)** la teoría que sostiene que la potencia dividida constitución entre los estados y el gobierno federal y que una interpretación terminante de esa división debe ser respetada

**steerage (tercera clase)** una área grande y espaciosa debajo de la cubierta del barco en la que viajaban muchos inmigrantes pobres (p. 211)

**stereotype (estereotipo)** una concepción fija en la que cree un grupo de personas (p. 200)

**Stono Rebellion (rebelión Stono)** una revuelta de esclavos en Carolina del Sur en 1739

**Strategic Arms Reduction Treaty (START) (tratado para la reducción de armas estratégicas)** el acuerdo firmado en 1991 que establecía una reducción cuantiosa del armamento nuclear de norteamericanos y soviéticos (p. 717)

**Strategic Defense Initiative (SDI) (Iniciativa de Defensa Estratégica)** propuesta del Presidente Reagan para crear un sistema de defensa contra un ataque nuclear (p. 705)

**strict construction (interpretación estricta)** la creencia en que el gobierno no debería hacer nada que la Constitución no diga explícitamente que puede hacer

**strike (huelga)** parar de trabajar para forzar al patrón a cumplir ciertas exigencias, como un salario más alto o mejores condiciones de trabajo

**Student Nonviolent Coordinating Committee (SNCC) (Comité No Violento de Coordinación Estudiantil)** una organización estudiantil a favor de los derechos civiles fundada en 1960 (p. 567)

**subsidy (subsidio)** un pago del gobierno para fomentar el desarrollo de ciertas industrias clave (p. 206)

**suburb (suburbio)** una comunidad residencial que rodea una ciudad (p. 218)

**suffrage (sufragio)** derecho a votar

**supply-side economics (economía de suministro indirecto)** la teoría que defiende que las reducciones de impuestos aumentarán la inversión y por lo tanto fomentarán el crecimiento económico (p. 703)

**Sussex pledge (la promesa de Sussex)** en 1916, una promesa del gobierno alemán de que sus submarinos avisarían a los barcos antes de atacar (p. 315)

**synagogue (sinagoga)** casa judía de oración

# T

**Taft-Hartley Act (Ley Taft-Hartley)** una ley de 1947 que permitía que el Presidente ordenara que volvieran al trabajo los trabajadores en huelga de ciertas industrias (p. 524)

**tariff (tarifa)** un impuesto sobre los bienes extranjeros importados en un país (pp. 68, 784)

**Tariff of 1828 (Tarifa de 1828)** un impuesto elevado sobre bienes manufacturados; llamada la "Tarifa de la Abominación" por los sureños

**teach-in (sesión de instrucción)** una sesión especial de conferencia y debate sobre un tema polémico (p. 627)

**Teapot Dome scandal (escándalo del Teapot Dome)** un escándalo durante la administración Harding referente a la concesión de derechos de prospección petrolera en tierras del gobierno a cambio de dinero (p. 345)

**telecommunications (telecomunicaciones)** comunicación a larga distancia por medios electrónicos (p. 1058)

**televangelism (televangelismo)** el uso de la televisión por organizaciones religiosas, especialmente para recaudar fondos (p. 702)

**temperance movement (movimiento de la templanza)** una campaña organizada para eliminar el consumo de alcohol (p. 224)

**tenant farming (agricultor arrendatario)** sistema de labranza en el que un agricultor alquila tierras de cultivo a un hacendado (p. 138)

**tenement (casa de vecindad)** un edificio de apartamentos lleno de gente, con pobres condiciones sanitarias, de seguridad y de comodidad (p. 218)

**Tennessee Valley Authority (Autoridades del Valle del Tennessee)** un proyecto federal para proporcionar corriente eléctrica, control de inundación y oportunidades recreativas en el valle del río Tennessee (p. 406)

**Tet Offensive (Ofensiva Tet)** el ataque que en 1968 lanzaron fuerzas norvietnamitas y del Victcong contra Vietnam del Sur (p. 621)

**Texas War for Independence (guerra de la Independencia de Texas)** la exitosa revuelta de los texanos contra el gobierno mexicano en 1835–1836 (p. 78)

**Thirteenth Amendment (Decimotercera Enmienda)** la enmienda constitucional, ratificada en 1865, que abolió la esclavitud (p. 116)

**38th parallel (paralelo 38)** la línea de latitud que dividía a Corea del Norte y Corea del Sur (p. 500)

**Three-Fifths Compromise (Compromiso de las Tres Quintas Partes)** el compromiso en la Convención Constitucional que establecía que las tres quintas partes de los esclavos de un estado contaran para propósitos de representación

**totalitarian (totalitario)** que describe una forma de gobierno que controla todos los aspectos de la vida de sus ciudadanos (p. 429)

**trade deficit (déficit comercial)** la cantidad de dinero que se pierde cuando una nación gasta más en importación de lo que gana con la exportación (p. 785)

**trade surplus (excedente comercial)** la cantidad de dinero que se gana cuando una nación gana más con la exportación de lo que gasta en importación (p. 785)

**Trail of Tears (Sendero de Lágrimas)** el desalojo forzoso de los cheroquís en 1838-1839 y su traslado a tierras al oeste del río Misisipí (p. 75)

**trans-Appalachia (transapalaches)** el área al oeste de los Montes Apalaches

**transcendentalism (trascendentalismo)** un movimiento filosófico a mediados del S. XIX que enfatizaba el descubrimiento espiritual y la clarividencia en lugar de la razón

**transcontinental railroad (ferrocarril transcontinental)** un ferrocarril que iba de costa a costa (p. 152)

**transistor (transistor)** un pequeñísimo circuito que amplifica, controla y genera señales eléctricas (p. 512)

**Treaty of Ghent (Tratado de Ghent)** el acuerdo firmado en 1814 que puso fin a la guerra de 1812

**Treaty of Greenville (Tratado de Greenville)** un tratado frimado en 1795 por los Estados Unidos y varios pueblos indígenas norteamericanos por el que los indios norteamericanos cedían el control de casi todo Ohio

**Treaty of Guadalupe Hidalgo (Tratado de Guadalupe Hidalgo)** un tratado firmado en 1848 por los Estados Unidos y México, que ponía final a la guerra Mexicana

**Treaty of Paris (1763) (Tratado de París de 1763)** el tratado que terminó la guerra Franco-india y por el cual Francia renunció en favor de Gran Bretaña a sus pretensiones sobre los territorios norteamericanos

**Treaty of Paris (1783) (Tratado de París de 1783)** el tratado que puso fin a la guerra de la Independencia y en el cual Gran Bretaña reconoció la independencia de Norteamérica (p. 31)

**Treaty of Tordesillas (Tratado de Tordesillas)** un tratado firmado por Portugal y España en 1494 en el que se repartían el mundo no cristiano

**triangular trade (comercio triangular)** el comercio entre las Américas, Europa y África (p. 24)

**Truman Doctrine (Doctrina Truman)** la declaración del Presidente Truman en 1947 que decía que los Estados Unidos apoyarían a las naciones amenazadas por el comunismo (pp. 490, 795)

**trust (sociedad de fidecomiso)** un grupo de compañías independientes que se sitúan bajo el control de una junta directiva (p. 161)

**trustee (depositario)** alguien en quien se deposita la confianza para que se encargue de un negocio

**Turner's Rebellion (Rebelión de Turner)** una fracasada revuelta de esclavos dirigida por Nat Turner en 1831

**Turner thesis (Tesis de Turner)** el razonamiento que hizo Frederick Jackson Turner en 1893, que decía que la frontera había dado forma al estilo de vida norteamericano (p. 198)

**turnpike (carretera de peaje)** una carretera en la que los usuarios deben pagar peaje

**Twenty-first Amendment (Vigesimoprimera Enmienda)** la enmienda constitucional, ratificada en 1933, que terminó con la Prohibición (p. 391)

# U

**U-boat** un submarino alemán (p. 314)

**Underground Railroad (Ferrocarril Subterráneo)** una red de rutas de escape que facilitaba protección y transporte a los esclavos que huían hacia el norte en busca de libertad

**undocumented immigrant (inmigrante indocumentado)** inmigrante que ha entrado ilegalmente en los Estados Unidos (p. 753)

**Union (Unión)** los Estados Unidos como entidad nacional; o, durante la guerra Civil, el Norte

**United Farm Workers (UFW) (Trabajadores Agrícolas Unidos)** un sindicato organizado por César Chávez para organizar a los braceros mexicanos en el oeste (p. 598)

**Upper South (Alto Sur)** los estados de Virginia, Carolina del Norte, Tennessee y Arkansas

**utopian community (comunidad utópica)** una pequeña sociedad dedicada a la perfección de las condiciones sociales y políticas

**U-2 incident (incidente U-2)** el derribo de un avión espía norteamericano sobre la Unión Soviética en 1960 (p. 506)

# V

**vaudeville (vodevil)** un espectáculo de variedades que presentaba números cómicos, musicales y de baile (p. 236)

**Versailles Treaty (Tratado de Versalles)** el tratado de 1919 que terminó la primera guerra mundial (p. 330)

**vertical consolidation (consolidación vertical)** hacerse con el control de los numerosos y distintos negocios que componen todas las fases del desarrollo de un producto (p. 161)

**veto (veto)** impedir que se convierta en ley (p. 41)

**vice (vicio)** comportamiento inmoral o corrupto (p. 224)

**victory garden (huerta de la victoria)** una huerta casera creada para incrementar la producción alimentaria durante la segunda guerra mundial (p. 466)

**Viet Cong (Vietcong)** fuerza formada por guerrillas comunistas en Vietnam del Sur que, con apoyo norvietnamita, luchó contra el gobierno de Vietnam del Sur en la guerra del Vietnam (p. 619)

**Vietnamization (vietnamización)** la política de reemplazar a las fuerzas militares norteamericanas por las de Vietnam del Sur (p. 635)

**Vietnam Veterans Memorial (Monumento Conmemorativo de los Veteranos de Vietnam)** el monumento en Washington, D.C., construido para honrar a los caídos en la guerra del Vietnam (p. 638)

**vigilante (vigilante)** un ciudadano que toma la ley en sus manos (p. 324)

**Virginia and Kentucky Resolutions (Resoluciones de Virginia y Kentucky)** resoluciones aprobadas en 1798 que atacaban la Ley de Extranjería y Sedición por ser anticonstitucionales

**Volunteers in Service to America (VISTA) (Voluntarios en Servicio a Norteamérica)** un programa federal organizado para mandar voluntarios a ayudar a las personas en las comunidades pobres (p. 547)

**Voting Rights Act of 1965 (Ley de Derechos Electorales de 1965)** una ley que se proponía reducir los impedimentos para el voto de los afroamericanos, en parte por medio del aumento de la autoridad federal para censar votantes (p. 579)

# W

**Wagner Act (Ley de Wagner)** una ley aprobada en 1935 que ayudaba a los sindicatos al legalizar la negociación colectiva y establecer la Mesa Nacional de Relaciones Laborales (p. 409)

**Wannsee Conference (Conferencia de Wansee)** la conferencia celebrada en 1942 en Alemania relativa al plan para asesinar a los judíos europeos (p. 453)

**war bond (bono de guerra)** un bono de ahorro del gobierno que se vende para recaudar dinero para la guerra (p. 463)

**War of 1812 (guerra de 1812)** la guerra entre los Estados Unidos y Gran Bretaña (p. 72)

**war of attrition (guerra de desgaste)** una guerra en la que uno de los lados causa continuas pérdidas al enemigo para disminuir su resistencia (p. 89)

**War Powers Act (Ley de los Poderes de Guerra)** una ley de 1973 que limita el poder del Presidente para desplegar tropas en el extranjero (p. 678)

**War Refugee Board (Oficina de Refugiados de Guerra)** una agencia federal creada en 1994 para tratar de ayudar a las personas amenazadas de muerte por los nazis (p. 454)

**Warren Commission (Comisión Warren)** la comisión presidida por el juez presidente Earl Warren que investigó el asesinato del Presidente Kennedy (p. 544)

**Warsaw Pact (Pacto de Varsovia)** una alianza militar entre la Unión Soviética y naciones de Europa del este formada en 1955 (pp. 495, 797)

**Watergate scandal (escándalo Watergate)** el escándalo que supuso el descubrimiento de actividades ilegales que finalmente produjeron la renuncia del Presidente Nixon en 1974 (p. 666)

**welfare capitalism (capitalismo del bienestar)** una estrategia laboral en la que las compañías satisfacen algunas de las necesidades de sus trabajadores sin intervención de los sindicatos (p. 376)

**Whiskey Rebellion (rebelión del Whisky)** los desórdenes de 1794 causados por la oposición a un impuesto sobre el whisky

**Whitewater affair (asunto Whitewater)** acusaciones contra el Presidente Clinton en las que se alegaba su participación en transacciones comerciales ilegales antes de convertirse en presidente (p. 727)

**wildcat strike (huelga no autorizada)** una huelga organizada por los trabajadores en vez de por los dirigentes sindicales (p. 462)

**Wilderness Road** un camino construido en 1770 que se convirtió en la ruta principal para atravesar los Montes Apalaches

**Woodstock festival (festival de Woodstock)** un festival de 1969 en el norte del estado de Nueva York (p. 632)

**work ethic (ética del trabajo)** sistema de valores que pone énfasis en la importancia del trabajo arduo para desarrollar la personalidad y conseguir el éxito (p. 772)

**World Trade Organization (WTO) (Organización Mundial del Trabajo)** una organización internacional formada en 1995 para fomentar la expansión del comercio mundial (p. 737)

**World Wide Web (Red Informática Mundial)** organización de redes globales de computadores por medio de la cual los usuarios pueden acceder a la información (p. 805)

**writ of habeas corpus (orden de hábeas corpus)** una protección legal que requiere que un tribunal determine si una persona ha sido encarcelada legalmente (p. 98)

# X

**XYZ Affair (Asunto XYZ)** en 1798, la controversia causada por las exigencias de los franceses en recibir sobornos de los negociadores norteamericanos

# Y

**Yalta Conference (Conferencia de Yalta)** la reunión en 1945 entre Churchill, Stalin y Roosevelt en la que los líderes hablaron de planes para el mundo de la posguerra (p. 443)

**yellow journalism (periodismo amarillo)** un tipo de información periodística que da importancia a relatos sensacionalistas de crimen y escándalo (p. 238)

# Z

**Zimmermann note (nota de Zimmermann)** una nota de un diplomático alemán en la que en 1917 se proponía una alianza con México (p. 316)

# Biographical Dictionary

## A

**Adams, Abigail** First Lady, 1797–1801; as the wife of Patriot John Adams, she urged him to promote women's rights at the beginning of the American Revolution

**Adams, John Quincy** Sixth President of the United States, 1825–1829; proposed greater federal involvement in the economy through tariffs and improvements such as roads, bridges, and canals

**Adams, John** Second President of the United States, 1797–1801; worked to relieve increasing tensions with France; lost reelection bid to Jefferson in 1800 as the country moved away from Federalist policies

**Addams, Jane** Cofounder of Hull House, the first settlement house, in 1889; remained active in social causes through the early 1900s (p. 225)

**Agnew, Spiro** Vice President under President Richard Nixon until forced to resign in 1973 for crimes committed before taking office; known for his harsh campaign attacks (p. 668)

**Allen, Richard** African American religious leader; helped found the African Methodist Episcopal Church (AME) in 1816

**Anthony, Susan B.** Political activist and women's rights leader in the late 1800s (p. 301)

**Arthur, Chester A.** Twenty-first President of the United States, 1881–1885; signed 1883 Pendleton Act, which instituted the Civil Service (p. 207)

**Askia, Muhammad** Ruler of the African empire of Songhai, 1493–1528; promoted Islamic culture

**Austin, Stephen** Leader of first American group of Texas settlers in 1822

Susan B. Anthony

## B

**Bakke, Allan** Student who won a suit against the University of California in 1978 on the grounds that the affirmative action program had kept him out (p. 694)

**Baldwin, James** African American author and spokesperson for the civil rights movement during the 1960s (p. 580)

**Banks, Dennis** Native American leader in 1960s and 1970s; helped organize American Indian Movement (AIM) and the 1973 Wounded Knee occupation (p. 602)

**Beecher, Catharine** Author whose 1841 book *A Treatise on Domestic Economy* argued that women should support reform from the home

**Beecher, Lyman** Revivalist during the Second Great Awakening; feared the rise of selfishness in the United States

**Begin, Menachem** Israeli leader during the 1970s; began the Middle East peace process by reaching the 1978 Camp David Accords with Egypt (p. 685)

**Bell, Alexander Graham** Inventor; developed the telephone in 1876; one of the founders of American Telephone & Telegraph (AT&T) (p. 154)

**Bellamy, Edward** Author of the novel *Looking Backward* (1888), which proposed nationalizing trusts to eliminate social problems (p. 285)

**Bethune, Mary McLeod** African American educator, New Deal worker; founded Bethune Cookman College in the 1920s, advised the National Youth Administration (p. 406)

**Beveridge, Albert J.** Indiana senator in the early 1900s; saw United States imperialism as a duty owed to "primitive" societies (p. 262)

**Booth, John Wilkes** Southern actor who assassinated President Abraham Lincoln in 1865 (p. 117)

**Brady, James** Press Secretary to President Reagan who was paralyzed by a gunshot during a 1981 assassination attempt; the 1994 law requiring a five-day waiting period before purchase of a gun was named for Mr. Brady (p. 763)

**Breckinridge, John C.** Presidential candidate of the southern wing of the Democratic party in 1860

**Brown, John** Abolitionist crusader who massacred proslavery settlers in Kansas before the Civil War; hoped to inspire slave revolt with 1859 attack on Virginia arsenal; executed for treason against the state of Virginia

**Bruce, Blanche** African American senator from Mississippi during Reconstruction (p. 135)

**Bryan, William Jennings** Advocate of silver standard and proponent of Democratic and Populist views from the 1890s through the 1910s; Democratic candidate for President in 1896, 1900, and 1908 (p. 194)

**Buchanan, James** Fifteenth President of the United States, 1857–1861; supported by the South; attempted to moderate fierce disagreement over expansion of slavery

**Bush, George H. W.** Forty-first President of the United States, 1989–1993; continued Reagan's conservative policies; brought together United Nations coalition to fight the Persian Gulf War (p. 714)

**Byrd, William** Wealthy plantation owner in colonial Virginia whose diary gives a vivid picture of colonial life

## C

**Calhoun, John C.** Statesman from South Carolina who held many offices in the federal government; supported slavery, cotton exports, states' rights; in 1850 foresaw future conflicts over slavery

**Carnegie, Andrew** Industrialist who made a fortune in steel in the late 1800s through vertical consolidation; as a philanthropist, he gave away some $350 million (p. 159)

**Carson, Rachel** Marine biologist, author of *Silent Spring* (1962), which exposed harmful effects of pesticides and inspired concern for the environment (p. 606)

**Carter, James Earl, Jr.** Thirty-ninth President of the United States, 1977–1981; advocated concern for human rights in foreign policy; assisted in mediating the Camp David Accords (p. 680)

**Castro, Fidel** Revolutionary leader who took control of Cuba in 1959; ally of Soviet Union through the 1980s (p. 505)

**Catt, Carrie Chapman** Women's suffrage leader in the early 1900s; helped secure passage of Nineteenth Amendment in 1920; headed National American Woman Suffrage Association (p. 303)

**Champlain, Samuel de** French explorer who founded the city of Quebec in 1608

**Chavez, Cesar** Latino leader from 1962 to his death in 1993; organized the United Farm Workers (UFW) to help migratory farm workers gain better pay and working conditions (p. 597)

**Churchill, Winston** Leader of Great Britain before and during World War II; powerful speechmaker who rallied Allied morale during the war (p. 431)

**Clark, William** Leader, with Meriwether Lewis, of expedition through the West beginning in 1804; brought back scientific samples, maps, and information on Native Americans

**Clay, Henry** Statesman from Kentucky; accused by Jackson of giving votes to John Q. Adams in return for post as Secretary of State; endorsed government promotion of economic growth; advocate of Compromise of 1850

**Cleveland, Grover** Twenty-second and twenty-fourth President of the United States, 1885–1889, 1893–1897; supported railroad regulation and a return to the gold standard (p. 193)

**Clinton, Bill** Forty-second President of the United States, 1993–2001; defeated George Bush after overcoming numerous political obstacles; advocated economic and health-care reform (p. 723)

**Columbus, Christopher** Explorer whose voyage for Spain to North America in 1492 opened the Atlantic World

**Coolidge, Calvin** Thirtieth President of the United States, 1923–1929; promoted big business and opposed social aid (p. 343)

**Coughlin, Father Charles E.** "Radio Priest" who supported and then attacked President Franklin Roosevelt's New Deal; prevented by the Catholic Church from broadcasting after he praised Hitler (p. 413)

**Coxey, Jacob S.** Populist who led Coxey's Army in a march on Washington, D.C., in 1894 to seek government jobs for the unemployed (p. 209)

**Custer, George Armstrong** General who directed army attacks against Native Americans in the 1870s; commanded army forces killed in 1876 at Little Bighorn in Montana (p. 181)

## D

**Davis, Jefferson** President of the Confederate States of America; ordered attack on Fort Sumter, the first battle of the Civil War

**Dewey, George** Officer in United States Navy, 1861–1917; led a surprise attack in the Philippines during the Spanish-American War that destroyed the entire Spanish fleet (p. 266)

W.E.B. Du Bois

**Diem, Ngo Dinh** Leader of South Vietnam, 1954–1963; supported by United States, but not by Vietnamese Buddhist majority; assassinated in 1963 (p. 618)

**Dix, Dorothea** Advocate of prison reform and of special institutions for the mentally ill in Massachusetts before the Civil War

**Dole, Robert** Senator from Kansas, 1969–1996; challenged Bill Clinton for the presidency in 1996 (p. 727)

**Douglas, Stephen** Illinois senator who introduced the Kansas-Nebraska Act, which allowed new territories to choose their own position on slavery; debated Abraham Lincoln on slavery issues in 1858

**Douglass, Frederick** African American abolitionist leader who spoke eloquently for abolition in the United States and Britain before the Civil War

**Du Bois, W.E.B.** African American scholar and leader in early 1900s; encouraged African Americans to attend colleges to develop leadership skills (p. 235)

## E

**Edison, Thomas A.** Inventor; developed the light bulb, the phonograph, and hundreds of other inventions in the late 1800s and early 1900s (p. 154)

**Ehrlichman, John** Adviser on domestic policy to President Richard Nixon; deeply involved in Watergate (p. 654)

**Einstein, Albert** Physicist who fled Nazi persecution and later encouraged President Roosevelt to develop the atomic bomb (p. 448)

**Eisenhower, Dwight D.** Thirty-fourth President of the United States, 1953–1961; leader of Allied forces in World War II; as President, he promoted business and continued social programs (p. 503)

**Ellington, Duke** African American musician, bandleader, and composer of the 1920s and 1930s (p. 360)

**Ellsberg, Daniel** Defense Department official; leaked Pentagon Papers to *The New York Times* in 1971, showing government lies to public about Vietnam (p. 665)

**Equiano, Olaudah** Antislavery activist who wrote an account of his enslavement

## F

**Father Divine** African American minister; his Harlem soup kitchens fed the hungry during the Great Depression (p. 386)

**Fillmore, Millard** Thirteenth President of the United States, 1850–1853; promoted the Compromise of 1850 to smooth over disagreements about slavery in new territories

**Finney, Charles Grandison** Revivalist during the Second Great Awakening; emphasized religious conversion and personal choice

**Fitzgerald, F. Scott** Novelist who depicted the United States and the world during the 1920s in novels such as *The Great Gatsby* (p. 362)

**Fitzhugh, George** Southern author who criticized northern industrialists for exploiting workers in his 1857 book *Cannibals All!*

**Ford, Gerald R.** Thirty-eighth President of the United States, 1974–1977; succeeded and pardoned Nixon; failed to establish strong leadership (p. 675)

**Ford, Henry** Pioneering auto manufacturer in the early 1900s; made affordable cars for the masses using assembly line and other production techniques (p. 349)

**Franklin, Benjamin** Colonial inventor, printer, writer, statesman; contributed to the Declaration of Independence and the Constitution

**Frémont, John C.** Explorer, military officer, and politician; led United States troops in 1846 Bear Flag Revolt when the United States took California from Mexico; ran for President as a Republican in 1856

**Friedan, Betty** Feminist author; criticized limited roles for women in her 1963 book *The Feminine Mystique* (p. 520)

## G

**Garfield, James A.** Twentieth President of the United States, 1881; his assassination by a disappointed office seeker led to the reform of the spoils system (p. 207)

**Garrison, William Lloyd** White leader of radical abolition movement based in Boston; founded *The Liberator* in 1831 to work for an immediate end to slavery

**Garvey, Marcus** African American leader from 1919 to 1926 who urged African Americans to return to their "motherland" of Africa; provided early inspiration for "black pride" movements (p. 370)

**Gates, Bill** Founder of Microsoft; revolutionized personal computing, investigated for questionable business practices (p. 744)

**George III** King of England during the American Revolution

**George, Henry** Author of *Progress and Poverty* (1879) linking land speculation and poverty; proposed a single tax based on land value (p. 285)

**Gingrich, Newt** Representative from Georgia, 1979–1998; called on Republican congressional candidates in 1994 elections to endorse "Contract with America" (p. 726)

**Gorbachev, Mikhail** Soviet leader whose bold reforms led to the breakup of the Soviet Union in the late 1980s (p. 711)

**Gore, Al** Senator from Tennessee; Vice President under President Bill Clinton, 1993–2001 (p. 725)

**Graham, Billy** Evangelist and presidential adviser; known for leading large-scale crusades, or religious rallies (p. 519)

**Grant, Ulysses S.** Eighteenth President of the United States, 1869–1877; commander of Union forces who accepted Lee's surrender in 1865 (p. 90)

*Newt Gingrich*

## H

**Haldeman, H. R.** Chief of Staff under President Richard Nixon; deeply involved in Watergate (p. 654)

**Hamilton, Alexander** Officer in the War for Independence: delegate to the Constitutional Convention; Federalist and first Secretary of the Treasury

**Handsome Lake** Leader of Seneca in late 1700s; encouraged blending of Native American and white American cultures

**Harding, Warren G.** Twenty-ninth President of the United States, 1921–1923; presided over a short administration marked by corruption (p. 344)

**Harrington, Michael** Author; wrote *The Other America* in 1962, which described areas of poverty in the otherwise prosperous United States (p. 542)

**Harrison, Benjamin** Twenty-third President of the United States, 1889–1893; signed 1890 Sherman Antitrust Act later used to regulate big business (p. 193)

**Harrison, William Henry** Ninth President of the United States, 1841; died after only a month in office

**Hayes, Rutherford B.** Nineteenth President of the United States, 1877–1881; promised to withdraw Union troops from the South in order to end dispute over his election; attacked spoils system (p. 142)

**Hearst, William Randolph** Newspaper publisher from 1887 until his death in 1951; used "yellow journalism" in the 1890s to stir up sentiment in favor of the Spanish-American War (p. 238)

**Hiss, Alger** Former State Department official investigated as a possible Communist spy by House Un-American Activities Committee after World War II; convicted of perjury in 1950 (p. 498)

**Hitler, Adolf** German leader of National Socialist (Nazi) party 1933–1945; rose to power by promoting racist and nationalist views (p. 430)

**Ho Chi Minh** Leader of the Communist party in Indochina after World War II; led Vietnamese against the French, then North Vietnamese against the United States in the Vietnam War (p. 617)

**Hollerith, Herman** 1890 census agent who devised a machine that used punch cards to tabulate data (p. 803)

**Hoover, Herbert** Thirty-first President of the United States, 1929–1933; worked to aid Europeans during World War I; responded ineffectively to 1929 stock market crash and Great Depression (p. 323)

**Houston, Sam** Leader of Texas troops in war for independence from Mexico in 1836; elected first president of independent Texas

**Humphrey, Hubert** Democratic presidential candidate in 1968; lost narrowly to Nixon in an election bid hurt by support for the Vietnam War and by third-party candidate George Wallace (p. 651)

**Hutchinson, Anne** Critic of Puritan leadership of Massachusetts Bay Colony; banished for her religious beliefs

## I

**Isabella** Ruler of Spanish Christian kingdoms with Ferdinand in late 1400s; sponsored Columbus's voyage to North America

## J

**Jackson, Andrew** Seventh President of the United States, 1829–1837; supported minimal government and the spoils system; vetoed rechartering of the national bank; pursued harsh policy toward Native Americans (p. 74)

**Jackson, Stonewall** Confederate general known for his swift strikes against Union forces; earned nickname Stonewall by holding his forces steady under extreme pressure at the First Battle of Manassas (p. 86)

**Jefferson, Thomas** Third President of the United States, 1801–1809; main author of the Declaration of Independence; a firm believer in the people and decentralized power; reduced the federal government (p. 69)

**Johnson, Andrew** Seventeenth President of the United States, 1865–1869; clashed with Radical Republicans on Reconstruction programs; was impeached, then acquitted, in 1868 (p. 127)

**Johnson, Lyndon B.** Thirty-sixth President of the United States, 1963–1969; expanded social assistance with his Great Society program; increased United States commitment during Vietnam War (p. 544)

**Jordan, Barbara** Member of Congress from Texas; first African American and woman to represent her state in Congress; gave keynote addresses at 1976 and 1992 Democratic National Conventions (p. 681)

**Joseph, Chief** Leader of Nez Percé; forced to give up his home by United States army, fled toward Canada; captured in 1877 (p. 182)

## K

**Kamiakin** Yakima chief who led Native Americans in 1855 war against Northwest settlers

**Kelley, Florence** Progressive reformer active from 1886 to 1920; worked in state and federal government for laws on child labor, workplace safety, and consumer protection (p. 288)

**Kennedy, John F.** Thirty-fifth President of the United States, 1961–1963; seen as youthful and inspiring; known for his firm handling of the Cuban Missile Crisis; assassinated in 1963 (p. 541)

**Kennedy, Robert F.** Attorney General under his brother, President John Kennedy, in the early 1960s; supported civil rights; assassinated while running for President in 1968 (p. 572)

**Keynes, John Maynard** British economist who believed that government spending could help a faltering economy; his theories helped shape New Deal legislation (p. 395)

**Khomeini, Ayatollah Ruholla** Islamic fundamentalist leader of Iran after the 1979 overthrow of the Shah; approved holding of American hostages (p. 687)

**Khrushchev, Nikita** Soviet leader from 1953 to 1964; opposed President Kennedy in the Cuban Missile Crisis (p. 553)

**King, Martin Luther, Jr.** African American civil rights leader from the mid-1950s until his assassination in 1968; used nonviolent means such as marches, boycotts, and legal challenges to win civil rights (p. 565)

**Kissinger, Henry** Secretary of State under Presidents Richard Nixon and Gerald Ford; used *realpolitik* to open relations with China, to end the Vietnam War, and to moderate Middle East conflict (p. 659)

## L

**Lafayette, Marquis de** French officer who assisted American forces in the War for Independence

**Lange, Dorothea** Photographed migrant farm workers during the Great Depression; inspired government aid programs and Steinbeck's *The Grapes of Wrath* (p. 384)

**Lee, Jason** First Methodist missionary to Oregon Country in 1834; built a mission school in Willamette Valley

**Lee, Robert E.** Brilliant general of Confederate forces during the Civil War (p. 93)

**Lenin, Vladimir I.** Revolutionary leader in Russia; established a Communist government in 1917 (p. 318)

**Levitt, William J.** Built new communities in the suburbs after World War II, using mass-production techniques (p. 514)

**Lewis, John L.** Head of United Mine Workers through World War II; used strikes during the war to win pay raises (p. 462)

**Lewis, Meriwether** Leader with William Clark of expedition through the West beginning in 1804; brought back scientific samples, maps, and information on Native Americans

**Lincoln, Abraham** Sixteenth President of the United States, 1861–1865; known for his effective leadership during the Civil War and his Emancipation Proclamation declaring the end of slavery in Confederate-held territory (p. 97)

**Lindbergh, Charles A.** Aviator who became an international hero when he made the first solo flight across the Atlantic Ocean in 1927 (p. 356)

**Little Turtle** Native American leader of the late 1700s; adopted policy of accommodation

**Lodge, Henry Cabot** Massachusetts senator of early 1900s; supported United States imperialism (p. 262)

**Long, Huey** Louisiana politician in 1930s; suggested redistributing large fortunes by means of grants to families; assassinated in 1935 (p. 413)

## M

**MacArthur, Douglas** United States general during the Great Depression, World War II, and Korean War; forced by Truman to resign in 1951 (p. 500)

**Madison, James** Fourth President of the United States, 1809–1817; called the Father of the Constitution for his leadership at the Constitutional Convention (p. 39)

**Mahan, Alfred T.** Author who argued in 1890 that the economic future of the United States rested on new overseas markets protected by a larger navy (p. 261)

**Malcolm X** African American leader during the 1950s and 1960s; eloquent spokesperson for African American self-sufficiency; assassinated in 1965 (p. 581)

James Madison

**Mann, Horace** School reformer and supporter of public education before the Civil War; devised an educational system in Massachusetts later copied by many states

**Mao Zedong** Leader of Communists who took over China in 1949; remained in power until his death in 1976 (p. 433)

**Marshall, George C.** Army Chief of Staff during World War II and Secretary of State under President Harry Truman; assisted economic recovery in Europe after World War II and established strong allies for the United States through his Marshall Plan (p. 440)

**Marshall, John** Chief Justice of the Supreme Court appointed by John Adams; set precedents that established vital powers of the federal courts (p. 69)

**Marshall, Thurgood** First African American Supreme Court justice; as a lawyer, won landmark school desegregation case *Brown* v. *Board of Education* in 1954 (p. 530)

**McCarthy, Eugene** Candidate in the 1968 Democratic presidential race who opposed the Vietnam War; convinced President Lyndon Johnson not to run again through his strong showing in the primaries (p. 634)

**McCarthy, Joseph R.** Republican senator from Wisconsin in the late 1940s and early 1950s; led a crusade to investigate officials he claimed were Communists; discredited in 1954 (p. 502)

**McClellan, George** Early Union army leader in the Civil War; careful organizer and planner who moved too slowly for northern politicians; ran against President Abraham Lincoln in the election of 1864 (p. 90)

**McKinley, William** Twenty-fifth President of the United States, 1897–1901; supported tariffs and a gold standard; expanded the United States by waging the Spanish-American War (p. 194)

William McKinley

**McNamara, Robert** Secretary of Defense under Presidents Kennedy and Lyndon Johnson; expanded American involvement in Vietnam War (p. 618)

**Meade, George G.** Union commander at Battle of Gettysburg in 1863; defended the high ground and forced Confederate army to attack, causing great casualties (p. 108)

**Means, Russell** Native American leader of 1960s and 1970s; helped organize American Indian Movement (AIM) and 1973 Wounded Knee occupation (p. 604)

**Metacom** Leader of Pokanokets in Massachusetts; also known by his English name, King Philip; led Native Americans in King Philip's War, 1675–1676

**Mitchell, John** Attorney General under President Richard Nixon; deeply involved in Watergate scandal (p. 654)

**Monroe, James** Fifth President of the United States, 1817–1825; acquired Florida from Spain; declared Monroe Doctrine to keep foreign powers out of the Americas

**Morse, Samuel F. B.** Artist and inventor; developed telegraph and Morse code in the 1830s

**Mott, Lucretia** Women's rights leader; helped organize first women's convention in Seneca Falls, New York, in 1848

**Mussolini, Benito** Italian fascist leader who took power in the 1920s; called *Il Duce* — "the leader"; known for his brutal policies (p. 429)

## N

**Nader, Ralph** Consumer advocate; published *Unsafe at Any Speed* in 1965 criticizing auto safety and inspiring new safety laws (p. 609)

**Nimitz, Chester** Leader of American naval forces in World War II Battle of Midway, during which several Japanese aircraft carriers were destroyed (p. 445)

**Nixon, Richard M.** Thirty-seventh President, 1969–1974; known for his foreign policy toward the Soviet Union and China and for illegal acts he committed in the Watergate affair that forced his resignation (p. 653)

## O

**O'Connor, Sandra Day** First woman Supreme Court justice; appointed by Reagan in 1981 (p. 710)

**Oppenheimer, J. Robert** Physicist who led American effort in World War II to develop first atomic bomb (p. 448)

## P

**Pahlevi, Muhammed Reza Shah** Leader of Iran, from 1941 until his overthrow in 1979; supported by the United States; brought modernization to his country along with repression and corruption (p. 687)

**Paine, Thomas** Author of political pamphlets during 1770s and 1780s; wrote *Common Sense* in 1776

**Paul, Alice** Women's suffrage leader of early 1900s; her Congressional Union used aggressive tactics to push the Nineteenth Amendment (p. 303)

**Penn, William** English Quaker who founded the colony of Pennsylvania in 1681 (p. 1)

**Perkins, Frances** Secretary of Labor 1933–1945 under President Franklin Delano Roosevelt; first woman Cabinet member (p. 406)

**Perot, H. Ross** Billionaire businessman who challenged Bill Clinton and George Bush for the presidency in 1992; strong opponent of NAFTA (p. 724)

**Pierce, Franklin** Fourteenth President of the United States, 1853–1857; signed the Kansas-Nebraska Act, which renewed conflicts over slavery in the territories

**Pinckney, Eliza Lucas** South Carolina plantation manager in the 1740s; promoted indigo as a staple crop

**Polk, James K.** Eleventh President of the United States, 1845–1849; led expansion of United States to southwest through war against Mexico

**Polo, Marco** Venetian traveler to China in the late 1200s; his book about the journey helped make Europeans aware of trade opportunities in eastern Asia

**Popé** Medicine man who led Pueblos and Apaches against Spanish rule in the Pueblo Revolt of 1680

**Prosser, Gabriel** Planned a slave revolt in Virginia in 1800; captured and executed after revolt failed

**Pulitzer, Joseph** Early 1900s newspaper publisher; used "yellow journalism" to stir up public sentiment in favor of the Spanish-American War (p. 238)

## R

**Randolph, A. Philip** Civil rights activist from the 1930s to the 1950s; planned the Washington march that pressured President Franklin Delano Roosevelt into opening World War II defense jobs to African Americans (p. 477)

**Reagan, Ronald** Fortieth President of the United States, 1981–1989; popular conservative leader who promoted supply-side economics and created huge budget deficits (p. 699)

**Riis, Jacob** Reformer who wrote *How the Other Half Lives,* describing the lives of poor immigrants in New York City in the late 1800s (p. 220)

**Robinson, Jackie** Athlete who in 1947 became the first African American to play baseball in the major leagues (p. 530)

**Rockefeller, Nelson** Vice President appointed by President Gerald Ford in 1974; the nation's only nonelected Vice President to serve with a nonelected President (p. 676)

**Roosevelt, Eleanor** First Lady 1933–1945; tireless worker for social causes, including women's rights and civil rights for African Americans and other groups (p. 396)

**Roosevelt, Franklin D.** Thirty-second President of the United States, 1933–1945; fought the Great Depression through his New Deal social programs; battled Congress over Supreme Court control; proved a strong leader during World War II (p. 396)

**Roosevelt, Theodore** Twenty-sixth President of the United States, 1901–1909; fought trusts, aided progressive reforms, built Panama Canal, and increased United States influence overseas (p. 265)

**Rosenberg, Julius and Ethel** Husband and wife convicted and executed in 1953 for passing atomic secrets to the Soviet Union; their guilt is still debated (p. 499)

**Rowson, Susanna Haswell** Author of *Charlotte Temple* (1794), a popular moralizing novel that encouraged women to look beyond appearances when choosing a husband

## S

**Sacajawea** Shoshone woman who served as guide and translator for Lewis and Clark on their exploratory journey through the West in the early 1800s

**Sacco, Nicola** Immigrant and anarchist executed, in a highly controversial case, for a 1920 murder at a Massachusetts factory (pp. 7, 342)

**Sadat, Anwar el-** Egyptian leader in the 1970s; began the Middle East peace process by reaching the 1978 Camp David Accords with Israel (p. 685)

**Salinger, J. D.** Author of 1951 novel *The Catcher in the Rye,* which criticized 1950s pressure to conform (p. 520)

**Santa Anna, Antonio López de** Mexican dictator who led government and troops in war against Texas; won the battle of the Alamo

**Schlafly, Phyllis** Conservative activist; led campaign during the 1970s and 1980s to block the Equal Rights Amendment (p. 593)

**Seward, William Henry** Republican antislavery leader during the 1860s; acquired Alaska in 1867 as Secretary of State (p. 260)

**Sherman, William Tecumseh** Union general in the Civil War; known for his destructive march from Atlanta to Savannah in 1864 (p. 113)

**Sirica, John J.** Washington judge who presided over the Watergate investigation in the 1970s; gave tough sentences to convicted participants and ordered President Richard Nixon to release secret tapes (p. 666)

**Sitting Bull** Chief Leader of Sioux in clashes with United States Army in Black Hills in 1870s (p. 181)

**Slater, Samuel** English textile worker who brought the Industrial Revolution to the United States by duplicating British textile machinery from memory

**Smith, John** Leader of the Jamestown, Virginia, colony in the early 1600s

**Smith, Joseph** Founder of Church of Jesus Christ of Latter-day Saints, or Mormons, in New York in 1830; killed by a mob in Illinois in 1844

**Spock, Benjamin** Pediatrician and author of *The Common Sense Book of Baby and Child Care* (1946), which encouraged mothers to stay home with their children rather than work (p. 520)

**Stalin, Joseph** Leader of the Soviet Union from 1924–1953; worked with Roosevelt and Churchill during World War II but afterwards became an aggressive participant in the cold war (p. 440)

**Stanton, Elizabeth Cady** Women's rights leader in the 1800s; helped organize first women's convention; wrote the Declaration of Sentiments on women's rights in 1848

**Starr, Ellen Gates** Cofounder of Chicago's Hull House, the first settlement house, in 1889 (p. 225)

**Steinem, Gloria** Journalist, women's rights leader since 1960s; founded *Ms.* magazine in 1972 to cover women's issues (p. 592)

**Stevenson, Adlai** Senator from Illinois and Democratic candidate for President in 1952 and 1956 against Eisenhower (p. 526)

**Stowe, Harriet Beecher** Author of the novel *Uncle Tom's Cabin* (1852), which contributed significantly to antisouthern feelings among Northerners before the Civil War (p. 7)

**Sumner, Charles** Abolitionist and senator from Massachusetts; beaten badly in the Senate by a southern congressman after making an antislavery speech

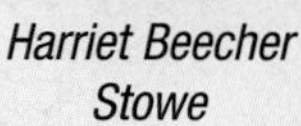

*Harriet Beecher Stowe*

## T

**Taft, William Howard** Twenty-seventh President of the United States, 1909–1913; continued progressive reforms of President Theodore Roosevelt; promoted "dollar diplomacy" to expand foreign investments (p. 275)

**Taney, Roger** Chief Justice of the Supreme Court who wrote an opinion in the 1857 Dred Scott case that declared the Missouri Compromise unconstitutional

**Taylor, Zachary** Twelfth President of the United States, 1849–1850; tried to avoid slavery issues

**Tecumseh** Native American leader in the late 1700s and early 1800s; led a pan-Indian movement that tried to unite several groups despite their differences

**Tenskwatawa** Native American leader of the early 1800s known as the Prophet; he called for a return to traditional ways and rejection of white values

**Thomas, Clarence** Conservative African American Supreme Court justice appointed in 1991; during his confirmation hearings he was charged with sexual harassment (p. 718)

**Thoreau, Henry David** Transcendentalist author known for his work *Walden* (1854) and other writings

**Travis, William** Leader in Texas's bid for independence from Mexico in 1836; died at the Alamo after appealing to the United States for help

**Truman, Harry S.** Thirty-third President of the United States, 1945–1953; authorized use of atomic bomb; signed Marshall Plan to rebuild Europe (p. 486)

Harry S. Truman

**Truth, Sojourner** Abolitionist and women's rights advocate before the Civil War; as a former slave, she spoke effectively to white audiences on abolition issues

**Tubman, Harriet** "Conductor" on the Underground Railroad, which helped slaves escape to freedom before the Civil War

**Turner, Frederick Jackson** Historian who wrote an essay in 1893 emphasizing the western frontier as a powerful force in the formation of the American character (p. 197)

**Turner, Nat** African American preacher who led a slave revolt in 1831; captured and hanged after the revolt failed

**Tweed, William Marcy** Boss of the Tammany Hall political machine in New York City; convicted of forgery and larceny in 1873 and died in jail in 1878 (p. 221)

**Tyler, John** Tenth President of the United States, 1841–1845; accomplished little due to quarrels between Whigs and Jacksonian Democrats (p. 854)

## V

**Van Buren, Martin** Eighth President of the United States, 1837–1841; Jacksonian Democrat; was voted out of office after the Panic of 1837 brought widespread unemployment and poverty (p. 853)

**Vance, Cyrus** Secretary of State under President Jimmy Carter; invited Israelis and Egyptians to Camp David in 1978 to begin Middle East peace process (p. 685)

**Vanzetti, Bartolomeo** Immigrant and anarchist executed, in a highly controversial case, for a 1920 murder at a Massachusetts factory (p. 342)

**Vesey, Denmark** African American who planned 1822 South Carolina slave revolt; captured and hanged after revolt failed

**von Steuben, Friedrich** Prussian officer who trained Washington's troops in the winter at Valley Forge

## W

**Walker, David** African American author of *Appeal to the Colored Citizens of the World* (1829), which called for an immediate end to slavery

**Walker, Madam C. J.** African American leader and businesswoman in the early 1900s; she spoke out against lynching (p. 245)

**Wallace, George C.** Third-party candidate for President in 1968; focused his campaign on issues of blue-collar anger in the North and racial tension (p. 652)

**Warren, Earl** Chief Justice of Supreme Court 1953–1968; investigated President Kennedy's assassination; led in many decisions that protected civil rights, rights of the accused, and right to privacy (p. 548)

**Washington, Booker T.** African American leader from the late 1800s until his death in 1915; founded Tuskegee Institute in Alabama; encouraged African Americans to learn trades (p. 234)

**Washington, George** First President of the United States, 1789–1797; led American forces in the War for Independence; set several federal precedents, including the two-term maximum for presidential office (p. 42)

**Webster, Noah** Author of the best-known American dictionary in the early 1800s; promoted a standard national language and public support for education

**Whitman, Narcissa Prentiss** Missionary; one of the first white women to cross the Rocky Mountains to Oregon in 1836

**Whitney, Eli** Inventor; developed the cotton gin in 1793, which rapidly increased cotton production in the South and led to a greater demand for slave labor

**Wilhelm, Kaiser** Emperor of Germany during World War I; symbol to the United States of German militarism and severe efficiency (p. 311)

**Wilson, Woodrow** Twenty-eighth President of the United States, 1913–1921; tried to keep the United States out of World War I; proposed League of Nations (p. 298)

## Y

**Yeltsin, Boris** Leader of Russia in late 1980s and 1990s; took over from Mikhail Gorbachev as reforms continued and Communist party control ended (p. 732)

**York, Alvin** American soldier who was awarded the Congressional Medal of Honor for bravery during World War I (p. 319)

**Young, Brigham** Mormon leader who supervised migration to Utah beginning in the 1840s; first governor when Utah became a United States territory

# Index

**Note:** Entries with a page number followed by a *c* indicate a chart or graph on that page; *m* indicates a map; and *p* indicates a picture.

## A

# B

## C

## D



## E

## F

## G

## I



## J

# K



# L

## N

## S

# T

## X



## Y



## Z



INDEX

# Acknowledgments

**Team Credits** The people who made up the *America: Pathways to the Present* team include: Tom Barber, Joyce Barisano, Wendy Bohannan, Bruce Bond, Melinda Boroson, Todd Christy, Patrick Connolly, Anthony DeAngelis, Anne Falzone, Elizabeth Good, Mary Ann Gundersen, Ed Hagenstein, Mary Hanisco, Michal Howden, Linda Johnson, Lynne Kalkanajian, John Kelley, Russ Lappa, Marilyn Leitao, Dotti Marshall, Grace Massey, Kathy Maxcey, Efrat Metser, Gabriela Pérez Fiato, Debra Reardon, Nancy Rogier, Luess Sampson-Lizotte, Suzanne Schineller, Angela Sciaraffa, Olena Serbyn Sullivan, Amit Shah, Carol Signorino, John Springer, Mark Staloff, Susan Swan, Kira Thaler-Marbit, Jean C. Thomas, Stuart Wallace.

### Cover Design

Bruce Bond

### Front Cover Photograph

Astronaut David R. Scott saluting the U.S. flag during the Apollo 15 mission, July/August 1971. NASA

### Picture Research

Pembroke Herbert and Sandi Rygiel/Picture Research Consultants, Inc.

**Geography and History Contributing Writers:** Carol Barrett, Department of Geography, University of Wisconsin at River Falls, River Falls, WI; Tom Baerwald, Program Director of Geography and Regional Science, National Science Foundation, Washington, D.C.; Peter Hugill, Department of Geography, Texas A&M University, College Station, TX

### Maps

**Horizon Design/Sanderson Associates:**

20, 24, 26, 29, 71, 72, 74, 77, 82, 90, 92, 108, 114, 121, 130, 134, 142, 153, 157, 181, 186, 189, 194, 219, 260, 266, 270, 274, 277, 279, 295, 304, 310, 319, 329, 355, 389, 396, 407, 431, 433, 434, 439, 446, 476, 487, 494, 501, 504, 517, 552, 554, 558, 572, 583, 618, 620, 637, 655, 681, 715, 731, 733, 788

**Olena Serbyn Sullivan:** xxix, 71

### Illustration

**Precision Graphics:**

40, 73, 116, 139, 159, 161, 162, 163, 164, 170, 187, 200, 206, 212, 213, 232, 234, 261, 272, 343, 344, 349, 377, 381, 382, 406, 442, 460, 462, 472, 489, 505, 512, 514, 515, 520, 543, 547, 548, 579, 590, 593, 599, 628, 655, 677, 705, 707, 741, 742, 756, 761, 776, 789

**Matthew Pippin**

79, 111, 156, 178, 321, 331, 348, 349, 438, 555, 692, 803, 804

### Photography

**Abbreviation Key** LOC = Library of Congress; RH/LS = photo by Rob Huntley/Lightstream; NA = National Archives; PRC = Picture Research Consultants, Inc.; FRENT = Collection of David J. and Janice L. Frent; BB = Brown Brothers; CP = Culver Pictures; WW = Wide World Photos; GL = Gamma Liaison; WC = Woodfin Camp & Associates; C&G = Chermayeff & Geismar/MetaForm photo by Karen Yamauchi; BS = Black Star; MP = Magnum Photos; CB = Corbis Bettmann; TL = Time-Life.

**Unit Openers** Page **17 T,** "Election Day in Philadelphia" by John Lewis Krimmel, 1815. Courtesy, Winterthur Museum; **17 B**, Wood Painted American Eagle, FE 37. Shelburne Museum; **25 T**, New York & Cuba Mail Steamship Company Dock scene. C/B; **257 B**,"Vote Yes" suffrage poster. Smithsonian Institution; **339 T**, Mother and Child during the Depression. LOC; **339 B**,"Kick Out Depression" button. FRENT; **427 T**, "Buy War Bonds" painting by N.C. Wyeth. PRC; **427 B**, Army Medal of Honor. U.S. Department of Defense; **539 T**, Selma March. (detail) by James H. Karales; **539 B**, Woodstock poster. The Image Works Archive; **647 B**, Statue of Liberty. Elsa Peterson/Stock Boston; **647 T**, Newly sworn in immigrants in Brooklyn. Lynn Johnson/BS; **751**, Flag and Confetti. C&G

**American Artifacts:**

**Abbreviation Key**: SI= Smithsonian Institution; OPPS=Office of Printing and Photographic Services, Smithsonian Institution; NPS=Courtesy of the National Park Service

**The Growth of Sports** FOOTBALL PLAYER, BASEBALL MUSIC, Larry Gates, SI; SKATING, Jim Wallace, SI; SKIING, FOOTBALL PANTS, BASEBALL, all by Rick Vargas, SI; BICYCLE, Alfred Harrell, SI; CYCLIST, Collection of Sally Fox

**African Americans' Great Migration** DOLL, Eric Long, SI; PLOW, Jeff Tinsley, SI; RECORD BOOK, Diane Penland, SI; HOME SCHOOLING, LOC; SUITCASE, Eric Long, SI; SOLDIERS, Courtesy of the National Archives & Records Administration; JOBS, Jeff Tinsley

**The Jazz Age** DUKE, Courtesy of John Hasse; TRUMPET, Jeffrey Ploskonka, SI; DRESS, Jeff Tinsley, SI; HYMIE, Danny Thompson, SI; SAXOPHONE, Diane Penland, SI; CLARINET, Diane Penland, SI; BAND, Missouri Historical Society, Block Brothers photo

**On the Home Front** Jeff Tinsley, SI all with exception of PROPAGANDA POSTERS, Richard Strauss, SI

**The Vietnam Veterans Memorial** VIETNAM MEMORIAL, Sandra Rogers, SI; STUFFED ANIMALS, Richard Strauss, SI; BOOTS, HELMET, LETTER , LETTER TO GARY, Eric Long, SI, NPS; DOGTAGS, Rick Vargas, SI

**The Information Age** SATELLITE, OPPS; FIBER-OPTIC, Courtesy of Intel Corporation, Jeff Tinsley, SI; LASER HEAD, OPPS; BAR CODES, MAD'S UPC, symbol cover is ©E.C. Publications, Inc. 1978. Used with permission from MAD Magazine; HAND HELD COMPUTER, Courtesy of Apple Computer, Inc. EARLY COMPUTER, Eric Long, SI; WATERGATE BUGS, Margaret McCullough, SI, courtesy of the National Archives & Records Administration

**Chapter 1** **18**, Chicago Historical Society; **19**, Courtesy of South Florida Science Museum. Photo by Randy Smith; **21**, Colonial National Historical Park; **22**, LOC; **23**, Museum of the City of New York; **25**, LOC; **30**, The Metropolitan Museum of Art, Gift of John S. Kennedy, 1897 (97.34); **35**, LOC; **36**, Independence National Historic Park; **38**, Collection of the Architect of the Capitol; **39**, LOC; **41**, Courtesy, American Antiquarian Society; **42**, LOC; **43 T**, The Brooklyn Museum 39.536.1 Gift of the Crescent-Hamilton Athletic Club; **43 B**, Museum of American Political Life. Photo by Sally Anderson-Bruce; **45**, Collection of the Architect of the Capitol; **67**; Locher/ *The Chicago Tribune;* **69**, © White House Historical Association/ Photo by National Geographic Society; **70 TL**, LOC: **70 TR**, LOC; **70 BL**, Courtesy of Bexar County & the Witte Museum, San Antonio; **70 BR**, Amon Carter Museum, Fort Worth, Texas; **76**, Peabody and Essex Museum; **81**, LOC; **83 L**, Kansas State Historical Society; **83 R**, WW.

**Chapter 2** **86**, West Point Museum; **87**, Collection of David & Kevin Kyle; **89**, LOC; **91**, Collection of Michael J. McAfee. Courtesy William Gladstone. Photo © Seth Goltzer; **93**, Museum of the Confederacy; **95**, West Point Museum Collections. Courtesy William Gladstone. Photo © Seth Goltzer; **97**, McLellan Lincoln Collection, John Hay Library, Brown University; **98**, LOC; **99**, Chicago Historical Society; **100**, LOC; **101**, LOC; **102**, Courtesy, American Antiquarian Society; **107**, Museum of the Confederacy; **109**, Photogoraph courtesy Historical Art Prints, Southbury, CT 06488; **110**, The Beverly R. Robinson Collection, U.S. Naval Academy Museum; **112**, Brown University Library; **117**, Virginia Historical Society; **118**, Anne S. K. Brown Military Collection, Brown University Library, Providence, RI; **119L**, Artist: Douglas Volk, Minnesota Historical Society; **119R**, Jay Syverson/Stock Boston; **120T**, Museum of the Confederacy; **120B**, Confederate Memorial Hall, New Orleans. From ECHOES OF GLORY; ARMS & EQUIPMENT OF THE CONFEDERACY. Photo by Larry Sherer © 1991Time-Life Books; **123,** CP.

**Chapter 3** **124**, LOC; **126**, Chicago Historical Society; **128 TL**, Collection of William Gladstone. Photograph by Seth Goltzer; **128 BL**, Collection of William Gladstone. Photograph by Seth Goltzer; **128 BR**, Collection of William Gladstone; **129**, Collection of William Gladstone; **132 TL**, FRENT; **132 TR**, M. Abramson/BS; **132 BL**, Radcliffe College Archives, Schlesinger Library; **132 BR**, C/B; **135**, LOC; **136**, Collection of Nancy Gewirz, Antique Textile Resource, Bethesda, Maryland; **137**, Courtesy of the Decorative and Industrial Arts Collection of the Chicago Historical Society; Acc. No. 1920.53; Photographer: John Alderson; **138**, The New-York Historical Society; **141**, Collection of State Historical Museum/Mississippi Department of Archives and History; **143**, LOC; **144**, LOC; **145 L**, LOC; **145 R**, Rick Friedman/ BS; **147**, LOC; **148**, LOC; **149**, NA.

**Chapter 4** **150**, The Oakland Museum History Department; **151**, Division of Political History, Smithsonian Institution, Washington, DC. #89-6626; **152**, Division of Community Life, Smithsonian Institution, Washington, D.C. #86-2200; **153**, Lightfoot Collection; **155 T**, C/B; **155 BL**, LOC; **155 BR**, WW; **158**, Museum of American Textile History; **159**, LOC; **160**, LOC; **165**, Putman County Historical Society, Cold Spring, N.Y.; **166 L**, LOC; **166 R**, Urban Archives, Temple University; **167**, Collection of Ralph J. Brunke; **168 L**, LOC; **168 R**, PRC; **171**, C/B; **172**, BB; **173 L**, Hagley Museum and Library; **173 R**, Paul Chesley/Photographers/Aspen; **175**, LOC.

**Chapter 5** **176**, National Cowboy Hall of Fame; **177**, The Oakland Museum History Department; **180**, © Justin Kerr, 1989; **182**, LOC; **184**, State Historical Society of Wisconsin; **185**, Western History Division, Denver Public Library, photo by L. C. McClure; **188**, The Oakland Museum History Department; **192**, East Carolina Manuscript Collection, J. Y. Joyner Library, East Carolina University; **193**, Kansas State Historical Society; **195**, LOC; **197**, Buffalo Bill Historical Center, Cody WY; **199 L**, Amon Carter Museum of Western Art; **199 R**, LOC; **201 L**, Denver Public Library; **201 R**, Bob Daemmrich Photography; **203**, LOC.

**Chapter 6** **204**, CP; **205,** Puck March 10, 1897; **207**, LOC; **208**, Union Pacific Railroad Museum; **209**, New York Public Library. Astor, Lenox and Tilden Foundation; **210**, LOC; **211**, National Park Service Collection, Gift of Angelo Forgione; **212**, BB; **213**, LOC; **215 T**, C&G; **215 B**, C&G; **216**, California Department of Parks and Recreation, courtesy Fred Wasserman; **217**, PRC/RH/LS; **218**, LOC; **220 T**, Museum of the City of New York, Gift of Joseph Varner Reed; **220 B**, BB; **221**, The Granger Collection, New York; **223**, Division of Political History, Smithsonian Institution, Washington. D.C. #88-8676; **224**, C&G; **225**, LOC; **226**, California Museum of Photography WX5266; **227 L**, Courtesy George Eastman House; **227 R**, Bob Daemmrich Photography; **229**, Puck 1909.

**Chapter 7** **230**, American Heritage; **232**, Nebraska State Historical Society; **233**, Sophia Smith Collection; **234**, BB; **235**, BB; **236**, Collection of Sally Fox; **237**, LOC; **238 L**, Chicago Historical Society; **238 TR**, Wood River Gallery, Mill Valley, California; **238 BR**, Wood River Gallery, Mill Valley, California; **239, C/B**; **242**, Frank Leslie's Illustrated Newspaper; **245**, National Portrait Gallery, Smithsonian Institution, Washington, DC. Art Resource, NY; **246**, Museum of American Political Life.Photo by Steve Laschever; **247**, Courtesy of The Maytag Company; **248**, PRC/RH/LS; **249**, Kansas State Historical Society; **251 L**, State Historical Society of North Dakota; **251 R**, Bob Daemmrich/Stock Boston; **253**, LOC; **254**, Kansas State Historical Society, **255**, Courtesy of Birmingham Public Library, Department of Archives & Manuscripts.

**Chapter 8** **258**, Courtesy of the U.S. Naval Academy Museum; **259**, The Oakland Museum History Department; **262**, LOC; **264**, C/B; 521 TL, NA; **265 TR**, Larry Burrows, Life Magazine; **265 BL**, NA; **265 BR**, Bill Gentile/SIPA Press; **267**, California Museum of Photography #24039; **268**, Courtesy of the Liliuokalani Trust and the Bishop Museum (detail); **269**, CP; **271**, PRC; **273**, BB; **274**, LOC; **275**, White House Historical Association; **276**, C/B; **278**, Courtesy of Fred and Kathryn Giampietro; **281 L**, LOC; **281 R**, WW; **283**, Puck, June 29, 1904.

**Chapter 9** **284**, C/B; **286**, Labor-Management Documentation Center, Cornell University; **287**, CP; **288**, Courtesy George Eastman House; **289**, C/B; **292**, CP; **293**, LOC; **296**, National Portrait Gallery, Smithsonian Institution, Washington, DC. Art Resource, NY; **297**, Joseph Keppler from PUCK.Theodore Roosevelt Collection, Harvard College Library; **298**, Museum of American Political Life; **299 T**, C/B; **299 B**, FRENT; **300** FRENT; **301**, Meserve Collection; **303**, Sophia Smith College Archives; **305 L**, Chicago Historical Society; **305 R**, Corporation for National Service; **307**, Courtesy of the League of Women's Voters of the United States.

**Chapter 10** **308** C/B; **309**, Collection of Colonel Stuart S.Corning, Jr. Photo ©RH/LS; **311**, Bayerisches Haupstaatsarchiv; **312**, CP; **314**, The Granger Collection; **315 L**, LOC; **315 R**, Boston Athenaeum; **316**, National Portrait Gallery, Smithsonian Institution, Washington, DC/Art Resource, NY; **317**, Collection of Colonel Stuart S.Corning, Jr. RH/LS; **318**, NA; **320**, BB; **322**, LOC; **324**, C/B; **325**, Wayne State University, Archives of Labor and Urban Affairs; **332**, LOC; **333 L**, Archive Photos/Lambert; **333 R**, C/B; **335**, Stock Montage; **336 T**, Collection of Colonel Stuart S. Corning, Jr.; **336 B**, U.S. Air Force; **337 T**, U.S. Air Force; **337 B**, C/B.

**Chapter 11** **340**, John Sloan Sixth Avenue Elevated at Third Street, 1928 (detail). Collection of Whitney Museum of American Art, Purchase 36.154. Photograph 1998: Whitney Museum of American Art, NY; **342**, FRENT; **344**, LOC; **345**, FRENT; **346**, LIFE Magazine December 10,1925; **347**, PRC/RH/LS; **350**, Courtesy Ford Archives; **351**, Lake County (IL) Museum/Curt Teich Postcard Archives; **352**, Saturday Evening Post, June 30, 1928, Curtis Archives; **353**, C/B; **354**, LOC; **355**, Schomburg Center for Research in Black Culture, The New York Public Library, Astor, Lenox and Tilden Foundations; **356**, CP; **357 L**, C/B; **357 R**, C/B; **358**, SuperStock; **359**, Division of Electricity/Smithsonian Institution; **360 L**, Nipper's Choice Phonographs, Keene, New Hampshire. Photograph by Wright Studio; **360 R**, C/B; **361 T**, Purchased with funds from the Edmundson Art Foundation, Inc. Des Moines Art Center Permanent Collections, 1958.2; **361 B**, C/B; **362 L**, Cartier Bresson/ Magnum Photos; **362 TM**, Beinecke Library, Yale University; **362 BM**, C/B; **362 R**, C/B; **366**, The Michael Barson Collection/Past Perfect. RH/LS; **367**, Chicago Historical Society; **368**, BB; **369**, C&G; **370**, BB; **371 L**, LOC; **371 R**, PRC; **373**, The Granger Collection, New York.

**Chapter 12** **374**, LOC; **375**, Courtesy of Speigel; **376**, Wood River Gallery, Mill Valley, California; **377**, Boston Athenaeum; **378**, C/B; **379**, LOC; **380**, C/B; **383**, Detroit News; **384**, Museum of the City of New York. Photograph by Bernice Abbott, Federal Arts Project; **385 L**, LOC; **385 R**, LOC; **386**, C/B; **388**, LOC; **391**, CP; **392**, C/B; **395**, C/B; **397 TL**, C/B; **397 TR**, FRENT; **397 BR**, Lyndon Baines Johnson Presidential Library; **398**, FDR Library; **399 L**, C/B; **399 R**, People Weekly © 1998 Steve Kagan; **401**, Reprinted from the Albany Evening News, 6/7/31 with permission of the Times Union, Albany, NY.

**Chapter 13** **402**, LOC; **403**, C/B; **404**, C/B; **405 T**, U.S. Forest Service; **405 B**, LOC; **407**, Franklin D. Roosevelt Library; **409**, LOC; **411**, Margaret Bourke-White LIFE Magazine © Time Warner; **412**, ©1935, 1963 by the Condé Nast Publications, Inc.; **415**, National Portrait Gallery, Smithsonian Institution, Washington, DC. Art Resource, NY; **416**, The Oakland Museum History Department; **417**, C/B; **418**, LOC; **419**, James Prigoff; **421 L**, PTC; **421 R**, David Hurn/MP; **423**, Franklin D. Roosevelt Library; **424**, NA; **425**, National Baseball Hall of Fame and Museum.

**Chapter 14** **428**, C/B; **429**, Collection of Chester Stott, RH/LS; **430**, Bilderdienst Suddeutscher Verlag; **431**, NA; **432**, LOC; **436**, Collection of Chester H. Stott, RH/LS; **437**, NA; **441 T**, National Portrait Gallery, Smithsonian Institution, Washington, DC. Art Resource. N.Y.; **441 B**, U.S. Army; **443**, U.S. Army; **445**, Navy Art Collection/ Gift of Abbott Laboratories; **446**, C/B; **448**, LOC; **449**, C/B; **450**, NA; **451**, US Holocaust Memorial Museum; **452 L**, Rijksinstituut voor Oorlogsdocumentatie, courtesy of U.S. Holocaust Memorial Museum Archives; **452 R**, Courtesy of U.S. Holocaust Memorial Museum Archives; **454**, US Holocaust Memorial Museum Archives; **455 L**, Yivo Institute for Jewish Research; **455 R**, C/B; **457**, Reprinted with permission of The Detroit News, a Gannett Newspaper, © 1993.

**Chapter 15** **458**, © The Curtis Publishing Company; **459**, Private Collection, RH/LS; **460**, NA; **461 T**, The Bancroft Library, Kaiser Pictorial Collections; **461 B**, NA; **463**, NA; **464**, LOC; **465**, C/B; **466**, National Museum of American History,Smithsonian Institution, Washington, D.C.; **467**, WW; **470**, Collection of Col. Stuart S. Corning,Jr. RH/LS; **471**, NA; **473**, Ellen Kaiper Collection, Oakland; **474**, Courtesy of the Norman Rockwell Family Trust and Curtis Archives; **475**, Collection of Jeff Ikler, RH/LS; **476**, LOC; **477 T**, LOC; **477 B**, National Portait Gallery, Gift of the Harmon Foundation/ Art Resource, NY; **478**, LOC; **479**, NA; **481 L**, LOC; **481 R**, Bob Daemmrich/ Stock Boston; **483**, Des Moines Register.

**Chapter 16** **484**, Collection of Whitney Museum of American Art, New York. Photography by Geoffrey Clements, NY; **485**, U.S. Army; **486**, Harry S. Truman Presidential Library; **488 L**, C/B; **488 R**, Courtesy of the J. N. Ding Darling Foundation; **490**, © 1949 Time Inc. Reprinted with permission; **493 T**, Bob Daemmrich/ Image Works; **493 BL**, C/B; **493 BR**, WW; **494**, Fenno Jacobs/BS; **498 T**, The Michael Barson Collection/Past Perfect, RH/LS; **498 B**, The Michael Barson Collection/Past Perfect. RH/LS; **499 L**, BB; **499 R**, Elliot Erwitt/MP; **500**, NA; **502**, C/B; **503 T**, C/B; **503 B**, The Michael Barson Collection/Past Perfect, RH/LS; **505**, © 1959 Newsweek Inc. All rights reserved. Reprinted by permission; **507 L**, Boeing Airplane Company; **507 R**, WW; **509**, From Herblock: A Cartoonist's Life (Macmillan Publishing, 1993).

**Chapter 17** **510**, © The Curtis Publishing Company; **511**, PRC; **512**, The McDonald's Corporation; **513**, Dan Weiner, Courtesy Sandra Weiner; **514**, Van Bucher/Photo Researchers; **516**, Collection of Robert and Bonnie Pope, RH/LS; **518**, Bill Ray LIFE Magazine © Time Warner; **519**, Leo Chopin/BS; **520**, The Michael Barson Collection/Past Perfect, RH/LS; **522**, PRC, RH/LS; **523**, Harry S. Truman Presidential Library; **524**, C/B; **525**, C/B; **526 T**, FRENT; **526 B**; Division of Political History, Smithsonian Institution, Washington, D.C. #91-13778; **527**, Dwight D. Eisenhower Library; **528**, From The Herblock's Special for Today (Simon & Schuster, 1958); **529**, FRENT; **530**, The Michael Barson Collection/Past Perfect, RH/LS; **531**, Grey Vielet LIFE Magazine © Time Warner; **532**, WW; **533 L**, C/B; **533 R**, Lonnie Duke/Tony Stone Images; **535**, ©The New Yorker Collection, 1954, Robert J. Day from cartoonbank.com. All Rights Reserved; **536**, NA; **537**, U. S. Naval Historical Center; **539 T**, (detail) by James H. Karales; **539 B**, The Image Works Archive.

**Chapter 18** **540**, John F. Kennedy Library; **541**, FRENT; **542**, John F. Kennedy Presidential Library; **544**, John F. Kennedy Presidential Library; **546**, Lyndon Baines Johnson Presidential Library; **549**, Supreme Court Historical Society; **551**, Courtesy Boeing Defense & Space Group; **553**, C/B; **557 L**, Courtesy of the Peace Corps; **557 R**, Courtesy of the Peace Corps; **559 L**, Y. Okamoto/LBJ Library; **559 R**, WW; **561**, ©1962 Herblock in The Washington Post.

**Chapter 19** **562**, Bob Adelman/MP; **563**, Dan Budnick/WC; **564**, C/B; **565**, C/B; **566**, WW; **567 T**, FRENT; **567 B**, Danny Lyon/MP; **568**, Dial Juvenile Books, 1968, a Division of Penguin Books USA, Inc.; **570**, Don Uhrbrock LIFE Magazine © Time Warner; **571 L**, Rapho/Photo Researchers; **571 R**, Danny Lyons/MP; **572**, C/B; **573**, WW; **574**, Charles Moore/BS; **575**, **Robert Phillips LIFE Magazine ©Time Warner**; **576 L**, Fred Ward/BS; **576 R**, Steve Schapiro/BS; **577 TL**, WW; **577 TR**, Bob Daemmrich Photography; **577 BL**, Bob Daemmrich Photography; **577 BR**, Bob Daemmrich/The Image Works; **578**, C/B; **579**, Eve Arnold/MP; **580**, C/B; **581**, Eve Arnold/MP; **582**, C/B; **583**, Charles Moore/BS; **584**, AP/Wide World Photos; **585 L**, C/B; **585 R**, Bob Mahoney/The Image Works; **587**, David Horsey/The Seattle-Post Intelligencer.

**Chapter 20** **588**, Ken Regan/Camera 5; **589**, Al Freni LIFE Magazine © Time Warner; **591 T**, Werner Wolff/ Black Star; **591 B**, © Bettye Lane; **592 T**, Bob Daemmrich Photography; **592 B**, Courtesy Lang Communications; **593**, C/B; **597**, Michael Nichols/MP; **598**, Craig Aurness/WC; **600**, George Bacon Collection, Hawaii State Archives; **601**, Eddie Adams/TIME Magazine; **602**, Jim Noelker/The Image Works; **603**, Rick Smolan/Against All Odds; **604 L**, Dirck Halstead/TIME Magazine; **604 R**, Dirck Halstead/TIME Magazine; **605**, C/B; 862, FRENT; **606**, FRENT; **607 T**, Alfred Eisenstaedt/LIFE Magazine © Time Warner; **607 B**, FRENT; **608 L**, Collection of Michael McCloskey; **608 R**, Ken Regan/Camera 5; **610**, C/B; **611 L**, M. Abramson/BS; **611 R**, Mike Orazzi; **612**, PRC; **615**, Mike Peters.

**Chapter 21** **616**, Larry Burrows; **617**, Courtesy United Nations, RH/LS; **618**, Dennis Brack/BS; **619**, C/B; **622**, Philip Jones Griffiths/MP, Zenith Electronics Corporation; **623**, C/B; **624 L**, Catherine Leroy/AP, print courtesy Time Inc. Picture Collection; **624 R**, Larry Burrows LIFE Magazine © Time Warner; **625**, Harry Breedlove; **626**, FRENT; **627**, The Bancroft Library, University of California; **629**, ©Lisa Law/The Image Works; **631**, The Oakland Museum History Department; **632**, © Lisa Law/The Image Works; **633**, Michael Frederick/The Image Works; **634**, Brad Markel/GL; **637**, FRENT; **638**, Thai Khad Chuon/C/B; **639 L**, WW; **639 R**, Bob Daemmrich/Tony Stone Images; **643**, From Herblock on All Fronts (New American Library, 1980); **644**, C/B; **645 L**, LOC; **645 R**, WW.

**Chapter 22** **648**, Nixon Presidential Materials Project; **649**, Courtesy of the Lyndon B. Johnson Presidential Library; **650 L**, Joseph Louw LIFE Magazine © Time Warner; **650 R**, Bill Eppridge LIFE Magazine © Time Warner; **651**, C/B; 908, FRENT; **653**, Roddey E. Mims/C/B; **654**, Nixon Presidential Materials Project; **656**, John Filo; **657**, Ted Cowell/BS; **658**, NASA; **659**, Dennis Brack/BS; **660**, Steve Northup, Time Magazine © Time Inc.; **661 T**, John Dominis LIFE Magazine © Time Warner; **661 B**, Sovfoto/Eastfoto; **662 T**, Rene Burri/MP; **662 B**, John T. Barr/GL; **663**, C/B; **664**, FRENT; **665 T**, Richard Ellis/Sygma; **665 B**, Dennis Brack/BS; **666**, WW; **669**, Roland Freeman/MP; **671 L**, Mark Godfrey/Image Works; **671 R**, WW; **673**, Tony Auth. Reprinted by permission: Tribune Media Services.

**Chapter 23** **674**, Robert Llewellyn; **675**, Dennis Brack/BS; **676 T**, WW; **676 B**, Copyright © 1974 by The New York Times Company; **678**, Gerald Ford Presidential Library; **679**, Hardin/BS; **680**, FRENT; **681**, Dennis Brack/BS; **682**, Jimmy Carter Presidential Library; **683**, Dennis Brack/BS; **685**, Jimmy Carter Presidential Library; **686**, C/B; **687**, Alain Minqam/GL; **688 L**, Peter Marlow/MP; **688 R**, FRENT; **690**, Dennis Brack/BS; **694 L**, WW; **694 R**, C/B; **695 L**, WW; **695 R**, PRC; **697**, Mike Peters/Dayton Daily News.

**Chapter 24** **698**, Sygma; **699**, FRENT; **700**, Diana Walker/Time Magazine; **701 TL**, C/B; **701 TR**, WW; **701 B**, Ken Hawking/Sygma; **702**, Les Schofer/Sygma; **704**, Charles Steiner/Sygma; **705**, C/B; **708**, Dick Halstead/GL; **710**, Zimberhoff/Sygma; **711**, WW; **714**, Atlan/Sygma; **715**, WW; **716**, R. Bossu/Sygma; **717 L**, Abbas/MP; **717 R**, Langevin/Sygma; **719 L**, David Woo/Sygma; **719 R**, Larry Downing/Sygma; **721**, Bob Englehard/The Hartford Courant.

**Chapter 25** **722**, National Center for Supercomputing Applications at the University of Illinois; **723**, John C. Sykes Jr.; **724**, Ira Wyman/Sygma; **726**, John Harrington/BS; **727** inset, The Liaison Agency Network; **727**, © Garse/SIPA Press; **728**, AP Photo/Eric Gay; **732**, C/B; **733**, Les Stone/Sygma; **735**, AP Photo/Boris Grdanoski; **736**, WW; **740**, JB Pictures Ltd.; **743**, B. Kraft/Sygma; **744**, Rick Maiman/Sygma; **745 L**, Doug Menuez/Stock Boston; **745 R**, Bob Daemmrich/Stock Boston; **747**, Mike Smith/Las Vegas Sun; **748**, C/B.

**Chapter 26** **752 T**, C&G; **752B**, Rebecca Cooney/NYT Pictures; **753**, Davies & Starr; **754**, BB; **755**, LOC; **756**, David Butow; **757**, ©1993 Time Inc., Reprinted by permission; **758**, Elsa Peterson/Stock Boston.

**Chapter 27** **760 T**, The New-York Historical Society; **760 B**, David J. Sams/Stock Boston; **761**, Boot Hill Museum, photo by Henry Groskinsky; **762**, North Carolina Museum of Art, Raleigh, Purchased with funds from the State of North Carolina; **763**, "The Cowboy" by Remington, 1902. Amon Cater Museum of Western Art; **764**, David Woo/GL; **765**, Dennis Brack/BS.

**Chapter 28** **767 B**, John Zoiner/Uniphoto; **768**, CP; **769 T**, Stock Montage; **769 B**, Museum of the City of New York; **770 T**, FRENT; **770 B**, LOC; **771**, Bob Daemmrich/Tony Stone Images; **772**, Barney Taxel/NYT Pictures.

**Chapter 29** **774 T**, PRC Archive; **774 B**, Gilles Mingasson/GL; **775**, David Hurn/MP; **777**, "Mother and Child" by Dorothea Lange (detail) LOC;

**778 T**, FRENT; **778 B**, Kingsport Press, Inc.; **779**, J. Pat Carter/GL; **780**, Leiderman/Rothco; **781**, John Harrington/BS.

**Chapter 30** 783 **T**, PRC Archive; **783 B**, Lisa Quinones/BS; **784**, Matthew McVay/ Tony Stone Images; **785**, William Campbell/Sygma; **786 T**, NA; **786 B**, LOC; **787 T**, BB; **787 B**, Museum of American Political Life; **790**, Int'l Brotherhood of Teamsters.

**Chapter 31** 792 **T**, Courtesy of Fred and Kathryn Giampietro; **792 B**, © B. Thouanel/ SIPA Press; **793 T**, Christopher Morris/BS; Klaus Reisinger/BS; **794 BOTH**, Collection of Col. Stuart S. Corning, Jr. RH/LS; **795 T**, WW; **795 B**, NA; **796**, Brad Markel/GL; ©1959 Newsweek, Inc. All rights reserved. Reprinted by permission; **798**, R. Bossu/Sygma.

**Chapter 32** **800**, David Chambers/Tony Stone Images; **801**, David Young Wolff/Tony Stone Images; **802**, National Center for Supercomputing Application at the University of Illinois; **804 L**, Courtesy Picture Tel; **804 M&R**, Div. of Political History, SI; **805 BL**, Courtesy Ford Archives; **805 BM**, NASA; **806**, C/B; **808**, Steve Dunwell/The Image Bank; **811**, Stock Connection©1995 Joe Sohn/Chromosohm.

**Reference Section** **812 TL clockwise**, Jim Pickerell; Franklin D. Roosevelt Library; Van Bucher/Photo Researchers; Collection of the Architect of the Capitol; C/B; **814**, Independence National Historic Park; **816**, Nichipor Collection, Courtesy of Minuteman National Historical Park. Rob Huntley/ Lightstream; **818**, Miriam and Ira D. Walsh Division of Art, Prints and Photographs, New York Public Library. Astor, Lenox and Tilden Foundations; **819**, Free Library of Philadelphia; **820**, Courtesy, American Antiquarian Society; **823**, LOC; **826**, PRC; **827**, LOC; **829**, Margaret Bourke-White LIFE Magazine © Time Warner; **830**, US Holocaust Memorial Museum; **832**, C/B; **834**, WW; **836**, Rick Reinhart/Impact Visuals; **837**, Paul Conklin; **857**, Corbis Sygma **858**, Jim Pickerell; **900**, Meserve Collection; **901**, Dwight D. Eisenhower Library; **902**, John Harrington/BS; **903**, WW; **904**, LOC; **905**, Radcliffe College Archives, Schlesinger Library; © 1949 Time Inc. Reprinted with permission.

## Primary Source Bibliography

**Chapter 1** **Samuel Maverick;** Cronon, William. Changes in the Land: Indians, Colonists, and the Ecology of New England. Hill and Wang, 1983, p. 139; **Morris Birkbeck:** Birkbeck, Morris. "Notes on a Journey in America from the Coasts of Virginia to the Territory of Illinois," Philadelphia, 1817, p. 34; **Reverend Walter Colton:** Three Years in California. S.A. Rollo, 1850, pp. 242–253.

**Chapter 2** **Mary Boykin Chesnut:** Woodward, C. Vann, et al., eds. *Mary Chesnut's Civil War.* Yale University Press, 1981, pp. 326, 327, 330, 333, 339; **Abraham Lincoln:** Ward, Geoffrey C. *The Civil War: An Illustrated History.* Alfred A. Knopf, 1990, p. 110; **Louis Wigfall:** McPherson, James M. *Battle Cry of Freedom.* Oxford University Press, 1988, p. 430; **Abraham Lincoln:** McPherson, p. 510; **Emancipation Proclamation:** Boorstin, Daniel, ed. *An American Primer.* University of Chicago Press, 1968, p. 431; **Frederick Douglass:** *Douglass' Monthly*, August, 1863; **soldier at Gettysburg:** E. B. Long, *The Civil War Day by Day.* Da Capo Press, 1971, p. 377; **Abraham Lincoln:** *Selected Speeches and Writings.* First Vintage Books, Library of America, p. 449; **Abraham Lincoln:** Lincoln, p. 450.

**Chapter 3** **Abraham Lincoln:** *Selected Speeches and Writings.* First Vintage Books, Library of America, p. 450; **Charlotte Forten:** "Life on the Sea Islands," *Atlantic Monthly,* Vol. 13 (May and June) 1864, pp. 588–589, 591–594, 666–667; **Lydia Child:** Foner, Eric. *Reconstruction: America's Unfinished Revolution 1863–1877.* Harper and Row, 1988, p. 473; **Ira Steward:** Levine, Bruce et al., eds. *Who Built America? Working People and the Nation's Economy, Politics, Culture, and Society.* Pantheon Books, 1989, p. 539.

**Chapter 4** **Andrew Carnegie:** Carnegie, Andrew. *The Empire of Business.* Doubleday, 1902, pp. 138–140, quoted in Kirkland, Edward Chase. *Dream and Thought in the Business Community, 1860–1900.* Cornell, 1956, pp. 156–157; **Resident of Lynn, Massachusetts:** Bureau of Labor, *Fourth Annual Report,* 1873, p. 306; **Frederick Winslow Taylor:** Taylor, Frederick W. *The Principles of Scientific Management.* W.W. Norton and Company, 1911, p. 39; **Samuel Gompers:** *Labor and the Employer.* Ayer Company Publishers, 1971, p. 118; **August Spies:** Kogan, B. R. "The Chicago Haymarket Riot," 1959 (a reproduction of the circular in the Chicago Historical Society collection).

**Chapter 5** **newspaper reporter:** Fite, Gilbert. *The Farmer's Frontier, 1865–1900.* University of New Mexico Press, 1974, p. 205; **newspaper report:** "Commercial and Financial Chronicle," September 21, 1879, quoted in Fite, p. 82; **Washington Gladden:** *The Annals of America.* Vol. 11, *1884–1894: Agrarianism and Urbanization.* Encyclopedia Britannica, 1968, p. 356.; **Tom Watson:** Woodward, C. Vann. *Tom Watson, Agrarian Rebel.* Oxford University Press, 1963, p. 220; **Frederick Jackson Turner:** Billington, Ray, ed. *Frontier and Section: Selected Essays of Frederick Jackson Turner.* Prentice Hall, 1961, p. 61; **Edward L. Wheeler:** *Deadwood Dick, The Prince of the Road.* Garland, 1979, p. 16.

**Chapter 6** **anonymous:** Kutler, Stanley I. *Looking for America: The People's History,* Vol. 2. W. W. Norton & Company, 1979, p. 178; **Fiorello LaGuardia:** *The Making of an Insurgent.* J. B. Lippincott Co., 1948, pp. 64–65; **Sadie Frowne:** Adapted from "The Story of a Sweatshop Girl: Sadie Frowne," Katzman and Tuttle. *Plain Folk: The Life Stories of Undistinguished Americans.* Illinois, University of Illinois Press, 1982; **Emily Dinwiddie:** "Some Aspects of Italian Housing and Social Conditions in Philadelphia," *Charities and the Commons,* Vol. 12, 1904, p. 490; **Jacob Riis:** *How the Other Half Lives.* Penguin, 1997, p. 6; **Martin Lomasney:** *The Boston Globe*, December 2, 1923, quoted in Zink, Harold. *City Bosses in the United States. A Study of Twenty Municipal Bosses.* Duke University Press, 1930, p. 83.

**Chapter 7** **Pauli Murray:** *Proud Shoes.* Harper and Row, 1956, pp. 269–270; **Booker T. Washington:** *Address of Booker T. Washington, principal of the Tuskegee Normal and Industrial Institute, Tuskegee, Alabama, delivered at the opening of the Cotton States and International Exposition, at Atlanta, Ga., September 18, 1895.* Daniel A. P. Murray Pamphlet Collection, Library of Congress, 1894, pp. 7–9; **W.E.B. Du Bois:** Du Bois, W.E.B. *The Negro Problem: A Series of Articles by Representative American Negroes of Today.* J. Pott & Company, 1903, pp. 33–75; **notice to performers:** Royle, Edwin Milton. "The Vaudeville Theatre," *Scribner's Magazine*, Vol. XXVI, October 1899, pp. 485–495.

**Chapter 8** **James G. Blaine:** LaFeber, Walter. *The New Empire: An Interpretation of American Expansion, 1860–1898.* Cornell University Press, 1963, p. 165; **Theodore Roosevelt:** Hart, Albert Bushnell, and Herbert Ronald Ferleger, eds. *Theodore Roosevelt Cyclopedia.* Roosevelt Memorial Association, 1941, p. 407; **Theodore Roosevelt:** Commager, Henry Steele, ed. *Documents of American History*, vol. 2, Eighth Edition. Appleton-Century Crofts, 1968, p. 34; **Carl Schurz:** "The Policy of Imperialism," 1899 address by Carl Schruz to Anti-Imperialist Conference in Chicago, October 17, 1899; **Bishop Alexander Walters:** "Wisconsin Weekly Advocate," August 17, 1899, quoted in Gatewood, Willard B., Jr. *Black Americans and the White Man's Burden, 1898–1903.* University of Illinois Press, 1975, p. 200.

**Chapter 9** **Edward Bellamy:** *Looking Backward.* River City Press, 1888, p. 56; **Upton Sinclair:** *The Jungle.* Doubleday, 1906, pp. 96–97; **Jane Addams:** "Why Women Should Vote." *Ladies Home Journal*, Vol. XXVII, January 1910, pp. 21–22; **Susan B. Anthony:** Sherr, Lynn. *Failure Is Impossible: Susan B. Anthony in Her Own Words.* Times Books, 1995, pp. 110–112.

**Chapter 10** **Arthur Zimmerman:** Leckie, Robert. *The Wars of America.* Harper and Row, 1968, p. 628; **Woodrow Wilson:** Cooper, John Milton, Jr. *Pivotal Decades: The United States, 1900–1920.* W. W. Norton and Company, 1990, p. 265; **Corporal Elmer Sherwood:** Berger, Dorothy and Josef, eds. *Diary of America.* Simon and Schuster, 1957, p. 536; **Herbert Hoover:** "Gospel of the Clean Plate." *Ladies Home Journal,* August 1917, p. 25; **Woodrow Wilson:** Commager, Henry Steele, ed. *Documents of American History,* vol. II, Eighth Edition. Appleton-Century-Crofts, 1968, p. 138; **Alice Lord O'Brian:** *No Glory: Letters from France, 1917–1919.* Airport Publishers, 1936, pp. 8, 141, 152–153.

**Chapter 11** **Henry Ford:** *My Life and Work.* Doubleday, 1923; **Preston Slosson:** *The Great Crusade and After, 1914–1928.* Macmillan, 1930, p. 157; **Edna St. Vincent Millay:** "First Fig." *Edna St. Vincent Millay: Selected Poems.* HarperCollins, 1991, p. 19; **Langston Hughes:** From COLLECTED POEMS by Langston Hughes Copyright (c) 1994 by the Estate of Langston Hughes reprinted by permission of Alfred A. Knopf, Inc.; **Alice Longworth:** *Crowded Hours: Reminiscences of Alice Roosevelt Longworth.* Charles Scribner's Sons, 1933, p. 324.

**Chapter 12** **Lincoln Steffens:** Leuchtenberg, William. *The Perils of Prosperity, 1914–1932.* University of Chicago Press, 1958, p. 202; **Broadway show tune:** Words by E. Y. Harburg, music by Jay Gorney. Harms, Inc., 1932. Renewed, permission from Warner Brothers Music; **Gordon Parks:** *Voices in the Mirror: An Autobiography.* Doubleday, 1990; **Wilson Ledford:** "How I Lived During the Depression." Interview taped and transcribed by Reuben Hiatt, November 7, 1982. Quoted in Snell, William R. ed., *Hard Times Remembered: Bradley County and the Great Depression.* Bradley County Historical Society, 1983, pp. 117–121; **Gerald W. Johnson:** "The Average American and the Depression." *Current History*, February 1932; **Kitty McCulloch:** Terkel, Studs. *Hard Times: An Oral History of the Great Depression.* Pantheon Books, 1970; **William Saroyan:** *Inhale and Exhale.* Random House, 1936, p. 81; **Herbert Hoover:** Myers, William S., ed. *The State Papers and Other Public Writings of Herbert Hoover.* Doubleday, Doran and Company, Inc., Vol. II, 1934, pp. 408–413; **Franklin D. Roosevelt:** *The New York Times,* September 24, 1932; **Roosevelt's Inaugural Address:** March 4, 1933.

**Chapter 13** **Harry Hopkins:** Dawley, Alan. *Struggles for Justice: Social Responsibility and the Liberal State.* Harvard University Press, 1991, p. 367; **federal official:** Markowitz, Gerald, and David Rosner, eds. "Slaves of the Depression." *Workers' Letters About Life on the Job.* Cornell, 1987, p. 154; **Franklin Roosevelt:** White, Walter. *A Man Called White: The Autobiography of Walter White.* Viking Press, 1948, pp. 179–180; **Sam E. Roberts:** Duram, James C., and Eleanor A. Duram. "Congressman Clifford Hope's Correspondence With his Constituents: A Conservative View of the Court-Packing Fight of 1937." *Kansas Historical Quarterly,* 37/1 (Spring 1971), p. 71; **Hiram W. Johnson:** Barnes, William R., and A. W. Littlefield. *The Supreme Court Issue and the Constitution, Comments Pro and Con by Distinguished Men.* Barnes & Noble, 1937, p. 49; **Walter Reuther:** Madison, Charles A. *American Labor Leaders, Personalities and Forces in the Labor Movement.* Ungar, 1950, p. 382; **Mrs. Renee Lohrback:** Blackwelder, Julia Kirk. *Women of the Depression: Caste and Culture in San Antonio, 1929–1939.* Texas A&M Press, 1984.

**Chapter 14** **Winston Churchill:** Baldwin, Hanson W. *The Crucial Years: 1939–1941.* Harper and Row, 1976, p. 127; **Franklin D. Roosevelt:** Commager, Henry Steele, ed. *Documents of American History*, vol. II, Eighth Edition. Appleton-Century-Crofts, 1968, p. 452; **Franklin D. Roosevelt:** Commager, Henry Steele, ed. *Documents of American History*, vol. II, Eighth Edition. Appleton-Century-Crofts, 1968, p. 449; **American GI:** Martin, Ralph. *The GI War.* Boston: Little, Brown and Co., 1967, p. 338; **Hiroshima survivor:** Cook, Haruko Taya, and Theodore Cook. *Japan at War: An Oral History.* The New Press, 1992, p. 397; **Leon Bass:** *Holocaust and Human Behavior.* Facing History and Ourselves National Foundation, p. 414.

**Chapter 15** **Leonard Williamson:** Hoopes, Roy. *Americans Remember the Home Front: An Oral Narrative.* Hawthorn Books, 1977, p. 115; **Want ad:** *Sporting News*, February 25, 1943; **Sheril Cunning:** Terkel, Studs. *"The Good War": An Oral History of World War Two.* Ballantine Books, 1984, p. 234; **Beatrice Clifton:** Gluck, Sherna Berger. *Rosie the Riveter Revisited: Women, the War, and Social Change.* Twayne Publishers, 1987, pp. 211, 219; **Lloyd Brown:** Blum, John Morton. *V Was for Victory: Politics and American Culture During World War II.* Harcourt Brace Jovanovich, 1976, p. 191; **Henry Murakami:** Harris, Mark Jonathan, et al. *The Homefront: America During World War II.* G. P. Putnam's Sons, 1984, p. 113.

**Chapter 16** **Winston Churchill:** *The Annals of America.* Vol. 16, *1940–1949: The Second World War and After.* Encyclopedia Britannica, 1968, p. 367; **George Kennan:** *The Annals of America.* Vol. 16, *1940–1949: The Second World War and After.* Encyclopedia Britannica, 1968, p. 444; **Harry Truman:** Commager, Henry Steele, ed. *Documents of American History*, vol. II, Eighth Edition. Appleton-Century-Crofts, 1968, p. 525; **George C. Marshall:** Commager, Henry Steele, ed. *Documents of American History*, vol. II, Eighth Edition. Appleton-Century-Crofts, 1968, p. 532; **MacArthur:** Phillips, Cabell. *The Truman Presidency: The History of a Triumphant Succession.* The Macmillan Company, 1966, p. 348; **John Foster Dulles:** Shafritz, Jay M. *HarperCollins Dictionary of American Govern-*